Also by Robert M. Parker, Jr.:

BORDEAUX: THE DEFINITIVE GUIDE
FOR THE WINES PRODUCED SINCE
1961

THE WINES OF THE RHÔNE VALLEY
AND PROVENCE

PARKER'S WINE BUYER'S GUIDE
1987–1988

PARKER'S WINE BUYER'S GUIDE
1989–1990

BURGUNDY: A COMPREHENSIVE GUIDE
TO THE PRODUCERS, APPELLATIONS,
AND WINES

BORDEAUX: A COMPREHENSIVE GUIDE
TO THE WINES PRODUCED FROM
1961–1990

PARKER'S WINE BUYER'S GUIDE Third Edition

ROBERT M. PARKER, JR.

A Fireside Book
Published by
Simon & Schuster

NEW YORK LONDON TORONTO SYDNEY TOKYO SINGAPORE

SIMON & SCHUSTER/FIRESIDE

Rockefeller Center
1230 Avenue of the Americas
New York, New York 10020

Portios of this book were previously published in the
author's bimonthly newsletter, The Wine Advocate.

Designed by Levavi & Levavi, Inc.
Maps by Jeanyee Wong
Drawings by Christopher Wormell
Manufactured in the United States of America

1   3   5   7   9   10   8   6   4   2
3   5   7   9   10   8   6   4   2   PBK

Library of Congress Cataloging-in-Publication Data
Parker, Robert M.
[Wine buyer's guide]
Parker's wine buyer's guide/Robert M. Parker, Jr.—3rd ed.
p.   cm.
"A Fireside book."
Includes index.
1. Wine and wine making.   I. Title.
TP548.P287   1994   93-25346
641.2'2—dc20   CIP

ISBN 0-671-79913-4
0-671-79914-2 PBK

ACKNOWLEDGMENTS

I would like to thank the following for their support and encouragement: Jean-Michel Arcaute, Jim Arsenault, Bruce Bassin, Ruth Bassin, Jean-Claude Berrouet, Michel Bettane, Bill Blatch, Jean-Eugene Borie, Monique Borie, Christopher Cannan, Dick Carretta, Henry Cavalier, Bob Cline, Linda Cunningham, Jean Delmas, Michael Dresser, Stanley Dry, Michael Etzel, Paul Evans, Joel Fleischman, Bernard Godec, Dan Green, Philip Guyonnet-Duperat, Josué Harari, Alexandra Harding, Brenda Hayes, Tom Hurst, Jean-Paul Jauffret, Nathaniel Johnston, Archie Johnston, Denis Johnston, Ed Jonna, Allen Krasner, Bob Lescher, Susan Lescher, Jim Lutfy, Eve Metz, Frank Metz, Jay Miller, President François Mitterrand, Gilbert Mitterrand, Kishin Moorjani, Christian Moueix, Jean-François Moueix, Jean-Pierre Moueix, Mitchell Nathanson, Bernard Nicolas, Jill Norman, Les Oenarchs-Bordeaux Chapter, Les Oenarchs-Baltimore Chapter, Daniel Oliveros, Bob Orenstein, Robert M. Parker, Sr., Allen Peacock, Frank Polk, Bruno Prats, Nicholas De Rabaudy, Martha Reddington, Dominique Renard, Dr. Alain Raynaud, Michel Rolland, Dany Rolland, Tom Ryder, Ed Sands, Bob Schindler, Jay Schweitzer, Ernie Singer, Jeff Sokolin, Elliott Staren, Sona Vogel, Jean-Claude Vrinat, Karen Weinstock, Joseph Weinstock, Jeanyee Wong, and Robin Zarensky.

For the girls . . . Maggie,
Sarah, CeCe, Dogus,
Maia-Song, and Joan

CONTENTS

HOW TO USE
THIS GUIDE

This book is both an educational and buying manual; it is not an encyclopedic listing of wine producers and growers. It is intended to make you a more formidable, more confident wine buyer by providing you sufficient insider's information to permit the wisest possible choice when a wine-buying decision must be made. The finest producers and growers of the world's greatest viticultural regions are evaluated, as well as most of the current and upcoming releases available in the marketplace. If you cannot find a specific vintage of a highly regarded wine, you still have at your fingertips a wealth of information and evaluations concerning the best producers for each viticultural area. At the heart of this book is an impartial and comprehensive consumer's guide to the world's finest, most consistent producers, and you should be confident in the knowledge that you will rarely make a mistake (unless, of course, the vintage is absolutely dreadful) if you go with a producer judged "outstanding" or "excellent."

However, to make the most of this guide, you must know how to use it.

Organization

The general organization of each specific viticultural region covered in this manual is as follows:
1. An overview of the viticultural region
2. A buying strategy for 1993–1994
3. A summary of the quality of recent vintages for the area
4. A quick reference chart to that area's best producers/growers
5. Tasting commentaries, a specific numerical rating for the wine, and a general retail price range for a 750-ml bottle of wine. (See the Wine Price Guide, on page 12, which explains the coding system.)

Viticultural Areas Covered

This guide covers the world's major viticultural regions. In Western Europe France receives the most detailed coverage, followed by Italy, Spain, Portugal, and Germany. In North America California receives significant coverage, reflecting its dominance in the marketplace. The wine regions that are represented most significantly in wineshops are given priority and much more detailed coverage than minor areas whose wines are rarely seen or exported to the United States. Consequently the sections dealing with Bordeaux, Burgundy, Champagne, Alsace, and the Rhône in France; Piedmont and Tuscany in Italy; California; and Germany receive more comprehensive coverage because those regions produce the world's greatest wines. In each section there is a thorough analysis of the region's producers, its overachievers and underachievers, as well as the region's greatest wine values.

Rating the Producers and Growers

Who's who in the world of wine becomes readily apparent after years of tasting and visiting the vineyards and wine cellars of the world's producers and growers. Great producers are, unfortunately, still quite rare, but certainly more growers and producers today are making better wine, with better technology and more knowledge. The charts that follow rate the best producers on a 5-star system, awarding 5 stars and an "outstanding" to those producers deemed to be the very best, 4 stars to those producers who are "excellent," 3 stars to "good" producers, and 2 stars or 1 star to those producers rated "average" and "below average." Since the book's aim is to provide you with the names of the very best producers, the content is dominated by the top producers rather than the less successful ones.

The few growers/producers who have received 5-star ratings are indeed those who make the world's finest wines; they have been selected for this rating for the following two reasons: they make the greatest wine of their particular viticultural region, and they are remarkably consistent and reliable even in mediocre and poor vintages. Ratings, whether specific numerical ratings of individual wines or classifications of growers, are always likely to create controversy not only among the growers, but among wine tasters themselves. But if done impartially, with a global viewpoint and firsthand, on-the-premises *(sur place)* knowledge of the wines, the producers, and the type and quality of the winemaking, such ratings can be reliable and powerfully informative. The important thing for readers to remember is that growers/producers who received either a 4-star or 5-star rating are to be searched out; I suspect few consumers will ever be disappointed with one of their wines. The 3-star-rated growers/producers are less consistent but can be expected to make average to above average wines in the very good to excellent vintages. Their weaknesses result from the fact that their vineyards are not as strategically placed, or because for financial or other reasons they are unable to make the severe selections necessary to make only the finest-quality wine.

The rating of the growers/producers of the world's major viticultural regions is perhaps the most important aspect of this book. Years of wine tasting have taught me many things, but the more one tastes the wines and assimilates the knowledge of the world's regions, the more one begins to isolate the handful of truly world-class growers and producers, those who seem to rise above the crowd in great as well as mediocre vintages. I always admonish consumers against blind faith in one grower or producer, or in one specific vintage, but an "outstanding" and/or "excellent" rating is as close to a guarantee of high quality in a producer or grower as you are likely to find.

Vintage Summaries

Although wine advertisements proclaiming "a great vintage" abound, I have never known it to occur that more than several viticultural areas of the world have a great vintage in the same year. Chances of a uniformly great vintage are extremely remote simply because of significantly different microclimates, soils, and so on, in every wine-producing region. It is easy to fall into the trap of thinking that because Bordeaux had a great vintage in 1982 and 1990, everyplace else in Europe did, too. Certainly in 1982 nothing could have been farther from the truth. Nevertheless, a Bordeaux vintage's reputation unfortunately seems to dictate what the world thinks about many other wine-producing areas. This obviously creates many problems, since in poor Bordeaux vintages the Rhône or Alsace or Champagne could have an excellent vintage, and in great Bordeaux vintages those same areas could have bad years because of poor climate conditions. To the casual observer, it seems every year is a top year for California, and this image is, of course, promoted by that state's publicity-conscious Wine Institute. It may be true that California rarely has a disastrous vintage, but tasting certainly proves that 1988 and 1989 are different in style and more irregular in quality than either 1984, 1985, 1986, 1987, or 1990. In this guide there are vintage summaries for each viticultural area because the vintages are very different in quantity and quality. Never make the mistake of assuming that one particular year is great everywhere or poor everywhere. I know of no year when that has happened.

Tasting Notes and Ratings

For many of the major viticultural areas, the growers/producers are listed alphabetically and their current wines are reviewed, scored, and commented upon. In this instance, great attention has been given to trying to provide an overview of the style and quality level of the wine's producer/grower. Such factors as whether the producer is steadily improving the wines' quality, resting on its allegedly superior reputation, or slipping in quality because of mismanagement, replanting, or simple negligence are issues that I deem important enough to bring to the attention of consumers.

Virtually all my tastings are done in peer-group, double-blind conditions—meaning that the same types of wines are tasted against each other and the producers' names are not known. The ratings reflect an independent, critical look at the wines. Neither price nor the reputation of the producer/grower affects the rating in any manner. I spend 3 months of every year tasting in vineyards both here and abroad. During the other 9 months of the year, 6- and sometimes 7-day work weeks are devoted solely to tasting and writing. I do not participate in wine judgings or trade tastings for many reasons, but principal among these are the following: (1) I prefer to taste from an entire bottle of wine, (2) I find it essential to have properly sized and cleaned professional tasting glasses, (3) the temperatures of the wine must be correct, and (4) I alone will determine the time allocated to the number of wines to be critiqued.

The numerical rating given is a guide to what I think of the wine vis-à-vis its peer group. Certainly wines rated above 85 are very good to excellent, and any wine rated 90 or above will be outstanding for its particular type. Although some would suggest that scoring is unfair to a beverage that has been extolled so romantically for centuries, the fact of the matter is that wine is no different from any other product being sold to a consumer—there are specific standards of quality that full-time wine professionals recognize, and there are benchmark wines against which all others can be judged. I know of no one with three or four different glasses of wine in front of him, regardless of how good or bad the wines might be, who cannot say, "I prefer this one to that one." Scoring wines is simply a matter of applying some sort of consistent numerical system to a professional's opinion. Scoring permits rapid communication of information to expert and novice alike.

The rating system I employ in my wine journal, *The Wine Advocate*, is the one that I have used in this buying guide. It is a 50–100-point scale; the most repugnant of all wines merits a 50, and the most glorious, perfect gustatory experience commands a 100. I prefer this system to the more widely quoted 20-point Davis scale (named after the University of California at Davis), because it permits much more flexibility in scoring. It is also easier to understand, since it corresponds with the grading system most of us became familiar with in school (it was inflicted upon me in law school), and it avoids the compression of scores from which the Davis scale suffers. It is not without problems, however. For example, readers will wonder what the difference is between 86 and 87. Both are very good wines, of course, and the only answer I can give is a simple one: when I tasted them side by side, I thought the 87-point wine was slightly better than the 86-point wine.

The score given for a specific wine reflects the quality of the wine at its peak of maturity. Wines from badly corked or defective bottles are retried, since a wine from a single bad bottle does not indicate an entirely spoiled batch. Many of the wines reviewed have been tasted several times, and the score represents a cumulative average of the wine's performance in all tastings. However, the written commentary that accompanies the ratings is a better source of information regarding the wine's style and personality, its relative quality level vis-à-vis its peers, and its relative value and aging potential. No numerical score can ever reveal these attributes.

Here is a general guide to interpreting the numerical ratings:

90–100 is equivalent to an A and should be given for an outstanding or special effort. Wines in this category are the very best produced for their type and, like a 3-star Michelin restaurant, are worth a special effort to find and try. There is a big difference between a 90 and a 99, but both are top marks. Few wines actually make it into this top category simply because there are not that many truly great wines.

80–89 is equivalent to a B in school, and such a wine, particularly one in the 85–89 range, is excellent. Many of the wines that fall into this range are great values, particularly if they sell for less than $15. Moreover, I would never hesitate to have any of these wines in my own personal collection; I am a conservative scorer.

70–79 represents a C, or average mark, but obviously 79 is a much more desirable rating than 70. Wines that receive scores between 75 and 79 are generally pleasant and straightforward, lacking in complexity, character, or depth. If priced under $6 a bottle, they warrant attention.

Below 70 is a D or F, depending on where you went to school. It is a sign of an unbalanced, flawed, or terribly dull or diluted wine that is of little interest.

In terms of awarding points, my scoring system gives a wine 50 points to start with. The wine's general color and appearance merit up to 5 points. Since most wines today have been well made thanks to modern technology and the increased use of professional oenologists, these tend to receive at least 4, often 5, points. The aroma and bouquet merit up to 15 points. Obviously the intensity of the aroma and bouquet are important, as is the wine's cleanliness. The flavor and finish merit up to 20 points, and again, intensity of flavor, balance, cleanliness, and depth and length on the palate are all important considerations when giving out points. Finally, the overall quality level or potential for further evolution and improvement—aging—merits up to 10 points. Wine tasting is part hedonistic and part technical. I lean toward the hedonistic side in awarding points, preferring wines that offer individuality, harmony, richness, and, above all, pleasure.

Scores help the reader gauge a professional critic's overall qualitative placement of a wine vis-à-vis its peers; here they are used only to enhance and complement the thorough tasting notes that are my primary means of communicating my judgments to you. Consequently the description of the wine's style, personality, and potential is more revealing than the score. No scoring system is perfect, but one that offers flexibility, if applied fairly and without prejudice, can quantify different levels of wine quality. If implemented properly, then, this guide will lead you to the finest wines as well as the very finest wine values. But no scoring system could ever convey the hedonistic oenological experience that might result when accompanied by ambience, gorgeous setting, excellent food, and fine company.

Quoted Prices

For a number of reasons no one suggested retail price for a particular wine is valid throughout the country. Take Bordeaux as an example. Bordeaux is often sold as "wine futures" 2 full years before the wine is bottled and shipped to America. This opening or base price can often be the lowest one will encounter for a Bordeaux wine, particularly if the vintage is reputed to be excellent or outstanding. Prices will always vary for Bordeaux, as well as for other imported wines, according to the quality of the vintage, the exchange rate of the dollar against foreign currencies, and the time of purchase by the retailer, wholesaler, or importer. Was the Bordeaux wine purchased at a low futures price in the spring following the vintage, or was the wine purchased when it had peaked in price and was very expensive?

Another consideration in pricing is that in many states, wine retailers can directly import the wines they sell and thereby bypass the middlemen, such as wholesalers, who usually tack on a 25% markup of their own. The bottom line in all this is that in any given vintage for Bordeaux, or any imported wine, there is no standard suggested retail price. Prices can differ by at least 50% for the same wine in the same city. However, in cities where there is tremendous competition among wineshops, the markup for wines can be as low as 10% or even 5%, versus the normal 50%–55%. This can result in significantly lower overall prices for wine, where in cities where there is little competition, the prices often charged are full retail and can be more expensive. I always recommend that consumers pay close attention to the wineshop advertisements in major newspapers. For example, *The New York Times'* Living Section and *The Wine Spectator* are filled with wine advertisements that are a barometer for the market price of a given wine. Readers should remember, however, that prices differ considerably, not only within the same state, but also within the same city. The approximate price range used reflects the suggested retail price with a 40%–60% markup by the retailer in most major metropolitan areas. Therefore, in many states in the Midwest and less populated areas, where there is little competition among wine merchants, the price may be higher. In marketplaces of brisk competition, such as Washington, D. C., New York, San Francisco, Boston, Los Angeles, Chicago, and Dallas, prices are often lower because of the discount wars that frequently occur. The reader and consumer must follow the advertisements in a major newspaper and shop around. Most major wine retailers feature sales in the fall and spring; summer is the slow season and generally the most expensive time to buy wine.

Following is the price guide I have used through the book.

WINE PRICE GUIDE

CODE
A: Inexpensive/less than $10
B: Moderate/between $10 and $15
C: Expensive/between $15 and $25
D: Very expensive/between $25 and $50
E: Luxury/between $50 and $75
EE: Superluxury/between $75 and $125
EEE: Over $125

ABOUT WINE

How to Buy Wine

On the surface, having made your choices in advance, you may believe that buying wine seems simple enough—you go to your favorite wine merchant and purchase a few bottles. However, there are some subtleties that must be appreciated to ensure that the wine is in healthy condition and unspoiled.

To begin with, take a look at the bottle of wine you are about to buy. Wine abuse is revealed by the condition of the bottle in your hand. If the cork has popped above the rim of the bottle and is pushed out on the lead or plastic capsule that covers the top of the bottle, look for another bottle to buy. Wines that have been exposed to very high temperatures expand in the bottle, thereby putting pressure on the cork and pushing it upward against the capsule. And it is the highest-quality wines, those that have not been overly filtered or pasteurized, that are most vulnerable to abusive transportation or storage conditions and will show the effects in this manner. A wine that has been frozen in transit or storage will likewise push out the cork, and although freezing is less damaging to a wine than boiling, both are hazardous to its health. Any cork protruding above the rim of the bottle is a bad sign: return the bottle to the shelf.

Another sign that a wine has been poorly stored is the presence around the rim of the bottle of seepage ("legs")—the sometimes sticky, dried residue of wine that has expanded and seeped around the cork and dripped onto the rim. This condition is almost always due to excessively high temperatures in transit or storage. Few merchants take the trouble to wipe off this evidence, so it can often be spotted, particularly in wines shipped during the heat of summer or brought into the United States through the Panama Canal in un-air-conditioned containers. In any case, avoid buying wine that shows dried seepage originating under the capsule and trickling down the side of the bottle.

Also be on the alert if a young wine (less than 4 years old) has more than one-half inch of airspace between the cork and the liquid level in the bottle; it may still be a very sound wine, but given the modern bottling operations that generally fill the bottle to within one-eighth inch of the cork, more than one-half inch airspace, or "ullage," is a suspicious sign—why take the risk if there are other bottles with better fills?

One final sign indicating poor storage conditions can generally be determined only after the wine has been decanted, though sometimes it can be spotted in the neck of the bottle. Wines that have been exposed to very high temperatures, particularly deep, rich, intense, red wines, will often form a heavy coat or film of coloring material on the inside of the glass. With a Bordeaux less than 3 years old, this coating generally indicates that the wine has been subjected to very high temperatures and has undoubtedly been damaged.

However, one must be careful here because this type of sediment does not always indicate a poor bottle of wine; vintage port regularly throws it, as do the huge, rich Rhône wines and Piedmontese wines.

On the other hand, two conditions consumers frequently think of as signs of a flawed wine are nothing of the kind. Many consumers return wine because of a small deposit or sediment in the bottom of the bottle. Ironically, this is actually the healthiest sign one could find in most bottles of wine. However, keep in mind that white wines rarely throw a deposit, and it is also rare to see a deposit in young wines under 2 to 3 years of age. The tiny particles of sandlike sediment that precipitate to the bottom of a bottle indicate that the wine has been made naturally and has not been subjected to a flavor- and character-eviscerating traumatic filtration. Such wine is truly alive and usually full of all its natural flavors.

Another reason wine consumers return bottles to retailers is the presence of small crystals called "tartrate precipitates." These crystals are found in all types of wines but appear most commonly in whites from Germany and Alsace. The crystals often shine and resemble little slivers of cut glass, but in fact they are harmless, tasteless, and a totally natural occurrence in many bottles of wine. They simply indicate that somewhere along its journey the wine was exposed to temperatures below 40°F in shipment and the cold has caused some tartaric crystals to precipitate. The crystals have no effect on the quality and normally signify that the wine has not been subjected by the winery to an abusive, sometimes damaging cold stabilization treatment for cosmetic purposes.

Fortunately, most of the better wine merchants, wholesalers, and importers are more cognizant today of the damage that can be done by shipping wine in unrefrigerated containers, especially in the middle of summer. However, far too many wines are still damaged by poor transportation and storage, and it is the consumer who suffers. A general rule is that heat is much more damaging to fine wines than cold. Remember, there are still plenty of wine merchants, wholesalers, and importers who treat wine no differently from beer or liquor, and the wine buyer must therefore be a bit knowledgeable before he or she buys a bottle of wine.

How to Store Wine

Wine has to be stored properly if it is to be served in a healthy condition. All wine enthusiasts know that subterranean wine cellars that are vibration-free, dark, damp, and kept at a constant 55°F are considered perfect for wine. However, few of us have our own castles and such perfect accommodations for our beloved wines. Although such conditions are ideal, most wines will thrive and develop well under other circumstances. I have tasted many old Bordeaux wines from closets and basements that have reached 65°–70°F in summer, and the wines have been perfect. In cellaring wine, keep the following rules in mind and you will not be disappointed with a wine that has gone over the hill prematurely.

First of all, in order to safely cellar wines for 10 years or more, keep them at 65°F and no higher. If the temperature rises to 70°F, be prepared to drink your red wines within 10 years. Under no circumstances should you store and cellar white wines more than 1–2 years at temperatures above 70°F. Wines kept at temperatures above 65°F will age faster but, unless the temperature exceeds

70°F, will not age badly. If you can somehow get the temperature down to 65°F or below, you will never have to worry about the condition of your wines. At 55°F, the ideal temperature according to the textbooks, the wines actually evolve so slowly that your grandchildren are more likely to benefit from the wines than you. Constancy in temperature is most essential, and any changes in temperature should occur slowly. White wines are much more fragile and much more sensitive to temperature changes and higher temperatures than red wines. Therefore, if you do not have ideal storage conditions, buy only enough white wine to drink over a 1–2-year period.

Second, be sure that your storage area is odor- and vibration-free, and dark. A humidity level above 50% is essential; 70%–75% is ideal. The problem with a humidity level over 75% is that the labels become moldy and deteriorate. A humidity level below 40% will preserve the labels but will dry out the corks, possibly shortening the potential lifetime of your wines. Low humidity is believed to be nearly as great a threat to a wine's health as high temperature. There has been no research to prove this, however, and limited studies I have done are far from conclusive.

Third, always bear in mind that wines from vintages that have produced powerful, rich, concentrated, full-bodied wines travel and age significantly better than wines from vintages that produced lighter-weight wines. It is often traumatic for a fragile, lighter-style wine from either Europe or California to be transported across the Atlantic or across the country, where the richer, more intense, bigger wines from the better vintages seem much less travel-worn after their journey.

Fourth, I always recommend buying a wine as soon as it appears on the market, assuming, of course, that you have tasted the wine and like it. The reason for this is that there are still too many American wine merchants, importers, wholesalers, and distributors who are indifferent to the way wine is stored. This attitude still persists, though things have improved dramatically over the last decade. The important thing to remember, after inspecting the bottle to make sure it appears healthy, is to stock up on wines as quickly as they come on the market and to approach older vintages with a great deal of caution and hesitation unless you have absolute faith in the merchant from whom you are buying the wine. Furthermore, you should be confident your merchant will stand behind the wine in the event it is flawed from poor storage.

The Question of How Much Aging

The majority of wines made in the world taste best when they are just released within 1–2 years of the vintage. Many wines are drinkable at 5, 10, or even 15 years of age, but based on my experience only a small percentage are more interesting and more enjoyable after extended cellaring than they were when originally released.

It is important to have a working definition of what the aging of wine actually means. I define the process as nothing more than the ability of a wine over time to (1) develop more pleasurable nuances, (2) expand and soften in texture (and in the cae of red wines, exhibit an additional melting away of tannins), and (3) reveal a more compelling aromatic and flavor profile. In short, the wine must deliver additional complexity, increased pleasure, and more interest as an older wine than it did when released. Only such a performance can justify the purchase of a wine in its youth for the purpose of cellaring it for future drinking. Unfortunately, just a tiny percentage of the world's wines falls within this definition of aging.

An unhealthy legacy of English wine critics is the fallacious belief that for a wine to be considered serious and profound it must have the ability to improve in the bottle. In France, the finest Bordeaux, northern Rhône Valley wines (particularly Hermitage and Côte Rôtie), a few red burgundies, some Châteauneuf-du-Papes, and, surprisingly, many of the sweet white Alsace wines and sweet Loire Valley wines do indeed age well and are frequently much more enjoyable and complex when drunk 5, 10, or even 15 years after the vintage. But virtually all other French wines, from Champagne to Côtes du Rhône, from Beaujolais to the "petits châteaux" of Bordeaux, to even the vast majority of red and white burgundies, are better in their youth.

The French have long adhered to the wine-drinking strategy that younger is better. Centuries of wine consumption, not to mention gastronomic indulgences, have taught the French something that Americans and Englishmen have failed to grasp: most wines are more pleasurable and friendly when young than old.

The French know that the aging and cellaring of wines, even those of high pedigree, are often fraught with more disappointments than successes. Nowhere is this more in evidence than in French restaurants, especially in Bordeaux, the region that boasts what the world considers the longest-lived dry red wines. A top vintage of Bordeaux can last for 20–30 years, sometimes 40 or more, but look at the wine lists of Bordeaux's best restaurants. The great 1982s have long disappeared down the throats of French men and women. Even the tannic, young, yet potentially very promising 1986s, which Americans have squirreled away for drinking in the next century, are now hard to find. Why? Because they have already been consumed. Many of the deluxe restaurants, particularly in Paris, have wine lists of historic vintages, but these are largely for rich tourists.

This phenomenon is not limited to France. Similar drinking habits prevail in the restaurants of Florence, Rome, Madrid, and Barcelona. Italians and Spaniards also enjoy young wines. This is not to suggest that Italy does not make some wines that improve in the bottle. In Tuscany, for example, a handful of Chiantis and some of the finest new-breed Tuscan red wines (i.e., the famed Cabernet Sauvignon called Sassicaia) will handsomely repay 8–15 years of cellaring. In the Piedmont section of northern Italy, no one will deny that a fine Barbaresco or Barolo improves after a decade in the bottle. But by and large, all of Italy's other wines are meant to be drunk young, a fact that Italians have long known and that you should observe as well.

With respect to Spain there is little difference, although a Spaniard's tastes differ considerably from the average Italian's or Frenchman's. In Spain, the intense aroma of smoky vanillin new oak is prized. As a result, the top Spanish wine producers from the most renowned wine region, Rioja, and other viticultural regions as well, tend to age their wines in oak barrels so that they can develop this particular aroma. Additionally, unlike French and Italian wine producers, or even their New World counterparts, Spanish wineries are reluctant to release their wines until they are fully mature. As a result, most Spanish wines are smooth and mellow when they arrive on the market. While they may keep for 5–10 years, they generally do not improve. This is especially true with Spain's most expensive wines, the Reservas and Gran Reservas from Rioja, which are usually not released until 5 to 8 years after the vintage.

All this impacts on the notion shared by most American wine enthusiasts, who, along with their English brethren, are the only wine consumers in the world to fret over the perfect moment to drink a bottle of wine. There is none. Most modern-day vintages, even ageworthy Bordeaux or Rhône Valley wines, can be drunk when released. Some of them will improve, but many will not. If you enjoy drinking a 1989 Bordeaux now, then who could be so foolish as to suggest that you are making an error because the wine will be appreciably better in 5–10 years?

In America and Australia, winemaking is much more dominated by technology. While a handful of producers still adheres to the artisanal, traditional way of making wine as done in Europe, most treat the vineyard as a factory and the winemaking as a manufacturing process. As a result, such techniques as sterile filtration are routinely utilized to produce squeaky clean, simplistic, sediment-free, spit-polished, totally stable wines with statistical profiles that fit neatly within strict technical parameters. Yet these same techniques will eviscerate wines of their flavors, aromas, and pleasure-giving qualities.

In both Australia and California, the alarming tendency of most Sauvignon Blancs and Chardonnays to collapse in the bottle and drop their fruit within 2–3 years of the vintage has been well documented. Yet some of California's and Australia's most vocal advocates continue to advise wine consumers to cellar and invest (a deplorable word when it comes to wine) in Sauvignon Blancs and Chardonnays. It is a doomed policy. If the aging of wine is indeed the ability of a wine to become more interesting and pleasurable with time, then the rule of thumb to be applied to American and Australian Sauvignon Blancs and Chardonnays is that they must be drunk within 12 months of their release unless the consumer has an eccentric fetish for fruitless wines with blistering acidity and scorchingly noticeable alcohol levels. Examples of producers whose Sauvignon Blancs and Chardonnays can last for 5–10 years and improve during that period can be found, but they are distressingly few in number.

With respect to red wines, a slightly different picture emerges. Take, for example, the increasingly fashionable wines made from the Pinot Noir grape. No one doubts the immense progress made in both California and Oregon in turning out fragrant, supple Pinot Noirs that are delicious upon release. But I do not know of any American producer who is making Pinot Noir that can actually improve beyond 10–12 years in the bottle. Under no circumstances is this a criticism.

Even in Burgundy there are probably no more than a dozen producers who make their wines in such a manner that they improve and last for more than a decade. Many of these wines can withstand the test of time in the sense of being survivors, but they are far less interesting and pleasurable at age 10 than when they were at 2 or 3. Don't be bamboozled by the public relations arm of the wine industry or the fallacious notion that red wines all improve with age. If you enjoy them young, and most likely you will, then buy only the quantities needed for near-term consumption.

America's most famous dry red wine, however, is not Pinot Noir but Cabernet Sauvignon, particularly that grown in California and to a lesser extent in Washington State. The idea that most California Cabernet Sauvignons improve in the bottle is a myth. Nonetheless, the belief that all California Cabernet Sauvignons are incapable of lasting in the bottle is equally unfounded. Today no one would be foolish enough to argue that the best California Cabernets cannot tolerate 15 or 20, even 25 or 30 years of cellaring.

I frequently have the opportunity to taste 20- to 30-year-old California Cabernet

Sauvignons, and they are delicious. But have they significantly improved because of the aging process? A few of them have, though most still tend to be relatively grapy, somewhat monolithic, earthy, and tannic at age 20. Has the consumer's patience in cellaring these wines for all those years justified both the expense and the wait? Lamentably, the answer will usually be no. Most of these wines are no more complex or mellow than they were when young.

Because these wines will not crack up and fall apart, there is little risk associated with stashing the best of them away, but I am afraid the consumer who patiently waits for the proverbial "miracle in the bottle" will find that wine cellaring can all too frequently be an expensive exercise in futility.

If you think it over, the most important issue is why so many of today's wines exhibit scant improvement in the aging process. While most have always been meant to be drunk when young, I am convinced that much of the current winemaking philosophy has led to numerous compromises in the winemaking process. The advent of micropore sterile filters, so much in evidence at every modern winery, may admirably stabilize a wine, but, regrettably, may also destroy the potential of a wine to develop a complex aromatic profile. When they are utilized by wine producers who routinely fertilize their vineyards excessively, thus overcropping, the results are wines that reveal an appalling lack of respect for the integrity of the vineyard, the specific personality of the vintage, and the intrinsic character of the grape.

The prevailing winemaking obsession is to stabilize wine so it can be shipped to the far corners of the world 12 months a year, stand upright in over-heated stores indefinitely, and never change or spoil if exposed to extremes of heat and cold or unfriendly storage conditions. For all intents and purposes, the wine is no longer alive. This may be okay for inexpensive jug wines, buy for the fine-wine market, where consumers are asked to pay $10–$20 or more for a bottle of wine, it is a winemaking tragedy. These stabilization and production techniques thus impact on the aging of wine because they preclude the development of the wine's ability to evolve and become a more complex, tasty, profound, and enjoyable beverage.

How to Serve Wine

There are really no secrets for proper wine service—all one needs is a good corkscrew, clean, odor-free glasses, a sense of order as to how wines should be served, and a knowledge of which wines need to be aired or allowed to breathe. The major mistakes most Americans, as well as most restaurants, make are 1) serving fine white wines entirely too cold, 2) serving fine red wines entirely too warm, and 3) giving too little attention to the glass into which the wine is poured. (A glass might contain a soapy residue or stale aromas picked up in a closed china closet or cardboard box.) All of these things can do much more to damage the impact of a fine wine and its subtle aromas than you might imagine. Many people tend to think that the wine must be opened and allowed to "breathe" well in advance of serving. Some even think a wine must be decanted, a rather elaborate procedure essential only if the wine needs to be separated from sediment that is present in the bottle. With respect to breathing or airing wine, I am not sure anyone has all the answers. Certainly no white wine requires advance opening and pouring, and red wines need only 15–30 minutes after being opened and poured into a clean, odor- and soap-free wine decanter. (There are, of course, certain wines that improve after 7–8 hours of "breathing," but these are quite rare.)

Although such topics seem to dominate much of the discussion in wine circles, a more critical aspect for me is the appropriate temperature of the wine and of the glass in which it is to be served. The temperature of red wines is very important, and in America's generously heated dining rooms, temperatures are often 75°–80°F, higher than is good for fine red wine. A red wine served at such a temperature will taste flat and flabby, its bouquet diffuse and unfocused. The alcohol content will also seem higher than it should be. The ideal temperature for most red wines is from 62° to 67°F; light red wine such as Beaujolais should be chilled to 55°F. For white wines, 55°–60°F is perfect, since most will show all their complexity and intensity at this temperature; if chilled to below 45°F, it will be difficult to tell, for instance, whether the wine is a Riesling or Chardonnay.

In addition, there is the all-important issue of the glasses in which the wine is to be served. An all-purpose, tulip-shaped glass of 8–12 ounces is a good start for just about any type of wine, but think the subject over carefully. If you go to the trouble and expense of finding and storing wine properly, shouldn't you treat the wine to a good glass? The finest glasses for both technical and hedonistic purposes are those made by the Riedel Company of Austria. I have to admit I was at first skeptical about these glasses. Georg Riedel, the head of his family's crystal business, claims to have created these glasses specifically to guide (by specially designed rims) the wine to a designated section of the palate. These rims, combined with the general shape of the glass, emphasize and promote the different flavors and aromas of a given varietal.

Over the last six months, I have tasted an assortment of wines in his glasses, including a Riesling glass, Chardonnay glass, Pinot Noir glass, and Cabernet Sauvignon glass, all part of his Sommelier Series. For comparative purposes, I then tasted the same wines in the Impitoyables glass, the INAO tasting glass, and the conventional tulip-shaped glass. The results were consistently in favor of the Riedel glasses. American Pinot Noirs and red burgundies performed far better in his huge 37-ounce, 9½-inch-high burgundy goblet (model number 400/16) than in the other stemware. Nor could any of the other glassware compete when one is drinking Cabernet and Merlot-based wines from his Bordeaux goblet (model number 400/00), a 32-ounce, 10½-inch-high, magnificently shaped glass. His Chardonnay glass was a less convincing performer, but I was astounded by how well the Riesling glass (model number 400/1), an 8-ounce glass that is 7¾ inches high, seemed to highlight the personality characteristics of Riesling.

George Riedel realizes that wine enthusiasts go to great lengths to buy wine in sound condition, store it properly, and serve it at the correct temperature. But how many connoisseurs invest enough time exploring the perfect glasses for their Pichon-Lalande, Méo-Camuzet, Clos Vougeot, or Maximin-Grunhauser Riesling Kabinett? His mission, he says, is to provide the "finest tools," enabling the taster to capture the full potential of a particular varietal. His glasses have convincingly proven his case time and time again in my tastings. I know of no finer tasting or drinking glasses than the Sommelier Series glasses from Riedel.

I have always found it amazing that most of my wine-loving friends tend to ignore the fact that top stemware is just as important as making the right choice in wine. When using the Riedel glasses, one must keep in mind that every one of these glasses has been engineered to enhance the best characteristic of a particular grape varietal. Riedel believes that regardless of size, the glasses work best when they are filled to no more than one-quarter of their capacity. If I were going to buy these glasses (the Sommelier Series tends to run $40–$70 a glass), I would unhesitatingly purchase both the Bordeaux and burgundy glasses. They outperformed every other glass by a wide margin. The magnificent 37-ounce burgundy glass, with a slightly flared lip, directs the flow of a burgundy to the tip and the center of the tongue, thus avoiding contact with the sides of the tongue, which deemphasizes the acidity, making the burgundy taste rounder and more supple. This is not just trade puffery on Riedel's part. I have done enough tastings to realize these glasses do indeed control the flow, and by doing so, they enhance the character of the wine. The large 32-ounce Bordeaux glass, which is nearly the same size as the burgundy glass, is more conical and the lip serves to direct the wine toward the tip of the tongue, where the taste sensors are more acutely aware of sweetness. This enhances the rich fruit in a Cabernet/Merlot-based wine before the wine spreads out to the sides and back of the palate, which picks up the more acidic, tannic elements.

All of this may sound absurdly high-brow or esoteric, but the effect of these glasses on fine wine is profound. I cannot emphasize enough what a difference they make.

If the Sommelier Series sounds too expensive, Riedel does produce less expensive lines that are machine-made rather than hand-blown. The most popular are the Vinum glasses, which sell for about $20 per glass. The Bordeaux Vinum glass is a personal favorite as well as a spectacular glass not only for Bordeaux, but for Rhône wines and white burgundies. There are also numerous other glasses designed for Zinfandel, Chianti, Nebbiolo-based wines, rosé wines, old white wines, and port wines, as well as a specially designed glass for sweet Sauternes-type wines.

For more complete information about prices and models, readers can get in touch with Riedel Crystal of America, P.O. Box 446, 24 Aero Road, Bohemia, NY 11716; telephone number (516) 567-7575. For residents or visitors to New York City, Riedel has a showroom at 41 Madison Avenue (at 26th Street).

And last but not least, remember: No matter how clean the glass appears to be, be sure to rinse it or your decanter with unchlorinated well or mineral water just before it is used. A decanter or wineglass left sitting for any time is a wonderful trap for room and kitchen odors that are undetectable until the wine is poured and they yield their off-putting smells. That, and soapy residues left in the glasses, has ruined more wines than any defective cork or, I suspect, poor storage from an importer, wholesaler, or retailer. I myself put considerable stress on one friendship simply because I continued to complain at every dinner party about the soapy glasses that interfered with the enjoyment of the wonderful Bordeaux wines being served.

Food and Wine Matchups

The art of serving the right bottle of wine with a specific course or type of food has become one of the most overly legislated areas, all to the detriment of the enjoyment of both wine and food. Newspaper and magazine columns, even books, are filled with precise rules that seemingly make it a sin not to choose the perfect wine to accompany the meal. The results have been predictable. Instead of enjoying a meal, most hosts and hostesses fret, usually needlessly, over their wine choices.

The basic rules of the wine/food matchup game are not difficult to master. These are the tried-and-true, allegedly cardinal principles, such as young wines before old wines, dry wines before sweet wines, white wines before red wines, red wines with meat and white wines with fish. However, there are exceptions to these general principles, and your choices are a great deal broader than you have been led to expect. One of France's greatest restaurant proprietors once told me that if people would simply pick their favorite wines to go along with their favorite dishes, they would all be a great deal happier. The famous Frenchman Henri Bérau stated it best: "The first condition of a pleasant meal depends, essentially, upon the proper choice of guests." White wine with fish, red wine with meat, may well have outlived its usefulness, but approach these new wine and food dictators as our ancestors would have dealt with snake-oil salesmen. Besides, has anyone ever been able to get both the wine and the food in his or her mouth at the same moment? My belief is that there are numerous combinations of wine and food that work reasonably well. Let me share some of my basic observations about the whole field. There are several important questions you should consider:

Does the food offer simple or complex flavors? Chardonnay and Cabernet Sauvignon, two grapes favored by America (and I suppose by the wine world as well), can produce majestic wines of exceptional complexity and flavor depth. However, as food wines they are remarkably one-dimensional. As complex and rewarding as they can be, they work well only with dishes with relatively straightforward and simple flavors. Cabernet Sauvignon marries beautifully with basic meat-and-potato dishes, filet mignon, lamb filets, steaks, and so on. Furthermore, as Cabernet Sauvignon and Merlot-based wines get older and more complex, they require increasingly simpler dishes to complement their complex flavors. Chardonnay goes beautifully with most fish courses, but when one adds different aromas and scents to a straightforward fish dish, from either grilling, or from ingredients in an accompanying sauce, Chardonnays are often competitive rather than complementary wines to serve. The basic rule, then, is this: Simple, uncomplex wines with complex dishes, and complex wines with simple dishes.

What are the primary flavors in both the wine and food? A complementary wine choice can often be made if one knows what to expect from the primary flavors in the food to be eaten. Creamy and buttery sauces with fish, lobster, and even chicken or veal work well with Chardonnay or white burgundies because of the buttery, vanillin aromas in the fuller, richer, lustier styles of Chardonnay. On the other hand, a mixed salad with an herb dressing and pieces of grilled fish or shellfish beg for an herbaceous, smoky Sauvignon Blanc or Sancerre or Pouilly-Fumé from the Loire Valley. For the same reason, a steak au poivre in a creamy brown sauce with its intense, pungent aromas and complex flavors requires a big, rich, peppery Rhône wine such as a Châteauneuf-du-Pape or Gigondas.

Is the texture and flavor intensity of the wine proportional to the texture and flavor intensity of the food? Did you ever wonder why fresh, briny, sea-scented oysters that are light and zesty taste so good with a Muscadet from France or lighter-style California Sauvignon Blanc or Italian Pinot Grigio? It is because these wines have the same weight and light texture as the oysters. Why is it that the smoky, sweet, oaky, tangy flavors of a grilled steak or loin of lamb work best with a Zinfandel or Rhône Valley red wine? First, the full-bodied, supple, chewy flavors of these wines complement a steak or loin of lamb cooked over a wood fire. Sauté the same steak or lamb in butter or bake it in the oven, and the flavors are less complex and then require a well-aged Cabernet Sauvignon or Merlot-based wine from California, Bordeaux, or Australia. Another poignant example of the importance of matching the texture and flavor intensity of the wine with the food is the type of fish you have chosen to eat. Salmon, lobster, shad, and bluefish have intense flavors and a fatty texture and therefore require a similarly styled, lusty, oaky, buttery Chardonnay to complement them. On the other hand, trout, sole, turbot, and shrimp are leaner, more delicately flavored fish and therefore mandate lighter, less intense wines such as non-oaked examples of Chardonnay from France's Mâconnais region or Italy's Friuli-Venezia Guilia area. In addition, a lighter-style champagne or German Riesling (a dry Kabinett works ideally) goes extremely well with trout, sole, or turbot but falls on its face if matched against salmon, shad, or lobster.

One further, classic texture and flavor matchup is that of a heavy, unctuous, rich, sweet Sauternes with foie gras. The extravagantly rich and flavorful foie gras cannot be served with any other type of wine, as it would overpower a dry red or a white. That both the Sauternes and the foie gras have intense, concentrated flavors and similar textures is exactly why the combination is so decadently delicious.

What is the style of wine produced in the vintage that you have chosen? Several of France's greatest chefs have told me they prefer off years of Bordeaux and Burgundy to great years and have instructed their sommeliers to buy the wines for the restaurant accordingly. Can this be true?

Yes, it can. From the chef's perspective, the food should be the focal point of the meal, not the wine. Many fear that a great vintage of Burgundy or Bordeaux, with wines that are exceptionally rich, powerful, and concentrated, takes attention away from their cuisine and makes it much more troublesome to match a wine with the food. Thus, many chefs prefer a 1987 Bordeaux on the table with their food as opposed to a superconcentrated 1982 or 1990. For the same reasons they would prefer a 1989 red burgundy over a 1990. Thus, the great vintages, although marvelous wines, are not always the ones to choose if the best matchup with food is desired. Lighter-weight yet tasty wines from so-so years can provide the superior complement to delicate and understated cuisine; save the great vintages for very simple food courses.

Is the food to be served in a sauce? Fifteen years ago, when eating at Michel Guerard's restaurant in Eugénie-les-Bains, I ordered a course where the fish was served in a red wine sauce. Guerard recommended a red Graves wine from Bordeaux since the sauce was made from a reduction of fish stock and a red Graves. The combination was successful and opened my eyes to the possibilities of fish with red wine. Since then I have had tuna with a green peppercorn sauce with California Cabernet Sauvignon (the matchup was great) and salmon sautéed in a red wine sauce that did justice to a young vintage of red Bordeaux. A white wine with any of these courses would not have worked. For the same reason I have enjoyed veal in a creamy Morilles sauce with a Tokay from Alsace. A corollary to this principle of letting the sauce dictate the type of wine you order is where the actual food is prepared with a specific type of wine. For example, coq au vin, an exquisite peasant dish, can be cooked and served in either a white wine or a red wine sauce. I have found that with coq au vin au Riesling, a dry Alsace Riesling is a simply extraordinary accompaniment. In Burgundy I have often had coq au vin in a red wine sauce consisting of a reduced burgundy wine, and here a red burgundy makes the dish even more special.

When you travel, do you drink locally produced wines with the local cuisine? It is no coincidence that the regional cuisines of Bordeaux, Burgundy, Provence, and Alsace in France and Tuscany and Piedmont in Italy seem to enhance and complement the local wines. In fact, most restaurants in these areas rarely offer wines from outside the local region. One always wonders which came first, the cuisine or the wine? Certainly America is beginning to develop its own regional cuisine, but except for California and the Pacific Northwest, few areas promote the local wines as appropriate matchups with the local cuisine. For example, in my backyard a number of small wineries make an excellent white wine called Seyval Blanc that is the perfect foil for both the oysters and blue channel crabs from the Chesapeake Bay. Yet few restaurants in the Baltimore-Washington area promote these local wines, which is a shame. Regional wines with regional foods should be a top priority when traveling not only in Europe, but in America's viticultural areas.

Have you learned the best and worst wine and food matchups? If wine and food combinations still perplex you, your best strategy may be to learn some of the greatest combinations as well as some of the worst. I can also add a few pointers I have learned through my own experiences, usually bad ones. Certain wine and food relationships of contrasting flavors can be sublime. Perhaps the best example is a sweet, creamy-textured Sauternes wine with a salty, aged Stilton or Roquefort cheese. This particular combination of two opposite sets of flavors and textures is sensational. Another great combination is Alsace Gewürztraminers and Rieslings with ethnic cuisine such as Indian and Chinese. The sweet-and-sour juxtapositions in Oriental cuisine and the spiciness of both cuisines seem to work beautifully with these two Alsatian wines.

One of the great myths about wine and food matchups is that red wines work well with cheese. The truth is they rarely ever work well together. So many cheeses, especially favorite wine cheeses such as Brie and double and triple creams, have such a high fat content that most red wines suffer incredibly when drunk with them. If you want to shock your guests but also enjoy wine with cheese, serve a white wine made from a Sauvignon Blanc grape, such as a Sancerre or Pouilly-Fumé, from France. The dynamic personalities of these two wines and their tangy, zesty acidity stand up well to virtually all types of cheese, but they go especially well with fresh goat cheeses.

Another myth is that dessert wines go best with desserts. Most people seem to like champagne or a sweet Riesling, sweet Chenin blanc, or a Sauternes with dessert. I find that dessert wines are best served *as* the dessert or after the dessert. Whether the dessert is cake, fruit tarts, ice cream or candy (except for chocolate-based desserts, which are always in conflict with any type of wine), I've always enjoyed dessert wines more as the centerpiece of attention than as accompaniment.

If wine and food matchups still seem too complicated for you, remember that in the final analysis, a good wine served with a good dish to good company is always in good taste. *À votre santé.*

What's Been Added to Your Wine?

Over the last decade people have become much more sensitive to what they put in their bodies. The hazards of excessive smoking, fat consumption, and high blood pressure are now taken seriously by increasing numbers of people, not just in America but in Europe as well. Although this movement is to be applauded, an extremist group, labeled by observers as "neo-Prohibitionists" or "new drys," have tried to exploit the individual's interest in good health by promoting the idea that consumption of any alcoholic beverage is an inherently dangerous abuse that undermines society and family. These extremist groups do not care about moderation; they want the total elimination of wine (one of alcohol's evil spirits) from the marketplace. Thus they have misrepresented wine and consistently ignored specific data that demonstrates that moderate wine drinking is more beneficial than harmful to individuals. Unfortunately, the law prohibits the wine industry from promoting the proven health benefits of wine.

Wine is one of the most natural of all beverages, but it is true that additives can be included in a wine (the neo-Prohibitionists are taking aim at these as being potentially lethal). Following are items that can be added to wine:

Acids Most cool-climate vineyards never need to add acidity to wine, but in California and Australia, hot-climate areas whose grapes often lack enough natural acidity, acid is often added to give balance to the wines. Most serious wineries add tartaric acid, the same type of acidity found naturally in wine. Less quality-oriented wineries dump in pure citric acid, which gives the wine a lemon-lime-sorbet taste.

Clarification Agents A list of items dumped into wine to coagulate suspended particles includes morbid names such as dried ox blood, isinglass, casein (milk powder), kaolin (clay), bentonite (powdered clay), and the traditional egg whites. These fining agents are designed to make the wine brilliant and particle-free; they are harmless, and top wineries either don't use them or use them minimally.

Oak Many top-quality red and white wines spend most of their lives aging in oak barrels. It is expected that wine stored in wood will take on some of the toasty, smoky, vanillin flavors of wood. These aromas and flavors, if not overdone, add flavor complexity to a wine. Cheap wine can also be marginally enhanced by the addition of oak chips that provide a more aggressive, raw flavor of wood.

Sugar In most of the viticultural regions of Europe except for southern France, Portugal, and Spain, the law permits the addition of sugar to the fermenting grape juice in order to raise alcohol levels. This practice, called "chaptalization," is most commonly performed in cool years where the grapes do not attain sufficient ripeness (in California and most of Australia, where the hot climate promotes ripening, chaptalization is unnecessary). Judicious chaptalization raises the alcohol level 1%–2%.

Sulfites All wines must now carry a label indicating whether they contain sulfites. Sulfite (also referred to as SO_2 or sulphur dioxide) is a preservative used to kill bacteria and microorganisms. It is sprayed on virtually all fresh vegetables and fruits, but a tiny percentage of the population is allergic to SO_2, especially some asthmatics. The fermentation of wine produces some sulfur dioxide naturally, but it is also added by burning a sulfur stick inside the oak barrel to kill any bacteria; it is added again at bottling to prevent the wine from oxidizing. Quality wines should never smell of sulfur (a burning match smell) because serious winemakers keep the sulfur level very low. Some wineries do not employ sulfites. When used properly, sulfites impart no smell or taste to the wine and, except for those who have a known allergy to them, are harmless to the general population. Used excessively, sulfites impart the aforementioned unpleasant smell and a prickly taste sensation. Obviously people who are allergic to sulfites should not drink wine, just as people who are allergic to fish roe should not eat caviar.

Tannin   Tannin occurs naturally in the skins and stems of grapes, and the content from the crushing of the grape skins and subsequent maceration of the skins and juice is usually more than adequate to provide sufficient natural tannin. Tannin gives a red wine grip and backbone, as well as acting as a preservative. However, on rare occasions tannin is added to a spineless wine.

Yeasts   Although many winemakers rely on the indigenous wild yeasts in the vineyard to start the fermentation, it is becoming more common to employ cultured yeasts for this procedure. There is no health hazard here, but increasing reliance on the same type of yeast for wines from all over the world leads to wines with similar bouquets and flavors.

Organic Wines

Organic wines, those that are produced without fungicides, pesticides, or chemical fertilizers, with no additives or preservatives, continue to gain considerable consumer support. In principle, organic wines should be as excellent as nonorganic. Because most organic wine producers avoid manipulating and processing their wines, the consumer receives a product that is far more natural than wines that have been manufactured and processed to death.

There is tremendous potential for huge quantities of organic wines, particularly from viticultural areas that enjoy copious quantities of sunshine and wind, the so-called Mediterranean climate. In France, the Languedoc-Roussillon region, Provence, and the Rhône Valley have the potential to produce organic wines if their proprietors desire. Much of California could do so as well. Parts of Australia and Italy also have weather conditions that encourage the development of organic vineyards.

Readers who want to pursue this further should read, *The Consumer's Guide to Organic Wine,* by Robert Johnson and Richard Pasichnyk and published in 1993 by Rowan and Littlefield Publishers, Inc.

Following is a list of producers just beginning to produce fine wines from organically cultivated vineyards:

Château Beaucastel Châteauneuf-du-Pape (Rhône)

Bellerose Vineyard (Sonoma)

Chapoutier (Rhône) *Note:* not yet completely organic, but this large firm will soon be

Clos de la Coulée de Sérrant—N. Joly (Savennières)

Daniel Combe (Rhône)

Coturri and Sons (California)

Domaine du Vas Deffens Coteaux Varois (France)

Fetzer Vineyard (Mendocino) *Note:* not all Fetzer wines are organically produced, so be sure to check the label

Frey Vineyards (Mendocino)
Pierre Frick (Alsace)
Domaine de la Gautière Vin de Pays (France)
Domaine Gramenon (Rhône)
Hallcrest Vineyards (Santa Cruz Mountains)
Hess Collection Winery (Napa)
Hidden Cellars (Mendocino)
Marcel Lapierre (Morgon-Beaujolais)
Leclerc-Briant (Champagne)
Domaine Leflaive (Puligny-Montrachet) *Note:* not yet fully organic, but moving in that direction
Leroy (Vosne-Romanée) *Note:* starting with the 1991 vintage
Mas Daumas-Gassac (France)
Pavie-Macquin (St.-Émilion)
Noel Pinguet-Domaine Huet (Vouvray)
Domaine Richeaume (Provence)
Domaine de la Romanée-Conti (Vosne-Romanée) *Note:* starting with the 1993 vintage
Domaine Terres Blanches Coteaux d'Aix-en-Provence Les Baux (France)
Topolos Winery (Sonoma)
Domaine de Torraccia (Corsica, France)

THE DARK SIDE OF WINE

The Growing International Neutralization of Wine Styles

Although technology allows winemakers to produce better and better quality wine, the continuing obsession with technical perfection is stripping wines of their distinctive character. Whether because of the excessive filtration of wines or excessive emulation of winemaking styles, it is, tragically, becoming increasingly difficult to tell an Italian Chardonnay from one made in France or California or Australia. When the world's corporate winemakers begin to make wines in the same way, designing them to offend the least number of people, wine will no doubt lose its fascinating appeal and individualism, becoming no better than most brands of whiskey, gin, Scotch, or vodka. One must not forget that the great appeal of wine is that it is a unique, distinctive, fascinating beverage, different every time one drinks it. Winemakers and the owners of wineries, particularly in America, must learn to preserve the individual character of their wines, even at the risk of alienating those consumers who may find them bizarre or unusual. It is the distinctive quality of wine that will ensure its future.

Destroying the Joy of Wine by Excessive Acidification and Filtration

Since the beginning of my career as a professional wine critic, I have tried to present a strong case against the excessive manipulation of wine. One look at the world's greatest producers and their wines will irrefutably reveal that the following characteristics are shared by all of them:

1. They are driven to preserve the integrity of the vineyard's character, the varietal's identity, and the vintage's personality.
2. They believe in low crop yields.
3. Weather permitting, they harvest only physiologically mature (versus analytically ripe) fruit.
4. Their winemaking and cellar techniques are simplistic in that they themselves are minimal interventionists, preferring to permit the wine to make itself.
5. Although they are not opposed to fining or filtrating unstable or unclear wine, they will absolutely refuse to strip (by excessive fining and filtration) a wine that is made from healthy, ripe grapes and is already stable and clear.

Producers who care only about making wine as fast as possible and collecting their accounts receivable quickly also have many things in common. Although they turn out neutral, vapid, mediocre wines, they are also believers in huge crop yields, with considerable fertilization to promote massive crops, as large as the vineyard can render (6 or more tons per acre, compared with modest yields of 3 tons per acre). Their philosophy is that the vineyard is a manufacturing plant and cost efficiency dictates that production be maximized. They rush their wine into bottle as quickly as possible in order to get paid. They believe in processing wine, such as centrifuging it initially, then practicing multiple fining and filtration procedures, particularly a denuding sterile filtration. This guarantees a wine that is lifeless, but stable—a product able to withstand temperature extremes and stand upright on a grocery store's shelf at the expense of its quality and individuality. These wineries harvest earlier than anybody else because they are unwilling to take risks, delegating all questions regarding wine to their oenologists, who rate security and stability over the consumer's goal of finding joy in wine.

The effect of this excessive manipulation, particularly overly aggressive fining and filtration, is dramatic. It destroys a wine's bouquet as well as its ability to express its *terroir* and varietal character. It also mutes the vintage's character. Fining and filtration can be lightly done, causing only minor damage, but most wines produced in the New World (California, Australia, and South America in particular) and most bulk wines produced in Europe are sterile-filtered. This stability and clarification procedure, which requires numerous prefiltrations to get the wines clean enough to pass through a micropore membrane filter, strips, eviscerates, and denudes a wine of much of its character.

Some wines can suffer such abuse with less damage. Thick, tannic, concentrated Syrah- and Cabernet Sauvignon–based wines may even survive these wine lobotomies, diminished in aromatic and flavor dimension but still alive. Wines such as Pinot Noir and Chardonnay are destroyed in the process.

Thanks to a new generation of producers, particularly in France, and aided by a number of specialist importers from America, there has been a recent movement against unnecessary fining and filtration. One only has to look at the extraordinary success enjoyed by such American importers as Kermit Lynch and Robert Kacher to realize how much consumer demand exists for producers to bottle a natural, unfiltered, uncompromised wine that is a faithful representation of its vineyard and vintage. Most serious wine consumers do not mind not being able to drink the last half ounce because of sediment. They know this means they are getting a flavorful, authentic, unprocessed wine that is much more representative than one that has been stripped at bottling.

Other small importers who have joined forces with Lynch and Kacher include Peter Weygandt of Weygandt-Metzler, Unionville, PA; Neal Rosenthal Select Vineyards, New York, NY; Eric Solomon of European Cellars, New York, NY; Louis/Dressner Selections, New York, NY; and Martine Saunier of Martine's Wines, San Rafael, CA. Because these (and other U.S.) importers often insist that their producers not filter those wines shipped to the United States, a richer, more ageworthy wine is now being sold in America than elsewhere in the world.

I am certain there would have been an even more powerful movement to bottle wines naturally with minimal clarification if the world's wine press had examined the effect of excessive fining and filtration. I find it difficult to criticize many American wine writers since the majority of them are part-timers. Few have either the time or resources to taste the same wines before and after bottling. Yet I remain disappointed that many of our most influential writers and publications have remained strangely silent, particularly in view of the profound negative impact filtration can have on the quality of fine wine. The English wine writing corps, which includes many veteran, full-time wine writers, has an appalling record on this issue, especially in view of the fact that many of them make it a practice to taste before and after bottling. Considering the number who care about the quality of wine, and the preservation of the character of the vineyard, vintage, and varietal, the reluctance of so many writers to criticize the wine industry undermines the entire notion of wine appreciation.

Even a wine writer of the stature of Hugh Johnson comes out strongly on the side of processed, neutral wines that can be shipped safely 12 months of the year. Readers may want to consider comments made by Johnson and his coauthor, James Halliday, in their book, *The Vintner's Art—How Great Wines Are Made*. Halliday is an Australian wine writer and winery owner, and Hugh Johnson, who may be this century's most widely read wine author, is a member of the board of directors of Château Latour and a merchant selling reproductions of antique wine paraphernalia. In their book they chastise American importer Kermit Lynch for his "romantic ideals," which they describe as "increasingly impractical." Johnson and Halliday assert that "the truth is that a good fifty percent of those artisan burgundies and Rhônes are bacterial time bombs." Their plea for compromised and standardized wines is supported by the following observation: "The hard reality is that many restaurants and many consumers simply will not accept sediment." This may have been partially true in America twenty years ago, but today the consumer not only wants, but demands a natural wine. Moreover, the wine consumer understands that sediment in a bottle of fine wine is a healthy sign. The authors' contention—that modern-day winemaking and commercial necessity require wines to be shipped 12 months a year and be durable enough to withstand months on retailers' shelves in both cold and hot temperature conditions—is highly debatable. America now has increasing numbers of responsible merchants, importers, and restaurant sommeliers who go to great lengths to guarantee the client a healthy bottle of wine that has not been abused. Astonishingly, Johnson and Halliday conclude that consumers cannot tell the difference between a filtered and nonfiltered wine! In summarizing their position, they state, "But leave the wine for 1, 2, or 3 months (one cannot tell how long the recovery process will take), and it is usually impossible to tell the filtered from the nonfiltered wine, provided the filtration at bottling was skillfully carried out." After 14 years of conducting such tastings, I find this statement not only unbelievable, but insupportable! Am I to conclude that all of the wonderful wines I have tasted from cask that were subsequently damaged by vigorous fining and filtration were bottled by incompetent people who did not know how to filter? Am I to think that the results of the extensive comparative tastings (usually blind) that I have done of the same wine, filtered versus unfiltered, were bogus? Are the enormous aromatic, flavor, textural, and qualitative differences that are the result of vigorous clarification techniques figments of my imagination? Astoundingly, the wine industry's reluctance to accept responsibility for preserving all that the best vineyards and vintages can achieve is excused rather than condemned.

If excessive fining and filtration are not bad enough, consider the overzealous additions of citric and tartaric acids employed by Australian and California oenologists to perk up their wines. You know the feeling—you open a bottle of Australian or California Chardonnay, and not only is there no bouquet (because it was sterile-filtered), but tasting the wine is like biting into a fresh lemon or lime. It is not enjoyable. What you are experiencing is the result of the misguided practice among New World winemakers of adding too much acidity as a cheap but fatal life insurance policy for their wines. Because they are unwilling to reduce their yields, because they are unwilling to assume any risk, and because they see winemaking as nothing more than a processing technique, acidity is added generously. It does serve as an antibacterial, antioxidant agent, thus helping to keep the wine fresh. But those who acidify the most are usually those who harvest appallingly high crop yields. Thus there is little flavor to protect! After 6–12 months of bottle age, what little fruit is present fades, and the consumer is left with a skeleton of sharp, shrill acid levels, alcohol, wood (if utilized), and no fruit—an utterly reprehensible way of making wine.

I do not object to the use of these techniques for bulk and jug wines, which the consumer is buying for value or because of brand-name recognition. But it is shameful for any producer to sell a wine as a handcrafted, artisan product at $20 or more a bottle, when the wine has been subjected to excessive acidification, fining, and filtration. Anyone who tells you that excessive acidification, fining, and filtration do not damage a wine is either a fool or a liar.

The Inflated Wine Pricing of Restaurants

Given the amount of money Americans spend eating at restaurants, it seems obvious that savvy restaurant owners could promote an enhanced awareness of wine by encouraging its consumption at restaurants. Unfortunately, most restaurants treat wine as a luxury item, marking it up an exorbitant 200%–500%, thereby effectively discouraging its consumption and reinforcing the mistaken notion that wine is only for the elite and the superrich.

The wine industry does little about this practice, being content merely to see its wines placed on a restaurant's list. But the consumer should revolt and avoid those restaurants that charge exorbitant wine prices, no matter how sublime the cuisine. I stopped going to New York's Le Bernardin years ago because of wine prices that reflect a 400%–500% markup, even though the food is spectacular. The Inn at Little Washington, Virginia, considered by many food critics to be this country's finest eating establishment, displays equally appalling markups. This is nothing more than legitimized mugging of the consumer.

Fortunately, things are slightly better today than they were a decade ago, as some restaurant owners now regard wine as an integral part of the meal and not merely as a device to increase the bill.

Collectors versus Consumers

I have reluctantly come to believe that many of France's greatest wine treasures—the first-growths of Bordeaux, including the famous sweet nectar made at Château d'Yquem; Burgundy's most profound red wines from the Domaine de la Romanée-Conti; and virtually all of the wines from the tiny white wine appellation of Montrachet—are never drunk, or should I say swallowed. Most of us who purchase or cellar wine do so on the theory that eventually every one of our splendid bottles will be swirled, sloshed, sniffed, sipped, and, yes, guzzled with friends. That, of course, is one of the joys of wine, and those of you who partake of this pleasure are true wine lovers. There are, however, other types of wine collectors—the collector-investor, the collector-spitter, and even the nondrinking collector. Needless to say, these people are not avid consumers.

Several years ago I remember being deluged with telephone calls from a man wanting me to have dinner with him and tour his private cellar. After several months of resisting, I finally succumbed. A very prominent businessman, he had constructed an impressive cellar beneath his sprawling home. It was enormous, and immaculately kept, with state-of-the-art humidity and temperature controls. I suspect it contained in excess of ten thousand bottles. Although there were cases of such thoroughbreds as Pétrus, Lafite-Rothschild, Mouton-Rothschild, and rare vintages of the great red burgundies such as Romanée-Conti and La Tâche, to my astonishment there were also hundreds of cases of 10- and 15-year-old Beaujolais, Pouilly-Fuissé, Dolcetto, and California Chardonnays—all wines that should have been drunk during their first 4 or 5 years of life. I diplomatically suggested that he should inventory his cellar, as there seemed to be a number of wines that mandated immediate consumption.

About the time I spotted the fifth or sixth case of what was clearly 10-year-old Beaujolais vinegar, I began to doubt the sincerity of my host's enthusiasm for wine. These unthinkable doubts (I was much more naive then than I am now) were amplified at dinner. As we entered the sprawling kitchen and dining room complex, he announced proudly that neither he nor his wife actually drank wine and then asked if I would care for a glass of mineral water, iced tea, or, if I preferred, a bottle of wine. On my sorrow-filled drive home that evening, I lamented the fact that I had not opted for the mineral water. For when I made the mistake of requesting wine with the meal, my host proceeded to grab a bottle of wine that one of his friends had suggested should be consumed immediately. It was a brown-colored, utterly repugnant, senile Bordeaux from perhaps the worst vintage in the last 25 years, 1969. Furthermore, the château chosen was a notorious underachiever from the famous commune of Pauillac. Normally the wine he chose does not merit buying in a good vintage, much less a pathetic one. I shall never forget my host opening the bottle and saying, "Well, Bob, this wine sure smells good."

Regrettably, this nondrinking collector continues to buy large quantities of wine, not for investment and obviously not for drinking. The local wine merchants tell me his type is not rare. To him, a collection of wine is like a collection of crystal, art, sculpture, or china, something to be admired, to be shown off, but never, ever to be consumed.

More ostentatious by far is the collector-spitter, who thrives on gigantic tastings where 50, 60, sometimes even 70 or 80 vintages of great wines, often from the same châteaux, can be "tasted." Important members of the wine press are invited (no charge, of course) in the hope that this wine happening will merit a major article in *The New York Times* or *Los Angeles Times* and the collector's name will become recognized and revered in the land of winedom. These collector-spitters relish rubbing elbows with famous proprietors and telling their friends, "Oh, I'll be at Château Lafite-Rothschild next week to taste all of the château's wines between 1870 and 1987. Sorry you can't be there." I have, I confess, participated in several of these events and have learned from the exercise of trying to understand them that their primary purpose is to feed the sponsor's enormous ego and often the château's ego as well.

I am not against academic tastings, where a limited number of serious wine enthusiasts sit down to taste 20 or 30 different wines (usually young ones), because that is a manageable number that both neophytes and connoisseurs can generally grasp. But to taste 60 or more rare and monumental vintages at an 8- or 12-hour tasting marathon is carrying excess to its extreme. Most simply, what seems to happen at these tastings is that much of the world's greatest, rarest, and most expensive wines are spit out. No wine taster I have ever met could conceivably remain sober, even if only the greatest wines were swallowed. I can assure you, there is only remorse in spitting out 1929 or 1945 Mouton-Rothschild.

Other recollections of these events have also long troubled me. I remember vividly one tasting held at a very famous restaurant in Los Angeles where a number of compelling bottles from one of France's greatest estates were opened. Many of the wines were exhilarating. Yet whether it was the otherworldly 1961 or opulent 1947, the reactions I saw on the faces of those 40 or so people, each of whom had paid several thousand dollars to attend, made me wonder whether it was 50 different vintages of France's greatest wines we were tasting or 50 bottles of Pepto-Bismol. Fortunately the organizer did appear to enjoy the gathering and appreciate the wines, but among the guests I never once saw a smile or any enthusiasm or happiness in the course of this extraordinary 12-hour tasting.

I remember another marathon tasting held in France by one of Europe's leading collector-spitters, which lasted all day and much of the night. Over 90 legendary wines were served, and midway through the afternoon I was reasonably certain there was not a sober individual remaining except for the chef and his staff. By the time the magnum of 1929 Mouton-Rothschild was served (one of the century's greatest wines), I do not think there was a guest left competent enough to know whether he was drinking claret or Beaujolais, myself included.

I have also noticed at these tastings that many collector-spitters did not even know that a bottle was corked (had the smell of moldy cardboard and was defective) or that a bottle was oxidized and undrinkable, adding truth to the old saying that money does not always buy good taste. Of course, most of these tastings are media happenings designed to stroke the host's vanity. All too frequently they undermine the principle that wine is a beverage of pleasure, and that is my basic regret.

The third type of collector, the investor, is motivated by the possibility of reselling the wines for profit. Eventually most or all of these wines return to the marketplace, and many of them wend their way into the hands of serious consumers who share them with their spouses or good friends. Of course they often must pay dearly for the privilege, but wine is not the only product that falls prey to such manipulation. I hate to think of wine being thought of primarily as an investment, but the world's finest wines do appreciate significantly in value, and it would be foolish to ignore the fact that more and more shrewd investors are looking at wine as a way of making money.

Unspeakable Practices

It is a frightening thought, but I have no doubt that a sizable percentage (between 10% and 25%) of the wines sold in America has been damaged because of exposure to extremes of heat. Smart consumers have long been aware of the signs of poor storage. They have only to look at the bottle (see pages 13–14).

The problem, of course, is that too few people in the wine trade take the necessary steps to assure that the wine is not ruined in shipment or storage. The wine business has become so commercial that wines, whether from California, Italy, or France, are shipped 12 months of the year, regardless of weather conditions. Traditionally, wines from Europe were shipped only in the spring or fall, when the temperatures encountered in shipment would be moderate, assuming they were not shipped by way of the Panama Canal. The cost of renting an air-conditioned or heated container for shipping wines adds anywhere from 20 to 40 cents to the wholesale cost of the bottle, but when buying wines that cost over $200 a case, the purchaser most likely will not mind paying the extra premium, knowing that the wine will not smell or taste cooked when opened.

Many importers claim to ship in reefers (the trade jargon for temperature-controlled containers), but only a handful actually do. America's largest importer of high-quality Bordeaux wine rarely, if ever, uses reefers and claims to have had no problems with their shipments. Perhaps they would change their minds if they had witnessed the cases of 1986 Rausan-Ségla, 1986 Talbot, 1986 Gruaud-Larose, and 1986 Château Margaux that arrived in the Maryland-Washington, D.C., market with stained labels and pushed-out corks.

Somewhere between Bordeaux and Washington, D.C., these wines had been exposed to torrid temperatures. It may not have been the fault of the importer, as the wine passed through a number of intermediaries before reaching its final destination. But pity the poor consumer who buys this wine, puts it in his cellar, and opens it 10 or 15 years in the future. Who will grieve for him?

The problem with temperature extremes is that the naturally made, minimally processed, hand-produced wines are the most vulnerable to this kind of abuse. Therefore many importers, not wanting to assume any risks, have gone back to their suppliers and demanded "more stable" wines. Translated into real terms, this means the wine trade prefers to ship not living wines, but vapid, denuded wines that have been "stabilized," subjected to a manufacturing process and either pasteurized or sterile-filtered so they can be shipped 12 months a year. Their corks may still pop out if subjected to enough heat, but their taste will not change, because for all intents and purposes these wines are already dead when they are put in the bottle. Unfortunately only a small segment of the wine trade seems to care.

Although some wine merchants, wholesalers, and importers are cognizant of the damage that can be done when wines are not protected, and take great pride in representing handmade, quality products, the majority of the wine trade continues to ignore the risks. They would prefer that the wines be denuded by pasteurization, cold stabilization, or a sterile filtration. Only then can they be shipped safely under any weather conditions.

Wine Producers' Greed

Are today's wine consumers being hoodwinked by the world's wine producers? Most growers and/or producers have intentionally permitted production yields to soar to such extraordinary levels that the concentration and character of their wines are in jeopardy. There remain a handful of fanatics who continue, at some financial sacrifice, to reject a significant proportion of their harvest so that only the finest-quality wine is sold under their name. However, they are dwindling in number. Fewer producers are prepared to go into the vineyard and cut bunches of grapes to reduce the yields. Fewer still are willing to cut back prudently on fertilizers. For much of the last decade production yields throughout the world continued to break records with each new vintage. The results are wines that increasingly lack character, concentration, and staying power. In Europe, the most flagrant abuses of overproduction occur in Germany and Burgundy, where yields today are 3 to almost 5 times what they were in the 1950s. It is misleading to argue that the vineyards are more carefully and competently managed, and that this results in larger crops. Off the record, many a seriously committed wine producer will tell you that "the smaller the yield, the better the wine."

If one wonders why the Domaine Leroy's burgundies taste richer than those from other domaines, consider the fact that its yields are one-third those of other Burgundy producers. If one asks why the best Châteauneuf-du-Papes are generally Rayas, Pegau, Bonneau, and Beaucastel, the answer is because their yields are one-half those of other producers of the appellation. The same assertion applies to J. J. Prüm and Müller-Cattoir in Germany: not surprisingly, they too have conservative crop yields that produce one-third the amount of wine of their neighbors.

Although I do not want to suggest there are no longer any great wines, or that most of the wines now produced are no better than the plonk peasants drank in the nineteenth century, I do wish to point out that overfertilization, modern sprays that prevent rot, the development of highly prolific clonal selections, and the failure to keep production levels modest have all resulted in yields that may well combine to destroy the reputations of many of the most famous wine regions of the world. Finding a flavorful Chardonnay from California today is not much easier than finding a concentrated red burgundy that can age gracefully beyond 10 years. The production yields of Chardonnay in California have often resulted in wines with only a faint character of the grape, that seem dominated almost entirely by acidity and/or the smell of oak barrels. What is appalling is that there is so little intrinsic flavor. Yet Chardonnays remain the most popular white wine in this country, so what incentive is there to lower yields?

Of course, if the public, encouraged by noncritical, indifferent wine writers, is willing to pay top dollar for mediocrity, then little is likely to change. On the other hand, if consumers start insisting that $15 or $20 should at the very minimum fetch a wine that provides far more pleasure, perhaps that message will gradually work its way back to the producers.

Wine Writers' Ethics and Competence

The problems just described have only occasionally been acknowledged by wine writers, who generally have a collective mind-set of never having met a wine they didn't like.

Wine writing in America has rarely been a profitable or promising full-time occupation. Historically, the most interesting work was done by the people who sold wine. There's no doubting the influence or importance of the books written by Alexis Lichine and Frank Schoonmaker. But both men made their fortunes by selling, rather than writing about, wine, even though both managed to write about wine objectively despite their ties to the trade.

There are probably not more than a dozen or so independent wine experts in this country who support themselves entirely by writing. Great Britain has long championed the cause of wine writers and looked upon them as true professionals. But even there, with all their experience and access to the finest European vineyards, most of the successful wine writers have been involved in the sale and distribution of wine. Can anyone name an English wine writer who criticized the performance of Lafite-Rothschild between 1961 and 1974 or Margaux between 1964 and 1977 (periods when the consumer was getting screwed)?

It is probably unrealistic to expect writers to develop a professional expertise with wine without access and support from the trade, but such support can compromise their findings. If they are beholden to wine producers for the wines they taste, they are not likely to fault them. If the trips they make to vineyards are the result of the winemaker's largesse, they are unlikely to criticize what they have seen. If they are lodged at the châteaux and their trunks are filled with cases of wine (as, sadly, is often the case), can a consumer expect them to be critical or even objective?

Beyond the foolish notion that a wine writer is going to bite the hand that feeds him, there is another problem: many wine writers lack the global experience essential to properly evaluate wine. Consequently, what has emerged from such inexperience is a school of wine writing that emphasizes evaluation of a wine's structure and acid levels rather than the level of pleasure a wine provides or is capable of providing in the future. The results are wine evaluations that read as though one were measuring the industrial strength of different grades of cardboard instead of a beverage that many consider nature's greatest gift to mankind. Balance is everything in wine, and wines that taste too tart or tannic rarely ever age into flavorful, distinctive, charming beverages. Although winemaking and wine technology are indeed better, and some of the most compelling wines ever made are being produced today, far too many mediocre wines are sitting on the shelves that hardly deserve their high praise.

There are, however, some interesting trends. The growth of *The Wine Spectator,* with its staff of full-time writers obligated to follow a code of ethics, has resulted in better and more professional journalism. It also cannot be discounted that this flashy magazine appears twice a month, good news for a wine industry frequently under siege by the antialcohol extremists. Some may protest the inflated ratings that *The Wine Spectator*'s tasting panel tends to bestow, but tasting is, as we all should know, subjective. The only criticism some might have is that their wine evaluations are the result of a committee's vote. Wines of great individuality and character rarely win a committee tasting because at least one taster will find something objectionable about them. Therefore, tasting panels, where all grades are averaged, frequently find wines of great individuality unusual. Can anyone name just one of the world's greatest red or white wines that is produced by the consensus of a committee? The wines that too often score the highest are those that are technically correct and designed to please the greatest number of people. Wouldn't most Americans prefer a hamburger from McDonald's than seared salmon served over a bed of lentils at New York City's famed Le Montrachet restaurant? The results of numerous California wine judgings support the same conclusion—many a truly great, individualistic, and original wine has no chance. The winners are too often fail-safe, technically correct, spit-polished, and clean examples of winemaking—in short, wines for fans of Velveeta cheese, Muzak, and frozen dinners. The opinion of an individual taster, despite that taster's prejudices and predilections (if reasonably informed and comprehensive), is always a far greater guide to the ultimate quality of the wine than that of a committee. At least the reader knows where the individual stands, while with a committee one is never quite sure.

Given the vitality of *The Wine Spectator* and a few other wine guides, it is unlikely that wine writers will have less influence in the future. The thousands and thousands of wines that come on the market, many of them overpriced and vapid, require consumer-oriented reviews from the wine-writing community. But until a greater degree of professionalism is attained, until more experience is evidenced by wine writers, until their misinformed emphasis on a wine's high acidity and structure is discredited forever, until most of the English wine media begin to understand and adhere to the basic rules against conflict of interest, until we all remember that this is only a beverage of pleasure, to be consumed seriously but not taken too seriously, then and only then will the quality of wine writing and the wines we drink improve. Will all of this happen, or will we be reminded of the words of Marcel Proust:

We do not succeed in changing things according to our desire, but gradually our desire changes. The situation that we hope to change because it was intolerable becomes unimportant. We have not managed to surmount the obstacle as we are absolutely determined to do, but life has taken us round to it, let us pass it, and then if we turn round to gaze at the road past, we can barely catch sight of it, so imperceptible has it become.

WINE TRENDS IN THE MARKETPLACE

Some General Observations about American Wines

1. California had a terrific vintage for white and red wines in 1990 and a very good one in 1991. Additionally, 1992 was an abundant year of good quality. These 3 consecutive quality crops should encourage sharp consumer interest, especially if the producers keep prices reasonable.
2. Zinfandel, the red, full-blooded type, is California's hottest wine. It has more personality than most California Cabernets, is easier to drink because it is more opulent, not to mention less tannic, and is moderately priced, rarely costing more than $15 a bottle.
3. California continues to lead the world in making uninteresting, highly processed wines that are excessively acidified and have little aromas and stripped, washed-out flavors because the wines are eviscerated by multiple filtrations. Many of that state's most famous wineries—Inglenook, Sterling, Buena Vista, Rutherford Hill, Chappellet, and Sebastiani—to name some of the best known, have put blind faith in oenology and the latest state-of-the-art equipment designed to give the consumer a spit-polished, sterile, stable, uniform, superclean product that is not likely to offend anyone—or for that matter, provide any joy. Winemaking in the New World has gone amok, placing commercial expedience and practicality over the consumer's desire to find pleasure. Consumers need to reject $15 Chardonnays and $20 Cabernets that have no bouquets, shrill levels of added acidity, and harsh tannins that attack the palate—and demand products that provide pleasure. My pick as the most exciting wine region of California in the upcoming years is Santa Barbara. Exceptional Pinot Noir and Chardonnay, in addition to highly promising Syrah, Mourvedre, Viognier, and Cabernet Franc, should cause an explosion of interest in this area.
4. The Pacific Northwest will become an increasingly reliable source of high-quality wine. Oregon continues to have too many thin, poorly made wines,

and although considerable potential exists in that state, most of it remains unrealized. However, Washington State is surging in popularity as more and more consumers discover the values and pleasures of its wines. Moreover, prices are lower than for California wines of similar quality.

5. The American wine industry will continue to suffer from excessive production and a shortage of buyers. This will result in increased bankruptcies, consolidations, and the dumping of excess stock. The good news for consumers is that sales will be plentiful and quality will have to improve.

Some General Observations about European Wines

1. All of Europe enjoyed 2 historic as well as great vintages in 1989 and 1990. Most of Europe had mediocre years in 1991 and 1992. The message could not be clearer—buy the 1989s and 1990s!
2. France's Bordeaux, red burgundy, Alsace, Loire Valley, Hermitage, and Châteauneuf-du-Pape, Italy's Piedmont and Tuscany, and all of Germany's wine regions had a very great vintage in 1990. The 1990s from the top producers of these regions are must-buys.
3. The days of purchasing Bordeaux or burgundy futures are over. There is no need for a consumer to put up money in advance of the wine's delivery, as the marketplace continues to be bloated with fine wine.
4. Europe's hottest red wines are from France's Rhône Valley.
5. For under $10 a bottle, the red wines from France's Languedoc-Roussillon region represent the greatest wine values in the world.
6. The 1992 European vintage is not the catastrophe that the wine media reported. Although heavy rains did cause major flooding, much of the rain was highly localized. Top quality will emerge from Germany, Alsace, parts of the Loire Valley, and Burgundy's Côte de Beaune. Moreover, other areas, especially the Rhône Valley and Bordeaux, were not damaged as heavily by harvest rains as initially believed. Quality is frightfully uneven, but pleasant surprises will abound.
7. Europe's finest white wine values continue to be those from France's Côte de Gascogne and from small, unheralded estates in Germany, many of which are represented by America's foremost German wine specialist, Terry Theise of Washington, D.C.
8. Look for the popularity of small specialist importers such as the firms listed below (many of them sell regionally, not nationally) to increase as consumer demand for unprocessed, authentic, unfiltered wines grows. Moreover, America's largest national importers are reluctant to deal with producers who do not make enough wine to sell nationally. And, lamentably, they do not want to make the effort and pay the additional cost to ship natural, unfiltered wines in temperature-controlled containers and trucks.

AMERICA'S LEADING SPECIALTY IMPORTERS

American B.D. Company, Hawthorne, NJ; 201-423-1200
American Estates, Summit, NJ; 908-273-5060
Arborway Imports, Lexington, MA; 617-863-1753
Blanchon Cellars, Ft. Washington, PA; 215-646-4866
Robert Chadderdon Selections, New York, NY; 212-757-8185
Châteauneuf Imports, Glendale, CA; 818-548-1200

Classic Wine Imports, Boston, MA; 617-731-6644
Empson (USA), Inc., Alexandria, VA; 703-684-0900
Estate Wines, San Rafael, CA; 415-492-9411
European Cellars, New York, NY; 212-924-4949
Europvin, Watertown, MA; 617-924-7620
J & R Selections, Ltd., Mount Pleasant, MI; 517-772-3695
Hand Picked Selections, Warrenton, VA; 703-347-3471
Ideal Wines, Medford, MA; 617-395-3300
Robert Kacher Selections, Washington, DC; 202-832-9083
Langdon-Shiverick, Chagrin Falls, OH; 216-247-6868
Louis/Dressner Selections, New York, NY; 212-319-8768
Kermit Lynch Selections, Berkeley, CA; 415-524-1524
Martine's Wines, San Rafael, CA; 415-485-1800
Marc de Grazia Wines, Michael Skurnik Selections, Westbury, NY;
    516-338-5900
New Castle Imports, Myrtle Beach, SC; 803-497-8625
Paterno Imports, Chicago, IL; 312-247-7070
Select Vineyards, New York, NY; 212-249-6650
Stacole Imports, Boca Raton, FL; 407-998-0029
Terry Theise Selections, Washington, DC; 202-526-8000
Vias Imports, Inc., Great Neck, NY; 516-487-2300
Vin Divino, Chicago, IL; 312-281-3363
Vineyard Brands, Chester, VT; 802-875-2139
Vinifera Imports, Ronkonkoma, NY; 516-467-5907
Viva Vino Imports, Eddystone, PA; 215-872-1500
Weygandt-Metzler, Unionville, PA; 215-932-2745
Winebow, Inc., HoHoKus, NJ; 201-445-0620
Wines of France, Mountainside, NJ; 908-654-6173
World Shippers and Importers, Philadelphia, PA; 215-732-2018

Some General Observations about the Wines of the Southern Hemisphere

1. Too much cheap, diluted wine continues to arrive from Australia and South America, especially from Chile.
2. Qualitatively, Argentina has surpassed Chile, with bodegas such as Weinert and Etchart producing world-class Merlot, Cabernet, and Malbec, often at eye-popping prices of $10.
3. Terrific values from South America can still be found, but be careful, the quality has dropped significantly in Chile as the world has taken an active interest in these wines.
4. Australia is making a comeback with copious quantities of low-priced, fruity, exuberant wines that are ready to drink when released. But again, caution is advised, as many Australian wines are cooked in transit thanks to importers indifferent to proper transportation and storage.
5. New Zealand has a handful of excellent wines (the Cloudy Bay Sauvignon Blanc and Chardonnay are exquisite), but this cool-climate viticultural area is not the promised paradise that so many wine writers, particularly the English, have proclaimed. The reasons are obvious—New Zealand rivals Chile when it comes to the number of paid junkets given to wine writers.

The Greatest Wines I Tasted . . .

THE BEST YOUNG AMERICAN CABERNET SAUVIGNON/MERLOT BLENDS

Dalla Valle 1990 Maya (California)
Dominus 1990, 1991 (California)
Forman 1990 (California)
Girard 1990 Cabernet Sauvignon Reserve (California)
La Jota 1990, 1991 (California)
Laurel Glen 1990, 1991 (California)
Leonetti Cellar 1987 Cabernet Sauvignon Reserve (Washington state)
Leonetti Cellar 1989 Cabernet Sauvignon (Washington state)
Robert Mondavi 1990, 1991 Cabernet Sauvignon Reserve (California)
Newton 1990, 1991 Merlot (California)
Joseph Phelps 1990 Insignia (California)
Ravenswood 1990 Pickberry (California)
Philip Togni 1990, 1991 (California)
Woodward Canyon 1988 Cabernet Sauvignon (Washington state)
Woodward Canyon 1988 Charbonneau (Washington state)

THE BEST YOUNG AMERICAN CHARDONNAY

Au Bon Climat 1991 Reserve Sanford & Benedict (California)
Au Bon Climat 1991 Reserve Bien Nacido (California)
Basignani 1991 (Maryland)
Calera 1989, 1990, 1991 Mount Harlan (California)
Edna Valley 1990 (California)
El Molino 1990 (Napa)
Forest Hill 1990, 1991 (California)
Harrison 1990 (California)
Kistler 1990, 1991 Durrel Vineyard (California)
Kistler 1990, 1991 Dutton Ranch Vineyard (California)
Kistler 1990, 1991 Kistler Vineyard (California)
Kistler 1990, 1991 McCrea Vineyard (California)
Marcassin 1990, 1991 Hyde Vineyard (California)
Marcassin 1990, 1991 Lorenzo Vineyard (California)
Newton 1990, 1991 Unfiltered (California)
Peter Michael 1990 (California)
Patz and Hall 1990 (California)
Ridge Vineyards 1990 Howell Mountain (California)
Signorello 1990 (California)
Signorello 1990 Founder's Reserve (California)
Talbot 1990 Diamond T Ranch (Monterey)
Marimar Torres 1990 Don Miguel Vineyard (California)
Williams-Selyem 1991 Allen Vineyard (Sonoma)

THE BEST YOUNG AMERICAN ZINFANDEL

Au Bon Climat 1991 Sauret (California)
Caymus 1990 (Napa)
Cline 1990 Reserve (Contra Costa)
Coturri 1990, 1991 Chauvet Vineyard (California)
Dry Creek 1991 Old Vines (California)

Elyse 1991 Howell Mountain (California)
Elyse 1990 Morisoli Vineyard (California)
Frey 1990 (Mendocino)
Hop Kiln 1990 Primativo-Old Vines (California)
Limerick Lane Cellars 1990 (Russian River)
Château Montelena 1990 (Napa)
Peachy Canyon 1990 Westside (Paso Robles)
Rafanelli 1990 (Sonoma)
Ravenswood 1991 Belloni (California)
Ravenswood 1990, 1991 Cooke Vineyard (California)
Ravenswood 1990, 1991 Dickerson Vineyard (California)
Ravenswood 1990, 1991 Old Hill Vineyard (California)
Ridge 1990 Geyserville (California)
Ridge 1990, 1991 Lytton Springs (California)
Rosenblum 1990, 1991 Michael Marston Vineyard (California)
Rosenblum 1990 Samsel Vineyard (California)
Edmunds St.-John 1990 Mount Veeder Vineyard (California)
Storybook Mountain 1990 Reserve (California)
Topolos 1990, 1991 Rossi Ranch (Russian River)
Williams-Selyem 1989, 1990 Martinelli Vineyard (California)

THE BEST YOUNG AMERICAN SAUVIGNON BLANC AND SEMILLON

Caymus 1990, 1991 Conundrum (California)
L'Ecole #41 1990 (Washington)
Flora Springs 1990 Soliloquy (California)
Hidden Cellars 1990 Alchemy (California)
Kalin 1990 Reserve (California)
Signorello 1990 Semillon (California)

THE BEST YOUNG AMERICAN PINOT NOIR

Au Bon Climat 1990, 1991 La Bauge au Dessus (California)
Au Bon Climat 1991 Sanford & Benedict (California)
Calera 1989 Jensen Vineyard (California)
Calera 1989, 1990 Mills Vineyard (California)
Calera 1989, 1990 Reed Vineyard (California)
Calera 1989, 1990 Selleck Vineyard (California)
Domaine Drouhin 1991 (Oregon)
Evesham Wood 1989, 1990, 1991 Cuvée J (Oregon)
Kalin 1987, 1988 Cuvée DD (California)
Lane Tanner 1991 Sanford & Benedict (California)
Panther Creek 1990 Canary Vineyard (Oregon)
Panther Creek 1990, 1991 Carter Vineyard (Oregon)
Panther Creek 1990, 1991 Reserve (Oregon)
Ponzi 1988, 1989, 1990, 1991 Reserve (Oregon)
Sokol Blosser 1990 Redland Vineyard (Oregon)
St.-Innocent 1990 O'Connor Vineyard (Oregon)
St.-Innocent 1990 Seven Springs Vineyard (Oregon)
Saintsbury 1990 Reserve (California)
Sanford 1990, 1991 Sanford & Benedict (California)

Williams-Selyem 1989, 1990 Allen Vineyard (California)
Williams-Selyem 1989, 1990 Rochioli Vineyard (California)

THE BEST YOUNG EUROPEAN RED WINES

Elio Altare 1988, 1989, 1990 Barolo Vigna Arborina (Italy)
L'Angélus 1989, 1990 (Bordeaux)
Beaucastel 1989 Châteauneuf-du-Pape (Rhône)
Beaucastel 1989, 1990 Hommage à Jacques Perrin (Rhône)
Henri Bonneau 1989, 1990 Cuvée des Celestins (Rhône)
Les Cailloux 1989, 1990 Centenaire (Rhône)
Chapoutier 1989, 1990 Châteauneuf-du-Pape Barbe Rac (Rhône)
Chapoutier 1990 Côte Rôtie La Mordorée (Rhône)
Chapoutier 1989, 1990 Hermitage Le Pavillon (Rhône)
Chave 1989, 1990 Hermitage (Rhône)
Domaine de Chézeaux 1990 Chambertin (Burgundy)
Domaine de Chézeaux 1990 Clos St.-Denis (Burgundy)
Domaine de Chézeaux 1990 Griottes-Chambertin (Burgundy)
Clerico 1988, 1989, 1990 Barolo Ginestra (Italy)
Clinet 1989 (Bordeaux)
J. J. Confuron 1990 Romanée St.-Vivant (Burgundy)
La Conseillante 1989, 1990 (Bordeaux)
Corino 1988, 1989, 1990 Barolo-Vigna Giachini (Italy)
Claude et Maurice Dugat 1990 Charmes-Chambertin (Burgundy)
Claude et Maurice Dugat 1990 Griottes-Chambertin (Burgundy)
L. Einaudi 1988 Barolo (Italy)
L'Évangile 1990 (Bordeaux)
La Fleur de Gay 1989 (Bordeaux)
Angelo Gaja 1988, 1989 Barbaresco Sori San Lorenzo (Italy)
Angelo Gaja 1988, 1989 Barbaresco Sori Tilden (Italy)
Bruno Giacosa 1988, 1989 Barbaresco Santo Stefano (Italy)
A. F. Gros 1990 Richebourg (Burgundy)
Anne et François Gros 1990 Clos de Vougeot-Maupertuis (Burgundy)
Guigal 1988, 1989, 1990, 1991 Côte Rôtie La Landonne (Rhône)
Guigal 1988, 1989, 1990, 1991 Côte Rôtie La Mouline (Rhône)
Guigal 1988, 1989, 1990, 1991 Côte Rôtie La Turque (Rhône)
Haut-Brion 1989 (Bordeaux)
Paul Jaboulet Ainé 1989, 1990 Hermitage La Chapelle (Rhône)
Louis Jadot 1990 Bonnes Mares (Burgundy)
Louis Jadot 1990 Chambertin (Burgundy)
Louis Jadot 1990 Chambertin Clos de Bèze (Burgundy)
Louis Jadot 1990 Gevrey-Chambertin Clos St.-Jacques (Burgundy)
Jayer-Gilles 1990 Echézeaux (Burgundy)
Lafleur 1989, 1990 (Bordeaux)
Latour 1990 (Bordeaux)
Leroy 1990 Chambertin (Burgundy)
Leroy 1990 Clos de la Roche (Burgundy)
Leroy 1990 Latricières-Chambertin (Burgundy)
Leroy 1990 Richebourg (Burgundy)
Leroy 1990 Romanée St.-Vivant (Burgundy)
Leroy 1990 Vosne-Romanée Les Beaumont (Burgundy)

Leroy 1990 Vosne-Romanée Les Brûlées (Burgundy)
Lynch-Bages 1989 (Bordeaux)
Marcoux 1989, 1990 Châteauneuf-du-Pape Vieilles Vignes (Rhône)
Margaux 1990 (Bordeaux)
La Mission Haut-Brion 1989 (Bordeaux)
Montrose 1989, 1990 (Bordeaux)
Ornellaia 1988 (Italy)
Palmer 1989 (Bordeaux)
Pertimali 1985, 1988 Brunello di Montalcino (Italy)
Pichon-Longueville Baron 1989, 1990 (Bordeaux)
Ponsot 1990 Chambertin (Burgundy)
Ponsot 1990 Clos de la Roche Vieilles Vignes (Burgundy)
Ponsot 1990 Clos St.-Denis (Burgundy)
Ponsot 1990 Griottes-Chambertin (Burgundy)
Rayas 1989, 1990 Châteauneuf-du-Pape (Rhône)
Domaine de la Romanée-Conti 1990 Romanée-Conti (Burgundy)
Domaine de la Romanée-Conti 1990 La Tâche (Burgundy)
Joseph Roty 1990 Charmes-Chambertin Vieilles Vignes (Burgundy)
Emmanuel Rouget 1990 Vosne-Romanée Cros Parantoux (Burgundy)
Salvioni 1985 Brunello di Montalcino (Italy)
Sandrone 1988, 1989 Barolo Boschis (Italy)
Aldo and Ricardo Seghesio 1988 Barolo-La Villa (Italy)
Philippo Sobrero 1982 Barolo (Italy)
Henri Sorrel 1989, 1990 Hermitage Le Gréal (Rhône)
Le Tertre Roteboeuf 1989 (Bordeaux)
Vega Sicilia 1968 Unico (Spain)
Roberto Voerzio 1988, 1989 Barolo Brunate (Italy)
Roberto Voerzio 1988, 1989 Barolo Cerequio (Italy)

THE BEST YOUNG EUROPEAN DRY WHITE WINES
Amiot-Bonfils 1989, 1990 Chassagne-Montrachet Les Caillerets (Burgundy)
Amiot-Bonfils 1989, 1990 Puligny-Montrachet Les Demoiselles (Burgundy)
Coche-Dury 1989, 1990 Corton-Charlemagne (Burgundy)
Coche-Dury 1989, 1990 Meursault-Perrières (Burgundy)
Coche-Dury 1989, 1990 Meursault-Rugiers (Burgundy)
Fernand Coffinet 1989 Bâtard-Montrachet (Burgundy)
Colin-Deleger 1989, 1990 Chassagne-Montrachet Les Demoiselles
    (Burgundy)
Jean Collet 1989, 1990 Chablis Valmur (Burgundy)
Faiveley 1989, 1990 Corton-Charlemagne (Burgundy)
Haut-Brion Blanc 1989 (Bordeaux)
Louis Jadot 1989 Chevalier-Montrachet Les Demoiselles (Burgundy)
Louis Jadot 1989 Corton-Charlemagne (Burgundy)
Louis Jadot 1989 Le Montrachet (Burgundy)
Comte Lafon 1989 Meursault-Charmes (Burgundy)
Comte Lafon 1989 Meursault-Perrières (Burgundy)
Comte Lafon 1989 Montrachet (Burgundy)
Lamy-Pillot 1989 Montrachet (Burgundy)
Louis Latour 1989 Bâtard-Montrachet (Burgundy)
Louis Latour 1989 Chevalier-Montrachet Les Demoiselles (Burgundy)

Louis Latour 1989 Corton-Charlemagne (Burgundy)
Louis Latour 1989 Le Montrachet (Burgundy)
Laville-Haut-Brion 1989 (Bordeaux)
Leflaive 1989, 1990 Chevalier-Montrachet (Burgundy)
Leroy 1989 Meursault Les Narvaux (Burgundy)
Leroy 1989 Puligny-Montrachet Les Folatières (Burgundy)
Niellon 1989, 1990 Bâtard-Montrachet (Burgundy)
Niellon 1989, 1990 Chevalier-Montrachet (Burgundy)
Ramonet 1989 Bâtard-Montrachet (Burgundy)
Ramonet 1989 Chassagne-Montrachet Les Caillerets (Burgundy)
Ramonet 1989 Chassagne-Montrachet-Les Ruchottes (Burgundy)
Ramonet 1989, 1990 Montrachet (Burgundy)
Raveneau 1989, 1990 Chablis Les Clos (Burgundy)
Raveneau 1989, 1990 Chablis Monte de Tonnerre (Burgundy)
Domaine de la Romanée-Conti 1989, 1990 Montrachet (Burgundy)
Sauzet 1989 Bâtard-Montrachet (Burgundy)
Domaine Weinbach 1990 white wines (Alsace)
Zind-Humbrecht 1989, 1990, 1991 white wines (Alsace)

THE BEST SPARKLING WINES
Bollinger 1985 Grand Année (France)
Bollinger 1985 Vieilles Vignes (France)
Gosset 1985 Grand Millesime (France)
Krug 1982 (France)
Lassalle 1986 Blanc de Blancs (France)
Lassalle 1985 Cuvée Angeline (France)
Lassalle N. V. Rosé (France)
Dom Pérignon 1985 (France)
Joseph Perrier 1985 Cuvée Royale (France)
Joseph Perrier N. V. Rosé (France)
Pol Roger 1985 Blanc de Chardonnay (France)
Pol Roger 1985 Brut (France)
Pol Roger 1985 Rosé (France)
Pol Roger 1985 Winston Churchill (France)
Salon 1982 (France)

The Best American Wine Values

Bel Arbors Zinfandel (California)
Carmenet Colombard Old Vines (California)
Cline Côtes d'Oakley (California)
Columbia Crest (Washington)
Dry Creek Fumé Blanc (California)
Edmunds St.-John Port o' Call (California)
Estancia (California)
Daniel Gehrs Le Chenay, La Chenière (California)
Geyser Peak Semchard (California)
Hess Select Chardonnay (California)
Kendall-Jackson Chardonnay Vintner's Reserve (California)
Liberty School (California)

Marietta Old Vine Red Lot 121 (California)
Mirassou White Burgundy (California)
Monterey Vineyards line of classic wines (California)
Mountain View Winery red wines (California)
Napa Ridge Chardonnay and Chardonnay Reserve (California)
Pedroncelli (California)
R. H. Phillips Chardonnay (California)
Preston Chenin Blanc (California)
Preston Cuvée de Fumé (California)
Château Ste.-Michelle white wines (Washington state)
Ivan Tamas Chardonnay, Fumé Blanc,
    Trebbiano (California)
Trentadue Carignane (California)
Trentadue Old Patch Red (California)

The Best European Wine Values

Gilbert Alquier (France)
Domaine de L'Arjolle (France)
Pierre d'Aspres (France)
Domaine des Astrucs (France)
Doña Baissas (France)
Domaine Le Bosc (France)
Campuget (France)
Domaine de Capion (France)
Château Capitoul (France)
Caves Coop d'Aléria Reserve du Président (France)
Domaine de Champagna (France)
Domaine de Clairfont (France)
Commanderie de la Bargemone (France)
Domaine de Couroulu (France)
Daniel Domergue (France)
Georges Duboeuf (France)
Domaine de l'Espiguette (France)
Bodegas Farina (Spain)
Fonseca (Portugal)
Domaine de la Gautière (France)
Gournier (France)
Domaine Gramenon (France)
Domaine des Grands Devers (France)
Château Grinou (France)
Guigal (France)
Château Haut-Fabregues (France)
Paul Jaboulet Ainé (France)
Domaine de Jougla (France)
Domaine de Joy (France)
Maître d'Estournel (France)
Mas des Bressandes (France)
Mas de Rey (France)
Elio Monte Montepulciano d'Abruzzo (Italy)

Monte Antico (Italy)
Domaine la Noble (France)
Château les Palais (France)
Château de Paraza (France)
Domaine de Pouy (France)
Château Rouquette sur Mer (France)
St.-Estève (France)
Domaine la Salle (France)
Domaine Salvat (France)
Taja Monastrell (Spain)
Domaine du Tariquet (France)
Taurino Salice Salentino (Italy)
Château Tayac (France)
Château Val-Joanis (France)
Abbaye de Valmagne (France)
Vidal-Fleury (France)
La Vieille Ferme (France)

The Best Southern Hemisphere Wines

Brown Brothers (Australia)
Caballero de la Cepa (Argentina)
Los Vascos (Chile)
Cousino Macul (Chile)
Etchart (Argentina)
Henschke (Australia)
Lindemans (Australia)
Montrose (Australia)
Navarro Correas (Argentina)
Penfolds (Australia)
Rosemount (Australia)
Santa Monica (Chile)
Seppelt (Australia)
Pascual Toso (Argentina)
Undurraga (Chile)
Weinert (Argentina)

THE WINES OF WESTERN EUROPE

1. FRANCE

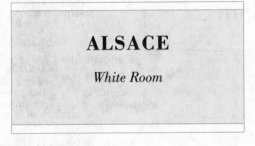

ALSACE

White Room

True connoisseurs of wine must find it appalling that so many importers trip over each other trying to find yet another excessively priced, overcropped, generally insipid Italian Chardonnay or French red burgundy that provides little joy, while ignoring the treasures of this fairy-tale viticultural area in the most beautiful wine-producing region of France. Every time I serve a dry Riesling, Gewürztraminer, Pinot Blanc, or Tokay-Pinot Gris blind to my guests, they are ecstatic about its quality. Why then have these wines failed to earn the popularity they so richly deserve?

For consumers who love wine with food, Alsace produces a bevy of dry, surprisingly flavorful, personality-filled wines that generally offer superb value for the dollar. Alsace also makes it easy for the consumer to understand its wines. As is done in California, the wines are named after the grape varietal used to make them. Additionally, one of Alsace's 51 Grand Cru vineyards can be annexed to the name of the varietal. When that occurs it usually means the wine sells at a price two to three times higher than wines that do not come from Grand Cru vineyards.

Another remarkable aspect of Alsace wines is how long-lived a top Riesling, Gewürztraminer, or Tokay-Pinot Gris can be. Ten to 20 years of longevity is not out of the question for the totally dry regular cuvées and Grands Crus, while the rich, opulent Vendange Tardive and the supersweet, luxuriously priced dessert wines called Sélection de Grains Nobles can survive and benefit from even longer bottle age.

If you would like to experience for yourself the extraordinary merit these wines possess, there has rarely been a more propitious moment to go shopping. With three glorious vintages in a row, prices are stable and the odds of finding something delicious, perhaps even profound, are stacked in favor of the consumer.

To help readers' appreciation and understanding of Alsace, I have briefly profiled the region's grape varieties and included some comments about the more expensive and rarer Vendange Tardive and Sélection de Grains Nobles. I have also provided a brief overview of the Grands Crus of Alsace.

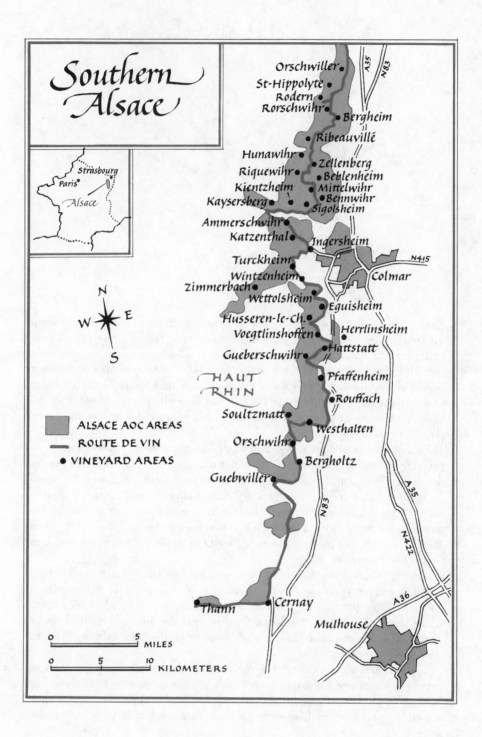

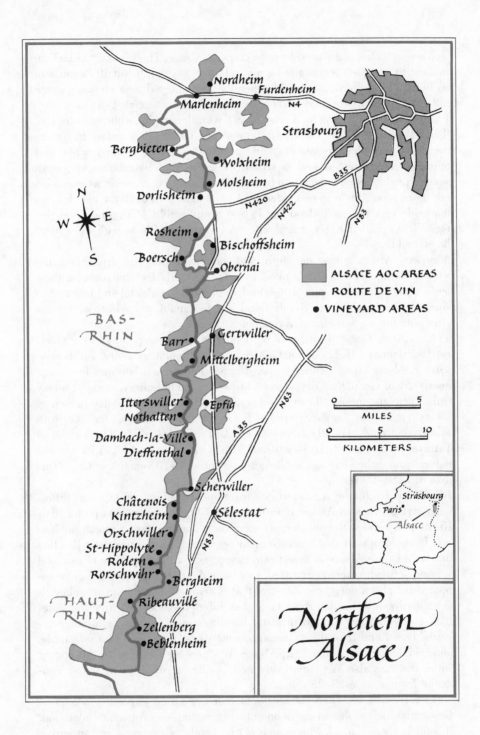

Nordheim
Furdenheim
Marlenheim
N4
Strasbourg
Bergbieten
Wolxheim
Molsheim
Dorlisheim
N420
N422
B35
N83
Rosheim
Bischoffsheim
Boersch
Obernai

ALSACE AOC AREAS
ROUTE DE VIN
VINEYARD AREAS

N
W E
S

BAS-
RHIN

Barr
Gertwiller
Mittelbergheim

N83

Itterswiller
Epfig
Nothalten
Dambach-la-Ville
Dieffenthal
A35

MILES
0   5

KILOMETERS
0   5   10

Scherwiller

Châtenois
Kintzheim
Sélestat
Orschwiller
N83
St-Hippolyte
Rodern
Rorschwihr
Bergheim

HAUT-
RHIN
Ribeauvillé

Zellenberg
Beblenheim

Strasbourg
Paris
Alsace

Northern Alsace

THE GRAPES AND FLAVORS OF ALSACE

Sylvaner   This is my least favorite grape of Alsace. The wines often lack an interesting bouquet, tending to be neutral, even vegetal, to smell. Because of its high acidity, Sylvaner should generally be employed as a blending grape rather than being permitted to stand by itself. Aging potential: 1–5 years.

Pinot Blanc   Looking for a crisp, dry, flavorful, complex white wine for less than $15? Pinot Blanc has always represented an excellent value. In Alsace the finest examples have an engaging bouquet of honeyed, stony, apple- and orange-scented fruit, as well as stylishly elegant, applelike flavors. Although several producers have begun to barrel-ferment this wine, the finest examples are those where there is no evidence of wood aging. Pinot Blanc also has remarkable versatility with food and is best drunk within 4–5 years of the vintage. Wines called Klevner and Pinot Auxerrois are Pinots with even more breed and finesse.

Muscat   Alsace's most delightful and seductively fragrant dry white table wine is Muscat. Terribly underrated, even ignored, this dry wine makes a glorious accompaniment to spicy dishes and, in particular, Oriental and Indian cuisine. Medium bodied yet vividly floral and perfumed, dry Alsatian Muscats offer pure finesse and charm. Aging potential: 3–5 years.

Tokay-Pinot Gris   Capable of producing wines as compelling as the greatest Chardonnays, Tokay-Pinot Gris reaches its height as a dry, full-bodied wine in Alsace. It is a super grape, which, when picked late and fermented nearly dry or completely dry, offers a huge perfume of buttery, creamy, smoky fruit; unctuous, intense flavors; and considerable power and palate presence. Its style mandates the same types of food (rich fish dishes and the like) with which one would normally serve a Grand Cru white burgundy. The Vendange Tardive Tokay-Pinot Gris wines from Alsace can contain 14%–15% alcohol naturally, and they can age well. Aging potential: 4–10 years; Vendange Tardive wines: 5–20 years.

Riesling   Irrefutably a great white wine grape, Riesling produces very differently styled wines in Alsace than it does in Germany. Alsatians prefer their Riesling dry and with considerably more body than do most German producers. It would appear that some German consumers also prefer their Riesling dry, as they are Alsace's largest purchasers, accounting for 57% of the total volume of Riesling that is exported. In Alsace the Rieslings have a floral component but also a deep *gout de pétrol* that is nearly impossible to articulate. It is an earthy, minerallike, flinty taste that differs considerably from the slatelike, steely character found in many Rieslings from Germany's Mosel vineyards. Less floral than their German counterparts, with more of a pineapple, honeyed, orange peel character, Alsace Rieslings are medium- to full-bodied wines that can also age remarkably well. Aging potential: 3–15 years; Vendange Tardive wines: 5–25 years.

Gewürztraminer   There is no doubt that one's first exposure to a great Gewürztraminer seems to cause one of two reactions—revulsion or adoration. It is intensely perfumed, with aromas of rose petals, lychee nuts, and superripe pineapples. The word subtleness is rarely used when discussing the merits of Gewürztraminer, and though I am unequivocally in the corner of this controversial grape, it is best drunk by itself as an aperitif or with pungent fish and pork dishes. In France great restaurants applaud its choice when diners are having foie gras or a rich cheese such as Muenster. This full-bodied, generally alcoholic wine (13.5%–14% alcohol is not uncommon) is capable of exceptional longevity. If the only Gewürztraminer you have tasted was from California or Oregon, you have not really tasted Gewürztraminer—no matter what the label or winemaker might say. Aging potential: 5–15 years; Vendange Tardive wines: 8–25 years.

Pinot Noir   Yes, Alsace does make red wine, but I have never been able to understand why. Although some exceptions do exist, their Pinot Noirs are generally expensive, feeble, and insipid wines, with washed-out flavors, even in the best vintages.

A NOTE ABOUT VENDANGE TARDIVE AND SÉLECTION DE GRAINS NOBLES WINES

The late harvested Vendange Tardive wines of Alsace are made from fully ripened (not overripe) fruit and are powerful, rich, large-scale wines that range in alcohol content from 14.3% to 16%. The levels of concentration and extract can be majestic. Depending on the wine producer, a Vendange Tardive wine can be fermented completely dry or left with a slight degree of residual sugar. The best of these wines are superlative expressions of winemaking and can provide thrilling as well as provocative drinking. They also age extremely well. A little-known fact is that these wines frequently age longer and more gracefully than France's Premier and Grand Cru white burgundies. Any late-harvested wine will have the designation "Vendange Tardive" on the label.

The wines called Sélection de Grains Nobles represent the sweet, nectar-like, albeit rare and luxury-priced segment of the Alsatian wine hierarchy. These wines are often riveting because their sumptuous levels of fruit extract are unencumbered by aromas of new oak. Alsatian winemakers, as a general rule, eschew new wood casks. A Sélection de Grains Nobles can easily last 15–30 years. Many of these wines now cost over $100—for a half bottle!

RECENT VINTAGES

1992—Alsace fared far better than most of southern France in this vintage. The harvest was the earliest since 1976, and the producers reported very high yields, with a lot of ripeness and richness, but wines that are extremely low in acidity. It is hard to predict how much of the Vendange Tardive and sweet dessert wines will be made, but it is unlikely to be as much as was produced in 1990 and 1989. There should be a lot of near-term drinking wines that are forward and overblown but ripe, juicy, and succulent. With prices dropping, this could turn out to be a more interesting vintage for consumers than initially believed.

1991—This is Alsace's toughest vintage since 1987. Nevertheless, some producers, such as Domaine Weinbach and Zind-Humbrecht, made wines that do not taste as if they came from a mediocre- to below-average-quality year. Most wines are relatively light, overly acidic, and slightly green, in complete contrast with the soft, fruity 1992s.

1990—Amazingly, this vintage is even more consistent in quality than 1989. There were fewer Vendange Tardive and Sélection de Grains Nobles wines produced, which should be good news for consumers looking for the drier Alsatian wines. I was impressed with the quality of all the varietals, but top marks must go to the glorious Rieslings, which are superior even to the 1989s. The Gewürztraminers, which were so stunningly perfumed and rich in 1989, are slightly less intense in 1990 but perhaps better balanced and less overwhelming. All things considered, this is a top-notch vintage that looks to be every bit as good as such previous great vintages as 1989, 1985, and 1983.

1989—This vintage most resembles 1983 in that the wines are superripe, strong, forceful, and heady, with exceptional perfume and, at times, mind-boggling richness. The vintage produced amazing quantities of Vendange Tardive and Sélection de Grains Nobles wines. In fact, at the sweeter end of the spectrum, 1989 is probably unequaled by any recent Alsace vintage. Even the totally dry wines tend to be massive. There is plenty of great wine from which to pick, although most wines' aging potential will have to be monitored given the relatively low acidity.

1988—This is a very good vintage that suffers only when compared with those of 1989 and 1990. The very dry, stylish wines may lack the concentration and sheer drama of the 1989s and 1990s, but they are nevertheless elegant, suave, and graceful. Most of the top Rieslings and Gewürztraminers will easily last for a decade or more.

1987—This vintage is surprisingly good, particularly in view of its so-so reputation. Some producers, such as Zind-Humbrecht, made superb wines in 1987. Overall, the quality is at least good and in many cases excellent. Hardly any Vendange Tardive or Sélection de Grains Nobles were made in this vintage because of fall rains.

1986—A patchy vintage, but Zind-Humbrecht and Domaine Weinbach made many glorious wines in 1986. Given a choice, I would be buying wines from 1988–1990 rather than taking a gamble with a 1986.

Older Vintages

To the extent one can still find any of the wines, the 1985 vintage is one of the four or five best for Alsace in the last 15 years. The wines are rich, with decent acidity, and are evolving gracefully in the bottle. They should provide delicious drinking and, in the case of the better Tokay-Pinot Gris, Rieslings, and Gewürztraminers, are capable of lasting for at least another decade. The 1984 and 1982 vintages get my vote as the two worst of the decade and are of no interest. Another great vintage for Alsace was 1983. I bought nearly 20 cases of the 1983s and have drunk them with immense pleasure since their release. Despite their low acidity and relatively intense, concentrated style, they have displayed no signs of cracking up. Many of the bigger-style Rieslings and Gewürztraminers are still improving.

To the extent anyone is lucky enough to find well-stored bottles of 1976s, 1971s, or 1967s, these can provide remarkable evidence of the aging potential of Alsace's top wines. I suspect the only places they may appear are at auctions and probably at alluring prices.

The Significance of Alsace's Grand Cru System

Alsace, like Burgundy, has developed a complicated Grand Cru system that is still the subject of considerable controversy. There is no doubt that many of the best hillside vineyards in Alsace have been included in the Grand Cru classification. However, there is no qualitative justification for excluding the monopole (single-proprietor) vineyards from being considered as Grands Crus. For this reason, irrefutably superb sites such as the Clos Sainte Hune, Clos Windsbuhl, and Clos des Capucins are deprived of such status. Moreover, some of the region's top producers—Hugel, Beyer, and Trimbach—have refused to indicate any Grand Cru designation on their top *cuvées* of wine, despite the fact that the bulk of their reserve wines are made from Grand Cru vineyards. Add to these problems the fact that the politicians of each wine village in Alsace have effectively persuaded authorities to give them their "own" Grand Cru. The political concessions have already resulted in a whopping 51 Grands Crus, which is nearly 20 more than what is permitted in Burgundy's Côte d'Or.

In spite of its weaknesses, the Grand Cru system provides an incentive for producers to achieve the best from the most privileged hillside vineyards. Because so few Alsace producers use new oak, one can also argue that these vineyards do indeed have their own special *terroir* character that is strongly reflected in the wine. My experience has been that the *terroir* character of a number of the Grands Crus is more forcefully expressed in Alsace's wines than in the Grands Crus of Burgundy, where the signature of the winemaker usually takes priority.

To help readers understand the Grands Crus, which will, for better or worse, become of increasing significance, I have listed the major Grands Crus in alphabetical order, along with the best producers from each Grand Cru. Additionally I have attempted to summarize some of the more relevant characteristics of each vineyard from information provided to me by the Alsace Wine Information Bureau.

THE GRANDS CRUS OF ALSACE

Altenberg de Bergbieten   SIZE: 66.7 acres; RELEVANT FACTS: hillside vineyard with a full southeast exposure and gypsum, clay, and gravelly soils; PRIVILEGED VARIETALS: Riesling and Gewürztraminer are considered superb, but Tokay-Pinot Gris and Muscat are also grown on these slopes; BEST PRODUCER: Frederick Mochel

Altenberg de Bergheim   SIZE: 64.2 acres; RELEVANT FACTS: Limestone and marl dominate the soil of this hillside vineyard, which is renowned for its superb Riesling and, to a lesser extent, its Gewürztraminer. PRIVILEGED VARIETALS: Riesling and Gewürztraminer; BEST PRODUCERS: Marcel Deiss, Charles Koehly, Gustave Lorentz

Brand   SIZE: 140 acres; RELEVANT FACTS: This gorgeous hillside vineyard behind the village of Turckheim has a south-southeast exposure. The soil is deep granite, laced with black mica. PRIVILEGED VARIETALS: Riesling, Tokay-Pinot Gris, and Gewürztraminer; BEST PRODUCERS: Zind-Humbrecht, Dopff "Au Moulin," Pierre Sparr, Albert Boxler

Eichberg   SIZE: 142.3 acres; RELEVANT FACTS: This vineyard, located south of the village of Eguisheim at the foot of the hillside in the village of Husseren-les-Châteaux (look for the three towers that dominate the hill), has a southeast exposure and a particularly dry and hot microclimate. The soil is rich clay and limestone. PRIVILEGED VARIETALS: Gewürztraminer, Riesling, and Tokay-Pinot Gris; BEST PRODUCERS: Kuentz-Bas, Scherer

Geisberg   SIZE: 21 acres; RELEVANT FACTS: A steep, terraced vineyard over-looking the charming village of Ribeauvillé, Geisberg is known for its very gravelly and limestone mixed soils and its powerful, elegant wines. PRIVILEGED VARIETAL: Riesling; BEST PRODUCER: Trimbach (Cuvée Frédéric Émile)

Gloeckelberg   SIZE: 57.8 acres; RELEVANT FACTS: Located near the villages of Saint Hippolyte and Rodern, this moderate-size vineyard has a south and southeast exposure with round, relatively acidic soil composed of sand, gypsum, and gravel. PRIVILEGED VARIETALS: Tokay-Pinot Gris, followed by Gewürztraminer; BEST PRODUCER: Charles Koehly

Goldert   SIZE: 111.9 acres; RELEVANT FACTS: One of the more striking vineyards in Alsace, located north of the village of Gueberschwihr, Goldert is situated at a relatively high altitude with deep calcareous soil and an east-southeasterly exposure. It is particularly renowned for its well-drained soils, which produce superb Gewürztraminer and Muscat. PRIVILEGED VARIETALS: Gewürztraminer, followed by Muscat; BEST PRODUCERS: Ernest Burn, Zind-Humbrecht

Hatschbourg   SIZE: 116.8 acres; RELEVANT FACTS: Located south of Colmar, near the village of Voegtlinshoffen, this hillside vineyard has a south-southeast exposure and a calcareous, marllike soil that provides excellent drainage. PRIVILEGED VARIETALS: Gewürztraminer, followed by Tokay-Pinot Gris and Riesling; BEST PRODUCERS: Joseph Cattin, Gerard Hartmann

Hengst   SIZE: 187.2 acres; RELEVANT FACTS: This relatively large vineyard, south of the village of Wintzenheim, has a south-southeast exposure. The soils, a combination of marl and calcareous, tend to produce rich, full-bodied wines. PRIVILEGED VARIETALS: Gewürztraminer, followed by Tokay-Pinot Gris and Riesling; BEST PRODUCERS: Josmeyer, Zind-Humbrecht, Albert Mann, Barmes-Buecher

Kanzlerberg   SIZE: 8.1 acres; RELEVANT FACTS: This tiny vineyard near the village of Bergheim, just west of the Grand Cru Altenberg, has a very heavy, clay/limestone soil intermixed with gypsum and marl. Powerful wines emerge from this gem of a vineyard. PRIVILEGED VARIETALS: Tokay-Pinot Gris and Gewürztraminer; BEST PRODUCER: Gustave Lorentz

Kastelberg   SIZE: 14.3 acres; RELEVANT FACTS: This steeply terraced vineyard in the very northern part of Alsace's viticultural region, near Andlau, is composed of deep layers of schist and quartz, the perfect soil base for Riesling. PRIVILEGED VARIETAL: Riesling; BEST PRODUCERS: Marc Kreydenweiss, Klipfel

Kessler   SIZE: 70.4 acres; RELEVANT FACTS: Steep, terraced vineyards composed of red sandstone, clay, and sand are situated in the very southern part of Alsace's viticultural region, with a stunning southeast exposure. PRIVILEGED VARIETALS: Gewürztraminer and Tokay-Pinot Gris, followed by Riesling; BEST PRODUCERS: Schlumberger, Dirler

Kirchberg de Barr   SIZE: 98 acres; RELEVANT FACTS: Located in the northern section of Alsace's viticultural region, behind the village of Barr, this vineyard has a southeast exposure and a soil base of calcareous marl with underlying beds of limestone and gravel. PRIVILEGED VARIETALS: Gewürztraminer, Riesling, and Tokay-Pinot Gris; BEST PRODUCERS: Emile Boeckel, A. Willm

Kirchberg de Ribeauvillé   SIZE: 28.2 acres; RELEVANT FACTS: The stony, claylike soil, with a south-southwest exposure, produces relatively full-bodied wines that require some time in the bottle to develop their bouquets. PRIVI-

LEGED VARIETALS: Riesling and Muscat, followed by Gewürztraminer; BEST PRO-
DUCER: Trimbach

Kitterlé SIZE: 63.7 acres; RELEVANT FACTS: Perhaps the most striking terraced vineyard in Alsace, Kitterlé, which sits on the photogenic, steep slopes
overlooking the town of Guebwiller, has three different exposures, south,
southeast, and southwest. The soils consist of red sandstone, with plenty of
quartz intermixed with lighter, sandier, gravelly soil, which produces wines of
extraordinary richness and aging potential. PRIVILEGED VARIETALS: Gewürztraminer, Riesling, and Tokay-Pinot Gris; BEST PRODUCER: Schlumberger (astonishing wines from this vineyard)

Mambourg SIZE: 3.2 acres; RELEVANT FACTS: One of the tiniest of the
Grands Crus, Mambourg, a hillside vineyard overlooking the village of Sigol-
sheim, has a calcareous and marllike soil that produces very low yields. This
heavy soil base is ideal for Gewürztraminer. PRIVILEGED VARIETALS: Gewürztraminer, followed by Tokay-Pinot Gris, Muscat, and Riesling; BEST PRODUCER:
Sparr

Mandelberg SIZE: not yet completely delimited; RELEVANT FACTS: Located
near the village of Mittelwihr, this hillside vineyard has a marl-and-limestone
soil base. PRIVILEGED VARIETALS: Gewürztraminer, followed by Riesling

Marckrain SIZE: not yet completely delimited; RELEVANT FACTS: Calcareous-
marl soil with clay makes up this vineyard located just south of the village of
Bennwihr. The heavy soil produces relatively rich, fragrant, full-bodied wines.
PRIVILEGED VARIETALS: Gewürztraminer, Tokay-Pinot Gris

Moenchberg SIZE: 29.5 acres; RELEVANT FACTS: Light, red sandstone inter-
mixed with limestone make up the soils of this hillside vineyard in northern
Alsace, between the villages of Andlau and Eichhoffen. PRIVILEGED VARIETAL:
Riesling; BEST PRODUCERS: Ostertag, Kreydenweiss

Muenchberg SIZE: 25 acres; RELEVANT FACTS: Light gravelly, sandy, nutri-
ent-poor soil is ideal for producing closed but highly concentrated wines. PRIV-
ILEGED VARIETAL: Riesling; BEST PRODUCERS: Julien Meyer, André Gresser

Ollwiller SIZE: 86.5 acres; RELEVANT FACTS: Located in the most southern
sector of Alsace's viticultural region, near the village of Wuenheim (situated
midway between Guebwiller and Thann), this hillside vineyard with a southeast exposure has soils made up of red sandstone and clay. PRIVILEGED
VARIETALS: Riesling and Gewürztraminer

Osterberg SIZE: not yet completely delimited; RELEVANT FACTS: With stony,
claylike soils, the Osterberg vineyard is located near the village of
Ribeauvillé). PRIVILEGED VARIETALS: Riesling, Gewürztraminer, and Tokay-
Pinot Gris; BEST PRODUCER: Trimbach

Pfersigberg SIZE: not yet completely delimited; RELEVANT FACTS: Gravelly
soils with rich deposits of magnesium make up this vineyard located near the
village of Eguisheim within view of the three ruined towers that dominate the
hillside above Husseren-les-Châteaux. PRIVILEGED VARIETALS: Gewürztraminer, Tokay-Pinot Gris, Riesling, and Muscat; BEST PRODUCERS: Kuentz-
Bas, Scherer

Pfingstberg SIZE: not yet completely delimited; RELEVANT FACTS: With its
southeast exposure and location in the southern part of Alsace's viticultural region, just to the north of Guebwiller, the red sandstone– and mica-based soils
produce classic, long-lived wines. PRIVILEGED VARIETALS: Gewürztraminer,
Tokay-Pinot Gris, and Riesling; BEST PRODUCER: Albrecht

Praelatenberg   SIZE: not yet completely delimited; RELEVANT FACTS: This hillside vineyard, located beneath the formidable mountaintop château of Haut-Koenigsbourg, possesses a heavy but well-drained soil consisting of gravel and quartz. PRIVILEGED VARIETALS: Riesling, followed by Gewürztraminer and Muscat

Rangen   SIZE: 46.4 acres; RELEVANT FACTS: One of the greatest of the Grands Crus, this vineyard, located at the very southern end of the viticultural region of Alsace, on steeply terraced hillsides with a full southerly exposure, has a soil base composed of volcanic rocks, schist, and numerous outcroppings of rocks. PRIVILEGED VARIETALS: Tokay-Pinot Gris, Gewürztraminer, and Riesling; BEST PRODUCERS: Zind-Humbrecht, Bernard Schoffit, Bruno Hertz, Meyer-Fonne

Rosacker   SIZE: 44.5 acres; RELEVANT FACTS: Located north of the village of Hunawihr, near two of the greatest enclosed vineyards (called "clos"), the Clos Windsbuhl and Clos Sainte Hune, this hillside vineyard with its east-southeast exposure is planted on calcareous, magnesium-enriched, heavy soil, with some sandstone. PRIVILEGED VARIETALS: Riesling, followed by Gewürztraminer; BEST PRODUCER: Mittnacht Klack

Saering   SIZE: 66 acres; RELEVANT FACTS: The Saering vineyards, with their east-southeasterly exposure, form part of the same striking hillside that contains the famous Kitterlé vineyard. Both overlook the bustling town of Guebwiller. The soil at Saering is heavy, sandy mixed gravel and chalk, which is perfect for Riesling. PRIVILEGED VARIETAL: Riesling; BEST PRODUCERS: Schlumberger, Jean-Pierre Dirler

Schlossberg   SIZE: 197 acres; RELEVANT FACTS: Steep, terraced, sandy, gravelly, mineral-rich soils dominate this vineyard located behind the charming village of Kaysersberg in the direction of Kientzheim. This is one of the largest Grands Crus, so quality varies enormously. PRIVILEGED VARIETAL: Riesling; BEST PRODUCERS: Domaine Weinbach, Pierre Sparr, Albert Mann

Schoenenbourg   SIZE: not yet completely delimited; RELEVANT FACTS: This outstanding as well as scenically beautiful, steep vineyard behind the walled village of Riquewihr is rich in marl, gypsum, sandstone, and fine, gravelly soil. PRIVILEGED VARIETALS: Riesling, followed by Muscat and some Tokay-Pinot Gris; BEST PRODUCERS: Hugel—its top cuvées usually contain high percentages of Riesling from the Schoenenbourg vineyard—Deiss, Beyer, Mittnacht Klack

Sommerberg   SIZE: 66.7 acres; RELEVANT FACTS: One of the steepest hillside vineyards in Alsace, Sommerberg is composed of hard granite and black mica and has a full southerly orientation. The vineyard is located behind the village of Niedermorschwihr. PRIVILEGED VARIETAL: Riesling; BEST PRODUCERS: Albert Boxler, Jean Geiler

Sonnenglanz   SIZE: 81.5 acres; RELEVANT FACTS: The southeasterly exposure and sloping hillside location, with vines planted on relatively heavy soil in a particularly dry microclimate, make Sonnenglanz one of the most favorable vineyard sites for Tokay-Pinot Gris and Gewürztraminer. PRIVILEGED VARIETALS: Tokay-Pinot Gris and Gewürztraminer; BEST PRODUCER: Bott-Geyl

Spiegel   SIZE: 45.2 acres; RELEVANT FACTS: Located between Guebwiller and Bergholtz in the southern area of Alsace, the Spiegel vineyards are on sandy soils with a full easterly exposure. PRIVILEGED VARIETALS: Tokay-Pinot Gris and Gewürztraminer; BEST PRODUCER: Dirler

Sporen SIZE: not yet completely delimited; RELEVANT FACTS: This great vineyard for Gewürztraminer, planted on deep, rich soils with a great deal of phosphoric acid, overlooks the splendid, pretty-as-a-postcard village of Riquewihr. The wines that emerge are among the richest and longest lived in the region, although they need time in the bottle to develop. PRIVILEGED VARIETALS: Gewürztraminer, followed by Tokay-Pinot Gris; BEST PRODUCERS: Hugel—its top cuvées of Gewürztraminer are made almost entirely from the Sporen vineyard—Mittnacht Klack, Dopff "Au Moulin"

Steinert SIZE: 93.8 acres; RELEVANT FACTS: Stony limestone soils located on a sloping hillside in a particularly dry area of Alsace produce very aromatic wines. PRIVILEGED VARIETALS: Gewürztraminer, followed by Tokay-Pinot Gris and Riesling

Steingrubler SIZE: not yet completely delimited; RELEVANT FACTS: Another hillside vineyard with a sandy soil at the top slopes and richer, less well-drained soils at the bottom of the slopes, Steingrubler has a reputation for producing wines of great longevity. PRIVILEGED VARIETALS: Riesling and Gewürztraminer

Steinklotz SIZE: 59.3 acres; RELEVANT FACTS: The most northerly Grand Cru Alsace vineyard, located near the village of Marlenheim, Steinklotz's south-southeasterly-oriented vineyard is planted on very gravelly calcareous soils. PRIVILEGED VARIETALS: Tokay-Pinot Gris, followed by Riesling and Gewürztraminer

Vorbourg SIZE: not yet completely delimited; RELEVANT FACTS: This vineyard, located near the village of Rouffach in the southern sector of Alsace's viticultural region, is composed of limestone- and marl-enriched soils spread over the hillside, with a south-southeast exposure. Ideal ripening conditions exist in this relatively hot, dry microclimate. PRIVILEGED VARIETALS: Riesling, Gewürztraminer, Tokay-Pinot Gris, and Muscat; BEST PRODUCER: Muré

Wiebelsberg SIZE: 30 acres; RELEVANT FACTS: This spectacularly situated hillside vineyard, overlooking the village of Andlau, is planted on well-drained sandstone, sandy soils. PRIVILEGED VARIETAL: Riesling; BEST PRODUCERS: Marc Kreydenweiss, Boeckel

Wineck-Schlossberg SIZE: not yet completely delimited; RELEVANT FACTS: Located west of the city of Colmar in the foothills of the Vosges Mountains, near the village of Katzenthal, this relatively obscure Grand Cru vineyard is planted on deep granite soils, producing very long-lived, subtle wines. PRIVILEGED VARIETALS: Riesling, followed by Gewürztraminer

Winzenberg SIZE: not yet completely delimited; RELEVANT FACTS: Located in the northern Bas-Rhin sector of Alsace, with a south-southeast exposure and a granite, mica-infused soil base, Winzenberg is one of the least known Alsace Grands Crus. PRIVILEGED VARIETALS: Riesling, followed by Gewürztraminer

Zinnkoepflé SIZE: not yet completely delimited; RELEVANT FACTS: This stunningly beautiful, steep hillside vineyard, oriented toward the south-southeast, and planted on deep beds of sandstone in the southern part of Alsace's viticultural region near Soultzmatt, produces very powerful, spicy, rich wines. PRIVILEGED VARIETALS: Gewürztraminer, followed by Riesling and Tokay-Pinot Gris

Zotzenberg SIZE: not yet completely delimited; RELEVANT FACTS: This vineyard, located north of Epfig just south of Barr, has an easterly and southerly exposure and is planted on marl- and limestone-based soils. The gradual slop-

ing hillside is best known for its Gewürztraminer and Riesling. PRIVILEGED VA-
RIETALS: Gewürztraminer and Riesling

THE MOST FAMOUS CLOS OF ALSACE

Some of Alsace's greatest wines come not from Grand Cru vineyards, but
from vineyards entitled to be called "clos" (meaning enclosed or walled vineyards). The most famous of these clos include the spectacular Clos des Capucins (12.6 acres) just outside the village of Kaysersberg, owned by the
remarkable Madame Faller of Domaine Weinbach. Extraordinary Riesling,
Gewürztraminer, and Tokay-Pinot Gris that are often far superior to most
Grands Crus emerge from this vineyard. The Clos Gaensbroennel (14.8 acres),
located near the northerly village of Barr, has provided me with some of the
most remarkable and long-lived Gewürztraminers I have had the pleasure to
taste. Clos Gaensbroennel is owned by Willm. Perhaps the best known clos in
all of Alsace is Clos Sainte Hune (3.08 acres), which is owned by the famous
firm of Trimbach in Ribeauvillé. It is planted entirely with Riesling. Rieslings
that emerge from this vineyard, often referred to as the Romanée-Conti of Alsace, can easily last and evolve in a graceful manner for 15–20 or more years.

Other exceptional clos include the Clos Saint Imer (12.5 acres), owned by
Ernest Burn. As the tasting notes evidence, the Riesling, Gewürztraminer, and
Tokay-Pinot Gris that come from this spectacularly placed clos near the village
of Gueberschwihr rank among the very finest in all of Alsace.

Near Rouffach is one of the largest enclosed Alsace vineyards, the Clos
Saint Landelin (39.5 acres), owned by the firm of Muré. Rich, full-bodied, opu-
lent Gewürztraminer, Riesling, Tokay-Pinot Gris, and even a splendid dry
Muscat are made from this enclosed hillside vineyard's grapes.

Zind-Humbrecht also owns and/or controls the production of two well-
known vineyards entitled to the clos designation. Its most famous, which it also
owns, is the Clos Saint-Urbain (12.5 acres). This sensationally located, steeply
terraced vineyard, planted on granite soils with a full southeasterly exposure
near the village of Thann, makes astonishingly rich, long-lived Gewürztraminer, Riesling, and Tokay-Pinot Gris. The latter wine, for my money, is the
Montrachet of Alsace. The other great clos that is farmed by the Humbrechts
(they do not own it) is the Clos Windsbuhl (11.1 acres). Located on a steep
hillside behind the magnificent church of Hunawihr, and adjacent to the
renowned Trimbach vineyard of Clos Sainte Hune, Clos Windsbuhl is planted
on a limestone and stony soil, with an east-southeast exposure. Majestic
Gewürztraminer is produced, as well as small quantities of Tokay-Pinot Gris
and Riesling.

Though I am less familiar with the following vineyards, I have been impressed with the Clos Zisser (12.5 acres), owned by the Domaine Klipfel and
planted entirely with Gewürztraminer. Other well-known clos with which I
have less experience include proprietor Jean Sipp's Clos du Schlossberg
(3 acres) outside the village of Ribeauvillé. Last, Marc Kreydenweiss has consistently made some of the finest dry Muscat from the Clos Rebgarten (0.5
acre), which is planted on sandy, gravelly soil just outside the village of
Andlau.

The wines from these clos are every bit as sensational as, and in many cases
greatly superior to, many of the Grands Crus. *In vino politiques?*

1993–1994 BUYING STRATEGY

Alsace's wines do not move briskly through the marketplace, so stocks of top vintages such as 1985, 1989, and 1990 can easily be found in many top wine shops. Be sure they have been well stored. The 1991s and 1992s will not be as rich as the 1989s and 1990s, but they will be far less expensive. From the top producers, they are good wines for consumption between now and 1997. However, if you are an Alsace fanatic, 1989 and 1990 are two superlative vintages.

RATING ALSACE'S BEST PRODUCERS

* * * * * (OUTSTANDING PRODUCERS)

Albert Boxler
Ernest and J. et F. Burn
Jean-Pierre Dirler
Hugel (Cuvée Jubilee)
Josmeyer (single-vineyard cuvées)
Mittnacht Klack

Charles Schleret
Bernard and Robert Schoffit
Domaine Trimbach (top cuvées)
Domaine Weinbach
Zind-Humbrecht

* * * * (EXCELLENT PRODUCERS)

J. B. Adam
Lucien Albrecht
Marcel Deiss
Dopff "Au Moulin" (single-vineyard
    cuvées)
Sick Dreyer
Pierre Frick
Hugel (Cuvée Tradition)
Josmeyer (regular cuvées)
Marc Kreydenweiss
Kuehn

Kuentz-Bas
Albert Mann
Julien Meyer
Meyer-Fonne
Muré—Clos Saint Landelin
Domaine Ostertag
Rolly-Gassman
Jean Schaetzel
Schlumberger
Pierre Sparr (single-vineyard cuvées)

* * * (GOOD PRODUCERS)

Barmes-Buecher
J. M. Baumann
Jean-Claude Beck
Jean-Pierre Becker
Leon Beyer
Emile Boeckel
Bott Frères
Joseph Cattin
Cave de Pfaffenheim
Cave Vinicole Turckheim
Dopff "Au Moulin" (regular cuvées)
Jean Geiler

Gérard et Serge Hartmann
Seppi Landmann
Gustave Lorentz
Muré–Clos Saint Landelin (regular
    cuvées)
Preiss-Henny
André Scherer
Maurice Schoech
Pierre Sparr (regular cuvées)
Domaine Trimbach (regular cuvées)
Willm

* * (AVERAGE PRODUCERS)

Bott-Geyl
Cave Vinicole de Bennwihr
Cave Vinicole de Hunawihr
Cave Vinicole Kientzheim
Cave Vinicole d'Obernai
Dopff et Irion

Robert Faller
Hubert Hartmann
Bruno Hertz
Jean-Pierre Klein
Charles Koehly et Fils
Preiss Zimmer

Albert Seltz   Wolfberger
Louis Sipp   Wunsch et Mann
Bernard Weber

J. B. ADAM (AMMERSCHWIHR)* * * *

1990 Gewürztraminer Kaefferkopf	C	89
1989 Gewürztraminer Kaefferkopf	C	85
1990 Gewürztraminer Réserve	C	87
1989 Gewürztraminer Réserve	C	85
1990 Gewürztraminer Vendange Tardive	D	92
1989 Gewürztraminer Vendange Tardive	D	89
1990 Muscat Réserve	C	86
1989 Muscat Réserve	C	84
1990 Pinot Blanc Réserve	B	82
1989 Pinot Blanc Réserve	B	85
1990 Riesling Kaefferkopf C.J.B.	C	86
1989 Riesling Kaefferkopf C.J.B.	B	83
1990 Riesling Kaefferkopf Vendange Tardive	C	90
1989 Riesling Kaefferkopf Vendange Tardive	C	91
1990 Riesling Réserve	C	83
1989 Riesling Réserve	C	82
1989 Riesling Sélection de Grains Nobles	E	90
1990 Tokay-Pinot Gris Cuvée Jean Baptiste	C	84
1989 Tokay-Pinot Gris Cuvée Jean Baptiste	C	86
1990 Tokay-Pinot Gris Réserve	C	79
1989 Tokay-Pinot Gris Réserve	C	84
1989 Tokay-Pinot Gris Sélection de Grains Nobles	E	99
1990 Tokay-Pinot Gris Vendange Tardive	D	90
1989 Tokay-Pinot Gris Vendange Tardive	D	90

Located in Ammerschwihr, Adam is an interesting, high-quality firm that is both a vineyard owner (33 acres) and a *négociant*, buying grapes for vinification. The wines are generally understated and backward yet capable of considerable aging, as evidenced by the Riesling and Pinot Gris offerings that often need a good 4–5 years to open up. I was astounded by a 1961 Tokay-Pinot Gris Réserve that was still in remarkable condition. That being said, my ratings may look conservative, but that is because these are tightly knit, delicate wines that can often be deceptive when tasted very young. I thought the 1989 Pinot Blanc Réserve was superior to the 1990. The 1989 had a lovely, grapefruit- and orange-scented nose, excellent freshness, and a tasty, medium-bodied finish. The 1990 was slightly lighter and less interesting. Adam produces a bevy of Rieslings, all of which are backward and closed. The 1989 Riesling Réserve was crisp and light. Although it did not reveal much depth or character, I did enjoy its understated, mineral, applelike style. Slightly better was the 1989 Riesling Kaefferkopf C.J.B. The Kaefferkopf vineyard produces very backward, high-strung, tightly knit Rieslings that need at least 4–5 years before they begin to blossom. The 1990 Riesling Réserve displayed an austere, earthy, green character, high acidity, and a crisp, zesty finish. The 1990 Riesling Kaefferkopf C.J.B. was delicate, backward, green, and unforthcoming. I suspect it will be better with another 2–3 years in the bottle. My notes may appear conservative, but I have to rate the wines the way they taste, and no matter how much I coaxed these Rieslings, they did not seem to have significant extraction of flavor. Adam produces two different cuvées of Tokay-Pinot Gris. The 1989 and 1990 Tokay-Pinot Gris Réserves were delicate, light, understated wines that were polite rather than blockbusters. The 1989, which displayed a subtle, creamy, buttery nose and pleasant, fresh fruit flavors, should be drunk over the next 2–4 years. The 1990 was understated to the point of being watery and shallow. The 1989 Tokay-Pinot Gris Cuvée Jean Baptiste exhibited fine honeyed, buttery, creamy flavors, medium body, decent acidity, and an attractive, alcoholic finish. Drink it over the next 5–6 years. In contrast, the 1990 Cuvée Jean Baptiste, which was quite closed, was light but tasty and full of finesse. The 1990 Gewürztraminer Réserve exhibited excellent character as well as a rich, dramatic bouquet of roses and smoked meats. In the mouth it was dry and stylish, with good fruit, fine acidity, and a long finish. It should drink nicely for the next 5–6 years. The 1989 Gewürztraminer Réserve was lighter and more backward but did not appear to have the requisite stuffing and intensity that the 1990 possessed. Adam produces a Grand Cru Gewürztraminer, and the 1990 Gewürztraminer Kaefferkopf had a lanolinlike and paraffin-scented nose, waxy, petrollike flavors, plenty of extraction, and a chewy texture. Drink this sumptuous style of Gewürztraminer over the next 5–8 years. The 1989 Gewürztraminer Kaefferkopf, much like the 1989 Réserve, is lighter, with less concentration and not much of a finish. Among the other dry wines from Adam, I enjoyed the 1990 Muscat Réserve, which displayed a floral-scented nose and dry, crisp, tart flavors. It should drink nicely for the next few years. The 1989 Muscat Réserve was leaner, more acidic, extremely dry and austere, but not as aromatically profound as the 1990. Adam's late harvest selections were superb. His style is to produce wines that most consumers would consider dry, but they do have a slight degree of residual sugar. The 1990 Riesling Kaefferkopf V.T. possessed a beautiful nose of honeyed apples as well as lovely, lush, medium- to full-bodied flavors that lingered on the palate. It would be an ideal wine for serving with smoked salmon. The 1989 Riesling Kaefferkopf V.T. exhibited more evidence of botrytis in its peachy, apricot-scented nose, and it was slightly drier in the mouth than the 1990. A long, ripe, medium-bodied wine with fine concentration and balance, it should drink well for the next 10–15 years. I thought both of the late harvest Tokay-Pinot Gris wines were superb. The 1990 Tokay-Pinot Gris V.T. was an elegant, powerful wine, with a gorgeously intense combination of buttery, smoky fruit, medium to full body, and a dry, long finish. The 1989 Tokay-Pinot Gris V.T. was more alcoholic and heady in its perfumed, spicy, exotic, smoky nose and long, glycerin-infused flavors. It was also slightly off-dry. Both of these wines should continue to evolve for at least another decade. Adam did not miss a step with the 1990 Gewürztraminer V.T., a stunningly rich, fabulously endowed, sumptuous wine, with flavors that are the essence of lychee nuts and smoked meats. In the mouth the wine is full bodied, long, and slightly off-dry. It should last for at least 10–15 more years. The 1989 Gewürztraminer V.T. is slightly sweeter and exhibits more evidence of botrytis, with a super abundance of fruit but not quite the aromatic complexity or stunning precision of flavors that the 1990 possesses. I tasted two very limited-production Sélection de Grains Nobles from Adam. The 1989 Riesling S.D.G.N. (of which 150 liters were made) was an extremely elegant, botrytised wine with a penetrating fragrance of honey and apples and medium-sweet, long, intense flavors. The real sensation was the 1989 Tokay-Pinot Gris S.D.G.N. It boasts 100 grams of residual sugar per liter and was made from grapes that yielded a mere 8 hectoliters per hectare. An extraordinary sweet wine, it exhibited a sensational leafy, honeylike fragrance, full-bodied, unctuous flavors, staggering depth, and fine acidity to give everything lift and balance. After another 5–6 years in the bottle, it may merit a perfect score. Unfortunately, a steep price and very limited availability will make it nearly impossible to afford and/or find.

LUCIEN ALBRECHT (ORSCHWIHR)* * * *

1990 Gewürztraminer Cuvée Martine	C	87
1989 Gewürztraminer Cuvée Martine	C	86
1988 Gewürztraminer Sélection de Grains Nobles	E	93
1988 Gewürztraminer Vendange Tardive	D	90
1990 Riesling Pfingstberg	C	87
1990 Tokay-Pinot Gris Pfingstberg	C	89
1989 Tokay-Pinot Gris Réserve	C	88

Although I was unmoved by Albrecht's wines in 1985 and 1986, I have been impressed with every vintage since. I did not taste his Pinot Blanc (Auxerrois) or any of his selections from the Bollenberg vineyard, but I did admire the eight wines he presented for tasting. The 1990 Riesling Pfingstberg is dry, with a delicate, earthy, flower-scented nose, medium body, excellent fruit, and a clean, stylish, very tasty, well-defined finish. Not a blockbuster Riesling, it is, however, rich and subtle—not an easy combination to master. Drink it over the next 5–7 years. The 1990 Tokay-Pinot Gris Pfingstberg had a classy nose of cream, honeyed fruit and spices. In the mouth it had that wonderful clarity all of Albrecht's wines possess, a taste that reminded me of smoked nuts, and a lovely, long, very dry, authoritative finish. I would not be surprised to see this wine turn out to be outstanding with another 1–2 years of bottle age. The 1989 Tokay-Pinot Gris Réserve is also a gorgeous wine, although softer, with a creamier, more honeyed, apricot- and peachlike aroma and flavors suggesting that Albrecht harvested some botrytis-affected grapes. Although the wine exhibits plenty of richness, it is softer and less well defined than the crisper 1990. The 1990 Gewürztraminer Cuvée Martine is a wine for those who like their Gewürztraminer in an elegant, graceful, nonblockbuster style. With the telltale rose petal, lychee nut, spicy fragrance, this is a classy, diplomatic Gewürztraminer that has more flexibility with an assortment of foods than the normal in-your-face style of wine that often emerges from this flashy varietal. The 1989 Gewürztraminer Cuvée Martine is deep, ripe, and bigger, but I did not think it was a better wine. It lacked a bit of acidity and came across as somewhat heavy-handed when compared with the lighter, more polished 1990. I thought Albrecht's 1988 Gewürztraminer Vendange Tardive was outstanding, with rich, alcoholic, chewy flavors, a great deal of lychee nut fruit, a sweet, spicy nose, and plenty of weight, richness, and good balance in the mouth. Drink this super Gewürztraminer over the next 7–10 years. Last, the 1988 Gewürztraminer Sélection de Grains Nobles was decadently rich, with an almost essence or eau de vie character that reminded me of pears. Beautifully balanced by fresh acidity, this unctuous, spectacularly rich wine should drink well for the next 2 decades.

BARMES-BUECHER (WETTOLSHEIM)* * *

1988 Gewürztraminer Steingrubler Sélection de Grains Nobles	E	88
1990 Pinot Blanc	A	86
1990 Riesling Herrenweg	B	86

This was my first look at the wines of Barmes-Buecher, all of which performed admirably in my tastings. The 1990 Pinot Blanc revealed itself to be a relatively full-bodied, chunky, opulent, tasty wine, with a lot of fruit and glycerin. I would opt for drinking this crowd pleaser over the next 1–2 years. The 1990 Riesling Herrenweg displayed an interesting, flowery, stony nose, and in the mouth I was impressed by the bone-dry, light, but unmistakable flavors of green melons and cantaloupe. Drink this vivid, very distinctive Riesling over the next 4–5 years. The 1988 Gewürztraminer Steingrubler S.D.G.N. was another unusual but altogether delicious wine. A bouquet reminiscent of Dijon mustard was followed by an extremely sweet, buttery, honeyed style of wine that did not reveal as much Gewürztraminer varietal character as one might expect. Nevertheless it was an unctuous, thick, honeyed wine for drinking over the next decade.

DOMAINE J. M. BAUMANN (RIQUEWIHR)* * *

1990 Gewürztraminer	B	86
1990 Gewürztraminer Sporen	C	88
1990 Riesling Birgélé	C	85
1990 Riesling Schoenenbourg	C	88
1990 Tokay-Pinot Gris Birgélé	B	84

I found the Baumann wines to be representative of a very dry, understated, polite style of winemaking. The 1990 Riesling Birgélé was elegant, stylish, crisp, and fresh. I am not sure it will make old bones, but I enjoyed it. The 1990 Riesling Schoenenbourg, from that famous Grand Cru vineyard, displayed a flowery, applelike bouquet, bracingly dry, crisp, concentrated flavors, fine acidity, and excellent length. It is still relatively young and unevolved, but my instincts tell me this graceful wine should drink well for at least another 7–8 years. I have a strong preference for this Riesling, which exhibits more richness and intensity than Baumann's 1990 Tokay-Pinot Gris Birgélé. Almost too polite, this light, austere, skinny wine was pleasant but lacked flavor authority and power. The 1990 Gewürztraminer possessed a seductive nose of lychee nuts, spices, and honeyed fruit, very dry, crisp, graceful flavors, and a medium-bodied, fresh finish. By comparison, the 1990 Gewürztraminer Sporen was the biggest, most unctuous and compelling wine that I tasted from Baumann. Medium to full bodied, with a nose of cherries, grapefruit, and spices, it was ripe yet possessed good acidity and a long finish. I would not be surprised to see this wine develop even more character over the next 7–8 years.

JEAN-CLAUDE BECK (DAMBACH-LA-VILLE)* * *

1990 Gewürztraminer Fronholtz Vieilles Vignes	C	90
1990 Riesling Pierre à Feu	B	78
1990 Riesling Frankstein	B	86
1990 Sylvaner	A	72
1990 Tokay-Pinot Gris Frankstein	C	?

Beck's neutral, somewhat green and bland 1990 Sylvaner was hardly inspirational. Nor was I moved by his 1990 Riesling Pierre à Feu or his 1990 Tokay-Pinot Gris Frankstein. The delicate 1990 Riesling Pierre à Feu was thin and tasted as if it had been made from overcropped grapes. The 1990 Tokay-Pinot Gris Frankstein may turn out to be an adequate wine, but an overwhelming smell of sulphur made evaluation impossible. Beck's 1990 Riesling Frankstein had an attractive, moderately intense, apple/peach-like aroma, delicate, dry, understated, but flavorful fruit flavors, and a crisp finish. The 1990 Gewürztraminer Fronholtz Vieilles Vignes was superb. A polished, brilliantly focused, graceful, yet authoritatively flavored Gewürztraminer, it offered up aromas of pineapples, grapefruit, and herbs as well as an almost perfumelike fragrance. Medium bodied and rich, this impeccably balanced wine should evolve gracefully over the next decade.

JEAN-PIERRE BECKER (ZELLENBERG)* * *

1990 Gewürztraminer Froehn Vendange Tardive	D	90
1989 Gewürztraminer Froehn Vendange Tardive	D	82
1989 Riesling Froehn	C	79
1990 Riesling Froehn Vendange Tardive	C	83
1990 Sylvaner "F" (Froehn)	B	85
1990 Tokay-Pinot Gris Rimelsberg Vendange Tardive	C	86
1989 Tokay-Pinot Gris Rimelsberg Vendange Tardive	C	85

Becker's wines tend to be relatively dry and austere, even his broad assortment of late harvest Vendange Tardive offerings. The very dry 1990 Sylvaner "F" (from the Grand Cru Froehn vineyard) displays excellent character for this varietal, with a spicy, floral bouquet and surprisingly intense, well-balanced flavors. Drink it over the next 1–3 years. The 1990 Riesling Froehn V.T. surprised me with its tartness, high acidity, and very dry, austere finish. The 1989 Riesling Froehn was severe and excessively lean, without the requisite depth of fruit necessary to offset its shrill acidity. On the other hand, Becker's

1990 Tokay-Pinot Gris Rimelsberg V.T. had a rich, off-dry, creamy palate; deep, spicy, almost cherrylike flavors; and a corpulent finish. If tasted blind, this could understandably be mistaken for a red wine. The 1989 Tokay-Pinot Gris Rimelsberg is leaner and lighter, without the depth or intensity of the 1990. With respect to the Gewürztraminers, the 1989 Gewürztraminer Froehn V.T. was fat and ripe but relatively monolithic and simple. However, the 1990 Gewürztraminer Froehn V.T. was a beauty, with medium-sweet flavors, super concentration of lychee nut and peach, honeyed-apricot fruit, full body, and an unctuous, long, rich, explosive finish. It should drink well for the next 7–8 years.

LÉON BEYER (EGUISHEIM)* * *

1990 Gewürztraminer Cuvée des Comtes d'Eguisheim	C	90
1990 Gewürztraminer Sélection de Grains Nobles	E	86
1990 Pinot Blanc de Blanc	A	85
1990 Riesling Cuvée Particulière	B	84
1989 Riesling Cuvée Particulière	B	86
1989 Tokay-Pinot Gris Sélection de Grains Nobles	E	87

The Beyer firm, which has owned vineyards adjacent to the charming village of Eguisheim since 1580, makes some of the longer-lived wines of Alsace. They are not known for their up-front, in-your-face fruit, frequently require time in the bottle, and can be easily underestimated when they are young. One of Beyer's consistently top wines is its Riesling Cuvée Particulière, which comes almost entirely from the Grand Cru Schoenenbourg vineyard. Among the others is the Gewürztraminer Cuvée des Comtes d'Eguisheim, which is capable of lasting for 15–20 years. For great value (well under $10 a bottle), keep an eye out for the excellent, medium-bodied, rich, dry 1990 Pinot Blanc de Blanc. Crisp but concentrated and full of finesse and character, it should drink well for 4–5 years. The 1990 Riesling Cuvée Particulière was extremely backward, crisp, and bone dry, with a pleasant apple- and flowerlike fragrance. It clearly needed a good 2–3 years of bottle age. The 1989 Riesling Cuvée Particulière was riper, fuller, and altogether a bigger wine, with an essence of minerals and wet stones in its applelike flavors. Again, this dry, medium-bodied, impeccably made wine will perform much better after another 2–3 years in the bottle. I thought Beyer's 1990 Gewürztraminer Cuvée des Comtes d'Eguisheim was sensational, with the rich, spicy, earthy, minerallike fragrance and taste that the Alsatians call "petrollike." This rich, medium- to full-bodied, beautifully etched Gewürztraminer was powerful, but crisp and well balanced. It should provide delicious drinking over the next 12–15 years. Among the two Sélection de Grains Nobles wines I tasted, the 1989 Tokay-Pinot Gris S.D.G.N. was extremely fat, alcoholic, chewy, and dense, although I did not see much evidence of botrytis, nor the striking complexity exhibited by the best examples of Sélection de Grains Nobles. The same can be said for the 1989 Gewürztraminer S.D.G.N. Oily, even furry, on the palate, powerful, with huge flavors, it is a bit heavy-handed and thick without the underlying acidity and structure needed to provide freshness and focus.

EMILE BOECKEL (MITTELBERGHEIM)* * *

1989 Gewürztraminer Vendange Tardive		C	86
1990 Riesling Wiebelsberg		C	85
1989 Riesling Wiebelsberg Vendange Tardive		C	87
1989 Riesling Zotzenberg		C	87

Boeckel continues to produce sound, occasionally very good, wines. I particularly admire some of the old-style labels used on certain bottlings that feature an Alsatian lady dressed in the traditional peasant clothing peering out the window of one of Alsace's charming timbered houses. Readers may remember that last year I gave high marks to several Boeckel wines. This year I was reassured by the overall quality of several of their new releases. The 1990 Riesling Wiebelsberg is a medium-bodied, extremely backward, austere, bone-dry Riesling made in an almost nervous, tense style that will require some bottle age. Nevertheless one has to admire its stony, minerallike fragrance and crisp, well-balanced flavors. It should last for up to a decade. The 1989 Riesling Zotzenberg was also bone dry but differed from the Riesling Wiebelsberg in its almost petrollike, mothball sort of fragrance, dry yet concentrated, crisp, tightly knit flavors, medium body, and long finish. This is not a wine that will appeal to everyone, for its unusual character will surely make it controversial, but I found it interesting, if a tad eccentric. The 1989 Riesling Wiebelsberg V.T. exhibited some of the honeyed peach and apricot fragrance that is attributable to the noble rot that attacks the grapes. However it, too, had a kinky, mothball sort of fragrance and medium-bodied, ripe, well-balanced flavors. Drink this distinctive, relatively intense wine over the next 7–8 years. The 1989 Gewürztraminer V.T. was surprisingly dry for a late harvest wine, but it exhibited good richness, an earthy, floral fragrance, and tropical fruits (oranges, bananas, pineapples) in its flavors. It should be drunk over the next 4–5 years.

BOTT FRÈRES (RIBEAUVILLÉ)* * *

1990 Gewürztraminer Cuvée Exceptionnelle		C	87
1990 Gewürztraminer Réserve Personnelle		C	86
1990 Pinot Blanc		A	81
1990 Riesling Cuvée Exceptionnelle		C	83
1990 Riesling Réserve Personnelle		C	82

This reliable firm, which owns 37 acres of vineyards around the town of Ribeauvillé, produces wines that are meant not to be aged, but rather consumed in their first 4–5 years of life. I thought the 1990s were good, although less impressive than Bott's 1989s and 1988s. The 1990 Pinot Blanc was crisp, with a subtle bouquet of apples and oranges. Although there was decent concentration in the mouth, the wine tailed off in the finish. The 1990 Riesling Réserve Personnelle was dry and austere, with a floral-scented nose and fresh, light-bodied, crisp flavors. The 1990 Riesling Cuvée Exceptionnelle had more character and fragrance in its flowery bouquet. Although light in the mouth, it was tasty and medium bodied, with a slightly longer finish. Drink this dry, ideal food wine over the next 1–3 years. The 1990 Gewürztraminer Cuvée Exceptionnelle was rich and graceful but not made in the same blockbuster style as so many Alsace Gewürztraminers. It exhibited a lush, petrol-tasting fruitiness, some viscosity, and a soft finish. The 1990 Gewürztraminer Réserve Personnelle was oilier and much heavier, with a lychee nut–, rose petal–scented nose and fat, alcoholic, somewhat flabby, but adequate flavors. It should provide considerable enjoyment if drunk over the next 1–2 years.

BOTT-GEYL (BEBLENHEIM)* *

1989 Gewürztraminer Sonnenglanz	C	62
1989 Gewürztraminer Vendange Tardive	C	75
1990 Pinot Blanc	A	86
1990 Riesling Réserve	B	78
1989 Tokay-Pinot Gris Réserve	B	55
1990 Tokay-Pinot Gris Sonnenglanz	C	73

With the exception of a deliciously stony, concentrated, well-balanced, tasty 1990 Pinot Blanc, the offerings from Bott-Geyl performed miserably in my tastings of Alsace wines. Although the 1990 Riesling Réserve was pleasant, it was green, light, and lacking concentration. The 1990 Tokay-Pinot Gris Sonnenglanz was diluted to the point of being insipid. The 1989 Tokay-Pinot Gris Réserve was defective, with a nose of shoe polish and varnish. The 1989 Gewürztraminer Sonnenglanz was also very odd, with thin, watery flavors and a bizarre bouquet that defied articulation. The 1989 Gewürztraminer V.T. was sweet, cloying, thick, and overweight. Save for the tasty Pinot Blanc, these were disappointing wines.

ALBERT BOXLER ET FILS
(NIEDERMORSCHWIHR)* * * * *

1989 Gewürztraminer Brand	C	93
1990 Riesling Brand	C	92
1990 Riesling Sommerberg	C	90
1989 Riesling Sommerberg	C	90
1990 Tokay-Pinot Gris Brand	C	92
1989 Tokay-Pinot Gris Brand	C	91
1989 Tokay-Pinot Gris Sélection de Grains Nobles	E	92
1988 Tokay-Pinot Gris Sélection de Grains Nobles	E	91
1990 Tokay-Pinot Gris Sommerberg	C	91

Albert Boxler's wines were among the highlights of my Alsace tastings, so I am happy to see these wines are now being represented in America. It appears that just about everything that emerges from the cellars of this 25-acre domaine is profound. Additionally, although these are great wines for drinking young, they give every indication of being capable of lasting for up to a decade or more. Boxler is highly respected in Alsace for his holdings in two of the great Grand Cru vineyards, Sommerberg and Brand. His 1990 Riesling Sommerberg is a lemony, tightly knit, highly extracted, beautifully elegant, poised Riesling loaded with fruit and glycerin and held together by superb acidity and a strong sense of *terroir*. Drink this riveting, very dry Riesling over the next decade. Even more alluring is the 1990 Riesling Brand, which had a huge smoky, flinty nose as well as roasted, dry, intense, impeccably well-balanced, rich flavors that are solidly constructed around a core of deep fruit and fine acidity. This medium-bodied, dry Riesling has considerable presence and an amazingly long finish. Drink it over the next decade. The 1989 Riesling Sommerberg is another exquisite example of just how phenomenal Boxler's Rieslings can be. Bone dry, with a stylish, intense, lemony, apple blossom–, mineral-scented nose, this rich, wonderfully poised, medium-bodied, suave Riesling would be perfect with fish or poultry dishes and should continue to evolve and drink beautifully for another decade.

Boxler hardly misses a beat when he turns to Tokay-Pinot Gris. His 1990 Tokay-Pinot Gris Sommerberg, although slightly less dry than the Rieslings, is extremely rich, with a smoky, nutlike bouquet and explosively rich, creamy flavors that display superb extraction and fine acidity, giving everything brilliant focus. This terrific Tokay-Pinot Gris should drink well for 10–12 years. The 1990 Tokay-Pinot Gris Brand was even more dramatic, with a buttery, smoky, nutty bouquet, full-bodied, intensely concentrated flavors, and a great finish. Drink this beauty with scallops and lobster. Boxler's 1989 Gewürztraminer Brand was one of the great dry Gewürztraminers I tasted from Alsace, with a smoky, lychee nut–, petrollike fragrance, fabulously rich, full-bodied, surprisingly racy flavors, and a tidal wave of fruit in its long, opulent finish. Again, it offers a decade's worth of aging potential. The 1989 Tokay-Pinot Gris S.D.G.N., which was extremely rich and long, with honeyed, opulent fruit flavors, was very sweet but was balanced by zesty acidity and an overall sense of structure. The 1988 Tokay-Pinot Gris S.D.G.N. was slightly less sweet than the 1989 but still deep and honeyed, with almost fruitcakelike flavors. Both wines should last for at least 15 or more years.

ERNEST OR J. ET F. BURN (GUEBERSCHWIHR)* * * * *

1990	Gewürztraminer Clos Saint Imer Goldert	C	93
1989	Gewürztraminer Clos Saint Imer Goldert Cuvée La Chapelle	C	91
1988	Gewürztraminer Clos Saint Imer Goldert Vendange Tardive	D	92
1990	Riesling Clos Saint Imer Goldert	C	90
1988	Riesling Clos Saint Imer Goldert Vendange Tardive	C	90
1990	Tokay-Pinot Gris Clos Saint Imer Goldert	C	90
1989	Tokay-Pinot Gris Clos Saint Imer Goldert La Chapelle	C	91

Any Alsatian willing to speak candidly (and there are not many) will acknowledge that the Clos Saint Imer vineyard of Ernest Burn produces some of that region's greatest wines. I was swept away by all of the wines I tasted from this property. For starters there is the dry, intense, blazingly clear, apple- and mineral-scented masterpiece of a wine, the 1990 Riesling Clos Saint Imer Goldert. Extremely fresh, lovely, and dry, with gobs of silky flavor as well as plenty of acidity and precision, this is a wonderfully precise wine for drinking over the next decade. The 1988 Riesling Clos Saint Imer Goldert V.T. was also outstanding. Surprisingly dry, it offers a classic example of the mineral, wet stone, apple, apricot, and cinnamon toast flavors that can emerge from this vineyard. This superconcentrated, dry, rich wine with amazing length should drink beautifully for the next 10–12 years. The three Gewürztraminers I tasted were all remarkable. The 1990 Gewürztraminer Clos Saint Imer Goldert had a huge nose of roses, intense lemon/lychee nut flavors, the amazing smokiness that comes with the great examples of this grape, and a taste so superb that I had a hard time spitting it out. It should go on and on for at least 10–15 or more years. The 1989 Gewürztraminer Clos Saint Imer Goldert, which Burn has called Cuvée La Chapelle (after the small chapel that overlooks the Goldert vineyard), exhibits a deeper color than the 1990 and, once again, the phenomenal rose petal, smoky, lychee nut flavors as well as an unbelievably exciting, dizzyingly complex, sensational palate. The overall impression is one of dryness and great concentration and focus. Wow! Drink this beauty over the next decade. The 1988 Gewürztraminer Clos Saint Imer Goldert V.T. is medium sweet and unbelievably rich, with some evidence of botrytis as well as gobs and gobs of concentration. I dare anyone to drink it with food, but who could resist this wine either before or after a meal! Burn made two stunning Tokay-Pinot Gris from Goldert's deep calcareous soils. The 1990 Tokay-Pinot Gris Clos Saint Imer Goldert is surprisingly delicate and civilized when compared with his flamboyant Gewürztraminers. With buttery, smoky, nutty, creamy flavors and an opulent texture, this beautiful, stylish Tokay should drink well over the next decade. The slightly off-dry 1989 Tokay-Pinot Gris Clos Saint Imer Goldert Cuvée La Chapelle is even richer. The heady flavors and underlying spice and acidity give it lift and focus. This big, in-your-face style of Tokay-Pinot Gris should be drunk over the next 7–8 years.

JOSEPH CATTIN (VOEGTLINSHOFFEN)* * *

1988 Gewürztraminer Sélection de Grains Nobles	E	92
1990 Pinot Blanc	A	75
1990 Riesling	B	76
1990 Riesling Vendange Tardive	C	86

It is a shame that I did not see any of Cattin's best selections from the great Hatschbourg vineyard. Several years ago I bought a case of his 1985 Gewürztraminer Hatschbourg, and today it is one of my favorite wines. His 1990 Pinot Blanc was undistinguished in its light, straightforward, delicate, but essentially indifferent winemaking style. The 1990 Riesling, although fresh and light, lacked fruit and personality. Far better was the 1990 Riesling V.T., which offered up a wonderfully citrusy, orange-scented nose, super fruit, richness on the palate, and a ripe, long, off-dry finish. I thought Cattin's 1988 Gewürztraminer S.D.G.N. was a knockout example of a sweet Gewürztraminer. A huge, smoky, meaty, Oriental spice–scented nose was followed by impressively endowed, medium-sweet flavors buttressed by good, crisp acidity. Drink this beauty over the next 15 years.

CAVE DE PFAFFENHEIM (PFAFFENHEIM)* * *

1989 Gewürztraminer Steinert	B	83
1988 Gewürztraminer Sélection de Grains Nobles	D	82
1990 Muscat Cuvée Diana	B	84
1990 Riesling Cuvée Jupiter	B	72
1989 Tokay-Pinot Gris Steinert	B	82

As cooperative wines go, these are acceptable. The 1990 Riesling Cuvée Jupiter is lean, light, fresh, and a bit innocuous, but adequate. My favorite wine from this producer was the 1990 Muscat Cuvée Diana, with its big, flowery bouquet and dry, crisp, light-bodied flavors. The 1989 Tokay-Pinot Gris Steinert was smoky and buttery but finished abruptly on the palate. The 1989 Gewürztraminer Steinert was pleasant but very light and made in a relatively boring style for a Gewürztraminer from a Grand Cru vineyard. Last, the 1989 Gewürztraminer S.D.G.N. was off-dry, decently fruity, but one-dimensional rather than complex.

CAVE VINICOLE (KIENTZHEIM)* *

1989 Gewürztraminer Altenberg	B	84
1990 Gewürztraminer Furstentum	B	85
1988 Gewürztraminer Vendange Tardive	C	82
1990 Riesling	A	75
1989 Riesling Réserve	B	72
1990 Riesling Schlossberg	B	78
1989 Riesling Schlossberg	B	75
1988 Tokay-Pinot Gris Sélection de Grains Nobles	D	75

I was unimpressed with the general level of quality of these wines from this cooperative in Kientzheim-Keisersberg. All the Rieslings were extremely acidic, lacking in fruit, and obviously produced from crop yields that were too high. The best of this group was the 1990 Riesling Schlossberg, but even that wine, despite its whiff of minerals and wet stones, was a relatively undistinguished effort. The best wine of the entire Cave Vinicole selection was the 1990 Gewürztraminer Furstentum. Without the eviscerated, stripped feel that the other wines possessed, it offered a delicate scent of roses followed by a medium-bodied, fruity wine with some concentration and character. Although the 1989 Gewürztraminer Altenberg was tightly knit, it too was stripped and entirely too processed. The same thing can be said for the 1988 Gewürztraminer V.T., which was one-dimensional and lacking complexity and richness of fruit. The 1988 Tokay-Pinot Gris S.D.G.N. was sticky and sweet to the point of being cloying. If you like the aroma of overripe pears, this wine did offer that type of bouquet. Unimpressive!

CAVE VINICOLE (TURCKHEIM)* * *

1990 Gewürztraminer Brand	C	87
1988 Gewürztraminer Sélection de Grains Nobles	D	85

1990 Pinot Blanc (Klevner) Médaille d'Or	A	85
1990 Riesling Brand	B	85
1989 Riesling Heimbourg	B	84
1989 Riesling Sporen	B	79
1990 Tokay-Pinot Gris Hengst	B	75

As cooperatives go, these were respectable wines. In fact, several of them were very good, including a tasty, generously endowed, fruity, pure 1990 Pinot Blanc (Klevner) Médaille d'Or. Drink this charmer over the next 2–3 years. I was not too impressed with the 1989 Riesling Sporen, which was made in a relatively light, straightforward style, although some attractive floral scents did redeem it. More interesting was the backward, concentrated 1989 Riesling Heimbourg, which is promising for the long term, and the well-made, earthy, rich, petrol-scented 1990 Riesling Brand. The 1990 Tokay-Pinot Gris Hengst was soft and one-dimensional. However, I was very impressed with the 1990 Gewürztraminer Brand, which exhibited an intense, lychee nut, smoky, earthy nose and ripe, full-bodied, soft flavors. All of these wines should be drunk over the next 2–3 years. The 1988 Gewürztraminer S.D.G.N. was unctuous, thick, rich, and sweet but lacked complexity. Drink this well-made wine over the next 10–12 years.

CAVE VINICOLE DE BENNWIHR (BENNWIHR)* *

1988 Gewürztraminer Sélection de Grains Nobles	D	62
1988 Gewürztraminer Vendange Tardive	C	85
1989 Riesling Rebgarten	B	74

The 1989 Riesling Rebgarten was extremely green and austere and will need considerable time in the bottle if it is ever going to develop any interest. I am nearly certain that there is not enough fruit to cover the wine's high acidity. The 1988 Gewürztraminer V.T. was sweet and thick, with an unctuous texture and just barely enough acidity to keep it from tasting cloying and sticky. Not the sort of Gewürztraminer Vendange Tardive that would marry well with food, it is best drunk either before or after a meal. The 1988 Gewürztraminer S.D.G.N. exhibited no evidence of botrytis, offering cloying, heavy, flabby fruit flavors without enough acidity or complexity for balance. If these three wines are typical of the Cave Vinicole de Bennwihr, I would be wary of their other offerings.

CAVE VINICOLE DE HUNAWIHR (HUNAWIHR)* *

1990 Pinot Blanc	A	75
1990 Riesling	A	82
1988 Tokay-Pinot Gris Vendange Tardive	B	69

The delicate, light, somewhat watery Pinot Blanc is acceptable, but clearly the 1990 Riesling, with its flowery bouquet and dry, light-bodied, crisp flavors, is a more successful wine. The 1988 Tokay-Pinot Gris V.T. was very disappointing; it had already taken on a staleness to its bouquet. I am at a loss for words to describe the bizarre, odd flavors.

CAVE VINICOLE D'OBERNAI (OBERNAI)* *

1990 Gewürztraminer	A	83
1990 Pinot Blanc	A	78
1990 Riesling	A	77

These co-op wines all possessed some character, were fresh, cleanly made, and representative of their types. The 1990 Pinot Blanc was light and correct, but unexciting. The same could be said for the 1990 Riesling, which offered up vague hints of green apple–like fruit, a floral scent, and light flavors. The best of the trio was a competent, soft, rose petal–scented, peach-flavored, slightly exotic, chunky 1990 Gewürztraminer. All of these wines should be drunk over the next 2–3 years.

MARCEL DEISS (BERGHEIM)* * * *

1989 Gewürztraminer Altenberg Sélection de Grains Nobles	EE	95
1988 Gewürztraminer Altenberg Sélection de Grains Nobles	EE	91
1990 Gewürztraminer Altenberg Vendange Tardive	D	87
1990 Gewürztraminer Bergheim Vendange Tardive	D	86
1989 Gewürztraminer Bergheim Vendange Tardive	D	91
1990 Gewürztraminer Mittelwihr	C	82
1989 Gewürztraminer Mittelwihr	C	87
1989 Gewürztraminer Quintessence	EE	94
1990 Gewürztraminer Saint Hippolyte	C	85
1989 Gewürztraminer Saint Hippolyte	C	87
1990 Muscat d'Alsace Bergheim	B	82
1989 Muscat d'Alsace Bergheim	B	84
1990 Pinot Blanc Bennwihr	B	86
1989 Pinot Blanc Bennwihr	B	85
1990 Pinot Blanc Bergheim	B	86
1989 Pinot Blanc Bergheim	B	85
1989 Pinot Blanc Bergheim Vieilles Vignes	B	88
1989 Pinot Gris Quintessence	EE	95
1990 Pinot Noir Burlenbeg Vieilles Vignes	C	85
1989 Pinot Noir Burlenbeg Vieilles Vignes	C	86
1990 Riesling Altenberg Vendange Tardive	D	86
1989 Riesling Altenberg Vendange Tardive	D	90
1988 Riesling Altenberg Vendange Tardive	D	91
1990 Riesling Bennwihr	C	84
1989 Riesling Bennwihr	C	85

1990 Riesling Burg Vendange Tardive	D	88
1989 Riesling Burg Vendange Tardive	D	92
1988 Riesling Burg Vendange Tardive	D	89
1990 Riesling Engelgarten	C	84
1989 Riesling Engelgarten	C	85
1990 Riesling Engelgarten Vieilles Vignes	C	90
1989 Riesling Engelgarten Vieilles Vignes	C	88
1988 Riesling Grasberg	C	88
1990 Riesling Grasberg Vendange Tardive	D	85
1989 Riesling Grasberg Vendange Tardive	D	92
1988 Riesling Grasberg Vendange Tardive	D	89
1989 Riesling Quintessence	EE	93
1989 Riesling Schoenenbourg Sélection de Grains Nobles	E	92
1988 Riesling Schoenenbourg Sélection de Grains Nobles	E	91
1990 Riesling Schoenenbourg Vendange Tardive	D	92
1990 Riesling Saint Hippolyte	C	86
1989 Riesling Saint Hippolyte	C	86
1990 Tokay-Pinot Gris Bergheim	C	85
1989 Tokay-Pinot Gris Bergheim	C	88

The young, intense, energetic Jean-Michel Deiss has become one of the new Alsace superstars, as evidenced by the fact that 70% of his production is now exported and he has had to allocate many of his top wines. Along with Leonard and Olivier Humbrecht, Deiss is perhaps the greatest proponent of *terroir* in Alsace. In Burgundy the fragmentation of the Premier Cru and Grand Cru vineyards, plus the very personal signatures of the greatest winemakers, make much of the *terroir* argument absurd. If you really want to pursue *terroir*, go see Deiss, whose low yields and scrupulous winemaking result in wines that reflect the different soil bases from which he works. His wines are vividly different, and he makes no bones about saying the role of the winemaker is marginal, merely to guide the healthy grapes through the winemaking process to reflect their *terroir* and vintage. Although it is mind-boggling to contemplate the number of wines he produces, tasting them is a delight. Deiss believes that 1989 is the greatest vintage for Alsace wines since 1959, and he scoffs at those who claim 1990 is just as great. The bevy of Pinot Blancs are all at least very good, with the Pinot Blancs from Bennwihr exhibiting a bit more of the orange blossom, crisp, lighter, more delicate style, and the Pinot Blancs from Bergheim offering richer, softer, more creamy-textured wines. All of them will make ideal drinking over the next 3–5 years for their purity and wonderfully crisp, elegant textures. Best of all is the 1989 Pinot Blanc Bergheim Vieilles Vignes, a pure, silky, rich, fragrant wine of considerable grace and style. It should drink nicely for 5–7 years. Interestingly, all of Deiss's wines are kept in contact with their lees until bottling. I did not think Deiss's Muscats were up to the quality level of some of his competitors', particularly those from Rolly-Gassmann. Although they were light, delicate, and floral, they were lacking a bit in concentration, particularly for a wine from this producer. His Tokay-Pinot Gris, a grape of which he is not a great fan, are made in a relatively lightweight, smoky, buttery style, with less alcohol than many of the blockbuster Pinot Gris from the likes of Kuentz-Bas or Zind-Humbrecht. His 1990 Tokay-Pinot Gris Bergheim is a refreshingly lighter style of this wine, with good fruit. But the real winner is his 1989 Tokay-Pinot Gris Bergheim, with its buttery, smoky, nutty bouquet, good acid, rich, medium-bodied, fleshy flavors, and creamy, long finish. It begs for salmon from the Pacific Northwest to complement its textures and flavors. If it is not already evident by the number of different Rieslings Deiss makes, this is the grape that excites him the most. His lightest, greenest, and easiest to understand is the 1990 Riesling Bennwihr, which is a tart, fresh, light, apple-flavored and -scented wine that can be gulped down easily while waiting for your entrée to reach the table. The 1989 Riesling Bennwihr is slightly longer and riper, with excellent acidity as well as an underlying mineral character. Deiss is the first to admit that his Bennwihr Rieslings are the most straightforward, which can easily be seen when tasting his Rieslings from Saint Hippolyte. These are bigger, more lemon/lime, steely Rieslings, with more flavor extraction, glycerin, and body. Nevertheless the overall impressions are of wines with crisp acidity, wonderful purity of flavor, and a stony essence of *terroir* character. I thought both the 1989 and 1990 Riesling Saint Hippolytes were equal in quality, although the 1990 did taste slightly more voluminous in the mouth. Between the 1989 and 1990 Riesling Engelgarten, I had a slight preference for the 1989, with its big bouquet of Mandarin oranges. Overall I felt it was a more exciting wine, with good acidity and a certain tartness, and, like most of Deiss's wines, was very young and backward, needing some time in the bottle. The 1990 was extremely tight, almost unapproachable, and I suspect my rating will turn out to be conservative. There is a special *cuvée* produced from the Engelgarten vineyard called Cuvée Vieilles Vignes. The 1990 Riesling Engelgarten Vieilles Vignes (from vines that are over 50 years old) is a rich, chewy, deep, extremely young and backward, but highly promising wine of wonderful intensity and at least 10–15 years of potential longevity. The 1989 Riesling Engelgarten Vieilles Vignes exhibits a bouquet of ripe oranges, has crisp acidity, medium body, and a long, rich, intensely concentrated palate. But it is oh, so backward. Give it at least 4–5 years to open up. Deiss's other Rieslings included a 1988 Riesling Grasberg made from a vineyard planted on limestone soil. It exhibits a great deal of botrytis, a real mineral character, and that petrol essence of earth one finds in so many Alsace Rieslings. Extremely dry, rich, and full, it should drink superbly over the next decade.

I get the impression that Deiss has little use for Gewürztraminer. Although I was slightly disappointed in the fluid, flabby, somewhat soft 1990 Gewürztraminer Mittelwihr, the 1989 Gewürztraminer Mittelwihr was terrific, with an exotic, lychee nut–, rose-scented nose, dramatic, full-bodied flavors, and excellent fruit and length. The 1990 Gewürztraminer Saint Hippolyte was spicy and ripe but had nowhere near the excitement of most of the Rieslings. The 1989 Gewürztraminer Saint Hippolyte appeared to be a far greater wine than the 1990, with its spicy, intense nose and excellent, rich, medium- to full-bodied, dry flavors. Both of these Gewürztraminers should drink well for the next 4–6 years.

One last comment about another of the totally dry wines from Deiss: he is considered by almost all his peers to produce the finest Pinot Noir in Alsace. Longtime readers know that I find most Alsace Pinot Noirs to be unbelievably boring and insipid. Although I must agree that Deiss makes the best Alsatian Pinot Noir, I am not moved enough to recommend it to readers. Nevertheless the 1989 Pinot Noir Vieilles Vignes, aged in 50% new oak from the Vosges mountains, has excellent color, 13.9% alcohol, and offers deep, somewhat simple, but ripe, rich cherry flavors married nicely to the smoky oak. If you are going to drink one Alsace Pinot Noir, let it be that from Marcel Deiss.

The 1989 Riesling Grasberg V.T. is a sensational example of essentially dry, superconcentrated, exotic Riesling. The huge bouquet of minerals, apricots, and oranges is followed by a stunningly proportioned, crisp, pure wine loaded with extract, brilliantly focused, and capable of lasting 10–12 years. In comparison, the 1990 Riesling Grasberg V.T. is much lighter and, although certainly good, lacked the flavor dimension, focus, and presence on the palate of the compelling 1989. Deiss produced two profound Vendange Tardive Rieslings from the marl-dominated soils of the Burg vineyard. The 1990 Riesling Burg V.T. displays a very steely, floral-scented nose, medium body, and long, tightly knit flavors and is less precocious and evolved than the Grasberg Riesling. The 1989 Riesling Burg V.T. is terrific. Slightly sweeter than Deiss's other Vendange Tardive wines, it possesses a honeyed, orange, essence of mineral character, dense, opulent fruit flavors, and a long, glycerin-laden finish. Deiss claims both these wines have 10–20 years of longevity. I did a mini vertical tasting of the Riesling Altenberg, a Grand Cru vineyard planted on clay/limestone-based soils. The 1990 Riesling Altenberg V.T. exhibited a very stony, lemony nose and appeared surprisingly light and unfocused in the mouth, without the extract one normally sees in Deiss's wines. Perhaps it is presently in an ungracious state of development. The 1988 Riesling Altenberg V.T. appears to be a more complete and intense wine. The rich, honeyed, almost cherry blossom–scented fragrance was followed by ripe, lemon/lime, steely flavors, fine acidity, and a slightly off-dry character. I suspect most tasters would consider this wine to be dry, given its high acidity and backward style. It should last for at least a decade. Deiss talks about his favorite vineyard, the Schoenenbourg, as having "the malady of Schoenenbourg." What he means is that the wine is impossibly closed when young and needs a minimum of 5–7 years in the bottle to begin to display its superb fruit and character. The Schoenenbourg vineyard, a marl- and gypsum-dominated *terroir*, produced a 1990 Riesling Schoenenbourg V.T. with great concentration of stony, applelike fruit that erupts with a searingly rich, tightly strung character, almost that of the essence of apricots, stones, and apples. The wine has impressive extract, but it is frightfully backward. Give it at least 5 years before even thinking about drinking it. The 1990 Gewürztraminer Bergheim V.T. was sweet and ripe but somewhat monolithic by the standards of Deiss's other wines. I preferred his superb 1989 Gewürztraminer Bergheim V.T. with its admirably focused nose of lychee nuts and meaty, smoky fruit. In the mouth it had super concentration, plenty of length, and a full-bodied yet tightly knit structure. Deiss also made a 1990 Gewürztraminer Altenberg V.T. that I thought was very good— deep, ripe, medium sweet, and displaying good acidity. Deiss, much like such producers as Dopff "Au Moulin" and to a lesser extent Ostertag, believes in almost excessively dry, high-acid Sélection de Grains Nobles wines. His 1989

Riesling Schoenenbourg S.D.G.N., which is relatively sweet by his standards, is packed with smoky, mineral, apricot- and applelike fruit, is medium bodied, and has very high acidity and great extraction of fruit. Do not touch it for at least 10–15 years. The 1988 Riesling Schoenenbourg S.D.G.N. has even higher extraction, exceptionally high acidity, and comes across as essentially dry, although there is plenty of sweetness to the wine. It should last for two decades. The 1989 Gewürztraminer Altenberg S.D.G.N., which has 100 grams of residual sugar per liter, represents a blockbuster, tightly knit, highly focused, superconcentrated style of Gewürztraminer made in a medium-sweet format. It will last for decades. The 1988 Gewürztraminer Altenberg S.D.G.N. is also a great wine, although not quite as powerful and packed with fruit as the 1989; it is capable of another 10–15 years of aging. In 1989 Deiss also made what he calls Quintessence. Aptly named, these releases have mind-boggling concentration and extract levels, as well as amazingly high acidity levels. Lord only knows how long they will last and how expensive they will be when ultimately released. They are equivalent to German Trockenbeerenauslese wines in terms of sweetness, although that fact is well concealed behind mouth-searing acidity. A thrill to taste, but made in such limited quantities, I have to wonder about the true commercial viability of wines such as these.

JEAN-PIERRE DIRLER (BERGHOLTZ)* * * * *

1989 Gewürztraminer Sélection de Grains Nobles	E	94
1989 Gewürztraminer Spiegel	C	88
1989 Muscat Saering	C	87
1989 Riesling Kessler	C	88
1990 Sylvaner Cuvée Vieilles Vignes	B	78

This family has been making wine in the southern area of Alsace's viticultural region since 1871. Dirler is well known for his very stylish, flavorful wines from such Grand Cru vineyards as Kessler, Saering, and Spiegel. Although his Sylvaner is also highly acclaimed, I was not taken with the 1990 Sylvaner Cuvée Vieilles Vignes, which tasted too neutral and green to elicit much enthusiasm. However, the rest of the Dirler offerings were all top class, beginning with a very fine, bone-dry, lemony, flinty, character-filled 1989 Riesling Kessler. Possessing loads of extract, this wine may ultimately merit an outstanding score with another 1–2 years of bottle age. I was also impressed by the flowery, gorgeously aromatic, still delicate, bone-dry 1989 Muscat Saering. I had a number of top dry Muscats on my recent trip to Alsace, and this was one of the more memorable examples. It should be drunk over the next 1–2 years, as the fragrance of Muscat tends to dissipate quickly. The two Gewürztraminers I tasted from Dirler included a rich, opulent, impeccably well-balanced, full-bodied 1989 Gewürztraminer Spiegel. Gewürztraminers from the sandy soils of this vineyard tend to be meaty and powerful, which is exactly what Dirler achieved in 1989. There is also a great deal of finesse in this beauty. Drink it over the next 5–10 years. Last, Dirler's 1989 Gewürztraminer S.D.G.N. is a great wine—decadently rich, gorgeously perfumed (peaches, apricots, lychee nuts, and smoke), with a fine, long, zesty finish. Based on what I have tasted from this producer, he deserves more attention from lovers of Alsace wines.

DOPFF "AU MOULIN" (RIQUEWIHR)
REGULAR CUVÉES* * * SINGLE-VINEYARD CUVÉES* * * *

N.V.	Crémant d'Alsace Brut Sauvage	B	86
N.V.	Crémant d'Alsace Cuvée Julien	B	85
1990	Gewürztraminer	B	85
1990	Gewürztraminer Brand	C	87
1989	Gewürztraminer Brand	C	85
1988	Gewürztraminer Brand	C	86
1990	Gewürztraminer Brand Vendange Tardive	D	90
1990	Gewürztraminer Sélection de Grains Nobles	E	92
1988	Gewürztraminer Sélection de Grains Nobles	E	?
1990	Gewürztraminer Sporen Vendange Tardive	D	94
1988	Gewürztraminer Vendange Tardive	D	87
1990	Muscat Réserve	B	85
1990	Riesling	B	72
1990	Riesling Schoenenbourg	C	87
1989	Riesling Schoenenbourg	C	86
1988	Riesling Schoenenbourg	C	90
1990	Riesling Sélection de Grains Nobles	E	90
1988	Riesling Sélection de Grains Nobles	E	87
1990	Riesling Vendange Tardive	D	85
1988	Riesling Vendange Tardive	D	88
1990	Sylvaner	A	75
1990	Tokay-Pinot Gris	B	84
1988	Tokay-Pinot Gris Sélection de Grains Nobles	E	85
1990	Tokay-Pinot Gris Vendange Tardive	D	87

Dopff "Au Moulin" is unquestionably one of the leading Alsace growers/*négo-ciants.* Its cellars, located just outside of the walled city of Riquewihr, produce 2.5 million bottles of wine a year. One-third of this domaine's production is estate-bottled from the family's 175 acres of vineyards, which includes some superb holdings in such Grand Crus as Schoenenbourg, Brand, and Sporen. Monsieur Dopff, the force behind this empire, has been the mayor of Riquewihr for over 30 years. He is one of the region's, if not the country's, leading personalities. The style of wine produced is one that emphasizes dryness as well as longevity. One Dopff "Au Moulin" specialty is the production of a sparkling wine called Crémant d'Alsace. They make a number of different cuvées, and one of my favorites is the N.V. Cuvée Julien, made from Pinot Blanc. It exhibits a fresh, lovely, dry, applelike fruitiness, good effervescence, and a lingering persistence on the palate. Given its price, it is a shame more of this wine is not made available to American consumers, many of whom can no longer afford French Champagne. Those looking for a bone-dry, austere, yeasty, toasty, Champagne-like wine should try the N.V. Brut Sauvage (the current release is all from the 1987 vintage, although there is no year shown on the bottle), which receives no dosage and is a dead ringer for a good bottle of Champagne. As for the other dry wines, the 1990 Sylvaner left me unmoved, although it was typical of a great majority of Alsatian Sylvaners in its green, neutral, meagerly endowed character. The other regular cuvées included a somewhat angular, compact, lean 1990 Riesling and a light, fresh, decently made 1990 Tokay-Pinot Gris. Among the generic cuvées from Dopff "Au Moulin," I thought the best was the 1990 Gewürztraminer, which exhibited a wonderfully intense nose of peaches, flowers, and pears, followed by surprisingly deep, robust, muscular flavors and a dry finish. I also found the 1990 Muscat Réserve to be a good example of this underrated varietal. Dry, with the stunning floral fragrance Muscat offers, this medium-bodied, well-made, wonderfully pure wine should be drunk over the next 1–2 years. I tasted three vintages of the Riesling Schoenenbourg. My favorite was the 1988, but that could simply be because it has had more time in the bottle to develop. On potential, Monsieur Dopff feels that both 1989 and 1990 will be superior. The 1990 is bone dry, austere, extremely floral, and pure, as well as concentrated, but also closed and unevolved. It is a wonderfully precise, tightly knit Riesling, but it needs at least another 2–3 years in the bottle. The 1989 was also dry, with that curious mothball sort of fragrance that I find in some Alsace wines, a floral, tasty, tightly knit, rich palate, and an austere finish. My favorite of this trio, the 1988 Riesling Schoenenbourg, revealed beautiful peach-, floral-, and applelike scents in its bouquet, a rich, medium-bodied, very concentrated taste, and a crisp, bone-dry, stylish finish. Among the dry Gewürztraminers, the top-of-the-line 1990 Gewürztraminer Brand exhibited a distinctive nose of butterscotch, smoky bacon, and peaches that was followed by rich, full-bodied, exotic flavors and a long, dry finish. It is not for those looking for a more timid example of wine from this flashy varietal. The 1989 Gewürztraminer Brand was not nearly as rich as the 1990. Surprisingly, it was much lighter and more polite, exhibiting some of the smoky, lychee nut character one finds in top Gewürztraminers. The 1988 Gewürztraminer Brand had the heady, super-intense, flamboyant Gewürztraminer fragrance, followed by lush, full-bodied, rich fruit and a dry, long, spicy finish. It is quite noticeable with the wines from Dopff "Au Moulin" that the Vendange Tardive wines are much drier than those of their colleagues. For example, the 1990 Riesling V.T. would easily be mistaken by most tasters for a completely dry wine. It is very crisp, with a tart, applelike fragrance and underlying stony, mineral, and petrollike fruit flavor. It should last for at least a decade. I did not taste the 1989 Riesling V.T., but the 1988 Riesling V.T. is a potentially outstanding wine. With a huge fragrance of flower and mineral scents, steely, ripe, medium- to full-bodied flavors, and a long, surprisingly dry finish, it should drink well for at least 10–15 years. The 1990 Tokay-Pinot Gris V.T. exhibited fine ripeness in the dry style of this domaine and a big, creamy, buttery finish, without any sense of heaviness or flabbiness. I tasted two truly magnificent late harvest Gewürztraminers from Dopff "Au Moulin." The 1990 Gewürztraminer Brand V.T. exhibited a smashing nose of lychee nuts, smoke, and grapefruit, followed by full-bodied, impeccably well-balanced and well-delineated flavors that exploded in a long, dry finish. One of the most riveting Gewürztraminers I tasted from Alsace was the 1990 Gewürztraminer Sporen V.T. It is an essentially dry, superbly concentrated, rich, full-bodied wine bursting with the essence of minerals, peaches, and lychee nuts. The finish lasted well over a minute. Drink this stunning Gewürztraminer over the next 10–15 years. Last, the 1988 Gewürztraminer V.T. had fatter and thicker flavors, without the elegance, finesse, or complexity of the two 1990 Gewürztraminers from the Brand and Sporen vineyards. Although most Sélection de Grains Nobles wines are very rich, unctuous, and sweet, Dopff "Au Moulin" has a tendency to pick grapes at Sélection de Grains Nobles sugar levels but vinify them dry, which makes for wines that are more austere and less forthcoming than those from other producers. The 1990 Riesling S.D.G.N. displayed an enticing bouquet of ripe pears and grapefruit, long, deep, finely etched flavors, and a full-bodied, off-dry format. It should drink well for 15 or more years. Monsieur Dopff thinks it will last 30–40 years. The 1988 Riesling S.D.G.N. was almost bone dry. Although it was a lovely wine, I am not sure I would pay the price asked for it. The 1988 Tokay-Pinot Gris S.D.G.N. was relatively thick and slightly dull, without sufficient finesse or elegance. I was struck by the enormous richness and impeccable balance of the 1990 Gewürztraminer S.D.G.N. It was the best of all of these superlate harvest wines. What made it so outstanding was its great balance and precision despite its intensity and weight. The 1988 Gewürztraminer S.D.G.N. was simply bizarre, with a thin texture, somewhat diluted character, and strange palate impression. I do not know what to make of this very dry, unusual style of Sélection de Grains Nobles.

DOPFF ET IRION (RIQUEWIHR)* *

1989 Gewürztraminer Sélection de Grains Nobles	E	85
1990 Gewürztraminer Les Sorcières	B	87
1990 Pinot Blanc Cuvée René Dopff	A	77
1990 Riesling Schoenenbourg	C	72
1989 Riesling Schoenenbourg	C	70
1989 Riesling Sélection de Grains Nobles	E	?
1990 Tokay-Pinot Gris Sporen	C	71

It is hard to understand the disappointing performance of these offerings from Dopff et Irion. If this firm is going to compete with the better Alsace producers, quality must certainly be given a higher priority. The 1990 Pinot Blanc Cuvée René Dopff is extremely light, almost watery, with decent acidity, but without any real fruit or character. The quality of the 1990 Riesling Schoenenbourg is inexcusable for a wine from such a top-class vineyard. Extremely green, as if the grapes were picked before they were ripe, this acidic, relatively harsh wine begs for some stuffing. The 1989 Riesling Schoenenbourg fares no better, given its underripe, vegetal, disappointing flavors. The 1990 Tokay-Pinot Gris from the Sporen vineyard (which is a terrific vineyard for Gewürztraminer and Tokay) is extremely light, watery, medium bodied, and barely acceptable. Whatever Dopff et Irion did wrong with these wines was not apparent in its 1990 Gewürztraminer Les Sorcières. By far the best of this mediocre group, this smoky, rich, full-bodied, concentrated wine has gobs of fruit, luscious texture, and a long, chewy, lip-smacking, heady finish. It will not be a long-lived Gewürztraminer but should last for at least 5–6 years. The 1990 Riesling S.D.G.N. had a very bizarre smell of straw and was disappointing on the palate as well. On the other hand, the very sweet and somewhat cloying 1989 Gewürztraminer S.D.G.N. was a thick, ripe, butterscotch- and ripe pineapple–flavored wine that will make tasty nectar for drinking over the next 7–8 years.

SICK DREYER (AMMERSCHWIHR)* * * *

1990 Gewürztraminer Kaefferkopf	C	89
1990 Klevner	B	85
1990 Riesling Kaefferkopf	B	86
1990 Riesling Kaefferkopf Cuvée J. Dreyer	C	90
1990 Tokay-Pinot Gris	B	87

These impressive wines were all made in a very natural, dry, seemingly unmanipulated style. The 1990 Klevner exhibited excellent ripeness, a rich, plump, apricot-, orange-, applelike fruitiness, and good, fresh acidity. A generous amount of glycerin and character give it a degree of opulence. Drink it over the next 2–3 years. The 1990 Riesling Kaefferkopf was slightly tart and backward, but it took no genius to recognize the solid inner core of rich, highly extracted fruit and the long, dry, excellent finish. It should drink well for at least 10–12 years. Dreyer's 1990 Riesling Kaefferkopf Cuvée J. Dreyer was a classic Riesling in the dry, rich, medium-bodied style that Alsace does so well. Extremely intense, with lots of minerals and flinty, applelike Riesling fruit, this blazingly clear expression of Riesling possesses outstanding depth and complexity. Drink it over the next 10–12 years. There is also a fine, dry, creamy, spicy, somewhat soft, but richly concentrated 1990 Tokay-Pinot Gris. Another top-notch wine is Dreyer's 1990 Gewürztraminer Kaefferkopf. The richest and most opulent of these offerings, it needs some swirling to reveal its delicate rose petal bouquet and its pineapple, grapefruit, and smoky, lychee nut fruit flavors. This graceful, medium-bodied Gewürztraminer displays plenty of crisp acidity that should ensure at least 6–8 years of longevity.

ROBERT FALLER ET FILS (RIBEAUVILLÉ)* *

1990 Riesling Geisberg	C	88
1989 Riesling Geisberg	C	82

After immersing myself for one week in tasting Alsace's last three vintages, I feel that 1990 is definitely *the* vintage for Riesling. When comparing the two Riesling Geisbergs from Robert Faller, one can see that there is just much more to the 1990. The wine is dry, with a floral bouquet that leaps from the glass. In the mouth it is medium bodied, with a lot of extract and a very crisp, stony finish. The 1989 is also dry, but more citrusy and tart, without the inner core of fruit and depth the 1990 possesses.

PIERRE FRICK (PFAFFENHEIM)* * * *

1990 Gewürztraminer	B	88
1989 Gewürztraminer Steinert	C	88

1989 Pinot Blanc	A	87
1990 Riesling	B	86
1989 Riesling Vendange Tardive	C	88
1989 Riesling Vendange Tardive Amethyeste	C	90
1990 Tokay-Pinot Gris	B	86

Pierre Frick is one of a handful of Alsace producers who has opted to cultivate his vineyards with no herbicides or pesticides. Additionally there is minimal sulphuring in the winery and no chaptalization. Such a philosophy can often result in wines that are a bit closed and difficult to assess when young, but that certainly did not seem to be the case with Frick's excellent array of 1989s and 1990s. His 1989 Pinot Blanc should prove to be one of the best of the vintage. One taste reveals gobs of tropical fruit aromas such as lemons and oranges, followed by a honeyed, applelike fruitiness, fresh acidity, and an excellent, well-delineated finish. It is hard to believe so many consumers neglect to try wines such as these, preferring instead to grab a bottle of highly manufactured, sterile, charmless Chardonnay. Frick's 1990 Riesling is dry, with a very finely etched nose of minerals, flowers, and lemons. In the mouth the wine exhibits lovely fruit, medium body, good dryness, and a crisp, wet stone–like finish. Drink it over the next 5–6 years. The 1990 Tokay-Pinot Gris is a polite, delicate, understated example of this varietal, which can sometimes border on being overbearing and heavy. I liked it for its polish and lovely creamy, buttery fruit intertwined with good acidity, and for its well-knit style. Although it is not likely to win many blind tastings, it is a tasty, well-made Tokay that may turn out to be underrated. Drink it over the next 5–7 years. The 1990 Gewürztraminer has a wonderfully seductive, meaty, smoky, lychee nut–scented nose, full body, excellent balance, and a crisp, almost kinetic sort of finish. Drink this big, exceptionally well-delineated Gewürztraminer over the next 7–8 years. Frick's 1989 Gewürztraminer Steinert, from the well-drained soils of this vineyard near Pfaffenheim, is a surprisingly delicate, understated wine from an aromatic perspective, but in the mouth one sees its authoritative, rich, grilled nut, meaty, fruit flavors and its almost yeasty, breadlike taste. It is an enthralling Gewürztraminer to drink over the next 7–8 years. With respect to the two offerings of Riesling V.T., the 1989 Riesling V.T. tastes dry and has an intriguing nose of flint and apples, medium body, fine concentration, and a zesty, rich finish. The 1989 Riesling Amethyeste V.T. is even more concentrated, with a fascinating level of ripeness, fruit, and acidity and a backward feel to it, but loads of personality and potential. Drink it over the next 5–15 years.

JEAN GEILER (INGERSHEIM)* * *

1990 Gewürztraminer Florimont	B	86
1988 Gewürztraminer Vendange Tardive	C	77
1990 Pinot Blanc Auxerrois Réserve	B	85
1990 Riesling Reserve	B	81
1990 Riesling Steinweg	B	83

These wines, attractively made and packaged at the co-op called Cave Vini-cole Ingersheim, are generally well made. The 1990 Pinot Blanc Auxerrois Réserve is a classy, fresh-tasting, delicately scented, medium-bodied wine with a great deal of fruit and character. Drink it over the next 1–2 years. The 1990 Riesling Steinweg is backward and austere, but I sense plenty of extrac-tion and a good, dry, stony finish. I suspect it will merit a higher score in an-other 2–3 years. The 1990 Riesling Réserve is fresh, well made, a bit high strung, acidic, and tart. I am not sure much more character will emerge with cellaring. Geiler's 1990 Gewürztraminer Florimont exhibits excellent purity of fruit, the telltale lychee nut– and rose petal–scented nose, medium body, and a smoky texture buttressed by decent acidity. Drink it over the next 3–4 years. The only disappointing offering from Geiler is the dull, off-dry, simple-scented 1988 Gewürztraminer V.T.

GERARD ET SERGE HARTMANN (VOEGTLINSHOFFEN)* * *

1989 Gewürztraminer Hatschbourg Vendange Tardive	C	83
1989 Muscat Réserve	B	84
1990 Pinot Blanc	A	75
1989 Pinot Blanc Médaille d'Or	A	86
1989 Riesling	B	78
1989 Tokay-Pinot Gris Hatschbourg Vendange Tardive	C	84

I have had some wonderful wines from this estate in past years, but I was less than moved by the quality of these releases. The best of the lot was an excel-lent, tasty, very perfumed, dry, medium- to full-bodied 1989 Pinot Blanc Mé-daille d'Or. It was certainly superior to the short, diluted 1990 Pinot Blanc. As for the 1989 Riesling, which won a prize from the famous Confrerie Saint Eti-enne in Alsace, I found it austere and acidic to the point of being shrill. The flavors were green, and the fruit was insufficient to back up the nasty acidity. The dry, very floral and delicate 1989 Muscat Réserve is a tasty, well-made wine. The 1989 Tokay-Pinot Gris Hatschbourg V.T. is ripe and chunky, with decent acidity, but it lacks complexity and tastes as if the grapes were picked before they were ripe physiologically. It is a good rather than profound wine from one of the great Grand Cru vineyards. The 1989 Gewürztraminer Hatschbourg V.T. is heavy-handed, excessively ripe, cloying to taste, and in need of some acidity for focus and balance.

HUBERT HARTMANN (ORSCHWIHR)* *

1988 Gewürztraminer Sélection de Grains Nobles	E	79
1990 Pinot Blanc Cuvée Printanière	A	76
1990 Riesling	A	74

The 1990 Pinot Blanc Cuvée Printanière is a straightforward, tart, lean wine that is acceptable for uncritical quaffing. The 1990 Riesling is short and acidic with inadequate fruit. Even the 1988 Gewürztraminer S.D.G.N. lacks complex-ity and comes across as flabby, unstructured, and cloying.

BRUNO HERTZ (EGUISHEIM)* *

1986	Gewürztraminer Vendange Tardive	C	75
1989	Muscat	B	85
1990	Pinot Blanc	B	84
1989	Riesling Rangen	B	77
1990	Tokay-Pinot Gris	B	82

The 1990 Pinot Blanc from this estate has an interesting Wheat Thins sort of nose, tasty, round, soft flavors, and an easy-to-like personality. Drink it over the next 1–2 years. The 1989 Riesling Rangen, from an extraordinary vineyard near the village of Thann, is a wishy-washy wine, with light, nondescript flavors and an almost flaccid, short finish. It is hard to understand what could have gone wrong. I found a great deal of charm in the 1989 Muscat, with its floral, perfumed bouquet and dry, flowery, fresh, enthralling flavors. It should be drunk over the next 1–2 years. The 1990 Tokay-Pinot Gris, most of which I assume came from the great Rangen vineyard, is elegant but somewhat one-dimensional in its straightforward, medium-bodied, creamy, peachy flavors. Last, the 1986 Gewürztraminer V.T. is a puzzling wine to taste given its lightness, relatively high alcohol, and lack of fruit extraction and personality. I expected more quality than this from Bruno Hertz.

HUGEL (RIQUEWIHR)
CUVÉE JUBILEE* * * * * CUVÉE TRADITION* * * *

1989	Gewürztraminer Cuvée Jubilee	C	90
1989	Gewürztraminer Cuvée Tradition	C	88
1983	Gewürztraminer Vendange Tardive	D	94
1989	Gewürztraminer Vendange Tardive	D	92
1990	Pinot Blanc Cuvée Les Amours	A	87
1989	Pinot Blanc Cuvée Les Amours	A	85
1989	Riesling Cuvée Jubilee	C	87
1990	Riesling Cuvée Tradition	B	85
1989	Riesling Cuvée Tradition	B	76
1989	Riesling Vendange Tardive	D	92
1983	Riesling Vendange Tardive	D	92
1989	Tokay-Pinot Gris Cuvée Jubilee	C	87
1989	Tokay-Pinot Gris Vendange Tardive	D	92

Mention Hugel and most wine consumers, regardless of whether they are from Singapore, Stockholm, or San Francisco, will no doubt recognize the name. This firm, which has been family-owned since 1639, is undoubtedly one of the best known and finest houses of Alsace. Today, the eleventh generation of Hugels produces only 100,000 cases of wine. The firm is both a vineyard owner (they own 62 acres) and *négociant,* buying hand-picked fruit and vinifying the wines in their cellars in Riquewihr. It is no secret that the Hugels have been vociferously opposed to the Grand Cru system in Alsace. With some degree of accuracy, they claim that many Grand Cru vineyards are political creations made to satisfy the local politicians of each wine village. Furthermore, they argue, the authorities permitted many Grands Crus to incorporate adjacent vineyard acreage that was not within the historic *lieux-dit* boundaries of the specific vineyard. Last, the Hugels point to the fact that their top-of-the-line wines, at one time called Réserve Personnelle and now called Jubilee, are produced primarily from Grand Cru vineyard fruit. For example, virtually all of their Gewürztraminer for the Cuvée Jubilee emanates from the great Sporen vineyard behind the town of Riquewihr. Nearly all of the Riesling grapes for their top cuvées come from the Schoenenbourg vineyard. Of course, both of these vineyards are Grands Crus. The Hugels, much like their good friends the Trimbachs in Ribeauvillé, are never in a hurry to rush their wines to the marketplace. For example, their 1983 Vendange Tardive wines were just released in 1991. It is the quality of these wines, which are among the longest lived of the entire Alsace region, with bottles from the nineteenth century still in beautiful condition, that makes Hugel so outstanding. Despite the fact that 85% of Hugel's production is exported, the United States accounts only for a mere 6%—another distressing sign that our country remains more loyal to prestigious labels and recognizable brand names than to high quality. Hugel consistently makes one of the finest Pinot Blancs. As good as the 1989 Pinot Blanc Cuvée les Amours is, consumers should be making reservations for the 1990 Pinot Blanc Cuvée les Amours, with its huge, flinty, fresh-scented nose and excellent, ripe, medium-bodied flavors. This delicious wine should drink beautifully for the next 4–5 years. The 1990 Riesling Cuvée Tradition is crisp, tasty, elegant, and understated. With another 2 years in the bottle it will undoubtedly merit a higher score. I had no problem pegging the 1990 Gewürztraminer Cuvée Tradition. It is a gorgeous pineapple- and lychee nut–scented wine with deep, intense flavors, a rich, full-bodied, muscular palate, and a crisp, stylish, well-built finish. Drink it over the next 10–12 years. The 1989 Riesling Cuvée Tradition appeared as backward as the 1990, with its austere, mineral-scented nose and fresh, medium-bodied flavors. Although it was not singing when I tasted it, I would not be surprised to see this wine blossom with another 4–5 years in the bottle. The 1989 Riesling Cuvée Jubilee displays beautiful, rich, dry Riesling fruit, an aroma of green herbs, a charcoallike smokiness, and a wonderful, pure, finely delineated, medium-bodied, dry, surprisingly long finish. Despite the fact that this wine is relatively closed, it should last for at least 12–15 years. The Hugels believe that all of their top-of-the-line Rieslings require at least 5–6 years of bottle age before they should be drunk. The 1989 Tokay-Pinot Gris Cuvée Jubilee is in need of at least 6–7 years of bottle age. Very dry and intense, with an exotic, kinky, creamy, smoky fruitiness and a long, heady, alcoholic finish, it should last for up to 15 or more years. The 1989 Gewürztraminer Cuvée Jubilee offers up a huge, meaty, smoky, bacon fat–scented nose, wonderfully constructed, rich, full-bodied flavors, plenty of glycerin, good acidity, and a lot of class and character. It should be at its best between 1994 and 2010. I say this because I own both the 1983 and 1985 Réserve Personnelle (the same as the Jubilee bottling), and both of those bottlings are just beginning to open up and display their multidimensional personalities. There are a number of superb Vendange Tardive bottlings in 1989 that should age well for 25–30 years or more. The 1989 Riesling V.T. exhibited that steely, earthy, petrollike nose, rich, highly extracted flavors with a touch of peach/apricot fruit suggestive of botrytis, and a slightly off-dry yet dazzling finish. It brought to mind the famous expression "an iron fist in a velvet glove." Drink it between 1995 and 2015. The 1989 Tokay-Pinot Gris V.T. possessed a nose that reminded me of smoked pork, followed by rich, toasty, honeyed, superconcentrated flavors, an unctuous texture, but enough acidity to provide lift and balance. Although it is still amazingly young and unevolved, it is so delicious. I have a few bottles left of the 1976 Tokay-Pinot Gris V.T., which, when I serve it blind to friends, is often mistaken for a Grand Cru burgundy. In fact, it is in far better condition than most white burgundies of a similar age. No doubt the 1989 version of this wine will last for at least 20 or more years. The 1989 Gewürztraminer V.T., with its 13.8% alcohol, is not for the shy. It will probably be a monumental Gewürztraminer in another 5–10 years. At present this wine reveals an extraordinary amount of rose-scented fruit, backed up by meaty, smoked ducklike flavors as well as a hint of lychee nuts and mint. The lavishly endowed personality of this wine makes it a dramatic style of Gewürztraminer that is hard to ignore. Despite the impression that the wine is relatively young and closed, it is impossible to resist. Last, the Hugel firm has just released its 1983 Vendange Tardive wines. The 1983 Gewürztraminer V.T. is just beginning to open up yet has 15–20 years of evolution ahead of it. It is a great bottle of Gewürztraminer, aromatic, structured, yet dramatic and unbelievably rich and long. Drink it with either a rich salmon dish, Muenster cheese, or foie gras. The 1983 Riesling V.T. is a very dry, rich, amazingly backward wine bursting with steely, green apple, petrollike flavors. This riveting example of a 10-year-old Riesling is just beginning to exhibit subtle signs of evolution. I also tasted a bevy of Sélection de Grains Nobles wines from Hugel, all of which would score in the upper 90s. They were remarkable, but they will not be released for at least 5–6 years. As unbelievable as it sounds, some of them had as much as 350 grams of residual sugar per liter! Along with the Hugels, I suspect their 1989 Sélection de Grains Nobles offerings in Gewürztraminer and Tokay-Pinot Gris will be among the greatest they have ever produced.

JOSMEYER—JOSEPH MEYER (WINTZENHEIM)
SINGLE-VINEYARD CUVÉES* * * * * STANDARD CUVÉES* * * *

1990 Chasselas "H" Vieilles Vignes	B	84
1990 Gewürztraminer Les Archenets	C	88
1989 Gewürztraminer Les Archenets	C	92
1990 Gewürztraminer Cuvée de Folastries	C	87
1989 Gewürztraminer Cuvée de Folastries	C	90
1989 Gewürztraminer Hengst	C	91
1990 Gewürztraminer Sélection de Grains Nobles	E	86
1989 Gewürztraminer Sélection de Grains Nobles	E	96
1990 Gewürztraminer Vendange Tardive	D	88
1989 Gewürztraminer Vendange Tardive	D	88

1989 Muscat Les Fleurons	B	87
1990 Pinot Auxerrois "H" Vieilles Vignes	B	87
1989 Pinot Auxerrois "H" Vieilles Vignes	B	90
1990 Pinot Blanc Les Lutins	B	85
1989 Pinot Blanc Les Lutins	B	87
1990 Pinot Blanc Mise du Printemps	A	85
1989 Riesling Hengst	B	87
1989 Riesling Hengst Cuvée de la Sainte Martine	C	90
1990 Riesling Hengst Vendange Tardive	C	90
1990 Riesling Le Kottabe	C	85
1989 Riesling Le Kottabe	C	84
1990 Riesling Les Pierrets	C	85
1989 Riesling Les Pierrets	C	87
1990 Tokay-Pinot Gris Cuvée du Centenaire	C	87
1989 Tokay-Pinot Gris Cuvée du Centenaire	C	88
1989 Tokay-Pinot Gris Sélection de Grains Nobles	E	93
1990 Tokay-Pinot Gris Vendange Tardive	D	86

Jean Meyer, one of Alsace's finest winemakers, has an extraordinary appreciation of his vineyards' *terroirs*. His wines tend to begin life slowly, but based on
the 1967s and 1971s I drank recently, they age magnificently. Josmeyer produces close to 30,000 cases of wine, of which a piddling 1,000–2,000 are
shipped to the United States—in a top year! No wonder we will never become a
wine-drinking country when so many consumers and retailers pass up such
high-quality, reasonably priced wines as Josmeyer's Pinot Blancs and his
Chasselas. The 1990 Chasselas "H" comes from a Grand Cru vineyard called
Hengst. Since under Alsace's laws this varietal is not allowed to have Grand
Cru status, Meyer simply uses the letter "H" on the label. The wine, which is
made from vines over 30 years in age, is fleshy, light, and richly fruity and provides an ideal introduction to this house's style. Josmeyer is the greatest proponent of Pinot Blanc and Pinot Auxerrois in Alsace. The 1990s were somewhat
closed and tight, but one could see they possessed plenty of fruit, although I
doubt they will achieve the level of quality reached in 1989. For starters there
is the wonderfully exuberant, floral, fresh, lively, deceptively easy-to-drink
1990 Pinot Blanc Mise du Printemps. This wine, which is meant to be drunk
within its first several years of life, is renowned for its purity and lightness of
flavor. If I were in the restaurant business, I would be encouraging customers
to choose it. The other Pinot Blancs include a deliciously elegant, fruity, crisp,
tangerine-tasting 1990 Pinot Les Lutins. The 1989 is softer but also richer and
creamier, with a great deal more glycerin and ripeness. If you like your Pinots
more vibrant, go for the 1990; if you like them richer and more substantial, the
1989 may make more sense. Josmeyer's Pinot Auxerrois "H" Vieilles Vignes
is, to my way of thinking, the greatest expression of Pinot Blanc in Alsace. The
1990 was remarkably closed and structured, but with swirling, the rich,

mango, honeyed, apple, and stony fruit emerges. However, there is no doubting that the 1989 is a richer, fuller, more concentrated wine, with great presence on the palate, impeccable structure, and the lightness and freshness that make this wine such a turn-on. Both of these offerings should drink beautifully for the next 5–6 years. I was pleased with the explosively flowery nose of the 1989 Muscat Les Fleurons. This crisp, very dry, seductive wine exhibits gobs of delicate fruit, light to medium body, and a long, zesty finish. Drink this beauty over the next several years. Josmeyer produces a bevy of Rieslings that begin at the bottom of the hierarchy with the Riesling Le Kottabe and proceed upward in quality and price to his top-of-the-line Grand Cru Rieslings from the Hengst vineyard. In both 1989 and 1990 the Riesling Le Kottabe was the lightest of these offerings, flowery, crisp, with good acidity, but without the profound character one finds in Josmeyer's other wines. It is a Riesling that can be drunk without a great deal of introspection. The 1990 Riesling Les Pierrets exhibits a stony, citric fragrance, along with some orange- and mango-flavored fruit, zesty acidity, and a good, solid core of depth, although it is still relatively closed. On the other hand, the 1989 Riesling Les Pierrets is already singing loudly from the glass. There is an essence of what the French call *gout de pétrol*, a hard-to-describe, stony, earthy, gasoline-related smell. The 1989 is rich and loaded with fruit, fuller than the 1990, with a spicy, stony, flowery finish. Although the 1990 Riesling Hengst was impossibly closed when I tasted it, it should be of high quality given the overall balance, weight, and ripeness I believe I detected. There is no denying the exceptional quality of the 1989 Riesling Hengst Cuvée de la Sainte Martine. Intensely concentrated and full bodied, it displays superb acidity and the essence of apple and apricot fruit in its concentrated, profound flavors. This dry Riesling should make for profound drinking over the next 10–15 years. There is also a regular cuvée of 1989 Riesling Hengst that was made from grapes harvested earlier than those in the Cuvée de la Sainte Martine. It is also an excellent wine, with a more pronounced stony, petrollike nose, long, excellent, dry, exceptionally fresh, pure flavors, and a medium-bodied finish. It should drink nicely for the next 5–7 years. In both 1989 and 1990 Josmeyer produced a Tokay-Pinot Gris Cuvée du Centenaire. The 1990 exhibited good ripeness, smoky fruit, and a densely packed character, although it was still closed. On the other hand, the 1989 displayed much more of a buttery, creamy character, as well as rich, full-bodied, dry, bacon flavors. What is so admirable about both of these wines is that they have the necessary acidity to balance their weight and potential richness. Among the other totally dry wines were a bevy of terrific Gewürztraminers, particularly from the 1989 vintage. The 1990 Gewürztraminer Cuvée de Folastries offered up an exotic, lychee nut fragrance, good acidity, dry, medium-bodied flavors, and plenty of length. Josmeyer claims this dramatic Gewürztraminer should be drunk over the next 5–6 years. The 1989 Gewürztraminer Cuvée de Folastries had a gorgeous, almost kinky nose of flowers, Oriental spices, and smoke; meaty, baconlike flavors; and a dramatic, terrific finish. It should also be drunk over the next 5–6 years. The 1990 Gewürztraminer Les Archenets exhibited a more smoky, roasted character, riper, more unctuous fruit flavors, and fuller body, with plenty of glycerin, even in the more suave 1990 vintage. In 1989 this wine was almost the essence of lychee nuts, bacon fat, and smoky, roasted flavors. Some tasters will no doubt be overwhelmed by this huge, rich, powerful Gewürztraminer, but I adored it. Drink it over the next 7–8 years. I did not taste the 1990 Gewürztraminer Hengst, but the 1989 was a superrich, backward, deeply concentrated, fabulously dry, large-scale Gewürztraminer for cellaring up to a decade or more. It is much less evolved than the other 1989s, but wow, what potential this Gewürztraminer has! Drink it between 1993 and 2003.

Among the Vendange Tardive offerings from Josmeyer, I thought the 1990 Tokay-Pinot Gris V.T. was ripe, rich, slightly off-dry, but not as well focused as many of the other wines from this estate. Far greater, even profound, was the 1990 Riesling Hengst V.T. This wine, with its huge aroma of flowers and oranges, followed by deep, fleshy, crisp flavors, with superb concentration, should make for quite a glass of Riesling over the next 10–12 years. It was surprisingly dry for a Vendange Tardive offering. The 1990 Gewürztraminer V.T. was smoky, with an intense lychee nut character, excellent medium- to full-bodied flavors, and a fine purity. As the score denotes, as excellent as it was, I actually preferred all the drier Gewürztraminers. I thought the 1989 Gewürztraminer V.T. was sweeter, rich and ripe, blatantly full bodied, but perhaps a trifle cloying, although I admired its depth and layers of fruit. Both the 1988 and 1989 Gewürztraminer V.T.'s should be drunk over the next 7–9 years. Among the supersweet, nectarlike wines, the 1990 Gewürztraminer S.D.G.N. was closed and not that evolved or compelling. There is plenty of depth, and I suspect it will be outstanding, but it was completely unevolved. The same cannot be said for the otherworldly 1989 Gewürztraminer S.D.G.N. This opulent, oily, chewy wine, with great sweetness as well as focus, is the type of superextracted Gewürztraminer that very few of us ever get a chance to taste. Although prices for these nectarlike cuvées of Alsatian wines are outrageously high, they should drink well for 30 or more years. The 1989 Tokay-Pinot Gris S.D.G.N. was just as sweet, with a huge, butter, honeyed aroma, and sweet, nectarlike flavors. It should last for at least 15–30 years. As much as I admire these sweet wines, I feel Josmeyer's strengths lie with the drier cuvées that age magnificently.

JEAN-PIERRE KLEIN (SAINT HIPPOLYTE)* *

1989	Gewürztraminer Schlossreben	B	85
1989	Riesling Schlossreben	B	82
1988	Riesling Schlossreben Vendange Tardive	C	72
1989	Tokay-Pinot Gris Geisberg	B	74
1988	Tokay-Pinot Gris Geisberg Vendange Tardive	C	74

I kept going back to the Riesling selections from Klein's Schlossreben vineyard, giving them plenty of chances to air out and prove that there was more to them than I suspected. The 1989 Riesling Schlossreben offered whiffs of wet stones, but in the mouth it was relatively green, tough-textured, extremely dry, and in need of an infusion of fruit and character. The 1988 Riesling Schlossreben V.T. was vegetal and disappointing; my rating may actually be generous. The 1989 Tokay-Pinot Gris Geisberg had extremely high acidity and was light, watery, and indifferent. The 1988 Tokay-Pinot Gris Geisberg V.T. offered more of a buttery, smoky character in the nose, but on the palate it was out of balance and exaggerated, with cloying flavors, resulting in a heavy-handed, sloppily made wine. The only interesting wine among this group was the 1989 Gewürztraminer Schlossreben. I liked it for its buttery, smoky, rose petal–scented fragrance, its good acidity, and its straightforward, chunky flavors. Overall, Klein's wines were unexciting, and several were disappointing.

CHARLES KOEHLY ET FILS (RODERN)* *

1990	Muscat	A	79
1990	Riesling Altenberg Vendange Tardive	C	84
1986	Tokay-Pinot Gris Altenberg Vendange Tardive	C	82

Koehly's wines are extremely austere, tightly knit, backward, and bone-dry, requiring some time to coax from the glass. Although they should age well, many tasters will find their style intimidatingly lean and backward. That being said, the 1990 Riesling Altenberg V.T. is a tart, crisp, elegant, bone-dry, tightly knit wine that may merit a higher score with another 2–3 years in the bottle. It is hard to hide the perfume of a top Muscat, but Koehly almost does that in this backward, very tart, austere, extremely dry 1990 Muscat that requires drinking over the next 2–3 years. Even his 1986 Tokay-Pinot Gris Altenberg V.T. is a lean, compact, reserved wine that has yet to open and evolve.

MARC KREYDENWEISS (ANDLAU)* * * *

1990	Clos du Val	B	86
1990	Gewürztraminer Kritt Sélection de Grains Nobles	E	90
1989	Gewürztraminer Kritt Sélection de Grains Nobles	E	98
1990	Gewürztraminer Kritt Vendange Tardive	D	91
1989	Gewürztraminer Kritt Vendange Tardive	D	89
1990	Klevner Kritt	B	90
1990	Pinot Blanc Kritt	B	89
1990	Riesling Andlau	B	87
1989	Riesling Kastelberg	B	89
1990	Riesling Kastelberg Sélection de Grains Nobles	E	92
1990	Riesling Kastelberg Vendange Tardive	D	87
1990	Riesling Wiebelsberg	C	88
1989	Riesling Wiebelsberg	C	87
1989	Riesling Wiebelsberg Vendange Tardive	D	90
1990	Tokay-Pinot Gris Moenchberg Sélection de Grains Nobles	E	93
1989	Tokay-Pinot Gris Moenchberg Sélection de Grains Nobles	E	98
1990	Tokay-Pinot Gris Moenchberg Vendange Tardive	D	90
1989	Tokay-Pinot Gris Moenchberg Vendange Tardive	D	89

There has been a long tradition of bottling at the Domaine Kreydenweiss. Marc Kreydenweiss's grandfather, Monsieur Gresser, was one of the first in Alsace to believe in estate bottling. The domaine, located in the Bas Rhin, or the northern half of Alsace's viticultural area, produces gorgeously balanced wines, full of character, that are consistently among the best in Alsace. Kreydenweiss exploits three Grand Cru vineyards—Kastelberg, Wiebelsberg, and Moenchberg—all of which are on steep hillsides overlooking the picture postcard–like beauty of the town of Andlau. Kreydenweiss keeps his yields to under 35 hectoliters per hectare. Unlike most of his peers, who prefer 1989, he believes 1990 is the best vintage he has ever produced. His wines are aged in oak *foudres sur-lies* for at least 8 months. Beginning in 1991, Kreydenweiss will be producing his wines from organically farmed vineyards with no pesticides, herbicides, or fungicides, as well as minimal or no use of sulphur in the winemaking process. Kreydenweiss is an absolute genius with Pinot Blanc/Klevner, and his 1990 Pinot Blanc Kritt is one of the best wines from this varietal. It is rich, full, opulent, explosively fruity, yet fresh and lively, and should continue to drink well for the next 2–3 years. The 1990 Klevner Kritt is even more stunning, with a honeyed, orange blossom–scented nose, gorgeously rich, medium-bodied fruit flavors, superpurity and focus, and a long, zesty finish. In 1990 Kreydenweiss introduced what must be one of the first proprietary white wines ever made in Alsace, called Clos du Val. The 1990, a blend of 70% Riesling and 30% Pinot Gris, exhibits an attractive floral, mineral-scented nose and polite, medium-bodied flavors. Although I liked all of his single-varietal wines much better, no one will be disappointed by this wine. Riesling is a specialty of this house. The 1990 Riesling-Andlau displays an excellent flowery-scented nose, dry, rich, medium-bodied flavors with a hint of botrytis, and a long, surprisingly full-bodied, even powerful finish. The other totally dry Riesling was the 1989 Riesling Kastelberg. This steep vineyard is composed of very stony soil and is known for its particular type of schist, which is unique in Alsace. The wine often has a resemblance to a top-class Chablis, given its gunflint, stony, smoky bouquet. With this Riesling one gets citron and green apples in a backward, concentrated, intense style that needs a considerable amount of time to reveal its full merits. Kreydenweiss suggests that it is capable of lasting for 2 decades. Among the other dry Rieslings, the 1990 Riesling Wiebelsberg exhibits excellent fruit, rich, ripe, citrusy, stony flavors, and a long, crisp, medium-bodied finish. The 1989 Riesling Wiebelsberg has more of a floral character and tastes leaner and more backward. It is clearly in need of at least 3–4 years of bottle age. Kreydenweiss made several Vendange Tardive Rieslings in each of the last few vintages. The 1989 Riesling Wiebelsberg V.T. possesses a spicy, orange blossom–scented nose, excellent medium-bodied, surprisingly dry flavors, and a long, crisp finish. The 1990 Riesling Kastelberg V.T., which displays an essence of slate, minerallike fruitiness and a floral-scented nose, is very backward, with tightly knit flavors; it needs several more years of cellaring. Kreydenweiss's 1990 Tokay-Pinot Gris Moenchberg V.T. is an excellent example from this vintage. Slightly off-dry, with a honey, creamy, nutty, almost vanillin-scented nose, rich, full-bodied, complex flavors, and a great deal of glycerin and alcohol (14%), this big wine should have at least a decade of aging potential. The 1989 Tokay-Pinot Gris Moenchberg V.T. exhibits a smoky, butter-cream nose, fat, chewy, dense flavors, 15% alcohol, and an off-dry yet explosively rich, lusty finish. It, too, should last for up to a decade. I also adored the two Gewürztraminers from the Kritt vineyard. The 1990 Gewürztraminer Kritt V.T. displays a fragrant, perfumed nose, dramatic, intense flavors, plenty of richness, opulence, and body, and an explosively long, exceptionally well-balanced finish. I had a hard time spitting out this wine. It should drink well for at least a decade. The 1989 Gewürztraminer Kritt V.T. is also dramatic and rich, although slightly less poised and perhaps more heavy-handed than the beautifully wrought 1990. The other wines I tasted from Kreydenweiss were all Sélection de Grains Nobles. I am afraid they will be appallingly expensive and difficult to find in the marketplace. Several of them were among the greatest sweet wines I tasted during my recent trip to Alsace. The 1989 Riesling Kastelberg S.D.G.N. is abundantly endowed with honeyed, apple- and peach-like fruit, plenty of botrytis, good acidity, and a long, superrich, medium-sweet finish. The 1990 Gewürztraminer Kritt S.D.G.N. exhibits an intense rose petal fragrance and is surprisingly graceful, suave, and civilized for a Gewürztraminer, with good acidity as well as a well-defined, medium-sweet finish. Although it is an excellent wine, it lacks the excitement of the other Sélection de Grains Nobles wines. The 1990 Tokay-Pinot Gris Moenchberg S.D.G.N., with 15% alcohol and 150 grams per liter of residual sugar, displays superb ripeness and enormous quantities of fruit. What is so striking about this wine is its superb balance. Nearly perfect, the 1989 Tokay-Pinot Gris Moenchberg S.D.G.N. boasts 13% alcohol and 15% residual sugar. It possesses an awesome nose of flowers, peaches, apricots, and honey. In the mouth there is the taste of a once-in-a-lifetime sort of nectar. Deep yet gorgeously balanced, with penetrating, fresh acidity, this is a wine of fabulous concentration and extraordinary length and presence on the palate. Amazingly, it does not taste heavy. The 1989 Gewürztraminer Kritt S.D.G.N. is, to my way of thinking, the essence of Gewürztraminer, a profoundly rich wine that has to be tasted to be believed. It exudes some almost undefinable scents of Oriental spices and a concentrated essence of lychee, with stunning acidity and an avalanche of fruit, all presented in what is a perfectly balanced, decadently sweet, nectarlike wine. This is a true winemaking tour de force; it should continue to drink well for 20–30 years.

KUEHN (AMMERSCHWIHR)* * * *

1990	Gewürztraminer Cuvée Saint Hubert	B	90
1989	Gewürztraminer Cuvée Saint Hubert	B	88
1990	Riesling Baron de Schielé	B	83
1988	Riesling Vendange Tardive	C	87

The vineyards of Kuehn are now owned by and the wines made at the Cave Vinicole Ingersheim. I remember having some sensational Gewürztraminers from Kuehn in my young student days, and I was glad to see that 20 years later these particular wines are still authoritatively flavored. The 1990 Riesling Baron de Schielé is a stony, high-acid, fresh, grapefruit-flavored wine that should provide interesting drinking over the next 3–4 years. Although I would have liked to see more fruit and depth, this is certainly a quaffable wine. Far more interesting is the 1988 Riesling V.T., with its exotic nose of petrol and earthy, spicy, peach, and mineral flavors. Drink this big, full-bodied, slightly off-dry Riesling over the next 7–8 years. Although the 1990 Gewürztraminer Cuvée Saint Hubert has gobs of rose petal–scented fragrance and a smoky, lychee nut aroma, in the mouth it is a meaty, rich, full-bodied, opulent wine wit plenty of power and an impeccable sense of balance. Drink it over the next 5–7 years. Interestingly, the 1989 Gewürztraminer Cuvée Saint Hubert is more tightly knit, more structured, and has a deeper color than the 1990, but it does not quite have the 1990's sheer drama and expressiveness. I would opt for drinking this relatively big Gewürztraminer over the next 5–6 years.

KUENTZ-BAS (HUSSEREN-LES-CHÂTEAUX)* * * *

1989 Gewürztraminer Cuvée Tradition	B	85
1990 Gewürztraminer Eichberg	C	89
1989 Gewürztraminer Eichberg	C	88
1990 Gewürztraminer Eichberg Cuvée Caroline Vendange Tardive	C	92
1989 Gewürztraminer Eichberg Cuvée Caroline Vendange Tardive	C	94
1988 Gewürztraminer Pfersigberg	C	90
1990 Gewürztraminer Pfersigberg Cuvée Caroline Vendange Tardive	C	89
1989 Gewürztraminer Pfersigberg Cuvée Jeremy Sélection de Grains Nobles	E	91
1988 Muscat d'Alsace Cuvée Tradition	A	83
1989 Muscat d'Alsace Réserve Personnelle	B	85
1990 Pinot Blanc Cuvée Tradition	A	85
1989 Pinot Blanc Cuvée Tradition	A	84
1990 Riesling Cuvée Tradition	B	85
1989 Riesling Cuvée Tradition	B	84
1989 Riesling Pfersigberg	B	87
1988 Riesling Pfersigberg	B	87
1990 Riesling Pfersigberg Cuvée Caroline Vendange Tardive	C	90
1989 Riesling Pfersigberg Cuvée Caroline Vendange Tardive	C	89
1990 Riesling Réserve Personnelle	B	86
1989 Riesling Réserve Personnelle	B	83
1988 Riesling Réserve Personnelle	B	86
1989 Tokay-Pinot Gris Cuvée Jeremy Sélection de Grains Nobles	E	89
1989 Tokay-Pinot Gris Cuvée Tradition	B	85
1989 Tokay-Pinot Gris Réserve Personnelle	B	86
1990 Tokay-Pinot Gris Réserve Personnelle	B	86
1989 Tokay-Pinot Gris Réserve Personnelle Cuvée Caroline Vendange Tardive	E	90

Kuentz-Bas, located in the hillside village of Husseren-les-Châteaux, is a vineyard owner, possessing 30 acres of vineyards and producing 30,000 cases of estate-bottled wines (called Réserve Personnelle), and a *négociant*, producing a bevy of wines under their other label (Cuvée Tradition). Their philosophy is that the Cuvée Tradition wines are to be drunk in their first 3–4 years of life. The Réserve Personnelle and Grand Cru wines are vinified to last 10–15 or more years. This old firm, founded in 1795, consistently produces very good wines. Prices for the Cuvée Tradition wines are, along with those of Pierre Sparr, the most reasonable of Alsace. Both the 1989 and 1990 Pinot Blanc Cuvée Traditions are fresh, flowery, light- to medium-bodied wines, with an attractive purity. The 1990 displays slightly more fruit, but both should be drunk over the next few years. The 1988 Muscat d'Alsace Cuvée Tradition is fresh and perfumed, crisp, light, and slightly short. The 1989 Muscat Réserve Personnelle exhibits a more penetrating fragrance and slightly more fruit to its dry, crisp, medium-bodied flavors. Both should be consumed over the next several years. Included in the dry Rieslings I tasted from Kuentz-Bas was a 1989 Riesling Cuvée Tradition, which was dry, austere, light, and one-dimensional, but quaffable. The 1990 Riesling Cuvée Tradition displayed a more intense floral nose and steely, apple- and apricotlike flavors in a medium-bodied, dry format. The 1990 Riesling Réserve Personnelle is a bigger-style wine, still totally dry, with 12.3% alcohol, more glycerin, and wet stone, flowery, subtle peach flavors and aromas. It should drink nicely for 7–8 years. The 1989 Riesling Réserve Personnelle, although one-dimensional in comparison with the 1990, was still cleanly made and pure, with fresh apple-like fruit. The 1988 Riesling Réserve Personnelle is clearly more concentrated and complex than the 1989, exhibiting excellent stony, apple- and apricotlike ripeness, dry, medium-bodied flavors, and a long, tart, crisp finish. Moving up the ladder of quality and price for Riesling, a 1989 Riesling Pfersigberg gave up scents of cantaloupes and green melons. It had a spicy, rich, velvet-textured palate, and long, dry, peachy, orangelike flavors. The 1988 Riesling Pfersigberg was also dry, but more steely, and had that unmistakable Alsatian smell and taste of petrol, which is hard to articulate but is an earthy, almost gasoline and/or paraffin wax sort of smell that is much more attractive than it sounds. Both of these wines should last for 7–8 years. Included in the two Vendange Tardive wines I tasted (Kuentz-Bas uses the designation Cuvée Caroline for its Vendange Tardive offerings) was a 1990 Riesling Pfersigberg Cuvée Caroline V.T. that was medium sweet, rich, and full bodied, with a pronounced orange, mango, sweet apple character and a long, crisp finish. A terrific wine, it would be ideal with Oriental dishes or as an aperitif. The 1989 Riesling Pfersigberg Cuvée Caroline V.T. also exhibited a bouquet of intensely ripe oranges and tropical fruits. Although it seemed slightly drier, it would still be considered an off-dry, sweet wine, with medium- to full-bodied flavors and a fresh, lively finish. Both of these wines should last for up to a decade. The 1989 Tokay-Pinot Gris Cuvée Tradition is an elegant, light, forward, creamy, smoky wine that has a taste of Wheat Thins. This medium-bodied, dry offering would be perfect with grilled fish or salmon. The 1989 Tokay-Pinot Gris Réserve Personnelle displays the textbook peachy, spicy, nutty flavors that make Tokay so reminiscent of a top white burgundy such as Meursault. This tasty mouthful of wine should drink well for another 5–7 years. The 1990 Tokay-Pinot Gris Réserve Personnelle has more lemony acidity and is higher strung, without the flesh and glycerin of the 1989. Kuentz-Bas made a superb 1989 Tokay-Pinot Gris Cuvée Caroline V.T. This big, rich, relatively alcoholic, apricot-scented, smoky, creamy-textured wine offered up superb ripeness, long, luscious, intensely concentrated flavors, and a big, explosive finish. Given its distinctive and robust personality, it would be a perfect partner for rich fish dishes or strongly flavored veal and pork dishes. This estate's Gewürztraminer, a specialty of Kuentz-Bas, is consistently excellent. The 1989 Gewürztraminer Cuvée Tradition is a graceful, elegant, well-made wine, with good body and freshness as well as a telltale, subtle scent of rose petals. It is a more manageable Gewürztraminer, well suited for serving with fish or chicken. The 1989 Gewürztraminer Eichberg is much more closed, but one can sense its more muscular style and richer, more concentrated, higher alcohol personality. It is a big yet still elegant Gewürztraminer for drinking over the next 7–8 years. The 1988 Gewürztraminer Pfersigberg, from limestone-based vineyards situated in a hotter microclimate, is much fuller and more opulent, with a huge nose of grapefruit, roses, and lychee nuts. This big, sensationally concentrated, dramatic Gewürztraminer should last for 10 or more years. The 1990 Gewürztraminer Eichberg is dry, with a powerful, unevolved, smoky, exotic fruit fragrance and a luscious, richly flavored, full-bodied personality. It, too, should last for up to a decade. Kuentz-Bas made a number of Vendange Tardive wines from Gewürztraminer in both 1989 and 1990. The 1990 Gewürztraminer Eichberg Cuvée Caroline V.T. is profound, with sensational scents of smoke, lychee nuts, roses, and peaches. In the mouth it is ripe and long, with considerable power, highly extracted flavors, and a dazzling finish. For a Vendange Tardive wine, it is surprisingly dry. The 1990 Gewürztraminer Pfersigberg Cuvée Caroline V.T. is a fruitier, slightly sweeter wine, with tremendous extract but without the complexity of the Eichberg. The greatest Gewürztraminer I tasted from the cellars of Kuentz-Bas was the 1989 Gewürztraminer Eichberg Cuvée Caroline V.T. This is a compelling, rich, full-bodied, slightly sweet Gewürztraminer, with spectacular flavors, an unbelievable amount of spicy, lychee nut, grapefruit, and peach flavors and a bacon fat–like taste to go along with its opulence. It is a wine to have with one of the specialty cheeses from Alsace, particularly the well-known, smoky, fat-tasting Muenster. The Sélection de Grains Nobles wines are called Cuvée Jeremy, and the 1989 Gewürztraminer Pfersigberg Cuvée Jeremy S.D.G.N. is a very sweet, big, muscular, opulent wine bursting with fruit and character. It should drink well for at least 10–20 years. I thought the 1989 Tokay-Pinot Gris Cuvée Jeremy S.D.G.N. was also excellent but less complex and enthralling than the Gewürztraminer. I was told that only 50% of the grapes for the Tokay-Pinot Gris were affected by botrytis, whereas 100% of the Gewürztraminer grapes were affected.

SEPPI LANDMANN (SOULTZMATT)* * *

1989 Gewürztraminer Vallé Noble	C	87
1988 Gewürztraminer Zinnkoepfle Sélection de Grains Nobles	E	76
1988 Riesling Zinnkoepfle Sélection de Grains Nobles	E	86
1989 Riesling Zinnkoepfle Vendange Tardive	D	86

1990 Sylvaner Vallé Noble	A	85
1989 Tokay-Pinot Gris Vallé Noble Vendange Tardive	D	62

This was an odd assortment of wines, with the 1990 Sylvaner Vallé Noble, the least expensive offering, faring as well as, and in some cases better than, the more prestigious bottlings. It would be worthwhile investing in a few bottles of this Sylvaner for its freshness, elegance, and medium-bodied, tasty personality. Dry and full of fruit, it exhibits considerably more character than one normally finds from this varietal. The 1989 Riesling Zinnkoepfle V.T. was also excellent, although made in an extremely dry, austere style for a Vendange Tardive wine. Crisp and elegant, with stylish apple- and underripe apricot–like fruit, this medium-bodied, refreshing Riesling should age nicely for 7–8 years. The 1989 Tokay-Pinot Gris Vallé Noble V.T. was a very disjointed, clumsy, bizarre-tasting, nearly vulgar wine. Who knows what went wrong with this undrinkable wine, but it does not deserve to be in the bottle. Landmann redeemed his reputation with his excellent 1989 Gewürztraminer Vallé Noble, which displayed gobs of smoky, lychee nut, meaty fruit, medium body, an overall elegant personality, and a dry, long, nicely balanced finish. It should drink well for the next 5–6 years. Among the two off-dry Sélection de Grains Nobles wines, the 1988 Riesling Zinnkoepfle S.D.G.N., which exhibited an enthralling nose that reminded me of eau de vie of pear, was made in an extremely high-acid, off-dry style. The wine did reveal a slight amount of oxidation, but I liked its honey- and pearlike flavors. Although not great, it is a fine wine, albeit considerably overpriced given its Sélection de Grains Nobles designation. The 1988 Gewürztraminer Zinnkoepfle S.D.G.N. was ripe and honeyed, but one-dimensional, simple, and cloying. Drink it over the near term, although it should last for 10 or more years.

GUSTAVE LORENTZ (BERGHEIM)* * *

1990 Gewürztraminer Altenberg	C	90
1987 Gewürztraminer Vendange Tardive	D	76
1990 Riesling Altenberg	C	87
1990 Tokay-Pinot Gris Altenberg	C	?

This is only a small selection from the Lorentz firm, which from time to time makes superb wines. When I remember the exceptional 1983s, I am surprised by the inconsistency exhibited by this firm's wines since that vintage. However, with the exception of the Tokay-Pinot Gris and the late harvest Gewürztraminer, the 1990s from Lorentz performed well. The 1990 Riesling Altenberg displays loads of flowery, stony fruit, very good acidity, a dry taste, and an inner core of concentrated Riesling fruit. It should age marvelously for at least a decade. I also thought Lorentz's 1990 Gewürztraminer Altenberg was superb, with its spicy, nutty, exotic fruit-scented nose and long, opulent, admirably endowed flavors infused with considerable glycerin, as well as enough acidity to provide freshness and lift. This is a larger-scale, muscular, yet extremely well-balanced Gewürztraminer for drinking over the next decade. I do not know what happened to the 1990 Tokay-Pinot Gris Altenberg, which had a bizarre, troubled nose and disjointed, odd flavors. I would prefer to reserve judgment until I see another bottle. The 1987 Gewürztraminer V.T. is extremely vegetal, austere, and very dry, without the underlying fruit necessary to balance the wine's high acidity and greenness.

ALBERT MANN (WETTOLSHEIM)* * * *

1989 Gewürztraminer Furstentum Sélection de Grains Nobles	E	92
1989 Gewürztraminer Hengst Sélection de Grains Nobles	E	93
1988 Gewürztraminer Sélection de Grains Nobles	E	86
1990 Gewürztraminer Steingrubler	C	91
1989 Gewürztraminer Steingrubler Vendange Tardive	D	89
1989 Muscat	A	79
1990 Pinot Blanc Auxerrois	A	87
1989 Pinot Blanc Auxerrois	A	86
1990 Riesling Hardt	B	80
1989 Riesling Pfleck Vendange Tardive	C	90
1988 Riesling Pfleck Vendange Tardive	C	89
1990 Riesling Schlossberg	C	87
1989 Riesling Schlossberg	C	90
1989 Tokay-Pinot Gris Hengst Vendange Tardive	D	90
1988 Tokay-Pinot Gris Sélection de Grains Nobles	E	91
1990 Tokay Pinot Gris Vieilles Vignes	C	89

Albert Mann's wines, along with those of Ernest Burn and Meyer-Fonne, proved to be among my most interesting discoveries on my recent trip to Alsace. These wines are generally superb in quality, with dramatic personalities, plenty of concentration, and impeccable balance. Mann's 1990 and 1989 Pinot Blanc Auxerrois were both bottled unfiltered. One can sense that there was little removed from either of these rich, honeyed, apple, gorgeously fruity, medium-bodied, elegant wines. The 1990 may have slightly more fragrance, but both are top-notch examples of how good this varietal can be. Drink them both over the next 2–3 years. Although I was unimpressed with the 1989 Riesling Hardt because of its forbiddingly high acidity and austere nature, as well as a thinness that suggested a lack of intensity, there is no doubting Mann's 1990 Riesling Schlossberg is a top-notch wine. This steely, elegant, high-toned, high-acid, rich wine, with admirable extraction, is totally unevolved and needs another 2–3 years of cellaring. For those who want more up-front fruit, take a serious look at the 1989 Riesling Schlossberg. One of the great dry 1989 Rieslings, it is superconcentrated, with an essence of mineral character combined with scents of green apples and underripe apricots. Both are medium-bodied, beautifully balanced, concentrated wines with very impressive fin-ishes. The 1989 had more to it. The 1989 Muscat exhibited a light-intensity, floral nose, but it was lean and relatively hard and attenuated, although still pleasant and cleanly made. I preferred Mann's creamy, smoky, nutty 1990 Tokay-Pinot Gris Vieilles Vignes. This wine displayed plenty of depth and lush, full-bodied, buttery opulence, decent acidity, and a terrific finish. It may merit an outstanding score in another 1–2 years. The other great dry wine produced by this domaine was the 1990 Gewürztraminer Steingrubler. This smoky, rose petal–scented, meaty, flashy Gewürztraminer displays gobs of fruit, a dry, full-bodied finish, and impressive length. Big and well balanced (not an easily obtainable combination for Gewürztraminer), it should drink well for at least 10–12 years. Mann's late harvest selections were no less impressive. His 1988 Riesling Pfleck V.T. possessed a sensational floral nose intertwined with the smell of ripe apricots. In the mouth it was long and medium bodied, quite dry for a Vendange Tardive wine, with a crisp, stony, terrific finish. It has 7–8 years of aging potential. As good as Mann's 1988 Riesling Pfleck V.T. was, his 1989 Riesling Pfleck V.T. was even better. It is a real beauty, with its intense combination of oranges and apples in the bouquet. In the mouth this is a relatively full-bodied, surprisingly dry Riesling with 13.5% natural alcohol, super fruit, a lot of body and glycerin, and that crisp, elegant finish that defines the classic Riesling. It should drink beautifully for the next 8–12 years. The 1989 Tokay-Pinot Gris Hengst V.T. was another wonderful, slightly off-dry, superb expression of this varietal. Extremely deep, with a waxy, creamy, buttery nose, smoky, opulent flavors, and good acidity, it begs for grilled salmon or a classic, creamy scallop dish. It should last for 8–10 years. Also impressive was the 1989 Gewürztraminer Steingrubler V.T. Rich, opulent, and full bodied, this is another notable expression of Gewürztraminer in a relatively full, muscular, well-balanced style. Mann is another producer who has made, by his standards, an enormous quantity of Sélection de Grains Nobles wines. I thought the 1988 Gewürztraminer S.D.G.N. was ripe, medium sweet, but very good rather than sublime. The 1989 Gewürztraminer Furstentum S.D.G.N. was sensational, given its superb balance and the fact that it managed to keep its enormous weight and richness from coming across as flabby or cloying. This is a superextracted, moderately sweet Gewürztraminer, with an intoxicating perfume of smoke, lychee nuts, and exotic fruits. In the mouth there is zesty acidity, essential to keep the wine in balance. Similarly, the 1988 Tokay-Pinot Gris S.D.G.N., in spite of its enormous weight and richness, is balanced by crisp acidity. The 1989 Gewürztraminer Hengst S.D.G.N. was every bit as sensational as his offering of Gewürztraminer from the Furstentum vineyard. In fact, it was even more opulent, with a baked orange, roasted nut, smoky character apparent in the wine's bouquet. In the mouth there is sensational Trockenbeerenauslese richness, good acidity, and an explosive finish. Do not be surprised to see this wine last for another 20–30 years.

JULIEN MEYER (NOTHALTEN)* * * *

1989 Gewürztraminer Vendange Tardive	C	93
1989 Muscat Petite Fleur	C	90
1990 Pinot Blanc Les Pierres Chaudes	B	87
1989 Pinot Blanc Les Pierres Chaudes	B	89
1990 Riesling Muenchberg	C	86
1989 Riesling Muenchberg	C	90
1990 Sylvaner Zellberg	B	87
1989 Sylvaner Zellberg	B	89

Julien Meyer, whose wines were all of exceptionally high quality, clearly merits representation in America. One is not likely to find better Sylvaner than the 1990 or 1989 Sylvaner Zellberg. Both were opulent, surprisingly rich, multidimensional wines. The 1990 exhibited a very floral bouquet, followed by surprisingly intense, well-balanced flavors. The 1989 displayed astonishing flavor concentration and character for a Sylvaner. These are winemaking tours de force for a grape that I generally find of little interest. Both the 1990 and 1989 Pinot Blanc Les Pierres Chaudes were also superlative efforts. The 1990 offered a seductive nose of cantaloupe, ripe oranges, and apples that was followed by a wine with surprisingly good acidity, a wet stone–, mineral–, applelike fruitiness, medium body, and an excellent finish. The 1989 was similar, but softer and more opulent and intense. Pinot Blanc just does not get much better than this. Drink both these wines over the next 2–3 years. The 1990 Riesling Muenchberg offered up a fine inner core of stony, citric, applelike fruit, a dry, medium-bodied taste, and a crisp, somewhat austere, but interesting finish. It may merit a higher score with another 2 years of bottle age. The 1989 Riesling Muenchberg was outstanding. The huge bouquet of rich apricot, banana, and peach fruit was reminiscent of a top Condrieu. In the mouth the wine was broadly flavored, dry, with layers of multidimensional fruit. Drink this glorious, impeccably well-balanced wine over the next decade. Meyer also exhibited a sure touch with his 1989 Muscat Petite Fleur, an intensely floral-scented, completely dry wine with great fruit and a crisp, zesty personality. Last, the 1989 Gewürztraminer V.T. possessed a slight sweetness. The wine is a knockout—rich, loaded with smoky, exotic fruit flavors, full bodied, superbly balanced, and a total joy to drink. It should evolve nicely over the next 7–10 years.

MEYER-FONNE (KATZENTHAL)* * * *

1990 Gewürztraminer Schlossberg	C	91
1989 Gewürztraminer Schlossberg Vendange Tardive	D	93
1990 Pinot Blanc	A	86
1990 Riesling Kaefferkopf	C	86
1990 Riesling Schlossberg	C	84
1990 Tokay-Pinot Gris	B	87
1989 Tokay-Pinot Gris Cuvée Saint-Urbain	C	79

With only one exception, these were impressive wines that, I am glad to report, are being imported into the United States. The 1990 Pinot Blanc ranks with some of the best of the vintage, with its floral, elegant nose, fresh, perfumed fruitiness, and distinct taste of oranges. Medium bodied, dry, and zesty, it should be drunk over the next 1–2 years. I am sure the 1990 Riesling Schlossberg will ultimately merit a higher score, but at present it is backward and tightly knit. However, it is a fine, elegant, flowery, medium-bodied, crisp, dry Riesling with considerable character; it is just frightfully unevolved. The 1990 Riesling Kaefferkopf exhibited a more cinnamon, earthy nose, some wonderful lemony, citrusy, applelike fruit, excellent concentration, and a rich, dry, tightly knit finish. It should evolve gracefully for at least a decade. The 1990 Tokay-Pinot Gris was much more seductive in its smoky, wood fire–like nose, creamy, buttery texture, and ripe, heady, intoxicatingly fruity aftertaste. I would opt for drinking this luscious Tokay over the next 5–6 years. Perhaps the following wine was in an awkward state of development, since it is the only wine from this producer that did not show well, but the 1989 Tokay-Pinot Gris Cuvée Saint-Urbain was extremely high in acidity, very awkward, and rough around the edges, and although exhibiting a nice inner core of fruit, it appeared clumsy and disjointed. Additionally, since the Saint-Urbain vineyard is one of the world's greatest sites for Tokay-Pinot Gris, I wonder if I have misread this wine? Meyer-Fonne made two sensational Gewürztraminers. The 1990 Gewürztraminer Schlossberg displays a dazzling bouquet of Oriental spices, lychee nuts, and exotic tropical fruits. In the mouth the wine is full bodied and superextracted, yet with enough acidity to hold together. Dry, rich, and luscious, this is a great Gewürztraminer for imbibing over the next 6–10 years. Meyer-Fonne's 1989 sublime, off-dry Gewürztraminer Schlossberg V.T. offers up more of rose petal aromas to go along with its intensely spicy, exotic character. In the mouth there is great extraction of fruit, huge body, and enough glycerin to coat your palate. This superbly rendered, off-dry (slightly sweet) Gewürztraminer, which was one of the highlights of my tastings, should be drunk over the next 10–12 years.

MITTNACHT KLACK (RIQUEWIHR)* * * * *

1990 Gewürztraminer Rosacker	C	90
1989 Gewürztraminer Rosacker	C	88
1990 Gewürztraminer Sporen	C	92
1988 Gewürztraminer Vendange Tardive	D	88
1990 Riesling Rosacker	C	88
1989 Riesling Schoenenbourg Vieilles Vignes	C	90
1988 Riesling Sélection de Grains Nobles	E	90
1989 Tokay-Pinot Gris	B	85

Superb performances by virtually all of this small producer's wines made for a wonderful discovery during my extensive tastings in Alsace. These are the first offerings I have tasted from Mittnacht Klack (not to be confused with Mittnacht Frères in Hunawihr), and they are wines of vivid purity of flavors, intense perfumes, and strikingly rich, well-focused personalities. I would have to rank Mittnacht Klack's performance in 1989 and 1990 with the best in Alsace. The 1990 Riesling Rosacker offered up a superb fragrance of flowers, citrus, and stones. In the mouth it was dry, with layers of crisp fruit, medium body, and a long, admirably extracted finish. It should drink well for at least a decade. The 1989 Riesling Schoenenbourg Vieilles Vignes is a classic expression of Riesling, with an intense, stony, petrollike nose; great, expressive, citrusy, apple- and minerallike flavors; and an explosively long, dry, intense finish. This is marvelous Riesling! Drink it over the next 10–12 years. I was also fond of the 1989 Tokay-Pinot Gris because of its suave, graceful, elegant, creamy, buttery, Wheat Thins–like fruitiness, as well as its crisp acidity. It should be consumed over the next 4–5 years. Mittnacht Klack has produced several profound Gewürztraminers, including the 1990 Gewürztraminer Rosacker. It smelled more like a rose than any Gewürztraminer I have ever had; the intensity of the perfume was so powerful that I was sure I could still smell it after the glass was removed. The wonderfully deep, elegant, spicy, dry, medium- to full-bodied flavors exhibited fine acidity, admirable purity, and great winemaking. Drink this beauty over the next decade. Even more profound was the 1990 Gewürztraminer Sporen. This superb hillside vineyard, located just behind the village of Riquewihr, is known for its great Gewürztraminers. The firms of Hugel and Dopff "Au Moulin" produce their top cuvées of Gewürztraminer from this vineyard. This spectacularly rich, dry, full-bodied, intensely concentrated, beautifully well-knit Gewürztraminer, with its bacon, lychee nut, smoky, opulent flavors, buoyed by fine fresh acidity and a dazzlingly long, dry finish, was one of the most memorable wines I tasted. Unfortunately I was not able to taste the 1989 Sporen. Though closed, the 1989 Gewürztraminer Rosacker offered plenty of extract, much of which is hidden behind a layer of crisp acidity. Considering the tightly knit character of this wine, I would opt for laying it away for 1–2 years and then drinking it over the following 10–12 years. With respect to the two late-harvest selections I saw, the 1988 Gewürztraminer V.T. displayed an interesting nose of pears and smoke, along with wonderfully pure flavors, was slightly off-dry rather than sweet, with fine balance and a long, heady finish. It should drink well for at least a decade. Mittnacht Klack's 1988 Riesling S.D.G.N. was, surprisingly, not that sweet, but crisp and elegant, with the emphasis on finesse instead of power and sweetness. I liked it, but I suspect most people who are inclined to shell out such big bucks for these nectarlike wines prefer those that deliver the most bang for their dollar.

MURÉ—CLOS SAINT LANDELIN (ROUFFACH)
SINGLE-VINEYARD CUVÉES* * * * REGULAR CUVÉES* * *

1988 Gewürztraminer Vorbourg Vendange Tardive	D	86
1989 Muscat Vorbourg Vendange Tardive	D	89
1989 Riesling Vorbourg	C	88
1989 Riesling Vorbourg Sélection de Grains Nobles	E	90
1989 Riesling Vorbourg Vendange Tardive	D	89
1989 Tokay-Pinot Gris Vorbourg	C	?
1989 Tokay-Pinot Gris Vorbourg Sélection de Grains Nobles	E	86
1989 Tokay-Pinot Gris Vorbourg Vendange Tardive	D	86

The Muré family is the sole owner of the 39-acre steeply terraced vineyard of Clos Saint Landelin. Their wines, which are often put through a malolactic fermentation, possess a distinctive style that in blind tastings tends to evoke considerable controversy. There is no doubting their richness, but on occasion I find them heavy-handed and thick. Nevertheless, I was generally impressed with the current offerings, none of which can be called wimpish wines. The 1989 Riesling Vorbourg exhibited an intriguing bouquet of mint, oranges, and flowery scents. In the mouth there was super depth and obvious glycerin. The wine is made in a very big, rich, dry, full-bodied style. This is one Riesling that can stand up to a lobster dish. Drink it over the next decade. The 1989 Tokay-Pinot Gris Vorbourg tasted funky and may have been aged in new oak casks in view of the strong vanillin scents I detected. I am not sure how to rate this wine because of its bizarre nature, but there is no doubting its extract levels and tons of thick, honeyed fruit. The other wines I tasted from Muré were all late harvest wines. The 1989 Riesling Vorbourg V.T. was superextracted, rich, full-bodied, and off-dry, with an abundance of honeyed apricot-, apple-, and peachlike fruit. It should last for at least a decade. The 1989 Tokay-Pinot Gris Vorbourg V.T. was massive, thick, and unctuous in the mouth. At present it lacks complexity. However, that should emerge after the wine spends some time in the bottle. This big, chewy, off-dry Tokay should last for at least 2 decades. With its gorgeous fruit salad aroma and deep, off-dry, heady flavors, the 1989 Muscat Vorbourg V.T. was a total joy to drink. Given its precarious balance, I would opt for consuming it over the next 2–3 years. Muré's 1989 Gewürztraminer Vorbourg V.T. was another thick, opulently styled, lavishly rich wine that could have used more acidity to provide clarity and length. For those who like almost syrupy Gewürztraminer, this medium-sweet wine will be immensely satisfying. Drink it either before or after a meal. The two super-sweet wines I tasted included a stunning 1989 Riesling Vorbourg S.D.G.N. This wine exhibited a great deal of peach- and apricot-scented and -flavored botrytis-affected fruit, aromas of baked apples, and a medium- to full-bodied, viscous, supersweet style. It should make delicious early-term drinking. Although the 1989 Tokay-Pinot Gris Vorbourg S.D.G.N. lacked some complexity and came across as one-dimensional, it is hard to ignore its extract levels, high alcohol, and heady, smoky, butterscotchlike aromas. Drink it over the next decade.

DOMAINE OSTERTAG (EPFIG)* * * *

1985 Crémant d'Alsace	B	85
1989 Gewürztraminer Epfig	B	90
1990 Gewürztraminer Epfig Sélection de Grains Nobles	E	92
1990 Gewürztraminer Epfig Vendange Tardive	D	91
1990 Gewürztraminer Fronholtz Sélection de Grains Nobles	E	95
1989 Gewürztraminer Fronholtz Sélection de Grains Nobles	E	90
1989 Gewürztraminer Fronholtz Vendange Tardive	E	79
1990 Muscat Fronholtz (Ottonel)	B	89
1989 Muscat Fronholtz (Ottonel)	B	90
1990 Pinot Blanc Barriques	B	86
1989 Pinot Blanc Barriques	B	78
1990 Pinot Gris Barriques	B	87
1989 Pinot Gris Barriques	B	88
1990 Pinot Noir Fronholtz	C	77
1990 Riesling Epfig	B	82
1989 Riesling Epfig	B	83
1990 Riesling Epfig Sélection de Grains Nobles	E	94

1989 Riesling Fronholtz	C	91
1990 Riesling Fronholtz Barriques Vendange Tardive	C	90
1990 Riesling Fronholtz Sélection de Grains Nobles	E	94
1989 Riesling Heissenberg	C	90
1990 Riesling Heissenberg Barriques Sélection de Grains Nobles	E	94
1990 Riesling Heissenberg Barriques Vendange Tardive	D	92
1989 Riesling Muenchberg	C	92
1990 Riesling Muenchberg Sélection de Grains Nobles	E	96
1990 Riesling Muenchberg Vendange Tardive	D	85
1990 Riesling Muenchberg Vieilles Vignes Sélection de Grains Nobles	E	98
1990 Riesling Muenchberg Vieilles Vignes Vendange Tardive	D	93
1989 Riesling Muenchberg Vieilles Vignes Vendange Tardive	D	93
1990 Sylvaner Vieilles Vignes	A	87
1989 Sylvaner Vieilles Vignes	A	86
1990 Tokay-Pinot Gris Barriques Sélection de Grains Nobles	E	92
1990 Tokay-Pinot Gris Muenchberg Vendange Tardive	D	91
1989 Tokay-Pinot Gris Muenchberg Vendange Tardive	D	92
1989 Tokay-Pinot Gris Sélection de Grains Nobles	E	93

Domaine Ostertag is located in the northern sector of Alsace's viticultural region in the village of Epfig. The owner, André Ostertag, has created a storm of controversy since he began to rejuvenate the wines from his family's 25 acres of vineyards. Although he is to be admired for his open, forward thinking, his diatribes against his fellow producers for their excessive reliance on filtration and pervasive use of herbicides, fungicides, and pesticides have not been widely applauded by his peers. Additionally, his belief in conservative yields and, above all, his belief in using small oak casks (many of them new) in which to vinify and age his wines, have made him either the most admired or disliked Alsatian vigneron, depending on one's view. Of course, the most important thing is what shows up in the finished bottle of wine, which is how Ostertag, as well as any other producer, must be judged. On that basis, the quality of the wines since 1987, except for a few bizarre examples where the oak overwhelms the fruit, have generally been impressive. Ostertag credits the revolution in his cellars to the Domaine Comte Lafon in Burgundy. Because of the Lafon influence, he has chosen a low-tech, artisanal, unfiltered style of winemaking. When I visited him in June, he had just returned from Vin Expo in Bordeaux, where he was one of ten vignerons asked to give a speech about the most important factors in producing high-quality wine. Nine of the ten speakers said technology was of the utmost significance, leaving André Ostertag alone to claim it was the vineyard that was most important. Because of the criticism he has received, he was in no mood to defend his colleagues, claiming that more than 25% of the region's vineyards are now harvested by machine and that most vineyards are pulled up after they reach the age of 25 because the vines are no longer as productive. Moreover, he continues to feel that too many producers are obsessed with processing their wines. How did Ostertag's wines taste in 1989 and 1990? With respect to the dry wines, which were all bottled unfiltered, Ostertag makes one of the more interesting wines from the generally neutral Sylvaner grape. Both his 1989 and 1990 Sylvaner Vieilles Vignes (from vines that average between 25 and 30 years old) display a much more floral character than the Sylvaner grape normally provides. Ostertag claims that Sylvaner does indeed have an interesting bouquet if yields are kept low. Both wines have a great deal of fruit, elegance, surprising body and length, and true character. The 1990, perhaps because it is fresher, does appear to have an edge in fruit and fragrance. Both wines should be drunk over the next 2–4 years. With respect to Ostertag's Pinot Blancs Barriques, which are brought up in small Vosges oak barrels, I did not find either the 1989 or 1990 vintage to be as striking as his 1988. The 1990 was delicate, with round, apple, spicy flavors, good crisp acidity, and a fresh finish. In contrast, the 1989 appeared slightly dull and flat in the mouth, displaying more evidence of its oak aging, which verged on being intrusive. Ostertag's 1989 and 1990 Pinot Gris Barriques offer a much better marriage of fruit and wood than the Pinot Blanc. Both wines exhibited attractive creamy, buttery, almost bacon-scented aromas, good structure, subtle yet rich, medium-bodied flavors, crisp acidity, and long finishes. The 1990 is slightly lighter with fresher acidity, whereas the 1989 is a rounder, fuller, more opulently styled wine. Both would be marvelous accompaniments to a bevy of seafood and poultry dishes. Moreover I suspect the 1989 will drink well for 5–7 years and the 1990 for 1–2 years longer. The dry Muscats from Alsace are terribly underrated. Ostertag made two of the best dry Muscats I have ever tasted in 1989 and 1990 from the Fronholtz vineyard. What makes these wines so riveting is that they are bone dry but have a gorgeous, flowery, seductive bouquet and precise yet rich, elegant flavors. The 1989 was even fuller and richer than the beautifully etched 1990. Both wines would be ideal as an aperitif wine or, surprisingly, with rich pork or sausage dishes.

I have always felt that of all his wines, Ostertag is most committed to his Rieslings. That was certainly evident with his three vineyard-designated 1989 Rieslings, all of which were outstanding. The 1989 Riesling Fronholtz (140 cases produced) had a rich, intense, almost exotic tropical fruit character and long, dry, applelike flavors buttressed nicely by fine acidity. Surprisingly intense yet impeccably balanced, this beauty should drink well over the next 5–7 years. The 1989 Riesling Muenchberg is even more profound, with an extraordinary perfume of minerals, wet stones, flowers, and apples. Amazingly backward yet superbly concentrated, with a great deal of precision to its character, this Riesling will be at its peak in 5–7 years and should last for up to 2 decades. The 1989 Riesling Heissenberg was aged in small oak casks because Ostertag felt that the wine was less structured and needed the backbone that the oak barrels can provide. This cinnamon, flowery, exotically scented wine is dry, with rich fruit flavors, decent acidity, and a long, dry aftertaste. Among these three 1989 Rieslings, it has the least potential for long-term aging and should be consumed over the next 4–5 years. Both the 1989 and 1990 Riesling Epfig are more straightforward, flowery, fresh Rieslings that are dry, with an attractive applelike character. Both should be consumed over the next 4–5 years for their freshness rather than their profound flavors. Among the other completely dry wines I tasted from Ostertag was a sensational 1990 Gewürztraminer Epfig. The huge bouquet of this wine included scents of roses, bacon fat, and tropical fruit. In the mouth it displayed wonderfully rich, crisp, medium- to full-bodied texture, gorgeous ripeness, and plenty of length. This beauty should drink well for the next 5–8 years. Ostertag also produces a tiny bit of Crémant d'Alsace that is a blend of Riesling and Pinot Blanc kept 3 months on its lees. The 1985, which had no sugar added, is a fresh, lively, crisp wine that is ideal for drinking over the next 2–3 years. Ostertag also makes a small quantity of Pinot Noir, and as with most Alsace reds, I found his 1990 Pinot Noir Fronholtz to be compact and narrowly constructed, with adequate fruit. While tasting through the bevy of Vendange Tardive wines produced by Ostertag, I was struck by the fact that they are significantly less alcoholic as well as less sweet than those of his colleagues. Ostertag believes these wines are best drunk not with food, but while listening to classical music or the music he prefers, jazz. Among the five Rieslings, the 1990 Riesling Fronholtz Barriques V.T. (aged in small oak casks) possesses gobs of extract, superb acidity, fabulous precision, and a wonderful inner core of rich, lemony, apple- and minerallike fruit. Most tasters would consider this to be a dry wine, although technically it is not. It will easily last for 15–20 years. The 1990 Riesling Heissenberg Barriques V.T. was also aged in small oak casks, but it is a much more exotic, cinnamon-, fruitcake-scented wine. Compared with the Fronholtz, it is dramatic, even flamboyant, as well as slightly sweeter. It offers a magnificent glass of Riesling that must be served on its own before a meal. Drink it over the next 10–15 years. The 1990 Riesling Muenchberg V.T. had an intense, flowery nose followed by lemony, applelike flavors. It finished with less authority and was not as well delineated as Ostertag's other Rieslings. Still a beauty, it was not as profound as his other wines. Ostertag's 1990 Riesling Muenchberg Vieilles Vignes V.T. is a staggering example not only of Riesling, but also of a drier-styled V.T. wine. The huge perfume of wet stones, minerals, apples, and floral-scented fruit is followed by a wine with great stuffing, fabulous precision and presence on the palate, and a long, superb finish. The wine's extract level and fine acidity suggest it will last for 15–20 more years. The 1989 Riesling Muenchberg Vieilles Vignes V.T. is equally superb, perhaps even more opulent, denser, and more muscular. Exceptionally well balanced, with a stunning array of orange, apple, and lemon fruit interlaced with the essence of mineral scents, this head-turning effort is more developed than the 1990 but should also last for 10–15 more years. Ostertag has produced a 1989 and 1990 Tokay-Pinot Gris Muenchberg V.T. wine. Both are essentially equivalent in quality, but the 1990 is an off-dry, creamy, buttery, smoky-scented wine with only 12% alcohol. The 1989 has 13.7% alcohol and is a slightly fuller, denser, sensationally rich, off-dry wine that makes a weighty impression on the palate. Both wines should last for 10–15 more years. Among the two Gewürztraminer V.T.'s I tasted, the 1990 Gewürztraminer Epfig V.T. (14.5% alcohol) was a powerful wine with exceptional richness and a bouquet filled with aromas of lychee nuts, roses, and an almost honeyed, banana sort of fruitiness. Full bodied, opulent, and deep, it should continue to drink well for another 10–12 years. The 1989 Gewürztraminer Fronholtz V.T. was lower in alcohol, and the extract level appeared suspect when compared with the other efforts from Ostertag. It displayed a monolithic, slightly cloying, dull taste that caused me to mark it down. Leaving it in the glass only appeared to emphasize its weaknesses. I would opt for drinking it over the near term. As should be already evident, there were immense quantities of Sélection de Grains Nobles (the decadently sweet wines of Alsace) made in 1989. Ostertag's first experience with Sélection de Grains Nobles was with the 1989 vintage, and all the grapes for these wines were 100% affected by the noble rot *(botrytis cinerea)*. Like other conscientious producers, Ostertag picks these grapes berry by berry rather than bunch by bunch, and the results are spectacular, although the commercial viability of such sweet wines, because of their frightfully high prices, is to my thinking dubious. As the numerical scores indicate, these are dazzling wines. What is so admirable about the Sélection de Grains Nobles wines from Alsace is that the best of them have 20–30 years of aging potential but can also be drunk at an extremely young age. Quantities of these wines are limited; usually only 50–100 cases are produced. The 1990 Riesling Epfig S.D.G.N. had a light golden color; a honeyed, waxy, superb nose; great richness; a viscous, unctuous, tropical fruit sweetness; and superb length. It should continue to drink well for the next 20 years. The 1990 Riesling Fronholtz S.D.G.N. was also light golden in color, with a stunning, almost baked apple–scented nose, opulent, thick, honeyed flavors, just enough acidity to give freshness, and a super sweetness. Both the 1990 Riesling Muenchberg S.D.G.N. and the 1990 Riesling Muenchberg Vieilles Vignes S.D.G.N. were much lighter in color, with an essence of liquid mineral character that added another dimension to their fabulous richness and extraordinary depth and sweetness. The Vieilles Vignes had even more precision and extraction than the regular cuvée. Both should last for 20 or more years. The 1990 Riesling Heissenberg Barriques S.D.G.N., which was aged in new oak casks, was extraordinarily dramatic and exotic. It was clearly more obvious, open, and evolved than the other sweet Rieslings. It is the best wine of this lot to drink over the next 7–10 years. Ostertag also made a 1990 Tokay-Pinot Gris Muenchberg Barriques S.D.G.N. that was aged in new oak, which, if you agree with Ostertag, gives the wine more framework and structure. There is no oak in evidence, as it has been completely absorbed by the phenomenal richness and sweetness of the wine. It possesses a creamy, cherry fruitiness, strikingly rich yet structured flavors, and a long, heady, sweet, alcoholic finish. I feel the 1989 Tokay-Pinot Gris Muenchberg Barriques S.D.G.N. is even greater than the 1990, no doubt because 1989 is one of those unreal vintages, in terms of the quantity and quality of Alsace's decadently sweet wines. This monument to the Pinot Gris grape, a fabulously rich, nectarlike, viscous wine, is bursting with smoky, buttery, applelike flavors and has fine acidity and a nice touch of toasty new oak that frames up this enormously concentrated wine. Although drinkable young, it should last for 15 or more years. There were three Sélection de Grains Nobles Gewürztraminers in 1989 and 1990. The 1990 Gewürztraminer Epfig S.D.G.N. was a powerful, somewhat drier wine than the other S.D.G.N.'s, with a lychee nut–, rose-scented nose and awesome flavor extraction. The 1990 Gewürztraminer Fronholtz S.D.G.N. also had intense aromas of lychee nuts, roses, and tropical fruits, was slightly sweeter, rich, and surprisingly well balanced. The 1989 Gewürztraminer Fronholtz S.D.G.N. was less profound than the 1990, as well as less delineated. However, it was still so enormously sweet and rich that one bottle could easily serve 20–30 people. As an afterthought, I have intentionally limited my tasting notes on the Sélection de Grains Nobles wines. I realize that the prices of these wines preclude their purchase save for a tiny percentage of readers. Moreover, the greatness of Alsace's white wines lies with its dry and slightly off-dry wines. Despite the extraordinary quality of these nectars, as a consumer advocate I find it hard to be enthusiastic about such microquantities of wines that sell for $75–$200 a bottle.

PREISS-HENNY (MITTELWIHR)* * *

1990 Gewürztraminer	B	76
1989 Gewürztraminer Cuvée Preiss	B	86
1989 Gewürztraminer Sélection de Grains Nobles	D	84
1988 Gewürztraminer Sélection de Grains Nobles	E	55
1990 Riesling	B	78
1990 Riesling Cuvée Preiss	B	85
1989 Riesling Sélection de Grains Nobles	E	85
1988 Riesling Sélection de Grains Nobles	E	52

Preiss-Henny's 1990 Riesling offered austere, dry, tart, vaguely floral aromas in a light-bodied format. The 1990 Riesling Cuvée Preiss had more to it. There were some pleasing flavors of green apples, a nice whiff of flowers and minerals, and a dry, medium-bodied finish. The 1990 Gewürztraminer was a disappointment. Its bland, insipid, one-dimensional qualities are hard to find in Alsatian Gewürztraminer. The 1989 Gewürztraminer Cuvée Preiss displayed more ripeness, some interesting peach and lychee nut fruitiness, good body, and a solid finish. As for the sweeter Sélection de Grains Nobles offerings, the 1989 Riesling S.D.G.N. was extremely dry and austere, making it acceptable, if unexciting. I found the 1989 Gewürztraminer S.D.G.N. slightly off-dry, tasting more like a Vendange Tardive wine than a Sélection de Grains Nobles. Both the 1988 Riesling S.D.G.N. and the 1988 Gewürztraminer S.D.G.N. were bizarre wines to say the least. The Riesling had a vegetal, mothball-like fragrance and tart, lean, almost nasty flavors. As hard as I tried, I could find little pleasure in either smelling or drinking it. The Gewürztraminer was even more bizarre, with an odd fragrance that smelled artificial and bone-dry, eccentric flavors that I am unable to define. Its finish was thin and acidic.

PREISS ZIMMER (TURCKHEIM)* *

1990 Gewürztraminer Comte de Beaumont	B	82
1990 Riesling Comte de Beaumont	B	72
1990 Riesling Sporen	B	84

Here are three unexciting wines from Preiss Zimmer. The 1990 Riesling Comte de Beaumont was lean and citrusy, with a vague hint of underlying fruit. The 1990 Riesling from the great Sporen vineyard exhibited more ripeness but was light and appeared to have been made from yields that were entirely too high. What a shame! Last, although the 1990 Gewürztraminer Comte de Beaumont had the most intensity of these three wines, as well as a remote suggestion of roses and lychee nuts in its nose, there was not a great deal to its simple, straightforward flavors.

ROLLY-GASSMANN (RORSCHWIHR)* * * *

1989 Gewürztraminer Kappelweg	C	90
1989 Muscat Moenchreben	B	90
1989 Pinot Blanc Auxerrois Moenchreben	B	87
1989 Riesling Kappelweg	C	90
1989 Tokay-Pinot Gris Réserve	C	87

The 1989 Pinot Blanc Auxerrois Moenchreben has that wonderful freshness and crispness that characterize this varietal, as well as excellent fruit and a honeyed, orange blossom–, applelike bouquet, all of which come together to represent the epitome of elegance and character. Drink it over the next 2–4 years. Rolly-Gassmann's 1989 Riesling Kappelweg is another classic example of the steely, citrusy, highly extracted, dry, medium-bodied Riesling that is produced so frequently in Alsace. It has a deep inner core of mineral, applelike fruit, with an overall impression of beautiful balance, freshness, and purity. I would opt for drinking it over the next 7–8 years. I have already alluded to the sublime combination of foie gras and the 1988 Muscat Moenchreben from Rolly-Gassmann, but I have to believe the 1989 Muscat Moenchreben is an even greater wine. It may be the finest dry Muscat I have ever tasted from Alsace. The bouquet was penetrating and fragrant enough to fill a room. In the mouth there is super fruit, good acidity, a lot of flavor, and an overwhelming sense of delicacy and finesse. This great, dry Muscat would make an ideal aperitif wine. The only limitation to a wine such as this is that it needs to be drunk within its first 2–3 years of life. The 1989 Tokay-Pinot Gris Réserve is also a successful wine. It was more alcoholic and obvious and a bigger, fatter, more buttery-style wine than Rolly-Gassmann's other efforts. The only Gewürztraminer I tasted was the 1989 Gewürztraminer Kappelweg, which was a beautifully well-focused, spicy wine with an abundant richness, graceful, full-bodied personality, and gobs of flavor in its well-focused, crisp finish. This big, impeccably balanced, rich Gewürztraminer would work wonderfully with both Oriental cooking and pungent, spicy, smoky dishes of all types.

JEAN SCHAETZEL (AMMERSCHWIHR)* * * *

1988 Gewürztraminer Kaefferkopf Cuvée Catherine	C	78
1990 Gewürztraminer Sélection de Grains Nobles	E	90
1989 Gewürztraminer Sélection de Grains Nobles	E	90
1989 Gewürztraminer Vendange Tardive	D	90
1990 Riesling Kaefferkopf Cuvée Nicolas	C	85
1989 Riesling Kaefferkopf Cuvée Nicolas	C	90
1990 Riesling Kaefferkopf Vendange Tardive	D	88
1990 Tokay-Pinot Gris Sélection de Grains Nobles	E	78

Over the years I have been generally impressed with the wines of Jean Schaetzel. He was one of the first Alsace producers to recognize the positive marketing response from using designer glass bottles for his wines, a trend that I am sure will be increasing. Virtually all of Schaetzel's cuvées come in extremely long, narrow, smoky green glass, with beautifully designed labels. Not that that has any effect on the quality, but these are usually extremely well-made wines that deserve more attention from the American marketplace. The 1990 Riesling Kaefferkopf Cuvée Nicolas is a lighter-style, very elegant, fresh, floral, dry wine ideal for drinking over the next 4–6 years. The 1989 Riesling Kaefferkopf Cuvée Nicolas exhibits all the same characteristics as the 1990, but greater depth and a more penetrating fragrance of flowers and minerals as well as a long, tasty, richer, yet still dry finish. This beauty should drink well for the next 7–8 years. Schaetzel produced a 1990 Riesling Kaefferkopf V.T. that was slightly off-dry, with a very floral, citrusy, applelike fragrance; rich, highly extracted, orangelike flavors; and a pure, very clean finish. It is an elegant yet authoritatively flavored Riesling. The 1989 Gewürztraminer V.T. displayed super fruit, a honeyed, bacon, lychee nut character, exceptionally rich, off-dry, full-bodied flavors, and an overall sense of balance and elegance. It should drink beautifully for the next 5–7 years. I was disappointed in Schaetzel's 1988 Gewürztraminer Kaefferkopf Cuvée Catherine. Although it possessed a big, spicy, exotic nose, the flavors were flat and the finish tailed off. As for the sweetest wines from this estate, I was unimpressed with the 1990 Tokay-Pinot Gris S.D.G.N. Although light, with decent acidity, it was flabby, one-dimensional, and simple. On the other hand, the 1989 and 1990 Gewürztraminer S.D.G.N. had superb honeyed, medium-sweet personalities, great concentration of fruit, and long, spicy, well-balanced finishes. The 1990 was more elegant because of higher acidity, whereas the 1989 was heavier and thicker. Both should easily last for 20 or more years.

ANDRÉ SCHERER (HUSSEREN-LES-CHATEAUX)* * *

1989 Gewürztraminer Eichberg Vendange Tardive	D	87
1988 Gewürztraminer Eichberg Vendange Tardive	D	82
1989 Gewürztraminer Pfersigberg	C	89
1990 Riesling Cuvée Jean Baptiste	C	72
1990 Riesling Pfersigberg	C	85
1989 Riesling Pfersigberg	C	82

My introduction to the wines of André Scherer began with a mediocre 1990 Riesling Cuvée Jean Baptiste that was tart, excessively acidic, and lacking in concentration. I was more pleased with the stylish, floral, dry, well-made 1990 Riesling Pfersigberg and austere but interesting, tightly knit, slightly attenuated 1989 Riesling Pfersigberg. Gewürztraminer appears to be the most interesting wine produced here. The 1989 Gewürztraminer Pfersigberg was big, dry, boldly flavored, spicy, exotic, powerful, rich, and loaded with glycerin and intense flavors. It should make luscious drinking over the next 5–6 years. The 1989 Gewürztraminer Eichberg V.T. was slightly off-dry, with a very ripe, intensely concentrated feel on the palate, but it lacked the aromatic dimension and complexity of the drier 1989 Gewürztraminer Pfersigberg. The 1988 Gewürztraminer Eichberg V.T. is a lean, straightforward Vendange Tardive.

CHARLES SCHLERET (TURCKHEIM)* * * * *

1989 Gewürztraminer Cuvée Exceptionnelle	C	91
1986 Gewürztraminer Prix d'Excellence Vendange Tardive	D	87
1989 Muscat	B	86
1990 Pinot Blanc	B	85
1990 Riesling	B	87
1989 Tokay-Pinot Gris Cuvée Exceptionnelle	C	93
1990 Tokay-Pinot Gris Médaille d'Or	C	90

Although very well known in Alsace, outside France Charles Schleret is probably the least known of this region's great winemakers. His basic cuvées are wonderful wines, but his Cuvée Exceptionnelle ranks among the greatest wines of Alsace. Schleret's 1990 Pinot Blanc is excellent, with subtle, fresh, apple- and orangelike fruit, medium body, and good acidity. Drink this dry wine over the next 2–4 years. The graceful 1990 Riesling offers up a tasty combination of apple-, mineral-, and floral-scented aromas and flavors. In the mouth the word that best describes this wine is "elegant." It suggests consumption over the next 4–5 years. The 1989 Muscat is another top success. Light, but extremely dry and floral, it is a total treat to smell and sip. I thought Schleret made two of the great Tokay-Pinot Gris I tasted on my recent trip. The 1990 Tokay-Pinot Gris Médaille d'Or is full of charm. Extremely well focused, it exhibits deep, intense, creamy, smoky, honeyed flavors, a dry finish, good acidity, and superb richness and depth. Compare it with your favorite Grand Cru white burgundy and see which you prefer. The Tokay-Pinot Gris 1989 Cuvée Exceptionnelle represents the essence of Pinot Gris, without the sweetness or heaviness this varietal sometimes offers. My notes contain such superlatives as "fabulous," "spectacular," and "great," intertwined with other positive descriptions such as "elegant," "impeccable balance," and "superconcentration." This great Tokay-Pinot Gris should drink beautifully for the next 10–15 years. Bravo! Schleret hardly misses a beat with his superlative 1989 Gewürztraminer Cuvée Exceptionnelle. What is so remarkable is that its honeyed, smoky, lychee nut, meaty character is combined with good acidity, an exceptional sense of balance and harmony, as well as a long, intense, dry, explosive finish. This is a Gewürztraminer worth buying by the case. Last, the 1986 Gewürztraminer Prix d'Excellence V.T., a surprisingly dry (for a Vendange Tardive), rich wine that is loaded with fruit flavors, remains amazingly young and unevolved, despite the fact that it is now 5 years old. Schleret makes some of Alsace's purist wines, and I highly recommend that consumers search out his releases.

SCHLUMBERGER (GUEBWILLER)* * * *

1989 Gewürztraminer Cuvée Anne	D	92
1988 Gewürztraminer Cuvée Anne	D	93
1989 Gewürztraminer Cuvée Christine	D	92
1989 Gewürztraminer Kessler	C	90
1989 Gewürztraminer Kitterlé	C	92
1989 Pinot Blanc Princes Abbes	A	87

1990 Pinot Blanc Princes Abbes	A	85
1990 Riesling Kitterlé	C	89
1989 Riesling Kitterlé	C	90
1986 Riesling Kitterlé	C	87
1989 Riesling Princes Abbes	B	86
1989 Riesling Saering	C	87
1989 Sylvaner	A	86
1989 Tokay-Pinot Gris	B	85
1989 Tokay-Pinot Gris Cuvée Clarisse Schlumberger	C	94
1989 Tokay-Pinot Gris Kitterlé	C	90

It remains a mystery as to why this superb firm, owners of 345 acres, 172 of which represent Grands Crus, which produces some of the most extraordinary wines of France, is not better known in the American marketplace. Perhaps they have never had an importer willing to promote the wines to the extent they justify. Tasting through the Schlumberger wines at their cellars in Guebwiller left me immensely impressed yet perplexed by the lack of success this firm has enjoyed—at least on these shores. This is an old, classic house, with everything still fermented in wood cuvées, 5–6 months of lees contact, and average yields of 40 hectoliters per hectare that are unbelievably conservative. For the Grands Crus that Schlumberger owns—the sandy soils of Kitterlé, the clay, heavier soils of Kessler, or the chalky soils of Saering—the yields do not exceed 30 hectoliters per hectare! The firm is currently run by the shy but serious Eric Beydon-Schlumberger, who appears to be very content with the low profile the Schlumberger firm maintains. As for the wines, the basic level, which generally carries the designation Princes Abbes, are up-front, ready-to-drink offerings when released and usually possess 4–6 years of aging potential. The 1989 Sylvaner displayed surprisingly good character for this varietal, excellent fruit, ripeness, and an enjoyable bouquet. Drink it over the next 1–2 years. The 1989 Pinot Blanc Princes Abbes was one of the best I tasted in Alsace, with a honeyed, rich, opulent nose of oranges, deep, full-bodied, luscious flavors, and excellent depth and length. The 1990 Pinot Blanc Princes Abbes, which was slightly lighter, with more of a mineral character than the bigger, richer 1989, was also a tasty, generous glass of wine. Both of these wines would be huge commercial successes in the United States if someone would promote their virtues. I also enjoyed the 1989 Riesling Princes Abbes for its big, mineral- and apple-scented nose and earthy, petrollike, rich, medium-bodied, dry flavors. It, too, should drink well for another 5–7 years. Among the Grand Cru Rieslings, the 1989 Riesling Saering exhibited super focus, excellent extraction of flavors, a dry, minerallike character, and a spicy nose. The 1989 Riesling Kitterlé could not have been more different given its exotic, peach-, apricot-, lusciously scented nose and opulent, lusty fruit flavors. The 1990 Riesling Kitterlé offered up a sensational nose of minerals and citrus, a powerful, concentrated texture, and an explosively rich, dry, long finish. This is superb Riesling that should last for at least a decade. The 1986 Riesling Kitterlé is just beginning to open up and display finely focused, apple, orange, and apricot fruit flavors, medium body, and a dry, elegant finish. Schlumberger is highly renowned in Alsace and in its two best foreign markets, Belgium and Germany, for Tokay-Pinot Gris. The 1989 Tokay-Pinot Gris (regular cuvée) offered spicy, buttery, fruit flavors, medium body, good freshness, and a crisp finish. The 1989 Tokay-Pinot Gris Kitterlé was a superb example of this varietal, exhibiting Meursault-like, buttery, hazelnut fruitiness, medium to full body, deep, concentrated flavors, and plenty of power and flavor extraction in the finish. For its size, the wine was extremely well balanced, and it should drink well for at least another 10 years. Should you be lucky enough to run across a bottle, for the first time since 1964, the Schlumbergers have made a 1989 Tokay-Pinot Gris Cuvée Clarisse. These grapes, picked at ripeness that would qualify them for a Sélection de Grains Nobles rating, were vinified dry. The result is like drinking a Montrachet-style Tokay-Pinot Gris. Exceptionally rich, with layer upon layer of concentrated, creamy, smoky, buttery fruit, this massive yet impeccably well-balanced wine lingers and lingers on the palate. Despite its alcohol level of 14.5%, it is never tiring or heavy to drink. This is a great white wine! Drink it over the next 15–20 years. Although I admire all the wines from Schlumberger, I have a soft spot for their phenomenal Gewürztraminers from the Kessler and Kitterlé vineyards. I saw only the 1989s, but both are superb expressions of this varietal, and textbook examples of the rich, powerful, blockbuster style of dry Gewürztraminer. The 1989 Gewürztraminer Kessler exhibits a huge bouquet of roses and grapefruit, followed by superbly concentrated, beautifully wrought flavors that possess fine acidity. This large-scale wine is totally dry, with great presence on the palate and a big, spicy, rich finish that must last for well over 30 seconds. I thought the 1989 Gewürztraminer Kitterlé, with its almost essence of lychee nuts and smoky, exotic flavors, was even more sensational. In the mouth it is chewy and meaty, with superb extraction of flavor, enough acidity to provide clarity and lift, and a blockbuster sort of finish. Both of these wines should drink well for the next 10–15 years. This firm rarely makes much Vendange Tardive wine, but their regular cuvée of late harvest Gewürztraminer is known as Cuvée Christine. The 1989 Gewürztraminer Cuvée Christine is a dense, almost thick, chewy wine, slightly sweet, full bodied, and overall a big, chunky mouthful of wine. It still needs plenty of time to develop and should last for at least 15 or more years. The dessert-style 1989 Gewürztraminer known as Cuvée Anne is even more enthralling than the Cuvée Christine. The 1989 Cuvée Anne, a Sélection de Grains Nobles, exhibited excellent acidity, a huge opulence of buttery, pineapple, smoky fruit, and a long, opulent finish. It will not be released for at least 2 years, as the 1988 Gewürztraminer Cuvée Anne has just arrived on the market. That wine does not have the weight of the 1989 but is a richly fruity, smoky, lychee nut–flavored wine for drinking over the next 15 or more years.

MAURICE SCHOECH (AMMERSCHWIHR)* * *

1989 Gewürztraminer	B	84
1988 Gewürztraminer Sélection de Grains Nobles	E	87
1989 Tokay-Pinot Gris	B	81

Although made in a light style, the 1989 Tokay-Pinot Gris was fresh, dry, crisp and will be a pleasant wine to drink over the next 2–4 years. I was surprised that the 1989 Gewürztraminer was so flowery, but I liked its elegance and attractive, round, up-front style. It should be drunk over the near term. Last, the 1988 Gewürztraminer S.D.G.N. possessed plenty of ripeness, a big, unctuous, smoky, exotic fruit character on the palate, and soft acidity. It did not appear to have the balance necessary to last more than 10 years, but it was concentrated and exhibited plenty of botrytis.

DOMAINE SCHOFFIT (COLMAR)* * * * *

1990	Chasselas Vieilles Vignes	A	86
1989	Gewürztraminer Rangen Clos Saint Théobald	C	90
1989	Muscat Vendange Tardive	D	92
1990	Riesling Rangen Clos Saint Théobald	C	88
1989	Riesling Rangen Clos Saint Théobald	C	86
1990	Sylvaner Cuvée Prestige	A	86
1989	Tokay-Pinot Gris Rangen Clos Saint Théobald	C	87
1990	Tokay-Pinot Gris Rangen Clos Saint Théobald Sélection de Grains Nobles	E	88

I was impressed with all of these offerings from Schoffit, another high-quality yet relatively unknown Alsace producer. For starters there is a richly fruity, charming, aromatic, concentrated, dry 1990 Chasselas Vieilles Vignes. Chasselas is not considered to be one of the noble varietals of Alsace, but you would never know that by tasting this wine made from 25-year-old vines. Drink it over the next 1–2 years. Schoffit also produced one of the better Sylvaners I tasted. The 1990 Sylvaner Cuvée Prestige offered a surprisingly intense, floral-, herb-, and mineral-scented nose, round, excellent, concentrated flavors, and a dry, medium-bodied finish. It is a charming Sylvaner (I rarely use that adjective in conjunction with this varietal) for drinking over the next 2–3 years. Schoffit is the owner of the tiny Clos Saint Théobald, which is situated within the larger Grand Cru vineyard of Rangen in the southern part of Alsace, near the town of Thann. His 1990 Riesling Rangen Clos Saint Théobald is an elegant, crisp wine with an inner core of steely, apple- and apricot-scented and -flavored fruit, superb acidity, and a dry, crisp, long finish. Just now beginning to open up, it should last for a decade. I thought the 1989 Riesling Rangen Clos Saint Théobald was also elegant, but less concentrated and complete when compared with the 1990. Although the 1989 Tokay-Pinot Gris Rangen Clos Saint Théobald was another very rich wine, it lacked the acidity necessary for long-term cellaring. Fat, muscular, and rich, it seemed to lack the balance necessary for a higher score. There is no doubting its up-front, opulent, luscious style, but I would opt for drinking it over the next 5–6 years. The 1989 Gewürztraminer Rangen Clos Saint Théobald is superb stuff. Deep, full bodied, and stuffed with the smoky, creamy, lychee nut, meaty fruit that Gewürztraminers possess, this slightly off-dry, chewy wine should drink beautifully for the next decade. The 1989 Muscat V.T. is a stunning wine, with a spring flower fragrance that can fill a room. In the mouth it is just barely off-dry, with superb delicacy to its flavors. This wine is fresh, lively, surprisingly light for its flavor intensity, but gorgeously perfumed, and just a knockout wine to drink. Consume it over the next several years. The 1990 Tokay-Pinot Gris Rangen Clos

Saint Théobald S.D.G.N. is an admirably well-balanced, rich, medium-sweet wine that should be drunk at the end of a meal. With plenty of crisp acidity, it is never tiring or cloying to drink. Schoffit made exceptional 1991s that are among the finest white wines I have tasted. Yields in 1991 were under 2 tons per acre!

ALBERT SELTZ (MITTELBERGHEIM)* *

1989 Sylvaner Sélection de Grains Nobles	E	74
1989 Sylvaner Vieilles Vignes Zotzenberg	A	86

Here are two interesting offerings from Albert Seltz. There is no question that the 1989 Sylvaner Vieilles Vignes Zotzenberg ranks with the best I tasted from the 1989 and 1990 vintages. Made from vines over 25 years old, it exhibits excellent concentration, a floral, earthy, herb-scented nose, and an intense, dry, crisp finish. It should drink well for the next 3–4 years. I do not think I have ever seen, much less tasted, a Sélection de Grains Nobles made from Sylvaner. Seltz's 1989 Sylvaner S.D.G.N. is a decent wine, somewhat neutral in terms of its nose, but in the mouth there is a subtle element of oxidation that reminded me of sherry. Off-dry and lean, it is nevertheless an adequate offering.

LOUIS SIPP (RIBEAUVILLÉ)* *

1990 Gewürztraminer	B	84
1989 Gewürztraminer Osterberg	B	85
1988 Gewürztraminer Vendange Tardive	C	76
1990 Pinot Blanc	A	84
1989 Pinot Blanc Réserve Personnelle	A	86
1990 Riesling	A	72
1990 Riesling Kirchberg	B	75
1989 Riesling Kirchberg	B	74

By all appearances, the Sipps have a flourishing business in the tourist village of Ribeauvillé. They claim to sell nearly 25% of their production directly to the hordes of foreigners that descend on this picture postcard village. I find their wines to be acceptable but rarely exciting. The 1990 Pinot Blanc is fresh and light, with decent fruit, light body, and a crisp finish. The 1989 Pinot Blanc Réserve Personnelle is a much more interesting wine, with richer, more honeyed-style, dry, medium-bodied flavors as well as excellent length and balance. The Rieslings were disappointing, particularly given the fact that the Sipps own nearly 15 acres of the Grand Cru vineyard Kirchberg, which has very pebbly, calcareous soils and is renowned for well-structured Rieslings that develop great finesse. Unfortunately I could not find such characteristics in the three Rieslings I tasted from Sipp. The 1990 Riesling was lean, tart, short, and barely acceptable. The 1990 Riesling Kirchberg was extremely austere, and as hard as I tried to find the underlying depth and character, it came across as malnourished, overcropped, and uninteresting. Nor did a year of bottle aging help the 1989 Riesling Kirchberg, a decent, but acidic, light, barely quaffable wine that exhibited little potential for further evolution. Sipp's Gewürztraminers appeared much better. The 1990 Gewürztraminer was a spicy, tasty, ripe, round, floral-scented wine that offered decent fruit and simple flavors. More interesting was the 1989 Gewürztraminer Osterberg, which had more structure and fruit, as well as the potential to evolve for another 5–6 years. Last, the 1989 Gewürztraminer V.T. was one-dimensional and bland—a sin for a Gewürztraminer!

PIERRE SPARR (SIGOLSHEIM)
SINGLE-VINEYARD CUVÉES* * * * REGULAR CUVÉES* * *

N.V. Crémant d'Alsace	B	87
1990 Gewürztraminer Brand	C	90
1989 Gewürztraminer Brand	C	85
1988 Gewürztraminer Brand Vendange Tardive	C	85
1990 Gewürztraminer Carte d'Or	B	85
1989 Gewürztraminer Mambourg	C	86
1990 Gewürztraminer Réserve	B	88
1989 Gewürztraminer Réserve	B	87
1990 Pinot Blanc Réserve	A	85
1990 Riesling Carte d'Or	A	84
1989 Riesling Mambourg	B	86
1990 Riesling Réserve	B	77
1989 Riesling Réserve	B	85
1989 Riesling Schlossberg	C	88
1990 Tokay-Pinot Gris Carte d'Or	B	85
1990 Tokay-Pinot Gris Réserve	B	87
1989 Tokay-Pinot Gris Tête de Cuvée	B	87
1989 Tokay-Pinot Gris Vendange Tardive	C	84

Among all of Alsace's wine producers, none has tried harder to penetrate the fickle, difficult, and, frankly, provincial American marketplace than the Sparr family and their nearby neighbors, the Trimbachs from Ribeauvillé. Sparr's wines, I am told, are actually less expensive in the American market than they are in France because they want to encourage consumers to give them a try. They have often been terrific values, and I have enjoyed numerous Pinot Blancs, Tokays, and Gewürztraminers from this firm. Their newest releases include an excellent, fresh, dry, honeyed, orange, citrusy 1990 Pinot Blanc Réserve. Continuing the success Sparr has always had with this varietal, it makes for a delicious, inexpensive wine for drinking over the next 2–4 years. But Sparr's greatest value is the excellent Crémant d'Alsace, an exuberant, fresh, tasty sparkling wine that competes favorably with many Champagnes. Priced under $15 a bottle, this is a smashing sparkling wine value. If Sparr's 1990 Riesling Réserve was a bit tart, lean, and green, that charge cannot be leveled against their stony, highly perfumed, dry, medium-bodied, admirably extracted 1989 Riesling Réserve and 1989 Riesling Mambourg. The Mambourg is slightly richer, but both are classy wines. They should last for at least 7–10 years. The 1989 Riesling Schlossberg may ultimately turn out to be outstanding. Still relatively closed, this concentrated, bone-dry wine exhibits the intense mineral, dried apricot fruit, petrollike fragrance so commonly found in Alsace Rieslings. Medium bodied and crisp, this wine should evolve effortlessly over the next decade. The 1990 Tokay-Pinot Gris Réserve was also excellent, with solidly built, creamy, smoky flavors, medium body, and a rich, dry finish. However, the 1990 Tokay-Pinot Gris Carte d'Or (Sparr's least expensive designation) is nearly as good. For a blockbuster style of rich, intense, chewy Tokay that begs for grilled salmon, check out the 1989 Tokay-Pinot Gris Tête de Cuvée, which is bone dry but smoky, spicy, and a heck of a mouthful of full-bodied Tokay. Drink it over the next decade. My feeling that Sparr's best wines are the Gewürztraminers appeared to be borne out with the current releases. The 1990 Gewürztraminer Carte d'Or was fresh, light, tasty, and capable of 4–5 years of evolution. The 1990 Gewürztraminer Réserve displayed a lovely nose of rose petals, rich, dry, full-bodied flavors, a luscious, chewy texture, and a crisp finish. The 1989 Gewürztraminer Réserve was similar but more backward and structured than the 1990. Even better was the 1990 Gewürztraminer Brand, with its intense, lychee nut–, rose petal–, Oriental spice–scented fragrance, exotic, kinky, full-bodied, unctuous flavors, good acidity, and an explosively rich, heady, long finish. For whatever reason, the 1989 Gewürztraminer Brand (a superb vineyard for Gewürztraminer) came across as too perfumed, somewhat artificial, and much more acidic and lean than the 1990. Although there were pleasant aspects to the wine, I sensed it was going through an awkward stage of development. Unfortunately I did not have a chance to see another bottle. Last, the 1989 Gewürztraminer Mambourg was opulently fruity, soft, alcoholic, and chewy; it should be drunk over the next 5–6 years. Among the late harvest wines, the 1989 Tokay-Pinot Gris V.T. was ripe and thick, but uncomplicated and simple. I marginally preferred the 1988 Gewürztraminer Brand V.T., which had an interesting apricot and peach jam–like nose, long, slightly sweet, spicy, viscous flavors, and enough acidity to provide framework and balance.

DOMAINE TRIMBACH (RIBEAUVILLÉ)
TOP CUVÉES* * * * * REGULAR CUVÉES* * *

1990 Gewürztraminer Réserve	C	87
1989 Gewürztraminer Réserve	C	86
1990 Gewürztraminer Seigneurs de Ribeaupierre	C	90
1989 Gewürztraminer Seigneurs de Ribeaupierre	C	90
1989 Gewürztraminer Sélection de Grains Nobles	E	88
1989 Gewürztraminer Sélection de Grains Nobles Hors Choix	E	97
1990 Gewürztraminer Vendange Tardive	D	91
1989 Gewürztraminer Vendange Tardive	D	87
1990 Pinot Blanc	A	85
1989 Pinot Blanc Sélection	A	84

1990	Riesling	B	84
1990	Riesling Clos Sainte Hune	D	92
1989	Riesling Clos Sainte Hune Vendange Tardive	D	93
1989	Riesling Clos Sainte Hune Vendange Tardive Hors Choix	E	97
1990	Riesling Cuvée Frédéric Émile	C	91
1989	Riesling Cuvée Frédéric Émile	C	90
1988	Riesling Cuvée Frédéric Émile	C	89
1990	Riesling Cuvée Frédéric Émile Sélection de Grains Nobles	E	93
1989	Riesling Cuvée Frédéric Émile Sélection de Grains Nobles	E	96
1990	Riesling Cuvée Frédéric Émile Vendange Tardive	D	92
1989	Riesling Cuvée Frédéric Émile Vendange Tardive	D	94
1990	Riesling Réserve	B	86
1989	Riesling Réserve	B	87
1989	Sylvaner Sélection	A	86
1990	Tokay-Pinot Gris Réserve	B	86
1989	Tokay-Pinot Gris Réserve	B	87
1990	Tokay-Pinot Gris Réserve Personnelle	C	86
1989	Tokay-Pinot Gris Sélection de Grains Nobles	E	89
1989	Tokay-Pinot Gris Sélection de Grains Nobles Hors Choix	E	95

The wines of the Trimbach family, along with those of their neighbors in Riquewihr, the Hugels, are the best-known Alsace wines in the American marketplace, and probably the world. The Trimbachs, who can trace their origins as a winemaking family to 1626, are today both vineyard owners and *négociants,* producing a range of wines that are the most elegant and restrained of the region. For that reason, and the fact that most of their top cuvées need 3–5 years to develop, this is not a firm that rushes to release its wines. Most of the 1989s and 1990s reviewed below, particularly the late harvest offerings, will probably not be released for at least 3–4 years. The quality is consistently very fine, although the wines rarely have the sheer drama and concentration of those from Zind-Humbrecht or Domaine Weinbach. Hubert Trimbach states that he wants all of the estate wines from the firm's 53 acres of vineyards, as well as those wines made from grapes they buy, "to have vitality, long life, and finesse." It is hard to argue with that attitude when it comes to tasting the 1990 Pinot Blanc. This elegant, dry, lightweight wine is ideal for casual quaffing over the next 2–3 years. The regular cuvée of 1990 Riesling is also very light, with lemony, applelike flavors, crisp acidity, and a dry finish. I was impressed with Trimbach's 1989 Sylvaner Sélection, an excellent, surprisingly intense, tangy wine with much more personality and fruit than one normally finds in Sylvaner. Drink it over the next 3–4 years. There is also a 1990 Pinot Blanc Sélection that was surprisingly soft for a Trimbach wine, but with good ripeness, honey, lemony, orangelike flavors and a decent finish. It should be drunk over the next 1–2 years.

Wines that have the word *Réserve* or *Sélection* on the label tend to be *cuvées* that are meant to be slightly richer and longer lived than the standard offerings named after the varietal. I thought Trimbach's 1989 and 1990 Riesling Réserves were both high-class, flinty, floral-, apricot-, apple-scented wines with medium body, plenty of lively acidity, and excellent concentration. The 1990 was slightly more austere and more closed, where the 1989 appeared softer and more obvious. Both should drink well for 7–8 years. One of the classic dry Alsace Rieslings is Trimbach's Riesling Cuvée Frédéric Émile. The average yearly production is only 3,000 cases, but it is one of the firmest and longest-lived Rieslings made, often needing 3–4 years after the vintage to reveal its floral, herbal aromas and honeyed richness. I did a mini vertical tasting back to 1983 and found the 1983 to be still amazingly rich, incredibly young, bone dry, and just beginning to evolve. Among the more recent vintages, there is a superb 1985 that may be still languishing on retailers' shelves, a good 1986, and three excellent to outstanding wines in 1988, 1989, and 1990. The 1988 Riesling Cuvée Frédéric Émile was extremely understated and backward, almost steely in a dramatic sense, but dry, with wonderful purity of fruit and apple, orange, citrusy flavors. It should drink well for the next decade. The 1989 Riesling Cuvée Frédéric Émile, which is also bone dry, has more depth to it as well as some evidence of botrytis in the apricot/peach fruitiness I detected in both the nose and taste. It is more austere at the moment than the 1988, but full of charm, and long, with an inner core of highly extracted fruit. Perhaps the best example of this wine since the glorious 1983 is the 1990 Riesling Cuvée Frédéric Émile. It is a richer, bigger, more complete wine than the 1989 or 1988, with super extraction of fruit, a very dry, crisp finish, and, most impressively, it blossoms and opens considerably in the glass after 30 minutes of airing. This is a superb, penetrating, brilliantly focused Riesling for drinking over the next 10–15 years. I have never thought of Trimbach as being one of Alsace's leading specialists in Tokay-Pinot Gris, but the 1989 and 1990 Tokay-Pinot Gris Réserves were stylish, elegant, graceful wines, with a creamy, buttery texture and smoky fruit allied with relatively high acidity, medium body, and an understated personality. Both should be drunk over the next 5–7 years. I had a slight preference for the richer, more opulent 1989. The style of Gewürztraminer sought by Trimbach is, not surprisingly, one of elegance rather than pure muscle and blockbuster opulence. Both the 1989 and 1990 Gewürztraminer Réserves were beautifully poised, more grapefruit than lychee nut– and smoke-scented wines, with crisp acidity and plenty of fruit in their dry, medium-bodied formats. The lighter 1990 had more elegance, where the 1989 was riper, displayed some evidence of botrytis, and finished with more glycerin and alcohol. Trimbach's top-of-the-line, dry Gewürztraminer is the Seigneurs de Ribeaupierre. Both the 1989 and 1990 are outstanding, with the 1990 exhibiting exceptional elegance, a rich, superbly concentrated feel on the palate, crisp acidity, wonderful purity of flavors, and a medium-bodied, authoritative finish. The 1989 Gewürztraminer Seigneurs de Ribeaupierre displayed more of a lychee nut, smoky character to go along with its intense grapefruity character. It is a medium- to full-bodied, larger-scale wine than Trimbach normally produces. More up-front, more obvious, and more flattering to taste than the 1990, it should therefore be drunk over the next 6–8 years. The Trimbach family turns out what many people consider to be the greatest expression of dry Riesling in France. It emerges from a tiny

3.06-acre vineyard called the Clos Sainte Hune. This vineyard, which is solely owned by the Trimbachs and therefore not entitled to Grand Cru status, is situated in the middle of the Rosacker Grand Cru vineyard. The clay- and limestone-based soil produces Rieslings of extraordinary perfume and unbelievable aging potential. The Trimbachs generously put on a vertical tasting of this Riesling (only 500–600 cases are produced each year) back to 1964. Yes, the greatest wines of the tasting were the 1967 and 1964, which are just becoming drinkable—after more than 20 years of cellaring! I have mixed feelings about extolling such a wine because it is almost impossible to find in the marketplace, but for those lucky enough to visit Alsace or find it on a wine list, it is probably best cellared, even in the lighter-weight vintages, for it appears to require at least 10 years before it begins to evolve. Of the recent vintages, the 1990 Riesling Clos Sainte Hune was very closed, but one could sense its super extraction of fruit, long, dry, tightly knit flavors, and medium-bodied, austere finish. It had a very strong mineral character. The 1989 Riesling Clos Sainte Hune V.T. was essentially a dry wine but was powerful, with extraordinary richness and a pronounced essence of mineral taste combined with scents of apples and apricots. There is even a strong smell of paraffin in the nose that makes this wine even more intriguing. The Trimbachs also produced a 1989 Riesling Clos Sainte Hune V.T. Hors Choix. The grapes were picked at almost Sélection de Grains Nobles ripeness but vinified dry. This is an amazingly rich, ripe, yet dry wine with extraordinary intensity and length as well as a finish that must last up to several minutes. Neither the 1990 nor the 1989s will be released for several more years. The current release of this wine is the 1985, which is a more evolved, marvelously rich, flinty, apple- and petrol-scented wine with superb acidity, wonderful ripeness and purity, and a terrifically long, dry finish. It should drink well for at least 20 years. Should you happen to be lucky enough to find any Clos Sainte Hune offered at auction or languishing on some obscure retailers' shelves, the other great vintages for this phenomenal Riesling are 1983 (rated 94), 1976 (rated 93), the famed 1967 (rated 96), and 1964 (rated 93). When Trimbach makes Vendange Tardive Rieslings, they can be some of the greatest in Alsace. For example, who can forget the riveting 1983 Riesling Cuvée Frédéric Émile V.T.? It would appear that Trimbach has again hit the jackpot with two compelling late harvest Rieslings in 1989 and 1990. The 1989 and 1990 Riesling Cuvée Frédéric Émile V.T. are both sensational, rich, concentrated, slightly off-dry, intense wines, with exotic ripeness, superb firmness and length, and exceptional extract, aromatic purity, and complexity. These will both be great, long-lived, late-harvest Rieslings that will prove amazingly flexible with food given their near dryness. On the down side, the small quantities produced will not be released for several years, and if you have to make the difficult choice between the two, the 1990 has more of the highly desirable mineral, or petrollike, character, intertwined with wonderfully intense aromas and flavors of apricots, whereas the 1989 is richer, fuller, and dazzling from beginning to end. Both should last for at least 10–15 years. Another great late-harvest wine was the 1990 Gewürztraminer V.T. Trimbach thinks it is the finest since the 1971. What is so impressive with this wine, in addition to its purity, is the impeccable balance it exhibits despite its power, high extraction, and massive, smoky, meaty, apricot- and peachlike flavors. This superb Gewürztraminer, ideal for drinking with richly sauced fish dishes, should drink well for at least 15 or more years. On the other hand, the 1989

Gewürztraminer V.T. was cloying, flat, and flabby, without enough balancing acidity. I tasted six Sélection de Grains Nobles offerings from Trimbach, four of which were extraordinary. The only less-than-profound wine was the 1989 Gewürztraminer S.D.G.N., which was supersweet, huge and fat in the mouth, and opulent, but perhaps not with enough acidity to give the wine the desired clarity and structure I had hoped to find. Nevertheless, it is still an excellent wine. Both the 1989 and 1990 Riesling Cuvée Frédéric Émile S.D.G.N. should prove to be monumental efforts. The 1990, with its 80 grams per liter of residual sugar, is a lighter wine, but with super ripeness, medium sweetness, and an almost essence of apricot flavor. The 1989, with 110 grams per liter of residual sugar, is a titan of a wine, with a smashingly intense nose of apples, minerals, and peaches, extraordinary richness and fullness, an off-dry to medium-sweet taste, and great acidity and clarity to its immense flavors. Three hundred bottles were produced of a 1989 Gewürztraminer S.D.G.N. Hors Choix. This is a nearly perfect wine, with a nectarlike richness, superb poise and balance, and a bouquet that soars from the glass. Its penetrating acidity and massive fruit flavors come together to make this a dazzling example of sweet Gewürztraminer that is fabulous and exciting to taste. Nearly as good is the 1989 Tokay-Pinot Gris S.D.G.N. Hors Choix. With an astounding 200 grams of residual sugar per liter, this thick, honeyed, extraordinary, rich wine would seemingly appear to be too heavy and cloying. But fine acidity balances everything. I would not be surprised to see this compelling sweet wine drink well for 25–30 years.

BERNARD WEBER (MOLSHEIM)* *

1990	Pinot Blanc	A	77
1989	Pinot Blanc	A	78
1990	Riesling	A	65
1989	Riesling Bruderthal	B	70
1990	Sylvaner	A	73
1989	Sylvaner	A	75

This was an unimpressive group of wines that were excessively high in acidity and lacking in concentration and character. Most of the wines appeared to be the product of overcropping and/or too early a harvest, plus an indifferent philosophy in the cellars. Caveat emptor!

DOMAINE WEINBACH (KAYSERBERG)* * * * *

1990	Gewürztraminer Cuvée Laurence	D	92
1989	Gewürztraminer Cuvée Laurence	D	90
1990	Gewürztraminer Cuvée Théo	D	92
1989	Gewürztraminer Cuvée Théo	D	93
1990	Gewürztraminer Réserve Personnelle	D	90
1990	Gewürztraminer Sélection de Grains Nobles	EE	92
1989	Gewürztraminer Sélection de Grains Nobles	EE	97

1990	Gewürztraminer Vendange Tardive	E	93
1990	Muscat Réserve Personnelle	C	89
1989	Muscat Réserve Personnelle	C	86
1990	Pinot Blanc d'Alsace	B	87
1989	Pinot Blanc Réserve	B	85
1990	Riesling Clos Sainte Catherine	D	94
1989	Riesling Clos Sainte Catherine	D	87
1990	Riesling Cuvée Théo	D	92
1989	Riesling Cuvée Théo	D	88
1990	Riesling Réserve Personnelle	D	89
1990	Riesling Schlossberg	D	92
1989	Riesling Schlossberg	D	90
1990	Riesling Sélection de Grains Nobles	EE	93
1989	Riesling Sélection de Grains Nobles	EE	99
1990	Riesling Vendange Tardive	D	93
1990	Sylvaner Réserve	B	85
1990	Tokay-Pinot Gris Réserve Personnelle	D	88
1990	Tokay-Pinot Gris Sélection de Grains Nobles	EE	93
1989	Tokay-Pinot Gris Sélection de Grains Nobles	EE	89
1989	Tokay-Pinot Gris Sainte Catherine	E	93
1990	Tokay-Pinot Gris Sainte Catherine Vendange Tardive	E	90
1990	Tokay-Pinot Gris Vendange Tardive	E	85

I have had the pleasure of meeting some extraordinary women winemakers in France, but those who transcend reality because of the sheer force of their personalities and brilliance of their wines must include the likes of Burgundy's Lalou Bize-Leroy, Pouilly Fuissé's Madame Ferret, and Alsace's Madame Colette Faller of Domaine Weinbach. I have been buying and drinking Domaine Weinbach's wines with enormous pleasure and regularity since they were first imported. It is an extraordinary domaine of 58 acres, including the monopole vineyard of Clos des Capucins (12.5 acres), located in front of Madame Faller's home. Under Alsace wine laws, monopole vineyards, regardless of how great they are, are not allowed to be considered for Grand Cru status. It seems to me that if the Grand Cru system is to ever have complete credibility, the single-owned monopole vineyards must be included. In any event, my visit and tasting with Madame Faller were among the highlights of my recent trip to France. Her extraordinary joie de vivre and dynamic personality would provide an interesting visit even if she made mediocre wines. Of course she does not, as her wines, along with those of Zind-Humbrecht and a handful of other producers, are the most strikingly rich and compelling wines of the region. In fact, it is Madame Faller's willingness to take unbelievable risks in extremely late harvesting that allows her to make so many exciting wines. Late harvest rains can also be her undoing. Fortunately that was not the case in either 1989 or 1990, her two best back-to-back vintages in memory. The vinification techniques at Domaine Weinbach are totally classic. There is no centrifuging, the vinification is normal, and all the wine is aged on its lees in large *foudres* for 9 months prior to bottling. The wines, which are so irresistible young, have proven they can also stand the test of time. For example, bottles of the 1983 vintages of Riesling, Gewürztraminer, and Pinot Gris that I own are still improving. Madame Faller's 1990s rival, and in some cases surpass, her glorious 1989s. For example, the 1990 Sylvaner Réserve is one of the most elegant examples of this varietal to be found in Alsace. Crisp and richly fruity, with a floral, perfumed nose and excellent ripeness, this dry, medium-bodied Sylvaner should be drunk over the next 2–3 years. The 1990 Pinot Blanc d'Alsace exhibits the characteristic elegance found in all of Domaine Weinbach's wines, as well as zesty acidity and that wonderfully intense, concentrated, honeyed, apple- and orangelike fruit so characteristic of a good Pinot Blanc. Among the dramatic Rieslings in 1990, the 1990 Riesling Réserve Personnelle exhibits fine body, a delicate, floral-, mineral-scented nose, dry, medium-bodied, concentrated flavors, and a pure, clean finish. Drink it over the next 5–7 years. Moving up the ladder in quality is the 1990 Riesling Schlossberg, a wine of remarkable finesse and elegance. Dry, delicate, subtle, and deliciously fruity, with an inner core of flowery as well as minerallike fruit, it should drink well for the next 7–8 years. The 1990 Riesling Cuvée Théo is even richer, with more glycerin and alcohol. Still dry, and crammed with extract, it is more powerful but still subtle and elegant. For me, the top Riesling from the Domaine Weinbach is the Clos Sainte Catherine, and the 1990 Riesling Clos Sainte Catherine is hard to resist. The gorgeously floral-, peach-, and apricot-scented nose is followed by a full-bodied, wonderfully intense, impeccably balanced, gloriously poised wine of great presence, extraction, elegance, and beauty. Dry yet loaded with fruit, this is an impeccable Riesling for enjoying over the next decade. The 1990 Riesling V.T. is a powerful, extraordinarily concentrated, dense, chewy Riesling that loses none of its finesse despite its enormous size and presence on the palate. Although it is off-dry, it displays an uncanny balance and fresh acidity. Who can ignore its luxurious quantity of mineral, peach-, apricot-, and apple-flavored fruitiness? Already dazzling, it should improve for at least another 5–7 years and last for 12–15 years.

Muscat is a wine that has a tendency to be ignored, even by Alsace wine enthusiasts. Do not make that mistake. The 1990 Muscat Réserve Personnelle is one of the best dry Alsatian Muscats, rivaling the 1988 and 1989 from Rolly-Gassmann. With its perfumed fragrance (the essence of flowers), the wine exhibits plenty of fruit, is light and lively, and provides a memorable drinking experience. It should be consumed over the next 1–3 years. Among the three 1990 drier-style Tokays I tasted from Domaine Weinbach, the 1990 Tokay-Pinot Gris Réserve Personnelle offers lively acidity, a creamy, buttery fruitiness, medium to full body, and an elegant finish. It is not a blockbuster in the style of the 1989s from this domaine, but it is still flavorful and authoritative. The 1990 Tokay-Pinot Gris Sainte Catherine V.T. is rich, still somewhat closed and unevolved, but full bodied, with layers of extract and the smoky, buttery, nutty richness that makes these wines so similar to a top-class white burgundy. I was slightly disappointed in the 1990 Tokay-Pinot Gris V.T. Although it was unctuous and thick, it appeared to be a bit simple and bordered on cloying.

I have a soft spot for this domaine's Gewürztraminers. Along with the Gewürztraminers from Zind-Humbrecht, they represent the most exciting level this varietal can reach in Alsace. The 1990 Gewürztraminer Réserve Personnelle is outstanding, not only for its pronounced aromas of roses, but also for its deep, rich, meaty flavors of lanolin, lemon, grapefruit, and nuts. In the mouth it is full bodied and impeccably well balanced and should continue to drink well for at least a decade. The 1990 Gewürztraminer Cuvée Théo displays a more honeyed, floral note to go along with its exotic, lychee nut–, lanolin-, grape-fruit-, and bananalike fruitiness. It is explosive in the mouth, with full body and sensational concentration, and ends with an enormously rich, dry finish. The 1990 Gewürztraminer Cuvée Laurence is, in essence, a declassified Ven-dange Tardive. It is off-dry, with big, dense, chewy, essence of lychee nut fruit flavors, plenty of heady alcohol, and a lusty, smoked meat sort of finish. This wine could be mistaken for a red wine from an aromatic perspective. The 1990 Gewürztraminer V.T. is very sweet and could easily pass for many producers' Sélection de Grains Nobles. I would serve it either before a meal or as dessert at the end. There is a huge amount of fruit in this rich, very concentrated wine with just barely enough acidity to hold it together. Of all the Gewürztraminers, it is the one that will have to be monitored most closely during the aging process. As for Domaine Weinbach's 1989 releases, the 1989 Pinot Blanc Réserve is a perfect example of why these wines deserve greater consumer recognition. The fresh, stony, flinty nose is followed by a wine with good body, a honeyed, applelike fruitiness, enough acidity for freshness, and a heady, plump, alcoholic finish. Drink this delicious Pinot Blanc over the next 2–3 years. The best dry Rieslings included the 1989 Riesling Clos Sainte Cather-ine, with its bouquet of flowers and honeyed citrus fruit. In the mouth it is dry and medium to full bodied, with good extraction of fruit and a wonderfully pure finish. It is more delicate than the 1989 Riesling Cuvée Théo, which has had some of its Riesling character muted by the hot summer and harvest condi-tions. Nevertheless, for those who like their Riesling highly extracted, rich, full bodied, and dry, this big, interesting wine has some of the citrusy, steely qual-ity of Riesling but is far too rich and muscular to satisfy Riesling purists. Re-gardless, I adored it. It should drink well for at least 5–7 years. The 1989 Riesling Schlossberg has retained all its Riesling character. The delicate flo-ral-, mineral-, and lemon/apple-scented bouquet is enthralling. In the mouth it is light but has wonderful freshness and a great sense of presence despite lack-ing the weight of the Cuvée Théo or the honeyed qualities of the Sainte Cather-ine. It is long but crisp and should fill out and evolve further with another 2–3 years of bottle age. It is a beauty!

If Pinot Blanc is often ignored as one of Alsace's best wine values, so is Muscat. Nowhere in the world is Muscat so frequently vinified to total dryness and offered in a medium-bodied, dry, yet fragrant style. The 1989 Muscat Réserve Personnelle, a light- to medium-bodied, intensely perfumed, crisp, delicious wine, is a delight to drink. But given the fragility of its perfume, it should be consumed over the next 1–2 years. The 1989 Tokay-Pinot Gris Sainte Catherine is a compelling yet big, ripe, rich, full-bodied wine that needs some time in the bottle. When I tasted it, I found it sensational but needing a year or more to develop. Its size and power are reminiscent of a top Meursault or Chassagne-Montrachet. The wine is capable of at least a decade of development. The 1989 Gewürztraminer Cuvée Laurence displays an explosively rich, smoky, honeyed, lychee nut character, big, deep, massive, fruit flavors, considerable body, and plenty of alcohol in its whoppingly long, gutsy finish. It is a dramatically intense Gewürztraminer. The big, bold 1989 Gewürztraminer Cuvée Théo is incredibly exotic, smoky, rich, and powerful. Totally dry and extraordinarily well balanced for its massive size and concentration, it is drinkable now, although it should easily last for up to a decade. Madame Faller also produces some of Alsace's greatest Sélection de Grains Nobles. However, they are not cheap. Prices for these wines range between $100–$200 a bottle, so despite their fabulous quality there is a highly restricted marketplace for them. With that in mind, here are some brief notes on Domaine Weinbach's Sélection de Grains Nobles. The 1990 Riesling S.D.G.N. is stuffed with fruit, exhibits exquisite richness, an interesting pear- and pineapple-scented nose, fine acidity, and long, unevolved flavors. In contrast, the 1990 Gewürztraminer S.D.G.N. is very rich, fragrant, up-front, and opulent, almost to the point of being cloying. Nevertheless it is a huge, adequately balanced wine for drinking over the next 15 years. The 1990 Tokay-Pinot Gris S.D.G.N., which is made from grapes that were 100% affected by botrytis, is the biggest, sweetest, and chewiest of these wines. Spectacular in its smoky, creamy, nectarlike richness, it should drink beautifully for 25–30 years. Among the 1989s, there are 500 bottles of the 1989 Riesling S.D.G.N., which is one of the greatest sweet wines I have ever tasted from Alsace. Oozing with fruit, it also displays remarkable acidity and lightness, despite record-breaking sugar and extract levels. It should also mature gracefully for 30 or more years. I found the 1989 Tokay-Pinot Gris S.D.G.N. to be excellent. Although fat, creamy, and sweet, it lacked the polish and finesse of the 1989 Riesling S.D.G.N. Last, the 1989 Gewürztraminer S.D.G.N. is another superextracted, honeyed wine, with extraordinary precision to its massive flavors. Here is another example of a sweet wine that needs no new oak to frame it. It should last for 30 or more years.

Madame Faller clearly ranks among the most talented winemakers in the world.

WILLM (BARR)* * *

1990 Gewürztraminer	A	79
1989 Gewürztraminer Clos Gaensbroennel	C	89
1989 Gewürztraminer Cuvée Émile Willm	B	82
1990 Pinot Blanc Cordon d'Alsace	A	81
1990 Riesling	A	74
1989 Riesling Cuvée Émile Willm	B	83
1989 Riesling Kirchberg	C	85
1990 Tokay-Pinot Gris	B	74
1989 Tokay-Pinot Gris (aged in new oak casks)	B	72
1989 Tokay-Pinot Gris Cuvée Émile Willm	C	80

I wish I could have been more impressed with these wines from Willm, which are now made by the cooperative known as the Cave Vinicole Eguisheim. With the exception of the opulent, rich, full-bodied, concentrated 1989 Gewürz-traminer Clos Gaensbroennel and the stylish, elegant, stony, citrusy 1989 Riesling Kirchberg, the wines ranged from standard quality to just barely above average. Even wines that have been noticeably successful in the past, such as Willm's Pinot Blanc, were light and lacking concentration and charac-ter. Although the 1990 Pinot Blanc was pleasant and fresh, it was not up to the quality produced by many of the best firms. The 1990 Riesling was tart, green, and attenuated. The 1990 Riesling Cuvée Émile Willm was light, delicate, flo-ral, and tasty and should be consumed over the next 2–4 years. The three Tokay-Pinot Gris offerings were all disappointing. The 1990 regular cuvée of Tokay-Pinot Gris was watery and thin. The adequate 1989 Tokay-Pinot Gris Cuvée Émile Willm exhibited more fruit, but the 1989 Tokay-Pinot Gris New Oak Casks was excessively woody to the point of obliterating the wine's fruit. Relatively speaking, the best of these wines was the 1990 Gewürztraminer, which was tasty, soft, and light (drink it over the next 1–2 years), the 1989 Gewürztraminer Cuvée Émile Willm, which was plump, but monolithic and soft, and the aforementioned excellent, perhaps even outstanding, 1989 Gewürztraminer Clos Gaensbroennel, which should evolve gracefully over the next 5–7 years.

WOLFBERGER (EGUISHEIM)* *

1990 Gewürztraminer	B	75
1985 Gewürztraminer Sélection de Grains Nobles	E	55
1988 Gewürztraminer Vendange Tardive	D	65
1990 Pinot Blanc	A	70
1990 Riesling	B	69

These were probably the worst group of wines I tasted in Alsace. The dry wines were simply highly acidic, watery, and thin, with green, vegetal tastes. As for the late-harvest wines, the 1988 Gewürztraminer V.T. was thick, cloying, and flat, and the 1985 Gewürztraminer S.D.G.N. was undrinkable because of its bizarre, funky character.

WUNSCH ET MANN (WETTOLSHEIM)* *

1990 Pinot Blanc	A	62
1990 Riesling Steingrubler	B	73
1988 Tokay-Pinot Gris Sélection de Grains Nobles	D	82

It is hard to understand the light, watery, thin 1990 Pinot Blanc, but even more disappointing was the 1990 Riesling from the Grand Cru Steingrubler vine-yard. It was completely diluted, thin, and uninteresting. Even the 1988 Tokay-Pinot Gris S.D.G.N. was monolithic, flabby, and, although sweet, lacking character.

ZIND-HUMBRECHT (WINTZENHEIM)* * * * *

1990 Gewürztraminer Clos Saint-Urbain Rangen	D	97
1989 Gewürztraminer Clos Windsbuhl	E	100
1990 Gewürztraminer Clos Windsbuhl Vendange Tardive	E	92

1990	Gewürztraminer Goldert Vendange Tardive	E	92
1989	Gewürztraminer Goldert Vendange Tardive	E	91
1990	Gewürztraminer Heimbourg Sélection de Grains Nobles	EE	92
1990	Gewürztraminer Heimbourg Vendange Tardive	E	95
1989	Gewürztraminer Heimbourg Vendange Tardive	E	99
1990	Gewürztraminer Hengst Vendange Tardive	E	93
1989	Gewürztraminer Hengst Vendange Tardive	E	96
1990	Gewürztraminer Herrenweg Turckheim	D	95
1989	Gewürztraminer Herrenweg Turckheim	D	90
1989	Gewürztraminer Herrenweg Vendange Tardive	E	97
1990	Gewürztraminer Rangen Sélection de Grains Nobles	EE	99–100
1989	Gewürztraminer Wintzenheim	D	94
1990	Pinot d'Alsace	B	89
1989	Pinot d'Alsace	B	87
1990	Pinot Noir	C	78
1989	Pinot Noir	C	82
1990	Riesling Brand	D	94
1990	Riesling Brand Vendange Tardive	E	95
1989	Riesling Brand Vendange Tardive	E	97
1990	Riesling Clos Hauserer Vendange Tardive	E	93
1990	Riesling Clos Saint-Urbain Rangen	D	94
1989	Riesling Clos Saint-Urbain Rangen	D	93
1990	Riesling Clos Windsbuhl Sélection de Grains Nobles	EE	90
1990	Riesling Clos Windsbuhl Vendange Tardive	E	91
1990	Riesling Gueberschwihr	D	86
1990	Riesling Herrenweg Turckheim	D	89
1989	Riesling Herrenweg Turckheim	D	90
1990	Riesling Herrenweg Vendange Tardive	E	92
1990	Riesling Turckheim	D	90
1989	Riesling Turckheim	D	88
1990	Riesling Wintzenheim	D	90
1990	Tokay-Pinot Gris Clos Jebsal Vendange Tardive	E	88
1989	Tokay-Pinot Gris Clos Jebsal Vendange Tardive	E	91
1990	Tokay-Pinot Gris Clos Saint-Urbain Rangen	E	96

1989 Tokay-Pinot Gris Clos Saint-Urbain Rangen	D	96
1990 Tokay-Pinot Gris Clos Windsbuhl Vendange Tardive	E	94
1989 Tokay-Pinot Gris Clos Windsbuhl Vendange Tardive	E	96
1989 Tokay-Pinot Gris Heimbourg Sélection de Grains Nobles	EE	99
1989 Tokay-Pinot Gris Rangen Clos Saint-Urbain Sélection de Grains Nobles	EE	99–100
1989 Tokay-Pinot Gris Rottenberg Sélection de Grains Nobles	EE	90
1990 Tokay-Pinot Gris Rottenberg Vendange Tardive	E	94
1990 Tokay-Pinot Gris Vieilles Vignes	D	93
1989 Tokay-Pinot Gris Vieilles Vignes	D	92

There are only a handful of cellars that produce a range of wines as riveting as that of Leonard and Olivier Humbrecht. In fact, I would rank Zind-Humbrecht's performance in 1989 and 1990 with the most memorable I have ever witnessed. Anyone traveling to Europe should make a special effort to visit and taste in these cellars. There is no one in Alsace who is any more dedicated to the concept of terroir, that fuzzy, albeit appealingly intellectual notion that a wine should reflect its soil, than Leonard and Olivier Humbrecht. This father-and-son team is obsessed with preserving what they consider the uniqueness of the many different vineyard sites they own. It has become fashionable to expound upon the theory of terroir, primarily by people who do more talking than tasting. However, in sipping through the Zind-Humbrecht wines, I found the notion of terroir persuasive. The results are wines faithful to their soils, as well as vivid and intense, with a longevity and compelling character rarely seen anywhere else in the world. These are the wines of true genius. At Humbrecht, I tasted through the 1989s again, and they are among the greatest dry wines from Alsace I have ever had the pleasure to taste. The 1989 Pinot Blanc is so perfumed and loaded with fruit that it could be confused with a Premier Cru white burgundy. However, it is Alsace Pinot Blanc at its most decadent and most profound. The wonderfully intense bouquet of honey, oranges, and apples is gorgeous. In the mouth the wine exhibits great fruit, a long, surprisingly intense, medium-bodied texture, and an opulent, nearly explosive, dry finish. This great Pinot Blanc will age for 4–5 years. Please give it a try! I tasted four dry 1989 Rieslings, ranging from excellent to profound. The 1989 Riesling Turckheim has surprisingly good acidity for the superripe 1989 vintage, a moderately intense, smoky, mineral-scented nose, rich, intense, beautifully etched apple- and minerallike flavors, and a long, dry finish. It is a glorious Riesling for drinking over the next 4–6 years. The 1989 Riesling Herrenweg Turckheim is slightly more concentrated, with fine, crisp acidity, and a super bouquet of citrusy, minerallike, exotic fruit. In the mouth there is great clarity to the wine's intense, full-bodied, yet impeccably pure, dry flavors. The finish is exceptional. This superb Riesling should drink well for the next 5–7 years. The 1989 Riesling Wintzenheim is equally profound, but more exotic, with a smoky, almost bacon- and lychee nut–scented nose. In the mouth it is firm, yet impressively rich, full, dry, long, and well balanced in the finish. Much like the Herrenweg Turckheim, it should be drunk over the next 5–7 years. The Riesling Clos Saint-Urbain is one of the most extraordinary and compelling dry Rieslings I have ever tasted from Alsace. Wines such as these almost make a mockery of a critic's attempt to articulate their aromas and flavors. The essence of the Riesling grape expresses itself in this wine with an intense nose offering aromas of citrus, minerals, smoke, gunflint, and ripe fruit. In the mouth the wine has an incredibly extracted inner core of fruit, buttressed beautifully by good acidity. There is remarkable length, and an overall sense of perfect harmony to this wine's elements. It is an impeccably balanced, elegant Riesling for drinking over the next 10–12 years.

I tasted two of the dry cuvées of 1989 Zind-Humbrecht Pinot Gris. With this grape Leonard Humbrecht and his son, Olivier, often obtain a level of concentration and opulence that one usually finds only in a great Grand Cru white burgundy such as Chevalier Montrachet or Montrachet itself. The 1989 Tokay-Pinot Gris Vieilles Vignes has a medium golden color and an almost thick-looking appearance because of the high glycerin and extraordinary extract it possesses. The honeyed nose of buttery nuts, smoke, and superrich fruit is unforgettable. In the mouth it is gloriously, even decadently, rich and full bodied, with a lavish texture and an extraordinary finish. It is the only 1989 I tasted from Zind-Humbrecht that has relatively low acidity, and therefore I would opt for drinking it over the next 4–5 years. Those consumers fortunate enough to find any of the 1989 Tokay-Pinot Gris Clos Saint-Urbain should buy as much as they can afford. This wine, although much more backward than the Tokay Vieilles Vignes, is a monumental example of what extraordinary heights this grape can reach in what appears to be an irrefutably great Alsatian vintage. The acidity is much higher than in the Vieilles Vignes, yet the wine is every bit as concentrated and may actually be even longer on the palate. One can sense this is a massive wine, held together by impeccable acidity yet ready to burst loose. The buttery, smoky bouquet is followed by a brilliantly balanced, full-bodied, amazingly extracted wine that never tastes heavy or out of balance because of its acidity and overall sense of harmony. This riveting wine should drink well for 10–15 or more years. The exotic, dramatic, and flamboyant Gewürztraminer, the world's love-it-or-leave-it grape, has undoubtedly had the kind of vintage where all of its flashy personality can be abundantly displayed. The three dry 1989 Gewürztraminers I tasted from Zind-Humbrecht included an exotic, lychee nut–, rose-scented 1989 Gewürztraminer Herrenweg Turckheim. Its bouquet soars from the glass, as do the in-your-face, no-holds-barred flavors. Yet there is plenty of acidity for focus, and the overall impression is one of great personality and character, as well as impeccable balance. Even better is the 1989 Gewürztraminer Wintzenheim. The huge, bacon fat–scented, honeyed aroma alone caused me to get out the checkbook to reserve a case. In the mouth the wine is full bodied, beautifully extracted, with rich flavors and a dry, long, spicy finish. This compelling Gewürztraminer should, like the Herrenweg Turckheim, drink beautifully for 5–7 years. The most memorable Gewürztraminer I have tasted is the 1989 Gewürztraminer Clos Windsbuhl. It is also one of the most compelling white wines I have ever had. Not only is it extraordinarily concentrated, but there is enough acidity to hold everything together and give the wine a sense of vibrancy and brilliant focus. In the Humbrecht cellars, it was more closed and structured than when I tasted it on these shores. The spicy, floral, smoky, mineral- and superripe fruit–scented aroma is followed by layer upon layer of fruit that tease and seduce the taster. The finish must last well over a minute. This full-bodied, perfectly rendered, dry white wine has a presence in the glass that only a few Grand Cru white burgundies possess. Given its exceptional harmony, acidity, and overall balance, this is a Gewürztraminer that will improve for the next 4–6 years, and where well stored, it will be drinkable over a span of 10–20 years. The other totally dry wine I tasted, the 1989 Pinot Noir, had an alcohol level approaching 15%, was aged in two-thirds new oak casks, and was made from clones that Humbrecht had acquired from Louis Latour's famed Corton-Grancey vineyard. It is a super effort for Alsace, but, as with most Alsace Pinot Noirs, it is relatively compact.

As phenomenal as the 1989 dry wines from Zind-Humbrecht are, the 1990s are in many cases nearly as profound. The 1990 Pinot Blanc is a superb rival to the glorious 1989. Amazingly concentrated, with an exotic orange and apple blossom fragrance, and rich, gorgeously poised and refreshing flavors, this medium-bodied Pinot Blanc is about as delicious a Pinot as one is likely to find from Alsace. Among the dry 1990 Rieslings, there is a flowery, crisp, lively, bone-dry 1990 Riesling Turckheim, a more concentrated, mineral-scented and -flavored, steely 1990 Riesling Herrenweg Turckheim, and a similar but even more mineral-dominated, backward, austere 1990 Riesling Gueberschwihr. At the top level, the extraordinary dry Rieslings Zind-Humbrecht made in 1990 include the 1990 Riesling Rangen Clos Saint-Urbain. The poor volcanic soil of this superbly situated steep vineyard with a full southerly exposure has produced an awesomely full-bodied, dry, smoky, rich, compelling Riesling of phenomenal depth and precision of flavor. It is one of the greatest expressions of dry Riesling I have ever tasted from Alsace and a worthy rival to the spectacular 1989. It should drink well for the next 15–20 or more years. The 1990 Riesling Brand is more floral, but very deep and rich, with impeccably precise flavors, good acidity, and a smashingly long finish. Zind-Humbrecht's two dry 1990 Tokay-Pinot Gris wines were both sensational but slightly less staggering than the otherworldly 1989s. The 1990 Tokay-Pinot Gris Vieilles Vignes, made from 40- to 50-year-old-vines situated in both Turckheim and Wintzenheim, is another smoky, creamy, buttery, rich wine, with gobs of fruit, wonderfully precise acidity, and a long, full-bodied, explosively rich finish. Most people would mistake this great wine for a Grand Cru from Chassagne-Montrachet. The taste of the 1990 Tokay-Pinot Gris Rangen Clos Saint-Urbain reinforces the fact that no one makes greater Tokay-Pinot Gris than Humbrecht. This is an extraordinary wine, perhaps slightly less perfumed than the surreal 1989 but exhibiting great presence on the palate, wonderful balance, and a fabulously waxy, earthy, flowery, exotic nose of smoke and superrich fruit. In the mouth there is enough acidity to provide precision to its enormously rich, hefty flavors. Time and time again I am reminded that this wine ought to be considered the Montrachet of Alsace.

As the tasting notes indicate, the 1989 Gewürztraminers from Zind-Humbrecht were otherworldly. But his 1990s are also terrific. The 1990 Gewürztraminer Herrenweg Turckheim is even more sensational than the 1989. With yields of only 22–25 hectoliters per hectare, this wine has a riveting bouquet of smoky lychee nuts, cloves, and allspice. In the mouth it exhibits some of the most concentrated Gewürztraminer fruit anyone is ever likely to confront. All of this is buttressed by fine acidity and an uncanny sense of balance despite the enormous size of this full-bodied, in-your-face style of Gewürztraminer. It should drink well for at least 15 or more years. The only thing that can be said about the 1990 Gewürztraminer Clos Saint-Urbain Rangen is that it is an utterly profound wine. It shares similar characteristics with the Gewürztraminer Herrenweg Turckheim, but it is even more extracted, with a honeyed richness and a smashingly long finish. It should last 10–15 years. The other totally dry wine I tasted from Zind-Humbrecht was the 1990 Pinot Noir. It had excellent color and good, spicy, berry fruit, but it seemed a bit simple and short.

It is difficult to imagine the extract levels in Zind-Humbrecht's Vendange Tardive wines given the immense concentration he attained with his dry wines. His Vendange Tardives, which are never shy, are wines to have either before a meal with foie gras (assuming anyone in our country of cholesterol counters still eats this sort of food) or, as André Ostertag says, should be drunk while listening to your favorite music. There is a gorgeous array of Vendange Tardive wines from both the 1989 and 1990 vintages from Zind-Humbrecht. For starters, the 1990 Riesling Clos Windsbuhl V.T. exhibits spectacular fruit, as well as elegance allied with surprising power—not an easy task to accomplish. Drink this rich, aromatic, wonderfully precise, and well-balanced wine over the next 12–15 years. The 1990 Riesling Herrenweg V.T. has even greater dimension. Consider its penetrating mineral, exotic fruit aromas, and dense but superbly balanced, honeyed fruit flavors backed up by zesty acidity. Again, 10–15 years is not an unrealistic time frame over which to drink this wine. I was knocked out by the extraordinary 1990 Riesling Clos Hauserer V.T., which comes from a 3-acre vineyard at the foot of the famous Grand Cru Hengst. The bouquet of oranges and tropical fruit, combined with an intense mineral character and fine acidity, makes for one heck of a glass of medium-bodied, superbly concentrated Riesling. The top award in the 1990 Vendange Tardive category goes to the 1990 Riesling Brand V.T. Only slightly off-dry, with amazingly high acidity and a level of extraction that one rarely encounters, it is a riveting example of how great Riesling can be when made from a low-yielding vineyard by an immensely talented winemaker. Phenomenal mineral-, apple-, orange-, and honeylike fruit is forcefully held in balance by the crisp acids. Among the 1989 Riesling Vendange Tardive wines from Zind-Humbrecht is a great 1989 Riesling Brand V.T. This is the essence of Riesling, and the mineral, stony soils of Brand have turned out an awesomely profound wine with extraordinary perfume, great precision of flavors, and wonderful fresh acidity that somehow manages to pull together the enormous component parts of this wine. Most consumers would probably consider it a dry wine, but it is a Vendange Tardive wine that should last for 15–20 or more years. With respect to the Tokay-Pinot Gris Vendange Tardive offerings in 1989 and 1990, Zind-Humbrecht has produced five wines, four of which are compelling and one excellent. The excellent wine, which may turn out to be outstanding with another 2–3 years in the bottle, is the 1990 Tokay-Pinot Gris Clos Jebsal V.T. It comes across as slightly more monolithic, fat, honeyed, rich, and dense but lacking the clarity and focus of the other Zind-Humbrecht wines. The 1989 Tokay-Pinot Gris Clos Jebsal V.T. seems to have all of the characteristics of the 1990, but with more depth, greater precision, more perfume, and a longer finish. Off-dry and full bodied, this offering should drink well for the next 10–20 years. I am convinced that the Clos Windsbuhl vineyard, located just behind the striking church of Hunawihr near Trimbach's famed Clos Sainte Hune vineyard, is a formidable site for top wines. A certain look and feel to the vineyard makes the greatness of the wines more understandable. Zind-Humbrecht has produced two truly profound Tokay-Pinot Gris wines in 1989 and 1990 from this vineyard. The 1989 and 1990 Tokay-Pinot Gris Clos Windsbuhl V.T. wines are must purchases for those who admire the style of Zind-Humbrecht and who agree with me that Tokay-Pinot Gris makes one of the world's finest yet relatively unknown grapes. The 1990 has a huge bouquet of nuts, honey, cream, and smoke, rich, multidimensional flavors, full body, and an explosively rich, off-dry finish. It should last for 10–20 more years. The 1989 is even more exotic, more layered, and one of the most sensational examples of Pinot Gris I have ever had the pleasure to taste. So concentrated and unctuous is it, I am not sure with what I would drink this wine, but believe me, I would consume it—any time, any place! Who can ignore its smoky, waxy, buttery fruit and thrill-a-sip texture and length? Still somewhat unevolved, it has at least 20 or more years of graceful evolution. The 1990 Tokay-Pinot Gris Rottenberg V.T. is another honeyed, intense, yet impeccably well-balanced monster of a wine with extraordinary extraction and flavor yet plenty of acidity for balance and focus. Smoky, rich, and overwhelming to taste, it has the potential to last for up to 30 or more years. There is little more one could ask for from the late harvest Gewürztraminers produced by this firm. The 1990 Gewürztraminer Clos Windsbuhl V.T. is relatively closed but elegant, with a rich, rose petal–, lychee nut–scented nose, opulent but well-structured flavors, and a super finish. Give it 2–3 years in the bottle to open and then drink it over the next decade. The 1989 and 1990 Gewürztraminer Goldert V.T. are essentially equivalent in quality. The 1990 is almost the essence of lychee nuts, very rich and fat, with a marvelous off-dry finish and a heady, pungent, intoxicating aroma. The 1989 is more floral and herbaceous, with more tropical fruit flavors as well as surprisingly high acidity and tightness. Nevertheless, the intense fragrance of roses remains apparent. It is capable of lasting for 15 or more years. Both the 1989 and 1990 Gewürztraminer Heimbourg V.T. are legendary efforts that should be considered among the greatest wines made from this varietal. I would not be surprised if the 1990, which is extremely sweet, was a declassified Sélection de Grains Nobles. It is a dessert-style Gewürztraminer, with an extraordinary honeyed, lychee nut fruitiness, viscous, thick flavors, and enough acidity and structure to give the wine a refreshing zestiness on the palate. The 1989 blew me away. The huge, smoky, bacon fat–, almost plum- and violet-scented nose is a real turn-on. In the mouth there was extraordinary richness, an off-dry character that was much less sweet than the 1990, and a dazzling finish crammed with fruit and glycerin. This spectacular wine must be tasted to be believed. The 1990 Gewürztraminer-Hengst V.T. is another classic. With a bouquet reminiscent of cherry jam, one could almost take this for a red wine. In the mouth it is off-dry, with sensational concentration, good acidity, and an almost roasted, smoky, mineral quality. It should last for at least 10–20 years. The 1989 Gewürztraminer Hengst V.T. had a great deal more botrytis in its nose, as evidenced by the apricot-, peachlike scents, as well as lively acidity, a magnificently rich, mineral, oily palate impression, and, once again, an astounding finish. Medium sweet, it is probably best drunk by itself either before or after a meal and should last for at least 10–20 years. The 1989 Gewürztraminer Herrenweg V.T. had a huge, earthy, smoky, bacon fat aroma, dense, sensationally rich, off-dry, deeply extracted flavors, and a super glycerin-laden finish. More forward than some of the other wines, it should provide riveting drinking over the next 10–15 years. Zind-Humbrecht also made some outstanding Sélection de Grains Nobles wines in both 1989 and 1990. Most of them will not be released for at least 2–3 years, but if you have the discretionary income and love the decadently sweet, honeyed character of these wines, there are a number that are not to be missed. Most of these wines were produced in lots of 100 cases or less, so availability is limited. The 1990 Riesling Clos Windsbuhl S.D.G.N. is extremely high in acidity, with amazing tartness and crispness on the palate. One could sense this wine's huge ripeness and inner core of honeyed apple and tropical fruits. It is almost criminal to drink a wine in such a state of infancy, so I would cellar it for at least another 5–10 years. The 1990 Gewürztraminer Rangen S.D.G.N. may well be the perfect sweet wine. I would be willing to put it in a blind tasting against the greatest vintages of d'Yquem just to prove how underrated and how magnificent these nectars from Alsace can be. From its smoky, ripe, lychee nut–, rose petal–scented nose to its fabulous concoction of fruit flavors, wonderful acidity, freshness and length, this is an unforgettable sweet wine. Drink it between 1998 and 2020. Although less complex, the 1990 Gewürztraminer Heimbourg S.D.G.N. remains a titan of a wine. With 200 grams of residual sugar per liter, it is about as sweet as wine can be. Yet the balance is striking. Leonard Humbrecht claims it will easily keep for 40–50 years. The 1989 Tokay Heimbourg S.D.G.N. is another eerily perfect wine. How it balances such remarkable intensity, richness, and sweetness yet still retains its impeccable sense of elegance, freshness, and lightness is mind-boggling. Interestingly, the Humbrechts vinify all their Sélection de Grains Nobles Tokays in new oak casks. The fact that there is not a whiff of new oak to be found in these wines may suggest just how highly extracted they are. Another celestial example of late harvest Tokay is the 1989 Tokay Rangen Clos Saint-Urbain S.D.G.N. One hundred cases of this wine with 250 grams per liter of residual sugar were produced. The bouquet almost fills the room with its smoky, floral, paraffin-scented, rich fruit. In the mouth there is mind-boggling richness, extraordinary balance, and a finish that must last several minutes. Last, the 1989 Tokay Rottenberg S.D.G.N. is very sweet and somewhat cloying when compared with these otherworldly wines, but is still impressive, rich, and full. Given its lower acidity and more obvious commercial style, it should probably be drunk in its first decade of life.

I have often contemplated why the wines of Zind-Humbrecht are so remarkable. There is no secret. The yields from his vineyards are extremely conservative, usually well under 30 hectoliters per hectare for the dry wines and under 10 hectoliters per hectare for the Vendange Tardive and sweet wines. The Humbrechts are also great proponents of extended lees contact. No new oak casks are used except for their Pinot Noir and a few of the Sélection de Grains Nobles wines, but all of the foudres in their cellar are equipped with rotors that are used to stir the lees, which the Humbrechts believe enhances the flavor and gives a certain "nutritional" value to their wines. I shall never forget the level of quality of Zind-Humbrecht's 1989s and 1990s for such brilliance is rarely encountered. Obviously the Vendange Tardive and Sélection de Grains Nobles wines are beyond the financial grasp of most American wine consumers. But even excluding the Vendange Tardive and Sélection de Grains Nobles wines, which admittedly have a small audience, there is enough compelling dry Pinot Blanc, Riesling, Tokay-Pinot Gris, and Gewürztraminer to please even the most finicky connoisseur. These are prodigious wines, and they deserve to be in every conscientiously stocked wine cellar in the world.

BORDEAUX

Harvest Moon

The Basics

TYPES OF WINE

Bordeaux is the world's largest supplier of high-quality, age-worthy table wine, from properties usually called châteaux. Production in the 1980s and 1990s varied between 25 adn 65 million cases of wine a year, of which 75% was red.

Red Wine   Much of Bordeaux's fame rests on its production of dry red table wine, yet only a tiny percentage of Bordeaux's most prestigious wine comes from famous appellations such as Margaux, St.-Julien, Pauillac, and St.-Estèphe, all located in an area called the Médoc, and Graves, Pomerol, and St.-Emilion, From these areas the wine is expensive yet consistently high in quality.

White Wine   Bordeaux produces sweet, rich, honeyed wines from two famous areas called Sauternes and Barsac. An ocean of dry white wine is made, most of it insipid and neutral in character, except for the excellent dry white wines made in the Graves area.

GRAPE VARIETIES

Following are the most important types of grapes used in the red and white wines of Bordeaux.

RED WINE VARIETIES

For red wines, three major grape varieties are planted in Bordeaux, as well as two minor varieties, one of which—Petit-Verdot—will be discussed below. The type of grape used has a profound influence on the style of wine that is ultimately produced.

Cabernet Sauvignon   A grape that is highly pigmented, very astringent, and tannic and that provides the framework, strength, dark color, character, and longevity for the wines in a majority of the vineyards in the Médoc. It ripens late, is resistant to rot because of its thick skin, and has a pronounced blackcurrant aroma that is sometimes intermingled with subtle herbaceous scents that with aging take on the smell of cedarwood. Virtually all Bordeaux châteaux blend Cabernet Sauvignon with other red grape varieties. In the Médoc the average percentage of Cabernet Sauvignon in the blend is 40–85%; in Graves, 40–60%; in St.-Émilion, 10–50%; and in Pomerol, 0–20%.

Merlot   Utilized by virtually every wine château in Bordeaux because of its ability to provide a round, generous, blushy, supple, alcoholic wine, Merlot ripens, on an average, one to two weeks earlier than Cabernet Sauvignon. In the Médoc this grape reaches its zenith, and several Médoc châteaux use high percentages of it (Palmer and Pichon-Lalande), but its fame is in the wines it renders in Pomerol, where it is used profusely. In the Médoc the average percentage of Merlot in the blend is 5–45%; in Graves, 20–40%; in St.-Émilion, 25–60%; and in Pomerol, 35–98%. Merlot produces wines lower in acidity and tannin than Cabernet Sauvignon, and as a general rule wines with a high percentage of Merlot are drinkable much earlier than wines with a high percentage of Cabernet Sauvignon but frequently age just as well.

Cabernet Franc   A relative of Cabernet Sauvignon that ripens slightly earlier, Cabernet Franc (called Bouchet in St.-Émilion and Pomerol) is used in small to modest proportions in order to add complexity and bouquet to a wine. Cabernet Franc has a pungent, often very spicy, sometimes weedy, olivelike aroma. It does not have the fleshy, supple character of Merlot, nor the astringence, power, and color of Cabernet Sauvignon. In the Médoc the average percentage of Cabernet Franc used in the blend is 0–30%; in Graves, 5–25%; in St.-Émilion, 25–66%; in Pomerol, 5–50%.

Petit-Verdot   A useful but generally difficult red grape because of its very late ripening characteristics, Petit-Verdot provides intense color, mouth-gripping tannins, and high sugar and thus high alcohol when it ripens fully, as it did in 1982 and 1983 in Bordeaux. When unripe it provides a nasty, sharp, acidic character. In the Médoc few châteaux use more than 5% in the blend, and those that do are generally properties such as Palmer and Pichon-Lalande, which use high percentages of Merlot.

WHITE WINE VARIETIES

Bordeaux produces both dry and sweet white wine. Usually only three grape varieties are used: Sauvignon Blanc and Semillon, for dry and sweet wine, and Muscadelle, which is used sparingly for the sweet wines.

Sauvignon Blanc   Used for making both the dry white wines of Graves and the sweet white wines of the Sauternes/Barsac region, Sauvignon Blanc renders a very distinctive wine with a pungent, somewhat herbaceous aroma and crisp, austere flavors. Among the dry white Graves, a few châteaux employ 100% Sauvignon Blanc, but most blend it with Semillon. Less Sauvignon Blanc is used in the winemaking blends in the Sauternes region than in Graves.

Semillon   Very susceptible to the famous "noble rot" called botrytis, which is essential to the production of excellent sweet wines, Semillon is used to provide a rich, creamy, intense texture to both the dry wines of Graves and the rich, sweet wines of Sauternes. Semillon is quite fruity when young, and wines with a high percentage of Semillon seem to take on weight and viscosity as they age. For these reasons, higher percentages of Semillon are used in making the

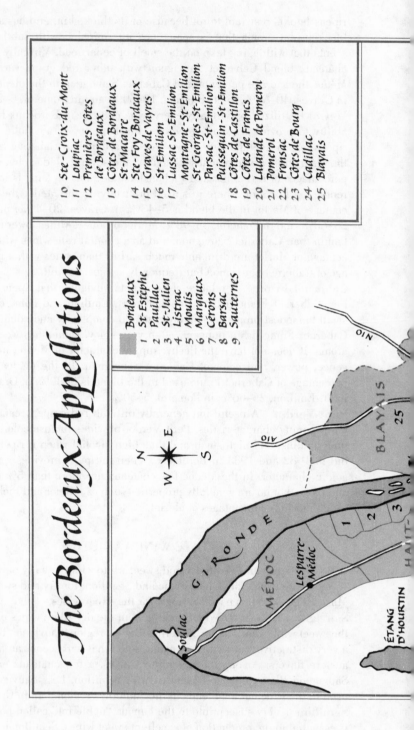

The Bordeaux Appellations

Bordeaux
1 St-Estèphe
2 Pauillac
3 St-Julien
4 Listrac
5 Moulis
6 Margaux
7 Cérons
8 Barsac
9 Sauternes
10 Ste-Croix-du-Mont
11 Loupiac
12 Premières Côtes de Bordeaux
13 Côtes de Bordeaux
14 St-Macaire
15 Ste-Foy-Bordeaux
16 Graves de Vayres
17 St-Emilion
   Lussac St-Emilion
   Montagne-St-Emilion
   St-Georges-St-Emilion
   Parsac-St-Emilion
   Puisseguin-St-Emilion
18 Côtes de Castillon
19 Côtes de Francs
20 Lalande de Pomerol
21 Pomerol
22 Fronsac
23 Côtes de Bourg
24 Cadillac
25 Blayais

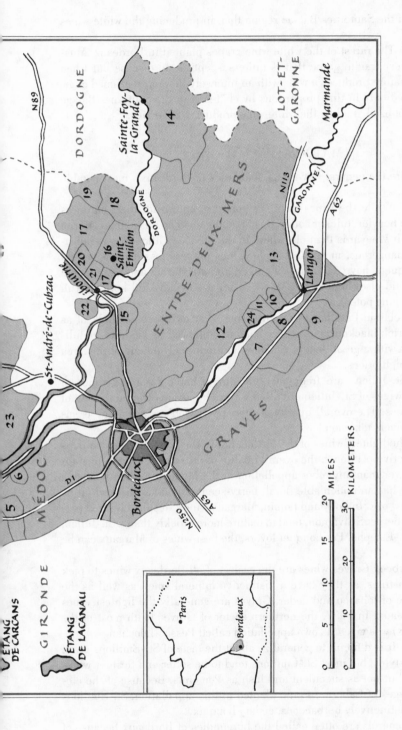

MILES
KILOMETERS

ÉTANG
DE CARCANS

ÉTANG
DE LACANAU

GIRONDE

MÉDOC

DORDOGNE

LOT-ET-
GARONNE

ENTRE-DEUX-MERS

GRAVES

Bordeaux

Sainte-Foy-
la-Grande

Saint-
Emilion

Libourne

St-André-de-Cubzac

Langon

Marmande

DORDOGNE

GARONNE

Paris

Bordeaux

N89

N113

A62

A63

N250

D1

5

6

23

22

15

20

21

17

16

19

18

17

13

24

11

10

8

9

7

12

14

sweet wines of the Sauternes/Barsac region than in producing the white wines of Graves.

Muscadelle   The rarest of the white wine grapes planted in Bordeaux, Muscadelle is a very fragile grape that is quite susceptible to disease but when healthy and mature produces a wine with an intensely flowery, perfumed character. It is used only in tiny proportions by châteaux in the Sauternes/Barsac region. It is not used at all by the white wine producers of Graves.

MAJOR APPELLATIONS

Following are the general flavor characteristics of Bordeaux's most notable types of wines.

St.-Estèphe   While the wines of St.-Estèphe are known for their hardness because of the heavier, thicker soil in this area, the châteaux have more Merlot planted in their vineyards than elsewhere in the Médoc. Although generalizations can be dangerous, most St.-Estèphe wines possess less expressive and flattering bouquets, have a tougher character, and are sterner and more tannic than those found elsewhere in the Médoc. They are usually full bodied, with considerable aging potential.

Pauillac   A classic Pauillac seems to define what most people think of as Bordeaux—a rich blackcurrant, cedary bouquet, followed by medium- to full-bodied flavors with a great deal of richness and tannin. The fame of this area equates with high prices.

St.-Julien   St.-Juliens are frequently indistinguishable from the wines of Pauillac. The wines of St.-Julien are filled with rich curranty fruit and smell of cedar and spices. The overall quality of this appellation's winemaking is superb, so consumers take note!

Margaux   The lightest wines of the Médoc, but in the great vintages perhaps the most seductive. Although the overall quality of the winemaking in this appellation is lower than any other appellation in the Médoc, in a top vintage a great Margaux has an undeniable floral, berry-scented bouquet backed up by the smell of new oak. In body and tannin, Margaux wines, despite elevated percentages of Cabernet Sauvignon, tend to mature more quickly than a St.-Julien, Pauillac, or St.-Estèphe. For bouquet lovers, the best wines of Margaux can be compelling.

Graves   Textbook Graves wines are the easiest of all Bordeaux wines to pick out in blind tastings, as they have a distinctive mineral smell as well as the scent and taste of tobacco and cedar. Graves are generally the lightest wines made in Bordeaux. In 1987, the northern sector of Graves (with most of the major châteaux) was given its own appellation called Pessac-Léognan.

St.-Émilion   It is difficult to generalize about the taste of St.-Émilions given the divergent styles, but most St.-Émilions tend to be softer and fleshier wines than Médocs, but not as succulent and lush as Pomerols. Because of the elevated percentages of Cabernet Franc planted in this appellation, St.-Émilions often have a distinctively herbaceous, cedary bouquet.

Pomerol   Pomerols are often called the burgundies of Bordeaux because of their rich, supple, more monolithic personalities, but they age extremely well and are undeniable choices for hedonists, as they provide oodles of rich blackcurrant, black cherry, sometimes blackberry, fruit. In the great vintages an exquisite opulence can be found in these wines.

White Graves   The top-notch white Graves are aged in oak and made from the Sauvignon Blanc and Semillon grapes. They often start off life excessively oaky but fill out beautifully with age and develop creamy, rich flavors that marry beautifully with the oak. Other white wines of Bordeaux are often totally neutral and insipid in character and taste simply of acidity and water.

Sauternes/Barsac   Depending on the vintage and degree of the noble rot (botrytis) that affects the grapes, the wines can taste either fat, ripe, and lacking in character in those years when there is little botrytis, or wonderfully exotic with a bouquet of honeyed tropical fruits and buttered nuts in those great vintages where there has been plenty of the noble rot.

AGING POTENTIAL

St.-Estèphe: 8–35 years   St.-Émilion: 8–25 years
Pauillac: 8–40 years   Pomerol: 5–30 years
St.-Julien: 8–35 years   White Graves: 5–20 years
Margaux: 8–30 years   Sauternes/Barsac: 10–50+ years
                              Red Graves: 8–30 years

OVERALL QUALITY LEVEL

Of all the great viticultural regions of the world, Bordeaux consistently produces wine of the highest quality. Although one-dimensional, innocuous wines can be found, bad wine is rare. For the world's top producers of Cabernet Sauvignon, Merlot, and Cabernet Franc, Bordeaux remains the point of reference.

THE MOST IMPORTANT INFORMATION TO KNOW

For the wine consumer trying to develop a degree of expertise when buying the wines of Bordeaux, the most important information to know is which châteaux are producing the best wines today. A review of the top categories of châteaux in Bordeaux will reveal which producers maintain a high commitment to quality. However, consumers should also familiarize themselves generally with the styles of wines from the different appellations. Some tasters will prefer the austere, sterner style of Bordeaux represented by St.-Estèphe or Pauillac, whereas others will love the lavish lushness and opulence of a Pomerol. It has been my experience that Graves wines, with their distinctive mineral scent and tobacco bouquet, are often the wines least favored by neophytes, but with more experience this character becomes one that is admired by connoisseurs. Be aware that the famous official classifications of wine quality in Bordeaux are all out of date and should be only of academic interest to the consumer. These historic classifications of wine quality were employed both to promote more wines and to establish well-delineated quality benchmarks, but because of negligence, incompetence, or just plain greed, some of these châteaux produce mediocre and poor wines that hardly reflect their placement in these classifications. A more valid guideline to the quality of Bordeaux wines is the classification of châteaux on the following pages. These reflect the overall quality of the wines rather than their historical pedigree.

1994–1995 BUYING STRATEGY

Thanks to a bevy of high-quality vintages from recent years, Bordeaux lovers wanting to guarantee the lowest-possible price for their favorite wines no longer have to buy them as futures, two years in advance of delivery. Although there exist a few successes in the generally mediocre vintages of 1991 and 1992, neither merits buying before consumers have had a chance to taste the wines and decide which deserve attention. The best 1990s, which have now arrived in the marketplace, are great wines, with many of them (particularly Médoc first-growths, St.-Estèphe, Pomerol, and St.-Émilion) rivaling and even eclipsing the more heralded, as well as more expensive, 1989s. Readers who desire a young, great vintage should try 1990.

Most of the top 1989s are in short supply, and their prices are 25–40% higher than their 1990 siblings, making 1989 a potentially overvalued vintage. With the exception of the two great wines of the vintage—La Mission-Haut-Brion and Haut-Brion—prices are stable.

Perhaps the best vintage for maximizing your buying power is the 1988. These wines were dumped by many major importers because sales were slow and they needed to raise cash to pay for their 1989s and 1990s. Many of the best 1988s continue to languish on retailers' shelves. Although they lack the drama and fleshiness of the best 1989s and 1990s, there are some excellent, even outstanding, wines available that from an aromatic and flavor perspective are more typical (some say more classic) than the 1989s and 1990s.

It is also worth looking at older vintages, such as 1986, 1985, and 1983. Because of the saturated marketplace, these wines have not budged in price over the last few years. However, do not expect the good times to continue. The so-so years of 1991 and 1992 will cause prices of Bordeaux wines to rise once existing stocks of the best 1990s, 1989s, 1988s, 1987s, 1986s, and 1985s have been depleted. But until then it is a buyer's market with considerable price reductions for all but the most glamorous wines.

VINTAGE SUMMARIES

1992—When I was in Bordeaux in January 1993 to finish my tastings of the 1990s from bottle, I had the opportunity to sample numerous wines (most of them just assembled) from this maligned vintage. It is too early to discuss any possible patterns of quality, but all the wines I tasted were light, very fruity, and soft, with surprising charm and roundness. They will certainly be wines to drink young, but by no means is this a catastrophe in Bordeaux. If the prices fall, and I predict they will, this vintage will find its place in the market after the wines are bottled and released. It was a huge crop, so those properties that make the most severe selections will probably turn out the best wines. This is not a vintage to purchase as a wine future.

1991—Pomerol and St.-Émilion experienced a poor vintage, much worse than 1987 and probably inferior to 1984. For example, these well-known estates have completely declassified their 1991s and will produce no wine under the château name: Ausone, Beauséjour-Duffau, Bon Pasteur, Canon, Canon-La-Gaffelière, Cheval Blanc, Fonroque, Haut-Bailly, Latour à Pomerol, Magdelaine, Pétrus, Trotanoy, and Vieux Château Certan. Many other prominent estates, particularly in St.-Émilion and Pomerol, were still considering whether to declassify.

As dismal as the vintage is in St.-Émilion and Pomerol, some surprisingly good wines have emerged from Graves and those Médoc vineyards adjacent to the Gironde. Readers will be surprised by the quality of many of these wines, which even include a handful that may merit outstanding scores. There are not abundant quantities of the 1991s, and the prices should be low in order to stimulate some consumer interest. One appellation that stands out for consistently good wines is St.-Estèphe, followed by Pauillac. These wines offer soft, ripe, forward fruit in a medium-bodied format and, much like the 1987s, should be drunk in their first ten years of life. The best wines I tasted in January 1993 (several months prior to bottling), with an approximate score shown in parentheses, include the following: Calon-Ségur (86–87), Domaine de Chevalier (85–87), Cos d'Estournel (88–90), La Dame de Montrose (86–87), Haut-Brion (87–90), Lafite-Rothschild (87–89), Latour (89–90), Léoville-Barton (86–87), Léoville-Las Cases (87–89), Lynch-Bages (86–88), Margaux (88–91), La Mission-Haut-Brion (86–88), Montrose (89–92), Palmer (86–88), Phélan-Ségur (85–86), Pichon-Longueville Baron (88–80), Pichon-Longueville, Comtesse de Lalande (87–90).

1990—Most of the great Bordeaux vintages of this century are the result of relatively hot, dry years. For that reason alone, 1990 should elicit considerable attention. The most revealing fact about the 1990 vintage is that it is the second-hottest of the century, barely surpassed by 1947. It is also the second-sunniest vintage, eclipsed only by 1949 in the post–World War II era. The amount of sunshine and the extraordinarily hot summers Bordeaux has enjoyed during the decade of the 1980s is frequently attributed to the so-called greenhouse effect and consequent global warming, about which the scientific community has been so concerned. Yet consider the Bordeaux weather for the period between 1945 and 1949. Amazingly, that era was even more torrid than 1989–1990. One might wonder if there was concern then about the ice caps of the North and South poles melting.

The weather in 1990 was auspicious because of its potential to produce great wines, but weather is only one part of the equation. The summer months of July and August were the driest since 1961, and August was the hottest since 1928, the year records were first kept. September (the month that most producers claim "makes the quality") was not, weatherwise, a particularly exceptional month. Among the great hot-year vintages, 1990 was the second wettest, surpassed only by 1989. As in 1989, the rain fell at periods that should give rise to concern. For example, on September 15 a particularly violent series of thunderstorms swung across Bordeaux, inundating much of the Graves region. On September 22–23 there was modest rainfall over the entire region. On October 7 and October 15 light showers were reported throughout the region. Most producers have been quick to state that the rain in September was beneficial. They argue that the Cabernet Sauvignon grapes were still too small and their skins too thick. Many Cabernet vines had shut down and the grapes refused to mature because of the excessive heat and drought. The rain, suggest the producers, promoted further ripening and alleviated the blocked state of maturity.

There is no doubting that the weather in 1990 put even more stress on the Bordeaux vineyards than the heat and drought of 1989. One of the keys to understanding this vintage is that many of the greatest wines of 1990 have emerged from those vineyards planted on the heavier, less-well-drained, less desirable vineyard soils. For example, in my tasting notes, I observed that the heavier soils from such appellations as St.-Estèphe, Fronsac, and the hillside vineyards of St.-Émilion produced richer, more concentrated, and more complete wines than many of the top vineyards planted on the fine, well-drained, gravel-based soils of Margaux and Graves. Yet an irony of the vintage is that Châteaux Margaux and Latour, both exceptionally stony, well-drained vineyards, produced monumental wines.

The crop size was enormous in 1990, approximately equivalent to the quantity of wine produced in 1989. In reality, more wine was actually made, but because the French authorities intervened and required significant declassification, the actual declared limit matches 1989, which means that for both vintages the production is 30% more than in 1982. Unoffically, however, many châteaux made much stricter selections in 1990 than in 1989, and the actual quantity of wine declared by the top producers under the "grand vin" label is often significantly less than in 1989.

Across almost every appellation, the overall impression one gets of the dry red wines is of extremely low acidity (as low as, and in some cases even lower than, in 1989), high tannins (in most cases higher than in 1989), and voluptuous, thick, rich cherry flavors that are extremely ripe, occasionally roasted. Because the tannins are soft (as in 1982, 1985, and 1989), it is likely that these wines will provide considerable enjoyment when they are young, but they will also have excellent aging potential, given that they are, generally speaking, the most concentrated and opulent wines since 1961 and 1982. In fact, I fully expect many of the 1990s to close up in 1–2 years.

The strengths in this vintage include three of the four Médoc first-growths. Astoundingly, it can be safely said that (with the exception of the rather fluid Mouton-Rothschild) Margaux, Latour, and Lafite-Rothschild have made richer, fuller, more complete wines in 1990 than in 1989. Elsewhere in the Médoc, particularly in St.-Julien and Pauillac, a bevy of large-scale, superrich, but soft, round, voluptuously textured wines with high alcohol, high tannin, and extremely low acidity have made. The strongest left-bank appellation in 1990 is St.-Estèphe. Virtually every château enjoyed sensational quality, with Montrose emerging as a wine of legendary proportions.

On the right bank, Pomerol, which I thought had enjoyed a less successful vintage than in 1989, has turned out to have had a great vintage. It barely eclipses 1989. Properties sitting on the St.-Émilion border, such as L'Évangile, La Conseillante, and Bon Pasteur, all managed to produce wines that will be among the most riveting of the vintage. The L'Évangile and Bon Pasteur 1990s are markedly superior to their 1989s. Pétrus, which made an extraordinary 1989, has fashioned a 1990 that Jean-Pierre Moueix feels is the most unctuous and concentrated wine since the 1947. And I agree. St.-Émilion, never a consistent appellation, has produced perhaps its most homogeneous and greatest vintage of the century, with all three sectors of the appellation—the plateau, the vineyards at the foot of the hillsides, and the vineyards on sandy, gravelly soil. It is interesting to note that both Cheval Blanc and Figeac made far greater 1990s than 1989s. The St.-Émilions will probably prove, along with the St.-Estèphes, to be the longest-lived and most concentrated wines in this vintage, with 15–25 or more years of longevity.

The dry white wines of Graves, as well as generic white Bordeaux, have enjoyed an excellent, perhaps even an outstanding, vintage that is superior to 1989. Poor judgment in picking the 1989s too soon was not repeated with the 1990s, which have more richness and depth than most 1989s.

TOP WINES FOR 1990

L'Angélus 96, L'Arrosée 92, Ausone 94+, Beauséjour-Duffau 98, Bon Pasteur 92, Calon-Ségur 90, Canon-La-Gaffelière 93, Certan de May 92, Cheval Blanc 95, Domaine de Chevalier 90, Clinet 92, Clos Fourtet 90, La Conseillante 98, Cos d'Estournel 92, La Dominique 93, L'Église-Clinet 90, L'Évangile 96, Figeac 94, Les Forts de Latour 90, La Gaffelière 90, Gazin 90, Grand-Mayne 90, Grand-Puy-Lacoste 90, Haut-Bailly 91, Haut-Brion 94, Haut-Marbuzet 94, Lafite-Rothschild 94+, Lafleur 98, Lagrange 93, Larcis-Ducasse 90, Latour 98, Léoville-Barton 94, Léoville-Las Cases 94+, Léoville-Poyferré 92, Lynch-Bages 93, Magdelaine 92, Margaux 100, La Mission-Haut-Brion 92, Montrose 100, Pape-Clément 93, Pavie 90, Pavie-Decesse 90, Pavie-Macquin 90, Petit-Village 90, Petrus 100, Pichon-Longueville Baron 95, Le Pin 95, Rausan-Ségla 92, St.-Pierre 90, Sociando-Mallet 90, Le Tertre-Roteboeuf 94, Troplong-Mondot 94, Vieux Château Certan 94

1989—The general news media, primarily ABC television and *The New York Times*, were the first to reveal that several châteaux began their harvest during the last days of August, making 1989 the earliest vintage since 1893. An early harvest generally signifies a torrid growing season and below average rainfall—almost always evidence that a top-notch vintage is achievable. In his annual *Vintage and Market Report*, Peter Sichel reported that between 1893 and 1989, only 1947, 1949, 1970, and 1982 experienced a similar weather pattern, but none of these years were as hot as 1989.

Perhaps the most revealing and critical decision (at least from a qualitative perspective) was the choice of picking dates. Never has Bordeaux enjoyed such a vast span of time (August 28–October 15) over which to complete the harvest. Some châteaux, most notably Haut-Brion and the Christian Moueix–managed properties in Pomerol and St.-Émilion, harvested during the first week of September. Other estates did not finish their harvesting until mid-October. During the second week of September, one major problem developed. Much of the Cabernet Sauvignon, while analytically mature and having enough sugar to produce wines with potentially 13% alcohol, was actually not ripe physiologically. Many châteaux, never having experienced such growing conditions, became indecisive. Far too many deferred to their oenologists, who saw technically mature grapes that were quickly losing acidity. The oenologists, never ones to take risks, advised immediate picking. As more than one proprietor and *négociant* said, by harvesting the Cabernet too early, a number of châteaux lost the chance to produce one of the greatest wines of a lifetime. This, plus the enormous crop size, probably explains the good yet uninspired performance of so many wines from the Graves and Margaux appellations.

There was clearly no problem with the early-picked Merlot, as much of it came in between 13.5% and a whopping 15% alcohol level—unprecedented in Bordeaux. Those properties that crop-thinned, Pétrus, La Fleur Pétrus, and Haut-Brion, had yields of 45–55 hectoliters per hectare, and superconcentration. Those that did not crop-thin had yields as preposterously high as 80 hectoliters per hectare.

Contrary to the reports of a totally "dry harvest," there were rain showers on September 10, 13, 18, and 22 that did little damage unless a property panicked and harvested the day after the rain. Some of the lighter-styled wines might very well be the result of jittery châteaux owners who unwisely picked after the showers.

Overall production was, once again, staggeringly high. Although the enormous hype from spectators outside Bordeaux bordered on irresponsible, the Bordelais had a far more conservative view of the 1989 vintage. Consider the following. England's Hungerford Wine Company, run with great flair by Nicholas Davies, recently sent out a questionnaire to 200 major Bordeaux proprietors. Their comments were fascinating. When asked to compare the 1989 vintage with another vintage, the most popular comparison (25% of those polled) was with 1982. Fourteen percent compared it with 1985, 10% with 1986, 8% with 1988, 7% with 1961, and 6% with 1947. Only Peter Sichel, president of Bordeaux's prestigious Union des Grands Crus (who appears far too young to remember), compared it with 1893. In this same intriguing survey, the proprietors, when asked for a general qualitative assessment, responded in the following manner: 64% rated it excellent, 17% rated it very good, 4% said it was the vintage of the century, and 10% rated it superb (meaning, I suppose, better than excellent, but not vintage-of-the-century material). The other 5% were unsure of what they had produced.

In general, the wines are the most alcoholic Bordeaux I have ever tasted, ranging from 12.8% to over 14.5% for many Pomerols. Acidities are extremely low and tannin levels surprisingly high. Consequently, in looking at the structural profile of the 1989s, one sees wines 1–2% higher in alcohol than the 1982s or 1961s; with generally lower acidity levels than the 1990s, 1982s, 1961s, and 1959s, yet with high tannin levels. Fortunately, the tannins are generally ripe and soft, à la 1982, rather than dry and astringent as in 1988. This gives the wines a big, rich, fleshy feel in the mouth not dissimilar to the 1982s. The top 1989s have very high glycerin levels, but except for the likes of Haut-Brion, La Mission-Haut-Brion, Clinet, and La Fleur de Gay, they are not as concentrated as the finest 1990s and 1982s. Margaux is clearly the least-favored appellation, much as it was in 1982. In Graves, except for Haut-Brion, La Mission-Haut-Brion, and Haut-Bailly, the wines are relatively light and undistinguished. In St.-Émilion the 1982s are more consistent as well as more deeply concentrated. Some marvelously rich, enormously fruity, fat wines were made in St.-Émilion in 1989, but there is wide irregularity in quality, and, of course, 1990 is significantly richer and fuller. However, in the northern Médoc, primarily St.-Julien, Pauillac, and St.-Estèphe, as well as in Pomerol, many exciting, full-bodied, and very alcoholic and tannic wines have been made. The best of these seem to combine the splendidly rich, opulent, fleshy texture of the finest 1990s and 1982s. However, the softness of the tannins, very high pHs (3.7–4.0 is the norm in this vintage), and low acidity, characteristics that caused a number of American critics to malign and erroneously dismiss the 1982s, are even more evident in the 1989s. Furthermore, the 1989s were made from much higher yields (20–40% more wine per acre) than the 1982s. This has caused more than one *négociant* to suggest, in a pejorative sense, that the best 1989 red Bordeaux has more in common with Côte-Rôtie or California than classic claret. Such statements are pure nonsense. The best of these wines are powerful, authoritative examples of their types; they do not taste like Côte-Rôtie or California Cabernet. However, because these wines are so individualistic and forward, I expect the vintage, much like 1982, to be controversial.

Like the 1982, this is a vintage that will probably be enjoyable to drink over a broad span of years. Despite high tannin levels, the low acidities combined with the high glycerin and alcohol levels give the wines a fascinatingly fleshy, full-bodied texture. Although there is considerable variation in quality, the finest 1989s from Pomerol, St.-Julien, Pauillac, and St.-Estèphe will, in specific cases, rival some of the greatest wines in 1982 and 1986.

TOP WINES FOR 1989

L'Angélus 94, Ausone 92, Beychevelle 91, Branaire-Ducru 91, Canon 92, Cantemerle 91, Cassagne-Haut-Canon-La-Truffière 90, Chasse-Spleen 91, Domaine de Chevalier 91, Clerc-Milon 90, Clinet 99, La Conseillante 97, La Dominique 93, Ducru-Beaucaillou 90, Domaine de L'Église 90, La Fleur de Gay 95, La Fleur Pétrus 91, La Gaffelière 90, Le Gay 92, Grand-Mayne 91, Haut-Bailly 90, Haut-Brion 100, Lafite-Rothschild 92, Lagrange 90, La Lagune 90, Latour 90, Léoville-Las Cases 95, Lynch-Bages 96, Magdelaine 90, Margaux 90, Meyney 90, La Mission-Haut-Brion 99, Montrose 94, Mouton-Rothschild 90, Palmer 96, Pavie-Macquin 90, Pétrus 98, Pichon-Longueville Baron 96, Pichon-Longueville, Comtesse de Lalande 92, Le Pin 91, Rausan-Ségla 90, Soutard 90, Le Tertre-Roteboeuf 94, Trottevielle 90

1988—The 1988 season produced a good but rarely thrilling vintage of red wines, and one of the greatest vintages of this century for the sweet wines of Barsac and Sauternes.

The problem with the red wines is that there is a lack of superstar performances on the part of the top châteaux. This will no doubt ensure that 1988 will always be regarded as a good rather than excellent year. Although the 1988 crop was large, it was exceeded in size by the 1989 and 1990 vintages. The average yield in 1988 was between 45–50 hectoliters per hectare, which was approximately equivalent to the quantity of wine produced in 1982. The wines tend to be well-colored, extremely tannic, and firmly structured, but all too often they exhibit a slight lack of depth and finish short, with noticeably green, astringent tannins.

These characteristics are especially evident in the Médoc, where it was all too apparent that many châteaux, apprehensive about the onset of rot and further rain, as in 1987, panicked and harvested their Cabernet Sauvignon too early. Consequently they brought in Cabernet that often achieved only 8-9% sugar readings. Those properties that waited (too few indeed) made the best wines.

In Pomerol and St.-Émilion the Merlot was harvested under ripe conditions, but because of the severe drought in 1988, the skins of the grapes were thicker and the resulting wines were surprisingly tannic and hard. In St.-Émilion many properties reported bringing in Cabernet Franc at full maturity and obtaining sugar levels that were higher than ever before. However, despite such optimistic reports, much of the Cabernet Franc tasted fluid and diluted in quality. Therefore St.-Émilion, despite its reports of a very successful harvest, exhibits great irregularity in quality.

The appellation of Graves probably produced the best red wines of Bordeaux in 1988.

Although there is no doubt that the richer, more dramatic, fleshier 1989s have taken much of the public's attention away from the 1988s, an objective look at the 1988 vintage will reveal some surprisingly strong performances in appellations such as Margaux, Pomerol, Graves, and in properties in the northern Médoc that eliminated their early-picked Cabernet Sauvignon or harvested much later. The 1988 vintage is not a particularly good one for the Crus Bourgeois, which harvested too soon. The lower prices they receive for their wines do not permit the Crus Bourgeois producers to make the strict selection that is necessary in years such as 1988.

The one appellation that did have a superstar vintage was Barsac and Sauternes. With a harvest that lasted until the end of November and textbook weather conditions for the formation of the noble rot, Botrytis cinerea, 1988 is already considered by European authorities to be the finest since 1937. Almost across the board, including the smaller estates, the wines have an intense smell of honey, coconut, oranges, and other tropical fruit. It is a remarkably rich vintage with wines of extraordinary levels of botrytis and great concentration of flavor, yet the rich, unctuous, opulent textures are balanced beautifully by zesty, crisp acidity. It is this latter component that makes these wines so special and the reason they have an edge over the 1989s.

One must also remember that the 1988 Bordeaux vintage offers wines that, in general, are priced 25-40% below the same wines in 1989. It is a vintage where the best wines will be ready to drink in 4–5 years but will last 15–25 years. For the sweet wines of Barsac/Sauternes, 30–40 more years of aging potential is not unrealistic.

TOP WINES FOR 1988

L'Angélus 91, Ausone 91, Bon Pasteur 89, Calon-Ségur 91, Canon-La-Gaffelière 90, Certan de May 93, Cheval Blanc 88, Domaine de Chevalier 90, Clerc-Milon 89, Clinet 90, Clos des Jacobins 89, Gombaude-Guillot Cuvée Spéciale 89, Gruaud-Larose 89, Haut-Bailly 89, La Fleur de Gay 93, Fourcas-Loubaney 88, Haut-Brion 91, Lafite-Rothschild 94, Lafleur 93, Larmande 90, Latour 89, Léoville-Barton 88, Léoville-Las Cases 92, La Louvière 89, Lynch-Bages 90, La Mission-Haut-Brion 90, Monbrison 90, Mouton-Rothschild 89, Pape-Clément 92, Petit-Village 92, Pétrus 94, Pichon-Longueville Baron 90, Pichon-Longueville, Comtesse de Lalande 90, Le Pin 90, Rausan-Ségla 92, Talbot 89, Le Tertre-Roteboeuf 91, Troplong-Mondot 89

1987—In spite of all the dreadful reports about this vintage, it will no doubt be shocking for some to learn that Bordeaux had another large crop, and the better wines are more appealing and of higher quality than this decade's two other mediocre years, 1980 and 1984. It is a year in which the September heat and sunshine saved the vintage. The results of two weeks of intensive tastings revealed that the early-picked Merlot was ripe, healthy, and rendered good, fruity, soft, commercial, but pleasant wines. The harvest rains virtually ruined the Cabernet Franc and early-picked Cabernet Sauvignon, but the very late harvesters did salvage some decent Cabernet Sauvignon from their vineyards. Overall, the 1987 clarets will require drinking very young, between now and

1996, but they can be charming wines of medium body. Fortunately they have none of the vegetal, austere characteristics of years such as 1984 and 1980. The top successes are in Graves, Pomerol, and the classified growths of the Médoc, which were able to make very severe selections. The dry white wines of Bordeaux, harvested under excellent conditions, are very good, better than the 1986s and, although lighter, are not far behind the tasty 1985 whites. For the sweet white wines of Sauternes and Barsac, it was certainly a very difficult year for them.

All things considered, 1987 provided some surprisingly pleasant, soft, clean, fruity wines that should be drunk before the end of this century.

TOP WINES FOR 1987

Certan de May 87, Clinet 90, La Conseillante 86, Ducru-Beaucaillou 83, L'Évangile 85, La Fleur de Gay 90, Gruaud-Larose 84, Haut-Brion 87, Latour 86, Léoville-Las Cases 87, Margaux 86, La Mission-Haut-Brion 87, Mouton-Rothschild 88, Palmer 86, Le Pin 88, Pétrus 87, Pichon-Longueville, Comtesse de Lalande 87, Talbot 85

1986—In the Médoc, from Margaux to St.-Estèphe, the overall quality level of the 1986 vintage is very good and sometimes exceptional. The amount of wine produced at many classified châteaux was exceptionally large but the selection process extremely severe, resulting in wines that are dense as well as very powerful and rich. The wines are marked by the Cabernet Sauvignon grape, which flourished in this vintage, and have the highest level of tannins ever measured. Three things stand out about this vintage: 1) the extraordinary potential for 25–35 years of longevity of many wines as a result of their fierce tannins and concentration; 2) deep color, concentrated flavors, and high tannins; 3) the sobering thought that only a few of the top wines will be enjoyable to drink before the year 2000. In short, this vintage is very complementary to the fruity, soft, medium-bodied 1985s. But before you get excited about the top 1986 Médocs, be sure to ask yourself if you have the patience to forget these tannic behemoths for a decade or more. The vintage closely resembles 1966 and 1975, but winemaking is significantly better now; no doubt some 1986s will provide disheartening drinking in 8–10 years because of their sharp, aggressive tannins, but in 2005 a dozen or so will challenge the greatest 1982s and probably outlive the legends of that extraordinary vintage. Although the Médoc was clearly the favored area in this vintage, especially Pauillac and St.-Julien, there are some very fine Graves, good Pomerols, and a number of St.-Émilions that are much deeper and richer than their counterparts in 1985. Sweet wine lovers will no doubt rejoice over the 1986 Barsacs and Sauternes. While less powerful than the 1983s, they are more aromatic and complex because the essential botrytis was more in evidence in 1986 than in 1983.

TOP WINES FOR 1986

L'Angélus 89, L'Arrosée 93, Beychevelle 92, Calon-Ségur 89, Canon 91, Certan de May 92, Chasse-Spleen 90, Cheval Blanc 93, Domaine de Chevalier 90, La Conseillante 89, Cos d'Estournel 95, La Dominique 90, Ducru-Beaucaillou 94, L'Église-Clinet 92, Figeac 90, La Fleur de Gay 90, Grand-Puy-Lacoste 90,

Gruaud-Larose 97, Haut-Brion 92, Haut-Marbuzet 90, Lafite-Rothschild 99, Lafleur 95, Lagrange 92, La Lagune 90, Latour 90, Léoville-Barton 92, Léoville-Las Cases 97, Lynch-Bages 92, Margaux 98, Meyney 91, La Mission-Haut-Brion 90, Montrose 91, Mouton-Rothschild 100, Palmer 90, Pape-Clément 91, Pavie 90, Pétrus 88, Pichon-Longueville, Comtesse de Lalande 96, Le Pin 90, Rausan-Ségla 96, St.-Pierre 90, Sociando-Mallet 90, Talbot 96, Vieux Château Certan 93

1985—Overall, 1985 is a lovely vintage of wines that are medium bodied, very fragrant, soft, and in large part destined to be consumed over the next 15 years until the hard and powerful 1986s have shed some tannins. The record-setting crop in the Médoc in 1985 has effectively prevented most of these wines from reaching greatness. As charming, round, forward, and even opulent as the 1985 Médocs are, any extensive tasting of them will reveal two weaknesses: 1) they lack grip and are low in acidity and tannin; and 2) the famous first-growths, except for Haut-Brion, Mouton-Rothschild, and Margaux, have performed well below the super-seconds. At their best, wines such as the extraordinary Cos d'Estournel, Lynch-Bages, Léoville-Barton, Ducru-Beaucaillou, Léoville-Las Cases, and Margaux may turn out to be modern-day versions of their 1953s, but for most of the Médocs, this vintage tastes like watered-down 1982s or riper, fruitier 1979s. As for Pomerol and St.-Émilion, there are some undeniable superstars to be found. Certainly Pétrus, Lafleur, Certan de May, Cheval Blanc, and L'Arrosée made their finest wines since 1982. L'Évangile made as great a wine as its 1982, and L'Église-Clinet made the finest wine I have ever tasted from this property. Yet once past most of the famous names, I have to admit to a degree of disappointment with other Pomerols and St.-Émilions that seem to show, in various degrees, the problems caused by an excessively abundant crop. Both the red and white Graves are excellent, but the Barsacs and Sauternes lack character and complexity.

Overall, 1985 will be remembered as a very good vintage that will provide early drinkability. Although nowhere near the quality of the stupendous 1982s, or many of the powerful, rich 1986 Médocs, 1985 should prove to be as good as 1983 and certainly better than 1978, 1979, and 1981. No one who bought the top wines (for drinking) will regret the purchase.

TOP WINES FOR 1985

L'Arrosée 94, Canon 90, Certan de May 94, Chasse-Spleen 90, Cheval Blanc 94, La Conseillante 94, Cos d'Estournel 95, Ducru-Beaucaillou 91, L'Église-Clinet 95, L'Évangile 95, La Fleur de Gay 89, Gombaude-Guillot Cuvée Spéciale 93, Gruaud-Larose 90, Haut-Brion 92, Lafleur 96, Léoville-Las Cases 92, Lynch-Bages 93, Margaux 91, La Mission-Haut-Brion 92, Mouton-Roth-schild 92, Petit-Village 89, Pétrus 89, Pichon-Longueville, Comtesse de La-lande 90, Le Pin 94, Rausan-Ségla 89, Sociando-Mallet 90, Soutard 90, Talbot 89, Le Tertre-Roteboeuf 90

1984—The late pickers in the Graves and Médoc harvested surprisingly sound Cabernet Sauvignon and produced wines that have adequate ripeness, color, medium body, and moderate tannins. Because the Merlot crop was largely ruined by the summer's poor weather, Pomerol and St.-Émilion are not appellations in which to search out good 1984s, although several exceptions exist, most notably L'Arrosée. The 1984s are compact, narrowly constructed wines that lack a certain lushness, charm, and fruitiness, but for those consumers who like their Bordeaux on the austere side, there are some wines to consider. Pichon Lalande is one of the best wines of the vintage. Prices, initially absurdly high for a vintage of such mediocre quality, have since been significantly discounted as the wine traders sought to reduce inventories. Don't spend more than $12–$15 for a 1984, regardless of châteaux.

TOP WINES FOR 1984

L'Arrosée 86, Domaine de Chevalier 85, Cos d'Estournel 84, Figeac 84, Gruaud-Larose 83, Haut-Brion 84, Latour 84, Lynch-Bages 84, Margaux 86, La Mission-Haut-Brion 82, Mouton-Rothschild 85, Pichon-Longueville, Comtesse de Lalande 86, Le Pin 87

1983—Twenty years ago the torrid heat, prevalent precipitation, and tropical humidity that persisted throughout the month of August 1983 would have spelled ruin for a vintage. But thanks to modern sprays the onslaught of rot was avoided, and the growers were rewarded with a stunningly perfect, albeit hot, month of September and a glorious October. The late harvesters fared the best, and this was an excellent Médoc year with a superior Cabernet Sauvignon. In particular, the appellation of Margaux, a perennial underachiever in the Bordeaux firmament, had its best vintage since 1961, while such notoriously inconsistent châteaux as Brane-Cantenac, Durfort-Vivens, Rausan-Ségla, and Kirwan made better wines than they had in years. The early cask tastings of the 1983s not only showed the strength of the vintage in the Médoc, but also revealed wines that, while ripe and full, were much more noticeably tannic than the opulent 1982s. The crop was again enormous, overall about 8% less than in 1982, but in the major Médoc appellations the production per hectare was surprisingly higher than in 1982, and the better châteaux ended up putting much more wine under their second labels than in 1982.

After recently retasting the 1983s, I was surprised to note the wines have not closed up as much as one would expect. The tannins, once thought much more aggressive than the 1982s, seem to be falling away rather quickly, whereas the higher level of tannins in the 1982s, initially concealed by the extraordinary fleshiness and opulence of fruit of those wines, is becoming more apparent. At present most 1983s taste much less concentrated and structured for the long haul than the 1982s.

Overall, this vintage has matured more quickly than the 1982s. The strengths of the vintage are clearly in the Margaux appellation, followed by St.-Julien and Pauillac. The Pomerols and St.-Émilions are certainly good but rarely have the succulent excitement that these wines can attain in top years. The Graves can also be fine. I find the overall personality of most of the St.-Estèphes to be boring. However, for the Barsacs and Sauternes 1983 was a much-needed top vintage, although 1986, 1988, 1989, and 1990 are shaping up as even better years for that much-neglected region. Ten years after the vintage, 1983 looks to be a very good year. Yet save for a handful of wines, it rarely achieves greatness. In the context of the vintages of the 1980s, it is clearly superior to 1981 and, in appellations such as Margaux and Sauternes, is better than 1982 and 1985; but overall it will have to take a backseat to 1982, 1985, 1986, 1988, and 1989. One caveat: The top 1983s remain realistically priced, as they were purchased when the dollar was twice its current strength. Consequently some true bargains can still be found.

TOP WINES FOR 1983

d'Angludet 89, L'Arrosée 88, Ausone 93, Canon 89, Cantemerle 91, Cheval Blanc 95, Domaine de Chevalier 90, La Conseillante 88, Ducru-Beaucaillou 87, L'Évangile 92, La Fleur de Gay 90, Gruaud-Larose 90, Haut-Brion 90, Haut-Marbuzet 88, Lafite-Rothschild 92, Lafleur 94, Latour à Pomerol 88, Léoville-Las Cases 90, Léoville-Poyferré 90, Lynch-Bages 88, Margaux 98, La Mission-Haut-Brion 90, Mouton-Rothschild 90, Palmer 97, Pavie 88, Pétrus 89, Pichon-Longueville, Comtesse de Lalande 93, Le Pin 95, Rausan-Ségla 92, Talbot 91

1982—Although the 1982s remain the most concentrated, complex, and interesting wines since the 1961 vintage, questions still continue to arise about their potential longevity vis-à-vis other great vintages of this century—1929, 1945, and 1961. I have had a chance in the last year to see most of the 1982s on several occasions, and I believe unequivocally that these are the most exhilarating wines of this generation. Despite a handful of writers who have steadfastly remained critical of this vintage, the majority point of view is that 1982 is clearly the greatest Bordeaux vintage since 1961. There is, however, no question that many wines can be drunk early with an extraordinary degree of pleasure—that is, except for the 1929s, unparalleled for any of the other great Bordeaux vintages of this century. However, I find most of the 1982 Médocs from St.-Julien, Pauillac, and St.-Estèphe to be firming up considerably, and despite their dense black/purple color, fragrant, opulent bouquets, and intense richness on the palate, they remain very undeveloped and little different from the way they tasted from the cask. Most of the Médocs, including all of the first-growths and the super-seconds (except for the soft, somewhat unstructured Palmer), will not be ready until the end of the 1990s, which is somewhat longer than I estimated originally. Saying this, I fear, will not prevent many of them from being drunk much earlier.

The Pomerols and St.-Émilions are also beginning to show more structure, but it is simply hard to resist the opulent, exotic pleasures of wines such as Cheval Blanc, Canon, L'Évangile, Le Pin, and Trotanoy, despite the fact they seem little evolved from their days in the cask. Of course one hears from the likes of Harry Waugh and Jean-Pierre Moueix that most of the 1947 Pétrus and 1947 Cheval Blanc was also drunk within the first 7–8 years of that historic vintage, but for the life of me I cannot think those wines, no matter how decadently rich and tasty, could have been more enjoyable in 1954–1955 than today (I recently gave both perfect scores in a blind tasting in Bordeaux). All this being said, I suspect the debate concerning the longevity issue of the 1982 clarets will go on for another 20–30 years. But if the ultimate criteria for the greatness of a wine or vintage are the degree to which it can provide hedonistic enjoyment and the span of years over which it can be drunk with pleasure, then 1982 has no modern-day peer. I, for one, started drinking the Cru Bourgeois (except for Sociando-Mallet and Poujeaux) in 1990–1992, then moved to the

Pomerols and St.-Émilions in 1992–1995, and will start on the Graves, St.-Juliens, Pauillacs, and St.-Estèphes from 1995 onward. The 1982 Margaux wines are very forward and can be drunk in 1–2 years. All of the top 1982s, where purchased in good health and stored properly, will drink gorgeously for another 10–25 years, perhaps longer. Despite their precociousness, their great fruit and depth will enable them to outlive all of the recent vintages except the 1986s. Finally, this vintage over the long term will be remembered above all for the following wines that are likely to be considered in the same mythical or legendary category in which we now look back on wines such as the 1929 and 1945 Mouton-Rothschild; 1928, 1945, and 1961 Latour; 1945, 1947, and 1961 Pétrus; 1947 Cheval Blanc; 1900 Margaux; and 1953 and 1959 Lafite-Rothschild.

TOP WINES FOR 1982

L'Arrosée 92, Ausone 94, Beychevelle 92, Bon Pasteur 98, Branaire-Ducru 91, Calon-Ségur 92, Canon 93, Certan de May 98, Cheval Blanc 100, La Conseillante 91, Cos d'Estournel 97, La Dominique 91, Ducru-Beaucaillou 94, Duhart-Milon-Rothschild 92, L'Évangile 96, Figeac 92, Les Forts de Latour 92, Grand-Puy-Lacoste 94, Gruaud-Larose 97, Haut-Brion 93, Haut-Marbuzet 93, Lafite-Rothschild 100, Lafleur 96, La Lagune 93, Latour 99, Latour à Pomerol 93, Léoville-Barton 93, Léoville-Las Cases 100, Léoville-Poyferré 92, Lynch-Bages 93, Margaux 100, Meyney 90, La Mission-Haut-Brion 94, Montrose 89, Mouton-Rothschild 100, Pavie 92, Petit-Village 93, Pétrus 98, Pichon-Longueville Baron 90, Pichon-Longueville, Comtesse de Lalande 99, Le Pin 99, Sociando-Mallet 92, Talbot 95, La Tour-Haut-Brion 94, Trotanoy 97, Vieux Château Certan 91

1981—I have found many of the wines from the 1981 vintage lacking generosity and richness, but for admirers of the lighter-styled, less intense, and less powerful Bordeaux vintages, a number of fine choices may be found, particularly in the appellations of St.-Julien, Pauillac, and Pomerol. In St.-Estèphe, Margaux, Graves, and St.-Émilion, the wines are patchy in quality. This vintage, which looked so promising and potentially great, was diluted by the rains that caught everybody off guard just as the harvest was ready to commence. This is not a very pleasant vintage for the Crus Bourgeois. Most of the 1981s are fully mature and will keep, where well stored, for 3–10 years thereafter.

TOP WINES FOR 1981

Certan de May 90, Cheval Blanc 89, La Conseillante 91, Ducru-Beaucaillou 90, Gruaud-Larose 88, Lafite-Rothschild 93, Latour 88, Léoville-Las Cases 88, Margaux 90, La Mission-Haut-Brion 90, Pétrus 88, Pichon-Longueville, Comtesse de Lalande 89, Le Pin 93, St.-Pierre-Sevaistre 88

1980—Sandwiched between a succession of fine vintages, the 1980 Bordeaux crop has been a forgotten stepchild. However, the adventurous wine enthusiast can probably tell a few tales about some surprisingly soft, supple wines that were much tastier than any critic led the public to believe.

The 1980 harvest was late and suffered from a poor summer, particularly the terrible flowering that diminished the size of the Merlot crop. The weather improved dramatically in September, which allowed the grapes to mature; however, the vintage that commenced on October 14 met with rain once again.

The resulting wines are light, some are rather diluted and disappointing, but a number of sound, fruity, supple wines were produced that, if well chosen, offer immediate drinkability and charm. A very fine wine was made at Margaux, which continued its record of producing one of the finest wines of the vintage since the Mentzelopoulos family took over this estate in 1977. If the vintage was decidedly uninspiring for red wines, the late-harvest sweet wines of Barsac and Sauternes turned out quite well, with most properties picking into late November under ideal weather conditions. Most 1980s are fully mature now.

TOP WINES FOR 1980

Domaine de Chevalier 84, Lafite-Rothschild 83, Latour 83, Léoville-Barton 83, Margaux 88, Pétrus 86, Pichon-Longueville, Comtesse de Lalande 84

1979—The 1979 harvest has provided one of the most useful vintages of Bordeaux wines. Not only was the crop enormous, but the quality was quite good. I thought the wines were a trifle light when I first did my cask tastings of this vintage in late March 1980, particularly when tasted against the fuller-bodied, richer 1978s. However, the wines have continued to put on weight and richness during their time in both cask and bottle, and although not big, rich, or full bodied, the 1979s are graceful, nicely concentrated, well-balanced wines that are very pleasing.

The weather conditions that led up to the 1979 harvest were hardly exceptional. The summer was unusually cold but quite dry. The harvest did not start until early October. The weather during the harvest was mixed, with generally good weather interlaced with showery periods. The grapes were considered healthy and mature in all regions of Bordeaux. The initial reaction was that 1979 was a "Merlot year," and therefore the top successes were in that region. Time, however, has proven that the top wines seem to be concentrated in the appellations of Margaux, St.-Julien, and Pauillac.

The 1979 red wines have shown consistently well in tastings. They are not powerful, but rather fruity, medium-bodied wines with good concentration and moderate tannins. Most are fully mature and ready to drink between 1993 and 2005. The top wines will of course last longer.

The late harvest permitted enough botrytis to form so that some successful sweet white wines were made. However, most of the Barsacs and Sauternes were not nearly as good as the 1980s.

TOP WINES FOR 1979

Ausone 87, Canon 86, Certan de May 92, Domaine de Chevalier 85, Cos d'Estournel 86, L'Évangile 88, Giscours 88, Gruaud-Larose 88, Haut-Bailly 87, Haut-Brion 93, Lafite-Rothschild 90, Lafleur 96, Latour 87, Léoville-Las Cases 86, Margaux 93, La Mission-Haut-Brion 91, Palmer 91, Pavie 85, Pétrus

89, Pichon-Longueville, Comtesse de Lalande 92, Le Pin 93, St.-Pierre-Sevaistre 85, du Tertre 89, Trotanoy 86

1978—This turned out to be an excellent vintage for the red wines of the Médoc and Graves, a good vintage for the red wines of St.-Émilion and Pomerol, and a fair vintage for the sweet white wines of Barsac and Sauternes. Extremely poor weather throughout the spring, June, July, and the first part of August had many growers thinking of a repeat of the poor vintage of 1977. However, in mid-August the weather became sunny, hot, and dry. For the next 9 weeks this weather continued virtually uninterrupted except for some light rain. The harvest commenced very late, October 7, and the grapes were brought in under ideal conditions. The astonishing turnaround in the weather and the resulting product caused Harry Waugh, the peripatetic English wine authority, to dub 1978 the "miracle vintage," a name that has stuck.

The top red wines of 1978 have almost always come from the Médoc and Graves. The wines of Pomerol and St.-Émilion, with a few exceptions, seem noticeably less successful, although they are certainly good. The 1978s at first appeared intensely fruity, very deeply colored, moderately tannic, and medium to full bodied. In style and character they seemed to resemble the lovely wines of the 1970 vintage, only slightly lighter and more herbaceous. Most of the top wines of 1978 are fully mature, and should be drunk by 2000.

Unfortunately, this was a difficult year for the sweet wines in Sauternes and Barsac, and most lack the honeyed botrytis character.

TOP WINES FOR 1978

Ausone 88, Cheval Blanc 87, Domaine de Chevalier 92, Ducru-Beaucaillou 90, Les Forts de Latour 87, Giscours 90, Grand-Puy-Lacoste 88, Gruaud-Larose 87, Haut-Brion 92, Lafite-Rothschild 88, Lafleur 90, La Lagune 88, Latour 93, Léoville-Las Cases 92, Margaux 94, La Mission-Haut-Brion 94, Palmer 91, Pétrus 88, Pichon-Longueville, Comtesse de Lalande 93, Prieuré-Lichine 86, Talbot 87, La Tour-Haut-Brion 93

1977—This is the worst vintage for Bordeaux between 1973 and 1991. A wet, cold summer played havoc with the crop. In addition, the Merlot crop was devastated by a spring frost. Although warm, dry weather arrived prior to the harvest, there was just not enough of it to save the vintage, although given the raw materials, several wines did turn out to be relatively decent. Unfortunately, 1977 was also a very poor year for the sweet wine producers. Most of the wines are rather high in acidity, with herbaceous, vegetal aromas and flavors. Personally I cannot recommend any of them.

1976—The 1976 was a very highly publicized vintage that has never quite lived up to its reputation. All the ingredients were present for a superb vintage. The harvest date of September 13 was the earliest since 1945. The weather during the summer had been torrid, as the average temperatures for the months of June through September were exceeded only by the hot summers of 1949 and 1947. However, with many vignerons predicting a "vintage of the century," very heavy rains fell between September 11 and 15, bloating the grapes.

The crop that was harvested was very large, the grapes were very ripe, and although the wines had good tannin levels, the acidity levels were low and the pH dangerously high. The top wines of 1976 now offer wonderfully soft, supple, fruity drinking and certainly can be said to have more charm than their more publicized siblings (the 1975s).

However, many 1976s, which lacked color from the beginning and were very fragile, have taken on a disturbing brown cast, while others have lapsed into premature senility. For the red wines, the vintage is strongest in St.-Julien, Pauillac, St.-Estèphe, and Margaux. It is weakest in Graves.

For the sweet wines, this is an excellent vintage—providing rich, intense, full-bodied wines with plenty of botrytis and character.

With few exceptions, the following wines are ideal for drinking over the next 4–5 years because few will still be alive thereafter.

TOP WINES FOR 1976

Ausone 93, Beychevelle 85, Branaire-Ducru 87, Cos d'Estournel 86, Ducru-Beaucaillou 85, Figeac 86, Haut-Brion 86, Lafite-Rothschild 96, La Lagune 87, Latour à Pomerol 86, Montrose 86, Pétrus 87, Talbot 86

1975—The 1975 vintage was conceived in a climate in which Bordeaux had just had three large, generally poor or mediocre crops—1972, 1973, and 1974. The 1975 crop was small as a result of spring frosts and because many growers zealously pruned their vines for fear of another big crop like 1974. July, August, and September were hot, but not excessively so. However, the latter two months were punctuated by several huge thunderstorms that delivered enormous amounts of rainfall. In fact, the rainfall in the critical months of August and September was approximately the same as that of Bordeaux's worst vintages—1969, 1968, and 1965. This caused some observers to question those who claimed that 1975 was the best Bordeaux vintage after 1961.

The harvest began on September 22 and continued until mid-October in good weather except for a hailstorm that ravaged the central Médoc communes of Avensan, Moulis, Arcins, and Lamarque.

The vintage has been highly touted, but my conclusion is that although some very great wines were produced, 1975 is much more irregular in quality than initially believed.

The wines continue to be tannic, full bodied, and backward yet show signs of opening up over the next 2–3 years. The top wines have the richness and depth of fruit and dark color to go along with the high level of dry, sometimes astringent tannins. Other wines surprisingly lack color and seem to have an excess of tannin. Certainly the 1975 vintage will provide some of the longest-lived Bordeaux wines in the last three decades, but unfortunately it will also provide a significant number of disappointments.

Of all the major communes, the wines of Pauillac and Pomerol appear to be most successful. The top wines have the potential to last another 10–15 years.

With regard to the Sauternes, this was an excellent vintage, with just about every estate producing a fine wine.

TOP WINES FOR 1975

Branaire-Ducru 92, Calon-Ségur 87, Chasse-Spleen 90, Cheval Blanc 90, L'Enclos 89, L'Évangile 95, Figeac 89, La Fleur Pétrus 90, Le Gay 90, Giscours 91, Gloria 87, Gruaud-Larose 90, Haut-Bages-Libéral 89, Lafite-Rothschild 96, Lafleur 100, La Lagune 88, Langoa-Barton 88, Latour 92, Léoville-Barton 90, Léoville-Las Cases 92, Meyney 90, La Mission-Haut-Brion 100, Mouton-Rothschild 90, Palmer 91, Pétrus 98, Pichon-Longueville, Comtesse de Lalande 92, Sociando-Mallet 90, La Tour-Haut-Brion 98, Trotanoy 94, Vieux Château Certan 90

1974—While the crop size was large in 1974 as a result of a good flowering and a dry, sunny May and June, the weather from late August through October was rainy. Despite the persistent soggy conditions, some surprisingly good wines were made in Graves, which is clearly the vintage's most successful appellation. Most 1974s are rather hard, tannic, hollow wines that lack flesh and richness. Three exceptions are Trotanoy, La Mission-Haut-Brion, and Latour; the last two were still young when last drunk in 1993.

The vintage was terrible in the Barsac and Sauternes regions and many properties declassified their entire crop.

1973—At one time in the mid-1970s, the 1973s had some value as agreeably light, soft, simple Bordeaux wines. Today, except for a handful of wines such as Latour and Pétrus, these wines have faded into oblivion.

The 1973 Bordeaux vintage was another in which the summer had been just fine and all of Bordeaux was set for a big crop of good-quality grapes. However, as so often happens in the region, in the course of the three weeks that followed the harvest commencement date of September 25, the heavens opened up and a good vintage was turned into a rain-bloated crop of mediocre grapes. The crop size was large, but the wines lacked color, extract, acidity, and backbone. The great majority of wines were ready to drink when released in 1976, and by 1979 many of them were beginning to fall apart. Nevertheless, there were some good, round, fruity wines that had some concentration to them. However, buying any 1973 now would be extremely dangerous unless it was Pétrus (clearly the wine of this vintage) or Latour.

As a general rule, the sweet wines of Barsac and Sauternes turned out a little better, but most of them should have been drunk by now.

TOP WINES FOR 1973

Beychevelle, Ducru-Beaucaillou, Giscours, Latour, Latour à Pomerol, Montrose, Les-Ormes-de-Pez, Pétrus, La Tour-Haut-Brion, and Trotanoy were successful for the vintage, but only Pétrus would still merit interest in 1993–1994

1972—The 1972 summer months were unusually cool and cloudy, with an abnormally rainy August. Although September brought dry, warm weather, it was too late to salvage the crop. This vintage produced the worst wines of the decade—acidic, green, raw, and vegetal-tasting. Their high acidity has indeed kept many of them alive, but their deficiencies are too great for mere age to overcome. As with any poor vintage, some châteaux managed to produce wines far better than their neighbors. In 1972 there were only a half dozen or so wines worthy of consumer interest and then only at very low prices. Certainly no one appellation in 1972 did better or worse than the others.

1971—Unlike 1970, 1971 was a rather small vintage because of a poor flowering in June that caused a significant reduction in the Merlot crop. By the end of the harvest, the crop size was a good 40% less than the huge crop of 1970.

Early reports on the vintage have proven to be overly enthusiastic. Some experts, relying on the small production yields when compared with 1970, even claimed the vintage was better than 1970. This has proven totally false. Certainly the 1971s were forward and delicious, as were the 1970s when first released, but unlike the 1970s, the 1971s lacked the great depth of color, concentration, and tannic backbone. The vintage was rather mixed in the Médoc, but it was certainly a fine year for Pomerol, St.-Émilion, and Graves.

Buying 1971s now is quite dangerous. There are only a few wines that are not fully mature, and even such superb wines as Pétrus, Latour, Trotanoy, La Mission-Haut-Brion and Haut-Brion, all examples of very well preserved wines from this vintage, are not likely to improve. Yet when the top 1971s have been well cellared, they can provide delicious drinking.

Originally, 1971 was portrayed as one of the really fine years that gets overlooked because of the publicity and hoopla given to the vintage that preceded it—in this case, the marvelous 1970. This is a very irregular vintage, with a handful of really sensational wines to go along with a horde of mediocre wines. The sweet wines of Barsac and Sauternes were extremely successful, and contrary to their red siblings, the white wines have aged beautifully and will easily outlast the great majority of reds produced in 1971.

TOP WINES FOR 1971

La Dominique 91, Haut-Brion 88, Latour 91, La Mission-Haut-Brion 87, Montrose 86, Mouton-Rothschild 86, Palmer 86, Pétrus 95, Talbot 86, Trotanoy 93

1970—Of all vintages between the two great harvests of 1961 and 1982, 1970 has proven to be the best. The wines are more attractive and charming than the austere 1966s and hard, tannic, big 1975s. The 1970 vintage was unusual in that it consisted of high volume and very high quality. It was splendidly uniform and consistent throughout Bordeaux, with every appellation able to claim its share of superstars. It was also an outstanding year for the lesser growths of Bordeaux.

Weather conditions during the summer and fall of 1970 were perfect. There was no hail, no weeks of drenching downpours, no frost, and no spirit-crushing deluge at harvest time. Everything went well, and the Bordeaux châteaux harvested one of the biggest and healthiest crops of grapes ever.

From the earliest days, the wines showed great color, an intense richness of fruit, full body, and good tannin. However, because the wines showed so well young, some writers began to say that they were precocious, a product of the "nouvelle vinification," and would not last until 1980. History has recorded that some of the greatest Bordeaux vintages—1929, 1947, 1949, 1953, and 1961—all showed extremely well young, causing many so-called experts to falsely assume they would not last. Like these older vintages, the 1970s have slowed down in development, and in 1993 many of the top wines have just reached their mature plateau.

The sweet wines were not as good as the 1971s but certainly successful.

The 1970s will provide one of the greatest levels of enjoyment of high-quality Bordeaux for years to come. In the last 35 years only four vintages, 1990, 1989, 1982, and 1961, can lay claim to being better than this marvelous vintage.

TOP WINES FOR 1970

Chasse-Spleen 90, Domaine de Chevalier 89, La Conseillante 92, Cos d'Estournel 87, Ducru-Beaucaillou 91, Figeac 90, La Fleur-Pétrus 87, Giscours 87, Gloria 87, Gruaud-Larose 87, Haut-Bailly 87, Haut-Batailley 87, Haut-Marbuzet 88, Lafleur 87, Lafon-Rochet 87, La Lagune 87, Latour 99, Latour à Pomerol 90, Léoville-Barton 87, Lynch-Bages 95, Magdelaine 88, La Mission-Haut-Brion 94, Montrose 94, Mouton-Rothschild 92, Les-Ormes-de-Pez 88, Palmer 95, Pétrus 98, Pichon-Longueville, Comtesse de Lalande 90, Rausan-Ségla 86, St.-Pierre-Sevaistre 87, Sociando-Mallet 87, Trotanoy 93

1969—After Bordeaux suffers through a disastrous vintage as it did in 1968, there has always been a tendency to lavish false praise on the next vintage. No doubt after a horrible year in 1968, Bordeaux badly wanted a fine vintage in 1969, but despite some overly optimistic proclamations by leading Bordeaux experts at the time of the vintage, 1969 turned out to be one of the least attractive vintages for Bordeaux wines in the last two decades.

The crop was small, and although the summer was sufficiently hot and dry to ensure a decent maturity, torrential September rains dashed everyone's hopes for a good vintage (except investors, who irrationally moved in to buy these insipid, nasty, acidic, sharp wines). Consequently the 1969s, along with being extremely unattractive wines, were quite expensive when they first appeared on the market.

I can honestly say I have never tasted a 1969 red wine I didn't dislike. Harsh and hollow, with no flesh, fruit, or charm, it is hard to imagine that any of these wines could have turned out palatable.

In the Barsac and Sauternes region, a few proprietors managed to produce acceptable wines.

1968—This was another of the very poor vintages Bordeaux had to suffer through in the 1960s. The culprit, as usual, was heavy rains (it was the wettest year since 1951), which bloated the grapes. However, there have been some 1968s that I found much better than anything produced in 1969, a vintage with a "better" reputation. Should anyone run across these wines today, caveat emptor would certainly apply, as I doubt that any of the wines would have much left to them.

1967—Even though 1967 cannot be considered a great or even a very good vintage, it was a large vintage of soft, quick-maturing wines that provided agreeable drinking between 1970 and 1978. Most 1967s should have been

consumed by the start of the 1980s, although a handful of wines such as Latour, Pétrus, Trotanoy, and Palmer should continue to give pleasure for another
2–3 years.

The strongest wines of 1967 were produced in the right-bank communes of
Pomerol and St.-Émilion, as well as in Graves and the Sauternes.

Should one find some of the top wines itemized below in large-format bottles
(magnums, double magnums, and so forth), they could well provide lovely
drinking.

TOP WINES FOR 1967

Latour 88, La Mission-Haut-Brion 85, Palmer 86, Pétrus 93, Trotanoy 91

1966—Although there is general agreement that 1966 is the best vintage of
the 1960s after 1961, it has not developed as well as many of its proponents
would have liked. The wines, now coming up on their thirtieth birthday, have
never really blossomed out. Many remain rather austere, lean, unyielding tannic wines that seem to be in danger of losing their fruit before their tannin.
This seems rather surprising in view of the early reports on the vintage, which
called the wines precocious, charming, and early-maturing. Yet if the vintage
is not as consistent as believed, 1966 produced some wonderfully rich, well-
balanced, medium-weight classic wines. The Médoc is clearly the strongest region for the top wines of this vintage, but there are many successes in Pomerol
as well. It was a mediocre year for the wines of Barsac and Sauternes.

With regard to the climatic conditions that shaped the vintage, the flowering
in June went slowly, July and August were intermittently hot and cold, and
September was dry and sunny. A large crop was harvested under sound
weather conditions.

Most 1966s should continue to drink well for another decade, although I
worry that the less balanced wines will dry out. This is a very good vintage, but
selection is extremely important.

TOP WINES FOR 1966

Beychevelle 86, Branaire-Ducru 88, Calon-Ségur 87, Ducru-Beaucaillou 87,
Gruaud-Larose 88, Lafleur 94, Latour 95, Latour à Pomerol 87, Léoville-Las
Cases 90, La Mission-Haut-Brion 91, Montrose 86, Mouton-Rothschild 90,
Palmer 96, Pape-Clément 88, Pétrus 89, Pichon-Longueville, Comtesse de La-
lande 88

1965—This, a vintage produced in rot and rain, is considered by most experts to be one of the worst in the post–World War II era. Its wet summer was
bad enough, but its real undoing was the incredibly wet and humid September,
which caused the rot to voraciously devour the vineyards. Obviously these
wines should be avoided. I myself have had little experience tasting them.

1964—One of the most intriguing vintages of Bordeaux, 1964 produced a
number of splendid, generally underrated and underpriced wines in Pomerol,
St.-Émilion, and Graves, where many proprietors had the good fortune to have
harvested their crops before the rainy deluge began on October 8. Because of

this downpour, which caught many Médoc châteaux with unharvested vine-yards, 1964 has never been regarded as a top Bordeaux vintage. Although the vintage can be notoriously bad for the properties of the Médoc and the late-harvesting Barsac and Sauternes estates, it is excellent to outstanding for the three appellations of Pomerol, St.-Émilion, and Graves.

The summer had been extremely hot and dry, and when the harvest com-menced, many proprietors thought that a great vintage was in the making. Since the Merlot grape ripens first, the harvest began in the areas where this is planted in abundance, St.-Émilion and Pomerol. When the rains came, not all of the Médoc properties were still picking. Consequently there were some ex-cellent wines made in the Médoc, but because of such famous failures as Lafite-Rothschild, Mouton-Rothschild, Lynch-Bages, Calon-Ségur, and Mar-gaux, many wine enthusiasts have apprehensively shied away from the vintage.

The successful wines are quite rich, full bodied, and concentrated, being more deeply colored and significantly richer than the leaner, more austere 1966s. Although most of the 1964s are now at full maturity, they will certainly hold another 5 years. Incredibly, I have enjoyed the best wines of 1964 more than the best wines of 1966, a vintage with a much greater reputation.

TOP WINES FOR 1964

L'Arrosée 87, Batailley 87, Cheval Blanc 95, Domaine de Chevalier 90, La Conseillante 88, Figeac 92, Gruaud-Larose 87, Haut-Brion 90, Lafleur 89, La-tour 90, La Mission-Haut-Brion 92, Montrose 92, Pape-Clément 88, Pétrus 97, Soutard 90, Trotanoy 90, Vieux Château Certan 90

1963—Bordeaux's châteaux have never been able to decide whether 1963 or 1965 was the worst vintage of the 1960s. As in 1965, rain and rot ruined the harvest.

1962—It might be expected that 1962, coming after the great vintage of 1961, would be underrated, which it has been; also, it is probably the most un-dervalued Bordeaux vintage of the last three decades. Elegant, supple, very fruity wines, the 1962s were neither too tannic nor big, but consistently plea-surable and charming. Because of their balance, they have kept longer than anyone ever imagined, and although all the 1962s now require drinking up, the well-cellared top wines of the vintage can be kept for several more years.

The crop size was large in 1962 due to a hot and sunny summer with just enough rain. The wines drank well when young, and it surprised everyone that they still were going strong when they passed their tenth birthday in 1972.

This was an especially good year for the sweet wines of Barsac and Sauternes, which are now at their decadently rich best.

TOP WINES FOR 1962

Cantemerle 86, Gruaud-Larose 87, Haut-Brion 88, Lafleur 88, Lascombes 87, Latour 93, Lynch-Bages 89, Montrose 88, Mouton-Rothschild 90, Palmer 89, Pétrus 87, Trotanoy 88

1961—Until the advent of the 1982 vintage, there was little one could offer to refute the argument that 1961 was the finest vintage in the post–World War II era. Even though the 1982s are styled differently, the best of them will be able to hold their own with the finest 1961s. The 1961s have sensational concentration, the magnificent, penetrating bouquets of ripe fruit, rich, deep, long flavors, and outstanding deep colors. Even though they are now 32 years old, the top wines can age for at least another decade, and the very best wines will still be marvelous by the year 2000.

The weather pattern was nearly perfect in 1961, with spring frosts reducing the crop size and then sunny, hot weather throughout the summer and harvest, resulting in splendid maturity levels for the grapes. The small harvest guaranteed high prices for these wines, and at today's prices, the 1961s are liquid gold.

The vintage was excellent throughout all appellations of Bordeaux except for the Barsacs and Sauternes, which have benefited greatly from the vintage's reputation but are in reality quite mediocre. Some of the St.-Émilions are also not what they might have been because the vineyards there had not fully recovered from the killer freeze of 1956.

TOP WINES FOR 1961

L'Arrosée 94, Beychevelle 88, Canon 88, Cantemerle 92, Cheval Blanc 93, Cos d'Estournel 92, Ducru-Beaucaillou 96, Figeac 89, Gruaud-Larose 96, Haut-Bailly 96, Haut-Brion 96, Latour 100, Latour à Pomerol 100, Léoville-Barton 92, Lynch-Bages 94, Magdelaine 91, Malescot St.-Exupéry 92, Margaux 93, La Mission-Haut-Brion 99, Montrose 95, Mouton-Rothschild 92, Palmer 96, Pape-Clément 93, Pétrus 100, Pichon-Longueville, Comtesse de Lalande 95, Pontet-Canet 94, La Tour-Haut-Brion 95, Trotanoy 98

RATING BORDEAUX'S BEST PRODUCERS OF DRY RED WINES

Note: Where a producer has been assigned a range of stars, ***/**** for example, the lower rating has been used for placement in this hierarchy.

* * * * *(OUTSTANDING PRODUCERS)

Ausone (St.-Émilion)
Canon (St.-Émilion)
Certan de May (Pomerol)
Cheval Blanc (St.-Émilion)
Domaine de Chevalier (Graves)
Clinet (Pomerol)
La Conseillante (Pomerol)
Cos d'Estournel (St.-Estèphe)
Ducru-Beaucaillou (St.-Julien)
L'Évangile (Pomerol)
Figeac (St.-Émilion)
La Fleur de Gay (Pomerol)
Gruaud-Larose (St.-Julien)
Haut-Brion (Graves)
Lafite-Rothschild (Pauillac)

Lafleur (Pomerol)
Latour (Pauillac)
Léoville-Las Cases (St.-Julien)
Lynch-Bages (Pauillac)
Château Margaux (Margaux)
La Mission-Haut-Brion (Graves)
Mouton-Rothschild (Pauillac)
Palmer (Margaux)
Pétrus (Pomerol)
Pichon-Longueville Baron (Pauillac)
Pichon-Longueville, Comtesse de
    Lalande (Pauillac)
Le Pin (Pomerol)
Le Tertre-Roteboeuf (St.-Émilion)

* * * *(EXCELLENT PRODUCERS)

L'Angélus (St.-Émilion)

Bon Pasteur (Pomerol)

Canon-La-Gaffelière (St.-Émilion)

La Dominique (St.-Émilion)

L'Église-Clinet (Pomerol)

La Fleur Pétrus (Pomerol)

Grand-Puy-Lacoste (Pauillac)

Haut-Bailly (Graves)

Haut-Marbuzet (St.-Estèphe)

Lagrange (St.-Julien)

La Lagune (Ludon)

Latour à Pomerol (Pomerol)

Léoville-Barton (St.-Julien)

La Louvière (Graves)

Montrose (St.-Estèphe)****/*****

Pape-Clément (Graves)

Pavie (St.-Émilion)

Petit-Village (Pomerol)

Rausan-Ségla (Margaux)****/*****

Sociando-Mallet (Haut-Médoc)

Talbot (St.-Julien)

Troplong-Mondot (St.-Émilion)

Trotanoy (Pomerol)

Vieux Château Certan (Pomerol)

* * *(GOOD PRODUCERS)

d'Angludet (Margaux)

d'Armailhac (Pauillac)

L'Arrivet-Haut-Brion (Graves)

L'Arrosée (St.-Émilion)***/****

Bahans Haut-Brion (Graves)

Balestard-La-Tonnelle (St.-Émilion)

Batailley (Pauillac)

Beau Séjour-Bécot (St.-Émilion)

Beaumont (Haut-Médoc)

Beauséjour (Duffau-Lagarrosse)
   (St.-Émilion)***/****

Bel-Air (Lalande-de-Pomerol)

Belair (St.-Émilion)

Bertineau-St.-Vincent (Lalande-de-
   Pomerol)

Beychevelle (St.-Julien)

Le Boscq (Médoc)

Boyd-Cantenac (Margaux)

Branaire-Ducru (St.-Julien)

Brane-Cantenac (Margaux)

Cadet-Piola (St.-Émilion)

Calon-Ségur (St.-Estèphe)***/****

Canon (Canon-Fronsac)

Canon de Brem (Canon-Fronsac)

Canon Moueix (Canon-Fronsac)

Cantemerle (Macau)

Cantenac-Brown (Margaux)

Cap-de-Mourlin (St.-Émilion)

de Carles (Fronsac)

Les Carmes-Haut-Brion (Graves)

Cassagne-Haut-Canon-La-Truffière
   (Canon-Fronsac)

Certan-Giraud (Pomerol)

Chambert-Marbuzet (St.-Estèphe)

Chantegrive (Graves)

Chasse-Spleen (Moulis)***/****

Chauvin (St.-Émilion)

Citran (Haut-Médoc)

Clerc-Milon (Pauillac)

Clos du Clocher (Pomerol)

Clos Fourtet (St.-Émilion)

Clos des Jacobins (St.-Émilion)

Clos La Madeleine (St.-Émilion)

Clos du Marquis (St.-Julien)

Clos de L'Oratoire (St.-Émilion)

Clos René (Pomerol)

Clos Saint-Martin (St.-Émilion)

La Clotte (St.-Émilion)

Corbin (St.-Émilion)

Corbin-Michotte (St.-Émilion)

Cormeil-Figeac (St.-Émilion)

Cos Labory (St.-Estèphe)

Coufran (Haut-Médoc)

Couvent-des-Jacobins (St.-Émilion)

La Croix (Pomerol)

La Croix du Casse (Pomerol)

La Croix de Gay (Pomerol)

Croque-Michotte (St.-Émilion)

Curé-Bon-La-Madeleine
   (St.-Émilion)

Dalem (Fronsac)

Dassault (St.-Émilion)

La Dauphine (Fronsac)

Duhart-Milon-Rothschild (Pauillac)

Durfort-Vivens (Margaux)

Domaine de L'Église (Pomerol)

L'Enclos (Pomerol)

de Ferrand (St.-Émilion)

de Fieuzal (Graves)

Fonbadet (Pauillac)

Fonplégade (St.-Émilion)
Fonroque (St.-Émilion)
Fontenil (Fronsac)
Les Forts de Latour (Pauillac)
Fourcas-Loubaney (Listrac)
Franc-Mayne (St.-Émilion)
La Gaffelière (St.-Émilion)***/****
Le Gay (Pomerol)
Gazin (Pomerol)
Giscours (Margaux)***/****
Gloria (St.-Julien)
Gombaude-Guillot
    (Pomerol)***/****
Grand-Mayne
    (St.-Émilion)***/****
Grand-Puy-Ducasse (Pauillac)
La Grave Trigant de Boisset
    (Pomerol)
Gressier Grand-Poujeaux
    (Moulis)***/****
La Gurgue (Margaux)
Haut-Bages-Libéral (Pauillac)
Haut-Batailley (Pauillac)
Haut-Corbin (St.-Émilion)
Haut-Sociondo (Blaye)
Hortevie (St.-Julien)
d'Issan (Margaux)
Jonqueyrès (Bordeaux Supérieur)
Le Jurat (St.-Émilion)
Labégorce-Zédé (Margaux)
Lafon-Rochet (St.-Estèphe)
Lamarque (Haut-Médoc)
Lanessan (Haut-Médoc)***/****
Langoa-Barton (St.-Julien)
Larcis-Ducasse (St.-Émilion)
Larmande (St.-Émilion)***/****
Larruau (Margaux)
Lascombes (Margaux)
Léoville-Poyferré (St.-Julien)
Liversan (Haut-Médoc)
Magdelaine (St.-Émilion)***/****
Malescot St.-Exupéry (Margaux)
Marquis-de-Terme (Margaux)
Maucaillou (Moulis)***/****
Mazeris (Canon-Fronsac)
Meyney (St.-Estèphe)***/****
Monbrison (Margaux)***/****
Moulin-Haut-Laroque (Fronsac)
Moulin-Rouge (Haut-Médoc)

Les-Ormes-de-Pez (St.-Estèphe)
Les Ormes-Sorbet (Médoc)
Parenchère (Bordeaux Supérieur)
Pavie-Decesse
    (St.-Émilion)***/****
Pavie-Macquin
    (St.-Émilion)***/****
du Pavillon (Canon-Fronsac)
Pavillon Rouge de Margaux
    (Margaux)
Les Pensées de Lafleur (Pomerol)
Peyredon-Lagravette (Listrac)
de Pez (St.-Estèphe)
Pey-Labrie (Canon-Fronsac)
Phélan-Ségur (St.-Estèphe)***/****
Pibran (Pauillac)
Picque-Caillou (Graves)
de Pitray (Côtes de Castillon)
Pontet-Canet (Pauillac)***/****
Potensac (Médoc)
Pouget (Margaux)
Poujeaux (Moulis)***/****
Prieuré-Lichine (Margaux)
Reserve de la Comtesse (Pauillac)
Roc des Cambes (Côtes de Bourg)
Rocher-Bellevue-Figeac
    (St.-Émilion)
Rolland-Maillet (St.-Émilion)
Rouet (Fronsac)
St.-Pierre (St.-Julien)***/****
de Sales (Pomerol)
Siran (Margaux)
Soutard (St.-Émilion)***/****
Tayac Prestige (Côtes de Bourg)
Terrey-Gros-Cailloux (St.-Julien)
du Tertre (Margaux)
Tertre-Daugay (St.-Émilion)
La Tonnelle (Blaye)
La Tour de By (Médoc)
La Tour-Haut-Brion (Graves)
Tour Haut-Caussan
    (Médoc)***/****
Tour du Haut-Moulin
    (Haut-Médoc)***/****
La Tour-du-Pin-Figeac-Moueix
    (St.-Émilion)
La Tour St.-Bonnet (Médoc)
La Tour Seguy (Bourg)

Les Tourelles de Longueville
  (Pauillac)
Trottevieille (St.-Émilion)

La Vieille-Cure (Fronsac)
La Violette (Pomerol)

RATING BORDEAUX'S BEST PRODUCERS OF
DRY WHITE WINES

* * * * *(OUTSTANDING PRODUCERS)

Domaine de Chevalier (Graves)
de Fieuzal (Graves)

Haut-Brion (Graves)
Laville-Haut-Brion (Graves)

* * * *(EXCELLENT PRODUCERS)

Clos Floridene (Graves)
Couhins-Lurton (Graves)
La Louvière (Graves)

Pavillon Blanc de Château Margaux
  (Bordeaux)
La Tour-Martillac (Graves)

* * *(GOOD PRODUCERS)

L'Arrivet-Haut-Brion (Graves)
Bouscaut (Graves)
Caillou Blanc de Talbot (Bordeaux)
Carbonnieux (Graves)
Domaine Challon (Bordeaux)
Chantegrive (Graves)
Ferrande (Graves)
Haut-Gardère (Graves)
Loudenne (Bordeaux)
Blanc de Lynch Bages (Bordeaux)
Malartic-Lagravière (Graves)

Château de Malle (Graves)
Château Millet (Graves)
Numéro 1 (Bordeaux)
Pape-Clément (Graves)
Pirou (Graves)
Pontac-Monplaisir (Graves)
Rahoul (Graves)
Respide (Graves)
Rochemorin (Graves)
Thieuley (Bordeaux)

RATING BORDEAUX'S BEST PRODUCERS OF
SAUTERNES/BARSACS

* * * * *(OUTSTANDING PRODUCERS)

Climens (Barsac)
Coutet-Cuvée Madame (Barsac)
Fargues (Sauternes)
Raymond-Lafon (Sauternes)

Rieussec (Sauternes)
Suduiraut-Cuvée Madame
  (Sauternes)
d'Yquem (Sauternes)

* * * *(EXCELLENT PRODUCERS)

Coutet regular *cuvée* (Barsac)
Doisy-Dubroca (Barsac)
Gilette (Sauternes)
Guiraud (Sauternes)
Haut-Claverie (Sauternes)

Lafaurie-Peyraguey (Sauternes)
Rabaud-Promis (Sauternes)
Suduiraut (Sauternes)
La Tour Blanche (Sauternes)

＊＊(GOOD PRODUCERS)

Bastor-Lamontagne (Sauternes)   de Malle (Sauternes)
Doisy-Daëne (Barsac)   Rayne-Vigneau (Sauternes)
Doisy-Védrines (Barsac)   Sigalas Rabaud (Sauternes)
Lamothe-Guignard (Sauternes)

Getting a Hand on Secondary Label

Secondary wines with secondary labels are not a recent development. Léoville-Las Cases first made a second wine (Clos du Marquis) in 1904, and in 1908 Château Margaux produced its first Le Pavillon Rouge du Château Margaux.

Yet a decade ago, about the only second labels most Bordeaux wine enthusiasts encountered were those from Latour (Les Forts de Latour), Margaux (Le Pavillon Rouge du Château Margaux), and perhaps that of Lafite-Rothschild (Moulin des Carruades). Today virtually every classified growth, as well as many Crus Bourgeois and numerous estates in Pomerol and St.-Émilion, have second labels for those batches of wine deemed not sufficiently rich, concentrated, or complete enough to go into their top wine, or "grand vin." This has been one of the major developments of the 1980s, fostered no doubt by the enormous crop sizes in most of the vintages. A handful of cynics have claimed it is done largely to keep prices high, but such charges are nonsense. The result has generally been far higher quality for the château's best wine. It allows a château to declassify the production from young vines, from vines that overproduce, and from parcels harvested too soon or too late into a second, or perhaps even a third, wine that still has some of the quality and character of the château's grand vin.

The gentleman who encouraged most châteaux to develop second wines was the famed oenologist Professor Emile Peynaud. Over the last decade the number of second wines has increased more than tenfold. Some properties, such as Léoville-Las Cases, have even begun to utilize a third label for wines deemed not good enough for the second label!

Of course all this complicates buying decisions for consumers. The wine trade has exacerbated matters by seizing the opportunity to advertise wine that "tastes like the grand vin" for one-half to one-third the price. In most cases there is little truth to such proclamations. I find that in general second wines have only a vague resemblance to their more esteemed siblings. Some second wines, such as those of the first-growths, particularly Les Forts de Latour and Bahans Haut-Brion, are indeed excellent, occasionally outstanding (taste the 1982 Les Forts de Latour or 1989 Bahans Haut-Brion), and can even resemble the style and character of the grand vin. But a strong caveat emptor applies here, particularly to those consumers who routinely purchase the second labels of Bordeaux châteaux thinking they are getting something reminiscent of the property's top wine.

In an effort to clarify the situation, the following chart rates secondary wines on a 1- to 5-star basis. Although it is generally true that the stricter the selection, the better the top wine, it is also important to remember that most second wines are rarely worth the price asked.

Note: Where a second wine merits purchasing, the vintage is listed.

EXPLANATION OF THE STARS

*****—The finest second wines

 ****—Very good second wines

  ***—Pleasant second wines

   **—Average quality second wines

    *—Of little interest

Secondary Labels

GRAND VIN	SECOND WINE
Andron-Blanquet	St.-Roch*
L'Angélus	Carillon de L'Angélus**
d'Angludet	Domaine Baury**
d'Arche	d'Arche-Lafaurie**
L'Arrosée	Les Côteaux du Château L'Arrosée**
Balestard-La-Tonnelle	Les Tourelles de Balestard**
Bastor-Lamontagne	Les Remparts du Bastor**
Beau Séjour-Bécot	Tournelle des Moines**
Beaumont	Moulin-d'Arvigny*
Beauséjour (Duffau-Lagarrose)	La Croix de Mazerat**
Belair	Roc-Blanquant*
Beychevelle	Amiral de Beychevelle**
	Reserve de L'Amiral**
Bonalgue	Burgrave*
Bouscaut	Valoux*
Branaire-Ducru	Duluc**
Brane-Cantenac	Château Notton**
	Domaine de Fontarney**
Broustet	Château de Ségur**
La Cabanne	Compostelle*
Cadet-Piola	Chevaliers de Malta**
Caillou	Petit-Mayne*
Calon-Ségur	Marquis de Ségur**
Canon	Clos J. Kanon**
Canon-La-Gaffelière	Côte Migon-La-Gaffelière**
Cantemerle	Villeneuve de Cantemerle**
Cantenac-Brown	Canuet**
	Lamartine**
Carbonnieux	La Tour-Léognan**
Certan-Giraud	Clos du Roy**
Chambert-Marbuzet	MacCarthy**
Chasse-Spleen	L'Ermitage de Chasse-Spleen**
Chauvin	Chauvin Variation*
Cheval Blanc	Le Petit Cheval**
Climens	Les Cyprès de Climens**
Clos Fourtet	Domaine de Martialis**
Clos Haut-Peyraguey	Haut-Bommes**
Clos René	Moulinet-Lasserre**
Colombier-Monpelou	Grand Canyon*
Corbin-Michotte	Les Abeilles**
Cos d'Estournel	Marbuzet***
Couvent-des-Jacobins	Beau-Mayne***
La Croix	Le Gabachot**
Croizet-Bages	Enclos de Moncabon*
Dauzac	Laborde*
Doisy-Védrines	La Tour-Védrines**
La Dominique	Saint-Paul de la Dominique**

GRAND VIN	*SECOND WINE*
Ducru-Beaucaillou	La Croix**
Duhart-Milon-Rothschild	Moulin de Duhart**
Durfort-Vivens	Domaine de Curé-Bourse*
L'Église-Clinet	La Petite L'Église**
de Fieuzal	L'Abeille de Fieuzal**
Figeac	Grangeneuve**
Fonplégade	Château Côtes Trois Moulins**
La Gaffelière	Clos la Gaffelière**
	Château de Roquefort**
Giscours	Cantelaude**
Gloria	Haut-Beychevelle Gloria**
	Peymartin**
Grand-Mayne	Les Plantes du Mayne**
Grand-Puy-Ducasse	Artigues-Arnaud**
Grand-Puy-Lacoste	Lacoste-Borie**
Gruaud-Larose	Sarget de Gruaud-Larose***
Guiraud	Le Dauphin**
Haut-Bailly	La Parde de Haut-Bailly***
Haut-Batailley	La Tour d'Aspic**
Haut-Brion	Bahans Haut-Brion***** (1990, 1989, 1988, 1987)
Haut-Marbuzet	Tour-de-Marbuzet**
d'Issan	Candel**
Labégorce-Zédé	Château de l'Amiral**
Lafite-Rothschild	Moulins de Carruades**** (1990, 1989)
Lafleur	Les Pensées de Lafleur***** (1990, 1989, 1988)
Lafon-Rochet	Le Numéro 2 de Lafon-Rochet***
Lagrange	Les Fiefs de Lagrange***
La Lagune	Ludon-Pomiès-Agassac**
Lanessan	Domaine de Sainte-Gemme**
Langoa-Barton	Lady Langoa**** (1989)
Larmande	Château des Templiers**
Lascombes	Segonnes**
	La Gombaude**
Latour	Les Forts de Latour***** (1990, 1989, 1982, 1978)
Léoville-Barton	Lady Langoa**** (1989)
Léoville-Las Cases	Clos du Marquis***** (1990, 1989, 1988, 1986, 1985, 1982)
	Grand Parc***
Léoville-Poyferré	Moulin-Riche**
La Louvière	L de Louvière**** (1989)
	Coucheray**
	Clos du Roi**
Lynch-Bages	Haut-Bages-Averous**** (1989)
Malescot St.-Exupéry	de Loyac*
	Domaine du Balardin*
de Malle	Château de Sainte-Hélène**
Château Margaux	Pavillon Rouge du Château Margaux*** (1990)
Marquis de Terme	Domaine des Gondats**
Maucaillou	Cap de Haut**
	Franc-Caillou**
Meyney	Prieuré de Meyney***
Monbrison	Cordat***
Montrose	La Dame de Montrose**** (1990, 1989)
Palmer	Réserve du Général***
Pape-Clément	Le Clémentin du Pape-Clément***
Phélan-Ségur	Franck Phélan***
Pichon-Longueville Baron	Les Tourelles de Pichon***

GRAND VIN	SECOND WINE
Pichon-Longueville,	
Comtesse de Lalande	Reserve de la Comtesse***
Pontet-Canet	Les Hauts de Pontet**
Potensac	Gallais-Bellevue**
	Lassalle**
	Goudy-la-Cardonne**
Poujeaux	La Salle de Poujeaux**
Le Prieuré	Château l'Olivier**
Prieuré-Lichine	Clairefont**
Rabaud-Promis	Domaine de l'Estremade**
Rahoul	Petit Rahoul**
Rausan-Ségla	Lamouroux**
Rieussec	Clos Labère***
St.-Pierre	Clos de Uza**
	St.-Louis-le-Bosq**
de Sales	Chantalouette**
Siran	Bellegarde**
	St.-Jacques**
Smith-Haut-Lafitte	Les Hauts-de-Smith-Haut-Lafitte*
Sociando-Mallet	Lartigue-de-Brochon**
Soutard	Clos de la Tonnelle**
Talbot	Connétable de Talbot***
Tertre-Daugay	Château de Roquefort***
La Tour Blanche	Mademoiselle de Saint-Marc***
La Tour de By	Moulin de la Roque*
	La Roque de By*
Tour Haut-Caussan	La Landotte**
La Tour-Martillac	La Grave-Martillac**
Troplong-Mondot	Mondot***
Vieux Château Certan	Clos de la Gravette***

The Best Wine Values in Bordeaux

(The top estates for under $20 a bottle)

St.-Estèphe   Marbuzet, Meyney, Les-Ormes-de-Pez, Phélan-Ségur, Tronquoy-Lalande

Pauillac   Fonbadet, Grand-Puy-Ducasse, Pibran

St.-Julien   Clos du Marquis, Gloria, Hortevie

Margaux and the Southern Médoc   d'Angludet, La Gurgue, Labégorce-Zédé

Graves   Bahans Haut-Brion, La Louvière, Picque-Caillou

Moulis and Listrac   Fourcas-Loubaney, Gressier Grand-Poujeaux, Maucaillou, Poujeaux

Médoc and Haut-Médoc   Beaumont, Le Boscq, Lanessan, Latour St.-Bonnet, Moulin-Rouge, Potensac, Sociando-Mallet, La Tour de By, Tour Haut-Caussan, Tour du Haut-Moulin, Vieux-Robin

Pomerol   Bonalgue, L'Enclos

St.-Émilion   Grand-Mayne, Grand-Pontet, Haut-Corbin, Pavie-Macquin

Fronsac and Canon-Fronsac   Canon (Moueix), Canon de Brem, de Carles, Cassagne-Haut-Canon-La-Truffière, Dalem, La Dauphine, Fontenil, La Grave, Mazeris, Moulin-Haut-Laroque, Moulin-Pey-Labrie, du Pavillon, Pez-Labrie, Rouet, La Vieille-Cure

Lalande-de-Pomerol   Bel-Air, Bertineau-St.-Vincent, du Chapelain, Les Hauts-Conseillants, Grand-Ormeau, Siaurac

Côtes de Bourg   Brûlesécaille, Guerry, Haut-Maco, Mercier, Roc des Cambes, Tayac-Cuvée Prestige

Côtes de Blaye   Bertinerie, Pérenne, La Rose-Bellevue, La Tonnelle

Bordeaux Premières Côtes and Supérieurs   La Croix de Roche, Dudon-Cuvée Jean Baptiste, Fontenil, Haux Frère, Jonqueyrès, Plaisance, de Plassan, Prieuré-Ste.-Anne, Recougne, Reynon

Côtes de Castillon   Pitray

Barsac/Sauternes   Bastor-Lamontagne, Doisy-Dubroca, Haut-Claverie, de Malle

Loupiac   Bourdon-Loupiac, Clos-Jean, Loupiac-Gaudiet, Ricaud

Entre-Deux-Mers (dry white wines)   Bonnet, Bonnet-Cuvée Réservée, Tertre-Launay, Turcaud

Bordeaux Premières Côtes and Generic Bordeaux (dry white wines)   Alpha, Bauduc-Les Trois-Hectares, Blanc de Lynch-Bages, Caillou Blanc du Château Talbot, Cayla-Le-Grand-Vent, Clos-Jean, De la Cloisère du Carpia, Numéro 1-Dourthe, Reynon-Vieilles Vignes, Roquefort-Cuvée Spéciale, Sec de Doisy-Daëne, Thieuley

Buying Bordeaux Wine Futures:
The Pitfalls and Pleasures

The purchase of wine, already fraught with pitfalls for consumers, becomes immensely more complex and risky when one enters the wine futures' sweepstakes.

On the surface, buying wine futures is nothing more than investing money in wine at a predetermined "future price" long before it is bottled and shipped to this country. You invest your money in wine futures on the assumption that the wine will appreciate significantly in price between the time you purchase the future and the time the wine has been bottled and imported to America. Purchasing the right wine, from the right vintage, in the right international financial climate, can result in significant savings. On the other hand, it can be quite disappointing to witness the wine's arrival 12–18 months later at a price equal to or below the future price and to discover the wine to be inferior in quality as well.

For years, future offerings have been limited largely to Bordeaux wines, although they are seen occasionally from other regions. In Bordeaux, during the spring following the harvest, the estates or châteaux offer for sale a portion of their crops. The first offering, or *première tranche,* usually gives a good indication of the trade's enthusiasm for the new wine, the prevailing market conditions, and the ultimate price the public will have to pay.

Those brokers and *négociants* who take an early position on a vintage frequently offer portions of their purchases to importers/wholesalers/retailers to make available to the public as a "wine future." These offerings are usually made to the retail shopper during the first spring after the vintage. For example, the 1990 Bordeaux vintage was being offered for sale as a "wine future" in April 1991. Purchasing wine at this time is not without risk. Although 90% of the quality of the wine and the style of the vintage can be ascertained by professionals tasting the wine in its infancy, increased interest in Bordeaux wine futures has encouraged a soaring number of journalists—some qualified, some not—to judge young Bordeaux wines. The results have been predictable. Many writers serve no purpose other than to hype the vintage as great and have written more glowing accounts of a vintage than the publicity firms doing promotion for the Bordeaux wine industry. (Of course, those writers who fail to admit or recognize greatness where warranted are no less inept and irresponsible.) Consumers should read numerous points of view from trusted professionals and ask the following questions: (1) Is the professional taster experienced in tasting young as well as old Bordeaux vintages? (2) How much time does the taster actually spend tasting Bordeaux during the year, visiting the properties, and thinking about the vintage? (3) Does the professional taster express his viewpoint in an independent, unbiased form, free of trade advertising? (4) Has the professional looked deeply at the weather conditions, harvesting conditions, grape variety ripening profiles, and soil types that respond differently depending on the weather?

When wine futures are offered for sale, there is generally a great deal of enthusiasm for the newest vintage from both the proprietors and the wine trade. "The greatest wines ever made are the ones that are available for sale" is a French saying that many wine producers and merchants live by. The business of the wine trade is to sell wine, so each year consumers are inundated with the latest claims of "great wines from a great vintage at great prices." This has undermined the credibility of many otherwise responsible retailers.

In short, there are only four valid reasons to buy Bordeaux wine futures.

1. Are you buying top-quality, preferably superb wine from an excellent—better yet, a great vintage?

Even in the greatest vintages there are disappointing appellations, as well as mediocre wines. At the same time, vintages that are merely good to very good can produce some superb wines. Knowing the underachievers and overachievers is paramount in making a good buying decision. In looking at the last 20 years, the only irrefutably great vintages have been 1982 for Pomerol, St.-Émilion, St.-Julien, Pauillac, and St.-Estèphe; 1983 for selected St.-Émilions and Pomerols, as well as the wines from Margaux; 1985 for the wines of Graves; 1986 for the northern Médocs from St.-Julien, Pauillac, St.-Estèphe, and the sweet wines from Barsac/Sauternes; 1988 for the Barsacs and Sauternes; 1989 for selected Pomerols, St.-Émilions, St.-Juliens, Pauillacs, and St.-Estèphes; and 1990 for the first-growths and a handful of Pomerols and St.-Émilions. There is no reason to buy wines as futures except for the top performers in a given vintage because prices generally will not appreciate in the period between the release of the future prices and the bottling of the wines. The exceptions are always the same—top wines and great vintages. If the financial climate is such that the wine will not be at least 25–30% more expensive when it arrives in the marketplace, most purchasers are better off investing their money elsewhere.

Recent history of the 1975 and 1978 Bordeaux future offerings provides a revealing prospectus to "futures" buyers. Purchasers of 1975 futures have done extremely well. When offered in 1977, the 1975 future prices included $140–$160 per case for such illustrious wines as Lafite-Rothschild and Latour, and $64–$80 for second-growths, including such proven thoroughbreds as Léoville-Las Cases, La Lagune, and Ducru-Beaucaillou. By the time these wines arrived on the market in 1978, the vintage's outstanding and potentially classic quality was an accepted fact, and the first-growths were retailing for $325–$375 per case; the lesser growths, $112–$150 per case. Buyers of 1975 futures have continued to prosper, as this vintage is now very scarce and its prices have continued to escalate to $900–$1,200 a case for first-growths and $350–$550 for second- through fifth-growths. Presently, the 1975 prices have come to a standstill because of doubts about how gracefully many of the wines are evolving. I would not be surprised to see some prices drop—another pitfall that must always be considered.

The 1978 Bordeaux futures, offered in 1980, present a different picture: 1978 was another very good vintage year, with wines similar in style but perhaps less intense than the excellent 1970 vintage. Opening prices for the 1978 Bordeaux were very high and were inflated because of a weak dollar abroad and an excessive demand for the finest French wines. Prices for first-growths were offered at $429–$499, prices for second- through fifth-growths at $165–$230. Consumers who invested heavily in Bordeaux have purchased good wine, but when the wines arrived on the market in spring 1981, the retail prices for these wines were virtually the same as future price offerings. Thus consumers who purchased 1978 futures and invested their money to the tune of 100% of the case price could have easily obtained a better return by investing in any interest-bearing account.

With respect to the vintages 1979, 1980, 1981, 1982, 1983, 1985, 1986, 1988, 1989, and 1990, the only year that has represented a great buy from a futures perspective is 1982 and possibly 1990. The 1980 vintage was not offered to the consumer as a wine future because it was of mediocre quality. And the enthusiast who purchased the 1979 and 1981 wines on a future basis no doubt was able, within two years after putting up the money, to buy the wines when they arrived in America at approximately the same price. Although this was not true for some of the highly rated 1981s, it was true for the 1979s. On the other hand, the 1982s have jumped in price at an unbelievable pace, outdistancing any vintage in the last twenty years. The first-growths of 1982 were offered to consumers in late spring 1983 at prices of $350–$450 for wines such as Lafite-Rothschild, Latour, Mouton-Rothschild, Haut-Brion, and Cheval Blanc. By March 1985 the Cheval Blanc had jumped to $650–$800, the Mouton to $800–$1,000, and the rest to $700. Today, prices for first-growths range from a low of $1,500 a case for Haut-Brion to $1,800–$2,400 a case for any of the three Pauillac first-growths. This is a significant price increase for wines so young, but it reflects the insatiable worldwide demand for a great vintage. Rare, limited-production wines like the Pomerols have skyrocketed in price. Pétrus has clearly been the top performer in terms of increasing in price; it jumped from an April 1983 future price of $600 to a 1991 price of $5,000. This is absurd given the fact that the wines will not be close to maturity for a decade. Other top 1982 Pomerols such as Trotanoy, Certan de May, and L'Évangile have doubled and tripled in price. Trotanoy, originally available for $280, now sells (when you can find it) for at least $1,000. Both Certan de May and L'Évangile have jumped from $180 to $750.

The huge demand for 1982 Bordeaux futures and tremendous publicity surrounding this vintage led many to assume that subsequent years would similarly escalate in price. That has not happened, largely because Bordeaux has had too many high-quality, abundant vintages in the 1980s. The only exceptions have been the first-growths of 1986, a great, long-lived, so-called classic year whose wines have continued to accelerate in price.

2. Do you believe you will be paying less for the wine as a future than when it is released in 2–3 years?

Many factors must be taken into consideration to make this determination. In certain years Bordeaux may release its wines at lower prices than it did the previous year (the most recent examples are 1986 and 1990). But one very important consideration is the international marketplace. In 1993 the American dollar is beginning to rebound but is still generally weak; moreover, our country is just now coming out of its recession. Other significant Bordeaux buying countries, such as England, have unsettled and troublesome financial problems as well. Even France is in a recession, at least according to all the economic experts. Newer marketplaces, such as Japan, are experiencing financial apprehension and increasing banking problems. Even Germany, which has become a major Bordeaux player, has experienced an economic downturn as a result of trying to revitalize East Germany's moribund economy. Consequently, the saturated marketplace is a matter of fact. The only three countries that appear to be in a healthy enough economic position to afford top-class Bordeaux are Belgium, Denmark, and Switzerland. Of course, this situation may change at some point in time, but even so, the international marketplace (along with the perceived reputation of a given vintage and the rarity of a particular estate) must always be considered before determining whether a wine will cost more when released than it does as a future.

3. Do you want to be guaranteed of getting top, hard-to-find wine from a renowned producer who makes only small quantities of wine?

Even if the vintage is not irrefutably great, or you cannot be assured that prices will increase, a handful of small estates, particularly in Pomerol and St.-Émilion, produce such limited quantities of wine, and have so many followers worldwide, that you would be wise to buy a case as a future if only to secure for yourself the wines that have pleased you in the past. In Pomerol, limited-production wines such as Le Pin, Clinet, La Conseillante, L'Évangile, La Fleur de Gay, Lafleur, Gombaude-Guillot, and Bon Pasteur have produced many popular wines during the 1980s that are very hard to find in the marketplace. In St.-Émilion some of the less renowned yet modestly sized estates such as L'Angélus, L'Arrosée, Canon, Grand-Mayne, Pavie-Macquin, La Dominique, Le Tertre-Roteboeuf and Troplong-Mondot produce wines that are not easy to find after bottling. Consequently admirers throughout the world frequently reserve and pay for these wines as futures. Limited-production wines from high-quality estates merit futures buying even in good to very good years.

4. Do you want to buy wine in half bottles, magnums, double magnums, jeroboams, or imperials?

One of the advantages of buying wine futures is that you can request your merchant to have the wines bottled to your specifications. There is a surcharge for such bottlings, but if you have children born in a certain year, or you want the luxury of buying half bottles (a sensible size for daily drinking), the only way to do this is by buying the wine as a future.

Should you decide to enter the futures market, be sure you know the other risks involved. The merchant you deal with could go bankrupt, leaving you and hundreds of other unsecured creditors hoping to recoup a few cents on your investment. Another risk is that the supplier the merchant deals with could go bankrupt or be fraudulent. You may get a refund from the wine merchant, but you will not get your wine. Therefore be sure to deal only with a financially solvent wine merchant who has sold wine futures before. Finally, buy wine futures only from a wine merchant who has received confirmed commitments as to the quantities of wine to be shipped. Some merchants sell Bordeaux futures to consumers before they have received commitments from suppliers. Be sure to ask for proof of the merchant's allocations.

For many Bordeaux wine enthusiasts, buying wine futures of the right wine, in the right vintage, at the right time, guarantees the receipt of liquid gems worth four or five times the price paid. However, only a handful of vintages over the last twenty years have appreciated that significantly in their first two or three years. In 1993–1994 the marketplace remains saturated. The fact that Bordeaux has had two back-to-back mediocre years, 1991 and 1992, for the first time since the early seventies, has eliminated the need to buy wine futures. The 1990s, already in the pipeline, merit considerable attention from serious Bordeaux collectors since many of the wines are extraordinary. Moreover, vintages such as 1988 were being significantly discounted at the time this book went to press. Even fashionable years such as 1985 and 1986 can represent top bargains.

For the next 1–2 years, consumers should be looking back to bargains that exist from inventories of already bottled Bordeaux, rather than investing their money in wine futures. At the time of this writing, futures buying makes no sense except perhaps for parents who may desire to buy a child's birth year wine in magnums or double magnums.

THE DRY RED WINES OF BORDEAUX

ANDRON-BLANQUET (ST.-ESTÈPHE)* *

1990	C	74
1989	C	82
1988	C	74

This perennial underachiever appears unable to muster the necessary motivation to produce high-quality wine. The 1988, which is light and lacking the charming fruitiness of the 1989, finishes short and is too acidic. The 1989 is surprisingly light but intensely fruity in a straightforward, jammy, medium-bodied style. The 1990 is the most disappointing wine from St.-Estèphe I tasted. Lean, short, and hard, it possesses insufficient fruit.

L'ANGÉLUS (ST.-ÉMILION)* * * *

1990	D	96
1989	D	94
1988	C	91

I do not think anyone can doubt that L'Angélus is one of the up-and-coming superstars, not only in St.-Émilion, but in all of Bordeaux. The 1988 L'Angélus is a rich, almost lusty St.-Émilion, with a full-throttle bouquet of licorice, spicy new oak, cassis, olives, and minerals. In the mouth it is full bodied, deep, and concentrated, with excellent extract and a long, heady, moderately tannic finish. **Anticipated maturity: Now–2006.** The 1989 is opaque black/ruby/purple, with a huge bouquet of smoky vanillin oak, olives, cassis, and grilled nuts. In the mouth it has sensational extract, full body, superb balance, and a fascinating long finish that must last for at least one minute. This is a great wine that was put in the bottle without fining or filtering—rather amazing in high-tech Bordeaux! An absolutely splendid effort that should not be missed, L'Angélus is the wine of St.-Émilion in 1989! **Anticipated maturity: 1995–2008.** The 1990 has a saturated purple color and a texture akin to port. Even more exotic, concentrated, and voluptuous than the 1989, it exhibits terrific concentration as well as a dazzling bouquet of coffee, mocha, herbs, black fruits, oak, and smoke. In the mouth there is layer upon layer of extract and perhaps slightly more tannin than the 1989. This massive wine was bottled unfiltered. A monumental effort! **Anticipated maturity: 1995–2008.**

PAST GLORIES: 1986 (89)

PAST MEDIOCRITIES . . . OR WORSE: Just about anything made in the sixties or seventies

D'ANGLUDET (MARGAUX)* * *

1990	C 85
1989	C 87
1988	C 81

The 1988 d'Angludet is a sinewy, surprisingly light wine, medium bodied, low in extract levels and tannins, and exhibiting straightforward, solid, but unexciting flavors. **Anticipated maturity: Now–1998.** The 1989 d'Angludet is one of this property's best wines since their excellent 1983. It does not, however, appear to have the stuffing necessary to surpass that wine. It is fat, plump, intensely fruity, with a good ruby color, supple texture, high alcohol, and soft tannins. **Anticipated maturity: Now–2002.** D'Angludet's 1990 rivals its 1989. More noticeably tannic than the 1989, without that vintage's sweet fruit and opulence, the 1990 is nevertheless a fine wine. It exhibits deep color, rich, herbaceous fruit, medium body, and plenty of substance in its finish. It should be at its best between 1995 and 2005.

PAST GLORIES: 1983 (89)

ANTHONIC (MOULIS)* *

1990	B 84
1989	C 84

Loosely knit and supple, but pleasant and ripe, the 1989 is a smooth, silky-textured wine that should be drunk over the next 3–4 years. The 1990 is a ripe, solidly made, concentrated wine that should age well for at least 7–8 years. Though it lacks complexity, there is good stuffing and character.

D'ARMAILHAC (PAUILLAC)* * *
Note: Formerly called Mouton-Baronne-Philippe

1990	D	85
1989	D	87
1988	C	84

When compared with the 1989, the 1988 Mouton-Baronne-Philippe is much lighter, more compact, noticeably hard and lean, and has a short finish. **Anticipated maturity: Now–1998.** The château feels the 1989 vintage of Mouton-Baronne-Philippe is its best wine in over three decades. It exhibits a very forward, creamy richness, gobs of velvety fruit, a heady alcohol content, and a fat, lush finish. **Anticipated maturity: Now–2000.** The 1990 d'Armailhac is dark ruby/purple, with an expressive nose of smoked nuts, cassis, smoke, and chocolate. This velvety-textured, round, agreeable wine lacks structure and length on the palate. It is charming, but less concentrated than the 1989. **Anticipated maturity: 1994–2003.**

L'ARRIVET-HAUT-BRION (GRAVES)* * *

1990	C	86
1989	C	73
1988	C	85

Although the 1988 is light, it exhibits a good ruby color; an earthy, fruity nose; round, ripe, charming flavors; and soft tannins in the finish. It will be ideal for drinking over the next 6–7 years. The medium-bodied 1989 has a suspiciously light color, and the tart green tannins are astringent and excessive. Frankly, there is not much to this wine. The reassuringly good 1990 is expressive of the Graves appellation. Deep ruby-colored, with a smoky, herbal, cedary nose, the wine is supple, delicious, and medium bodied, with gobs of cherry fruit in the smooth finish. Anticipated maturity: Now–1999.

L'ARROSÉE (ST.-ÉMILION)* * */* * * *

1990	D	92
1989	D	85
1988	D	83

After a succession of wonderful vintages (1982, 1983, 1985, and 1986), L'Arrosée lost the magic touch in 1988 and 1989. The 1988 is not up to its previous standards. Medium bodied, spicy, and fruity, with good depth but not much length, it lacks complexity and intensity, indicating that either the grapes were harvested too early or the production was too abundant. **Anticipated maturity: Now–2000.** The 1989 is a tasty, amply endowed wine, but it is terribly low in acidity, diffuse, muddled, and lacking the great extract and compelling fragrance that this property so often obtains. **Anticipated maturity: Now–1999.** A super-concentrated effort from L'Arrosée, the 1990 is pure power, glycerin, and concentration. The wine reveals gobs of sweet tannins, a smoky, herb- and cassis-scented nose, and a sumptuous texture and superb concentration. Backward but approachable, this is a reassuringly out-

standing wine that is one of the many stars of this vintage. **Anticipated maturity: 1995–2020.**
PAST GLORIES: 1986 (93), 1985 (94), 1983 (88), 1982 (92), 1961 (94)

AUSONE (ST.-ÉMILION)* * * * *

1990	EEE	94+
1989	EEE	92
1988	EEE	91

The 1988 Ausone may need 20 years to reach its peak. Unlike a number of 1988s where the balance between tannin and fruit favors the former (always a troubling sign), Ausone offers plenty of juicy red and black fruit extract in a medium-bodied, superbly concentrated, intense and powerful format. **Anticipated maturity: 2008–2040.** In 1989 Ausone, Bordeaux's and perhaps France's most cerebral wine, harvested its splendidly situated microvineyard between September 7 and 19. Their first *cuvée* of Merlot reached 14.6% alcohol naturally, the highest anyone at the château could ever remember. The result is a wine with remarkable strength yet stunning balance because of its extremely high tannin content. It is the tannin that gives focus and definition to the wine's intense core of exotic black fruits. This is a medium- to full-bodied, backward 1989, possessing a haunting underlying mineral character that seems to be a characteristic of this property's greatest vintages. On potential this is certainly the finest Ausone since the 1982. **Anticipated maturity: 2015–2035.** I predict that within the next 25 years the 1990 will become the best Ausone since the 1982 and 1983. With its excellent richness, an exotic, kinky, Oriental spice component, and a rich, mineral character, as well as admirable concentration and length, I prefer it to the impressive 1989. It should only be purchased for your children. **Anticipated maturity: 2010–2040.**
PAST GLORIES: 1983 (93), 1982 (94), 1976 (93)
PAST MEDIOCRITIES . . . OR WORSE: 1971 (78), 1970 (69), 1961 (74)

BAHANS HAUT-BRION (GRAVES)* * *

1990	C	87
1989	C	89
1988	C	86

The 1988, a classic expression of Graves, offers up the telltale aromas of tobacco and black fruit. Medium bodied, soft, and round, this seductive wine should drink well for 5–6 years. The 1989 is one of the best second wines I have ever tasted. What makes it so admirable is that it resembles the great 1989 Haut-Brion. Although it is less tannic and not nearly as concentrated, it is no light-bodied wine. A gorgeous nose of roasted, sweet black fruits and tobacco is followed by a wine with silky texture, medium to full body, and a long, intense finish. Drink this beauty over the next 9–11 years. Thirty-five percent of the crop went into the 1990. Highly perfumed, it exhibits good ripeness, tasty, rich, sweet fruit, soft tannins, elegance, and low acidity. Drink it over the next 7–8 years.

BALESTARD-LA-TONNELLE (ST.-ÉMILION)* * *

1990	C	87
1989	C	86
1988	B	83

Balestard's 1988 is a narrowly constructed, compact, monolithic wine that should be consumed over the next 5–8 years. It certainly will last, but again, the problem is the lack of balance between the excessive tannins and the amount of fruit present. **Anticipated maturity: Now–2000.** The 1989 is a jammy, raspberry- and blackberry-scented wine that is fat and lacks acidity but has high alcohol and a chunky, fleshy, mouth-filling feel. **Anticipated maturity: Now–2005.** The big, fat, oaky, chocolatey, herb-scented 1990 is admirable for its density, high alcohol, and in-your-face style. **Anticipated maturity: 1994–2002.**

BATAILLEY (PAUILLAC)* * *

1990	C	86
1989	C	87
1988	B	85

Typically stern, tough, closed, and difficult to penetrate, the 1988 Batailley displays a dark ruby color; a reticent bouquet of minerals, smoked nuts, black-currants, and oak; medium body; and an elevated tannin level. **Anticipated maturity: 1997–2008.** The 1989 has gone into a hard, tannic, tough stage that suggests considerable patience will be necessary. The ruby/purple color is sound, and the bouquet of toasty, smoky oak, chocolate, and superripe cassis is followed by a medium-bodied, rich, extracted wine with ferocious tannins and good acidity. This is a large-scale, more traditionally styled wine that will need at least a decade of bottle age. **Anticipated maturity: 2000–2018.** The 1990 offers medium-dark ruby color, as well as an open-knit, fragrant, spicy, sweet nose. In the mouth the wine is decidedly less structured and tannic when compared with the 1989, but more soft, elegant and, at least for now, more flattering. A clone of Batailley's 1962? **Anticipated maturity: 1995–2010.**

BEAU SÉJOUR-BÉCOT (ST.-ÉMILION)* * *

1990	C	88
1989	C	87
1988	C	85

The 1988 Beau Séjour-Bécot has an aggressive oak-scented bouquet that, with airing, seems to step back and allow the ripe, curranty fruit to emerge. The wine appears to have good to very good concentration. **Anticipated maturity: Now–2004.** A high percentage of new oak tends to work well in a vintage such as 1989, where the underlying concentration and jammy, low-acid fruit character need the structure of oak to give the wine definition and focus. The 1989 has a dizzyingly high alcohol level; luscious, concentrated, rich, jammy, sweet, black cherry fruit; an opulent texture; and plenty of soft tannins in the finish. **Anticipated maturity: Now–2002.** The 1990 is a highly successful effort, with an opaque, dark ruby/purple color; a big, spicy, oaky, vanillin, and black cherry–scented nose; medium to full body; good tannin and grip; and a surprisingly long, structured finish. **Anticipated maturity: 1995–2005.**

BEAU-SITE (ST.-ESTÈPHE)* *

1990	B	84
1989	B	85
1988	B	77

Medium-dark ruby, with a tight but emerging bouquet of herbs, oak, and red fruits, the 1988 Beau-Site is a lean, austere, medium-bodied St.-Estèphe with abundant astringent tannins to resolve. The 1989 is probably the best wine produced at Beau-Site since 1982. Deep ruby/purple in color, with a moderately intense bouquet of superripe cassis fruit, minerals, and spicy oak, this medium-bodied, moderately tannic, concentrated wine has more power and opulence than most vintages of Beau-Site. Drinkable young, it should age gracefully for up to a decade. **Anticipated maturity: Now–2000.** The 1990 is an easygoing, round, fruity wine that exhibits soft tannins and a velvety feel. **Anticipated maturity: Now–2002.**

BEAUMONT (HAUT-MÉDOC)* * *

1990	A	85
1989	A	85

A smart purchase for shrewd consumers looking for an attractive wine, the deeply colored, richly oaky, black raspberry– and cherry-scented 1989 Beaumont displays fat, ripe flavors, moderate tannins, low acidity, and a luscious, alcoholic finish. Drink it over the next 4–5 years. The 1990 is a woody but rich wine that reveals more oak, but it is equally rich, with an attractive plumpness. **Anticipated maturity: Now–2000.**

BEAUREGARD (POMEROL)* *

1990	C	87

This muscular, chunky, full-bodied wine offers considerable weight and intensity. Although it was jammy and lacking individuality and complexity from barrel, it has developed considerable personality. It is the finest Beauregard in years. Drink it over the next 7–8 years.

BEAUSÉJOUR (DUFFAU-LAGARROSSE) (ST.-ÉMILION)* * */* * * *

1990	D	98
1989	D	88
1988	D	87

The 1988 has excellent depth and fullness, with a spicy, earthy, rich bouquet filled with aromas of licorice, plums, spices, new oak, and subtle herbs. Exceptionally concentrated, with sound acidity and moderate alcohol, this beautifully made, complex wine should reach maturity by the mid-1990s and last through the first decade of the next century. Given the very fine 1989 and outstanding 1990 produced, this property may be on a hot streak. Although the 1989 has a promising, understated bouquet of black cherry fruit, minerals, and spicy oak, it is surprisingly restrained for the vintage. Nevertheless, the ruby/purple color, the velvety, extracted, almost sweet, alcoholic flavors, and good tannins in the finish are clearly reminiscent of a vintage where tremendous ripeness was attained. It is not a blockbuster, but an extremely well-balanced, concentrated, impressive effort that still has some baby fat to shed. **Anticipated maturity: Now–2007.** The blockbuster 1990, a superstar of the vintage, is unquestionably the finest wine I have ever tasted from Beauséjour-Duffau. An opaque black/ruby color is followed by a bouquet that offers up intense, lingering aromas of herb-scented cassis, licorice, minerals, sweet plums, and new oak. In the mouth there is outstanding extraction of fruit, superlative depth and power, a formidable unctuosity and density, and an overall sense of elegance and finesse—an exceedingly difficult combination to produce in a wine. This profound St.-Émilion is a must buy, but move quickly, as the production of 3,000 cases is among the smallest of the St.-Émilion Premiers Grands Crus. **Anticipated maturity: 1995–2008.**

BEL-AIR (LALANDE-DE-POMEROL)* * *

1990	B	85
1989	B	85

A surprisingly old-style, dense, thick, rustic, wine, the 1989 Bel-Air possesses gobs of fruit, plenty of mouth-coating glycerin, and some tough tannins in the long finish. Alcoholic and precocious, the chunky yet flattering and supple 1990 should drink well for at least another 5–7 years. It is less structured and more loosely knit than the fine 1989, but more expansive and mouth-filling.

BELAIR (ST.-ÉMILION)* * *

1990	D	89
1989	D	88
1988	D	85

The 1988 is a lean, austere wine, with an inner core of curranty fruit, fine tannins, and a general sense of elegance and grace. **Anticipated maturity: 1995–2010.** The 1989 exhibits a huge, smoky, roasted, exotic bouquet of plums and Oriental spices. The wine exhibits surprisingly crisp acidity and plentiful but soft tannins. The formidable level of alcohol and sensationally extracted, multidimensional fruit flavors make this a brilliant effort. **Anticipated maturity: 1995–2010.** From the barrel, the 1990 was typically backward, stern, and firm. Now in bottle, it has emerged somewhat from its tannic armor and is more interesting. There is sweet, nearly overripe fruit, plenty of mineral/stony scents, and evidence of new oak underlying this medium-weight wine's backward personality. The aromas of overripe cherries and prunes are vaguely reminiscent of the great Pomerol, Lafleur. **Anticipated maturity: 1997–2012.**

BERLIQUET (ST.-ÉMILION)* *

1989	C	82
1988	C	79

This compact, relatively attenuated 1988 St.-Émilion could use more fat, depth, and charm. It is spicy, but lean and anorexic, with a short, tannic finish. **Anticipated maturity: Now–1995.** Medium ruby, with a spicy, earthy, ripe berry–scented bouquet, the medium-bodied 1989 exhibits adequate acidity and grip for the vintage, but it lacks concentration and depth. **Anticipated maturity: Now–1998.**

BERTINEAU-ST.-VINCENT (LALANDE-DE-POMEROL)* * *

1989	B	86

A huge nose of saddle leather, chocolate, and black cherries is followed by an opulently textured, intense, robustly styled wine with plenty of extract and a long finish. Drink it over the next 5–7 years.

BEYCHEVELLE (ST.-JULIEN)* * *

1990	D	85
1989	D	91
1988	D	84

Relatively light and lacking concentration, with an underripe, green streak to its flavors, the 1988 Beychevelle will age well, but it lacks the depth and ripeness to provide excitement. **Anticipated maturity: 1994–2002.** In 1989 Beychevelle produced a compellingly elegant wine that rivals its 1986 and 1982, the two other superstars made at this beautiful estate during the 1980s. An exquisite bouquet of superripe fruit, vanillin, flowers, and licorice is followed by a delicious array of flavors that swell and expand on the palate. Rich and concentrated, yet suave and graceful, the 1989 Beychevelle is extremely long, with a hefty dosage of soft tannins. **Anticipated maturity: Now–2008.** The vintage's extraordinarily high yields have taken a toll on the 1990's extract. It exhibits moderately dark color and a nice perfume of berry fruit, herbs, and smoky new oak. In the mouth there is more acidity than in many 1990s, but the overall mouth-feel is one of lightness, medium body, and a lack of concentration. **Anticipated maturity: 1994–2002.**

PAST GLORIES: 1986 (92), 1982 (92)

BON PASTEUR (POMEROL)* * * *

1990	D	92
1989	D	88
1988	C	89

Bon Pasteur's 1988 is a sure bet. Deep, opaque ruby (darker than the 1989), with a huge bouquet of chocolate, plums, currants, and herbs, this full-bodied, admirably extracted wine should prove to have considerable longevity. **Anticipated maturity: Now–2008.** The 1989 is rich, opulent, and intense, with a huge, smoky, plumlike bouquet. The scents of coffee and mocha can also be detected in this full-bodied, soft, and seductive wine. **Anticipated maturity: Now–2001.** With time, the 1990 should prove to be the finest Bon Pasteur since the glorious 1982. The intense opaque color is impressive. Even more so is the huge nose of superripe black cherry fruit, mocha, tobacco, and toasty new oak. In the mouth it is deep and intense, with medium to full body, excellent depth, a sweet, expansive texture, fine overall balance, and more structure and tannin than the 1989. Very impressive! **Anticipated maturity: 1995–2005.**

PAST GLORIES: 1982 (98)

LE BOSCQ (MÉDOC)* * *

1990	Vieilles Vignes	A	86
1989	Vieilles Vignes	A	85

The big aroma of chocolate-covered berries is followed by a deep, ripe wine gushing with fruit, low acidity, and a full-bodied, velvety texture. The 1989 Le Boscq should be drunk over the next 3–4 years. Rich and fat, with gobs of flavor and glycerin, as well as a chewy texture, the deep, medium- to full-bodied 1990 is bursting with fruit and character. It is a delicious Bordeaux for consuming over the next 5–6 years.

BOURGNEUF-VAYRON (POMEROL)* *

1990	C	87
1989	C	84
1988	C	82

The 1988 lacks the fruit and heady qualities of the 1989 Bourgneuf-Vayron, but it is a respectable, straightforward, medium-bodied Pomerol for drinking over the next 5–7 years. Bourgneuf's 1989 is a chunky, ripe, foursquare style of wine that has abundant quantities of fruit, good body, and soft tannins in its alcoholic finish. **Anticipated maturity: Now–1998.** With a deep ruby color and a huge plummy, spicy bouquet that borders on overripeness, the lush, rich, chewy-textured 1990 is the most impressive Bourgneuf in years. **Anticipated maturity: Now–2002.**

BOUSCAUT (GRAVES)* *

1990	C	78
1989	C	82
1988	C	83

The 1988 Bouscaut is a spicy, well-made, medium-bodied wine that is ideal for drinking over the next 5–6 years. The 1989 Bouscaut is similar to the 1988—light, medium bodied, and correct—but it has more alcohol, extremely high tannins that appear excessive for its straightforward, fruity personality, and a great deal of oak. If it fills out and develops a midpalate (unlikely), this offering may merit a higher score. **Anticipated maturity: Now–1998.** Deep in color, with an appealing smoky, oaky, ripe berry–scented nose, the 1990 Bouscaut possesses less substance and aging potential.

BOYD-CANTENAC (MARGAUX)* * *

1990	C	86
1989	C	86

The 1989 Boyd-Cantenac is a thick, unctuous, heavyweight wine, low in acidity but enormously rich, fruity, and full. It has high alcohol and plenty of tannin, so it should age well yet be drinkable early. **Anticipated maturity: Now–2003.** A successful wine, the 1990 exhibits an impressive deep black/ruby color; a spicy, rich, jammy nose; ripe, rich flavors; medium to full body; and plenty of tannin in the low acid finish. **Anticipated maturity: 1996–2008.**

BRANAIRE-DUCRU (ST.-JULIEN)* * *

1990	C	88
1989	C	91
1988	C	81

The 1988 Branaire is light, angular, and pleasant, but one-dimensional. Drink this acceptable claret between now and 1998. Reminiscent of the 1982, the 1989 has a forward, expansive bouquet of ripe plums and minerals that leaps from the glass. In the mouth the wine is pure silk. Luscious to the point of opulence, this medium-bodied wine is bursting with chocolatey, blackcurrant fruit. Aging in oak casks has given it the definition it needed, as well as some tannic firmness, but this is a lusty Branaire to consume early. **Anticipated maturity: Now–2005.** What I enjoy so much about the 1990 is its open-knit, fragrant nose of chocolate, raspberries, vanillin, and toast. Although similar to the 1989—plump, expansive, and round, with no rough edges—it does not possess as much concentration and length. **Anticipated maturity: 1994–2005.**
PAST GLORIES: 1982 (91), 1975 (92)

BRANE-CANTENAC (MARGAUX)* * *

1989	D	88
1988	C	77

Dark ruby-colored, the 1988 is intensely herbaceous, suggesting that the Cabernet Sauvignon was harvested too early. Medium bodied and lacking concentration and class, it is another undistinguished effort from this perennial underachiever. Drink it over the next 3–4 years. I found the 1989 Brane-Cantenac to be similar to its 1982, only higher in alcohol and lower in acidity, with a loosely structured yet powerful, concentrated, fruity taste. Lots of new oak has given the wine much needed form and focus. Although lacking in finesse, this wine offers a big, succulent mouthful of juicy fruit along with a blast of alcohol in the finish. **Anticipated maturity: Now–2004.**

LA CABANNE (POMEROL)* *

1990	C	84
1989	C	84
1988	C	82

La Cabanne tends to produce ready-to-drink, easygoing, lighter-style Pomerols. The 1988 La Cabanne is a light, oaky wine with a sound, unexciting character. Drink it over the next 3–5 years. Because of the vintage, the 1989 carries more fruit, alcohol, and tannin than usual. Exhibiting some toasty new oak scents and a good dark ruby color, this generously fruity, soft, medium-bodied Pomerol should drink well young. **Anticipated maturity: Now–1997.** The sweet, fruity, oaky aromas of the 1990 are followed by a wine with good depth, soft texture and an adequate finish. **Anticipated maturity: Now–2000.**

CADET-PIOLA (ST.-ÉMILION)* * *

1990	C	87
1989	D	87
1988	C	86

Typically, the 1988 Cadet-Piola possesses excruciatingly high tannin levels, but the big, rich, black cherry flavors intertwined with new oak, scents of chocolate, and Provençal herbs gives me some basis for saying that the wine has the requisite depth to stand up to the tannin. Medium to full bodied, it should age well for up to two decades. **Anticipated maturity: 1995–2010.** The 1989 is an impressive wine with a thick black/ruby color. The nose is closed, but on the palate the wine is an overwhelmingly muscular, hard, tough-textured, tannic behemoth that needs at least 7–10 years of cellaring. The muscular, backward style is typical of Cadet-Piola. **Anticipated maturity: 1996–2010.** The 1990 is a classic Cadet-Piola—highly structured, deep in color, forbiddingly backward, and nearly impenetrable. Black/ruby/purple-colored, extremely tannic and hard, it appears to possess the requisite concentration to balance out its tough personality. This is not a wine for those who lack patience. **Anticipated maturity: 1997–2010.**

CALON-SÉGUR (ST.-ESTÈPHE)* * */* * * *

1990	D	90
1989	D	89
1988	C	91

The 1988 Calon-Ségur outshines both the 1990 and the 1989. Deeply colored, superbly balanced, rich, and full bodied, it appears to be a worthy candidate for 20–25 years of longevity. A classic example of this château's wine, it is surprisingly powerful for the vintage. **Anticipated maturity: 1998–2020.** This property has turned in a distinguished effort in 1989. It has an impressive deep ruby color, a sweet, chewy, dense texture, full body, plenty of alcohol, and gobs of soft tannins. Quite precocious, it will have a life span of at least 15 years. **Anticipated maturity: 1996–2010.** The 1990 has put on weight since I last tasted it. Dark ruby-colored, with a fragrant bouquet of spicy, oaky, cherry, and herblike fruit, this is an admirably concentrated, surprisingly approachable, extremely well-balanced wine with great depth and purity of fruit. **Anticipated maturity: 1995–2010.**

PAST GLORIES: 1986 (89), 1982 (92), 1953 (92), 1949 (95), 1947 (94), 1945 (92), 1928 (94)

PAST MEDIOCRITIES . . . OR WORSE: 1970 (80), 1964 (75), 1961 (83)

CAMENSAC (HAUT-MÉDOC)* *

1990	B	?
1989	B	?

A damp, cardboard smell is apparent in both the 1989 and 1990. This component makes judgment impossible.

CANON (CANON-FRONSAC)* * *

1990	B	89
1989	B	87

The 1989 Canon exhibits a big, jammy, sweet, herb, leather, and fruity nose. In the mouth the wine is long, intense, expansively flavored, wonderfully pure, and well focused with considerable concentration and depth. It should last for at least 10–15 more years. The impressive 1990 displays a deep, dark ruby color, and the nose offers up aromas of roasted nuts, black fruits, and herbs. In the mouth the wine is full bodied, rich, concentrated, and tannic. It is easily a candidate for 12–20 years of cellaring. I would not want to touch a bottle for another 4–5 years.

CANON (ST.-ÉMILION)* * * * *

1990	D	88
1989	D	92
1988	D	87

The 1988's deep ruby/purple color is impressive, and the spicy, mineral-, tar-, and cassis-scented bouquet is captivating. Although there is an elevated level of tannins, this wine possesses excellent concentration, plenty of length, and a sense that the yields were conservative, as there is good inner strength and depth. This is a less generous style of Canon, but it should age well for two or more decades. **Anticipated maturity: 1996–2012.** The 1989 is deep ruby/purple in color, with a rich, spicy, new oaky, blackcurrant bouquet of moderate intensity. This full-bodied, rather burgundian-textured wine is tannic and deeply endowed. **Anticipated maturity: Now–2008.** The 1990 is not up to the quality of the 1989. Powerful and backward, it displays astringent tannins and a tough-textured personality. Offering a bouquet of black raspberry fruit intertwined with aromas and flavors of coffee and chocolate, this tannic, medium-bodied wine will require considerable patience. **Anticipated maturity: 2000–2025.**
PAST GLORIES: 1986 (91), 1985 (90), 1983 (89-T), 1982 (93), 1961 (88), 1955 (88)
PAST MEDIOCRITIES . . . OR WORSE: 1975 (65), 1970 (84)

CANON DE BREM (CANON-FRONSAC)* * *

1990	B	89
1989	B	87

An impressive effort, the well-structured, medium- to full-bodied, concentrated 1989 displays an opulent nose of black cherries, herbs, and earth. Concentration, moderate tannins, and a long finish are present in the mouth. Drink it over the next 12–15 years. The perfumed, large-scale, forceful 1990 has superb depth, terrific richness, a sense of elegance a robust personality, deep, chewy flavors, and copious amounts of sweet tannin in the finish. Drink it between 1996 and 2005. A sleeper!

CANON-LA-GAFFELIÈRE (ST.-ÉMILION)* * * *

1990	C	93
1989	C	89
1988	C	90

This splendidly perfumed 1988 offers up a veritable smorgasbord of aromas, ranging from smoky, toasty, new oak, to jammy blackcurrants and Oriental spices. In the mouth it is full bodied, seductively round, expansively flavored, with a luscious and velvety finish. This gorgeously made, highly extracted wine should drink well for the next 8–10 years. **Anticipated maturity: Now–2004.** The 1989 is an aggressively powerful, extremely alcoholic, rich, broadly flavored, oaky wine that will probably need to be drunk within its first 10–15 years of life. Its high alcohol, high tannins, yet extremely low acidity give it a seductive, precocious feel in the mouth now, but the tannins and the heady alcohol content should allow it to age well. **Anticipated maturity: Now–2002.** The fabulous 1990 is a more classically structured and balanced wine. The color is an impressive dark ruby/purple, and the bouquet, while reticent, offers up aromas of herbs, sweet black fruits, and smoky oak. In the mouth there is thrilling density, a backward, deep, concentrated, well-structured feel, and plenty of length and extract. This is another great wine from this up-and-coming estate. **Anticipated maturity: 1995–2010.**

CANON-MOUEIX (CANON-FRONSAC)* * *

1990	C	89

More forward and slightly less tannic than Canon, this is a rich, impressively constituted wine with oodles of unctuous black cherry fruit wrapped nicely by spicy oak. Full bodied yet supple, this wine should be consumed over the next 8–10 years. Another very impressive 1990 from Canon-Fronsac!

CANTEMERLE (MACAU)* * *

1990	C	86
1989	C	91
1988	C	86

The 1988 Cantemerle possesses adequate hard, dry tannins, but unlike many Médocs, there is sufficient fruit. The classy bouquet of black fruits, minerals, and spices is hard to resist. Medium bodied and elegant, with plummy, mineral, and herb flavors, this stylish wine should be at its best between now and the end of the century. I believe the 1989 Cantemerle is this estate's finest wine since its monumental 1953. This ruby/purple wine has an explosive bouquet of crushed blackberry fruit and violets and an opulent, lush texture bolstered by good alcohol levels and soft tannins. **Anticipated maturity: 1994–2010.** The 1990 offers soft, seductive, fragrant aromas that are obvious and pleasing. This medium-bodied wine, with lush fruit, soft tannins, low acidity, and a charming finish, is already drinking well. **Anticipated maturity: Now–1999.**

PAST GLORIES: 1983 (91), 1961 (90), 1959 (89), 1953 (94)
PAST MEDIOCRITIES . . . OR WORSE: 1986 (82), 1975 (84)

CANTENAC-BROWN (MARGAUX)* * *

1990	C	87
1989	C	85?
1988	C	82

The 1988 Cantenac-Brown is attenuated, with an elevated level of tannin. This spicy, medium-bodied wine is well made, but it is not as impressive as I originally believed. **Anticipated maturity: Now–2000.** For those who like an affable style of wine that is easy to drink, the 1989 offers generous amounts of soft, easygoing blackcurrant fruit, medium body, some hollowness, and a smooth finish. It is deceptively easy to drink, but essentially unexciting. **Anticipated maturity: Now–2001.** Slightly more structured and richer than the 1989, the opulent 1990 may lack some comlexity, but it offers gobs of rich, expansive, concentrated fruit in a full-bodied format. I especially admire the big, dramatic bouquet of smoke and cassis. **Anticipated maturity: Now–2003.**

CAP-DE-MOURLIN (ST.-ÉMILION)* * *

1990	B	87
1989	C	86
1988	B	85

Cap-de-Mourlin's 1988 has a lean, toughly knit texture. The tannins are high, but the wine is concentrated. **Anticipated maturity: Now–2004.** The 1989 exhibits plenty of toasty, smoky, new oak and is full bodied, with high alcohol, low acidity, and a rich, jammy, long finish. The abundant tannins are soft. **Anticipated maturity: Now–2006.** If you are looking for a light wine with elegance and finesse, the blockbuster 1990 should be avoided. It is a big, beefy, rustic wine with more than enough tannin to ensure a decade's worth of aging potential. The tannin is adequately balanced by copious quantities of fat cassis fruit, sweet oak, and gobs of glycerin and alcohol. **Anticipated maturity: 1994–2003.**

CARBONNIEUX (GRAVES)* *

1990	C	85
1989	C	83
1988	B	83

The 1988 Carbonnieux is an elegant, lighter-style wine displaying charm, medium body, sweet strawberry fruit, and plenty of oak. It is not a big wine, but it is stylish, flavorful, and graceful. Drink it over the next 6–7 years. The 1989 is straightforward, pleasant, oaky, medium bodied, and tannic. It is a serviceable, attractively fruity, middle-weight wine, but not distinguished. **Anticipated maturity: Now–2000.** As for the 1990, behind the intensely oaky nose there appears to be good extract; a forward, even flattering personality; and a charming, moderately endowed finish.

DE CARLES (FRONSAC)* * *

1990	B	86
1989	B	86

The 1989 reveals an attractive deep ruby color as well as a spicy, beautifully scented nose of black cherries, herbs, and minerals. In the mouth there are smooth, elegant, concentrated flavors, medium body, and a fleshy, round, gentle finish. Drink it over the next 6–7 years. The 1990 possesses an impressive deep, relatively opaque color, and the nose offers up rustic aromas of black fruits and leather. This low-acid, fat-textured wine is loaded with glycerin and fruit. **Anticipated maturity: Now–2000.**

LES CARMES-HAUT-BRION (GRAVES)* * *

1990	C	86
1989	C	86
1988	C	87

This obscure but interesting property in the suburb of Pessac, not far from Haut-Brion, produces excellent wines that deserve a greater following. The 1988 Les Carmes-Haut-Brion has a big, smoky, hickory- and plum-scented bouquet; concentrated, soft, but structured flavors; and a long finish. An attractive textbook Graves with the characteristic cigar-box, mineral-scented aromas and flavors, it should be drunk over the next 4–6 years. The smoky, tobacco, minerallike bouquet of the 1989 is enticing. The palate reveals a ripe, roasted, open-knit fruitiness with a finish that is alcoholic and soft. **Anticipated maturity: Now–1997.** The 1990 reveals a classic Graves nose of sweet, weedy tobacco, roasted black fruits, and minerals. In the mouth it is medium bodied, spicy, and rich, with adequate structure and a smooth, luscious texture. Drink it over the next 10–12 years.

CARRUADES DE LAFITE (PAUILLAC)* *

1990	C	86
1989	C	85
1988	C	86

Well made and actually more complete and deeper than both the 1989 and 1990, the 1988 shares some of the classic lead-pencil, mineral, curranty character that is evidenced in the "grand vin." Spicy and tannic, with fine depth, this wine should evolve well for 7–10 years. I lament the fact that few "second" wines actually resemble their more esteemed siblings. Why? As severe as the selection can be for the grand vin, little selection is employed for most second wines, as diluted *cuvées*, young vines, and whatever is tossed into these blends. With that warning in mind, the 1989 is a *deuxième* wine that displays some of Lafite's personality. The vanillin, smoky, lead-pencil nose is unmistakable. In the mouth there is real focus, character, and elegance. This tasty Lafite lookalike will drink handsomely for 6–12 or more years. The 1990 offers soft, spicy, cedary, lead-pencil-scented fruit that is followed by a medium-bodied, spicy wine with good character, depth, and light tannins in a surprisingly long finish. It should drink nicely for 7–8 years.

CASSAGNE-HAUT-CANON-LA-TRUFFIÈRE (CANON-FRONSAC)* * *

1990	B	82
1989	B	90

The black-colored 1989 exhibits exceptional concentration, a wonderfully pure, vivid nose of jammy cassis, spicy new oak, herbs, and licorice. There is an expansive, sweet richness, superstuffing, and delineation to the wine's flavors, as well as a long, intense, beautifully structured, opulent finish. This is a stunning wine! **Anticipated maturity: 1995–2005.** The 1990 Cassagne-Haut-Canon-La-Truffière exhibits a dense, almost black color, as well as huge tannins that appear astringent and rough. The wine finishes slightly hollow and tough.

CERTAN-GIRAUD (POMEROL)* * *

1990	D	87
1989	D	87
1988	D	85

This fine, although somewhat schizophrenic (consistently inconsistent) estate tends to harvest late, thus producing jammy, alcoholic wines. Ripe, medium bodied, fleshy, but simple, Certan-Giraud's 1988 is an attractive wine that should provide tasty drinking over the next 3–6 years. The 1989 looks much better. Black/ruby in color, with an intoxicatingly intense nose of cassis, this velvety, large-scale, rich, alcoholic wine has low acidity but high tannins. **Anticipated maturity: Now–2001.** The 1990, rather diffuse and fruity from the barrel, is markedly more impressive from the bottle. Rich, dense, and well endowed, it is an opulent, chewy, loaded wine that reminds me of the 1982. Consume it over the next 10–12 years.

CERTAN DE MAY (POMEROL)* * * * *

1990	EE	92
1989	EE	87
1988	EE	93

The 1988's dark ruby/purple color is thick and opaque (in contrast with the relatively translucent 1989). What first overwhelms the taster is the spectacular spicy, cedary, toasty, black raspberry fragrance. The wine has that exotic, kinky, irresistible grilled or smoked meat character in the nose. This wine is crammed with black fruits that exhibit a subtle herbaceous quality. The 1988 has superb extraction of fruit, is full bodied, and is a rich, classic Pomerol. **Anticipated maturity: 1994–2010.** The 1989 is excellent, more loosely knit than usual, with an herbaceous, cassis, smoky, roasted bouquet. Although the wine exhibits plenty of extraction, it falls short of the quality of this property's wines in years such as 1982, 1985, 1986, and 1988. It has put on weight in the cask, but I doubt that it will ultimately be outstanding. **Anticipated maturity: 1994–2006.** The full-bodied 1990 exhibits a distinctive nose that offers huge, herbaceous, cassis scents intertwined with aromas of roasted nuts and peanut butter. This dense, concentrated wine reveals super extraction, soft tannins, and a voluptuous, even thick finish. **Anticipated maturity: 1995–2010.**

PAST GLORIES: 1986 (92), 1985 (94), 1982 (98), 1981 (90), 1979 (92)

CHAMBERT-MARBUZET (ST.-ESTÈPHE)* * *

1990	C	89
1989	C	86
1988	B	83

Abnormally light, fragrant, and evolved, the 1988 is surprisingly shy and subdued. It should be drunk up. The 1989 Chambert-Marbuzet exhibits plenty of toasty new oak, has an exotic bouquet of black fruits and spices, is exuberantly fruity, soft, and medium bodied, and finishes with a whopping blow of alcohol and smooth tannins. It is flashy but lacking some substance in the midpalate. Drink it over the next 6–7 years. **Anticipated maturity: Now–1995.** Richly oaky and very spicy, the fleshy 1990 is oozing with ripe fruit. Authoritatively flavored and full bodied, this is the finest Chambert-Marbuzet yet made. It will offer sensual drinking for another 5–9 years.

CHANTEGRIVE (GRAVES)* * *

1990	C	85
1989	C	85
1990 Cuvée Edouard	C	86
1988 Cuvée Edouard	C	85

This well-run property has turned out a ripe, perfumed, tasty, medium-bodied 1988 Cuvée Edouard that is fully mature. The nose and flavors of smoked nuts, tobacco, and red fruits is a delight. **Anticipated maturity: Now–1995.** As for the 1989, a big, pruny, plummy, spicy nose is followed by a light- to medium-bodied wine with luscious fruit and some shortness in the finish. Overall it is a pleasing wine that should make for pleasant drinking over the next 2–3 years. With respect to the 1990, vanillin aromas from new oak are followed by a richly fruity, medium-bodied, nicely concentrated, low-acid wine that is delicious for drinking over the next 5–6 years. The 1990 Cuvée Edouard is enhanced by more obvious toasty new oak and sweeter, riper fruit. The tannins are more present, and although this wine is drinkable now, it should age well for 7–8 years.

CHASSE-SPLEEN (MOULIS)* * */* * * *

1990	C	88
1989	C	91
1988	C	86

Chasse-Spleen made a good, elegant 1988. Displaying a generous, intense, smoky, blackcurrant bouquet and chewy, medium-bodied flavors, it has a surprisingly long, spicy, soft finish. **Anticipated maturity: Now–2001.** Make no mistake about it, the 1989 Chasse-Spleen is the finest wine this property has produced since its great 1949. This is a spectacularly rich, powerful, authoritative example of the vintage that can compete with and even surpass

many of the most famous names. Layer upon layer of concentrated, sweet, expansive, blackcurrant fruit is wrapped in a frame of toasty new oak and decent acidity. An awesome wine! **Anticipated maturity: 1996–2015.** The 1990 has evolved well and is displaying far greater intensity, medium to full body, herb- and black cherry–scented flavors, soft tannins, and good ripeness and richness. It is not as superconcentrated as the brilliant 1989, but it is an immensely attractive, well-made wine. Drink it over the next decade.
PAST GLORIES: 1986 (90), 1985 (90), 1975 (90), 1970 (90), 1949 (92)

CHAUVIN (ST.-ÉMILION)* * *

1990	C	88
1989	C	86
1988	C	84

Medium-dark ruby, with a spicy, plum-, and subtle herb-scented bouquet, the medium-bodied 1988 Chauvin has good extracted flavor, a nice, spicy, vanillin oakiness, and tightly knit flavors. **Anticipated maturity: Now–2002.** In 1989, for the first time, the renowned Libourne oenologist, Michel Rolland, had full charge of overseeing the winemaking. The result is a broad-flavored, hedonistic, concentrated, deeply extracted, luscious wine. **Anticipated maturity: Now–1996.** The explosively rich, fruity, unctuous 1990 exhibits plenty of velvety, smooth tannins, excellent concentration, and medium to full body. This admirably endowed, opulent, sumptuous Chauvin is the finest wine made at this estate in decades. **Anticipated maturity: Now–2005.**

CHEVAL BLANC (ST.-ÉMILION)* * * * *

1990	EE	95
1989	EE	89
1988	EE	88

The 1988 Cheval Blanc exhibits fine ripeness and a cool, almost menthol, plummy bouquet intertwined with aromas of smoke, tobacco, and new oak. In the mouth there are some aggressive tannins, but the wine does not possess the depth one expects from renowned estates. It is a very good Cheval Blanc, but I had expected more. **Anticipated maturity: Now–2002.** The 1989 is an excellent wine, but, again, I had expected more power, depth, and intensity. The big, exotic, precocious, forward bouquet displays aromas of herbs, tobacco, sweet blackcurrants, mint, and the telltale smoky character that sets Cheval Blanc apart. The wine tastes like candy, given its expansive, sweet palate impression. There is excellent depth, but a surprisingly quick finish. **Anticipated maturity: Now–2005.** Will the 1990 turn out to be a replay of Cheval Blanc's glorious 1983? It appears to be the most complete Cheval produced since their historic duo of 1982 and 1983. Richer and longer in the mouth than the lightish 1988, and significantly deeper and more complete than the 1989, the 1990 exhibits deeper color than recent vintages of Cheval, as well as a profound menthol aroma intermingled with scents of truffles, mocha, toast, and sweet black fruits. This expansive, typical, exotic example of Cheval Blanc is captivating because of its opulence and rich, velvety finish. It already provides immense pleasure. An attention grabber! **Anticipated maturity: Now–2010.**

PAST GLORIES: 1986 (93), 1985 (94), 1983 (95), 1982 (100), 1981 (89), 1975 (90), 1961 (93), 1955 (90), 1953 (94), 1949 (100), 1948 (96), 1947 (100), 1945 (91)
PAST MEDIOCRITIES . . . OR WORSE: 1971 (84), 1970 (85), 1966 (85)

DOMAINE DE CHEVALIER (GRAVES)* * * * *

1990	D	90
1989	D	91
1988	D	90

Domaine de Chevalier produced one of the finest wines of this vintage in 1988. Dark ruby, with an unevolved but generous bouquet of smoky new oak, cassis, and flowers, this fleshy, generously endowed wine is the finest effort from this property since their 1983. **Anticipated maturity: 1995–2008.** Domaine de Chevalier has called its 1989 comparable to the 1970, 1961, and 1945. A densely concentrated, tannic, medium-bodied, rich, and stylish wine, it is loaded with toasty, vanillin scents and flavors. **Anticipated maturity: 1996–2015.** Although this is a difficult wine to effectively evaluate young, I am confident that the 1990 has fine depth and intensity. It is oaky, with plenty of structure, excellent depth, and an extremely long, rich finish. Given its elevated level of both new oak and tannins, it will need some time in the cellar. At this stage it reminds me of the stylish yet rich 1983. **Anticipated maturity: 1997–2008.**
PAST GLORIES: 1986 (90), 1983 (90), 1978 (92), 1970 (89), 1964 (90), 1959 (89), 1953 (92)
PAST MEDIOCRITIES . . . OR WORSE: 1982 (67?), 1975 (68), 1971 (67)

CISSAC (HAUT-MÉDOC)* *

1990	B	79
1989	B	82

Though the 1989 Cissac is a nicely extracted wine, with good ripe fruit and some of the opulence so prevalent in this vintage, it is oaky. If the oak becomes less noticeable, do not be surprised to see this wine merit a higher score. Tough, hard tannins almost overwhelm the 1990's narrow, medium-bodied fruitiness. Despite the good spice and ripeness, this is an austerely styled wine.

CITRAN (HAUT-MÉDOC)* * *

1989	C	88
1988	B	86

Starting with the 1988 vintage, Citran has established itself as one of the stars among the Médoc Crus Bourgeois. Dark ruby/purple, with a smoky, roasted bouquet of cassis and lavish amounts of new oak, this cunningly made, ripe, overtly commercial wine will prove to be a crowd pleaser because of its direct, forward, plump character. **Anticipated maturity: Now–1996.** The 1989 is terrific. Purple-colored, with a huge nose of cassis, licorice, and smoky oak, this fleshy, huge wine is loaded with fruit, glycerin, and tannin. It should drink beautifully for 10–12 years.

CLERC-MILON (PAUILLAC)* * *

1990	C	86
1989	D	90
1988	D	89

The 1988 is deep in color, with a moderately intense bouquet of herbs, smoke, and blackcurrants. The hardness it revealed when it was young has melted away, and at present, a rich, creamy texture offers up considerable roasted fruit flavors complemented by lavish amounts of oak. The 1989 Clerc-Milon is a wonderfully hedonistic wine. Deep ruby, with an intense, roasted, smoky bouquet of plums and currants, this full-bodied wine is packed with fruit, chewy and opulent as well as soft and alcoholic. This sensually styled wine should be at its best between 1993 and 2010. Not as concentrated, opulent, and velvety as the 1989, the 1990 is still a sexy and smooth wine, with a fragrant nose of cassis, smoke, vanillin, roasted nuts, and exotic scents. This luscious wine, with a creamy texture and excellent color, falls off on the palate, much like its siblings, d'Armailhac and Mouton-Rothschild. It should offer delicious drinking for another 8–10 years.

CLINET (POMEROL)* * * * *

1990	E	92
1989	EE	99
1988	D	90

The 1988 is a dazzling example of Clinet. Its color is a deep black/purple, and the bouquet exhibits the classic Pomerol scents of truffles, plums, subtle herbs, and new oak. The wine has extraordinary extraction of fruit and a full-bodied, tannic finish. **Anticipated maturity: Now–2010.** The black/purple-colored 1989 is one of the blockbusters of the vintage. The bouquet gushes with aromas of black raspberries, licorice, chocolate, and minerals. In the mouth the weight, concentration, and highly extracted style have resulted in a massive wine with a whopping finish. **Anticipated maturity: 1995–2015.** The 1990's opaque, dark ruby/purple color and spicy, oaky, floral-, licorice-, black raspberry–scented nose are top flight. There is fine ripeness, medium to full body, a sense of elegance. An impressively pure, rich, authoritative example of Clinet, it is less massive yet more elegant than the 1989. **Anticipated maturity: 1995–2005.**
PAST MEDIOCRITIES . . . OR WORSE: Anything prior to 1985 should be approached with considerable caution

CLOS DU CLOCHER (POMEROL)* * *

1990	D	87
1989	D	88
1988	C	85

The 1988 is a ripe, fleshy, chewy wine with some oak in evidence. Those looking for a forward, plump style of Pomerol should check it out. **Anticipated maturity: Now–1999.** The 1989 Clos du Clocher is the finest example of this property's wines I have tasted. It offers a deep purple/ruby color, with a penetrating blackberry and vanillin fragrance. Highly extracted fruit is buttressed by supporting tannins, yet the acidity is low. This concentrated wine will provide impressive drinking early but should have the potential to last for 10–12 years. Although one might quibble over the 1990's loose-knit structure and limited aging potential, there is no doubting the impressive color; big, deep, rich, chewy, chocolatey, herb, and cassis flavors; and lusty, heady, pleasing finish. Drink this beauty over the next 7–9 years. It makes for quite an unctuous, heady mouthful of wine.

CLOS L'ÉGLISE (POMEROL)* *

1990	D	87
1989	D	76
1988	D	72

The 1988, which is similar to the 1989 but with less alcohol and body, should be consumed over the next 4–5 years. The 1989 is light, intensely herbaceous, and short on the palate. **Anticipated maturity: Now–1999.** The 1990 is the best wine in years from this estate. It exhibits an excellent bouquet of cassis, spicy new oak, and subtle herbs. In the mouth it is medium bodied, with an attractive ripeness, elegance, and a fleshy, surprisingly rich, long finish. Drink it over the next 7–10 years.

CLOS FOURTET (ST.-ÉMILION)* * *

1990	C	90
1989	C	86
1988	C	79

The 1988's fruit has faded, and the tannins have become hard, lean, and aggressive. The 1989 is an alcoholic, exuberantly styled, easy-to-drink wine, but its lack of grip, definition, and tannin may give some concern. **Anticipated maturity: Now–1998.** The 1990 is shaping up as the finest effort in decades from this well-known producer. It reveals an impressively deep black/ruby color and a dramatic nose of black fruits, smoke, roasted nuts, flowers, and herbs. Medium to full bodied, with a succulent texture and impressive concentration, this tannic and structured Clos Fourtet has a heady, concentrated, multidimensional finish. Bravo! **Anticipated maturity: 1995–2010.**

CLOS DES JACOBINS (ST.-ÉMILION)* * *

1990	D	86
1989	D	86
1988	C	89

The 1988 Clos des Jacobins is a beautifully made, deep ruby-colored wine, with a bouquet of spring flowers, olives, smoky blackcurrants, and licorice. In the mouth there is plenty of rich, concentrated, opulent fruit, modest tannins, and good length. I prefer it to the 1989. **Anticipated maturity: Now–2003.** The 1989 exhibits a smooth, lush texture, abundant ripeness, and a short finish. Because of the high alcohol and low acidity, this wine must be drunk young. **Anticipated maturity: Now–2000.** A rival to the fleshy 1989, the

1990 exhibits soft tannins; a big, herb- and blackberry-scented nose; fat, luscious flavors; low acidity; and plenty of length and fruit that conceal the tannins. **Anticipated maturity: Now–2002.**

CLOS DU MARQUIS (ST.-JULIEN)* * *

1990	C	88
1989	C	88
1988	C	85

The second wine of Léoville-Las Cases, the 1988 Clos du Marquis has good fruit, a spicy, oaky character, medium body, and a fine core of black cherry fruit. Firm and capable of supporting 8–10 years of cellaring, it is a good effort, but the 1989 and 1990 are superior. The 1989's complex bouquet of toasty new oak and cassis is followed by a surprisingly rich, deep, well-built wine that resembles the great Léoville-Las Cases. This beauty will support considerable cellaring. If you can neither afford Léoville-Las Cases nor wait for it to lose all its tannins, consider this offering from Clos du Marquis. **Anticipated maturity: Now–2005.** The 1990 is equal to the 1989. The saturated color, intense black cherry, oaky nose, and dense, rich, medium- to full-bodied flavors reveal fine concentration and balance. Drink it over the next 5–12 years.

CLOS DE L'ORATOIRE (ST.-ÉMILION)* * *

1990	C	88

An impressive wine, this sleeper of the vintage has an opaque, deep ruby/purple color, a jammy nose of superripe fruit and oak, and a full-bodied, intensely flavored taste. This big wine should develop more finesse and age gracefully for 10–15 years.

CLOS RENÉ (POMEROL)* * *

1990	C	88
1989	C	85
1988	C	86

The 1988 Clos René, which has more tannin than the 1989, as well as more structure, is a rich, complete wine. **Anticipated maturity: Now–1999.** Clos René's 1989 reveals an alluring bouquet of superripe, almost sweet, jammy, cassis fruit. In the mouth the pleasant impression is dampened by a wine that is slightly light, alcoholic, soft, and fruity. **Anticipated maturity: Now–1996.** As for the 1990, superripe aromas of prunes and plums are followed by a meaty, full-throttle style of wine with considerable power, low acidity, fleshy fruit, and a smooth-as-silk texture. It is the most impressive Clos René in years. Drink it over the next 10–15 years.

CLOS SAINT-MARTIN (ST.-ÉMILION)* * *

1990	C	89
1989	C	86
1988	C	86

This tiny estate is beginning to make much better wines. The intense bouquet of herbs, black fruits, spices, and new oak offered in the 1988, is followed by a rich, supple, generously endowed wine that adroitly marries power with finesse. **Anticipated maturity: Now–1997.** As for the 1989, there are enough ripe tannins to warrant aging for 10–15 years, but considering this wine's harmony and luscious richness on the palate, most readers will probably prefer to drink it in its first decade of life. **Anticipated maturity: Now–2002.** Dark in color, with a pure as well as dramatic bouquet, the 1990 displays massive extraction of fruit, full body, deep, multidimensional flavors, and a long, spicy finish. The considerable depth of fruit nearly obscures the significant tannins. **Anticipated maturity: 1995–2010.**

LA CLOTTE (ST.-ÉMILION)* * *

1990	C	89

On the rare occasions I get to taste this wine, I am always impressed by its opulence and character. The 1990 is a knockout. The seductive nose of jammy, berry fruit, herbs, and vanillin grabbed my attention. Superconcentrated, with layer upon layer of fruit, this multidimensional wine is loaded! Drink it over the next decade.

LA CLUSIÈRE (ST.-ÉMILION)* *

1990	C	89
1989	C	77?
1988	C	79

Although the 1988 is slightly better than the 1989, it is still overwhelmingly tannic and mean-spirited, with an aggressive nature to its tannins that seems to obliterate any charm. The 1989's alcohol level is high, and the green, harsh, unripe tannins suggest that the grapes may have been analytically but not physiologically mature. It is a sinewy, charmless wine. In total contrast, the 1990 is the most impressive La Clusière that I have tasted. Deep ruby-colored, with a bouquet that soars from the glass with scents of ripe raspberries and vanillin, this opulent wine offers layers of rich, sweet fruit, loads of glycerin, and a long, velvety finish. It is already delicious, but the necessary depth and balance are present for another 10–12 years of evolution.

COLOMBIER-MONPELOU (PAUILLAC)* *

1990	C	81
1989	C	78
1988	B	78

The 1988 Colombier-Monpelou possessed a very oaky nose, but not enough depth or body to warrant interest. From cask, the 1989 Colombier-Monpelou exhibited meager flavors and a light, washed-out character. Although the wine now tastes better, it is clearly made in a fruity, soft, forward style. The 1990 is a straightforward, round, commercial, soft, fruity wine with decent concentration, but no great complexity or depth, and a short finish. Drink it over the next 4–6 years.

LA COMMANDERIE (ST.-ESTÈPHE)* *

1990	C	85

The 1990 exhibits high alcohol, plummy, black fruits, and a silky style. Drink it over the next 5–7 years.

LA CONSEILLANTE (POMEROL)* * * * *

1990	EE	98
1989	EE	97
1988	D	86

La Conseillante's 1988 suffers in comparison with the 1989 and 1990, but it is a fleshy, soft, charming, velvety-textured, medium-bodied wine for drinking over the next 7–9 years. **Anticipated maturity: Now–1999.** The 1989 and the 1990 are this property's greatest efforts since its 1949. The 1989's awesome bouquet of plums, exotic spices, and vanillin is followed by a wine that has brilliant definition and remarkable freshness and depth of fruit, as well as grace and elegance. Fabulously long, pure, sweet, and expansive, with an explosive finish, this wine should be at its best between 1996 and 2015. It was aged in 100% new oak because of its richness. **Anticipated maturity: 1996–2010.** How much fun millionaires will have debating the virtues of the 1989 versus the 1990 La Conseillante! Deep ruby/purple, with a sexy nose of exotic spices, sweet black fruits, and new oak, the 1990 displays La Conseillante's creamy/velvety texture, gobs of rich fruit, exceptional concentration, and a suave, superb finish that goes on and on. It will provide memorable drinking young yet should age beautifully for 20 or more years. A stunning performance, it is even more profound than the dazzling 1989. **Anticipated maturity: 1994–2012.**
PAST GLORIES: 1986 (89), 1985 (94), 1983 (88), 1982 (91), 1981 (91), 1970 (92), 1953 (90), 1949 (94), 1947 (91)
PAST MEDIOCRITIES . . . OR WORSE: 1978 (75), 1976 (72), 1975 (83)

CORBIN (ST.-ÉMILION)* * *

1989	C	87
1988	C	74

The 1988 Corbin is light and diluted, with a weedy, indifferent character. The 1989 has extremely low acidity and soft tannins, but the overall impression is one of power, an opulent, even unctuous texture, and precocious drinkability. If you like this big, overripe, Australian style of wine, and intend to drink it within its first decade of life, it will undoubtedly provide an enticing level of exhilaration. **Anticipated maturity: Now–1997.**

CORBIN-MICHOTTE (ST.-ÉMILION)* * *

1990	D	87
1989	D	86
1988	C	83

Corbin-Michotte's 1988 is a medium-bodied, pleasant, correct wine, with decent acidity and length. Drink it over the next 4–6 years. The 1989, which appears to be a sleeper of the vintage, is vastly superior. It is a black/purple-colored wine, oozing with extract. Full bodied, richly perfumed, with the scent of superripe plums and minerals, it has an alcohol level of nearly 14%, relatively low acidity, but high tannins. It is a decadently rich wine, even for the vintage. **Anticipated maturity: Now–2002.** The 1990 is similar to the 1989. Ripe but slightly deeper, it is a wine to consume over the next 7–8 years.

CORDEILLAN-BAGES (PAUILLAC)* *

1990	C	81
1989	C	84

From a small vineyard adjacent to the luxury hotel in Pauillac of the same name, this medium-bodied 1989 has a light intensity; fruity, spicy nose; lean, compact flavors (young vines?); and a short finish. A pleasant but one-dimensional wine, it should be drunk over the next decade. Soft, fruity, and well made, but lacking personality, grip, concentration, and a finish, the 1990 should be drunk over the next 2–4 years.

CORMEIL-FIGEAC (ST.-ÉMILION)* * *

1990	C	85
1989	C	85
1988	C	81

Medium-deep ruby, with a spicy, herbaceous bouquet, cedary, round flavors, and moderate tannins, the 1988 has medium body, adequate ripeness, and a short finish. **Anticipated maturity: Now–1995.** With respect to the 1989, fleshy, superripe aromas of jammy plums and herbs emerge from the glass. The wine is medium to full bodied, corpulent, and generously endowed, with low acidity and some firm tannins in the finish. **Anticipated maturity: Now–2001.** Although lacking some complexity, the 1990 offers a bouquet filled with gobs of rich, succulent black fruits and herbs, and dense, chunky, chewy, curranty fruit flavors intertwined with the taste of herbs. Not the most complex wine from St.-Émilion in 1990, it is nevertheless an attractive offering. Drink it over the next 7–8 years.

COS D'ESTOURNEL (ST.-ESTÈPHE)* * * * *

1990	D	92
1989	D	89
1988	D	87

Although tannic and austere, the 1988 has an intriguing bouquet of exotic spices and black fruits. It will outlive the 1989. **Anticipated maturity: 2000–2020.** The 1989 is a medium-bodied, rich, concentrated wine displaying an impressive color and a nose of superripe black fruits, toasty oak, and licorice. The finish is long, alcoholic, and lush. There is every possibility that this wine will turn out to be as good as the château's memorable 1953. **Anticipated maturity: Now–2008.** The deep ruby/purple-colored 1990 offers a moderately intense bouquet of pure black raspberry fruit wrapped nicely in toasty new oak. Rich, concentrated, and similar in style to the opulent 1985, this impressively made, well-structured wine should provide fine near-term drinking yet evolve gracefully for several decades. It is obviously richer and longer than the 1989. **Anticipated maturity: 1996–2012.**

PAST GLORIES: 1986 (95), 1985 (95), 1982 (97), 1961 (92), 1959 (92), 1953 (95), 1928 (97)

PAST MEDIOCRITIES . . . OR WORSE: 1975 (77), 1966 (85), 1964 (72)

COS LABORY (ST.-ESTÈPHE)* * *

1990	C	89
1989	C	89
1988	C	84

The 1988 Cos Labory is a pleasant, well-colored, tannic, medium-bodied wine, with fine balance and length. It should provide decent rather than inspired drinking. **Anticipated maturity: Now–2000.** Smart money will go after the 1989 and 1990. The 1989 is black/ruby in color, with a huge bouquet of cassis, layers of extract, a very high tannin level, and a hefty level of alcohol. **Anticipated maturity: 1995–2015.** The 1990 is nearly black in color, with a reticent, spicy, licorice-, mineral-, and cassis-scented nose. In the mouth there is great extraction; rich, full-bodied, chewy texture; and a splendidly long, moderately tannic finish. Bravo! **Anticipated maturity: 1996–2010.**

COUFRAN (HAUT-MÉDOC)* * *

1990	B	86
1989	B	85

Given the opulence of the vintage, I expected more flesh and intensity to the 1989 Coufran. It exhibits structure, deep color, and plenty of depth, but neither the softness nor silky texture I have come to expect. **Anticipated maturity: Now-2000.** Medium bodied and soft in tannins, the plump, sweet, ripe 1990 reveals concentration and a succulent personality. It offers delicious ripe fruit in an easy-to-understand format. Drink it over the next 4–6 years.

COUVENT-DES-JACOBINS (ST.-ÉMILION)* * *

1990	C	85
1989	C	86

The 1989 is a deeply colored, intensely perfumed, full-bodied wine with layers of extract, an unctuous, plummy fatness, high alcohol, and low acidity. **Anticipated maturity: Now–1997.** Jammy, herb, and berry aromas dominate the 1990's spicy bouquet. In the mouth there is fine ripeness, a lush, silky, fruity personality, and a smooth, heady, sweet, but unstructured finish. Although it will not make old bones, the 1990 Couvent-des-Jacobins will provide rewarding drinking early on. **Anticipated maturity: Now–1997.**

LE CROCK (ST.-ESTÈPHE)* *

1990	B	87
1989	B	83
1988	B	82

The 1988 Le Crock is similar in quality to the 1989, but it is totally different in style. Leaner, smaller-scaled, and neither as tannic nor as alcoholic, it should be drunk over the next 5–6 years. The 1989 has more fruit than usual, good ruby color, a blackberry fruitiness, soft texture, medium body, low acidity, but high tannins. It lacks complexity but should offer serviceable drinking over the next 4–5 years. **Anticipated maturity: Now–1996.** Another excellent wine from St.-Estèphe, the 1990 is also the finest Le Crock I have tasted. Deep ruby/purple-colored, with a spicy, rich nose, and dense, muscular, full-bodied flavors, this big wine will age impressively. **Anticipated maturity: 1996–2006.**

LA CROIX (POMEROL)* * *

1990	C	87
1989	C	85
1988	C	82

The 1988 La Croix has a soft, fruity, agreeable character and a round texture. Drink it over the next 2–4 years. The 1989, a rich, unctuous, highly extracted wine, reveals layer upon layer of earthy, spicy fruit, and a long, alcoholic finish. The wine lacks grip and structure, but there is no doubting the overwhelmingly big, intense flavors. A full-throttle, rustic style may not appeal to some tasters. **Anticipated maturity: Now–2005.** The 1990, disappointing from cask, is far more impressive from the bottle. A rich, unctuous wine, with an old-style personality and thick, fruity flavors, this mouth-filling wine will make uncomplex but satisfying drinking over the next 10 years.

LA CROIX DU CASSE (POMEROL)* * *

1990	C	89
1989	D	87
1988	C	86

The 1988 La Croix du Casse exhibits deep, well-endowed, full-bodied, admirably extracted flavors with good tannins, crisp acidity, and a satisfying, moderately long finish. **Anticipated maturity: Now–2000.** The 1989 is a black/ruby/purple color, with a big, rich, expansive bouquet filled with aromas of ripe plums, chocolate, cedar, and toasty new oak. It offers splendid concentration, medium-bodied flavors, and plenty of alcohol and soft tannins in the finish. It should provide delicious drinking over its first decade of life. **Anticipated maturity: Now–1998.** The 1990 is this estate's finest effort to date. It offers deep ruby/black color; an expansive, sweet, cassis-scented nose; soft, luscious, opulent, superbly endowed flavors; super length; low acidity; and a lush as well as long finish. It should be drunk within its first 7–9 years of life.

LA CROIX DE GAY (POMEROL)* * *

1990	D	86
1989	D	87
1988	D	86

The 1988 displays a great deal of new oak, has good concentration, a smooth, velvety, nearly opulent texture, and a sweet, smooth-as-silk finish. **Anticipated maturity: Now–1998.** The 1989 La Croix de Gay is unusually deep, concentrated, and full bodied, with excellent tannin and extract levels. The acidity is low, but the high tannins and elevated alcohol level should allow this wine to age well for 6–15 years. It is the most impressive young La Croix de Gay I have tasted, reflecting this estate's increasing attention to detail and commitment to excellence. **Anticipated maturity: 1995–2005.** Nearly lavish aromas of sweet, toasty, vanillin oak and ripe berry fruit soar from the glass of the seductive 1990. In the mouth one could wish for more depth, but overall this is a richly fruity, soft, elegant, yet still interesting Pomerol that should drink beautifully for another 7–8 years.

CROIZET-BAGES (PAUILLAC)*

1989	C	73
1988	C	74

Life is too short to drink Croizet-Bages. The 1988 Croizet-Bages is straightforward, pleasant, soft, but shallow. **Anticipated maturity: Now–1995.** Unfortunately, insipidness is the rule at this property. How anyone could produce such a light, overtly herbaceous, innocuous wine in 1989 escapes logic. **Anticipated maturity: Now–1997.**

CROQUE-MICHOTTE (ST.-ÉMILION)* * *

1989	D	87
1988	C	85

The 1988 Croque-Michotte has an attractive, spicy, cedary, berry-scented bouquet touched judiciously by toasty, vanillin oak. In the mouth the wine is medium bodied, with decent acidity, moderate tannins, and a generous personality. **Anticipated maturity: Now–2000.** The deep ruby/purple-colored 1989 offers an intense bouquet of jammy cassis, herbs, new oak, and minerals. In the mouth it is explosively fruity, lush, and medium to full bodied, with a great deal of glycerin and an almost thick texture. Drink it over the next 7–8 years. **Anticipated maturity: Now–1998.**

DALEM (FRONSAC)* * *

1990	B	86
1989	B	85

The gentle, round, seductive 1989 offers a spicy, oaky, fruity nose; sweet, generous flavors; medium body; and a silky finish. Drink it over the next 4–5 years. The 1990 exhibits more depth and weight, plenty of sweet, rich cassis fruit, a subtle mineral component, and a medium-bodied, long, soft finish. Drink it over the next 7–8 years.

DASSAULT (ST.-ÉMILION)* * *

1990	C	87
1989	C	84
1988	C	85

Dassault's 1988 displays a ripe, sweet, plummy fruit character and a soft finish, but there is enough tannin to ensure longevity of 6–8 years. This wine would make an excellent choice for restaurants. The 1989 is a loosely structured, grapey, expansively flavored, soft, and alcoholic wine that lacks structure. However, it will offer a deliciously smooth glass of wine if drunk young. **Anticipated maturity: Now–1996.** The 1990 is the strongest effort I can recall from Dassault. A precocious bouquet of sweet, plummy fruit, licorice, and black cherries is followed by a wine bursting with fruit. Drink this succulent, fat, chewy 1990 over the next 7–8 years.

LA DAUPHINE (FRONSAC)* * *

1990	B	88
1989	B	86

Almost burgundian in its superripe nose of prunes, black cherries, and flowers, the 1989 is seductive, with abundant glycerin and alcohol, as well as an element of overripeness. Drink this luscious offering over the next 6–7 years. The predominant aroma of the 1990 is one of sweet, expansive, ripe black fruits. The wine is gloriously rich and fleshy, with an opulent texture, low acidity, and a silky, authoritative finish. It is one of the finest La Dauphines to date. **Anticipated maturity: Now–2001.**

DAUZAC (MARGAUX)* *

1990	C	74
1989	C	76
1988	C	83

The 1988 Dauzac has a deep color, medium body, and an attractive bouquet of spicy, herbal, red currant fruitiness bolstered by the smell and taste of new oak. Will the hard tannins in the finish melt away before the fruit fades? **Anticipated maturity: Now–2000.** The unstructured, diffuse, shockingly light 1989 has some pleasant jammy, berry fruit in evidence but little else. Soft and low in acidity, it should be drunk over the next 4–7 years. The 1990 is hard, austere, malnourished, and disappointing, especially in the context of a great vintage.

LA DOMINIQUE (ST.-ÉMILION)* * * *

1990	C	93
1989	C	93
1988	C	87

In some ways it is a shame that the 1989 La Dominique is such a show-stopping effort, for it overwhelms the 1988. The 1988 is a more typical (or as the Bordelais would have you believe, more classic) effort, with an alluring and

precocious, big bouquet of plummy fruit and sweet, vanillin-scented oak. This wine offers exuberantly rich, fruity, opulent flavors, medium to full body, and a long, satiny finish. Drink it over the next 8–10 years. The 1989 is the most massive wine I tasted from this vintage in St.-Émilion. The frightening thing is that despite an alcohol level that would make a grower in Châteauneuf-du-Pape jump with joy, there is not a trace of hotness in the wine's nose, flavors, or finish, largely because of the extraordinary intensity and concentration. In 1989 the wine was stored in 100% new oak, and that, plus its stupendous levels of extract, makes for one of the most dramatic and flamboyant wines of St.-Émilion, a breathtaking wine of great flavor dimension, complexity, and aging potential. **Anticipated maturity: 1996–2008.** The 1990 is an equally flamboyant, impressively endowed wine. It offers a black/ruby/purple color; a big nose of spices, herbs, and smoky black raspberries; rich, alcoholic, sumptuous flavors; and a long, smooth, soft finish. It is an impressive, large-scale wine that may turn out to resemble the great 1971 made at this estate. **Anticipated maturity: Now–2005.**
PAST GLORIES: 1986 (90), 1982 (91), 1971 (90), 1970 (88), 1955 (89)
PAST MEDIOCRITIES . . . OR WORSE: 1985 (74), 1975 (79)

DUCRU-BEAUCAILLOU (ST.-JULIEN)* * * * *

1990	D	89+
1989	D	90
1988	D	88

The 1988 Ducru is a medium-bodied wine, without the profound depth and sheer intensity of fruit of the 1989. Possessing high tannins and good ripeness, with an overall sense of compactness and toughness, it recalls the style of the best 1966 Médocs. **Anticipated maturity: 1996–2008.** In 1989 Ducru-Beaucaillou made another exceptional wine. It tastes like a hypothetical blend of their 1986 and 1982. Less powerful and concentrated than the 1982, but not nearly as backward nor as tannic as the 1986, the 1989 is one of the Médoc's most elegantly rendered wines. Dark ruby, with a more perfumed, toasty character than usual, this medium-bodied, earthy, currant- and mineral-flavored wine exhibits plenty of depth, surprising acidity for the vintage, firm tannins, and an understated yet authoritative style that makes it a benchmark for its type. **Anticipated maturity: 1998–2020.** The 1990 Ducru-Beaucaillou is a dark ruby-colored wine that is similar to both the 1986 and 1985, given its forward bouquet of oak, minerals, and cassis, attractive ripeness, firm tannins, excellent concentration and density, and powerful, tannic, long finish. It is one of the more closed 1990s. **Anticipated maturity: 1999–2015.** A few examples of the 1990 Ducru have revealed the scent of cardboard intermingled with the wine's rich mineral and cassis aromas. Other bottles have been totally clean.
PAST GLORIES: 1986 (94), 1985 (91), 1982 (94), 1981 (90), 1978 (90), 1970 (91), 1961 (96)

DUHART-MILON-ROTHSCHILD (PAUILLAC)* * *

1990	C	88
1989	C	88
1988	C	88

The 1988 Duhart-Milon exhibits a bouquet of ripe fruit, spices, cedar, and herbs. The wine is rich, full bodied, admirably concentrated, and long, with plenty of tannin. **Anticipated maturity: 1995–2010.** The 1989 has an intense bouquet of creamy blackcurrant fruit and exotic spices. There is even a touch of the famous Pauillac lead-pencil smell. Medium bodied, rich, and alcoholic, this voluptuous-styled wine has all the components necessary to seduce tasters for the next 8–12 years. **Anticipated maturity: 1994–2008.** The 1990, with its lead pencil– and cassis-scented nose, is firm and unevolved, but there appears to be more on the palate, and the finish is longer. There is a strong, weedy, cassis, Cabernet character to the wine, as well as a sense of elegance, balance, rich extract, and tannin. **Anticipated maturity: 1997–2007.**

PAST GLORIES: 1982 (92)

PAST MEDIOCRITIES . . . OR WORSE: 1975 (75), 1970 (70)

DURFORT-VIVENS (MARGAUX)* * *

1989	C	86
1988	C	76

Medium ruby, with a spicy, dusty, very herbaceous bouquet, the 1988 Durfort-Vivens has an astringent, pervasive vegetal character. No doubt the Cabernet Sauvignon was picked before it had attained maturity, resulting in a short, compact, and attenuated wine. **Anticipated maturity: Now–1998.** The 1989 Durfort-Vivens has proven to be admirably concentrated, low in acidity, tannic, meaty, and potentially very good. **Anticipated maturity: 1994–2005.**

DOMAINE DE L'ÉGLISE (POMEROL)* * *

1990	C	82
1989	D	90

The firm of Borie-Manoux has become deadly serious about the quality of its top wines. There is no better evidence of this than in the splendidly rich, highly extracted, immensely impressive 1989 Domaine de L'Église. Black/ruby in color, with fabulous, highly extracted flavors suggestive of prunes and black plums, gobs of soft tannin as well as alcohol, yet decent acidity for the vintage, this rich, broad-shouldered Pomerol is the most massive wine I have yet tasted from the Domaine de L'Église. It is very soft and therefore should be appealing young. **Anticipated maturity: 1994–2015.** Sadly, overproduction and superripe fruit resulted in a soft, low-acid, medium-weight 1990. Although round and tasty, it is essentially one-dimensional and lacking grip and depth. **Anticipated maturity: 1994–2000.**

L'ÉGLISE-CLINET (POMEROL)* * * *

1990	D	90
1989	D	88
1988	D	88

The 1988 is medium bodied and admirably concentrated, with a nose of smoky oak and plums. It should be at its best between 1993 and 2002. The 1989 is a

rich, velvety, alcoholic wine that is disarmingly seductive and smooth. It has a good tannin level when analyzed, but the high alcohol and low acidity give it a precocious character. Gloriously fruity, this sumptuous, velvety-textured wine will provide immense satisfaction. **Anticipated maturity: Now–2000.** As for the 1990, the saturated dark ruby color is nearly opaque. The lovely aroma of smoke, new oak, cassis, leather, chocolate, and black fruits is followed by a wine with excellent ripeness that is soft and superconcentrated, with a huge, silky textured finish. It is the finest L'Église-Clinet since the 1985 and 1986. **Anticipated maturity: Now–2007.**
PAST GLORIES: 1986 (92), 1985 (95)

L'ENCLOS (POMEROL)* * *

1990	C	89
1989	C	87
1988	B	83

The 1988 L'Enclos is a straightforward, fruity, soft-textured wine, with adequate concentration; an attractive, spicy, plummy, mocha-scented bouquet; decent concentration; and a moderately long finish. It is already drinking well and can be expected to evolve pleasantly, if uninspiringly, for another 4–5 years. The 1989 offers a hedonistic mouthful of plush, concentrated, blackberry- and violet-scented fruit, full bodied and silky smooth. The masses of rich fruit nearly obscure some sizable tannins in the finish. This beautifully made, intensely perfumed wine should provide delicious drinking for the next 10–12 years. The 1990 is even more structured and richer than the 1989. Very dark in color, with enticing tobacco-, plum-, and coffeelike aromas and flavors presented in a superripe, full-bodied format, this is the finest L'Enclos since the 1982. Drink it over the next 5–15 years.

L'ÉVANGILE (POMEROL)* * * * *

1990	EE	96
1989	EE	89
1988	D	87

L'Évangile's 1988 possesses this château's characteristic blackberry, plumlike nose, along with considerable grace, charm, depth, and harmony. It is precocious and should continue to drink well for 10–12 years. Deep ruby/garnet, with a superripe, portlike nose of licorice, black fruits, and spring flowers, the gorgeously rich, opulent 1989 makes a fat, expansive impact on the palate. Extremely low in acidity, alcoholic, and rich, this big, beefy wine will require drinking in its first 12–15 years of life. **Anticipated maturity: 1994–2005.** The 1990 could prove to be one of the finest L'Évangiles in the post–World War II era, rivaling the superb wines this renowned estate produced in 1947, 1950, 1975, 1982, and 1985. This is a blockbuster, black/ruby/purple-colored wine, with a restrained but promising nose of black fruits, toffee, new oak, and minerals. In the mouth there is exceptional richness, full body, an unctuous, nearly portlike texture, and great length and depth. The fruit's massive richness obscures a considerable amount of tannin. This is one of the most tannic Pomerols of the vintage. This riveting wine resembles in weight and force the pre-1976 vintages of its neighbor, Pétrus. **Anticipated maturity: 1997–2015.**

PAST GLORIES: 1985 (95), 1983 (92), 1982 (96), 1975 (95), 1961 (97), 1950 (92), 1947 (98)

PAST MEDIOCRITIES . . . OR WORSE: 1981 (73), 1970 (84)

DE FERRAND (ST.-ÉMILION)* * *

1990	C	87
1989	C	85
1988	C	79

The 1988's tannins are green, excessively hard, and dry and tend to overwhelm the wine's concentration. Though there is some decent black cherry fruit, it will undoubtedly lose the battle in its struggle against the tannin. **Anticipated maturity: Now–2002.** The 1989 appears to have the structure and concentration necessary to support the tannin. It is a dark ruby/purple-colored wine, closed for a 1989 but still easy to recognize as big and muscular. This impressively sized specimen will need plenty of time in the cellar. **Anticipated maturity: 1996–2008.** The 1990 may prove to be the best de Ferrand since its fine 1985. Although it appeared diffuse and soft when I first tasted it, it has taken on considerable structure and has developed fine intensity, medium to full body, excellent ripeness, and good definition and focus. **Anticipated maturity: Now–2001.**

FEYTIT-CLINET (POMEROL)* *

1990	C	86
1989	C	84
1988	C	84

The 1988 Feytit-Clinet is a straightforward, spicy, ripe Pomerol that displays fresh acidity, giving its flavors more precision and clarity. It also possesses an elegant, plummy bouquet and a long, lush, spicy finish. Although not a big Pomerol when measured against the heavyweights of the appellation, Feytit-Clinet is a charming, stylish wine that should be at its best between 1994 and 2003. The 1989 exhibits a moderately intense, ripe, spicy, straightforward bouquet, medium to full body, lots of extract, and high, surprisingly hard tannins. **Anticipated maturity: Now–2002.** The medium-bodied 1990 Feytit-Clinet reveals toasty, vanillin-scented, superripe aromas, gobs of rich, unctuous fruit, and a soft, chewy, smooth finish. It is one of the best examples of Feytit-Clinet in years. **Anticipated maturity: Now–1998.**

DE FIEUZAL (GRAVES)* * *

1990	C	82
1989	C	87
1988	C	86

The 1988 de Fieuzal is an extracted, darkly colored wine with an excellent nose of sweet curranty fruit, medium body, and a compact, very tannic (nearly astringent) finish. The wine has closed up since its bottling and appears to need considerable time in the bottle. Will the fruit hold up? **Anticipated maturity: 1996–2010.** The concentrated, black/purple-colored 1989 is the most powerful and large-scale offering among the Graves wines from the Léognan area. It displays smoky, concentrated, blackcurrant fruit, medium body, gobs of tannin, and a long finish. **Anticipated maturity: 1994–2010.** The 1990's nose is closed, but it does offer tons of sweet vanillin oak and black fruit flavors intermingled with herbaceous scents. There are gobs of tannin, but the midpalate is hollow, and there is an absence of flesh. The finish is overly woody and hard. **Anticipated maturity: 1996–2005.**

FIGEAC (ST.-ÉMILION)* * * * *

1990	E	94
1989	E	86
1988	D	83

Figeac's 1988 offers a moderate ruby color, high tannins, and a tart, lean, austere, overtly herbaceous character. The wine is light, with a surprisingly short finish. **Anticipated maturity: Now–1997.** The 1989 has consistently displayed a lack of richness, suggesting high crop yields and too short a vatting time. My experience has taught me that Figeac is among the most perplexing wines to evaluate young and often can do a 180-degree turnabout in quality. Medium ruby, with an olive-, herb-, vanillin-, and berry-scented bouquet, this medium-bodied wine exhibits soft tannins and a precocious personality. Seductive and forward it may be, but some additional stuffing and extract could have resulted in a sublime wine. **Anticipated maturity: Now–2002.** The exceptional 1990 is the first great Figeac since the splendid 1982. When Figeac gets everything right, as it did in 1990, the result is one of the most compelling wines in Bordeaux. The huge nose of new saddle leather, herbs, black fruits, and smoke is followed by a wine with exceptional concentration, excellent balance and depth, and a smooth-as-silk finish. Ripe tannins and sweet fruit combine to produce a splendidly opulent, rich Figeac that should drink well for two decades. This is undoubtedly one of the most impressive notes I have ever given an infant vintage of Figeac. I should also note that the 1990 Figeac bears more than a casual resemblance to its renowned neighbor, Cheval Blanc. **Anticipated maturity: 1995–2010.** A fabulous wine!
PAST GLORIES: 1986 (90), 1983 (87), 1982 (94), 1970 (90), 1964 (92), 1961 (89), 1959 (91), 1953 (93)
PAST MEDIOCRITIES . . . OR WORSE: 1988 (83), 1979 (83), 1966 (85)

LA FLEUR (ST.-ÉMILION)* *

1990	C	86
1989	C	83
1988	C	82

The 1988 is light in color, with soft, round, fruity flavors that provide immediate appeal. It should be drunk over the next 3–4 years. The tannins are a little unripe and hard, but the wine exhibits an attractive fruitiness, medium body, and some heady alcohol in the finish. **Anticipated maturity: Now–1996.** Continuing with the increased quality that has been evident over the last several vintages, the 1990 offers a decadent nose of sweet vanillin oak, jammy berry fruit, and flowers. It is all silky fruit, with a fat, chewy texture and soft tannins. Drink it over the next 5–7 years. Not complex, but very delicious.

LA FLEUR DE GAY (POMEROL)* * * * *

1990	EE	89
1989	EE	95
1988	EE	93

Only limited quantities (1,000–1,500 cases) of the super 1988 are available. It is, however, worth whatever arm-twisting and retailer-browbeating one must do to latch on to a few bottles. The 1988's black/ruby/purple color makes it one of the darkest-colored wines of the vintage. The bouquet is now shut down compared to the terrific fragrance and opulence it displayed when young. However, it takes no real talent to detect scents of smoky, toasty oak, black plums, allspice, and Oriental spices, as well as gobs of superripe fruit. Extremely concentrated on the palate, but structured, with considerable tannin, this massive, full-bodied, more aggressive La Fleur de Gay will not have the sumptuous appeal of many Pomerols, but give it 4–5 years to mellow and it will provide a dazzling glass of decadent Pomerol. **Anticipated maturity: 1994–2010.** The 1989 offers a veritable smorgasbord of heavenly delights. The dark ruby/purple color is opaque, suggesting low yields and superconcentration. In the mouth there is only one word to describe the texture and intensity, and that is explosive. It is amazingly concentrated and more structured and tannic than many 1989 Pomerols. In spite of the low acidity, the tannins tend to keep down the level of enjoyment. Nevertheless, it is so crammed with ripe fruit that I suspect many will find it irresistible when young. The problem with this wine, much like many of the finest Pomerols, is that the production is minuscule. **Anticipated maturity: 1995–2008.** The 1990 is reminiscent of the 1983, only lighter. Unquestionably inferior to the 1989, 1988, and 1987, it offers a pleasant color; a sweet perfume of ripe fruit and aggressive, spicy, oak; medium body; good concentration, soft tannins; and low acid in the moderately long finish. **Anticipated maturity: 1995–2003.**
PAST GLORIES: 1987 (90), 1986 (90), 1985 (89), 1983 (90)
PAST MEDIOCRITIES . . . OR WORSE: 1982 (83)

LA FLEUR GAZIN (POMEROL)* *

1990	C	85
1989	C	78
1988	C	84

Initially the 1988 was tannic, austere, and lean, lacking both fruit and character. However, in the bottle the wine has come alive, offering much richer fruit, a sexy, oaky component, and lush texture. **Anticipated maturity: Now–1998.** The performance of the 1989 La Fleur Gazin suggests that the vineyard was harvested too early. The attenuated, higher-than-normal acidity levels, and green, hard, unripe tannins are not enjoyable. However, the wine does possess noticeable alcohol, and is otherwise well made. **Anticipated maturity: Now–2000.** The 1990 has gained weight and now offers meaty, soft, fat flavors, rich, plummy fruit, and a juicy finish. **Anticipated maturity: Now–1998.**

LA FLEUR PÉTRUS (POMEROL)* * * *

1990	D	88
1989	D	91
1988	D	85

The 1988 is a tasty, attractive, ripe, agreeable wine with adequate depth, medium body, and enough length and tannin to warrant drinking over the next decade. **Anticipated maturity: Now–2000.** In 1989 50% of the grapes were cut off to reduce the crop size and to augment the wine's intensity. The results may be the finest La Fleur Pétrus since the 1950 and 1947. Dark, opaque ruby, with a tight yet expressive bouquet of exotic spices, mocha, and deep, superripe black cherry fruit, this medium-bodied wine has an inner core of depth and length. Its admirable intensity of flavor is backed by a formidable degree of alcohol and tannin. **Anticipated maturity: 1996–2009.** The 1990 is less concentrated than other top Pomerols. The bouquet offers aromas of tobacco, coffee, mocha, and red fruits intertwined with scents of new oak. In the mouth the wine is medium bodied, moderately concentrated, and admirably pure, with moderate tannins and crisp acidity—unusual for a 1990. Drink it over the next 10–12 years.

PAST GLORIES: 1982 (90), 1975 (90), 1970 (88), 1952 (91), 1950 (95), 1947 (96)

FONBADET (PAUILLAC)* * *

1990	C	87
1989	C	83
1988	C	75

The 1988 tastes tart and lean, and its lack of fruit is cause for concern. **Anticipated maturity: Now–1996.** The 1989 is surprisingly light, soft, alcoholic, and will no doubt be short-lived because of its low acidity. There is plenty of fruit, but the overall effect is of a flabby, unstructured wine. **Anticipated maturity: Now–1998.** The best Fonbadet since the powerful 1982, the 1990 reveals an opaque, dark ruby color and a pure, spicy nose of black fruits and earthy, trufflelike aromas. In the mouth there is excellent ripeness, a sweet, rich texture, plenty of tannin and glycerin, and a long, powerful finish. **Anticipated maturity: 1994–2003.**

FONPLÉGADE (ST.-ÉMILION)* * *

1990	C	88
1989	C	85
1988	C	78

The 1988 Fonplégade does not possess the ripeness and fruit necessary to stand up to its lean, sinewy, attenuated character. The astringent, dry tannins in the finish also suggest that the balance between fruit and tannin is suspect. **Anticipated maturity: Now–1996.** The 1989 is a generously fruity, alcoholic wine that should last for up to a decade. But it lacks the extra dimension of concentration and complexity the top wines of the appellation achieved in this vintage. The wine is round, supple, and already a delight to drink. **Anticipated maturity: Now–1997.** The 1990 has excellent concentration, plenty of tannin, a saturated color, decent acidity, and a full-bodied robustness that characterizes this well-made St.-Émilion. This may turn out to be the finest Fonplégade in decades. Drink it over the next 8–12 years.

FONROQUE (ST.-ÉMILION)* * *

1990	C	88
1989	C	86
1988	C	83

The 1988 Fonroque displays underlying ripe fruit, spicy new oak, good acidity, and some aggressive tannins in the finish. It is a pleasant but undistinguished wine. **Anticipated maturity: Now–2000.** The 1989 is excellent, exhibiting the size, richness, and heady alcohol content of the vintage, as well as an opulent, fleshy texture. This larger-scale Fonroque should make delicious drinking for the next 5–9 years. **Anticipated maturity: Now–2000.** The 1990 is a big, chewy, sweet, opulent St.-Émilion with good body and intensity, as well as a deep mouth-feel. There are gobs of fruit, plenty of spices and herbs, and a nice touch of sweet vanillin from the new oak. Drink it over the next decade. It is the finest Fonroque in decades.

FONTENIL (FRONSAC)* * *

1990	B	88
1989	B	87

The impressive 1989, made from an estate owned by Libourne's husband-and-wife oenologist team of Dany and Michel Rolland, is one of the up-and-coming stars of the appellation. The color is deep ruby/purple, and the nose is spicy, with evidence of new oak and ripe cassis. In the mouth there is excellent definition, medium to full body, fine intensity, and a long, deep, well-structured finish. It should easily last for 10–12 years. The 1990 Fontenil is a highly extracted, rich, ageworthy wine. The color is deep, opaque ruby/purple, and the nose offers up aromas of toasty new oak, black fruits, herbs, and spices. In the mouth considerable density and a rich, medium- to full-bodied texture are followed by a long, moderately rich, elegant finish. The 1990 Fontenil should be at its best by the mid-1990s and last through the first decade of the next century.

LES FORTS DE LATOUR (PAUILLAC)* * *

1990	D	90
1989	D	87
1988	D	84

The medium-bodied, somewhat austere, noticeably oaky and tannic 1988 Forts de Latour possesses good aging potential but lacks charm, complexity, and concentration. Nevertheless, it is an elegant, understated wine. **Anticipated**

maturity: Now–2002. As for the 1989, once past the bouquet of black fruits, cedar, and oak, it is round, generously endowed, surprisingly supple (even for the second wine of Latour), and low in acidity, with a fleshy, heady finish. **Anticipated maturity: 1994–2004.** The rich, well-endowed 1990 possesses round, generous, surprisingly concentrated flavors. It will make ideal drinking over the next 10–15 years. Over one-half of the crop was relegated to this, the most complete second wine made at this property since the glorious 1982. **Anticipated maturity: Now–2005.**
PAST GLORIES: 1982 (92)

FOURCAS-DUPRÉ (LISTRAC)* *

1990	B	77
1989	C	83

The light-intensity, ripe nose of the 1989 is followed by a medium-bodied, adequately concentrated wine with decent acidity and freshness. Drink it over the next 4–5 years. The thin, spicy aromas of the 1990 are followed by a straightforward, compact wine of no great distinction.

FOURCAS-LOUBANEY (LISTRAC)* * *

1990	B	88
1989	B	85
1988	B	88

Black/ruby in color, with a full-intensity bouquet of superpure blackcurrants, herbs, and toasty new oak, this wine is splendidly concentrated for a 1988, has excellent balance and a long finish. **Anticipated maturity: Now–2005.** Soft and forward, with excellent color and a big, plummy, oaky nose, the 1989 lacks the concentration and grip of the 1990 and 1988, yet it offers a generous, amply endowed mouthful of wine. Drink it over the next 4–6 years. The 1990 is deep in color, with a rich nose of cassis and oak. Dense, concentrated, medium to full bodied, and tannic, it is an immensely impressive wine. **Anticipated maturity: 1996–2008.**

FRANC-MAYNE (ST.-ÉMILION)* * *

1990	C	89
1989	C	87
1988	C	79

The attractive, spicy, intensely herbaceous nose of the 1988 Franc-Mayne is followed by a wine that is relatively hollow, attenuated, vegetal, and short in the finish. The color is sound, but the overall impression is uninspiring. **Anticipated maturity: Now–1998.** The purple-colored 1989 is a spicy, jammy-scented wine with oodles of ripe cassis fruit, a soft yet expansive texture, low acidity, and high alcohol in the finish. This decadent mouthful of juicy, succulent St.-Émilion should be drunk in its first 5–7 years of life. **Anticipated maturity: Now–2000.** Significantly richer than the top-notch 1989, the low-acid 1990 exhibits sensational ripeness and depth, a chewy, black cherry fruitiness, a viscous texture, and a dazzling finish. This is an explosively rich wine that might merit a higher rating in a few years. **Anticipated maturity: 1994–2007.**

Note: Some bottles of the 1989 and 1990 have exhibited an annoying smell of cardboard.

LA GAFFELIÈRE (ST.-ÉMILION)* * */* * * *

1990	D	90
1989	D	89
1988	C	87

The 1988 La Gaffelière is a well-made, elegant, understated, charming, well-balanced wine that has avoided the excesses of tannin so prevalent in many 1988s. The interplay between the herb-tinged raspberry fruit and new oak is admirable. **Anticipated maturity: Now–2000.** The 1989 displays an enthralling bouquet of black cherries, spring flowers, minerals, and toasty new oak. Medium to full bodied, it possesses good acidity for the vintage, soft tannins, and a long, velvety, rich finish. This is a stylish yet authoritative La Gaffelière. **Anticipated maturity: 1996–2010.** The deep ruby-colored 1990 offers up abundant aromas of sweet new oak, ripe berry fruit, and floral scents. In the mouth this stylish, medium-weight, beautifully proportioned wine has excellent concentration, decent acidity, moderate tannins, and a considerable sense of elegance and richness. It is the finest La Gaffelière since the 1970 and 1947. **Anticipated maturity: Now–2008.**

PAST GLORIES: 1982 (87), 1953 (89), 1947 (88)

PAST MEDIOCRITIES . . . OR WORSE: 1981 (72), 1978 (67), 1975 (79), 1971 (68), 1966 (78)

LE GAY (POMEROL)* * *

1990	D	89
1989	D	92
1988	D	86

The 1988 Le Gay is moderately rich, full bodied, deep, and oaky. It should reach maturity, optimistically, by the turn of the century. **Anticipated maturity: 1997–2010.** Have you been longing for the post–World War II style of heavyweight, thick, mouth-coating wine that modern-day winemakers eschew? The 1989 Le Gay will give you a déjà vu of the late 1940s. This Herculean-size wine (from old vines and yields that were one-fourth those of other Pomerols) is fascinating. The opaque purple/black color, the savage, animal, roasted black-currant-scented nose, the spectacular depth, the thick, concentrated flavors, and the mouth-shattering tannins are the stuff of which legends are made . . . in the last century. However, patience will be required. **Anticipated maturity: 2005–2030.** Although the 1990 does not possess the weight or richness of its predecessor, it does offer a huge nose of black fruits, prunes, and damp earth. In the mouth the wine exhibits none of the ferocious tannins that Le Gay routinely possesses, medium to full body, and a concentrated finish. Le Gay has produced a civilized wine with more up-front appeal than usual. **Anticipated maturity: 1996–2010.**

PAST GLORIES: 1975 (90)

GAZIN (POMEROL)* * *

1990	D	90
1989	D	88
1988	D	87

After years of mediocrity, Gazin has begun to move in the right direction. The turnaround started with the 1988, which is a wonderfully seductive, rich, sweet, broad-flavored, hedonistic wine, with light tannins, a rich, savory texture, and a satiny, alcoholic finish. Moreover, who can ignore the big bouquet of herbs, mocha, and sweet fruit? **Anticipated maturity: Now–2003.** The 1989 Gazin possesses an intense bouquet of toasty new oak, intertwined with aromas of rich, jammy, plump fruit, and flowers. The chewy texture suggests opulence, even unctuousness. The finish, with its elevated alcohol level and low acidity, should provide immense gratification for those who prefer sensual over intellectual wines. **Anticipated maturity: 1994–2005.** There is something about the 1990 Gazin, particularly in its sweet, oaky, plummy, coffee-scented bouquet, that reminds me of modern-day vintages of Pétrus (i.e., 1985). This is not a blockbuster Pomerol, but one that stresses elegance allied with excellent ripeness, medium body, and a fleshy yet graceful, silky finish. It should be drinkable in 3–4 years and last up to two decades. It is the most impressive Gazin in over three decades.

GISCOURS (MARGAUX)* * */* * * *

1990	C	86
1989	C	87
1988	C	78

The 1988 Giscours is an extremely overripe wine, with aromas of prunes, peaches, and apricots. Loosely structured, sweet and flabby, this plump wine does not have the tannin necessary to give it grip. It should be drunk over the next 4–5 years. The 1989 Giscours is the first reassuringly fine wine made at this property since the 1983. It exhibits a black/ruby color and a big, forceful bouquet of overripe plums and licorice. In the mouth the wine has the telltale succulent character of the vintage, a chewy texture, excellent concentration, high alcohol, low acidity, and a long, opulent finish. It should prove seductive and heady to nearly everyone. **Anticipated maturity: Now–2008.** The robust, exotic, rich, full-bodied 1990 offers low acidity, plenty of tannin, and excellent richness and fruit. **Anticipated maturity: 1994–2005.** After some so-so efforts, it is nice to see this property rebound with two fine efforts in 1989 and 1990.

PAST GLORIES: 1979 (88), 1978 (90), 1975 (91)

GLORIA (ST.-JULIEN)* * *

1990	C	84
1989	C	86
1988	C	85

The 1988 is an unabashedly fruity, exuberant, herb- and cassis-scented wine, with a smooth texture and easy-to-understand and -enjoy flavors. No wonder

Gloria is called a beginner's Bordeaux. **Anticipated maturity: Now–1997.**
The 1989 Gloria is a fat, plump, deliciously agreeable wine with a considerable alcoholic kick in the finish. Fruity, with soft tannins, it will be a fine wine
to drink over the next 7–10 years. **Anticipated maturity: Now–2000.** Surprisingly light, as well as lacking a midpalate and flavor extraction, the 1990
Gloria is still a pleasant, middle-of-the-road, commercial wine that should be
drunk over the next 5–7 years.

GOMBAUDE-GUILLOT (POMEROL)* * */* * * *

1990	C	85
1989	C	86
1988	C	84
1989 Cuvée Spéciale New Oak	D	87
1988 Cuvée Spéciale New Oak	D	89

The 1988 regular *cuvée* of Gombaude-Guillot has a ruby color, with a spicy
bouquet and medium-bodied, adequately concentrated flavors. The finish has
some sharp tannins. The overall impression is that of a wine with adequate
rather than great depth. As for the 1988 Cuvée Spéciale, this luxury *cuvée*,
aged in 100% new oak, surprisingly does not exhibit as much of a smoky,
vanillin character in the nose as one might suspect. Rich and full bodied, with
intense aromas and flavors of blackcurrants, plums, and minerals, this beauty
should have a graceful evolution. **Anticipated maturity: Now–2003.** The
1989 regular *cuvée* displays moderate ruby/purple color and an aroma of
roasted black plums and cassis. In the mouth it is concentrated and medium
bodied, with a silky opulence of fruit seen only in the best examples from this
vintage. Long, but low in acidity, with moderate tannins, this is a smooth
Pomerol. Curiously, I had rated it significantly higher prior to bottling. **Anticipated maturity: 1994–2005.** The 1989 Cuvée Spéciale, aged in 100% new
oak, is richer and packed with fruit, although the difference between the two
wines is less noticeable in 1989 than in prior vintages. Full bodied, sweet, and
silky, it will be a Pomerol to drink over the first 7–10 years of life.

Last, with an attractive medium ruby color and a pronounced nose of cherries, smoke, and herbs, the round, exceptionally soft, fleshy 1990 regular *cuvée*
is low in acidity. However, it exhibits fine ripeness and gobs of up-front, chewy
fruit and glycerin. Drink it over the next 5–8 years.
PAST GLORIES: 1985 Cuvée Speciale (93)

GRAND-MAYNE (ST.-ÉMILION)* * */* * * *

1990	C	90
1989	C	91
1988	B	87

The 1988 Grand-Mayne is a big, alcoholic, obvious wine displaying an intense,
vanillin-scented, black plum–like fruitiness and fleshy, chewy flavors. **Anticipated maturity: Now–2003.** The 1989 has an almost overwhelming bouquet of sweet, jammy black fruits and spices intertwined with the toasty scent
of new oak barrels as well as a pronounced scent of Provençal herbs. The

wine's exuberance and opulence are nicely framed by plenty of smoky oak. Quite a flamboyant, intensely flavored, rich, full-bodied wine, the 1989 Grand-Mayne should provide thrilling drinking over the next decade. **Anticipated maturity: Now–2005.** The black/purple hue of the 1990 makes it one of the most impressively colored St.-Émilions of the vintage. In addition, aromas of black cherries, smoky new oak, herbs, and anise are appealing. In the mouth there is excellent concentration, gorgeous purity and extraction of fruit, full body, plenty of tannin, and a structured, graceful finish. If you have not yet caught on to how fine this property's wines have become over recent vintages, do not wait any longer: prices can only go up. **Anticipated maturity: 1995–2007.**

GRAND-PONTET (ST.-ÉMILION)* *

1990	C	89
1989	C	84
1988	C	82

The 1988 Grand-Pontet has an indifferent bouquet of new oak and some vague spicy, ripe fruit. On the palate it is soft, woody, nicely concentrated, but one-dimensional. Drink it over the next 3–4 years. The 1989 is lighter than many wines from this vintage. Displaying some dilution in the midpalate, it is an alcoholic, chunky, softly styled St.-Émilion. **Anticipated maturity: Now–1997.** Lusciously fruity, with tons of sweet, smoky new oak, the 1990's unctuous flavors ooze from the glass. The wine has copious quantities of fruit, a silky, full-bodied feel, and an opulent, splendidly long finish. For drinking over the next 6–10 years, it will provide considerable pleasure. This is a sleeper of the vintage!

GRAND-PUY-DUCASSE (PAUILLAC)* * *

1990	C	84
1989	C	87
1988	B	85

The 1988 Grand-Puy-Ducasse is a lighter-weight version of the 1989, less alcoholic but more tannic and compact. Nevertheless, it has fine fruit and attractive ripeness. Drink it over the next 3–5 years. The 1989 is forward, with a cedary, ripe, moderately intense bouquet. Not a blockbuster, but spicy and delicious, with abundant quantities of chocolate- and cassis-flavored fruit, this may be the finest wine from this property in decades. **Anticipated maturity: Now–2002.** The 1990 is light and delicate, but pleasant in a one-dimensional, fruity way. **Anticipated maturity: Now–1999.**

GRAND-PUY-LACOSTE (PAUILLAC)* * * *

1990	D	90
1989	D	89
1988	D	85

The 1988 effort from this estate is deep ruby, has a reticent bouquet, an austere, firm, tannic framework, and medium body. The wine has noticeable

richness and depth, as well as high tannins. **Anticipated maturity: 1995– 2005.** The 1989 is a classic Pauillac. A penetrating bouquet of intense black-currants, sweet vanillin oak, and roasted aromas is followed by a medium- to full-bodied wine that exhibits wonderful ripeness and length. This is a gener-ously constituted, soft, admirably made wine. **Anticipated maturity: 1994– 2015.** The 1990 resembles a more powerful combination of this estate's 1978 and 1985. Forward, with low acidity, its delicious sweet cassis fruit soars from the glass. It offers chewy, dense, alcoholic, plump, and delicious flavors pre-sented in a full-bodied format. This is a hedonistic offering from one of the most underrated Pauillac producers. Will the 1990 turn out to be the finest Grand-Puy-Lacoste since the 1982? **Anticipated maturity: 1995–2010.**
PAST GLORIES: 1986 (90), 1982 (94), 1970 (90)

LA GRAVE TRIGANT DE BOISSET (POMEROL)* * *

1990	C	89
1989	C	87
1988	C	86

The 1988 boasts an intense, new oak-dominated bouquet, some spicy, medium-bodied, ripe fruit, moderate tannins, sound acidity, and moderate al-cohol in the finish. It does not have the ampleness of the 1989, but those who like a more restrained, polite style of Pomerol may prefer the 1988. **Antici-pated maturity: Now–2001.** The 1989 is more concentrated, alcoholic, and structured than the 1988. The excellent bouquet of spicy, toasty oak, black cherries, and plums is followed by a medium-bodied wine, with a heady alco-hol content, plenty of tannin, and good concentration. **Anticipated maturity: Now–2002.** The 1990 is the finest La Grave Trigant de Boisset I have tasted. Deep ruby, with a fragrant bouquet of sweet black fruits, toast, and mocha, this voluptuously textured wine gushes with fruit. Deep, juicy, and creamy, it makes for a gorgeously soft mouthful of wine. **Anticipated maturity: Now–2001.**

GRESSIER GRAND-POUJEAUX (MOULIS)* * */* * * *

1989	C	88
1988	C	87

Opaque ruby/purple, with a reticent but emerging bouquet of chocolate, cassis, and cedar, the 1988 is medium to full bodied, typically backward and rustic but filled with character. **Anticipated maturity: 1996–2008.** The dark, opaque ruby/purple color of the 1989 suggests a serious level of extract and in-tensity. The bouquet remains tight, but with swirling, delicious aromas of tar, spices, coffee, and blackcurrants. In the mouth the wine is packed with fruit, has high levels of glycerin, outstanding concentration, and plenty of tannin in the finish. Although the acidity is low, the tannins are high. My guess is that this rustic, old-style wine needs another 8–10 years of cellaring. **Anticipated maturity: 1999–2015.**

GRUAUD-LAROSE (ST.-JULIEN)* * * * *

1990	D	88
1989	D	88
1988	C	89

The 1988 Gruaud-Larose is probably a 30-year wine. Surprisingly powerful, rich, concentrated, long, and full bodied for a 1988, and reminiscent of the 1975 only less savage, it appears to be a more complete wine than either the 1989 or 1990. **Anticipated maturity: 2000–2025.** In 1989 Gruaud-Larose produced another tannic, nearly impenetrable wine. Medium ruby/purple in color, ferociously tannic, but deep and backward, this vintage of Gruaud may evolve for 20–30 years, but does it have the requisite depth of fruit to balance out the tannins? This wine could well behave similarly to the stubbornly tannic, still charmless 1975. A wine to purchase for your grandchildren? **Anticipated maturity: 2000–2025.** As for the 1990, although the nose is still closed, it does offer woodsy, herb, and black fruit aromas. In the mouth there is power, a structured, medium- to full-bodied taste profile, and fine stuffing and depth. Nevertheless, I cannot help but wonder if Gruaud-Larose is intentionally producing less of a blockbuster style. I hope not. **Anticipated maturity: 1997–2015.**

PAST GLORIES: 1986 (97), 1985 (90), 1983 (90), 1982 (97), 1961 (96), 1953 (90), 1949 (93), 1928 (98)

LA GURGUE (MARGAUX)* * *

1990	C	83
1989	C	86
1988	C	85

The 1988 is moderately deep ruby, with an impressive bouquet of spring flowers, blackcurrants, and licorice. This medium-bodied, surprisingly soft and intense 1988 will make tasty drinking for the next 4–6 years. The late Bernadette Villars fashioned a lovely 1989 La Gurgue. Bursting with ripe plums and blackcurrants, impressively rich, heady, and alcoholic, this velvety, low-acid wine already provides delicious drinking. **Anticipated maturity: Now–1997.** Lighter, with plummy, tasty black fruit flavors, the 1990 does not exhibit much grip, and the finish is short. It should be consumed within its first 4–5 years of life.

HANTEILLAN (HAUT-MÉDOC)* *

1990	B	85
1989	B	74

The 1989 Hanteillan is tasty and light, with good ripeness, medium body, and a pleasant yet dry, hard finish. **Anticipated maturity: Now–1997.** Rather than tasting typically lean and austere, Hanteillan's 1990 is exhibiting more midpalate and richness than usual. For me it is the property's finest effort to date. **Anticipated maturity: Now–2000.**

HAUT-BAGES-AVEROUS (PAUILLAC)* *

1990	C	86
1989	C	85
1988	B	81

Soft, diluted, somewhat flabby, and lacking focus, this medium-bodied 1988 (the second wine of Lynch-Bages) should be drunk over the next 1–2 years. The 1989 is an excellent second wine, displaying rich cassis fruit, good, spicy, new oak, and a delicious, medium- to full-bodied, corpulent texture. Drink it over the next 4–5 years. The 1990 is extremely fat and fruity, as well as attractively ripe and soft. This highly commercial yet delicious medium-bodied wine should be drunk over the next 4–6 years. It would make an ideal wine for restaurants.

HAUT-BAGES-LIBÉRAL (PAUILLAC)* * *

1990	C	87
1989	C	84
1988	C	81

The 1988 exhibits some greenness to its tannins, is medium bodied, spicy, offers some currant fruit, and finishes abruptly. Drink it over the next 4–5 years. **Anticipated maturity: Now–1998.** The 1989 Haut-Bages-Libéral tastes surprisingly light. It has a brilliant ruby/purple color, decent acidity, and moderate tannin, but it finishes short. It is a good effort but is atypically restrained and subdued for a 1989 Pauillac. **Anticipated maturity: Now–1999.** Deeply colored, with a sweet, plummy, oaky nose, the 1990 represents a major improvement over the indifferent 1989. Opulent and rich, this low-acid, fleshy wine lacks grip, but it does offer a big, meaty mouthful of juicy Pauillac. **Anticipated maturity: 1994–2005.**
PAST GLORIES: 1986 (90), 1985 (89), 1982 (92), 1975 (88)

HAUT-BAILLY (GRAVES)* * * *

1990	D	91
1989	D	90
1988	C	89

The 1988 is full and rich, with that profound, mineral, spicy, sweet oaky, curranty aroma; gentle, yet full-bodied, creamy-textured flavors; and a long, smooth, marvelous finish. This wine may well turn out to be outstanding with another 3–4 years in the bottle. **Anticipated maturity: Now–2003.** The 1989 is made in a more forceful style. Ruby/purple-colored, with a jammy nose of ripe blackberries and new oak, this medium-bodied, alcoholic wine has low acidity but high tannins. The overall impression is one of bigness and strength, without heaviness. This should prove to be an uncommonly graceful, long-lived, and pure expression of the Haut-Bailly style. **Anticipated maturity: 1994–2012.** Impressively deep ruby in color, with a big, authoritative nose of superripe fruit and subtle new oak, the medium-bodied, stylish 1990 offers plenty of glycerin and ripeness, as well as a sense of balance and finesse. It

looks to be another classy Haut-Bailly that should rival the fine 1983 and 1989. **Anticipated maturity: 1995–2005.**
PAST GLORIES: 1983 (87), 1979 (87), 1964 (88), 1961 (93)
PAST MEDIOCRITIES . . . OR WORSE: 1982 (?), 1975 (67), 1971 (75)

HAUT-BATAILLEY (PAUILLAC)* * *

1990	C	88
1989	C	87
1988	C	83

The 1988 Haut-Batailley is a lightweight, lean, closed, hard-edged wine that lacks charm and finesse. The tannin level appears excessive for the fruit component. **Anticipated maturity: Now–1998.** The 1989 Haut-Batailley has a gorgeous amount of up-front, satiny fruit, and is lush and ripe as well as long. The palate impression is almost one of sweet, jammy fruit because of its super-richness. **Anticipated maturity: Now–2006.** The 1990 offers a forward, smoky, sweet oaky nose intertwined with bold and lavish aromas of blackcurrants. Medium bodied, with low acidity, light tannins, and layers of ripe fruit, this finesse-style wine should provide superlative drinking for more than a decade. It is the finest Haut-Batailley since 1982.

HAUT-BRION (GRAVES)* * * * *

1990	E	94
1989	E	100
1988	E	91

The 1988 Haut-Brion is built along the lines of the 1966, but it is more concentrated and powerful. The dense bouquet of tobacco, ripe, black fruits, and spicy oak has just begun to develop. Medium bodied, rich, and tannic, with a good inner core of fruit, this wine will have to be cellared until the end of this century. **Anticipated maturity: 2000–2025.** The 1989 Haut-Brion is the wine of the vintage! Significantly more concentrated than the great 1986 and 1982, this is a monumental wine that Jean Delmas says is reminiscent of, but even superior to, the heroic 1959. Opaque, deep ruby/purple, with a roasted tobacco, cassis, smoky aroma, the 1989 has phenomenal depth and an opulent texture remotely suggestive of the 1982, but with far greater extract levels, length, and a dazzling finish. Charged with copious quantities of lavishly ripe fruit and soft tannins, the 1989 Haut-Brion appears destined to become a legend, as well as to drink sublimely for 20–30 years. I say that because of its superb inner core of rich, concentrated, gloriously ripe fruit. **Anticipated maturity: 1996–2015.** The 1990 is another outstanding effort. Although it does not have the heavy weight or awesome richness of the 1989, it is filled with wonderfully sweet, roasted, spicy fruit, as well as enticing fatness and glycerin, all packaged in a medium- to full-bodied format. The superb, fragrant bouquet of cassis, tobacco, new oak, and minerals is already revealing great complexity. Despite the fact that the wine does not make as powerful an impact on the palate as the 1989, it is still an exceptionally fine, archetypal Haut-Brion. More forward than the 1988, it most closely resembles a hypothetical blend of the 1985 and 1983. I have noticed that it improves and expands considerably with 60–70 minutes of airing. **Anticipated maturity: 1996–2010.**

PAST GLORIES: 1986 (92), 1985 (91), 1983 (90), 1982 (93), 1979 (93), 1978 (92), 1975 (90), 1964 (90), 1961 (96), 1959 (97), 1953 (94), 1949 (94), 1945 (99), 1928 (90?)

PAST MEDIOCRITIES . . . OR WORSE: 1970 (84), 1966 (86)

HAUT-CORBIN (ST.-ÉMILION)* * *

1990	C	87
1989	C	87
1988	C	86

Although the 1988 Haut-Corbin does not have nearly the size or alcohol levels of the 1989, it is perhaps a more classic wine, with deep ruby/purple color; a big, spicy, herbaceous, licorice-, and cassis-scented bouquet; medium body; and plenty of tannin in its relatively long finish. **Anticipated maturity: Now–2001.** The 1989 is a chewy, intense, full-bodied wine with considerable power. The overwhelming character offers a huge amount of ripe black fruit, buttressed by toasty new oak and the scent and taste of herbs. There is plenty of alcohol in the finish. Long, rich, spicy, and intensely flavored, it should continue to age well for another decade. **Anticipated maturity: Now–2001.** The 1990 exhibits a cedary, Médoc-like nose, excellent color, good density and extraction of fruit, an appealing purity, and moderate tannin in a fine finish. **Anticipated maturity: 1994–2003.**

HAUT-MAILLET (POMEROL)* *

1990	C	85
1989	C	84
1988	B	76

Haut-Maillet's 1988 is light and medium bodied and has a short finish. Drink it over the next 2–3 years. Aged in 50% new oak casks, the 1989 possesses an attractive bouquet of vanillin and black cherry and plummy fruit. In the mouth there is adequate extraction of fruit, full body, plenty of alcohol, and low acidity. **Anticipated maturity: Now–1998.** The 1990 exhibits good color, a superripe, plum- and mocha-scented nose, alcoholic, round, rich, fruity flavors, and a soft finish. Drink it over the next 5–6 years.

HAUT-MARBUZET (ST.-ESTÈPHE)* * * *

1990	C	94
1989	C	88
1988	C	88

The 1988 is less dramatic than the 1989, but it is still a dark ruby-colored, flashy, seductive, full-bodied, amply endowed, and generously oaked wine. Its tannins are slightly more aggressive than fans of this property's wines usually expect, but the wine exhibits plenty of extract and size. **Anticipated maturity: Now–2003.** The 1989 displays an intense, smoky, oaky, curranty bouquet; lush, creamy, broad flavors; excellent ripeness; plenty of alcohol; and 6–8 years of drinking potential. Once again, this property has produced one of the sexiest wines of the vintage. It is impossible to resist. **Anticipated maturity: Now–2002.** The 1990 is a classic example of Haut-Marbuzet's exotic style. Huge aromas of olives, sweet new oak, and lavishly rich fruit are followed by a decadently rich, opulently styled wine that offers up gobs of sweet, herb-flavored fruit. Full bodied, high in alcohol, with soft tannins, this gorgeous multidimensional wine should drink well for another decade. **Anticipated maturity: Now–2005.** It is the finest Haut-Marbuzet since the other-worldly 1982.

PAST GLORIES: 1986 (90), 1985 (88), 1983 (88), 1982 (94)

HAUT-SARPE (ST.-ÉMILION)* *

1990	C	88
1989	C	81
1988	C	79

The 1988 Haut-Sarpe displays some attractive ripeness on the palate but finishes with some mean-spirited, aggressive tannins that suggest this wine should be consumed within its first 4–7 years of life for its exuberance rather than overall balance. The 1989 is compact, lacks dimension and flavor breadth, and has very good color but seems to have been made from grapes that were picked a bit too green and unripe. **Anticipated maturity: Now–2000.** Haut-Sarpe's 1990 is a spicy, traditionally styled wine with full body, mouth-watering tannins, lavish quantities of black cherry fruit, a thick, chewy texture, and a long, spicy finish. **Anticipated maturity: 1996–2009.** It is the best example from this estate in years.

HAUT-SOCIONDO (BLAYE)* * *

1990	A	85

This excellently run property has once again produced a powerfully scented, rich, cherry- and herb-flavored wine with good fruit, ripeness, and a long, smooth, silky finish. Drink it over the next 4–5 years.

HORTEVIE (ST.-JULIEN)* * *

1990	C	86
1989	C	87
1988	B	85

This property continues to benefit from the utilization of small new oak barrels in which to age their wine. The result is a more structured product that can support the superripe fruit and high alcohol that Hortevie frequently achieved during the 1980s. The 1988 is typical of the vintage—tannic, lean, austere, and in need of 2–3 years of cellaring. It is well made, but lighter and less complete than either the 1989 or 1990. It should drink well from now until the end of the decade. The 1989 is an excellent wine, rich, powerful, concentrated, and alcoholic, with a long, heady finish. It should prove to be this property's finest wine since 1982. **Anticipated maturity: Now–2000.** The 1990 is a rich, velvety textured, deliciously jammy wine that will make ideal drinking over the next 7–8 years. Although it lacks complexity and grip, it is plump and tasty. **Anticipated maturity: Now–1999.**

D'ISSAN (MARGAUX)* * *

1990	C	85
1989	C	83
1988	C	75

The 1988 is unacceptably light, sinewy, and lacking fruit. Moreover, this medium-bodied wine has excessive acidity and tannin. D'Issan is normally a light, delicate wine, so it is foolish to expect the power of a blockbuster wine, but this is a disappointment. The 1989 is a fruity, straightforward, smooth, agreeable yet simple wine. Ripe, with low acidity, it should be drunk over the next 4–6 years. The 1990 d'Issan is a lighter-bodied, fragrant wine with medium ruby color, spicy, sweet berry scents, medium body, moderate tannin, and decent concentration. Tasty and supple in a lighter, more delicate style, it should have 10–15 years of positive evolution in the bottle.

JONQUEYRÈS (BORDEAUX SUPÉRIEUR)* * *

1990 Vieilles Vignes	A	89

For its price and class, this is an absolutely amazing wine. Nearly black in color, and made from 75–80% Merlot and the rest Cabernet Sauvignon, the wine offers a huge nose of licorice, currants, and flowers, followed by profoundly rich, concentrated flavors, soft tannins, and a lush, amazingly long finish. The 1990 Jonqueyrès will make delicious drinking for at least a decade.

LE JURAT (ST.-ÉMILION)* * *

1990	C	84
1989	C	86
1988	C	86

A successful effort, the 1988 exhibits soft tannins as well as sufficient herb-scented, black cherry fruit. Medium bodied, with good color, this lush wine should be drunk between now and 1997. The 1989 should prove to be the finest wine produced at Le Jurat in recent memory. Black/ruby in color, with a huge bouquet of smoky, ripe, superrich black fruits, this intensely concentrated, alcoholic, large-scale wine has a supple, lush texture, plenty of soft tannins in the finish, and surprising length. **Anticipated maturity: Now–2005.** The herbaceous 1990 exhibits black cherry aromas and flavors that are presented in a medium-bodied format. This wine should be drunk over the next 4–6 years.

KIRWAN (MARGAUX)* *

1990	C	78
1989	C	83
1988	C	79

The 1988 Kirwan is a cleanly made, shallow, vaguely fruity, narrowly constructed, lean wine, with some hard tannins in the finish. Drink it over the next 3–4 years. Kirwan's wines improved during the 1980s, so I was disappointed that the 1989 did not excite me more. Elegant, charming, and soft, but lacking some intensity and character, it represents a good short-term claret for drinking between now and 1999. The 1990 is a finesse-style, light-bodied, tannic wine with medium color saturation. Though it finishes short on the palate, it should evolve and perhaps improve over the next 7–8 years.

LABÉGORCE-ZÉDÉ (MARGAUX)* * *

1990	B	88
1989	B	87
1988	B	78

Lacking substance and length, the 1988 Labégorce-Zédé possesses a slightly hollow, underripe character, as well as excessively herbal, nearly vegetal flavors. The dark-colored 1989 offers an intense aroma of plums and licorice. This full-bodied, large-scale wine has layers of fruit, soft, ripe, abundant tannins, and an impressively long finish. **Anticipated maturity: Now–2005.** Similar to the 1989, but even richer and denser, the opaque, lavishly rich, spicy, oaky 1990 exhibits excellent fruit and length. It is an authoritative, boldly flavored wine that should drink well for the next 10–15 years.

LAFITE-ROTHSCHILD (PAUILLAC)* * * * *

1990	E	94+
1989	E	92
1988	E	94

Broodingly backward and in need of considerable bottle age, the 1988 is a classic expression of Lafite. Deeper in color than the 1989, the 1988 has the telltale Lafite bouquet of cedar, subtle herbs, dried pit fruits, minerals, and cassis. Extremely concentrated, with brilliantly focused flavors and huge tannins, this backward yet impressively endowed Lafite-Rothschild may well turn out to be the wine of the vintage! **Anticipated maturity: 2000–2035.** The forward 1989 offers the telltale fragrance of lead pencils, cedar, and currant fruit and, for Lafite, unusually high glycerin and alcohol. The wine is easy to taste and appreciate, as it is rich, medium bodied, expansive, and more supple and obvious than usual. Speculating when it might be in full blossom is no easy chore given its sexy, sensual yet light style. It is somewhere between the 1953 and 1976 in stylistic terms. **Anticipated maturity: 1997–2020.** The 1990 appears to be a synthesis in style of the backward, tannic 1988 and more forward, softer 1989. The nose is not yet as seductive as the 1989's, but the wine exhibits a deeper, thicker, ruby/purple color and cuts a fuller, more complete profile on the palate. It not only rivals the seductiveness of the 1989, but it is also a far richer and more tannic wine. Although it needs at least a decade of cellaring, it should last for 30 or more years. An impressive wine, the 1990 Lafite is this estate's finest since the 1982 and 1986. **Anticipated maturity: 2000–2030.**

PAST GLORIES: 1986 (99), 1983 (92), 1982 (100), 1981 (93), 1976 (96), 1975 (96), 1959 (96), 1953 (97), 1899 (96)
PAST MEDIOCRITIES . . . OR WORSE: 1971 (60), 1970 (79), 1966 (84), 1961 (84), 1955 (84), 1949 (86), 1945 (77)

LAFLEUR (POMEROL)* * * * *

1990	E	98
1989	E	96
1988	E	93

Lafleur, one of the greatest wines of Bordeaux, is also one of the most difficult to find, as only 1,000 cases are produced. The 1988 Lafleur is a legitimate superstar of the vintage. The slow-to-emerge bouquet offers up aromas of cherries, cassis, minerals, spring flowers, and oak. Deeply colored, with a powerful, even massive mouth-feel, this wine represents the essence of old vines and low yields. The finish is dazzling, but 10–15 years of patience are essential. **Anticipated maturity: 2000–2030.** The 1989 is super, but the exotic, dense, kinky style that Lafleur usually exhibits is more refined. Dark ruby/purple in color, superconcentrated, and closed, it has a great deal of tannin and alcohol in the finish. This is a wine to be drinking during the first two and a half decades of the next millennium. **Anticipated maturity: 2000–2030.** The thick purple color of the 1990 is accompanied by a bouquet that offers up aromas of minerals, licorice, flowers, overripe black and red fruits (especially cherries), and prunes. The wine possesses gobs of tannin and glycerin, as well as exceptional concentration and richness. More viscous and weighty than the phenomenal 1989, the 1990 appears destined for 3 decades of life. Of the many great wines made at this estate, the 1990 has the potential to rival the 1979, 1975, 1950, and 1947. **Anticipated maturity: 2000–2030.**
PAST GLORIES: 1986 (95), 1985 (96), 1983 (94), 1982 (96), 1979 (96), 1978 (90), 1975 (100), 1966 (94), 1962 (95), 1961 (98?), 1955 (92), 1950 (100), 1949 (94), 1947 (100)
PAST MEDIOCRITIES . . . OR WORSE: 1981 (?), 1976 (78), 1971 (83)

LAFON-ROCHET (ST.-ESTÈPHE)* * *

1990	C	89
1989	C	88
1988	C	85

The 1988 has medium body, good ripe fruit, and commendable harmony. Surprisingly concentrated for the vintage, this excellent dark ruby-colored yet monolithic wine should age nicely for 10–20 years. Drink it between now and 2003. The 1989 Lafon-Rochet is a more tannic and brawny wine. Dark ruby, with an intense bouquet of overripe cassis, this chewy, well-endowed, full-bodied wine may be reminiscent of the excellent 1970. It is a traditionally made, surprisingly big wine. **Anticipated maturity: 1996–2015.** The 1990, a stunning effort, offers further proof of just how successful 1990 turned out to be for St.-Estèphe. Very dark ruby, with a tightly knit nose of black fruits, this massively endowed wine is as powerful and concentrated a Lafon-Rochet as I have ever tasted. Patience will be required with this offering. **Anticipated maturity: 1998–2022.**

LAGRANGE (POMEROL)* *

1990	C 86
1989	C 75
1988	C 76

The 1988 is shallow, insipid, and undistinguished. The 1989 is typically rough-edged, lean, austere, and too tannic for graceful aging. **Anticipated maturity: Now–2000.** The 1990 has turned out well, in fact, much better than I had thought possible. Deep ruby-colored, with a roasted cherry–scented bouquet and fat, jammy, chunky, flavors, this corpulent Pomerol will make delicious drinking over the next 5–6 years.

LAGRANGE (ST.-JULIEN)* * * *

1990	C 93
1989	C 89
1988	C 86

The 1988 exhibits a dark ruby/purple color and a closed but spicy, reticent bouquet vaguely suggestive of cedar, plums, and green olives. This medium-bodied, surprisingly hard and tannic wine will need 4–6 years of bottle age to soften. Also dark ruby/purple, with an intense, nearly roasted bouquet of cassis, herbs, chocolate, and smoky new oak, the full-bodied, unctuous 1989 is deeply extracted, tannic, powerful, low in acidity, but undeniably impressive in a thick, alcoholic style that will make some Bordeaux purists shudder. **Anticipated maturity: 1995–2010.** The 1990 is a stunning success for Lagrange and the finest wine made under Japanese ownership. It boasts a saturated deep purple color and a powerful aroma that suggests spicy new oak and superripe red and black fruits. The wine exhibits extremely high tannins; low acidity, spectacular richness, balance, and purity; full body; and an explosive finish. Given the muscular style and low acidity of this wine, it should be drinking well by the mid-1990s and last for 15 or more years. It bears a strong resemblance to the 1990 Léoville-Las Cases.

PAST GLORIES: 1986 (92), 1985 (89)
PAST MEDIOCRITIES . . . OR WORSE: 1978 (80), 1975 (70), 1971 (65), 1970 (84)

LA LAGUNE (LUDON)* * * *

1990	C 89
1989	C 90
1988	C 85

La Lagune's 1988 has a streak of herbaceousness and tart, aggressive tannins that appear to have the upper hand in the wine's balance. Medium bodied, spicy, and straightforward, it lacks the flesh and chewy opulence of top vintages of La Lagune, but it should prove to be long-lived. One question remains: Is there enough fruit? **Anticipated maturity: Now–2005.** The hedonistic, rich, opulent, velvet-textured 1989 displays a moderately dark ruby color, a big, intense bouquet of ripe plums and prunes, a richly concentrated, oaky fruitiness, medium to full body, plenty of glycerin, and soft tannins. This sensual, alluring wine will drink well for the next 10–15 years. **Anticipated maturity: Now–2008.** Made from superripe fruit, the 1990 exhibits low acidity; excellent concentration; a smoky, nutty, sweet berrylike fruitiness; a round, generous texture; and a fat, lush finish. It lacks some grip but should provide delicious, complex drinking over the next decade. It tastes more like Burgundy than Bordeaux.

PAST GLORIES: 1986 (90), 1982 (93), 1978 (88), 1976 (88)
PAST MEDIOCRITIES . . . OR WORSE: 1966 (84), 1961 (60)

LAMARQUE (HAUT-MÉDOC)* * *

1990	A	87
1989	B	85

Spicy, with new oak intermingled with aromas of black cherries and herbs, the 1989 is fleshy in the mouth, with good intensity, an attractive ripeness, and a solid, structured finish. Drink it over the next 6–7 years. The 1990, the finest Lamarque in years, is an attractive, oaky, blackcurrant-scented wine, supple, concentrated, powerful, and long. Drinkable now, it should mature over the next 6–10 years.

LANESSAN (HAUT-MÉDOC)* * */* * * *

1990	C	88
1989	B	87
1988	B	86

The 1988 Lanessan is a full, rich, concentrated wine. Deep and ripe, with a complex bouquet of menthol, cedar, and blackcurrants intertwined with subtle scents of oak, this plump, highly concentrated, full-bodied wine should drink beautifully for 10–15 years. **Anticipated maturity: Now–2008.** Lanessan's 1989 is herbaceous but also fat, richly fruity, and soft. A weighty, rich, full-bodied wine, it offers gorgeous amounts of fruit, glycerin, and tannin. **Anticipated maturity: Now–2004.** The 1990 is opaque with a huge, peppery, spicy, black cherry nose intermingled with aromas of Provençal herbs. In the mouth there is excellent richness, a density and thickness to the texture, and tannin and glycerin in the long finish. It should drink well for 10–12 or more years.

LANGOA-BARTON (ST.-JULIEN)* * *

1990	C	87
1989	C	86
1988	C	85

The 1988 Langoa-Barton has some ripeness in its aroma but is austere, compact, and medium bodied. It should age well given the abundant tannins and firm framework. Drink it between now and the year 2000. The 1989 is a medium-bodied, pretty wine, but not as tannic, powerful, and concentrated as other St.-Juliens. The bouquet offers a pleasing tobacco, spice, and currant mélange. Well balanced, with a nice marriage of oak and red fruits, this wine displays surprisingly decent acidity. **Anticipated maturity: Now–2005.** The elegant, medium-bodied, tannic 1990 exhibits attractive ripe fruit as well as moderate depth and intensity. **Anticipated maturity: 1995–2005.**

LARCIS-DUCASSE (ST.-ÉMILION)* * *

1990	C	90
1989	C	86
1988	C	87

Larcis-Ducasse made an excellent wine in 1988—full bodied, rich, with impressive ripeness and length and at least 20 years of potential evolution. This is an admirable, old-style wine that will appeal to those who have patience. **Anticipated maturity: 1996–2010.** The 1989, although filled with tannin and structured for aging up to 30 years, does not have quite the inner core of depth and intensity of the 1988. This is an imposingly backward style of wine that may ultimately merit a higher score—provided the fruit does not dry out before the tannin fades. **Anticipated maturity: 1998–2010.** The 1990 is a wine of impressive richness, with a spicy, cedary, cassis-scented nose, a creamy, velvety texture, and rich, full-bodied flavors. There are layers of fruit supported by moderate tannins. A little more concentration and this wine could have been monumental. **Anticipated maturity: 1995–2008.**

LARMANDE (ST.-ÉMILION)* * */* * * *

1990	C	88
1989	C	88
1988	C	90

A consistent overachiever, Larmande has produced a thrilling 1988. Black/ruby/purple in color, with a superbouquet of plums, minerals, and spicy new oak, this rich, highly extracted, lusciously put together St.-Émilion has gorgeous extract levels. Deep, full bodied, impeccably pure, and well balanced, it should drink well for the next 10–15 years. **Anticipated maturity: Now–2002.** Also a flattering wine, the 1989 is nearly as structured and concentrated as the 1988. If you like wonderfully round, hedonistic, soft, alcoholic, luscious St.-Émilions, this superripe, heady, and voluptuously textured wine will offer many thrills. **Anticipated maturity: Now–2001.** The charming, personable 1990 Larmande displays fine color, excellent ripe plum and cassis fruit, full body, and considerable tannin in the finish. The telltale signs of the 1990 vintage—high levels of hard tannins, plenty of succulent, chewy fruit, and exceptionally low acidity—are all present. **Anticipated maturity: 1994–2003.**

LAROSE-TRINTAUDON (HAUT-MÉDOC)* *

1990	A	86
1989	B	82

The oaky, ripe fruit of the 1989 is followed by a medium-bodied, soft, low-acid wine that should drink nicely for another 4–5 years. The 1990 is significantly better. Dark ruby-colored, with a rich, lush, fragrant bouquet, this exuberantly fruity wine offers good body and balance. An excellent restaurant wine, it should be drunk over the next 5–6 years.

LASCOMBES (MARGAUX)* * *

1990	C	86
1989	C	85
1988	C	85

Deep ruby/purple, with a moderately intense bouquet of cedar, plums, and currants, the 1988 Lascombes is a spicy, robustly styled Margaux. Medium to full bodied and well balanced, it is not as excessively tannic as many 1988 Médocs tend to be. **Anticipated maturity: 1994–2002.** Lascombes's 1989 has an aroma of roasted peanuts. A muscular, tannic wine, it exhibits a powerful, rich, alcoholic finish. I would not be surprised to see this wine turn out much better than my rating. **Anticipated maturity: Now–2002.** Exhibiting good tannin, the exotic, orange-scented 1990 offers up ripe aromas of tropical fruits, cassis, and new oak. Rich, medium to full bodied, with excellent concentration, low acidity, and a velvety, even voluptuous mouth-feel, this wine should provide delicious drinking over the next 8–10 years.

PAST GLORIES: 1966 (88), 1959 (90)

PAST MEDIOCRITIES . . . OR WORSE: 1981 (72), 1979 (76), 1978 (76)

LATOUR (PAUILLAC)* * * * *

1990	EEE	98+
1989	EEE	90
1988	EE	89

The 1988 Latour is deep in color, has a complex mineral, hickory wood, leafy, and blackcurrant-scented bouquet, a medium body, and nicely extracted flavors, but ferocious tannins in the finish. Patience will most definitely be required. Developing more richness and character than I had previously anticipated, it is certainly more classic and typical of Latour than several of the property's more recent vintages (such as 1983, 1985, and 1989). **Anticipated maturity: 2000–2025.** The 1989 Latour is deep ruby/purple, with a penetrating bouquet of cassis. This elegant, medium-bodied, surprisingly approachable wine is bursting with fruit and extract. The finish is admirably long and persistent. The high tannins are largely obscured by the wine's fine fruit and depth. For lovers of Latour, this is an understated, remarkably restrained style of wine. **Anticipated maturity: 1997–2015.** Unquestionably the 1990 is the finest, most archetypal Latour since the 1982 and 1970. In fact, the 1990 signals a return to the more forceful, opaque, powerful, brute-strength style for which Latour was famous during most of this century. The flirtation, intentional or otherwise, with a lighter style of wine is not apparent in this blockbuster. The 1990 exhibits tight but highly promising aromas of minerals, roasted nuts, and superripe, rich cassis fruit. It is an exceptionally powerful wine, with massive intensity and plenty of glycerin, as well as extraordinary extract and mouth-searing tannins that explode on the palate. Along with Montrose, Margaux, and Pétrus, Latour is a strong favorite for the wine of the vintage! A triumph! **Anticipated maturity: 2000–2035.**

PAST GLORIES: 1986 (91), 1982 (99), 1978 (93), 1975 (92), 1971 (91), 1970 (99), 1966 (95), 1964 (90), 1962 (93), 1961 (100), 1959 (95), 1949 (98), 1945 (99?), 1928 (95), 1924 (94), 1900 (89), 1899 (93), 1870 (90)

PAST MEDIOCRITIES . . . OR WORSE: Virtually none in top vintages, although the 1985, 1983, 1979, and 1976 are below the château's extraordinarily high standards.

LATOUR À POMEROL (POMEROL)* * * *

1990	D	88
1989	E	87
1988	D	87

The 1988 Latour à Pomerol exhibits an oaky, soft, fruity, tea- and berry-scented bouquet and rich, ripe, admirably concentrated flavors that display some sweetness and length. This is a luscious style of wine for drinking over the next 7–9 years. The 1989 Latour à Pomerol possesses a deep ruby/purple color and a full-intensity bouquet of spices, new wood, plums, and cassis. This expansively flavored, seemingly sweet (because of the fruit's ripeness), full-flavored wine has considerable tannin in the finish. **Anticipated maturity: 1995–2015.** The 1990 is superripe, supple, and already delicious. Made in an unctuous, richer, more meaty style than the 1989, it exhibits fine ripeness, a generous fruitiness, and flattering, sweet, plummy, oaky flavors. **Anticipated maturity: Now–2004.**

PAST GLORIES: 1983 (88), 1982 (93), 1970 (90), 1961 (100), 1959 (94), 1947 (100)

PAST MEDIOCRITIES . . . OR WORSE: 1978 (83), 1975 (67), 1971 (82)

LÉOVILLE-BARTON (ST.-JULIEN)* * * *

1990	C	94
1989	C	88
1988	C	88

The 1988 Léoville-Barton is a classic example of the vintage. The tannins are hard, but the wine exhibits plenty of depth, an inner core of juicy cassis fruit, firm structure, and very good length. This is an excellent wine, with plenty of rich, deep, curranty fruit to balance out the tannins. **Anticipated maturity: 1996–2012.** Léoville-Barton's 1989 is an elegantly wrought, admirably concentrated wine. It reveals considerable tannin, an inner core of sweet, expansive, curranty fruit, low acidity, and a moderately long finish. **Anticipated maturity: 1996–2010.** The 1990 is a dense, full-bodied, tannic, and concentrated wine with significant potential. It should turn out to be among the richest and most complex St.-Julien proprietor Anthony Barton has yet fashioned. It is sweeter and more unctuous than the 1986 and more concentrated than the 1985. A classic wine, as well as a notable bargain, it will age effortlessly. **Anticipated maturity: 1996–2020.**

PAST GLORIES: 1986 (92), 1985 (92), 1982 (93), 1975 (90), 1961 (92), 1959 (94), 1953 (93), 1949 (94), 1948 (96), 1945 (98)

PAST MEDIOCRITIES . . . OR WORSE: 1979 (75), 1971 (70), 1966 (84)

LÉOVILLE-LAS CASES (ST.-JULIEN)* * * * *

1990	EE	94+
1989	EE	95
1988	E	92

The 1988 is one of the true stars of the vintage. The full-intensity bouquet of black cherries and toasty new oak is high class. Beautifully balanced, medium-bodied, concentrated flavors exhibit impressive ripeness and high tannins. The rich and full 1988 Léoville-Las Cases avoids the harsh, dry, astringent taste of many 1988s. **Anticipated maturity: 1995–2020.** Michel Delon has also produced an enthralling 1989. In weight, texture, and character it resembles a synthesis of his 1982 and 1986. Opaque, deep ruby/purple (one of the thickest wines in color), this superbly extracted wine has an awesome bouquet of black and red fruits nicely interspersed with scents of vanillin. Rich, opulent, long, and mouth-filling, Léoville-Las Cases is packed with fruit and is large framed yet astonishingly well balanced. **Anticipated maturity: 1998–2020.** The structured, dense 1990 possesses a black/ruby color and dazzling concentration, as well as fine acidity. It exhibits a pure nose of black cherries, as well as cassis, aromas of lead pencil and new oak, and gorgeously rich, long, classic flavors. This is another backward, classic wine made for long-term cellaring. **Anticipated maturity: 2000–2020.**

PAST GLORIES: 1986 (97), 1985 (92), 1983 (90), 1982 (100), 1981 (88), 1978 (92), 1975 (92), 1966 (90)

PAST MEDIOCRITIES . . . OR WORSE: 1971 (73), 1970 (77), 1961 (84)

LÉOVILLE-POYFERRÉ (ST.-JULIEN)* * *

1990	D	92
1989	C	87
1988	C	82

The 1988 Léoville-Poyferré, which is austere and supercharged with tannin, exhibits leanness and a lack of fruit and charm. It will age well, but will it ever provide much pleasure? **Anticipated maturity: 1994–2006.** If the tannins had not been so forbiddingly high, I would have been more supportive of this château's 1989. Dark ruby, but not as opaque or purple as some 1989s tend to be, this medium-bodied, tough-textured wine looks to be a long-distance runner, but will the fruit hold up? **Anticipated maturity: 1998–2020.** The 1990 (40% of the crop was declassified) is the most impressive Poyferré produced since 1983 and 1982. Black/purple, with a tight but promising aroma of jammy black fruits, herbs, and new wood, this well-endowed, brilliant wine offers gobs of tannins and extract. Full bodied and chewy, with superb purity, this wine will repay long cellaring. Bravo! **Anticipated maturity: 1996–2025.** P.S. Poyferré's second wine, the 1990 Moulin Riche, is very good. I rated it 86.

PAST GLORIES: 1983 (90), 1982 (92)

PAST MEDIOCRITIES . . . OR WORSE: 1976 (75), 1975 (?), 1970 (65), 1962 (67)

LIVERSAN (HAUT-MÉDOC)* * *

1990	B	85
1989	B	85
1988	B	86

The 1988 exhibits a deep ruby/purple color, a wonderful bouquet of spicy oak, black cherries, and cassis, excellent richness, depth, and superlative length. **Anticipated maturity: Now–2000.** Medium dark ruby, with a moderately intense bouquet of vanillin, spices, and black fruits, the supple, fruity 1989 is a Cru Bourgeois for drinking over the next 4–5 years. Deep ruby/purple, with a tight but promising bouquet of cassis and spicy oak, the medium-bodied 1990 exhibits fine depth, a firm structure, and a good, clean, authoritative finish. It should drink nicely for at least 7–8 years.

LA LOUVIÈRE (GRAVES)* * * *

1990	C	89
1989	C	87
1988	C	89

The finest La Louvière I have tasted, the 1988 is a concentrated, well-balanced wine possessing a delectable roasted, cassis fruitiness that expands on the palate. Impressively concentrated, with an opulent texture and velvety tannins, this complete wine should provide delicious drinking over the next decade. **Anticipated maturity: Now–2002.** Deep, nearly opaque, with a spicy, overripe nose of jammy black fruits, tobacco, and prunes, the full-bodied 1989 is already delicious. **Anticipated maturity: 1994–2005.** The 1990 has turned out to be a fuller-bodied, more deeply concentrated wine than the 1989. Although more tightly knit and less charming at the moment, it is a more complete wine, with greater length and aging potential. The wine is opaque black/purple-colored, with fragrant bouquet of toast and cassis. **Anticipated maturity: 1995–2006.**

LYNCH-BAGES (PAUILLAC)* * * * *

1990	D	93
1989	D	96
1988	D	90

Undoubtedly, the 1988 Lynch-Bages is the biggest wine produced in the northern Médoc in this vintage. The saturated black/ruby/purple color suggests excellent ripeness and plenty of concentration. The oaky bouquet exhibits roasted black raspberries and currants, as well as an earthy, robust character. The wine is full bodied and rich, with an attractive cedary, herbaceous, black fruit character. This fleshy, broad-shouldered wine characterizes the style of the château. **Anticipated maturity: Now–2010.** The 1989 is the finest young Lynch-Bages I have ever tasted. Its opaque black/purple color suggests a level of concentration one rarely sees in Bordeaux. Some might accuse this wine of being too extracted, too weighty, and too unclaretlike, but that is what the great old Lynch-Bages vintages of 1970, 1961, and 1955 all offered. A powermonger that wants to grab all your attention, this bruiser is a superwine and undoubtedly one of the finest ever made at this property. **Anticipated maturity: 1996–2015.** The 1990 Lynch-Bages offers a sweet, superripe nose and lavishly rich, low acid, chewy flavors. It is obviously not as concentrated and massive as the extraordinary 1989, but it does possess fabulous richness and a huge, full-bodied, velvet-textured taste. There is plenty to like and enjoy in this offering, which reminds me of a richer, more concentrated 1985. What a glorious mouthful of claret! **Anticipated maturity: 1994–2010.**

PAST GLORIES: 1986 (92), 1985 (93), 1983 (88), 1982 (93), 1970 (95), 1962 (89), 1961 (94), 1959 (94), 1957 (88), 1955 (92), 1953 (90), 1952 (91)

PAST MEDIOCRITIES . . . OR WORSE: 1979 (79), 1978 (82), 1976 (72), 1975 (79), 1971 (58), 1966 (84)

LYNCH-MOUSSAS (PAUILLAC)* *

1989	C	79
1988	C	80

Light, yet fruity and medium bodied, with good concentration, the soft, somewhat one-dimensional 1988 should be drunk over the next 4–6 years. The 1989 is pleasant and cleanly made, but uncommonly light and soft for such a well-placed vineyard. Drink it over the next 4–5 years. **Anticipated maturity: Now–1996.**

MAGDELAINE (ST.-ÉMILION)* * */* * * *

1990	E	92
1989	E	90
1988	D	87

The bouquet of the 1988 Magdelaine is understated, but the wine exhibits fine ripeness and intensity, along with attractive cherry fruit intertwined with toasty new oak. **Anticipated maturity: 1995–2005.** The 1989 remains the finest young Magdelaine I have tasted. Deep ruby/purple in color, with a restrained but blossoming bouquet of chocolatey, superextracted, roasted, plummy fruit, this wine has an extra dimension to its flavors and excellent length yet remains understated and well balanced. There is considerable tannin in the finish, but the alcohol seems less exaggerated than in many St.-Émilions, and the acidity is sound. **Anticipated maturity: 2000–2025.** The 1990 Magdelaine is the most sumptuous example I have tasted of this wine. The nose reveals interesting herb, berry, mineral, and vanillin scents. Copious, even lavish quantities of sweet tobacco-, coffee-, and orange tea–like flavors can be found in this superripe Merlot-based wine. The acidity is adequate, and the moderate tannins are firm. Magdelaine represents a different expression of St.-Émilion that tasters often find too austere. The opulent, even decadent 1990 is an exception. **Anticipated maturity: 1995–2008.**

PAST GLORIES: 1982 (90), 1961 (91)

PAST MEDIOCRITIES . . . OR WORSE: 1986 (?), 1985 (82), 1981 (80), 1979 (84)

MALARTIC-LAGRAVIÈRE (GRAVES)* *

1990	C	73
1989	C	82
1988	C	77

The 1988 Malartic-Lagravière is lean, austere, light bodied, and too polite. A little excess would have been appreciated. **Anticipated maturity: Now–2000.** The 1989 is extremely subtle, light to medium bodied, forward, yet structured enough to last until the end of the century. **Anticipated maturity: 2000–2007.** The 1990 is an excessively introverted, shy style of wine, as well as frightfully light colored. The weedy nose and flavors are also surprising.

MALESCASSE (HAUT-MÉDOC)* */* * *

1990	B	86
1989	B	81

Reticent from an aromatic perspective, the austere, medium-bodied 1989 exhibits pleasant fruit but finishes dry and lean. Nevertheless, there is some charm to be found. Drink it over the next 5–6 years. The 1990 is sweet, richly fruity, medium bodied, dense, and chewy. It, too, should be drunk over the next 5–6 years.

MALESCOT ST.-EXUPÉRY (MARGAUX)* * *

1990	C	89
1989	C	86
1988	C	84

The 1988 Malescot's bouquet offers a stylish mix of oak, herbs, and blackcurrants. Medium bodied, austere, yet backed up with sufficient fruit to age well, this elegantly wrought wine should be at its best between now and 2005. The 1989 displays the big, ripe, heady bouquet typical of so many wines of this vintage. It is ripe, richly fruity, and expansive on the palate, with some generous alcohol in the finish. **Anticipated maturity: Now–2002.** I have never been so impressed with a young vintage of Malescot as I am with the 1990. Although it can often lack ripeness and intensity, the rich suave 1990 exhibits an attractive bouquet of sweet ripe cherries, herbs, and new oak, medium body, a lovely balanced feel on the palate, and a supple finish. Drinkable young, it should evolve well for 12–18 years.

PAST GLORIES: 1961 (92), 1959 (90)

PAST MEDIOCRITIES . . . OR WORSE: 1986 (82), 1985 (74), 1983 (83), 1981 (78), 1978 (78), 1975 (76), 1966 (67)

MARBUZET (ST.-ESTÈPHE)* */* * *

1990	B	86
1989	B	85
1988	B	80

Initially, the 1988 Marbuzet was excessively tannic, but it has dropped much of its tannin and is now tasting softer. It is ideal for consuming over the next

3–4 years. The 1989 Marbuzet is richly fruity, supple, fragrant, and perfect for drinking over the next 5–7 years. **Anticipated maturity: Now–1997.** The rich, soft, oaky, forward, open-knit yet concentrated flavors of the 1990 offer immediate appeal. This excellent second wine will provide delicious drinking over the next 4–6 years. Restaurants take notice!

CHÂTEAU MARGAUX (MARGAUX)* * * * *

1990	EEE	100
1989	EEE	90
1988	EE	88

The 1988 Margaux has a classic bouquet of violets and blackcurrants intertwined with the vanillin scents of new oak. Medium bodied, decently concentrated, but extremely hard and tannic, this surprisingly tough-textured, stern wine should outlive the 1989, but will it ever provide as much charm and pleasure? The astringent nature of the tannins in the finish gives me cause for concern. **Anticipated maturity: 2000–2015.** The aggressively oaky 1989 reveals excellent color, deep, ripe aromas of cassis, medium to full body, soft tannins, and low acidity. Although forward, it is still capable of 20 or more years of evolution. I do wonder about the overt smell of raw oak in this wine. **Anticipated maturity: 1996–2015.** More than any other recent vintage, the 1990 reminds me of what Château Margaux's classic 1953 might have tasted like at age 3. Not a heavyweight in the style of the 1982, the 1990 exhibits an ethereal bouquet of flowers, cassis, smoke, new oak, and Asian spices. The tannins are significant but tender, and the wine is expansive, with remarkable finesse, richness, and a smooth-as-silk finish. The wine's exceptional richness and harmony are hallmarks. This vintage gets my nod as the most classic example of Margaux made under the Mentzelopoulos administration. The 1990 is a majestic vintage for Château Margaux, as well as one of the greatest wines of this superb vintage. **Anticipated maturity: 1997–2020.**
PAST GLORIES: 1986 (98), 1985 (92), 1983 (96), 1982 (100), 1981 (90), 1979 (92), 1978 (94), 1961 (93), 1953 (96), 1947 (92), 1945 (94), 1928 (97), 1900 (100)
PAST MEDIOCRITIES . . . OR WORSE: 1976 (70), 1975 (68), 1971 (70), 1970 (76), 1966 (83), 1964 (78)

MARQUIS D'ALESME-BECKER (MARGAUX)* *

1990	C	79
1988	C	80

Medium ruby, with a straightforward, curranty, plummy bouquet, the relatively light, medium-bodied, straightforwardly styled 1988 should be consumed over the next 4–6 years. Where is the famed Margaux fragrance and velvety, enthralling texture? Deep in color, with a woody, nondescript nose, the spicy, hard, medium-bodied 1990 exhibits more tannin than ripe fruit. It possesses too much structure and too little fruit for my taste. Drink it in its first 7–8 years of life.

MARQUIS-DE-TERME (MARGAUX)* * *

1990	C	87
1989	C	89
1988	C	86

Deep ruby/purple, with a spicy, oaky, relatively intense bouquet, the 1988 Marquis-de-Terme has good body, fine extract levels, a moderately high level of tannin, and good aging potential. **Anticipated maturity: Now–2005.** The 1989 is an excellent wine, dark ruby, medium to full bodied, fleshy, and chewy, with low acidity and high alcohol. The expansive, superripe, nearly sweet-tasting flavors give this wine immense crowd appeal. It should develop quickly. **Anticipated maturity: Now–2004.** Spicy new oak and copious quantities of black fruits dominate the nose of the 1990. The wine exhibits medium body, an expansive, lush richness, plenty of extract and glycerin, fine tannins, and a smooth finish. **Anticipated maturity: 1995–2002.**

MAUCAILLOU (MOULIS)* * */* * * *

1989	C	87
1988	B	86

The 1988 Maucaillou is an extremely attractive, oaky, plump, elegant, richly fruity, medium-bodied wine that should drink beautifully for the next 4–6 years. The 1989 has a generous level of gorgeous black raspberry fruit in its bouquet, followed by wonderfully rich, fleshy, highly extracted fruit flavors and a velvety texture. It is pure seduction and finesse in the finish. **Anticipated maturity: Now–2001.**

MAZERIS (CANON-FRONSAC)* * *

1990	C	87

I have admired the wines of Mazeris for their vivid purity of sweet black raspberry fruit. The 1990 continues to suggest that this characteristic is the most dominant personality trademark of Mazeris. There is fine intensity, good sweetness and richness on the palate, medium body, moderate tannins, and an impressive finish that is neither too heavy nor oaky. **Anticipated maturity: 1995–2005.**

MEYNEY (ST.-ESTÈPHE)* * */* * * *

1990	B	88
1989	C	90
1988	B	88

If you lack patience, you will want no part of the 1988 Meyney. Tannic yet packed with fruit, the 1988 will need at least 5 years of cellaring. **Anticipated maturity: 1998–2015.** The 1989 is one of the finest Meyneys ever produced. The opaque black/ruby color, a bouquet of minerals and damson plums, the alcoholic, massive flavors and the mouth-coating tannins all combine to create a sensory overload. The 1989 will prove uncommonly long-lived as well as profoundly flavored. **Anticipated maturity: 1995–2020.** Though not as rich as the 1989, the 1990 is still a fine effort from this perennial overachiever.

It offers deep ruby/purple color; a fine nose of black fruits, herbs, and oak; ripe, generous, tannin-dominated flavors; good concentration; and a moderately long, tough finish. **Anticipated maturity: 1996–2010.**
PAST GLORIES: 1986 (91), 1982 (90), 1975 (90)

LA MISSION-HAUT-BRION (GRAVES)* * * * *

1990	EE	92
1989	EEE	99
1988	D	90

Perhaps the high quantity of Merlot (45% in this vintage's blend) has helped provide the 1988 with significant opulence and depth of fruit. The 1988 has turned out to be a beautifully made, deep, full-bodied, concentrated, rich, well-structured wine that will last for 15–20 years. It is a big, deep, soft, concentrated wine. **Anticipated maturity: 1994–2012.** The 1989 La Mission-Haut-Brion irrefutably ranks with the finest wines made at this château. It is a thick, muscular, sensationally concentrated wine. Once past the roasted cassis and smoky, chocolatey nose, the wine is superbly extracted with plum and tar-like flavors framed with generous quantities of new oak. The 1989 is voluptuous, unctuous, and massively concentrated. Nevertheless, it should drink reasonably well given its heady alcohol content and soft tannins. It is clearly a La Mission that will last for at least several decades. **Anticipated maturity: 1995–2015.** The 1990 reveals excellent weight and richness, as well as surprising opulence. The color is an opaque, deep ruby/purple, and the nose offers up forceful scents of toasty vanillin oak intertwined with aromas of black fruits, minerals, smoke, and hickory. In the mouth there is wonderful richness, a sweet, expansive palate, a chewy texture, and a deep, persistent, splendidly rich finish. **Anticipated maturity: 1995–2010.**
PAST GLORIES: 1986 (90), 1985 (92), 1983 (90), 1982 (94), 1981 (90), 1979 (91), 1978 (94), 1975 (100), 1970 (94?), 1966 (89), 1964 (91), 1961 (100), 1959 (100), 1958 (94), 1957 (93), 1955 (100), 1953 (93), 1952 (93), 1950 (90), 1949 (100), 1947 (94), 1946 (90), 1945 (94), 1937 (88), 1929 (98)
PAST MEDIOCRITIES . . . OR WORSE: Virtually none, although the 1976 is somewhat of a disappointment, and of course, many bottles of the 1970 are plagued by excessive volatile acidity.

MONBRISON (MARGAUX)* * */* * * *

1990	C	88
1989	C	89
1988	C	90

Sadly, the brilliant winemaker behind the recent success of Monbrison, Jean-Luc Vonderheyden, died in 1992. His pursuit of excellence will be hard to forget. The 1988 Monbrison is a special wine. The dazzling bouquet of new oak, smoke, superripe blackcurrants, Provençal herbs, and minerals is first class. Black/ruby in color, this highly extracted, rich, concentrated, medium- to full-bodied wine surpasses the quality of most of the Margaux classified growths. **Anticipated maturity: 1994–2005.** The black/purple-colored 1989 is fabulous. It reveals none of the problems that many Margaux châteaux encountered in 1989. Although extremely tannic and backward, it displays good acidity, stupendous concentration and length, and the potential to age for 20 or more years. **Anticipated maturity: 1994–2010.** The softer 1990 is a lovely, rich, complex wine with an impressive dark ruby/purple color, a smoky, floral, cassis-scented nose, medium- to full-bodied flavors, and a nicely extracted, elegant finish. **Anticipated maturity: 1994–2007.**

MONTROSE (ST.-ESTÈPHE)* * * */* * * * *

1990	E	100
1989	D	94
1988	C	83

The surprisingly light 1988 Montrose lacks richness and depth. **Anticipated maturity: Now–2000.** Montrose produced a brilliant 1989. Some of Bordeaux's cognoscenti claim it is the greatest wine produced at the estate since 1959. Dark ruby/purple, with an intense aroma of crushed raspberries, minerals, wood, and iron, the 1989 has a full-bodied, highly extracted feel on the palate, plus gobs of soft tannins, low acidity, and high alcohol in its explosive finish. It is one of the vintage's superstars. **Anticipated maturity: 1998–2025.** The 1990 has turned out to be even better than the extraordinary 1989. Dense black/purple-colored, with a tight yet potentially sensational bouquet of new saddle leather, black fruits, Oriental spices, new oak, and minerals, the 1990 exhibits profound concentration of fruit, a spectacularly intense midpalate, and massive power. One of the superstars of this superb vintage, Montrose is also one of the most awesomely concentrated, forceful, and monumental wines made in Bordeaux over recent decades. **Anticipated maturity: 2000–2045.**

PAST GLORIES: 1986 (91), 1982 (89), 1970 (94), 1964 (92), 1961 (95), 1959 (96), 1955 (90), 1953 (93)

PAST MEDIOCRITIES . . . OR WORSE: 1988 (83), 1985 (85), 1983 (83), 1981 (84), 1979 (82), 1978 (84)

MOULIN DU CADET (ST.-ÉMILION)* *

1990	C	86
1989	B	85
1988	B	75

The 1988 Moulin du Cadet is a hard, austere, malnourished, skinny wine lacking charm and character. Avoid it. There is a significant difference between the 1989 and 1988 Moulin du Cadet. The 1989 possesses rich, sweet, expansive flavors and exhibits good concentration and length. **Anticipated maturity: Now–1996.** The medium-bodied 1990 gushes with fruit. Fat and supple, this tasty, disarming wine should be drunk over the next 3–5 years.

MOULIN-HAUT-LAROQUE (FRONSAC)* * *

1990	C	86

Proprietor Jean-Noel Hervé consistently produces one of the best wines in Fronsac. His 1990, although not as powerful or impressive as the 1989, is a rich, intense, concentrated wine, with extremely low acidity, a weighty feel on the palate, and plenty of depth and texture. Although the 1990 will not be as long-lived or as profound as the 1989, it should provide delicious drinking over the next 10–12 years.

MOULIN-ROUGE (HAUT-MÉDOC)* * *

1990		B	87
1989		A	87
1988		A	85

Not as sumptuous as the 1989 or 1990, the 1988 Moulin-Rouge still delivers plenty of up-front, rich, supple, curranty fruit, a silky texture, and a satisfyingly long finish. **Anticipated maturity: Now-1995.** The 1989 is an immensely appealing, sweet, expansive, full-bodied, opulent wine that is crammed with delicious black raspberry and blackcurrant fruit. The overall impression is one of an unctuous, fleshy quality. Drink it over the next 4–6 years. Absolutely delicious! The 1990's fat, ripe, succulent aromas are followed by expansive, round flavors. There is a sweet taste because of the fruit's superripeness. Very similar to the 1989, this delicious, forward, seductive wine will make excellent drinking over the next 5–7 years.

MOULINET (POMEROL)* *

1990		C	83
1989		C	85
1988		B	79

Moulinet's 1988 will last longer than the 1989 but will never provide as much pleasure given its undernourished, lean, compact, short flavors. The 1989 is about as good a wine as Moulinet is capable of producing. It is a big, jammy, ripe, hedonistic wine lacking complexity but offering straightforward, chunky, luscious fruit, medium body, with a soft texture and alcoholic finish. **Anticipated maturity: Now–1997.** An easygoing, lighter-styled, medium-bodied wine, Moulinet's 1990 exhibits soft tannins, noticeable alcohol, and little concentration or grip. At its best, it is charming and pleasant. Drink it over the next 5–6 years.

MOUTON-ROTHSCHILD (PAUILLAC)* * * * *

1990		EEE	87
1989		EEE	88
1988		EEE	89

The 1988 Mouton has an attractive aroma of exotic spices, minerals, coffee, blackcurrants, and sweet oak. Much like the 1989, the bouquet is staggering, but the flavors are distinctly less profound. In the mouth it is a much firmer, tougher, more obviously tannic wine than the 1989, with medium body and outstanding ripeness. A beautifully made 1988 that will last 20–25 years, its short finish keeps it from being sublime. The 1988 is somewhat reminiscent of the 1985, but with more tannin. **Anticipated maturity: 1997–2020.** The 1989's perfume of Oriental spices, soy sauce, leather, toasty oak, mocha, and blackcurrants is amazingly developed for such a young wine. The wine continues to reveal an aggressively woody note and lacks weight and depth in the mouth. Moreover, the finish is surprisingly brisk given the up-front fragrance. This is a wine I overrated from cask. It is comparable stylistically to the ready-to-drink 1985, but lighter and more blatantly oaky. It should be drinkable early, and I suspect most admirers of the flashy, dramatic style of wine made at Mouton will want to consume it between 1996 and 2010. The 1990, also impressive from barrel, is a disappointment from the bottle. Although less evolved than the 1989, it is excessively oaky, with a Jack Daniel's, whiskey barrel–like smell. It is medium-bodied, somewhat hollow, and frankly embarrassed when tasted beside the likes of Latour and Margaux. I tasted it from the bottle 3 times with identical impressions. What a shame! The 1990's label by the late Francis Bacon is stunning. **Anticipated maturity: 1999–2010.**

PAST GLORIES: 1986 (100), 1985 (92), 1983 (90), 1982 (100), 1970 (92?), 1966 (90), 1962 (90), 1961 (92?), 1959 (99), 1955 (97), 1952 (87), 1949 (91), 1947 (97), 1945 (100)

PAST MEDIOCRITIES . . . OR WORSE: 1981 (83), 1979 (84), 1978 (86)

NENIN (POMEROL)* *

1990	C	84
1989	C	78

The 1989 Nenin is frightfully light and simple for the vintage, resembling a generic Bordeaux rather than one of the better-known estates of Pomerol. It possesses soft tannins, meager fruitiness, and innocuous character. **Anticipated maturity: Now–1996.** The 1990, which exhibits surprisingly good color, is a wine with attractive mineral, floral, and black fruit aromas, medium body, moderate tannins, and a plump, tough-textured finish. **Anticipated maturity: 1994–2001.**

OLIVIER (GRAVES)**

1990	C	85
1989	C	84

Olivier's 1989 is one of the best efforts in some time from this perennial underachiever. The bouquet is dominated by gobs of spicy new oak and a sweet, almost Beaujolais-like, red fruit character. In the mouth it is medium bodied, light, and soft. It is a pleasant, picnic-style claret that requires consumption over the next 3–4 years. As for the 1990, an attractively ripe, oaky, black cherry–scented nose is followed by a wine with medium body, soft, smooth flavors, low acidity, and some tannin. Although there is something slick about its style, it is an enjoyable, cleanly made, chunky wine that is ideal for drinking over the next 5–6 years.

LES-ORMES-DE-PEZ (ST.-ESTÈPHE)* * *

1990	B	89
1989	C	86
1988	B	85

The 1988 is a tasty, surprisingly forward wine that should drink well for up to a decade. The opulent and intense 1989 is full bodied and softly tannic. It should provide robust drinking for at least a decade. **Anticipated maturity: Now–2000.** The dark, almost opaque ruby/purple-colored 1990 exhibits excellent depth, plenty of stuffing and focus, and a long, ripe, alcoholic finish. This lavishly rich, full-bodied offering is supple and stunning, as well as a notable value. Drink it over the next 10–15 years.

LES ORMES-SORBET (MÉDOC)* * *

1990	B	86

An oaky, cassis-scented nose is followed by sweet, rich, superripe flavors, low acidity, and firm tannins. The 1990 Les Ormes-Sorbet should prove to be an attractive wine for drinking over the next 5–6 years.

PALMER (MARGAUX)* * * * *

1990	E	87
1989	E	96
1988	D	87

Palmer's 1988 offers a promising sweet bouquet of ripe plums, has dense, rich, concentrated fruit, medium body, and an expansive, lush, heady finish. This is one of the best and most delicious wines of the Margaux appellation in 1988. **Anticipated maturity: Now–2006.** Palmer's 1989 is magnificent. It remains a wine of immense seduction. The bouquet roars from the glass, offering aromas of black fruit, spring flowers, licorice, and sweet oak. The expansive, rich, fat texture owes its opulence to the high percentage of Merlot used by this property. Opaque, deep ruby/purple, this full-bodied, satiny wine has considerable alcoholic clout, is low in acidity, but splendidly concentrated and abundantly full of velvety tannins. It will be fascinating to follow this wine's evolution. **Anticipated maturity: 1994–2012.** The 1990 is an attractively sweet and ripe wine, with some of the opulence of the magnificent 1989. The finish is shorter, but the wine is rich, with a juicy, succulent, medium-weight, fragrant style. Already delicious, it should age well for 10–15 years.
PAST GLORIES: 1986 (90), 1983 (97), 1979 (91), 1978 (91), 1975 (90), 1970 (96), 1966 (96), 1961 (98), 1959 (93), 1949 (93), 1945 (97), 1928 (96)
PAST MEDIOCRITIES . . . OR WORSE: 1981 (81)

PAPE-CLÉMENT (GRAVES)* * * *

1990	D	93
1989	D	88
1988	C	92

Possessing the quintessential Graves elegance and perfume, the 1988 is impressively deep in color for a Graves, with a thrillingly fragrant nose of roasted chestnuts, tobacco, currants, and earthy stones. One notices that this is an atypically backward, full Pape-Clément, but there is wonderful ripeness and high, velvety tannins. The finish is all smoky-scented black cherries. **Anticipated maturity: Now–2008.** In 1989 Pape-Clément produced a charming, forward, medium-bodied wine with plenty of charm, good color, medium body, soft tannins, and an alluring weedy, mineral-laced, blackcurrant fruitiness. **Anticipated maturity: Now–2003.** The 1990 is a textbook example of how

elegant yet authoritatively flavored Pape-Clément can be. The deep ruby-colored, multidimensional 1990 possesses an enthralling nose of tobacco, roasted nuts, and sweet black fruits. There is excellent concentration, as well as a sense of expansiveness, finesse, and complexity. It may prove to be the finest wine made at Pape-Clément in more than two decades. **Anticipated maturity: 1996–2008.**
PAST GLORIES: 1986 (91), 1961 (93)
PAST MEDIOCRITIES . . . OR WORSE: 1982 (59), 1981 (65), 1978 (72), 1976 (62)

PARENCHÈRE (BORDEAUX SUPÉRIEUR)* * *
1990	A	86

The 1990 Parenchère, one of the best Bordeaux Supérieur estates, is a worthy successor to their fine 1989. A big, spicy, rich, cassis-and-earthy nose is followed by a wine with surprising extraction of flavor, moderate tannins, and a creamy, long finish. Drink it over the next 7–8 years.

PATACHE D'AUX (MÉDOC)* */* * *
1990	A	85
1989	A	85

The sweet, black cherry– and herb-scented nose of the 1989 is followed by a wine with good concentration; round, soft tannins; noticeable glycerin and alcohol; and a fine finish. Drink it over the next 2–3 years. With respect to the 1990, big, herbaceous, cedarlike aromas jump from the glass. In the mouth the wine is spicy and medium bodied, with good fruit and a soft, decent finish. Drink it over the next 5–6 years.

PAVEIL-DE-LUZ (MARGAUX)* *
1990	B	72

The impressive color of this wine leads one to believe there is real concentration present. Such is not the case. The wine exhibits a watery, diluted mid-palate, as well as a light-bodied, short, clipped finish. Drink it over the next 5–6 years.

PAVIE (ST.-ÉMILION)* * * *
1990	C	90
1989	D	89
1988	C	86

The backward 1988 Pavie is a structured, tannic wine, balanced nicely by elegant, ripe, tobacco- and black cherry–scented fruit, good acidity, and a long, spicy, tannic finish. **Anticipated maturity: 1995–2005.** The 1989 is a deep, dark ruby-colored wine with excellent ripeness, a firm, fleshy texture, and an attractive yet alcoholic finish. The wine has considerable extract and is among the most powerful Pavies produced in the last two decades. **Anticipated maturity: 1996–2010.** The 1990 is an impressive, even blockbuster Pavie. Densely colored, with a reticent but emerging bouquet of black cherries, herbs, and oak, it is a classic *vin de garde,* with at least 25–30 years of aging

potential. Unmistakable power is accompanied by fine extract, a viscous, thick texture, and impeccable balance. **Anticipated maturity: 1999–2015.**
PAST GLORIES: 1986 (90), 1983 (88), 1982 (92)
PAST MEDIOCRITIES . . . OR WORSE: 1975 (72), 1970 (83)

PAVIE-DECESSE (ST.-ÉMILION)* * */* * * *

1990	C	90
1989	C	88
1988	C	86

The 1988 Pavie-Decesse has fine concentration, good length, an enticing bouquet of earthy, mineral, and exotic fruit, but tremendous tannin in the finish. Cellaring is most definitely needed. **Anticipated maturity: 1997–2009.** The 1989 Pavie-Decesse is a dense, tannic, full-bodied, rich, and, not surprisingly, backward wine for the vintage. It displays an herbaceous, mineral-scented, black cherry fruitiness, full body, and crisp acidity. **Anticipated maturity: 1995–2010.** The 1990 offers powerful aromas of sweet fruit, minerals, and herbs that are followed by a low acid wine with a big, chewy texture, gobs of tannin, and plenty of extract and depth. This is an exceptionally powerful wine that should prove to be sensational. **Anticipated maturity: 1997–2010.**

PAVIE-MACQUIN (ST.-ÉMILION)* * */* * * *

1990	C	90
1989	C	90
1988	B	87

The wines of this estate, which have come on strong in the late 1980s, merit considerable consumer interest. The 1988 Pavie-Macquin is an excellent wine. Deep in color, with a spicy, black fruit–scented bouquet caressed gently by sweet vanillin oak, this medium-bodied, concentrated, classy wine offers considerable generosity as well as finesse and length. It should be drunk over the next 8–10 years. The 1989 Pavie-Macquin is one of the sleepers of the vintage. The opaque, deep ruby/purple color suggests old vines and sensational extract. The implications drawn from the wine's color are fulfilled in the mouth. Fabulously concentrated, with wonderful purity of raspberry flavor and fine balance, this massive, highly extracted, medium-bodied wine should last for up to 20 years. It is a real beauty. **Anticipated maturity: 1995–2015.** The 1990 Pavie-Macquin is another successful wine. The intense bouquet of raspberries and smoky oak is followed by a wine with super richness, a graceful, elegant, suave style, and an expansiveness and sweetness to its concentrated, medium-bodied flavors. I continue to see a Burgundian (Musigny?) character in this wine. **Anticipated maturity: 1994–2003.**

DU PAVILLON (CANON-FRONSAC)* * *

1990	C	87
1989	C	86

The 1989 offers up aromas of olives, cedar, chocolate, and cassis. These are followed by a wine with a savory fatness, low acidity, and good richness and depth. Drink it over the next 7–8 years. The dense-colored 1990 du Pavillon is one of the most impressive wines of Fronsac. It boasts a purple color, a pure bouquet of cassis, terrific richness, medium to full body, and tremendous levels of fruit in the tannic finish. The wine exhibits considerable weight, plenty of structure, and decent acidity. I would opt for drinking it between 1995 and 2003. A sleeper!

PAVILLON ROUGE DE MARGAUX (MARGAUX)* * *

1990	D	87
1989	D	85

This is the second wine of Margaux. The 1989's finish is abrupt, but there is a black fruit character that is accompanied by copious quantities of toasty oak. Drink it over the next 3–6 years. The 1990 is a lovely wine, with a fragrant bouquet; soft, medium-bodied, smooth-as-silk flavors; fine concentration; enough acidity for focus; and a fine finish. Drink it over the next decade.

LES PENSÉES DE LAFLEUR (POMEROL)* * *

1990	D	89
1989	D	89

Can a second wine (of the famous Château Lafleur) be this delicious? The unbelievable length to which the proprietors go in order to eliminate anything less than sublime from their grand vin is evidenced by this 1989 from Lafleur. Amazingly rich, with incredibly deep, dense, cassis, mineral, and exotic flavors, this full-bodied, well-structured, highly concentrated wine should continue to evolve for at least two decades. **Anticipated maturity:1995–2010.** The 1990 is also a knockout. With plenty of tannin and a sense of overripe, jammy, cherry, kirsch-flavored fruit, the 1990 displays considerable power and a fleshy richness. It exhibits surprising individuality, including an exotic, even flamboyant personality. **Anticipated maturity: Now–2002.**

PETIT-VILLAGE (POMEROL)* * * *

1990	D	90
1989	D	88
1988	D	92

The 1988 will not be a long-lived Petit-Village. Prospective purchasers should consider the fact that it will probably have to be drunk within its first decade of life. But oh, what pleasure it will provide! There is no doubting the sumptuous, seductive character of this superconcentrated yet velvety 1988. Its dark ruby/purple color suggests ripeness and extract. The huge aroma of exotic spices, bacon fat, jammy plums, and smoky, toasty new oak is a complete turn-on. This heady, concentrated, splendidly extracted Pomerol is all velvet and suppleness. **Anticipated maturity: Now–2000.** The 1989's sweet, round, in-your-face, obvious style is also delicious. Its huge, chocolate-, plum-, and sweet oak–scented bouquet roars from the glass. Expansive, fat, hedonistic flavors coat the palate with plump, ripe fruit. There is a glaring lack of acidity and structure, but this generous wine is for consuming over the next 5–7 years. **Anticipated maturity: Now–1997.** The 1990 is another in-your-face, ostentatious, superdelicious wine. The rich, oaky, smoky, alcoholic, lusciously rich, hedonistic wine makes for a wonderful drink. The wine is now revealing far more weight and tannin than it did from barrel. Drink this voluptuous, opulently textured, decadently smooth and ripe Pomerol over the next 8–12 years. PAST GLORIES: 1985 (89), 1982 (93)

PÉTRUS (POMEROL)* * * * *

1990	EEE	100
1989	EEE	98
1988	EEE	94

The 1988 Pétrus is dark ruby/purple, with a thickness to the color that suggests a high glycerin content. The nose is muted, but it does offer intense smells of jammy black fruits intermingled with aromas of coconut, tea, super-ripe oranges, and some vanillin oakiness. In the mouth this firmly structured, full-bodied, massive Pétrus is charged with both extract and tannin. It will need at least 8–10 years of cellaring. **Anticipated maturity: 2002–2030.** The proprietors think the 1989 is the finest Pétrus since the 1947. Black/purple, with the intense, dramatic bouquet of superconcentrated blackcurrants, tobacco, tea, and plums, this wine makes an unforgettable palate impression. The 1989 exhibits great extraction of fruit, a dense, huge, massive texture, and a fabulous black fruit, spice, and herb-scented nose that is touched by aromas of new oak. Almost thick, this wine is also extremely tannic. My guess is that despite its high alcohol, glycerin, and low acidity, it will need at least 10 years after bottling to fully reveal its considerable potential. **Anticipated maturity: 2000–2035.** The 1990 is an awesomely dense, rich, concentrated wine with tons of tannin, gobs of glycerin, and an exotic coffee-, tobacco-, herb-, and superripe berry-scented nose and flavors. It is the most powerful, intense, and concentrated Pétrus to emerge from this estate since 1961. I could not bring myself to spit this one out. Another legend! **Anticipated maturity: 2000–2025.**

PAST GLORIES: 1986 (89), 1985 (89), 1982 (98), 1979 (89), 1975 (98), 1971 (95), 1970 (99), 1967 (92), 1964 (97), 1961 (100), 1950 (99), 1949 (91), 1948 (98), 1947 (100), 1945 (98)

PAST MEDIOCRITIES . . . OR WORSE: Virtually none, although the 1983, 1981, and 1978 have not lived up to my initial expectations.

PEYREDON-LAGRAVETTE (LISTRAC)* * *

1990	B	86
1989	B	85

Softer than the 1990, but admirably concentrated and smooth as silk, with plenty of body, glycerin, and alcohol, the charming, low-acid, concentrated 1989 should make delicious drinking for at least 4–5 years. The 1990 reveals an impressive deep, opaque color; a big, spicy, herb, and black cherry nose; and rich, opulent flavors that exhibit fine balance and plenty of depth. **Anticipated maturity: 1994–2004.**

DE PEZ (ST.-ESTÈPHE)* * *

1989	B	86
1988	B	83

The 1988 is a typical effort from de Pez, with a reserved and polite bouquet of moderately ripe blackcurrants, minerals, and wood. The wine is medium bodied, slightly astringent, austere, and restrained. It lacks flesh and appears compact. **Anticipated maturity: Now–2000.** The 1989, which is opulently rich and more precocious than usual, possesses layers of cassis fruit intertwined with scents of herbs and toasty oak. Surprisingly fleshy for de Pez, with low acidity, this full-bodied effort will drink well young but boasts the requisite depth and balance to last for 12–15 years. **Anticipated maturity: 1994–2005.**

PEY-LABRIE (CANON-FRONSAC)* * *

1990	B	87
1989	B	86

Dark ruby, with a spicy, mineral-, licorice-, and floral-scented nose, the 1989 displays good ripe fruit, a medium-bodied texture, and a long, moderately tannic, admirably endowed finish. **Anticipated maturity: Now–2003.** Powerful and rich, with an impressive opaque ruby/purple color, the medium- to full-bodied, cassis-scented 1990 displays gobs of extract. **Anticipated maturity: 1995–2005.**

PHÉLAN-SÉGUR (ST.-ESTÈPHE)* * */* * * *

1990	C	89
1989	C	88
1988	B	87

The 1988 Phélan-Ségur is a textbook example of a St.-Estèphe. A toasty, blackcurrant-scented bouquet is followed by a medium-bodied wine with fine balance, excellent richness, good body, and surprising length. It is a beautiful wine for drinking over the next decade. The rich, full-bodied 1989 offers power and finesse. Deep ruby/purple, with gobs of red and black fruits in its aroma, this concentrated, impressively rich, expansive-tasting wine should prove to be at its best between now and 2003. **Anticipated maturity: 1995–2003.** The 1990 is darkly colored, with a big, sweet, opulent, nearly explosive nose. This full-bodied wine displays excellent intensity and extract, plenty of ripe tannins, and a long, rich, authoritative finish. **Anticipated maturity: Now–2003.** This is a super bargain!

PIBRAN (PAUILLAC)* * *

1990	C	88
1989	C	87
1988	B	86

The 1988, a plump, tasty, ripe, amply endowed Pauillac, lacks complexity, but it does have gobs of sweet fruit and offers immediate appeal. **Anticipated maturity: Now–1996.** This excellent Pauillac Cru Bourgeois has turned in a strong effort in 1989. It is deep ruby/purple, with a fine nose of smoky new oak followed by copious quantities of cassis fruit wrapped in plenty of new oak. The low-acid finish is fat and mouth-filling. Drink it over the next 5–7 years. The 1990 Pibran is a clone of the 1989, although slightly fatter and richer. Drink it over the next 6–9 years.

PICHON-LONGUEVILLE BARON (PAUILLAC)* * * * *

1990	D	95
1989	D	96
1988	D	90

The 1988 Pichon Baron promises to be one of the half-dozen superstars of this vintage. Surprisingly large scale for a 1988, with an oaky, cassis- and licorice-scented nose, it is deep in color, rich, softly tannic, medium to full bodied, and should reach maturity early on but keep for 15–20 years. **Anticipated maturity: 1994–2010.** The 1989 is this property's finest wine in at least three decades. It is one of the most opaque wines of the vintage, with a black/purple color suggesting exceptional extract and superripeness. The aroma reminded me of essence of cassis and plums intertwined with the scent of smoky new oak. Spectacularly rich and ripe, with layer upon layer of compelling extract, this well-balanced, full-bodied, low-acid wine has the requisite tannin and depth to age well for two or more decades. **Anticipated maturity: 1995–2020.** The dark ruby/purple color of the 1990 Pichon Baron is followed by a huge nose of black fruits, vanillin, and spices. This full-bodied, highly extracted wine is fabulously concentrated and admirably pure. There are lavish quantities of ripe, rich fruit, and, fortunately, the wine has taken on more structure than it revealed in cask. Who can ignore its sexy perfume of new oak, overripe cassis fruit, and Asian spices? It is slightly less focused than the 1989, but who cares? This rich, complete wine is, once again, one of the stars of the vintage. Moreover, the price is reasonable. **Anticipated maturity: 1996–2020.**
PAST GLORIES: 1986 (88), 1982 (88), 1959 (89), 1953 (89)
PAST MEDIOCRITIES . . . OR WORSE: 1981 (83), 1978 (82), 1975 (64), 1970 (73), 1966 (82)

PICHON-LONGUEVILLE, COMTESSE DE LALANDE
(PAUILLAC)* * * * *

1990	D	87
1989	D	92
1988	D	90

Dark ruby, with a full-intensity bouquet of new oak, black fruits, vanillin, and spring flowers, this silky smooth, full-bodied 1988 has excellent extraction of fruit, plenty of glycerin, and a sense of elegance. Seductively precocious, it should drink superbly over the next 10–15 years. **Anticipated maturity: Now–2008.** The 1989 has a dark purple color, with a bouquet of sweet cassis, plumlike fruit, and roasted nuts. The wine is formidably concentrated, expansive, seductive, and generous. The finish must last for up to a minute. The tannin level is high, but the tannins are soft. **Anticipated maturity: Now–**

2012. The 1990 is less well endowed. It displays medium-dark ruby color and an attractive bouquet of vanillin from new oak, ripe blackcurrants, and spices. The wine is not as concentrated as usual, but it does exhibit medium body, some glycerin, and fine ripeness, as well as an overall sense of grace. A stylish wine, it could have benefited from more length and intensity. In the context of the vintage, it is marginally disappointing. **Anticipated maturity: Now–2000.**

PAST GLORIES: 1986 (96), 1985 (90), 1983 (94), 1982 (99), 1981 (89), 1979 (92), 1978 (93), 1975 (90), 1961 (95), 1945 (96)

PICQUE-CAILLOU (GRAVES)* * *

1990	B	86
1989	B	76
1988	B	86

The 1988 is, along with the 1985, Picque-Caillou's wine of the decade. Deep ruby, with a pronounced earthy, currany aroma, this fleshy, even opulent wine is loaded with fruit; it should drink well for 6–7 years. The disappointing 1989 is overripe, with a cooked, smoked component. **Anticipated maturity: Now–1995.** Fortunately, this property rebounded in 1990 with a rich, smoky, oaky, tobacco- and earth-scented wine. Lovely, rich, round fruit and good depth accompany a smooth finish in this textbook, lighter-weight Graves. Drink it over the next 5–6 years.

LE PIN (POMEROL)* * * * *

1990	EEE	95
1989	EEE	91
1988	EE	90

This exotic and kinky wine has Bordeaux enthusiasts searching for adjectives to describe its character. The 1988 is very oaky, concentrated, and rich, with a deep inner core of black fruits (plums and prunes) that linger on the palate. It has more aggressive tannins than the 1989, but also more extract and structure. **Anticipated maturity: Now–2003.** The 1989, which is already drinkable, raising doubts about its longevity, offers a gloriously hedonistic mouthful of wine. With very low acidity, as well as masses of new oak and fruit, this wine defines the word *decadent*. Drink this yummy wine young. **Anticipated maturity: Now–2000.** The 1990 is a more focused and more richly extracted wine, with impressive persistence and depth. It also exhibits a flamboyant nose of exotic spices, black fruits, and smoky new oak. The voluptuous texture that has turned this wine into a cult item is present, along with a smashingly intense, opulent finish with enough tannin to suggest that 10–15 years of aging is possible. But who can resist it now? This is the finest Le Pin since the 1982 and 1983. And remember, I have a tendency to underestimate this wine when it is young! **Anticipated maturity: Now–2007.**

PAST GLORIES: 1987 (89), 1986 (90), 1985 (94), 1983 (95), 1982 (99), 1981 (93), 1980 (89), 1979 (93)

PLAGNAC (MÉDOC)* *

1990	A	84
1989	A	85

The 1989 possesses a nose of spicy, earthy, berry fruit intermingled with the scent of minerals. Round, medium bodied, slightly herbaceous, luscious, and soft, it should be drunk over the next 4–5 years. The 1990 is a fruity, soft, straightforward wine with surprising character and plenty of up-front appeal. Drink it over the next 4–5 years.

PLINCE (POMEROL)* *

1990	C	82
1989	C	85
1988	C	80

The 1988 Plince comes across as sinewy and charmless. However, because of its high tannin level, it will age decently, lasting through the first 4–5 years of the next century. The 1989 reveals the superripe, plum and black fruit character of the vintage. It is a surprisingly intense and extracted wine, with a good amount of tannin in the finish and an alcohol level of 13–13.5%. It is one of the most impressive wines I have tasted from this vineyard. **Anticipated maturity: 1993–2000.** Straightforward, chunky, chewy fruit is offered in the medium-bodied, uncomplicated, monolithic 1990. With low acidity, this fat wine is too simple to merit higher marks. **Anticipated maturity: Now–1997.**

LA POINTE (POMEROL)* *

1989	C	74
1988	C	76

The 1988 La Pointe is light, medium bodied, and one-dimensional. Drink it over the next 4–5 years. Medium ruby, with some dilution in color evident at its edges, this light-bodied, simple, fruity, alcoholic 1989 leaves a great deal to be desired. It should be drunk over the next 3–5 years.

PONTET-CANET (PAUILLAC)* * */* * * *

1990	D	89
1989	D	89
1988	C	83

The 1988 Pontet-Canet typifies many of the Médocs in this vintage with its fine color, narrowly constructed personality, and green tannins. Relatively lean and austere, this wine will age well, but it will always lack charm and flesh. The 1989 exhibits an impressive deep ruby/purple color, a highly scented nose of exceptionally ripe cassis fruit and licorice, full body, an excellent midpalate, and a rich, intense, relatively tannic finish. **Anticipated maturity: 2000–2015.** The 1990 is as impressive as the similarly styled 1989. Dense purple in color, with a huge, smoky, cassis-scented nose, this well-constituted wine is very tannic, admirably deep, and in need of 5–8 years of cellaring. **Anticipated maturity: 1997–2020.**

PAST GLORIES: 1986 (88), 1982 (87), 1961 (94), 1945 (93), 1929 (90)
PAST MEDIOCRITIES . . . OR WORSE: 1979 (80), 1978 (82), 1971 (81), 1970 (82), 1966 (77)

POTENSAC (MÉDOC)* * *

1990	B	86
1989	B	87
1988	B	85

Displaying an attractive ripeness in the nose, the 1988 Potensac is soft, elegant, and well made in the mouth. There is some pleasant new oak in evidence, but the wine's roundness and precociousness suggest it should be consumed early in life. The 1989 Potensac is a big, intense, alcoholic wine with exceptional ripeness, full body, and a long, chewy, fleshy finish. **Anticipated maturity: Now–1999.** Potensac's 1990 is almost as good as their 1989. It is deeply colored, with plenty of body, an attractive, pure, curranty, earthy nose, medium to full body, a classic structure, and a long finish. Drink this impressive wine over the next decade.

POUGET (MARGAUX)* * *

1990	C	82
1989	C	85
1988	C	79

The 1988 Pouget is compact and one-dimensional. **Anticipated maturity: Now–1997.** Fat, chunky, and beefy, the 1989 lacks complexity but does offer a generous mouthful of wine. Low acidity, soft tannins, and very high alcohol suggest that this wine should be drunk early. **Anticipated maturity: Now–1997.** Although there is considerable muscle, depth, and power in the 1990, there is also a tough texture due to the high level of astringent tannin— giving the wine a relatively hard, charmless taste.

POUJEAUX (MOULIS)* * */* * * *

1990	C	86
1989	B	86
1988	C	87

The 1988 Poujeaux is a beautiful wine, superior in my opinion to both the 1989 and 1990. The oaky, classic, curranty bouquet exhibits both intensity and ripeness. The wine offers plenty of toasty new oak, medium body, good acidity, excellent depth and definition, and firm tannins in the finish. **Anticipated maturity: Now–2005.** The 1989 is an excellent wine, exhibiting a moderately intense bouquet of toasty new oak, spicy, blackcurrant fruit, medium to full body, and attractive ripeness and heady alcohol in the finish. **Anticipated maturity: Now–2003.** Oaky, with good fruit, the well-made, medium-bodied, moderately tannic, attractive 1990 will provide fine drinking over the next 10–12 years.

LE PRIEURÉ (ST.-ÉMILION)* *

1990	C	84
1989	C	82
1988	C	79

The 1988 Prieuré is a straightforward, extremely light, medium-bodied wine lacking concentration and a finish. Le Prieuré's 1989 is a soft, commercial wine with round, agreeable, curranty fruit flavors and some endearing fatness and charm. **Anticipated maturity: Now–1996.** The supple, smooth, seductive, medium-bodied 1990 will provide delicious drinking if consumed in its first 5–6 years of life.

PRIEURÉ-LICHINE (MARGAUX)* * *

1990	C	89
1989	C	88
1988	C	86

The 1988 is a light- to medium-bodied, perfumed and well-balanced wine that avoids the green tannins and astringence of many 1988s. Medium-dark ruby, with an attractive bouquet of wood, currants, herbs, and minerals, this stylish wine is tasty and elegant. It should drink well for 8–12 years. The 1989 Prieuré-Lichine is one of the richest and fullest wines this property has made. Substantial in size, with gobs of ripe currant fruit, full body, soft, plentiful tannins, and a heady alcohol degree, this velvety wine should prove charming in its youth but easily last for 15 or more years. **Anticipated maturity: Now–2005.** The deeply colored 1990, also rich, deep, and expansively flavored, offers a spicy, cedary, fruitcake-scented nose; splendidly ripe, sweet, expansive flavors; excellent depth and length; and a full-bodied, lush finish. It is even bigger than the 1989. **Anticipated maturity: 1995–2005.**
PAST GLORIES: 1986 (88)
PAST MEDIOCRITIES . . . OR WORSE: 1981 (75)

PRIEURS DE LA COMMANDERIE (POMEROL)* *

1990	C	79
1989	C	83
1988	B	76

The 1988 is diluted and excessively oaky, as well as having a color that seems extremely advanced for the vintage. The 1989 lacks acidity and tannin, has flabby, unstructured flavors, and finishes with entirely too much alcohol and oak taste. **Anticipated maturity: Now–1996.** Medium ruby, with a pronounced oaky nose and light-bodied, ripe flavors, the 1990 exhibits an appealing softness but not much personality. Drink it over the next 4–5 years.

PUY-BLANQUET (ST.-ÉMILION)* *

1990	C	84
1989	C	82
1988	B	80

The 1988 exhibits some ripeness, richness, and length on the palate in a medium-bodied, somewhat charming and graceful style. **Anticipated maturity: Now–2002.** The 1989 Puy-Blanquet has a streak of greenness that suggests the grapes were picked before they were fully ripe. In the mouth the hardness and toughness of the tannins that were so apparent from the barrel sample have mellowed. The result is a fruity, round, easygoing, herb- and currant-flavored wine for drinking over the near term. **Anticipated maturity: Now–2003.** The moderately ruby-colored 1990 exhibits a fragrant, spicy, cherry-scented nose intertwined with strong herb and earth aromas. In the mouth the wine reveals something Puy-Blanquet usually lacks—an inner core of sweet, ripe fruit. Although it is not complicated and the finish could be longer, it is a good effort. **Anticipated maturity: Now–2000.**

RAHOUL (GRAVES)* *

1989	C	85
1988	B	77

Compact, oaky flavors and a short, empty finish to the 1988 fail to elicit my interest. The 1989, the best recent vintage I have had of Rahoul's red wine, exhibited a big, smoky, black cherry aroma, medium body, and a soft, exotic finish, although the alcohol was extremely noticeable and the acids suspiciously low. Drink it over the next 4–7 years.

RAUSAN-SÉGLA (MARGAUX)* * * */* * * * *

1990	C	92
1989	D	90
1988	C	92

Rausan-Ségla now rivals Palmer as the second-best wine of the Margaux appellation. Quality has soared, in large part because of the brutal selection process that ensures only the best juice from the vineyard's oldest vines gets into the final blend. The 1988 Rausan-Ségla is black/ruby in color, intensely concentrated, full bodied, and tannic, with an admirable purity of fruit (black raspberries). A backward, large-scale wine, it is impressively built for the long haul. **Anticipated maturity: 1997–2012.** The 1989 is a seductive, jammy, concentrated wine offering a huge bouquet of blackberries and raspberries. Voluptuous on the palate, with layer upon layer of fruit and extract, this silky-textured, flamboyantly styled wine should provide terrific drinking when young. **Anticipated maturity: Now–2012.** Dark ruby/purple, with a gloriously sweet, raspberry-scented nose, the full-bodied 1990 displays intensely concentrated flavors touched generously by lavish quantities of sweet new oak. With plenty of richness, superb extraction of flavor, and great definition and length, as well as considerable tannin, the 1990 should prove to be another outstanding Rausan-Ségla. **Anticipated maturity: 1997–2020.**
PAST GLORIES: 1986 (96), 1983 (92)
PAST MEDIOCRITIES . . . OR WORSE: 1981 (65), 1979 (72), 1978 (74), 1975 (75)

RAUZAN-GASSIES (MARGAUX)* *

1990	C	73
1988	C	72

Dusty, hard, even harsh flavors are obliterated by the abrasive tannins in the 1988. The impression created is one of hollowness, with only a skeleton of acidity, wood, and tannin. **Anticipated maturity: Now–1999.** Soft bodied, light, and fruity, the 1990 exhibits some tannin in the finish but lacks depth and complexity. Drink it over the next 10–12 years.

RÉSERVE DE LA COMTESSE (PAUILLAC)* * *

1989	C	83

Aside from the slightly short finish (remember, this is a second wine), the 1989 is a smooth, elegant, ripe, tasty wine that reveals a vague kinship to its big sister. Richly fruity and supple, this is a 1989 to drink over the next 3–5 years.

ROC DES CAMBES (CÔTES DE BOURG)* * *

1990	B	89
1989	B	88

Absolutely delicious, the 1989 Roc des Cambes reveals an impressive, opaque, dark ruby/purple color. The fragrant, chocolatey, sweet, berry-scented nose, deep, dense, full-bodied flavors, low acidity, and a long, lush finish make for a convincingly satisfying glass of wine. **Anticipated maturity: Now– 1998.** The 1990 is another explosively rich, deep, intense wine with gobs of fruit, a lavish texture, and a heady, long finish. Small yields and superripe grapes appear to be the secret ingredients to this exciting wine. Drink it over the next decade.

ROCHER-BELLEVUE-FIGEAC (ST.-ÉMILION)* * *

1990	B	86
1989	B	84
1988	B	86

Rocher-Bellevue-Figeac's 1988 is a flattering, ripe wine gushing with fruit. Deep ruby/purple, rich, and intense, in a medium-bodied format, this rich, nicely concentrated, complex wine should be at its best between now and 1998. The 1989 offers a dark ruby color, fat, forward, generously endowed flavors with plenty of glycerin and alcohol, low acidity, and soft tannins. It is a juicy, jammy mouthful of Merlot. **Anticipated maturity: Now–1996.** The 1990, made from 100% Merlot, may be the best example from this property since its fine 1985. Densely colored, with low acidity, this wine possesses copious quantities of black fruits intermingled with scents and flavors of herbs. The overripe character only adds to this wine's up-front appeal. Drink it over the next 5–7 years.

ROLLAND-MAILLET (ST.-ÉMILION)* * *

1989	B	86

Produced by Libourne's famous oenologist, Michel Rolland, this St.-Émilion is a rich, sweet, expansive wine with flavors of black cherries and roasted nuts. Full-bodied, chewy, and dense, it makes for a meaty mouthful of wine. **Anticipated maturity: 1993–2000.**

ROUET (FRONSAC)* * *

1990	B	85

An attractively clean, ripe, spicy nose is followed by a medium-bodied wine with good flavor concentration, decent acidity, and moderate tannins in its finish.

ROUGET (POMEROL)* */* * *

1990	C	85
1989	C	84
1988	C	84

A modest success for the vintage, the 1988 Rouget exhibits some black cherry fruit partially hidden behind the tannins, medium body, and a blossoming bouquet of earthy fruit intertwined with the scents of minerals and herbs. **Anticipated maturity: 1994–2006.** The 1989 is an abundantly rich, medium-bodied wine, with dusty tannins, plenty of alcohol, fine ripeness, and a long, hard, tannic finish. It will never be elegant, but for a more rough-and-tumble style of Pomerol, it should provide interesting drinking. **Anticipated maturity: Now–2006.** The 1990 exhibits more sweet fruit and fat than usual. It is medium bodied and surprisingly forward, with a soft, alcoholic finish. Drink it over the next 6–7 years.

ST.-PIERRE (ST.-JULIEN)* * */* * * *

1990	D	90
1989	D	89
1988	C	87

The 1988 St.-Pierre is a richly fruity, substantial wine, a characteristic missing in many of the more compact, austere Médoc 1988s. Deep ruby, medium bodied, with an attractively long, well-balanced finish, it is a classic example from this vintage. **Anticipated maturity: Now–1999.** The 1989 is dark ruby/purple, with a smashing aroma of jammy, super ripe blackcurrants and new oak. This full-bodied, opulent wine offers a luscious, heady mouthful of low-acid wine. The high alcohol, combined with the wine's fragile balance, will have to be monitored carefully. **Anticipated maturity: Now–2010.** The lusty, richly oaky, deep, spicy 1990 appears designed to immediately impress both critics and consumers. The color is dark, the big, vanillin, smoky aromas are intermingled with decadent quantities of black fruits, and the finish is lush, chewy, and soft. **Anticipated maturity: 1996–2007.**

PAST GLORIES: 1986 (90), 1983 (87), 1982 (88), 1981 (88)

DE SALES (POMEROL)* * *

1990	C	89
1989	C	85
1988	C	84

The forward 1988 will provide attractive drinking over the next 4–6 years. The 1989 is surprisingly full bodied for a de Sales, with a deep, intense, black cherry–scented bouquet intertwined with the scents of vanillin and toast. In the mouth the wine displays fine ripeness, full body, a heady alcohol content, and a long, tannic, rich finish. **Anticipated maturity: Now–2003.** The bold, rich 1990 has a bouquet similar to the 1989, with its sweet, forward, leathery, spicy, toffee-, caramel-, and berry-scented nose. There is plump, ripe fruit, medium body, fine flesh, and a long finish. It is the biggest de Sales I have tasted. Drink it over the next 7–12 years.

SÉNÉJAC (HAUT-MÉDOC)* *

1990	A	86
1989	A	82

Pleasant aromas of ripe fruit, spicy oak, and earthy scents arise from the 1989 Sénéjac. In the mouth the wine exhibits the "hot year" ripeness obtained in this vintage, soft tannins, and low acidity. Drink it over the next 3–4 years. The 1990 has turned out to be a rich, fruity, medium-bodied wine with plenty of extract, muscle, and tannin. Drink it over the next 6–8 years.

SIAURAC (LALANDE DE POMEROL)* */* * *

1990	B	87

This plummy, sweet, round, velvety-textured wine is bursting with fruit. Fat, concentrated, and opulent, Siaurac is one of the stars of this appellation.

SIRAN (MARGAUX)* * *

1990	C	87
1989	C	86
1988	C	85

Deep ruby in color, with a spicy, blackcurrant-scented bouquet, the full-bodied 1988 exhibits good depth and structure, but it will need 4–5 years in the bottle to shed its toughness. **Anticipated maturity: 1995–2005.** The 1989 is a graceful, medium-bodied wine displaying the vintage's soft, silky texture, plenty of alcohol, low acidity, and aging potential of 4–8 years. It is hard not to admire its sweet, round, gentle nature. **Anticipated maturity: Now–2000.** The deeply colored 1990 reveals a tightly knit nose that offers aromas of black fruits, smoky oak, and earth. In the mouth there is medium body, excellent ripeness, good acidity, and plenty of length in the moderately tannic finish. It should age nicely for 10–15 or more years.

SMITH-HAUT-LAFITTE (GRAVES)* *

1990	C	86
1989	C	81
1988	C	75

Lean, tart, malnourished flavors reflect indifferent winemaking in the 1988. Moreover, it is too light and lacking in charm and balance. Caveat emptor! The 1989 is an example of a wine with a delicate, fruity character that was overwhelmed by excessive use of new oak. The flavors of oak have crushed much of the wine's finesse and elegance. **Anticipated maturity: Now–1997.** New owners, plus the hiring of renowned oenologist Michel Rolland, have already resulted in higher quality. For example, the 1990 is a surprisingly strong effort from this perennial underachiever. The color is dark ruby, and the nose offers attractive, seductive aromas of sweet red fruits, vanillin, and spices. In the mouth there is a smooth, velvety texture, fine ripeness, succulent fruit, attractive glycerin, and a heady, lush finish. This sexy, easy-to-drink Graves should provide delicious drinking for another 5–7 years.

SOCIANDO-MALLET (HAUT-MÉDOC)* * * *

1990	C	90
1989	C	88
1988	C	87

The 1988 Sociando-Mallet is medium bodied, somewhat lighter than one might expect, but concentrated and spicy, with a sense of balance. It should last for 12–15 years. Sociando-Mallet's 1989 reveals a dark ruby/purple color with an aroma of blackcurrants, licorice, minerals, and toasty new oak. There are nicely concentrated flavors, moderately high tannins, and a long finish. Typical of the property, this wine has the components and depth to last up to 20 years. **Anticipated maturity: 1995–2010.** The 1990 gets my nod as the best wine produced at this estate since the 1982. Dense and concentrated, it possesses an opaque black/purple color. The nose offers up pure, vibrant aromas of black cherries and raspberries as well as minerals and spicy new oak. The wine's richness and mouth-searing tannins culminate in an intense, even dazzlingly long finish. A knockout! **Anticipated maturity: 2000–2020.**

SOUDARS (HAUT-MÉDOC)* */* * *

1990	B	85
1989	B	78

Surprisingly light, flaccid and unstructured, the soft 1989 Soudars offers unexciting, simple fruit flavors. Drink it over the next 1–2 years. Soft, fat, and lacking acidity, the chunky, immensely fruity, pleasant 1990 should be drunk in its first 4–5 years of life.

SOUTARD (ST.-ÉMILION)* * */* * * *

1990	C	88
1989	C	90
1988	C	87

Backward, dense, concentrated, and unforthcoming, the powerful, herbaceous, vanillin- and blackcurrant-scented 1988 Soutard has plenty of extract, although it is buried beneath considerable quantities of tannin. It is a worthy candidate for 20 or more years of cellaring. **Anticipated maturity: 1998–2020.** As one might expect, Soutard's 1989 is also a backward wine. Impressively opaque ruby/purple, with a spicy, vanillin-scented, plum-and-licorice bouquet, this full-bodied, muscular, densely concentrated wine needs at least 7–10 years of bottle aging. Look for it to last at least 20 or more years. **Anticipated maturity: 2000–2020.** The 1990, which is close in quality to the 1989, is a typical Soutard, with its massive proportions, gobs of tannin, highly structured, old-style, intense concentration, and powerful, tannic, rich finish. **Anticipated maturity: 1996–2020.**
PAST GLORIES: 1985 (90), 1982 (88), 1964 (90), 1955 (88)

TAILHAS (POMEROL)* *

1990	C	82

A monochromatic nose of ripe fruit is followed by rich, fat, low-acid flavors that come across as slightly flabby. Drink this chunky wine over the next 3–5 years.

TAILLEFER (POMEROL)* *

1990	C	81
1989	C	85
1988	C	82

The 1988 Taillefer is straightforward and light bodied, with a hint of ripe fruit and toasty vanillin oak, but not much of a finish. Drink it up within 3–4 years. The 1989 Taillefer is less weighty and powerful than many Pomerols in this vintage but does possess richly fruity, velvety flavors in a medium-bodied texture, with a good deal of alcohol and some surprisingly tough tannins in the finish. **Anticipated maturity: Now–1998.** Although the color is solidly dark and the nose fruity, the 1990 is light bodied, and the quickly fading finish reveals too much alcohol. This is a near-termer in its drinking potential.

TALBOT (ST.-JULIEN)* * * *

1990	C	85
1989	C	88
1988	C	89

The 1988 Talbot is dark ruby, with a well-focused personality brimming with spicy, chocolatey, blackcurrant, leathery, herbal fruit buttressed by good acidity and high tannins. In the mouth the wine has a gamelike, smoky, beefy character. If the tannins fade a little and the fruit takes over, this will be an outstanding wine. **Anticipated maturity: 1995–2015.** The 1989 is more elegant, with none of the herb, meaty, leathery aromas of the 1988. Opaque black/ruby, with a pronounced bouquet of black fruits and spices, this extracted, medium- to full-bodied wine is voluptuous on the palate, with a fine finish. The 1989 Talbot promises to drink well during its first decade of life but keep for up to 20 years. **Anticipated maturity: 1994–2015.** The

medium-colored 1990 is an elegant, structured, more restrained style of wine than usual. There is ripeness and length, but the wine lacks the outstanding depth and flavor dimension of other top vintages of Talbot. Is the style being changed? **Anticipated maturity: Now–2008.**
PAST GLORIES: 1986 (96), 1985 (89), 1983 (91), 1982 (95), 1953 (90), 1949 (90), 1945 (94)
PAST MEDIOCRITIES . . . OR WORSE: 1975 (84), 1970 (78), 1966 (77)

TAYAC (CÔTES DE BOURG)* * *

1990	B	75
1990 Cuvée Prestige	C	87
1989 Cuvée Prestige	C	89
1990 Cuvée Réservée	B	86
1989 Cuvée Réservée	B	87
1990 Rubis	A	85
1989 Rubis	A	86

The 1989 Cuvée Prestige offers a sweet nose of overripe black fruits, leather, and spices, followed by a rich, full-bodied, opulently textured wine bursting with fruit and glycerin. It will last for 10–15 years. Spicy and rich, with excellent concentration, medium to full body, moderate tannins, and a fine inner core of fruit, the boldly styled 1989 Cuvée Réservée should drink well for at least 7–10 years. The 1989 Rubis, made from nearly 90% Merlot, exhibits a spicy, berry-, herb-, and coffee-scented nose; ripe, medium- to full-bodied flavors; and good length and chewiness in its finish. Drink it over the next 4–6 years.

The 1990 regular *cuvée* is a lightweight, medium-bodied, pleasant, but undistinguished effort. Drink it over the next 4–5 years. The 1990 Rubis, made primarily from Merlot, is soft, with a big, berry-scented nose, lush, superripe flavors, and a long, smooth-as-silk finish. Drink it over the next 5–6 years. The 1990 Cuvée Reservée is a denser, more tannic, structured wine. Because of that, it is less charming than the Rubis. Nevertheless, it will handsomely repay aging given its firm, tannic framework and long finish. The 1990 Cuvée Prestige is, not surprisingly, the biggest and richest of these wines, with a deeper color, more density and extraction of flavor, and more tannin. It will require patience. Although it does not have the splendid opulence of the 1989, it should turn out to be an impressive bottle of wine that will last for 8–15 years.

TERREY-GROS-CAILLOUX (ST.-JULIEN)* * *

1990	B	86
1989	B	85
1988	B	78

The 1988 Terrey-Gros-Cailloux tastes surprisingly light, straightforward, and undistinguished. The 1989 exhibits an attractive ripe fruit but tastes too one-dimensional and simple to merit higher marks. **Anticipated maturity: Now–1997.** The 1990 is rich, chunky, and loaded with ripe, fat, berry- and herb-flavored fruit. Bold and spicy, with considerable body, it will drink well for the next 6–9 years.

DU TERTRE (MARGAUX)* * *

1990	C	87
1989	C	86
1988	C	86

The 1988 du Tertre is a good example for the vintage. Medium-deep ruby, with a curranty, smoky, oak-dominated nose, this wine continues to bear a resemblance to the château's excellent 1979. It will drink well young, but keep. **Anticipated maturity: 1994–2003.** The 1989 du Tertre is a charming, soft, medium-bodied wine that lacks concentration and structure. It is evolved, perfumed (jammy blackcurrants), low in acidity, and ideal for drinking during its first 6–8 years of life. **Anticipated maturity: Now–1998.** The 1990 represents a strong effort for this property. It is surprisingly dark in color, with medium body, fine structure, plenty of depth and richness, and an interesting bouquet of olives, smoky oak, and overripe black fruits. This wine reminds me somewhat of a lighter version of the 1979. **Anticipated maturity: 1996–2008.**

TERTRE-DAUGAY (ST.-ÉMILION)* * *

1990	C	86
1989	C	87
1988	C	86

This long-time underachiever is finally beginning to resurrect its image. The 1988 offers an attractive aroma of dried herbs and black fruits integrated nicely with the smell of toasty new oak. It is medium bodied and spicy, with good acidity and aggressive tannins. This well-made, amply endowed St.-Émilion should drink well for the next 8–10 years. The 1989 is the best wine produced at the property in years. Concentrated, full bodied, with a heady alcohol content, this lavish, richly fruity, broad-shouldered wine should be drunk in its first decade of life. **Anticipated maturity: Now–2005.** The 1990 exhibits fine concentration, a deep, dark ruby color, low acidity, a multidimensional personality, and a long, luscious finish. For drinking over the next 8–10 years, it will provide considerable enjoyment.

LE TERTRE-ROTEBOEUF (ST.-ÉMILION)* * * * *

1990	C	94
1989	D	94
1988	C	91

The 1988 wine from the "hill of the belching beef" is extraordinary and, once again, superconcentrated, with a dazzling level of extract and a powerful, full-bodied, concentrated finish. Approachable now, the 1988 Le Tertre-Roteboeuf will benefit from 2–3 years of bottle age and should keep well. **Anticipated maturity: 1995–2010.** The 1989 Le Tertre-Roteboeuf is one of the most concentrated wines of the vintage. That tells you something about François

Mitjavile and his refusal to let yields soar to limits that many of his famous neighbors are permitting. This rich, concentrated wine is opaque black/purple in color, with a splendid aroma of roasted chestnuts, black fruits, exotic spices, and minerals. The new oak frames this awesomely structured and massively concentrated wine. The results reveal winemaking genius. When will it be ready? Given its massive size and low acidity, I anticipate earlier rather than later. **Anticipated maturity: 1995–2010.** The 1990 is another immensely impressive wine. Now in the bottle, it has turned out to be as concentrated as the 1989. It reveals an opaque, dark ruby/purple/black color, as well as an intense bouquet of crushed black raspberry fruit, smoke, oak, licorice, and minerals. The wine boasts sensational concentration, massive richness, a chewy, thick, unctuous texture, and a rivetingly long, alcoholic, tannic finish. **Anticipated maturity: Now–2010.**

LA TONNELLE (BLAYE)* * *

1990	A	85

For years, shrewd consumers have been stocking up on this soft, often opulently styled wine with excellent fruit and an easygoing, attractive, silky texture. The 1990 continues a line of successes that began with the lovely 1982. Drink it over the next 4–5 years.

LA TOUR DE BY (MÉDOC)* * *

1990	B	85
1989	A	86

The 1989 exhibits excellent deep ruby color and a big nose of sweet fruit and oak, followed by a wonderfully lush, concentrated, moderately tannic wine that is admirably endowed, and well balanced. Drink it over the next 6–7 years. Excellent! The 1990 is a worthy rival to the 1989. Moderate oaky aromas are followed by a ripe, fruity, medium-bodied wine that is soft enough to offer immediate drinking and deep enough to last for 5–7 years.

LA TOUR-HAUT-BRION (GRAVES)* * *

1990	C	86
1989	D	88
1988	C	83

The 1988 La Tour-Haut-Brion has the telltale aggressive, hard tannins so prominent in this vintage, good body, and adequate persistence on the palate. Not charming, but austere and forceful, it should be at its best between 1995 and 2003. The 1989 La Tour-Haut-Brion is excellent. Primarily a Cabernet Sauvignon–based wine (85% Cabernet, 15% Merlot), it exhibits a bold bouquet of herbs, smoke, and cassis, plenty of ripeness, medium to full body, and a big, alcoholic, low-acid finish. **Anticipated maturity: Now–2000.** Less concentrated than the 1989, the soft, fruity, earthy 1990 exhibits the mineral, tobacco, roasted character one finds in wines from the northern viticultural region of Graves. Plump and fleshy, it should be drunk over the next 7–10 years.
PAST GLORIES: 1982 (94), 1978 (93), 1975 (98), 1970 (87), 1966 (88), 1961 (95), 1959 (92), 1955 (94), 1953 (96), 1949 (97), 1947 (95)
PAST MEDIOCRITIES . . . OR WORSE: 1986 (82), 1983 (84)

TOUR HAUT-CAUSSAN (MÉDOC)* * */* * * *

1990	B	88
1989	B	88
1988	B	86

The 1988 has an elegant, cedary, spicy, currant bouquet, medium-bodied, stylish, well-balanced flavors, and soft tannins, as well as the depth and overall equilibrium to last 4–7 years. **Anticipated maturity: Now–1996.** The 1989 is a more dramatic, alcoholic wine than the 1988, displaying some new oak in its nose, a robust, low-acid taste, and enough tannin to support a decade's worth of aging. It is a surprisingly big, forceful wine that will reward those shrewd enough to buy it. **Anticipated maturity: Now–2000.** As for the 1990, powerful aromas of ripe fruit and minerals are followed by a deep, nearly massive wine with significant glycerin, tannin, body, and depth. This brooding giant of a Cru Bourgeois should drink well for at least 10–15 years. It may turn out to be just as impressive as the 1989.

TOUR DU HAUT-MOULIN (HAUT-MÉDOC)* * */* * * *

1990	B	87
1989	B	88
1988	B	87

The 1988 Tour du Haut-Moulin is a substantial wine with brilliant definition, aggressive tannins, and gobs of blackcurrant fruit intermixed with scents of minerals and spices. The finish is impressive. This is one of the stars among the Crus Bourgeois. **Anticipated maturity: Now–1998.** The 1989 is low in acidity, opulent, and alcoholic, yet highly extracted, flamboyant, and dramatic. The rich, full flavors marry well with the new oak. **Anticipated maturity: Now–1996.** A traditional style of winemaking is evident in the dense, powerful, backward yet well-structured and concentrated 1990. The color is impressive, and the nose reluctantly offers up sweet aromas of fruit, earth, and minerals. There is enough power and intensity to suggest this wine will still be going strong at age 10.

LA TOUR-MARTILLAC (GRAVES)* *

1990	C	85
1989	C	80?

There was clearly an attempt on the part of the proprietors to make a denser, richer wine in 1989. But in doing so, they appeared to have extracted an unpleasant level of tannin. There is plenty of new oak, but the overall impression is one of toughness, lack of charm, and excessively astringent tannin levels. **Anticipated maturity: 1995–2000.** Although not a blockbuster, the 1990 is a light- to medium-bodied, elegant Graves, with a fragrant, earthy, berry- and mineral-scented nose, as well as ripe flavors. Exceptionally easy to drink, it exhibits soft tannins, good depth, and an overall sense of finesse and balance. Drink it over the next 7–8 years.

LA TOUR-DE-MONS (MARGAUX)* *

1990	B	85

This is a competent effort from a property that has potential but has yet to regain the magic it displayed in the forties, fifties, and sixties. The 1990 reveals an impressive dark ruby color, a sweet, floral, fruity nose, medium-bodied, silky-textured flavors, low acidity, and good length. If more structure and personality emerge, it may merit a higher score.

LA TOUR-DU-PIN-FIGEAC-MOUEIX (ST.-ÉMILION)* * *

1990	C	89
1989	C	88
1988	C	87

The 1988 from this estate is a worthy competitor with the 1989, with excellent extract, more elegance but less power, and a rich, toasty, plummy bouquet intertwined with scents of licorice, toast, and spring flowers. Full bodied and intense for a 1988, it should be at its best between now and 2004. The 1989 is a concentrated, powerful, full-bodied wine, with gobs of extract and a penetrating bouquet of black fruits, new oak, and subtle herbs. A powerhouse of a wine, it is well balanced, with decent acidity for the vintage and a super finish. **Anticipated maturity: 1994–2003.** The seductive, impressive, black/ruby-colored 1990 is another exhilarating St.-Émilion. Densely colored, this wine's huge bouquet of jammy fruits (plums and raspberries), meaty, full-bodied texture, and lavish quantities of fruit all combine to make this an impressive effort. **Anticipated maturity: 1994–2008.**

LA TOUR ST.-BONNET (MÉDOC)* * *

1990	B	87+
1989	A	86

La Tour St.-Bonnet's 1989 is atypically powerful and rich, with a dense ruby/purple color, superb extract, a long, rich finish, and wonderful structure, particularly for a wine of its pedigree. It is hard to ignore the intense bouquet of cassis and minerals. **Anticipated maturity: Now–2000.** The 1990 is a super effort that merits considerable interest given the reasonable price. Powerful and full bodied, this macho wine is loaded with extract, flavor, and tannin. If more complexity develops, this wine might deserve an even higher rating. **Anticipated maturity: 1994–2004.**

LA TOUR SEGUY (BOURG)* * *

1990	B	86
1989	B	85

The impressively dense color of the 1989 is followed by a wine that reluctantly offers up aromas of superripe cassis. In the mouth, the wine exhibits excellent richness, surprisingly good acidity for a 1989, and plenty of tannin, power, and structure. **Anticipated maturity: Now–2002.** Deep purple in color, with a straightforward, enjoyable, ripe nose of cassis and minerals, the 1990 displays excellent ripeness, a robust constitution, plenty of stuffing, and moderate tannins. Drink it over the next 10 years. A sleeper!

LES TOURELLES DE LONGUEVILLE (PAUILLAC)* * *

1990	C	87
1989	C	85
1988	B	85

The second wine of Pichon Baron, the 1988 Les Tourelles de Longueville is surprisingly soft for the vintage, with rich, round, fat flavors suggestive of oak, cassis, herbs, and minerals. It is a delightful wine for drinking over the next 4–5 years. The highly competent 1989 is displaying fine toasty new oak, soft, plump, up-front cassis fruit, a lovely chewy texture, soft tannins, and alarmingly low acidity. It is ideal for drinking over the next 3–4 years. Fat, alcoholic, plump, and concentrated, the rich, complex 1990 is oozing with fruit, has full body, and surprising length. This excellent second wine will make for a tasty mouthful over the next 5–6 years.

TROPLONG-MONDOT (ST.-ÉMILION)* * * *

1990	C	94
1989	C	91
1988	C	89

The 1988 Troplong-Mondot is a beautifully made, elegant wine with a deep ruby/purple color; a fascinating bouquet of plums, spicy new oak, and minerals; rich, multidimensional flavors; and fresh acidity. This is another example of a young proprietor committed to making a strict selection. **Anticipated maturity: Now–2007.** The 1989 exhibits a medium-bodied, enormously rich, powerful, concentrated feel on the palate, with highly extracted flavors of black raspberries and vanillin. Tannic, yet voluptuous because of its low acidity, this is a stunning, intensely fragrant and compelling wine. A remarkably classy wine. **Anticipated maturity: 1994–2008.** The awesome 1990 is a must buy given its reasonable price. Fabulously concentrated, it exhibits an impressively opaque dark ruby/purple color and a rich, penetrating bouquet of minerals, herbs, anise, spicy new oak, and black fruits. Also present is a lovely combination of power, finesse, and graceful, medium- to full-bodied, lavishly endowed, chewy, focused flavors. The acidity is sound, and the wine reveals moderate, sweet tannins. It is considerably richer and more tannic than the outstanding 1989. Drink it over the next 10–20 years.

TROTANOY (POMEROL)* * * *

1990	E	89
1989	E	88
1988	E	86

The very good 1988 possesses an attractive plum-and-vanillin nose. On the palate the wine exhibits fine concentration, firm, relatively hard tannins, and a spicy, long finish. Although it is tasty, I would have preferred a more exciting style. **Anticipated maturity: 1995–2008.** The 1989 displays a ruby/purple color and a promising aroma of ripe cassis fruit gently kissed by oak. This broad-shouldered Trotanoy may reassure some of the disappointed fans of this property that the indifferent results in 1983, 1985, and 1986 were a fluke. I suspect the 1989 Trotanoy will drink well in spite of the high tannin level. I could not help but notice the weedy, herbaceous component to the wine's fruit since bottling. **Anticipated maturity: 1994–2010.** The 1990 confirms the recent trend of this property to produce lighter, finesse-filled wines that are designed for early drinking, rather than the massive, blockbuster style of Trotanoy that was previously in fashion. The Moueix family disagrees, feeling the 1990 is a return to a bigger style. Certainly it is the richest Trotanoy since the 1982. The 1990 exhibits a deep color, a spicy, sweet, currant nose, moderate tannins, medium body, and excellent concentration. **Anticipated maturity: 1995–2003.**

PAST GLORIES: 1982 (97), 1975 (94), 1971 (93), 1970 (93), 1967 (91), 1964 (90), 1961 (98), 1959 (92), 1945 (96)

PAST MEDIOCRITIES . . . OR WORSE: 1983 (81)

TROTTEVIEILLE (ST.-ÉMILION)* * *

1990	D	88
1989	D	90
1988	C	86

This famous St.-Émilion estate has made considerable progress during the 1980s. The 1988 Trottevieille is a very good but tannic, backward style of wine that needs 5–6 years in the bottle to shed its toughness. There is plenty of ripe, extracted fruit, the color is dark ruby, and there is a feeling of weight and length, but the tannins dominate the wine. **Anticipated maturity: 1996–2008.** The 1989 is an immensely impressive wine, exhibiting an opaque, black color and a sensational bouquet of licorice, chocolate, and superripe plums. In the mouth the wine displays immense size, enormous concentration, a tremendous level of tannins, and an intense, alcoholic, long, opulent, low-acid finish. **Anticipated maturity: 1996–2015.** The 1990 is at least very good. A backward, oaky, tannic wine in need of some bottle age, this full-bodied St.-Émilion exhibits plenty of power and guts. **Anticipated maturity: 1996–2005.**

VERDIGNAN (HAUT-MÉDOC)* */* * *

1990	A	84
1989	A	85

The chunky, fat 1989 Verdignan offers gobs of berry fruit and spices, as well as fine glycerin and alcohol in its lusty finish. Drink it over the next 3–4 years. A typically good Cru Bourgeois with fine fruit, medium body, some tannin, and a nice, lush finish, the 1990 Verdignan should be drunk over the next 4–5 years.

LA VIEILLE-CURE (FRONSAC)* * *

1990	B	88
1989	B	86

The 1989's open-knit, fragrant nose of sweet fruit, earth, and vanillin is followed by a fleshy, chewy wine with excellent richness and a Pomerol-like succulence and intensity. Drink this delicious, well-made, well-balanced wine over the next 10–12 years. The delicious 1990 is a dead ringer for a top Pomerol. Deeply colored, it displays a fragrant black fruit scent and plump, almost sweet, supple, rich, full-bodied flavors that suggest a high Merlot content. It has excellent color, a chewy texture, and a velvety yet well-delineated finish. Drink it over the next 7–8 years. Impressive and well priced!

VIEUX CHÂTEAU CERTAN (POMEROL)* * * *

1990	D	94
1989	E	89
1988	D	91

The 1988 is a classic Vieux Château Certan. The huge bouquet of cassis, herbs, and new oak is followed by a wine that is medium bodied, with deep, black cherry flavors wrapped intelligently in toasty oak. Extracted, deep, yet impeccably balanced, this well-delineated Pomerol should age well for 20–25 years. **Anticipated maturity: 1994–2010.** The 1989 Vieux Château Certan is a very good wine, with dark ruby/purple color, a big, spicy, herb- and cassis-scented bouquet, medium body, and a long, relatively opulent finish. **Anticipated maturity: 1994–2005.** Deeply colored, with a marvelously fragrant nose of herbs, berry fruit, oak, and exotic spices, the compelling 1990 Vieux Château Certan displays surprising opulence and ripeness, more unctuosity than usual, and admirable structure and definition. The acid is lower, yet the extract level is much higher in the 1990 than in the 1989. This is a superlative, medium- to full-bodied, multidimensional wine. **Anticipated maturity: 1994–2010.**
PAST GLORIES: 1986 (93), 1983 (88), 1982 (91), 1964 (90), 1959 (93), 1950 (96), 1948 (95), 1947 (95), 1945 (96)
PAST MEDIOCRITIES . . . OR WORSE: 1971 (74), 1970 (80), 1966 (74)

VIEUX CLOS ST.-ÉMILION (ST.-ÉMILION)* */* * *

1990	B	89

This little-known estate has turned in an exemplary effort. A deeply colored, full-bodied, viscous wine, it offers gobs of sweet, roasted, curranty fruit, a velvety texture, soft tannins, and a succulent finish. Another hedonistic, rich St.-Émilion! **Anticipated maturity: Now–2002.**

VIEUX-ROBIN (MÉDOC)* */* * *

1990	A	86
1989	A	85

Vieux-Robin is turning out to be one of the best Cru Bourgeois estates in the Médoc. The oaky 1989 offers lusty, full-bodied, lush black cherry and cassis fruit, low acidity, and a juicy, succulent, silky-smooth finish. Drink it over the next 2–3 years. The 1990, their best wine to date, displays superb richness as well as a huge nose of ripe, plummy fruit. In the mouth it is a deep, medium- to full-bodied, impressively endowed wine that should drink well for at least another 7–8 years.

VILLEMAURINE (ST.-ÉMILION)* *

1990	C	75
1989	C	80
1988	C	78

The 1988 Villemaurine exhibits abundant quantities of high tannin, a large, oaky, yet simple, ripe, plummy bouquet, and plenty of alcohol and size in the finish. **Anticipated maturity: Now–2002.** Black/purple in color, the 1989 displays a spicy, earthy, herb- and cassis-scented nose. It is a big, chewy, monolithic wine that is impressively tannic but lacking dimension. **Anticipated maturity: 1995–2003.** Unbelievably dominated by new oak, the 1990 is light with inadequate depth and character.

LA VIOLETTE (POMEROL)* * *

1990	D	86

Dark ruby/purple, with a surprisingly intense nose of flowers, plums, and licorice, this wine displays fine concentration, low acidity, moderate tannin, medium to full body, and a long, nearly lavish finish. It will require early consumption. **Anticipated maturity: Now–2000.**

VRAYE–CROIX–DE–GAY (POMEROL)* *

1990	D	86

This vineyard, superbly situated on the plateau of Pomerol, is a classic example of the perennial underachiever. The dark ruby color and fragrant, floral-, cassis-, coffee-, and tobacco-scented nose of the 1990 offer some personality. **Anticipated maturity: 1994–2002.**

THE DRY WHITE WINES OF BORDEAUX

L'ARRIVET-HAUT-BRION (GRAVES)* * *

1990	C	86
1989	C	77

The 1990 is a major improvement on this property's mediocre 1989. It is ripe, with a mineral, flowery, waxy nose and rich, dry, medium-bodied flavors that exhibit fine concentration and a judicious use of toasty new oak. Drink it over the next 7–8 years. Unfortunately, new wood dominates much of the 1989's fruit and character. In the mouth there is light body and decent concentration, but, again, the predominant characteristic is that of new oak. What a shame.

BOUSCAUT (GRAVES)* *

1990	C	84
1989	C	71

Bouscaut's 1990 exhibits soft, lightly honeyed flavors and some attractive ripe, herb-tinged, flowery fruit to go along with the new oak. The wine is pleasant, medium bodied, and ideal for drinking over the next 4–5 years. As for the

1989, dull, sterile, nearly nonexistent aromas are followed by thin, stripped, high-strung flavors that lack charm, flesh, and character. This wine should be drunk now.

CARBONNIEUX (GRAVES)* * *

1990	C	87
1989	C	84

Carbonnieux's 1990 appears to be a more ambitious effort than many recent vintages. Possessing the low acidity that marks the 1990 vintage, the wine has a fragrant, rich nose followed by a deep, concentrated wine with a chewy texture, enough acidity for focus, and a clean aftertaste. Drink it over the next 7–8 years. The 1989 Carbonnieux offers an attractive, smoky, oaky bouquet, some scents of honey and herbs, and soft, agreeable, round, fruity flavors. The low acidity suggests the wine should be drunk over the next 2–3 years.

CHANTEGRIVE (GRAVES)* * *

1990 Cuvée Caroline	C	87
1989 Cuvée Caroline	C	86

This is the luxury *cuvée* of the well-known Graves estate of Chantegrive. In both 1989 and 1990 it was made and aged in new oak, and the results are wines with wonderfully fresh, toasty, fig- and melon-scented noses, medium body, and luscious, soft fruit. Both vintages require consumption over the next 2–3 years.

DOMAINE DE CHEVALIER (GRAVES)* * * * *

1990	E	92
1989	E	87

It is typical for Domaine de Chevalier's personality and fruit to go into hiding after bottling. However, there is no doubting that the 1990 is a superbly extracted, rich wine, loaded with intensity and fatness as well as a honeyed, rich, Sauvignon/Semillon character. A bigger wine than the 1989, the 1990 should prove to have 20 years of potential longevity. The 1989 does not have the concentration of the 1988, and given my high expectations, I am disappointed (in the context of other Domaine de Chevaliers) by its showings to date. There is plenty of intense vanillin oakiness in the bouquet, as well as some faint scents of minerals, herbs, and underripe apricots. However, the wine is medium bodied and lacks concentration and depth. Perhaps there is more here than presently meets the palate or the nose. **Anticipated maturity: Now–1998.** PAST GLORIES: 1985 (93), 1983 (93), 1970 (93), 1962 (93)

CLOS FLORIDENE (GRAVES)* * * *

1990	C	90
1989	C	88

The 1990 is a dry, lavishly rich, honeyed wine with a super perfume of figs and melons. It exhibits a multidimensional texture and a huge bouquet. Although the 1990 is the best example of Clos Floridene I have tasted, there is no doubting the seductive charm of the 1989. The big, honeyed, melony, flowery, herbaceous-scented nose is followed by relatively rich, yet vividly fresh, lively flavors that exhibit good body, plenty of extract, and a long, luscious finish. It should be drunk over the next 2–3 years.

DE FIEUZAL (GRAVES)* * * * *

1990	D	92
1989	D	87

The huge, oaky, fig, herb, and melony nose of the 1990 is followed by a wine with super extraction, rich, medium- to full-bodied, concentrated flavors, and a glycerin-imbued, long, lush finish. The 1990 is the best dry white wine from de Fieuzal since their marvelous 1985. Like many 1989 white Graves, de Fieuzal does not quite have the grip and delineation one expects because of this vintage's low acidity. Nevertheless, this has still turned out to be one of the most successful dry white wines of the vintage. It is a rich, honeyed, smoke-scented wine with wonderfully ripe apple- and melonlike flavors. It should be drunk over its first 4–5 years of life.
PAST GLORIES: 1985 (93)

HAUT-BRION (GRAVES)* * * * *

1990	E	89
1989	E	97

Haut-Brion's 1990 is a lighter-bodied, more delicate and elegant example than their blockbuster 1989. A sweet, waxy, flowery nose is followed by a medium-bodied wine with good concentration but without the depth and spectacular intensity of the 1989. Whether the 1989 ultimately turns out to be better than the great 1985 remains to be seen, but there is no doubting this is the most immense and large-scale Haut-Brion Blanc I have ever tasted. Jean Delmas, administrator of the Dillon properties, felt the 1989 fully replicated the fleshy, chewy texture of a great Grand Cru white Burgundy. Only 600 cases were made of this rich, alcoholic, sumptuous wine. It is amazingly full and long in the mouth, with a very distinctive mineral, honeyed character. The low acidity would seemingly suggest a shorter life than normal, but I am convinced this wine will last 10–30 years or more. It is a real show stopper! **Anticipated maturity: 1996–2020.**
PAST GLORIES: 1985 (97)

HAUT-GARDÈRE (GRAVES)* * *

1990	C	86
1989	C	86

This is an up-and-coming estate, with its vineyards located just across the street from de Fieuzal. The 1990 possesses more honeyed richness than its older sibling, but the two wines are qualitative equals. The 1990 should be drunk over the next 4–5 years. The 1989 has an attractive stony, mineral, honeyed nose, medium body, good flavor extraction, and more character than many of the more famous classified growths. Drink it over the next 4–6 years.

LAVILLE-HAUT-BRION (GRAVES)* * * * *

1990	E	91
1989	E	95

Although the 1990 Laville-Haut-Brion may not possess the pure power and richness of the 1989, it is one of the finest dry white wines of the vintage. Meaty and chewy, with a lot of alcohol, superb extraction, and a long, unctuous, thick, honeyed finish, it should drink well for 15–20 years. The 1989 is an absolutely magnificent bottle of white Graves with extraordinary depth of flavor and that honeyed, rich (glycerin levels must be absurdly high) texture that comes only from tiny yields. The bouquet is a bit more subdued after bottling, but there is no doubting the melony, fig, herb, and waxy components that make this such an exhilarating wine to smell. In the mouth there are massive extract levels. I am confident that this may turn out to be the greatest Laville-Haut-Brion made in the last 20–30 years. How interesting it will be for millionaires to compare this wine with the great 1989 Haut-Brion Blanc! **Anticipated maturity: 1996–2020.**
PAST GLORIES: 1985 (93), 1983 (90), 1975 (90), 1966 (92), 1962 (88), 1947 (93), 1945 (96)

LA LOUVIÈRE (GRAVES)* * * *

1990	C	90
1989	C	88

I admired the ripe, waxy, melon- and tropical fruit–scented nose of the 1990. It exhibits gobs of fruit, medium to full body, and a dry, pure, crisp finish. Drink it over the next 7–8 years. The 1989 is a relatively fat, open-knit, richly fruity La Louvière that lacks some grip and delineation. Yet there is no doubting its lavish, rich fruitiness, easygoing texture, and ability to provide considerable pleasure. It will not be long-lived, and it is best drunk over the next 5–6 years.

MALARTIC-LAGRAVIÈRE (GRAVES)* * *

1990	D	77
1989	D	75

The decision to use 100% Sauvignon Blanc, ferment the wine in stainless steel, and then age the wine for 7–8 months in vat is something I find curious. I say that because this property often produces a white wine with a shrill character that comes across as too lemony and tart. No doubt, given its high acidity, the wine will hold up. But if the question is the degree of pleasure it is capable of providing, Malartic-Lagravière fails to please. Both the 1989 and 1990 are too tart. Both wines share a light straw/green color, are reserved, and have unimpressive depth and length. **Anticipated maturity: Now–1995.**

OLIVIER (GRAVES)* *

1990	C	82
1989	C	78

Both the 1990 and 1989 are light, tart, malnourished wines. The 1989 displays some faint new oak smells in the background, but it is a straightforward, dry, fruity white Graves that hardly merits its reputation as a classified growth. Drink it over the next 2–3 years. The 1990 exhibits more fat and fruit.

ROCHEMORIN (GRAVES)* * *

1990	C	84
1989	C	78

As much as I admire the honeyed, herbal, and fruity 1990, I felt the 1989 from this Graves estate was relatively light and innocuous. Drink it over the next 2–3 years.

SMITH-HAUT-LAFITTE (GRAVES)* *

1990	C	83
1989	C	74

The 1990 reveals adequate ripeness, good fruit, some body, and a short but pleasant finish. Drink it over the next 5–6 years. The 1989 is glaringly deficient in acidity. It comes across as a flat, flabby wine, with excessive wood and not enough fruit. It should be consumed immediately.

LA TOUR-MARTILLAC (GRAVES)* * * *

1990	C	90
1989	C	88

This property is making more impressive wines. The 1990 is a deep, intense, powerful, ripe wine, with super extraction and huge, honeyed, herb- and figlike flavors that last and last. Drink this impressive dry white wine over the next 7–10 years. Although the 1989 is not as concentrated as the 1987, 1988, or 1990, it still possesses an immensely attractive lemony, grassy, oaky nose; medium-bodied, soft, richly fruity flavors; and good length. It will not have extended aging potential given its low acidity, but it will provide great enjoyment if consumed before 1996.

THE SWEET WHITE WINES OF BORDEAUX
BARSAC AND SAUTERNES

D'ARCHE (SAUTERNES)* *

1989	C	?
1988	C	88

The 1988 d'Arche is a beautifully made, intense wine with a gorgeous nose of honeyed pineapple fruit. In the mouth it is unctuous and full bodied, with great sweetness and presence as well as a long, rich, nearly viscous finish. **Anticipated maturity: 1993–2005.** The 1989 has consistently tasted muddled, out of focus, too low in acidity, and excessively alcoholic and heavy-handed. Wines such as this sometimes turn around in the bottle and develop more structure. But after tasting this wine four different times, I am at a loss to understand its lack of definition. Judgment reserved.

BASTOR-LAMONTAGNE (SAUTERNES)* * *

1989	B	87
1988	B	87

The excellent 1988 displays a great deal of botrytis, as evidenced by its honeyed pineapple- and orange-scented nose. In the mouth it is full, wonderfully pure, focused, and long, with moderate sweetness. This Sauternes could actually serve as a good aperitif as well as a dessert wine. **Anticipated maturity: Now–2000.** Very typical of the vintage, the 1989 Bastor-Lamontagne is extremely low in acidity, ripe, with surprisingly evolved, medium-gold color and a great deal of fruit. Deep yet elegant and spicy, with some attractive vanillin notes, this is a classy, more boldly flavored wine than usual. It will no doubt have to be drunk quite early. **Anticipated maturity: Now–1995.**

BROUSTET (BARSAC)* *

1990	C	85
1989	C	86
1988	C	88

The 1988 Broustet has the advantage of having fine acidity, an emerging complexity, and an uplifting bouquet of honeyed apricot/peach fruit, which, along with some vibrant acidity, gives its powerful, rich, intense flavors a sense of balance and focus. It is the best Broustet I have ever tasted. **Anticipated maturity: Now–2008.** The 1989 should be consumed in its first decade of life since it offers a big, fat, plump, juicy mouthful of wine. Surprisingly elegant for a 1989, but extremely alcoholic and not that complex, it is a sweeter wine than the 1988 but lacks the flavor dimension and character of the previous vintage. **Anticipated maturity: Now–2002.** The 1990 is a straightforward, attractive, pineapple- and tropical fruit–scented wine with good viscosity, adequate acidity, and a plump, alcoholic finish. Drink it over the next 10–12 years.

CAILLOU (BARSAC)* *

1990	C	85
1989	C	87
1988	C	87

A totally different style from the 1989, the 1988 is a more elegant, crisper, more focused Barsac, with lovely waxy, pineapplelike fruitiness, medium body, good grip, and an overall zesty, lively feel. Although not a match for the 1989 in terms of weight and alcohol, it is every bit as good. **Anticipated maturity: Now–2006.** The excellent 1989 reveals a lot of sweetness and much more fruit (decadent amounts of pineapple), body, and glycerin than one normally finds in Caillou, in an opulent, almost lavishly rich style. As is typical in this vintage, the acidity is low. The wine should probably be consumed over the next 10–15 years. **Anticipated maturity: Now–2005.** The supersweet, chunky 1990 displays gobs of nearly cloying sweet flavors of orange, pineapple, and coconut. The acidity is appallingly low, but the alcohol seems to be holding it together—at least for the moment. Drink the 1990 Caillou early, preferably within its first 10 years of life.

CLIMENS (BARSAC)* * * * *

1990	D	92
1989	D	90
1988	D	96

Climens made such a spectacular 1986 that it is hard to believe the 1988 may ultimately turn out to be superior. What makes Climens so stunning is its penetrating acidity, combined with fabulous richness and complexity. The 1988 reveals layer upon layer of honeyed pineapple- and orange-scented and -flavored fruit, vibrant acidity, high levels of botrytis, and a fabulously long yet well-focused finish. It is a great wine, but don't bet the farm that it will turn out to be better than their profound 1986. However, it is vastly superior to both the 1989 and 1990. **Anticipated maturity: 1998–2015.** For whatever reason, the 1989 is merely outstanding rather than dazzling. Although it lacks the complexity of the 1988, it is a plump, muscular, rich, intense, full-bodied, and sweeter-than-usual wine. For a 1989, it even possesses good acidity. If more complexity and grip develop, my rating will look stingy. **Anticipated maturity: 1995–2010.** The 1990 may turn out to be better than the 1989, but I doubt it will rival the 1986 or 1988. It is a more powerful example of Climens than those vintages. Climens is one 1990 that possesses crisp acidity to give focus to the superrich, honeyed, citrusy, tropical fruit, and coconut flavors. It is all finesse, but the multidimensional personality is unmistakable. The 1990 is another superlative wine from what is probably my favorite estate of the region. Drink it over the next 20–25 years.

PAST GLORIES: 1986 (96), 1983 (92), 1980 (90), 1975 (89), 1971 (94), 1959 (90), 1949 (94), 1947 (94?), 1937 (92), 1929 (90)

CLOS HAUT-PEYRAGUEY (SAUTERNES)* *

1990	C	86
1989	C	82
1988	C	86

The 1988 is a graceful style of wine, with an attractive vanillin, apricot-scented bouquet, medium body, good acidity, abundant botrytis levels, and plenty of delineation to its plump, round, attractive flavors. **Anticipated maturity: Now–1997.** The thick, cloying, excessively sweet 1989 lacks acidity and comes across as fat, unfocused, and just a bit heavy and too obvious. There is plenty of fruit, but it lacks complexity. **Anticipated maturity: Now–1995.** This property produced an attractive wine in 1990. The intense nose of honeyed pineapple is followed by a wonderfully rich, elegant wine with decent acidity and plenty of glycerin and sweetness that is all framed nicely by the wine's acids and a touch of new oak barrels. The finish is spicy, long, and refreshing. Drink this charmer over the next 10–15 or more years.

COUTET (BARSAC)* * * */* * * * *

1990	D	83
1989	D	89
1988	D	93

1989 Cuvée Madame	E	96
1988 Cuvée Madame	E	98

Coutet appears to be on a hot streak at the moment. Even the 1988 regular *cuvée* is a deliciously full, huge wine for Coutet, with gobs of botrytis, a full-bodied, opulent texture, zesty acidity, and spectacular length. It is the finest regular *cuvée* of Coutet I have ever tasted. A classic! **Anticipated maturity: 1996–2012.** The 1989 Coutet has more finesse and acidity than many wines from the vintage. It exhibits plenty of new oak, as well as opulent, unctuous fruit. The bouquet is not as compelling as in the 1988, but there is plenty of honeyed, nearly chewy richness and intensity. It is a relatively powerful wine for Coutet, and probably 1–2% higher in alcohol than the 1988. It will probably have to be drunk within its first 20 years of life. **Anticipated maturity: 1995–2015.** The 1990 Coutet offers a spicy, oaky, coconut-, and citrus-scented nose that is followed by medium-bodied, elegant flavors that lack botrytis. I wish the finish exhibited more fruit rather than high alcohol.

As wonderful as the 1988 regular *cuvée* is, it pales in comparison with the limited-production, luxury *cuvée* called Cuvée Madame. This wine exhibits a mind-blowing richness, a fabulous bouquet that seems to soar from the glass, astonishing intensity, impeccable balance, and a remarkable finish. This is true nectar! **Anticipated maturity: 1997–2020.** The 1989 Cuvée Madame is one of the richest and fullest examples of this wine I have ever tasted. This medium/light gold-colored wine exhibits a huge bouquet of coconuts, mocha, peaches, and vanillin. Unctuous and crammed with fruit, this gloriously extracted wine has less grip and focus than the nearly perfect 1988, but the concentration is akin to the essence of Coutet. The finish is spectacular in this sweet, decadent wine. **Anticipated maturity: 1996–2015.**
PAST GLORIES: Cuvée Madame—1986 (96), 1981 (96), 1971 (98)

DOISY-DAËNE (BARSAC)* * *

1990	C	84
1989	C	86
1988	C	88
1990 L'Extravagance	E	94

The 1988 Doisy-Daëne is a medium-weight wine, exhibiting a great deal of botrytis in a lemony-, pineapple-, and apricot-scented nose. In the mouth it is crisp, with brilliant focus to its component parts, a wonderful sweetness buoyed by fresh acidity, and a long, harmonious finish. **Anticipated maturity: Now–2005.** The 1989 is a surprisingly restrained, elegant example of the vintage. Although it does not possess the depth of the 1988, there are abundant ripe, obvious, honeyed fruit flavors and decent acidity. This is an admirable example of balancing power and finesse. **Anticipated maturity: Now–2007.** Heavy-handed, with a big, chunky nose of tropical fruits, the full-bodied, alcoholic regular bottling of Doisy-Daëne lacks both acidity and botrytis. In 1990 this property also made 100 cases (4 barrels) of a deluxe *cuvée* called l'Extravagance. It is a phenomenal wine, with sensational extraction of flavor; a wonderful, honeyed, botrytis character; deep, rich, multidimensional flavors; and a fabulous finish. Should any readers be lucky enough to run across a bottle, it will be worth the extra effort and cost necessary to obtain it.

DOISY-DUBROCA (BARSAC)* * * *

1988	C	92

Do you want to taste a clone of the great Climens that sells for one-half the price? This sensational wine, which bears an uncanny resemblance to Climens, possesses great richness, crisp acidity, and an impeccable balance between power and finesse. The huge, botrytis-filled bouquet of oranges, pineapples, melons, and honey is superb. A winemaking tour de force! **Anticipated maturity: Now–2010.**

DOISY-VÉDRINES (BARSAC)* * *

1990	C	82
1989	C	88
1988	C	85

The 1988 is an elegant, stylish wine, with good richness, medium body, an underlying sweetness, and high acidity that brings everything into focus. Endowed with plenty of botrytis, the wine has a deep, long, alcoholic finish, but it is less impressive than many wines from this vintage. The 1989 is clearly superior. **Anticipated maturity: Now–2006.** The 1989 is unctuous and viscous, with a chewy, heavyweight style, low acidity, mammoth size, and splendidly concentrated fruit suggestive of superripe, honeyed pineapple. Perhaps it comes down to personal taste, but in this case the 1989 seems to have even more complexity and botrytis than the excellent 1988. **Anticipated maturity: Now–2010.** A crisp, citrus-scented wine, the 1990 Doisy-Védrines tastes watery and diluted. It lacks the richness one has come to expect from this generally well-run estate. If some more fruit emerges, it may become a stylish but uninspiring example of a sweet wine from the Barsac/Sauternes region.

FILHOT (SAUTERNES)* *

1989	C	86
1988	C	84

The 1988 Filhot typifies the unexciting style of wines produced at this château. There is a very obvious, fruity, ripe, attractive bouquet devoid of complexity. In the mouth this off-dry, slightly sweet, monolithically styled, soft, fruit, round, foursquare wine is pleasant, but it lacks any real distinction, focus, or character. **Anticipated maturity: Now–1996.** The 1989 appears to be taking on a very mature look at an alarmingly fast pace. The color is already medium gold, and the wine, while exhibiting very low acidity, is extremely sweet, with a big, pineapple-scented bouquet. There is an attractive purity, but softness and lack of grip suggest this is a wine that needs to be consumed in its first decade of life. **Anticipated maturity: Now–2000.**

GUIRAUD (SAUTERNES)* * * *

1990	D	88
1989	D	90
1988	D	91

The 1988 Guiraud marks this estate's finest effort to date. Extraordinarily rich, concentrated, and oaky, this wine is full-bodied and fabulously long, but ever so precise and clear. The huge bouquet of toasty vanillin-scented new oak, pineapples, coconuts, and buttery oranges is a joy to experience. In the mouth there is very little with which to find fault. Spectacularly concentrated and potentially long-lived, Guiraud is another dazzling star of the vintage. **Anticipated maturity: 1996–2025.** The 1989 offers huge, penetrating aromas of vanillin-scented, smoky new oak and superripe pineapple that soar from the glass. In the mouth this is a terrific, rich, full-bodied, in-your-face style of Sauternes that goes right to the edge of being almost too massive and overbearing. Fortunately there is enough acidity to give it grip and focus. It will have to be monitored during its evolution, given its precarious balance, but there is no denying the sumptuous appeal of this very sweet, alcoholic, honeyed wine. **Anticipated maturity: 1996–2010.** The 1990's deep color is more evolved than in other 1990 Sauternes, and in the mouth the 1990 Guiraud is heavy and oaky, with a roasted character to the fruit. Although there is plenty of viscosity, alcohol, and wood, I found this wine consistently chunky, very rich, powerfully impressive, but too spicy for my taste.

LAFAURIE-PEYRAGUEY (SAUTERNES)* * * *

1990	D	90
1989	D	92
1988	D	94

Probably the greatest wine this estate has ever produced, the 1988 reveals stunning levels of botrytis and extract. It is a massively rich, concentrated wine that never tastes heavy or thick. The length is mind-boggling, as is the splendid combination of power and elegance. A superlative effort, this wine belongs in any serious Sauternes lover's cellar. **Anticipated maturity: 1995–2015.** The 1989 started off life relatively heavy, fat, and perhaps too alcoholic and low in acidity. It has taken on much more structure and is clearly one of the top wines of the vintage. An explosive nose of honeyed apricot/orange fruit is followed by viscous, thick, rich, huge, mouth-filling flavors that coat the palate. There is barely enough acidity to give the wine a certain grip and focus. This heavyweight, old-style Sauternes will no doubt last because of its hefty alcohol content. But it will be drinkable very young, and its aging will have to be monitored carefully. **Anticipated maturity: 1994–2005.** In 1990 this property once again turned out one of the better wines of the vintage. An attractive nose of ripe apricots, honeyed peaches, and spicy new oak is followed by a wine with deep, rich, chewy, multidimensional flavors, good viscosity, and enough acidity to frame the wine and provide balance. Lafaurie-Peyraguey should prove to be one of the best 1990s from the Sauternes/Barsac region. Drink it over the next 20 years.

PAST GLORIES: 1986 (92), 1983 (92)

LAMOTHE-DESPUJOLS (SAUTERNES)* *

1990	C	84
1989	C	76
1988	C	72

It is hard to understand what could have happened at Lamothe-Despujols in such a superb vintage as 1988. The 1988 is dull, muted, and lacking fruit, freshness, and character. **Anticipated maturity: Now.** Very thick, heavy, excessively alcoholic, with no grip, focus, or delineation to its flavors, drinking this cloyingly sweet, chunky, overdone 1989 is akin to being hit on the head with a sledgehammer. **Anticipated maturity: Now–1999.** The 1990 reveals an attractive nose of tropical fruits, particularly oranges. It is followed by a flavorful, medium-bodied wine with good fat, chewiness, and sweetness, but not a great deal of finesse. Drink it over the next decade.

LAMOTHE-GUIGNARD (SAUTERNES)* * *

1990	C	86
1989	C	87
1988	C	89

The 1988 Lamothe-Guignard is all finesse, with a wonderfully intense bouquet of pineapples, bananas, mangoes, honey, and toasty oak. In the mouth the wine displays splendid concentration, medium body, and vivid clarity and precision to its flavors because of excellent acidity. It should drink beautifully for 10–15 years. It does not have the weight of the 1989, but oh, what charm! **Anticipated maturity: Now–2008.** There is a remarkable contrast in styles between the 1988 and 1989 vintages of Lamothe-Guignard. The 1989 is a blockbuster in a heavy, brawny, outrageously alcoholic, unctuous style that is impressive at first but may become tiring. It is an extremely powerful, intense wine, but it comes across as a bully when compared with the charm of the 1988. Nevertheless, this wine has many admirers. **Anticipated maturity: Now–2002.** The 1990 is a relatively heavy-handed style of wine with some noticeable new oak, thick, low-acid, ripe flavors; a honeyed, chewy texture; and plenty of hot alcohol in the finish. If it pulls itself together, it should provide lusty drinking for at least a decade.

DE MALLE (SAUTERNES)* * *

1990	C	89
1989	C	86
1988	C	87

Except for the splendid 1990, the 1988 is the best example I have ever tasted of a sweet wine from Château de Malle. The wonderfully perfumed bouquet of pineapples and honeyed, buttery, applelike fruit is intense and persistent. In the mouth the wine has the precision that is so much a characteristic of the 1988 vintage, as well as an attractive hint of toasty new oak that frames the rich, concentrated, highly extracted, moderately sweet, honeyed flavors. This well-balanced wine should drink beautifully for the next 10–15 years. **Anticipated maturity: Now–2005.** The lovely, moderately intense bouquet of vanillin spices and pineapples is followed by a wine with excellent acidity for a 1989, good grip and definition, and a medium-bodied, crisp finish. This will be a Sauternes to drink early in life, but it should last well. The 1990 de Malle is one of the stars of the vintage. **Anticipated maturity: Now–2003.** The best young de Malle I have ever tasted, the 1990 is a Climens look-alike. It exhibits a fresh, orange, citrusy, honeyed nose touched subtly by new oak. In the mouth there is wonderful richness, zesty acidity to provide definition, and a crisp, rich, authoritative yet stylish finish. It should drink well for at least 10–15 or more years. If the price is right, this might be worth the plunge.

NAIRAC (BARSAC)* *

1990	C	82
1989	C	85
1988	C	?

The 1988 has consistently tasted dull and muted, with its fruit suppressed by excessive oak. It is hard to understand why this wine has tasted so backward and unexpressive from both cask and bottle. Judgment reserved. When I first tasted the 1989 Nairac from cask, it appeared to be excessively oaky, as well as a bit too fat and alcoholic. However, it has evolved gracefully in the cask and now exhibits plenty of toasty vanillin-scented new oak, an opulently rich nose and texture, long, heady, unctuous flavors, and enough acidity for grip and focus. It will evolve quickly, as its color is already a deep medium gold. **Anticipated maturity: Now–2003.** Nearly all my tastings of young vintages of Nairac suggest that the wine is too oaky, as the toasty, vanillin aromas tend to obliterate the wine's fruit. Although there is good ripeness, as well as plenty of glycerin and alcohol, the oak has the upper hand at the moment. If everything comes together, the 1990 Nairac should be a good, though not exciting, bottle of wine.

RABAUD-PROMIS (SAUTERNES)* * * *

1990	C	87
1989	D	89
1988	D	93

What a turnaround this famous old estate has made. The 1986 was the best Rabaud-Promis in decades, and the 1988 promises to be superior. Full bodied, splendidly rich, chewy, and unctuous, and well delineated, with excellent acidity, this wine offers a spectacularly heady, long, concentrated finish, a real show stopper. The 1988 Rabaud-Promis promises to be one of the sweetest and most powerful wines of the vintage. Magnificent! **Anticipated maturity: 1996–2020.** The 1989 is opulent, with superb intensity, but the alcohol is high in the finish, and the wine comes across as large scale, very oaky, and rich. A little more acidity would have improved the focus and could have made this wine sublime. Those who like their Sauternes lusty and obvious will drool over this wine. I still prefer their 1988. **Anticipated maturity: 1995–2012.** Although the 1990 Rabaud-Promis is not up to the quality of the 1986, 1988, and 1989, this medium- to full-bodied wine displays good richness, plenty of spicy new oak and tropical fruit flavors, and an alcoholic, rich finish. Drink it over the next 10–15 years.

RAYMOND-LAFON (SAUTERNES)* * * * *

1990	E	93
1989	E	92

In several blind tastings against Premiers Crus Classés held in France, the 1989 Raymond-Lafon came out first. It is a remarkably rich, exotic, unctuously styled wine with sensational extract, a very sweet, concentrated palate, and a long, heady finish. Its predominant character at the moment is that of honeyed pineapples interwoven with scents of spring flowers and new oak. It is a great 1989 with the acidity to provide the necessary delineation. **Anticipated maturity: 1995–2020.** The spectacularly sweet, opulent 1990 exhibits a stunning nose of coconuts and pineapples. In the mouth there is phenomenal richness, as well as enough acidity and botrytis to give it the extra dimension missing in so many 1990s. The finish is all fruit, glycerin, and moderately high alcohol. Drink this stunning 1990 between 1995 and 2015. This may be the wine of the vintage for Sauternes.
PAST GLORIES: 1986 (92), 1983 (93), 1980 (90), 1975 (90)

RAYNE-VIGNEAU (SAUTERNES)* */* * *

1990	D	85
1989	D	?
1988	D	90

The 1988 is the best wine I have tasted from this property. An intense, honeyed, pear, flower, and apricot fragrance is reminiscent of Muscat de Beaumes de Venise. In the mouth there is exceptional richness, super focus because of fine acidity, a wonderful touch of toasty new oak, and an elegant, very positive, crisp finish. This beautifully made, authoritatively tasting, yet impeccably well-balanced Sauternes is vastly superior to the 1989 and 1990. **Anticipated maturity: Now–2006.** During its first two years of life, the 1989 consistently tasted muted and uninteresting, lacking richness and concentration. In 1992 the wine began to pull itself together, exhibiting thick, glycerin-filled, heavy flavors and gobs of alcohol and sweetness. **Anticipated maturity: 1995–2005.** A slightly artificial, canned fruit cocktail–scented nose in the 1990 is followed by a wine with good ripeness, low acidity, and a heavy, alcoholic finish. It will have to be drunk young—let's say within its first decade of life.

RIEUSSEC (SAUTERNES)* * * * *

1990	D	90
1989	D	94
1988	D	95

The 1988 is a profound Rieussec. An utterly mind-blowing performance for this château, it offers a hauntingly perfect bouquet of great precision and persistence. In the mouth the wine reveals remarkable clarity, stunning power and depth, and a finish that must last several minutes. It is a winemaking tour de force and one of the greatest young Sauternes I have had the pleasure of tasting. **Anticipated maturity: 1998–2015.** The 1989 Rieussec is also one of the stars of the vintage. It is a fat, rich, very broad-shouldered wine, with great depth and richness and considerably more alcohol than the 1988. Although I did not detect as much botrytis as I would have hoped, it is still a massive, blockbuster of a wine. Its evolution should be fascinating to follow. **Anticipated maturity: 1998–2015.** As for the 1990, a huge nose of honeyed pears and tropical fruit is followed by a deep, rich, full-bodied wine with great presence on the palate, enough acidity to provide grip and focus, and a spectacularly long, lusty finish that is neither too alcoholic nor heavy—a common problem with many 1990s. Is it as superb as the 1988 or 1989? I doubt it, but it is still one of the stars of the vintage. **Anticipated maturity: 1995–2015.**

ROMER DU HAYOT (SAUTERNES)* *

1989	B	86
1988	B	85?

The 1988 Romer du Hayot exhibits a rich, concentrated bouquet filled with evidence of botrytis and fully mature fruit. In the mouth it is medium to full bodied, with good acidity and plenty of length and concentration. Ideally it should be drunk over the next 10–12 years. I should note that several samples of this wine had an inexcusable fecal aroma. **Anticipated maturity: Now–1998.** The 1989 is too alcoholic, very sweet and cloying, but fat and deep, with a lack of acidity creating a certain diffusiveness among its component parts. Nevertheless, among those who love lusty, slightly out-of-balance, thick Sauternes, this wine will have its admirers. **Anticipated maturity: Now–1997.**

SIGALAS RABAUD (SAUTERNES)* * *

1990	D	88
1989	C	89
1988	D	90

The 1988 is the richest Sigalas Rabaud I have yet to taste, with unctuous, fleshy, highly extracted flavors; great length; a stunningly perfumed, fragrant bouquet of honey, melons, and oranges; and a big, rich, vibrant finish. A top success, it is one of the finest wines from this château in years. **Anticipated maturity: 1994–2007.** Not surprisingly, the 1989 is sweeter and more alcoholic than the 1988, with a candied fruit salad character. It is a bit monolithic when compared with the 1988, but nevertheless impressive, if only because of its size and weight, which are atypically considerable for Sigalas Rabaud. **Anticipated maturity: 1994–2005.** The 1990 is one of the few wines of the vintage that actually displays copious quantities of botrytis as well as elegance. A honeyed, fruity nose is followed by seductive, rich, well-balanced flavors of peaches, apricots, and coconuts. The acidity is better than in most 1990s, and the finish is long and convincingly rich without being heavy. Drink it over the next 10–15 years.

SUAU (BARSAC)* *

1990	C	82
1989	C	83
1988	C	79

The 1988 Suau is a light, relatively shallow wine with good acidity. It should be consumed over the next 4–5 years. The 1989 is sweet, alcoholic, richly fruity, and heavy. It just does not possess much style. **Anticipated maturity: Now–1997.** The 1990 offers an attractive nose of ripe apricots, followed by a medium- to full-bodied, simple wine with a lot of sweetness and chunkiness but not much finesse. It should drink well for at least 10–12 or more years.

SUDUIRAUT (SAUTERNES)* * * */* * * * *

1990	D	87
1989	D	89
1988	D	92
1989 Cuvée Madame	E	96

The 1988 Suduiraut is one of the biggest, densest wines of the vintage. At present its explosive power and richness seem well harnessed by the wine's superb balance and good acidity. The nose remains suppressed, but on the palate, the formidable, even massive power and extraordinary concentration cannot be hidden. It is one of the most backward wines of the vintage, as its fabulous length attests. **Anticipated maturity: 2000–2030.** The 1989 regular *cuvée* is a blockbuster, heavyweight, oily, almost overdone version of Sauternes. There is no denying its opulence, high alcohol, and almost cloying sweetness. It is undoubtedly the most massive wine I have ever tasted from Suduiraut. Is it another 1959 in the making? **Anticipated maturity: 2000–2020.** As for the Cuvée Madame, it is an extraordinary Sauternes. Fabulously concentrated, with an unctuous texture and what must be nearly 14–15% natural alcohol, this mammoth-size Sauternes should prove to be one of the monumental efforts of the vintage. For those who prefer power and finesse, the 1988 may take preference; for those who want pure brute strength and unbelievable size, the 1989 Cuvée Madame is without equal. **Anticipated maturity: 2000–2025.** The 1990 regular *cuvée* offers an intriguing nose of eau-de-vie of pears that is followed by an alcoholic, ripe, intensely rich, viscous, slightly overbearing wine. If the 1990 Suduiraut pulls itself together, it could turn out to be an outstanding wine. For the moment, I have rated it conservatively. **Anticipated maturity: 1995–2010.**

LA TOUR BLANCHE (SAUTERNES)* * * *

1990	D	91
1989	D	92
1988	D	92

Perhaps the most remarkable story in Barsac/Sauternes is the tremendous progression in quality made by La Tour Blanche. This property has always been capable of turning out good wine, but never in their history have they produced such enthralling wines as the 1988, 1989, and 1990. This is one example where the 1989 is greater than the 1988. The 1988 is astonishingly rich and deep, with a pervasively intense nose of botrytis, new oak, and honeyed oranges and melons. In the mouth it is extremely full bodied and powerful, with great persistence and intensity of flavor, as well as a fascinating balance between acidity and power. **Anticipated maturity: 1996–2015.** Explosive, with a fabulous bouquet of oranges, mangoes, and coconut, the decadently rich, full-bodied, monstrous-size 1989 has enough acidity for balance. It is one of the greatest wines of the 1989 Barsac/Sauternes vintage. **Anticipated maturity: 1996–2030.** The 1990 reveals a subtle touch of toasty new oak, as well as honeyed, ripe flavors. In the mouth the wine emphasizes stylish, rich fruit flavors and elegance rather than blockbuster alcohol and viscosity. There is a sense of depth, overall gracefulness, and finesse to this moderately rich, classy example of Sauternes. Though it does not have the power or botrytis of the 1989, or the finesse of the 1988, it is still an admirable example of La Tour Blanche. **Anticipated maturity: 1995–2010.**

D'YQUEM (SAUTERNES)* * * * *

1988	E	98
1987	E	88
1986	E	98
1985	E	89

Millionaires will have considerable fun comparing the evolution of the 1988 d'Yquem with the 1986. Both are superrich, honeyed, botrytised wines, although the 1988 appears to be more backward than the 1986. The 1988 exhibits a similarity to the monumental 1975 produced at d'Yquem. Both the 1988 and 1986 have 40–50 years of positive evolution, although one suspects that most of the production will be consumed within the next several years. The 1987, from a difficult vintage, is a medium-weight d'Yquem, with enticing oaky, tropical fruit aromas, but the unctuousness and profound depth of flavor so obvious in the 1986 and 1988 are not present in the 1987. If you are going to drink d'Yquem as an aperitif, a vintage such as 1985 makes sense. It should last for 15–20 or more years. Although the 1985 is a big, rich wine, it lacks botrytis and, therefore, complexity. It is full bodied, with a great deal of depth and that oaky, smoky, almost coconut, orange/honeyed richness, but I could not detect the complexity one normally associates with d'Yquem. It should last for 20–30 years.

PAST GLORIES: 1983 (96), 1982 (92), 1981 (90), 1980 (93), 1976 (96), 1975 (99), 1971 (92), 1967 (96), 1962 (90), 1959 (96), 1945 (98), 1937 (99), 1921 (100)

NOTE: If you are not among the rich and famous who can afford Yquem, consider Château de Fargues. It often tastes better than Yquem when young, and also keeps for 15–25 years. It is owned by the same family that produces Yquem, and made in exactly the same manner. The top vintages include 1986 (93), 1983 (92), 1980 (91), 1976 (90), and 1975 (91).

BURGUNDY AND BEAUJOLAIS

There is no reason, but the truth is plain to see.

The Burgundy Minefield

Even the most enthusiastic burgundy connoisseurs admit that the wines of Burgundy are too expensive, too variable in quality, too quick to fall apart, and too difficult and trouble-some to find. Why, then, are they so cherished?

Although it is tempting for those who have neither the financial resources nor the enthusiasm for these wines to conclude that burgundies are purchased only by wealthy masochists, the point is that burgundy at its best is the world's most majestic, glorious, and hedonistic Pinot Noir and Chardonnay. Burgundy has somehow defied definition, systemization, or even standardization. No matter how much research and money is spent trying to taste and understand the complexity of the wines of Burgundy and its myriad vineyards, to a large extent they remain a mystery.

Perhaps this is best shown in the analogy between several famous Bordeaux vineyards and a handful of renowned Burgundy vineyards. Take the famous St.-Julien vineyard of Ducru-Beaucaillou in the heart of the Médoc. It is 124 acres in size. Compare it with its famous neighbor about 10 miles to the south, Château Palmer in Margaux, with a vineyard of 111 acres in size. Any consumer who buys a bottle of a specific vintage of Ducru-Beaucaillou or Palmer will be getting exactly the same wine. Of course it may have been handled differently or subjected to abuse in transportation or storage, but the wine that left the property was made by one winemaking team, from one blend, and the taste, texture, and aromatic profile of a specific vintage should not be any different whether drunk in Paris, Vienna, Tokyo, New York, or Los Angeles.

Compare that situation with the famous Grand Cru from Burgundy's Côte de Nuits, Clos Vougeot. Clos Vougeot has 124 acres, making it approximately the same size as Ducru-Beaucaillou. Yet although there is only one proprietor of the latter vineyard, Clos Vougeot is divided among 77 different proprietors. Many of these proprietors sell their production to *négociants,* but in any given vintage there are at least three dozen or more Clos Vougeots in the marketplace. All of them are entitled to Grand Cru status, they vary in price from $50 to $200+ a bottle, but less than one-half dozen are likely to be compelling wines. The remainder range in quality from very good to dismal and insipid. Clos Vougeot is the most cited as a microcosm of Burgundy—infinitely confusing, distressingly frustrating—yet in the hands of a few top producers majestic wines do indeed emanate.

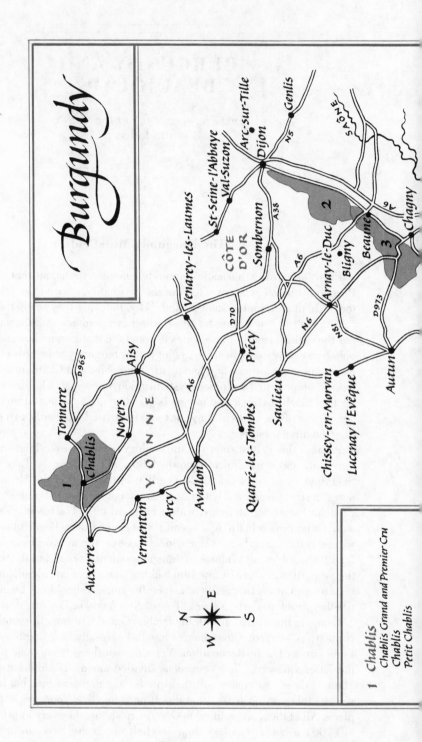

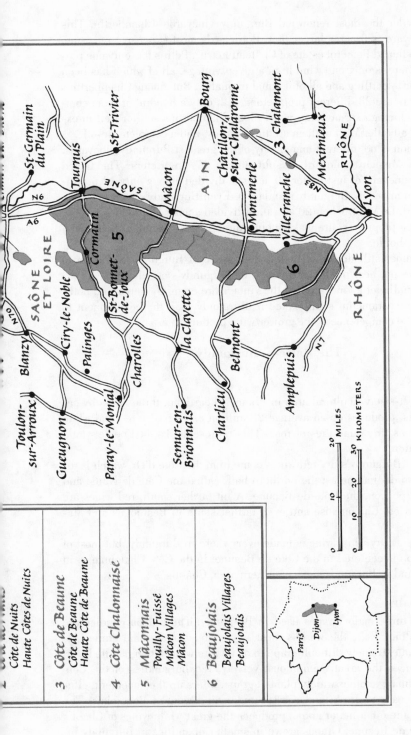

Côte de Nuits
Hautes Côtes de Nuits

3 Côte de Beaune
   Côte de Beaune
   Haute Côte de Beaune

4 Côte Chalonnaise

5 Mâconnais
   Pouilly-Fuissé
   Mâcon Villages
   Mâcon

6 Beaujolais
   Beaujolais Villages
   Beaujolais

St-Germain
du Plain

St-Trivier

Toulon-
sur-Arroux

Gueugnon

Blanzy

Ciry-le-Noble

Palinges

Paray-le-Monial

Charolles

St-Bonnet-
de-Joux

Cormatin

Cluny

Semur-en-
Brionnais

la Clayette

Charlieu

Belmont

Amplepuis

Tournus

Mâcon

Montmerle

Villefranche

Bourg

Châtillon-
sur-Chalaronne

Chalamont

Meximieux

Lyon

SAÔNE
ET LOIRE

SAÔNE

AIN

RHÔNE

RHÔNE

N6

A6

N79

N70

N7

N83

N6

MILES
0   10   20

KILOMETERS
0   10   20   30

Paris

Dijon

Lyon

Also consider the most renowned Burgundy vineyard—Chambertin. This 32-acre vineyard is 3 acres larger than Bordeaux's most expensive red wine, that from the famed Pomerol estate of Château Pétrus. Pétrus has only one producer, and there is only one wine from a given vintage, all of which has been blended prior to bottling and all of it equal in quality. But among Chambertin's 32 acres, there are 23 different proprietors, with only a handful of them committed to producing extraordinary wine. Most Chambertins sell for well in excess of $150 a bottle. Most of them are thin, watery, and a complete rip-off.

The situation is no different among any of the greatest Burgundy vineyards. The 24-acre Musigny vineyard is split among 17 proprietors. The famed Richebourg vineyard of just under 20 acres is divided among *only* 12 proprietors (a low number by Burgundy standards). Even Burgundy's greatest white wine vineyard, Le Montrachet (20 acres), is divided among 15 producers. Only 5 or 6 of these proprietors are making outstanding wines, yet all of them fetch $200–$300 a bottle.

Any consumer still driven to make some sense of Burgundy will have to learn who are the best producers in each of Burgundy's appellations, for although the quality of a vineyard and the vintage are certainly important, nothing is of more paramount significance in Burgundy than the commitment to quality and the competence of the grower/wine producer.

The Basics—Burgundy

TYPES OF WINE

This modest-size viticultural area in France's heartland, three hours by car south of Paris, produces on an average 22 million cases of dry red and white wine as well as tiny quantities of rosé. This represents 3% of France's total wine production.

Red Wine   Burgundy's dry red wines come from the Côte d'Or, which is divided into two distinct areas: the northern half, called the Côte de Nuits, and the southern portion, the Côte de Beaune. A bit farther south, red wines are made in the Côte Chalonnaise and even farther south in Beaujolais and Mâconnais.

White Wine   Dry white wine is made everywhere in Burgundy, but most of the production is centered in the Côte de Beaune, in the Côte Chalonnaise, in Mâconnais, and in Burgundy's most northern area, Chablis.

GRAPE VARIETIES

There are three major grapes used in Burgundy. The red burgundies are made from Pinot Noir, the world's most fickle and troublesome grape. Although it is an extremely difficult grape to make into wine, when handled with care it produces the great, sumptuous, velvety, red burgundies of the Côte d'Or. The Gamay, another widely planted grape, offers up the succulent, effusively fruity, easy-to-drink, and easy-to-understand wine of Beaujolais. The Chardonnay, the other major grape, produces the great white wines of Chablis and the Côte de Beaune. Grapes grown in smaller quantities in Burgundy include the Aligoté grape—planted in less hospitable sites—and the Pinot Blanc and Pinot Beurrot, also called Pinot Gris (planted in minute quantities).

FLAVORS

When it is great, Pinot Noir produces the most complex, hedonistic, and remarkably thrilling red wine in the world, but the problem is that only a tiny percentage of Burgundy's wines attain this level. At its best, the bouquet is filled with red fruits and exotic spices, and the taste is broad, expansive, round, lush, and soft. Great burgundy always tastes sweeter than Bordeaux and has a significantly lighter color. Rarely does young burgundy have more than a medium cherry color. Gamay is drunk not for its complexity, but for its heady, direct, ripe, soft, fleshy, exuberant fruitiness and easygoing texture. Chardonnay can range from stony and mineral-scented with high acidity in Chablis, to buttery, smoky, creamy, decadently rich, and tasting of sautéed almonds and hazelnuts in a great Côte de Beaune white burgundy, to refreshingly light, lemony, floral, and thirst-quenching in the wines of Mâconnais.

AGING POTENTIAL

Red Wines
Côte de Nuits: 2–15 years
Côte de Beaune: 2–15 years
Beaujolais: 1–5 years
White Wines
Chablis: 1–10 years
Côte de Beaune: 4–10 years
Mâconnais: 1–4 years

OVERALL QUALITY LEVEL

No matter which appellation one looks at in Burgundy, the range in quality from watery, poorly made, incompetent wines to majestic wines of great flavor and dimension is enormous. Burgundy is filled with precarious pitfalls for the uninformed consumer, as the number of poor and mediocre wines, although significantly less than in years past, still greatly exceeds the amount of fine wines made.

THE MOST IMPORTANT INFORMATION TO KNOW

Consult the guide to Burgundy's best producers below to avoid buying poor and mediocre wine. Many pitfalls await uninformed consumers seeking out the wines of Burgundy.

RECENT VINTAGES

1992—This is an inconsistent vintage, with some top-notch successes as well as disappointments. Most Beaujolais, Mâconnais, Chalonnaise, and Côte de Beaune producers completed their harvest before any major rains arrived. In the Côte de Nuits nearly half the crop had been harvested before the first significant rain fell. That rainfall was followed by 4–5 days of hot dry weather, then more rain. The quality will vary from outstanding *cuvées* of splendidly opulent, rich wine to *cuvées* diluted by the rain. One can only buy burgundy by knowing the finest growers, but 1992 will be a particularly difficult vintage to handicap in black-and-white terms given the immense potential for a wide range of wines.

With respect to the white wines, with the exception of Chablis, which had to be harvested after the rains, most should be soft, fat, and fleshy—in short, very delicious. The growers who kept their yields down should produce superb wines; those who had excessive yields will turn out loosely knit, short-lived wines. In either case, the whites will have to be drunk young.

1991—As in 1987, some surprisingly good wines were produced in 1991. The red wines are soft, up-front, and neither acidic nor vegetal, two nasty characteristics of poor vintages. The wines lack weight and generosity, and given the saturated, depressed state of the international marketplace following the great success Burgundy enjoyed between 1985 and 1990, the 1991s will be difficult to sell unless they are released at much lower prices than previous vintages.

The white wines vary in quality from dismal to well above average. All of them are soft and destined to be consumed in the first 5–6 years following the vintage.

1990—This is a very good vintage for white burgundies, but only a handful of producers achieved greatness because the yields were entirely too high to obtain the requisite concentration. Those growers who pruned back meticulously to restrict their yields, and who picked physiologically mature fruit, have made stunning wines. There is the potential for high-class wines in Chablis, above-average quality wines in Meursault, and good to excellent wines in Puligny-Montrachet and Chassagne-Montrachet. One appellation that appears to have enjoyed considerable success is Corton-Charlemagne. At the top levels, the red wines are the finest red burgundies I have ever tasted. I have never seen a vintage that is as darkly colored, with such sumptuous, rich, thick fruit. Moreover, many of the wines possess excellent structure and moderate levels of sweet tannins. The 1990 is one of those rare red burgundy vintages that will offer an exceptionally broad window of drinkability. Qualitatively, it towers above the 1988 and 1985 vintages.

1989—Here is a spectacular vintage for white burgundy that may ultimately prove to be the best year for the white wines of Corton-Charlemagne, Meursault, Puligny-Montrachet, and Chassagne-Montrachet in more than 20 years. The 1989 red burgundies are delicious, forward, ripe wines that are flattering at present and in many cases better balanced and more complex than the 1988s. Not surprisingly, most growers prefer their 1989s to the 1988s. I would opt for drinking them sooner (over the next 6–9 years) than later.

1988—The question about this vintage is, why have so many wine writers, above all the English press (who judge Burgundy as if it is Bordeaux), rated this vintage so highly? A handful of great wines have been produced that can be compared to the superb red burgundies of 1969. But what about the high yields and astringent level of tannins of the 1988s? It will be an aging race between the fruit and the tannin. In Pinot Noir, highly tannic wines usually age poorly. Burgundy enthusiasts who have stashed away quantities of 1988s are likely to be more disappointed than pleased by what they find in 5–6 years. Most Burgundy growers have already begun to express concerns about the high level of tannins, which are astringent, green, and dry rather than soft, sweet, and mature as in 1985 and 1990. The lean, austere 1988 white burgundies recall the 1981s. If they develop along similar lines, they will be more acidic and alcoholic than fruity in 5–6 years.

1987—From the top estates, delicious, supple red wines were made, which is amazing given the fact that most producers had to harvest under heavy rain. Although some good buys may be found, consumers remain apprehensive about the vintage's reputation. This is a mediocre year for white wines.

1986—This is a great year for white burgundy and an unexciting one for red burgundy. Most of the red wines possess structure and tannin but are hollow on the midpalate. They lack the succulence and chewiness found in the burgundies of such top years as 1985 and 1990, making them dubious choices. Although the wines have held up reasonably well, I have noticed a number of examples that appear to have dropped their tannin in the last 1–2 years and are now taking on amber at the edge. I would steer clear of the 1986 red burgundies unless you have access to the few gems of this vintage.

1985—Initially proclaimed as Burgundy's "vintage of the century," the white wines continue to provide rich, sumptuous drinking. The top whites should last for another 5–7 years. Today, the red wines present a mixed bag of impressions. Some of the larger-scale red wines appear closed, muted, monolithic, and one-dimensional. Yet they continue to exhibit a healthy deep ruby color and plenty of depth and weight. The lighter reds have taken on some amber at the edge, are soft and fruity, but have not developed the aromatic complexity I would have expected. Certainly 1985 can be an outstanding vintage, but as it has matured, the overall quality is mixed.

1984—All of us remember 1984, which, like 1980, was declared by several wine writers to be a major catastrophe long before they ever tasted the wines. In 1980 the source of information was the *négociant* Louis Latour, who had all sorts of problems with the vintage and indeed made poor wine that year. As all burgundy lovers know, 1980 has turned out some of the most delicious and best-balanced wines of the last 10–15 years, and some of the wines from the Côte de Nuits are superb. Well, 1984 did not turn out to be as good as 1980, but many of the good growers have made wines that were better balanced and richer than the 1982s. The vintage was late, and everyone had to chaptalize because the natural alcohol contents were only 9%–10%. However, the resulting red wines are often quite elegant, very cleanly made, fruity, soft, and agreeable. The yields were low because of a poor flowering. There is the normal irregularity, but the wines of the Côte de Nuits are better colored and richer than those of the Côte de Beaune. The good 1984s will be at their best between now and 1994. They will certainly not be long-lived but when well chosen will be very pleasant wines.

1983—At the time of harvest, before any wine could be tasted, a number of critics were calling this vintage one of the greatest ever, solely on the basis of some astonishing levels of sugars in the very ripe grapes. Others based their praise on actual tasting notes. After a comprehensive tasting of the wines, one of England's most experienced Burgundy writers, Clive Coates, said, "This is the sort of Burgundy vintage the world has been anxiously waiting for. They have a concentration of ripe fruit which is exhilarating. These are wines of depth, character, complexity, and length." For about 15% of the red burgundies, the latter assessment was correct, but as I advised my readers in August 1984, over three-fourths of the red burgundies I tasted were flawed either from the rampant rot that plagued the grapes or the hailstorm that wreaked havoc on some of the Côte d'Or's most famous vineyards. Ten years after the harvest, it is safe to say that 1983 is largely a failure as a red wine vintage. Far too many wines smell and taste of rot and/or are unbelievably tannic and astringent. However, the great 1983s, from producers such as Roumier, the Domaine de la Romanée-Conti, Henri Jayer, Maume, Hubert Lignier, Mongeard-Mugneret, Faiveley, and Ponsot, should provide some of the longest-lived wines of the last three decades. Yet this is a vintage to approach with great caution, and the knowledge that even its finest wine will require cellaring until the late 1990s.

BURGUNDY'S GREATEST RED WINES

Bertrand Ambroise Nuits St.-Georges Les Vaucrains
Bertrand Ambroise Corton-Rognet
Comte Armand Pommard-Clos des Epeneaux
Robert Arnoux Vosne-Romanée Les Suchots
Fougeray de Beauclair Bonnes Mares
Pierre Bourée Charmes-Chambertin
Pierre Bourée Clos de la Roche
Philippe Charlopin-Parizot Clos St.-Denis
Jean Chauvenet Nuits St.-Georges Les Vaucrains
Domaine Chézeaux Chambertin
Domaine Chézeaux Clos St.-Denis
Domaine Chézeaux Griotte-Chambertin
Chopin-Groffier Clos Vougeot
J. J. Confuron Romanée St.-Vivant
J. Confuron-Cotetidot Clos Vougeot
J. Confuron-Cotetidot Echézeaux
Claude et Maurice Dugat Charmes-Chambertin
Claude et Maurice Dugat Gevrey-Chambertin Lavaux
   St.-Jacques
Claude et Maurice Dugat Griotte-Chambertin
Dujac Bonnes Mares
Dujac Clos de la Roche
Dujac Clos St.-Denis
Michel Esmonin Gevrey-Chambertin Clos St.-Jacques
Faiveley Chambertin Clos de Bèze
Faiveley Corton Clos des Cortons
Armand Girardin Pommard Les Epenots
Armand Girardin Pommard Les Rugiens
Machard de Gramont Pommard Le Clos Blanc
Jean Grivot Clos Vougeot
A. F. Gros Echézeaux
A. F. Gros Richebourg
Anne et François Gros Clos Vougeot Le Grand Maupertuis
Anne et François Gros Richebourg
Domaine Jean Gros Clos Vougeot
Domaine Jean Gros Richebourg
Domaine Jean Gros Vosne-Romanée Clos des Réas
Domaine Gros Frère et Soeur Clos Vougeot de Musigni
Domaine Gros Frère et Soeur Richebourg
Haegelen-Jayer Clos Vougeot

*Hospices de Beaune Beaune Nicolas Rolin
*Hospices de Beaune Corton Charlotte Dumay
*Hospices de Beaune Mazis-Chambertin
*Hospices de Beaune Pommard Dames de la Charité
*Hospices de Beaune Savigny-Lès-Beaune Arthur Girard
*Hospices de Beaune Volnay Santenots Jehan de Massol
Louis Jadot Beaune Clos des Ursules
Louis Jadot Bonnes Mares
Louis Jadot Chambertin Clos de Bèze
Louis Jadot Corton-Pougets
Louis Jadot Gevrey-Chambertin-Clos St.-Jacques
Henri Jayer Richebourg
Henri Jayer Vosne-Romanée Les Brûlées
Henri Jayer Vosne-Romanée Cros Parantoux
Jayer-Gilles Echézeaux
Jayer-Gilles Nuits St.-Georges Les Damodes
Jayer-Gilles Nuits St.-Georges Les Hauts Poirets
Michel Lafarge Volnay Clos du Château des Ducs
Michel Lafarge Volnay Clos de Chênes
Domaine Comte Lafon Volnay Champans
Domaine Comte Lafon Volnay Santenots
Domaine Lecheneaut Clos de la Roche
Domaine Lecheneaut Nuits St.-Georges Les Cailles
Philippe Leclerc Gevrey-Chambertin Les Cazetiers
Philippe Leclerc Gevrey-Chambertin Combe aux Moines
Domaine Lejeune Pommard Les Rugiens
Leroy Chambertin
Leroy Clos de la Roche
Leroy Clos Vougeot
Leroy Latricières-Chambertin
Leroy Mazis-Chambertin
Leroy Nuits St.-Georges Les Boudots
Leroy Richebourg
Leroy Romanée St.-Vivant
Leroy Savigny-Lès-Beaune Les Narbantons
Leroy Vosne-Romanée Les Beaux Monts
Leroy Vosne-Romanée Les Brûlées
Domaine Hubert Lignier Charmes-Chambertin
Domaine Hubert Lignier Clos de la Roche
Domaine Maume Mazis-Chambertin
Domaine Jean Méo-Camuzet Clos Vougeot
Domaine Jean Méo-Camuzet Richebourg
Domaine Jean Méo-Camuzet Vosne-Romanée Les Brûlées
Mongeard-Mugneret Richebourg
A. Mussy Pommard Epenots
Philippe Naddef Mazis-Chambertin
Ponsot Chambertin

* The Hospices de Beaune wines are sold in cask to different buyers. Between 1978 and 1987 the quality of the Hospices' wines was superb, but since 1988 the wines have lacked richness, structure, and concentration.

Ponsot Clos de la Roche Vieilles Vignes
Ponsot Clos St.-Denis Vieilles Vignes
Ponsot Griotte-Chambertin
Ponsot Latricières-Chambertin
Domaine Pothier-Rieusset Pommard Rugiens
Pousse d'Or Volnay-Clos de la Bousse d'Or
Domaine de la Romanée-Conti Grands-Echézeaux
Domaine de la Romanée-Conti Richebourg
Domaine de la Romanée-Conti Romanée-Conti
Domaine de la Romanée-Conti Romanée-St.-Vivant
Domaine de la Romanée-Conti La Tâche
Joseph Roty Charmes-Chambertin
Joseph Roty Mazis-Chambertin
Emmanuel Rouget Echézeaux
Emmanuel Rouget Vosne-Romanée Cros Parantoux
Georges Roumier Bonnes Mares
Georges Roumier Chambolle-Musigny Les Amoureuses
Georges Roumier Ruchottes-Chambertin
Domaine Armand Rousseau Chambertin
Domaine Armand Rousseau Chambertin Clos de Bèze
Domaine Armand Rousseau Gevrey-Chambertin Clos
    St.-Jacques
Christian Serafin Charmes-Chambertin
Christian Serafin Gevrey-Chambertin Les Cazetiers
Château de la Tour Clos Vougeot
Château de la Tour Clos Vougeot Vieilles Vignes
Truchot-Martin Charmes-Chambertin Vieilles Vignes
Comte de Vogüé Musigny Vieilles Vignes (prior to 1973 and after 1989)

Rating the Red Burgundy Growers, Producers, and Négociants

No one will ever have a great deal of success selecting a burgundy without a thorough knowledge of the finest growers and *négociants*. The most meticulous producers often make better wine in mediocre vintages than many less dedicated growers and producers make in great vintages. Knowing the finest producers in Burgundy is unquestionably the most important factor contributing to your success in finding the best wines.

The following is a guide to the best red and white burgundy producers. Consistency from year to year and among the producers' total range of wines were the most important considerations. One should be cognizant of the fact that many lower-rated producers may make specific wines that are qualitatively above their placement herein.

Note: Where a producer has been assigned a range of stars, * * */* * * * for example, the lower rating has been used for placement in this hierarchy.

RATING BURGUNDY'S RED WINE PRODUCERS

* * * * * (OUTSTANDING PRODUCERS)

Claude et Maurice Dugat (Gevrey-
Chambertin)
Domaine Dujac (Morey St.-Denis)
Domaine Henri Jayer (Vosne-
Romanée)
Domaine Comte Lafon (Meursault)
Philippe Leclerc (Gevrey-
Chambertin)

Leroy (Vosne-Romanée)
Domaine Hubert Lignier (Morey
St.-Denis)
Domaine de la Romanée-Conti
(Vosne-Romanée)
Georges Roumier (Chambolle-
Musigny)

* * * * (EXCELLENT PRODUCERS)

Bertrand Ambroise (Prémeaux)
Domaine de l'Arlot (Prémeaux)
Comte Armand (Pommard)
Robert Arnoux (Vosne-Romanée)
Denis Bachelet (Gevrey-Chambertin)
Barthod-Noëllat (Chambolle-
Musigny)
Fougeray de Beauclair (Marsannay)
Pierre Bertheau (Chambolle-
Musigny)
Besancenot-Mathouillet (Beaune)
Pierre Boillot (Meursault)
Bourée Père et Fils (Gevrey-
Chambertin)
Georges Bryczek (Morey St.-Denis)
Alain Burguet (Gevrey-Chambertin)
Jacques Cacheux-Blée et Fils
(Vosne-Romanée)
Guy Castagnier (Morey St.-Denis)
Château de Chambolle-Musigny
(Chambolle-Musigny)
Jean Chauvenet (Nuits St.-Georges)
Georges et Michel Chevillon (Nuits
St.-Georges)
Robert Chevillon (Nuits St.-Georges)
Chézeaux (Gevrey-
Chambertin)****/*****
Georges Chicotot (Nuits St.-Georges)
Daniel Chopin-Groffier (Prémeaux)
Bruno Clair (Marsannay)
J. Confuron-Cotetidot (Vosne-
Romanée)
Bernard et Pierre Dugat (Gevrey-
Chambertin)
Maurice Ecard et Fils (Savigny-Lès-
Beaune)

René Engel (Vosne-Romanée)
M. Frédéric Esmonin (Gevrey-
Chambertin)
Michel Esmonin (Gevrey-
Chambertin)
Faiveley (Nuits St.-Georges)
Jean Faurois (Vosne-Romanée)
Jean Garaudet (Pommard)
Michel Gaunoux (Pommard)
Pierre Gelin (Fixin)
Jacques Germain (Chorey-Lès-
Beaune)
Armand Girardin (Pommard)
Machard de Gramont (Nuits St.-
Georges)
Jean Grivot (Vosne-Romanée)
A. F. Gros (Pommard)
Anne et François Gros (Vosne-
Romanée)
Domaine Jean Gros (Vosne-
Romanée)****/*****
Domaine Gros Frère et Soeur (Vosne-
Romanée)
Haegelen-Jayer (Vosne-Romanée)
Hospices de Beaune (Beaune)
Hospices de Nuits (Nuits
St.-Georges)
Louis Jadot (Beaune)
Domaine Robert Jayer-Gilles
(Magny-Lès-Villers)****/*****
Domaine Joblot (Givry)
Michel Juillot (Mercurey)
Domaine Michel Lafarge (Volnay)
Domaine Lecheneaut (Nuits
St.-Georges)
René Leclerc (Gevrey-Chambertin)

Lejeune (Pommard)

Domaine Maume (Gevrey-Chambertin)

Domaine Jean Méo-Camuzet (Vosne-Romanée)****/*****

Alain Michelot (Nuits St.-Georges)

Mongeard-Mugneret (Vosne-Romanée)

Hubert de Montille (Volnay)

Domaine Albert Morot (Beaune)

Mugneret-Gibourg (Vosne-Romanée)

André Mussy (Pommard)

Pernin-Rossin (Vosne-Romanée)

Ponsot (Morey St.-Denis)****/*****

Domaine Pothier-Rieusset (Pommard)

Pousse d'Or (Volnay)

Daniel Rion (Nuits St.-Georges)

Joseph Roty (Gevrey-Chambertin)

Emanuel Rouget (Nuits St.-Georges)

Domaine Armand Rousseau (Gevrey-Chambertin)

Christian Serafin (Gevrey-Chambertin)

Jean Tardy (Vosne-Romanée)

Tollot-Beaut et Fils (Chorey-Lès-Beaune)

Château de la Tour (Vougeot)

J. Truchot-Martin (Morey St.-Denis)

Comte Georges de Vogüé (Chambolle-Musigny)

* * * (GOOD PRODUCERS)

Pierre Amiot et Fils (Morey St.-Denis)

Pierre André (Aloxe-Corton)

Marquis d'Angerville (Volnay)

Ballot-Millot (Meursault)

Philippe Batacchi (Gevrey-Chambertin)

Château de Beauregard (Fuissé)

Adrien Belland (Santenay)

Joseph Belland (Santenay)

Bertagna (Vougeot)

Domaine Denis Berthaut (Fixin)

Pierre Bitouzet (Savigny-Lès-Beaune)

Bitouzet-Prieur (Volnay)

Simon Bize et Fils (Savigny-Lès-Beaune)

Marcel Bocquenet (Nuits St.-Georges)

Henri Boillot (Pommard)

Jean Boillot (Volnay)

Lucien Boillot et Fils (Gevrey-Chambertin)

Bonnot-Lamblot (Savigny-Lès-Beaune)

Bordeaux-Montrieux (Mercurey)

Bouchard Père et Fils (Beaune)

Jean-Marc Bouley (Volnay)

Denis Boussey (Monthélie)

Jean-Claude Brelière (Rully)

Michel Briday (Rully)

Camus (Gevrey-Chambertin)

Luc Camus (Savigny-Lès-Beaune)

Capitain-Gagnerot (Ladoix-Serrigny)

Capron-Manieux (Savigny-Lès-Beaune)

Domaine Sylvain Cathiard (Vosne-Romanée)

Ceci (Vougeot)

Émile Chandesais (Fontaines)

Chandon de Briailles (Savigny-Lès-Beaune)

Chanson Père et Fils (Beaune)

Maurice Chapuis (Aloxe-Corton)

Philippe Charlopin-Parizot (Marsannay)

Jean Chartron (Puligny-Montrachet)

F. Chauvenet (Nuits St.-Georges)

Michel Clair (Santenay)

Georges Clerget (Vougeot)

Michel Clerget (Vougeot)

Yvon Clerget (Volnay)

Coche-Bizouard (Meursault)

J. F. Coche-Dury (Meursault)***/****

Domaine Les Colombiers (Saint-Véran)

Jean-Jacques Confuron (Prémeaux)

Coquard-Loison-Fleurot (Flagey-Echézeaux)

Domaine Edmond Cornu (Ladoix-Serrigny)

Coron Père et Fils (Beaune)

Coste-Caumartin (Pommard)

Marius Delarche (Pernand-Vergelesses)

Jean-Pierre Diconne (Auxey-Duresses)

Doudet-Naudin (Savigny-Lès-Beaune)

Joseph Drouhin (Beaune)

Drouhin-Larose (Gevrey-Chambertin)

Dubreuil-Fontaine (Pernand-Vergelesses)

Duchet (Beaune)

Bernard Fèvre (Saint-Romain)

Fichet (Volnay)

René Fleurot-Larose (Santenay)

Domaine de la Folie (Rully)

Domaine Forey Père et Fils (Vosne-Romanée)

Domaine du Gardin-Clos Salomon (Givry)

Philippe Gavignat (Nuits St.-Georges)

Lucien Geoffroy (Gevrey-Chambertin)

François Gerbet (Vosne-Romanée)

Jacques Girardin (Santenay)

Bernard Glantenay (Volnay)

Michel Goubard (Saint-Desert)

Bertrand de Gramont (Nuits St.-Georges)

Alain Gras (St.-Romain)

Pierre Guillemot (Savigny-Lès-Beaune)

Heresztyn (Gevrey-Chambertin)

Alain Hudelot-Noëllat (Vougeot)

Paul et Henri Jacqueson (Rully)

Jaffelin (Beaune)

Georges Jayer (Vosne-Romanée)

Domaine Jacqueline Jayer (Vosne-Romanée)

Lucien Jayer (Vosne-Romanée)

Jeannin-Naltet Père et Fils (Mercurey)

Jean-Luc Joillot-Porcheray (Pommard)

Philippe Joliet (Fixin)

François Labet (Vougeot)

Labouré-Roi (Nuits St.-Georges)

Lafouge (Auxey-Duresses)

Laleure-Piot Père et Fils (Pernand-Vergelesses)

Lamarche (Vosne-Romanée)

Hubert Lamy (Saint-Aubin)

Louis Latour (Beaune)

Olivier Leflaive Frères (Puligny-Montrachet)

François Legros (Nuits St.-Georges)

Domaine Lequin-Roussot (Santenay)

Thierry Lespinasse (Givry)

Georges Lignier (Morey St.-Denis)

Loron et Fils (Pontanevaux)

Château de la Maltroye (Chassagne-Montrachet)

Manière-Noirot (Vosne-Romanée)

Marchand-Grillot et Fils (Gevrey-Chambertin)

Tim Marshall (Nuits St.-Georges)

Joseph Matrot (Meursault)

Meix Foulot (Mercurey)

Prince Florent de Mérode (Ladoix-Serrigny)

Michel (Vosne-Romanée)

Jean Michelot (Pommard)

Domaine Modot (Chambolle-Musigny)

Moillard (Nuits St.-Georges)

Daniel Moine-Hudelot (Chambolle-Musigny)

Domaine de la Monette (Mercurey)

Bernard Morey (Chassagne-Montrachet)

Denis Mortet (Gevrey-Chambertin)

Gérard et René Mugneret (Vosne-Romanée)

Philippe Naddef (Couchey)

André Nudant et Fils (Ladoix-Serrigny)

Domaine Parent (Pommard)

Parigot Père et Fils (Meloisey)

Pavelot-Glantenay (Savigny-Lès-Beaune)

Domaine des Perdrix (Prémeaux-Prissey)

Domaine Les Perrières (Gevrey-Chambertin)

Domaine des Pierres Blanches (Beaune)

Château de Pommard (Pommard)

Domaine Jacques Prieur (Meursault)

Prieur-Brunet (Santenay)
Henri Prudhon (Saint-Aubin)
Michel Prunier (Auxey-Duresses)
Ramonet (Chassagne-Montrachet)
Remoissenet Père et Fils (Beaune)
Henri Remoriquet (Nuits
    St.-Georges)
Bernard Rion Père et Fils (Vosne-
    Romanée)
Antonin Rodet (Mercurey)
Michel Rossignol (Volnay)
Philippe Rossignol (Gevrey-
    Chambertin)
Régis Rossignol-Changarnier
    (Volnay)
Rossignol-Trapet (Gevrey-
    Chambertin)
Rougeot (Meursault)

Domaine Roux Père et Fils (Saint-
    Aubin)
Château de Rully (Rully)
Daniel Senard (Aloxe-Corton)
Bernard Serveau (Morey St.-Denis)
Servelle-Tachot (Chambolle-
    Musigny)
Robert Sirugue (Vosne-Romanée)
Thevenot-Le-Brun et Fils (Marey-
    Lès-Fussey)
Gérard Thomas (Saint-Aubin)
Jean Trapet (Gevrey-Chambertin)
Domaine des Varoilles (Gevrey-
    Chambertin)
Michel Voarick (Aloxe-Corton)
Domaine Joseph Voillot (Volnay)
Leni Volpato (Chambolle-Musigny)

* * (AVERAGE PRODUCERS)

Bernard Amiot (Chambolle-Musigny)
Amiot-Servelle (Chambolle-Musigny)
Arlaud Père et Fils (Nuits
    St.-Georges)
Arnoux Père et Fils (Chorey-Lès-
    Beaune)
André Bart (Marsannay)
Albert Bichot (Beaune)
Domaine Billard-Gonnet (Pommard)
Domaine de Blagny (Blagny)
Jean-Marc Boillot (Pommard)
Jean-Claude Boisset (Nuits
    St.-Georges)
Bouchard-Aîné et Fils (Beaune)
Marc Brocot (Marsannay)
Lucien Camus-Bauchon (Savigny-
    Lès-Beaune)
Chanzy Frères-Domaine de
    l'Hermitage (Bouzeron)
Clos Frantin-Bichot (Vosne-
    Romanée)**/***
Domaine Clos des Lambrays (Morey
    St.-Denis)
Michel Clunny et Fils (Brochon)
Claude Cornu (Magny-Lès-Villers)
Gérard Creusefond (Auxey-Duresses)
Pierre Damoy (Gevrey-Chambertin)
David et Foillard (St.-Georges-de-
    Reneins)

Denis Père et Fils (Pernand-
    Vergelesses)
Dufouleur Père et Fils (Nuits
    St.-Georges)
Dupont-Tisserandot (Gevrey-
    Chambertin)
René Durand (Comblanchien)
Jacques Durand-Roblot (Fixin)
Dureuil-Janthial (Rully)
Jean-Claude Fourrier (Gevrey-
    Chambertin)
Gay Père et Fils (Chorey-Lès-
    Beaune)
Geantet-Pansiot (Gevrey-
    Chambertin)
Domaine Geisweiler et Fils (Nuits
    St.-Georges)
Maurice et Jean-Michel Giboulot
    (Savigny-Lès- Beaune)
Girard-Vollot et Fils (Savigny-Lès-
    Beaune)
Domaine Henri Gouges (Nuits
    St.-Georges)
Robert Groffier (Morey St.-Denis)
Jean Guitton (Bligny-Lès-
    Beaune)
Antonin Guyon (Savigny-Lès-
    Beaune)
Hubert Guyot-Verpiot (Rully)

Château Philippe Le Hardi (Santenay)
Domaine des Hautes- Cornières (Santenay)
André l'Heritier (Chagny)
Huguenot Père et Fils (Marsannay)
Frederick Humbert (Gevrey-Chambertin)
Lucien Jacob (Échevronne)
Jessiaume Père et Fils (Santenay)
Henri Lafarge (Bray)
Lahaye Père et Fils (Pommard)
René Lamy-Pillot (Santenay)
Henri Latour (Auxey-Duresses)
Lumpp Frères (Givry)
Lupé-Cholet (Nuits St.-Georges)
Lycée Agricole et Viticole (Beaune)
Henri Magnien (Gevrey-Chambertin)
Michel Magnien (Morey St.-Denis)
Maillard Père et Fils (Chorey-Lès-Beaune)
Maldant (Chorey-Lès-Beaune)
Michel Mallard et Fils (Ladoix-Serrigny)
Yves Marceau-Domaine de la Croix Gault (Mercurey)
P. de Marcilly Frères (Beaune)
Jean Marechal (Mercurey)
Mazilly Père et Fils (Meloisey)
Louis Menand Père et Fils (Mercurey)
Mestre Père et Fils (Santenay)
Pierre Millot-Battault (Meursault)
P. Misserey (Nuits St.-Georges)
Château de Monthélie (Monthélie)
Monthélie-Douhairet (Monthélie)
Jean Moreau (Santenay)
Gabriel Muskovac (Pernand-Vergelesses)
Newman (Morey St.-Denis)
Patriarche Père et Fils (Beaune)
Pavelot (Pernand-Vergelesses)
Henri Perrot-Minot (Morey St.-Denis)

Domaine de la Poulette (Corgoloin)
Domaine du Prieuré (Rully)
Domaine du Prieuré (Savigny-Lès-Beaune)
Prosper-Maufoux (Santenay)
Maurice Protheau et Fils (Mercurey)
Roger Prunier (Auxey-Duresses)
Domaine Max Quenot Fils et Meuneveaux (Aloxe-Corton)
Domaine Charles Quillardet (Gevrey-Chambertin)
Gaston et Pierre Ravaut (Ladoix-Serrigny)
Rebougeon-Mure (Pommard)
Henri Rebourseau (Gevrey-Chambertin)
La Reine Pedauque (Aloxe-Corton)
Louis Remy (Gevrey- Chambertin)
Henri Richard (Gevrey- Chambertin)
Maurice Rollin Père et Fils (Pernand-Vergelesses)
Hervé Roumier (Chambolle-Musigny)
Roy Frères (Auxey-Duresses)
Roy Père et Fils (Gevrey-Chambertin)
Fabien et Louis Saier (Mercurey)
Maurice et Hervé Sigaut (Chambolle-Musigny)
Suremain (Mercurey)
Taupenot Père et Fils (Saint-Romain)
Tortochot (Gevrey- Chambertin)
Domaine Louis Trapet (Gevrey-Chambertin)
G. Vachet-Rousseau (Gevrey-Chambertin)
Henri de Villamont (Savigny-Lès-Beaune)
Émile Voarick (Saint-Martin- Sous-Montaigu)
Alain Voegeli (Gevrey- Chambertin)
André Ziltener Père et Fils (Gevrey-Chambertin)

Where Are Burgundy's Red Wine Values?

The glamour appellations of the Côte de Nuits and the Côte de Beaune offer exorbitant prices as well as irregular quality. If values are to be found, consumers must look beyond the most prestigious names and most renowned appellations, searching out some of the less highly acclaimed appellations. Following are some appellations and producers to check out in the Côte de Nuits, Côte de Beaune, and possibly the best source of red and white burgundies, the Côte Chalonnaise, located just south of the Côte d'Or.

Marsannay (Côte de Nuits)   You are not likely to find great wines from this appellation, but good producers can produce wines that are far above the normal quality level, which means something better than the compact, straightforward, hard, charmless Pinot Noirs that often emanate from Marsannay. Look for the following Marsannays that can still be purchased for under $20 a bottle:

Régis Bouvier-Marsannay Clos du Roy, Marsannay Vieilles Vignes; Marc Brocot-Marsannay; Bruno Clair-Marsannay, Marsannay Les Longerois, Marsannay Vaudenelles; Jean-Pierre Guyard-Marsannay Les Recilles; Louis Jadot-Marsannay; Philippe Naddef-Marsannay

Fixin (Côte de Nuits)   It may be situated next to the famed appellation Gevrey-Chambertin, but Fixin has never overcome its reputation of producing exceptionally robust, sturdy, muscular wines that are short on finesse. However, some producers excel in producing wines with serious flavor and balance.

The best wines include André Bart-Fixin Les Hervelets; Denis Berthaut-Fixin Les Arvelets, Fixin Les Clos, Fixin Les Crais; Bruno Clair-Fixin; Faiveley-Fixin; Pierre Gelin-Fixin-Clos du Chapitre, Fixin Les Hervelets, Fixin Clos Napoléon; Philippe Joliet-Fixin-Clos de la Perrière; Mongeard-Mugneret-Fixin

Ladoix (Côte de Beaune)   Ladoix is Burgundy's least-known appellation, making it one of the more attractive places to shop, but you must know the right addresses. Amazingly, the best Pinot Noirs here cost less than Pinot Noirs from California and Oregon. This is not an appellation to buy blindly, as the wines can be dusty and earthy, with too little fruit.

The best wines include Capitain-Gagnerot-Ladoix, Ladoix Les Micaudes; Chevalier Père et Fils-Ladoix Premier Cru; Edmond Cornu-Ladoix, Ladoix Premier Cru; Michel Mallard-Ladoix Les Joyeuses; André Nudant-Ladoix Premier Cru; Gaston et Pierre Ravaut-Ladoix Les Corvées

Savigny-Lès-Beaune (Côte de Beaune)   Savigny-Lès-Beaune has a good reputation for light, berry-scented (primarily cherry) wines that at their worst can have an overwhelming rusty, earthy undertone. The vineyards on the northern hillsides overlooking the Rhoin River, which cuts this appellation in half, produce the finest wine. Most sell for between $18 and $25 a bottle. They are not as inexpensive as Marsannay or Ladoix, but at their best they exhibit considerably more complexity and a compelling Pinot Noir perfume.

The best wines include Simon Bize-Savigny-Lès-Beaune aux Vergelesses, Savigny-Lès-Beaune aux Guettes, Savigny-Lès-Beaune Premier Cru; Bonnot-Lamblot-Savigny-LèsBeaune Les Dominodes; Capron-Manieux-Savigny-Lès-Beaune Les Lavières; Chandon de Briailles-Savigny-Lès-Beaune Les Lavières; Chanson-Savigny-Lès-Beaune Les Dominodes; Bruno Clair-Savigny-Lès-Beaune Les Dominodes; Doudet-Naudin-Savigny-Lès-Beaune Les Guettes; Joseph Drouhin-Savigny-Lès-Beaune Premier Cru; Maurice Ecard-Savigny-Lès-Beaune Les Serpentières, Savigny-Lès-Beaune Les Narbantons; J. M.

Giboulot-Savigny-Lès-Beaune Les Serpentières; Machard de Gramont-Savigny-Lès-Beaune Les Guettes; Pierre Guillemot-Savigny-Lès-Beaune Les Serpentières, Savigny-Lès-Beaune Les Jarrons; Hospices de Beaune-Savigny-Lès-Beaune Cuvée Arthur Girard, Savigny-Lès-Beaune Cuvée Fouquerand, Savigny-Lès-Beaune Cuvée Forneret; Louis Jadot-Savigny-Lès-Beaune Les Dominodes; Albert Morot-Savigny-Lès-Beaune Les Vergelesses-Clos la Bataillère; Pavelot-Glantenay-Savigny-Lès-Beaune Les Dominodes, Savigny-Lès-Beaune Les Guettes; Jean Pichenot-Savigny-Lès-Beaune; Tollot-Beaut-Savigny-Lès-Beaune Les Lavières

Monthélie (Côte de Beaune) The vineyards of Monthélie are adjacent to Volnay, yet the wines could not be more different. The old-style Monthélies are plagued by excessive tannin and body, but a younger generation of winemakers is bringing out the wines' fruit and character, hoping that consumers will make the 1–2 minute trek from the neighboring villages of Volnay and Pommard to take a look at this hilltop village, where most red burgundies can still be bought for under $20–$25 a bottle.

The best wines include Eric Boussey-Monthélie; J. F. Coche-Dury-Monthélie; Louis Deschamps-Monthélie Les Mandenes; Gérard Doreau-Monthélie Les Champs Fulliot; Jean Garaudet-Monthélie; Hospices de Beaune-Monthélie-Cuvée Lebelin; Louis Jadot-Monthélie; Jehan-Changarnier-Monthélie; Comte Lafon-Monthélie; Pernin-Rossin-Monthélie; Henri Potinet-Ampeau-Monthélie; Eric de Suremain-Monthélie-Château de Monthélie, Monthélie-Sur la Velle

Auxey-Duresses (Côte de Beaune) Auxey-Duresses has often been described as the poor person's Volnay. Such comments are pejorative and tend to irritate the local *vignerons,* who are proud of their spicy, robust, black cherry–scented and –flavored wine that often possesses surprising aging potential. The key is to pick ripe fruit. If the fruit is not ripe, the tannins tend to be green and the acids can reach shrill levels.

The best wines include Robert Ampeau-Auxey-Duresses Ecussaux; Jean-Pierre Diconne-Auxey-Duresses; Hospices de Beaune-Auxey-Duresses-Cuvée Boillot; Domaine Jessiaume-Auxey-Duresses Ecussaux; Domaine Lafouge-Auxey-Duresses La Chapelle; Leroy-Auxey-Duresses; Duc de Magenta (Jadot)-Auxey-Duresses; Maroslavic-Leger-Auxey-Duresses Les Bréterins; Pernin-Rossin-Auxey-Duresses; Michel Prunier-Auxey-Duresses-Clos du Val; Roy Frères-Auxey-Duresses-Le Val; René Thevenin-Auxey-Duresses-Clos du Moulin aux Moines

Chassagne-Montrachet (Côte de Beaune) The down side to Chassagne-Montrachet's fame as one of Burgundy's great white wine villages is that few people pay attention to the tasty, bing cherry, almond, earthy fruitiness their red wines possess. There are Premiers Crus that can be bought for $25 a bottle, making this an interesting market. Most red Chassagnes also have the virtue of lasting for 10 years in a top vintage.

The best wines include Jean-Noël Gagnard-Chassagne-Montrachet-Clos de la Maltroye, Chassagne-Montrachet-Clos St.-Jean; Duc de Magenta (Louis Jadot)-Chassagne-Montrachet-Clos de la Chapelle; Château de la Maltroye-Chassagne-Montrachet-Clos du Château, Chassagne-Montrachet-Clos St.-Jean, Chassagne-Montrachet-Clos de la Boudriotte; Paul Pillot-Chassagne-Montrachet-Clos St.-Jean; Domaine Ramonet-Chassagne-Montrachet-Clos de la Boudriotte; Domaine Roux-Chassagne-Montrachet-Clos St.-Jean

Saint-Romain (Côte de Beaune)   Although this quaint village is off the beaten track, it is only a 10-minute drive from either Meursault or Volnay and worth the extra effort to visit. Some tasty, bargain-priced burgundies can be found, as white burgundy is Saint-Romain's claim to fame—today.

The best wines include Bernard Fèvre-Saint-Romain; Alain Gras-Saint-Romain; Taupenot Père et Fils-Saint-Romain; René Thévenin-Monthélie Saint-Romain

Saint-Aubin (Côte de Beaune)   Saint-Aubin is a true burgundy lover's paradise. Filled with young, talented, ambitious growers, it produces a number of wines that sell for well under $25 a bottle. The red wines can be surprisingly robust, full, concentrated, and chewy.

The best wines include Jean-Claude Bachelet-Saint-Aubin Derrière la Tour; Raoul Clerget-Saint-Aubin Les Frionnes; Marc Colin-Saint-Aubin; Lamy-Pillot-Saint-Aubin; Langoureau (Gilles Bouton)-Saint-Aubin en Remilly; Henri Prudhon-Saint-Aubin Sentiers de Clou, Saint-Aubin Les Frionnes; Domaine Roux Père et Fils-Saint-Aubin; Gérard Thomas-Saint-Aubin Les Frionnes

Rully (Côte Chalonnaise)   Like any appellation, one has to be careful, but the spicy, cherry, strawberry, dusty aromas and flavors of a good Rully can be purchased for prices in the midteens.

The best wines include Michel Briday-Rully; Domaine de la Folie-Rully-Clos de Bellecroix; H. & P. Jacqueson-Rully Les Cloux, Rully Les Chaponnières; Domaine de la Rénarde-Rully Premier Cru; Antonin Rodet-Rully; Château de Rully-Rully; Domaine de Rully St.-Michel-Rully Les Champs Cloux, Rully-Clos de Pelleret

Mercurey (Côte Chalonnaise)   Mercurey prices have risen to $25 a bottle now that the world has begun to discover the progress Mercurey producers have made. This is an up-and-coming source of good wines.

The best wines include Château de Chamirey-Mercurey; Charton et Trébuchet-Mercurey-Clos des Hayes; Faiveley-Mercurey-Clos du Roi, Mercurey-Clos des Myglands, Mercurey La Framboisière, Mercurey La Croix Jacquelet, Mercurey Les Mauvarennes; Michel Juillot-Mercurey-Clos des Barraults, Mercurey-Clos Tonnerre; Domaine de Meix Foulot-Mercurey Les Veleys, Mercurey-Clos du Château de Montaigu; Domaine de la Monette-Mercurey; Domaine de Suremain-Mercurey-Clos Voyen Mercurey Clos l'Évêque

Givry (Côte Chalonnaise)   Givry has two of the finest winemakers in all of Burgundy, Monsieur Joblot and Monsieur Lespinasse. Both are making wines that compete with some of the finest of the Côte d'Or. They have caused a popular boom in this backwater appellation.

The best wines include Jean Chofflet-Givry; Domaine Joblot-Givry-Clos du Cellier-aux-Moines, Givry-Clos du Bois Chevaux, Givry-Clos de la Servoisine; Louis Latour-Givry; Gérard Mouton-Givry; Domaine Veuve Steinmaier-Givry-Clos de la Baraude; Domaine Thenard-Givry-Clos Saint-Pierre, Givry-Cellier-aux-Moines, Givry Les Bois Chevaux; Thierry Lespinasse-Givry en Choué

Santenay (Côte de Beaune)   It is amazing that Santenay continues to have problems overcoming its image as the last of the Côte d'Or appellations. Over 99% of its wine is red, all of it made from the Pinot Noir grape. The wine trade still bristles when reminded of a quotation from one of Britain's leading wine merchants: "Life is too short to drink Santenay." That has not been the case for some time, but Santenay remains unfashionable. That is a boon for thrifty consumers looking for a solid, frequently delicious bottle of Pinot Noir for $15–$25 a bottle. Although many Santenays can be excessively tannic, hollow, and pleasureless, the good producers make a wine that is medium weight by Burgundy standards, with a pronounced bouquet of strawberry and cherry fruit allied to a mineral, almost almondlike smell.

The best wines include Bernard Bachelet-Santenay; Adrien Belland-Santenay-Clos des Gravières, Santenay La Comme; Marc Colin-Santenay; Joseph Drouhin-Santenay; Jean-Noël Gagnard-Santenay Clos de Tavannes; Jessiaume Père-Santenay Gravières; Lequin-Roussot-Santenay Premier Cru; Château de La Maltroye-Santenay La Comme, Santenay Les Gravières; Bernard Morey-Santenay-Grand Clos Rousseau; Jean-Marc Morey-Santenay-Grand Clos Rousseau; Domaine de la Pousse d'Or-Santenay Clos Tavannes; Prieur-Brunet-Santenay La Maladière, Santenay La Comme; Remoissenet-Santenay Les Gravières

BURGUNDY'S GREATEST WHITE WINES

Amiot-Bonfils Chassagne-Montrachet Les Caillerets
Amiot-Bonfils Le Montrachet
Amiot-Bonfils Puligny-Montrachet Les Demoiselles
Robert Ampeau Meursault Les Charmes
Robert Ampeau Meursault Les Perrières
Domaine de la Bongrand (Jean Thevenet) Mâcon-Clessé
Roger Caillot Bâtard-Montrachet
Chandon des Briailles Corton
Maurice Chapuis Corton-Charlemagne
J. F. Coche-Dury Corton-Charlemagne
J. F. Coche-Dury Meursault Les Perrières
J. F. Coche-Dury Meursault Les Rougeot
Fernand Coffinet Bâtard-Montrachet
Marc Colin Montrachet
Colin-Deleger Chassagne-Montrachet Les Demoiselles
Jean Collet Chablis Vaillons
René et Vincent Dauvissat Chablis Les Clos
Marius Delarche Corton-Charlemagne
Joseph Drouhin Beaune-Clos des Mouches
Joseph Drouhin Montrachet-Marquis de Laguiche
Marcel Duplessis Chablis Les Clos
Faiveley Corton-Charlemagne
J. A. Ferret Pouilly-Fuissé-Hors Classé
Château Fuissé Pouilly-Fuissé Les Vieilles Vignes
Jean-Noël Gagnard Bâtard-Montrachet
Jean-Noël Gagnard Chassagne-Montrachet Les Caillerets
Guffens-Heynen Pouilly-Fuissé-Clos des Petits Croux
Guffens-Heynen Pouilly-Fuissé-Les Croux
Guffens-Heynen Pouilly-Fuissé La Roche
Hospices de Beaune Corton-Charlemagne-Cuvée Françoise de Salins
Hospices de Beaune Meursault-Les Charmes-Cuvée Albert-Grivault
Hospices de Beaune Meursault-Cuvée Goureau

Hospices de Beaune Meursault-Cuvée Loppin
Hospices de Beaune Meursault-Les Genevrières-Cuvée Baudot
Hospices de Beaune Meursault-Les Genevrières-Cuvée Philippe le Bon
Louis Jadot Chevalier-Montrachet Les Demoiselles
Louis Jadot Corton-Charlemagne
Louis Jadot Montrachet
François Jobard Meursault Les Genevrières
Domaine Comte Lafon Meursault Les Charmes
Domaine Comte Lafon Meursault Les Perrières
Domaine Comte Lafon Montrachet
René Lamy-Pillot Le Montrachet
Louis Latour Bâtard-Montrachet
Louis Latour Chevalier-Montrachet Les Demoiselles
Louis Latour Corton-Charlemagne
Domaine Leflaive Bâtard-Montrachet
Domaine Leflaive Chevalier-Montrachet
Domaine Leflaive Le Montrachet
Domaine Leflaive Puligny-Montrachet Les Combettes
Domaine Leflaive Puligny-Montrachet Les Pucelles
Leroy Corton-Charlemagne
Leroy Meursault Les Narvaux
Leroy Puligny-Montrachet Les Folatières
A. Long-Depaquit Chablis Les Clos
A. Long-Depaquit Chablis Les Preuses
A. Long-Depaquit Chablis Valmur
Bernard Morey Chassagne-Montrachet Les Embrazées
Michel Niellon Bâtard-Montrachet
Michel Niellon Chassagne-Montrachet Les Vergers
Michel Niellon Chevalier-Montrachet
Paul Pernot Bâtard-Montrachet
Ramonet Bâtard-Montrachet
Ramonet Chassagne-Montrachet Les Caillerets
Ramonet Chassagne-Montrachet Les Ruchottes
Ramonet Le Montrachet
François et Jean-Marie Raveneau Chablis Blanchots
François et Jean-Marie Raveneau Chablis Les Clos
François et Jean-Marie Raveneau Chablis Montée de Tonnerre
François et Jean-Marie Raveneau Chablis Valmur
Remoissenet Père et Fils Corton-Charlemagne-Diamond Jubilée
Domaine de la Romanée-Conti Le Montrachet
Étienne Sauzet Bâtard-Montrachet

RATING BURGUNDY'S WHITE WINE PRODUCERS

(excluding the Mâconnais producers)

* * * * * (OUTSTANDING PRODUCERS)

J. F. Coche-Dury (Meursault)

René et Vincent Dauvissat (Chablis)

Domaine Comte Lafon (Meursault)

Domaine Leflaive (Puligny-Montrachet)

Leroy and Domaine d'Auvenay (Vosne-Romanée)

Michel Niellon (Chassagne-Montrachet)

Domaine Ramonet (Chassagne-Montrachet)

François et Jean-Marie Raveneau (Chablis)

Domaine de la Romanée- Conti (Vosne-Romanée)

Étienne Sauzet (Puligny-Montrachet)

* * * * (EXCELLENT PRODUCERS)

Amiot-Bonfils (Chassagne-Montrachet)

Robert Ampeau (Meursault)

Domaine de l'Arlot (Prémeaux)

Charles et Paul Bavard (Puligny-Montrachet)

Blain-Gagnard (Chassagne-Montrachet)

Pierre Boillot (Meursault)

Bonneau du Martray (Pernand-Vergelesses)

Roger Caillot et Fils (Meursault)

Fernand Coffinet (Chassagne-Montrachet)

Marc Colin (Chassagne-Montrachet)

Colin-Deleger (Chassagne-Montrachet)

Jean Collet (Chablis)

Jean Dauvissat (Chablis)

Jean Defaix (Chablis)

Georges Déleger (Chassagne-Montrachet)

Joseph Drouhin (Beaune)

Druid Wines (Morey St.-Denis)

Domaine Marcel Duplessis (Chablis)

Faiveley (Nuits St.-Georges)****/*****

Fontaine-Gagnard (Chassagne-Montrachet)

Jean-Noël Gagnard (Chassagne-Montrachet)

Château Grenouilles (Chablis)

Albert Grivault (Meursault)

Louis Jadot (Beaune)

François Jobard (Meursault)

Hubert Lamy (Saint-Aubin)

P. Lamy (Charraque)

Roger Lassarat (Vergisson)

Louis Latour (Beaune)

A. Long-Depaquit (Chablis)

Domaine du Duc de Magenta (Chassagne-Montrachet)

Manciat-Poncet (Charnay-Lès-Mâcon)

Château de Meursault (Meursault)

Louis Michel/Domaine de la Tour Vaubourg (Chablis)

Michelot-Buisson (Meursault)

Bernard Morey (Chassagne-Montrachet)

Jean-Marc Morey (Chassagne-Montrachet)

Marc Morey (Chassagne- Montrachet)

Pierre Morey (Meursault)

Paul Pernot (Puligny-Montrachet)****/*****

Prieur-Brunet (Santenay)

Remoissenet Père et Fils (Beaune)

Guy Robin (Chablis)

Guy Roulot (Meursault)

Domaine de Rully St.-Michel (Rully)

Château de la Saule (Montagny)

Philippe Testut (Chablis)

Verget (Vergisson)

A. P. de Villaine (Bouzeron)

Robert Vocoret et Fils (Chablis)

*** *(GOOD PRODUCERS)*

Château Bader-Mimeur (Chassagne-Montrachet)
Ballot-Millot et Fils (Meursault)
Bitouzet-Prieur (Volnay)
Étienne Boileau (Chablis)
A. Buisson-Battault (Meursault)
Louis Carillon (Puligny- Montrachet)
La Chablisienne (Chablis)
Jean Chartron (Puligny- Montrachet)
Chartron et Trébuchet (Puligny-Montrachet)
Anne-Marie Chavy (Puligny-Montrachet)
Henri Clerc et Fils (Puligny-Montrachet)
Julien Coche-Debord (Meursault)
Cooperative La Chablisienne (Chablis)
Jean Defaix (Milly)
Jean-Paul Droin (Chablis)
Paul Droin (Chablis)
P. Dubreuil-Fontaine et Fils (Pernand-Vergelesses)
Domaine de l'Eglantière (Maligny)
William Fèvre/Domaine de la Maladière/Ancien Domaine Auffray (Chablis)
René Fleurot-Larose (Santenay)
Domaine de la Folie (Rully)
Gagnard-Delagrange (Chassagne-Montrachet)
Château Génot Boulanger (Meursault)
Maison Jean Germain (Meursault)

Jean-Paul Jauffroy (Meursault)
Michel Juillot (Mercurey)***/****
Lafouge (Auxey-Duresses)
Laleure-Piot (Pernand- Vergelesses)
René Lamy-Pillot (Santenay)
Laroche (Chablis)
Latour-Giraud (Meursault)
Olivier Leflaive Frères (Puligny-Montrachet)***/****
Lequin-Roussot (Santenay)
Château de la Maltroye (Chassagne-Montrachet)
Joseph Matrot (Meursault)
Michelot-Buisson (Meursault)***/****
J. Moreau et Fils (Chablis)
Perrin-Ponsot (Meursault)
Paul Pillot (Chassagne- Montrachet)
Louis Pinson (Chablis)
Jacques Prieur (Meursault)
Henri Prudhon (Saint-Aubin)
Château de Puligny- Montrachet (Puligny- Montrachet)
Rapet Père et Fils (Pernand-Vergelesses)
Guy Robin (Chablis)
Antonin Rodet (Mercurey)
Ropiteau Frères (Meursault)
Roux Père et Fils (Saint-Aubin)
Château de Rully (Rully)
Gérard Thomas (Saint-Aubin)
Jean Vachet (Saint-Vallerin)
Domaine de Vauroux (Chablis)

** *(AVERAGE PRODUCERS)*

Bachelet-Ramonet (Chassagne-Montrachet)
Billaud-Simon (Chablis)
Blondeau-Danne (Meursault)
Guy Bocard (Meursault)
Boisson-Vadot (Meursault)
Boyer-Martenot (Meursault)
Bressand (Pouilly-Fuissé)
Xavier Bouzerand (Monthélie)
Michel Bouzereau (Meursault)
Hubert Bouzereau-Gruère (Meursault)

Chanzy Frères-Domaine de l'Hermitage (Bouzeron)
Chevalier Père et Fils (Buisson)
Chouet-Clivet (Meursault)
Darnat (Meursault)
Michel Dupont-Fahn (Meursault)
Gabriel Fournier (Meursault)
René Guerin (Vergisson)
Domaine l'Heritier-Guyot (Dijon)
Patrick Javillier (Meursault)
Lamblin et Fils (Maligny)
Domaine des Malandes (Chablis)

Maroslavac-Léger (Chassagne-
   Montrachet)
M. Millet (Montagny)
Raymond Millot et Fils (Meursault)
René Monnier (Meursault)
Henri Morconi (Puligny-Montrachet)
Bernard Moreau (Chassagne-
   Montrachet)
Mosnier-Sylvain (Chablis)
Jean Pascal et Fils (Puligny-
   Montrachet)

Baron Patrick (Chablis)
Michel Pouhin-Seurre (Meursault)
Prosper Maufoux (Santenay)
A. Regnard et Fils (Chablis)
La Reine Pedauque (Aloxe-Corton)
Riger-Briset (Puligny- Montrachet)
Simonnet-Febvre et Fils (Chablis)
J. Thevenet-Machal (Puligny-
   Montrachet)

Where Are Burgundy's White Wine Values?

Jean-Claude Bachelet Saint-Aubin Les Champlots
Michel Briday Rully-Grésigny
Château de Chamirey Mercurey
Charton et Trébuchet Rully Chaume
Charton et Trébuchet Saint-Aubin
Charton et Trébuchet Saint-Aubin La Chatenière
Raoul Clerget Saint-Aubin Le Charmois
Marc Colin Saint-Aubin La Chatenière
Joseph Drouhin Mâcon La Forêt
Joseph Drouhin Rully
Faiveley Bourgogne
Faiveley Mercurey-Clos Rochette
Faiveley Rully
Domaine de la Folie Rully-Clos de Bellecroix
Domaine de la Folie Rully-Clos St.-Jacques
Jean Germain St.-Romaine Clos Sous le Château
Alain Gras St.-Romaine
Jacqueson Rully-Grésigny
Louis Jadot Bourgogne Blanc
Robert Jayer-Gilles Bourgogne Hautes-Côtes de Beaune
Robert Jayer-Gilles Bourgogne Hautes-Côtes de Nuits
Michel Juillot Mercurey
Louis Latour Mâcon Lugny
Louis Latour Montagny
Louis Latour Saint-Véran
Lequin-Roussot Santenay Premier Cru
Moillard Montagny Premier Cru
Bernard Morey Saint-Aubin
Jean-Marc Morey Saint-Aubin Le Charmois
Prieur-Brunet Santenay-Clos Rousseau
Henri Prudhon Saint-Aubin
Antonin Rodet Bourgogne Blanc
Antonin Rodet Montagny
Château de Rully Rully
Domaine de Rully St.-Michel Rully Les Cloux
Domaine de Rully St.-Michel Rully Rabourcé

Château de la Saule Montagny
Gérard Thomas Saint-Aubin Murgers des Dents de Chien
Jean Vachet Montagny Les Coeres
Aubert de Villaine Bourgogne Aligoté
Aubert de Villaine Bourgogne Le Clous

And Don't Forget . . .

Virtually all of the best producers of inexpensive Chardonnay from the vast region known as the Mâconnais are rated in subsequent pages, but the wines that come from this huge region, particularly the Mâcon-Villages wines (made from Chardonnay), can be super bargains. At their best they offer wonderfully fresh aromas and flavors of apples and lemony fruit.

RATING THE MÂCONNAIS WHITE WINE PRODUCERS

(MâconVillages, Saint-Véran, Pouilly-Fuissé,
Pouilly-Loché, and Beaujolais Blanc)

* * * * * (OUTSTANDING PRODUCERS)

Daniel Barraud Pouilly-Fuissé Cuvée Vieilles Vignes
Domaine de la Bongrand (Jean Thevenet) Mâcon-Villages
André Bonhomme Mâcon-Villages
J. A. Ferret Pouilly-Fuissé
André Forest Pouilly-Fuissé Cuvée Vieilles Vignes
Château Fuissé Pouilly-Fuissé Cuvée Vieilles Vignes
Guffens-Heynen Mâcon-Villages
Guffens-Heynen Pouilly-Fuissé Clos des Petits Croux
Guffens-Heynen Pouilly-Fuissé Les Croux
Guffens-Heynen Pouilly-Fuissé La Roche
Roger Lasserat Saint-Véran Cuvée Prestige
Manciat-Poncet Mâcon-Villages
René Michel Mâcon-Villages
Domaine du Vieux St.-Sorlin Mâcon-Villages

* * * * (EXCELLENT PRODUCERS)

Auvigue-Burrier-Revel Mâcon-Villages
Daniel Barraud Mâcon-Vergisson La Roche
Daniel Barraud Pouilly-Fuissé La Verchere
Château de Beauregard Pouilly-Fuissé
Domaine des Chazelles Viré
Chenevière Mâcon-Villages
Corsin Pouilly-Fuissé
Château Fuissé Pouilly-Fuissé
Emilian Gillet Mâcon-Viré
Domaine des Granges (J. F. Cognard) Mâcon-Villages
Thierry Guérin Pouilly-Fuissé Clos de France
Louis Jadot Mâcon-Villages
Roger Lasserat Pouilly-Fuissé
Roger Lasserat Pouilly-Fuissé Clos de France
Roger Lasserat Pouilly-Fuissé Cuvée Prestige
Roger Lasserat Saint-Véran Fournaise
Louis Latour Mâcon-Lugny-Les Genevrières

Manciat-Poncet Pouilly-Fuissé
Gilles Noblet Pouilly-Fuissé
Talmard Mâcon-Villages

Jean-Claude Thevenet Saint-Véran
Clos de l'Hermitage

* * * (GOOD PRODUCERS)

Château de Beauregard Saint-Véran
André Besson Saint-Véran
Domaine de Chervin (Albert Goyard) Mâcon-Villages
Cooperative Clessé Mâcon-Clessé
Cooperative Igé Mâcon-Igé
Cooperative Lugny Mâcon-Lugny
Cooperative Prissé Mâcon-Prissé
Cooperative Viré Mâcon-Viré
Corsin Pouilly-Fuissé
Corsin Saint-Véran
Louis Curvieux Pouilly-Fuissé
Joseph Drouhin Mâcon-Villages-La Forêt
Georges Duboeuf Beaujolais Blanc
Georges Duboeuf Mâcon-Villages
Georges Duboeuf Saint-Véran
Château Fuissé Saint-Véran
Domaine de la Greffière (Henri Greuzard) Mâcon-Villages
Henry-Lucius Grégoire Saint-Véran
Thierry Guérin Saint-Véran
Louis Jadot Beaujolais Blanc
Louis Jadot Pouilly-Fuissé
Edmond Laneyrie Pouilly-Fuissé

Louis Latour Pouilly-Fuissé
Bernard Léger-Plumet Pouilly-Fuissé
Bernard Léger-Plumet Saint-Véran
Jean-Jacques Litaud Pouilly-Fuissé
Loron et Fils Mâcon-Villages
Roger Luquet Pouilly-Fuissé
Roger Luquet Saint-Véran
Domaine de la Maison (Georges Chagny) Saint-Véran
Maurice Martin Saint-Véran
Mathias Pouilly-Fuissé
Domaine de Montbellet Mâcon-Villages
Domaine des Pierres Rouge Saint-Véran
Domaine du Prieuré (Pierre Janny) Mâcon-Villages
Domaine de Roally (Henri Goyard) Mâcon-Villages
Domaine Saint-Martine Saint-Véran
Jacques Sumaize Saint-Véran
Roger Sumaize Pouilly-Fuissé
Trenel Fils Mâcon-Villages
Trenel Fils Pouilly-Fuissé

BEAUJOLAIS

"C'est Si Bon"

What is the most successful and lucrative wine produced in Burgundy? The answer is Beaujolais. This wine is made from vineyards strung across a number of enchanted mountainsides that mark the beginning of what is known as France's Massif Central. The region of Beaujolais is 34 miles long from north to south and 7 to 9 miles wide. The granite mountainsides range in height from 2,300 feet to more than 3,400 feet and provide a backdrop for what is one of

France's two most beautiful viticultural regions (the other being Alsace). Nearly 4,000 growers make a living in this idyllic area. Some of them sell tiny portions of their crops locally, but most prefer to sell to one of the large firms that dominate the business.

The only grape permitted by law to be used in making Beaujolais is the Gamay, or Gamay Noir à Jus Blanc, its official name. It seems to thrive in the stony, schistose soils of the region. Most red wine grapes have trouble producing high-quality crops in granite-based soils, but Gamay seems to be a natural. The compelling characteristic of Gamay is its youthful, fresh, exuberant, crunchy fruit, which the *vignerons* of Beaujolais have learned to maximize through an unusual method called carbonic maceration. In this style of vinification, the grapes are not pressed but simply dumped unceremoniously into a vat in full bunches. Grapes at the very bottom of the vat burst because of the weight on top of them. That juice begins to ferment, warming up the vat and causing fermentation in the unbroken grapes actually to begin inside their skins. The advantage of this technique is that a wine's perfume and fruity intensity are largely related to what is inside the grape skin. The acid and tannin are extracted primarily from the breaking and pressing of the skins.

This interesting fermentation method results in fruity, exuberant, intensely perfumed wines that are ideal when chilled and drunk in the so-called nouveau style. Today Beaujolais Nouveau is a phenomenon in the export markets, but it only started in the late 1970s. Beaujolais Nouveau, which can be released only on the third Thursday in November, accounts for nearly half of the enormous production of this region. Moreover, it is one of France's most successful export items: to satisfy a seemingly insatiable thirst for this wine, hundreds of thousands of cases are airfreighted each season to such far-flung locations as Sydney, Tokyo, Hong Kong, Seoul, San Francisco, New York, Stockholm, London, and, of course, Paris.

The Nouveau hysteria and incredible profits taken by the wine trade from the sales of Nouveau have fostered the inevitable backlash: there are now those who disparage not only the wine, but those who consume it. This is all nonsense, because there is no doubting that in vintages such as 1992, delicious, zesty, exuberant, fresh, vibrantly fruity Beaujolais Nouveau is made. The only limitation is that the wine should be drunk within 3–4 months of its release. Beaujolais Nouveau has become useful for introducing people to the glories of red wine and has also weaned people off some of the sugary white zinfandels and cloying liebfraumilchs that dominate the marketplace. A few arrogant wine snobs would have you believe Beaujolais Nouveau is not fashionable, but that is ludicrous.

However, to think of Beaujolais only in terms of the Nouveau is to do this fascinating region a great injustice. In addition to Beaujolais Nouveau, there is Beaujolais Supérieur, which generally comes on the market about a month after Beaujolais Nouveau. There is also Beaujolais-Villages, which is an appellation unto itself, spread out over most of the Beaujolais appellation, where 39 communes have been selected by the legislature for producing some of the better wines of the region. Many of the top producers make a Beaujolais-Villages Nouveau because it has a more firm, robust character and can last 3–4 months longer than the straight Beaujolais Nouveau. If you are drinking Nouveau for its up-front, exuberant, fresh, unabashed fruitiness, then a good

Beaujolais Nouveau will often be more pleasing than a Beaujolais-Villages Nouveau.

The glories of Beaujolais, aside from its narrow, winding roads, sleepy valleys, photogenic hillsides, and quaint, old villages, are the ten Beaujolais crus. These wines all come from a village or group of villages in the northern end of the Beaujolais region, with each cru believed to have a style of its own.

RATING THE BEAUJOLAIS PRODUCERS

* * * * * (OUTSTANDING PRODUCERS)

Domaine Bachelard—Georges
   Duboeuf (Fleurie)
René Berrod (Moulin-à-Vent)
René Berrod-Les Roches du Vivier
   (Fleurie)
Guy Braillon (Chénas)
Domaine des Brureaux (Chénas)
Domaine des Champs Grilles—J. G.
   Revillon (St.-Amour)
Chauvet—Georges Duboeuf (Moulin-
   à-Vent)
Michel Chignard-Lès-Moriers
   (Fleurie)
Clos de la Roilette—F. Coudert
   (Fleurie)
Domaine de la Combe-Remont—
   Georges Duboeuf (Chénas)

Jean Descombes—Georges Duboeuf
   (Morgon)
Château des Deduits—Georges
   Duboeuf (Fleurie)
Diochon (Moulin-à-Vent)
Domaine des Grandes Vignes—J. C.
   Nesme (Brouilly)
Domaine des Héritiers-Tagent—
   Georges Duboeuf (Moulin-à-Vent)
Jacky Janodet (Moulin-à-Vent)
Château de Moulin-à-Vent—Jean-
   Pierre Bloud (Moulin-à-Vent)
Domaine des Terres Dorées—J. P.
   Brun (Beaujolais-Villages)
Domaine de la Tour du Bief—
   Georges Duboeuf (Moulin-à-Vent)
Jacques Trichard (Morgon)

* * * * (EXCELLENT PRODUCERS)

L. Bassy (Côte de Brouilly)
Alain Bernillon (Côte de Brouilly)
Bouillard (Chiroubles)
Georges Boulon (Chiroubles)
Georges Brun (Morgon)
Domaine de la Bruyère (Moulin-à-
   Vent)
Louis Champagnon (Chénas)
Cheysson-Les-Fargues (Chiroubles)
Guy Cotton (Côte de Brouilly)
Domaine des Darroux— Georges
   Duboeuf (Chénas)
Guy Depardon (Fleurie)
Desmeures—Georges Duboeuf
   (Chiroubles)
Georges Duboeuf (Régnié)
Jean Durand (Régnié)
Château de Grand Pré—Pierre
   Ferraud (Fleurie)

Domaine du Granite Bleu—Georges
   Duboeuf (Beaujolais-Villages)
Château des Jacques (Moulin-à-
   Vent)
Janin (St.-Amour)
Château de Javernand—Georges
   Duboeuf (Chiroubles)
Hubert Lapierre (Chénas)
Manoir des Journets—Georges
   Duboeuf (Chénas)
Domaine des Mouilles—Georges
   Duboeuf (Juliénas)
Château de Nervers—Georges
   Duboeuf (Brouilly)
J. C. Nesme (Côte de Brouilly)
Domaine des Nugues—Gérard Gelin
   (Beaujolais-Villages)
Georges Passot (Chiroubles)
André Pelletier (Juliénas)

Domaine Pirolette—Georges
Duboeuf (St.-Amour)

Domaine Ponchon— J. Durand
(Régnié)

Domaine du Potet—Georges Duboeuf
(Régnié)

Domaine de la Princess Lieven—
Georges Duboeuf (Morgon)

Domaine des Quatre Vents—
Georges Duboeuf (Fleurie)

Joel Rochette (Régnié)

Jean-Paul Ruet (Brouilly)

Jean-Paul Ruet (Régnié)

Jean-Louis Santé (Chénas)

Domaine de la Seigneurie de Juliénas—Georges Duboeuf (Juliénas)

Domaine de la Sorbière—J. C. Pivot
(Beaujolais- Villages)

Domaine de la Teppe—Chanut
Frères (Moulin-à-Vent)

Trenel et Fils (*cuvées* may be five-star
quality, but the overall level is at
least four-star)

Georges Trichard (St.-Amour)

Domaine Vatoux—Georges Duboeuf
(Morgon)

Château des Vierres—Georges
Duboeuf (Beaujolais-Villages)

Château des Vignes—Georges
Duboeuf (Juliénas)

* * * (GOOD PRODUCERS)

M. Gabriel Aligne (Moulin-à-Vent)

M. Gabriel Aligne (Régnié)

Ernest Aujas (Juliénas)

Paul Beaudet (virtually all *cuvées*)

Antoine Beroujon (Brouilly)

Château de Bluizard—Georges
Duboeuf (Brouilly)

Domaine de Boischampt (Juliénas)

Domaine de la Boittière (Juliénas)

Château Bonnet (Chénas)

Domaine des Caves—Georges
Duboeuf (Moulin-à-Vent)

Château de la Chaize (Brouilly)

Louis Champagnon (Moulin-à-Vent)

Domaine de la Chanaise (Morgon)

Château des Chénas (Chénas)

Paul Cinquin (Régnié)

Clos du Fief (Juliénas)

Clos du Fief (St.-Amour)

Robert Condemine (Brouilly)

Pierre Cotton (Brouilly)

Deplace Frères-Domaine du Crêt des
Bruyères (Régnié)

Claude Desvignes (Morgon)

Joseph Drouhin (virtually all *cuvées*)

Domaine des Ducs (St.-Amour)

Pierre Ferraud (Régnié)

Pierre Ferraud (other *cuvées*)

Sylvain Fessy-Cuvée André Gauthier
(Morgon)

Domaine de la Gerarde (Régnié)

Gonon (Juliénas)

Domaine de la Grand Cour
(Brouilly)

Domaine de la Grand Cour (Fleurie)

Domaine de la Grand Cru (Fleurie)

Domaine de Grande Grange—
Georges Duboeuf (Beaujolais-
Villages)

Claude et Michel Joubert (Juliénas)

Marcel Joubert (Brouilly)

Château de Juliénas (Juliénas)

Château des Labourons (Fleurie)

André Large (Côte de Brouilly)

Domaine de Lavant (Brouilly)

Lémonon—Loron et Fils (Moulin-à-
Vent)

Bernard Meziat (Chiroubles)

Giles Meziat (Chiroubles)

Domaine du Paradis—Georges
Duboeuf (St.-Amour)

Georges Passot (Morgon)

Jean Patissier (St.-Amour)

Pavillon de Chavannes (Côte de
Brouilly)

Domaine du Petit Pressoir (Côte de
Brouilly)

Alain Pierre (Régnié)

Domaine des Pillets (Morgon)

Domaine des Pins (St.-Amour)

Domaine de Pizay (Morgon)

Domaine du Prieuré—Georges
Duboeuf (Brouilly)

Château de Raousset (Chiroubles)

Michel et Jean-Paul Rampon
  (Régnié)
Remont—Pierre Ferraud (Chénas)
Domaine de la Roche—Georges
  Duboeuf (Brouilly)
André Ronzière (Brouilly)
Claude et Bernard Roux (Régnié)
Francis Saillant (St.-Amour)
René Savoye (Chiroubles)
Savoye (Morgon)

Domaine de la Source (Chiroubles)
Château Thivin (Côte de Brouilly)
Michel Tribolet (Fleurie)
Château des Tours (Brouilly)
René et Bernard Vassot (Régnié)
Lucien et Robert Verger (Côte de
  Brouilly)
Domaine des Versaudes—Georges
  Duboeuf (Morgon)

* * (AVERAGE PRODUCERS)

Château de Corcelles
Jaffelin
Loron
Moillard
Mommessin
Robert Pain

Pasquier-Desvigne
Piat
Roger Rocassel
Paul Spain
Louis Tête

A Note on Recent Vintages and
General Characteristics of the 10 Beaujolais Crus

Although examples of old bottles of Beaujolais that have retained their fruit can be found (in 1991 I drank a bottle of 1929 Moulin-à-Vent at New York's superb restaurant Le Montrachet with its sommelier, Daniel Johnes, that was marvelously intact), most Beaujolais should be consumed within several years of the vintage. If you are going to take a gamble on aging Beaujolais, it should be Moulin-à-Vent. It comes down to a matter of personal taste, but if you are buying these wines for their vibrant, up-front, exuberant, unabashed fruitiness, then drink them young!

A quick overview of the top Beaujolais crus, from north to south, begins with St.-Amour.

St.-Amour is a wine known for its good color, but it can be lacking in body and length, as the vineyards often fail to achieve maximum ripeness except in exceptionally hot, dry years such as 1989. When good, the wines exhibit a blackberry, raspberry fruitiness, medium body, and soft textures.

Juliénas is one of the larger appellations for top Beaujolais. There are many fine producers from Juliénas, so the competition for top-quality wine is intense. The finest examples display the exuberant, rich, fresh fruitiness of Beaujolais, backed up by plenty of body, intensity, and relatively high alcohol.

The smallest Beaujolais cru, Chénas, produces wines with a kinship to the full-bodied wines of its neighbor, Moulin-à-Vent. A top Chénas displays a deep, robust, intense color and a muscular, rich, concentrated style. It is a fuller, more chunky style of Beaujolais that occasionally lacks perfume and elegance. Given its rusticity, many wines of Chénas can age for 4–5 years.

Moulin-à-Vent is often referred to as the king of Beaujolais, and it is certainly the most expensive. Moulin-à-Vent costs $3–$5 more than other Beaujolais. Moulin-à-Vent produces the most powerful, concentrated, and ageworthy Beaujolais. Although highly prized, in many ways it is atypical, resembling a medium-weight red burgundy from the Côte d'Or rather than an effusively fruity Beaujolais. The wines can easily last for more than 10 years, particularly those from the best producers.

The same people who call Moulin-à-Vent king of Beaujolais refer to Fleurie as its queen. With one of the bigger vineyard acreages, Fleurie may be the quintessential example of Beaujolais—heady, perfumed, rich, without the weight, body, or tannin of the bigger wines from Moulin-à-Vent or Chénas. At its best it is a pure, lush, silky, fruity wine that is undeniably seductive and disarming.

Chiroubles' vineyards sit at the highest altitude of Beaujolais. The wines are considered the most ethereal and fragrant of all the Beaujolais crus. Much of its character is derived from its penetrating, pervasive fragrance. The down side is that Chiroubles can lack body, mature very quickly, and almost always must be drunk within 1–2 years of the vintage.

Morgon has a reputation of being among the more robust and ageworthy of the Beaujolais crus. There is considerable variation in style, given its large size. Many wines are quite full and rich, while others are dull and hollow. A great Morgon will have exotic flavors of overripe cherries, peaches, and apricots as well as a taste of kirsch.

The newest of the Beaujolais crus, Régnié, offers many different styles. Most of the local cognoscenti claim a classic Régnié possesses an intense smell of cassis and raspberries. It is a relatively light- to medium-bodied wine that needs to be drunk within 3 years of the vintage.

Brouilly, another large Beaujolais cru, produces relatively light, aromatic, fruity wines that are often no better than a Beaujolais-Villages. However, in the hands of the best producers, the wines have an additional degree of charm and fruit, making them ideal Beaujolais.

In contrast, the Côte de Brouilly is composed of vineyards on better-drained and exposed slopes. The wines tend to be more alcoholic than those from Brouilly, with more body and glycerin.

As for the generic Beaujolais and Beaujolais-Villages, again, the producer is most important. One of the best values in the marketplace is a top-quality Beaujolais or Beaujolais-Villages.

With respect to vintages, in both 1991 and 1992 most Beaujolais producers were able to harvest before the late summer and early fall rains did any damage. The 1991s tend to be more classic Beaujolais in their fragrance. They should be consumed by mid-1994 at the latest. The 1992s are soft, fleshy, fat, atypical, heady wines that will need to be consumed before the end of 1995. Neither vintage is up to the spectacular quality of the 1989s, which should have been consumed several years ago.

RED BURGUNDY

BERTRAND AMBROISE (PRÉMEAUX)* * * *

1990	Corton-Rognet	E	94+
1989	Corton-Rognet	E	90
1989	Côte de Nuits-Villages	C	87
1990	Nuits St.-Georges	D	85

1989 Nuits St.-Georges	D	84
1990 Nuits St.-Georges Rue de Chaux	E	90+
1989 Nuits St.-Georges Rue de Chaux	E	87
1990 Nuits St.-Georges Les Vaucrains	E	92+
1989 Nuits St.-Georges Les Vaucrains	E	90

Bertrand Ambroise is one of the up-and-coming superstars of Burgundy. His winemaking achieves maximum extraction and produces wines of almost massive intensity, with huge tannins, very full body, and the potential for significant longevity. In short, he does not believe in making soft, up-front, precocious wines that are immediately flattering. His 1990s are the best wines Ambroise has yet produced. His 1990 Nuits St.-Georges is a tarry, tough-textured, backward wine with admirable extraction of fruit, as well as a macho, powerful style. The 1990 Nuits St.-Georges Rue de Chaux displays a saturated dark purple color and a tight but promising nose of sweet blackberries, toasty oak, vanillin, and licorice. In the mouth this dense, medium- to full-bodied, highly concentrated wine also possesses loads of round, sweet tannins. I suggest 5–6 years of cellaring, followed by a window of drinkability of 10–15 years. Although the 1990 Nuits St.-Georges Les Vaucrains is similarly styled, the color is nearly black, and the wine is massively concentrated and exceptionally backward. It is a throwback to the old-style, heavy-duty, superconcentrated, formidable red burgundies that have not existed since 1959. Cellar this blockbuster wine for 5–6 years; it should last for two decades or more. You may want to splurge on a few bottles of Ambroise's 1990 Corton-Rognet. Again, the color is black. After coaxing, the nose reveals scents of black cherries, minerals, and truffles. The wine is nearly too extracted. There are gobs of fruit and considerable tannin. A minimum of 10 years of cellaring will be required for this full-bodied, massively constituted red burgundy to reach its apogee. **Anticipated maturity: 2000–2025.** The 1989 Côte de Nuits-Villages is dark in color, with plenty of rich, ripe, blackberry fruit. This intense, medium-bodied, surprisingly concentrated and interesting Pinot Noir possesses a soft, silky texture and a long finish. Drink it over the next 4–6 years. The 1989 Nuits St.-Georges (from 60-year-old vines) exhibits more tannin, with plenty of intense fruit and a firm, tough texture. The 1989 Nuits St.-Georges Rue de Chaux offers a fragrant bouquet of licorice, plums, and herbs that is followed by long, ripe, intense, spicy flavors and loads of tannin and glycerin in its heady finish. It should keep for 10–15 years. The superb 1989 Nuits St.-Georges Les Vaucrains is an explosively rich wine, with a fabulous perfume of Oriental spices, black fruits, and new oak. In the mouth there is intensity, purity, and remarkable balance. Drink this beauty between 1994 and 2010. Unfortunately only 75 cases were produced for the world. The 1989 Corton-Rognet, from Ambroise's youngest vineyard (18-year-old vines), displays opaque black/ruby/purple color and a sensational perfume of minerals, road tar, and black fruits. In the mouth there is a chewy, intense concentration that one usually associates with extremely old vines. The yields were modest, and almost 100% new oak was used, giving the wine a super color, stability, and intensity. The finish is long, tannic, and formidable. Drink this wine between 1996 and 2010. These offerings are reasonably priced for such high quality. OTHER THOUGHTS: Excellent ageworthy 1988s were made by Ambroise.

BERNARD AMIOT (CHAMBOLLE-MUSIGNY)* *

1990 Chambolle-Musigny	D	84
1990 Chambolle-Musigny Les Charmes	D	86
1990 Chambolle-Musigny Les Chatelots	D	84
1990 Chambolle-Musigny Premier Cru	D	82

Despite the alarmingly light ruby color, much akin to a rosé, the fragrant, seductive 1990 Chambolle-Musigny Les Charmes offers admirable finesse. The
huge nose of berry fruit, alcohol, and flowers is followed by a round, sweet wine
with an alcoholic finish.
OTHER THOUGHTS: Light, rather feeble 1987s, 1988s, and 1989s also fail to in-
spire confidence.

AMIOT-SERVELLE (CHAMBOLLE-MUSIGNY)* *

1990 Chambolle-Musigny	D	80
1990 Chambolle-Musigny Les Amoureuses	EE	87
1990 Chambolle-Musigny Les Charmes	EE	84
1990 Chambolle-Musigny Derrière La Grange	E	84
1990 Chambolle-Musigny Premier Cru	EE	82
1990 Clos Vougeot	EE	86

This domaine has received numerous accolades from the European press. Although I enjoyed the two 1990 offerings, I was surprised by their shallow, light
colors and forward, ready-to-consume personalities. None of the wines from
Amiot-Servelle appear destined to last more than 7–8 years. The two best
wines include the 1990 Clos Vougeot, which exhibits a light ruby color, an attractive flower- and berry-scented nose, medium body, a round texture, and an
excellent long, lusty finish. Drink it over the next 5–6 years. The 1990 Chambolle-Musigny Les Amoureuses is deeper colored, with an elegant floral,
cherry-scented nose, medium body, soft tannins, low acidity, and a lush, gentle
finish. I would opt for consuming it over the next 6–7 years.
OTHER THOUGHTS: Disappointing 1989s and 1988s.

DOMAINE DE L'ARLOT (PRÉMEAUX)* * * *

1990 Côte de Nuits-Villages	D	84
1989 Côte de Nuits-Villages	D	84
1990 Nuits St.-Georges-Clos de l'Arlot	D	89
1989 Nuits St.-Georges-Clos de l'Arlot	D	87
1990 Nuits St.-Georges-Clos des Forêts	D	91
1989 Nuits St.-Georges-Clos des Forêts	D	89

The red winemaking at this estate is identical with that of Jacques Seysses of
the Domaine Dujac. Consequently the wines are light colored, with superbly
fragrant bouquets, silky textures, and gobs of jammy, sweet fruit. In a vintage
such as 1990, they possess a more saturated color than in 1989 or 1988 but remain seductive and compelling. The 1990 Nuits St.-Georges-Clos de l'Arlot of-

fers a gorgeous nose of sweet, earthy, raspberry fruit and smoky new oak. There is a candylike sweetness, a succulent, soft texture, and an intense, honeyed finish to this beautiful wine. The richer 1990 Nuits St.-Georges-Clos des Forêts displays a deeper dark ruby color and a big, sweet, expansive nose of jammy black fruits, smoke, underbrush, and damp earth. There is superb richness, a velvety texture, and a long, unctuous finish. Neither of these offerings will be particularly long-lived. The 1989 Côte de Nuits-Villages is a soft, berry-scented, oaky wine with low acidity and a round, straightforward finish. Drink it over the next 3–4 years. The 1989 Nuits St.-Georges-Clos de l'Arlot reveals a seductively elegant nose of sweet berry fruit, toast, vanillin, and smoke, a generous, satiny smooth texture, and fine concentration. The 1989 Nuits St.-Georges-Clos des Forêts is slightly deeper, with a big, smoky, rich nose, stylish, long, superripe fruity flavors, a velvety texture, and a long, heady, alcoholic finish. This beauty should be consumed over the next 10–12 years.

OTHER THOUGHTS: Wines of great elegance and finesse; very good 1988s.

COMTE ARMAND (POMMARD)* * * *

1990 Pommard-Clos des Epeneaux	E	94+

This is a monster wine. The color is black/purple, and the nose offers up sweet aromas of licorice, minerals, and superripe black fruits intertwined with the smell of toasty vanillin new oak. There is awesome concentration, a thick, glycerin-imbued, full-bodied, chewy texture, and mouth-searing tannins in the explosively long finish. It should keep for 25–30 years.

OTHER THOUGHTS: These wines are frequently too tannic, but if you are young, rich, and an optimist, why not?

ROBERT ARNOUX (VOSNE-ROMANÉE)* * * *

1990 Bourgogne Rouge	B	83
1990 Clos Vougeot	D	87
1990 Nuits St.-Georges des Corvées-Paget	D	84
1990 Nuits St.-Georges Les Poisets	D	90
1990 Romanée St.-Vivant	EEE	94
1990 Vosne-Romanée Les Chaumes	D	86
1990 Vosne-Romanée Les Suchots	E	93

Unquestionably, the 1990s are Robert Arnoux's finest wines since his 1978s and 1980s. Arnoux's 1990 Nuits St.-Georges Les Poisets offers up a compelling bouquet of smoke, herbs, sweet black fruits, and minerals. There is excellent richness, full-bodied lusciousness, velvety texture, and a heady finish. Drink it over the next 7–9 years. The 1990 Vosne-Romanée Les Chaumes is spicy, ripe, long, medium bodied, round, and precocious. Drink it over the next 4–5 years. The extraordinary 1990 Vosne-Romanée Les Suchots exhibits an explosively complex, rich nose of Oriental spices, sweet black fruit, and vanillin. The color is a deep ruby/purple. The wine's dense, full-bodied, rich, layered texture is all sweetness, jammy fruit, and glycerin. This decadent red burgundy should continue to drink well for 7–10 years. Slightly less impressive, but still rich and full-bodied, is the 1990 Clos Vougeot. Arnoux also made a terrific, although absurdly priced, 1990 Romanée St.-Vivant. The wine flaunts a black fruit character, toasty new oak, and gobs of Oriental spices. The predominant fruit flavor is of superripe black cherries. It should drink well for 10–12 years. These are exciting Pinot Noirs.

OTHER THOUGHTS: A highly regarded producer who was off form for most of the 1980s.

BALLOT-MILLOT ET FILS (MEURSAULT)* * *

1990	Beaune Les Epenottes	D	85
1989	Pommard Les Pézerolles	D	90
1990	Volnay Taillepieds	D	88
1989	Volnay Taillepieds	D	87

The medium-weight, spicy, fruity 1990 Beaune Les Epenottes exhibits a deep color, an attractive fragrance of red fruits, and a moderately long finish. Drink it over the next 4–5 years. The 1990 Volnay Taillepieds offers more dimension from both aromatic and flavor perspectives. The wine displays a deep ruby color, an excellent nose of red and black fruits, spices, and vague floral notes. It is rich and medium bodied, with sweet, expansive, chewy fruitiness, soft tannins, and low acidity. Drink it over the next 7–8 years. The 1989 Volnay Taillepieds offers an opaque, deep ruby color; a sweet, jammy nose of raspberries and new oak; delicious, opulent, creamy-textured fruit flavors; and plenty of extraction. There is enough acidity, tannin, and depth to hold this wine together for at least 7–8 years. The 1989 Pommard Les Pézerolles exhibits a stunningly intense nose of black fruits, vanillin, and minerals. In the mouth there is superb ripeness, gobs of rich, velvet fruit, soft tannins, and a long, explosively rich finish. This is a beautiful wine for drinking over the next decade. OTHER THOUGHTS: An underrated performer turning out stylish, ripe, elegant wines.

BARTHOD-NOËLLAT (CHAMBOLLE-MUSIGNY)* * * *

1990	Bourgogne Rouge	B	85
1989	Bourgogne Rouge	B	82
1990	Chambolle-Musigny	C	86
1989	Chambolle-Musigny	C	85
1990	Chambolle-Musigny aux Beaux Bruns	D	87
1989	Chambolle-Musigny aux Beaux Bruns	D	85
1990	Chambolle-Musigny Les Charmes	D	87
1989	Chambolle-Musigny Les Charmes	D	86
1990	Chambolle-Musigny Les Cras	D	86+
1989	Chambolle-Musigny Les Cras	D	87
1990	Chambolle-Musigny Les Varoilles	D	86+
1989	Chambolle-Musigny Les Varoilles	D	86

Identical wines from this excellent Chambolle-Musigny estate appear under the name of Barthod-Noëllat, as well as the daughter's name, Ghislaine Barthod. For starters, one of the better generic Bourgognes I have tasted is the 1990, which displays surprisingly dark color and a lovely nose of berry fruit nicely touched by spicy oak. It is elegant, medium bodied, and soft. Drink it over the next 4–5 years. Barthod's excellent 1990 Chambolle-Musigny is tasty and forward, displaying a pleasant concoction of red fruits, toasty oak, and floral scents. It should be drunk over the next 5–6 years. The 1990 Chambolle-Musigny aux Beaux Bruns exhibits a medium-bodied, elegant, sweet, black fruit–scented nose; spicy, oaky, nicely concentrated flavors with firm tannins; decent acidity; and a long, structured, rich finish. Drink it between 1995 and 2004. The leaner-style 1990 Chambolle-Musigny Les Cras (from a vineyard close to Bonnes Mares) offers a lighter color and is less concentrated in the mid-palate and finish. It is a stylish, compact, and less flattering wine. Also tannic and closed, but with excellent potential, is the 1990 Chambolle-Musigny Les Varoilles. It is a medium-weight, impeccably clean wine that, at present, is dominated by its oak and tannins. Do not look for it to be ready to drink for 3–4 years. A wine that admirably supports its name is the densely colored 1990 Chambolle-Musigny Les Charmes. The fragrant, sweet nose of flowers, cherry fruit, and smoky oak is followed by a wine with excellent depth, crisp acidity, and a medium-bodied, tasty, well-structured, long finish. It, too, needs 2–3 years of cellaring; it should keep for 10–12 years. The 1989s also present a strong lineup. There is a reasonably priced, pleasantly ripe, crisp, elegant 1989 Bourgogne Rouge and a 1989 Chambolle-Musigny with stylish, clean, pure berry fruit intelligently enhanced by new oak and a moderately tannic finish. The 1989 Chambolle-Musigny Les Varoilles is the lightest and most flattering of the Premiers Crus. The 1989 Chambolle-Musigny Les Cras, one of the two deepest and most concentrated wines, with more muscle, power, and tannin than the other *cuvées,* offers up finely etched Pinot aromas. Drink it between 1994 and 2003. The deepest-colored wine is the 1989 Chambolle-Musigny aux Beaux Bruns. Dominated by mineral scents, it is the most rustic and masculine of these wines. Drink it over the next 10–12 years. The 1989 Chambolle-Musigny Les Charmes clearly deserves its name. One of the most elegant wines, it exhibits beautifully crafted berry fruit intertwined with aromas of sweet vanillin oak. Drink it over the next 7–8 years.

OTHER THOUGHTS: Recent vintages showed considerable improvement under the daughter's direction.

PHILIPPE BATACCHI (GEVREY-CHAMBERTIN)* * *

1990	Clos de la Roche	E	87+
1990	Côte de Nuits-Villages	D	78
1990	Fixin	D	78
1990	Gevrey-Chambertin	D	80+
1990	Gevrey-Chambertin Les Evocelles	D	85+
1990	Morey St.-Denis Premier Cru	D	82+

The black-colored 1990 Gevrey-Chambertin Les Evocelles, with its chunky, rich, closed personality, possesses plenty of aging ability, but how much charm and finesse will emerge is impossible to judge. I hope my score looks conservative in 7–8 years when this wine should be fully mature. The even bigger, thicker, richer, chewy 1990 Clos de la Roche may ultimately turn out to be an outstanding wine. At present it is backward, dense, and tannic. These appear to be wines for die-hard optimists, but there is impressive raw material and fascinating stuffing.

OTHER THOUGHTS: The Pinot Noir that tastes like Petite Sirah?

FOUGERAY DE BEAUCLAIR (MARSANNAY)* * * *

1990 Bonnes Mares	E	93
1990 Côte de Nuits-Villages	C	85
1990 Marsannay-Les Dessus des Longeroies	C	87
1990 Marsannay-Les Favières	D	85
1990 Marsannay-Les St.-Jacques	C	87
1990 Vosne-Romanée Les Damodes	D	86

The 1990 Marsannay-Longeroies reveals a saturated black/purple color, an attractive fragrance of black cherries and damp earth, and dense, ripe, medium- to full-bodied flavors with considerable tannin. It should drink well over the next 5–7 years. The 1990 Marsannay-Les Favières is nearly as densely colored, but with less sweet fruit. The tannins appear more prominent. It should drink well for a decade. The 1990 Marsannay-Les St.-Jacques is the sweetest and oakiest of the three Marsannays. There is commendable depth of fruit, which confirms the ripeness and concentration achieved. It, too, should last for up to a decade. The 1990 Côte de Nuits-Villages is an attractive, straightforward, dense, muscular Pinot Noir, with full body and spicy, ripe fruit. The 1990 Vosne-Romanée Les Damodes, although not as rich or tannic as the Marsannays, may develop more elegance and fragrance. It should keep for a decade. The super 1990 Bonnes Mares offers up a big, expansive nose of sweet black fruits, new oak, and flowers. The wine is opulent and succulent, with medium to full body, superb depth of flavor, brilliant focus and delineation, and a round, generously endowed, velvety-textured finish. It should drink well for the next 7–10 years.

OTHER THOUGHTS: This producer should be closely watched, as the wines look promising.

BITOUZET-PRIEUR (VOLNAY)* * *

1990 Volnay	D	84
1990 Volnay Les Aussy	D	86+
1990 Volnay Caillerets	D	86+
1990 Volnay Clos des Chênes	E	85+
1990 Volnay Pitures	D	87
1990 Volnay Taillepieds	D	87

The rich, deep ruby color of the 1990 Volnay Taillepieds is followed by a sweet, fragrant nose of red and black fruits and an elegant, medium-bodied personality with fine depth and ripeness. Drink this exceptionally well-balanced wine over the next 10–12 years. The slightly fatter 1990 Volnay Pitures offers less elegance but more up-front richness, as well as additional glycerin and body. Both the Volnay Les Aussy and Volnay Caillerets were tightly knit, backward, and tannic. The 1990 Volnay Les Aussy, made from 37-year-old vines, displays fine length, richness, ripeness, and weight, but the tannins dominate. It should drink well between 1995 and 2005. The 1990 Volnay Caillerets, which is even more tannic, is powerful and authoritative on the palate, with tremendous extract. Closed and unevolved, it needs 4–5 years of cellaring.

OTHER THOUGHTS: Good, but rather chunky, firm, tannic wines that lack excitement.

JEAN BOILLOT (VOLNAY)* * *

1990	Beaune Clos du Roi	D	87
1990	Beaune Les Epenottes	D	87
1990	Nuits St.-Georges Les Cailles	D	82
1990	Savigny-Lès-Beaune Les Lavières	D	84
1990	Volnay Caillerets	D	85
1990	Volnay-Chevrets	D	86
1990	Volnay Fremiets	D	89

Jean Boillot's red burgundies offer attractive richness, good structure, a generous lashing of toasty new oak, and 5–8 years of longevity. Both the 1990 Beaune Les Epenottes and 1990 Beaune Clos du Roi are medium-bodied, elegant wines with supple fruitiness, opulent textures, ripe tannins, and low acidity. The dark ruby-colored 1990 Volnay-Chevrets is made in a seductive style, with medium weight and forward, ripe, plummy fruit. Drink it over the next 5 years. The most concentrated of all Jean Boillot's wine, the 1990 Volnay Fremiets, is voluptuous and fat, with gobs of chewy, sweet, expansive Pinot fruit. The 1990 Volnay Caillerets is the lightest. With less concentration and more tannin, it should turn out to be a pleasant, medium-weight, straightforward, tasty 1990 that should be cellared for 1–2 years.

OTHER THOUGHTS: Unrealized potential for even higher quality.

JEAN-MARC BOILLOT (POMMARD)* *

1990	Beaune Les Montrevenots	D	87
1989	Beaune Les Montrevenots	D	75
1990	Bourgogne	C	82
1990	Pommard	D	83
1990	Pommard Les Jarolières	E	87
1989	Pommard Les Jarolières	E	77
1990	Pommard Les Rugiens	E	87+
1990	Pommard Les Saucilles	E	86
1990	Volnay	D	86

1989 Volnay	D	74
1990 Volnay Carelle	E	84
1990 Volnay Les Pitures	E	85
1989 Volnay Les Pitures	E	80
1990 Volnay Le Ronceret	E	86

Most of these wines are made in a modern-day, clean, fruity, attractive style. The 1990 Volnay exhibits an excellent deep ruby color, a lovely floral- and red fruit–scented nose, sweet, ripe fruit, medium body, and soft tannins in the finish. Drink it over the next 5–6 years. The impressively dark-colored 1990 Beaune Les Montrevenots displays a charming, rich nose full of aromas of superripe red fruits, herbs, and toasty new oak. This voluptuously textured wine reveals both elegance and richness. Drink it over the next 5–6 years. The 1990 Volnay Le Ronceret also possesses a deep ruby color, an excellent black cherry–scented nose, and sweet, ripe, medium-bodied flavors. It can be cellared for 5–6 years. The 1990 Volnay Les Pitures is a more muscular, tannic, structured wine with a leaner, sleeker texture and less fruit. The wine exhibits weight and depth, but 3–4 years of cellaring might be beneficial. The 1990 Pommard Les Saucilles is tannic and closed, but enough sweet, ripe fruit is evident in the wine's medium-bodied format to warrant a recommendation. Boillot's two finest wines include an excellent 1990 Pommard Les Jarolières. This dark ruby/purple-colored wine, made from 56-year-old vines, offers up a fragrant nose of spicy wood, underbrush, and black fruits. There is a sweet, black cherry component, excellent density and richness, moderate tannins, and a long, full-bodied finish. Approachable now, this wine should age well for up to a decade. The 1990 Pommard Les Rugiens (from a vineyard planted in 1912) has an exotic, earthy, extroverted style. It possesses wonderful extraction of fruit, a rich, generous feel, and a long, lusty finish. It should age gracefully for 7–10 years.

Not everyone made charming, fruity, and supple 1989s. All of these 1989s from Jean-Marc Boillot lack concentration, have excessive tannin for the amount of fruit, and come across as anorexic, malnourished wines of little interest or charm. Caveat emptor.

OTHER THOUGHTS: Modern-day, squeaky-clean Pinot Noir for technocrats.

LUCIEN BOILLOT ET FILS (GEVREY-CHAMBERTIN)* * *

1990 Bourgogne	B	77
1990 Gevrey-Chambertin	C	86
1989 Gevrey-Chambertin Les Cherbaudes	C	85
1990 Gevrey-Chambertin Les Corbeaux	D	88
1990 Gevrey-Chambertin Les Evocelles	D	87
1989 Gevrey-Chambertin Les Evocelles	D	86
1990 Nuits St.-Georges Les Pruliers	D	88
1989 Nuits St.-Georges Les Pruliers	D	87
1990 Pommard Les Fremiers	D	87

1990 Volnay	D	84
1990 Volnay Les Angles	D	86
1989 Volnay Les Angles	D	84

The 1990 Gevrey-Chambertin displays attractive ripeness, medium to full body, an earthy, black fruit–scented nose, and a spicy, moderately tannic finish. Drink it over the next 5–6 years. Boillot's three best wines include an extremely fine 1990 Gevrey-Chambertin Les Evocelles. Its superripe nose of black fruits, licorice, and toast is followed by a wine with excellent intensity, medium to full body, low acidity, and powerful tannins in the finish. I would opt for drinking it between 1994 and 2003. The 1990 Gevrey-Chambertin Les Corbeaux is more supple and less structured yet is still impressively full, generously endowed, and spicy. Drink it between now and 2004. The 1990 Nuits St.-Georges Les Pruliers exhibits copious quantities of up-front, sweet black fruits intertwined with aromas of truffles, toasty oak, and earth. Ripe and lush, it is delicious now but promises to last for 7–8 years. The 1989 Volnay Les Angles is the lightest, with a lovely, fragrant bouquet, plenty of ripe berry fruit, and a pleasing finish. Drink it over the next 4–5 years. Slightly richer and more enticing is the 1989 Gevrey-Chambertin Les Evocelles. It displays the telltale, meaty, smoky nose of a good Gevrey-Chambertin, round, generously endowed flavors, a smooth texture, and a spicy finish. This wine should drink well for at least 3–5 years. The 1989 Gevrey-Chambertin Les Cherbaudes reveals a seductively fragrant, full-intensity nose; admirably endowed, plump, chunky flavors; an earthy, smoky fruitiness; and a low-acid, light-tannin finish. It will make delicious drinking for 5–6 years. The best of Boillot's 1989s is the 1989 Nuits St.-Georges Les Pruliers. The smoky, earthy, plum-scented nose is followed by a fullbodied wine with seductive quantities of juicy, succulent fruit, low acid, and some noticeable yet soft tannin and alcohol in the impressive finish. Drinkable now, it should continue to improve for 2–3 years and last for up to a decade. The 1990 Volnay Les Angles is round, voluptuous, and supple, with attractive fruit, medium body, and plenty of charm and finesse. It should be drunk over the next 5–7 years. The 1990 Pommard Les Fremiers possesses more structure, alcohol, grip, and tannin. However, there is adequate sweet fruit to balance the wine's structural components. Less precocious than the Volnay, it will benefit from 1–3 years of cellaring and should last for up to a decade.

OTHER THOUGHTS: This Boillot has thrown out his filters, and what a coincidence—higher quality.

PIERRE BOILLOT (MEURSAULT)* * * *

1990 Meursault Les Caillerets	D	90
1990 Pommard	D	89

Both of these wines are full bodied and intensely concentrated, with sweet, expansive textures and long, luscious, lusty finishes. Boillot's intense 1990 Meursault Les Caillerets is more structured than his Pommard. It should drink well for the next 7–8 years.

OTHER THOUGHTS: Explosive, ripe, rich wines for hedonists.

BOUCHARD PÈRE ET FILS (BEAUNE)* * *

1990	Aloxe-Corton	D	78
1990	Beaune-Marconnets	D	87
1990	Beaune Les Teurons	D	85
1990	Chambertin	EE	85
1990	Le Corton	EE	89
1990	Volnay Les Caillerets Cuvée Carnot	D	88
1990	Volnay Fremiets-Clos de la Rougeotte	D	84
1990	Volnay Taillepieds	D	88

After years of indifferent performances, Bouchard's 1990s exhibit encouraging signs of improvement. The best wines include a big, beefy, tannic, dense, masculine 1990 Le Corton, which should keep for another 10–15 years; the 1990 Volnay Les Caillerets Cuvée Carnot, a dense, chewy, richly concentrated, full-bodied wine that will age for more than a decade; the 1990 Volnay Taillepieds, another rich, stylish, deeply colored, concentrated wine that will keep for a decade; and a spicy, tannic, well-structured, chewy 1990 Beaune-Marconnets, which can be drunk now or cellared for 8–10 years. The other wines display considerable body and excellent color but monolithic, straightforward personalities.

OTHER THOUGHTS: After sleeping through the last several decades, this huge firm is beginning to get the message that quality, not reputation, sells.

JEAN-MARC BOULEY (VOLNAY)* * *

1990	Beaune Les Reversées	D	79
1989	Beaune Les Reversées	D	85
1990	Bourgogne Rouge	C	75
1989	Bourgogne Rouge	C	84
1990	Hautes-Côtes de Beaune	C	76
1989	Hautes-Côtes de Beaune	B	82
1990	Pommard	C	72
1989	Pommard	C	84
1990	Pommard Les Fremiers	D	86
1989	Pommard Les Fremiers	D	87
1990	Pommard Les Pézerolles	D	87
1989	Pommard Les Pézerolles	D	87
1990	Pommard Les Rugiens	D	86+
1990	Volnay	C	78
1989	Volnay	C	85
1990	Volnay Les Carelles	D	86

1989 Volnay Les Carelles	D	85
1990 Volnay Clos des Chênes	D	87
1989 Volnay Clos des Chênes	D	87
1990 Volnay Le Ronceret	D	80
1989 Volnay Le Ronceret	D	85

Readers who like concentrated, tannic, oaky wines will admire Bouley's 1990s. He is aiming for maximum extraction as well as a gutsy style of Pinot Noir, perhaps at the expense of charm and finesse. The atypical, oaky 1990 Volnay Clos des Chênes offers thick, chewy, tannic flavors. **Anticipated maturity: 1996–2007.** The 1990 Volnay Les Carelles possesses terrific color; plenty of hard tannins; good richness, grip, and body; and a spicy, unevolved finish. The 1990 Pommard Les Pézerolles may turn out to be one of Bouley's finest 1990s. It is a chewy, concentrated wine with a ruby/purple color, plenty of toasty new oak, and a robust, powerful finish that lasts for nearly a minute. The oodles of sweet fruit are tightly knit to lavish quantities of new oak and aggressive tannins. **Anticipated maturity: 1996–2008.** The supple 1990 Pommard Les Fremiers exhibits a spicy, oaky, plummy fragrance, medium body, low acidity, and high tannins. Drink it over the next 10 years. The deeply colored 1990 Pommard Les Rugiens is medium to full bodied and tannic, but the nose offers mostly aromas of new oak, earth, and black fruits. The wine is weighty on the palate, with excellent ripeness, but the huge tannins in the finish suggest a wait of 5–6 years is warranted. **Anticipated maturity: 1997–2007.** Bouley's 1989s are also oaky, surprisingly powerful, and tannic, particularly for the vintage. His less expensive wines include a solidly made, robust, fruity, rustic 1989 Bourgogne. I was less impressed with the monolithic 1989 Hautes-Côtes de Beaune. Bouley's 1989 Beaune Les Reversées is light, with a berry fragrance backed up by substantial quantities of new oak. Though it displays surprisingly good color, it finishes short. The 1989 Volnay exhibits a sweet, plummy nose, good, deep ruby color, elegant, moderately rich fruit flavors, medium body, and a crisp finish. Approachable now, it should mature nicely for 4–5 years. The similarly styled, although bigger and more tannic, 1989 Volnay Le Ronceret exhibits the same degree of ripeness, copious amounts of new oak, and generous tannins in the finish. The 1989 Volnay Clos des Chênes is a powerful style of Volnay that purists may find too burly. It reveals gobs of extract and plenty of tannin, glycerin, and depth. Drink it between 1995 and 2006. In contrast, the 1989 Volnay Les Carelles is an elegant, softer wine, with sweet fruit, a nice touch of spicy oak, and fine length. It will be ready to drink within 3–4 years and should keep for up to a decade. The 1989 Pommard exhibits richness and ripeness in a forceful style. Although it lacks complexity, it offers mouth-filling fruit. The 1989 Pommard Les Pézerolles offers up an intriguing chocolatey, black fruit–, oak-, and herb-scented nose, black cherry flavors, plenty of body and alcohol, and enough tannin to support 10–12 years of aging. The 1989 Pommard Les Fremiers, a powerful, rich, authoritative wine, displays admirable extraction of flavor, obvious oak, and plenty of tannin. It needs several years of cellaring.

OTHER THOUGHTS: If all Burgundians used this much new oak, the world's forests would be even more endangered.

BOURÉE PÈRE ET FILS (GEVREY-CHAMBERTIN)* * * *

1989 Beaune Les Epenottes	C	86
1989 Chambertin	E	86+
1989 Chambolle-Musigny Les Charmes	D	86
1989 Charmes-Chambertin	E	87
1989 Clos de la Roche	E	88
1989 Corton	E	87
1989 Côte de Nuits-Villages	B	84
1989 Echézeaux	E	90
1989 Gevrey-Chambertin Les Cazetiers	D	87
1989 Gevrey-Chambertin Clos de la Justice	D	87
1989 Gevrey-Chambertin Lavaux St.-Jacques	D	88
1989 Latricières-Chambertin	E	86
1989 Mazis-Chambertin	E	87
1989 Pernand-Vergelesses-Les Vergelesses	C	83
1989 Pommard Les Epenots	D	86
1989 Santenay Les Gravières	C	86
1989 Volnay-Santenots	D	86

The Bourée firm, run by the Vallet family, continues to be an underestimated source of traditional burgundies. The red burgundies, which usually spend 2 years in old casks, are rarely racked and are bottled unfiltered barrel by barrel. Like many of the better 1989s, Bourée's red wines from this charming vintage are round and soft textured, with admirable finesse and fruit. Almost all of them will have to be drunk before the turn of the century. The 1989 Côte de Nuits-Villages possessed low acidity, a spicy, earthy, fruity nose, decent color, and a round, gentle finish. The richer 1989 Santenay Les Graviéres exhibited more fat, a fragrant, spicy, herb- and berry-scented nose, and lush flavors. It reminded me of a 1985. Drink it over the next 5–7 years. The cherry-scented 1989 Pernand-Vergelesses-Les Vergelesses was an elegant, lighter-bodied wine that avoided the hardness of so many wines from that village. I also found generous amounts of ripe cherry fruit in Bourée's 1989 Volnay-Santenots. It was a wine with excellent suppleness, spicy fruit, medium body, and low tannins and acidity, making it ideal for consumption over the next 5–6 years. Even better was the 1989 Beaune Les Epenottes, a rich, supple, velvety-textured wine bursting with an attractive earthy, cherry, raspberry fruitiness. It will make delicious drinking over the next 5–7 years. More tannic, with more glycerin, alcohol, and body, is the 1989 Pommard Les Epenots. The return to sweet, fat, gorgeously ripe, gentle, low-acid fruit can be seen in the fleshy 1989 Corton. From the Côte de Nuits comes a gentle, light ruby-colored 1989 Morey St.-Denis that is ideal for current drinking. One of their specialties is a deep, structured Gevrey-Chambertin Clos de la Justice. The 1989 will make delicious drinking over the next 5–6 years. Bourée's 1989 Chambolle-Musigny Les Charmes offers a floral-scented, intense bouquet, round, gentle, harmonious flavors, and an easygoing finish. Again, the words *expansive* and *soft* are applicable. The 1989 Gevrey-Chambertin Les Cazetiers displays a more cinnamon, oaky, smoky personality, ripe fruit, decent body, and noticeable tannins. The 1989 Gevrey-Chambertin Lavaux St.-Jacques exhibits a deep ruby color and a gorgeous nose of raspberry fruit intertwined with aromas of smoke, earth, and spicy oak. It offers excellent ripeness, plenty of concentration, a sweet, expansive texture, and a long, lush finish. The 1989 Charmes-Chambertin displays a perfumed nose of red fruits, flowers, and herbs. It is already a delight to drink. Although the 1989 Mazis-Chambertin is more savage, smoky, and rustic, it reveals tender tannins and low acidity. Bourée's Clos de la Roche can be absolutely terrific. The 1989 exhibits a spicy, earthy, herb- and mineral-scented character. It will require drinking over the next 5–6 years. The 1989 Latricières-Chambertin offers up a richly fruity nose, soft tannins, and a smooth texture. Drink it over the next 5–6 years. The gorgeously scented, full-bodied, elegant 1989 Echézeaux is loaded with aromas and flavors of red and black fruits as well as flowers. This beauty should be consumed over the next 7–8 years. Last, the 1989 Chambertin, which should turn out to be nearly as good as the Echézeaux, is atypically closed and hard for a 1989. It will need at least 5–6 years to shed its considerable tannins.

OTHER THOUGHTS: Traditional old-style, powerful wines routinely emerge from these cellars. They age as well as any in Burgundy. From barrel the 1990s looked super, even richer than Bourée's top-level 1985s.

CACHEUX-BLÉE ET FILS (VOSNE-ROMANÉE)* * * *

1990 Echézeaux	E	89
1990 Vosne-Romanée	C	82
1990 Vosne-Romanée Les Suchots	D	87

Cacheux's light ruby-colored 1990 Vosne-Romanée Les Suchots exhibits more flavor than its light color suggests. Spicy, with an attractive cherry-, almond-, and oak-scented nose, this medium-bodied, soft wine should be drunk over the next 5–6 years. The 1990 Echézeaux reveals a more intense fragrance of flowers and berry fruit, complemented nicely by toasty new oak and imbued with copious quantities of glycerin, body, and richness. Its soft tannins and low acidity make it delicious to drink now and over the next 7–8 years.

OTHER THOUGHTS: A serious, shy producer who merits more recognition.

SYLVAIN CATHIARD (VOSNE-ROMANÉE)* * *

1990 Vosne-Romanée Les Malconsorts	D	85
1989 Vosne-Romanée Les Malconsorts	D	87
1989 Vosne-Romanée en Orveaux	D	85
1989 Vosne-Romanée aux Reignots	D	83

The 1990 Vosne-Romanée Les Malconsorts is a light, medium-weight wine with decent color, a tasty, up-front, berry fruitiness, some evidence of new oak, and a gentle, moderately long finish. Drink it over the next 4–5 years. The 1989 offerings are all light yet stylish red burgundies for drinking now. The best of this trio is the concentrated and impressive 1989 Vosne-Romanée Les Malconsorts. It exhibits an attractive medium-ruby color, a floral, richly fruity, spicy nose, medium body, decent extract, and soft tannins. It is much richer, deeper, and more complete than the 1989 Vosne-Romanée aux Reignots and the tannic and hard 1989 Vosne-Romanée en Orveaux.

OTHER THOUGHTS: Good but uninspiring wines.

CECI (VOUGEOT)* * *

1989	Chambolle-Musigny Les Echanges	D	87
1989	Clos Vougeot	E	88
1989	Gevrey-Chambertin Clos de la Justice	D	85
1989	Morey St.-Denis	C	86
1989	Vougeot-Clos du Village	D	86

Drink the attractive, wonderfully ripe, round, sweet, generously endowed 1989 Morey St.-Denis over the next 4–5 years. The 1989 Vougeot-Clos du Village offers a seductive nose of red fruits, spices, and new oak. It is a generously endowed, expansively flavored, ripe, rich wine that should be drunk over the next 5–6 years. The 1989 Gevrey-Chambertin Clos de la Justice is a smokier, meatier wine, with more tannin. I also enjoyed the floral, supple, satiny-smooth-textured 1989 Chambolle-Musigny Les Echanges. It revealed ripe, rich fruit, soft tannins, and a good finish. Ceci's 1989 Clos Vougeot possesses a deep, opaque, ruby/purple color and a super nose of flowers, jammy red fruits, and sweet, toasty new oak. Fat and crammed with ripe fruit, it displays plenty of glycerin, moderate alcohol, and soft tannins. Drink this undeniably hedonistic wine over the next 5–7 years.

OTHER THOUGHTS: After some shaky performances in the early 1980s, the quality has been good.

CHANDON DE BRIAILLES (SAVIGNY-LÈS-BEAUNE)* * *

1990	Corton Les Bressandes	E	87
1989	Corton Les Bressandes	E	85
1990	Corton-Clos du Roi	E	88
1989	Corton-Clos du Roi	E	86
1989	Corton Les Maréchaudes	C	85
1990	Pernand Île des Vergelesses	C	82
1989	Pernand Île des Vergelesses	C	84
1990	Savigny-Lès-Beaune	C	80
1990	Savigny-Lès-Beaune Les Fourneaux	C	84
1990	Savigny-Lès-Beaune Les Lavières	C	84
1989	Savigny-Lès-Beaune Les Lavières	C	83

This is a source of undeniably charming, lighter-style red burgundies that emphasize finesse and elegance rather than power. My favorite 1990s include a light ruby-colored, cherry-scented 1990 Corton Les Bressandes with medium body, a satiny texture, and gobs of cherry fruit in its long, alcoholic finish. It is delicious to drink, and although I do not believe it will age particularly well, it should drink nicely for another 4–6 years. The domaine's richest and most extracted 1990 is the Corton-Clos du Roi, which exhibits an ostentatious bouquet of toasty new oak, jammy black cherries, and herbs, excellent richness, medium body, and copious quantities of glycerin and alcohol in the soft finish. It should last another 5–6 years. The 1989 Savigny-Lès-Beaune Les Lavières, which displays the color of a white zinfandel, is delicate and flavorful, with a smooth aftertaste. Drink it over the next 2–3 years. The 1989 Pernand Île des Vergelesses is deeper and more earthy. The flavor, intensity, and fragrance move up a notch with the 1989 Corton Les Maréchaudes. This medium ruby-colored wine offers rich flavors and a burst of cherry fruit intertwined with smells of sweet oak and leather. Drink it over the next 3–4 years. The similarly styled 1989 Corton Les Bressandes is soft and fragrant and best drunk over the next 4–5 years. The medium ruby-colored 1989 Corton-Clos du Roi offers up aromas of vanillin, strawberries, black cherries, and herbs. Displaying a good combination of fruit and oak, this velvety wine should be drunk over the next 4–7 years.

OTHER THOUGHTS: Fabulous potential, but multiple filtrations and a fining take a toll.

PHILIPPE CHARLOPIN-PARIZOT (MARSANNAY)* * *

1990	Chambertin	E	87
1989	Chambertin	E	86
1990	Charmes-Chambertin	E	87
1989	Charmes-Chambertin	E	86
1990	Clos St.-Denis	E	92
1989	Clos St.-Denis	E	89
1990	Gevrey-Chambertin Vieilles Vignes	D	86
1989	Gevrey-Chambertin Vieilles Vignes	D	84
1990	Marsannay Monchenevoy	C	85
1989	Marsannay Monchenevoy	C	83
1990	Morey St.-Denis	C	84
1989	Morey St.-Denis	C	79
1990	Vosne-Romanée	D	86

These wines are clean, fruity, and well made, but they lack the extra dimension of richness necessary to make old bones and provide profound drinking. They can be tasty and enjoyable—provided the purchaser consumes them in their youth. The 1990 Marsannay Monchenevoy exhibits fine color, a pleasant ripe berry–scented nose, a soft texture, and round tannins. Drink it over the next 4–5 years. The 1990 Gevrey-Chambertin Vieilles Vignes reveals a fine fragrance of berry fruit, earth, and toasty oak. It is medium bodied, seductive, and ideal for drinking now. The 1990 Vosne-Romanée offers surprising ripeness (nearly overripeness), soft tannins, and a supple texture. Drink it over the next 4 years. The 1990 Charmes-Chambertin displays a sweet, fragrant, jammy nose, medium-bodied, concentrated flavors, and a generous finish. Ready to drink, it should last for 4 or more years. The 1990 Clos St.-Denis's saturated color is followed by a bouquet that explodes from the glass with aromas of sweet black raspberries, cedar, herbs, new oak, and spices. Its layered texture, admirable opulence, and superb concentration are notable. Drink it over the next decade. Charlopin's 1990 Chambertin is good but unexciting. It is an elegant wine, with a leafy, cedary, animal, berrylike fragrance, medium body, good rather than great concentration, and a soft, supple finish. The bargain-priced 1989 Marsannay Monchenevoy offers excellent fruitiness, a berry-scented nose, good body and length, and the potential to last another 4–5 years. The 1989 Morey St.-Denis is light and straightforward. The 1989 Gevrey-Chambertin Vieilles Vignes exhibits decent color, a pleasant, meaty, smoky, spicy character, and enough body and tannin to support 4–5 years of aging. The 1989 Charmes-Chambertin reveals a deeper color, a perfumed, rich, berry-scented nose, noticeable tannin, and zesty acidity. It should last for 8–10 years. The 1989 Clos St.-Denis is again the star. A deep ruby/purple-colored wine with a fragrance of Oriental spices, black fruits, new oak, and minerals, it is rich and full bodied, with considerable opulence, elegance, and enough glycerin, tannin, and alcohol to warrant holding back a few bottles for 10–12 years. The 1989 Chambertin is a medium-weight wine, with good ripeness but high tannin.

OTHER THOUGHTS: Young *vigneron* continues to experiment but still refuses to throw away his filters.

JEAN CHAUVENET (NUITS ST.-GEORGES)* * * *

1990	Nuits St.-Georges	C	86
1989	Nuits St.-Georges	C	79
1990	Nuits St.-Georges Les Bousselots	D	90
1989	Nuits St.-Georges Les Bousselots	D	86
1990	Nuits St.-Georges Les Vaucrains	D	92
1989	Nuits St.-Georges Les Vaucrains	D	87

Chauvenet's 1990 Nuits St.-Georges displays wonderful sweetness, a ripe, black fruit character, medium body, an opulent texture, and a long finish. Drink it over the next 5–6 years. The 1990 Nuits St.-Georges Les Bousselots possesses a dark color and a huge nose of black cherries and black raspberries. Moreover, the wine exhibits jammy ripeness, low acidity, superb concentration, and a heady, rich, luxurious finish. This wine should drink well for the next 10–12 years. The enormous truffle-, black raspberry-, peppery-, and clove-scented nose of the 1990 Nuits St.-Georges Les Vaucrains is exceptional. This full-bodied, rich, expansive wine is crammed with extract. The finish is deep, spicy, and moderately tannic. Drink it between 1994 and 2007. Chauvenet's 1989s include a tannic, austerely styled 1989 Nuits St.-Georges. The 1989 Nuits St.-Georges Les Bousselots offers up abundant quantities of supple, ripe, juicy, succulent fruitiness. The wine possesses glycerin, medium body, good purity, and a tender finish. Drink it over the next 5–6 years. The 1989 Nuits St.-Georges Les Vaucrains exhibits an earthy, black truffle–scented nose intertwined with black fruit aromas. It is sweet, expansive, and richly fruity, with soft tannins and a heady finish. Drink it over the next 7–8 years.

OTHER THOUGHTS: Vivid, pure, rich, concentrated wines that have explosive levels of fruit.

ROBERT CHEVILLON (NUITS ST.-GEORGES)* * * *

1990	Bourgogne Rouge	C	82
1990	Nuits St.-Georges	D	80
1990	Nuits St.-Georges Les Cailles	D	88
1989	Nuits St.-Georges Les Chaignots	D	85
1989	Nuits St.-Georges La Perrière	D	78
1990	Nuits St.-Georges Les Roncières	D	81
1989	Nuits St.-Georges Les St.-Georges	D	88
1990	Nuits St.-Georges Les Vaucrains	D	90+
1989	Nuits St.-Georges Les Vaucrains	D	88

Chevillon's wines are user-friendly, exhibiting authentic Pinot aromas and flavors. If they rarely dazzle, they usually don't disappoint. The elegant, fruity 1990 Nuits St.-Georges Les Roncières offers moderately intense aromas of blackberries and toasty oak. It is medium bodied, soft, and ideal for drinking over the next 5–7 years. A more serious wine, the 1990 Nuits St.-Georges Les Cailles is deeply colored, with a rich, spicy, herb- and black cherry–scented nose, medium body, good structure and definition, decent acidity, and rich flavors. Drink it between 1994 and 2002. Chevillon's 1990 Nuits St.-Georges Les Vaucrains is a blockbuster red burgundy, with sensational concentration, a saturated purple color, a huge, smoky, peppery, overripe plum-scented nose, and medium-bodied, unctuous, thick flavors that nearly conceal the tannin. Although it can be drunk now, it will be even more enthralling after 2–3 years in the cellar. It should last for a decade. The 1989 Nuits St.-Georges La Perrière offers sweet, earthy fruit in its nose, a ripe, tasty palate, and low acidity in the finish. Drink it over the next 3–4 years. The 1989 Nuits St.-Georges Les Chaignots is tightly knit and structured, with some of the smoky, earthy Nuits character in the nose, but it is too tight and hard. At least 2–3 years of cellaring is recommended. The two best *cuvées* I have ever tasted from Chevillon include the 1989 Nuits St.-Georges Les Vaucrains, with its huge, oaky, earthy, smoky nose, ripe, concentrated flavors, medium body, soft tannins, and decent acidity. It should drink deliciously for at least a decade. The 1989 Nuits St.-Georges Les St.-Georges exhibits a more opaque color, more black fruits than smoky earth aromas, and deep, rich, concentrated flavors. Drink it between 1994 and 2000.

OTHER THOUGHTS: Excellent producer, but my experience suggests that the wines, so flashy in cask, rarely live up to their potential when fully mature.

CHÉZEAUX (MOREY ST.-DENIS)* * * */* * * * *

1990	Chambertin	EEE	95
1990	Chambolle-Musigny Les Charmes	E	87
1990	Clos St.-Denis	EE	98

1990 Gevrey-Chambertin	D	87
1990 Gevrey-Chambertin Premier Cru	E	89
1990 Griotte-Chambertin	EEE	98

All of these offerings possess exceptional concentration and that rich mid-palate and length that so many modern-day burgundies frequently lack (primarily because of early picking, high yields, short macerations, and excessive fining and filtration). The 1990 Gevrey-Chambertin boasts an opaque dark ruby/garnet color, a huge nose of jammy black fruits, herbs, and licorice, and a long, opulent, splendidly concentrated finish. Drink it over the next 7–8 years. The 1990 Gevrey-Chambertin Premier Cru offers an earthy, smoked meat, animal sort of nose. This full-bodied wine has exceptional richness, black cherry flavors, gobs of glycerin, and a dense, powerful, moderately tannic finish. It should last for at least 7–10 years. The 1990 Chambolle-Musigny Les Charmes is a lighter-style, more elegant wine. More floral, with a medium to dark ruby color, this round, generously endowed, lush Pinot should be drunk over the next 7–8 years. The 1990 Griotte-Chambertin rivals that made by Maurice and Claude Dugat. Nearly black in color, the wine offers up extraordinarily rich aromas of black cherries, flowers, and truffles. The wine is stunningly rich, viscous, and chewy, with full body, tons of glycerin, and a super finish. Drink it between 1995 and 2010. Even more flattering is the mind-blowing 1990 Clos St.-Denis. The bouquet soars from the glass, offering a veritable smorgasbord of aromas from new oak and black plums to cinnamon, coffee, and beef. The wine is softer and less powerful than the Griotte-Chambertin but awesomely rich, with a nectarlike essence. The 1990 Chambertin does not possess the unctuous, weighty richness and fragrance of either the Griotte or Clos St.-Denis, but it is still a generously endowed, amazingly rich wine, with a broad-shouldered, flashy, expansive texture, profound concentration, and a sweet fragrance of jammy black fruits, earth, and minerals. It should last for 2 decades.

OTHER THOUGHTS: Awesome wines in the best vintages (1980, 1985, 1990), shameful ones in other years (1984, 1986, 1987).

CHOPIN-GROFFIER (PRÉMEAUX)* * * *

1989 Chambolle-Musigny	C	87
1990 Clos Vougeot	E	92
1989 Clos Vougeot	E	94
1990 Nuits St.-Georges	D	86
1989 Nuits St.-Georges	D	87
1990 Nuits St.-Georges Les Chaignots	D	90
1989 Nuits St.-Georges Les Chaignots	D	90
1990 Vougeot	D	88
1989 Vougeot	D	89

Chopin's wines boast extraordinary purity of fruit and that wonderfully vibrant fragrance that only Pinot Noir can achieve. Chopin's 1990s are loaded with luscious, sweet, succulent fruit that will provide immensely seductive drinking over the next decade. For starters there is an elegant, berry-scented, ripe, medium- to full-bodied, soft, and tasty 1990 Nuits St.-Georges. The stunning 1990 Nuits St.-Georges Les Chaignots reveals a beautifully fragrant nose of black fruits, herbs, licorice, and damp earth. The finish displays sweet, jammy Pinot fruit, a touch of toasty new oak, and gobs of glycerin and alcohol. Drink it over the next 7–8 years. The 1990 Vougeot possesses more noticeable tannin, but who can ignore the brilliantly defined bouquet of red and black fruits, sweet oak, and fruitcake? It will benefit from 1–2 years of cellaring and should drink well for at least a decade. Chopin's 1990 Clos Vougeot offers up masses of ripe, jammy black fruit intermingled with scents of toast, smoke, and vanillin. This splendidly rich, full-bodied wine displays cascades of fruit that I am sure conceal considerable tannin. As tempting as it might be to drink this wine now, past experience indicates this wine will improve for 5–7 years. It should last for 12–15 years. Chopin's 1989s are smashing successes. The 1989 Nuits St.-Georges exhibits abundant quantities of superripe berry fruit touched gently by sweet, vanillin, new oak. The wine is all velvet and silk, with low acidity and a round, generous finish. Drink it over the next 7–8 years. The lighter 1989 Chambolle-Musigny is more velvet textured. The color is dark ruby, and the nose offers floral, berry, and sweet, earthy smells. It will not make old bones, but for drinking over the next 5–6 years, it offers a hedonistic mouthful. The 1989 Vougeot raises the extraction level and offers abundant, lavish quantities of sweet, jammy, ripe, black fruits. This gorgeously structured, smooth, ripe, concentrated wine suggests immediate drinkability. Drink this beauty over the next decade. The 1989 Nuits St.-Georges Les Chaignots possesses an earthy, trufflelike *terroir* character in its black fruit–dominated nose. There is explosive richness, great ripeness and length, and spectacular purity and focus. Drink this charming, powerful, and concentrated wine over the next 10–12 years. The 1989 Clos Vougeot is magnificent. The color is dark ruby, the nose redolent with smells of blackberries, spices, new oak, and minerals. This is a wine of lavish concentration and presence, a fabulous finish, and a multidimensional personality. Drink it over the next 10–12 years.

OTHER THOUGHTS: The wines taste as if Henri Jayer made them—brilliant for near- and midterm drinking.

BRUNO CLAIR (MARSANNAY)* * * *

1990 Chambertin-Clos de Bèze	E	87
1989 Chambertin-Clos de Bèze	E	90
1990 Gevrey-Chambertin Les Cazetiers	E	88
1989 Gevrey-Chambertin Les Cazetiers	E	88
1990 Gevrey-Chambertin-Clos de Fonteny	D	86
1989 Gevrey-Chambertin-Clos de Fonteny	D	86
1990 Gevrey-Chambertin-Clos St.-Jacques	C	89
1989 Gevrey-Chambertin-Clos St.-Jacques	E	89
1990 Marsannay Casse-Tête	D	86

1990	Marsannay Les Longeroies	C	84
1989	Marsannay Les Longeroies	C	85
1990	Marsannay-Vaudenelles	C	84
1989	Marsannay-Vaudenelles	C	76
1990	Morey St.-Denis	C	83
1989	Morey St.-Denis	C	85
1989	Savigny-Lès-Beaune Les Dominaudes	C	85
1990	Vosne-Romanée Les Champs Perdrix	D	81
1989	Vosne-Romanée Les Champs Perdrix	D	75

Bruno Clair's stylish, elegant 1990s include a soft, tasty, fruity 1990 Marsannay Casse-Tête. It should provide easy drinking early on and last for 7–8 years. Clair's 1990 Gevrey-Chambertin-Clos de Fonteny is a sweet, round, spicy wine with a dark fruit character, medium body, and moderate tannins. Drink it over the next 7–8 years. Richer, with higher levels of tannins and more opulence and fragrance is the 1990 Gevrey-Chambertin Les Cazetiers. Seductive, full, and rich, it will make delicious drinking for the next decade. Bruno Clair's best 1990 is his Gevrey-Chambertin-Clos St.-Jacques. A huge nose of black cherries, herbs, new oak, and minerals zooms from the glass. Deep and medium to full bodied, with low acidity, moderate tannins, and fine extract, this wine should continue to drink well for 7–10 years. The 1990 Chambertin-Clos de Bèze is medium bodied and relatively restrained, with good ripeness, attractive levels of extract, and moderate tannins. Although the 1989 Marsannay-Vaudenelles is light and high in acidity, behind the tartness is decent fruit. Drink it over the next 2–3 years. The 1989 Marsannay Les Longeroies exhibits deeper color and more ripeness, as well as an interesting, earthy, berry-scented nose. Medium bodied and spicy, it is ideal for current consumption. The 1989 Morey St.-Denis is an elegant, tasty, round wine, with soft tannins, decent acidity, and an attractive minerallike, berry fruitiness backed up by a subtle touch of new oak. I was disappointed with the 1989 Vosne-Romanée Les Champs Perdrix, as it displayed some oxidized, old tea aromas. It requires immediate consumption. The 1989 Savigny-Lès-Beaune Les Dominaudes is deeply colored, and the nose exhibits aromas of flowers, earth, and black fruits. Drink it over the next 4–7 years. The 1989 Gevrey-Chambertin-Clos de Fonteny reveals richness, a sense of elegance, medium body, and soft tannins. The 1989 Gevrey-Chambertin Les Cazetiers is deeper and more dominated by the scent of minerals and animal smells. With big, ripe berry fruit flavors, and soft tannins in the finish, it should drink well for 7–8 years. The 1989 Gevrey-Chambertin-Clos St.-Jacques exhibits a gorgeous nose of superripe red fruits. There is excellent concentration, plenty of charm, the smooth, supple concentration that the 1989s so frequently offer, and plenty of glycerin, alcohol, and fruit. Drink it over the next 7–8 years. The biggest, most backward wine from Bruno Clair is the 1989 Chambertin-Clos de Bèze. The nose smells of vanilla, black cherries, and flowers. The wine displays more tannin than the other offerings, as well as noticeable body and length. It is capable of lasting for up to a decade.

OTHER THOUGHTS: Thoughtful, impeccable winemaker needs to take more risks if greatness is to be achieved.

YVON CLERGET (VOLNAY)* * *

1990	Bourgogne Rouge	C	75
1990	Pommard Les Rugiens	D	85+
1990	Volnay Les Caillerets	D	85
1990	Volnay Carelle Sous La Chapelle	D	77
1990	Volnay-Clos du Verseuil	D	82+
1990	Volnay Premier Cru	D	78
1990	Volnay Santenots	D	85+

The three finest wines I tasted include a stylish, elegant, spicy, but woody and tannic, 1990 Volnay Santenots. It exhibits adequate ripeness, medium weight, and plenty of structure and grip. It will benefit from 5–6 years of cellaring and has the potential to last for more than a decade. The 1990 Volnay Les Caillerets also displays significant tannin. In addition to an attractive red fruit nose intertwined with aromas of oak and earth, there is fine ripeness, a medium-bodied feel in the mouth, and considerable hardness in the finish. The tough-textured 1990 Pommard Les Rugiens is medium to full bodied, with a hard, astringent finish. It should be cellared for at least 5 years.
OTHER THOUGHTS: Why do other people see more in these wines than I?

CLOS FRANTIN-BICHOT (BEAUNE)* */* * *

1990	Chambertin	E	87
1989	Chambertin	E	79
1990	Clos Vougeot	E	86
1989	Clos Vougeot	E	84
1990	Echézeaux	E	85
1989	Echézeaux	E	75
1990	Grands Echézeaux	E	87
1989	Grands Echézeaux	E	83
1990	Vosne-Romanée	E	81
1990	Vosne-Romanée Les Malconsorts	E	85
1989	Vosne-Romanée Les Malconsorts	E	79

The 1990 Vosne-Romanée Les Malconsorts is a sweet, round, agreeable, medium-bodied wine, with an attractive, light perfume and a straightforward finish. The light, soft 1990 Echézeaux is fruity and clean, with a short finish. The 1990 Clos Vougeot exhibits more depth, as well as an attractive deep ruby color, acceptable intensity, and a moderately long and tannic finish. Drink it between 1994 and 2000. The 1990 Grands Echézeaux offers up aromas of spice and superripe plums. The wine is medium bodied, with fine richness, a chewy, glycerin-imbued texture, and moderate tannins in the good to very good finish. Drink it over the next 7–8 years. Bichot's 1990 Chambertin reveals a medium to dark ruby color and an attractive nose of new oak and black cherries. On the palate the wine is ripe, with good richness, spicy oak, and a pleasant finish. Drink it over the next 7–8 years. All the 1989s lacked noses and were compact, sterile, and innocuous, with little or no complexity. The best of the group included a compact, still ripe, fruity 1989 Clos Vougeot and a tasty, expansive, sweet 1989 Grands Echézeaux. Even that wine displayed a muted nose, no doubt from having been nearly destroyed at bottling.

OTHER THOUGHTS: An extraordinary estate with fabulous vineyards and a great winemaker are all negated by *négociant* Bichot's insistence on sterile filtering these gems at bottling.

COCHE-BIZOUARD (MEURSAULT)* * *

1989 Auxey-Duresses	C	85
1989 Meursault Rouge	C	87
1989 Monthélie Les Duresses	C	87
1989 Pommard La Platière	D	88

The 1989 Meursault Rouge ranks with the finest red wines I have ever tasted from this appellation, which is more renowned for its nutty, buttery, opulent white wines. It exhibits a deep opaque color and amazingly rich, red fruit flavors backed up by lavish quantities of vanillin-scented new oak. Soft and luscious, it is ideal for drinking over the next 5–7 years. The 1989 Auxey-Duresses avoids the toughness, hardness, and sometimes overwhelmingly earthy character of this appellation. It is a round, generously endowed, supple Pinot Noir, supported nicely by new oak. Drink it over the next 5–6 years. The 1989 Monthélie Les Duresses is a delicious wine. The deep ruby/purple color is followed by a nose of sweet, ripe Pinot fruit married with generous amounts of new oak. The wine displays layer upon layer of Pinot fruit, soft acids, and good tannins in its long, heady, lusciously ripe finish. The 1989 Pommard La Platière is terrific. This wine is extremely backward, powerful, and concentrated. It exhibits a promising nose of new oak, herbs, black fruits, and minerals. Drink it between 1994 and 2005.

OTHER THOUGHTS: Monsieur Coche has made enormous progress in red-wine making.

J. F. COCHE-DURY (MEURSAULT)* * */* * * *

1989 Auxey-Duresses	C	87
1990 Bourgogne	C	85
1990 Meursault	C	87
1989 Volnay	C	85

The excellent 1989 Auxey-Duresses exhibits a deep, opaque, ruby color, a richly fruity nose, solid glycerin-laden flavors, good body, and a long finish. It should continue to drink well for 7–8 years. The 1989 Volnay is tight and backward. It did display promising perfume, richness, and personality and may well evolve into something special with 2–3 more years of bottle age, making my rating look conservative. Jean-François Coche-Dury's 1990 Bourgogne is a gentle, soft, richly fruity wine that will make delicious drinking over the next 3–4 years. The bigger, richer 1990 Meursault possesses a saturated purple color, a lovely perfume of plums and toasty oak, and a long, luscious, opulent finish. Drink it over the next 7–8 years.

OTHER THOUGHTS: The king of white burgundy deserves greater red wine vineyards given his unlimited talent.

JEAN-JACQUES CONFURON (PRÉMEAUX)* * *

1990	Nuits St.-Georges Les Chaboeufs	D	93
1990	Romanée St.-Vivant	EE	96

The exceptionally concentrated 1990 Nuits St.-Georges Les Chaboeufs boasts an opaque black/purple color and a sensational nose of roasted black cherries and spicy, toasty new oak. It tastes as if it were the essence of Pinot Noir. There are considerable tannins in the long, impressive finish. It will keep for 12–15 years. Confuron's 1990 Romanée St.-Vivant offers up a huge nose of flowers, licorice, sweet oak, and extraordinarily ripe black cherries and black raspberries. The wine is closed, but its huge, weighty, massive extraction of fruit, decent acidity, and blazingly well-defined personality make for a compelling example of Pinot Noir. Drink it between 1995 and 2012.

OTHER THOUGHTS: The dreadful wines of the early 1980s are history—an estate to watch.

J. CONFURON-COTETIDOT (VOSNE-ROMANÉE)* * * *

1990	Bourgogne Rouge	C	82
1990	Chambolle-Musigny	D	86
1990	Clos Vougeot	E	92
1990	Echézeaux	E	91
1990	Gevrey-Chambertin	D	85
1990	Nuits St.-Georges	D	87
1990	Nuits St.-Georges Premier Cru	D	90
1990	Vosne-Romanée	D	85
1990	Vosne-Romanée Les Suchots	D	87

The hedonistic, rich, plummy, sweet 1990 Nuits St.-Georges is ideal for drinking over the next 5–6 years. It boasts admirable richness and density as well as soft tannins. The 1990 Vosne-Romanée is lighter and more elegant, yet not as concentrated. The 1990 Gevrey-Chambertin is more woody, but extremely ripe and tasty, with excellent fruit and a long, medium-bodied, concentrated finish. Along with the Nuits St.-Georges, the best of the villages wines is the 1990 Chambolle-Musigny. It reveals a deep ruby color, a big, jammy, flowery nose, and ripe, medium-bodied, unctuously textured flavors. It should drink well for 7–8 years. Confuron's Vosne-Romanée Les Suchots exhibits a relatively light color for a 1990. The nose offers up sweet aromas of herbs and cherries. There is medium body, a round texture, and a supple finish. Drink it over the next 7–8 years. Confuron's Nuits St.-Georges Premier Cru generally takes a backseat to the Vosne-Romanée Les Suchots. The 1990 is a wine of extraordinary richness, with a dark, almost saturated ruby/purple color. Huge aromas of jammy plums, minerals, and spices jump from the glass. Highly extracted, with an opulent texture, this outstanding wine exhibits low acidity and soft tannins. It will keep for 10–12 years. The 1990 Echézeaux is slightly lighter than the Nuits St.-Georges Premier Cru, but its beautiful ruby/purple color, its sweet nose of cassis, herbs, and flowers, and its long, heady, admirably endowed finish make for a sumptuous mouthful. Drink it over the next decade. The dark ruby-colored 1990 Clos Vougeot possesses a huge nose of black fruits and spicy oak. There is formidable intensity, medium to full body, soft tannins, low acidity, and a finish that must last for nearly a minute. It can be drunk now or cellared for 10–12 years.

OTHER THOUGHTS: Monsieur Confuron has the vineyards and the proper wine-making philosophy, but his personality can make a visit painful.

DOMAINE EDMOND CORNU (LADOIX-SERRIGNY)* * *

1990 Aloxe-Corton	C	82
1990 Aloxe-Corton Les Moutottes	D	85
1990 Chorey-Lès-Beaune Les Bons Ores	C	84
1990 Corton Les Bressandes	E	89
1990 Ladoix	C	79
1990 Ladoix Les Corvées	D	87+
1990 Savigny-Lès-Beaune	C	77

The saturated color of the 1990 Ladoix Les Corvées is followed by a nose that offers up aromas of roasted red and black fruits, spicy oak, and herbs. Rich and full bodied, with oodles of ripe fruit, this lush, expansively flavored wine should drink well for up to a decade. Cornu's 1990 Aloxe-Corton Les Moutottes is a slightly harder wine, with less concentration and a more austere style. Although well made, with good ripeness and balance, it requires 1–2 years of cellaring; it should last for 7–8 years. Cornu's finest wine is his Corton Les Bressandes. The 1990 possesses a deep ruby color, a sweet nose of black fruits, dense, full-bodied, black cherry and curranty flavors, high tannins, and a spicy, long, well-balanced finish. Approachable now, it should be cellared for 2–3 years. It will evolve gracefully for at least 10–15 years.

OTHER THOUGHTS: Reliable producer trying hard in some little-known appellations.

COSTE-CAUMARTIN (POMMARD)* * *

1990 Pommard	C	86
1989 Pommard	C	82
1990 Pommard-Clos des Boucherottes	C	90
1989 Pommard-Clos des Boucherottes	C	87
1990 Pommard Les Fremiers	C	87
1989 Pommard Les Fremiers	C	86

The 1990 Pommard possesses a thick, deep ruby color and a spicy, earthy nose with cherry notes in the background. Full bodied, dense, and powerful, with formidable levels of tannin, this chunky, robust wine should be at its best between 1995 and 2006. The 1990 Pommard Les Fremiers is nearly black in color, with a nose of smoked meat, earth, and black fruits. Spicy, with gobs of tannin as well as impressive quantities of fruit, this rough-and-tumble wine needs at least 4–5 years of cellaring. **Anticipated maturity: 1996–2007.** The outstanding 1990 Pommard-Clos des Boucherottes exhibits an opaque, saturated ruby/purple color and a splendid but unevolved nose of jammy black cherry fruit intertwined with aromas of cloves, saddle leather, and damp earth. Awesomely concentrated, full bodied, and intense, with mouth-searing tannins, this large-scale, forceful wine needs 5–8 years of cellaring. **Anticipated maturity: 1997–2010.** With respect to the 1989 vintage, the 1989 Pommard-Clos des Boucherottes appears to have the best potential, but keep in mind that a 10-year wait is in order for this wine to shed its considerable tannins. If the fruit holds up, it may well turn out to be an outstanding wine.

OTHER THOUGHTS: Old-style, rustic, brutally tannic wines that should be bought only by those capable of deferring their gratification.

MARIUS DELARCHE (PERNAND-VERGELESSES)* * *

1990 Corton Les Rénardes	E	92
1990 Pernand-Vergelesses Les Vergelesses	D	86

Delarche's 1990 Corton Les Rénardes is sensational, with a stunning perfume of black cherries, toasty new oak, minerals, and spices. Exceptionally full bodied, with dazzling concentration and plenty of extract and glycerin, this broad-shouldered, macho wine possesses soft tannins and a long, rich, juicy finish. Approachable now, it should age beautifully for at least 12–15 years.

OTHER THOUGHTS: Uneven producer tends to score big with his Corton Les Rénardes in top years such as 1985 and 1990.

JOSEPH DROUHIN (BEAUNE)* * *

1990 Aloxe-Corton	C	82
1990 Beaune-Clos des Mouches	D	88
1990 Charmes-Chambertin	EE	90
1990 Chorey-Lès-Beaune	B	86
1990 Clos Vougeot	EE	88
1990 Pommard	C	80
1990 Pommard Les Epenots	E	87
1990 Savigny-Lès-Beaune	C	80
1990 Savigny-Lès-Beaune Les Serpentières	D	86
1990 Volnay	C	83
1990 Volnay Clos des Chênes	D	89

The supple 1990 Chorey-Lès-Beaune is an ideal wine for restaurants looking for a soft, authentic red burgundy with plenty of jammy cherry and strawberry fruit. Drink it over the next 4–5 years. The medium ruby-colored 1990 Savigny-Lès-Beaune Les Serpentières has a closed nose of earthy, cherry, dried pit

fruit aromas. Medium bodied, with fine extract and fruit, as well as more noticeable tannins, this wine can be drunk now, although it would benefit from
1–2 years of cellaring. It should last for 8–10 years. Drouhin does a marvelous
job with his Beaune-Clos des Mouches. The 1990, which is one of the best he
has made during the last decade, exhibits a medium dark ruby color. The nose
reveals copious quantities of red and black fruits nicely married with smoky,
toasty new oak. The wonderful sweet, jammy fruit of the 1990 vintage is abundantly displayed. The velvety finish includes some round tannins. This wine
will continue to improve for 5–7 years. Slightly more impressive is the 1990
Volnay Clos des Chênes. The darkest colored of all the Drouhin 1990 Côte de
Beaunes, this is an impeccably made, exceptionally rich wine with excellent
delineation to its flavors and impressive intensity. The wine's black cherry
fruit is nicely supported by toasty new oak. The spicy, earthy 1990 Pommard
Les Epenots exhibits plenty of power, as well as more tannin, body, and ripe
fruit. This wine should evolve gracefully for another 7–8 years. The best wine
is the 1990 Charmes-Chambertin, a superrich, elequant, supple wine to drink
over the next 6–12 years.
OTHER THOUGHTS: A classic study in "play it safe" winemaking results in very
good but rarely sublime wines.

DUBREUIL-FONTAINE ET FILS (PERNAND-VERGELESSES)* * *

1990 Corton Les Bressandes	E	89
1990 Corton-Clos du Roi	E	90+
1990 Pernand-Vergelesses Île de Vergelesses	D	85
1990 Pommard Les Epenots	D	86+
1990 Savigny-Lès-Beaune Les Vergelesses	D	86

The 1990 Pernand-Vergelesses Île de Vergelesses exhibits an excellent
plummy color, a big, spicy, oaky, earthy nose, fine flavor extraction, and a
chunky, chewy finish. Slightly more impressive is the 1990 Savigny-Lès-
Beaune Les Vergelesses. The color has a purple hue, and the sweet nose of
cherries, oak, and herbs is enticing. This medium-bodied wine displays fine
structure, concentration, and balance, as well as soft tannins and low acid in
the lusty finish. Rich, heady, and lusty, the 1990 Corton Les Bressandes offers
a deep ruby color, a multidimensional, rich, medium- to full-bodied palate, a
viscous texture, and an attractive sweet, expansive, satiny smooth finish. The
dark-colored 1990 Pommard Les Epenots is closed, giving up vague aromas of
sweet new oak and ripe, earthy, plummy fruit. This broad-shouldered, well-
endowed wine reveals considerable tannin. The 1990 Corton-Clos du Roi exhibits a saturated dark ruby/purple color. Its promising nose of jammy black
cherries and smoky new oak and its full-bodied, thick, ripe, concentrated flavors suggest 3–5 years of cellaring is warranted.
OTHER THOUGHTS: Elegance and finesse are these wines' virtues.

BERNARD ET PIERRE DUGAT (GEVREY-CHAMBERTIN)* * * *

1990 Charmes-Chambertin	E	87
1990 Gevrey-Chambertin Vieilles Vignes	D	85

Bernard Dugat's 1990 Gevrey-Chambertin Vieilles Vignes possesses attractive jammy fruit, a pleasant, medium-bodied, round texture, surprising evidence of toasty new oak, and a juicy finish. Drink it over the next 4–5 years. The Charmes-Chambertin reveals spicy oak in its elegant, well-defined, berry-scented nose. In the mouth the wine is medium bodied, with fine concentration, soft acids, and a spicy, moderately tannic finish. It will benefit from 1–2 years of cellaring and should keep for up to a decade.

OTHER THOUGHTS: Stylish, rich wines that exhibit a sure hand.

CLAUDE ET MAURICE DUGAT (GEVREY-CHAMBERTIN)* * * * *

1990 Charmes-Chambertin	E	96
1990 Gevrey-Chambertin Lavaux St.-Jacques	D	92
1990 Gevrey-Chambertin Premier Cru	D	89
1990 Griotte-Chambertin	E	99

The 1990 Gevrey-Chambertin Premier Cru boasts a terrific saturated color as well as a fragrant nose of jammy black fruits, smoke, roasted nuts, and cinnamon. Full yet wonderfully supple, this medium- to full-bodied, lusciously textured wine should be drunk over the next 7–8 years. The 1990 Gevrey-Chambertin Lavaux St.-Jacques reveals a fabulous, opaque, dark ruby/purple color. The nose offers up the essence of Pinot Noir in its bouquet of black fruits, minerals, flowers, and a woodsy, damp underbrush aroma. The subtle vanillin scent of new oak can be detected, but what one finds in abundance is an extraordinary, voluptuous, rich, superconcentrated wine with low acidity, gobs of fruit and glycerin, and a phenomenally long finish. The Charmes-Chambertin and Griotte-Chambertin are magnificent. The 1990 Charmes-Chambertin is so concentrated, voluptuous, and chewy that the overall impression is one of layer upon layer of sweet, jammy Pinot fruit crammed into a wine that fills and coats the mouth with such purity and intensity that it has to be tasted to be believed. Approachable now, it should drink well for the next 10–12 years. The 1990 Griotte-Chambertin is even richer and longer. The phenomenally sweet, opulent extraction of fruit is complemented lightly by toasty new oak. The result is a massive yet exceptionally concentrated, supple wine that exhibits a whoppingly long finish. It will last for 10–15 years.

OTHER THOUGHTS: Only the Domaine de la Romanée-Conti makes more flamboyant and exciting red burgundies than these Dugats.

DOMAINE DUJAC (MOREY ST.-DENIS)* * * * *

1990 Bonnes Mares	E	94
1989 Bonnes Mares	E	87
1990 Charmes-Chambertin	E	91
1989 Charmes-Chambertin	E	89
1990 Clos de la Roche	E	93
1989 Clos de la Roche	E	90
1990 Clos St.-Denis	E	93
1989 Clos St.-Denis	E	89

1990 Echézeaux	E	89
1989 Echézeaux	E	87
1990 Gevrey-Chambertin aux Combottes	E	90
1989 Gevrey-Chambertin aux Combottes	E	89
1989 Morey St.-Denis	D	86

The 1990 Gevrey-Chambertin aux Combottes is medium to dark ruby in color, with a superripe, expansive bouquet of jammy fruit, cinnamon, and roasted nuts. It is voluptuously textured, with round, juicy, succulent fruit and a spicy, velvety, full-bodied finish. Drink it over the next 7–8 years. The 1990 Charmes-Chambertin has a slightly deeper ruby color and a stunningly complex, open nose of herbs, black fruits, and smoky oak. Densely concentrated and full bodied, it is elegant, fat, and rich. I found Dujac's 1990 Echézeaux to possess an attractive raspberry- and floral-scented nose, medium-bodied, soft, stylish flavors, low acidity, and light tannins. Drink it over the next 7–8 years. The 1990 Clos St.-Denis exhibits a complex, sweet, earthy, berry, herb, and smoky nose, voluptuous, rich, chewy flavors, and a well-defined, long finish that reveals a moderate tannin level beneath the copious quantities of sweet fruit. Unquestionably the 1990 Clos de la Roche is darker in color, bigger framed, and fuller bodied. Again, the nectar, honeylike texture of the 1990 vintage is well displayed. The wine is superbly concentrated, with a huge fragrance and long, moderately tannic, sweet flavors. The 1990 Bonnes Mares enjoys the most saturated, deep ruby color and a tightly knit, closed nose, which, with coaxing, offers up smells of meat, soy, sweet black fruits, and toasty vanillin oak. It is splendidly rich and well delineated, with full body, exceptional extraction of flavor, impeccable balance, and a long, deep finish. It should be at its best between 1995 and 2008. The 1989 Morey St.-Denis exhibits an expansive, sweet, berry- and toast-scented nose, round, moderately endowed flavors, and a smooth, velvety finish. The 1989 Gevrey-Chambertin aux Combottes shares the same sweet, vanillin, superripe berry fruit nose, with open-knit, round, generously endowed flavors and a soft, low-acid finish. Since there is not much tannin, I would opt for drinking it now. The meatier, more structured 1989 Charmes-Chambertin is deeper in color, with more tannin in the finish. The 1989 Clos de la Roche exhibited a smoked meat, earthy, ripe nose, superb richness on the palate, low acidity, and a long, moderately tannic, clean finish. Drinkable now, it should continue to evolve for at least 7–8 years. The 1989 Clos St.-Denis offered aromas of smoky fruit, new oak, and a pleasant trufflelike earthiness. In the mouth it was round, generously endowed, supple, and fruity. Drink it over the next 5–7 years. Dujac's 1989 Echézeaux, the lightest cuvée, is an elegant, understated, soft-textured wine that should make delicious drinking over the next 3–4 years. The 1989 Bonnes Mares exhibited a tight but spicy bouquet of earthy, berry-flavored fruit, decent acidity, and firm tannins in the wine's finish.

OTHER THOUGHTS: Never judge Pinot Noir by its color; Dujac's pale-colored Pinots pack dramatic bouquets and explosive flavors in top years such as 1969, 1978, 1985, 1989, and 1990.

MAURICE ECARD ET FILS (SAVIGNY-LÈS-BEAUNE)* * * *

1990 Savigny-Lès-Beaune Les Jarrons	D	87
1990 Savigny-Lès-Beaune Les Narbantons	D	88
1990 Savigny-Lès-Beaune Les Peuillets	D	85
1990 Savigny-Lès-Beaune Les Serpentières	D	90

Over the years, Ecard has produced stylish and underrated red burgundies. His 1990s are excellent. The 1990 Les Narbantons exhibits a deep, dark ruby color, an intense nose of spices and black cherries, a structured, long, ripe finish, and enough tannin and acidity to suggest it will age for 10–12 years. The 1990 Les Serpentières is as good a red burgundy as you can find in Savigny-Lès-Beaune. The huge nose of jammy red and black fruits, spices, and minerals is followed by a deep, superbly rich, powerful wine with decent acidity and a long, fleshy, rich finish. It should drink well for at least 12–15 years. The 1990 Savigny-Lès-Beaune Les Peuillets is a straightforward, attractive, moderately endowed wine. More of the appellation's earthy undertone is present, but I enjoyed its ripe fruitiness, medium body, and crisp finish. Drink it over the next 5–6 years. Ecard's 1990 Savigny-Lès-Beaune Les Jarrons displays a smoky, herb- and berry-scented nose, suave, graceful, fleshy flavors, medium body, and an excellent finish. Forward enough to be drunk, it should age gracefully for another 7–8 years.

OTHER THOUGHTS: A name to trust when looking for authentic Pinot Noir on a budget.

DOMAINE RENÉ ENGEL (VOSNE-ROMANÉE)* * * *

1990 Clos Vougeot	E	88
1989 Clos Vougeot	E	86
1990 Echézeaux	E	86
1989 Echézeaux	E	86
1990 Grands Echézeaux	E	90
1989 Grands Echézeaux	E	89
1990 Vosne-Romanée	D	82
1989 Vosne-Romanée	D	84
1990 Vosne-Romanée Les Brûlées	D	87
1989 Vosne-Romanée Les Brûlées	D	87

Although the 1990 Vosne-Romanée Les Brûlées is less dramatic than many wines from this vineyard, it exhibits fine richness, soft tannins, elegance, and a round, generous, fleshy finish. I would opt for drinking it over the next 6–7 years. The 1990 Echézeaux is typically light and well delineated, with excellent ripeness, medium body, and a floral-, raspberry-, and cherry-scented nose with subtle oak in the background. It, too, requires drinking in its first 6–7 years. I was immensely impressed with the lavish black cherry and plum fruitiness of the 1990 Clos Vougeot. It is a fuller-bodied wine, unctuous, yet medium bodied, with fine power and definition. The best wine from Engel is his elegant, soft, deeply colored 1990 Grands Echézeaux. Soft, fragrant, and evolved, with the color already showing some lightening at the edge, it should be drunk over the next 5–6 years. The light 1989 Vosne-Romanée offers sweet, opulent, soft fruit. One of the stars for Engel in 1989 is the smoky, intense, richly fruity, generously endowed 1989 Vosne-Romanée Les Brûlées. Drink this beauty over the next 5–6 years for its gorgeous, lavish amounts of fruit and spice. Engel's 1989 Echézeaux is stylish and light bodied, with a medium ruby color and a subtle, pleasant perfume of red fruits and flowers. I saw the same lightness and lack of depth in the 1989 Clos Vougeot. Although there is good berry fruit, the wine's midrange does not possess enough depth. The 1989 Grands Echézeaux reveals a much deeper color, a big, raspberry, spicy nose, and soft, velvety-textured, smooth flavors. The acidity is low, and there is elevated alcohol, but this is a delicious, up-front, flattering style of red burgundy. OTHER THOUGHTS: A very good estate that has the potential to produce great wines. But will it?

M. FRÉDÉRIC ESMONIN (GEVREY-CHAMBERTIN)* * * *

1989	Gevrey-Chambertin Estournelles St.-Jacques	E	84
1990	Gevrey-Chambertin Lavaux St.-Jacques	E	86
1990	Griotte-Chambertin	E	86
1989	Griotte-Chambertin	E	83
1990	Mazis-Chambertin	E	87
1989	Mazis-Chambertin	E	85
1990	Ruchottes-Chambertin	E	85
1989	Ruchottes-Chambertin	E	84

The 1990 Gevrey-Chambertin Lavaux St.-Jacques is a backward, moderately tannic wine with a closed nose but good weight and fine length and substance. Drink it between 1996 and 2003. Among the Grands Crus, the 1990 Ruchottes-Chambertin enjoys fine depth, a spicy, earthy, leathery nose, moderate tannins, average to slightly above average concentration, and a ripe, alcoholic finish. Drink it between 1995 and 2004. The 1990 Mazis-Chambertin appears to be the best of these 1990s, with the deepest color, a closed nose, a highly extracted, rich, broad-shouldered feel in the mouth, and 4–12 years of aging potential. The 1990 Griotte-Chambertin offers an attractive, captivating nose of sweet cherries, elegant, round, medium-bodied flavors, soft tannins, low acidity, and surprisingly hard tannins in an otherwise round, soft finish. In the 1989 Mazis-Chambertin and 1989 Ruchottes-Chambertin I detected that artificial earth smell that I associate with the Kisselguhr filtration system. All four of the 1989 offerings were light, compact, brilliantly polished wines that lacked flavor dimension and ampleness on the palate.

OTHER THOUGHTS: A treasure chest of superlative vineyards will lead Esmonin to fame if he jettisons his filters.

MICHEL ESMONIN (GEVREY-CHAMBERTIN)* * * *

1990	Côte de Nuits-Villages	B	82
1989	Côte de Nuits-Villages	B	78
1990	Gevrey-Chambertin	D	85

1989 Gevrey-Chambertin	D	85
1990 Gevrey-Chambertin-Clos St.-Jacques	E	92
1989 Gevrey-Chambertin-Clos St.-Jacques	E	90

This tiny domaine is a terrific source for Gevrey-Chambertin-Clos St.-Jacques. The 1990 offers a gorgeous nose of black cherries, herbs, new oak, and minerals that is intense and persistent. In the mouth the wine is full bodied, with superb richness, blazingly clear definition, and a long, authoritative, yet elegant finish. Drink it between 1995 and 2010. Esmonin's 1990 Gevrey-Chambertin offers up a pleasant pure cherry-scented nose, as well as delicious, medium-bodied, elegant flavors. Drink it over the next 4–5 years. The 1989 Côte de Nuits-Villages is an agreeable wine, with ripeness, a light-bodied, moderately concentrated personality, and a short finish. The 1989 Gevrey-Chambertin is excellent, with a classy, ripe cherry–scented nose, a good touch of toasty vanillin new oak, medium body, and supple, fleshy, concentrated flavors. Drink it over the next 5–7 years. The 1989 Gevrey-Chambertin-Clos St.-Jacques exhibits a wonderful deep color as well as an enticing nose of flowers, red and black fruits, spicy new oak, and minerals. It is crammed with opulently rich, superripe fruit, decent acidity, and a long, lingering, explosive finish. There are enough tannins to suggest that laying this wine away for 3–4 years may result in something even more profound. It should last for 12–15 years.

OTHER THOUGHTS: A tiny but super producer who makes a Clos St.-Jacques better than most producers' Grands Crus.

FAIVELEY (NUITS ST.-GEORGES)* * * *

1990 Beaune Les Bressandes	D	90
1990 Beaune Les Champs Pimonts	D	88
1989 Beaune Les Champs Pimonts	D	86
1990 Bourgogne	B	87
1990 Chambertin-Clos de Bèze	EE	90+
1989 Chambertin-Clos de Bèze	EE	90
1990 Chambolle-Musigny La Combe d'Orveau	E	87
1990 Chambolle-Musigny Les Fuées	E	92
1990 Charmes-Chambertin	EE	93
1989 Chassagne-Montrachet	E	90
1990 Clos de la Roche	EE	89
1989 Clos de la Roche	EE	86
1990 Clos Vougeot	EE	90+
1989 Clos Vougeot	EE	86
1990 Corton-Clos des Cortons	EE	93+
1989 Corton-Clos des Cortons	EE	90

1990	Côte de Beaune-Villages	C	86
1989	Echézeaux	E	90
1990	Gevrey-Chambertin Les Cazetiers	E	88+
1989	Gevrey-Chambertin Les Cazetiers	E	89
1990	Gevrey-Chambertin Combe aux Moines	E	88+
1989	Gevrey-Chambertin Combe aux Moines	E	86
1990	Gevrey-Chambertin Les Issarts	D	88
1990	Gevrey-Chambertin Les Marchais	D	86
1990	Latricières-Chambertin	EE	90
1990	Mazis-Chambertin	EE	92
1990	Mercurey-Clos des Myglands	C	87
1989	Mercurey-Clos des Myglands	C	86
1990	Mercurey-Clos du Roy	D	89
1989	Mercurey-Clos du Roy	C	85
1990	Mercurey Domaine de la Croix Jacquelet	C	86
1989	Mercurey Domaine de la Croix Jacquelet	C	85
1990	Mercurey La Framboisière	C	87
1989	Mercurey La Framboisière	C	85
1990	Mercurey Les Mauvarennes	C	86
1990	Morey St.-Denis Clos des Ormes	E	88
1989	Morey St.-Denis Clos des Ormes	E	89
1990	Nuits St.-Georges Les Argillats	D	87
1990	Nuits St.-Georges Les Chaignots	E	88
1990	Nuits St.-Georges Clos de la Maréchale	D	89
1989	Nuits St.-Georges Clos de la Maréchale	D	87
1990	Nuits St.-Georges Les Damodes	E	87
1989	Nuits St.-Georges Les Damodes	E	85
1990	Nuits St.-Georges Les Porets St.-Georges	E	88
1989	Nuits St.-Georges Les Porets St.-Georges	E	87
1990	Nuits St.-Georges Les St.-Georges	E	92
1990	Nuits St.-Georges La Vigneronde	E	90
1990	Pommard Les Chaponnières	E	93
1989	Pommard Les Chaponnières	E	87
1989	Rully	C	87
1990	Rully Les Villeranges	C	86

1989 Rully Les Villeranges	C	79
1990 Volnay Clos des Chênes	E	90

The 1990 Gevrey-Chambertin Les Marchais is a tannic, dense, dark ruby-colored, impressively built, and concentrated wine. It should last for 10 years or more. Faiveley's 1990 Nuits St.-Georges-Les Argillats is a fatter, softer-textured wine, with a lovely plum-, herb-, and cassis-scented nose, round, generous, velvet-textured flavors, soft tannins, low acidity, and plenty of glycerin and alcohol in the finish. The 1990 Gevrey-Chambertin Les Issarts is a leafy, beefy, spicy wine. Its rustic, earthy nose is followed by long, opulent, ripe flavors with significant fatness and richness. It promises to age well for 7–10 years. The 1990 Gevrey-Chambertin Les Cazetiers reveals a similar leathery, beefy aroma, but there are more black fruit scents. It is savagely tannic, full bodied, with gobs of extract and a deep, muscular, spicy finish. Only a masochist would want to drink it now. It requires cellaring and should last for 10–15 years. Another tough, tannic, backward wine is the 1990 Gevrey-Chambertin Combe aux Moines. It reveals more of a red fruit character, as well as loads of tannin, fine concentration, and a sense of balance and grace. Drink it between 1996 and 2003. The 1990 Morey St.-Denis Clos des Ormes's big, perfumed nose of jammy berry fruit, sweet oak, cedar, and herbs is captivating. This wine is soft, generously endowed, and medium to full bodied, with a velvet-textured, lush finish. Drink it over the next 7–8 years. The 1990 Nuits St.-Georges Clos de la Maréchale possesses a deep, saturated ruby/purple color; a huge, up-front nose of minerals, roasted black fruits, herbs, and meat; super depth of fruit; an unctuous, velvety texture; and a lusty, fat, glycerin-imbued finish. It should provide pleasure for 10–12 years. The less powerful 1990 Nuits St.-Georges Les Porets St.-Georges is a medium-bodied wine, with a rich, spicy nose and a more linear, compact style. Faiveley's 1990 Nuits St.-Georges Les Damodes, which offers up a thick, fragrant nose of black cherries, herbs, and minerals, is full bodied, rich, monolithic, tannic, and hard. The fruit is present, but this is a 1990 that requires 4–5 years of cellaring; it should keep for a decade or more. I admire the sweet anise, earthy, trufflelike aromas of the 1990 Nuits St.-Georges Les Chaignots. This succulent, soft-textured, medium-bodied wine displays wonderful depth of fruit, an admirable chewy texture, and a long finish. It will provide flattering drinking over the next 7–10 years. The seductive 1990 Nuits St.-Georges La Vigneronde offers huge black cherry and black raspberry fruit aromas kissed gently by sweet, smoky new oak. The finish is all glycerin, alcohol, and jammy, concentrated fruit. The profound 1990 Nuits St.-Georges Les St.-Georges's color is a saturated purple/black. The nose offers up intense smells of cloves, new oak, smoke, and black cherries. Dense, full bodied, and moderately tannic, this superbly structured, concentrated wine should drink well through the first decade of the twenty-first century. The 1990 Chambolle-Musigny La Combe d'Orveau is elegant, soft, sweet, round, and graceful. Prudence suggests drinking it over the next 6–7 years. Faiveley's 1990 Chambolle-Musigny Les Fuées exhibits a huge, sexy, floral, raspberry, black cherry nose, as well as fabulous richness, a soft, unctuous texture, and round, sweet tannins. A hedonistically, decadently styled wine, it should drink well for the next 10–12 years. The attractive 1990 Clos de la Roche displays a moderately intense, earthy, red fruit–scented nose, an elegant, light style, and a soft finish. Drink it over the next 10–12 years.

The 1990 Latricières-Chambertin is similar in style. Heady, with more alcohol and glycerin than many of the other Grands Crus, this ripe, medium- to full-bodied, velvety-textured wine should provide delicious drinking over the next 7–8 years. If you are looking for a more rustic wine, with more muscle and structure, Faiveley's Clos Vougeot and Mazis-Chambertin should be considered. The tightly knit 1990 Clos Vougeot exhibits a deep ruby color, followed by a reticent but promising bouquet of jammy black cherries and new oak. It is full bodied, rich, and powerful, with gobs of fruit, glycerin, and tannin. Even more savage and ferociously tannic, but potentially superior, is the 1990 Mazis-Chambertin. It possesses the darkest, most saturated ruby/purple color of any of the Grands Crus, as well as a fuller-bodied, more concentrated style. Faiveley's 1990 Charmes-Chambertin exhibits a seductive, already developed bouquet of smoked duck, sweet, jammy black fruits, and spicy new oak. The wine is fat and sweet, with low acidity and light tannins. The finish is like eating candy. Drink this beauty over the next 8–10 years. The 1990 Chambertin-Clos de Bèze reluctantly offers up aromas of black cherries, new oak, and earth. There is a suggestion of opulence and weight, but the wine is tight, tannic, and in need of at least 4–6 years of cellaring. It should age well for 15 or more years.

Faiveley produces one of the best *cuvées* of generic red burgundy. The 1990 Bourgogne is thick and rich, with a full-bodied, almost unctuous texture. Drink it over the next 10 or more years. The 1990 Rully Les Villeranges offers an earthy, spicy nose. It is an elegant, soft wine with excellent concentration and a dried cherry fruit aroma and flavor. The 1990 Mercurey Domaine de la Croix Jacquelet reveals a deep ruby color, a big, sweet nose of red currants, wonderful ripeness, crisp acidity for focus, and a medium-bodied, fleshy finish. It should drink well for the next 5–7 years. The 1990 Mercurey Les Mauvarennes exhibits slightly more toasty oak in its sweet, cherry-scented nose. It combines both elegance and richness in a tasty, generously endowed, medium-bodied format. Drink it over the next 7–8 years. The 1990 Mercurey La Framboisière, with its dark purple color and fragrant, full-intensity nose of raspberries and cherries, possesses gobs of fruit, a sweet, expansive, chewy texture, soft tannins, low acidity, and a spicy, opulent finish. It will make delicious drinking over the next decade. Slightly more structured and broader, with more of an earthy character, is the 1990 Mercurey-Clos des Myglands. Sweet, round, and muscular, with gobs of fruit, moderate tannins, and plenty of body, glycerin, and alcohol, this is a mouth-filling wine. The 1990 Mercurey-Clos du Roy possesses a dark ruby/purple color and closed but promising aromas of black fruits, minerals, toasty oak, and flowers. Full bodied and rich, with authoritative power and moderate tannins, this classic Mercurey should drink well for the next 10–12 years.

In the Côte de Beaune, Faiveley has fashioned an attractive, richly fruity, soft, generously endowed 1990 Côte de Beaune-Villages. The opulent, jammy, cherry- and toasty oak–scented 1990 Beaune Les Champs Pimonts has excellent extraction of fruit, medium body, a deep, supple texture, soft tannins, and a lush finish. The floral, roasted, cherry nose of the 1990 Beaune Les Bressandes is followed by full-bodied, voluptuously textured, rich flavors and a fat, luscious, heady finish. Drink this hedonistic burgundy over the next 7–8 years. Faiveley's 1990 Pommard Les Chaponnières is sensational. A sweet, oaky, plummy, jammy nose jumps from the glass. The saturated color suggests intensity. Full bodied and immensely rich, with a chewy, almost unctuous texture and a deep, dramatic, even flamboyant finish, this wine is supple enough to be drunk now and will continue to provide fascinating drinking over the next decade. The 1990 Volnay Clos des Chênes is a more elegant, finesse-style wine, with a fragrant, floral- and berry-scented nose, soft, satiny-textured flavors, and a graceful, well-balanced finish. Faiveley's Corton-Clos des Cortons is often their most backward wine. The 1990 offers a nearly opaque purple color and a tight but promising nose of blackcurrants, toasty new oak, Oriental spices, and minerals. Dense and rich, with a high level of soft tannins, this full-bodied, massively endowed wine needs at least 6–8 years of cellaring and should keep for 20–25 years.

Faiveley's 1989s are nearly as good as their 1990s. The stylish, delicious 1989 Mercurey La Framboisière is a soft, generously endowed red burgundy for drinking over the next 5–6 years. Both the 1989 Mercurey Domaine de la Croix Jacquelet and 1989 Mercurey-Clos des Myglands exhibit intriguing aromas of almonds, cherries, and smoke. The wines reveal attractive concentration, a ripe cherry fruitiness, and spicy, medium-bodied finishes. The Clos des Myglands possesses more glycerin, body, and length. Drink them both over the next 5–6 years. The 1989 Rully Les Villeranges is compact. The 1989 Beaune Les Champs Pimonts offers sweet, round, black cherry fruit, a scent of herbs and vanillin, and a gentle, velvety, medium-bodied texture. For a more smoky, black fruit character, try the 1989 Nuits St.-Georges Les Damodes. It is gentle in the mouth, with soft tannins, low acidity, and plump, ripe, fruity flavors. The more concentrated 1989 Nuits St.-Georges Les Porets St.-Georges exhibits an intriguing mineral, smoky, earthy, berrylike fruitiness; ripe, medium-bodied flavors; soft tannins; and a heady finish. Drink it over the next 5–6 years. The 1989 Nuits St.-Georges Clos de la Maréchale displays a classic Nuits St.-Georges nose of damp earth, smoke, and minerals. It should last for up to a decade. The 1989 Morey St.-Denis Clos des Ormes possesses an exotic bouquet of Oriental spices, minerals, and plumlike fruit. It is an impressively constituted wine with gobs of fruit, an opulent, full-bodied finish, and tender tannins. I had a definite preference for the 1989 Gevrey-Chambertin Les Cazetiers over the 1989 Gevrey-Chambertin Combe aux Moines. The latter wine was more monolithic and one-dimensional. Les Cazetiers exhibited a generous spicy, earthy, smoky nose; gorgeously rich, ripe, fruity flavors; and fine concentration and length. The 1989 Pommard Les Chaponnières was an interesting, full-bodied, chunky wine, with good fruit, structure, and character. Faiveley's 1989 Echézeaux offered up a beautiful perfume of flowers, minerals, Oriental spices, and black fruits. The wine has super stuffing, a lavish, velvety texture, and a soft, generous finish. The 1989 Clos de la Roche was round and generous, with a rustic, earthy, leathery, cedary nose and attractive cherry fruit. I thought the 1989 Clos Vougeot to be chunky and admirably concentrated, but monolithic and lacking flavor dimension and aromatic complexity. The superb 1989 Chambertin-Clos de Bèze, with its sweet, berry-scented nose intertwined with aromas of caramel, vanillin, and smoky oak, is a seductive, rich wine. Flavors of superripe berry fruit, coffee, and chocolate, along with the explosive finish, are hard to ignore. The wine possesses the balance and depth necessary to evolve for at least a decade. The most backward of all the 1989 Faiveley wines, with the deepest, dark ruby/purple color, is the Corton-Clos des Cortons. The closed but emerging nose of cassis, licorice, herbs, and spicy new oak is followed by black cherry and mineral flavors that exhibit fine acidity and tannin in the heady, robust finish. Drink it between 1995 and 2005.

OTHER THOUGHTS: Although Faiveley is a great firm and a leading vineyard owner, its wines are expensive, so search out their terrific wines from Mercurey. On the dark side, reports continue to circulate that Faiveley's wines tasted abroad are less rich than those tasted in the cellars—something I have noticed as well. Ummm . . . !

JEAN FAUROIS (VOSNE-ROMANÉE)* * * *

1990 Clos Vougeot	E	89
1990 Vosne-Romanée Les Chaumes	D	86

The 1990 Vosne-Romanée Les Chaumes reveals an intriguing nose of prune, raspberry fruit, sweet, graceful, round flavors, soft tannins, and an elegant, low-acid, expansive finish. It will not make old bones, so drink it over the next 5–7 years. The 1990 Clos Vougeot possesses an attractive dark ruby color as well as an alcoholic, roasted fruit– and black cherry–scented nose. The wine is excellent rather than dazzling, with medium to full body, fine concentration, light tannins, low acidity, and a heady, lusty finish. Drink it over the next 7–8 years.

OTHER THOUGHTS: Faurois retired after 1990, so this is it.

DOMAINE FOREY PÈRE ET FILS (VOSNE-ROMANÉE)* * *

1990 Echézeaux	E	89
1990 Nuits St.-Georges Les Perrières	D	82
1990 Vosne-Romanée	D	84
1990 Vosne-Romanée Les Gaudichots	D	88

Forey's famed Vosne-Romanée Les Gaudichots offers a seductive perfume of spicy new oak and minerals. The 1990 is medium bodied and soft, with ripe tannins and a long, rich finish. Drink it between 1994 and 2002. Although light for a 1990, Forey's Echézeaux exhibits a flowery, plummy, vanillin, smoky fragrance; soft, medium-bodied flavors; fine concentration; and a sweet, round finish. Drink it over the next decade.

OTHER THOUGHTS: Good but unspectacular wines.

JEAN GARAUDET (POMMARD)* * * *

1990 Beaune-Clos des Mouches	C	84
1989 Beaune-Clos des Mouches	C	85
1989 Beaune Hautes-Côtes de Beaune	B	84
1990 Bourgogne Hautes-Côtes de Beaune	B	82
1990 Pommard Les Charmots	D	89
1989 Pommard Les Charmots	D	87
1990 Pommard Les Noizons	D	87

The 1989 Beaune Hautes-Côtes de Beaune is an inexpensive introduction to the classy, pure, ripe fruity style of Garaudet. Exhibiting a round, supple texture and a smooth finish, it should be drunk over the next 3–4 years. The 1989 Beaune-Clos des Mouches reveals an elegant, cherry- and herb-scented nose intertwined with aromas of new oak. In the mouth there is good fatness, decent acidity, moderate tannins, and an ample finish. It should mature nicely for 4–5 years. The 1990 Pommard Les Charmots reveals a saturated, deep ruby/purple color and a fragrant nose of black fruits and toasty new oak. It is full bodied, with excellent richness. The 1989 offers a deep ruby color, a big, explosive nose of toasty new oak and ripe berry fruit, a spicy, attractively endowed palate, medium body, soft tannins, and decent acidity. Garaudet has also fashioned a graceful, supple, and rich 1990 Pommard Les Noizons. Drink this attractive wine over the next 5–7 years.

OTHER THOUGHTS: Why did Garaudet make better 1987s and 1988s than 1989s and 1990s?

J. M. GAUNOUX (POMMARD)* * * *

1990 Corton Les Rénardes	E	88
1989 Pommard Les Charmots	D	87
1989 Pommard Les Grands Epenots	D	89
1990 Pommard Les Perrières	D	87
1989 Pommard Les Rugiens	D	90

The delicious 1990 Pommard Les Perrières possesses a fragrant nose of jammy red and black fruits and toasty new oak. Round and generously endowed, with a lush texture, this chewy wine should drink well for the next 7–8 years. The 1990 Corton Les Rénardes is slightly more muscular and broad-shouldered. It, too, is forward and fat, with a big, spicy, mineral- and black cherry–scented nose and lusty, rich, alcoholic flavors. Drink it over the next 7–8 years. The terrific 1989 Pommards are superconcentrated and bursting with rich berry fruit. They possess an up-front seductiveness but have the potential to be cellared for another 6–8 years. They are explosively rich, full, intense wines with soft tannins, low acidity, and oodles of beautiful berry fruit. The 1989 Pommard Les Charmots is the most forward of this trio. The 1989 Pommard Les Grands Epenots and 1989 Pommard Les Rugiens are larger-scaled, with plenty of depth and intensity. These offerings will provide satisfying drinking over the next 5–8 years.

OTHER THOUGHTS: This guy knows how to make in-your-face, decadent, supple, lusty Pinot Noir!

PHILIPPE GAVIGNAT (NUITS ST.-GEORGES)* * *

1989 Côte de Nuits-Villages	B	84
1989 Nuits St.-Georges	C	72
1989 Nuits St.-Georges Les Argillats	D	88

This young producer turned out a deep, highly extracted, rich, beautiful Nuits St.-Georges Les Argillats. Although it exhibits some subtle new oak, its beauty lies in the abundantly pure, ripe, opulent Pinot fruit. There is decent acidity and soft tannins.

OTHER THOUGHTS: It is too soon to know for sure where this producer is going.

JACQUES GERMAIN (CHOREY-LÈS-BEAUNE)* * * *

1990 Beaune Les Cent Vignes	D	87
1990 Beaune Les Teurons	D	88

Both wines reveal a deep ruby color and bouquets filled with aromas of cherries and a judicious use of spicy new oak. The slightly fleshier and more evolved 1990 Beaune Les Cent Vignes exhibits zesty acidity and moderate tannins in its long finish. Approachable now, it should age gracefully for at least a decade. The 1990 Beaune Les Teurons is slightly more concentrated, with a firmer, more structured palate. The generous quantities of black cherry fruit offered in a medium-bodied format are hard to ignore. I should also note that both wines enjoy excellent purity and balance. Each will age effortlessly through the next decade.

OTHER THOUGHTS: Classic red burgundies that are pure, impeccably well balanced, and made to last.

ARMAND GIRARDIN (POMMARD)* * * *

1990 Beaune-Clos des Mouches	D	90+
1989 Beaune-Clos des Mouches	D	90
1990 Pommard Les Charmots	D	90+
1989 Pommard Les Charmots	D	90
1990 Pommard Les Epenots	D	92+
1989 Pommard Les Epenots	D	92
1990 Pommard Les Rugiens	D	94+
1989 Pommard Les Rugiens	D	92

Armand Girardin's 1990s, all veritable monsters given their phenomenal extraction, have the potential for 15–25 years of longevity. They are classic, old-style, huge, unctuous wines that represent the essence of Pinot Noir. Girardin's black-colored 1990 Beaune-Clos des Mouches exhibits a promising nose that exudes aromas of licorice, earth, black fruits, and Oriental spices, as well as gobs of mouth-filling fruit and glycerin imbued with formidable tannin levels. This massive wine will last for 2–3 decades! The 1990 Pommard Les Charmots is another opaque, black-colored wine. With considerable coaxing, the nose offers up vague aromas of black cherries, licorice, tar, and sweet oak. Magnificently concentrated, sweet, expansive, and mammoth, this full-bodied, tannic wine should be cellared for 7–10 years. It should last through the first quarter of the next century. My notes for the 1990 Pommard Les Epenots from both the barrel and the bottle began with similar warnings: "Don't touch it for at least 10 years." It is phenomenally extracted, with an opaque black/purple color, chewy, viscous levels of Pinot fruit, and a thick, chewy finish. **Anticipated maturity: 2002–2030.** A similar description can be attached to the 1990 Pommard Les Rugiens, which is even richer than Les Epenots! Les Rugiens is a 25–40-year wine—a rarity in Burgundy. Also monstrously endowed, with portlike Pinot Noir fruit, this is a wine of extraordinary concentration, majestic stature, and prodigious potential for longevity. **Anticipated maturity: 2002–2035+.** Like his 1990s, Girardin's 1989s represent some of the most powerful, concentrated, densest Pinot Noirs I have tasted. The 1989 Beaune-

Clos des Mouches is a broodingly opaque-colored wine packed with spicy, chocolatey, black cherry fruit. It offers gobs of glycerin and tannin as well as a huge, powerful finish. Drink it between 1996 and 2005. The opaque black/purple-colored 1989 Pommard Les Charmots is sweeter and riper on the palate, with a sensational perfume of minerals, exotic spices, new oak, and black fruits. Drink it between 1994 and 2008. I was bowled over by the 1989 Pommard Les Epenots. The color is nearly black, and the bouquet offers up staggering aromas of black cherries, subtle herbs, and spicy new oak. There is purity of flavor, mouth-coating glycerin, extraordinary flavor extraction, and velvety tannins. This wine needs several years of cellaring; it should last for 15–20 years. For readers who may own it, Girardin's 1989 Pommard Les Rugiens is unevolved and impenetrable. Bury it in the cellar for at least 5–7 years.

OTHER THOUGHTS: Is Girardin's secret fantasy to produce red Hermitage?

JACQUES GIRARDIN (SANTENAY)* * *

1990 Chassagne-Montrachet Morgeot	?	83
1989 Chassagne-Montrachet Morgeot	D	86
1990 Santenay-Beauregard	D	85
1989 Santenay-Beauregard	D	87
1990 Santenay-Clos de la Confrérie-Cuvée Prestige	D	87
1990 Savigny-Lès-Beaune Les Gollardes	?	76

If you want oodles of pure fruit in a medium-bodied, ripe, succulent style that will offer delicious drinking over the next 4–5 years, consider Jacques Girardin's 1990 Santenay-Beauregard. If you want the same opulence of fruit, as well as lavish quantities of sweet, toasty new oak, then the 1990 Santenay-Clos de la Confrérie-Cuvée Prestige merits consideration. The latter wine, which is larger-scaled and more ambitiously styled, should age for 7–8 years. Girardin's 1989 Chassagne-Montrachet Morgeot reveals excellent color and a rich, sweet nose of red fruits, herbs, and new oak. Drink this undeniably charming wine over the next 2–3 years. Even better is the 1989 Santenay-Beauregard. It possesses pure, sweet, ripe, opulent Pinot fruit that is presented in a medium-bodied, decadent style.

OTHER THOUGHTS: Very tasty, supple wines for early drinking are the rule.

BERNARD ET LOUIS GLANTENAY (VOLNAY)* * *

1990 Pommard Les Rugiens	D	90
1990 Volnay	D	84
1990 Volnay Les Brouillards	D	87
1990 Volnay Les Caillerets	D	88+
1990 Volnay Clos des Chênes	D	90+
1990 Volnay Santenots	D	89

The densely colored 1990 Volnay Les Brouillards offers a nose of *surmaturité*, meaning that aromas such as peaches are present with those of jammy black cherries and herbs. The wine is deep and concentrated, with significant tannin, glycerin, and alcohol in the lusty finish. Glantenay's 1990 Volnay Santenots is an extremely tannic, powerful, authoritatively flavored, full-bodied wine that will repay cellaring. More closed than the Les Brouillards, it exhibits none of the late harvest apricot/peach, exotic fruitiness in its nose or flavors. **Anticipated maturity: 1996–2010+.** The 1990 Volnay Clos des Chênes is purple/black-colored, with a huge, jammy, apricot/black raspberry/black cherry–scented nose that is supported by lavish quantities of smoky new oak. This massive wine will require a good 4–5 years of cellaring and has the potential to last for 10–15 or more years. The tannic, hard, closed 1990 Volnay Les Caillerets offers more promise than pleasure. It is the most tightly knit of Glantenay's 1990s. I would cellar it for at least 4–5 years. Not surprisingly, the 1990 Pommard Les Rugiens displays a wealth of lavish, black cherry fruit in its nose. Along with dramatic levels of toasty new oak, it boasts viscous, thick, rich flavors that are high in alcohol and low in acidity. This is a large-scale, forceful, old-style, tannic red burgundy that will handsomely repay cellaring. **Anticipated maturity: 1996–2008.**

OTHER THOUGHTS: A producer on the move up, but let's hope he does not get carried away with too much new oak and power.

MICHEL GOUBARD (SAINT-DESERT)* * *

1990 Bourgogne Mont Avril	B	85
1990 Bourgogne Mont Avril Futs de Chêne	B	85

Michel Goubard is well known in France for his tasty yet inexpensive white and red burgundies. Although not the richest, most complex red burgundies, they offer pure fruit and authentic Pinot Noir character for a modest price. The 1990 Bourgogne Mont Avril exhibits an attractive medium ruby color, a peppery, spicy, red currant–scented nose, medium bodied, soft flavors, and enough tannin and acidity to support 3–5 years of aging. More oak and less red fruit is evident in the 1990 Futs de Chêne. The wine also has slightly more tannin, grip, and structure. It should age well for 3–4 years.

OTHER THOUGHTS: Burgundy on a budget.

DOMAINE HENRI GOUGES (NUITS ST.-GEORGES)* *

1990 Nuits St.-Georges	C	82
1989 Nuits St.-Georges	C	81
1989 Nuits St.-Georges Les Chaignots	D	83
1990 Nuits St.-Georges Clos des Porrets	D	77
1989 Nuits St.-Georges Clos des Porrets	D	83
1990 Nuits St.-Georges Les Pruliers	D	81
1989 Nuits St.-Georges Les Pruliers	D	85
1990 Nuits St.-Georges Les St.-Georges	E	85
1989 Nuits St.-Georges Les St.-Georges	E	87
1990 Nuits St.-Georges Les Vaucrains	E	85
1989 Nuits St.-Georges Les Vaucrains	E	86

The 1990 Nuits St.-Georges Les Vaucrains offers a vague, earthy, truffle-scented, closed nose. It displays a medium ruby color, tightly knit, tart flavors, medium body, and a restrained, understated style. It should last for 6–8 years. The 1990 Nuits St.-Georges Les St.-Georges possesses a subtle, spicy, red fruit–scented nose touched lightly by oak. It is lean, elegant, and understated, with a tannic finish. The 1989 Nuits St.-Georges is soft, light, and pleasant. The light ruby-colored 1989 Nuits St.-Georges Les Chaignots exhibits a classic "Nuits" bouquet of stony, earthy fruit. It is tasty and soft, with decent concentration, an elegant personality, and a pleasing finish. The austere and tannic 1989 Nuits St.-Georges Clos des Porrets needs another 1–2 years in the bottle to fully reveal its ripeness, smoky, earthy nose, and pleasant berry fruitiness. The 1989 Nuits St.-Georges Les Pruliers displays a spicy, plummy, oaky nose and tasty, well-balanced, ripe fruity flavors. The body is light, but this wine should evolve over the next 3–5 years. One of the two best *cuvées* from Gouges in 1989 is the Nuits St.-Georges Les Vaucrains. It offers an excellent, intense nose of herbs, black fruits, and earth; an attractive, smoky, cherry fruitiness; soft tannins; and good body. The darkest-colored, richest, and most ageworthy of all the Gouges *cuvées* is the 1989 Nuits St.-Georges Les St.-Georges. Deeply colored, with a promising bouquet of black fruits and spices, this medium-bodied wine displays fine concentration, decent acidity, fine definition and purity of flavor, and a long, spicy finish. Drink it between 1993 and 2003.

OTHER THOUGHTS: The onetime benchmark for red burgundy continues to make pleasant but essentially shallow, one-dimensional wines.

MACHARD DE GRAMONT (NUITS ST.-GEORGES)* * * *

1990 Beaune Les Chouacheux	D	90
1990 Beaune Les Epenottes	D	88
1990 Chambolle-Musigny Les Noizeres	D	84
1990 Nuits St.-Georges Les Damodes	D	89
1990 Nuits St.-Georges Les Hauts Poirets	D	90+
1990 Nuits St.-Georges en la Perrière Noblot	D	87
1990 Nuits St.-Georges Les Vallerots	D	81
1990 Pommard Le Clos Blanc	D	89+
1990 Savigny-Lès-Beaune Les Guettes	C	86

With respect to the selections from the Côte de Nuits, the 1990 Nuits St.-Georges Les Damodes reveals a black/purple color and a wonderful rich nose of flowers, spices, and superjammy plums. There is superb depth, plenty of tannin, and a long, unctuous finish. It should last for 10–12 years. Gramont's magnificent 1990 Nuits St.-Georges Les Hauts Poirets has a black/ruby color, exceptional concentration, a viscous texture, and mouth-coating glycerin and tannin levels. This wine should keep for 12–15 years. Although the 1990 Nuits St.-Georges en la Perrière Noblot is also ripe, concentrated, and tasty, it is slightly softer, with less power and length. Drink it over the next 7–8 years. The 1990 Savigny-Lès-Beaune Les Guettes exhibits a deep ruby color and an attractive, moderately intense nose of black cherries, herbs, and spices.

Medium bodied, with a sweet, expansive fruitiness, firm structure, good acidity, and a long finish, it should drink well for the next decade. I was seduced by the huge, sweet, cherry, and oaky nose of the 1990 Beaune Les Epenottes. Classy, rich, and opulent, with low acidity and copious quantities of generous sweet fruit, this is a wine to drink over the next 6–7 years. I thought the 1990 Beaune Les Chouacheux to be stunning. Densely colored, superconcentrated, and succulent, it possesses an expansive texture and a long finish. I would not be surprised to see the 1990 Pommard Le Clos Blanc turn out to be just as compelling. It is a bigger, more structured and forceful wine, with reserves of rich fruit and a generous, full-bodied, viscous mouth-feel. There are soft tannins, plenty of richness, and enough structure and grip to give it 10–15 years of aging potential.

OTHER THOUGHTS: Serious wine estate turning out lusty, rich, powerful wines that can stand up to cellaring.

ALAIN GRAS (SAINT-ROMAIN)* * *

1990 Auxey-Duresses	C	86
1990 Saint-Romain	C	87

The excellent 1990 Saint-Romain offers a fragrant nose of jammy black cherries, minerals, and smoke, a medium-bodied texture, and generous, fat, chewy Pinot Noir flavors. Drink it over the next 4–5 years. The 1990 Auxey-Duresses possesses more tannin and grip, a spicy, earthy character, rich fruit, glycerin, and heady alcohol in the finish. It should drink well for 5–6 years.

OTHER THOUGHTS: Jump on the Alain Gras bandwagon before the entire world discovers him.

ROBERT GROFFIER (MOREY ST.-DENIS)* *

1989 Bonnes Mares	E	85
1989 Bourgogne Rouge	B	76
1989 Chambolle-Musigny Les Amoureuses	E	81
1989 Chambolle-Musigny Les Hauts-Doix	D	77
1989 Chambolle-Musigny Les Sentiers	D	79
1989 Gevrey-Chambertin	C	78

I was disappointed with the light, insipid 1990s produced by Groffier. The 1989s were only slightly better. However, several wines had that artificial earth smell that I associate with the Kisselguhr filtration system, which these wines have had to endure prior to bottling. Producers need to recognize that this filtration system often results in wines that have a phony smell of earth. All of these 1989s are weak, light wines that will have to be drunk over the next 4–6 years. Given their fragility, and the fact that I tasted them in France, one wonders how they will fare after the transatlantic voyage. The best cuvées included the shallow but pleasant and elegant 1989 Chambolle-Musigny Les Amoureuses and the denser 1989 Bonnes Mares. Although the Bonnes Mares was clearly the better wine, both of these wines should be drunk over the next 3–4 years.

OTHER THOUGHTS: A perplexing estate to follow—super 1988s, disappointing 1985s, 1989s, and 1990s.

A. F. GROS (POMMARD)* * * *

1989 Bourgogne Hautes-Côtes de Nuits	B	84
1990 Bourgogne Hautes-Côtes de Nuits	B	85
1990 Echézeaux	EE	94
1989 Echézeaux	EE	87
1990 Richebourg	EEE	95
1989 Vosne-Romanée-Mazières	D	86
1989 Vosne-Romanée-Clos des Réas	D	86

It is difficult to find high-quality generic burgundy, but this 1990 Bourgogne Hautes-Côtes de Nuits exhibits fine sweetness, excellent ripeness, and a medium-bodied, generous texture. Drink it over the next 4–5 years. The profound 1990 Echézeaux displays a super nose of sweet black raspberries, toasty new oak, and violets. There is full body, a generous yet gentle, expansive richness, an unctuous texture, and an explosively long finish. Drink it over the next 9–10 years. The 1990 Richebourg rivals the best of the vintage, with an explosive nose of minerals, black fruits, flowers, and smoky new oak. This is great stuff—smashingly rich, voluptuous, opulent, and full bodied, with layer upon layer of sweet black fruits that are bolstered and defined by new oak and adequate acidity. Drink it over the next 10–12 years. The 1989s are stylish, elegant wines, with good color, attractive, supple fruit, and fine depth. Even the 1989 Bourgogne Hautes-Côtes de Nuits displayed nicely focused, ripe berry fruit and a medium-bodied format. The floral, plummy, sweet bouquet of the 1989 Vosne-Romanée-Mazières is a turn-on. The attractive suppleness and smooth, satiny-textured flavors enhance its appeal. Drink it over the next 4–5 years. The 1989 Vosne-Romanée-Clos des Réas is tighter and more tannic. Although deeply colored, with considerable promise, it is closed. The 1989 Echézeaux displays fine deep ruby color, a rich, plummy, floral-scented nose, medium body, admirable concentration, and a spicy, long, soft finish. It should drink well for a decade.

OTHER THOUGHTS: This relatively new domaine has been a fast learner. The Richebourg is otherworldly.

ANNE ET FRANCOIS GROS (VOSNE-ROMANÉE)* * * *

1989 Chambolle-Musigny La Combe d'Orveau	D	85
1990 Clos Vougeot Le Grand Maupertuis	EE	96
1989 Clos Vougeot Le Grand Maupertuis	EE	?
1990 Richebourg	EEE	93
1989 Richebourg	EEE	94
1990 Vosne-Romanée	D	88
1989 Vosne-Romanée	D	86

The 1990 Vosne-Romanée offers deep color, rich, red cherry fruit, excellent richness, soft tannins, and a lush, long finish. Drink it over the next 5–6 years. The 1990 Richebourg is all finesse. The intensely aromatic nose of flowers and black fruit is followed by a medium-bodied wine with a silky, chewy texture, loads of fruit and concentration, abundant glycerin, and moderate alcohol as well as tannin. It should last for up to a decade. The 1990 Clos Vougeot Le Grand Maupertuis is a superstar. This wine exhibits a sweet, jammy, toasty, black fruit–scented nose, opulent, sumptuous flavors that boast superb extraction of flavor, and a profoundly long, velvety finish. It should age well for another 10–12 years. The delicious, sweet, oaky, spicy 1989 Vosne-Romanée makes good drinking now. The elegant 1989 Chambolle-Musigny La Combe d'Orveau, which offers abundant ripe fruitiness, should be consumed over the next 4–5 years. The 1989 Clos Vougeot was disappointing, offering up raisiny, pruny, overripe fruit. The 1989 Richebourg was a superb wine, with gorgeous, medium dark ruby color and a penetrating fragrance of sweet plums, toasty new oak, and minerals. Wonderfully round, with an opulent texture and considerable persistence on the palate, it will have to be drunk over the next 6–7 years.

OTHER THOUGHTS: Another Gros, another great Richebourg.

DOMAINE JEAN GROS (VOSNE-ROMANÉE)* * * */* * * * *

1989 Bourgogne Hautes-Côtes de Nuits	B	75
1989 Bourgogne Rouge	B	76
1990 Richebourg	EEE	92
1989 Richebourg	EEE	90
1989 Vosne-Romanée	D	82
1990 Vosne-Romanée-Clos des Réas	D	90
1989 Vosne-Romanée-Clos des Réas	D	88

The 1990 Vosne-Romanée-Clos des Réas exhibits a deep ruby color; a sweet, earthy, leathery, black raspberry–scented nose; rich, medium- to full-bodied flavors; expansive texture; and soft tannins and low acidity in the long finish. Drink it over the next 10–12 years. The 1990 Richebourg is lighter than expected, but an outstanding example. The color is medium dark ruby, and the nose reveals a ripe black fruit character intertwined with floral elements. This finesse-filled, medium-bodied wine should be drunk over the next 7–8 years. Other wines include a light, fluid, soft, undistinguished 1989 Bourgogne Rouge and a simple, compact, clipped 1989 Bourgogne Hautes-Côtes de Nuits. The 1989 Vosne-Romanée, although floral, fruity, and soft, lacked staying power. There were no problems to be found with the superb, deep ruby-colored, beautifully perfumed 1989 Vosne-Romanée-Clos des Réas. This fragrant, rich, medium-bodied wine is bursting with creamy berry fruit and spicy new oak. It displays an opulent feel and a beautiful marriage of finesse and power. Drink it over the next decade. The 1989 Richebourg has a sweet, floral, black fruit, oaky nose intertwined with scents of minerals. It is superopulent, with striking concentration, a beautiful, fascinating texture, low acidity, and tender tannins.

OTHER THOUGHTS: Classic expressions of Pinot Noir at the top levels.

DOMAINE GROS FRÈRE ET SOEUR (VOSNE-ROMANÉE)* * * *

1990 Bourgogne Hautes-Côtes de Nuits	C	85
1989 Bourgogne Hautes-Côtes de Nuits	C	78
1989 Clos Vougeot	E	90
1990 Clos Vougeot de Musigni	E	93
1990 Grands Echézeaux	EE	90
1989 Grands Echézeaux	EE	86
1990 Richebourg	EEE	94
1989 Richebourg	EEE	90
1990 Vosne-Romanée	D	87
1989 Vosne-Romanée	D	82

Gros Frère et Soeur has made a tasty, richly fruity, cherry-scented and -flavored, ripe, generously endowed 1990 Bourgogne Hautes-Côtes de Nuits. The 1990 Vosne-Romanée, with its big nose of overripe black fruits and prunes and dense, rich, medium-bodied flavors, also offers considerable attraction. It is a delicious, succulent style of Vosne-Romanée. The 1990 Grands Echézeaux possesses a sweet, jammy nose of black cherries, raspberries, peaches, and toasty new oak. Intense, with medium to full body, outstanding concentration, and a long, spicy, high alcohol, chewy finish, this wine should last for 10–12 years. The 1990 Clos Vougeot de Musigni is an exquisite wine. The dark ruby/purple color, huge, flowery, sweet, black cherry aromas, and supercrammed, fabulously rich palate may be the making of a legend. There are tons of glycerin and alcohol, as well as moderate tannin levels, in this super-rich, hedonistic wine. Drink it over the next 10–15 years. The 1990 Richebourg is also an amazingly rich, voluptuous, chewy wine. This opulent, viscous, well-endowed wine will provide magical drinking over the next 10–12 years. Bernard Gros's lower-level 1989s, particularly the Bourgogne Hautes-Côtes de Nuits and Vosne-Romanée, were light, fluid wines that exhibited decent fruit. Although the 1989 Grands Echézeaux was light, it did offer sexy black fruit aromas intertwined with scents of flowers. It was medium bodied, elegant, round, and delicate. The 1989 Clos Vougeot reveals exotic aromas of sweet black fruit, oranges, apricots, and new oak. A lush, medium-bodied wine with a velvety texture, low acidity, and a luscious finish, it should drink well for 5–7 years. The 1989 Richebourg, although not a blockbuster, displays superb elegance. The ripe, intense bouquet of smoky new oak, black fruits, and minerals is followed by a medium-bodied, well-balanced wine with adequate acidity, soft tannins, and a lush, round finish. Drink it over the next 5–8 years. OTHER THOUGHTS: Among the most decadent and controversial wines of Burgundy.

PIERRE GUILLEMOT (SAVIGNY-LÈS-BEAUNE)* * *

1989 Savigny-Lès-Beaune Les Jarrons	C	85
1989 Savigny-Lès-Beaune Les Serpentières	C	87

The 1989 Les Jarrons exhibits an earthy, ripe, berry-scented nose intermingled with the scent of herbs. Medium bodied, with good fleshy fruit and some tannin, this wine should provide delicious drinking over the next 5–6 years. Even richer, fuller, and more loaded is the 1989 Les Serpentières. The wine displays more of a truffle, earthy character in the nose, with plenty of red fruit extraction on the palate. Drink this beauty over the next 6–7 years.

OTHER THOUGHTS: Solid, ageworthy, rather rustic wines that merit attention.

HAEGELEN-JAYER (VOSNE-ROMANÉE)* * * *

1990 Chambolle-Musigny	D	86
1990 Clos Vougeot	E	92
1990 Echézeaux	E	90
1990 Vosne-Romanée	E	86

The 1990 Chambolle-Musigny offers an attractive plum color and a sweet, earthy nose of black fruits and herbs. Full bodied, with rustic tannins, admirable acidity, and a full, chewy texture, this uncomplex wine has plenty of depth, weight, and character. Drink it over the next decade. Although it may lack some complexity, Haegelen-Jayer's 1990 Vosne-Romanée is a big, rough-and-tumble, broad-shouldered wine with plenty of spicy, earthy, black fruits and herbal, chewy, full-bodied flavors, with noticeable tannin in the finish. The 1990 Clos Vougeot reveals a dense, saturated garnet color, aromas of smoked meats, black fruits damp earth, and spices, and full body. This rich, chewy, fleshy-textured wine needs 2–3 years of cellaring and should last for 15 years. The garnet-colored 1990 Echézeaux exhibits more aromatic dimension but neither the depth nor muscle of the Clos Vougeot. The nose is dominated by floral and black raspberry notes. In the mouth the wine is medium to full bodied, with soft tannins, excellent concentration, and a long, rich, alcoholic finish. Drinkable now, it should continue to evolve gracefully over the next decade.

OTHER THOUGHTS: Full-throttle, concentrated, sometimes massive, old-style Pinot Noir that can last for decades emerge from these fine cellars.

PAUL ET HENRI JACQUESON (RULLY)* * *

1990 Mercurey Les Naugues	C	85+
1989 Mercurey Les Naugues	C	83
1990 Rully Les Chaponnières	C	86
1989 Rully Les Chaponnières	C	86
1990 Rully Les Cloux	C	88
1989 Rully Les Cloux	C	87

The dark-colored 1990 Rully Les Chaponnières is medium bodied, with a spicy, earthy, berry-scented nose, decent acidity, and plenty of glycerin, alcohol, and fruit. Drink it over the next 5–6 years. The Mercurey Les Naugues is a difficult wine to evaluate because of its considerable tannin as well as an underlying, earthy, mineral character that tends to dominate. The closed 1990, which displays plenty of guts and stuffing, is tougher in texture than the Rullys. Jacqueson's top wine is the excellent Rully Les Cloux. The 1990 is bursting with copious quantities of red and black fruits. It possesses a gorgeous richness, an aromatic, spicy, oaky, almost plummy-scented nose, and long, rich, supple flavors. I would not be surprised to see the wine close up and age for 8–10 years. The 1989 Rully Les Chaponnières offers a deep ruby/purple color, big, ripe, berry- and mineral-scented aromas, spicy new oaky flavors, a generous texture, and fine depth and ripeness. It should drink well for 7–8 years. Even more interesting is the 1989 Rully Les Cloux. This wine exhibits a terrific black raspberry– and mineral-scented nose, fine stuffing and richness, an opulent texture, and a finesse-filled finish.

OTHER THOUGHTS: One of the stars of Rully.

LOUIS JADOT (BEAUNE)* * * *

1990 Aloxe-Corton	C	85
1990 Beaune Les Avaux	D	92
1989 Beaune Les Avaux	D	87
1990 Beaune Les Boucherottes	D	92
1989 Beaune Les Boucherottes	D	87
1990 Beaune Les Bressandes	D	91
1990 Beaune Les Chouacheux	D	92
1990 Beaune-Clos des Couchereaux	D	90
1990 Beaune-Clos des Ursules	D	93+
1989 Beaune-Clos des Ursules	D	90
1990 Beaune Les Grèves	D	90
1990 Beaune Premier Cru	D	87
1990 Beaune Les Teurons	D	92
1990 Beaune Les Touissaints	D	90
1990 Bonnes Mares	E	96
1989 Bonnes Mares	E	90
1989 Bourgogne Rouge	B	84
1990 Chambertin	EEE	95
1990 Chambertin-Clos de Bèze	EEE	96
1989 Chambertin-Clos de Bèze	EEE	93
1990 Chambolle-Musigny	D	85
1990 Chambolle-Musigny Les Amoureuses	D	92
1989 Chambolle-Musigny Les Amoureuses	D	90
1990 Chapelle-Chambertin	E	91
1990 Charmes-Chambertin	E	88
1990 Chassagne-Montrachet Morgeot-Clos de la Chapelle	D	89
1990 Clos Vougeot	D	90+

1989	Clos Vougeot	D	89
1990	Corton	D	90
1990	Corton Dr. Peste (Hospices de Beaune)	EE	87
1990	Corton Les Pougets	E	93+
1989	Corton Les Pougets	E	92
1989	Côte de Beaune-Villages	B	82
1990	Echézeaux	E	90
1990	Fixin	C	84
1990	Gevrey-Chambertin	C	84
1990	Gevrey-Chambertin-Clos St.-Jacques	EE	96
1989	Gevrey-Chambertin-Clos St.-Jacques	EE	92
1990	Gevrey-Chambertin Estournelles St.-Jacques	E	91
1990	Gevrey-Chambertin Lavaux St.-Jacques	E	92
1989	Gevrey-Chambertin Lavaux St.-Jacques	D	92
1990	Griotte-Chambertin	EE	89
1990	Marsannay	C	84
1989	Marsannay	C	87
1990	Mazis-Chambertin	E	93
1990	Monthélie	C	85
1990	Musigny	EEE	93
1989	Musigny	EEE	89
1990	Nuits St.-Georges	D	81
1990	Nuits St.-Georges Les Boudots	D	91
1990	Nuits St.-Georges-Clos des Corvées	D	90
1990	Pernand-Vergelesses-Clos de la Croix Pierre	C	86
1990	Pommard	D	86+
1990	Pommard Les Arvelets	D	88
1990	Pommard Les Grands Epenots	D	91+
1990	Romanée St.-Vivant	E	94
1990	Ruchottes-Chambertin	EE	93
1989	Ruchottes-Chambertin	EE	93
1990	Savigny-Lès-Beaune	C	85
1990	Savigny-Lès-Beaune Les Dominaudes	C	88
1990	Volnay	D	87
1990	Volnay Les Santenots	D	90

1990 Vosne-Romanée	D	86
1990 Vosne-Romanée Les Suchots	D	88

The excellent 1990 Chambolle-Musigny offers sweet, elegant, ripe berry flavors, fine body, soft tannins, and a voluptuous mouth-feel. Even better is the robust, ripe, earthy, rich 1990 Vosne-Romanée. The 1990 Nuits St.-Georges Les Boudots is black-colored, with a sweet, truffle-, licorice-, and raspberry-scented nose and rich, full-bodied, opulent flavors. Drink it between 1995 and 2010. The 1990 Nuits St.-Georges-Clos des Corvées reveals more toasty new oak in its nose as well as scents of flowers, black fruits, and minerals. It possesses a dense, fleshy texture as well as a lush finish. Drink it over the next 12–15 years. The delicious 1990 Vosne-Romanée Les Suchots is ripe and full bodied, with excellent extraction. I would suggest drinking it between 1995 and 2008. The superb 1990 Chambolle-Musigny Les Amoureuses offers a huge nose of jammy black cherries, herbs, spices, and spring flowers that is followed by a superconcentrated, velvety-textured, full-bodied wine with masses of fruit. It is capable of lasting for 12–15 years.

The 1990 Gevrey-Chambertin Estournelles St.-Jacques exhibits a rich, spicy, meaty nose intertwined with aromas of jammy black cherries and cocoa. Superconcentrated and full bodied, with a sweet expansiveness, chewy glycerin, and a dense, long finish, this magnificent, rich wine should be at its best between 1996 and 2010. The less muscular 1990 Gevrey-Chambertin Lavaux St.-Jacques is more flattering and seductive. The perfumed fragrance of flowers, black cherries, and new oak is captivating. There is wonderful ripeness, medium to full body, plenty of glycerin, and an expansive, chewy texture. Jadot produced a profound 1990 Gevrey-Chambertin-Clos St.-Jacques. The color is a saturated dark ruby. The nose explodes from the glass, offering a mélange of scents, including black raspberries, toasty new oak, cloves, vanilla, and candy. In the mouth there is astonishing richness, a thick, well-defined texture, and a flamboyant, moderately tannic finish. Jadot's Griotte-Chambertin and Charmes-Chambertin were excellent, but not as concentrated as others. The light- to medium-bodied 1990 Griotte-Chambertin possesses a sweet cherry fruitiness, soft, round, generously endowed flavors, low acidity, and light tannins. Drink it over the next 10–12 years. The 1990 Charmes-Chambertin is similarly styled, although lighter and more loosely knit. It, too, should be drunk over the next 10–12 years.

Jadot's 1990 Clos Vougeot is a wine with considerable power and mouth-searing tannins. Its dense, saturated color, full body, and high tannin suggest it should be cellared until the turn of the century. The 1990 Echézeaux's attractive black cherry, black raspberry, floral nose is elegant and open-knit. This medium-bodied, soft, graceful wine possesses admirable charm and style as well as a precocious fruitiness. Drink it over the next 7–8 years. The 1990 Chapelle-Chambertin's tannins are ferocious, but the wine reveals the sweet, dense, concentrated fruit necessary to balance them out. With coaxing, aromas of roasted nuts, vanillin, and sweet, jammy fruit emerge. **Anticipated maturity: 2000–2020.** The opaque, saturated, dark-colored 1990 Ruchottes-Chambertin offers up a huge nose of grilled meats, black fruits, herbs, and cinnamon. Full bodied, with masses of fruit, glycerin, and alcohol, this large-scale, broad-shouldered wine makes a powerful impact. **Anticipated maturity: 1996–2012.** The 1990 Mazis-Chambertin is a blockbuster, with deep purple color and a huge nose of pure black fruits, smoke, herbs, meats, and toasty new oak. Phenomenally dense, concentrated, and powerful, with full body and mouth-watering tannins, this huge wine should be at its best between 1996 and 2015. The 1990 Musigny's nose consists primarily of sweet black cherries and new oak. There is a soft, velvety texture, medium body, low acidity, and gentle tannins in the finish. Drink it over the next 12 years. The 1990 Romanée St.-Vivant shares the full-bodied, sweet, expansive style many of the Jadot red burgundies possess. The tannins are more noticeable in the long, spicy finish. **Anticipated maturity: 1997–2012.** The 1990 Bonnes Mares is the sweetest and most open-knit, with layer upon layer of fruit, huge body, yet a sense of elegance and precision to its lavish richness and huge, perfumed personality. It is more developed than either the Chambertin-Clos de Bèze or Chambertin. The 1990 Chambertin-Clos de Bèze gets my nod as the wine in the Jadot portfolio that should hit the highest peak in quality and pleasure. It needs at least 5–7 years in the cellar and has the potential to last for 25 or more years. The color is a saturated dark ruby/purple, and the closed nose offers sweet, jammy aromas framed by noticeable smoky new oak. The magnificent richness, highly structured and delineated style, and explosively rich finish all make for a show-stopping impression. The slightly rounder 1990 Chambertin is not as tannic or as weighty as the Clos de Bèze. I would not touch a bottle for 5 years. It should mature and improve for 15–20 years.

At the bottom of the Beaune hierarchy is the 1990 Savigny-Lès-Beaune. It exhibits a deep ruby color, a ripe, jammy nose, good body, and soft tannins. Jadot's 1990 Monthélie displays a pure, black fruit nose to go along with its spicy, herbal scents. Medium to full bodied, with moderate tannins and crisp acidity, this chunky wine will drink well for up to a decade. The 1990 Pernand-Vergelesses-Clos de la Croix Pierre displays more finesse and less tannin, although it possesses just as much earthiness as the Monthélie. A medium- to full-bodied wine that warrants 2–3 years of cellaring, it will keep for 10–12 years. The 1990 Savigny-Lès-Beaune Les Dominaudes exhibits an opaque, dark ruby color, a huge, sweet, licorice-, black cherry–, and truffle-scented nose, dense, full-bodied flavors that are oozing extraction, and considerable tannin. Although it reveals tons of fruit, it should be cellared for 2–4 years. Impressive! The 1990 Volnay is sweet, ripe, fragrant, and seductive in an elegant, graceful style. The more tannic and tough 1990 Pommard displays excellent richness and a full-bodied, spicy, moderately tannic finish. The 1990 Aloxe-Corton is spicy and rich, with significant tannins. The 1990 Chassagne-Montrachet Morgeot-Clos de la Chapelle reveals a dark ruby color and a nose that offers an intense and alluring concoction of jammy red and black fruits, herbs, and smoky new oak. Rich and full bodied, with a wonderful inner core of concentrated Pinot fruit, this medium-bodied wine possesses elegance, structure, and power. It should last for another 10–12 years. The 1990 Volnay Les Santenots has an exquisite bouquet of minerals, black fruits, and oak. Full bodied and intensely concentrated, with tremendous density and length, this wine displays a sweet, long finish. The wine's grip and tannin suggest 12–15 years of longevity is possible. The 1990 Pommard Les Arvelets offers up a flamboyant nose of earthy red and spicy black fruits; a round, generously endowed, satiny smooth taste; and a lusty, heady, alcoholic finish. The 1990 Pommard Les Grands Epenots, a massive, chewy, opaque wine with a promising nose of black cherries, earth, and sweet oak, is stupendously concentrated and explosively rich.

Among the most forward, succulent, and juicy of the Beaune Premiers Crus are the Beaune Les Grèves, Beaune-Clos des Couchereaux, Beaune Les Touissaints, Beaune Les Bressandes, and Beaune Les Chouacheux. These wines are all more developed and seemingly less tannic than the Beaune Les Teurons, Beaune Les Boucherottes, Beaune Les Avaux, and Beaune-Clos des Ursules. The 1990 Beaune Les Grèves is also the most elegant and seductive. Juicy, fragrant, and undeniably seductive, it coats the mouth with sweet Pinot fruit. The 1990 Beaune-Clos des Couchereaux reveals an intense and dramatic nose of red and black fruits, oak, and flowers. Long, rich, and succulent, with gobs of fruit, it should drink well for the next 7–10 years. The 1990 Beaune Les Touissaints is fatter and heavier, displaying that expansive, sweet, chewy fruit that makes this vintage special. The nose soars from the glass with aromas of jammy black cherries and herbs. The finish is velvety and impressive. Drink it over the next 7–10 years. The 1990 Beaune Les Bressandes tastes rich and full, with more alcohol than the Touissaints, Couchereaux, and Grèves. It offers a concoction of red fruits and a multidimensional, layered texture with superb concentration. It should age beautifully for 10–15 years. The 1990 Beaune Les Chouacheux is terrific, with full body, a huge perfume of black fruits and flowers, and super length. The 1990 Beaune Les Teurons possesses more structure but shares the same voluptuous, spectacularly concentrated personality. I was thrilled by the purity and intensity of the 1990 Beaune Les Boucherottes. An exceptional wine with the precociousness of the other wines, it possesses more layers and dimension than many of its peers. The 1990 Beaune Les Avaux is another wine that tastes like sweet candy. An opulent, decadently rich, medium- to full-bodied wine bursting with jammy fruit, this fleshy, juicy wine will continue to drink well for another 10–12 years. Not surprisingly, the most structured and backward is the 1990 Beaune-Clos des Ursules. One of the treasures of the Jadot domaine, it possesses an opulent texture, denser and richer fruit flavors, more grip and structure, and noticeable tannins. The bouquet of roasted red and black fruits, toasty oak, and minerals is terrific. This wine needs 3–4 years, perhaps longer. It should evolve and improve for 15–25 years.

Jadot's 1990 Corton Dr. Peste, from the Hospices de Beaune, is dominated by toasty new oak. It lacks the density and richness of Jadot's other wines. The 1990 Corton from Jadot is an authoritative, full-bodied, monolithic wine; it offers exceptional richness and a powerful finish. **Anticipated maturity: 1997–2010.** Another backward yet spectacular wine is Jadot's Corton Les Pougets. This is a specialty of the house and is often among the finest red wines from the Corton appellation. The 1990 is a massive wine, with extraordinary richness, a viscous texture, and astonishing chewiness in its glycerin-dominated, high-alcohol, tannic finish. It needs at least 4–5 years of cellaring and should last for 20–30 years.

The generic 1989 Bourgogne Rouge offers a big, spicy, ripe nose, round, solidly built, expansive flavors, and good acidity. The 1989 Côte de Beaune-Villages is a pleasant, elegant, fruity wine with a short finish. The 1989 Beaune Les Boucherottes offers up a nose of smoky Pinot fruit (berries, herbs, and spices), a smooth-as-silk texture, wonderful concentration, and a volup-

tuous finish. Drink it over the next 7–12 years. The 1989 Beaune-Clos des Ursules possesses a huge, smoky, meaty nose and rich, seductively soft flavors,
with enough acidity to provide clarity. Drink it over the next decade. The 1989
Corton Les Pougets, one of the vintage's few blockbuster wines, is dense ruby
in color, with a superb, smoky, earthy, rich, fruity nose, full body, gobs of glycerin and richness, and a long finish. It can be cellared for up to 15 years. The
1989 Beaune Les Avaux is an elegant, richly fruity, supple Pinot. The 1990
Pommard Les Grands Epenots makes for a fleshy, meaty mouthful of wine. The
big, sweet, fragrant nose is followed by deep, chunky, enjoyable flavors of
plums, herbs, chocolate, and nuts. The acid is low, but this wine is loaded with
glycerin and fruit. The 1989 Chambolle-Musigny Les Amoureuses offers a fragrant bouquet of flowers, berries, and vanillin as well as a sweet, expansive,
opulent palate. Drink it over the next 10–12 years. The 1989 Musigny is backward, with a tight but promising, flowery, berry fragrance, rich, medium-bodied flavors, abundant tannin and acidity, and an impressive finish. Jadot's
1989 Clos Vougeot is an attractive, rich, full-bodied wine with an enticing
coffee-, berry-, and roasted nut–scented nose, rich, medium- to full-bodied flavors, soft tannins, and a heady, alcoholic finish. It will last for 12–15 years.
The 1989 Bonnes Mares is a surprisingly big, muscular, tannic wine, with gobs
of fruit, a saturated color, and a mineral element to its deep, savage, red fruit
character. It needs at least 3–4 years of cellaring and may keep for 12–15
years. The 1989 Gevrey-Chambertin-Clos St.-Jacques is, again, rich and
dense, with a terrific perfume of red fruits, vanillin, and spicy oak. The wine is
full bodied, with outstanding concentration, moderate tannins, decent acidity,
and a long finish. Drink it between now and 2006. The 1989 Gevrey-Chambertin Lavaux St.-Jacques is more developed and forward, with a huge, sweet,
wonderful fragrance of berry fruit and new oak. Drink this gorgeous wine over
the next 10–12 years. Jadot's 1989 Ruchottes-Chambertin exhibits a huge
bouquet of smoky, herbal, meaty Pinot fruit that is followed by deep, fabulously concentrated flavors, body, and admirable length. The 1989 Chambertin-Clos de Bèze reveals spectacular ripeness, a huge, concentrated,
superripe, perfumed nose of oak and berry fruit, long, rich flavors, fine structure, crisp acidity, and a lusty finish.
OTHER THOUGHTS: The Gageys, father André (supposedly retired) and son
Pierre-Henri, along with their gifted oenologist, Jacques Lardière, prove that
sometimes "nice" guys do finish first.

LUCIEN JAYER (VOSNE-ROMANÉE)* * *

1990 Echézeaux	E	85
1990 Vosne-Romanée Les Beaux Monts	E	85

The 1990 Echézeaux is fruity, soft, and delicious but clearly destined to be
drunk over the next 4–5 years. The 1990 Vosne-Romanée Les Beaux Monts
exhibits more tannin, but it lacks color saturation and finishes without the intensity and richness one would expect from this producer.
OTHER THOUGHTS: Onetime great producer appears to be stumbling.

DOMAINE ROBERT JAYER-GILLES
(MAGNY-LÈS-VILLERS)* * * */* * * * *

1990 Côte de Nuits-Villages	D	90
1989 Côte de Nuits-Villages	D	87
1990 Echézeaux	EE	96
1989 Echézeaux	EE	92
1989 Hautes-Côtes de Beaune	C	84
1990 Hautes-Côtes de Nuits	C	88
1989 Hautes-Côtes de Nuits	C	87
1990 Nuits St.-Georges Les Damodes	E	94
1989 Nuits St.-Georges Les Damodes	E	92
1990 Nuits St.-Georges Les Hauts Poirets	D	92

The 1990 Hautes-Côtes de Nuits enjoys a saturated ruby/purple color and a big nose of cassis, minerals, and new oak. There is excellent definition, medium to full body, and a concentrated, long, luscious finish. Drink it over the next 7–8 years. Robert Jayer's 1990 Côte de Nuits-Villages has a saturated black/purple color and intense black cherry, herb, and sweet oaky aromas. This wine reveals superrichness, medium to full body, wonderful purity and clarity, and a long, soft, tannic finish. Drink it over the next 10–12 years. Jayer's 1990 Nuits St.-Georges Les Hauts Poirets offers aromas of jammy black cherries and new oak, great ripeness, medium to full body, soft tannins, and admirable length. It should drink well for the next 10–15 years. Jayer's 1990 Nuits St.-Georges Les Damodes is a magnificent wine. The nearly black color is followed by a nose with aromas of *sur-maturité* in the pruny, black cherry scents intertwined with copious quantities of toasty new oak and roasted meats. The wine exhibits great extraction of flavor, full body, and a sweet, rich, viscous finish. The significant tannins are balanced by the wine's awesome concentration. Drink it between 1995 and 2010. Although softer, the 1990 Echézeaux shares the same deep black/purple color, with a more compelling and open nose of spring flowers, minerals, black fruits, and toasty oak. Deep, sweet, and much less tannic than the Les Damodes, this seductive wine makes for an opulent mouthful of Grand Cru Pinot Noir. Drink it over the next 10–15 years. Jayer's 1989 Hautes-Côtes de Beaune is an attractive, ripe, generously fruity, oaky wine that should be consumed over the next 3–4 years. The superb 1989 Hautes-Côtes de Nuits is an amazing wine with a huge nose of smoky, black fruits, minerals, and licorice. It exhibits excellent concentration, a black cherry personality, and long, medium-bodied, spicy flavors, and it is capable of lasting for 7–8 years. The 1989 Côte de Nuits-Villages is another stunningly fine wine for its pedigree. The color is deep ruby, and the bouquet offers up aromas of toast, black plums, herbs, and minerals. There is amazing ripeness, a rich, beautifully extracted midpalate, and a long, smooth-as-silk finish. This Côte de Nuits-Villages can last for 10 years. Jayer's best-kept secret is the microscopic quantities of his Nuits St.-Georges Les Damodes. The 1989 delivers an opaque, black/ruby/purple color and a huge bouquet of flowers, black fruits, and spicy new oak. The wine is full bodied, with superb flavor definition and depth as well as moderate tannins in the long, rich, impressive finish. It should keep for up to 20 years. Last, Jayer's 1989 Echézeaux, although not as massive as his Nuits St.-Georges Les Damodes, is a concentrated, fragrant, seductive wine with layers of fruit. Possessing an intense perfumed character dominated by the smell of black fruits, spices, new oak, and minerals, it is rich and luscious, softer than Les Damodes, brilliantly balanced, concentrated, and opulent in its long finish. This is a terrific Echézeaux for drinking over the next 10–15 years.

OTHER THOUGHTS: Since 1985, an array of fabulous wines has emanated from these cellars.

DOMAINE JOBLOT (GIVRY)* * * *

1990 Givry-Clos du Cellier-aux-Moines	C	92
1989 Givry-Clos du Cellier-aux-Moines	C	90
1990 Givry-Clos de la Servoisine	C	91
1989 Givry-Clos de la Servoisine	C	88

Joblot is the uncontested king in the Givry appellation. The 1990 Servoisine offers a spectacularly opaque, deep purple color and an intense, relatively unevolved nose of plums, roasted nuts, minerals, and spicy new oak. The wine is crammed with richness as well as a multidimensional texture and has an explosively long finish. The 1990 Clos du Cellier-aux-Moines reveals a slightly denser color and, from an aromatic perspective, is more closed. The wine is thicker, richer, and slightly more concentrated, and the tannins are also more pronounced. The 1989 Givry-Clos de la Servoisine possesses a saturated, deep ruby color and a huge nose of ripe berry fruit intertwined with aromas of smoke, vanillin, and minerals. In the mouth there is explosive ripeness, a supple, silky texture, and a long finish. The 1989 Givry-Clos du Cellier-aux-Moines has an opaque dark ruby/purple color. The nose offers abundant aromas of berries, toast, and minerals. There is impressive concentration, fine acidity, soft, moderate tannins, and an explosive finish.

OTHER THOUGHTS: Memorize this name for gorgeous, value-priced, sumptuous Pinot Noir.

JEAN-LUC JOILLOT (POMMARD)* * *

1989 Hautes-Côtes de Beaune	C	87
1990 Pommard Les Noizons	D	85

Although the monolithic 1990 Pommard Les Noizons reveals excellent color and spicy, ripe fruit aromas, it has a chunky, medium-bodied feel that lacks complexity and personality. Drink it over the next 7–8 years. The 1989 Hautes-Côtes de Beaune is a fine value in Pinot Noir. This wine exhibits a supersaturated, deep color; a big nose of ripe berry, Pinot fruit; lush, intense flavors; and a heady finish.

OTHER THOUGHTS: Can't say much about Joillot.

MICHEL JUILLOT (MERCUREY)* * * *

1990 Aloxe-Corton Les Caillettes	D	89
1990 Bourgogne	C	79

1990 Corton Les Perrières	E	91
1990 Mercurey	C	82
1990 Mercurey Les Champs Martins	D	86
1990 Mercurey-Clos des Barraults	D	87
1990 Mercurey-Clos Tonnerre	D	82
1990 Mercurey Vieilles Vignes	C	86

Juillot has turned out an attractive, although tannic, medium-bodied 1990 Mercurey Vieilles Vignes. It offers a dusty, cherry fruitiness, firm structure, and surprising weight and intensity. Approachable now, it will last for 7–8 years. The deep ruby-colored 1990 Mercurey-Clos des Barraults offers up a spicy, black cherry– and mineral-scented nose, medium- to full-bodied flavors, excellent concentration, and a moderately long finish. The 1990 Mercurey Les Champs Martins, which is slightly lighter than the Clos des Barraults, is a beautifully rendered, richly fruity, medium-bodied wine. It should continue to drink well for the next 5–7 years. Juillot's 1990 Aloxe-Corton Les Caillettes exhibits a deep ruby color and a sweet, plummy nose with hints of vanillin and minerals. It is a full-bodied, impressively endowed and structured wine that enjoys serious concentration, a subtle touch of toasty new oak, and a dense, tannic finish. Drink it over the next 10–12 years. The 1990 Corton Les Perrières displays an explosively rich nose of toasty new oak and roasted black fruits such as plums and prunes. Sweet, expansive, chewy, and well endowed, this full-bodied, structured, deep wine has at least 12–15 years of aging potential.

OTHER THOUGHTS: Serious winemaker can turn out fine Mercureys and Cortons.

FRANÇOIS LABET (VOUGEOT)* * *

1990 Beaune-Clos des Couchereaux	C	82+
1990 Beaune-Clos des Monsnières	C	79
1990 Hautes-Côtes de Beaune	B	85
1990 Hautes-Côtes de Nuits	C	83

These are all attractive, round, ripe, straightforward Pinot Noirs with good concentration, soft tannins, and satiny finishes. Drink them over the next 2–4 years. Oddly enough the least expensive wine, the Hautes-Côtes de Beaune, performed better than the others.

OTHER THOUGHTS: Labet is intent on making better wines, so keep an eye on him.

MICHEL LAFARGE (VOLNAY)* * * *

1990 Bourgogne	B	84
1990 Bourgogne Passe-Tout-Grains	B	85
1990 Pommard Les Pézerolles	E	92
1990 Volnay-Clos du Château des Ducs	E	91

Lafarge's 1990 Bourgogne Passe-Tout-Grains possesses richness, ripeness, and a soft, supple texture. Drink it over the next 4–5 years. The 1990 Volnay-

Clos du Château des Ducs reveals a splendidly saturated dark ruby/purple color, a huge nose of pure black and red fruits, medium to full body, superb concentration, soft tannins, and a super finish. It should drink well for at least 10–15 years. The 1990 Pommard Les Pézerolles behaves like a Pommard in its full-bodied, pumped-up, rich style, but there is grace, charm, and finesse. The deep, saturated ruby/purple color is followed by a promising nose of jammy red and black fruits, earth, and toasty oak. Full bodied and rich, this substantial yet stylish and seductive wine should continue to drink well for 10–12 years. OTHER THOUGHTS: Textbook red burgundies full of fruit and character from a can-do-no-wrong producer.

DOMAINE COMTE LAFON (MEURSAULT)* * * * *

1990 Volnay Champans	E	91
1989 Volnay Champans	E	88
1990 Volnay Clos des Chênes	E	88
1989 Volnay Clos des Chênes	E	86
1990 Volnay Santenots	E	93
1989 Volnay Santenots	E	91

The 1990 Volnay Clos des Chênes is a wine with a thick, dark ruby color as well as a huge nose of superripe, jammy cherries, spices, and minerals. It should keep for several decades. The 1990 Volnay Champans reveals an even more saturated, opaque ruby/purple color. The sensational nose offers up aromas of overripe cherries and plums, as well as toasty, smoky oak and roasted herbs. Boldly flavored and superconcentrated, this rich, dense wine manages to retain an extraordinary degree of elegance. The finish is long, moderately tannic, and pure. **Anticipated maturity: 1997–2015.** Lafon's largest production in red wine is Volnay Santenots. It is also the estate's best red wine. The black/ruby-colored 1990 Santenots offers up aromas of minerals, black cherries, flowers, and oak. There is magnificent richness, considerable body, glycerin, and extraction, as well as tons of tannin and alcohol. The tannins are soft, so the textural impact is chewy and voluptuous. This is a beautifully concentrated, multidimensional wine that should drink well for 15–20 years. The 1989 Volnay Clos des Chênes offers a beautiful nose of vibrant berry fruit, herbs, and spicy oak; a beautiful, rich, soft, voluptuous texture; and a long, heady finish. Delicious now, this wine should continue to evolve for 10–12 more years. The 1989 Volnay Champans is a more backward style of wine, with formidable stuffing, an intense but reticent bouquet of spicy oak, red fruits, and minerals, beautiful balance, superb concentration of fruit, and plenty of tannin. It should last for 12–15 years. The glorious 1989 Volnay Santenots is an unbelievably concentrated, magnificently deep wine bursting with red and black fruits. Displaying a sensationally fragrant nose and a finish that must last for a minute, this wine is powerful and packed with fruit yet manages to carry off its large-scale size with considerable elegance. Drink it between 1996 and 2010. OTHER THOUGHTS: Although the fantastic reputation for whites is justified, this estate also makes terrific reds.

LAFOUGE (AUXEY-DURESSES)* * *

1989 Auxey-Duresses-Clos du Val	C	85
1989 Auxey-Duresses La Chapelle	C	86

These are two highly competent examples of how good Auxey-Duresses can sometimes be. These wines, which possess good tannin, body, and plenty of ripe, dusty, cherry fruit, as well as a certain pervasive earthiness in their flavors, will last for up to a decade. They represent clean, well-knit, full, chunkier styles of red burgundy.

OTHER THOUGHTS: Thrifty consumers take note!

LALEURE-PIOT PÈRE ET FILS (PERNAND-VERGELESSES)* * *

1990 Chorey-Lès-Beaune-Les Champs Longs	C	85
1990 Corton Les Bressandes	E	88
1990 Corton Rognet	E	88
1990 Pernand-Vergelesses	C	83
1990 Pernand-Vergelesses Les Vergelesses	C	81
1990 Savigny-Lès-Beaune Les Vergelesses	C	85

Consumers shopping for a decent value should check out the 1990 Chorey-Lès-Beaune-Les Champs Longs. Ripe and sweet, it can be drunk over the next 3–4 years. The 1990 Savigny-Lès-Beaune Les Vergelesses is a solid, sturdy wine, with more tannin as well as a pervasive, earthy stemminess. Medium bodied, with a deep red fruit (cherries) character, this wine should be drunk before 2003. The 1990 Corton Rognet exhibits a saturated dark color, excellent concentration, medium to full body, and that sweet inner core of ripe fruit that is a hallmark of the 1990 red burgundy vintage. I would opt for drinking this wine over the next decade. The 1990 Corton Les Bressandes is even softer and fatter, with a huge black cherry–, sweet toasty oak–, and herb-scented nose. Round, voluptuous, and chewy, with multidimensional flavors and layer upon layer of fruit, this hedonistic wine merits consumption over the next 7–9 years.

OTHER THOUGHTS: An irregular performer that warrants attention in the top years—1985 and 1990.

LAMARCHE (VOSNE-ROMANÉE)* * *

1989 Clos Vougeot	EE	87
1989 Echézeaux	EE	86
1989 Vosne-Romanée Les Chaumes	EE	85
1989 Vosne-Romanée La Grande Rue	EE	88
1989 Vosne-Romanée Les Suchots	EE	86

The 1989 Vosne-Romanée Les Chaumes exhibits good color, a fine texture, soft tannins, and depth and ripeness. Drink it over the next 5–7 years. The 1989 Vosne-Romanée Les Suchots displays more new oak in the nose and is more tannic and structured. It could last for up to 8 years. The 1989 Echézeaux possesses a deep ruby color, an elegant, flowery, spicy, raspberry-

and oak-scented nose, admirable concentration, decent tannin, and fresh acidity. Drink it between 1994 and 2000. The 1989 Clos Vougeot offers a deep ruby color, a sweet, oaky, black fruit–scented nose, ripe, medium-bodied flavors, and a long finish. Drink it over the next 7–8 years. The deeply colored, backward 1989 Vosne-Romanée La Grande Rue is concentrated, with a tight but blossoming bouquet of black fruits, minerals, Oriental spices, and new oak. There is beautiful harmony among its admirably endowed components, crisp acidity, plenty of soft tannins, and abundant quantities of fruit. Drink it over the next 10–12 years.

OTHER THOUGHTS: Famous old firm continues to show signs of a comeback, but the quality is still not proportional to the greatness of the domaine's vineyards.

RENÉ LAMY-PILLOT (SANTENAY)* *

1990 Blagny Premier Cru	C	83
1990 Chassagne-Montrachet	C	84
1990 Chassagne-Montrachet Boudriotte	D	86
1990 Chassagne-Montrachet Champs Morgeot	C	77
1990 Saint-Aubin Les Castets	D	85

Lamy's 1990 Saint-Aubin Les Castets displays a fragrant, berry, earthy, spicy Pinot nose; medium body; lush, sweet, expansive flavors; and a supple finish. Drink it over the next 4–5 years. Deeper colored, with more spice, tannin, body, and concentration, the 1990 Chassagne-Montrachet Boudriotte is a larger-scale wine, with excellent concentration as well as plenty of grip and structure. It needs 2–4 years of cellaring and should last for 10–12.

OTHER THOUGHTS: Far better whites than reds.

DOMAINE LECHENEAUT (NUITS ST.-GEORGES)* * * *

1990 Clos de la Roche	EE	94
1990 Nuits St.-Georges Les Cailles	D	91+
1990 Nuits St.-Georges Les Damodes	D	90

The 1990 Nuits St.-Georges Les Damodes exhibits a dark ruby/purple color and a huge nose of roasted nuts, black plums, and cherries. This sumptuous, intensely concentrated, full-bodied wine displays low acidity, sweet tannins, and gobs of glycerin, extract, and alcohol. Drink it over the next decade. The 1990 Nuits St.-Georges Les Cailles is slightly harder and more tannic. The deep, nearly opaque dark ruby color is followed by a wine with a spicy; vanillin- and black cherry–scented nose; rich, medium- to full-bodied flavors; and an impressively constituted, rich, structured finish. It should drink well for 15 years or more. Domaine Lecheneaut's 1990 Clos de la Roche is an exotic wine, with a huge nose of cinnamon, smoke, tobacco, and black fruits. It offers admirable density and richness and a chewy, fleshy texture endowed with significant glycerin and extract. Considerable tannin lurks under the lavish quantities of fruit. Drink this profound wine over the next 10–12 years.

OTHER THOUGHTS: If the exquisite 1990s are indicative, this is a blossoming superstar.

PHILIPPE LECLERC (GEVREY-CHAMBERTIN)* * * * *

1990 Bourgogne Les Bons Batons	C	88
1990 Chambolle-Musigny Les Babillaires	D	87
1989 Gevrey-Chambertin	C	84
1990 Gevrey-Chambertin Les Cazetiers	E	90
1989 Gevrey-Chambertin Les Cazetiers	E	86
1990 Gevrey-Chambertin Les Champeaux	E	89
1990 Gevrey-Chambertin Combe aux Moines	E	92+
1989 Gevrey-Chambertin Combe aux Moines	E	86

Leclerc's 1990 Bourgogne Les Bons Batons offers up a huge, sweet nose of black cherries and herbs, followed by unctuous, thick flavors and a full-bodied, lusty finish. Short on finesse, it delivers gobs of richness and character. Leclerc's 1990 Chambolle-Musigny Les Babillaires displays sweet, surprisingly graceful and elegant aromas of flowers and red fruits. This lush, opulently styled wine is medium to full bodied, with admirable sweet fruit and enough new oak to give it definition. Drink it over the next decade. There is a heavy overlay of oak in the 1990 Gevrey-Chambertin Les Champeaux. The deep ruby/purple color and the big, toasty, herb-, prune-, and plum-scented nose make for a dramatic impression. There is lovely richness, medium to full body, and that unctuous thickness that Leclerc often obtains. Drink it over the next decade. The 1990 Gevrey-Chambertin Les Cazetiers offers an opaque dark ruby/garnet color; a sweet, roasted nut, meaty, vanillin- and black raspberry–scented nose; immense body and richness; and a blockbuster finish. It should be drinkable in 2–3 years and last for 12–15. The star in 1990 is the Gevrey-Chambertin Combe aux Moines. This opaque dark purple/black-colored wine exhibits a tight but promising bouquet of black fruits, truffles, herbs, cloves, and smoke. There is astonishing richness, massive body, gobs of glycerin and extract, and a thick, chewy finish. Drink it over the next 20 years. The 1989 Gevrey-Chambertin is round and tasty, although light. The 1989 Gevrey-Chambertin Les Cazetiers is smooth and supple, with an attractive herb and berry fragrance, good, smoky, medium-bodied flavors, and a round finish. It should drink nicely over the next 5–8 years. The 1989 Gevrey-Chambertin Combe aux Moines exhibits more tannin and glycerin.

OTHER THOUGHTS: Burgundy's answer to a Hell's Angels motorcycle gang member is brilliant and focused in his cellars.

RENÉ LECLERC (GEVREY-CHAMBERTIN)* * * *

1990 Gevrey-Chambertin Clos Prieur	D	85
1990 Gevrey-Chambertin Combe aux Moines	E	91
1990 Gevrey-Chambertin Lavaux St.-Jacques	E	89+

Leclerc's 1990 Gevrey-Chambertin Clos Prieur reveals a dense, plummy color; a big, pruney, earthy nose; long, deep, overripe flavors; full body; and plenty of alcohol, glycerin, and tannin. Drink it over the next 7–8 years. The 1990 Gevrey-Chambertin Lavaux St.-Jacques reveals a highly saturated, opaque, ruby/purple color; a sweet, roasted nut, cassis, smoky nose; and unctuous, concentrated, full-bodied, powerful flavors. This enormous style of Pinot Noir will drink well for the next 10–12 years. The thrilling 1990 Gevrey-Chambertin Combe aux Moines possesses a huge nose of sweet black fruits, coffee, mushrooms, and tar. A rich, expansive-flavored wine with a viscous texture and superb length, it has 10–15 years of cellaring potential.

OTHER THOUGHTS: This up-and-down performer has been on target since the mid-1980s.

OLIVIER LEFLAIVE FRÈRES (PULIGNY-MONTRACHET)* * *

1990 Pommard Les Rugiens	D	85
1990 Volnay-Clos de la Barre	D	87
1990 Volnay Fremiers	D	85

The excellent 1990 Volnay-Clos de la Barre has a deep ruby color, an earthy, black cherry– and herb-scented nose, excellent concentration, moderate tannins, crisp acidity, and a fine finish. It will last for 10–12 years. The lighter 1990 Volnay Fremiers is tasty and elegant. Drink it over the next 4–6 years. Leflaive's 1990 Pommard Les Rugiens is a medium-bodied, solidly made, tangy style of Pommard with spicy fruit and adequate depth, body, and power. Drink it over the next 5–6 years.

OTHER THOUGHTS: The *négociant* with the magic name is making considerable strides in red wine quality.

DOMAINE LEJEUNE (POMMARD)* * * *

1990 Bourgogne	B	87
1990 Pommard Les Argillières	D	90
1989 Pommard Les Argillières	D	90
1990 Pommard Les Rugiens	D	93
1989 Pommard Les Rugiens	D	94

The 1990 Bourgogne has a deep ruby color; an attractive nose of red and black fruits, smoke, and herbs; and a ripe, long finish. Drink it over the next 4–5 years. The 1990 Pommard Les Argillières offers a stunning nose of spring flowers, toasty new oak, and black fruits. Deep, full bodied, and concentrated, with considerable tannic clout, this lusty, full-throttle Pommard should evolve gracefully for 10–15 years. The rich and multidimensional 1990 Pommard Les Rugiens is a saturated dark ruby/purple color. The wine's tight nose opens with airing to reveal jammy aromas of black cherries and red currants intertwined with roasted scents of oak. Superbly concentrated, this deep, broodingly backward Pommard is a magnificent head turner. **Anticipated maturity: 1997–2010.** The 1989 Pommard Les Argillières offers a spectacular nose of sweet, jammy fruit, new oak, and flowers. The finish is spectacularly long and velvety. Drink this beauty over the next 7–8 years. The 1989 Pommard Les Rugiens exhibits a compelling nose of oak, black fruits, spices, and minerals. Its staggering concentration culminates in a huge, lavishly rich aftertaste that lasts for well over a minute. The acidity is low, and the tannins, while moderate in quantity, are soft. Drink it over the next decade.

OTHER THOUGHTS: Oh, how I have underestimated these wines in the past. I am now a true believer in Lejeune!

LEROY (VOSNE-ROMANÉE)* * * * *

1989 Auxey-Duresses	C	87
1990 Bourgogne Rouge	C	86
1989 Bourgogne Rouge	C	85
1990 Chambertin	EEE	100
1989 Chambertin	EEE	90
1990 Chambolle-Musigny Les Fremières	E	90
1989 Chambolle-Musigny Les Fremières	E	87
1990 Clos de la Roche	EEE	100
1989 Clos de la Roche	EEE	93
1990 Clos Vougeot	EEE	94
1989 Clos Vougeot	EEE	89
1990 Corton Les Rénardes	EE	90
1989 Corton Les Rénardes	EE	87
1989 Gevrey-Chambertin	E	86
1990 Gevrey-Chambertin aux Combottes	EE	93
1989 Gevrey-Chambertin aux Combottes	EE	90
1990 Latricières-Chambertin	EEE	96
1989 Latricières-Chambertin	EEE	94
1989 Musigny	EEE	91
1990 Nuits St.-Georges Les Allots	E	92
1989 Nuits St.-Georges Les Allots	E	89
1990 Nuits St.-Georges aux Bas de Combe	E	90
1989 Nuits St.-Georges aux Bas de Combe	E	86
1990 Nuits St.-Georges Les Boudots	EE	94
1989 Nuits St.-Georges Les Boudots	EE	93
1990 Nuits St.-Georges Les Lavières	E	90
1989 Nuits St.-Georges Les Lavières	E	86
1990 Nuits St.-Georges Les Vignes Rondes	EE	92
1989 Nuits St.-Georges Les Vignes Rondes	EE	90
1990 Pommard Les Trois Follots	E	87
1990 Pommard Les Vignots	E	90+
1989 Pommard Les Vignots	E	86
1990 Richebourg	EEE	98
1989 Richebourg	EEE	92

1990 Romanée St.-Vivant	EEE	96
1989 Romanée St.-Vivant	EEE	92
1990 Savigny-Lès-Beaune Les Narbantons	D	92
1989 Savigny-Lès-Beaune Les Narbantons	D	87
1990 Vosne-Romanée Les Beaux Monts	EE	98
1989 Vosne-Romanée Les Beaux Monts	EE	91
1990 Vosne-Romanée Les Brûlées	EE	96
1989 Vosne-Romanée Les Brûlées	EE	90
1990 Vosne-Romanée Clos des Réas	E	92
1989 Vosne-Romanée Clos des Réas	E	88
1990 Vosne-Romanée Les Genevrières	E	89
1989 Vosne-Romanée Les Genevrières	E	87

There is no question that in the cellars of Leroy one can taste the summits that Pinot Noir can achieve. The perfectionist proprietor, Lalou Bize-Leroy, has long been fanatical about the quality of her wines. Most of the following wines will not peak for at least 10–15 years, and Lalou Bize-Leroy believes the most concentrated wines will last 40–60 years. The 1990 Nuits St.-Georges aux Bas de Combe offers a ripe nose given its aromas of jammy black raspberries, prunes, and truffles. This sweet, forward wine exhibits copious quantities of rich fruit, glycerin, and tannins. The 1990 Nuits St.-Georges Les Lavières displays a seductive perfume of minerals, flowers, and sweet blackberries. The wine is well structured, with outstanding concentration, an opulent texture, and a firm, moderately tannic, long finish. It admirably combines power and elegance. **Anticipated maturity: 1994–2008.** The 1990 Nuits St.-Georges Les Allots exhibits a licorice, black fruit, earthy character; a supersaturated, deep purple color; deep, thick, rich, fruity flavors; full body; and a sweet, long, moderately tannic finish. Leroy's 1990 Nuits St.-Georges Les Vignes Rondes reveals a sensational nose of smoke, minerals, flowers, and black raspberries. Dense, with a blazingly well-defined personality, this rich, full-bodied, complex wine possesses considerable tannins as well as stunning concentration and length. **Anticipated maturity: 1995–2010+.** The most exotic and flashy of these five wines is the 1990 Nuits St.-Georges Les Boudots. The huge nose of roasted meats, pure black raspberries, and herbs soars from the glass. Full bodied, with layer upon layer of rich, unctuous Pinot fruit, this superconcentrated, voluptuously textured wine is so rich that the formidable tannin levels are nearly concealed. The finish goes on and on. **Anticipated maturity: 1995–2010+.** The 1990 Vosne-Romanée Clos des Réas possesses a sweet nose of nearly overripe fruit. Powerful and rich, with wonderful expansiveness and opulence, it will drink well for 10–15 years. The slightly lighter 1990 Vosne-Romanée Les Genevrières is elegant in a flattering, feminine style. It offers a beautiful red fruit character, a subtle touch of oak, and a long finish. Drink it over the next 10–12 years. The 1990 Vosne-Romanée Les Brûlées reveals a roasted nose of meat and smoky black fruit. A flashy and extroverted wine, it exhibits a broad-shouldered, expansive, succulent texture, with oodles of flavor and glycerin. This thrilling wine should last for 15 or more years. The more subtle 1990 Vosne-Romanée Les Beaux Monts offers authoritative and persistent aromas of black fruits, herbs, underbrush, and sweet oak. Displaying exceptional concentration of flavor and high levels of tannin, it should be cellared for 7–8 years and should last for 30 or more. The 1990 Chambolle-Musigny Les Fremières is elegant, sweet, soft, floral, and perfumed. Much more decadent and showy is the 1990 Gevrey-Chambertin aux Combottes. The sweet nose of coffee, caramel, black cherries, and earth is a turn-on. This full-bodied, voluptuously textured, superbly concentrated wine with no hard edges exhibits lavish quantities of jammy fruit buttressed nicely by new oak, decent acidity, and moderate tannins. It should last for 20–25 years. The dense ruby/purple-colored 1990 Clos Vougeot exhibits admirable weight, massive concentration of fruit, high tannins, and a long, tightly knit finish. The 1990 Latricières-Chambertin offers up a fragrant nose of truffles, cinnamon, cloves, smoked meat, and black fruits. It is all finesse and elegance, but with stunning concentration of fruit and a wonderfully long, impeccably proportioned finish. Despite its current appeal, it needs 7–8 years of cellaring. Like Leroy's other Grands Crus, it will last for 30–40 years. The black-colored 1990 Richebourg is amazingly closed, but the awesome concentration, sheer precision of flavors, and extraordinary fatness and intensity are mind-boggling. This is another wine to put away for at least a decade and then watch unfold for the next 20–35 years. There can be little doubt that Lalou Bize-Leroy makes Burgundy's finest Romanée St.-Vivant. With its dark ruby/purple color and huge, sweet nose of exotic spices, smoked meats, black cherries, and cloves, the 1990 is provocative and compelling. The wine is rich, long, and full bodied, with moderate tannins, a sensational midpalate that is crammed with fruit, and a deep, rich finish. It should reach its plateau of maturity in 6–7 years and last for 25–30.

The two best burgundies I tasted in the 1990 vintage were Lalou's 1990 Clos de la Roche and 1990 Chambertin. The Clos de la Roche offers a smorgasbord of aromas, ranging from scents of new saddle leather, black plums, black raspberries, minerals, and smoked duck to Oriental spices. In the mouth the first impression is one of an extraordinarily layered wine with a texture akin to biting into a chewy candy. It is sweet, rich, full, and dense, yet everything is so well defined. The finish lasts for over a minute. When should one consume a wine such as this? It should be at its best between 1996 and 2010. The Chambertin will probably need more time, but what is so extraordinary about this wine is the concentrated essence of Pinot Noir. There is a nectarlike, honeyed texture to the 1990 Chambertin, which is the richest, longest wine I have ever tasted from this renowned vineyard. The nose is closed yet also intense. Huge aromas of black fruits, minerals, subtle oak, and spices emerge with coaxing.

I suppose there is a natural tendency to overlook Madame Bize-Leroy's Côte de Beaune wines. Her sweet, round 1990 Bourgogne Rouge exhibits good color, an expansive texture, and a generous mouth-feel. Moreover, it will last for 10–15 years. The 1990 Savigny-Lès-Beaune Les Narbantons is awesome. The forceful bouquet, which is just beginning to form, soars from the glass, offering up aromas of minerals, toasty oak, and gobs of black fruit. It possesses magnificent richness, medium to full body, and a layered, multidimensional, chewy texture. **Anticipated maturity: 1996–2010+.** The 1990 Pommard Les Trois Follots is a good wine, with deep color and a spicy, earthy nose, but it does not possess the dimension, flavor, or length of the 1990 Pommard Les Vignots. The latter wine's tannins are considerable, but there is enough body and concentration of fruit to stand up to the wine's structure. Deep and spicy, it is among the more reasonably priced Leroy red burgundies. The 1990 Corton Les Rénardes is a frightfully backward, masculine, tough-textured wine that is loaded with concentration, glycerin, and tannin. It should last 25–30 years. Just how good the 1989 red burgundy vintage has turned out is exemplified by the comments of Madame Bize-Leroy, who compares 1989 with 1964, which produced gloriously opulent red burgundies. The 1989 Bourgogne Rouge is a tasty, round, ripe, chunky wine that should drink deliciously for 5–6 years. Even better is the excellent 1989 Auxey-Duresses, an expansively flavored, sweet, generously endowed, spicy wine that can easily sustain 10–15 years of aging. The elegant raspberry- and strawberry-scented 1989 Savigny-Lès-Beaune Les Narbantons has copious quantities of earthy fruit, soft tannins, decent acidity, and a round finish. Drink it over the next 12–15 years. The fine 1989 Pommard Les Vignots offers a spicy, mineral, and berry fruit character, tender tannins, and a round, straightforward finish. Drink it over the next decade. Leroy's 1989 Corton Les Rénardes combines an elegant, berry fruit character with a strong *terroir* element. There is a meaty texture to the wine, but the tannins are high. The wine is capable of lasting 15–20 years. The 1989 Nuits St.-Georges aux Bas de Combe is a forward, seductive style of red burgundy. It should make delicious drinking for at least a decade. Similarly styled was the 1989 Nuits St.-Georges Les Lavières. This wine exhibited medium body, silky tannins, and an attractive, rich berry fruit–scented nose, with some spicy new oak also in evidence. More serious and ambitious is the 1989 Nuits St.-Georges Les Allots. This earthy, smoky, black fruit–scented wine enjoys impressive intensity, a full-bodied, robust texture on the palate, and spicy, moderately tannic, rich flavors. It is capable of lasting 10–15 years. The 1989 Nuits St.-Georges Les Vignes Rondes was pure seduction. The huge nose of black fruits, spicy new oak, and flowers is followed by an opulently styled, satiny-textured, beautifully delineated wine that exhibits plenty of sweet Pinot fruit. Drink this beauty over the next 12–15 years. The terrific 1989 Nuits St.-Georges Les Boudots reveals a huge, exotic nose of smoked meats, tar, flowers, and black plums. It is a wine of stunning richness, with gobs of glycerin and extract. Approachable now, this beauty should hit its peak by the mid-1990s and last through the first decade of the next century. The 1989 Vosne-Romanée Clos des Réas revealed a sweet, soft, gentle aroma of black fruits and flowers intertwined with scents of minerals. The wine is generously endowed with seductive flavors, decent acidity, and a smooth finish. It should last for at least 10–12 years. The 1989 Vosne-Romanée Les Genevrières makes for a fine glass of wine. The bouquet offers a beautifully etched, floral, fruity nose. The wine exhibits a fine supple texture, soft tannins, and a long finish. The 1989 Vosne-Romanée Les Brûlées possesses an explosive nose of juicy black fruits, spring flowers, and spicy new oak. There are no hard edges, as the wine offers up abundant levels of velvety, succulent fruit, soft acids, and round, ripe tannins. This beauty should age magnificently for the next 15–20 years. Be sure to check out Leroy's 1989 Vosne-Romanée Les Beaux Monts, a staggeringly rich, profound bottle of Vosne-Romanée with chewy, intense flavors and sensational concentration. As for the 1989 Richebourg, it was much more closed and backward. Although less flattering and enjoyable, one has to be impressed with the profound deep ruby/purple color, the reticent yet promising bouquet of black fruits, minerals, and Oriental spices, and the long, highly structured, dense, tannic flavors. It should keep for 25–30 years. Leroy's 1989 Romanée St.-Vivant is another dense, earthy, chewy wine that possesses at least 25 years of aging potential. Although backward, it exhibits a multidimensional personality, layers of highly extracted fruit, excellent color, and a moderately long, spicy finish. The 1989 Chambolle-Musigny Les Fremières is an elegant, floral, feminine, easy-to-drink style of wine, with graceful flavors and a soft texture. I would opt for consuming it within its first 10 years of life. The 1989 Clos Vougeot offers up a lovely concoction of superripe red fruits in its perfumed nose. The wine has a good level of fruit extract, soft, tender tannins, low acidity, and a beautifully lush, opulent finish. Drink it over the next 10–15 years. The 1989 Musigny possesses an exquisite bouquet of fruit, oak, flowers, and minerals. Its fragrant personality, soft elegance, and finesse suggest drinking over the next 15–20 years. The 1989 Gevrey-Chambertin reveals surprisingly dense color, a big, smoked meat, leathery nose, and chocolatey, robust flavors. It is a chewy mouthful of burgundy. Drink it over the next 10–12 years. The 1989 Gevrey-Chambertin aux Combottes offers up a huge nose of Oriental spices, superripe cherries, toasty vanillin oak, and ground beef. It is a glorious glass of expansive, opulent red burgundy for drinking over the next 12–15 years. The 1989 Clos de la Roche was another fabulously rich, exotic wine. From its huge bouquet of earthy, cinnamon, smoked meat aromas, to its full-bodied, luxuriously rich, cherrylike flavors, this was a wine of great extraction of flavor and a compelling, multidimensional personality. With its almost raunchy aromas and flavors, this magnificent bottle of Clos de la Roche goes to the limit of exoticism. It will last for 25 years. Almost as spectacular and exotic was the 1989 Latricières-Chambertin. Here is another fat wine, crammed with gorgeous levels of superripe Pinot fruit intermingled with aromas of leather, cedar, cinnamon, and superripe cherries and raspberries. The length goes on and on. Though the acid is low, there is plenty of tannin to give structure, resulting in a rich and massive wine for drinking over the next 15–20 years. The closed 1989 Chambertin is a superb wine, but so impenetrable. Do not touch a bottle before the turn of the century.

OTHER THOUGHTS: Leroy is undeniably the greatest producer of long-lived, superrich wines, most of which continue to be the reference standard for their appellations.

GEORGES LIGNIER (MOREY ST.-DENIS)* * *

1990 Bonnes Mares	EE	90
1990 Chambolle-Musigny	D	83
1990 Clos de la Roche	E	87?
1990 Clos St.-Denis	E	89
1990 Gevrey-Chambertin	D	74
1990 Gevrey-Chambertin Les Combottes	D	87
1990 Morey St.-Denis	D	85
1990 Morey St.-Denis-Clos des Ormes	D	86

The 1990 Morey St.-Denis is a solid effort. This soft wine offers a generous berry fragrance, elegant, medium-bodied flavors, and a smooth finish. The

1990 Morey St.-Denis-Clos des Ormes reveals a deeper ruby color, more depth, a layered, chewy texture, and a long, alcoholic, fat finish. Precocious, it should be consumed over the next 4–5 years. Lignier's 1990 Gevrey-Chambertin Les Combottes is even deeper colored, with a textbook Gevrey nose of smoked meat, earthy spices, and sweet berry fruit. In the mouth this excellent wine displays medium body, a creamy texture, and a lovely fat, long, heady finish. It, too, should be drunk over the next 5–6 years. The 1990 Clos St.-Denis exhibits a super nose of herbs and jammy red and black fruits, intermingled with scents of Oriental spices. The wine is full bodied, loosely structured, alcoholic, rich, succulent, and delicious. It should last for 7–8 years. A wine that merits patience is the deeply saturated 1990 Clos de la Roche. Highly structured, with hard tannins, fine concentration, and a dry, austere, unflattering finish, it displays attractive weight and ripeness. Pinot Noir with this much tannin always makes me nervous. Lignier's best offering is his 1990 Bonnes Mares. This outstanding wine possesses the deepest color (a dark ruby/garnet), as well as a superb nose of Oriental spices, black fruits, toasty new oak, and cedar. The wine boasts moderate tannins, outstanding richness and concentration, a medium- to full-bodied, chewy texture, and a dramatic, smashingly long finish. It should last for up to a decade.

OTHER THOUGHTS: The superb potential in the barrel is blunted and traumatized by excessive fining and filtering.

DOMAINE HUBERT LIGNIER (MOREY ST.-DENIS)* * * * *

1990	Bourgogne Rouge	C	85
1990	Chambolle-Musigny Les Baudes	D	90
1989	Chambolle-Musigny Les Baudes	C	86
1989	Chambolle-Musigny Premier Cru	D	87
1990	Charmes-Chambertin	E	92
1989	Charmes-Chambertin	E	90
1990	Clos de la Roche	E	92
1989	Clos de la Roche	E	88
1990	Morey St.-Denis	D	86
1989	Morey St.-Denis	D	84
1989	Morey St.-Denis Premier Cru	D	86
1990	Morey St.-Denis Vieilles Vignes	D	87

Hubert Lignier has fashioned a tasty 1990 Bourgogne Rouge that exhibits the sweetness so typical of the vintage, as well as chewy, fleshy, wonderfully ripe flavors. Drink it over the next 4–5 years. His 1990 Morey St.-Denis offers up a spicy, sweet, fragrant nose, heady, alcoholic, medium-bodied flavors, low acidity, and a velvety, long finish. Drink it over the next 5–6 years. The 1990 Morey St.-Denis Vieilles Vignes displays a fragrant aroma of black raspberries and subtle vanillin. There is gorgeous fruit, medium body, and an opulent, satiny-smooth finish. Drink it over the next 7–8 years. The huge fragrance of anise, herbs, black fruits, and smoky new oak is captivating in the 1990 Chambolle-Musigny Les Baudes. Dense and concentrated, yet remarkably elegant and well delineated, this rich, medium-bodied wine possesses superb concentration, adequate acidity, and a long, flowing, graceful finish. Drink it over the next decade. The 1990 Charmes-Chambertin is forward, with a staggeringly intense nose of black fruits, new oak, and flowers. It is dense, rich, and full bodied, with soft tannins, low acidity, and that unctuous, chewy texture that so many 1990s possess. The 1990 Clos de la Roche shares a similarly sweet, earthy, black cherry– and mineral-scented nose and enjoys great concentration and opulence as well as more tannin, body, and structure. Both of these wines should last for 12–15 years. The 1989 Morey St.-Denis exhibits an elegant, soft, raspberry- and cherry-scented nose, light to medium body, and gentle flavors. It is ideal for current consumption. The 1989 Morey St.-Denis Premier Cru offers more ripeness, length, glycerin, and concentration as well as tender tannins and a forward, precocious style. Drink it over the next 5–6 years. The 1989 Chambolle-Musigny Les Baudes is a beautifully scented (flowers, berries, and herbs) wine, with a creamy texture, a honeyed, berrylike fruitiness, and a luscious, velvety, smooth finish. Drink it over the next 5–7 years. The 1989 Clos de la Roche is surprisingly large-scale and powerful. It reveals excellent concentration as well as muscle and power. The 1989 Charmes-Chambertin offers up a seductive nose of smoke, ripe berry fruit, and vanillin. The wine is pure seduction, with gobs of sweet, jammy fruit that caress the palate and a silky finish. Drink this beauty over the next 7–8 years.

OTHER THOUGHTS: Great 1985s and 1988s suggest this Lignier has had few equals over recent years.

CHÂTEAU DE LA MALTROYE (CHASSAGNE-MONTRACHET)* * *

1989 Chassagne-Montrachet	C	84
1989 Chassagne-Montrachet-Clos de la Boudriotte	D	86
1989 Chassagne-Montrachet-Clos de la Maltroye	D	85
1989 Chassagne-Montrachet-Clos St.-Jean	D	87
1989 Santenay La Comme	C	85

The 1989 Santenay La Comme offers a beautifully etched nose of bing cherry fruit, herbs, and almonds. There is plenty of body, fine concentration, and a soft, tender finish. Drink it over the next 2–3 years. The 1989 Chassagne-Montrachet is round, with good ripeness, a spicy, smoky nose, and medium-bodied, pleasant flavors. The 1989 Chassagne-Montrachet-Clos de la Boudriotte is the most forward, supple, and fleshiest and will probably be the shortest-lived. It is a lovely, elegant, berry fruit–scented and –flavored wine that provides delicious drinking. The 1989 Chassagne-Montrachet-Clos St.-Jean is sweeter, more opulent, and expansive, with more noticeable oak, excellent ripeness, and a long finish. The most tannic and full bodied is the 1989 Chassagne-Montrachet-Clos de la Maltroye. Ideally it needs several more years of cellaring, after which it should last for 5–6 years.

OTHER THOUGHTS: A wealthy estate that is just beginning to realize its full potential.

JOSEPH MATROT (MEURSAULT)* * *

1990 Auxey-Duresses	D	85
1990 Blagny-La Pièce Sous le Bois	E	89
1990 Meursault	D	86
1990 Volnay Santenots	E	88

The attractive cherry-scented nose of the 1990 Auxey-Duresses is followed by tasty, supple, medium-bodied flavors that exhibit no hard edges. The wine has good balance and a gentle touch of toasty new oak. The 1990 Meursault offers a seductive, intensely fragrant nose of sweet red and black fruits and lush, medium-bodied flavors that exhibit a satiny texture. I adored the forward, almost explosive combination of toasty new oak and opulent red and black fruits of the 1990 Volnay Santenots, a dramatic, almost decadently rich wine. Drink this lusty red burgundy over the next 5–6 years. Matrot's 1990 Blagny-La Pièce Sous le Bois reveals the deepest saturation of color of these wines. The toasty, smoky, black cherry– and herb-scented nose is followed by full-bodied, immensely flattering and tasty, thick Pinot Noir flavors. Chewy and fat, with gobs of extraction, this wine should be drunk over the next 7–8 years.

OTHER THOUGHTS: Tasty, fat, velvet-textured red wines now surpass the firm's whites.

DOMAINE MAUME (GEVREY-CHAMBERTIN)* * * *

1990 Bourgogne	B	82
1989 Bourgogne	B	79
1989 Charmes-Chambertin	E	89
1990 Gevrey-Chambertin	D	84
1990 Gevrey-Chambertin Les Champeaux	D	89+
1990 Gevrey-Chambertin Lavaux St.-Jacques	D	89
1989 Gevrey-Chambertin Lavaux St.-Jacques	D	87
1990 Gevrey-Chambertin en Pallud	D	89
1989 Gevrey-Chambertin en Pallud	D	78
1990 Gevrey-Chambertin Premier Cru	D	88+
1989 Gevrey-Chambertin Premier Cru	D	86
1990 Mazis-Chambertin	EE	93
1989 Mazis-Chambertin	EE	90

The 1990 Gevrey-Chambertin en Pallud appears to have the sweetest fruit, the 1990 Les Champeaux the most tannins, and the 1990 Lavaux St.-Jacques the most balance and length. None of these wines should be drunk before the late 1990s. All of them should last for 10–15 years into the next century. The top wine in 1990 is Maume's sensational Mazis-Chambertin. With a saturated dark purple color and a huge, unevolved fragrance of black raspberries, minerals, licorice, and pepper, this full-bodied, virile, superconcentrated, dense, old-style red burgundy exhibits mouth-searing tannins, enormous extraction of fruit, and enough body, glycerin, and alcohol to see it through 3 decades of cellaring.

Maume's successful 1989s are nearly as intense as his richer and fuller 1990s. The 1989 Bourgogne offers an interesting, smoky, ground beef aroma, ripe, rustic flavors, and soft tannins. The 1989 Gevrey-Chambertin en Pallud displays plenty of black fruits, spices, and earthy notes. Abundant tannins are present, and the finish is hard, tough, and coarse. Drink it between 1994 and 2005. The 1989 Gevrey-Chambertin Premier Cru exhibits a similar dusty, curranty, earthy, floral-scented nose that is followed by sweeter, more expansive flavors and a generously endowed finish. Plenty of alcohol and glycerin coat the mouth and ward off the tannic toughness. The 1989 Gevrey-Chambertin Lavaux St.-Jacques exhibits more new oak in its vanillin-, blackberry-, spicy-scented nose. Rich, with excellent concentration, low acidity, and firm tannins, it should be drunk between 1993 and 2005. The 1989 Charmes-Chambertin displays a fabulous, opaque black/ruby color and a huge nose of cassis, smoked meat, and licorice. The wine is concentrated, tannic, backward, and atypically massive for a 1989. It has the potential to last for 15 more years. The 1989 Mazis-Chambertin offers a superb nose of roasted plums, minerals, black truffles, and toasty new oak; gobs of fruit; mouth-searing tannins; plenty of extraction and flavor; and a whoppingly long finish. This big, forceful, rustic-style Mazis-Chambertin will keep for a decade or more.

OTHER THOUGHTS: Is this the way burgundy tasted in the nineteenth century?

MEIX-FOULOT (MERCUREY)* * *

1990 Mercurey	B	84
1990 Mercurey-Clos du Château Montaigu	C	90
1990 Mercurey Veleys	C	86

Yves de Launay's 1990 Mercurey Veleys exhibits an impressive, opaque dark ruby/purple color, full-bodied, powerful flavors, and considerable tannin. This big, broad-shouldered wine will keep for at least a decade. One of the finest Mercureys I have ever tasted is Launay's 1990 Mercurey-Clos du Château Montaigu. Aromas of roasted nuts, black cherries, herbs, and spices explode from the glass. Rich and full bodied, with superb concentration yet a considerable level of tannin, this Mercurey should last for up to 15 years.

OTHER THOUGHTS: An estate worth pursuing for long-lived red wines from Mercurey.

DOMAINE JEAN MÉO-CAMUZET (VOSNE-ROMANÉE)* * * */* * * * *

1990 Bourgogne Rouge	C	85
1989 Bourgogne Rouge	C	76
1989 Clos Vougeot	E	87
1990 Corton	E	92
1989 Corton	E	90
1990 Nuits St.-Georges	D	84
1990 Nuits St.-Georges aux Boudots	E	90
1989 Nuits St.-Georges aux Boudots	E	87

1990 Nuits StGeorges aux Murgers	E	88
1989 Nuits StGeorges aux Murgers	E	86
1990 Richebourg	EEE	92
1989 Richebourg	EEE	90
1989 Vosne-Romanée	C	76
1990 Vosne-Romanée aux Brûlées	EE	91
1989 Vosne-Romanée aux Brûlées	EE	89
1990 Vosne-Romanée Les Chaumes	E	86
1989 Vosne-Romanée Les Chaumes	E	82
1990 Vosne-Romanée Cros Parantoux	EE	90
1989 Vosne-Romanée Cros Parantoux	EE	89

This firm has made an attractive 1990 Bourgogne. It offers up superripe, jammy aromas of herbs and black cherries. Medium bodied, soft, and chewy, with low acidity and plenty of tasty Pinot fruit, it should be drunk over the next several years. The immensely impressive 1990 Corton reveals a dark ruby/purple color and a huge nose of smoky new oak, black fruits, herbs, and minerals. This stunningly proportioned Corton is already delicious, yet it should drink well for another 12–15 years. The soft, ripe, generously endowed, precocious-tasting 1990 Vosne-Romanée Les Chaumes should be drunk over the next 7–8 years. The 1990 Vosne-Romanée aux Brûlées exhibits a huge, roasted, smoky, black cherry– and raspberry-scented nose; luscious, full-bodied, opulent flavors; and loads of alcohol, glycerin, and soft tannins. It promises to last for at least a decade. The 1990 Vosne-Romanée Cros Parantoux's bouquet is filled with sweet, jammy red and black fruits buttressed by aromas of toasty new oak. This opulent, full-bodied wine reveals soft tannins as well as superb richness. It will benefit from 2–3 years of cellaring and should keep for 10–12 years. The 1990 Nuits StGeorges aux Murgers offers up a smoky, chocolate- and anise-scented nose, deep, rich, lovely flavors, and medium to full body. Drink it over the next 7–8 years. The 1990 Nuits StGeorges aux Boudots reveals a saturated deep ruby/purple color; a terrific nose of black fruits, minerals, licorice, and new oak; medium to full body; and a muscular, chunky finish with gobs of tannin, glycerin, and alcohol. It should keep for 12 years or more. The 1990 Richebourg boasts more fragrance as well as more of a floral component in its sweet aromas of black fruits, toasty new oak, minerals, and roasted fruits. With medium to full body, good tannins, crisp acidity, and a long, luscious finish, it can be drunk now or cellared for 10–12 years. The 1989s include a straightforward, herbaceous Bourgogne Rouge. The quality jumps with a floral, elegant, richly fruity, soft 1989 Vosne-Romanée Les Chaumes, and the earthier, smokier, richer 1989 Nuits StGeorges aux Boudots and 1989 Nuits St.-Georges aux Murgers. Neither Les Boudots nor aux Murgers will make old bones, but they will offer seductive drinking for at least 3–5 years. The stars of Méo-Camuzet in 1989 include a rich, wonderfully smoky, floral-scented, ripe, and concentrated 1989 Vosne-Romanée aux Brûlées and an equally superb 1989 Vosne-Romanée Cros Parantoux. Both of these wines exhibit excellent concentration, decent acidity, soft tannins, and gobs of rich, plummy, seductive Pinot fruit. The Vosne-Romanée aux Brûlées is more exotic, while the Cros Parantoux is classic. Both should drink well for at least 4–6 years. The 1989 Clos Vougeot exhibits ripe fruit, a nice smoky, toasty oakiness, fine concentration, and some soft tannins in its moderately long finish. It should be consumed over the next decade. The deeply colored, rich, sweet, expansively flavored, opulent 1989 Corton has the potential to last for 10–12 years. The dazzlingly perfumed, supple, wonderfully pure, elegant 1989 Richebourg offers sweet, juicy Pinot fruit. These wines are ideal for drinking over the next 7–8 years.

OTHER THOUGHTS: One of the new stars of Burgundy, this estate is making sensational Pinot Noir.

PRINCE FLORENT DE MÉRODE (LADOIX-SERRIGNY)* * *

1989	Aloxe-Corton Les Maréchaudes	D	86
1990	Aloxe-Corton Premier Cru	D	82
1990	Corton Les Bressandes	E	87
1989	Corton Les Bressandes	E	86
1990	Corton-Clos du Roi	E	90
1989	Corton-Clos du Roi	E	87
1990	Corton Les Maréchaudes	D	87
1989	Corton Les Maréchaudes	D	86
1990	Corton Les Rénardes	E	90
1989	Corton Les Rénardes	E	86
1990	Ladoix Les Chaillots	C	86
1989	Ladoix Les Chaillots	C	85
1990	Pommard-Clos de la Platière	D	87
1989	Pommard-Clos de la Platière	D	85

The delicate style of Mérode's wines aims to achieve seductive aromas and flavors in an elegant, soft style. The wines rarely possess much color, but this lightness of color can be deceiving. These wines are opulent and rich and meant for near-term drinking. Mérode's 1990 Ladoix Les Chaillots is all charm and finesse. Light ruby in color, with an attractively fruity nose intertwined with aromas of sweet oak and flowers, it is round and well balanced, with lovely fruit and a smooth, velvety-textured finish. Drink it over the next 3–4 years. The medium ruby color of the 1990 Corton Les Maréchaudes is followed by a cherry-scented nose and rich, concentrated flavors that exhibit soft tannins and low acidity. It is a stylish Corton for drinking over the next 5–6 years. The 1990 Corton Les Bressandes is deeper in color and has an elegant nose of black cherries, toasty new oak, and herbs. Medium bodied with a smooth texture, fine ripeness, and length, it should be drunk over the next 5–7 years. Far richer and more expansive is the medium ruby-colored 1990 Corton Les Rénardes. The nose explodes from the glass with aromas of black cherries, flowers, and toasty new oak. Opulent, heady, and rich, with significant glycerin, alcohol, and sweet fruit, this luscious wine will drink well for 6–7 years. The

1990 Corton-Clos du Roi displays the same weight, ripeness, and expansive perfume as the Corton Les Rénardes, yet it is more structured. The 1990 Pommard-Clos de la Platière displays the classic Pinot Noir nose of underbrush, red fruits, and herbs. An elegant wine by Pommard standards, it possesses generous richness, ample amounts of toasty new oak, and an alcoholic finish. Drink it over the next 5–6 years. The 1989s are soft, elegant, richly fruity, and ideal for drinking now. The 1989 Ladoix Les Chaillots is a strong effort, exhibiting an elegant, cherry fruitiness, sweet new oak, and a richly fruity, supple palate. Drink it over the next 3–4 years. The bigger-style 1989 Pommard-Clos de la Platière possesses an expansive, sweet, richly fruity nose and palate, soft tannins, and a silky finish. Drink it over the next 4–5 years. The 1989 Aloxe-Corton Les Maréchaudes offers an intense fragrance of flowers, sweet oak, and ripe berry fruit. Low in acidity, it requires consumption over the next 3–4 years. The 1989 Corton Les Maréchaudes exhibits similar sweet, oaky, black cherry–scented fruit aromas, followed by round, silky, fruity flavors. One of the richest, densest, chewiest wines is the 1989 Corton Les Rénardes. It is a deeper-colored, more spicy, structured wine that can handle up to 5–6 years of aging. The narrowly constructed 1989 Corton Les Bressandes displays good fruit. The 1989 Corton-Clos du Roi merits its name, as it is the best of the 1989s. The profound bouquet of spicy new oak, flowers, and super-ripe red fruits is followed by a wine with a multilayered texture, ripeness, glycerin, and length. The acids are sound and the tannins elevated but tender. Drink this wine over the next 7–9 years.

OTHER THOUGHTS: After living off his domaine's reputation for several decades, the prince de Mérode has finally gotten serious.

MICHAEL MODOT (CHAMBOLLE-MUSIGNY)* * *

1990 Chambolle-Musigny Les Charmes	D	87
1990 Chambolle-Musigny Premier Cru	D	86

The 1990 Chambolle-Musigny Premier Cru enjoys excellent color, a ripe, tasty, medium-bodied fruitiness, and a deep, long, moderately tannic yet elegant finish. It should keep for a decade. The 1990 Chambolle-Musigny Les Charmes exhibits a flowery, spicy, plummy-scented nose; dense, chewy, ripe, powerful flavors; medium body; and a long, lusty finish. Drink it between 1995 and 2005.

OTHER THOUGHTS: Based on the 1990s and 1989s, this is a name to look for.

MONGEARD-MUGNERET (VOSNE-ROMANÉE)* * * *

1990 Bourgogne	B	77
1990 Bourgogne Hautes-Côtes de Nuits	C	82
1990 Clos Vougeot	EE	90
1989 Clos Vougeot	EE	77
1989 Echézeaux	EE	87
1990 Echézeaux Vieilles Vignes	EE	89
1990 Fixin	B	81
1989 Fixin	B	75

1990 Grands Echézeaux	EE	89
1989 Grands Echézeaux	EE	87
1990 Nuits St.-Georges Les Boudots	D	82
1990 Richebourg	EEE	91
1989 Richebourg	EEE	89
1990 Savigny-Lès-Beaune Les Narbantons	C	81
1989 Savigny-Lès-Beaune Les Narbantons	C	74
1990 Vosne-Romanée	C	77
1989 Vosne Romanée	C	82
1990 Vosne-Romanée Les Orveaux	C	84
1989 Vosne-Romanée Les Orveaux	C	84

The 1990 Echézeaux Vieilles Vignes offers a light ruby color and a sweet, fragrant nose of berry fruit and toasty new oak. There is admirable sweetness and alcohol, excellent ripeness, and a long finish. Once past the glycerin, alcohol, and new oak, there is not much structure. Drink it over the next 4–5 years. The medium ruby color of the 1990 Clos Vougeot is followed by a wine with a big, jammy, highly scented nose of toasty oak, red and black fruits, and minerals. It is fat, alcoholic, and oaky, with low acidity, no apparent grip or tannin, but a decadent, lush finish. Drink it over the next 5–6 years. The 1990 Grands Echézeaux reveals a surprisingly light-ruby color as well as a heavy overlay of smoky new oak. The wine is sweet, with loads of glycerin and alcohol, fine ripeness, but not the extraction of fruit that low yields/old vines produce. The long, heady, voluptuous finish is a turn-on. Consumption over the next 5–6 years is advised. Mongeard's medium ruby–colored 1990 Richebourg is similarly styled, with tons of sweet new oak intermingled with scents of black fruits. There is plenty of round, gentle fruit, but little structure or definition. For drinking over the next 5–6 years, it will be dazzling. The 1989 Savigny-Lès-Beaune Les Narbantons is light, angular, and short. The 1989 Fixin is pleasant but uninteresting, and the 1989 Vosne-Romanée is tannic, round, fruity, clipped, and compact. The 1989 Vosne-Romanée Les Orveaux is better, with juicy, ripe black fruits in the nose to go along with aromas of sweet oak. It is soft, medium bodied, pleasant, and ideal for current drinking. The 1989 Echézeaux exhibits seductive, sweet, plummy fruit as well as aromas of minerals and spices. Round, with soft tannins and low acidity, it should be drunk over the next 2–3 years. The 1989 Grands Echézeaux offers good fruit, deep color, and a wonderfully velvety, ripe fruitiness and texture. It needs to be drunk up over the next 5–6 years. I was disappointed with Mongeard's 1989 Clos Vougeot, a diluted, hard, tannic, coarse wine lacking fruit. The 1989 Richebourg exhibits an enthralling bouquet of sweet, plummy fruit, minerals, spicy new oak, and flowers. It is round and expansive, with gentle tannins and an opulent finish. Drink it over the next 6–7 years.

OTHER THOUGHTS: One of my favorite *vignerons* has displayed distressing signs of slipping, but enough magic is still there to justify interest.

HUBERT DE MONTILLE (VOLNAY)* * * *

1990 Pommard Les Grands Epenots	E	89+
1990 Pommard Les Pézerolles	E	91+
1990 Pommard Les Rugiens	E	90+
1990 Volnay Champans	E	90
1990 Volnay Mitan	D	87+
1990 Volnay Taillepieds	E	?

This domaine's style of winemaking produces such tannic, high-acid, backward wines that a minimum of 10–15 years of cellaring is required. In terms of extraction and concentration, these offerings appear to possess the requisite depth to balance out their high acidity and hard tannins—I think. The 1990 Volnay Mitan exhibits an impressively dense color and excellent weight and richness, but the hard tannins and noticeable acidity in the finish blistered my palate. **Anticipated maturity: 2002–2030.** The opaque dark ruby/purple color of the 1990 Volnay Champans is followed by enticing aromas of black cherries, damp earth, and spices. It is deep and brutally tannic. **Anticipated maturity: 2005–2030.** I have reservations about the 1990 Volnay Taillepieds. This offering is so hard and lean that it would be foolish to suggest there is enough fruit and richness to survive the tannin. The 1990 Pommard Les Grands Epenots needs 10–15 years of cellaring. The color is an admirable dark ruby/purple. The nose is spicy and ripe, but tight. The wine displays terrific richness as well as harsh tannins and high acidity. **Anticipated maturity: 2003–2030.** The 1990 Pommard Les Pézerolles possesses the most weight, structure, and massiveness. The finish was so acidic and tannic that my gums ached. Last, the 1990 Pommard Les Rugiens reveals the classic purity that these wines display, as well as a deep, dark ruby/purple color, plenty of body and glycerin, formidable concentration, enormous tannin levels, crisp acidity, and a tight, hard, spicy, long finish. Only a masochist would consider drinking it before 2005.

OTHER THOUGHTS: Are these wines museum pieces or beverages? Are they even enjoyable?

BERNARD MOREY (CHASSAGNE-MONTRACHET)* * *

1990 Beaune Les Grèves	D	82
1990 Chassagne-Montrachet	C	77
1990 Saint-Aubin Le Charmois	C	85
1990 Santenay-Grand Clos Rousseau	D	87

The 1990 Santenay-Grand Clos Rousseau is a crowd pleaser. The huge nose of sweet, almost candied red fruits and toasty new oak is a real turn-on. Alcoholic, soft, and obvious, even ostentatious, this low-acid, loosely knit red burgundy is a joy to drink. However, it does not have enough concentration to merit an outstanding rating. It should be drunk over the next 2–4 years.

OTHER THOUGHTS: Morey's whites are far superior.

DOMAINE ALBERT MOROT (BEAUNE)* * * *

1990 Beaune Les Bressandes	C	88
1989 Beaune Les Bressandes	C	87
1990 Beaune Les Cent Vignes	C	86
1989 Beaune Les Cent Vignes	C	85
1990 Beaune Les Grèves	C	86
1989 Beaune Les Grèves	C	88
1990 Beaune Les Marconnets	C	89+
1989 Beaune Les Marconnets	C	89
1990 Beaune Les Teurons	C	90
1989 Beaune Les Teurons	C	89
1990 Beaune Les Toussaints	C	86
1990 Savigny Vergelesses-Clos la Bataillère	B	86
1989 Savigny Vergelesses-Clos la Bataillère	B	84

The 1990 Savigny Vergelesses-Clos la Bataillère exhibits a rich, black cherry, smoky nose, deep, fat, concentrated flavors, moderate tannins, crisp acidity, and a spicy finish. It should keep for 10–15 years. The 1990 Beaune Les Cent Vignes displays an impressive deep ruby color and a reticent but blossoming nose of sweet cherry fruit, toasty oak, and earth. Medium bodied, with fine ripeness, acidity, and noticeable tannin, this attractive, streamlined style of wine should be at its best between 1996 and 2010. The 1990 Beaune Les Grèves offers up a spicy, oaky, chocolate- and cherry-scented, seductive nose, medium body, and elegant, tasty, soft fruit flavors. It is capable of lasting 10–12 years. The 1990 Beaune Les Toussaints exhibits a slightly deeper color and is a more backward, fuller wine. The tannins are tougher, but behind the wine's structure are copious quantities of chocolatey, black cherry, spicy fruit. This medium-bodied wine should prove to be long-lived. **Anticipated maturity: 1996–2006.** The 1990 Beaune Les Bressandes reveals a sweet, smoky, black cherry–scented nose, rich, chewy flavors, and a tannic finish. Look for optimum drinking between 1995 and 2008. The full-bodied, dense 1990 Beaune Les Marconnets possesses a superripe nose and high tannins, as well as impressive extraction of fruit. This rich wine is capable of 15–20 years of longevity. The 1990 Beaune Les Teurons is powerful and muscular, with a leathery, black cherry–scented nose. It offers gobs of tannin and ripe fruit, superb definition and richness, and a long, concentrated finish. A wine such as this may keep for 2 decades. The 1989 Savigny Vergelesses-Clos la Bataillère offers deep color, a vibrant, clean, pure, ripe nose of berry fruit and herbs, an attractive cherry, smoky fruitiness, and an adequate finish. The 1989 Beaune Les Cent Vignes displays an impressively deep, opaque color; an attractive, smoky, tarlike, roasted cherry-scented nose; rich, concentrated fruit flavors; and a long finish. The bouquet of the 1989 Beaune Les Grèves reveals sweet, abundant aromas of black cherries, toasty new oak, and flowers. Loaded with ripe berry fruit, glycerin, and soft tannins, this wine should be drunk over the next 10–12 years. The 1989 Beaune Les Bressandes exhibits more structure and tannin, with the potential to last for 12–15 or more years. Abundant quantities of sweet cherry fruit, intertwined with aromas of herbs, new oak, spice, and fruitcake, are presented in a medium-bodied, tightly knit format. It should have considerable longevity. The superbly concentrated 1989 Beaune Les Marconnets has a dark ruby/purple color. The nose offers up aromas of black fruits, spicy oak, licorice, and flowers. Concentrated, with gobs of tannin, decent acidity, and a long finish, this larger-scale Beaune should be at its best between 1995 and 2010. The 1989 Beaune Les Teurons, which the proprietor calls a "Beaune to coat your bones," displays a huge, dark ruby color and a reticent but promising nose of smoked meat, leather, and black fruits. It boasts superb concentration, admirable tannin and structure, and a superlong finish. Expect it easily to live through the first decade of the next century.

OTHER THOUGHTS: Classic, tightly knit, reserved, and restrained Pinots admirably stand the test of time and open slowly—just like the proprietor, Mademoiselle Choppin. For connoisseurs only.

DENIS MORTET (GEVREY-CHAMBERTIN)* * *

1990	Bourgogne	B	84
1989	Bourgogne	B	84
1990	Chambertin	EE	91
1989	Chambertin	EE	87
1990	Chambolle-Musigny aux Beaux Bruns	D	88
1989	Chambolle-Musigny aux Beaux Bruns	D	87
1990	Clos Vougeot	E	90
1989	Clos Vougeot	E	87
1990	Gevrey-Chambertin	C	83
1989	Gevrey-Chambertin	C	86
1990	Gevrey-Chambertin Champeaux	D	86
1989	Gevrey-Chambertin Champeaux	D	87
1990	Gevrey-Chambertin-Clos Prieur	D	85
1989	Gevrey-Chambertin-Clos Prieur	D	87

The 1990 Gevrey-Chambertin-Clos Prieur exhibits an attractive medium-ruby color; a fragrant black fruit, spicy, flowery nose; lush flavors; good concentration; low acidity; and sweet tannins. Drink it over the next 6–7 years. The 1990 Gevrey-Chambertin Champeaux is slightly fuller, deeper, and more tannic. It is a wine to drink in its first 8–9 years of life. Mortet's 1990 Chambolle-Musigny aux Beaux Bruns exhibits elegant, flowery, velvety-textured flavors, a succulent finish, and 5–7 years of aging potential. The 1990 Clos Vougeot is an opulent, intensely rich wine, with great ripeness and extraction of fruit, superb length, medium to full body, ripe tannins, and a heady, lusty, long finish. It should drink well for at least a decade. Mortet's medium dark ruby-colored 1990 Chambertin offers spicy aromas of new oak, earthy black fruits, and smoke. This rich, voluptuously textured, luscious wine offers a sweet, expansive, chewy texture, as well as a rich, soft, full-bodied finish. Drink it over the next 10–12 years. The 1989 Bourgogne is a solid, plump, ripe, tasty wine with good fruit. Drink it over the next 1–3 years. The 1989 Gevrey-Chambertin offers an attractive, flattering, precocious, berry- and spice-scented bouquet and round, velvety flavors. Drink it over the next 2–3 years. The luscious 1989 Gevrey-Chambertin-Clos Prieur exhibits fine extraction of flavor, some spicy new oak in the nose, an overall sense of elegance, and round, gentle, berry fruitiness intertwined with aromas and flavors of herbs, vanillin, and berry fruit. It should be consumed over the next 6–7 years. The 1989 Gevrey-Chambertin Champeaux is a fuller, more masculine, smoky, meaty wine. The 1989 Chambolle-Musigny aux Beaux Bruns offers a delicate, floral nose, suave, berry fruit flavors, some new oak, and a gentle finish. It is ideal for drinking over the next 5–6 years. When compared with his other wines, Mortet's 1989 Clos Vougeot displays a slightly deeper color, a big, rich, berry-scented nose, less complexity, and more tannin, glycerin, and body. It is capable of lasting for 8–10 years. The 1989 Chambertin is deep ruby colored, with more alcohol evident. Meaty, with a smoky, leathery, spicy component, it displays good body, silky tannins, and a lush finish. It should be drunk over the next 7–8 years.

OTHER THOUGHTS: A young producer whose 1990s reached new heights in quality. Was it Mortet or the vintage?

MUGNERET-GIBOURG (VOSNE-ROMANÉE)* * * *

1990	Bourgogne Rouge	B	80
1989	Bourgogne Rouge	B	82
1990	Chambolle-Musigny Les Feusselottes	D	87
1989	Chambolle-Musigny Les Feusselottes	D	84
1990	Clos Vougeot	EE	88
1989	Clos Vougeot	EE	86
1990	Echézeaux	EE	87
1989	Echézeaux	EE	85
1990	Nuits St.-Georges Les Chaignots	D	84
1989	Nuits St.-Georges Les Chaignots	D	84
1990	Ruchottes-Chambertin	E	88
1989	Ruchottes-Chambertin	E	85
1990	Vosne-Romanée	C	82
1989	Vosne-Romanée	C	81

The 1990 Chambolle-Musigny Les Feusselottes offers an attractive, earthy, black cherry, herb, and oaky nose; lovely ripe, medium-bodied flavors; and a soft finish. Drink it over the next 10–12 years. The attractive, tasty 1990 Echézeaux is medium bodied with fine ripeness, but it is short. Drink it over the next 7–8 years. The 1990 Ruchottes-Chambertin exhibits a spicy, earthy, animal-scented nose, adequate ripeness, medium body, crisp acidity, and a moderately long, tannic finish. It remains closed and angular. **Anticipated maturity: 1996–2008.** The 1990 Clos Vougeot is tough, textured, austere, and lean. There is excellent ripeness, as well as plenty of weight and depth, but the wine is backward and unevolved. **Anticipated maturity: 2000–2010.** The competently made 1989 Bourgogne Rouge exhibits adequate color, a pleasant herb and berry fragrance, soft texture, and attractive fruit. Both the 1989 Vosne-Romanée, with its soft, diluted flavors, and the 1989 Nuits St.-Georges Les Chaignots, with its smoky, understated flavors, lack concentration and depth. The 1989 Chambolle-Musigny Les Feusselottes reveals an elegant style and graceful berry fruit flavors intermixed with aromas of flowers and toasty new oak. Drink this medium-bodied wine over the next 4–5 years. The 1989 Echézeaux displayed a light ruby color and an elegant, spicy, exotic, black fruit, Oriental spice, and toasty nose. The wine lacks some stuffing, but there is enough sweet, ripe, supple fruit to provide considerable enjoyment. I would opt for drinking it over the next 4–5 years. The 1989 Clos Vougeot is more tannic, with muscle and depth. Light in color, it reveals a spicy, raspberry- and black cherry–scented nose. Despite the tannin, it exhibits more richness in the finish than the other Mugneret offerings. This wine is capable of lasting for at least 10–12 years. The subtle 1989 Ruchottes-Chambertin lacks depth and intensity. The 1989 displays a medium ruby color, some earthy, meaty, smoky components, ripe, medium-bodied, tasty flavors, and a spicy finish. Drink it over the next 7–8 years.

OTHER THOUGHTS: A onetime sensational property that has slipped in quality since Dr. Georges Mugneret's death.

ANDRÉ MUSSY (POMMARD)* * * *

1990	Beaune Les Epenottes	D	91
1990	Beaune Les Montrevenots	D	92
1990	Bourgogne	B	87
1990	Pommard	D	88
1990	Pommard Les Epenots	E	92+
1990	Pommard Premier Cru	D	89

This is a terrific lineup of explosively ripe, rich, juicy wines bursting with fruit and character. The 1990 Bourgogne is a gloriously perfumed, expansive, sweet, fat-tasting wine, with its Pinot character screaming from the glass. Drink it over the next 4–5 years. The 1990 Beaune Les Epenottes is a dense, dramatic wine, with a huge nose of jammy red and black fruits, smoke, and earth. Full bodied and lavishly rich, this highly extracted yet lush wine is delicious. It possesses the requisite concentration and grip to last for 12–15 years. The 1990 Beaune Les Montrevenots is an ostentatious, hedonistic, luscious red burgundy the likes of which are few and far between. Its expansive, multidimensional flavors, texture, staggeringly perfumed bouquet, and lusty personality make for a remarkable tasting experience. It is a wine to drink over the next 7–8 years. The solid, medium- to full-bodied 1990 Pommard offers fine depth and richness as well as moderate tannins. It should last for 10–15 years. The well-structured 1990 Pommard Premier Cru possesses grip, body, and power. Closed and tight, with an impenetrable, brooding character, it offers 12–15 years of aging potential. The 1990 Pommard Les Epenots displays a saturated deep ruby color. The nose reveals powerful scents of red and black

fruits, minerals, smoke, and wood. It exhibits enormous richness, excellent definition, and a whoppingly long finish. **Anticipated maturity: 1996–2010.**
OTHER THOUGHTS: In the best years—1985, 1988, 1990—ravishing and sumptuous red burgundies from one of the most experienced winemakers in the Côte d'Or.

PHILIPPE NADDEF (COUCHEY)* * *

1989	Gevrey-Chambertin	C	84
1990	Gevrey-Chambertin Cazetiers	D	89
1989	Gevrey-Chambertin Cazetiers	D	86
1990	Gevrey-Chambertin Champeaux	D	87
1989	Gevrey-Chambertin Champeaux	D	86
1989	Marsannay	B	75
1990	Mazis-Chambertin	E	94
1989	Mazis-Chambertin	E	88

The seductive 1990 Gevrey-Chambertin Champeaux exhibits a roasted element and round, generous, supple flavors. Drink it over the next 7–8 years. The 1990 Gevrey-Chambertin Cazetiers, which possesses more finesse and elegance, reveals a rich, glycerin-dominated, fleshy fruitiness, medium body, soft tannins, and low acidity. Drink it over the next 7–8 years. Naddef's 1990 Mazis-Chambertin is thrilling. The opaque purple color is followed by a soaring nose of jammy black raspberry, minerals, and toasty new oak. This spectacularly concentrated wine displays definition, firm tannins, adequate acidity, and an explosively rich finish. It should keep for 12–15 years. The 1989 Marsannay is ripe and tasty, but innocuous and one-dimensional. The 1989 Gevrey-Chambertin offers a sweet, berry, oaky nose, ripe, round flavors, and soft tannins. Drink it over the next 3–4 years. The 1989 Gevrey-Chambertin Champeaux is an oaky, supple, fragrant wine with abundant quantities of red and black fruits. The low acidity and soft tannins suggest it should be consumed over the next 5–6 years. Naddef's 1989 Gevrey-Chambertin Cazetiers is more tannic and closed. It reveals a deeper color as well as a richer, more intense feel. The dark-colored 1989 Mazis-Chambertin offers a gorgeous nose of sweet oak, black raspberries, and minerals. Drink this concentrated, full-bodied, satiny-textured wine over the next 7–8 years.
OTHER THOUGHTS: Another young *vigneron* garnering plenty of attention.

ANDRÉ NUDANT ET FILS (LADOIX-SERRIGNY)* * *

1989	Aloxe-Corton La Coutière	C	85
1989	Aloxe-Corton Les Valozières	C	85
1989	Corton Les Bressandes	C	86
1989	Ladoix Les Buis	C	82

These are good examples of the 1989 vintage. Soft acidity, tender tannins, ripe, luscious fruit, and vivid purity and cleanliness combine to make these wines delicious and ideal for drinking over the next 4–5 years.
OTHER THOUGHTS: Clean, commercial wines are the norm.

PONSOT (MOREY ST.-DENIS)* * * */* * * * *

1990 Chambertin	EEE	93
1990 Chambolle-Musigny Les Charmes	E	90
1990 Clos de la Roche Vieilles Vignes	EEE	96
1990 Clos St.-Denis Vieilles Vignes	EEE	96
1990 Gevrey-Chambertin Cuvée de l'Abeille	D	87
1990 Griotte-Chambertin	EE	94
1990 Latricières-Chambertin	EE	92
1990 Morey St.-Denis Cuvée des Grieves	D	87

Ponsot has made terrific 1990s. Even the lower-level wines, such as the Morey St.-Denis and Gevrey-Chambertin, possess considerable depth, big, spicy, earthy, ripe aromas, medium to full body, and enough tannin and depth to warrant holding or drinking over the next 6–7 years. The finesse-filled 1990 Chambolle-Musigny Les Charmes possesses a fragrant nose of berries, herbs, and spices. Drink this lush burgundy over the next 7–8 years.

All Ponsot's Grands Crus are exceptionally rich, powerful wines with nearly overripe Pinot Noir fruit displayed in dramatic and lavish quantities. The 1990 Latricières-Chambertin is the most developed, with an exceptionally fragrant aroma of meat, herbs, and black fruits and a touch of macerated prunes to add complexity. Full bodied and expansive, it has low acidity and gobs of richness and tannin. The 1990 Griotte-Chambertin exhibits marvelous color, a beautifully pure perfume, and a stunningly opulent texture and finish. Both of these wines can be drunk now but promise to keep and improve for 10 more years. The top Grands Crus include a firm, backward, highly promising 1990 Chambertin. Neither as rich nor as full bodied as the 1990 Clos St.-Denis Vieilles Vignes or 1990 Clos de la Roche Vieilles Vignes, it displays admirable intensity and a generous, medium- to full-bodied, rich, firm taste and finish. The 1990 Clos St.-Denis Vieilles Vignes and the 1990 Clos de la Roche Vieilles Vignes are the superstars of this property. The Clos de la Roche has more of a mineral, meaty component to its nearly overripe aromas of prunes, oranges, black cherries, and black raspberries. Sensationally concentrated, with an unctuous texture, this thick, rich wine goes on in the mouth. It is Ponsot's best wine since his 1980. The Clos St.-Denis Vieilles Vignes reveals less of the animal side of Pinot Noir and more of the black fruit character. The aromas of overripeness in the Clos de la Roche are not apparent in the Clos St.-Denis. The latter wine is densely colored, with a huge perfume of black fruits, herbs, and truffles. Full bodied and rich, with a viscous, thick texture and spectacular length like the Clos de la Roche, the Clos St.-Denis is a red burgundy for drinking over the next 15–20 years.

OTHER THOUGHTS: If Ponsot were a baseball player, he would consistently lead the league in home runs and strikeouts. Phenomenal wines in 1980, 1985, and 1990, some brilliant 1983s, lousy wines in 1981, 1982, 1984, 1986, and 1987.

DOMAINE POTHIER-RIEUSSET (POMMARD)* * * *

1990 Beaune Boucherottes	C	87
1989 Beaune Boucherottes	C	82

1990 Bourgogne Vieilles Vignes	C	84
1989 Bourgogne Vieilles Vignes	C	82
1990 Pommard	C	84+
1989 Pommard	C	80
1990 Pommard-Clos des Vergers	D	88
1989 Pommard-Clos des Vergers	D	85
1990 Pommard Les Epenots	D	88+
1989 Pommard Les Epenots	D	86
1990 Pommard Les Rugiens	D	90+
1989 Pommard Les Rugiens	D	87
1990 Volnay	C	84
1989 Volnay	C	85

Pothier's 1990s are intensely rich, tannic, exceptionally well-endowed wines with the potential to last 15–25 or more years. The 1990 Beaune Boucherottes is a dense, ruby/purple-colored wine with a promising nose of truffles, black fruits, herbs, and licorice. It displays plenty of concentration as well as large doses of tannin and acidity. **Anticipated maturity: 1997–2010.** The classic 1990 Pommard-Clos des Vergers exhibits a striking nose of ripe apple skin, red and black fruits, and earth, with a tarlike note. Full bodied, dense, rich, and, at present, rustic and macho, this broad-shouldered wine merits 8–10 years of cellaring. **Anticipated maturity: 1998–2015.** If you think the Clos des Vergers is unevolved, consider the 1990 Pommard Les Epenots. Don't touch it for a decade. The dark ruby color is followed by a full-bodied wine with superconcentration. The promising aromas of baked apples, smoked nuts, black fruits, and cloves require coaxing from the glass. Meaty, chewy, and frightfully backward and dense, this is a wine to drink between the turn of the century and 2025. The biggest, most majestic wine is the 1990 Pommard Les Rugiens. It possesses a more saturated color, a larger and broader aromatic and flavor profile, and a formidably long, chewy, concentrated finish. It is a blockbuster, but backward and tannic. When I consider the wine's enormous weight and richness, I do not see it reaching full maturity before the turn of the century. The 1989s are atypically backward, tannic wines for the vintage. Pothier's 1989 Bourgogne Vieilles Vignes is a foursquare, chunky, spicy wine with good color, plenty of substance, but not much finesse. It will hold up for 5–6 years. The 1989 Volnay displays excellent richness, surprisingly deep color, good fruit, and plenty of tannin and body. It needs another several years to open. I was surprised by the tenderness, softness, and fragility of the 1989 Beaune Boucherottes. Although it displayed fine color, it was low in acidity and did not exhibit the structure one normally associates with Pothier's wines. The 1989 Pommard is a chunky, monolithic, spicy, robust wine offering more muscle than finesse or elegance. The 1989 Pommard-Clos des Vergers is backward, densely colored, with a reticent but evolving nose of smoky, chocolaty, berrylike fruit, plenty of body and tannin, but low acidity. The 1989 Pommard Les Epenots is an old-style, chunky, thick, extremely tannic wine that will repay 5–7 years of cellaring. The 1989 Pommard Les Rugiens, the deepest and richest of Pothier's 1989s, is extremely closed and dense, with hard tannins and surprisingly high acidity. With plenty of glycerin, extract, and body, this wine should last for 15 years.

OTHER THOUGHTS: This is the quintessential expression of Pommard—dense, rich, sturdy, tannic, and ageworthy.

POUSSE D'OR (VOLNAY)* * * *

1990 Santenay-Clos Tavannes	D	85
1990 Volnay Les Caillerets	D	86
1990 Volnay Les Caillerets-Clos des 60 Ouvrées	D	88+
1990 Volnay-Clos de la Bousse d'Or	E	87

The 1990 Volnay Les Caillerets offers an earthy, spicy, herb- and black fruit–scented nose; tight, but well-endowed, medium-bodied flavors; good weight and density; and moderate tannins in the sleek finish. Although closed, this wine displays excellent potential. **Anticipated maturity: 1996–2004.** The 1990 Volnay Les Caillerets-Clos des 60 Ouvrées is rich and aromatic, with an enticing fragrance of apple skins and meaty, earthy, black cherry–scented fruit. Still unevolved, it will keep for 10–15 years. For combining power, richness, and finesse in a medium-bodied, tightly knit framework, the 1990 Volnay-Clos de la Bousse d'Or ranks high. The wine's fragrance of spices, minerals, wood, and red and black fruits is just beginning to emerge. This deep ruby-colored wine also possesses a velvety-textured feel, fine richness, and a supple, pure finish. Except for the dry, austere tannins in the aftertaste, everything is in harmony. This wine should keep for at least a decade. The 1990 Santenay-Clos Tavannes offers a medium ruby color; a dusty, herb- and red fruit–scented nose; firm, lean, concentrated flavors; crisp acidity; and a compact finish. Drink it over the next decade.

OTHER THOUGHTS: Some of Burgundy's greatest wines emerged from this estate between 1964 and 1978, but some of that magic is now missing.

JACQUES PRIEUR (MEURSAULT)* * *

1990 Chambertin	EE	82
1990 Clos Vougeot	EE	78
1990 Meursault-Clos de Mazeray	D	86
1990 Musigny	EEE	87
1990 Volnay-Champans	E	79
1990 Volnay-Clos des Santenots	D	87
1990 Volnay Santenots	D	86

The 1990 Meursault-Clos de Mazeray exhibits an opaque color, a big, oaky, cherry-scented nose, and solid, full-bodied, muscular flavors. Although it comes across as chunky, perhaps even heavy-handed, the wine's suppleness and richness is admirable. Give it several years of cellaring and drink it between 1995 and 2005. The 1990 Volnay Santenots is also a dark, dense, ruby/purple-colored wine, with a big, oaky, herb, jammy cherry nose and rich, highly structured, full-bodied flavors that display considerable alcohol, tannin, and body. The wine needs 2–4 years of cellaring but should keep for a decade. The best of this trio, the 1990 Volnay-Clos des Santenots, exhibits a saturated dark ruby color, a rich, spicy, oaky, roasted black fruit–scented nose, and impressively endowed, fleshy flavors that are buttressed by significant tannins and alcohol. The finish is full and long. **Anticipated maturity: 1996–2008.**

OTHER THOUGHTS: They may be thick and rich, but these burgundies taste soul-less.

PRIEUR-BRUNET (SANTENAY)* * */* * * *

1990	Pommard La Platière	D	87
1990	Santenay La Maladière	D	86
1990	Volnay Santenots	D	87

Most consumers tend to ignore the wines of Santenay, but the 1990 Santenay La Maladière exhibits a seductive nose of strawberries and cherries, inter-twined with scents of herbs. This exuberantly fruity wine displays a silky tex-ture, excellent depth, soft tannins, and low acidity. Drink it over the next 5–6 years. The 1990 Volnay Santenots reveals a slightly deeper color, an even sweeter nose of black fruits and flowers, medium body, excellent definition, adequate grip, and a lusty, high-alcohol, low-tannin finish. Drink it over the next 6–7 years. The 1990 Pommard La Platière shares similar characteristics. It is slightly oakier, with a more roasted character. Full bodied, with fleshy, chewy flavors that exhibit plenty of glycerin, alcohol, and fruit, this is another corpulent 1990 for consuming over the next 6–7 years.

OTHER THOUGHTS: An underrated producer.

HENRI PRUDHON (SAINT-AUBIN)* * *

1990	Chassagne-Montrachet	C	85
1990	Saint-Aubin Les Frionnes	C	86
1990	Saint-Aubin Sentier de Clou	C	87

The 1990 Saint-Aubin Les Frionnes displays an attractive cherry and currant fruitiness with an underlying mineral scent. In the mouth it is robust yet sup-ple, with ripe fruit and a medium-bodied, slightly tannic finish. Drink it over the next 4–5 years. The 1990 Saint-Aubin Sentier de Clou is a robust, chewy wine with a generous perfume of smoky red fruits. Full bodied, with moderate tannins, this excellent wine should drink well for another 7–8 years. Prudhon told me it was made exclusively from 30–35-year-old vines. The 1990 Chas-sagne-Montrachet reveals a roasted, herb, nutty, earthy fruitiness, medium body, and considerable tannin in the finish. Although chunky and monolithic, it possesses good fruit and structure. It will be interesting to see how well it evolves.

OTHER THOUGHTS: A reliable producer of tasty wines.

DOMAINE RAMONET (CHASSAGNE-MONTRACHET)* * *

1990	Chassagne-Montrachet-Clos de la Boudriotte	D	87
1989	Chassagne-Montrachet-Clos de la Boudriotte	D	86

1990 Chassagne-Montrachet-Clos St.-Jean	D	85
1989 Chassagne-Montrachet-Clos St.-Jean	D	85

Ramonet does not get enough credit for the tasty, elegant red wines he produces. The 1990 Chassagne-Montrachet-Clos St.-Jean is medium bodied and elegant, with plenty of up-front, earthy, cherry fruit, soft tannins, and an attractive, spicy finish. Drink it over the next 3–4 years. The 1990 Chassagne-Montrachet-Clos de la Boudriotte, from a vineyard owned exclusively by the Ramonets, is not so humbly called "the Romanée-Conti of the Côte de Beaune" by Noël Ramonet. It is a fatter, deeper-flavored wine with copious amounts of sweet cherry fruit intertwined with aromas of herbs. More fleshy, with slightly higher alcohol and a soft, succulent finish, it should be drunk over the next 5–6 years. The lighter-style 1989 Chassagne-Montrachet-Clos St.-Jean is richly fruity, with a fragrant nose and round, graceful flavors. Drink it over the next 4–5 years. The 1989 Chassagne-Montrachet-Clos de la Boudriotte is a riper, deeper wine. It displays better color; an attractive, smoky, herb- and berry-scented nose; medium-bodied, lush flavors; and excellent ripeness and length. Drink it over the next 7–8 years.

OTHER THOUGHTS: If it is Ramonet, it must be a great and frightfully expensive, white burgundy.

HENRI REMORIQUET (NUITS ST.-GEORGES)* * *

1990 Bourgogne Hautes-Côtes de Nuits	B	82
1989 Bourgogne Hautes-Côtes de Nuits	B	80
1990 Nuits St.-Georges	B	83
1989 Nuits St.-Georges	B	81
1990 Nuits St.-Georges Les Allots	C	84
1989 Nuits St.-Georges Les Allots	C	85
1990 Nuits St.-Georges Les Bousselots	D	86+
1989 Nuits St.-Georges Les Bousselots	D	85
1990 Nuits St.-Georges Les Damodes	D	84
1989 Nuits St.-Georges Les Damodes	D	86
1989 Nuits St.-Georges Rue de Chaux	D	84
1989 Nuits St. Georges Rue de Chaux	D	89
1990 Nuits St.-Georges Les St.-Georges	D	87
1989 Nuits St.-Georges Les St.-Georges	D	86

Remoriquet's 1990 Nuits St.-Georges Les Bousselots is a soft, ripe, tasty wine with hard tannins in the finish. Rich, medium bodied, with an earthy, peppery, black fruit character, it should be drunk between 1996 and 2003. The richer, fuller 1990 Nuits St.-Georges Les St.-Georges reveals a saturated dark ruby color and a big, spicy, earthy, herb- and blackberry-scented nose. This full-bodied, tannic yet tasty wine will be at its best between 1995 and 2004. Remoriquet's 1989 Bourgogne Hautes-Côtes de Nuits and leaner, spicy, earthy, smoky 1989 Nuits St.-Georges are straightforward and solidly built. The 1989

Nuits St.-Georges Les Allots is ripe, tasty, elegant, and supple. A bigger, more earthy, smoky, tannic, and tough-textured 1989 Nuits St.-Georges Les Damodes; a large-scale, tannic, medium-bodied, ripe, concentrated 1989 Nuits St.-Georges Les Bousselots; a nearly superb, black-colored, rich, fruity, opulent, massive 1989 Nuits St. Georges Rue de Chaux; and a deeply colored, backward, tannic, concentrated 1989 Nuits St.-Georges Les St.-Georges round out his portfolio of 1989s. These 1989s should age gracefully for up to a decade.

OTHER THOUGHTS: More finesse and these wines would be top-notch.

BERNARD RION PÈRE ET FILS (VOSNE-ROMANÉE)* * *

1989 Chambolle-Musigny Les Echézeaux	D	82
1989 Chambolle-Musigny Les Gruenchers	D	80
1989 Clos Vougeot	E	89
1989 Nuits St.-Georges	C	72
1989 Nuits St.-Georges Les Murgers	D	85
1989 Vosne-Romanée	C	77
1989 Vosne Romanée Les Chaumes	D	82

The earthy, plummy, smoky 1989 Nuits St.-Georges Les Murgers exhibits meaty flavors, gobs of tannin, and fine concentration and length. It should be at its best between 1993 and 2005. The 1989 Clos Vougeot reveals superrichness, plenty of glycerin and body, and a heady, intense finish. Drink it between 1994 and 2005.

OTHER THOUGHTS: Muscular, dense wines that value tannin over elegance.

ANTONIN RODET (MERCUREY)* * *

1990 Aloxe-Corton Clos de la Boulotte	C	77
1990 Mercurey Château de Chamirey	C	85
1990 Château de Rully	C	86
1990 Pommard Les Grand Clos des Epenots	D	79

The attractive 1990 Château de Rully offers up a cedary, cherry- and herb-scented nose, medium- to full-bodied, spicy flavors, soft tannins, and a lush, fat, heady finish. Drink it over the next 5–7 years. The 1990 Mercurey Château de Chamirey displays an attractive plummy color, a superripe nose of black fruits and minerals, medium body, and an overall sense of elegance and balance. It should drink well for the next 5–7 years.

OTHER THOUGHTS: Keep an eye out for this firm's selections from Rully and Mercurey, as they are good wines at reasonable prices.

DOMAINE DE LA ROMANÉE-CONTI (VOSNE-ROMANÉE)* * * * *

1990 Echézeaux	EE	94
1989 Echézeaux	EE	90
1990 Grands Echézeaux	EEE	95
1989 Grands Echézeaux	EEE	92

1990 Richebourg	EEE	96
1989 Richebourg	EEE	93
1990 Romanée-Conti	EEE	98
1989 Romanée-Conti	EEE	96
1990 Romanée St.-Vivant	EEE	92
1989 Romanée St.-Vivant	EEE	94
1990 La Tâche	EEE	97
1989 La Tâche	EEE	96

The DRC 1990s are among the deepest-colored wines from this domaine that I have tasted in the last decade. Moreover they are firmly structured, with significant tannins from both the vintage and from the aging in 100% new oak barrels. For the fortunate few who have had the discretionary income to afford the other great vintages of the DRC from the 1980s—1980, 1983, 1985, 1988, and 1989—the question is, are the 1990s superior? It is too early to say, but the 1990s undoubtedly represent a classic, concentrated, long-lived style of wine. In addition, all of these wines should have a more graceful evolution and broader window of drinkability than the tannic 1988s, as well as potentially greater longevity than the succulent and opulent 1985s. All of these offerings are outstanding, with that telltale complex, exotic fragrance that the DRC routinely achieves. The 1990 Echézeaux's deep color is followed by a bouquet with well-developed aromas of spices, plums, black raspberries, and sweet new oak. The wine exhibits admirable toastiness, rich, medium to full body, moderate tannins, low acidity, and an impressive finish. **Anticipated maturity: 1995–2010.** The 1990 Grands Echézeaux is broader, with more black raspberry and black cherry elements in its smoky, exotic nose, as well as a longer, more opulent and fleshy finish. Its lifeline should be similar to the Echézeaux's. The DRC's 1990 Romanée St.-Vivant is a tougher wine to evaluate. I found the 1990 to have a pervasive earthy, cinnamon-, clove-, and sweet fruit–scented nose intermingled with scents of spicy new oak. Although closed, the wine exhibits great depth, medium to full body, and copious quantities of hard tannins in the structured, austere finish. **Anticipated maturity: 1999–2015.** The 1990 Richebourg is exceptionally fragrant, with aromas of sweet jammy raspberries, plums, Oriental spices, and new oak, all of which soar from the glass. It is crammed with fruit and boasts a fat, opulent texture reminiscent of the 1985. The finish is rich and authoritative. The 1990 La Tâche possesses a dramatic, rich, opulent, black fruit character. This expansive, broad-shouldered wine exhibits an impressive dark ruby color; the telltale DRC fragrance of minerals, spices, black fruits, and toasty new oak; full body; outstanding richness; multidimensional flavors; a layered texture; and a smashingly long, intense finish. The new oak and tannin levels are noticeable. **Anticipated maturity: 1997–2015+.** The 1990 Romanée-Conti should ultimately be the most compelling of the DRC wines. Normally it possesses a lighter color than either La Tâche or Richebourg, but in 1990 it boasts a surprisingly saturated color that is the equal of La Tâche and Richebourg. The nose offers up sweet, clove, cinnamon, and blackberry aromas intermingled with toasty, smoky new oak. Lavishly rich and full bodied, with abundant tannins, this profound, surprisingly large-scale, tannic wine carries more muscle than usual. **Anticipated maturity: 2000–2025.** The 1989s, which are much more flattering and precocious than the 1990s, represent one of the best vintages for the DRC during the 1980s. These are wines of tremendous ripeness, opulence, and richness, as well as considerable tannin. The 1989 Echézeaux displays the most evolved bouquet of Oriental spices, coffee, smoked meats, rich, pruny fruit, and sweet, expansive, opulent flavors. Although there is considerable tannin at the end of the palate, the overall impression is of glorious ripeness, an exotic fruit character, and enough structure and tannin to support several decades of aging. The 1989 Grands Echézeaux offers a pure, Oriental spice– and black fruit–scented nose intertwined with aromas of smoky new oak. In the mouth there is great depth of fruit, but the wine is tannic. It finishes on the palate with considerable power, tannin, and structure, an indication that it needs 5–6 years of cellaring. It should last for up to 2 decades. The 1989 Romanée St.-Vivant exhibits a cinnamon, smoky, earthy nose, superb extraction of fruit, plenty of glycerin, moderate tannin, and an explosively rich, long finish. Some tasters may find it rustic when compared with the two previous wines. The 1989 Richebourg offers a gloriously sweet, perfumed aroma of black fruits, new oak, and fruitcake. It boasts sensational extract and is crammed with expansively flavored, glycerin-infused, rich, ripe fruit. The intense ripeness and fruit character follow through in the wine's finish. This is a large-scale, rich, ripe, surprisingly seductive Richebourg. Drink it between 1995 and 2015. The backward 1989 La Tâche displays an impressively dark color, and with coaxing, some aromas of Oriental spice, black fruits, and new oak emerge. This highly structured, massive, stubbornly unevolved La Tâche should last for 30 or more years. The 1989 Romanée-Conti is one of the lighter-colored wines. It exhibits an ethereal fragrance of coffee, smoke, spices, leather, and smoked meats, is rich and intense, and possesses a remarkably sweet, long finish. Although it appears significantly less concentrated and structured than La Tâche, its length is every bit as impressive. It will last for decades.

OTHER THOUGHTS: The DRC has been on a hot streak since 1978—spectacular 1978s, 1979s, 1980s, 1983s, 1985s, and 1988s and remarkably good 1984s, 1986s, and 1987s. Only the 1981s are a letdown. These are Burgundy's most dramatic and ostentatious wines!

MICHEL ROSSIGNOL (VOLNAY)* * *

1989 Beaune Les Teurons	C	87
1989 Côte de Beaune-Villages Clos des Pierres Blanches	C	84
1989 Volnay	C	87
1989 Volnay Pitures	C	85

The 1989 Côte de Beaune-Villages is an exceptionally powerful, dense, tannic, and deeply colored wine. It is atypical for a 1989. The 1989 Beaune Les Teurons is a voluptuous, hedonistic, richly fruity, luscious red burgundy bursting with aromas of new oak, smoke, and roasted black cherry fruit. Long and luscious, it will make delicious drinking over the next 5–6 years. Rossignol's 1989 Volnay exhibits a perfumed nose of red fruits, spicy oak, and minerals. It is rich and deep, with soft tannins and a degree of opulence. The closed 1989

Volnay Pitures exhibits more tannin. Although some fragrance can be coaxed from the glass, the wine remains tight.
OTHER THOUGHTS: A fine winemaker continues to labor in the shadows.

PHILIPPE ROSSIGNOL (GEVREY-CHAMBERTIN)* * *

1989 Côte de Nuits-Villages	C	75
1989 Fixin Vieilles Vignes	C	85
1989 Gevrey-Chambertin	C	79

The 1989 Fixin Vieilles Vignes offers straightforward, deep, concentrated, plummy fruit allied with medium body, decent tannin, and refreshing acidity. The 1989 Côte de Nuits-Villages was too austere and tannic for my taste, and the 1989 Gevrey-Chambertin, while elegant and spicy, does not represent the value of the Bourgogne Rouge or Fixin Vieilles Vignes.
OTHER THOUGHTS: Little excitement can be found at this address.

ROSSIGNOL-TRAPET (GEVREY-CHAMBERTIN)* * *

1989 Beaune	C	84
1989 Beaune Les Teurons	D	?
1990 Chambertin	EE	86
1989 Chambertin	EE	86
1990 Chambertin Vieilles Vignes	EEE	88
1989 Chambertin Vieilles Vignes	EEE	87
1990 Chapelle-Chambertin	E	85
1989 Chapelle-Chambertin	E	86
1990 Gevrey-Chambertin	C	83
1989 Gevrey-Chambertin	C	77
1990 Gevrey-Chambertin Petite Chapelle	D	84
1989 Gevrey-Chambertin Petite Chapelle	D	78
1990 Latricières-Chambertin	EE	85
1989 Latricières-Chambertin	EE	85
1989 Morey St.-Denis	C	83
1989 Savigny-Lès-Beaune	B	81

The style of Rossignol-Trapet's wines is one of ripe, fruity wines, with medium body, soft tannins, and low acidity. They are not made for extended cellaring and should be consumed within their first 5–6 years of life. I enjoyed the 1990 Latricières-Chambertin for its spicy, rich, sweet, leathery nose and round, generously endowed, supple finish. It makes for a tasty mouthful of wine. The 1990 Chapelle-Chambertin is similarly ripe and tasty, with excellent fragrance. It is a seductive, lighter-style wine that requires consumption over the next 4–5 years. The medium ruby-colored, light 1990 Chambertin reveals a clipped, monolithic bouquet of grilled nuts and spicy fruit. Tasty, round, elegant, and sweet, with a supple finish, it should be drunk over the next 4–5 years. The 1990 Chambertin Vieilles Vignes exhibits a big nose of roasted nuts and sweet, jammy black fruits. This dramatic, medium-bodied wine exhibits abundant alcohol, a lusty, chewy, fat texture, and a sweet finish. Drink this flamboyant Chambertin over the next 8–10 years. The 1989s are also fruity, tasty wines that will be short-lived. Little excitement can be mustered for the understated, straightforward 1989 Savigny-Lès-Beaune, or the simple 1989 Beaune, or the bizarre-smelling 1989 Beaune Les Teurons. Nor could I muster much enthusiasm for the 1989 Gevrey-Chambertin, which was light, watery, and uninspiring. Sadly, the 1989 Gevrey-Chambertin Petite Chapelle was also austere, short, and clipped. The 1989 Morey St.-Denis exhibited excellent color, fruit, and substance, as well as a long finish. The 1989 Chapelle-Chambertin offers a fragrant nose of smoky, berry fruit and herbs that is followed by a rich, lush, succulent wine with low acidity, plenty of glycerin, and a long, spicy, supple finish. It should drink well for at least 7–8 years. The 1989 Latricières-Chambertin was richer, with a super fragrance of smoked meat, berry fruit, herbs, and new oak. It requires drinking over the next 5–7 years. The 1989 Chambertin is light, with a delicate nose of berry fruit, herbs, and smoked duck. Drink it over the next 5–7 years. The lovely 1989 Chambertin Vieilles Vignes exhibits medium ruby color; a big, smoky, spicy, fruitcake-scented nose; rich, expansive flavors; soft tannins; and low acidity. Drink this hedonistic wine over the next 7–8 years.

OTHER THOUGHTS: If the name says Trapet, it must mean great vineyards—which translates into good but unspectacular wine.

JOSEPH ROTY (GEVREY-CHAMBERTIN)* * * *

1990	Bourgogne Cuvée de Pressonière	B	80
1990	Bourgogne Grand Ordinaire	B	79
1990	Bourgogne Pinot Noir	B	81
1990	Charmes-Chambertin Vieilles Vignes	EEE	96
1990	Gevrey-Chambertin La Brunelle	D	79
1990	Gevrey-Chambertin Champs Chenys	D	86
1990	Gevrey-Chambertin Clos Prieur	D	84
1990	Gevrey-Chambertin Les Fontenys	E	86
1990	Griotte-Chambertin	EEE	91
1990	Marsannay	B	83
1990	Mazis-Chambertin	EEE	90

The wines that I enjoyed the most include a tannic, woody, ripe, deep ruby-colored 1990 Gevrey-Chambertin Champs Chenys. It possesses excellent ripeness and an attractive texture and finishes with hard tannins and a lot of wood. Hold it for at least 3–4 years. Although similarly styled, the lighter-colored 1990 Gevrey-Chambertin Les Fontenys tastes more elegant. It exhibits fine ripeness, medium body, spicy richness, elevated tannins, and gobs of toasty new oak. The 1990 Mazis-Chambertin reveals a nearly opaque deep ruby/purple color; a closed but promising nose of minerals, black fruits, licorice, and vanillin; and a superextracted, savagely tannic, medium- to full-bodied, tough-textured, concentrated finish. I would not touch a bottle for at least 6–7 years. Roty's 1990 Griotte-Chambertin is slightly lighter than the Mazis-Chambertin, as well as more elegant and softer, without the ferocious tannins so evident in the Mazis. It boasts medium to full body, superb extraction of flavor, and a seductive nose of black cherries, smoky oak, and minerals. This wine promises to last for 10–15 years. The spectacular 1990 Charmes-Chambertin Vieilles Vignes is the essence of Pinot Noir, with a saturated color, an intense nose of black fruits, flowers, and oak, and a phenomenal, portlike richness. It should keep for up to 20 years.

OTHER THOUGHTS: Superextracted, woody wines need time; Roty made terrific 1989s, 1985s, and 1980s; rather compact, oaky 1988s and 1987s.

EMMANUEL ROUGET (NUITS ST.-GEORGES)* * * *

1990	Echézeaux	EE	94
1989	Echézeaux	EE	91
1990	Nuits St.-Georges	D	87
1989	Nuits St.-Georges	D	86
1990	Vosne-Romanée	D	88
1989	Vosne-Romanée	D	86
1990	Vosne-Romanée Les Beaux Monts	E	90
1989	Vosne-Romanée Les Beaux Monts	E	88
1990	Vosne-Romanée Cros Parantoux	E	95
1989	Vosne-Romanée Cros Parantoux	E	90

The 1990 Nuits St.-Georges's bouquet leaps from the glass, offering up earthy, vividly pure red and black fruits. Medium bodied, lush, round, and already gorgeous, this wine should last for 5–7 years. The 1990 Vosne-Romanée reveals a deeper ruby/purple color, more toasty new oak, and a riper, richer, fuller-bodied impact. Its purity, intensity, and lavishly ripe fruit are captivating. The 1990 Vosne-Romanée Les Beaux Monts is superb, with a dark ruby/purple color, a huge fragrance of spring flowers, black raspberries, and toasty, smoky, new oak. The wine is medium to full bodied, with huge reserves of fruit, gobs of glycerin, and lusty quantities of alcohol in the long, rich, moderately tannic, sweet finish. Drink it over the next 10–12 years. The 1990 Vosne-Romanée Cros Parantoux is mind-boggling. The dense black/purple color is accompanied by a tightly knit, pure, intense nose of black fruits and smoky, new oak. This is the richest, most concentrated wine of the Rouget portfolio, and its extract level, purity, and delineation are profound. Drink it over the next 10–15 years. The 1990 Echézeaux offers up lavish quantities of sweet black fruits and floral, mineral, and toasty new oak scents. The wine boasts great intensity, medium to full body, gobs of black cherry and black raspberry fruit, and an opulent, glycerin-imbued, lusciously intense finish. It should drink well for the next 10–12 years. The 1989s from Nuits St.-Georges and Vosne-Romanée reveal remarkable clarity, ripe, berry fragrances, soft textures, good concentration, and a gentle touch of toasty new oak. Both require early consumption. The 1989 Vosne-Romanée Les Beaux Monts possesses a deeper color; a floral, black fruit–scented nose; lush, ripe, opulent flavors; excellent concentration; and a long, heady, spicy finish. The outstanding 1989 Vosne-Romanée Cros Parantoux is of Grand Cru quality. The deep ruby color is followed by a bouquet of sweet, jammy, black fruits, new oak, and flowers. In the mouth the wine displays superconcentration, low acidity, and tender tannins, as well as a gloriously rich, highly extracted, smooth-as-silk finish. Slightly superior is the 1989 Echézeaux. It exhibits a huge, flowery, cassis-scented nose intertwined with aromas of toasty new oak, superb richness, good acidity, a medium-bodied, multifaceted texture, and a silky finish. The latter three wines should drink well for another 6–8 years.

OTHER THOUGHTS: Under the tutelage of the great master of Pinot Noir, Henri Jayer, Rouget is quickly on his way to fame and fortune.

GEORGES ET CHRISTOPHE ROUMIER
(CHAMBOLLE-MUSIGNY)* * * * *

1990	Bonnes Mares	E	92
1989	Bonnes Mares	E	87
1990	Bourgogne Rouge	C	85
1989	Bourgogne Rouge	C	82
1990	Chambolle-Musigny	D	86
1989	Chambolle-Musigny	D	86
1990	Chambolle-Musigny Les Amoureuses	E	89
1989	Chambolle-Musigny Les Amoureuses	E	88
1990	Clos Vougeot	E	90
1989	Clos Vougeot	E	86
1990	Morey St.-Denis Clos de la Bussière	D	87
1989	Morey St.-Denis Clos de la Bussière	D	86
1990	Musigny	EE	91
1989	Musigny	EE	89
1990	Ruchottes-Chambertin	EE	90
1989	Ruchottes-Chambertin	EE	88

The round, ripe 1990 Bourgogne Rouge is a pleasingly fruity, tasty wine. The 1990 Chambolle-Musigny is also well made, with surprising intensity, a lovely floral- and berry-scented nose, and a smooth, attractive finish. Drink it over the next 5–7 years. The 1990 Morey St.-Denis Clos de la Bussière exhibits a deep, saturated dark ruby color, a broad nose of earthy black cherries and minerals, ripe, medium-bodied flavors, and a smooth finish. Drink it over the next 7–8 years. The Premier Cru, 1990 Chambolle-Musigny Les Amoureuses, is supple and elegant, with a flowery, finesse-filled bouquet, medium-bodied, concentrated flavors, low acidity, and light tannins in the velvety-textured finish. This rich Chambolle should be enjoyable young and last for 10–12 years. The superb, massive 1990 Clos Vougeot is full bodied, with plenty of glycerin, alcohol, and tannic clout. It should last for 20 years. The 1990 Ruchottes-

Chambertin reveals the smoky, earthy, gamey bouquet that is either adored or disliked. This sweet, full-bodied wine displays a kinky, earthy, black cherry, tarry fruitiness, admirable body, moderate tannins, and a long finish. Drink it between 1995 and 2010. Roumier's 1990 Bonnes Mares is a terrific red burgundy, with a dark ruby/garnet color; a big, spicy, plummy, earthy nose; rich, opulent, muscular, full-bodied flavors that exhibit terrific extraction of fruit; and a spicy, mineral, ironlike finish. Drink it between 1994 and 2008. Roumier's 1990 Musigny is lighter than the Bonnes Mares, with a classy, floral nose, fresh, elegant, medium-bodied flavors, and an expansive, velvet-textured finish. The 1989 Bourgogne Rouge is a pleasant, fruity, cleanly made wine with adequate ripeness. The 1989 Chambolle-Musigny offers up a delicious cherry-scented nose, ripe, moderately concentrated flavors, soft acids, and some tannins in the finish. It should mature for at least 5–6 years. The 1989 Morey St.-Denis Clos de la Bussière reveals more body and a big, rustic, leathery, gamey nose. The more savage aspect of the Pinot Noir grape is in evidence in this mineral-scented, smoky, meaty wine with abundant body and tannin. Drink it over the next decade. Roumier's 1989 Clos Vougeot reveals an attractive herb- and berry-scented nose, fat, straightforward, fruity flavors, good depth and glycerin, and some moderate tannins. I was impressed with the sweet, elegant, expansively flavored, fragrantly scented 1989 Chambolle-Musigny Les Amoureuses. It is burgundy at its most seductive and hedonistic level, without a hard edge. Drink this beauty over the next 6–7 years. The 1989 Ruchottes-Chambertin displays a big, mushroomy, meaty, smoky, Oriental spice–scented nose; rich, flattering, sweet, delicious flavors; soft tannin; and low acidity. There is plenty of alcohol, glycerin, and substance in this fleshy, dramatic wine. Drink it over the next 10–12 years. The 1989 Bonnes Mares offers up a spicy, herbal, fruity nose backed by subtle nuances of new oak, elegance, a rich, lush, berry fruitiness, and good acidity. It should be consumed over the next 7–8 years. Much more delicate and elegant is the 1989 Musigny. The wine's floral fragrance is impressive, as are the subtle, ripe, Pinot flavors intermingled with scents of new oak, herbs, and spices. The finish is long, and the overall impression is one of lightness, combined with considerable flavor authority—a difficult twosome to achieve. Drink this wine over the next 7–8 years.

OTHER THOUGHTS: The name Roumier is synonymous with classic old-style red burgundies. Don't miss the 1988s and 1983s, among the few great wines of these two vintages.

DOMAINE ARMAND ROUSSEAU (GEVREY-CHAMBERTIN)* * * *

1990	Chambertin	EEE	90+
1989	Chambertin	EEE	96
1990	Chambertin-Clos de Bèze	EEE	90
1989	Chambertin-Clos de Bèze	EEE	94
1990	Charmes-Chambertin	EE	84
1989	Charmes-Chambertin	EE	85
1990	Clos de la Roche	E	85
1989	Clos de la Roche	E	86

1990 Gevrey-Chambertin	C	80
1989 Gevrey-Chambertin	C	85
1990 Gevrey-Chambertin Les Cazetiers	C	82
1989 Gevrey-Chambertin Les Cazetiers	C	86
1990 Gevrey-Chambertin-Clos St.-Jacques	EE	90
1989 Gevrey-Chambertin-Clos St.-Jacques	EE	92
1990 Mazis-Chambertin	E	87
1990 Ruchottes-Chambertin-Clos des Ruchottes	E	87
1989 Ruchottes-Chambertin-Clos des Ruchottes	EE	90

At the top level, Rousseau consistently produces three profound wines—Gevrey-Chambertin-Clos St.-Jacques (as good as most producers' Grands Crus), Chambertin-Clos de Bèze, and Chambertin. That being said, I remain perplexed as to why Rousseau's other wines are so surprisingly light and fluid. His medium ruby-colored 1990 Mazis-Chambertin reveals a rich, sweet nose of black fruits, ground beef, and sweet oak. Soft and round, with low acidity and light tannins, it is an atypical Mazis. Drink it over the next 7–8 years. I was surprised by the lightness of the 1990 Clos de la Roche. The color is light ruby, and the nose is elegant, with a flowery, cherry fruitiness and a touch of earth. This attractive wine is round, simple, and fruity. It should be consumed over the next 6–7 years. The wine from Rousseau's *monopole* vineyard, Clos des Ruchottes, is denser. I was fond of the 1990's big, sweet, earthy, ripe fruit, and open-knit nose. There is also a lovely mélange of expansively flavored Pinot fruit, an attractive smokiness, and a lightly tannic, low-acid, ripe finish. Drink it over the next 6–7 years. The outstanding 1990 Gevrey-Chambertin-Clos St.-Jacques possesses a saturated deep ruby color and an explosive nose of black fruits, spicy new oak, flowers, and truffles. The wine is dense, seductive, and ripe, with low acidity, glycerin, and alcohol, making it a voluptuous, opulent mouthful. Drink it over the next decade. Both the Chambertin-Clos de Bèze and Chambertin are more closed, deeper-colored wines. I thought the 1990 Chambertin-Clos de Bèze to be lower in acidity and more forward. I am sure it will last for 15 or more years. It offers roasted black cherry and toasty new oak scents, outstanding concentration, full body, and a long, rich, moderately tannic finish. The 1990 Chambertin reveals an impressive dark ruby/purple color, a closed bouquet, and tight, hard tannins. This deep, broad-shouldered, full-bodied, intensely concentrated, chewy-textured wine should last through the first decade of the next century. The 1989 Gevrey-Chambertin is lean and compact, but it is capable of 5–10 years of aging. The 1989 Gevrey-Chambertin Les Cazetiers is a perfumed, richly fruity, yet firmly tannic wine that should evolve gracefully over 8–12 years. Rousseau's 1989 Charmes-Chambertin is a monolithic, straightforward, round, supple wine that lacks intensity. The 1989 Clos de la Roche is a bigger, more alcoholic wine, with greater size and more plumpness, glycerin, fat, and tannin. It will be at its best between 1994 and 2003. The 1989 Ruchottes-Chambertin-Clos des Ruchottes is superb. A huge nose of Oriental spices, saddle leather, superripe berry fruit, and new oak is splendid. There is profound richness, multidimensional flavors, plenty of new oak, and a terrific finish. This wine should last for

10–12 years. Rousseau's famed Gevrey-Chambertin-Clos St.-Jacques is a terrific wine in 1989, with a fabulous nose of black fruits, spicy new oak, and Oriental spices. The new oak holds its superconcentrated personality together. With low acidity, high tannin, and a wonderful purity and length on the palate, this magnificent 1989 will make splendid drinking between 1993 and 2006. The 1989 Chambertin-Clos de Bèze possesses an opaque dark ruby/purple color and a huge, unevolved bouquet of black fruits, herbs, licorice, and new oak. In the mouth it displays fascinating depth and fruit, superb extraction, good tannin, and decent acidity. It is a voluptuous, beautifully rendered wine that should drink well for at least 15 more years. Rousseau's 1989 Chambertin, a magnificent wine from this appellation, clearly lives up to its reputation as the "king of wines." A huge nose of sweet, gamey, smoky, earthy fruit, intermingled with scents of toasty new oak, is followed by a wine with sensational ripeness, staggering concentration, and flavors reminiscent of Peking duck lathered with green onions and plum sauce. It should mature brilliantly for 12–15 years.

OTHER THOUGHTS: This legendary producer makes three great wines—Clos St.-Jacques, Clos de Bèze, and Chambertin. The balance of the portfolio is uninspiring.

FABIEN ET LOUIS SAIER (MERCUREY)* *

1989 Clos des Lambrays	EEE	76
1989 Mercurey Champs Martin	C	72

This domaine is a disappointment. The 1989 Mercurey Champs Martin is light and thin, with sharp acidity and hard tannins. There is no depth, and the wine has been stripped at bottling. More inexcusable is the 1989 Clos des Lambrays. Its color is a pale light ruby, and the nose offers up insipid, innocuous, faded Pinot aromas marked by new oak and underripe fruit. It is clipped and short. Pity the poor purchaser who buys this wine based on its reputation.

OTHER THOUGHTS: These folks desperately need a wake-up call!

DANIEL SENARD (ALOXE-CORTON)* * *

1990 Aloxe-Corton Les Valozières	C	80?
1990 Corton Les Bressandes	E	84?
1990 Corton en Charlemagne	D	85+
1990 Corton-Clos des Meix	E	82?
1990 Corton-Clos du Roi	E	88+

The wines I tasted from Daniel Senard were extremely oaky, tannic, and backward and nearly impossible to judge. Will the wood and tannin outlive the fruit? The wines that appear to have the best chance of achieving harmony include the 1990 Corton en Charlemagne. A rare red wine, it exhibits an opaque dark purple color and a closed nose with vague aromas of ripe plums and prunes as well as gobs of smoky new oak. Full bodied and rich, but tough and hard, this wine needs at least a decade of cellaring. If the fruit holds up, it will be outstanding. Even richer and better balanced, particularly in its proportions of fruit, wood, and tannin, is the 1990 Corton-Clos du Roi. Nearly black in color and extremely oaky, this is a wine of enormous richness. It needs at least 7–8 years of cellaring and should last for 15–20.

OTHER THOUGHTS: A new style of wine is emerging from this estate—dense, rich, but oh so oaky!

CHRISTIAN SERAFIN (GEVREY-CHAMBERTIN)* * * *

1990 Charmes-Chambertin	E	92
1989 Charmes-Chambertin	E	89
1990 Gevrey-Chambertin	D	87
1989 Gevrey-Chambertin	D	82
1990 Gevrey-Chambertin Les Cazetiers	E	90+
1989 Gevrey-Chambertin Les Cazetiers	E	87
1990 Gevrey-Chambertin Le Fonteny	D	87+
1989 Gevrey-Chambertin Premier Cru	D	86
1990 Gevrey-Chambertin Vieilles Vignes	D	86+
1989 Gevrey-Chambertin Vieilles Vignes	D	86

The softest wine of Serafin's 1990 offerings, the dark-colored Gevrey-Chambertin, exhibits a sweet perfume of black fruits and damp earth. In the mouth it is medium bodied, with gorgeous fruit extraction, soft tannins, and a moderately long, round finish. Drink it over the next 5–6 years. The closed, tannic 1990 Gevrey-Chambertin Vieilles Vignes possesses higher acidity yet excellent concentration. It should last for well over a decade. The dark-colored, medium-bodied 1990 Gevrey-Chambertin Le Fonteny offers a tight but promising nose of spicy oak, ripe black fruits, and minerals. There is excellent concentration, surprisingly crisp acidity for a 1990, and a moderately long, fresh finish. It should be at its best between 1994 and 2002. Serafin's 1990 Gevrey-Chambertin Les Cazetiers has a saturated, opaque dark ruby/purple color and a tight but blossoming bouquet of herbs, black cherries, smoke, and roasted nuts. It is rich and full bodied, with excellent structure, mouth-watering tannins, and a long, concentrated, powerful finish. **Anticipated maturity: 1996–2010.** The 1990 Charmes-Chambertin is more open than the Les Cazetiers, with a roasted, cassis, almost prunelike character. This aspect of *surmaturité* is also noticeable in the splendidly opulent, rich, gamey black raspberry flavors. This rich, voluptuously textured, sweet, expansive wine makes a considerable impact on the palate, but the tannins are less noticeable. The finish is exceptionally long. Drink it between now and 2007. Serafin's fruity 1989 Gevrey-Chambertin exhibits a deep color, round, attractive flavors, and good body. The far superior 1989 Gevrey-Chambertin Vieilles Vignes possesses a bouquet of earth, roasted nuts, and black fruits, good tannin and body, a touch of new oak, and a spicy finish. Drink it between now and 2000. The 1989 Gevrey-Chambertin Premier Cru is also densely packed, but tight and unevolved, with good tannins and spicy new oak. There is a noticeable jump in quality with the 1989 Gevrey-Chambertin Les Cazetiers. This offering displays more new oak in the nose, more of a succulent, superripe, black fruit character, excellent concentration, plenty of tannin, and a long finish. Powerful and backward, it should last for 12–15 years. Serafin's 1989 Charmes-Chambertin offers a big, intense, flowery, curranty nose, excellent ripeness, medium to full body, rich, concentrated flavors, and a long, moderately smooth finish. The tannins are softer, but the wine enjoys excellent length.

OTHER THOUGHTS: The producer in Gevrey that other winemakers admire the most—classic expressions of Pinot Noir.

BERNARD SERVEAU (MOREY ST.-DENIS)* * *

1990	Chambolle-Musigny Les Amoureuses	E	88
1989	Chambolle-Musigny Les Amoureuses	E	85
1989	Chambolle-Musigny Les Chabiots	D	84
1989	Chambolle-Musigny Les Sentiers	D	79
1990	Morey St.-Denis Les Sorbès	D	86
1989	Morey St.-Denis Les Sorbès	D	76

Serveau generally produces a light, lacy style of Pinot Noir. The 1990 Morey St.-Denis Les Sorbès offers an excellent nose of cherry fruit, herbs, and damp earth. It is medium bodied, elegant, restrained, tasty, and gracious. Drink it over the next 4–6 years. The 1990 Chambolle-Musigny Les Amoureuses reveals a deep ruby color; a spicy, mineral, raspberry- and vanillin-scented nose; medium-bodied, attractively rich, supple flavors; and a spicy, clean, vividly pure finish. Drink it over the next 7–8 years.

Most of the 1989s are too tannic. A wine that did show well is the round, suave, and stylish 1989 Chambolle-Musigny Les Chabiots. One has to admire its sweet, gentle fruitiness and harmony. Drink it over the next 2–3 years. The 1989 Chambolle-Musigny Les Amoureuses exhibits better ripe-ness, a lusty, soft texture, low acidity, adequate concentration, and an attractive perfume. It should be drunk over the next 3–4 years.

OTHER THOUGHTS: Long known for silky, elegant wines, this estate may be heading down the slippery slope.

JEAN TARDY (VOSNE-ROMANÉE)* * * *

1989	Chambolle-Musigny	C	85
1989	Clos Vougeot	E	86
1989	Nuits St.-Georges au Bas de Combe	D	85
1989	Nuits St.-Georges Les Boudots	D	85
1989	Vosne-Romanée Les Chaumes	D	85

Tardy's 1989s are soft, fruity, pleasant wines. There is a charming 1989 Chambolle-Musigny; a supple, earthy 1989 Nuits St.-Georges au Bas de Combe; and a fruity, floral, easygoing, graceful 1989 Vosne-Romanée Les Chaumes. Tardy can make a superb Nuits St.-Georges Les Boudots. The 1989 is good, although lighter and less concentrated than in the past. The 1989 Clos Vougeot is a fruity, tasty, supple wine, but it lacks intensity. These are straightforward wines that should be drunk over the next 2–3 years.

OTHER THOUGHTS: I had expected more in 1989 and 1990, but Tardy is a name to be reckoned with.

CHÂTEAU DE LA TOUR (VOUGEOT)* * * *

1990 Clos Vougeot	E	90
1990 Clos Vougeot Vieilles Vignes	EE	94+

The 1990 regular *cuvée* of Clos Vougeot possesses a saturated deep ruby color. The nose offers lavishly rich, sweet aromas of black fruits and new oak. The wine enjoys exceptional concentration, a dense, expansive, opulent palate, plenty of glycerin, and a heady, lusty, intensely concentrated finish. It should evolve gracefully for a decade. The superconcentrated 1990 Clos Vougeot Vieilles Vignes represents the essence of Pinot Noir. More backward and less flattering, it is both massive and intense. The tannins are significant, and the extraction of fruit is mind-boggling. This huge, spectacularly concentrated wine has the potential to last 20 or more years.

OTHER THOUGHTS: The most important vineyard holding in the "Clos" is finally making wines worthy of its reputation.

JEAN TRAPET (GEVREY-CHAMBERTIN)* * *

1990 Chambertin	EEE	84
1989 Chambertin	EEE	87
1990 Chambertin Vieilles Vignes	EEE	88
1989 Chambertin Vieilles Vignes	EEE	88
1990 Chapelle-Chambertin	EE	84
1989 Chapelle-Chambertin	EE	?
1990 Gevrey-Chambertin	C	75
1989 Gevrey-Chambertin	C	84
1990 Latricières-Chambertin	EE	86
1989 Latricières-Chambertin	EE	86

Two 1990 wines of merit include a tannic, closed Latricières-Chambertin, which exhibits excellent deep ruby color, a spicy, meaty, berry-scented nose, moderate body, good definition and ripeness, and a moderately tannic, spicy finish. It will keep for 10–12 years. The other wine of interest is the 1990 Chambertin Vieilles Vignes. A smoky, roasted nose of ripe fruit and oak offers moderate intensity. The wine displays medium body, good concentration, low acidity, and firm tannins in the elegant finish. Drink it between 1994 and 2002. The 1989 Gevrey-Chambertin reveals some ripeness, a beefy midpalate, and fleshy flavors. It should be drunk over the next 5–6 years. I enjoyed the elegant 1989 Latricières-Chambertin. It displays a nice touch of new oak, a berry-scented nose, and supple flavors. Drink it over the next 5–6 years. Although there is plenty to like in the 1989 Chapelle-Chambertin in terms of concentration and extract, the nose exhibited a barnyard, fecal aroma that was off-putting. The 1989 Chambertin is backward and structured, with a good, spicy, smoky, meaty nose, and ripe, fruity flavors. It should drink well for a decade. The 1989 Chambertin Vieilles Vignes displays more depth, a pronounced, smoky, berry, meaty nose, and sweet, expansive flavors. Drink it between 1994 and 2002.

OTHER THOUGHTS: Oh, to have such great vineyards yet do so little to justify and protect their reputation!

TRUCHOT-MARTIN (MOREY ST.-DENIS)* * * *

1989	Chambolle-Musigny Les Sentiers	D	86
1990	Charmes-Chambertin Vieilles Vignes	D	92
1990	Clos de la Roche	E	89
1990	Gevrey-Chambertin aux Combottes	D	88
1990	Morey St.-Denis-Clos Sorbès	D	87

The 1990 Morey St.-Denis-Clos Sorbès reveals a medium ruby color; a spicy, rich, seductive nose; sweet, round, velvety flavors; an unctuous texture; and a generous, silky finish. Drink it over the next 5–7 years. The medium ruby/garnet-colored 1990 Gevrey-Chambertin aux Combottes exhibits a more earthy, leathery, animal, herbal component to its nose, as well as rich, long, intense, chewy flavors that coat the palate with glycerin, heady quantities of alcohol, and sweetness. Drink it over the next 5–6 years. The 1990 Clos de la Roche possesses the telltale earthy, mineral, leafy, leathery nose that so often emerges in wines from this Grand Cru vineyard; jammy, opulent fruit; some tannin and structure; and a spicy, leathery, intense, wet stone–like finish. This complex wine will be even more enjoyable to drink in 1–2 years; it should last for up to a decade. The 1990 Charmes-Chambertin Vieilles Vignes boasts a much deeper color than most Truchot wines. A super nose of jammy black raspberries, flowers, and sweet oak is followed by a wine with great richness, profound intensity, and opulence. The overall impression is one of elegance and precocious fruitiness and headiness. It should drink well for at least a decade. Truchot's delicious 1989s are ideal for drinking over the next 4–6 years. The 1989 Chambolle-Musigny Les Sentiers is a pretty wine, with a moderately intense bouquet of red fruits and flowers, graceful fruit flavors, soft tannins, and low acidity. It will make delicious drinking over the next 3–4 years. The 1989 Morey St.-Denis-Clos Sorbès reveals an even paler color, an understated mineral, fruity nose, and soft, round flavors that tail off in the finish. Drink it over the next 1–2 years. The 1989 Clos de la Roche exhibits a perfume of minerals, smoked meats, and superripe red fruits. The gorgeous level of fruit extraction is obvious in this satiny-textured, expansively-flavored, delicious wine. Drink it over the next 4–6 years. The 1989 Charmes-Chambertin Vieilles Vignes reveals the deepest color of Truchot's wines as well as a big, rich, smoky, black fruit–scented nose; soft, rich, opulent fruit flavors; and a moderately tannic, structured finish. For the record, Truchot-Martin's wines are all bottled unfiltered.

OTHER THOUGHTS: Gorgeously seductive wines that prove just how much flavor Pinot Noir can have in such light-colored wines.

COMTE DE VOGÜÉ (CHAMBOLLE-MUSIGNY)* * * *

1990	Bonnes Mares	EE	90+
1990	Chambolle-Musigny	D	87

1990 Chambolle-Musigny Les Amoureuses	E	85+
1990 Musigny Vieilles Vignes	EEE	94+

The 1990 Chambolle-Musigny is a notable success. The color is deep ruby/purple, and the nose offers up sweet aromas of black fruits, minerals, and toast. In the mouth it is round, gentle, and generous, with a lush yet elegant finish. Drink it over the next 6–7 years. I found the 1990 Chambolle-Musigny Les Amoureuses to be completely closed, with a compact, austere character. There is enough fruit and personality to merit a recommendation. It should keep for 10 or more years. Although the 1990 Bonnes Mares is closed, the dark ruby/purple color and the wine's terrific potential are evident. Full bodied, with a blossoming, black cherry nose complemented by a judicious use of toasty new oak, this wine exhibits wonderful richness, excellent definition, and a long, dense, concentrated finish. **Anticipated maturity: 1997–2010.** The 1990 Musigny Vieilles Vignes possesses a nearly opaque purple color as well as a closed but highly promising nose of cassis, licorice, new oak, flowers, and minerals. There is significant body, a formidable structure, outstanding richness and extraction of fruit, and a long, tannic finish. **Anticipated maturity: 1999–2020.**

OTHER THOUGHTS: One of the greatest names in Burgundy was a qualitative no-show between 1973 and 1988. The delicious 1989s and superb 1990s, I hope, signal a return to the glory days of the forties, fifties, and sixties.

WHITE BURGUNDY

AMIOT-BONFILS (CHASSAGNE-MONTRACHET)* * * *

1989 Chassagne-Montrachet Les Caillerets	D	93
1989 Chassagne-Montrachet Les Vergers	D	88
1989 Le Montrachet	EEE	98
1989 Puligny-Montrachet Champ Gain	D	90
1989 Puligny-Montrachet Les Demoiselles	E	93

Amiot-Bonfils remains one of the most underrated producers of white burgundies. The range of 1989 white wines I tasted was the finest I have ever experienced from Amiot. For starters, there is an opulent, superrich 1989 Chassagne-Montrachet Les Vergers. It would have merited an outstanding rating simply on the basis of its power and intensity, but I thought there was too much new oak showing in the nose and flavors. That may be absorbed given the wine's stunning concentration. Drinkable now, this wine will age gracefully for at least a decade. The brilliant 1989 Puligny-Montrachet Champ Gain displayed subtle spicy oak in the nose, wonderfully rich, stylish, concentrated flavors, plenty of glycerin and alcohol, and an explosively long finish. Connoisseurs who are able to defer their gratification should check out the 1989 Chassagne-Montrachet Les Caillerets, a spectacularly rich, structured wine that needs at least 1–2 years of bottle age. It is the most tightly knit of the Amiot-Bonfils Premiers Crus, may well be the most concentrated, and may ultimately warrant an even higher score. It is a beautifully made white burgundy built for extended cellaring of 10–12 years. The 1989 Puligny-Montrachet Les Demoiselles is another spectacular example of this superlative vintage for white burgundy. Immense on the palate, with oodles of ripe apple fruit intertwined with flavors of butter, oranges, and smoke, this offering has considerable structure. Given the sheer honeyed style of this wine, it can be drunk at an earlier age. Wow, these 1989 white burgundies are delicious! Last, there are only 25 cases of the Amiot-Bonfils 1989 Le Montrachet—for the world. Unbelievably spectacular, it clearly rivals the 1989 Montrachets produced by the likes of Ramonet and the Domaine de la Romanée-Conti. The nose exhibits a profound honeyed richness, the palate displays the very essence of Chardonnay, and the finish endures extraordinarily. It is nearly painful to drink, largely because the wine's rarity and price will probably make a repeat experience highly unlikely. However, for the handful of people who ever do lay their hands on a bottle, it should evolve gracefully for at least 2 decades.

RATINGS FOR THE 1990S: Chassagne-Montrachet Les Caillerets (92), Chassagne-Montrachet Les Vergers (89), Le Montrachet (92), Puligny-Montrachet Les Demoiselles (90)

DOMAINE DE L'ARLOT (PRÉMEAUX)* * * *

1990 Clos de l'Arlot	D	90
1989 Clos de l'Arlot	D	92

The Domaine de l'Arlot is also making superlative white wines. The 1990 Clos de l'Arlot exhibits an excellent buttery, stony richness, plenty of flesh and depth in the midpalate, and good acidity in the long, heady, alcoholic finish. The 1989 Clos de l'Arlot is superconcentrated, with a big, smoky, earthy, buttery nose, rich, concentrated, glycerin-laden flavors, and a whoppingly long, intense finish. Interestingly, the manager of Domaine de l'Arlot, Jean-Pierre de Smet, brought several cases of this wine to the 1991 Oregon Pinot Noir Festival, where it created a miniriot when word got out about how spectacular it was.

BALLOT-MILLOT ET FILS (MEURSAULT)* * *

1989 Meursault Les Charmes	D	84
1989 Meursault Les Genevrières	D	85

Neither white wine dazzled me. I may have caught the 1989 Meursault Les Charmes in an awkward period. The wine is completely closed, and is atypical of the 1989 vintage with its medium-bodied, crisp, lighter style. Although the 1989 Meursault Les Genevrières revealed more ripeness and intensity, it did not have the presence or complexity revealed by many wines in 1989, particularly those from Meursault, which had extremely low yields.

RATINGS FOR THE 1990'S: Meursault (78), Meursault Les Charmes (85)

DANIEL BARRAUD (POUILLY-FUISSÉ)* * * *

1990 Mâcon-Vergisson La Roche	B	86
1990 Pouilly-Fuissé La Verchere	C	86
1990 Pouilly-Fuissé Vieilles Vignes	D	90

The wines of Daniel Barraud offer excellent purity of flavor and plenty of concentration. The 1990 Mâcon-Vergisson La Roche exhibits a bouquet of stylish, floral fruit, fresh, medium-bodied, tasty flavors, and plenty of fruit. The 1990 Pouilly-Fuissé La Verchere is similar in style, with more of an apple/butter-scented nose, good, medium-bodied, fruit, and a crisp finish. The star of this trio is the 1990 Pouilly-Fuissé Vieilles Vignes, a superbly concentrated, rich, brilliantly balanced Chardonnay with an amazingly long finish. Drink this super wine over the next 3–4 years.

BITOUZET-PRIEUR (VOLNAY)* * *

1989 Meursault Les Charmes	E	87?
1989 Meursault-Clos du Cromin	D	90
1989 Meursault Les Perrières	E	92

The fact that Meursault had extremely small yields in 1989 is evident in the concentration levels of most producers' wines. Bitouzet-Prieur, a winemaker who turns out Meursaults of uncommon elegance and finesse, has produced blockbuster wines in 1989. Although the 1989 Meursault-Clos du Cromin is a backward style of Meursault, it is a stunning wine. The huge nose of smoky hazelnuts, butter, and citrus is followed by a tightly knit yet full-bodied style of Meursault that coats the palate. It should drink well for at least a decade. The 1989 Meursault Les Charmes is oaky. Although there is no doubting its massive feel on the palate, the oak was intrusive, raising concerns about what direction the wine might take. I admire its size and richness, but it is presently in an awkward, clumsy stage. Such a criticism cannot be leveled against the backward 1989 Meursault Les Perrières. This wine is the most backward of this trio, yet it is also the most concentrated, complete, and complex and displays a restrained underlying mineral, buttery richness. This big, rich, blockbuster-style, tightly knit Meursault should provide sensational drinking for the next 10–12 years.

RATINGS FOR THE 1990S: Meursault Les Charmes (84), Meursault-Clos du Cromin (78), Meursault Les Perrières (85)

ÉTIENNE BOILEAU (CHABLIS)* * *

1990 Chablis	B	85
1990 Chablis Mont de Milieu	?	82
1990 Chablis Montmains	D	87
1990 Chablis Les Vaillons	C	87
1990 Chablis Vaugiraut	C	78

Two offerings from Étienne Boileau stood out in my tastings. The Chablis Les Vaillons exhibits a textbook nose of minerals and fruit that is followed by a medium-bodied texture, good depth, and a well-delineated, crisp finish. The Chablis Montmains displays a lemony/lime, mineral character, admirable depth of fruit, and a crisp, long finish. Both wines should drink well for the next 4–5 years. The other offerings were pleasant but uninspiring. The generic Chablis is a good value for its quality level.

ANDRÉ BONHOMME (VIRÉ)* * * *

1990	Mâcon-Viré	B	86
1989	Mâcon-Viré	B	89

André Bonhomme, the top specialist of Mâcon-Viré, is making wines of extraordinary precision, elegance, and character. Should anyone happen to find the 1989 languishing on a retailer's shelves, snatch it up; it is the perfect expression of Chardonnay from the Mâconnais region. Loaded with fruit, it has an underlying elegance, crispness, and focus that is a joy to experience. It should continue to drink well for another 1–2 years. The 1990 is also top-notch, although it does not possess the intensity and sheer presence on the palate of the 1989. Nevertheless, it displays an alluring stony, floral, buttery, apple component to its nose and flavors that makes a good Mâcon rich and fresh to drink.

BOYER-MARTENOT (MEURSAULT)* *

1990	Bourgogne	B	85
1990	Meursault Les Charmes	D	86
1990	Meursault en l'Ormeau	C	82
1990	Meursault Les Perrières	D	87

Although I have been unimpressed with Boyer's wines in the past, the 1990s exhibit more character and fruit than I have previously found. The Bourgogne blanc is a well-packed, fruity, elegant wine, with good stuffing and plenty of Chardonnay character. The Meursault en l'Ormeau is stylish and correct, but restrained and straightforward. The Meursault Les Charmes is chewy and ripe, lacking complexity, but dense and flavorful. The best of this quartet is the deep, rich, medium- to full-bodied, mineral-scented Meursault Les Perrières. It possesses admirable intensity for a 1990, decent acidity, and a fine finish. It should be drunk over the next 4–5 years.

COOPERATIVE LA CHABLISIENNE (CHABLIS)* * *

1990	Chablis Blanchot	C	86
1990	Chablis Fourchaumes	C	86
1990	Chablis La Porte d'Or	B	85
1990	Chablis Les Preuses	D	87
1990	Chablis Vaudésir	D	87

This cooperative continues to show considerable competence in its philosophy of winemaking. Its Chablis is made in a modern, pure, clean style, with only certain wines being exposed to oak aging. The resulting wines possess wonderful crispness, pure fruit, and generally very good concentration. Its least expensive wine, the Chablis La Porte d'Or, is soft, ripe, and fruity, with enough Chablis character to justify its modest price. The Chablis Fourchaumes displays a steely character, an elegant personality, and crisp fruit. Drink it over the next 3–4 years. The Chablis Les Preuses is a bigger, richer, fatter wine with more body and alcohol. The soft, tasty Chablis Blanchot is ideal for consuming over the next 3–4 years. Last, the Chablis Vaudésir is ripe and dense, with considerable body and a ripe finish.

CHARTRON ET TRÉBUCHET (PULIGNY-MONTRACHET)* * *

1989 Batard-Montrachet	EE	87
1989 Beaune	C	87
1989 Chassagne-Montrachet	C	87
1989 Chevalier-Montrachet	EE	88
1989 Puligny-Montrachet-Clos du Cailleret	E	90
1989 Puligny-Montrachet-Clos des Pucelles	E	90
1989 Puligny-Montrachet Les Referts	E	90
1989 Rully Chaume	C	86
1989 Saint-Aubin en Remilly	C	86
1989 St.-Romain	C	86

The 1989 white burgundies from Chartron et Trébuchet are the best this rela-tively young *négociant* firm has yet produced. After tasting their entire line, I noted (and I have seen this in past vintages as well) that a number of their lower-level wines taste every bit as good as some of their Premiers Crus and Grands Crus. In fact, despite how good the Bâtard-Montrachet and Chevalier-Montrachet tasted, the Grands Crus do not seem to be significantly better and, perplexingly, are neither as interesting nor as rich as their best Premiers Crus. For reasonably good values in white burgundies, consumers should be looking for their nicely oaked, fleshy, flinty, medium-bodied, and elegant 1989 St.-Ro-main; their hazelnut-scented, toasty, rich, opulent, yet still graceful 1989 Saint-Aubin en Remilly; and their full-bodied, muscular, intensely flavored 1989 Rully Chaume. All three of these wines should make delicious drinking over the next 2–4 years. One of the surprises of my tastings was the wonderful performance of the 1989 Beaune. One rarely sees white wines from this appel-lation, the best known being Drouhin's Clos des Mouches, but Chartron et Trébuchet's 1989 Beaune had surprising richness and intensity; a big, beauti-ful, floral, buttery, apple-scented bouquet; full-bodied, rich, glycerin-laden flavors; and a long, opulent finish. It is a terrific wine that should drink beauti-fully over the next 4–5 years. I also liked their big, chewy, fat, muscular 1989 Chassagne-Montrachet. I am often disappointed with the villages wines from Puligny-Montrachet and Chassagne-Montrachet, but there is no doubting the quality of this tasty, full-bodied, generously endowed wine. It has all the big, buttery, hazelnut- and orange-flavored fruit anyone could want. Among the Premiers Crus, all the wines I tasted were good, but those that stood out in-cluded a superelegant, highly extracted, dense, deliciously ripe 1989 Puligny-Montrachet Les Referts; a structured, backward, highly concentrated, medium-bodied 1989 Puligny-Montrachet-Clos du Cailleret; and a buttery, somewhat steely, mineral-, orange-, apple-, and vanillin-scented 1989 Puligny-Montrachet-Clos des Pucelles. I thought all three of these Premiers Crus were every bit as good as the Grands Crus I tasted from Chartron et Trébuchet. I would opt for drinking them over the next 5–8 years.

RATINGS FOR THE 1990s: Bâtard-Montrachet (87), Bourgogne (83), Chassagne-Montrachet Les Morgeots (86), Chassagne-Montrachet St.-Marc (82), Chevalier-Montrachet (90), Meursault (82), Meursault-Charmes (84), Puligny-Montrachet (83), Puligny-Montrachet-Clos du Cailleret (88), Puligny-Montrachet-Clos des Pucelles (88), Puligny-Montrachet Les Folatières (85), Puligny-Montrachet Les Garennes (87), Puligny-Montrachet Les Referts (88)

J. F. COCHE-DURY (MEURSAULT)* * * * *

1989	Corton-Charlemagne	EE	98
1989	Meursault Les Perrières	D	97
1989	Meursault-Rougeot	D	93

Jean-François Coche-Dury is one of the greatest winemakers on planet Earth. He continues to produce dazzling wines from unbelievably tiny yields, taking the maximum risk by bottling his wines with no filtration. His spectacular 1989s are worth a special effort to obtain. The 1989 Meursault-Rougeot presents a huge nose of minerals and buttery tropical fruit, long, superrich flavors, good acidity and structure, and a dazzling finish. Drinkable now, it should evolve splendidly over the next 5–6 years. Coche-Dury's 1989 Meursault Les Perrières smells and tastes as if it were a Montrachet. If there is one Premier Cru vineyard in Burgundy that merits elevation to Grand Cru status, it must be Les Perrières in Meursault. The huge nose of minerals, lemons, apple blossoms, and buttered toast is followed by a wine with immense richness, massive structure, and layer upon layer of Chardonnay fruit. This wine is crammed with enough glycerin, extract, alcohol, and intensity to evolve for at least 10 or more years. However, it is impossible to resist at the moment, given its extreme richness. This is a winemaking tour de force! Coche-Dury's 1989 Corton-Charlemagne is unbelievably concentrated. It exhibits superb depth, good acidity, a penetrating earthy, mineral quality, and a finish that lasts over a minute. RATINGS FOR THE 1990s: Corton-Charlemagne (96), Meursault Les Narvaux (89), Meursault Les Perrières (93), Meursault-Rougeot (90)

FERNAND COFFINET (CHASSAGNE-MONTRACHET)* * * *

1989	Bâtard-Montrachet	EE	95
1989	Chassagne-Montrachet	D	88
1989	Chassagne-Montrachet Blanchot	D	90

Coffinet's 1989s are remarkably rich and complex. The 1989 Chassagne-Montrachet displays an intense, smoky, bacon fat–scented, buttery nose; ripe, long, superconcentrated flavors; full body; plenty of weight and thickness; and enough acidity for focus. Drink it over the next 5–7 years. The 1989 Chassagne-Montrachet Blanchot exhibits a huge nose of buttery, toasty, smoky, exotic fruit, super depth and richness, crisp acidity, and plenty of glycerin and alcohol in its long finish. In this spectacular vintage, here is a Premier Cru that tastes like a Grand Cru. Not surprisingly, Coffinet's 1989 Bâtard-Montrachet is a riveting example of a great white burgundy. The huge nose of bacon fat, ripe apple, and pineapple fruit, as well as aromas of toast and minerals, is followed by a wine with sensational concentration, staggering depth and length, and a Montrachet-like feel in the mouth. Drink this dazzling white burgundy over the next 10–12 years. RATINGS FOR THE 1990s: Bâtard-Montrachet (90)

COLIN-DELEGER (CHASSAGNE-MONTRACHET)* * * *

1989 Chassagne-Montrachet Les Chaumées-Clos St.-Abdon	D	87
1989 Chassagne-Montrachet Les Demoiselles	D	92
1989 Chassagne-Montrachet Morgeot Blanc	D	90
1989 Chassagne-Montrachet en Remilly	D	90

Colin-Deleger has made some lovely 1989s that offer wonderful tropical fruit aromas of superripe grapes; fat, unctuous, opulent textures that come from wine high in glycerin and low yields; and heady, alcoholic finishes. The most flamboyant, concentrated, and dramatic of these four offerings is the 1989 Chassagne-Montrachet Les Demoiselles. Its huge, buttery popcorn, grilled nut bouquet is followed by splendidly rich flavors that go on and on. I would opt for drinking it between 1992 and 1997. The wine I found closest to Les Demoiselles was the 1989 Chassagne-Montrachet en Remilly. It was also precocious, with wonderful opulence and a full-bodied personality. Both the 1989 Chassagne-Montrachet Les Chaumées-Clos St.-Abdon and the 1989 Chassagne-Montrachet Morgeot were more tightly knit and reserved. The 1989 Morgeot merits 1–2 years of cellaring, but it can be enjoyed for its smoky, hazelnut- and tropical fruit–scented bouquet and rich, fruit salad flavors presented in a medium- to full-bodied, graceful, elegant manner. Les Chaumées-Clos St.-Abdon is the lightest of these 1989s.

RATINGS FOR THE 1990S: Chassagne-Montrachet Les Chaumées-Clos St.-Abdon (85), Chassagne-Montrachet Les Demoiselles (90), Chassagne-Montrachet Morgeot Blanc (87), Chassagne-Montrachet en Remilly (86)

JEAN COLLET (CHABLIS)* * * *

1989 Chablis Les Vaillons	D	89
1989 Chablis Valmur	D	95

The huge mineral-scented nose of the 1989 Chablis Les Vaillons is followed by zesty, crisp, austere flavors, plenty of body, and a big, rich finish. I would not be surprised to see this wine merit a higher rating after another 2–3 years of bottle age. It will keep for at least a decade. Collet's 1989 Chablis Valmur is the quintessential example of a profound Chablis. It displays that unmistakable mineral, flinty, smoky smell, backed up by fabulously concentrated, high-extract flavors buttressed by zinging amounts of acidity. The finish is a blockbuster. But keep in mind, this wine is still an infant in terms of development. Drink it over the next 10–12 years.

DOMAINE DE LA COLLONGE (POUILLY-FUISSÉ)* * * *

1990 Pouilly-Fuissé	C	89

Gilles Noblet is one of the best producers in Pouilly-Fuissé, and this 1990 is a huge, rich, dramatic wine with gobs of fruit, full body, and plenty of alcohol in the finish. Drink it over the next several years.

CORSIN (POUILLY-FUISSÉ)* * * *

1990 Pouilly-Fuissé	C	87

This excellent Pouilly-Fuissé offers cherry notes in its bouquet. Dense, rich, and full bodied, it exhibits excellent concentration, adequate acidity for focus, and a lusty, alcoholic finish. Drink it over the next 1–2 years.

LOUIS CURVEUX (FUISSÉ)* * *

1990 Pouilly-Fuissé Les Menestrières	C	88

Another excellent 1990 Pouilly-Fuissé, this rich wine displays crisp acidity, plenty of body, and loads of fruit. Drink it over the next several years.

JEAN DAUVISSAT (CHABLIS)* * * *

1989 Chablis Les Vaillons	D	88
1989 Chablis Les Vaillons Vieilles Vignes	E	90

Both of these offerings are textbook Chablis, with vividly focused, pinpoint controlled, stony, mineral fruitiness and noses of citrus, steel, apple blossoms, and butter. Although the 1989 Les Vaillons regular *cuvée* is rich, with loads of fruit, it possesses a certain austerity and brilliance. The 1989 Les Vaillons Vieilles Vignes is similar, but riper from an aromatic perspective, as well as richer and longer in the mouth. Both are classic examples of Chablis that should drink beautifully for the next decade.

JEAN DEFAIX (MILLY)* * * *

1990 Chablis-Côte de Lechet	D	88
1990 Chablis Les Vaillons	D	87

These are gorgeous wines from Chablis, with an underlying mineral character, excellent crisp, lemony-apple-like Char-donnay fruit, and fine length and depth. The Chablis Les Vaillons possesses the most mineral scents and the Côte de Lechet a more orange, tropical fruit–like character. Both wines should drink beautifully for the next 5–6 years.

JEAN-PAUL DROIN (CHABLIS)* * *

1990 Chablis Fourchaume	D	85
1990 Chablis Montée de Tonnerre	D	87
1990 Chablis Montmains	D	79
1990 Chablis Les Vaillons	D	82
1990 Chablis Valmur	D	82
1990 Chablis Vosgros	D	82

Droin produces light, modern-style Chablis. With the exception of the Montée de Tonnerre and the Fourchaume, all of his 1990 offerings lack concentration and depth. They are crisp, pleasant, correct wines for drinking over the next 3–4 years. The Chablis Fourchaume displays some attractive wet stone components in its medium-bodied, fruity character. The best wine, the Chablis Montée de Tonnerre, offers a gunflint, smoky nose, medium body, excellent acidity, and good richness and depth. Drink it over the next 5–6 years.

JOSEPH DROUHIN (BEAUNE)* * * *

1989 Corton-Charlemagne	E	90
1989 Meursault	D	85
1989 Meursault Les Charmes	E	87
1989 Meursault Les Perrières	E	86
1989 Montrachet-Marquis de Laguiche	EEE	93
1989 Puligny-Montrachet	D	78
1989 Puligny-Montrachet Les Pucelles	D	84

The three Meursaults exhibited good ripeness, plenty of tasty, opulent fruit, and enough acidity to provide lift and freshness. Bearing in mind the low yields the Meursault appellation benefited from in 1989, these wines did not appear to be as powerful as many of their peers. However, they do exhibit the Drouhin touch of elegance and finesse. The 1989 Meursault Les Perrières is the most elegant and the 1989 Meursault Les Charmes the fullest and ripest. I was somewhat underwhelmed by Drouhin's lean, diluted 1989 Puligny-Montrachet, as well as the 1989 Puligny-Montrachet Les Pucelles. There is no question that Drouhin's 1989 Corton-Charlemagne is top-notch, with a big, citrusy, cinnamon-, baked apple–, and toasty oak–scented nose and ripe, intense flavors, all balanced by crisp acidity. The famous Montrachet from the Marquis de Laguiche is already delicious. The huge, smoky, tropical fruit–scented nose is followed by a wine that offers up gobs of honeyed, apple-, butter-, and orangelike flavors, good, lemony acidity, and a rich, creamy, well-evolved finish. Drink this beauty over the next decade.

DRUID WINES (MOREY ST.-DENIS)* * * *

1989 Meursault-Limozin	D	89

The 1989 Meursault-Limozin (made by Jacques Seysses of the Domaine Dujac) exhibits the vintage's telltale, superripe, sweet, buttery, tropical fruit–scented nose and a touch of new oak. In the mouth the wine is deep, rich, and fat, with barely enough acidity to hold it together. Nevertheless, there is plenty to like in this luscious, lavishly rich white burgundy for drinking over the next 5–6 years.

RATINGS FOR THE 1990S: Meursault Les Clous (88), Meursault-Limozin (89)

DUBREUIL-FONTAINE ET FILS (PERNAND-VERGELESSES)* * *

1989 Bourgogne Aligoté	B	86
1989 Corton-Charlemagne	EE	89

Bourgogne Aligoté is usually not this good. The 1989 from Dubreuil-Fontaine is an elegant, mineral-scented, fleshy wine with plenty of fruit and character. Drink it over the next year. The 1989 Corton-Charlemagne is extremely closed and tightly knit. Although it displays plenty of weight and potential, it requires at least 4–5 years of cellaring. My rating may look conservative by the mid-1990s. Drink it between 1995 and 2005.

GERARD DUPLESSIS (CHABLIS)* * * *

1989 Chablis	B	85
1989 Chablis Les Clos	D	92
1989 Chablis Montée de Tonnerre	C	89

The straight 1989 Chablis is a crisp, elegant, mineral-dominated, austere Chablis, tasty and impeccably clean. The nearly outstanding quality of the 1989 Chablis Montée de Tonnerre will not go unnoticed by Chablis aficionados for its hauntingly intense, essence of stone, and minerallike bouquet, followed by gobs of fruit in a backward, austere, highly concentrated, crisp style. It should easily last for 10–15 years. The magnificent 1989 Chablis Les Clos (from yields that did not exceed 25 hectoliters per hectare) exhibits enormous concentration and an explosively long finish. The wine is unbelievably backward and unevolved, yet what promise it holds for the future!

FAIVELEY (NUITS ST.-GEORGES)* * * */* * * * *

1989 Bourgogne Blanc-Cuvée Georges Faiveley	B	86
1989 Corton-Charlemagne	EE	96
1989 Meursault	D	90
1989 Montagny Premier Cru	C	86
1989 Puligny-Montrachet	E	91
1989 St.-Véran	B	86

Of the current releases, Faiveley produces, along with Leroy and Louis Jadot, the finest *cuvée* of generic white burgundy. The 1989 Bourgogne Blanc-Cuvée Georges Faiveley exhibits surprising intensity and richness, along with an attractive vanillin, buttery nose, ripe, rich, full-bodied flavors, and a long aftertaste. The 1989 St.-Véran is the first wine this firm has ever produced from that appellation. Floral and crisp, it is a more understated, elegant, and lighter style of wine than the Bourgogne Blanc. The 1989 Montagny Premier Cru possesses a stony, floral, applelike fruitiness in its aroma and taste. In the mouth there is vivid purity, good acidity, and an excellent crisp finish. Outstanding wines were produced by Faiveley from the village appellations of Meursault, Chassagne-Montrachet, and Puligny-Montrachet. The 1989 Meursault exhibited the telltale tropical fruit– and hazelnut-scented nose that highly extracted Meursaults can render. It is super in the mouth, with an unmistakable opulence buoyed by crisp acidity. Everything about the wine suggests it was made from either old vines or extremely low yields. Drink this big, bold, buttery, nutty style of Meursault over the next 5–6 years. The 1989 Puligny-Montrachet was even richer, with a buttery, floral, elegant nose, smoky, decadently rich flavors, decent acidity, and plenty of alcohol and stuffing in the long finish. Last, Faiveley, who makes tiny quantities of Corton-Charlemagne from one of the best vineyards on top of the Corton hill, has made an exquisite wine in 1989. Whether it turns out to be as magnificent as his 1986 remains to be seen. Only 1,672 bottles were made from minuscule yields of only 17 hectoliters per hectare. Extremely backward and nearly impenetrable, it does develop with 10–15 minutes of airing to reveal huge, stony, buttery, pineapple fruit flavors, spectacular concentration, glycerin, and intensity, and a phenomenally long finish that lasts over a minute. This is a Corton-Charlemagne to lay away for 10–15 years and drink through the first several decades of the next century—if you are lucky enough to find a bottle.

RATINGS FOR THE 1990S: Bourgogne (87), Chablis Vaillons (90), Chassagne-Montrachet (86), Corton-Charlemagne (93), Mercurey-Clos Rochette (89), Meursault (82), Puligny-Montrachet (90), Rully (87)

RENÉ FLEUROT-LAROSE (SANTENAY)* * *

1989 Bâtard-Montrachet	EE	89
1989 Chassagne-Montrachet-Clos de la Roquemaure	D	86
1989 Le Montrachet	EEE	89

Fleurot's 1989 Chassagne-Montrachet-Clos de la Roquemaure (a *monopole* vineyard) offered up a huge tropical fruit–scented nose of pineapples, coconut, and other exotic fruits. In the mouth it was ripe, rich, and full, with good acidity and plenty of length. It could easily evolve for another 8–10 years. Although both the 1989 Bâtard-Montrachet and the 1989 Le Montrachet were excellent wines, they were not profound, particularly for the vintage. Perhaps I caught them at an awkward or closed stage. The 1989 Bâtard-Montrachet exhibited an exotic nose, rich, deep, intense, full-bodied flavors, good glycerin and alcohol, and a modestly long finish. Drink it over the next 7–8 years. The 1989 Le Montrachet was deep and rich, but not celestial. It should be consumed over the next decade.

CHÂTEAU FUISSÉ (FUISSÉ)* * * * *

1990 Pouilly-Fuissé	C	87
1989 Pouilly-Fuissé	C	89
1990 Pouilly-Fuissé Les Vieilles Vignes	D	92
1989 Pouilly-Fuissé Les Vieilles Vignes	E	93
1989 St.-Veran	C	85

Although the 1989 St.-Véran exhibits a sort of bubble gum–like aroma that is too commercial in style for my taste, I have to admire its friendliness, superripe fruitiness, and lusciousness. Drink it over the next year. The 1989 Pouilly-Fuissé (regular *cuvée*) may be an outstanding wine. Exceptionally concentrated, opulent, and rich, with plenty of glycerin in the finish, it is a big mouthful of Chardonnay and the best regular *cuvée* of Pouilly-Fuissé I have tasted from this domaine in some time. The astonishingly rich 1989 Pouilly-Fuissé Les Vieilles Vignes could easily be confused for a top Côte d'Or Grand Cru for its layer upon layer of buttery, superripe, pineapple-scented and -flavored fruitiness, vivid purity and definition, plenty of lushness, and decadent levels of extract in the long, heady finish. Despite what the label says, I am convinced there must be 14% or more alcohol in this blockbuster Pouilly-Fuissé. Drink it over the next 5–7 years. Although the 1990 Pouilly-Fuissé (regular *cuvée*) is a more floral, delicate, restrained style of wine, it is no wimp. Rich and loaded with fruit, it exhibits an extra dimension in its flavors and a long, lush finish. The 1990 Pouilly-Fuissé Les Vieilles Vignes is a worthy rival to the powerful 1989. Rich, alcoholic, and heady, it displays gobs of fruit and sensational extraction of flavor. Many consumers tend to ignore Pouilly-Fuissé, but there are producers in this appellation, such as Château Fuissé and Madame Ferret, who are making wines that rival the best from Burgundy's Côte d'Or. Château Fuissé is one of them.

JEAN-NOËL GAGNARD (CHASSAGNE-MONTRACHET)* * * *

1989 Bâtard-Montrachet	EEE	92
1989 Chassagne-Montrachet	E	86
1989 Chassagne-Montrachet Les Caillerets	E	92
1989 Chassagne-Montrachet Morgeot	E	88
1989 Chassagne-Montrachet Premier Cru	E	90

Gagnard's 1989 Chassagne-Montrachet exhibits a moderately intense, oak-tinged, orange- and apple-scented bouquet, medium- to full-bodied, fleshy flavors, low acidity, and a powerful finish. The 1989 Chassagne-Montrachet Premier Cru is superior. The honeyed bouquet is intense, as are the deep, chewy, highly concentrated flavors. This big, stylish white burgundy is filled with aromas and flavors of hazelnuts, oranges, and apples. Unctuous and extremely rich with an explosive finish, it should drink well for 7–8 years. The 1989 Chassagne-Montrachet Morgeot is lighter and more backward, with higher acidity than the other offerings. More austere in character, yet admirably concentrated, it is made in a refined and polite style. For those who possess both the discretionary income and the requisite patience, the 1989 Chassagne-Montrachet Les Caillerets should provide memorable drinking in about 3–4 years and should keep for a decade or more. This wine is exceptionally rich and backward, but still bursting at the seams with buttery, smoky, honeyed apple, banana, pineapple, and orange fruit. Full bodied, strikingly well balanced, and focused, this is an exceptional wine. The 1989 Bâtard-Montrachet is loaded with power but is far less evolved. Exceptionally rich and full-bodied, with that unctuous, superconcentrated feel that the top white burgundies possess in the 1989 vintage, it has fine, lively acidity. I would give it at least 2 years in the bottle to develop more nuances and complexity.

RATINGS FOR THE 1990S: Bâtard-Montrachet (89), Chassagne-Montrachet Premier Cru (86), Chassagne-Montrachet Les Caillerets (89), Chassagne-Montrachet Morgeot (87)

CHÂTEAU GRENOUILLES (CHABLIS)* * * *

1990 Chablis Grenouilles	D	89

This is a classic, textbook example of Chablis with a penetrating fragrance of minerals and fruit. Elegant and powerful, this rich, medium-bodied wine exhibits good acidity and fine depth and character. Drink it over the next 7–8 years.

GUFFENS-HEYNEN (VERGISSON)* * * *

1990 Mâcon-Pierreclos en Chavigne	B	90
1990 Pouilly-Fuissé-Clos des Petits Croux	E	93
1990 Pouilly-Fuissé Les Croux	D	88
1990 Pouilly-Fuissé La Roche	E	89

Guffens's 1990 Mâcon-Pierreclos en Chavigne is a sensationally rich, stylish wine with great elegance and persistence on the palate and a long, crisp finish. Drink it over the next 4–5 years. The 1990 Pouilly-Fuissé Les Croux displays a rich, buttery nose, intense, ripe, long, applelike flavors, and plenty of extraction. The La Roche, which is dominated more by minerals than its butterlike element, offers undeniable elegance and finesse, as well as a medium- to full-bodied, long finish. Worth an effort to find is any of the microquantity of the 1990 Pouilly-Fuissé-Clos des Petits Croux, a spectacular Pouilly-Fuissé. Displaying a fabulous, tropical fruit– and buttery-scented nose, long, superextracted flavors, great balance, and good acidity, it has the potential to last for at least a decade.

LOUIS JADOT (BEAUNE)* * * *

1989 Bâtard-Montrachet	EE	93
1989 Bourgogne Blanc	B	85
1989 Chassagne-Montrachet Morgeot	D	91
1989 Chevalier-Montrachet Les Demoiselles	EEE	96
1989 Corton-Charlemagne	EE	95
1989 Mâcon-Villages La Fontaine	A	86
1989 Marsannay Blanc	B	84
1989 Meursault Les Perrières	E	90
1989 Le Montrachet	EEE	98
1989 Puligny-Montrachet-Clos de la Garenne	E	92

The 1989 Bourgogne Blanc offers an attractive buttery, apple nose and surprisingly bold, ripe, concentrated flavors. Among the other less expensive white wines, there is a delicious 1989 Mâcon-Villages that should be consumed over the next year given its ripeness and precociousness, and a buttery, rich 1989 Marsannay Blanc. For pure richness, intensity, and a buttery opulence, check out the 1989 Chassagne-Montrachet Morgeot from the Duc de Magenta. This terrific wine should evolve beautifully over the next decade. Full of finesse and slightly more stylish, but every bit as concentrated, is the buttery-scented 1989 Puligny-Montrachet-Clos de la Garenne. Jadot's 1989 Meursault Les Perrières is an intense, rich, buttery wine, with aromas of grilled nuts, apples, and oranges. It is softer and more flattering to drink than many of Jadot's other white burgundies. The 1989 Bâtard-Montrachet reveals superextraction of flavor and fine acidity. Although it is closed, the explosive length and ripeness suggest this will be a stupendous Bâtard-Montrachet for drinking between 1995 and 2010. The 1989 Corton-Charlemagne needs 7–10 years of cellaring and is capable of lasting 25–30. Normally one of the slowest Grand Crus to evolve, the 1989 should mature at a glacial pace. Spectacularly concentrated, its aromas of minerals, oranges, ripe pineapples, and buttery baked apples soar from the glass. Extremely long and full bodied, with blockbuster length and intensity, this is spectacular Corton-Charlemagne. The 1989 Chevalier-Montrachet Les Demoiselles is unevolved and needs 5–10 years of cellaring; it should last for 20–30 years. It is absolutely magnificent with its subtle yet authoritative bouquet of minerals and superripe fruit. With high acidity, formidable depth, and a chewy texture, it is the essence of Chardonnay. The superopulent, highly extracted Le Montrachet possesses density, balance, a haunting combination of minerals and ripe fruit, and a finish that exceeds 60 seconds. More developed and softer than the Chevalier-Montrachet and Corton-Charlemagne, it should last for at least 20–25 years.

RATINGS FOR THE 1990S: Beaune Les Grèves (82), Bourgogne Blanc (85), Chevalier-Montrachet Les Demoiselles (90), Corton-Charlemagne (88), Meursault Les Charmes (86), Meursault Les Gouttes d'Or (84), Meursault Les Perrières (87), Le Montrachet (90), Puligny-Montrachet Le Champ Gain (86), Savigny-Lès-Beaune (85)

JEAN-PAUL JAUFFROY (MEURSAULT)* * *

1990 Meursault Les Chevalières	C	85
1990 Meursault Le Meix Gagne	C	84
1990 Meursault Le Poruzot	D	88

Jauffroy is known for his old-style, rustic, full-bodied wines that lack finesse and elegance. They are not the most flattering wines to drink young, although I found the 1990 Meursault Le Poruzot to be loaded with potential given its superconcentration, rich, slightly oxidized style, and big, alcoholic, thick flavors. Wines such as this tend to be clumsy in their youth, but they age exceptionally well, so do not be surprised to see this wine still going strong at the turn of the century. The two other Meursaults, although good, are less impressively endowed.

FRANÇOIS JOBARD (MEURSAULT)* * * *

1989 Meursault-Blagny	D	90
1989 Meursault Les Charmes	D	91
1989 Meursault Les Genevrières	D	93
1989 Meursault Le Poruzot	D	90

The 1989 Meursault-Blagny is uncommonly elegant, with high acidity, wonderfully ripe fruit, fine balance, and a long finish. Unevolved and young, it promises to develop nicely for at least a decade. The 1989 Meursault Les Genevrières needs several years in the cellar and promises to last for 15 or more years. This brilliant wine exhibits extraordinary sweetness and ripeness of fruit, penetrating acidity, an exhilarating perfume of hazelnuts, lemon rind, oranges, and butter, and a sensational finish. Jobard's 1989 Meursault Le Poruzot is a tightly knit, understated, elegant wine. With plenty of apple blossom/lemony fruit, it has a long finish. Drink it over the next 10–12 years. It should make for superb drinking in 4–5 years and last for 10–15 years.

RATINGS FOR THE 1990S: Meursault (84), Meursault Les Genevrières (89), Meursault Le Poruzot (90)

MICHEL JUILLOT (MERCUREY)* * */* * * *

1990 Corton-Charlemagne	E	93
1990 Mercurey	C	83
1990 Mercurey Les Champs Martins	C	85

Juillot is equally adept at turning out fine white wines. His two offerings from Mercurey include a relatively straightforward, steely, brisk 1990 Mercurey and a more concentrated, more mineral, floral-dominated Mercurey Les Champs Martins. Both wines should be drunk over the next several years. Juillot fashions one of the great Corton-Charlemagnes, as his 1990 so dramatically proves. Medium golden in color, with a huge, smoky, earthy nose and honeyed fruit, this superconcentrated, full-bodied wine exhibits magnificent extract, good acidity, and fine length. Delicious now, it should age well for up to 7–10 years.

DOMAINE COMTE LAFON (MEURSAULT)* * * * *

1989 Meursault	D	87
1989 Meursault Les Charmes	E	98
1989 Meursault Clos de la Barre	D	91
1989 Meursault Les Désirées	D	90
1989 Meursault Les Genevrières	D	94
1989 Meursault Les Perrières	E	97
1989 Montrachet	EEE	96

The 1989 Meursault is powerful, alcoholic, and loaded with fruit and richness. Delicious to drink at present, it should be consumed over the next 6–7 years. The 1989 Meursault Les Désirées exhibits crisp acidity, a beautiful nose of tropical fruit, stones, and spices, and a textbook, rich, luscious finish. It should evolve for up to a decade. The 1989 Meursault Clos de la Barre offers a wonderful juxtaposition of power and elegance. The high acidity and formidable concentration level result in a hazelnut- and mineral-scented wine with gorgeous levels of extraction, admirable purity of flavor, and a long finish. It should be drunk between 1994 and 2005. I felt Lafon's 1989 Meursault Les Genevrières was more subtle and restrained. It is a beautiful Meursault, but some cellaring is essential. Do not be surprised to see it evolve for 10–15 years. The blockbuster 1989 Meursault Les Charmes exhibits decadent levels of richness, amazing amounts of glycerin, and an extraction level that is usually found in only the finest white burgundy Grands Crus. The huge nose of superripe apples, buttered toast, and nuts is followed by a wine of awesome richness and phenomenal length and poise. The 1989 Meursault Les Perrières, which is also compelling, is less dramatic and flamboyant than Les Charmes. It exhibits exceptional flavor extraction; the telltale mineral, cold steel, gunflint sort of nose that a textbook Les Perrières possesses; sensational fruit extraction; and a whoppingly long, crisp finish. Do not expect it to be fully mature for at least 5–6 years. It should evolve over the next two decades. The closed 1989

Montrachet offers up steely, mineral aromas reminiscent of the Meursault Les Perrières. There is awesome concentration, surprisingly high acidity, and exhilarating definition and length. Drink it after 2000.

RATINGS FOR THE 1990S: Meursault Les Charmes (92), Meursault Clos de la Barre (89), Meursault Les Désirées (87), Meursault Les Genevrières (89), Meursault Les Perrières (92), Montrachet (93)

RENÉ LAMY-PILLOT (SANTENAY)* * *

1989 Chassagne-Montrachet Grande Montagne	D	90
1989 Chassagne-Montrachet Morgeot	D	90
1989 Chassagne-Montrachet Premier Cru	D	84
N. V. Crémant de Bourgogne	B	86
1989 Montrachet	EEE	97

The N. V. Crémant de Bourgogne is a delicious sparkling wine that offers plenty of crisp, fresh flavors and a persistent effervescence. The 1989 Chassagne-Montrachet Premier Cru tasted monolithic but possessed decent fruit. The 1989 Chassagne-Montrachet Grande Montagne is an outstanding wine, with a huge, buttery, pineapple- and vanillin-scented nose; deep, intense, opulent flavors; crisp acidity; and an explosively long finish. This is a wine to drink over the next decade. The 1989 Chassagne-Montrachet Morgeot is also impressively rich, although it is more dominated by a cold steel, minerallike character. There is less power, more elegance and structure. Lamy's 1989 Montrachet displayed a huge bouquet of tropical fruit aromas, and in the mouth possessed enough glycerin to choke on. This unbelievably concentrated nectar had a finish that lasted over a minute.

RATINGS FOR THE 1990S: Chassagne-Montrachet Morgeot (85), Montrachet (93)

ROGER LASSARAT (VERGISSON)* * * *

1990 Pouilly-Fuissé Clos de France	C	86
1990 Pouilly-Fuissé Cuvée Prestige	D	87
1990 St.-Véran Cuvée Prestige	C	88
1989 St.-Véran Cuvée Prestige	C	87
1990 St.-Véran Fournaise	C	87

There are two cuvées of St.-Véran. The Fournaise, which is largely vinified in tank, is an elegant, wonderfully fruity, crisp wine, with zesty acidity and plenty of flowery, buttery, applelike fruit. The 1990 St.-Véran Cuvée Prestige, which is vinified 50% in stainless-steel tanks and 50% in small oak barrels, is a much riper, richer, more concentrated wine. The 1989 St.-Véran Cuvée Prestige is a fatter wine, with gobs of glycerin, a noticeably higher degree of alcohol, plenty of intensity, and an opulent, nearly viscous feel on the palate. The 1990 Pouilly-Fuissé Clos de France is a suave, stylish wine. The 1990 Pouilly-Fuissé Cuvée Prestige is rich and full bodied, with underlying elegance and plenty of length and character. The wine is aged in small oak casks, but the oak is almost concealed by the wine's concentration of fruit.

LOUIS LATOUR (BEAUNE)* * * *

1989 Bâtard-Montrachet	EE	96
1989 Chevalier-Montrachet Les Demoiselles	EE	97
1989 Corton-Charlemagne	E	95
1990 Mâcon-Chameroy	A	85
1990 Mâcon-Lugny Les Genevrières	A	87
1989 Montrachet	EEE	97
1989 Puligny-Montrachet Les Folatières	D	91
1989 St.-Véran	B	84

Both the Mâcon-Lugny and Mâcon-Chameroy are loaded with fruit and have a luscious character. The 1990 Mâcon-Chameroy is bursting with lemony/apple- and buttered popcorn–scented fruit, displays a clean, medium- to full-bodied texture, and offers a crisp, long finish. It should be drunk over the next 1–2 years. The 1990 Mâcon-Lugny Les Genevrières is opulent, rich, and full, with a big, flowery, buttery bouquet and lovely, honeyed, apple- and nutlike flavors. It should be drunk over the next 1–2 years. The 1989 St.-Véran is tasty but much simpler, with a commercial, fruit salad nose and flavors. The 1989 Puligny-Montrachet Les Folatières exhibits a super nose of butter, roasted nuts, and baked apples, followed by creamy, deep, dramatic flavors. The finish has just enough acidity to provide lift and clarity. The 1989 Bâtard-Montrachet is absolutely spectacular. The bouquet is bursting with flavors of oranges, smoky oak, toast, and butterscotch. In the mouth there is enormous richness, gobs of glycerin and extraction of flavor, and surprisingly high acidity in view of the wine's massiveness. Drink it over the next 10–15 years. The 1989 Corton-Charlemagne should also age gracefully for at least 10–15 years. It is more restrained, but it is huge, weighty, and high in extract. The 1989 Chevalier-Montrachet Les Demoiselles is another enormously weighty, blockbuster Chardonnay. The honeyed, creamy richness and huge aromas of smoke, flowers, tropical fruits and nuts are celestial. Drink this extraordinarily concentrated, beautifully crafted bottle of wine over the next 10–15 years. Latour's 1989 Montrachet is backward. Although the bouquet is unforthcoming, the wine is loaded with a steely acidity and massive richness and possesses a mind-blowing finish. It tastes like eau-de-vie of buttered apples and liquid popcorn. Drink it between 1996 and 2010. These are outstanding white burgundies by any standard of measurement.

RATINGS FOR THE 1990S: Bâtard-Montrachet (91), Chassagne-Montrachet (70), Chevalier-Montrachet (90), Corton-Charlemagne (89), Mâcon-Chameroy (82), Meursault (75), Meursault-Blagny (79), Montagny (82), Montrachet (90), Puligny-Montrachet (72)

DOMAINE LEFLAIVE (PULIGNY-MONTRACHET)* * * * *

1989 Bâtard-Montrachet	EE	93
1989 Bienvenues-Bâtard-Montrachet	EE	90
1989 Bourgogne Blanc	B	85
1989 Chevalier-Montrachet	EE	95

1989 Puligny-Montrachet	D	85
1989 Puligny-Montrachet Clavaillon	D	87
1989 Puligny-Montrachet Les Combettes	D	92
1989 Puligny-Montrachet Les Pucelles	D	90

The 1989 Bourgogne Blanc is as good as the 1989 Puligny-Montrachet. The Bourgogne Blanc has more fruit and substance, whereas the Puligny-Montrachet is leaner, more elegant, and dominated by a steely, minerallike fruitiness. The light 1989 Puligny-Montrachet Clavaillon is richly fruity and softer than usual. Drink it over the next 4–5 years. The 1989 Puligny-Montrachet Les Pucelles is a wine of irresistible finesse and elegance, crammed with fruit, personality, and pleasure. Unevolved and tight, 1–2 years of cellaring will coax out more of the wine's nuances and personality. It should have 10–12 years of evolution. The 1989 Puligny-Montrachet Les Combettes exhibits more of a buttery, hazelnut fragrance, wonderfully lush, rich, concentrated flavors, plenty of glycerin and body, and a long finish. It is capable of lasting another decade. The excellent 1989 Bienvenues-Bâtard-Montrachet is backward and unevolved. The 1989 Bâtard-Montrachet is more developed, richer, and very intense. It possesses a gorgeous aroma of oranges, flowers, butter, and minerals, as well as pure buttery fruit supported admirably by crisp acidity and a deft touch of toasty new oak. It should drink magnificently for at least 10–12 years. The 1989 Chevalier-Montrachet is the firmest and least forthcoming and needs time. The entire wine explodes at the end of the palate, suggesting 4–6 years of cellaring is required. This honeyed, creamy-textured wine possesses superb acidity for a 1989 and should prove to be capable of 10–15 or more years of longevity.

RATINGS FOR THE 1990s: Bâtard-Montrachet (91), Bienvenues-Bâtard-Montrachet (88), Chevalier-Montrachet (94), Puligny-Montrachet (85), Puligny-Montrachet-Clavaillon (87), Puligny-Montrachet Les Combettes (87), Puligny-Montrachet Les Folatières (87), Puligny-Montrachet Les Pucelles (88)

OLIVIER LEFLAIVE FRÈRES (PULIGNY-MONTRACHET)* * */* * * *

1990 Auxey-Duresses	C	86
1990 Bâtard-Montrachet	E	91
1990 Bourgogne Les Setilles	B	85
1990 Chassagne-Montrachet	C	82
1990 Chassagne-Montrachet Les Chaumées	D	88
1990 Chassagne-Montrachet Morgeot	D	90
1990 Corton-Charlemagne	E	93
1990 Mercurey	C	85
1990 Meursault	D	86
1990 Meursault Les Perrières	D	88
1990 Puligny-Montrachet	D	86
1990 Puligny-Montrachet Champ Canet	D	89

1990 Puligny-Montrachet Champ Gain	D	90
1990 Puligny-Montrachet Les Folatières	D	90
1990 Rully	C	86
1990 Saint-Aubin en Remilly	C	87
1990 St.-Romain	B	85

This firm, which started off by making straightforward, one-dimensional, commercially oriented wines, has improved the quality of its winemaking. Their 1990 white burgundies are head and shoulders above anything else they have produced to date. The entire line merits attention. The less expensive wines include a tasty, elegant 1990 Bourgogne Les Setilles. It offers attractive lemon/apple fruit and a delicious, crisp, medium-bodied finish. The 1990 St.-Romain is more steely, and the Auxey-Duresses more earthy, although it is surprisingly elegant and loaded with fruit for a white wine from this appellation. The 1990 Mercurey displays a floral, mineral component, and the Rully is medium bodied, fruity, clean, wonderfully fresh, and lively. All of these wines should be drunk over the next several years. Moving up a notch in quality is the 1990 Saint-Aubin en Remilly, a rich, steely, medium-bodied wine with excellent concentration, an attractive bouquet, and a zesty, long finish. It should drink well for the next 3–4 years. The 1990 Chassagne-Montrachet is somewhat one-dimensional, but the Puligny-Montrachet is one of the better generic examples I have tasted from this village. It exhibits a steely, floral, elegant nose, tasty, medium-bodied flavors, and a touch of tangerine in its finish. The Chassagne-Montrachet and the Meursault, a fresh, relatively light but tasty wine, should both be drunk over the next 2–3 years. Among the Premiers Crus there are many excellent wines. The 1990 Chassagne-Montrachet Les Chaumées is a fat, ripe, honeyed wine with aromas of butter, nuts, and apples. Spicy, deep, and rich, it should be drunk over the next 3–4 years. The outstanding 1990 Chassagne-Montrachet Morgeot is a super bottle of Chardonnay, with great concentration, a rich, wonderfully well-delineated personality, and gobs of fruit and extract. It's a beauty! The 1990 Meursault Les Perrières is fat, chewy, and luscious but lacking the complexity of the Chassagne-Montrachet Morgeot. The 1990 Puligny-Montrachet Champ Canet is a graceful, elegant wine with a gorgeous nose of flowers and steely, mineral-scented, applelike fruit. It is crisp, concentrated, and long in the mouth. Even better is the 1990 Puligny-Montrachet Champ Gain, a big, ripe, full-bodied wine that admirably combines power and elegance. I also liked the 1990 Puligny-Montrachet Les Folatières, a rich, well-knit, concentrated wine that displays excellent overall balance. The two Grands Crus are both outstanding. The 1990 Bâtard-Montrachet exhibits superb concentration for the abundant 1990 vintage, a rich, honeyed texture, and good acidity in the powerful, heady finish. It should drink well for 5–6 years. Although the 1990 Corton-Charlemagne should turn out to be the best of all these offerings, at present it is the most closed and least flattering. The nose reluctantly offers up aromas of pineapples, minerals, oranges, and toasty oak. In the mouth it is dense and chewy, with smashing concentration, good acidity, and an impressive finish. It should drink well for up to 10 years.

LEROY AND DOMAINE D'AUVENAY (VOSNE-ROMANÉE)* * * * *

1989 Bourgogne d'Auvenay	B	86
1989 Chassagne-Montrachet Les Chenevottes	E	91
1989 Meursault Les Narvaux	E	93
1989 Puligny-Montrachet Les Folatières	EE	98

Leave it to Lalou Bize-Leroy to produce some of the richest, most concentrated, and unctuous white burgundies anyone is ever going to taste. A good introduction to the style of Lalou Bize-Leroy is her modestly priced 1989 Bourgogne d'Auvenay. One of the best examples of this wine she has made, it exhibits an attractive floral, buttery nose, fat, ripe, generously endowed flavors, good glycerin and alcohol, and a long, robust finish. Drink it over the next decade. The 1989 Chassagne-Montrachet Les Chenevottes offers up a huge nose of buttery popcorn, tropical fruits, and spices. In the mouth there is great definition to its thick, lavishly rich flavors. This full-bodied, unctuously styled Chassagne should drink well young but last for 10–15 years. Lalou Bize-Leroy's 1989 Meursault Les Narvaux may be the best example I have yet to taste from this domaine. The huge nose of smoke, hazelnuts, oranges, and pineapples is breathtaking. In the mouth there is spectacular concentration, with a honeyed texture, adequate acidity, and a whopping alcoholic, rich finish. Drink this blockbuster white burgundy over the next 10 years. My highest marks go to the 1989 Puligny-Montrachet Les Folatières. It possesses an awesome bouquet of minerals, butter, and tropical fruits. There is extraordinary richness, amazing viscosity (oil of Chardonnay), and an intensity level that is rarely encountered. This monumental white burgundy should last for 20–25 years.

RATINGS FOR THE 1990S: Auxey-Duresses (87), Bourgogne d'Auvenay (84), Corton-Charlemagne (92), Meursault Les Narvaux (87), Meursault Les Perrières (87), Puligny-Montrachet Les Folatières (90)

CHÂTEAU DE LA MALTROYE (CHASSAGNE-MONTRACHET)* * *

1989 Chassagne-Montrachet Les Chenevottes	D	82
1989 Chassagne-Montrachet-Clos du Château	D	87
1989 Chassagne-Montrachet Les Crets	D	?
1989 Chassagne-Montrachet Les Grandes Ruchottes	D	85
1989 Chassagne-Montrachet Morgeot-Vigne Blanche	D	89
1989 Chassagne-Montrachet Premier Cru	D	?
1989 Santenay La Comme Blanc	C	88

For value, the best wine is the 1989 Santenay La Comme Blanc. This boldly flavored, rich, concentrated, forward wine exhibited a whiff of sulphur that did blow off. The 1989 Chassagne-Montrachet Premier Cru was impossible to judge. A touch of sulphur was also present in the 1989 Chassagne-Montrachet Les Chenevottes, as well as in the 1989 Les Crets. After fighting past the sulphur, one could see that the wines possess good stuffing, fine acidity, and plenty of power and length. The two wines that displayed less sulphur and were able to be evaluated included the excellent, rich, structured, backward 1989

Chassagne-Montrachet-Clos du Château and the 1989 Chassagne-Montrachet Morgeot-Vigne Blanche. Both of these wines are candidates for 10–15 more years of aging potential. My instincts say that the Morgeot-Vigne Blanche is the most complete of these wines.

MANCIAT-PONCET (CHARNAY-LÈS-MÂCON)* * * *

1990 Mâcon-Charnay	B	85
1990 Pouilly-Fuissé Les Crays Nonfiltered	C	88
1990 Pouilly-Fuissé La Roche	C	86
1990 Pouilly-Fuissé La Roche Vieilles Vignes	C	88

The ripe, richly fruity, aromatic 1990 Mâcon-Charnay is bursting with tropical fruit and exhibits crisp acidity and admirable purity. Drink it over the next several years. The 1990 Pouilly-Fuissé La Roche displays a well-delineated, richly fruity, mineral-scented nose, lovely, opulent flavors, decent acidity, and plenty of length and richness. The 1990 Pouilly-Fuissé La Roche Vieilles Vignes is richer as well as longer and fuller on the palate. Manciat-Poncet's richest and most complete wine is the 1990 Pouilly-Fuissé Les Crays. The alluring nose of spring flowers, minerals, and ripe apples/buttery fruit is followed by a wine with medium to full body and excellent ripeness and concentration. All of these Pouilly-Fuissés will drink well for at least 2–3 years.

LOUIS MICHEL ET FILS (CHABLIS)* * * *

1989 Chablis Les Clos	D	90
1989 Chablis Les Montmains	D	87
1989 Chablis Les Vaillons	D	87

In contrast with the more oaky, barrel-fermented style of such renowned producers as Raveneau and Dauvissat, Michel's Chablis are vinified and aged in stainless steel. Wines of extraordinary precision and purity, they offer an alternative to the more buttery, toastier styles of Chablis from other top producers. The stony, crisp, flinty 1989 Chablis Les Montmains and rich, mineral-dominated 1989 Chablis Les Vaillons both have weight and flesh in addition to crisp acidity. Their acidity should guarantee at least 5–7 years of evolution. The biggest and richest of these wines, the 1989 Chablis Les Clos, displays exhilarating, pure, clean aromas of tropical fruit, lemons, and minerals. Full bodied, with fine acidity and plenty of richness and length, it should be drunk over the next decade.

MICHELOT-BUISSON (MEURSAULT)* * */* * * *

1990 Bourgogne	C	78
1990 Meursault Les Charmes	D	87
1990 Meursault-Clos Le Cromin	D	87
1990 Meursault-Clos St.-Felix	D	87
1990 Meursault Les Genevrières	D	89
1990 Meursault Grands Charrons	D	?

1990 Meursault Le Limozin	D	85
1990 Meursault Sous La Velle	D	87
1990 Meursault Les Tillets	D	84

Michelot's wines appear under multiple labels, but the most commonly encountered is Michelot-Buisson. However, in many markets the wines can be found under the name Mestre-Michelot. I have been drinking Michelot wines for almost 15 years, and they are very tasty white burgundies if consumed within 3–4 years of the vintage. I have had bad luck in holding these wines more than 4–5 years. Michelot's intense, oaky style and fat, low-acid fruit work well initially, but the wines quickly become disjointed. The 1990s are all tasty wines, with the unctuous texture that Michelot likes, gobs of toasty new oak, plenty of alcohol, and a loose-knit character. The leanest is the Meursault Les Tillets; the most generous, intense, and complex, the Meursault Les Genevrières and Meursault Les Charmes; and the most disappointing, the somewhat oxidized and thin Meursault Grands Charrons. They should all be consumed before the end of 1995.

BERNARD MOREY (CHASSAGNE-MONTRACHET)* * * *

1989 Chassagne-Montrachet	D	87
1989 Chassagne-Montrachet Les Baudines	D	88
1989 Chassagne-Montrachet Les Caillerets	D	90
1989 Chassagne-Montrachet Les Embrazées	D	92
1989 Chassagne-Montrachet en Morgeot	D	89
1990 Saint-Aubin Les Charmois	B	87

Morey's best values include his charmingly fruity and bigger-than-usual 1990 Saint-Aubin Les Charmois. Offering a big mouthful of wine, this effort from Morey should be checked out by value seekers. The 1989 Chassagne-Montrachet displays a sweet, opulent feel, direct, hefty flavors, and enough acidity to pull everything into focus. Drink this fragile wine over the next 2–3 years. The 1989 Chassagne-Montrachet Les Baudines is similarly styled. The 1989 Chassagne-Montrachet Les Caillerets, a spectacularly rich, intense wine, is loaded with buttery popcorn–like fruit. The wine possesses a thick texture in the mouth and plenty of alcohol and glycerin in the nearly viscous finish. Drink this blockbuster Chardonnay over the next 4–7 years. The 1989 Chassagne-Montrachet en Morgeot, which is more stylish and elegant, with a mineral character, should provide attractive drinking over the next 3–4 years. Another blockbuster is the 1989 Chassagne-Montrachet Les Embrazées. Its aromas offer up a smorgasbord of tropical fruit, new oak, and butter, as well as the flavor of oranges and an unbelievable amount of glycerin, alcohol, and fruit extraction. Drink this decadent Chardonnay over the next 7–8 years.
RATINGS FOR THE 1990S: Chassagne-Montrachet (86), Chassagne-Montrachet Les Baudines (86), Chassagne-Montrachet Les Caillerets (87), Chassagne-Montrachet Les Embrazées (87), Chassagne-Montrachet en Morgeot (87)

MARC MOREY (CHASSAGNE-MONTRACHET)* * * *

1990 Bourgogne	B	80
1990 Chassagne-Montrachet Les Chenevottes	D	87
1990 Chassagne-Montrachet Virondot	D	88
1990 Puligny-Montrachet Les Pucelles	D	87

If the name is Morey, chances of getting good white burgundy are high, particularly if it is a Morey from the village of Chassagne-Montrachet. Although I thought Morey's generic Bourgogne blanc was straightforward and simple, his Puligny-Montrachet Les Pucelles offers up a lovely, floral, apple-scented nose, wonderful ripeness, and medium body allied to fine concentration and crisp acidity. Drink it over the next 4–5 years. The Chassagne-Montrachet Les Chenevottes is a more expansively flavored wine, with a spicy, almost oily texture, excellent concentration, and a ripe, nutty, chewy finish. Drink it over the next 3–4 years. The Chassagne-Montrachet Virondot is the richest and fullest of these offerings, with a big, spicy, buttery, honeyed nose, medium- to full-bodied flavors, adequate acidity, and a fleshy finish. It should be drunk over the next 2–3 years.

PIERRE MOREY (MEURSAULT)* * * *

1989 Meursault Les Genevrières	D	86
1989 Meursault Les Perrières	E	87
1989 Meursault Les Tessons	D	85

The 1989 Meursault Les Perrières exhibits an advanced color and frightfully low acidity, as well as obvious oak. Heavy-handed, thick, and superrich are the best adjectives for describing these wines.

MICHEL NIELLON (CHASSAGNE-MONTRACHET)* * * * *

1989 Bâtard-Montrachet	EE	96
1989 Chassagne-Montrachet	D	86
1989 Chassagne-Montrachet Les Vergers	D	90
1989 Chevalier-Montrachet	EE	93

The 1989 Chassagne-Montrachet, although somewhat top-heavy, is bursting with buttery popcorn–scented fruit. I would opt for consuming this chewy gem over the next 2–3 years. The 1989 Chassagne-Montrachet Les Vergers reveals a honeyed, tropical fruit richness redolent of pineapples, nuts, vanillin, and tangerines. There is sensational ripeness, surprisingly crisp acidity for such a large-scale wine, and spectacular length. The 1989 Bâtard-Montrachet is an enormous wine. It exhibits a buttery, coconut-scented nose, huge, opulent, glycerin-laden flavors, spectacular depth, and a mind-blowing finish. How I wish all Montrachets would taste this good! The 1989 Chevalier-Montrachet is more timid, but it is still large-scaled and rich, with higher acidity. Yet it does not display the dramatic intensity and flamboyance of either the Bâtard-Montrachet or the Chassagne-Montrachet Les Vergers.
RATINGS FOR THE 1990s: Bâtard-Montrachet (91), Chassagne-Montrachet (83), Chassagne-Montrachet Les Vergers (90), Chevalier-Montrachet (91)

PAUL PERNOT (PULIGNY-MONTRACHET)* * * */* * * * *

1989 Bâtard-Montrachet	EEE	94
1989 Bourgogne Blanc Champerrier	C	87
1989 Puligny-Montrachet Les Folatières	EE	90
1989 Puligny-Montrachet Les Pucelles	EE	89

The 1989 Bourgogne Blanc Champerrier is a deliciously round, medium- to full-bodied, ripe, seductive wine. The 1989 Puligny-Montrachet Les Pucelles offers wonderful fat, buttery, chewy flavors; a gorgeous floral-, vanillin-, and tangerine-scented bouquet; and an explosively rich, long, spicy finish. It promises to keep for another 1–2 years. I thought Pernot's 1989 Puligny-Montrachet Les Folatières was a slightly deeper wine. With an intriguing mineral scent, the wine has intense, buttery, applelike fruit in reserve and enough acidity to give it grip and focus. Both wines can be drunk over the next 7–8 years. The 1989 Bâtard-Montrachet offers a huge mouthful of massively extracted Chardonnay fruit. Still unevolved, it needs another year to develop more nuances. There can be no doubting its phenomenal concentration and rich, luscious, almost exotic mélange of tropical fruit flavors that have been married brilliantly with just enough new oak. The finish is sumptuous.
RATINGS FOR THE 1990S: Bâtard-Montrachet (86), Puligny-Montrachet Les Folatières (84), Puligny-Montrachet Les Pucelles (79)

DOMAINE PINSON (CHABLIS)* * *

1990 Chablis Les Clos	D	88
1990 Chablis Les Forêts	D	86
1990 Chablis Montmains	D	86
1990 Chablis Monts de Milieu	C	84

These sturdy, spicy wines represent a more traditional style of Chablis. The tasty Monts de Milieu is light and monolithic. The Les Forêts exhibits deeper fruit, more body, and good crispness. The Montmains displays a big, steely, mineral-scented nose; tons of fruit; a spicy, rich, medium-bodied personality; and good fruit and balance in the finish. Not surprisingly, Les Clos is the biggest, richest, most concentrated of these offerings. After 3–4 years of aging, it may merit an even higher score. The Montmains and Les Clos should drink well for the next 7–8 years.

JACQUES PRIEUR (MEURSAULT)* * *

1989 Chevalier-Montrachet	EEE	90
1989 Meursault-Clos de Mazeray	D	86
1989 Meursault Les Perrières	E	90
1989 Montrachet	EEE	90
1989 Puligny-Montrachet Les Combettes	D	89

The 1989 Meursault-Clos de Mazeray exhibits an attractive, lush, pineapple fruitiness, creamy texture, and a smoky, toasty finish. The 1989 Puligny-Montrachet Les Combettes offered a distinctive bouquet of roasted hazelnuts, butter, and oranges that was followed by rich, lush, citrusy, concentrated, massive fruit flavors. The 1989 Meursault Les Perrières was even more dominated by a smoky, buttery, toasty oak nose. In the mouth there was an intense essence of wet stones and minerals and a honeyed, full-bodied, pear-, pineapple-, and coconut-flavored finish. This intriguing wine should develop beautifully over the next decade. The extraordinarily backward 1989 Chevalier-Montrachet was among the least evolved of these five wines. Its multidimensional personality contained elements of lemon, honey, vanilla, and baked apples and a creamy richness. The wine had good acidity and a long, explosive finish. Do not touch a bottle for at least 5–6 years. It is capable of at least 2 decades of evolution. The 1989 Montrachet was even more backward. Though it possessed huge weight in the mouth and a phenomenal finish, the wine was dominated by a citrusy, lemonlike acidity, and the bouquet remained closed even after 60 minutes of coaxing. Readers should note that all of the above wines were from the Domaine Jacques Prieur; they are not the *négociant* bottlings.

HENRI PRUDHON (SAINT-AUBIN)* * *

1989 Saint-Aubin	C	85
1989 Saint-Aubin Les Perrières	C	88

The 1989 Saint-Aubin offers a whiff of sulphur, but it blows off in 5 minutes. Behind the sulphur is a full-bodied, stony-scented and -flavored wine, with good body, chunkiness, and mineral-infused Chardonnay fruit. The 1989 Saint-Aubin Les Perrières is very rich, full, and unctuous, with layer upon layer of Chardonnay fruit allied with subtle, toasty new oak and a minerallike character. This full-bodied, muscular, rich wine should make super drinking over the next 4–6 years.

DOMAINE RAMONET (CHASSAGNE-MONTRACHET)* * * * *

1989 Bâtard-Montrachet	EEE	93
1990 Bourgogne Aligoté	C	87
1989 Chassagne-Montrachet	D	88
1989 Chassagne-Montrachet Les Caillerets	E	93
1989 Chassagne-Montrachet Morgeot	D	90
1989 Chassagne-Montrachet Les Ruchottes	D	93
1989 Montrachet	EEE	97
1990 Saint-Aubin Le Charmois	D	87

From the charming village of Saint-Aubin, Ramonet produced an attractively elegant, ripe, and authoritatively flavored 1990 Saint-Aubin Le Charmois. Drink this tasty wine over the next 2–3 years. Ramonet's 1989 Chassagne-Montrachet is a gorgeously fruity, opulent, fat wine that is bursting at the seams with buttery tropical fruit flavors as well as gobs of glycerin and alcohol. Drink it over the next 4–5 years. Among the Chassagne-Montrachet Premiers Crus, the 1989 Chassagne-Montrachet Morgeot exhibited a smell of flowers, minerals, and buttery fruit. In the mouth it is deep and ripe, with structure and persistence. This tightly knit, superbly concentrated wine will last for at least

10–12 years. The 1989 Chassagne-Montrachet Les Caillerets is sensational. From its smoky, exotic nose of earth, butter, oranges, and tropical fruits to its layers of chewy, high-octane fruit, this unctuous, well-balanced, large-scale Chardonnay will make gorgeous drinking over the next decade. The Chassagne-Montrachet Les Ruchottes is always among the deepest and richest of all Ramonet's wines. The 1989's huge weight and richness in the mouth is obvious, but the tight bouquet needs coaxing to reveal its buttery tropical fruit scents and toasty new oak. The acidity is high, particularly for a low acid vintage such as 1989, and the length is sensational. This authoritative Chassagne-Montrachet Les Ruchottes should rival the magnificent 1986. The 1989 Bâtard-Montrachet offers up an interesting nose of vanillin, mint, butter, peach, and apricot fruit. In the mouth there is awesome concentration. Long, with good acidity and plenty of buttery fruit, this big, lusty, hefty Bâtard should drink gorgeously after another 3–4 years in the cellar. The 1989 Montrachet attained a natural alcohol level of 14.8%. So much for those oenologists' wines made within safe technical parameters! You can imagine this wine's unbelievable concentration and viscosity, yet it possesses exquisite balance. All things considered, I would wait 10 years before popping the cork. Ramonet's 1990 Bourgogne Aligoté exhibits surprising richness, an almost buttery, apple, hazelnut fruitiness, and good body.

RATINGS FOR THE 1990S: Bâtard-Montrachet (90), Bienvenues-Bâtard-Montrachet (89), Chassagne-Montrachet (86), Chassagne-Montrachet Les Ruchottes (88), Montrachet (93), Saint-Aubin Le Charmois (85)

RAVENEAU (CHABLIS)* * * * *

1989 Chablis Blanchots	D	92
1989 Chablis Les Clos	E	95
1989 Chablis Montée de Tonnerre	D	92
1989 Chablis Les Vaillons	D	88
1989 Chablis Valmur	D	93

The 1989 Chablis Les Vaillons possesses an intriguing stony, mineral scent, long, rich, austere flavors, and an intensity and precision to its finish that suggests it will mature for at least a decade. The 1989 Chablis Montée de Tonnerre exhibits a provocative, flinty, stony nose; huge, impeccably precise flavors of butter, stones, lemons, and oranges; super acidity; admirable ripeness and intensity; and an explosive finish. It should last through the first decade of the next century. The most opulent of all of these Chablis is the 1989 Chablis Blanchots. Although there is extraordinary intensity to this chewy, big, lusty Chablis, the tropical fruit–scented nose offers up less of the gunflint, cold steel/wet stone aromas Chablis is famous for. Since it is lower in acidity than the other Raveneau wines, I would opt for drinking it over the next decade. The 1989 Chablis Valmur is Chablis at its greatest—stony, rich, with high acidity, spectacular length, razor sharp precision, and terrific individuality. The most powerful, intense, and fullest bodied of all of these Chablis is the 1989 Chablis Les Clos. It combines the best characteristics of all the crus—the stones, the gunflint, the oranges, the butter, and the acidity, along with gobs of fruit, a spectacular density and extract, and a whoppingly long finish.

RATINGS FOR THE 1990S: Chablis Blanchots (92), Chablis Les Clos (96), Chablis Montée de Tonnerre (93), Chablis Les Vaillons (89), Chablis Valmur (93)

REMOISSENET PÈRE ET FILS (BEAUNE)* * * *

1989 Corton-Charlemagne Diamond Jubilée	E	93
1989 Meursault Les Genevrières-Hospices de Beaune Philip le Bon	E	93

The 1989 Corton-Charlemagne Diamond Jubilée is the most backward of the Corton-Charlemagnes I tasted—typifying the ageworthy Remoissenet style of white burgundy. It will stand up to a considerable amount of cellaring. I would not pull the cork on a bottle for at least 4–5 years; it should have 20–25 years of longevity. Similar comments apply to the 1989 Meursault Les Genevrières-Hospices de Beaune. This wine exhibits more creamy, toasty oak in the nose, excellent concentration, high acidity for a 1989, and plenty of power and richness in its long finish. This is a Meursault that may last for 10–15 or more years.

GUY ROBIN (CHABLIS)* * * *

1990 Chablis Montee de Tonnerre	D	91

Robin is an inconsistent producer who often makes absolutely wretched wines because of his liberal use of sulphur. Although I did not taste through his entire line of 1990s, this Chablis Montée de Tonnerre is an impressive, old-style Chablis with a slight hint of oxidation. It exhibits gobs of honeyed, mineral fruit, exceptional concentration, and a stunning finish. Even this wine is likely to be controversial given its hefty weight and old-style character. Drink it over the next decade.

ANTONIN RODET (MERCUREY)* * *

1990 Bourgogne Blanc	B	85
1989 Château de Chamirey Mercurey Blanc	C	87
1990 Château de Rully Blanc	C	86
1989 Château de Rully Blanc	C	87

Restaurants looking for white burgundies that offer richness, personality, and complexity should be giving wines such as these more attention. The wonderfully crisp, floral, buttery, fat 1990 Bourgogne Blanc is oozing with surprising amounts of flavor. Few would complain about the quality and reasonable prices of the Château de Rully and Château de Chamirey white wines. Of the two vintages of Château de Rully I tasted, the 1989 is richer, more lush and alcoholic, with more glycerin and a dramatic, up-front, buttery, minerallike fruitiness. The 1990 is more elegant and restrained, but it is impeccably precise in its flavors and long in the mouth. Minerals, apples, and floral scents dominate the 1989 Château de Chamirey Mercurey.

DOMAINE DE LA ROMANÉE-CONTI (VOSNE-ROMANÉE)* * * * *

1990 Montrachet	EEE	92
1989 Montrachet	EEE	99

Not surprisingly, the 1989 Montrachet is another awesome example from the Domaine de la Romanée-Conti. If pure, honeyed thickness and glycerin are what you are looking for, there is not a more concentrated Chardonnay produced in the world. There is nothing commercial about this 1989 Montrachet. If you have $500 to spend, here is a bottle that will offer an awesome nose of honeyed, buttery, apple fruit intertwined with aromas of smoked nuts and toasty new oak. In the mouth it is almost greasy because of its extraordinary viscosity, thickness, and richness. The finish is explosive, and although the alcohol must be over 14.5%, it cannot be detected because of the wine's phenomenal concentration. This wine may merit a perfect score in 5–10 years.

GUY ROULOT (MEURSAULT)* * * *

1989 Meursault Les Charmes	D	90
1989 Meursault Les Meix Chavaux	D	88
1989 Meursault Les Perrières	D	86?
1989 Meursault Les Tessons	D	90

The 1989 Meursault Les Meix Chavaux is a big, oaky, honeyed wine with plenty of nutty, rich fruit, a good deal of glycerin, and gobs of tropical fruit flavors. Drink it over the next 4–5 years. My favorite Meursault is the 1989 Meursault Les Tessons. It has a honeyed texture, exceptional concentration, and a bold, nutty, dramatic nose. Drink it over the next 5–6 years. Roulot's 1989 Meursault Les Charmes is similar in style, with more noticeable oak and honeyed, lemony/apple, tropical fruit aromas and flavors. Drink this big wine over the next 5 years. The 1989 Meursault Les Perrières is dominated by new oak. Although there is plenty of richness, the wine is heavy-handed, woody, and overdone.

RATINGS FOR THE 1990s: Meursault Les Charmes (87), Meursault Les Meix Chavaux (86), Meursault Les Tessons (86)

ROUX PÈRE ET FILS (SAINT-AUBIN)* * *

1989 Puligny-Montrachet Les Enseignières	C	85
1989 Puligny-Montrachet La Garenne	C	86
1989 Saint-Aubin Chatenière	C	85
1989 Saint-Aubin La Pucelle	C	85

Both 1989 Saint-Aubins possess that chalky, mineral, crisp character that comes from Chardonnay grown in that appellation's vineyards. Because of the supermaturity achieved by the grapes in 1989, there is more ripeness and glycerin than usual. Both wines represent solidly made, weighty, attractive white burgundies for drinking over the next 2–4 years. I had a slight preference for the 1989 Puligny-Montrachet La Garenne because it combines elegance with richness and displays more fruit and length than the fine, buttery, full-bodied 1989 Puligny-Montrachet Les Enseignières. Both wines should be drunk over the next 5–6 years.

DOMAINE DE RULLY SAINT-MICHEL (RULLY)* * * *

1990 Rully Les Clouds	C	84
1989 Rully Les Clouds	C	85
1990 Rully Rabourcé	C	85
1989 Rully Rabourcé	C	86

This excellent domaine in the Côte Chalonnaise produces not only tasty red wines, but also stylish, mineral-scented white wines that resemble a good Premier Cru from Chablis. The 1990s, which were lighter than the 1989s, were dominated by a stony component. The 1989s exhibit richer fruit and more glycerin, body, and alcohol. The 1989 Rully Rabourcé is a dead ringer for a top Premier Cru from the great Chablis vineyard of Montée de Tonnerre. These wines are easily capable of lasting for 4–5 years.

CHÂTEAU DE LA SAULE (MONTAGNY)* * * *

1989 Montagny	C	86
1989 Montagny Les Burnins	C	86

I did not see any significant difference between these two *cuvées* from the Château de la Saule and proprietor Alain Roy-Thevenin. Both wines exhibit a stony fruitiness, a chewy, fleshy texture, and admirable ripeness. They finish with crisp acidity and authority. These are fine examples of the Chardonnay grape from the underrated appellation of Montagny. They should continue to drink well for 4–5 years.

ÉTIENNE SAUZET (PULIGNY-MONTRACHET)* * * * *

1989 Bâtard-Montrachet	EE	95
1989 Puligny-Montrachet Champ Canet	E	86
1989 Puligny-Montrachet Les Combettes	E	92
1989 Puligny-Montrachet Les Referts	E	89

The 1989 Puligny-Montrachet Champ Canet, which is a superripe, lusty, chunky bottle of Chardonnay, lacks the usual Sauzet elegance and finesse, although there is plenty of depth. It should be consumed over the next 4–5 years. The 1989 Puligny-Montrachet Les Referts exhibits similar richness and intensity, but with better acidity. It comes across on the palate as a much more focused and profound bottle of Chardonnay. Drink it over the next 5–8 years. There is no ignoring the huge, oaky, roasted nut, creamy, butterscotchlike aromas of the luscious 1989 Puligny-Montrachet Les Combettes. The wine displays high alcohol, plenty of gorgeous exotic fruit flavors, and a heady, decadently rich, long finish. Drink it over the next 5–7 years.

The only Grand Cru I tasted was the superintense, full-bodied, buttery, baked apple– and smoke-scented 1989 Bâtard-Montrachet. This exquisite Bâtard is similar in style to that of a Louis Latour, although not as massive. Tons of fruit are held together by good acidity, and the finish is rich and explosively long.

JEAN THEVENET (QUINTAINE-CLESSÉ)* * * * *

1990 Mâcon-Clessé Cuvée Tradition	C	90
1989 Mâcon-Clessé Cuvée Tradition	C	91

Jean Thevenet makes the finest wine of the Mâconnais region. His wines have a formidable level of richness and intensity. The 1989 Mâcon-Clessé Cuvée Tradition reveals a huge nose of smoked nuts, pineapples, and apples. There is superb acidity, great richness and precision to its full-bodied flavors, and a whoppingly long, intense finish. The 1990 is similarly styled, but crisper acids and less fat make for an authoritative and slightly more elegant wine.

JEAN-CLAUDE THEVENET (MÂCON)* * * *

1990 Saint-Véran Clos de l'Hermitage Vieilles Vignes	C	88

This is an example of a truly riveting Saint-Véran that is loaded with buttery, rich Chardonnay fruit. Drink it over the next 4–5 years.

JACQUES THEVENOT-MACHAL (PULIGNY-MONTRACHET)* *

1989 Meursault Le Poruzot	D	80
1989 Puligny-Montrachet Les Charmes	D	79
1989 Puligny-Montrachet Les Folatières	D	84

The 1989 Puligny-Montrachet Les Charmes displays plenty of body and gobs of glycerin, but a sterile nose. The 1989 Meursault Le Poruzot exhibits good acidity, a muted, dull nose, full body, plenty of richness, and a honeyed, creamy nuttiness. Drink it over the next 2–4 years. The best of this trio, the 1989 Puligny-Montrachet Les Folatières, enjoys more of a floral-, mineral-, and tropical fruit–scented nose, superrich, creamy fruit, decent acidity to provide focus, and an alcoholic finish. Drink it over the next 5–7 years.

JEAN VACHET (SAINT-VALLERIN)* * *

1990 Montagny Les Coeres	C	85
1989 Montagny Les Coeres	C	86

Vachet's name is closely associated with the best Montagny. His 1989 and 1990 possess a wonderful, stony, cold steel–scented fruit and elegant, apple blossom–scented nose, with the 1989 having more glycerin, alcohol, and tangerinelike fruitiness. Drink them over the next 1–3 years.

VERGET (MÂCON)* * * *

1991 Bâtard-Montrachet	E	89
1991 Bourgogne	C	86
1991 Chablis Montmains	D	87
1991 Chassagne-Montrachet Morgeot	D	88
1991 Corton-Charlemagne	E	91

The highly talented Belgian winemaker Guffens-Heynen has formed this *négociant* business dedicated to buying only the finest grapes and vinifying the wines under his control. His talent is evidenced in these fine 1991s. The Bourgogne blanc exhibits a lot of class, plenty of ripe fruit, and a tasty, elegant personality. Drink it over the next several years. The Chablis Montmains offers a steely, crisp, mineral-scented nose, medium body, good depth and definition, and a long, zesty finish. It should drink well for 2–4 years. The rich, chewy, sweet-tasting Chassagne-Montrachet Morgeot reveals excellent ripeness for the vintage, a wonderful opulence to its fruit, and a long, lusty finish. Drink it over the next 1–2 years. The Corton-Charlemagne is full bodied and well defined, with considerable depth and intensity as well as enough acidity and body to carry it for 5 or more years. It is undoubtedly a success for the vintage. The Bâtard-Montrachet exhibits plenty of toasty oak in the nose, excellent delineation, crisp acidity, and admirable weight and ripeness. Still tight, it will benefit from another year of cellaring; it should last through the balance of this decade. Excellent wines also appearing under the Verget label include a Saint-Véran and Mâcon-Villages.

DOMAINE DU VIEUX ST.-SORLIN (MÂCON)* * * *

1990 Mâcon La Roche Vieilles Vignes Blanc	B	88

The 1990 Mâcon La Roche Vieilles Vignes displays gobs of floral, buttery, applelike fruit, crisp acidity, and excellent length and character. Drink it before 1994.

AUBERT DE VILLAINE (BOUZERON)* * * *

1990 Bourgogne Aligoté	B	89
1989 Bourgogne Aligoté	B	86
1990 Chardonnay	C	87
1989 Chardonnay	C	85

I loved this 1989 Bourgogne Aligoté for its crispness, opulent fruit, and surprising intensity. The 1990 is the best Aligoté I have ever tasted. The 1990 Chardonnay is excellent, with an apple-, lemon-, and vanilla-scented nose, spicy, medium-bodied flavors, and good purity and crispness. Not surprisingly, the 1989 Chardonnay is fatter, with an attractive ripeness. All of these wines should be drunk over the next 1–2 years.

CHAMPAGNE

After the Gold Rush

A decade ago champagne buyers never had it so good. The strong dollar, bumper crops of solid-quality wine in Champagne, and intense price competition by importers, wholesalers, and retailers combined to drive down prices. It was a wonderful buyer's market. A small mediocre crop in 1984, a top-quality but tiny crop in 1985, and a sagging American dollar caused champagne prices to soar. This was evident in 1990 as prices rose 30%–75%. But the international recession, the downsizing of the consumer's appetite for expensive products, including champagne, and a bevy of abundant crops have caused most Champagne houses to slice prices, except for their luxury *cuvées*. Thus 1994 will again represent a buyer's market for champagne as prices continue to fall after the dizzy heights they reached in 1990.

The Basics

TYPES OF WINES

Only sparkling wine (about 180 million bottles a year) is produced in Champagne, a viticultural area 90 miles northeast of Paris. Champagne is usually made from a blend of three grapes—Chardonnay, Pinot Noir, and Pinot Meunier. A champagne called Blanc de Blancs must be 100% Chardonnay. Blanc de Noirs means that the wine has been made from red wine grapes, and the term *crémant* signifies that the wine has slightly less effervescence than typical champagne.

GRAPE VARIETIES

Chardonnay   Surprisingly, only 25% of Champagne's vineyards are planted in Chardonnay.
Pinot Meunier   The most popular grape in Champagne, Pinot Meunier accounts for 40% of the appellation's vineyards.
Pinot Noir   This grape accounts for 35% of the vineyard acreage in Champagne.

FLAVORS

Most people drink champagne young, often within hours of purchasing it. However, some observers would argue that high-quality, vintage champagne should not be drunk until it is at least 10 years old. French law requires that nonvintage champagne be aged at least 1 year in the bottle before it is released, and vintage champagne 3 years. As a general rule, most top producers are just releasing their 1988s and 1986s in 1993 and 1994. The reason for this is that good champagne not only should taste fresh but also should have flavors akin to buttered wheat toast, ripe apples, and fresh biscuits. When champagne is made badly it tastes sour, green, and musty. If it has been abused in shipment or storage, it will taste flat and fruitless. A Blanc de Blancs is a more delicate, refined, lighter wine than champagnes that have a hefty percentage of Pinot Noir and Pinot Meunier, the two red grapes used.

AGING POTENTIAL

Champagne from such illustrious houses as Krug, Bollinger, and Pol Roger can age for 25–30 years, losing much of their effervescence and taking on a creamy, lush, buttery richness not far different from a top white burgundy. Krug's 1947, 1962, 1964, and 1971; Bollinger's 1966, 1969, and 1975 R.D.; and Pol Roger's 1928 and 1929 were exquisite when drunk in 1992. All are examples of how wonderful champagne can be with age. But readers should realize that each champagne house has its own style, and the aging potential depends on the style preferred by that producer. Below are some aging estimates for a number of the best-known brands currently available on the market. The starting point for measuring the aging potential is 1994, not the vintage mentioned.

1975 Bollinger R.D.: now plus 8 years
1979 Bollinger R.D.: now plus 5 years
1982 Bollinger R.D.: now plus 10 years
1982 Bollinger Vieilles Vignes: 5–30 years
1985 Bollinger Grande Année: now plus 15 years
1985 Gosset Grand Millésime: now plus 8 years
1979 Krug: now plus 15 years
1981 Krug: now plus 15 years
1982 Krug: 5–30 years
1982 Krug Clos du Mesnil: now plus 12 years
1985 Laurent-Perrier Grand Siècle: now plus 10 years
1982 Dom Pérignon: now plus 12 years
1985 Dom Pérignon: now plus 15 years
1979 Pol Roger Cuvée Winston Churchill: now plus 8 years
1982 Pol Roger Blanc de Chardonnay: now plus 8 years
1982 Pol Roger Cuvée Winston Churchill: now plus 20 years
1985 Pol Roger Brut: now plus 12 years
1985 Louis Roederer Cristal: now plus 10 years
1986 Louis Roederer Cristal: now plus 8 years
1982 Salon: now plus 15 years
1985 Taittinger Comtes de Champagne: now plus 15 years
1985 Veuve Clicquot La Grande Dame: 5–20 years

OVERALL QUALITY LEVEL

French champagne is irrefutably the finest sparkling wine in the world. Despite the hoopla and vast sums of money invested in California, there is no competition from any other wine-producing region if quality is the primary consideration. Nevertheless, the extraordinary financial success enjoyed by many of the big champagne houses has led, I believe, to a lowering of stan-

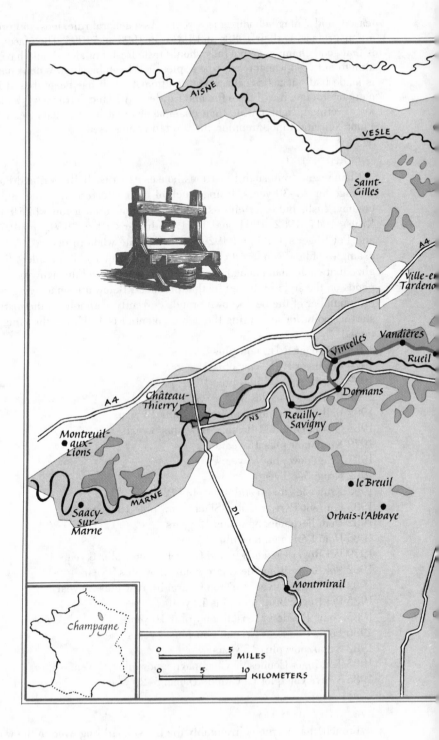

AISNE

VESLE

Saint-
Gilles

Ville-e
Tardeno

A4

Vincelles Vandières

Rueil

Château-
Thierry

Dormans

A4

Reuilly-
Savigny

N3

Montreuil-
aux-
Lions

MARNE

le Breuil

Orbais-l'Abbaye

Saacy-
sur-
Marne

D1

Montmirail

Champagne

0   5 MILES

0   5   10 KILOMETERS

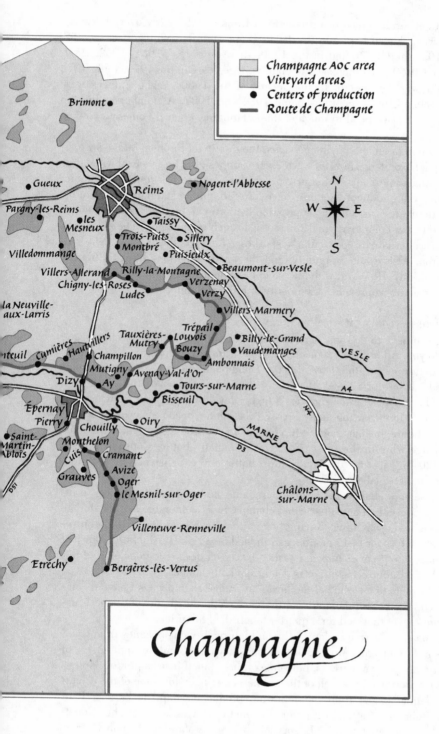

Champagne

dards. Commercial greed has driven most firms to call nearly every harvest a vintage year. For example, in the 1950s there were four vintage years, 1952, 1953, 1955, and 1959, and in the 1960s there were five, 1961, 1962, 1964, 1966, and 1969. This increased to eight vintage years in the 1970s (only 1972 and 1977 were excluded). In the decade of the 1980s, eight vintages were again declared, the exceptions being 1984 and 1987. A number of the top champagne houses need to toughen their standards when it comes to vintage champagne.

In addition to too many vintage years, the quality of the nonvintage *brut cuvées* has deteriorated. The wines, which are supposed to be released when they are showing some signs of maturity, have become greener and more acidic, suggesting that producers not only have lowered quality standards, but are releasing their wines as quickly as possible. Unfortunately, there is really no alternative to the complexity and finesse of French champagne. There are less expensive alternatives, particularly sparkling Loire Valley wines, some *crémants* from Alsace and Burgundy, and the sparkling wines from California, Spain, and Italy. However, with few exceptions none of the bubblies from these sources remotely approaches the quality of French champagne.

MOST IMPORTANT INFORMATION TO KNOW

First, you have to do some serious tasting to see which styles of champagne appeal to you. Additionally, consider the following guidelines:

1. The luxury or prestige *cuvées* of the Champagne houses are always overpriced (all sell for $75–$150 a bottle). The pricing plays on the consumer's belief that a lavish price signifies a higher level of quality. In many cases it does not. Moreover, too many luxury *cuvées* have become pawns in an ego contest between Champagne's top houses to see who can produce the most expensive wine in the most outrageous, dramatic bottle. Consumers often pay $20–$30 just for the hand-blown bottle and expensive, hand-painted, labor-intensive label.

2. Purchase your champagne from a merchant who has a quick turnover in inventory. More than any other wine, champagne is vulnerable to poor storage and bright shop lighting. Buying bottles that have been languishing on retailers' shelves for 6–12 months can indeed be a risky business. If your just purchased bottle of champagne tastes flat, has a deep golden color, and few bubbles, it either is too old or is dead from bad storage.

3. Don't hesitate to try some of the best nonvintage champagnes I have recommended. The best of them are not that far behind the quality of the best luxury *cuvées*, yet they sell for a quarter to a fifth of the price.

4. There has been a tremendous influx of high-quality champagnes from small firms in Champagne. Most of these wines may be difficult to find outside of major metropolitan markets, but some of these small houses produce splendid wine worthy of a search of the marketplace. Look for some of the estate-bottled champagne from the following producers: Baptiste-Pertois, Paul Bara, Bonnaire, Cattier, Drappier, Delamotte, Duval-Leroy, Michel Gonet, Guy Larmandier, Lassalle, Legras, Mailly, Serge Mathieu, Joseph Perrier, and Ployez-Jacquemart.

5. Several technical terms that appear on the label of a producer's champagne can tell you several things about the wine. *Brut* champagnes are dry but legally can have up to 1.2% sugar added (called *dosage*). Extra-dry cham-

pagnes are those that have between 1.2% and 2% sugar added. Most tasters would call these champagnes dry, but they tend to be rounder and seemingly fruitier than *brut* champagnes. The term *ultra brut, brut absolu,* or *dosage zéro* signifies that the champagne has had no sugar added and is bone dry. These champagnes are rarely seen but can be quite impressive as well as austere and lean-tasting.

1993–1994 BUYING STRATEGY

Prices have tumbled for the nonvintage *cuvées* and some vintage champagne, but the luxury *cuvées* remain appallingly expensive. The 1982 was a stunning vintage, but the wines have largely disappeared from the marketplace. Current vintages are 1985, 1986, and 1988. The vintage of choice is the magnificent 1985. If you love the sublime fizz offered by champagne, 1985 is a mandatory purchase. Keep in mind that it is often smart to seek out some of the smaller producers who do not have national importers, which often means that prices are more reasonable.

VINTAGE GUIDE

1992—This hugely abundant yet potentially high-quality vintage escaped most of the bad weather that plagued the southern half of France. If the quality turns out to be as high as is believed, and the quantity is as enormous as reported, this could continue to provide price stability—a good sign.

1991—A small, exceptionally difficult vintage that is unlikely to be declared a vintage year except by the greediest of producers. It rivals 1987 and 1984 as one of the three worst vintages for champagne in the last 15 years.

1990—A huge crop of ripe fruit was harvested. The 1990 has all the earmarks of the best champagne vintage since 1985. Reports are that the wines will be full, rich, aromatic, and destined to be drunk early because of low acidity. Such a large, high-quality crop will also keep prices stable.

1989—Another high-quality, abundant year should produce wines similar to the ripe, rich, creamy style of the 1982 champagnes.

1988—Not much champagne was made because of the small harvest, but this will undoubtedly be a vintage year; look for the 1988s to be leaner, more austere, and higher in acidity than the flamboyant 1989s and 1990s.

1987—A terrible year, the worst of the decade, definitely not a vintage year.

1986—This is a vintage year, producing an abundant quantity of soft, ripe, fruity wines.

1985—Along with 1982, 1985 appears to be the finest vintage of the 1980s, thanks to excellent ripeness and a good-size crop.

1984—A lousy year, but there were vintage champagnes from 1984 on the market. Remember what P. T. Barnum once said?

1983—A gigantic crop of good-quality champagne was produced. Although the wines may lack the opulence and creamy richness of the 1982s, they are hardly undersize. Most 1983s have matured quickly and are delicious in 1993. They should be drunk over the next 3–4 years.

1982—A great vintage of ripe, rich, creamy, intense wines. If they are to be criticized, it would be for their very forward, lower-than-normal acids that suggest they will age quickly. No one should miss the top champagnes from 1982—they are marvelously rounded, ripe, generously flavored wine.

1981—The champagnes from 1981 are rather lean and austere, but that has not prevented many top houses from declaring this a vintage year.

OLDER VINTAGES

The 1980 vintage is mediocre, 1979 is excellent, 1978 is tiring, 1976, once top-notch, is now fading, 1975 is superb, as are well-cellared examples of 1971, 1969, and 1964. When buying champagne, whether it is 3 years old or 20, pay the utmost care to the manner in which it was treated before you bought it. Champagne is the most fragile wine in the marketplace, and it cannot tolerate poor storage.

RATING CHAMPAGNE'S BEST PRODUCERS

* * * * * (OUTSTANDING PRODUCERS)

Bollinger (full bodied)
Gosset (full bodied)
Krug (full bodied)
Pol Roger (medium bodied)

Louis Roederer (full bodied)
Salon (medium bodied)
Taittinger (light bodied)
Veuve Clicquot (full bodied)

* * * * (EXCELLENT PRODUCERS)

Baptiste-Pertois (light bodied)
Paul Bara (full bodied)
Billecart-Salmon (light bodied)
Bonnaire (light bodied)
de Castellane (light bodied)
Cattier (light bodied)
Charbaut (light bodied)
Delamotte (medium bodied)
Drappier (medium bodied) since 1985
Alfred Gratien (full bodied)
Heidsieck Monopole (medium bodied)
Henriot (full bodied)
Jacquart (medium bodied)

Jacquesson (light bodied)
J. Lassalle (light bodied)
Laurent-Perrier (medium bodied)
Lechère (light bodied)
R. & L. Legras (light bodied)
Mailly (medium bodied)
Serge Mathieu (medium bodied)
Moët & Chandon (medium bodied)
Bruno Paillard (light bodied)
Joseph Perrier (medium bodied)
Ployez-Jacquemart (medium bodied)
Dom Ruinart (light bodied)
Jacques Selosse (light bodied)
Taillevent (medium bodied)

* * * (GOOD PRODUCERS)

Ayala (medium bodied)
Barancourt (full bodied)
Bricout (light bodied)
Canard Duchêne (medium bodied)
Deutz (medium bodied)
Duval-Leroy (medium bodied)
H. Germain (light bodied)
Michel Gonet (medium bodied)
Georges Goulet (medium bodied)
Charles Heidsieck (medium bodied)

Lanson (light bodied)
Guy Larmandier (full bodied)
Launois Père (light bodied)
Mercier (medium bodied)
Mumm (medium bodied)
Perrier-Jouët (light bodied)
Philipponnat (medium bodied)
Piper Heidsieck (light bodied)
Pommery and Greno (light bodied)

* * (AVERAGE PRODUCERS)

Beaumet-Chaurey (light bodied)

Besserat de Bellefon (light bodied)

Boizel (light bodied)

Nicolas Feuillatte (light bodied)

Goldschmidt-Rothschild (light bodied)

Jestin (light bodied)

Oudinot (medium bodied)

Rapeneau (medium bodied)

Alfred Rothschild (light bodied)

Marie Stuart (light bodied)

FINDING THE BEST CHAMPAGNES

THE BEST PRODUCERS OF NONVINTAGE BRUT

Bollinger

Charbaut

Delamotte

Drappier

Krug

Lechère

Bruno Paillard

Perrier-Jouët

Ployez-Jacquemart

Pol Roger

Louis Roederer

THE BEST PRODUCERS OF ROSÉ CHAMPAGNE

Billecart-Salmon

Bollinger Grande Année

Delamotte

Gosset

Heidsieck Monopole Diamant Bleu

Jacquesson

Krug

Laurent-Perrier Grand Siècle Cuvée Alexandre

Moët & Chandon Dom Pérignon

Perrier-Jouët Blason de France

Perrier-Jouët Fleur de Champagne

Pol Roger

Dom Ruinart

Taittinger Comtes de Champagne

Veuve Clicquot

THE BEST PRODUCERS OF 100% CHARDONNAY BLANC DE BLANCS

Baptiste-Pertois

Charbaut

Delamotte

Duval-Leroy

Jacquart

Jacquart Cuvée Spéciale

Jacquesson

Krug Clos de Mesnil

Lassalle

Lechere

R. & L. Legras

Bruno Paillard

Joseph Perrier Cuvée Royale

Pol Roger Blanc de Chardonnay

Salon

Taillevent

Taittinger Comtes de Champagne

THE BEST PRODUCERS OF LUXURY CUVÉES

Bollinger R.D.

Bollinger Grande Année

Bollinger Vieilles Vignes

Heidsieck Monopole Diamant Bleu

Lassalle Cuvée Angeline

Laurent-Perrier Grand Siècle

Moët & Chandon Dom Pérignon

Joseph Perrier Cuvée Josephine

Pol Roger Cuvée Winston Churchill

Louis Roederer Cristal

Taittinger Comtes de Champagne

Veuve Clicquot La Grande Dame

LOIRE VALLEY

Take Me to the River

The Basics

TYPES OF WINES

Most wine drinkers can name more historic Loire Valley châteaux than Loire Valley wines. That is a pity, because the Loire Valley wine-producing regions offer France's most remarkable array of wines. The region stretches along one-third of the meandering 635-mile Loire River, and the astonishing diversity of grapes planted in the valley is far greater than that in the more well-known wine growing regions of Burgundy or Bordeaux.

With sixty wine appellations and *vin délimité de qualité supérieure* (VDQS) areas, the vastness and complexity of the Loire Valley as a winemaking area is obvious. Dry white table wines dominate the production, as do the three major white wine grapes found in the Loire. The Sauvignon Blanc is at its best in Sancerre and Pouilly-Fumé. The Chenin Blanc produces dry, sweet, and sparkling white wines. It reaches its zenith in Vouvray, Savennières, Bonnezeaux, Coteaux du Layon, and Quarts de Chaume. Last, there is the Muscadet grape (its true name is Melon de Bourgogne), from which Muscadet wines are made.

Plenty of light, frank, fruity, herbaceous red wine is made from Gamay, Cabernet Franc, and Cabernet Sauvignon grapes in appellations with names such as Bourgueil, Chinon, St.-Nicholas-de-Bourgueil, Touraine, and Anjou. Rosés, which can be delicious but are frightfully irregular in quality, tend to emerge from Anjou, Sancerre, Chinon, and Reuilly.

GRAPE VARIETIES

Chenin Blanc, Sauvignon Blanc, Muscadet, and Gros Plant are the four dominant white wine grapes, but Chardonnay, especially in the VDQS region called Haut-Poitou, is frequently seen. For red wines, Gamay and Pinot Noir are seen in the VDQS vineyards, but the top red wine Loire appellations use virtually all Cabernet Sauvignon and Cabernet Franc.

A QUICK GUIDE TO THE DIVERSITY OF THE LOIRE VALLEY

Anjou   This large appellation is acclaimed for its rosé wines, which can range from dry to medium sweet. In the 1980s, red wine grapes such as Cabernet Sauvignon, Cabernet Franc, and Gamay began to receive considerable attention from bargain hunters looking for inexpensive, light-bodied, fruity red wines. In particular, Gamay has done well in Anjou, producing richly fruity wines. Cabernet Franc and Cabernet Sauvignon, although admired by many, are too vegetal for my taste.

With respect to white wines, Chenin Blanc, Chardonnay, and Sauvignon Blanc made with modern vinification methods can result in fragrant, fruity, light wines that are adored by consumers. There is even some sparkling wine, called Anjou Mousseux. Its principal virtue is its reasonable price under $12.

ANJOU PRODUCERS OF MERIT

Ackerman-Laurence
  (sparkling wines)**
Château de Chamboureau**
Clos de Coulaine**

Colombier**
Fougeraies**
Richou Rochettes **

Bonnezeaux   Only one grape is grown in this appellation, Chenin Blanc, which reaches extraordinary heights of richness, complexity, and aging ability in Bonnezeaux. This is a decadently rich, sweet wine that demonstrates what pinnacles Chenin Blanc can reach. These wines can live for decades. This Grand Cru appellation, technically within the larger Coteaux du Layon, made phenomenally rich, long-lived wines in 1989 and 1990.

BONNEZEAUX PRODUCERS OF MERIT

Domaine de la Croix des Loges
  (Christian Bonnin)****
Château de Fesles (this estate is in
  a class of its own)****

Domaine du Petit Val**/***

Bourgueil   If you ask a Parisian about Bourgueil, chances are it is one of his favorites. More popular in France than in America, Bourgueil is considered to make a fruity, raspberry-scented and -flavored wine that should be drunk in its first 5–6 years of life. The problem is that unless the vintage is exceptionally ripe, as it was in 1989 and 1990, the wines are strikingly vegetal.

BOURGUEIL PRODUCERS OF MERIT

Caslot-Galbrun***
Demont**
Pierre-Jacques Druet ****

Lamé-Delille-Boucard***

Cabernet d'Anjou   The name suggests a red wine, but in essence this is a rosé that tends to be herbaceous and sweet. I am not an admirer of these wines, but should you want to take the plunge, check out one of the following producers.

CABERNET D'ANJOU PRODUCERS OF MERIT

Bertrand**
Poupard**

Château de Tigné**
Verdier**

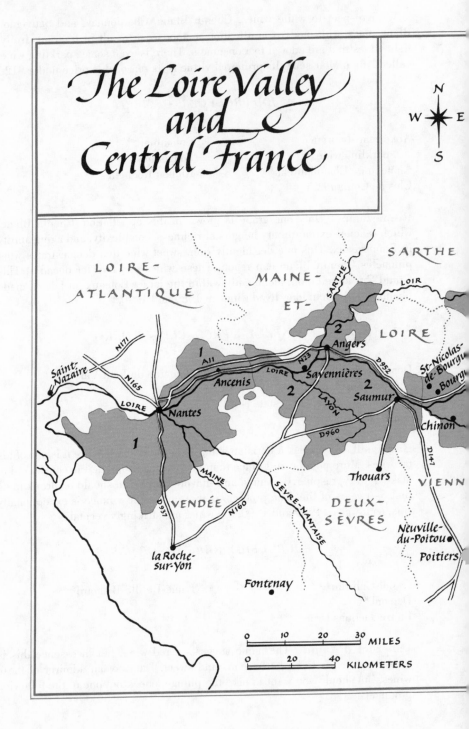

The Loire Valley and Central France

N W E S

SARTHE

LOIRE-ATLANTIQUE

MAINE-ET-LOIRE

LOIR

Saint-Nazaire

N171

A11

N165

1

N23

Angers

2

St-Nicolas-de-Bourgu

D952

Bourgu

LOIRE

Ancenis

LOIRE

Savennières

2

Saumur

2

N165

Nantes

LAYON

Chinon

D147

1

D960

D937

MAINE

VENDÉE

N160

SÈVRE-NANTAISE

Thouars

DEUX-SÈVRES

VIENN

la Roche-sur-Yon

Neuville-du-Poitou

Poitiers

Fontenay

| 0 | 10 | 20 | 30 | MILES |

| 0 | 20 | 40 | KILOMETERS |

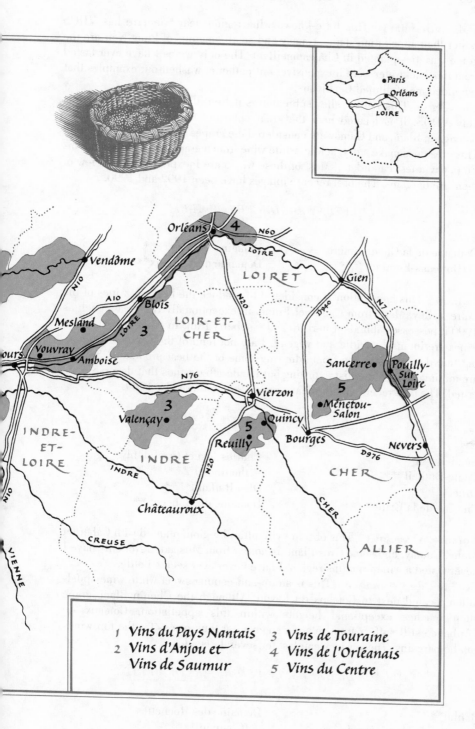

Paris
Orléans
LOIRE

Orléans
N60
LOIRE
LOIRET
Gien
Vendôme
N10
A10
Blois
Loire
LOIR-ET-
CHER
N20
Mesland
ours
Vouvray
Amboise
N76
Vierzon
Sancerre
Pouilly-
sur-
Loire
Ménetou-
Salon
N7
D940
INDRE-
ET-
LOIRE
3
Valençay
Quincy
5
Reuilly
Bourges
Nevers
N20
INDRE
INDRE
D976
N10
Châteauroux
CHER
VIENNE
CREUSE
ALLIER

1 Vins du Pays Nantais
2 Vins d'Anjou et
   Vins de Saumur
3 Vins de Touraine
4 Vins de l'Orléanais
5 Vins du Centre

Châteaumeillant This little-known wine region near Sancerre has VDQS rather than appellation status. Gamay and small amounts of Pinot Noir are the grape varieties planted in Châteaumeillant. The only wines I have ever tasted from this backwater were inexpensive, but pathetic, washed-out examples that reminded me of diluted Beaujolais.

Cheverny This Loire Valley subregion is not entitled to appellation status, only VDQS. It is located near the great châteaux of Chambord and Blois. Sauvignon Blanc and Gamay are considered the grapes with the most potential. This area does make a dry, acidic, white wine from a grape known as Romorantin (a trivia test candidate). Most of these wines are inexpensive, and a few of them are bargains. The best recent vintages have been 1992 and 1990.

CHEVERNY PRODUCERS OF MERIT

Domaine de la Gaudronnière
  (Dorléans-Ferrand)****

Domaine Gendrier***
Domaine de Veilloux***

Chinon This appellation is considered to produce the best red wines of the Loire Valley. Made from Cabernet Franc, in exceptionally ripe years such as 1990 it possesses abundant herb-tinged raspberry fruit. In other years Chinon wines are intensely acidic and vegetal. I am not fond of the wines of Chinon, but that does not stop me from admiring some of the best producers. Several are minimal interventionists, turning out handcrafted wines that deserve to be tasted. The best recent vintages have been 1990, followed by 1989.

CHINON PRODUCERS OF MERIT

Baudery***
Couly-Dutheil***
Druet***
Château de la Grille***

Charles Joguet (irrefutably
  the finest)****/*****
Olga Raffault****
Domaine du Roncée***

Coteaux d'Ancenis This obscure viticultural region, planted with Cabernet Franc, Gamay, and some Gros Plant, is not far from Muscadet. Not only have I never tasted a wine from this region, I have never ever seen a bottle.

Coteaux de l'Aubance This is an up-and-coming sweet white wine appellation located next to Coteaux du Layon. Although the Chenin Blanc grape often reaches exceptional heights within this appellation, Coteaux de l'Aubance still suffers from relative anonymity; thus prices for the top wines can be bargains. These wines can last for several decades.

COTEAUX DE L'AUBANCE PRODUCERS OF MERIT

Bablut***
Domaine de Haute-Perche
  (Papin)***
Domaine Didier Richou
  (particularly their Cuvée les
  Trois Demoiselles)****

Domaine des Rochettes
  (Chauvin)****

Coteaux du Giennois   This appellation just north of Sancerre should be an excellent region for good values, but to date the quality has been average. The best producer is Balland-Chapuis.

Coteaux du Layon   One of the Loire Valley's most renowned appellations, Coteaux du Layon produces decadently sweet wines from the Chenin Blanc grape that have been attacked by the same noble rot that is famous for the wines of Barsac and Sauternes in Bordeaux and the Sélection des Grains Nobles in Alsace. The spectacular vintages of 1989 and 1990, considered by most growers to be the finest since 1959 and 1947, caused much of the world to take notice of the excellent quality that often emerges from this region—at modest prices. Readers should be aware that some labels say Coteaux du Layon-Villages, which reflects the fact that the French government has allowed seven villages in Coteaux du Layon to affix their names to the wine. A top Coteaux du Layon can be drunk as an aperitif for its opulent peach and apricot fruitiness, but I feel it is best consumed after a meal by itself. The finest vintages are 1990, 1989, and, if you can still find any, 1986 and 1983.

COTEAUX DU LAYON PRODUCERS OF MERIT

Alfred Bidet***
Domaine de Brizé****
Domaine Cady Valette***
Clos de Ste.-Catherine
   (Baumard)*****
Jean-Louis Foucher***
Domaine Gaudard***
Guimonière***/****
Domaine des Hauts
   Perrays***/****
Jolivet***/****
Domaine des Maurières
   (Fernand Moron)****
Château Montenault
   (Clos de la Hersé)****

La Motte (André Sorin)***
Moulin-Touchais (a producer with an
   enormous array of vintages going
   back to the late 1940s that can
   still be purchased)***
Domaine Ogereau***
Château de Passavant
   (Jean David)***
Domaine des Rochettes****
Domaine de la Pierre Blanche
   (Vincent Lecointre)***
Domaine de la Pierre
   Saint-Maurille***
La Soucherie***
Domaine de Villeneuve***

Coteaux du Vendômois   Some pretty wretched red wines made from Pinot Noir, Gamay, and an oddity called Pineau d'Aunis, as well as some meager white wines from Chardonnay and Chenin Blanc, emerge from this VDQS region situated north of Tours. I cannot see any reason to get excited about this area.

Côte Roannaise   If you do not think the Loire Valley encompasses a huge area, this region, which is not an appellation but rather a VDQS, is closer to Lyons than it is to any Loire Valley château. The grape here is Gamay, although there are tiny quantities of Pinot Noir. Although these wines can rival Beaujolais, they are generally not shipped outside France, so American consumers have little access to them. Should you run across one of these wines, the following producers merit a look.

CÔTE ROANNAISE PRODUCERS OF MERIT

Chargros**   Domaine de Pavillon
Chaucesse**/***   (Maurice Lutz)***
Lapandéry**/***

Côtes d'Auvergne   This is another red wine VDQS making strawberry- and cherry-flavored, light, insipid wines from Gamay. Some Pinot Noir is also made, the best of which comes from Michel Bellard (***). Bellard makes not only a good red wine, but also a crisp, scented rosé.

Crémant de Loire   This is the Loire Valley's best appellation for both pink and white sparkling wine. If the American importers do a good job of getting the wines into the country without abusing them in transport, readers will enjoy these tasty, light, inexpensive sparkling wines. Many of these wines are non-vintage, so it is important to buy only the freshest stock, a determination often impossible to make until you pull the cork. Sparkling Loire wines have to be drunk within 1–2 years of their bottling.

CRÉMANT DE LOIRE PRODUCERS OF MERIT

Ackerman-Laurence***   Gratien and Meyer***
Domaine Gabillière***

Gros Plant du Pays Nantais   This region, entitled only to a VDQS, is planted with one of the meanest, nastiest white wine grapes in the world, the Gros Plant. It goes by different names in other parts of France, such as Picpoul and Folle Blanche. Normally used only as a blending agent to buttress other varietals that produce richer, low-acid wines, unripe Gros Plant can shatter your teeth with its acidity and greenness. The best advice is to stay away from it despite what appear to be superlow prices. Some of the big Muscadet producers (Métaireau and Sauvion, for example) have begun to tame some of Gros Plant's acidity, but you are much better off spending another dollar for Muscadet, unless you are a masochist.

Haut-Poitou   The production of this region, which is VDQS rather than an appellation, is dominated by the huge cooperative at Neuville. Thus, anyone can buy a *cuvée*, slap whatever name they want on it, and simply call it "Mr. Smith's Haut-Poitou." Nevertheless, the white wines, such as Sauvignon Blanc and Chardonnay, are light, fresh, floral, and tasty, which is surprising when you consider that this is a very inexpensive wine. The bad news is that the red wines, made from Cabernet Sauvignon, Cabernet Franc, and Gamay, are nasty, raw, lip-stinging wines with little flavor but plenty of acidity and vegetal characteristics. The cooperative is the only producer in this region of which I am aware.

Jasnières   This 47-acre appellation just north of Tours produces very dry, often excellent white wines from Chenin Blanc. They are not easy to find, but if you come across any, you are well advised to try them for their delicacy as well as rarity.

JASNIÈRES PRODUCERS OF MERIT

Gaston Cartereau****   J. B. Pinon***
Domaine de la Chanière****

Ménétou-Salon   Ménétou-Salon, a relatively small appellation of 250 acres, produces excellent white wines from Sauvignon Blanc and some herbal, spicy, light-bodied rosé and red wines from Pinot Noir. In my opinion, the wines to buy are the Sauvignons, which exhibit a pungent, herbaceous, earthy, curranty nose and crisp, rich, grassy flavors. The best recent vintage has been 1990, followed by 1982 and 1989.

MÉNÉTOU-SALON PRODUCERS OF MERIT

Domaine de Chatenoy***   Cuvée Pierre-Alexandre****
Domaine Chavet**** (many think he   Marc Lebrun***
   makes one of the greatest dry rosés   Henri Pellé***/****
   from Pinot Noir in France)

Montlouis   Montlouis is often regarded as the stepchild of its more famous southern neighbor, Vouvray. It is a good source for sparkling wines made from Chenin Blanc that can range from bone dry to honeyed, sweet, and sticky. They are less expensive than those from Vouvray. The white wines also range from dry to medium sweet. Quality from the top producers is generally good.

MONTLOUIS PRODUCERS OF MERIT

Domaine Berger***   Pierre Mignot***
Claude Levasseur***/****

Muscadet   This vast area is known for making inexpensive, fresh wines that must be consumed within several years of the vintage. There is generic Muscadet, but even better is the Muscadet de Sèvre-et-Maine, which is bottled *sur-lie* by the best producers. Muscadet, which possesses an enthralling crispness and freshness, works wonders with fresh shellfish. This vast area offers a tremendous range in quality, from insipid, vapid, hollow wines to wines with considerable personality. Readers should note the following chart to see who is producing the best Muscadet. Keep in mind that Muscadet is made from a grape called Melon de Bourgogne, which is also found in American wine from the likes of the Beaulieu winery in the Napa Valley and the Panther Creek winery in Oregon. The best recent vintages for Muscadet have been 1992 and 1990.

RATING MUSCADET'S BEST PRODUCERS

* * * * (EXCELLENT PRODUCERS)

Michel Bahuaud
André-Michel Bregeon
Château de Chasseloir
Chéreau-Carré
Joseph Drouard
Domaine du Fief Guérin
Marquis de Goulaine
Château de la Mercredière
Louis Métaireau

Domaine de la Mortaine
Domaine des Mortiers-Gobin
Château La Noë
Domaine La Quilla
Sauvion Cardinal Richard
Sauvion Château de Cléray
Domaine des Sensonnières
Domaine de la Vrillonnière

* * * (GOOD PRODUCERS)

Serge Batard
Domaine de la Botinière
Château de la Bretesche
La Chambaudière
Domaine des Dorices
Domaine de la Fevrie
Le Fief du Breil
Domaine de la Fruitière

Domaine de la Guitonnière
Domaine de la Grange
Domaine des Herbauges
Domaine de l'Hyvernière
Château de la Jannière
Château l'Oiselinière
Château de la Ragotière
Sauvion (other *cuvées*)

Pouilly-Fumé   Pouilly is the name of the village, and *fumé* means smoke. This appellation, renowned the world over for its richly scented, flinty (some say smoky), earthy, herbaceous, melony white wines that can range from medium bodied to full and intense, does indeed produce some of the world's most exciting wines from Sauvignon. The down side of this fame is the high prices fetched by the region's top producers of Pouilly-Fumé. Is a superb Pouilly-Fumé worth $40? Readers should also realize that most producers make numerous *cuvées* and often offer a luxury *cuvée* at prices of $25–$40 a bottle, which exceed the limit I will pay. The best recent vintages include excellent 1989s that should be drunk up, spectacular 1990s that should drink well until the end of the century, and light but good 1992s. The following list comprehensively covers the finest producers. By the way, a food that is heavenly with Pouilly-Fumé is goat cheese.

RATING POUILLY-FUMÉ'S BEST PRODUCERS

* * * * * (OUTSTANDING PRODUCERS)

J. C. Chatelain
Didier Dagueneau (Clos des
    Chailloux)
Didier Dagueneau (Cuvée Silex)

Serge Dagueneau
Château du Nozet-Ladoucette (Baron
    de L Pouilly-Fumé)
Michel Redde (Cuvée Majorum)

* * * * (EXCELLENT PRODUCERS)

Masson-Blondelet
Tinel-Blondelet

Château de Tracy

*** *(GOOD PRODUCERS)*

Henri Beurdin (Reuilly)

Gerard Cordier (Reuilly)

Paul Figeat

Henri Pellé (Ménétou)

Raymond Pipet (Quincy)

Michel Redde

Guy Saget

Jean Teiller (Ménétou-Salon)

Pouilly-sur-Loire This interesting appellation relies on the Chasselas grape, a lowly regarded varietal that can make fruity, soft wines when yields are restricted. Wines from this appellation should be inexpensive and consumed within 1 year of the vintage.

Quarts de Chaume This appellation produces what may be France's least-known great sweet wine. One hundred acres, planted entirely with Chenin Blanc, produce crisp, backward wines that are almost impenetrable when young. They open gradually to reveal a honeyed, splendid, floral, apricot, peachy richness that lingers and lingers. Quarts de Chaume is one of the greatest sweet wines, not only in France but in the world. Insiders have tended to keep its magical qualities a secret. The noble rot, which is the key to the compelling bouquet of sweet wine, frequently attacks the Chenin Blanc grown on the slopes of Quarts de Chaume appellation. The yields, limited to 22 hectoliters per hectare, are the lowest permitted in France. What does that tell you? Unlike Barsac and Sauternes, Quarts de Chaume is not aged in new oak casks. Consequently the full expression of Chenin Blanc, not influenced by oak, is vividly on display. Not much of this wine is produced, but, fortunately, a number of American importers have for years been selling the wines from this underrated appellation.

QUARTS DE CHAUME PRODUCERS OF MERIT

Domaine des Baumard*****

Château de Belle Rive****

Domaine Echarderie***/****

Domaine Suronde***/****

Quincy Another appellation dedicated to Sauvignon Blanc, Quincy, which is near the historic city of Bourges, takes Sauvignon to its most herbaceous—some would say vegetal—limit. This can be an almost appallingly asparagus-scented and -flavored wine in underripe years, but in top years, such as 1990, that character is subdued. Quincy wines are bone dry and can last for 5–6 years.

QUINCY PRODUCERS OF MERIT

Domaine Jérôme de la Chaise***

Domaine Jaumier***

Domaine Mardon***

Raymond Pipet***

Alain Thirot-Duc de Berri

(a co-op wine)***

St.-Nicolas-de-Bourgueil If I had to pick a favorite red wine–producing region of Loire, it would be this charming area. The red wines, which are all drinkable when released, are light, with intense perfumes of raspberry, curranty fruit flavors, followed by a soft, round, supple texture. They are currently in fashion in Paris, and prices are rising for wines that should never sell for more than $8–$10 a bottle. The red wine grapes used are Cabernet Franc and Cabernet Sauvignon. Small quantities of rosé are also produced.

ST.-NICOLAS-DE-BOURGUEIL PRODUCERS OF MERIT

Max Cognard***	Domaine des Ouches***
J. P. Mabileau***	Joel Taluau***

Sancerre   Sancerre and Vouvray are probably the best-known appellations of the vast Loire Valley viticultural region. Sancerre has been a highly fashionable wine for over 2 decades, and its success is based on its crisp acidity allied with rich, zesty, Sauvignon fruitiness. A small amount of red wine, which I find disappointing, is made from Pinot Noir; it, too, is called Sancerre. Sancerre's success is justifiable in view of the number of high-quality producers in this region. The only legitimate concern about Sancerre is the high price this wine fetches. The steep slopes of chalk and flint that surround Sancerre's best villages—Bué, Chavignon, and Verdigny—are undoubtedly responsible for the flinty, subtle, earthy character evident in so many of the top wines. There is no shortage of superlative Sancerre producers as evidenced by the following list. The finest recent vintages have been 1990, 1989, and 1992. White Sancerre and the limited quantities of rosés should be drunk within 2–3 years of the vintage, although some can last longer. Sancerre Pinot Noir can last for 4–5 years.

RATING SANCERRE'S BEST PRODUCERS

* * * * * (OUTSTANDING PRODUCERS)

Bailly-Reverdy	André Vatan
Paul Cotat (all three *cuvées*)	
Château du Nozet-Ladoucette (Comte Lafond Sancerre)	

* * * * (EXCELLENT PRODUCERS)

Lucien Crochet	H. Reverdy
Vincent Delaporte	Jean Reverdy
Gitton	Jean-Max Roger
Domaine la Moussière-Cuvée Edmond	Lucien Thomas
	Domaine Vacheron
André Neveu (all *cuvées*)	

* * * (GOOD PRODUCERS)

Henri Bourgeois	Château de Maimbray
Clos de la Poussie (Cordier)	Roger Neveu
Jolivet	

Saumur   White, red, and rosé wines all emerge from this Loire Valley appellation. Two related appellations are Saumur-Mousseux, an underrated area for producing fresh, lively, inexpensive sparkling wines, and Saumur-Champigny, which many feel produces good fresh red wines (although I do not agree). Consumers should be able to find some good values from the former appellation. Look for the sparkling wine *cuvées* from such producers as Ackerman-Laurence (**/***), Bouvet-Ladubay (**/***), Gratien and Meyer (**/****), and Langlois and Château (**/***). Unfortunately, many of these sparkling wine *cuvées* are beat up in transit to America, so what consumers encounter is oxidized and flat, unlike what is seen in France.

Savennières   Savennières, the Montrachet of the Loire Valley, produces dry Chenin Blanc that can age for 15–20 years and possess an intensity, richness, and complexity that one has to taste to believe. There are only 150 acres, but the production is limited to 30 hectoliters per hectare, and the minimum alcohol level is 12%. The results are sensationally rich, intense wines that develop a honeyed complexity and huge, floral, mineral bouquet after 7–8 years of cellaring. The wines start life relatively backward and tart, but if you are looking for a great dry white wine that can out-age most Chardonnays, check out a Savennières. The best recent vintages have been 1990 (one of the three greatest years since World War II), 1989, and 1983.

RATING SAVENNIÈRES BEST PRODUCERS

* * * * * (OUTSTANDING PRODUCERS)

Domaine des Baumard (Clos du Papillon)

Domaine des Baumard (Trie Spéciale)

Clos de la Coulée de Serrant (N. Joly)

Domaine du Closel (Clos du Papillon)

* * * * (EXCELLENT PRODUCERS)

Domaine des Baumard (regular *cuvée*)

Domaine des Baumard (Clos de St.-Yves)

Château de Chamboureau

Château d'Epiré

Roche aux Moines (Pierre and Yves Soulez)

* * * (GOOD PRODUCERS)

Château de la Bizolière

Clos de Coulaine

Touraine   This general appellation covers considerable acreage, so it is important to know the best producers, as generalizations about the wines cannot be made. Certainly the Sauvignon Blanc and Chenin Blanc range from plonk to delicious fruity, vibrant wines. The red wines can also range from disgustingly vegetal to richly fruity and aromatic. One constant is that any Touraine white or red wine should be consumed within 2–3 years of the vintage. The best recent vintages have been 1990, followed by 1992.

TOURAINE PRODUCERS OF MERIT (WHITE WINES)

Domaine de la Charmoise****

Domaine de la Charmoise M de Marionet*****

Domaine des Corbillières***

Vouvray   Vouvray vies with Sancerre for the best-known appellation of the Loire Valley. Unlike Sancerre, no rosé or red wine is produced in Vouvray, only white—and all from the Chenin Blanc grape, which can reach imposingly high acidity levels in the limestone and chalky/clay soils of these charming vineyards located east of Tours. A huge appellation (over 3,800 acres), Vouvray produces tasty, sparkling wines, wonderfully bone-dry, crisp, delicious dry wines, and some of the most spectacularly honeyed sweet wines one will ever taste. The sweet wines, indicated by the word *Moelleux* on the label, are the result of the noble rot and can last for 40–50 or more years. The greatest vintage for Vouvray sweet wines since 1959 or 1947 was 1990. A close second is 1989. Consumers who adore these wines should not wait too long to stock up. The following list identifies the top producers, but several deserve special mention, including Gaston Huet, whose three vineyard-designated sweet wines called Le Haut-Lieu, Le Mont, and Le Clos du Bourg are riveting examples of Vouvray. Another up-and-coming Vouvray superstar is Philippe Foreau, who makes wines from his estate (called Clos Naudin). Like most producers in this area, he fashions numerous *cuvées*, but the quality in vintages such as 1989 and 1990 has been extraordinary. Domaine Bourillon-Dorleans is another emerging superstar, especially for its decadently rich *cuvées* called Moelleux and Coulée d'Or.

RATING VOUVRAY'S BEST PRODUCERS

* * * * * *(OUTSTANDING PRODUCERS)*

Domaine Bourillon-Dorleans	Gaston Huet
Philippe Foreau Clos Naudin	

* * * * *(EXCELLENT PRODUCERS)*

Domaine de la Charmoise	Château Moncontour

* * * *(GOOD PRODUCERS)*

Marc Brédif	J. M. Monmousseau
Jean-Pierre Freslier	D. Moyer
Sylvain Gaudron	Prince Poniatowski-Le Clos Baudin

FLAVORS

There is an unbelievable variety in flavors and textures to the wines of the Loire Valley. Below is a quick summary of tastes of the major wines.

DRY WHITE WINES

Muscadet-sur-Lie   A classic Muscadet, sur-Lie has light body, tart, dry, fresh, stony, and delicate flavors, and refreshing acidity.
Savennières   A good Savennières is marked by a stony, lemon- and limelike bouquet with dry, austere yet floral, deep flavors and medium body.
Vouvray   Dry, very flowery and fruity, with crisp acidity for balance, a Vouvray is delightful as an aperitif wine.
Sancerre   Assertive aromas of fresh herbs, recently cut grass, wet stones, and currants dominate this crisp, intense, and flavorful wine.

Pouilly-Fumé Pouilly-Fumé is very similar in aromatic character to Sancerre, but on the palate it is a fuller, more opulent and alcoholic wine.

DRY RED WINES

Bourgueil Bourgueils are prized for their herb-tinged strawberry and cherry fruit in a light, soft, compact format.

Chinon Aggressively herbaceous aromas and cherry fruit age nicely into a cedary/curranty wine of character in a good Chinon.

Touraine Most wines of Touraine are light, soft, and fruity and dominated by herbaceous or vegetal bouquets.

SWEET WHITE WINES

Vouvray Buttery, overripe tropical fruit, honey, and flowers are the aromas and tastes in a sweet Vouvray. Crisp acidity gives a vibrance and a well-delineated character to these wines.

Coteaux du Layon, Quarts de Chaume, Bonnezeaux Although undistinguished when young, in great years these sweet wines age into honeypots filled with rich, ripe, decadent levels of fruit. They are probably the world's most undervalued great sweet wines.

AGING POTENTIAL

Dry White Wines
Muscadet: 1–3 years
Pouilly-Fumé: 3–5 years
Sancerre: 3–5 years
Savennières: 3–12 years
Vouvray: 2–6 years
Dry Red Wines
Bourgueil: 3–7 years
Chinon: 3–10 years
Touraine: 3–6 years
Sweet White Wines
Bonnezeaux: 5–20 years
Coteaux du Layon: 5–20 years
Quarts du Chaume: 5–20 years
Vouvray: 10–30 years

OVERALL QUALITY LEVEL

Poor to superb. The Loire Valley, with thousands of growers, is a minefield for the consumer who is not armed with the names of a few good producers. The producers chart lists the top proprietors. Avoid anything labeled Rosé d'Anjou.

MOST IMPORTANT INFORMATION TO KNOW

Learn the multitude of appellations and the different types of wines produced, and memorize a few of the top producers. Then and only then will you be able to navigate the turbulent waters of the Loire.

1993–1994 BUYING STRATEGY

If you can still find any of the great 1989s and 1990s from Vouvray, Savennières, Bonnezeaux, Coteaux du Layon, and Quarts de Chaume, move quickly to purchase them. Most insiders have long known that 1990, for both Savennières and the sweet wines of Loire, is one of the three or four greatest vintages in the post–World War II era. The 1991 vintage is disappointing, and 1992 is excessively abundant and average in quality. If you wish to drink the lighter wines from the Loire, look for the 1992s from Muscadet. Avoid anything older.

VINTAGE GUIDE

1992—The Loire Valley escaped most of the horrific downpours that plagued southern France, but the crop size was appallingly large. Reports of excessive yields from virtually every appellation were numerous. Growers had a chance to pick relatively ripe fruit that should have produced a good vintage, but only those who kept their yields low will produce good wines. This should be a vintage of far fewer sweet wines than in 1989 and 1990. There will be pleasant, straightforward, fruity wines that will have to be drunk young. The most successful appellations for white wines are Muscadet, Sancerre, and Pouilly-Fumé. Chinon is the most successful for red wines.

1991—This is a difficult vintage throughout the Loire Valley, with relatively acidic, lean, light-bodied wines that lack ripeness and flavor authority. Successes can be found, but overall, a small crop combined with inadequate ripeness produced ungenerous wines lacking fruit and charm.

1990—This is one of the all-time greatest vintages for just about every region of the Loire Valley, especially the sweet wine appellations and the great dry white wines of Savennières, Pouilly-Fumé, and Sancerre. The levels of richness and intensity of the 1990s are mind-boggling. Consumers lucky enough to find and afford the top cuvées of the decadently sweet wines from Bonnezeaux, Coteaux du Layon, Quarts de Chaume, and Vouvray, as well as some of the spectacularly full-bodied, awesomely rich, dry Savennières, will have treasures that will last in their cellars for 25–30 or more years. Most Muscadet should have been drunk by the beginning of 1993, but the top cuvées of dry Sancerre and Pouilly-Fumé should last through 1995.

The red wines are also surprisingly good (I have a strong bias against most of them because of their overt vegetal character), but because of the drought and superripeness they are less herbaceous than usual and offer copious quantities of red and black fruits.

1989—Somewhat similar to 1990, although yields were higher and there was less botrytis in the sweet wine vineyards, 1989 is an excellent, in many cases a superb, vintage for Vouvray, Quarts de Chaume, Coteaux du Layon, and Bonnezeaux. It is also a super vintage for Savennières. All the drier wines from Sancerre, Pouilly-Fumé, Touraine, and Muscadet should have been consumed by now, as they were exceptionally low in acidity.

1988—A good but unexciting vintage produced pleasant, textbook wines that admirably represent their appellation or region but lack the huge perfumes, richness, and depth of the finest 1989s and 1990s.

1987—A mediocre to poor year.

OLDER VINTAGES

The decadently rich dessert wines of the Coteaux du Layon, Bonnezeaux, Quarts de Chaume, and Vouvray from 1983, 1976, 1971, 1962, 1959, 1949, and 1947 can be spectacular wines. These wines are still modestly priced and are undoubtedly the greatest bargains in rich dessert wines in the world. Although it is not easy to find these older vintages, consumers should put this information to good use by stocking up on the 1989s and 1990s.

Savennières is probably the world's greatest buy in dry, full-bodied white wines. Older Savennières vintages to look for are 1986, 1985, 1978, 1976, 1971, 1969, 1962, and 1959. Occasionally, small quantities of these wines come up for auction. They are well worth the low prices being asked.

Gaston Huet's sweet Vouvrays from 1959 and 1962 remain in superb condition. Why don't more people realize just how fine these wines are? For red wines, Charles Joguet's best *cuvées* of red wine from his Chinon vineyards, unfiltered and as rich as a Loire Valley red can be, will easily last 10–15 years or more. For example, his 1978s are just now becoming fully mature. If you like an herbaceous, stemmy red wine, you will find that the Chinons of Jacques Druet and Olga Raffault will also last 10–12 more years.

LANGUEDOC-ROUSSILLON

The Art of the Possible

Great Wine Values for Tough Economic Times

Among all the French viticultural regions, none has made more progress than the vast region referred to as Languedoc-Roussillon. Bounded on the northeast by the Rhône Valley, on the east by the Mediterranean Sea, on the west by the hilly terrain known as the *massif central,* and on the south by the Pyrenees mountains of Spain, this sun-drenched region produces more than half of France's red table wine. Once known for its barely palatable, acidic, thick, alcoholic wines from huge industrial-oriented cooperatives that placed quantity before quality, the Languedoc-Roussillon region has undergone an amazing transformation since the mid-1980s. Moreover, some of America's most innovative importers are flocking to the region in search of delicious, bargain-priced white, red, and rosé wines.

There is no shortage of wine from which to choose, because the Languedoc-Roussillon area, with its 70,000 acres of vines, annually produces an ocean of 300 million cases. The finest vineyard sites generally tend to be planted on hillsides, with heavy soils that provide outstanding drainage. Excluding Corsica, Languedoc-Roussillon is the hottest viticultural region of France. Torrential rainstorms are common during the summer, but the amount of rainfall is small and the area, much like the southern Rhône, is buffeted by winds from both inland and the Mediterranean, thus creating an ideal climate for the sanitary cultivation of vineyards, with minimal need for fungicides, herbicides, and insecticides.

Most of the progress that has been made is attributable to two major developments. The advent of temperature-controlled stainless-steel fermentation tanks (an absolute necessity in this torridly hot region) has greatly enhanced the aromatic purity and fruit in the wines. Even more important, many of the indigenous grape varieties of this area, Carignan, Cinsault, and Terret Noir for red and rosé wines, and Clairette, Ugni Blanc, Picpoul, and Maccabeo for white wines, are used decreasingly in favor of widely renowned, superstar grapes such as Syrah, Mourvèdre, Cabernet Sauvignon, Merlot, and Grenache. White wine varietals making significant inroads include Chardonnay, Sauvignon Blanc, and Chenin Blanc. Since the mid-1980s, thousands of acres of these varietals have been planted.

Across this vast area, stretching from southwest of Avignon, where the appellations of Châteauneuf-du-Pape and Tavel end, to the Spanish border are well over 20 different viticultural regions producing an enormous array of dry white, rosé, and red table wine, as well as the famed *vins doux naturels*, sweet dessert wines that are slightly fortified. Much of the wine from the region either has just recently achieved *appellation contrôlée* status or remains entitled to VDQS status or nothing more than a *vin de pays* designation. As the following tasting notes indicate, some of the finest wines can legally be called only a *vin de pays*.

Following is a quick rundown of the major viticultural areas.

Costières de Nimes   This area, which received *appellation contrôlée* status in 1986, produces white, red, and rosé wines. The area takes its name from the extraordinary Roman city of Nimes. The vineyard area consists of a group of pebble-strewn slopes and a plateau region that lie in the Rhône delta. Seventy-five percent of the production is in red wine, 20% in rosé, and the remainder white. The two best estates are, irrefutably, Château de la Tuilerie and Château de Campuget. Other interesting domaines include the Domaine St.-Louis-la-Perdrix and Château Belle-Coste. The red wines are permitted to be made from a maximum of 50% Carignan. Other allowable grape varieties include Cinsault, Counoise Grenache, Mourvèdre, Syrah, Terret Noir, and two obscure red varietals called Aspiran Noir and Oeillade. White varietals are dominated by Clairette and Grenache Blanc, with small amounts of Picpoul, Roussanne, Terret Blanc, Ugni Blanc, Malvoisie, Marsanne, and Maccabeo also present.

Coteaux du Languedoc   This vast area (given *appellation contrôlée* status in 1985) includes vineyards in three French departments, Aude, Garde, and L'Hérault. It runs from Nimes in the north to Narbonne in the south. Consumers will find wines labeled merely with the appellation Coteaux du Languedoc, as well as those where the individual village names are affixed.

Two of the finest villages, St.-Chinian and Faugères, were elevated to their own *appellation contrôlée* status in 1982. The grape varieties are essentially the same as in the Costières de Nimes, although the more serious estates use higher percentages of Syrah, Mourvèdre, Grenache, and Counoise in their red wines, generally at the expense of Carignan and Cinsault. The best wines of St.-Chinian come from Domaine des Jougla and Cazal Viel, and the best wines of Faugères have consistently come from Haut-Fabrèges and Gilbert Alquier. Perhaps the greatest wine of the entire appellation of Coteaux du Languedoc (as well as the most expensive) is the Prieuré de St.-Jean de Bebian of Alain Roux. This wine, along with the Mas de Daumas Gassac, a *vin de pays*, are irrefutably the two greatest red wines of the Languedoc-Roussillon region.

Minervois   Minervois may have the best long-range potential of the appellations in the Languedoc-Roussillon area. To say that there are still many underachievers would not be unjust. This area of nearly 14,000 acres of vineyards is bounded on the west by the extraordinary fortified fortress city of Carcassonne and on the east by St.-Chinian. Minervois flourished under Roman rule but never recovered from the phylloxera epidemic that devastated France's vineyards in the late nineteenth century. The vineyards, the best of which tend to be located on gently sloping, south-facing, limestone hillsides sheltered from the cold north winds, endure the hottest microclimate of the region. Virtually all the wine production is red, although it is not surprising to see microquantities of a surprisingly tasty rosé emerge. The amount of white wine produced makes up less than 2% of the total production. Some of the best estates represented in America include Château de Paraza, Château de Gourgazaud, Daniel Domergue, Tour St.-Martin, Laville-Bertrou, Château Donjon, and Domaine Ste.-Eulalie.

Corbières   Corbières, which is located farther down the coast, south of Minervois, was recently elevated to *appellation contrôlée* status. It boasts the largest production area (over 57,000 acres) of the entire Languedoc-Roussillon region. Red wine accounts for 90% of the production, and the predominant varietal is the omnipresent Carignan, although the more serious estates have begun to employ increasing percentages of Syrah and Mourvèdre. The outstanding estates in Corbières include the brilliant Château Le Palais, Château Etang des Colombes, Domaine St.-Paul, Domaine de Villemajou, and the Guy Chevalier wines produced at a cooperative called Les Vignerons d'Octaviana.

Fitou   Fitou, the oldest of the *appellation contrôlée* regions of the Languedoc-Roussillon area (its AOC status was bestowed in 1948), represents two separate areas bounded on the north by Corbières. One region, representing low-lying vineyards near the coast, is planted on shallow, gravelly soil atop limestone beds. No one I have ever talked with believes top-quality wines can emerge from this particular sector. On the hillsides farther inland, the best vineyards are planted on sloping, well-drained, sandstone-and-limestone mixed soils. The ripest, fattest, fruitiest wines from Fitou generally emanate from this area. The grape varieties for Fitou are the same as in the other regions of Languedoc, with Carignan once again the dominant varietal, but the more serious producers are utilizing more Mourvèdre, Syrah, and Grenache. Some rosé wines are made in Fitou, but I have never seen a bottle of white. I do not believe any is permitted under the *appellation contrôlée* laws.

Côtes du Roussillon and Côtes du Roussillon-Villages   The Roussillon vineyards, all of which run from the Mediterranean Sea inland, surrounding

Perpignan, France's last urban bastion before the Spanish border, are known to have produced wines since the seventh century B.C. There is immense potential, not only for dry red table wines, but for the sweet, fortified wines that often excel in this windy, sun-drenched region. The best vineyards, which are entitled to the Côtes du Roussillon or Côtes du Roussillon-Villages appellation, stretch out over a semicircle of hills facing the Mediterranean Sea. These hillside vineyards, planted on expanses of limestone and granite, enjoy a phenomenally sunny, hot summer. Virtually all of the rainfall results from thunderstorms. It has always amazed me that these wines are still so reasonably priced given the amount of labor necessary to cultivate so many of the terraced vineyards of this region. The tiny amount of white wine produced is generally from such obscure varietals as Malvoise du Roussillon and Maccabeo. The red wines are generally produced from the ubiquitous Carignan, as well as Grenache, Syrah, and Mourvèdre. These are full-bodied, relatively rich wines, with a big, fleshy, peppery character. Despite their softness and easy drinkability when young, some wines are made that can last for up to a decade. The best estates in the Côtes du Roussillon and Côtes du Roussillon-Villages are Pierre d'Aspres, Cazes Frères, Château de Jau, Sarda-Malet, Domaine Salvat, and Domaine St.-Luc. There are also a bevy of cooperatives, none of which I have visited, but several have received high praise, particularly the cooperatives of Maury and Latour de France.

Collioure   This tiny appellation, the smallest in the Languedoc-Roussillon region for dry red wine, is located just to the south of the Côtes du Roussillon on an expanse of terraced, hillside vineyards called the Côtes Vermeille. Virtually all of the Collioure vineyards are located on these steeply terraced slopes, and the red wine is produced largely from a blend of Grenache, Carignan, Mourvèdre, Syrah, and Cinsault. Tiny yields are commonplace in Collioure, and as a result the wines tend to be relatively rich and full. They have never been discovered by American wine enthusiasts. The best Collioures come from the great Domaine du Mas Blanc of Dr. Parcé, also renowned for his fabulous fortified, portlike Banyuls. There are generally two *cuvées* of Collioure, one called Les Piloums and the other Cosprons Levants. Other interesting producers include the Celliers des Templiers and Thierry Parcé at the Domaine de la Rictorie.

Vins Doux Naturels   The Languedoc-Roussillon area abounds with some of the greatest values in sweet and fortified sweet dessert wines in Europe. The most famous are those from Banyuls (located on the coastline south of Perpignan) and Maury (located on the hillsides north of Perpignan). Both appellations require that these decadently rich, fortified wines be made from at least 50% Grenache. Wines entitled to the Banyuls Grand Cru designation must be composed of at least 75% Grenache.

Other areas producing sweet wines include Muscat de Rivesaltes, Muscat de Lunel, Muscat de Frontignan, and the two smaller appellations of Muscat de Mireval and St.-Jean de Minervois. Both the Muscat de Frontignan and Muscat de Mireval are located near L'Hérault. Muscat de Lunel is produced east of Nimes in the northern sector of the Languedoc-Roussillon.

The most famous of these wines are the great Banyuls from Dr. Parcé. They have a legendary reputation in France but remain, to my surprise, largely unknown in the United States.

Almost all of these wines can handle considerable aging and are remarkable for their value, particularly when compared with the soaring prices for vintage and tawny ports.

The Basics

TYPES OF WINE

The appellations, the wines, the estates, and the areas here are not well known to wine consumers; consequently there are some great wine values. The range in wines is enormous. There is sound sparkling wine such as Blanquette de Limoux, gorgeously fragrant, sweet muscats like Muscat de Frontignan, oceans of soft, fruity red wines, the best of which are from Minervois, Faugères, Côtes du Roussillon, Costières du Gard, and Corbières, and even France's version of vintage port, Banyuls. These areas have not yet proven the ability to make interesting white wines, except for sweet muscats.

GRAPE VARIETIES

Grenache, Carignan, Cinsault, Mourvèdre, and Syrah are the major red wine grapes planted in these hot regions. Small vineyards of Cabernet Sauvignon and Merlot are becoming more common.

With respect to white wine varietals, Chardonnay, Sauvignon Blanc, and Chenin Blanc can now be found in these areas, but the older white wine vineyards generally consist of such workhorse varietals as Ugni Blanc, Picpoul, Maccabeo, and two of the better traditional varietals, Marsanne and Roussanne.

FLAVORS

Until the late 1980s, this hot, frequently torrid part of France produced wines that never lacked ripeness but rather suffered from overripeness. However, the advent of a new generation of young, enthusiastic, and better-equipped winemakers, significant investment in temperature-controlled stainless-steel fermentation tanks, and more attention to harvesting the fruit before it becomes raisiny have resulted in soaring quantities of inexpensive, gorgeously ripe, perfumed, fruity wines. There are remarkable variations in style—from serious, relatively long-lived reds to those made by the carbonic maceration method and designed to be drunk within several years of the vintage. Top producers have begun to offer luxury *cuvées* (for now, still modestly priced) that have been aged in new oak barrels. Some of these *cuvées* are highly successful, while others are overwhelmingly oaky.

AGING POTENTIAL

The dry red wines of Mas de Daumas Gassac, St.-Jean de Bebian, and a few other top producers can age for 10–15 years. The longest-lived wines of the region are the portlike wines of Banyuls, which can last for up to 30 years when made by a great producer such as Dr. Parcé. Other red wines should be drunk within 5–7 years of the vintage.

The white wines should be drunk within several years of the vintage.

OVERALL QUALITY LEVEL

Long known for monotonous mediocrity, quality levels have increased significantly as wine market insiders have realized the potential for well-made, inexpensive wines from these areas. America's small specialist importers now make annual pilgrimages to these areas, looking for up-and-coming producers.

MOST IMPORTANT INFORMATION TO KNOW

Most consumers as well as retailers probably cannot name more than two or three Languedoc-Roussillon producers. However, if you are going to take advantage of some of the best-made wines that sell at low prices, it is important to learn the names of the finest producers, as well as their American importers.

1993–1994 BUYING STRATEGY

With the exception of Mas de Daumas Gassac, St.-Jean de Bebian, and Dr. Parcé's wines from Banyuls, do not buy anything older than 1990, unless it is one of the luxury *cuvées*. With the aforementioned producers, you can go back 10 years and feel confident you have bought a wine in good condition. For all other producers, the vintages of choice are 1990 and 1991, the former excellent and the latter considered to be the finest vintage for Languedoc-Roussillon in over 2 decades. The area was spared the rains that hit most other parts of France. The 1992 will be irregular in quality, with white wines being more consistent than reds.

Super Sparkling Wine Values

It is probably the least-known well-made sparkling wine of France, at least to the Anglo-Saxon world. From an appellation called Blanquette de Limoux, hidden in the Languedoc-Roussillon area just north of Spain's border, comes France's oldest sparkling wine, made a century before a monk named Dom Pérignon was credited with discovering the process of producing champagne. Made primarily from the Chardonnay, Chenin Blanc, and Mauzac grapes, the wines are qualitatively close to a high-quality, nonvintage champagne at one-third the price—most dry *brut* vintage sparkling wines from this appellation retail for $10 a bottle. The best are the St.-Hilaire Blanc de Blancs, the Maison Guinot, and the two top wines from the Coopérative Aiméry, the Cuvée Aldéric and Cuvée Sieur d'Arques.

The World's Greatest Wines with Chocolate

The late-harvested wines from Banyuls, made by Dr. Parcé at Mas Blanc, are some of the most unique in the world. One Banyuls labeled "dry" is an explosively rich, full-bodied, Grenache-based wine that should be drunk with hearty fare on cool fall and winter evenings. Another, a dry red wine called Collioure, is a complex table wine, impeccably made from a blend of 40% Syrah, 40% Mourvèdre, and 20% Grenache. And then there is Dr. Parcé's famous portlike sweet Banyuls made from very ripe Grenache. Complex, decadent, and the only wine I have found to work well with chocolate desserts, this is a spectacular offering that can age well for 20–25 years. The alcohol content averages 16%–18%. Parcé also makes a special *cuvée* of Vieilles Vignes (old vines) that is even more stunning. Dr. Parcé's sweet Banyuls usually sell for under $25 a bottle, making them a moderately priced alternative to vintage port. The other decadent wine to serve with chocolate is from Mas Amiel, a superlative producer from the obscure appellation of Maury. The French equivalent of a vintage port, Mas Amiel's wines are stunning in quality and remarkably low in price. Don't miss them.

Marvelous Muscats

Looking for a sweet, ripe, honeyed, aromatic, reasonably priced wine to serve with fresh fruit or fruit tarts? Then be sure to try the Muscat de Frontignan from the Château de la Peyrade, which sells for about $15 a bottle. It is a heady drink, but the Muscat's seductive charm and power is evident in this excellent wine. Another terrific sweet wine comes from Domaine Cazes, a splendid Muscat de Rivesaltes that sells for about $20.

RECENT VINTAGES

Heat and sun are constants in this region. Vintages are incredibly consistent, and the quality of most wines has more to do with the availability of modern technology to keep the grapes and grape juice from overheating in the frightfully hot temperatures. Nevertheless, recent vintages that stand out are 1991 (perhaps the most successful region in France), 1990, and 1989. Because of harvest rains, 1992 will be mixed, but most of the white wine varietals were harvested prior to the deluge. Moreover, the rains were highly localized, with some vineyards being inundated while others remained untouched. Vintages are significantly less important in an area such as Languedoc-Roussillon than in others because ripeness is rarely a problem. With each vintage since 1987 there has been a significant leap in quality.

FINDING THE WINES OF LANGUEDOC-ROUSSILLON

Unlike most other wines, the wines of Languedoc-Roussillon remain a specialized item. It will assist readers to have a list of the importers who have done most of the exploration of this area. Some of these importers are regional, and others are national:

Arborway Imports, Lexington, MA; 617-863-1753 (a regional importer dealing primarily in Massachusetts)

European Cellars, New York, NY; 212-924-4949 (the enthusiastic Eric Solomon, a top specialist for the wines of southern France, sells his wines nationally)

Hand Picked Selections, Warrenton, VA; 703-347- 3471 (perhaps the top importer in the country for specializing in wines that sell for under $10; owner Dan Kravitz represents a considerable number of wines from this region)

Ideal Wines, Medford, MA; 617-395-3300

Robert Kacher Selections, Washington, DC; 202-832-9083 (one of the first to exploit this region's potential, Robert Kacher brings in some of the finest wines from the Languedoc-Roussillon region)

Langdon-Shiverick, Chagrin Falls, OH; 216- 247-6868

Kermit Lynch Selections, Berkeley, CA; 510-524-1524 (this trailblazer, who has long represented many of France's small artisan producers, has plunged into Languedoc-Roussillon with considerable enthusiasm)

Wines of France, Mountainside, NJ; 908-654-6173 (Frenchman Alain Jun-
guenet, the first to see Languedoc-Roussillon's potential, has the most extensive portfolio of wines from this region, as well as some of its top estates)

RATING LANGUEDOC AND ROUSSILLON'S BEST PRODUCERS

* * * * * (OUTSTANDING PRODUCERS)

None

* * * * (EXCELLENT PRODUCERS)

Domaine l'Aiguelière-Montpeyrous
   (Coteaux du Languedoc)
Gilbert Alquier Cuvée les Bastides
   (Faugères)
Domaine d'Aupilhac (VDP)
Château La Baronne (Corbières)
Château Bastide-Durand (Corbières)
Domaine Bois Monsieur (Coteaux du
   Languedoc)
Château de Calage (Coteaux du
   Languedoc)
Château de Campuget Cuvée Prestige
   (Costières de Nimes)
Domaine Capion (VDP)
Domaine Capion Merlot (VDP)
Guy Chevalier La Coste (Corbières)
Guy Chevalier La Coste
   Cabernet/Syrah (L'Aude)
Guy Chevalier L'Église Grenache
   Noir (Corbières)
Guy Chevalier Le Texas Syrah
   (Corbières)
Domaine La Colombette (VDP)
Daniel Domergue
   (Minervois)* * * */* * * * *
Château Donjon Cuvée Prestige
   (Minervois)
Château des Estanilles (Faugères)
Château des Estanilles Cuvée Syrah
   (Faugères)
Château Helene Cuvée Helene de
   Troie (VDP)

Domaine de L'Hortus (Coteaux du
   Languedoc)* * * */* * * * *
Domaine Maris (Minervois)
Mas Amiel (Maury)
Mas Champart (Coteaux du
   Languedoc)
Mas de Daumas Gassac (L'Hérault)
   * * * */* * * * *
Mas Jullien-Les Cailloutis (Coteaux
   du Languedoc)
Château d'Oupia Cuvée des Barons
   (Minervois)
Château les Palais Cuvée Randolin
   (Corbières)
Dr. Parcé Mas Blanc
   (Banyuls)* * * */* * * * *
Château Routas Infernet (Coteaux
   Varois)
Château Routas Truffière (Coteaux
   Varois)
Domaine du Sacre Coeur (St.-
   Chinian)
Prieuré de St.-Jean de Bebian (vins
   de pays)* * * */* * * * *
Catherine de St.-Juery (Coteaux du
   Languedoc)
Domaine La Tour Boisee Cuvée
   Marie-Claude (Minervois)
Les Vignerons d'Octaviana Grand
   Chariot (Corbières)

* * * (GOOD PRODUCERS)

Abbaye de Valmagne (Coteaux du
   Languedoc)
Gilbert Alquier (Faugères)

Domaine de L'Arjolle (Côtes de
   Thongue)
Pierre d'Aspres (Côtes du Roussillon)

* * * (GOOD PRODUCERS)

Domaine des Astruc (VDP)

Château Belle-Coste (VDP)

Château de Blomac Cuvée Tradition (Minervois)

Château du Campuget (Costières de Nimes)

Domaine Capion Syrah (L'Hérault)

Château Capitoul (Coteaux du Languedoc)

Château de Casenove (Côtes du Roussillon)* * */* * * *

Cazal-Viel (St.-Chinian)

Cazal-Viel Cuvée Georges A. Aoust (St.-Chinian)

Cazes Frères (Roussillon)

Celliers des Templiers (VDP)

Domaine Dona Baissas (Côtes du Roussillon)

Château Étang des Colombes Cuvée du Bicentenaire (Corbières)

Château Fabas Cuvée Alexandre (Minervois)

Domaine des Gautier (Fitou)

Château de Gourgazaud (Minervois)

Domaine de Gournier (VDP)

Château Haut-Fabrèges (Faugères) * * */* * * *

Domaine Lalande (vins de pays d'Oc)

Château des Lanes (Corbières)* * */ * * * *

Laville-Bertrou (Minervois)

Château de Luc (Corbières)

Mas des Bressandes (vins de pays)

Mas Jullien Les Vignes Oubliés (Coteaux du Languedoc)

Mas de Ray Cuvée Caladoc (Bouches du Rhône)

Mas de Ray Cuvée Camargue (Bouches du Rhône)

Château Maurel Fonsalade (St.-Chinian)

Domaine La Noble (vins de pays)

Château les Palais (Corbières)* * */ * * * *

Prieuré Château les Palais (Corbières)

Château de Paraza-Cuvée Spéciale (Minervois)* * */* * * *

Dr. Parcé Mas Blanc Collioure Les Piloums (Banyuls)

Dr. Parcé Mas Blanc Collioure Cosprons Levants (Banyuls)

Château de Pena Côtes du Roussillon-Villages (Côtes du Roussillon)

Château de la Peyrade (Muscat-Frontignan)

Domaine Piccinini (Minervois)

Domaine de Pilou (Fitou)

Domaine de Pomaredes Merlot (VDP)

Château La Roque (Coteaux du Languedoc)

Château Rouquette sur Mer (Coteaux du Languedoc)

Château Routas Agrippa (Coteaux Varois)* * */* * * *

Château Routas Traditionel (Coteaux Varois)

Domaine Salvat (Côtes du Roussillon)

Sarda-Malet Black Label (Côtes du Roussillon)

Tour St.-Martin (Minervois)

Château de la Tuilerie (Costières de Nimes)

Bernard-Claude Vidal (Faugères)

* * (AVERAGE PRODUCERS)

Domaine des Bories (Corbières)

Domaine du Bosc (L'Hérault)

Domaine du Bosccaute (L'Hérault)

Château de Cabriac (Corbières)

Domaine de Capion (L'Hérault)

Domaine de Coujan (VDP)

Château L'Espigne (Fitou)

Château Étang des Colombes Cuvée Tradition (Corbières)

Domaine de Fontsainte (Corbières)

Château de Grezan (Faugères)

Château Hélène (VDP)

Château de Jau (Côtes du Roussillon)

Domaine des Jougla Cuvée Tradition (St.-Chinian)

Domaine des Jougla Cuvée White Label (St.-Chinian)

Château de Lascaux (Coteaux du Languedoc)

Domaine de la Lecugne (Minervois)

Domaine de Mayranne (Minervois)

Château Milhau-Lacugue (St.-Chinian)

Château La Mission Le Vignon (Côtes du Roussillon)

Caves de Mont Tauch (Fitou)

Domaine de Montmarin (Côtes de Thongue)

Château de Nouvelles (Fitou)

Château de Paraza (Minervois)

Cuvée Claude Parmentier (Fitou)

Château Pech-Rédon (Coteaux du Languedoc)

Domaine Perrière Les Amandiers (Corbières)

Qrmand de Villeneuve (Côtes du Roussillon)

Château de Queribus (Corbières)

Domaine de la Rictorie (Banyuls)

Domaine de la Roque (Coteaux du Languedoc)

Château de Roquecourbe (Minervois)

St.-André (L'Hérault)

Château St.-Auriol (Corbières)

Château St.-Laurent (Corbières)

Domaine Ste.-Eulalie (Minervois)

Sarda-Malet (Côtes du Roussillon)

Domaine du Tauch (Fitou)

Domaine de Villemajou (Corbières)

Château de Villerambert-Julien (Minervois)

Caves de Vins de Roquebrun (St.-Chinian)

Selected Tasting Notes

DOMAINE L'AIGUELIÈRE-MONTPEYROUS* * * *
1989 Coteaux du Languedoc   A   89

I had both the 1988 and 1989 wines from this up-and-coming star from the Coteaux du Languedoc. Made from old vines of Syrah and Cabernet Sauvignon, this offering is a splendidly rich, full-bodied wine with 10–15 or more years of aging potential. It reminded me of the superb wine produced by the Domaine de Trevallon in the Coteaux du Baux. The 1988, if you can still find it, is much more developed and evolved than the 1989, which is an impressive wine, with an opaque, deep ruby/purple color, a huge nose of ripe cassis, licorice, and herbs, and a long, concentrated, full-bodied taste. The finish is long, moderately tannic, and impressive. The 1989 should be at its best by 1993–1994 and continue to evolve gracefully for at least a decade. A name to watch!

CHÂTEAU DE BLOMAC* * *
1990 Cuvée Tradition   A   86

This wine exhibits an attractive, spicy, black raspberry–scented nose as well as rich, round, medium-bodied, supple flavors that display good extraction and balance. There is some heady alcohol in the velvety finish. Drink this delicious wine over the next 1–2 years.

CHÂTEAU DU CAMPUGET* * */* * * *
1990 Costières de Nimes   A   86

If you liked the chewy, spicy, fleshy 1989 from this estate, you are going to love the 1990. This innovative red wine blend (made from 15% Merlot, 20% Syrah, 25% Cabernet Sauvignon, and the rest Mourvèdre) has a dark ruby color, a big, in-your-face, ripe, fruity, spicy, plummy nose, lush, supple, velvety flavors, and a smooth-as-silk finish. This is the kind of wine to throw in the refrigerator for 20 minutes and drink as you would a Beaujolais. It is absolutely delicious.

DOMAINE CAPION* * *

1990 Vins du Pays d'Oc New Oak Cuvée	A	87
1990 Vins du Pays d'Oc Syrah	A	87

Domaine Capion has impressed me in the past, and the 1990 Syrah offers an excellent color, a big, smoky, herb- and black cherry–scented nose, ripe, medium- to full-bodied flavors, and a long, spicy, softly tannic finish. It should drink well for at least 4–5 years. Some readers might be surprised by the fact that I enjoyed the regular *cuvée* as much as the prestige *cuvée* aged in small oak barrels. The 1990 New Oak Cuvée is a more ambitiously styled wine, yet it is not any better. There are aromas of new oak and vanillin in the nose, as well as more structure and tannin because of the wood. Perhaps with aging the proprietor's decision to employ expensive new oak will justify the higher price.

DANIEL DOMERGUE* * * */* * * * *

1990 Minervois Campagne de Centeilles	A	87
1990 Minervois Clos Centeilles	B	89

Domergue has built a cult following in what is becoming an increasingly fashionable appellation for top-notch wines at bargain-basement prices—Minervois. These wines are so fashionable in France that the newest vintages are sold out immediately. I inserted both of these offerings in several blind tastings against some *négociant* 1989 red burgundies, and Domergue's wines were ranked surprisingly high. The 1990 Minervois Campagne de Centeilles exhibits a beautiful deep ruby/purple color, a big nose of herbs, black fruits, and spices, excellent depth, good acidity, soft tannins, and an elegant, graceful finish. The 1990 Minervois Clos Centeilles is even richer, with vivid purity, some evidence of spicy new oak, medium to full body, and a long, intense finish. These beautifully pure, hand-crafted wines will benefit from 2–3 years of cellaring.

CHÂTEAU DES ESTANILLES* * * *

1990 Faugères	B	90
1990 Faugères Cuvée Syrah	B	90

Made from 100% Mourvèdre and aged in new oak casks for 9 months, the 1990 Faugères offers an intensely aromatic, leathery, blackcurrant- and licorice-scented nose, amazingly ripe, rich, concentrated flavors, good acidity, firm tannins, and a smashingly long finish. Although approachable now, it should age well for up to a decade. The 1990 Faugères Cuvée Syrah, also made from 100% Syrah and aged for 14 months in new oak casks, is the poor man's Guigal Côte Rôtie La Mouline. It exhibits the same big, smoky, bacon fat, curranty nose as a fine Côte Rôtie. There is splendid ripeness and richness, medium to full body, and an explosively rich, long, gamey finish. In a blind tasting I would never think this wine was from Languedoc-Roussillon.

CHÂTEAU FABAS* * *

1988 Minervois Cuvée Alexandre		87

I have tasted only one vintage of this producer's wines, but wow, I was impressed. This *cuvée spéciale* was aged in small oak barrels and made with an exceptionally high percentage of Mourvèdre (60%), Syrah (30%), and Grenache (10%). The wine has a deep, almost opaque ruby/purple color, a huge bouquet of roasted herbs and cassis, luscious vanillin-tinged, opulent flavors, plenty of body and glycerin, and a long, heady finish. There is enough stuffing and tannin to warrant cellaring another 3–5 years.

CHÂTEAU HAUT-FABRÈGES* * */* * * *

1989 Faugères	A	87
1989 Faugères Cuvée Sélectionée	A	88

The 164 acres of the Haut-Fabrèges vineyards, owned by the Saur family, are all planted on south-facing slopes in the foothills of the Cévennes. Their average yield rarely exceeds 36 hectoliters per hectare, and their choice of red wine grapes includes 38% Grenache, 18% Cinsault, 20% Carignan, 14% Syrah, and 10% Mourvèdre. Their top *cuvée,* called Cuvée Sélectionée, is aged in oak and represents a blend of 40% Grenache, 30% Syrah, and 30% Mourvèdre. These offerings were among the stars in my tastings of the Languedoc-Roussillon wines. The 1989 Faugères is a deliciously ripe, luscious wine with gobs of plummy black fruits, a round, generously endowed, satiny texture, and a smooth, heady finish. It is all a bistro or country wine of France should be, and its purity and concentration make it a top choice for drinking over the next 3–4 years. The 1989 Faugères Cuvée Sélectionée is one of the best dry red table wines I have ever tasted from this region. There is a beautiful balance between the new oak and the complex, rich, full-bodied fruitiness. This intense wine is a knockout in the mouth, with impressive extraction of flavors, enough acidity to provide grip and focus, and an explosively rich, long finish. Like so many of the better wines I tasted from this region, it is a sensational bargain. Drink it over the next 5–6 years.

DOMAINE DE L'HORTUS* * * */* * * * *

1990 Coteaux du Languedoc	B	92

Only 2,300 bottles were produced of this 60% Mourvèdre/40% Syrah blend aged 14 months in new oak casks. The opaque black/ruby color is followed by a huge nose of black cherries, Provençal herbs, spices, and vanillin. There is super richness, beautiful definition and focus, and a long, moderately tannic, intense finish. This is a dazzling wine for the price.

MAS AMIEL* * * *

1990 Maury	B	86
1981 Maury Cuvée Spéciale	C	90
1979 Maury Cuvée Spéciale	C	90
1985 Maury Réserve	B	87
1983 Maury Réserve	C	90

N.V. Maury 15 Ans d'Age	C	92
N.V. Maury Vin Doux Naturel	B	87

This domaine, run by Charles Dupuy and encompassing over 326 acres of vineyards, sells virtually all of its production to private clients in Europe. Only 5% of the domaine's decadently rich, fortified wines are exports, which is a shame given their high quality and surprisingly modest prices. Mas Amiel is located inland in the appellation of Maury, west of Perpignan, surrounded by what is undoubtedly some of the most breathtaking scenery in this part of France. All of these offerings are fortified wines, meaning that 5%–10% pure alcohol has been added and the wines macerated after this fortification. Interestingly, the wines are stored in glass demijohns (all of which are 70 liters in size) and kept outside for a year before being moved to large oak *foudres,*where they can then be aged for up to 15 years. The placement of the wines in the frightfully torrid heat is believed to give these wines their particular style and complexity. These fortified wines, which resemble anything from a young vintage port to an older tawny, are made from a blend of 90% Grenache, 5% Macabeu, and 5% Carignan.

Given the current American obsession with avoiding alcohol, calories, and products that provide pleasure, I wonder about the demand for wines such as these (perhaps the most receptive marketplace for these amazing wines are with those who are adventurous or avowedly hedonistic). The general pattern from Mas Amiel is that wines such as the 1990 Maury, a black/ruby/purple wine, are meant to taste like young vintage port. The 1990 Maury is explosively rich and fruity, but hardly complex. No doubt it will last for 15–20 years given its strength and concentration. The Mas Amiel Réserves, which are 7 years old when released, are a good introduction to the distinctive style of the Maury appellation. I prefer the 1983 to the 1985 because it is an older wine and has had more time to develop a bouquet. Both exhibit the slightly oxidized, kinky, exotic nose of chocolate-covered raisins, overripe red fruits, and big, rich, alcoholic, spicy, nutty flavors. They can be cellared for decades or more.

The Cuvée Spéciales are wines that have been aged for at least a decade (1 year in glass demijohns baking in the relentless heat of the Languedoc-Roussillon sun and 9 years in big oak *foudres*). Both the 1981 and 1979 are rich, raisiny, pruny wines that in a blind tasting could easily be confused with 20-year-old, high-class tawny ports. They possess gobs of fruit, super bouquets of chocolate, raisins, and the roasted character that is so much a part of these wines. Given the labor costs, as well as the fact that these wines are aged by the winery 7–10 years before their release, it is hard to understand how the estate can make a profit selling them at such prices.

The best and oldest *cuvée* from Mas Amiel is the 15 Ans d'Age. With 15 years of aging, the fire and power of these fortified wines has been partially tamed and one begins to see, if you can believe it, a degree of elegance and finesse. Yes, the huge bouquet of chocolate, raisins, and roasted black fruits remains very much in evidence, but the exuberance and unbridled strength and headiness has mellowed.

Wines such as these of Mas Amiel, as well as the Banyuls of Dr. Parcé's famous Mas Blanc, must be the last of the unknown greats of France. Certainly great Parisian restaurants, particularly Taillevent, have thought enough of these wines to feature them on their illustrious wine lists. Perhaps that will in-

duce reluctant readers to give these portlike, bargain-priced, distinctive, fortified wines a chance.

MAS DE DAUMAS GASSAC* * * *

1990	C	91
1989	C	90
1988	C	88

This is the most famous *vin de pays* in France. And why shouldn't it be, given
the fact that the widely read French magazine *Gault-Milau* called it the
"Lafite-Rothschild of the Languedoc-Roussillon" area and the London *Times*
claimed it tasted like a "Latour"! Fame came almost instantly once the first
wine was released in 1978. The genius behind this domaine, located 18 miles
west of Monpellier, is Aimé Guibert, who, along with his wife, purchased the
estate in 1970. Told by the late Professor Henri Enjalbert of the University of
Bordeaux that his property was sitting on the very same type of porous soils
that made up the best parts of the Médoc, particularly the estates of Lafite-
Rothschild and Latour, Guibert began planting his estate with a variety of Bordeaux grapes such as Cabernet Sauvignon, Merlot, Cabernet Franc, and
Malbec. I recently did a vertical tasting of every Mas de Daumas Gassac red
made, and none of them were in danger of falling apart. The earlier vintages
were more muscular and have turned out slightly more rustic than I am sure
the proprietor would have preferred, but all have stood the test of time admirably. They still remain rich, full-bodied, impressively constituted big
wines.

The two recent vintages, 1988 and 1989, have sacrificed none of the splendid ripeness and admirable extraction of the earlier wines, yet they have added
a degree of finesse. There is no question that the older age of a vine makes for
a potentially finer wine, and the vineyards of Mas de Daumas Gassac are just
now reaching full maturity. Both the 1988 and 1989 are black/ruby/purple
wines with huge aromas of sweet black fruits, some vanillin from new oak,
herbs, and minerals. In the mouth the 1989 is more opulent and the 1988 more
structured, but both are full-bodied, intensely concentrated wines that can be
drunk in 4–5 years yet should evolve gracefully for 15–20 years. Although
prices have risen, this remains one of the most remarkable nonappellation
wines of France. The fact that it is better than many appellation wines must be
unsettling to the French authorities.

The white wine is also a knockout, but, unlike the red, it must be drunk
within 2–3 years of the vintage. It tastes amazingly like a Condrieu, although
the percentage of Viognier has rarely exceeded 40%. The 1990 white wine is a
blend of 30% Viognier, 30% Chardonnay, 20% Petit Manseng, 5% Muscat,
5% Marsanne, 5% Roussanne, and 5% Bourboulenc. This is an intensely fragrant, seductive wine, with a great deal of fruit, finesse, and complexity. My
experience is that it drinks beautifully for about 2 years and begins a rapid decline in its third year. The 1990 spent 40 days in new oak casks. Unfortunately, only 1,000 cases were made, but it is worth a special effort to find.

Much of the great progress enjoyed by the Languedoc-Roussillon wines in
the 1980s must certainly be attributable to the immense success and laudatory
publicity that Guibert's wines have justifiably received. The public has ac-

cepted them and the critics have swooned over them. Moreover, they appear to be improving with each new vintage. What else can anyone want?

MAS JULLIEN* * * *

1990	Coteaux du Languedoc Blanc	A	85
1990	Coteaux du Languedoc Blanc Les Vignes Oubliées	A	87
1988	Coteaux du Languedoc Les Cailloutis	A	87

The regular white wine offering, the 1990 Blanc, represents the crisp, fresh, floral, fruity style of modern-day white-wine making. Delicious, with depth, charm, and character, it should be consumed over the next year or 2. The 1990 Les Vignes Oubliées is a much richer, deeper-colored, more robust wine that cuts a fuller feel on the palate. Although it is more rustic, it offers more personality, as well as significant body and depth. This *cuvée* requires drinking with food. The 1988 Les Cailloutis is a vividly pure, wonderfully scented wine redolent with aromas of berries and raspberries. Medium bodied, with crisp acidity, and a long, zesty finish, it should drink beautifully for at least 5–6 years.

DR. PARCÉ MAS BLANC* * * */* * * * *

1989	Banyuls Rimage	D	92
1988	Banyuls Rimage	D	94
1986	Banyuls Rimage	C	94
1983	Banyuls Rimage	D	89
N.V.	Banyuls Solera Hors d'Age	D	91
1982	Banyuls Vieilles Vignes	D	92
1977	Banyuls Vieilles Vignes	D	90
1976	Banyuls Vieilles Vignes	D	93
1988	Collioure Cosprons Levants	C	86
1988	Collioure Les Piloums	C	86

It is probably difficult for Americans to understand that Dr. Parcé's 42-acre estate, which he runs with his son, produces wines that are legendary in France. In fact, many European connoisseurs are convinced that Dr. Parcé's Banyuls offer the same level of excitement as a great first-growth Bordeaux or Burgundy Grand Cru. Dr. Parcé, who is largely responsible for the creation of the *appellation contrôlée* status for Collioure in 1971, produces two *cuvées* of Collioure from his steep, terraced vineyards that overlook the Mediterranean. His vineyards for these two wines are planted with 60% Mourvèdre, 30% Syrah, and 10% Counoise. The results are intensely rich, spicy, exotic wines, with a great deal of flavor, density, and an almost wild and savage character that might be too much for neophytes to comprehend. Nevertheless, both the 1988 Collioures are loaded with fruit and are ideal choices for the spicy, aromatic, bistro cooking that is the rage in this country. Unfortunately, only 1,500 cases of his Collioures are produced.

Dr. Parcé is more renowned for his rich, fortified Banyuls, of which three *cuvées* are usually available. I have never had anything other than a superb

Banyuls from Dr. Parcé and have often tasted them side by side with some of my favorite mature vintage ports and 20- and 30-year-old tawnys. Although it may sound unlikely, I have a strong preference for the Banyuls. Banyuls is also the perfect wine to have with chocolate dishes, as I found out over a decade ago when Monsieur Durrbach of the Domaine de Trevallon and I dined together at his local restaurant, the Oustau de Baumanière, downing an assortment of Dr. Parcé's Banyuls with some exquisite chocolate desserts.

Younger vintages of Banyuls tend to be more explosively rich and fruity. Dr. Parcé is renowned for his vintage port–style Banyuls that are bottled early with a vintage and the designation *rimage.* They are meant to evolve and age in the bottle, which they do exceptionally well. The 1989 is a very rich, portlike wine with gorgeous extract levels and a huge, black raspberry–, licorice–, and tar-scented nose. It can be cellared for 20–30 years. I do not understand why the 1988 and 1986 are less expensive. Both are more intense, more powerful and concentrated wines. The 1988 reminds me of chocolate-covered candy. Opaque dark purple, with a super nose and blockbuster flavors, this full-bodied powerhouse should be at its best between the mid-1990s and the first several decades of the next century. The 1986 was similar in stature but did exhibit more tarlike, herb, and chocolate aromas in its bouquet. The intoxicating perfume of the 1983 Banyuls, which offers up aromas of chocolate, raisins, prunes, smoked nuts, and herbs, is something to behold. In the mouth there is that opulence and round, generous texture that clearly indicates this is a fortified wine with an alcohol content of 16%–17%. Most of these vintage-dated Banyuls are aged 8–10 years before they are released. The Cuvée Vieilles Vignes, of which the 1982, 1977, and 1976 are the current releases, seems always to have slightly more depth. These wines improve immensely after their release, which is normally after 7–10 years of aging in Dr. Parcé's cellars. I have bought and drunk cases of the great 1969, 1975, 1978, and 1982. Dr. Parcé and his fans claim that as rich as these wines are, they also work well with game and extremely strong cheeses. The rarest, most expensive, and perhaps most profound *cuvée* is the Solera Hors d'Age, which is stored in cask but kept in the open air, intentionally exposed to the enormous temperature extremes of this part of France. Evaporation continues to take place and younger wine is used to top off the *cuvée,* thus the designation *solera* on the label, indicating the same system of producing wine as used in Spain for that country's renowned sherries. *Cuvées* of Hors d'Age will never indicate a vintage, but they are incredibly rich and sweet and clearly best if served at the end of a meal.

Virtually every 3-star French restaurant has a selection of Dr. Parcé's Banyuls. Although many of these restaurateurs feel compelled to place internationally recognized superstar Bordeaux and burgundies on their wine lists, it has always seemed to me that Dr. Parcé's Banyuls and Collioures are stocked because of the restaurant's love and admiration for these distinctive, highly individualized products.

PRIEURÉ DE ST.-JEAN DE BEBIAN* * * *

1989	C	92
1988	C	89

Proprietor Alain Roux is one of the shining stars of the Languedoc-Roussillon region. He has 59 acres entitled to the appellation Coteaux du Languedoc. His vineyards are situated on the hillsides north of the ancient village of Pézénas, which insiders tell me will be France's next St.-Paul de Vence. Real estate speculators might want to take note. The vineyard is comprised of 30% Grenache, 17% Syrah, and 17% Mourvèdre. The remaining acreage is planted with Counoise, Muscardin, and Cinsault, essentially the same grape varietals as used in Châteauneuf-du-Pape. The soil, which has a preponderance of the football-size stones (a legacy of the Ice Age) found in Châteauneuf-du-Pape, is considered ideal for these varietals. Roux produces a wine with every bit as much extraction and character as the more renowned Mas de Daumas Gassac. Although his estate is not nearly as famous, his wines can be superb. It is interesting that he obtains such quality without using any of the fashionable Cabernet Sauvignon in the blend.

The 1989 is a blockbuster wine, opaque black/purple in color, with a huge bouquet of crushed red and black fruits, minerals, roasted herbs, and spices. In the mouth there is astonishing concentration, relatively low acidity, but staggering richness and length. It should be drinkable by the mid-1990s and last for 10–20 years thereafter. The 1988 is more streamlined but still a relatively big, spicy, rich, complex wine, with a great deal of extraction, higher acidity, and lower tannins. It will be at its best between 1994 and 2005.

Not surprisingly, Roux is a great friend and fan of Gérard Chave in Hermitage, the Perrin brothers of Beaucastel in Châteauneuf-du-Pape, and the idiosyncratic Jacques Reynaud of Château Rayas. Roux believes, perhaps correctly, that his wines merit comparison with these Rhône Valley legends. There is no doubt that he clearly deserves more attention for his brilliant wine-making efforts. This is another superstar of the Midi.

PROVENCE

La Vie en Rose . . . et rouge!

It is easy to regard Provence as just the dramatic playground for the world's rich and famous, for few wine lovers seem to realize that this vast viticultural region in southern France is at least 2,600 years old. For centuries tourists traveling through Provence have been seduced by the aromatic and flavorful thirst-quenching rosés that seem to complement the distinctive cuisine of the region so well. Yet today Provence is an exciting and diverse viticultural region that is turning out not only extremely satisfying rosés, but immensely promising red wines and a few encouraging whites.

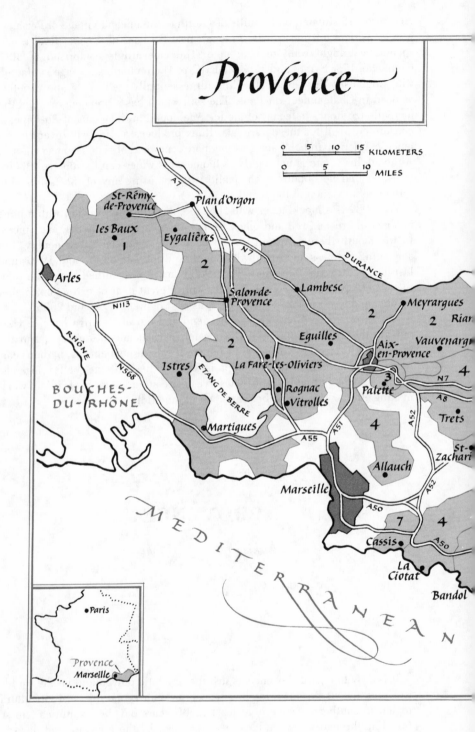

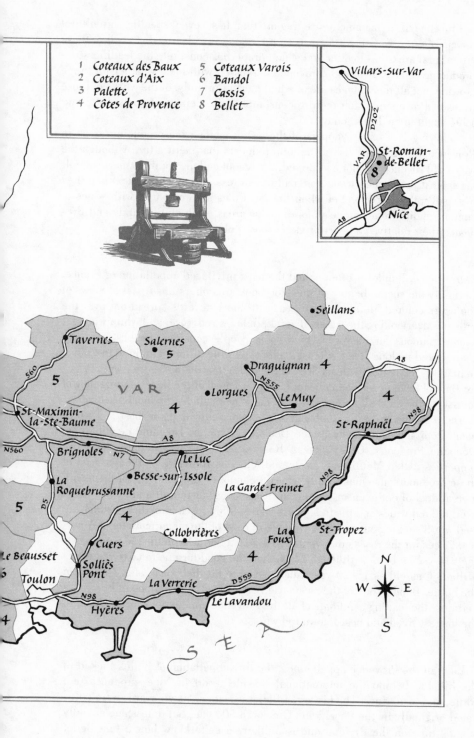

1 Coteaux des Baux
2 Coteaux d'Aix
3 Palette
4 Côtes de Provence
5 Coteaux Varois
6 Bandol
7 Cassis
8 Bellet

Villars-Sur-Var

St-Roman-
de-Bellet

Nice

Seillans

Tavernes
Salernes
5

VAR
4

Draguignan 4
Lorgues
Le Muy

4

St-Maximin-
la-Ste-Baume

St-Raphaël

Brignoles
Le Luc

La
Roquebrussanne
Besse-sur-Issole

La Garde-Freinet

5

4
Collobrières
La
Foux
St-Tropez

Cuers
4
Le Beausset
Solliès
Pont
La Verrerie
Toulon
Hyères
Le Lavandou

4

SEA

N
W   E
S

Provence is a mammoth-size region that has seven specific viticultural areas. The best way to get a grasp on the region is to learn what each of these viticultural areas has to offer and which properties constitute the leading wine-producing estates. Although Provence is blessed with ideal weather for grape growing, not all the vintages are of equal merit. Certainly, of the white and rosé wines of Provence, which require consumption in their youth, only 1992 and 1991 ought to be drunk today.

Following is a brief synopsis of the seven major wine-producing areas in Provence, along with a list of the top producers that merit a try. Although the wines of Provence are not overpriced, the recent collapse of the American dollar against the French franc has made them less attractive in price than they were several years ago. Yet when the top wines are compared with wines of similar quality from France's more famous areas, such as Burgundy and Bordeaux, their relative value as French wines is obvious.

Bandol

In France, Bandol is often called the most privileged appellation of France. Certainly the scenic beauty of this storybook area offers unsurpassed views of the azure-colored Mediterranean Sea, with the vineyards spread out over the hillsides overlooking the water. Bandol produces red, rosé, and white wines. It is most famous for its rosé, which some people consider the best made in France, and its long-lived, intense, tannic red wine, which is unique in France in that it is made from at least 50% of the little-known Mourvèdre grape. Prices for Bandol have never been cheap, largely because of the never-ending flow of tourists to the area who buy up most of the wine made by the local producers.

There seems to be no doubt among connoisseurs that the best red wines come from such producers as the Domaine Tempier, Domaine de Pibarnon, Domaine Pradeaux, Ott's Château Romassan, Château Vannières, and two properties called Moulin des Coste and Mas des Rouvière. Although most of these producers also make white wines, I cannot recommend any of them with a great deal of enthusiasm, as they always seem to taste dull and heavy. However, the red wines and the fresh, personality-filled rosés from these estates are well worth seeking out and are available in most of the major markets in America. Prices for the rosés now average $10–$15 a bottle, with the red wines costing $15–$25 a bottle. Although I have had the good fortune to taste red wines of Bandol as old as 15–20 years, most seem to hit their peak after 6 years in the bottle. Bandol, one of the most strictly regulated appellations in France, is certainly the leading candidate of all the Provence appellations for producer of the longest-lived and best-known red wines.

Bellet

Like all the Provence appellations, the tiny appellation of Bellet, tucked in the hillside behind the international seaside resort of Nice, produces red, white, and rosé wines. The history of Bellet is rich, as its vineyards were cultivated originally by the Phoenician Greeks in 500 B.C., but unless one actually spends time on the Riviera, one is unlikely ever to know how a fine Bellet tastes. Most of the wine produced in this microappellation of 100-plus acres never makes it outside of France, as the local restaurant demand is insatiable.

Only a handful of producers are making wine here, and the very best is the Château de Crémat, owned by the Bagnis family, a splendid estate of 50 acres that produces nearly 6,000 cases of wine. It is imported to the United States, but because of its high price ($15–$20 a bottle), few consumers know how it really tastes. Château de Crémat is a unique estate in Provence in that the white wine is of extremely high quality, and the local connoisseurs claim the rosé and red wines are the best made in this part of the French Riviera. The best recent vintages have been the 1990, 1989, and 1988, but I have tasted the red wines from Château de Crémat back through 1978, and they have shown no signs of decline. However, the wines of Bellet remain esoteric, enjoyed only by a handful of people with prices that seem steep for the quality.

Cassis

The tiny village of Cassis, located on the western end of France's famous Côte d'Azur, is one of the most charming fishing villages on the Riviera. Located on a secluded bay, it is dwarfed by the surrounding steep limestone cliffs. Hordes of tourists frequent the area, insuring that most of the wine made here is consumed at the local bistros along with the area's ubiquitous *soupe de poisson*. Although this appellation makes red wine as well as rosé, it is white wine that has made Cassis famous. The red wine tends to be heavy and uninteresting, and although the rosé can be good, it never seems to approach the quality level of its nearby neighbor, Bandol. The white, which is often a blend of little-known grapes such as Ugni Blanc, Clairette, and Bourboulenc, is a spicy, fleshy wine that often seems unattractive by itself, but when served with the rich, aromatic seafood dishes of the region, it takes on a character of its own. The estates of Cassis producing the best white wines include Clos Ste.-Magdelaine, La Ferme Blanche, and Domaine du Bagnol. Prices average $10–$15 for these white wines, which are not bad values, but they have a distinct character that requires fairly rich, spicy fish courses to complement their unique personality.

Coteaux d'Aix-en-Provence

This gigantic viticultural region, which extends primarily north and west of Aix-en-Provence, has numerous small estates making acceptable but generally overpriced wines that require drinking within the first 7–8 years of their lives. However, two of the very finest red wine producers in Provence are located here: Domaine Trevallon and the better-known Château Vignelaure. Both producers specialize in red wine, capable of aging 15–20 years, produced from a blend of two great red wine grapes, Cabernet Sauvignon and Syrah. Other estates have tried to imitate the wines made by Trevallon and Vignelaure, but no one has yet succeeded.

The Domaine Trevallon is owned by the ruggedly handsome Eloi Durrbach, who carved his vineyard out of the forbidding and lunarlike landscape near the medieval ghost town of Les Baux. Its first vintage was only in 1978, but that has been followed by other successful vintages that have produced compellingly rich, intense wines with enormously complex bouquets and significant concentration, as well as tremendous aging potential. The most recent vintage to be released is the 1990, a fabulously rich wine with a cascade of silky, concentrated cassis and blackberry fruit intermingled with scents of wild thyme.

Not surprisingly, proprietor Durrbach apprenticed at Château Vignelaure, the other great estate of the Coteaux d'Aix-en-Provence. Vignelaure's wines, although not as bold and striking as Trevallon's, are still elegant expressions of Provençal winemaking at its best. They are widely available in America.

Côtes du Lubéron

Virtually all the wine made in the Côtes du Lubéron is produced by one of the many cooperatives that dominate this region's production. However, this area, which is located in the northern area of Provence near the villages of Apt and Pertuis, has immense potential. The best estate in the Côtes du Lubéron is the Château de Mille, run with great meticulousness by Conrad Pinatel. However, there is also a new and extremely promising estate called Château Val-Joanis, launched in 1978 with an initial investment of $6 million to construct a 494-acre vineyard and château near the town of Pertuis. The Chancel family, great believers in the idea that top-quality wines will ultimately be produced from the Côtes du Lubéron, is behind this extraordinary investment. At present they are making a good, fresh white wine, a delicious, fragrant rosé, and an increasingly serious red wine. All sell for under $12 a bottle, making them outstanding values.

Côtes de Provence

The Côtes de Provence is the best-known and largest viticultural region of Provence, with just under 50,000 acres planted in vines. This appellation is famous for the oceans of dry, flavorful rosé wine that tourists gulp down with great thirst-quenching pleasure. There are many fine producers of Côtes de Provence wines, but the best include the very famous Domaines Ott, which is available on virtually every restaurant wine list in southern France, the Domaine Gavoty, the Domaine Richeaume, and the Domaine Saint-André de Figuière. All these estates, with the exception of the Domaine Richeaume, produce outstanding rosé wine. The Domaine Richeaume specializes in intense, rich, complex red wines that are surpassed only by the aforementioned wines from the Domaine Trevallon and Château Vignelaure. In addition, one of the best white wines produced in Provence is made by the Domaine Saint-André de Figuière. All these wines are currently available in most of the major metropolitan markets in the United States, but they are not inexpensive. The Ott wines, no doubt because of their fame in France, sell for fairly hefty prices, but I have never heard anyone complain regarding the quality of their superb rosés and underrated red wines. Certainly the white wine made by Saint-André de Figuière is not overpriced and is an especially fine representative example of just how good a white wine from Provence can be. Saint-André de Figuière also makes a delicious, supple red wine that is well worth trying. Should you find a bottle of the Domaine Richeaume's red wine, made by a fanatical German by the name of Henning Hoesch, it is well worth $15 to taste a bottle of Provence's finest examples of red wine. His serious, densely colored red wines are loaded with fruit, power, and tannin and seem easily capable of aging for over a decade, as they are usually made from a blend of Cabernet Sauvignon and Syrah, with some Grenache added at times.

Palette

Palette is a tiny appellation just to the east of Aix-en-Provence that in actuality consists of only one serious winemaking estate, Château Simone. Run by René Rougier, this tiny estate of 37 acres produces a surprisingly long-lived and complex red wine, a fairly oaky, old-style rosé wine, and a muscular, full-bodied white wine that behaves as if it were from the northern Rhône Valley. Simone's wines are not inexpensive, but they do age extremely well and have always had a loyal following in France.

Provence is one of France's oldest yet least-known viticultural regions. It remains largely unchartered territory for wine consumers. However, a taste of the best rosés, white wines, and red wines from its bold and innovative new vineyards is certain to cause many consumers to consider Provence more than just an expensive playground for the rich.

The Basics

TYPES OF WINE

A huge quantity of bone-dry, fragrant, crisp rosés is made as well as rather neutral but fleshy white wines and ever higher-quality red wines.

GRAPE VARIETIES

For red wines, the traditional grape varieties have been Grenache, Carignan, Syrah, Mourvèdre, and Cinsault. Recently, however, a great deal of Cabernet Sauvignon has been planted in the Côtes de Provence and Coteaux d'Aix-en-Provence. The most interesting red wines are generally those with elevated levels of either Syrah, Mourvèdre, or Cabernet Sauvignon. For white wines, Ugni Blanc, Clairette, Marsanne, Bourboulenc, and to a lesser extent Semillon, Sauvignon Blanc, and Chardonnay are used.

FLAVORS

There is immense variation because of the number of microclimates and different grapes used. Most red wines have vivid red fruit bouquets that are more intense in the Coteaux des Baux than elsewhere. In Bandol the smells of tree bark, leather, and currants dominate. The white wines seem neutral and clumsy when served without food, but when drunk with the spicy Provençal cuisine, they take on life.

AGING POTENTIAL

Rosés

1–3 years

White Wines

1–3 years, except for that of Château Simone, which can last for 5–10 years

Red Wines

5–12 years, often longer for the red wines of Bandol and specific wines such as Domaine Trevallon and Château Vignelaure

OVERALL QUALITY LEVEL

The level of quality has increased and in general is well above average, but consumers must remember to buy and drink the rosé and white wines only when they are less than 3 years old.

MOST IMPORTANT INFORMATION TO KNOW

Master the types of wines of each appellation of Provence, as well as the names of the top producers.

1993–1994 BUYING STRATEGY

There is a bevy of top vintages from which to choose, but the problem in America is finding these wines. Except for some of the Côtes du Ventoux wines, most wholesalers and retailers find that the wines have to be hand-sold and therefore are reluctant to stock them. Vintages of choice are 1989 and 1990. Both 1991 and 1992 are spotty, except for the rosés.

RATING PROVENCE'S BEST PRODUCERS

* * * * * (OUTSTANDING PRODUCERS)

Luigi–Clos Nicrosi (Corsica)
Château Pradeaux (Bandol)
Domaine Tempier La Migoua (Bandol)
Domaine Tempier La Tourtine (Bandol)

Domaine de Trevallon (Coteaux d'Aix-en-Provence)
Château Val-Joanis Cuvée Les Griottes (Côtes du Lubéron)

* * * * (EXCELLENT PRODUCERS)

Domaine Canorgue (Côtes du Lubéron)
Domaine Champagna (Côtes du Ventoux)
Château de Crémat (Bellet)
Commanderie de Bargemone (Côtes de Provence)
Commanderie de Peyrassol (Côtes de Provence)
Domaine de Féraud (Côtes de Provence)* * * */* * * * *
Domaine Le Gallantin (Bandol)
Domaine de la Garnaude Cuvée Santane (Côtes de Provence)
Domaines Gavoty (Côtes de Provence)
Domaine Hauvette (Coteaux d'Aix-les-Baux)
Domaine de L'Hermitage (Bandol)
Mas de la Dame (Coteaux d'Aix-en-Provence)
Mas de Gourgonnier (Coteaux d'Aix-en-Provence)

Mas de la Rouvière (Bandol)
Château de Mille (Côtes du Lubéron)
Moulin des Costes (Bandol)
Domaines Ott—all cuvées (Bandol and Côtes de Provence)
Domaine de Pibarnon (Bandol)
Domaine Ray-Jane (Bandol)
Domaine Richeaume (Côtes de Provence)
Domaine de Rimauresq (Côtes de Provence)
Saint-André de Figuière (Côtes de Provence)
Domaine St.-Jean de Villecroze (Coteaux Varois)
Château Ste.-Roseline (Côtes de Provence)
Château Simone (Palette)
Domaine Tempier (Bandol)
Château Val-Joanis (Côtes du Lubéron)
Château Vannières (Bandol)
La Vieille Ferme (Côtes du Lubéron)

* * * (GOOD PRODUCERS)

Domaine du Bagnol (Cassis)
Château Barbeyrolles (Côtes de Provence)
Château Bas (Coteaux d'Aix)
La Bastide Blanche (Bandol)

Domaine de Beaupré (Coteaux d'Aix-en-Provence)
Domaine La Bernarde (Côtes de Provence)
Domaine Caguelouf (Bandol)

Château de Calissanne (Coteaux d'Aix)

Castel Roubine (Côtes de Provence)

Cave Cooperative d'Aleria-Réserve du Président (Corsica)

Clos Catitoro (Corsica)

Clos Ste.-Magdelaine (Cassis)

Domaine de Curebreasse (Côtes de Provence)

Château Ferry-Lacombe (Côtes de Provence)

Domaine Fiumicicoli (Corsica)

Château de Fonscolombe (Coteaux d'Aix-en-Provence)

Domaine Frégate (Bandol)

Hervé Goudard (Côtes de Provence)

Château de l'Isolette (Côtes du Lubéron)

Domaine de Lafran-Veyrolles (Bandol)

Domaine La Laidière (Bandol)

Domaine Lecci (Corsica)

Domaine du Loou (Coteaux Varois)

Château Maravenne (Côtes de Provence)

Mas de Cadenet (Côtes de Provence)

Mas Ste.-Berthe (Coteaux d'Aix)

Domaine de la Noblesse (Bandol)

Domaine Orenga (Corsica)

Domaine de Paradis (Coteaux d'Aix)

Domaine Peraldi (Corsica)

Château de Rasque (Côtes de Provence)

Château Real-Martin (Côtes de Provence)

Château St.-Esteve (Côtes de Provence)

Château St.-Jean Cuvée Natasha (Côtes de Provence)

Château Sainte-Anne (Bandol)

Domaine des Salettes (Bandol)

Domaine de la Sanglière (Côtes de Provence)

Domaine de Terrebrune (Bandol)

Domaine de Torraccia (Corsica)

Toussaint Luigi–Muscatella (Corsica)

Château Vignelaure (Coteaux d'Aix-en-Provence)

Selected Tasting Notes

DOMAINE CHAMPAGNA* * * *

1990 Côtes du Ventoux   A   89

This is a sensational wine from the Côtes du Ventoux. Deep ruby/purple in color, it offers a huge bouquet of crushed black raspberries, smoke, and minerals. In the mouth there are lavish quantities of opulent fruit, plenty of body, and enough tannin and acid to provide the necessary framework. Although hard to resist gulping down, it is capable of at least 4–5 years of cellaring. This wine warrants purchasing by the case.

DOMAINE DE PIBARNON* * * *

1990 Bandol Rouge   C   93

This is one of the finest young Bandol reds I have tasted. The color is saturated dark ruby/purple, and the nose offers up intense aromas of cassis, olives, and spicy new oak. There is extravagant richness as well as layer upon layer of fruit, good structure, and a whoppingly long, extremely well delineated finish. This magnificent Bandol should age effortlessly for 10–15 or more years.

DOMAINE DE TREVALLON* * * * *

1990 Coteaux d'Aix-en-Provence   C   94

Five years ago in my book *The Wines of the Rhône Valley and Provence* I stated that "Domaine de Trevallon was one of the greatest discoveries in my life." Since the late 1970s I have been following the Durrbach family's wines, made near the medieval ghost town of Les Baux in the phantomlike, weird Val d'Enfer (Valley of Hell). The vineyard is planted with 60% Cabernet Sauvignon and 40% Syrah. I am convinced the 1990 is the best Trevallon to date. It possesses an opaque purple color, a huge nose of minerals and cassis, full-bodied, lusciously rich, beautifully balanced flavors, adequate acidity, moderate tannin, and plenty of glycerin. The finish is long and exhilarating. Still an infant in terms of its development, this wine already makes a gorgeous drink. Based on previous efforts, it should last for a decade or more—if you can keep your hands off it. The wine was bottled unfiltered, so expect considerable sediment to develop.

CHÂTEAU VAL-JOANIS* * * */* * * * *

1988 Côtes du Lubéron	A	87
1990 Côtes du Lubéron Cuvée Griottes	A	89

When I was doing research for my book on the Rhône Valley and Provence in the mid-1980s, I visited Château Val-Joanis in the beautiful Côtes du Lubéron and was amazed at the huge sculpturing of the mountainsides that the Chancel family had done in order to plant their vineyards. It was easy to see that as the vines became older, this would become one of the leading domaines of the region, largely because of Chancel's unwavering commitment to excellence. This 1988 vindicates his belief that the Syrah grape will bring fame to the Côtes du Lubéron. Although the 1988 regular *cuvée* tastes like a lighter-style Côte Rôtie, it costs $15–$20 less a bottle. The super bouquet of smoky bacon fat and raspberries is followed by a soft, medium-bodied, lushly textured wine with gobs of fruit. The fine satiny-smooth finish is also a treat. The wine is absolutely delicious, and the price makes it one of the great red wine bargains currently in the marketplace. I would opt for drinking it over the next 3–4 years, although I suspect it will keep longer where well stored.

The smashing 1990 was bottled unfined and unfiltered at the request of the American importer. The result is a wine with a huge, spicy, black cherry–scented nose, full-bodied, superconcentrated, supple flavors, and a long, ripe, concentrated finish. It reminds me of a top-notch Châteauneuf-du-Pape. This dazzling wine should drink well for at least 7–8 years.

LA VIEILLE FERME* * * *

1990 Côtes du Lubéron Blanc	A	85
1990 Côtes du Rhône Blanc Gold Label	A	86
1990 Côtes du Rhône Gold Label	A	86
1990 Côtes du Ventoux	A	86

The *négociant* wines of La Vieille Ferme are made by Jean-Pierre Perrin, the coproprietor of the renowned Château Beaucastel. They have consistently represented great values, so it is not surprising that their 1990s are extremely well made wines. The 1990 Côtes du Lubéron Blanc represents an innovative blend of Grenache Blanc, Roussanne, and Ugni Blanc. It offers up an attractive crisp, floral nose, dry, medium-bodied flavors, and refreshing zestiness in its lemony, citrusy finish. The white 1990 Côtes du Rhône Gold Label is made from 100% Bourboulenc. Not surprisingly, it is a richer, fuller, fleshier wine, with a floral- (roses?) and honey-scented nose, full-bodied flavors, good acidity, and excellent purity and freshness. Both of these wines should be drunk over the next year.

With respect to the red wines, the 1990 Côtes du Ventoux, a blend of 60% Grenache, 20% Syrah, 15% Mourvèdre, and 5% Cinsault, is richly fruity and supple, with great color, an excellent bouquet of cassis and herbs, and a long, tasty, round finish. Because it is perfect for casual sipping, restaurants would be smart to use it as a house wine given its wide commercial appeal. The 1990 Côtes du Rhône Gold Label, a serious blend of 40% Grenache, 20% Mourvèdre, 10% Syrah, 10% Cinsault, and the rest various other Rhône varietals, is a surprisingly big, bold, dramatically flavored, spicy, berry-scented wine, with admirable intensity, soft tannins, a heady alcohol and glycerin content, and a robust, spicy finish. I would not be surprised to see this wine evolve even more complexity and character over the next 4–5 years. By the way, should you run across any of the 1989s from La Vieille Ferme, they, too, are still drinking well and merit consideration.

Corsica

I have included this wild, savage, yet remarkably beautiful island in the chapter on Provence because the quality of its wines has increased significantly. There are several Corsican wines that should not be missed.

Unquestionably the finest wine in Corsica is made by Toussaint Luigi from his vineyard called Clos Nicrosi, near Rogliano. He makes a full-bodied, dry white wine with a peachy, apricot, nutty nose that is reminiscent of a white Hermitage. But the real joy from this estate is the Muscat called Muscatella. It is always offered in a nonvintage blend, and I have consistently rated it between 90 and 94. One of the most decadent, well-balanced, sweet Muscats made in the world, it offers a strong reason for consumers to take a look at Corsica.

Corsica is also capable of making some spectacular, inexpensive red wines. One of the best is the Réserve du Président made by the excellent cooperative called Cave Cooperative d'Aleria. A blend of Merlot, Grenache, Syrah, Cabernet Sauvignon, and Nieluccio (a varietal indigenous to Corsica), it is a medium- to full-bodied, deliciously fruity, exuberant wine that at $5 a bottle must be included among the world's greatest wine bargains. The coop released a delicious 1992 Chardonnay in summer 1993 for $5 a bottle—an amazing buy.

Other Corsican domaines to be taken seriously include the Domaine de Torraccia in Lecci de Porto Ecchio, Domaine Fiumicicoli and Clos Catitoro in Sartene, Domaine Peraldi in Mezzavia, Domaine Leccia in Poggio d'Oletta, and Domaine Orenga in Patrimonio. All of these estates tend to make regular cuvées of red, white, and rosé wines, the dry rosés being the best, followed by the reds. Some domaines also offer reserve cuvées that see some time in small oak barrels. The quality of these reserve wines has increased dramatically over the last few years.

THE RHÔNE VALLEY

L'effet que tu me fais

The Basics

TYPES OF WINE

In actuality, the Rhône Valley has two halves. The wines of the northern Rhône Valley, from famous appellations such as Côte Rôtie, Hermitage, and Cornas, are ageworthy, rich, full-bodied red wines from the noble Syrah grape. Minuscule quantities of fragrant and delicious white wine are made at Condrieu. White wine is also made at Hermitage, and good, but not great, red and white wines are made in the appellations of Crozes-Hermitage and St.-Joseph.

The southern Rhône, with its Mediterranean climate, primarily produces lusty, full-bodied, heady red wines, but some very fragrant underrated rosés are also made, as are better and better white wines. In the appellation of Muscat de Beaumes-de-Venise, a honeyed, perfumed, sweet white wine is made, and in Tavel, France's most famous rosé wine is produced.

GRAPE VARIETIES

RED WINE VARIETALS

Cinsault All the growers in Châteauneuf-du-Pape seem to use a small amount of Cinsault. It ripens very early, gives good yields, and produces wines that offer a great deal of fruit. It seems to offset the high alcohol of the Grenache and the tannins of the Syrah and Mourvèdre. Despite its value, it seems to have lost some appeal in favor of Syrah or Mourvèdre, but it is a valuable asset to the blend of a southern Rhône wine.

Counoise Very little of this grape exists in the south because of its capricious growing habits. However, I have tasted it separately at Château Beaucastel in Châteauneuf-du-Pape, where the Perrin family is augmenting its use. It had great finesse and seemed to provide deep, richly fruity flavors and a complex perfume of smoked meat, flowers, and berry fruit. The Perrins feel Counoise has as much potential as a high-quality ingredient in their blend as Mourvèdre.

Grenache A classic hot-climate grape varietal, Grenache is, for better or worse, the dominant grape of the southern Rhône. The quality of the wines it produces ranges from hot, alcoholic, unbalanced, and coarse to rich, majestic, very long-lived, and sumptuous. The differences are largely caused by the yield of juice per vine. Where Grenache is pruned back and not overly fertilized, it can do wondrous things. The sensational Châteauneuf-du-Pape Château Rayas is a poignant example of that. At its best it offers aromas of kirsch, blackcurrants, pepper, licorice, and roasted peanuts.

Mourvèdre   Everyone seems to agree on the virtues of the Mourvèdre, but few people want to take the risk and grow it. It flourishes in the Mediterranean appellation of Bandol, but only Château Beaucastel in Châteauneuf-du-Pape has made it an important part (one-third or more) of their blend. It gives great color, a complex, woodsy, leathery aroma, and superb structure and is resistant to oxidation. However, it ripens very late and, unlike other grape varietals, has no value until it is perfectly mature. When it lacks maturity, the growers say it gives them nothing, for it is colorless and acidic. Given the eccentricities of this grape, it is unlikely that anyone other than adventurous or passionately obsessed growers will make use of it. Its telltale aromas are those of leather, truffles, fresh mushrooms, and tree bark.

Muscardin   Muscardin provides wine with a great deal of perfume as well as a solid measure of alcohol and strength. Beaucastel uses Muscardin, but by far the most important plantings of Muscardin at a serious winemaking estate are at Chante Perdrix in Châteauneuf-du-Pape. The Nicolet family uses 20% in their excellent Châteauneuf-du-Pape.

Syrah   Syrah, one of the world's greatest red varietals and accountable for all of the northern Rhône wines, such as Hermitage, Cornas, Côte Rôtie, St.-Joseph, and Crozes-Hermitage is relegated to an accessory role in the south. However, its role in providing needed structure, backbone, and tannin to the fleshy Grenache is incontestable. Some growers believe it ripens too fast in the hotter south, but in my opinion it is a very strong addition to many southern Rhône wines. More and more of the Côtes du Rhône estates are producing special bottlings of 100% Syrah wines that show immense potential. The finest Syrah made in the southern Rhône is the Cuvée Syrah from the Château de Fonsalette, a wine that can last and evolve for 15–25 years. Its aromas are those of berry fruit, coffee, smoky tar, and hickory wood.

Terret Noir   Little of this grape is now found in the southern Rhône, although it remains one of the permitted varieties. It was used to give acidity to a wine and modify the strong character provided by the Grenache and Syrah. None of the best estates care to employ it anymore.

Vaccarese   It was again at Beaucastel where I tasted the wine produced from this grape, which the Perrins vinify separately. Although not as powerful and deep as Syrah, nor as alcoholic as Grenache, it has a unique character, with signature aromas of pepper, hot tar, tobacco, and licorice.

WHITE WINE VARIETALS

Bourboulenc   This grape offers plenty of body. The local cognoscenti also attribute the scent of roses to Bourboulenc, although I cannot yet claim the same experience.

Clairette Blanc   Until the advent of cold fermentations and modern equipment to minimize the risk of oxidation, the Clairette produced heavy, alcoholic, often deep yellow-colored wines that were thick and ponderous. Given the benefit of state-of-the-art technology, it produces soft, floral, fruity wine that must be drunk young. The superb white Châteauneuf-du-Pape of Vieux Télégraphe has 35% Clairette in it.

Grenache Blanc   Deeply fruity, highly alcoholic, yet low-acid wines are produced from Grenache Blanc. When fermented at cool temperatures and with the malolactic fermentation blocked, it can be a vibrant, delicious wine

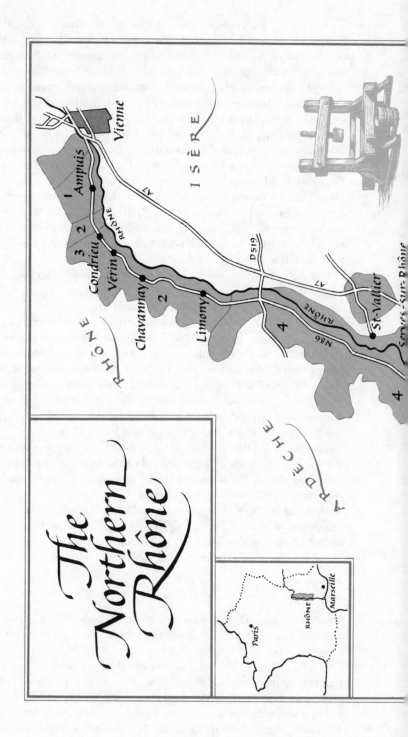

The Northern Rhône

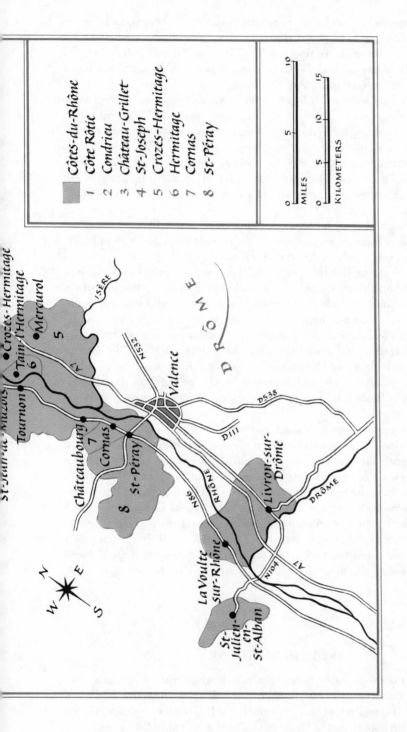

Côtes-du-Rhône
1 Côte Rôtie
2 Condrieu
3 Château-Grillet
4 St-Joseph
5 Crozes-Hermitage
6 Hermitage
7 Cornas
8 St-Péray

MILES
0   5   10
KILOMETERS
0   5   10   15

St-Jean-de-Muzols
Crozes-Hermitage
Tain-l'Hermitage
Mercurol
5
6
Tournon
Châteaubourg
7
Cornas
St-Péray
8
N532
Valence
ISÈRE
A7
DRÔME
D538
DIII
RHÔNE
N86
Livron-sur-Drôme
DRÔME
La Voulte-sur-Rhône
N304
A7
St-Julien-en-St-Alban

N
W   E
S

capable of providing wonderful near-term pleasure. The exquisite white Châteauneuf-du-Pape from Henri Brunier, Vieux Télégraphe, contains 25% Grenache Blanc; that of the Gonnet brothers' Font de Michelle, 50%. In a few examples such as these I find the floral scent of paper-white narcissus and a character vaguely resembling that of Condrieu.

Marsanne   When harvested fully ripe and its yields kept low, Marsanne can produce Hermitage white wines of extraordinary power and longevity. The Marsanne planted in the south produces rather chunky wines that must receive help from other varieties because they cannot stand alone. Wine writer Jancis Robinson often claims it smells "not unpleasantly reminiscent of glue."

Picardin   This grape has fallen out of favor largely because the growers felt it added nothing to their blends. Apparently its neutral character was its undoing.

Picpoul   Frankly, I have no idea what this grape tastes like. I have never seen it isolated or represented in such a hefty percentage as to be identifiable. Today it is seen very rarely in the southern Rhône.

Roussanne   For centuries this grape was the essence of white Hermitage in the northern Rhône, but its small yields and susceptibility to disease saw it largely replaced by Marsanne. Making somewhat of a comeback in the southern Rhône, it has the most character of any of the white wine varietals—aromas of honey, coffee, flowers, and nuts—and produces a wine that can be very long-lived, an anomaly for a white wine in the southern Rhône. The famous Châteauneuf-du-Pape estate Beaucastel uses 80% Roussanne in its white wine, which, not surprisingly, is the longest-lived white wine of the appellation. Since 1986 Beaucastel has also produced a 100% old-vine Roussanne that can be profound.

Viognier   Viognier produces a great and unique white wine that is synonymous with Condrieu and Château Grillet of the northern Rhône. Its sensational fragrance of spring flowers, apricots, peaches, and honey has caused prices of Condrieu to soar. In the south there is little of it, but experimental plantings have exhibited immense potential. The finest example in the southern Rhône is the Domaine Ste.-Anne in the Côtes du Rhône village of Gervais. St.-Estève is another domaine in the Côtes du Rhône that produces a good Viognier. Beaucastel began to utilize it in its white Coudoulet in 1991. Unfortunately Viognier is not a permitted varietal in Châteauneuf-du-Pape, where it could immensely enhance the neutral character of so many of that village's white wines.

APPELLATIONS

NORTHERN RHÔNE

Condrieu   This exotic, often overwhelmingly fragrant wine is low in acidity and must be drunk young, but it offers hedonistic aromas and flavors of peaches, apricots, and honey and an unbelievably decadent, opulent finish. The single-estate appellation of Château Grillet is adjacent to Condrieu.

Cornas   The impenetrable black/ruby color, the brutal, even savage tannins in its youth, the massive structure and muddy sediment in the bottle, are all characteristics of a wine that tastes as if it were made in the nineteenth century. Cornas wines are among the most virile and robust in the world, offering a powerful aroma of cassis and raspberries that develops with aging into chestnuts, truffles, licorice, and blackcurrants. These are among the most underrated great red wines of the world, but one must have patience with them.

Côte Rôtie   This is an immense, fleshy, rich, fragrant, smoky, full-bodied, stunning wine with gobs of cassis fruit frequently intertwined with the smell of frying bacon. Côte Rôtie is one of France's greatest wines and can last for 25 years or more where well stored.

Crozes-Hermitage   Despite this appellation's proximity to the more famous Hermitage, its red wines tend to be soft, spicy, fruity, chunky, vegetal, and rather one-dimensional rather than distinguished. The white wines vary enormously in quality and can be pleasant but are often mediocre and too acidic.

Hermitage   At its best, Hermitage is a rich, almost portlike, viscous, very full-bodied, tannic red wine that can seemingly last forever. It is characterized by a great peppery, cassis smell, often with a touch of Provençal herbs thrown in for complexity. The white Hermitage can be neutral, but the great examples display a bouquet of herbs, minerals, nuts, peaches, and a stony, wet-slate type of smell. Both red and white Hermitage possess legendary reputations for longevity. These wines can last for 25–30 years.

St.-Péray   Tiny quantities of still and sparkling white wines are made from this forgotten appellation of the Rhône Valley. Neither merits consumer interest, as the wines often are dull, heavy, and diffuse.

St.-Joseph   The northern Rhône's most underrated appellation for red and white wine. The reds and whites are juicy and best drunk young.

SOUTHERN RHÔNE

Châteauneuf-du-Pape   There is an enormous diversity to the styles of Châteauneuf-du-Pape. One, which resembles a Beaujolais, offers jammy, soft, fruity flavors and must be drunk quite young. A second type, in which the wine is vinified in a classic manner, can be very dense in color, quite rich and full bodied, and can last 15–20 years. It is often characterized by the smell of saddle leather, fennel, licorice, black truffles, pepper, nutmeg, and smoked meats. Wines made by both these methods and then blended together, and dominated by the Grenache grape, often smell of roasted peanuts and overripe bing cherries. White Châteauneuf-du-Papes are usually neutral and uninteresting, but a few examples have a floral- and tropical fruit–scented bouquet. Generally, they must be drunk extremely young.

Côtes du Rhône   The best Côtes du Rhône offer uncomplicated but deliciously succulent, crunchy, peppery, blackberry and raspberry fruit in a supple, full-bodied style that is meant to be consumed within 5–6 years of the vintage.

Gigondas   Gigondas offers up a robust, chewy, full-bodied, rich, generous red wine that has a heady bouquet and supple, rich, spicy flavors. A tiny quantity of a very underrated rosé wine is often made and should be tried by consumers looking for something special.

Muscat de Beaumes-de-Venise   This sweet, alcoholic, but extraordinarily perfumed, exotic wine offers up smells of peaches, apricots, coconut, and lychee nuts. It must be drunk in its youth to be fully appreciated.

Northern Rhône   **Southern Rhône**
Condrieu: 2–5 years   Châteauneuf-du-Pape (red):
Cornas: 5–15 years   5–20 years
Côte Rôtie: 5–25 years   Châteauneuf-du-Pape (white):
Crozes-Hermitage: 3–8 years   1–2 years
Hermitage (red): 5–30 years   Côtes du Rhône: 4–8 years
Hermitage (white): 3–15 years   Gigondas: 5–12 years
St.-Joseph: 3–8 years   Muscat de Beaumes-de-Venise:
                                            1–3 years
                                        Tavel: 1–2 years

In the northern Rhône appellations of Côte Rôtie, Hermitage, Condrieu, and Cornas, the general level of winemaking is excellent. In the other appellations, it is irregular. In the southern Rhône, Châteauneuf-du-Pape has the broadest range in quality, from superb to irresponsible and inept producers. Gigondas has the highest level of quality winemakers.

NORTHERN RHÔNE

Côte Rôtie—An Overview

Type of wine produced: Red wine only
Grape varieties planted: Syrah and a tiny quantity of Viognier (up to
                                    20% can be added)
Acres currently under vine: 345
Quality level: Exceptional, among the finest red wines in the
                                    world
Aging potential: 5–30 years
General characteristics: Fleshy, rich, very fragrant, smoky, full-bodied,
                                    stunning wines
Greatest recent vintages: 1991, 1989, 1988, 1987, 1985, 1983, 1978,
                                    1976, 1969
Price range: $25–$55, except for the single vineyard wines
                                    of Guigal, which retail, if one can find them,
                                    for $150. Beware of speculators, particularly
                                    the English wine trade, which often asks
                                    $250–$350 a bottle.

RATING THE CÔTE RÔTIE PRODUCERS

***** *(OUTSTANDING)*

Chapoutier Cuvée Mordorée   Guigal La Mouline
Marius Gentaz-Dervieux   Guigal La Turque
Guigal La Landonne   Jean-Paul and Jean-Luc Jamet

René Rostaing Côte Blonde
René Rostaing Côte Brune La
   Landonne

René Rostaing Côte Brune La
   Viaillère (since 1991)
L. de Vallouit Les Roziers

* * * * *(EXCELLENT)*

Gilles Barge
Pierre Barge
Bernard Burgaud
Chapoutier Côtes Blonde et Brune
Clusel-Roch Les Grandes Places
Henri Gallet
Vincent Gasse
Guigal Côtes Blonde et Brune

Robert Jasmin
Michel Ogier
René Rostaing (regular *cuvée*)
L. de Vallouit Vagonier
Vidal-Fleury La Chatillonne Côte
   Blonde
Vidal-Fleury Côte Blonde et Brune

* * * *(GOOD)*

Guy Bernard
Domaine de Bonserine
Emile Champet
Joel Champet La Viaillère
Chapoutier (regular *cuvée*)
Clusel-Roch (regular *cuvée*)
Delas Frères Seigneur de Maugiron

Albert Dervieux-Thaize *
Georges Duboeuf Domaine Ile
   Rousse
Pierre Gaillard
J. M. Gérin Champin de Siegneur
J. M. Grand Place
Paul Jaboulet Ainé Les Jumelles

   * Since 1991 Dervieux-Thaize has retired and the wines from his vineyards are now made by René Rostaing, a 5-star producer.

Condrieu—An Overview

Type of wine produced:	White wine only
Grape varieties planted:	Viognier
Acres currently under vine:	57
Quality level:	Exceptional, one of the rarest and most unique wines in the world
Aging potential:	1–4 years
General characteristics:	An exotic, often overwhelming tropical fruit fragrance inter-twined with floral aspects; a low-acid, very rich wine that is usually short-lived
Greatest recent vintages:	1991, 1990 (only for the sweeter Vendange Tardive wines), 1989 (they may already be getting old)
Price range:	$30–$60

RATING THE CONDRIEU PRODUCERS

* * * * * *(OUTSTANDING PRODUCERS)*

Dumazet
Guigal
André Perret

Philippe Pichon
Georges Vernay Coteaux du Vernon

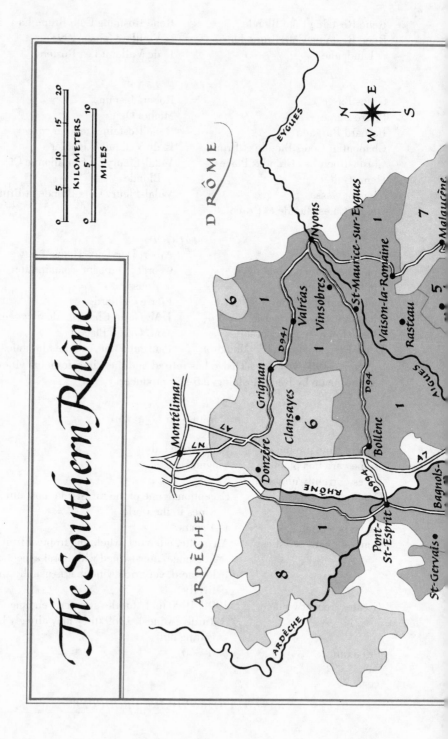

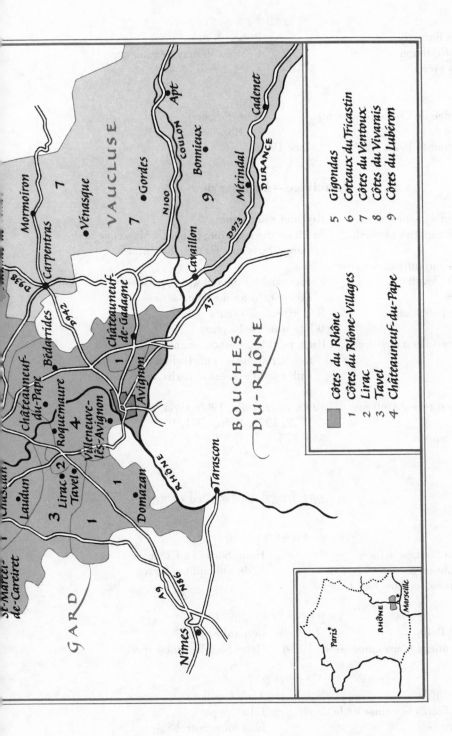

* * * * *(EXCELLENT PRODUCERS)

* * * *(EXCELLENT PRODUCERS)

Gilles Barge	Robert Niero
Yves Cuilleron	Georges Vernay (regular *cuvée*)
Delas Frères	

* * * (GOOD)

Domaine du Chêne (Rouvière)	Nero-Pinchon
Grillet *	Du Rozay

* Prior to 1979, *****; *** since 1979

Hermitage—An Overview

Type of wine produced:	Red and white wine
Grape varieties planted:	Syrah for the red wine; primarily Marsanne and some Roussanne for the white wine
Acres currently under vine:	330
Quality level:	Exceptional for the red wines, good to exceptional for the white wines
Aging potential:	Red wine: 5–30 years
	White wine: 3–15 years
General characteristics:	Rich, portlike, viscous, chunky, full-bodied, tannic red wines. Full-bodied white wines with a unique scent of herbs, minerals, and peaches
Greatest recent vintages:	1990, 1989, 1988, 1985, 1983, 1979, 1978, 1972, 1970, 1966, 1961, 1959
Price range:	$35–$75

RATING THE RED HERMITAGE PRODUCERS

* * * * *(OUTSTANDING)

Chapoutier Le Pavillon	Henri Sorrel Le Gréal
J. L. Chave	L. de Vallouit Greffières
Paul Jaboulet Ainé La Chapelle	

* * * *(EXCELLENT)

Albert Belle	Bernard Faurie
Chapoutier La Sizeranne (since 1989)	Henri Sorrel (regular *cuvée*)

* * *(GOOD)

Dard et Ribo	Alain Graillot
Delas Frères Marquise de la Tourette	J. L. Grippat
Desmeure	Jean-Marc Sorrel
Jules Fayolle et Fils	Vidal-Fleury
Ferraton Père et Fils Cuvée Les Miaux	

RATING THE WHITE HERMITAGE PRODUCERS

***** *(OUTSTANDING)*

Chapoutier Cuvée de l'Orvée   J. L. Chave

**** *(EXCELLENT)*

Paul Jaboulet Ainé Chevalier de   Guigal
  Stérimberg (since 1989)   Henri Sorrel Les Rocoules
J. L. Grippat

Crozes-Hermitage—An Overview

Type of wine produced: Red and white wine
Grape varieties planted: Marsanne and Roussanne for the white wine;
                                    Syrah for the red wine
Acres currently under vine: 2,840
Quality level: Mediocre to very good
Aging potential: White wine: 1–4 years
                                 Red wine: 3–10 years
General characteristics: Tremendous variability in the red wines; white
                                    wines are fleshy, chunky, solid, and rather
                                    undistinguished
Greatest recent vintages: 1990, 1989, 1988, 1985, 1983, 1978
Price range: $14–$25

RATING THE CROZES-HERMITAGE PRODUCERS

***** *(OUTSTANDING)*

Alain Graillot La Guiraude   Paul Jaboulet Ainé Thalabert

**** *(EXCELLENT)*

Albert Belle   Domaine du
Alain Graillot (regular *cuvée*)   Pavillon-Mercurol
Paul Jaboulet Ainé   L. de Vallouit L'Arnage

*** *(GOOD)*

Chapoutier Les Meysonniers   Delas Frères Marquise de la Tourette
Curson–Étienne Pochon   Ferraton Père et Fils
Dard et Ribo

St.-Joseph—An Overview

Type of wine produced: Red and white wine
Grape varieties planted: Marsanne and Roussanne for the white wine;
                                    Syrah for the red wine
Acres currently under vine: 1,580
Quality level: Good to excellent
Aging potential: White wine: 1–5 years
                                 Red wine: 1–6 years

General characteristics:	The red wines are the lightest, fruitiest, and most feminine of the northern Rhône. The white wines are perfumed and fleshy, with scents of apricots and pears
Greatest recent vintages:	1990, 1989, 1988, 1985, 1983, 1978
Price range:	$12–$20

RATING THE ST.-JOSEPH PRODUCERS

* * * * * (OUTSTANDING)

J. L. Chave

Domaine de Gachon—Pascal Perrier

J. L. Grippat Cuvée des Hospices

Paul Jaboulet Ainé Le Grand Pompée

André Perret Les Grisières

L. de Vallouit Les Anges

* * * * (EXCELLENT)

Chapoutier Deschants

Domaine du Chêne (Rouvière)

Bernard Faurie

Domaine de Fauterie

Alain Graillot

Domaine de Monteillet

André Perret (regular *cuvée*)

Pascal Perrier

Raymond Trollat

* * * (GOOD)

Pierre Coursodon

Yves Cuilleron

Dard et Ribo

Pierre Gaillard

J. L. Grippat (regular *cuvée*)

Cornas—An Overview

Type of wine produced:	Red wine only
Grape varieties planted:	Syrah only
Acres currently under vine:	240
Quality level:	Very good to exceptional
Aging potential:	5–15 years
General characteristics:	Black/ruby in color, tannic, full-bodied, virile, robust wines with a powerful aroma
Greatest recent vintages:	1990, 1988, 1985, 1983, 1979, 1978, 1976, 1969
Price range:	$15–$25

RATING THE CORNAS PRODUCERS

* * * * * (OUTSTANDING)

Auguste Clape   Noël Verset

* * * * (EXCELLENT)

Thierry Allemand

Chapoutier (since 1991)

Marcel Juge (Cuvée C)

Jacques Lemencier

Robert Michel Le Geynale

Alain Voge Cuvée Vieilles Vignes

*** *(GOOD)*

René Balthazar

Guy de Barjac

Jean-Luc Colombo

Delas Frères Chante Perdrix

Paul Jaboulet Ainé

Marcel Juge (regular *cuvée*)

Jean Lionnet

Robert Michel (regular *cuvée*)

Alain Voge Cuvée Barriques

SOUTHERN RHÔNE

Côtes du Rhône and Côtes du Rhône-Villages— An Overview

Type of wine produced: Red, white, and rosé wines

Grape varieties planted: Mostly Grenache, but Syrah, Mourvèdre, and Cinsault can be found. Most white wines are made from Grenache Blanc and Clairette, but great hopes have been raised by Viognier

Acres currently under vine: 115,000

Aging potential: Most wines must be drunk within 4 years of the vintage. Several, particularly Fonsalette and Coudoulet, can improve and last for 15 years

General characteristics: Tremendous diversity in styles, from light and fruity to deep, full bodied, tannic, and concentrated

Greatest recent vintages: 1990, 1989, 1988

Price range: $6–$20

RATING THE CÔTES DU RHÔNE PRODUCERS

***** *(OUTSTANDING)*

Coudoulet de Beaucastel

Daniel Brusset-Les Hauts de Montmirail

Domaine Gramenon Cuvée Cepes Centennaire

Domaine Gramenon Cuvée de Laurentides

Domaine de la Guichard

Jean-Marie Lombard

Rayas Fonsalette

Rayas Fonsalette Cuvée Syrah

Des Tours

**** *(EXCELLENT)*

Domaine de l'Amandier

Domaine de l'Ameillaud

Domaine des Anges

Domaine Les Aussellons

La Borie

Domaine André Brunel

Cabasse

De la Canorgue

Cave Jaume

Close de la Mure

Georges Duboeuf Domaine des Aires Vieilles

Georges Duboeuf Domaine des Moulins

Domaine de Couroulu

Domaine de l'Espigouette

Domaine Gramenon

Du Grand Moulas

Domaine Grand Prébois
Domaine des Grands Devers
Guigal
Paul Jaboulet Aîné Parallel 45
Domaine Mitan
Domaine des Moulins
Domaine de l'Oratoire St.-Martin
Domaine Pelaquié
Domaine de Piaugier Les Briguières
Domaine de Piaugier Montmartel
Plan Dei
Domaine de la Présidente
Rabasse-Charavin

Domaine de la Réméjeanne
Domaine Richard
St.-Estève
Domaine Saint-Gayan
Domaine Santa Duc
Domaine la Soumade
Domaine Ste.-Anne
Domaine Ste.-Apollinaire
Domaine des Treilles
Le Val des Rois
La Vieille Ferme Gold Label
Vieux Chêne (various wines)

* * * (GOOD)

D'Aigueville
Paul Autard
La Berthete
Roman Bouchard
Auguste Clape
Daniel Combe
Domazon
Estagnol
Domaine de Font-Sane Côtes du
    Ventoux
Domaine Les Gouberts

Malijay
Domaine de Mont-Redon
Domaines Mousset
Nero-Pinchon Ste.-Agathe
Domaine St.-Michel
Domaine St.-Pierre
Château du Trignon
Domaine de Verquière
Vidal-Fleury
La Vielle Ferme (other cuvées)

Châteauneuf-du-Pape—An Overview

Type of wine produced: 97% red; 3% white
Grape varieties planted: 13 (actually 14, if the white clone of Grenache is
                          included). In practice, Grenache, Syrah,
                          Mourvèdre, and Cinsault dominate for the red
                          wines; Grenache Blanc, and Clairette for the
                          whites
Acres currently under vine: 8,200
Quality level: Red wines: below average to exceptional; the
                          diversity of styles and range in quality of
                          wines produced in Châteauneuf-du-Pape is as
                          extreme as any major appellation in France.
                          White wines: quality tends to be mediocre
Aging potential: Red wines: 5–20 years. White wines: 1–2 years,
                          with the white wines of Beaucastel and Rayas
                          being the only major exceptions
General characteristics: Red wines: range from full bodied, generous,
                          rich, round, alcoholic, and long-lived to soft,
                          fruity, and Beaujolais-like. White wines: at
                          their best, they are floral, fruity, and clean;
                          most often they are tart, hollow, and boring

Greatest recent vintages: 1990, 1989, 1988, 1985, 1981, 1979, 1978, 1970, 1967

Price range: $10–$20, except for some of the luxury *cuvées*

RATING THE PRODUCERS OF CHÂTEAUNEUF-DU-PAPE

* * * * * *(OUTSTANDING)*

Beaucastel
Beaucastel Hommage à Jacques
   Perrin
Domaine de Beaurenard Cuvée
   Boisrenard
Henri Bonneau Cuvée des Celestins
Lucien et André Brunel-Les Cailloux
   Cuvée Centenaire
Chapoutier Barbe Rac

Clos du Mont-Olivet La Cuvée du
   Papet
De la Gardine Cuvée des
   Générations
Domaine de Marcoux Cuvée Vieilles
   Vignes
Domaine du Pegau
Rayas

* * * * *(EXCELLENT)*

Pierre André
Paul Autard
Paul Autard Cuvée la Côte Ronde
Lucien Barrot
Domaine de Beaurenard
Henri Bonneau Cuvée Marie Beurrier
Le Bosquet des Papes
Lucien et André Brunel-Les Cailloux
Cabrières Cuvée Prestige
Les Cailloux (regular *cuvée*)
Domaine Chante Cigale (only their
   unfiltered *cuvées*)
Domaine de Chante Perdrix
Chapoutier La Bernardine (since
   1989)
Domaine Gérard Charvin
Domaine Les Clefs d'Or
Clos du Caillou
Clos du Mont-Olivet
Clos des Papes
Cuvée du Belvedere
Cuvée du Vatican
Domaine Durieu Cuvée Lucile Avril
Eddie Féraud
Font de Michelle
Font de Michelle Cuvée Étienne
   Gonnet
De la Gardine

Domaine Grand Jean
Guigal
Domaine Haut des Terres Blanches
Paul Jaboulet Ainé Les Cèdres (prior
   to 1970 and after 1988)
Pierre Jacumin—Cuvée de
   Boisdauphin
Domaine de la Janasse Chaupoins
Domaine de la Janasse Cuvée
   Vieilles Vignes
Domaine de Marcoux (regular *cuvée*)
Domaine de Montpertuis Cuvée
   Tradition
Moulin-Tacussel
La Nerthe
De la Nerthe Cuvée des Cadettes (a
   5-star producer if the estate stops
   filtering)
Domaine Pontifical (François Laget)
Rayas Pignan
Domaine de la Roquette
Domaine Roger Sabon Cuvée
   Prestige
Domaine Saint-Benôit
Domaine de la Solitude (since 1990)
Domaine de la Vieille Julienne
Vieux Donjon
Domaine du Vieux Télégraphe

* * * *(GOOD)*

Jean Avril
Domaine Avril Juliette
Michel Bernard
Domaine Berthet Rayne
Domaine Bois de Boursan
Domaine de Bois Dauphin
Domaine Bouvachon Bovine
Cabrières Cuvée Tradition
Caves Perges
Caves St.-Pierre
Domaine des Chanssaud
Domaine du Chantadu
Domaine Chante Cigale (regular
    cuvées)
Domaine de la Charbonnière
Clos Bimard
Clos des Pontifes
Clos du Calvaire
Clos du Roi
Clos Saint-Jean
Clos Saint-Michel
Jean Comte de Lauze
Domaine la Crau des Papes
Edmond Duclaux
Domaine Durieu (regular *cuvée*)
Des Fines Roches
Font du Loup
Fortia
Lou Fréjau
Domaine du Galet des Papes
Domaine Les Gallimardes
Domaine du Grand Tinel
Domaine Grand Veneur

Domaine de la Janasse (regular
    cuvée)
Domaine Mathieu
Domaine de la Millière
Domaine de Montpertuis Cuvée
    Classique
Domaine de Mont-Redon
Domaine de Nalys
Domaine de Palestor
Père Anselme
Domaine du Père Caboche
Domaine du Père Pape Clos du
    Calvaire
Roger Perrin
Domaine de la Pinède
Domaine de la Présidente
Domaine des Relagnes—Cuvée
    Vigneronne
Domaine Riché
Domaine Roger Sabon (regular *cuvée*)
Domaine Roger Sabon Cuvée
    Réservée
Domaine de St.-Siffrein
Domaine Sénéchaux
Simian
Domaine de la Souco-Papale
Domaine Terre Ferme
Domaine Jean Trintignant
Domaine Raymond Usseglio
Vaudieu
Vidal-Fleury
Vieux Lazaret
Domaine du Vieux Calcernier

Gigondas—An Overview

Type of wine produced:	Red wine and a small quantity of rosé
Grape varieties planted:	Primarily Grenache, with some Syrah, Mourvèdre, and Cinsault
Acres currently under vine:	2,925
Quality level:	Average to exceptional
Aging potential:	5–15 years
General characteristics:	Robust, chewy, full-bodied red wines are mouth-filling and flavorful. At its best, the rare, underrated rosé is fresh and vibrant
Greatest recent vintages:	1990, 1989, 1985, 1979, 1978
Price range:	$12-$20

RATING THE PRODUCERS OF GIGONDAS

* * * * * *(OUTSTANDING)*

Daniel Brusset-Les Hauts de
  Montmirail
Edmond Burle
Domaine de Cayron
Domaine de Font-Sane Cuvée
  Spéciale Fut Neuf

Domaine Saint-Gayan
Domaine Santa Duc Cuvée Prestige
  Des Hautes Garrigues

* * * * *(EXCELLENT)*

Domaine le Clos des Cazaux
Domaine de Font-Sane (regular *cuvée*)
Les Gouberts Cuvée Florence
Domaine du Gour de Chaule
Guigal
Paul Jaboulet Aîné (before 1978 and
  after 1989)

Domaine de Longue-Toque
Moulin de la Gardette
Domaine des Pesquiers
Domaine de Piaugier
Domaine Raspail (Dominique Ay)
Redoitier
Domaine Santa Duc (regular *cuvée*)

* * * *(GOOD)*

Pierre Amadieu—Domaine Romane-
  Machotte
Domaine La Bastide St.-Vincent
Domaine des Bosquets
Domaine la Bouissière
Cave Co-op
Domaine des Epiers
Domaine la Fourmone—
  Roger Combe
Domaine Les Gouberts
  (regular *cuvée*)
Domaine Le Grande Romane

Domaine du Grapillon d'Or
Domaine de Joncuas
Domaine de la Mavette
Montmirail Cuvée Beauchamp
Domaine du Moutvac
L'Oustau Fauquet
Domaine Les Pallières
Raspail (Gabriel Meffre)
Domaine du Terine
Domaine Les Teysonnières
Domaine Les Tourelles
Château du Trignon

Muscat de Beaumes-de-Venise—An Overview

Type of wine produced:	A sweet, fortified wine—*vin doux naturel*
Grape varieties planted:	Muscat
Acres currently under vine:	576
Quality level:	Very good to outstanding
Aging potential:	1–4 years
General characteristics:	A sweet, decadently rich, intensely perfumed wine
Greatest recent vintages:	1991, 1990
Price range:	$15–$25

RATING THE MUSCAT DE BEAUMES-DE-VENISE
PRODUCERS

* * * * * (OUTSTANDING)

Chapoutier   Paul Jaboulet Aîné
Domaine de Coyeux   Vidal-Fleury
Domaine Durban

* * * * (EXCELLENT)

Domaine Castaud-Martin   Domaine St.-Sauveur

* * * (GOOD)

Cave Co-op

Vacqueyras—An Overview

Type of wine produced: Primarily red wine, with a small quantity of dry
                                  rosé
Grape varieties planted: Primarily Grenache
Acres currently under vine: 4,300
Quality level: Good, and improving
Aging potential: 3–8 years
General characteristics: Virtually identical with Gigondas
Greatest recent vintages: 1990, 1989, 1988
Price range: $8–$12

RATING THE VACQUEYRAS PRODUCERS

* * * * * (OUTSTANDING)

Des Tours

* * * * (EXCELLENT)

Domaine le Clos des Cazaux   Montmirail Deux Frères
Domaine le Couroulu   Domaine le Sang des Cailloux
Domaine la Fourmone—Roger Combe

* * * (GOOD)

Domaine des Amouriers   Domaine de la Monardière
Domaine de la Garrique   Domaine de Montvac
Paul Jaboulet Aîné   Château des Roques
Domaine de la Jaufrette   Vidal-Fleury
Domaine des Lambertins   Le Vieux Clocher

BUYING STRATEGY

To the extent you can still find well-preserved stocks, Rhône lovers should
be concentrating on buying as many of the top 1990s, 1989s, and 1988s as
they can afford. Given the irregularity of the quality of the 1991 and 1992 vin-

tages, it may be a long time before the Rhône Valley can again boast three consecutive vintages such as 1988, 1989, and 1990. It is probably too late to stock up on the finest 1989s, but the 1990s are arriving in the marketplace in 1993 and should continue to arrive throughout 1994. Much like 1989, 1990 is one of the three finest Rhône Valley vintages since 1961.

RECENT VINTAGES

1992—In the north it was a difficult year, as heavy and persistent September rains ruined the chance for an excellent vintage. It is still too early to evaluate, but if the northern Rhônes turn out to be as good as the soft, lighter-style 1987s, it will be welcome news. In the south the bad, even horrific deluges were localized. Consequently some areas were ruined (particularly the flat valley vineyards), but others were spared. The 1992 is an irregular vintage in the south that will undoubtedly fall below the great quality of 1989 and 1990 and the excellent quality of 1988.

1991—In the southern Rhône, the rains that came late in the year had a devastating impact on Châteauneuf-du-Pape. Many vineyards harvested diluted Grenache that had also begun to rot. Some of the top estates, such as Henri Bonneau and Rayas, will not produce a 1991, and others are not certain. Not everyone failed. Readers will no doubt be surprised by how good the 1991 Beaucastel is, but that is due to the fact that the Mourvèdre, Counoise, and Syrah, with their thicker skins, did not suffer from the rot and diluting rains to the extent that the Grenache did. For reasons that escape me, Gigondas seemed to have been impacted less by the terrible weather. At best it was an average-quality year in Gigondas and a disastrous year in Châteauneuf-du-Pape. Similarly, most of the Côtes du Rhône-Villages reported failed Grenache crops and very little wine of high quality.

In the northern Rhône, the 1991s from Côte Rôtie and Condrieu are better than the 1990s. In 1990 most of the steep, hillside vineyards were stressed by drought to the point where photosynthesis stopped in the vines, making it difficult for many grapes to fully achieve physiological maturity. Similarly, the 1991 Condrieus are superior to the 1990s, as the former vintage produced wines that are well balanced, with wonderful ripe fruit, decent acidity, and excellent freshness. The 1991 Côte Rôties display none of the hollowness that some of the 1990s possess. They are ripe, rich, and forward. In St.-Joseph, Crozes-Hermitage, and Hermitage, 1991 will not have the extraordinary quality of 1990, 1989, or 1988, but it should prove superior to 1987 and 1986. It is certainly a good vintage of forward, ripe, concentrated wines.

1990—This is a superlative vintage for most of the Rhône Valley. In the south the torridly hot, dry summer resulted in superripe grapes packed with sugar. At the top levels the wines are deeply colored, exceptionally powerful, with high levels of soft tannins and alcohol of 14–15% plus. The wines have a more roasted, extreme style than the more classic 1989s, but they are sumptuous, as well as loaded with concentrated fruit. It is unquestionably a great vintage in Châteauneuf-du-Pape, an excellent one in Gigondas, and a top-flight year in most of the Côtes du Rhône-Villages. The red wines from both Gigondas and Châteauneuf-du-Pape, despite higher alcohol than the 1989s, will probably mature more quickly than the 1989s because their acidity levels are lower and because the wines are so opulent and precocious. Nevertheless, the top *cuvées* of Châteauneuf-du-Pape should easily last for 15–20 years.

If you are a lover of Hermitage and Crozes-Hermitage, grab your wallet! In Hermitage 1990 looks to be even better than the great 1978 vintage. Gérard Chave, Michel Chapoutier, and Gérald Jaboulet all believe it is the finest year for this renowned appellation since 1961. The massive wines are almost black in color, with extraordinary extraction of fruit, high tannins, and a textural sweetness and succulence. Jaboulet's La Chapelle, Chave's Hermitage, and Chapoutier's luxury *cuvée* Le Pavillon are likely candidates for perfection, provided those who can both find and afford them wait the 15 or more years they will need to attain maturity. Even the wines of Crozes-Hermitage are superconcentrated. Those from Alain Graillot and Paul Jaboulet Aîné are especially exciting. Côte Rôtie is a mixed bag, with the top *cuvées* of Chapoutier, Guigal, and a handful of others looking excellent, sometimes extraordinary. Other wines are merely above average in quality. St.-Joseph and Cornas are at least good.

1989—This is unquestionably a great vintage for Châteauneuf-du-Pape and gets my nod as the finest for that appellation since 1978. In fact, it is 1978 that comes to mind when looking for a vintage of similar characteristics. The hot, dry weather produced small grapes with more noticeable tannins than the 1990s. However, when analyzed, most 1990s have the same tannin levels as the 1989s, but the 1989s taste more structured and more classically rendered. Given the stunning ripeness and reasonable yields, the 1989 Châteauneuf-du-Papes are nearly as powerful as the 1990s. They have low acidity, spectacular levels of fruit extraction, and a full-bodied, potentially long-lived style. It is a matter of personal taste whether one prefers the 1990s or the 1989s, but both are dazzling vintages. One really has to look to the individual domaine to determine who fared better in one vintage or the other. The 1989 vintage is more consistent in Gigondas and, again, that appellation's best overall year since 1978. For Rhône wine enthusiasts, these two years offer the best opportunities to replenish your cellars since 1978 and 1979.

Less massive, more supple and opulent wines were produced throughout the northern Rhône. The most successful appellations were Hermitage and Côte Rôtie. The least successful was Cornas. Côte Rôtie producers were ecstatic after the vintage, but only the best *cuvées* of Guigal and a few other wines have the requisite concentration and grip to live up to the initial hyperbole. Although the wines are flattering and will make delicious drinking over the next 10–15 years, this is an excellent rather than great vintage. In Hermitage it would be considered a great vintage except for the fact that 1990 surpassed it. The top *cuvées* are rich and full bodied, with 20 or more years of longevity. They also have a softness and are less massive on the palate, particularly when tasted next to the 1990s. The vintage is irregular in Cornas. The heat and drought appear to have caused problems for many vineyards in that appellation. As in Hermitage, Crozes-Hermitage enjoyed an excellent year.

1988—Although this is a very good vintage throughout the southern Rhône, it has been overshadowed by the thrilling quality of both 1989 and 1990. The 1988s do not possess the size, alcohol levels, or pure weight and drama of the 1989s or 1990s, but they are full-bodied, classically styled wines with slightly greener tannins and higher acidity. The 1988s should age gracefully, but they will rarely achieve the decadence, complexity, and pleasure that the top 1989s and 1990s will attain.

In the northern Rhône, Côte Rôtie enjoyed a superb vintage that equals 1985, 1983, and 1978. In fact, the 1988 Côte Rôties are significantly better than the 1989s, 1990s, and 1991s. The wines are superconcentrated, with great extraction of fruit, firm structure, and promising potential for longevity. Hermitage is at least excellent and sometimes superb (consider wines such as Sorrel's Le Gréal, Jaboulet's La Chapelle, and Chave's Hermitage). The wines of Cornas are very good, as are those of Crozes-Hermitage and St.-Joseph.

1987—This was a poor to mediocre year in the southern Rhône. In the northern Rhône, 1987 is a delicious vintage for Côte Rôtie, which enjoyed more success than any other northern Rhône Valley appellation. The wines are ripe and concentrated, with a velvety richness. Virtually everyone made good wine. The wines are delicious at present and should last another 5–6 years. The wines of Hermitage are smaller-scaled but clearly made from ripe fruit, with none of the nasty, herbal, vegetal character that comes from cool, wet, mediocre years. Chave, Sorrel, and Guigal all made tasty 1987s that should continue to drink well for another 7–8 years.

1986—The vintage in 1986 was extremely irregular, with medium-weight wines being produced. About 20% of the grapes in the Rhône Valley had not been harvested when the area was inundated with heavy rains on October 12, and the weather that followed over the next two weeks was equally miserable. However, the early pickers did exceptionally well, particularly in the southern Rhône, where quality is at least good, sometimes outstanding. Production was less than in the bountiful year of 1985, but because of the late harvest deluge, selection was critical, and one sees a great deal of irregularity in the range of quality. The wines are firmer, more tannic, and less fat and precocious than the 1985s. The top southern Rhônes from Châteauneuf-du-Pape and Gigondas appear to have outstanding cellaring potential.

Guigal is the star of the northern Rhône, with a number of stunning *cuvées*. In view of the amount of rain and potential for rot during the humid, wet harvest season, Guigal's achievement is remarkable. Jaboulet's La Chapelle is also surprisingly good, although narrowly constructed. In spite of these successes, 1986 is a vintage to approach with considerable caution.

1985—My tastings indicate that this vintage has produced excellent wines in the northern Rhône and very good wines in the south. For Côte Rôtie it is a great vintage. The wines are very deep in color, quite rich, but not particularly tannic. The overall impression is of wines fully ripe, rich in fruit, very opulent in style, and quite forward. Overall the vintage is very close in quality to 1978. In Côte Rôtie and Châteauneuf-du-Pape it is better than 1983. Everywhere it is certainly better than 1982, 1981, and 1980. The white wines are very powerful and rich but must be drunk young.

1984—A rather mediocre vintage of light- to medium-bodied wines that will offer straightforward, one-dimensional drinking over the near term. There are many surprisingly good wines from Châteauneuf-du-Pape and Gigondas, and the white wines of the entire region are quite good.

1983—An outstanding vintage in the north, a very good yet irregular vintage in the south. A hot, dry summer resulted in fully mature grapes loaded with sugar, flavor extract, and hard tannins. The wines of Hermitage, Crozes-Hermitage, and St.-Joseph are clearly the best since 1978 and 1961, neither as massive and rich as the 1978s nor as opulent as the 1985s, but more elegant and potentially very long-lived. The southern Rhônes should be moderately long-lived since they are ripe yet full of tannin. In Châteauneuf and Gigondas, 1983 is just behind 1978, 1981, and 1985 in quality.

PAST GREAT VINTAGES FOR THE NORTHERN RHÔNE: 1978, 1972 (Hermitage), 1970, 1966, 1961, 1959

PAST GREAT VINTAGES FOR THE SOUTHERN RHÔNE: 1981, 1979, 1978, 1970, 1967, 1961, 1957

The Rhône Valley

THIERRY ALLEMAND* * * *

1990 Cornas Vieilles Vignes (cream-colored label)	C	93

Allemand is an up-and-coming Cornas superstar, and his black/purple-colored 1990 is a dazzling example of the appellation. The nose offers up splendidly ripe aromas of bacon fat and cassis. Flamboyant and rich, with surprisingly soft tannins for a Cornas but fabulous concentration and a full-bodied, lush, long finish, it should drink gorgeously for at least 10–15 more years. Very impressive!

PIERRE AMADIEU—DOMAINE ROMANE-MACHOTTE* * *

1990 Gigondas	B	80
1989 Gigondas	B	79
1988 Gigondas	B	86

The 1990 Gigondas is light and somewhat stemmy, but soft and medium to full bodied, with some attractive spicy, cherry fruitiness. Drink it over the next 4–6 years. The 1989 Gigondas comes across as concentrated and simple. The 1988 is a much fuller, richer, more interesting wine, displaying evidence of some exposure to new oak casks. It is a full-bodied, peppery, herbaceous, black fruit–scented and -flavored wine with good balance, a nice chewy texture, and a long, heady finish. Drink it over the next 5–8 years.

PIERRE ANDRÉ* * * *

1990 Châteauneuf-du-Pape	C	88

Pierre André's 1990 red Châteauneuf-du-Pape reveals a deep ruby/purple color and a lovely mélange of sweet red and black fruits intermingled with strong aromas of olives and Provençal herbs. The wine is full bodied, fat, and succulent, with wonderful opulence, a velvety texture, and a smooth, ripe, luscious finish. It is a wine to drink over the next 7–8 years.

DOMAINE DES ANGES* * * *

1990 Clos de la Tour	B	89
1989 Clos de la Tour	B	87
1990 Côtes du Ventoux	A	85

The standard cuvée of 1990 Côtes du Ventoux offers up smoky aromas intermingled with scents of black fruits (plums and cassis). The wine is supple and medium bodied, with no hard edges and a tasty finish. Drink it over the next 2–3 years. The *cuvée spéciale*, Clos de la Tour, is made from 100% Grenache from old vines. The dark ruby-colored 1990 exhibits an explosively ripe, vividly scented nose, superb depth, medium to full body, and a long, spicy, moderately tannic finish. It has the potential to last for 10 years. The more elegant 1989 Clos de la Tour offers a more peppery-scented nose, with a truffle-like earthiness in the background. Rich, medium to full bodied, with melted tannins and a long, lush finish, it should be drunk over the next 5–6 years.

PAUL AUTARD* * * *

1990 Châteauneuf-du-Pape	C	87
1989 Châteauneuf-du-Pape	C	87
1988 Châteauneuf-du-Pape	C	88
1991 Châteauneuf-du-Pape Blanc	C	74
1990 Châteauneuf-du-Pape Cuvée la Côte Ronde	D	91
1990 Côtes du Rhône	A	84

Autard's white Châteauneuf-du-Pape is a neutral wine lacking in fruit. As for the red wines, the 1990 Côtes du Rhône is a medium-bodied, soft, fruity wine for drinking over the next 1–2 years. Autard's 1990 red Châteauneuf (standard *cuvée*) is an excellent bottle of wine. With a black/ruby/purple color and an intense nose of black cherries and smoke, it is packed with flavor, soft tannin, and a spicy, earthy fruitiness. This full-bodied, smooth, gutsy wine can handle cellaring of 7–9 years. The 1989 exhibits an impressive deep, dark ruby/purple color, a spicy, tight nose of cassis and herbs, plenty of richness, and fine structure. **Anticipated maturity: 1994–2006.** The more evolved 1988 offers a bouquet of tobacco, black raspberries, pepper, and Provençal herbs. Full bodied, round, and plump, oozing with ripeness and richness, and possessed of a long alcoholic finish, it should last for up to a decade. The 1990 Cuvée la Côte Ronde is a wine that has obviously seen some aging in new oak casks. The opaque ruby/purple color, multidimensional nose of black fruits, minerals, and toasty vanillin, and full-bodied, gloriously extracted flavors of chocolate, herbs, and coffee generously fill the mouth. As with most Châteauneuf-du-Papes, it can be drunk now or cellared safely for 10–12 plus years.

JEAN AVRIL* * *

1990 Châteauneuf-du-Pape	C	82

This pleasant, loosely knit, overripe, fat style of wine is meant to be drunk over the next 4–5 years. Although there is low acidity, high alcohol, and an absence of complexity, there is also plenty of fruit.

DOMAINE DE BABAN* *

1990 Châteauneuf-du-Pape	C	85

A deep medium-ruby color and a spicy, earthy nose is followed by a wine with good concentration, moderate tannins, and a correct but uninspiring finish. Drink it over the next 7–8 years.

GILLES BARGE* * * *

1991 Côte Rôtie	D	88
1990 Côte Rôtie	D	86
1989 Côte Rôtie	D	88
1988 Côte Rôtie	D	76

The excellent 1991 Côte Rôtie is dark ruby/purple, with a fragrant nose of underbrush, black fruits, and toast. This dense, concentrated, medium- to full-bodied wine exhibits soft tannins, low acidity, and gobs of rich fruit. Drink it over the next 10–12 years. The 1990 Côte Rôtie reveals spicy oak and black raspberry aromas in the nose, round, medium-bodied, ripe fruity flavors, soft tannins, and a pleasant finish. Drink it over the next 5–7 years. The excellent 1989 exhibits an attractive sweet raspberry-scented nose intermingled with the scents of earth and oak; fine ripeness; deep, intense, rich fruitiness; medium body; good glycerin; enough acidity to provide focus; and a soft, medium-bodied finish. It should drink well over the next 6–7 years. I was disappointed with the shallow, musty 1988 Côte Rôtie.

PIERRE BARGE* * * *

1991 Côte Rôtie	D	84
1990 Côte Rôtie	D	84
1989 Côte Rôtie	D	90
1988 Côte Rôtie	D	89

The 1991 Côte Rôtie appears slightly better than the 1990. Both are relatively light, elegant, soft, gentle wines that should be consumed over the next 5–6 years. The 1989 Côte Rôtie exhibits outstanding intensity and extraction of flavor. A huge, spicy, oaky, bacon fat–, and black fruit–scented nose zooms from the glass. There is plenty of depth, gobs of fruit, nice acidity, and a long, rich, moderately soft finish. This flattering and precocious-tasting Côte Rôtie should drink well over the next decade. The 1988 Côte Rôtie is the most structured and powerful. The bouquet consists of smoky, vanillin scents intermingled with rich black fruits such as plums and prunes. Full bodied and tannic, this offering should be at its best between now and 2008.

GUY DE BARJAC* * *

1990 Cornas	C	72
1989 Cornas	C	75
1988 Cornas	C	84

I am not sure what the problem is in Barjac's cellars, but it has been some time since he has made a memorable wine. The 1990 Cornas displays a stinky, odd, lees aroma. The 1989 Cornas continues to reveal a lack of richness and a disjointed personality. It will have to be drunk over the next 1–4 years. The 1988 Cornas offers a dark ruby color, soft, full-bodied, intense flavors, some of the chewy texture one finds in Cornas, and spice, tannin, and alcohol in the finish. It should be at its best between 1994 and 2003.

LUCIEN BARROT* * * *

1990	Châteauneuf-du-Pape	C	90
1989	Châteauneuf-du-Pape	B	90
1988	Châteauneuf-du-Pape	B	90

The 1989 is a sweeter, rounder, more velvety-textured wine than the superb 1988. As large-scale and rich as the 1988, it is a precocious, decadently hedonistic, flavorful Châteauneuf-du-Pape. The tannins are soft, but there is an abundance of rich, smoky, cedary, chocolaty fruit in this fleshy, powerful wine. It should drink magnificently for at least another 10 years. Barrot has fashioned a seductive 1990. The deep ruby/purple color is followed by a wine with a spicy, precocious, peppery, smoky, tar-, and berry-scented nose. I also detected the apricot and peach scents of super maturity, a velvety texture, and gobs of ripe, luscious fruit. For drinking over the next 10 years, this heady, fat, somewhat decadent style of Châteauneuf-du-Pape will prove hard to resist.

DOMAINE LA BASTIDE ST.-VINCENT* * *

1990	Gigondas	B	85
1989	Gigondas	B	85
1988	Gigondas	B	85
1990	Vacqueyras	A	86

These three Gigondas represent a straightforward, commercial style of Gigondas with plenty of up-front charm. The ripe black fruit nose, tasty, fat, chewy flavors, supple texture, and clean, smooth fruit are appealing. They should be drunk within 5–6 years of the vintage. The exotically scented (oranges, prunes, and jammy black cherries), nearly overripe 1990 Vacqueyras displays excellent richness, a medium- to full-bodied palate, and long, flowing, glycerin-dominated, richly fruity flavors. Drink it over the next 1–2 years.

BEAUCASTEL* * * * *

1990	Châteauneuf-du-Pape	D	94
1989	Châteauneuf-du-Pape	D	97
1988	Châteauneuf-du-Pape	D	92
1987	Châteauneuf-du-Pape	C	79
1990	Châteauneuf-du-Pape Blanc	D	88
1989	Châteauneuf-du-Pape Blanc	D	86
1990	Châteauneuf-du-Pape Roussanne Vieilles Vignes	E	90
1989	Châteauneuf-du-Pape Roussanne Vieilles Vignes	D	90
1988	Châteauneuf-du-Pape Roussanne Vieilles Vignes	D	90
1990	Côtes du Rhône Coudoulet	C	88
1989	Côtes du Rhône Coudoulet	C	88
1988	Côtes du Rhône Coudoulet	B	90
1991	Coudoulet Blanc	C	86

1990 Hommage à Jacques Perrin	EE	98
1989 Hommage à Jacques Perrin	EE	100

The 1990 Châteauneuf-du-Pape Blanc exhibits a great deal of strength and muscle in a full-bodied, well-balanced, ripe, heady, nicely textured style. Less concentrated than the 1989, it is still an impressive mouthful of wine. It tends to be best several years after bottling, at which time it closes up, not to emerge for 7–8 years. The 1989 Châteauneuf-du-Pape Blanc is surprisingly forward, round, richly fruity, ripe, and luscious, with at least 10–12 years of evolution ahead of it. The 1988 Châteauneuf-du-Pape Blanc reveals a spicy, almost peppery bouquet that suggests a red wine more than a white. It is fat, full bodied, deep, and rich, with excellent length.

As the first vintage for a white wine from Coudoulet, the 1991 is fragrant, tasty, and medium bodied, with some Viognier present. Drink it over the next 3–4 years. The 1990 Roussanne Vieilles Vignes has that distinctive bouquet of honey, smoky hazelnuts, and pineapples. Closed, but rich and full, with an intriguing texture, it will last for 10–20 years. The 1989 Roussanne Vieilles Vignes offers an expansive, intense bouquet of smoky hazelnuts, wet stones, and pineapples. It is full bodied, rich, and concentrated, but low in acidity. The 1988 Roussanne Vieilles Vignes possesses a bouquet of grilled almonds, buttery pineapple, and minerals, a more honeyed and richer texture than the 1989, and better acidity. It should drink and evolve for at least 12–15 years. The 1990 Coudoulet exhibits a meaty, leathery, peppery, cassis-scented nose, deep, supple, heady flavors, soft tannins, and low acidity. It reminded me of the perfumed, velvety-textured, smooth-as-silk 1989. Given how well Coudoulet ages, I would expect the 1990 to drink well in another 1–2 years and last for up to 12–15 years. The softer 1989 Coudoulet reveals a forward, fleshy personality, with peppery and plum scents, excellent flavor concentration, plenty of glycerin, and a smooth, spicy finish. It can be drunk over the next 12–15 years. The 1988 Côtes du Rhône Coudoulet has layer upon layer of rich, peppery, black-raspberry fruit, plenty of body, and a long finish. Beaucastel's 1990 Châteauneuf-du-Pape is opaque black/ruby/purple. Its perfume consists of smoked meats, coffee, hickory, Oriental spices, and black raspberries. The wine, while concentrated, full bodied, and extremely rich, displays hard tannins and comes across as a muscular example of Beaucastel. It should age for at least 30 years. The 1989 possesses an intense black/ruby/purple color. The nose offers a veritable smorgasbord of jammy cassis, Provençal herbs, Oriental spices, fruitcake, coffee, and hickory wood. The wine is sensationally concentrated and well balanced, with soft tannins and enough acidity to provide balance and freshness. It can be drunk now because of its lavish richness, yet it should age for at least 20–25 more years. The 1988 Châteauneuf-du-Pape is surprisingly supple and velvet-textured, with rich, full-bodied flavors, a big, fragrant bouquet of peppers and black raspberries, an opulent, full-bodied texture, and soft tannins. Drinkable now, it should continue to evolve for at least 12–15 years. The 1987 Châteauneuf, from what is certainly the worst vintage of the decade in the southern Rhône, is light, fruity, and correct.

The Perrins have decided that only in exceptional vintages will the Hommage à Jacques Perrin *cuvée* be produced. It possesses an increased percentage of Mourvèdre (60%), along with Grenache (20%), Counoise (10%), and

Syrah (10%). The 1990 is an awesome, superconcentrated, mammoth-size wine with black/purple color and a huge, fragrant perfume of smoked meat, black fruits, earth, and Oriental spices. Muscular and tannic, with tremendous amounts of glycerin and concentration, this super *cuvée* should reach its peak by the end of the century and last for 20–30 years. Production is extremely limited. The 1989 Hommage à Jacques Perrin is a profound wine. The dense, saturated, almost opaque black/purple color suggests superripeness and intensity. The nose offers up huge, smoky aromas filled with scents of minerals, licorice, black fruits, and even an intriguing floral component. The wine is exceptionally full bodied and tannic, as well as awesomely concentrated and magnificently well balanced. **Anticipated maturity: 1998–2015.**

RATINGS FOR OLDER VINTAGES OF BEAUCASTEL CHÂTEAUNEUF-DU-PAPE: 1986 (79–86?), 1985 (93), 1984 (76), 1983 (90), 1982 (81), 1981 (94), 1980 (86), 1979 (90), 1978 (91+), 1976 (73), 1973 (73), 1972 (88), 1971 (88), 1970 (94), 1969 (87), 1967 (89), 1966 (87), 1964 (83)

RATINGS FOR OLDER VINTAGES OF BEAUCASTEL CÔTES DU RHÔNE COUDOULET: 1986 (82), 1985 (90), 1984 (78), 1983 (87), 1981 (88), 1979 (86), 1978 (89)

DOMAINE DE BEAURENARD* * * */* * * * *

1990 Châteauneuf-du-Pape	C	90
1989 Châteauneuf-du-Pape	C	88
1988 Châteauneuf-du-Pape	C	87
1990 Châteauneuf-du-Pape Cuvée Boisrenard	D	96
1990 Côtes du Rhône	A	87

The 1990 Châteauneuf-du-Pape possesses an impressive dark ruby color, a huge bouquet of cloves, spice, cinnamon, black cherries, and tobacco, super-rich, soft, opulent fruit flavors, a silky texture, and a luscious finish. It will drink well for 8–10 years. The 1989 is medium to full bodied, round, generous, and perfumed (coffee, hickory, berry, and herbs dominate), with a supple, juicy finish. Drink it over the next 6–7 years. Although not as richly fruity, the 1988 is a delicious, amply endowed wine that should drink well for the next 5–6 years.

In 1990 a luxury *cuvée*, Boisrenard, was made. The 1990 is a massively rich, brilliantly well-delineated wine. The opaque ruby/purple color, the huge nose of sweet black fruits, toast, mocha, and tobacco, the multidimensional, layered texture, and the great extraction of flavor should propel this sumptuous wine through the first decade of the next century. **Anticipated maturity: Now–2010.**

Beaurenard's Côtes du Rhône is the type of wine that offers immediate gratification but can last for 4–5 years. The color is a healthy dark plum, and the nose is all sweet black fruits, roasted peanuts, and herbs. This expansive, round, wine offers a delightful, immensely satisfying drinking experience.

ALBERT BELLE* * * *

1990 Crozes-Hermitage Cuvée Louis Belle	C	90
1990 Crozes-Hermitage	C	87
1989 Crozes-Hermitage	C	87

1990 Hermitage	D	91

1989 Hermitage	D	91

The 1990 Crozes-Hermitage Cuvée Louis Belle possesses an opaque purple color. With swirling, the tight nose offers enticing aromas of herbs, tar, smoke, and black fruits. The wine exhibits the essence of black cherry fruit, is full bodied, dense, and rich, with considerable tannin and a formidable finish. This superb Crozes should carry its Syrah fruit for 10–15 years. **Anticipated maturity: 1996–2008.** The 1990 Crozes-Hermitage displays a black/ruby color and a sweet, fragrant, undeveloped bouquet of black fruits, herbs, and spices. It is rich, forward, deep, expansive, and long, with sound acidity and high, round tannin levels. This beauty should be at its best between 1993 and 2003. The 1989 Crozes-Hermitage exhibits an impressive deep color; good acidity, tannin, and fruit extraction; and a long, aggressive finish. It should drink well for at least the next decade. Belle's 1990 Hermitage offers an opaque color, followed by aromas of smoky oak, minerals, black fruits, herbs, and truffles; great extraction of fruit; a long, full-bodied, concentrated taste; plenty of power; high tannins; and adequate acidity. It should provide thrilling drinking for the next 15 or more years. The dark ruby/purple-colored 1989 possesses the sweet smells of cassis fruit, licorice, and roasted meats, explosive richness of fruit, superconcentration and length, and a voluptuous finish.

GUY BERNARD* * *

1991 Côte Rôtie	D	85

1990 Côte Rôtie	D	85

1988 Côte Rôtie	D	83

1987 Côte Rôtie	D	86

Bernard's 1987 is a soft, deliciously fruity, herb- and cassis-flavored wine, with some spicy, woody elements. The tannins are light, the acidity is sound, and the concentration is good. This is a delightful, elegant Côte Rôtie for drinking over the next 2–4 years. The 1988 should have been better. It displays an intensely herbaceous bouquet, with peppery, somewhat disjointed, yet ripe flavors. Although I admire the deep color, fine concentration, and extraction of the 1990, it tastes monochromatic. It is beefy, with a spicy, herbal, leathery nose and full-bodied, tannic flavors. The 1991 is reminiscent of the 1987 but with slightly richer fruit.

DOMAINE BOIS DE BOURSAN* * *

1990 Châteauneuf-du-Pape	C	85

1989 Châteauneuf-du-Pape	B	89

1988 Châteauneuf-du-Pape	B	86

The 1990 Châteauneuf offers up a vague but overripe nose of peaches, apricots, and black cherries. It is a tasty, soft, loosely knit wine that is ideal for drinking over the next 5 years. The 1989 Châteauneuf-du-Pape is better balanced, with an impressive deep, ruby/purple color and a reticent but blossoming bouquet of herbs, vanilla, red and black fruits, and a slightly resinous (pine trees?) component. Powerful, with plenty of richness, a dried-cherry fruit flavor, elevated tannins, and a heady, spicy, finish, it should last for 10–12 years. The supple 1988 exhibits an herbaceous, saltwater-scented bouquet, velvety textures, and a long finish. It should be drunk up.

DOMAINE DE BOIS DAUPHIN* * *

1990 Châteauneuf-du-Pape	C	82
1990 Châteauneuf-du-Pape Clos des Pontifes	C	88

The standard *cuvée* of 1990 Châteauneuf-du-Pape is a straightforward, soft, commercial, herb- and cherry-scented wine that hits the palate with no hard edges, offers medium to full body, plenty of alcohol, and a round, heady finish. Drink it over the next 3–4 years. The 1990 Clos des Pontifes is a much more impressively constituted wine. The dark ruby/purple color and perfumed nose of sweet, smoky oak, black cherries, and spices is followed by a generously endowed, full-bodied wine with alcoholic clout and a sweet, ripe, succulent finish. Forward and precocious, it should drink well for another 7–8 years.

HENRI BONNEAU* * * * *

1990 Châteauneuf-du-Pape Cuvée des Celestins	D	98
1989 Châteauneuf-du-Pape Cuvée des Celestins	D	98
1988 Châteauneuf-du-Pape Cuvée des Celestins	D	96
1990 Châteauneuf-du-Pape Cuvée Marie Beurrier	C	90
1989 Châteauneuf-du-Pape Cuvée Marie Beurrier	C	89
1988 Châteauneuf-du-Pape Cuvée Marie Beurrier	C	90

Henri Bonneau releases his lightest (actually, the word *light* is not in Bonneau's vocabulary) Châteauneuf-du-Pape *cuvée* under the name Marie Beurrier. Its power and strength overwhelm most other Châteauneuf-du-Papes. Most tasters will find the wine to be enormously rich and thick. The 1988 is a great bottle, with an exotic bouquet of herbs, chocolate, red fruits, and leather. It is velvety, rich, and a true old, heady, blockbuster style of Châteauneuf. Given its size, it should drink well for at least 10–15 years. The 1989 reveals a dark plummy color, a huge sweet nose reminiscent of brandy-soaked fruitcake, opulent, full-bodied flavors that exhibit excellent concentration, and a heady finish. This broad-shouldered wine can be drunk now or held for 5–10 years. The powerful, concentrated 1990 Marie Beurrier is nearly black in color, and the alcohol level is well over 15%. The huge nose suggests considerable *surmaturité* (maximum ripeness) in its cassis, peach, and apricot aromas. Thick, rich flavors viscously coat the palate, covering not only the alcohol, but some serious tannins. This full-bodied, exceptionally decadent wine will make for a sumptuous mouthful over the next 15 or more years. Bonneau's 1990 Châteauneuf-du-Pape Cuvée des Celestins promises to be a prodigious wine. It displays an opaque, black/ruby/purple color and an immensely spicy, chocolate, licorice, meaty nose, fine concentration, sweet, expansive flavors, fabulous length, and copious tannins in the finish. It will easily last for 20–25 years yet drink well early. **Anticipated maturity: 1996–2020.** The 1989 Cuvée des Celestins is extraordinary, with a degree of richness and dimension of flavor that are rare. The color is opaque black/plum-like, and the backward, unevolved nose offers exciting scents of Provençal herbs, black olives, truffles, cassis, smoke, and minerals. This mammoth wine reveals phenomenal extraction of flavor, huge body, and massive length. An immortal Châteauneuf-du-Pape, it should hit its peak in the late 1990s and last through the first two decades of the next century. The 1988 is also a wine of enormous depth, richness, and complexity. It can be drunk now (almost any southern Rhône can be consumed when released) and will last for 20–25 years.

RATINGS FOR OLDER VINTAGES OF HENRI BONNEAU CHÂTEAUNEUF-DU-PAPE CUVÉE DES CELESTINS: 1986 (94), 1985 (96), 1983 (90), 1979 (91), 1978 (100), 1970 (96)

DOMAINE DE BONSERINE* * *

1990 Côte Rôtie	D	85
1989 Côte Rôtie	D	85
1988 Côte Rôtie	C	88

The Domaine de Bonserine's 1990 Côte Rôtie is an attractive, medium-bodied, soft, fleshy wine with an elegant personality and round, graceful, yet generous flavors. It should be at its best between now and 2000. The 1989 Côte Rôtie displays an attractive bouquet of superripe raspberries, light tannins, a soft, medium-bodied, supple palate, and a low-acid finish. Drink it over the next 3–4 years. The 1988 Côte Rôtie is a large-scale, rich, intensely concentrated wine with the telltale bouquet of black raspberries, bacon fat, and new oak. Surprisingly backward and dense, this excellent effort should be at its best between 1994 and 2005.

LE BOSQUET DES PAPES* * * *

1990 Châteauneuf-du-Pape	C	92
1989 Châteauneuf-du-Pape	C	91
1988 Châteauneuf-du-Pape	C	89

The 1990 Châteauneuf-du-Pape's saturated, opaque purple color is followed by superripe aromas of black cherries, cassis, herbs, and pepper, a rich, full-bodied texture, and a long, moderately tannic, structured finish. Drink it over the next 10–15 years. The 1989 Châteauneuf-du-Pape displays a more structured, tannic, backward style. The opaque dark ruby/purple color and the huge bouquet of cassis, herbs, and spices are followed by a well-built, dense, concentrated wine that should last for 10–15 years. The 1988 offers a bouquet redolent with aromas of blackcurrants, tobacco, and cedar. This velvety-textured, full-bodied, admirably concentrated wine with flavors suggestive of fruitcake should drink well for up to a decade.

ROMAN BOUCHARD* * */* * * *

1988 Côtes du Rhône-Villages Eighth Generation	A	85
1990 Côtes du Rhône-Villages Valreas	B	87
1989 Côtes du Rhône-Villages Valreas	A	85
1988 Côtes du Rhône-Villages Valreas	A	86
1989 Côtes du Rhône-Villages Valreas Cuvée des Rois	A	85

The 1990 Valreas is excellent, with an herbal, peppery, spicy, rich nose, medium to full-bodied flavors, fine extraction of flavor (gobs of black cherries), and a long, moderately tannic finish. The 1989, lighter but similarly styled, is soft, opulently fruity, and ideal for near-term drinking. The 1988 Valreas exhibits an attractive dark ruby color; a big, spicy, cedary, herbaceous, roasted bouquet; ripe, amply endowed flavors; and a spicy, medium-bodied finish. The 1988 Côtes du Rhône-Villages Eighth Generation is slightly more peppery and spicy but is still wonderfully endowed with rich, round, soft fruit, good body, excellent depth, and a long, heady finish. The 1989 Côtes du Rhône-Villages Valreas Cuvée des Rois offers an enticing cherry and raspberry fruitiness, medium ruby color, velvety-textured, ripe cherry fruit, and a generous finish.

DOMAINE LA BOUISSIÈRE* * *

1989 Gigondas	B	85?
1988 Gigondas	B	82

The 1989 displays plenty of concentration, but there are significant levels of high tannins. Is there enough underlying fruit to support such astringent tannins? The 1988 has neither the concentration nor the tannin level of the 1989, as it was made in a softer, more forward style.

LUCIEN ET ANDRÉ BRUNEL-LES CAILLOUX* * * */* * * * *

1990 Châteauneuf-du-Pape	C	93
1989 Châteauneuf-du-Pape	C	93
1988 Châteauneuf-du-Pape	C	89
1991 Châteauneuf-du-Pape Blanc	C	85
1990 Châteauneuf-du-Pape Cuvée Centenaire	D	95
1989 Châteauneuf-du-Pape Cuvée Centenaire	D	96
1990 Côtes du Rhône Domaine André Brunel	A	86

As I have said many times, André Brunel is one of Châteauneuf-du-Pape's most forward-thinking, talented winemakers. The 1990 Côtes du Rhône Domaine André Brunel is an inexpensive introduction to Brunel's style; this robust, richly fruity, deeply colored wine offers a big, peppery, spicy, black fruit–scented nose, lusciously soft yet structured flavors, and plenty of guts and flesh in its long finish. The 1991 Châteauneuf-du-Pape Blanc exhibits much more character than most of its vapid peers. The citrusy, mineral-scented nose is pleasant, and the wine reveals good body, some glycerin, and enough acidity to provide focus. Drink it within 3 years of the vintage. The 1990 Les Cailloux exhibits a deep ruby/purple color, a ripe, peppery, black fruit– and herb-scented nose, soft tannins, and full-bodied, chewy, expansive flavors. It should provide memorable drinking between now and 2003. The black/purple-colored 1989 Les Cailloux offers a huge nose of leather, cedar, exotic spices, and red and black fruits and a long, concentrated, impressive finish. It will last for up to 2 decades. The 1988 is less concentrated, but its complex bouquet of peppers, spices, black fruits, and herbs is followed by a rich, medium-to full-bodied, velvety textured wine. It should drink well for the next 7–8 years. Brunel's *prestige cuvée,* the 1990 Cuvée Centenaire, reveals an

opaque dark ruby/purple color and a profound nose. A floral, sweet black raspberry character in the bouquet, combined with smoky new oak and minerals,
provides excitement. The wine is full bodied and exceptionally generous, with
a sweet taste due to its fabulous ripeness and richness. The finish is opulent,
voluptuous, and long. The 1990 offers more complexity and finesse in a more
up-front style. It should provide fabulous near-term drinking and last for
12–15 years. The extraordinary 1989 Cuvée Centenaire is rich and deep with
layers of concentrated fruit built into its massive framework. All of this comes
together in a remarkably well-balanced format for such a rich, full wine. What
is so impressive is the penetrating, explosive bouquet of minerals, licorice,
black fruits, and Oriental spices. This Châteauneuf-du-Pape is drinkable, but
it will improve for at least another 10–15 years. Fabulous!

DANIEL BRUSSET-LES HAUTS DE MONTMIRAIL* * * * *

1990	Cairanne Côtes du Rhône-Villages	A	86
1990	Gigondas Les Hauts de Montmirail	C	90
1989	Gigondas Les Hauts de Montmirail	C	93
1988	Gigondas Les Hauts de Montmirail	C	91
1987	Gigondas Les Hauts de Montmirail	B	79

For a wonderfully made Côtes du Rhône-Villages, check out Brusset's peppery, spicy, richly fruity 1990 Cairanne. This is an altogether seductive, round,
expansively flavored wine for current drinking. The black-colored 1990
Gigondas Les Hauts de Montmirail exhibits lavish quantities of toasty new oak,
along with superripe scents of cassis. Exceptionally rich, as well as round and
soft, this dramatic, full-throttle Gigondas is a real head turner. **Anticipated
maturity: Now–2002.** The 1989 Gigondas Les Hauts de Montmirail is a
spectacular wine for this appellation. Superrich, with a huge bouquet that
soars from the glass, it offers up aromas of cassis, vanillin, smoke, minerals,
and licorice. With huge extraction of flavor, plenty of tannin, and a sweet, expansive, superb finish, it should be drunk over the next 12–15 years. The 1988
is almost as good. The huge, mineral, toasty, blackcurrant-scented bouquet is
enthralling. This full-bodied wine has great presence, super depth and length,
slightly better acidity, and more definition than the 1989. The 1987 is an adequate wine given the deplorable vintage conditions. Brusset has turned out a
soft, fruity, spicy wine that should be drunk over the next 1–3 years.

BERNARD BURGAUD* * * *

1991	Côte Rôtie	D	91
1990	Côte Rôtie	D	88
1989	Côte Rôtie	D	90
1988	Côte Rôtie	D	92

The outstanding 1991 Côte Rôtie is a dense, opaque black/purple-colored
wine with a powerful nose of black fruits, herbs, and flowers. Full bodied, with
super extraction, it offers a rich, authoritative, well-structured taste and a velvety finish. With moderate tannins and terrific concentration, it should be
drinkable by the mid-1990s and last for 15 years. The 1990 Côte Rôtie ex-

hibits Burgaud's telltale opaque, dark ruby color, as well as an herbal, earthy, oaky nose intertwined with aromas of black cherries and black raspberries. It is one of the more concentrated 1990 Côte Rôties, with a thickness and richness surprising for the vintage. **Anticipated maturity: 1996–2010.** The 1989 exhibits a superb black/ruby/purple color. This huge, blockbuster, concentrated, intense Côte Rôtie has gobs of everything, including acidity, a tremendous tannin level, and outstanding concentration and intensity of fruit. **Anticipated maturity: Now–2007.** The 1988 may prove to be even longer-lived. The wine is splendidly concentrated, opaque in color, but tannic, structured, and in need of cellaring. It should prove to be a superb Côte Rôtie. **Anticipated maturity: 1996–2010.**

EDMOND BURLE* * * * *

1990 Gigondas Les Pallieroudas	B	92
1989 Gigondas Les Pallieroudas	B	93

This producer makes burly, almost black-colored, phenomenally extracted wines. These two offerings are similar—not surprising, since both 1989 and 1990 were dry, hot years. The colors are opaque black/purple, and the bouquets offer up sweet, smoky, ripe fruit that soars from the glass. Both wines are massively concentrated, yet opulent and silky given the sweetness and ripeness of the tannins. The finishes are voluptuous, long, and heady. The 1990 reveals a slightly more roasted black cherry/black raspberry component, whereas the 1989 is bursting with exhilarating levels of sweet black fruits intermingled with flavors of Provençal herbs. Undoubtedly the alcohol level of both wines is well over 14%. Both can be drunk now but should keep for 12–15 years.

CABRIÈRES* * */* * * *

1991 Châteauneuf-du-Pape Blanc	C	70
1990 Châteauneuf-du-Pape Cuvée Prestige	D	90
1989 Châteauneuf-du-Pape Cuvée Prestige	D	90
1988 Châteauneuf-du-Pape Cuvée Prestige	D	87
1990 Châteauneuf-du-Pape Cuvée Tradition	C	86
1988 Châteauneuf-du-Pape Cuvée Tradition	C	85

It would appear that the quality of this famous old estate is improving, though their white wines have tended to be one-dimensional and straightforward. The 1991 white is a technocrat's dream—no bouquet, high acid, clipped flavors, and a clean yet empty finish.

In top years Château Cabrières produces two red Châteauneuf-du-Papes—a Cuvée Tradition, which is their standard *cuvée*, and in high-quality vintages, a Cuvée Prestige. The latter wine represents 10% of their production. The 1990 Cuvée Tradition offers a superripe nose of apricot, peach, and black cherry fruit. The element of *sur-maturité*, a sweet, jammy apricot fruit character, is evident. Low in acidity, crammed with glycerin and rich fruit, this should be a seductive red wine for drinking over the next 5–7 years. The 1988 Cuvée Tradition is a delicious, ripe, herbaceous, black cherry–scented wine with considerable body and a velvety finish. The 1990 Cuvée Prestige has obviously seen some new oak given the subtle vanillin, smoky character in the fabulously dramatic, earthy, black fruit–scented, sweet nose. The wine displays full body, exquisite depth and richness, and fine grip and focus. This flashy, velvet-textured wine can be drunk young but will keep for 15 years. The 1989 Cuvée Prestige displays a huge, smoky, hickory, black cherry– and herb-scented nose that is followed by a rich wine adroitly blending power and finesse. There is expansive, sweet, ripe fruit, decent acidity for focus, and moderate tannin levels in the finish. **Anticipated maturity: Now–2006.** The 1988 Cuvée Prestige is similarly styled, but less tannic and alcoholic.

DE LA CANORGUE* * * *

1989 Côtes du Lubéron	A	87
1988 Côtes du Lubéron	A	86

I have a slight preference for the opulent, more fragrant 1989. The deep ruby/purple-colored 1988 offers up a clean bouquet of cassis, a relatively fleshy, medium- to full-bodied, spicy taste, and a soft finish. The 1989 is slightly lower in acidity, more alcoholic, and voluptuous and fleshy. Both wines should be drunk over the next 1–2 years.

DOMAINE DE CASSAU* */* * *

1990 Gigondas	B	85
1989 Gigondas	B	77

The 1990 gets my nod as being a more complete, more interesting, better-balanced wine than the 1989. It exhibits attractive black cherry fruit to go along with toasty new oak smells in its ripe, medium-bodied style. In contrast, the 1989 came across as extremely lean, tart, and made from underripe, immature fruit. Drink this straightforward, compact Gigondas over the next 3–4 years.

CAVE LE GRAVILLAS* */* * *

1989 Gigondas	B	73
1988 Gigondas	B	80

Neither the 1989 nor the 1988 exhibit depth, complexity, or concentration. Both are relatively light, soft, fruity wines meant for consumption in their first 5–6 years of life.

CAVES ST.-PIERRE* * *

1990 Châteauneuf-du-Pape Clefs des Prélats	B	78
1991 Châteauneuf-du-Pape Clefs des Prélats Blanc	B	74
1989 Châteauneuf-du-Pape Grande Cuvée	C	86
1988 Châteauneuf-du-Pape Grande Cuvée	C	85

This large cooperative has turned out a sterile, light- to medium-bodied white 1991 Châteauneuf-du-Pape with no bouquet and crisp, short flavors. The 1989 Châteauneuf-du-Pape Grande Cuvée displays plenty of richness, as well as a heady, alcoholic finish to go along with its fat, concentrated, peppery, blackcurrant flavors. Soft and forward, it will be ideal for drinking in its first 4–6 years of life. The 1988 is smooth, round, and generously flavored. It is low in acidity, so I would opt for drinking it over the next 1–2 years. The 1990 Clefs des Prélats offers soft, ripe fruit, medium body, and a spicy, adequate finish.

LES CAVES DES VIGNERONS DE GIGONDAS* */* * *

1989 Gigondas	B	74
1988 Gigondas Cuvée Pavillon de Beaumirail	C	88
1989 Gigondas Cuvée Seigneurie de Frontage	B	83

These wines are from the modern, well-run cooperative in Gigondas. The regular 1989 bottling is a straightforward, light, soft, fruity, innocuous wine. However, the 1989 Cuvée Seigneurie de Frontage is a more powerful, serious effort. Alcoholic, yet imbued with gobs of rich, chocolaty, berry fruit, this full-bodied, lush, velvety-textured wine should be drunk over the next 4–5 years. The impressive Cuvée Pavillon de Beaumirail offers a big, smoky, black cherry–scented bouquet, rich, full-bodied, intensely concentrated flavors, and a long, rich finish.

LES CAVES DES VIGNERONS DE VACQUEYRAS* *

1990 Gigondas	B	72
1989 Gigondas	B	78

This cooperative has produced a fluid, soft, Beaujolais-like 1990 Gigondas that should be drunk soon. The 1989 Gigondas is similarly round, fruity, and light, but there is some attractive olive-scented, black cherry fruit.

DOMAINE DE CAYRON* * * * *

1990 Gigondas	B	89+
1989 Gigondas	B	90
1988 Gigondas	B	90
1986 Gigondas	B	90
1985 Gigondas	B	91

Cayron's Gigondas is one of the most concentrated wines of the southern Rhône. The 1990 will last for 12–15 years. The black/ruby color, big, spicy, earthy, licorice nose, and opulent, fat, chewy flavors nearly conceal the considerable tannin levels. This in-your-face, full-throttle Gigondas should be quasi-civilized by 1995 and absolutely delicious by the late 1990s. The 1989 reveals even greater richness. The kinky, exotic, smoked meat fragrance, gobs of thick, chewy, chocolate- and hickory-flavored fruit, and mouth-coating glycerin and tannin levels make for an interesting, even provocative glass of wine. Drink it over the next 12–14 years. The 1988 is drinkable now, given its huge, peppery, fruitcake, herbaceous, olive, and smoky flavors and aromas. Expansive and nearly sweet, it is a thrill-a-sip Gigondas that should continue to turn heads, raise eyebrows, and horrify puritans for at least another 15 years. The heady 1985 is still sitting on some retailers' shelves, along with the 1986, which is slightly less concentrated and alcoholic than the 1985 but still wonderfully perfumed, rich, and intense.

LE CELLIER DES PRINCES* *

1990 Châteauneuf-du-Pape	B	82
1989 Châteauneuf-du-Pape	B	79
1988 Châteauneuf-du-Pape	B	83
1991 Châteauneuf-du-Pape Blanc	B	65

This huge *négociant* is the biggest producer of Châteauneuf-du-Pape. The 1991 white Châteauneuf-du-Pape expressed all that is wrong with modern-day winemaking. Completely devoid of a nose, with sanitized, superclean, nearly nonexistent flavors, this manufactured wine is incapable of providing any pleasure. All three vintages of red wine were ripe, full, richly fruity, slightly jammy, but solidly made. The 1989 and 1988 should be drunk over the next 3–4 years and the 1990 over the next 4–6.

EMILE CHAMPET* * */* * * *

1990 Côte Rôtie	D	85
1989 Côte Rôtie	D	90
1988 Côte Rôtie	D	91

Champet has turned out a full-bodied, fragrant, spicy, deep, highly extracted 1988 that should drink well for the next 12–14 years. His 1989 is similarly rich, with a huge, chocolaty, leathery, rustic nose, sweet, expansive, luscious flavors, softer tannins than the 1988, but a tasty finish. I would opt for drinking it over the next 10 years. As for the 1990, Champet has made a wine with an intensely leather-scented, almost smoked beef aroma, with medium body, plenty of tannin, but not the richness or persistence of either the 1989 or 1988. The 1990 will have to be drunk between now and 1998.

JOEL CHAMPET* * *

1990 Côte Rôtie	D	83
1991 Côte Rôtie La Viaillère	D	85
1990 Côte Rôtie La Viaillère	D	76
1989 Côte Rôtie La Viaillère	D	88
1988 Côte Rôtie La Viaillère	D	85

Champet's 1991 Côte Rôtie from the superb La Viaillère vineyard offers an attractive, sweet, black raspberry, herbal, earthy nose, medium-weight, moderately concentrated flavors, soft tannins, low acidity, and a forward, precocious personality. I found Champet's 1990 Côte Rôtie La Viaillère to be light, fluid, and one-dimensional, lacking in concentration and complexity. The same cannot be said for the sweet, expansive, glycerin-laden, nicely textured 1989 La Viaillère. It has surprising softness and a lush, velvety texture. This charmer should be drunk over the next 7–9 years. The 1988 displays a great deal of new oak in its spicy, smoky bouquet, but it does not reveal the same degree of ripeness, richness, or overall complexity and potential as the 1989. It should be drunk over the next 4–5 years. The 1990 Côte Rôtie is light and disjointed, but pleasant in a one-dimensional manner. Drink it over the near term.

DOMAINE DES CHANSSAUD* * *

1990 Châteauneuf-du-Pape	C	85
1989 Châteauneuf-du-Pape	C	76
1988 Châteauneuf-du-Pape	B	83
1990 Châteauneuf-du-Pape Blanc	C	85

Patrick Jaumes's 1990 white Châteauneuf-du-Pape is ripe, with an elegance and a floral-, fruit salad–scented nose, medium body, good glycerin, and a spicy, clean, fleshy finish. The 1990 red Châteauneuf-du-Pape offered up a sweet, almost apricot- and raspberry-jam-scented nose that was obviously the result of late harvested grapes. Expansive and slightly sweet, with round, soft flavors, it is ideal for drinking over the next 3–5 years. Both the 1989 and 1988 were ripe, full, richly fruity, slightly jammy, solidly made, representative examples of the appellation. Both should be drunk over the next 3–4 years.

DOMAINE DU CHANTADU* * *

1990 Châteauneuf-du-Pape	C	86
1989 Châteauneuf-du-Pape	C	82
1988 Châteauneuf-du-Pape	C	85

The 1990 Châteauneuf-du-Pape offered overripe aromas of oranges, apricots, and peaches; rich, soft tannins; medium to full body; and plenty of heady alcohol. Chantadu's 1989 Châteauneuf-du-Pape is a relatively commercial, open-knit, soft, direct style of Châteauneuf-du-Pape, with a bouquet of pepper, herbs, and berries; medium body; soft, ripe fruit; and a round, alcoholic finish. Drink it over the next 2–4 years. Last, the ripe, alcoholic 1988 has more focus to its heady, fleshy, chocolaty flavors. It is a very good example of a modern-style Châteauneuf-du-Pape that is ideal for drinking over the next 3–4 years.

DOMAINE CHANTE CIGALE* * */* * * *

1990 Châteauneuf-du-Pape	C	78–90?
1989 Châteauneuf-du-Pape	C	86–90*
1988 Châteauneuf-du-Pape	C	87
1991 Châteauneuf-du-Pape Blanc	C	68

The 1991 Châteauneuf-du-Pape Blanc reveals excessive sulphur in the nose, diluted flavors, and a stripped, sterile finish. As for the red wines, there are, lamentably, multiple *cuvées* for sale, ranging from soft and fruity to rich, full bodied, and unfiltered. Although all three *cuvées* of 1989 were at least good, that is not the case in 1990. One *cuvée* I tasted was outstanding and clearly superior to the best *cuvée* of 1989. It reveals a saturated, dark plummy color; a huge roasted, smoky, leathery, meaty nose; dense, superbly concentrated fruit flavors; and a long, full-bodied, sweet finish. It is a powerful, authoritatively flavored Châteauneuf-du-Pape that should drink well for a decade or more. Another *cuvée* being sold directly from the domaine to European clients exhibited an obviously sterile-filtered nose, short, clipped, eviscerated flavors, and a hollow, thin finish. The quality range of 12 points suggests an appalling lack of consistency. Should a producer not have some responsibility for putting a consistent product on the market? How can anyone have confidence in what they are buying, given such qualitative disparity? If you can find the best bottling, this is clearly a wine worth buying, but be sure to taste Chante Cigale's 1990 before making a commitment. The 1988 Châteauneuf-du-Pape from Chante Cigale offers a tobacco-scented, herbaceous, almost trufflelike nose, medium- to full-bodied flavors, fine tannin and acidity, but nowhere near the dramatic, flamboyant flavors of the 1989. Although soft enough to drink now, the 1988 should evolve nicely for 7–9 years.

DOMAINE DE CHANTE PERDRIX* * * *

1990	Châteauneuf-du-Pape	C	86
1989	Châteauneuf-du-Pape	C	93

After the success Chante Perdrix enjoyed with its glorious 1989, the 1990 is less exciting. Although undoubtedly a good Châteauneuf-du-Pape, it lacks the concentration, complexity, and aging potential of the 1989. The color is a medium-dark ruby, and the nose offers intense aromas of herbs, licorice, and red and black fruits. The wine is medium to full bodied, with an attractive, unctuous, fleshy texture, good rather than great depth, and a smooth, silky fin- ish. I would opt for drinking it over the next 5–6 years. The 1989 is spectacu- lar, a huge, massive wine oozing with extract and personality. It is a blockbuster wine for drinking over the next 10 years.

CHAPOUTIER* * * * *

1990	Muscat de Beaumes-de-Venise	C	90
1990	Châteauneuf-du-Pape Barbe Rac	E	97
1989	Châteauneuf-du-Pape Barbe Rac	E	93
1990	Châteauneuf-du-Pape La Bernardine	C	92?
1989	Châteauneuf-du-Pape La Bernardine	C	85?
1988	Châteauneuf-du-Pape La Bernardine	C	85
1990	Condrieu	D	88
1990	Cornas	C	89
1990	Côte Rôtie Côtes Brune et Blonde	D	89
1989	Côte Rôtie Côtes Brune et Blonde	D	90
1988	Côte Rôtie Côtes Brune et Blonde	D	92
1990	Côte Rôtie Cuvée Mordorée	E	94
1990	Côtes du Rhône-Villages Rasteau	B	86
1989	Côtes du Rhône	A	84
1991	Côtes du Rhône Belle Ruche	A	82
1990	Côtes du Rhône Belle Ruche	A	84
1991	Côtes du Rhône Blanc de Blancs	A	84
1990	Côtes du Rhône Blanc de Blancs	A	81

1991 Côtes du Rhône Rasteau	B	86
1990 Côtes du Rhône Rasteau	B	86
1991 Côtes du Rhône Rosé	A	86
1990 Côtes du Rhône Rosé	A	85
1990 Côtes du Ventoux	A	82
1989 Crozes-Hermitage Blanc	B	85
1991 Crozes-Hermitage Les Meysonniers Blanc	C	87
1990 Crozes-Hermitage Les Meysonniers	C	88
1989 Crozes-Hermitage Les Meysonniers	C	86
1988 Crozes-Hermitage Les Meysonniers	B	87
1988 Crozes-Hermitage Petite Ruche	B	85
1991 Hermitage Chante-Alouette	D	93
1990 Hermitage Chante-Alouette	D	93
1989 Hermitage Chante-Alouette	D	90
1988 Hermitage Chante-Alouette	D	87
1987 Hermitage Chante-Alouette	C	87
1986 Hermitage Cuvée Anniversaire	D	91
1991 Hermitage Cuvée de l'Orvée	E	93
1990 Ermitage Le Pavillon	E	100
1989 Ermitage Le Pavillon	E	100
1990 Hermitage La Sizeranne	D	93
1989 Hermitage La Sizeranne	D	93
1988 Hermitage La Sizeranne	D	90
1987 Hermitage La Sizeranne	C	86
1990 Hermitage Vin de Paille	E	96
1989 St.-Joseph Blanc	B	87
1990 St.-Joseph Deschants	B	86
1989 St.-Joseph Deschants	B	85
1988 St.-Joseph Deschants	B	87
1991 St.-Joseph Deschants Blanc	B	86
1990 St.-Joseph Deschants Blanc	B	87
1989 St.-Joseph Deschants Blanc	B	86
1990 Tavel Rosé	C	87

I have never experienced a more significant leap in quality and change in winemaking philosophy than that which has taken place in Chapoutier's cellars during the mid- to late-1980s. The 27-year-old Michel Chapoutier, who has taken over for his father, has totally revolutionized the winemaking at this estate, "going back to nature," as he says, cultivating the vineyard by organic methods and reducing yields to extremely conservative levels. The 1990 Condrieu is a dry, exceptionally flowery-scented wine, with aromas and flavors suggestive of ripe peaches and bananas. Drink it before the end of 1993. The 1991 Côtes du Rhône Blanc de Blancs offers up honeyed, fruity scents, relatively low acidity, and a rich, medium-bodied, crisp finish. Drink it over the next 2–3 years. Although heavier and not as fragrant, the 1990 Côtes du Rhône Blanc de Blancs is still attractive in a monolithic style. The 1989 Côtes du Rhône Blanc, organically made, is a wonderfully fresh, medium-bodied wine with good acidity and an underlying honeyed, apple ripeness. The 1991 Crozes-Hermitage Les Meysonniers Blanc offers up a more honeyed, pearlike nose and is made in a chunkier, more fruity style. Although fuller and slightly more ostentatious, it offers more power rather than finesse. The 1989 Crozes-Hermitage Blanc has a lovely, honeyed, apricot-scented bouquet, crisp acidity, medium body, and excellent freshness. The 1989 St.-Joseph Blanc has a wonderful flinty, mineral character similar to a Chablis. Dry, full bodied, relatively austere, but bursting with complexity and fruit, this wine should drink well for the next 4–5 years. Offering up a nose of minerals, cold steel, and tangerines, the 1991 St.-Joseph Deschants Blanc could also be mistaken for a top-class Chablis with its stony character, crisp, medium-bodied, fresh fruit, and excellent balance. It should drink well for 4–5 years. The 1990 displays the essence of flint in its bouquet. It is rich, long, deep, and extremely well balanced, with zesty acidity and a honeyed, pear- and apricotlike, nutty fruitiness. Drink it over the next 3–4 years. The 1989 St.-Joseph Deschants possesses the same flinty, earthy, mineral character.

Chapoutier has always made some of the finest and longest-lived white Hermitage. The 1991 Hermitage Chante-Alouette is a brilliantly well-focused, rich, full-bodied white wine with an enticing perfume of pears, flowers, and minerals, excellent honeyed richness and extraction, decent acidity, and a subtle touch of new oak that adds to the wine's dimension and structure. The 1990 Hermitage Chante-Alouette exhibits a slightly deeper color. The nose displays honeyed, hazelnut, stony, peachlike aromas. There is superb extraction of flavor, combined with surprisingly crisp, high acidity. This massive, extremely rich and intense white Hermitage should be drunk between now and 2010. The 1989 Hermitage Chante-Alouette displays a rich, buttery, hazelnut-scented nose, deep, heady flavors, and a lot of fatness in its chewy texture. It will evolve for 2 decades. The 1988 Chante-Alouette is less concentrated, more spicy than flowery, but has keeping qualities. The 1987 Hermitage Chante-Alouette has good acidity as well as a stony, peachlike bouquet. Medium bodied, it should continue to keep well for another 10–12 years. Chapoutier made a great 1986 Hermitage Cuvée Anniversaire, spectacularly rich, intense, and concentrated, yet firmly structured. A straw-colored wine, it has a bouquet of minerals, grilled hazelnuts, and gobs of spicy fruit. In the mouth it is full bodied, with a stony, minerallike, underlying fruitiness and a long, intense finish. Drinkable now, this wine should age for at least 15–20 or more years. A luxury Cuvée de l'Orvée was produced in 1991. Made from a patch of old vines, this spendidly rich white Hermitage possesses a bouquet that soars from the glass, offering up aromas that represent the essence of the grape and the vineyard—ripe pears, truffles, and a petroleum smell not unlike that of a great Alsace Riesling. The wine exhibits a Montrachet texture, a superconcentrated, unctuous feel, exceptional power and depth, and an amazingly long finish. It will last and improve for 25–30 years. Michel Chapoutier produced two stunning white dessert wines in 1990. His 1990 Beaumes-de-Venise is a delicate yet richly fragrant, subtle Muscat that is moderately sweet and possesses good acidity as well as a wonderful vibrancy, freshness, and purity to its flavors. Drink it before the end of 1994. Chapoutier also produced an astonishing 1990 Vin de Paille. The grapes spend 2½ months on straw mats before they are crushed and vinified, and the result is an unctuous, unbelievably rich, fabulously perfumed, honeyed wine with extraordinary balance for its massive size. Wines such as these can last 40–50 years.

Lamentably, most Americans have never appreciated the glories of a bonedry, yet full-flavored rosé from southern France. These smashing wines are ideal as aperitifs and have remarkable flexibility with an assortment of foods. The problem is that most of them arrive in this country beaten up in transit or are shipped long after their freshness and vibrancy have dissipated. Chapoutier has produced some gorgeously seductive dry rosés. The 1991 Côtes du Rhône Rosé offers a bouquet of red fruits and austere, dry, medium-bodied, crisp flavors. The 1990 Tavel Rosé is a more ambitious, fuller, bigger wine with a great deal of glycerin, a super strawberry- and cherry-scented nose, dramatic flavors, and even some tannin in the finish. I would not be surprised to see this rosé drink well for at least 2–3 years.

Nowhere has the revolution at Chapoutier been more evident than with the cultivation, vinification, *élevage,* and taste of this firm's red wines. The old, slightly oxidized style of Michel's father has been abandoned in favor of low yields, small casks, and a natural, artisanal style. The 1990 St.-Joseph Deschants has a black/ruby/purple color, a pronounced black cherry– and herb-scented nose, fine definition to its rich, medium-bodied flavors, and a spicy, tannic finish. The 1989 St.-Joseph Deschants displays a nose of spring flowers and black fruits in a ripe, tasty, softer style than the 1990. Both wines should drink well for the next 5–6 years. The 1988 St.-Joseph Deschants has a darker, more opaque color; an intense, spicy, black cherry, earthy bouquet; wonderfully deep, intense, supple flavors; and a long, heady finish. Drink this gorgeous bottle of St.-Joseph over the next 3–5 years. Both the 1989 and 1990 Crozes-Hermitage Les Meysonniers are very good wines bursting with fruit and admirably concentrated. The tasty, rich 1989 is slightly softer, but has an attractive nose of cassis, herbs, and minerals, and a medium-bodied finish. The 1990 is black/ruby in color, with 10–15 years of aging potential, a long, concentrated, complex taste, and a nearly explosive finish. The rich, full-bodied 1988 Crozes-Hermitage Les Meysonniers is also dark ruby, with an intense bouquet of black raspberries and cassis. The 1988 Crozes-Hermitage Petite Ruche, made from much younger vines, is still a good wine. Dark ruby/purple, with a slightly herbaceous, blackcurrant-scented bouquet, medium body, and spicy, more chocolaty and coffee flavors, this wine should be drunk over the next 3–4 years. Chapoutier has begun to produce a fruity, soft, pleasant wine from the Côtes du Ventoux. The 1990 is an attractive, medium-bodied, agreeable first effort. The 1991 Côtes du Rhône Belle Ruche reveals a solid, peppery, spicy nose, ripe, medium-bodied flavors, and a round, soft finish. Drink it over the next 2–3 years. The 1990 Côtes du Rhône Belle Ruche offers a big, herbal, black cherry, chocolate nose, rich, medium- to full-bodied flavors, and a generously long, supple finish. It should drink well for the next 4–5 years. The 1989 Côtes du Rhône Belle Ruche has a chunky, peppery, medium-bodied style.

The 1991 Côtes du Rhône Rasteau is a dark-colored wine, with more power and concentration than the Belle Ruche, as well as a soft, fleshy finish. Drink it over the next 2–3 years. The 1990 Côtes du Rhône Rasteau offers a roasted, chocolate, spicy, cherry nose and ripe, glycerin-laden flavors. It should drink well for at least another 5–6 years. In the past, Chapoutier's Châteauneuf-du-Pape La Bernardine was often a musty, diluted, disjointed, alcoholic wine. The 1990 Châteauneuf-du-Pape La Bernardine is significantly better than the 1989. The deep dark ruby/garnet color is followed by a huge nose of sweet, roasted, raspberry fruit intermingled with scents of peanuts, fruitcake, and spicy pepper. This rich, expansive, full-bodied wine exhibits an unctuous texture, concentration, and a long, moderately tannic finish. An intense, velvety wine, it should continue to provide exciting drinking for at least 12–14 years. I should note that numerous shallow-tasting bottles of this wine and the 1989 have shown up in the marketplace, giving rise to serious questions about bottle variation. The lighter 1989 Châteauneuf-du-Pape La Bernardine displays a big, spicy, berry-scented nose intermingled with the scent of herbs, almonds, and gobs of red fruits; voluptuous, nicely concentrated, supple flavors; and a long and heady finish. The 1988 Châteauneuf-du-Pape La Bernardine is full bodied and rich, with a heady bouquet of roasted peanuts and black fruits. Chapoutier's luxury *cuvée*, the 1990 Barbe Rac, is an awesome red wine. The opaque dark ruby/purple color is followed by powerful aromas of black raspberries, chocolate, roasted nuts, herbs, and earth. There is extraordinary richness, gobs of glycerin, a full-bodied, unctuous texture, and a finish that reveals stunning extraction of flavor and high tannins. My instincts suggest that 25–35 years of longevity is probable. The 1989 Châteauneuf-du-Pape Barbe Rac possesses a huge bouquet of herbs, licorice, chocolate, and berry fruit. It displays exceptional density, concentration, high tannins, and layers of richness. The wine does not taste alcoholic despite its considerable size and power. This is a sensational expression of Châteauneuf-du-Pape that should drink beautifully for 20–25 years. Chapoutier's 1990 Côte Rôtie is an attractive, forward, spicy, richly fruity wine that will have to be drunk over the next 6–7 years. The 1989 Côte Rôtie exhibits a beautiful bouquet of black raspberries, spices, olives, and a touch of new oak. Pure velvet, with a decadently rich, silky texture, soft tannins, and low acidity, it should drink well for the next 10–12 years. The 1988 Côte Rôtie Brune et Blonde displays a rich, smoky, bacon fat–scented bouquet backed up by copious quantities of black raspberries. The wine exhibits fine depth and precision and full body, with slightly more acidity and firmer tannins than the 1989. It is a super bottle of Côte Rôtie that should drink well for 10–15 years. The 1990 Côte Rôtie Mordorée is intended to rival the finest single-vineyard Côte Rôties made by the likes of Guigal. The saturated dark ruby/purple color is followed by an awesome nose that offers generous quantities of sweet black fruits, flowers, toasty new oak, and smoky bacon fat. There is superb concentration, a sweet, expansive texture, and a mindboggling, long finish. This lavishly rich Côte Rôtie, which is already delicious, is capable of lasting for 10–15 years.

Hermitage is the flagship wine of the Chapoutier firm. The 1987 Hermitage La Sizeranne is powerful and concentrated, with a dark ruby/purple color, a big, intense nose of cassis, herbs, and minerals, medium to full body, a velvety taste, and a heady finish. Drinkable now, it should continue to age well for 10–12 years. The 1988 La Sizeranne is a soft but concentrated Hermitage. The bouquet is slightly more floral and includes the scent of violets to go along with the superripe aromas of cassis and toasty oak. Generously endowed and full bodied, it will last for 10–15 years. The 1989 Hermitage La Sizeranne is a sensational, organically made, unfined, unfiltered wine. The dark ruby/purple color is opaque and dense. The bouquet offers aromas of cassis, minerals, smoky oak, and herbs. In the mouth this rich, powerful, highly concentrated, superripe wine exhibits brilliant delineation to its flavors as well as impressive presence and length. Still unevolved and backward, this beauty should be at its best between 1997 and 2015. The 1990 Hermitage La Sizeranne is even better. The wine's color is almost black. It possesses a superrich nose of Oriental spices, licorice, and cassis, fabulous concentration, high tannins, decent acidity, and muscular, rich flavors. It should last for 30 or more years. The prestige *cuvée* of 1989 Hermitage Le Pavillon, made from a parcel of old vines (averaging 70–80 years of age), has an opaque black/purple color and a hauntingly stunning bouquet of violets, cassis, minerals, and oak. This extraordinarily rich yet perfectly balanced wine will probably not be ready to drink for at least 5–10 years, but it will evolve for 3 decades or more. Only 600 cases of this magnificent wine were produced. The 1990 Hermitage Le Pavillon is as compelling as the 1989. It exhibits slightly less opulence, but more power and weight. Black in color, with an extraordinary perfume of licorice, sweet blackcurrants, smoke, and minerals, it coats the palate with layer upon layer of decadently rich, superconcentrated, nearly viscous Syrah flavors. There is amazing glycerin, a chewy, unctuous texture, and phenomenal length. The tannins, which are considerable when analyzed, are virtually obscured by the massive quantities of fruit. Do not open a bottle for at least 7–10 years. It should last for 30–40 years.

The 1990 Cornas reveals a dark purple, almost black color; a sweet, pure nose of cassis; fat, dense, full-bodied flavors; soft tannins; and a supple, velvety-textured finish. Drink it over the next 8–10 years.

DOMAINE DE LA CHARBONNIÈRE* * *

1990 Châteauneuf-du-Pape	C	87
1989 Châteauneuf-du-Pape	B	85
1988 Châteauneuf-du-Pape	C	87

The 1990 Châteauneuf-du-Pape displays a pleasing richness, attractive herb and black cherry scents, and ripe, round, supple cherry and cassis flavors. Drink it over the next 4–6 years. The understated, subdued 1989 Châteauneuf-du-Pape offers up a delicate bouquet of flowers and cherry fruit, spicy, herbaceous fruit flavors, medium body, soft tannins, and an austere finish. Drink it over the next 6–7 years. The 1988 Châteauneuf displays excellent extract; a rich, concentrated, broad, expansive, nearly sweet palate impression; and spicy, peppery, curranty flavors intertwined with flavors of thyme and pepper.

DOMAINE GÉRARD CHARVIN* * * *

1990 Châteauneuf-du-Pape	C	90

The huge, intensely fragrant nose of black cherries, apricots, and kirsch is at the limit of overripeness. This rich, thick, densely concentrated wine is loaded with extraction, gobs of tannin, and glycerin and what must be 14–15% natural alcohol. It should drink well for 12–15 years.

J. L. CHAVE* * * * *

1990 Hermitage	E	98+
1989 Hermitage	D	96
1988 Hermitage	D	94
1987 Hermitage	D	87
1991 Hermitage Blanc	D	90
1990 Hermitage Blanc	D	92
1989 Hermitage Blanc	D	92
1988 Hermitage Blanc	D	90
1987 Hermitage Blanc	D	87
1989 Hermitage Vin de Paille	EE	98
1986 Hermitage Vin de Paille	EE	97
1990 St.-Joseph	C	89
1989 St.-Joseph	C	88

Life is too short not to cellar and drink the wines of Gérard Chave, one of our planet's greatest winemakers. Many modern-day oenologists, who favor safety and security over character and quality, would be well advised to spend some time with Gérard Chave. He takes considerable risks in making wines that are meant, as he says, "not only to last, but to provide extraordinary pleasure." As the numerical scores indicate, there is not much difference between the vintages of white Hermitage, although they differ stylistically. The 1987 Hermitage Blanc is an excellent, round, ripe wine with an attractive honeyed, peachlike bouquet intertwined with the smell of spring flowers (acacias?). It is medium to full bodied, with beautiful clarity and a rich finish. It should continue to drink well for another 4–6 years. The 1988 Hermitage Blanc is more delicate, and less fat and flamboyant. It offers up an enticing bouquet of acacia flowers and honeyed fruit. The 1989 Hermitage Blanc is lower in acidity and more expansive and weighty, making for a huge, chewy mouthful of white wine. Less evolved than the 1989, the 1990 Hermitage Blanc is an explosively rich, powerful, fat, chewy white Hermitage bursting with fruit, with a wonderful purity and focus to its flavors as well as a dramatically long finish. It may ultimately turn out to be the best of these offerings. Chave's excellent 1991 Hermitage Blanc offers a floral-, apricot-, and figlike nose; luxurious, chewy, intense flavors; low acidity; and a long, fleshy finish. Chave believes it will drink beautifully for 10 or more years.

Chave has produced two recent vintages of his famous straw wine, a dessert-style white Hermitage called Vin de Paille. The grapes for these rare wines are harvested and then left on straw mats until they shrivel into raisins. The 1986 is one of the most extraordinary wines I have tasted. With its deep golden color and huge honeyed bouquet that offers a smorgasbord of decadent sweet fruits, this stunningly rich, intense, unctuous nectar must be tasted to be believed. It is nearly perfection and probably will last 20–30 years. As unbelievable as it may sound, the 1989 is even more honeyed, rich, and extracted. Chave's beautiful 1987 Hermitage is soft and elegant, but wonderfully round, rich, concentrated, and seductive. It can be drunk now, but it should be even more complex with 2–3 years of bottle age. It will not be long-lived. The vibrant and brilliantly pure 1988 Hermitage exhibits an opaque dark ruby/purple color and a huge fragrance of spring flowers, cassis, minerals, and spices. It is full bodied and extremely rich, with plenty of tannin and structure as well as 30 years of aging potential. The 1989 Hermitage's blazing expression of Syrah, its bouquet of hickory, coffee, cassis, tar, and ripe blackberry fruit, and its astonishing opulence are dazzling. The 1990 Hermitage looks to be even better, further evidence of just how remarkable that vintage is for Hermitage. It boasts an opaque dark ruby/purple color. Since bottling the nose has closed, but supersweet, overripe aromas of cassis and minerals emerge with swirling. The wine is massive, with an animallike, peppery, powerful Syrah character brilliantly displayed in a multidimensional, multilayered fashion. The tannin level is high, and the finish is exquisite. **Anticipated maturity: 2005–2040+.** Chave also makes splendid albeit tiny quantities of St.-Joseph. The 1989, which is now in the bottle, is a hedonistic, exuberantly rich, fruity wine, bursting with scents and flavors of cassis and Provençal herbs. Drink this lovely wine over the next 5–7 years. The 1990 St.-Joseph, which is richer and more gorgeously scented than even the 1989, promises to be even more exciting!

RATINGS FOR OLDER VINTAGES OF J. L. CHAVE HERMITAGE: 1986 (86), 1985 (92), 1984 (78), 1983 (93+), 1982 (94), 1981 (77), 1980 (76), 1979 (89), 1978 (98), 1976 (76), 1972 (89), 1969 (73), 1967 (93), 1955 (94)

DOMAINE DU CHÊNE—M. AND D. ROUVIÈRE* * * *

1991 Condrieu	D	88
1990 Condrieu Julien Vendange Tardive	D	92
1991 Condrieu Château de Virieu	C	88
1990 St.-Joseph	C	87
1988 St.-Joseph	B	86
1990 St.-Joseph Annais	C	88
1989 St.-Joseph Annais	C	86
1988 St.-Joseph Annais	C	87

The 1991 Condrieu exhibits structure, finesse, medium to full body, that heavenly, almost honeysuckle, peach, apricotlike perfume, and a long, luscious finish. The 1991 Condrieu Château de Virieu is a powerhouse, with little subtlety but gobs of heady, peachy, apricot fruit presented in a full-bodied, fat, chewy format. It needs to be consumed before the end of 1993. For Viognier decadence, consider the 1990 Condrieu Julien. A wine made from late-harvested fruit in a medium-sweet style, it is a powerful, thick, chewy, superconcentrated

Condrieu. Drink it over the next 1–2 years. The 1988 St.-Joseph is a deep, chewy, intense, medium- to full-bodied wine with serious extract. The 1990 St.-Joseph displays a dense, dark ruby color, a spicy, vanillin, black cherry–scented nose, excellent ripe fruit, moderate tannins, and a medium-bodied, well-focused finish. Still rough around the edges, it should drink well for the next 5–7 years. The 1990 St.-Joseph Annais has a forceful nose of vanillin and toasty, smoky oak that is backed up by rich aromas of black fruits, particularly raspberries and cherries. Ripe and medium to full bodied, with moderate tannins, a structured, well-endowed taste, and a spicy finish, it can be kept for 5–8 years. The 1989 St.-Joseph Annais exhibits a great deal of toasty, smoky, new oak, plenty of ripe raspberry and black cherry fruit, and medium body. It should drink well for 4–6 years. The 1988 Annais is even more concentrated, displaying a fascinating bouquet of smoky oak and black raspberries. A full-bodied, intensely concentrated wine with good acidity and excellent length, it should last for 7–8 years.

AUGUSTE CLAPE* * * * *

1990 Cornas	C	91
1989 Cornas	C	88
1988 Cornas	C	89
1987 Cornas	C	86
1991 Côtes du Rhône	B	85
1990 Côtes du Rhône	B	86
1991 Le Vin des Amis	A	87

The 1990 Cornas is outstanding. The color is an opaque black/purple, and the nose offers up rich, ripe aromas of black fruits, licorice, and spices. Supercon-centrated, with a full-bodied, highly extracted, mouth-filling taste, this Cornas possesses moderate tannins, adequate acidity, and a smashingly long finish. It is also relatively refined for a Cornas, displaying no signs of the rustic tannins or funky, earthy smells so many can possess. Enjoy it over the next 12–15 years. The 1989 Cornas is a wine with a dark ruby/purple color, an attractive berry nose, substantial flavor authority, but less extraction of flavor and softer tannins than one normally expects from a Clape Cornas. Stylistically it reminds me of a beefed-up 1982. It should drink well for at least 12–15 years. The 1988 Cornas is a more tender style of Cornas. Lighter, softer, and not nearly as rich and full, it should drink well over the next decade. Shrewd consumers looking for a terrific bargain should consider Clape's 100% Syrah-based wine called Le Vin des Amis. Made from Syrah vines planted at the foot of the Cor-nas hills, this purple-colored wine exhibits a big, peppery, cassis-scented nose, excellent flavors, medium to full body, soft tannins, low acidity, and a lush finish. The 1991 Côtes du Rhône is a tasty, soft, purple-colored, medium-bodied wine. The 1990 Côtes du Rhône is rich, full, and intense. It displays excellent purity and focus to its big, peppery, cassis flavors. This will make a robust mouthful of wine for drinking over the next 7–8 years.

RATINGS FOR OLDER VINTAGES OF AUGUSTE CLAPE CORNAS: 1986 (84+), 1985 (91), 1984 (85), 1983 (90+), 1982 (85), 1981 (86), 1980 (82), 1979 (89), 1978 (92), 1976 (92)

DOMAINE LES CLEFS D'OR* * * *

1990 Châteauneuf-du-Pape	C	88
1989 Châteauneuf-du-Pape	C	91
1988 Châteauneuf-du-Pape	C	90
1991 Châteauneuf-du-Pape Blanc	C	75

Les Clefs d'Or's white Châteauneuf-du-Pape has been consistently good, but its 1991 is unexciting. A vague nose of flowers is followed by a wine with high acidity, average flavor extraction, and a short finish. The 1990 red Châteauneuf-du-Pape exhibits the power, richness, and structure of a top year. Backward, with an interesting and penetrating bouquet of blackberries, spring flowers, earth, and herbs, it possesses plenty of fat and tannin. It has the potential to last for 2 decades. The 1989 offers a huge bouquet of sweet, nearly overripe raspberry fruit intermingled with scents of licorice and flowers. It is exceptionally rich, with gobs of glycerin, plenty of tannin, and a long, well-structured, impressive finish. It should last for 15 or more years. The 1988 is a superb wine, one of the stars of that excellent vintage. The bouquet smells of plums, blackberries, violets, and other spring flowers. Fat, ripe, concentrated, and full bodied, it is an opulently styled, gorgeously textured, fleshy Châteauneuf-du-Pape for drinking over the next 10 years.

CLOS BIMARD* * *

1990 Châteauneuf-du-Pape	C	86
1989 Châteauneuf-du-Pape	C	86

The 1990 exhibits a spicy, herb-tinged, black cherry–scented nose, tannic, medium- to full-bodied flavors that display fine concentration, and enough extract and balance to evolve over the next 7–12 years. The 1989 offers a deep purple color, ripe, chewy, blackberry and black cherry flavors, plenty of glycerin, noticeable tannin, and a full-bodied, backward, tightly structured, firm finish. It will require cellaring. **Anticipated maturity: 1996–2008.**

CLOS DU CAILLOU* * * */* * * * *

1990 Châteauneuf-du-Pape	C	92
1989 Châteauneuf-du-Pape	C	86
1988 Châteauneuf-du-Pape	C	91
1991 Châteauneuf-du-Pape Blanc	C	84

The 1990 is a lavishly built, blockbuster Châteauneuf-du-Pape, with enormous quantities of sweet red and black fruits. The bouquet of black raspberries and flowers is both intense and captivating. The wine is crammed with highly extracted, rich fruit and possesses a chewy, enticing texture and a rich, tannic finish. It should make a sumptuous Châteauneuf-du-Pape for drinking over the next 10–12 years. Claude Pouizin's 1989 is richly fruity, round, and generous. It is a chunky, generously endowed wine for drinking over the next 5–7 years. If you can still find any, the 1988 is a terrific, rich, full wine that will continue to drink well for another 7–8 years. The attractive 1991 white Châteauneuf-du-Pape is certainly a success for the vintage. It is a cleanly made, fruity, tasty, fresh style, with subtle floral, melony, underripe peach flavors. It requires immediate consumption.

DOMAINE LE CLOS DES CAZAUX* * * *

1990	Gigondas Cuvée de la Tour Sarrazine	B	87
1989	Gigondas Cuvée de la Tour Sarrazine	B	83
1990	Vacqueyras Cuvée Saint-Roch	B	87
1990	Vacqueyras Cuvée Templiers	B	89

Clos des Cazaux is probably the top estate of Vacqueyras. The 1990 Cuvée Templiers, made of virtually 100% Syrah, has an inky purple color, a huge nose of cassis and smoke, authoritative, full-bodied flavors, soft tannins, and stunning length. It should last for 7–9 years. The 1990 Cuvée Saint-Roch is also a generously endowed wine, with a plump, unctuous texture, excellent purity and definition, and a long finish. It requires consumption over the next 4–6 years. The 1990 Gigondas Cuvée de la Tour Sarrazine offers a more noticeable herbal, peppery streak in its flavors, medium to full body, fine richness, and more tannin and structure. Drink it over the next 6–8 years. The 1989 Gigondas Cuvée de la Tour Sarrazine has diluted fruit flavors and a decent finish.

CLOS DU MONT-OLIVET* * * */* * * * *

1990	Châteauneuf-du-Pape	C	90
1989	Châteauneuf-du-Pape	C	92
1988	Châteauneuf-du-Pape	C	90
1991	Châteauneuf-du-Pape Blanc	C	79
1990	Châteauneuf-du-Pape La Cuvée du Papet	D	92
1989	Châteauneuf-du-Pape La Cuvée du Papet	D	95

Clos du Mont-Olivet can be one of the longest-lived Châteauneuf-du-Papes, having the potential to mature over a span of 15–20 years. This domaine still employs the reprehensible practice of bottling its wine as it is sold, resulting in a vintage often being bottled over a 4–10 year span. The key is to buy the newest Clos du Mont-Olivet vintage as soon as it is released. The quality of the 1990s merits serious consideration, but move quickly; do not wait for second and third bottlings to appear in subsequent years. The later bottlings are more austere and not as fresh. The three newest vintages of Clos du Mont-Olivet reaffirm that their wines are attention grabbers, with dense, saturated color and superextraction of red fruits, herbs, coffee, and tobacco. The 1990 red Châteauneuf-du-Pape should prove to have 15 or more years of longevity. It is a concentrated, back-strapping, muscular wine. The color is a dark ruby/purple. With swirling, a spicy, peppery nose of cassis fruit and herbs is apparent. Full bodied and impressively endowed, this large-scale wine requires cellaring. The 1989 is even richer, with a wonderful, spicy, black olive– and cassis-scented nose, chocolaty, dusty, chewy flavors, plenty of tannin, gobs of glycerin, and a powerful, tannic finish. The 1988 has a fabulous bouquet of Oriental spices, black cherries, cedar, chocolate, and coffee. Full bodied, with an intense, rich, well-balanced finish, it should last for at least 12–15 years.

The 1990 Cuvée du Papet, a luxury *cuvée,* reveals a dark ruby color, a sweet, herbal, cherry-scented bouquet, an enormously rich, expansive, highly extracted finish, and enough alcohol and glycerin to provide an unctuous texture. It should drink well for 10–15 or more years. The 1989 Cuvée du Papet offers up huge aromas of Provençal herbs, roasted nuts, and sweet, jammy, exotic fruits. Its decadence and opulence must be tasted to be believed. This unctuous, wonderfully rich wine makes for splendid drinking, but it promises to last for 20–25 years. It is an astonishing, old-style, traditionally made Châteauneuf-du-Pape, the likes of which are rarely seen in today's high-tech world, where wines are so often made within strictly formulated parameters.

The white Châteauneuf-du-Pape from Clos du Mont-Olivet has never been one of my favorites. Their 1991 white displays a bouquet redolent of bananas. The wine has good body but lacks fruit.

CLOS DE LA MURE* * * *

1990 Côtes du Rhône	A	86

Proprietor Michel has turned out an absolutely luscious Côtes du Rhône in 1990. It possesses a deep color, a huge bouquet of ripe berry fruit, herbs, and black cherries, full-bodied, spicy, supple flavors, and a rich, intense finish. Drink it over the next 2–3 years.

CLOS DES PAPES* * * *

1990 Châteauneuf-du-Pape	C	92
1989 Châteauneuf-du-Pape	C	91
1988 Châteauneuf-du-Pape	C	88
1991 Châteauneuf-du-Pape Blanc	C	74
N.V. Le Petit Vin d'Avril	A	84

The 1991 Châteauneuf-du-Pape Blanc is standard fare—a bland, high-tech, denuded wine that has some perfume but very little fruit, depth, or length. Drink it over the next year. Proprietor Paul Avril's red wines are among the most classic of the appellation, but they are also among the least flattering to taste when young. In top years, such as 1989 and 1990, they are meant to last for 15–20 years. Both the 1989 and 1990 are rich, tannic wines that are significantly less developed and forward than the 1988. The 1990 Châteauneuf-du-Pape is Avril's finest wine since his terrific 1978. It exhibits an impressive opaque, dark ruby/purple color, a pronounced nose of sweet cassis and black cherry fruit, an attractive, expansive sweetness and ripeness on the palate, and a powerful, long finish. Although backward, it should age gracefully for 15–20 years. The 1989 Châteauneuf-du-Pape displays a dark ruby color and a reticent and extremely closed bouquet of herbs, red and black fruits, minerals, and spring flowers. With coaxing, the wine opens. It is full bodied, muscular, tannic, and backward, with excellent concentration. The 1988 is less concentrated and much more evolved. It displays a huge, peppery, spicy nose, intense, richly fruity flavors, medium to full body, and moderate tannins in the finish. Drink this finesse-style wine between now and 2004. Avril also produces a tasty nonvintage wine called Le Petit Vin d'Avril. This chunky, full-bodied, quaffable red wine offers considerable value.

RATINGS FOR OLDER VINTAGES OF CLOS DES PAPES CHÂTEAUNEUF-DU-PAPE: 1986 (77), 1985 (88), 1983 (87), 1982 (72), 1981 (89), 1979 (88), 1978 (93), 1970 (90)

CLOS DU ROI* * *

1990 Châteauneuf-du-Pape	C	74

A brilliantly polished ruby color, a vague, peppery nose, and faded, short, eviscerated flavors suggest this is another wine that has been traumatized by a sterile filtration. Technocrats might applaud its structure, cleanliness, and blandness.

CLOS SAINT-MICHEL* * *

1990 Châteauneuf-du-Pape	C	79
1989 Châteauneuf-du-Pape	C	87
1991 Châteauneuf du-Pape Blanc	B	80
1990 Châteauneuf-du-Pape Cuvée Reservée	C	86

I was unimpressed with the disjointed, soft, flabby, yet fruity 1990. Far more interesting is the 1989, a heady, opulent wine with decadent levels of black fruits, gobs of glycerin, and a plush, velvety texture. Drink this head-turning, in-your-face style of Châteauneuf-du-Pape over the next 5–6 years. The 1990 Cuvée Reservée offers a huge nose of roasted peanuts and ripe, jammy cassis fruit, making for an uncomplex but enticing introduction. This deeply colored wine exhibits dense, thick, chewy, mouth-filling flavors that are full of alcohol and glycerin. The 1991 white Châteauneuf-du-Pape is fruity, soft, ripe, and medium bodied, with a clean finish. Although uninspiring, it is acceptable and merits consumption.

CLUSEL-ROCH* * */* * * *

1990 Côte Rôtie	D	80
1989 Côte Rôtie-Les Grandes Places	E	94
1989 Côte Rôtie	D	90
1988 Côte Rôtie	D	92

The 1989 Côte Rôtie is one of the finest efforts of the vintage. The wine exhibits a healthy dark ruby/purple color as well as a sweet nose of bacon fat, black raspberries, earth, and flowers. There is medium to full body, excellent purity and balance, and a moderately tannic, generous finish. Drink it over the next 10–12 years. The 1989 Les Grandes Places is richer and more sumptuous. It also has more tannin and depth. Drink it between 1995 and 2008. The superconcentrated, tannic 1988 Côte Rôtie is more closed than the 1989, but its impressive extraction of fruit is admirable. The nose offers aromas of smoked meats, black fruits, and herbs. It is full bodied, with terrific concentration as well as a long, powerful finish. Drink it between 1995 and 2008. The 1990 Côte Rôtie is herbaceous, medium bodied, and lacking concentration.

JEAN-LUC COLOMBO* * *

1991 Cornas Les Ruchets	D	88
1990 Cornas Les Ruchets	D	85
1989 Cornas Les Ruchets	D	79
1988 Cornas Les Ruchets	D	89
1987 Cornas Les Ruchets	D	87

Colombo, an oenologist and consultant as well as grower/producer, was the first in Cornas to begin using new oak casks to try to tame some of the rustic, savage elements in the wines produced from the sun-drenched amphitheater of vines that overlooks the city of Valence. Colombo's first vintage, the 1987, has now reached full maturity. The big, bacon fat and cassis scents of Syrah, as well as vanillin from new oak, are obvious. The wine is civilized for a Cornas, with medium body and rich, complex flavors. The tannins have melted away. This is clearly a modern-style Cornas. The 1988 is less appealing from an aromatic perspective. Its nose is more closed, but in the mouth the wine displays greater extraction of flavor and a more solid inner core of fruit, as well as more tannin and glycerin in the finish. It is an elegant, stylish wine. The 1988 should last for a decade or more. Colombo's 1989 is an excessively oaky, medium-bodied wine that is out of balance. There is some concentration, but the oak obliterates the fruit. Although the streamlined, compact 1990 Cornas Les Ruchets is good, it lacks generosity, and its international style has a degree of vagueness. It should be drunk over the next 7–8 years. The excellent 1991 Cornas Les Ruchets displays a dark ruby color, a big, spicy, berry-scented nose with a subtle touch of vanillin, medium to full body, a sweet, expansive texture, and ripe tannins in the finish. Drink it over the next 10–12 years.

DANIEL COMBE* * *

1990 Côtes du Rhône Vignoble de la Jasse	A	86
1990 Vin de Pays Vignoble de la Jasse	A	86

The 1990 Côtes du Rhône is a lusciously soft, round, fruity wine, with some mature aromas of cedar, Provençal herbs, chocolate, and berries. It is medium bodied, low in acidity, light in tannin, and ideal for current drinking. The 1990 Vin de Pays is a well-endowed, richly fruity, supple wine bursting with aromas of red and black fruits. It goes down the gullet easily! Drink it before the end of 1994.

JEAN COMTE DE LAUZE* * *

1990 Châteauneuf-du-Pape	C	81
1989 Châteauneuf-du-Pape	C	86
1988 Châteauneuf-du-Pape	C	84
1991 Châteauneuf-du-Pape Blanc	B	69

The undistinguished 1991 Châteauneuf-du-Pape Blanc is watery, thin, and short, with no substance, fruit, or character. The 1990 red Châteauneuf-du-

Pape is a round, sweet, commercial wine, with light intensity, albeit pretty cherry aromas and a soft, medium-bodied finish. It should be drunk over the next 3–4 years. The 1989 offers up a pronounced peppery, herbal, smoky nose, some tannin and structure, medium to full body, and a decent finish. **Anticipated maturity: 1994–2000.** The 1988 is robust and round, but one-dimensional and a little rustic and coarse. It should drink well for 3–4 years.

DOMAINE LA CRAU DES PAPES* * *

1990 Châteauneuf-du-Pape	C	85+

I hope this wine can throw off some of its high tannins without losing its fruit and drying out. It is a big, beefy, solid Châteauneuf-du-Pape with admirable body, but the chalky quality and astringency of the tannins concern me.

YVES CUILLERON* * * *

1991 Condrieu	D	89
1991 Condrieu Vieilles Vignes	D	92
1989 St.-Joseph	C	84
1988 St.-Joseph	C	87

The 1991 Condrieu (regular *cuvée*) exhibits a beautiful nose of spring flowers and apricots. It is followed by ripe, medium- to full-bodied, elegant flavors that are presented in a rich, well-balanced format. Drink it up. The 1991 Condrieu Vieilles Vignes offers a flowery, apricot/peachy scent as well as a pronounced aroma of cherries. In the mouth the wine displays marvelous depth, a full, unctuous, chewy texture, enough acidity to provide definition, and gobs of fruit and alcohol in the lusty finish. It should be drunk before the end of 1995. The 1989 St.-Joseph is a straightforward, monolithic, spicy, gamey style of St.-Joseph that leans toward the rustic style of winemaking. There is plenty of tannin and grip, but it may be lacking some fruit. The 1988 St.-Joseph is more impressive, with a deep ruby/purple color and an intense, unevolved bouquet of cassis and raspberries. It exhibits excellent concentration, medium to full body, some attractive fatness, a velvety texture, and moderate tannins in its long, ripe finish. It should drink well for another 5–7 years.

CURSON–ÉTIENNE POCHON* * *

1990 Crozes-Hermitage	C	86
1989 Crozes-Hermitage	C	86
1988 Crozes-Hermitage	C	85
1990 Crozes-Hermitage Blanc	C	81
1989 Crozes-Hermitage Blanc	C	74

I am not impressed with Curson's white wines, which tend to be straightforward and clean but lacking soul and personality. The 1990 white Crozes-Hermitage displays more character than the insipid 1989, which is light and watery. The

1990 red Crozes-Hermitage exhibits an opaque black/purple color, a huge nose of herbs and overripe cassis, fine richness, plenty of tannin, a combination of elegance and fatness, and a long, spicy, roasted finish. This wine could be confused with a medium-weight Hermitage. The 1989 Crozes-Hermitage shares similar substance and richness, but the acids are lower. Much like the 1990, this chewy, rich Hermitage should be drunk within its first 8–10 years of life. The 1988 possesses a black/ruby color as well as a wonderfully up-front, seductive bouquet of black fruits and toasty new oak. It offers good rather than great concentration and lacks length and a finish.

CUVÉE DU BELVEDERE* * * *

1990 Châteauneuf-du-Pape	C	87?
1989 Châteauneuf-du-Pape	C	88
1988 Châteauneuf-du-Pape	C	88

The best two wines I have tasted from proprietor Robert Girard are his sensational 1978 and his glorious 1983. His 1989 offers a graceful, rich, plummy bouquet intertwined with scents of raspberries and chocolate. Elegant, with rich fruit, good structure, and noticeable tannins, this well-balanced Châteauneuf-du-Pape will drink well for the next 10–12 years. The 1990 is variable, some bottles tasting far richer than others. The best examples reveal a medium-deep ruby color, an intensely fragrant bouquet of jammy raspberries, flowers, and earth, and an opulent, fleshy, satiny-smooth finish. Drink it over the next 6–8 years. The 1988 reveals the big, bold, dramatic bouquet that Girard routinely obtains. Luscious, rich, and full bodied, it should be drunk over the next 5–6 years.

RATINGS FOR OLDER VINTAGES OF CUVÉE DU BELVEDERE CHÂTEAUNEUF-DU-PAPE: 1986 (87), 1985 (86), 1983 (90), 1981 (85), 1978 (91)

CUVÉE DU VATICAN* * * *

1990 Châteauneuf-du-Pape	C	87
1989 Châteauneuf-du-Pape	C	86

Despite their up-front, dizzyingly alcoholic style, these two wines can stand the test of time. The 1990 exhibits an intensely spicy, cherry-, roasted nut–, and kirsch-scented nose; sweet, alcoholic, supple, chewy flavors; plenty of ripeness; and sweet tannins in the long, succulent, lusty finish. This is a decadently styled, exotic Châteauneuf-du-Pape that merits drinking over the next 7–8 years. The 1989 displays much of the same personality. It is a lusty, heady, rich Châteauneuf-du-Pape, with the smell of peaches and apricots, a generous amount of fruit, and a soft, lush, hot finish. Drink it over the next 6–7 years. Readers should note that this is an estate that bottles its wines as they are sold, so be sure to purchase the earlier bottlings.

DARD ET RIBO* * *

1988 Crozes-Hermitage	B	87
1988 Hermitage	C	85
1988 St.-Joseph	B	85

The 1988 St.-Joseph exhibits a pure, black raspberry fruitiness, medium body, soft acidity, and a nicely concentrated, satiny finish. The 1988 Hermitage is moderately concentrated, smooth, and forward, with a subtle vanillin character. It lacks the flavor dimension and concentration of the finest Hermitages. The 1988 Crozes-Hermitage is spicy, rich, full bodied, and crammed with intense cassis fruit intertwined with flavors of Provençal herbs. This impressive Crozes appears to have more extract and character than the Hermitage. Drink the Crozes over the next 2–3 years.

DELAS FRÈRES* * * *

1988 Châteauneuf-du-Pape	C	80
1991 Condrieu	E	90
1990 Cornas Chante Perdrix	C	86
1989 Cornas Chante Perdrix	C	79
1988 Cornas Chante Perdrix	C	81
1990 Côte Rôtie	E	84
1989 Côte Rôtie	E	84
1988 Côte Rôtie	E	88
1989 Côte Rôtie Seigneur de Maugiron	E	87
1988 Côte Rôtie Seigneur de Maugiron	E	89
1989 Côtes du Rhône-Villages	A	85
1990 Côtes du Ventoux	A	82
1990 Crozes-Hermitage	B	84
1989 Crozes-Hermitage	B	84
1989 Gigondas	B	84
1989 Hermitage	D	84
1990 Hermitage Marquise de la Tourette	E	89
1989 Hermitage Marquise de la Tourette	E	88
1988 Hermitage Marquise de la Tourette	E	88
1990 Hermitage Marquise de la Tourette Blanc	E	89
1989 Hermitage Marquise de la Tourette Blanc	E	87
1988 Hermitage Marquise de la Tourette Blanc	E	87
1987 Hermitage Marquise de la Tourette Blanc	E	78
1990 St.-Joseph	B	85
1989 St.-Joseph	B	86
1988 St.-Joseph	B	78
1989 Vacqueyras	A	84

The best wines of Delas are their northern Rhônes, particularly those from their vineyards. The southern Rhône *cuvées* tend to be a mixed bag of commercially acceptable but uninteresting products. Of the four vintages of Hermitage Marquise de la Tourette, the 1990 exhibited the most intensity, an unctuous, chewy constitution, rich, honeyed, apple-, and nutlike flavors, and a heady finish. I would not be surprised to see this wine evolve for 20 years. The 1989 white Marquise de la Tourette was much lighter, exhibiting medium body and attractive, fleshy, chunky flavors. The 1988 white Marquise de la Tourette displayed fine acidity, an unctuous, honeyed, pineapple- and peachlike character, the elusive scent of wet stones, and a fine finish. It should drink well for at least 10–15 years. The 1987 Hermitage Marquise de la Tourette Blanc is a light, straightforward, relatively innocuous wine, but it is cleanly made and quaffable. The 1991 Condrieu is an opulently styled, rich, full-bodied, fleshy wine that should be drunk before the end of 1994. The lightest *cuvée* of red wine, the 1990 Côtes du Ventoux, exhibited a fruity, carbonic maceration style and a pleasant smoothness. It is best consumed by 1995. The 1989 Côtes du Rhône-Villages is a rich, heady, full-bodied, complex, impressively concentrated wine. I found little difference in style or character between the Crozes-Hermitage and St.-Joseph. The 1990 Crozes-Hermitage appeared to be denser and fuller than the 1989, which had considerable tannin. It was a big, herbaceous, one-dimensional wine. Both the 1990 and 1989 St.-Josephs were more flattering, with less tannin and toughness, more of the attractive black fruit character, and softer textures. The 1988 St.-Joseph was light and straightforward. Delas is widely known for its Cornas, which it ages in small oak barrels. Its 1990 Cornas Chante Perdrix was forward and precocious, with soft tannins and some sweetness and ripeness. It possessed a long, supple finish. The 1989 Cornas Chante Perdrix was dangerously close to being excessively woody. The wine possessed plenty of ripe berry fruit and a peppery, spicy nose intermingled with the strong scents of vanillin. Drink this forward, soft, supple Cornas over the next 3–5 years. The 1988 Cornas Chante Perdrix was surprisingly light bodied, a bit diluted, and too oaky. Although the 1990 Côte Rôtie is light and lacking concentration and depth, it does possess smoky, sweet fruit, medium body, and a short finish. It is a lighter-style Côte Rôtie for drinking over the next 6–7 years. In 1989 the regular *cuvée* of Côte Rôtie is straightforward, soft, and commercial. It should be drunk over the next 2–4 years. The 1988 Côte Rôtie is concentrated, with more acidity and harder tannins, and should drink well for the next 5–7 years. The 1989 Côte Rôtie Seigneur de Maugiron is more ambitious, exhibiting a great deal of toasty new oak, an attractive bacon fat nose intermingled with aromas of ripe prunes, and a long, rich, opulent finish. It should last for another 7–8 years. The 1988 Côte Rôtie Seigneur de Maugiron is the most complete of these wines, full bodied, harmonious, concentrated, and fragrant. Drink it over the next 8–10 years. The 1990 Hermitage Marquise de la Tourette should make a superb bottle of wine in about 7–8 years. Black/purple in color, it possesses a huge, spicy, licorice, toasty, smoky nose, superrich cassis flavors, good acidity, and plenty of tannin. **Anticipated maturity: 1996–2012.** The 1989 Hermitage (regular *cuvée*) is light to medium bodied, tasty, and straightforward, with a fragrant smell of minerals and cassis. The 1989 Hermitage Marquise de la Tourette exhibits far greater flavor extraction and plenty of hard tannins in the finish. Although not as concentrated as the 1990, it appears to be more tannic and structured. The promising 1988 Hermitage Marquise de la Tourette, although closed, tannic, and hard, offers an attractively ripe, new oak– and cassis-scented nose. It is rich, but the tannins dominate. It should last for 2 decades. Less impressive are the soft, straightforward, commercially oriented, one-dimensional 1988 Châteauneuf-du-Pape, the 1989 Vacqueyras, and the 1989 Gigondas.

ALBERT DERVIEUX-THAIZE* * */* * * *

1989	Côte Rôtie Côte Blonde La Garde	D	84
1988	Côte Rôtie Côte Blonde La Garde	D	85?
1989	Côte Rôtie Côte Brune Fongent	D	78
1989	Côte Rôtie Côte Brune La Viaillère	D	86?
1988	Côte Rôtie Côte Brune La Viaillère	D	90
1987	Côte Rôtie Côte Brune La Viaillère	D	86

Albert Dervieux's style has always been among the most traditional of Côte Rôties, producing firmly structured, tannic, sometimes coarse, rustic, and aggressive wines. That being said, the 1989 Côte Rôtie Fongent is extremely light, with an almost metallic character as well as a stinky, lees smell. The 1989 Côte Rôtie Côte Blonde La Garde is soft and light and lacks concentration and grip. Drink it over the next 5–6 years. The supple 1988 La Garde is exceptionally tannic, with the tannins possessing a coarse, astringent edge that is troubling. There is good ripeness and underlying concentration, but the tannins may ultimately overwhelm the fruit. The 1989 Côte Rôtie Côte Blonde La Viaillère, usually the most backward and impressive of Dervieux's wines, has plenty of weight. Yet the huge, aggressive, astringent tannins are a problem. The superb 1988 La Viaillère is extremely intense, very muscular, and tannic, with loads of concentration, powerful aromas of roasted black fruits and earthy, mineral scents that blossom from the glass. Do not touch a bottle until 1998. Last, the powerful, backward 1987 La Viaillère is a rough-textured, deeply concentrated, tannic, masculine wine that will keep for 7–10 years.

LOUIS DREVON* *

1989	Côte Rôtie	C	77
1988	Côte Rôtie	C	75

Both of these wines represent unimpressive performances. The 1989 is soft, with a touch of raspberries and new oak in the nose. It exhibits round, light, undistinguished flavors. The surprisingly insipid 1988 is similarly styled. Drink both of them over the next 3–4 years.

GEORGES DUBOEUF* * * *

1990	Côte Rôtie Domaine Ile Rousse	C	89
1989	Côte Rôtie Domaine Ile Rousse	C	92

1988 Côte Rôtie Domaine Ile Rousse	C	93
1990 Côtes du Rhône Domaine des Aires Vieilles	A	85
1990 Côtes du Rhône Domaine des Moulins	A	87
N.V. Fleur de Rosé	A	86

In recent years Georges Duboeuf has expanded his Beaujolais empire to include selected Rhône Valley estates. His most noteworthy achievement is the wonderfully fresh, dry, crisp Fleur de Rosé, a refreshingly dry rosé with tons of floral, cherry, and strawberry fruit. This bargain-priced, perfect summer wine should be drunk within 6–7 months of its release, so be sure to ask your favorite wine merchant when the wine will arrive. Duboeuf's Côtes du Rhône estates include the Domaine des Moulins, of which the 1990 is a surprisingly dark ruby-colored wine with fine extract, unexpected density, and a rich, chewy, full style. The 1990 Côtes du Rhône Domaine des Aires Vieilles offers a lusty glassful of good, spicy, herb- and berry-scented Côtes du Rhône. Duboeuf, through a rigorous selection process and the use of 15% new oak casks, has fashioned a powerful, tannic, backward 1988 Côte Rôtie Domaine Ile Rousse that needs at least another 5–7 years of aging. The 1989 Ile Rousse has lower acidity and is much more supple and precocious. Black/purple in color, with a supersmoky, bacon fat–, and cassis-scented bouquet, this rich, sumptuous style of Côte Rôtie will make excellent drinking over the next 10–15 years. The 1990 Côte Rôtie Domaine Ile Rousse is less concentrated than the 1989, but rich, full, and tannic and displaying some attractive black raspberry aromas and flavors, intermingled with scents of vanillin from aging in new oak casks. The wine still has tannin to shed. **Anticipated maturity: 1994–2006.**

EDMOND DUCLAUX* * *

1990 Châteauneuf-du-Pape	C	86
1989 Châteauneuf-du-Pape	C	86

An exotic, overripe cherry fruit character in the 1990 reminded me of the great wine made at Rayas, although it did not have the concentration or complexity of Rayas. Nevertheless, this deep, tannic wine should age nicely for the next 5–10 years. The 1989 was tightly knit, with considerable tannin, a good, spicy, ripe, herb and berry fruit character, and a medium-bodied, austere finish.

DOMAINE DURBAN* * * * *

1991 Muscat de Beaumes-de-Venise	C	90
1990 Muscat de Beaumes-de-Venise	C	89

Both of these wines offer sexy bouquets of pineapples, honey, and tropical fruits. They display the opulent, moderately sweet, unctuous quality of a top Beaumes de Venise, but there is enough acidity to buttress the hefty, thoroughly satisfying flavors. The 1991 is not nearly as viscous and weighty as riper, hotter years tend to be. These are among the least known of the world's great dessert wines, but they must be drunk within 4–5 years of the vintage.

DOMAINE DURIEU* * */* * * *

1990 Châteauneuf-du-Pape		C	87
1989 Châteauneuf-du-Pape		C	79
1988 Châteauneuf-du-Pape		C	86
1990 Châteauneuf-du-Pape Cuvée Lucile Avril		D	88+

The 1988 exhibits fine tannin; is medium to full bodied, spicy, and heady; and possesses an earthy, cinnamon- and raspberry-scented bouquet and juicy, tannic flavors. It should drink well between now and 1996. Paul Durieu produced a so-so 1989, not easy to accomplish in such a super vintage. His 1989 is a green, hard, meagerly endowed wine, lacking richness and character. He produced two *cuvées* in 1990. The 1990 regular *cuvée* displays a dark ruby color; spicy, earthy, sweaty, leathery aromas; meaty, sweet, expansive, full-bodied flavors, and a long, lush, alcoholic finish. Drink it over the next 6–9 years. The 1990 Cuvée Lucile Avril exhibits a huge nose of smoked meats, leather, ripe black cherry fruit, and herbs. The wine is full bodied, intense, alcoholic, and tannic. Impressive but rustic, it should be cellared for 4–5 years. It exhibits the stuffing and structure necessary to last for 12–15 years.

DOMAINE DE L'ESPIGOUETTE* * * *

1990 Côtes du Rhône-Villages		A	83
1989 Côtes du Rhône-Villages		A	86
1990 Côtes du Rhône-Villages Plan de Dieu		A	87
1990 Vin de Pays		A	85

The 1990 Vin de Pays is a surprisingly deep, big, chunky wine with gobs of flavor, and a chocolaty, roasted, black cherry–scented bouquet. This fabulous value should drink well for at least another 2–3 years. Proprietor Bernard Latour's 1990 Côtes du Rhône-Villages is solid, ripe, peppery, and spicy. Among Latour's two best Côtes du Rhônes is the 1990 Côtes du Rhône-Villages Plan de Dieu, a big, meaty, chocolaty, robust wine, with aromas of roasted cassis and nuts, chewy, intensely concentrated flavors, and a long, robust, heady finish. Drink this beauty over the next 3–4 years. The 1989 Côtes du Rhône-Villages is similarly styled, deep, chunky, muscular, and delicious.

DOMAINE DE FAUTERIE* * * *

1990 St.-Joseph		C	87

This wine's dark ruby/purple color displays ripeness and a highly pigmented color. The nose offers up pure aromas of black fruits. Rich, full bodied, and chewy, with plenty of soft tannins, adequate acidity, and a fleshy, mouth-filling finish, this well-balanced wine is tempting to drink now. It should continue to improve for 2–5 years and last for a decade.

JULES FAYOLLE ET FILS* * *

1989 Crozes-Hermitage Les Pontaix		B	?
1988 Crozes-Hermitage Les Pontaix		B	76
1990 Hermitage Les Dionnières		C	?

| 1989 Hermitage Les Dionnières | D | 87 |
| 1988 Hermitage Les Dionnières | D | 85 |

The 1988 Hermitage Les Dionnières displays excellent deep ruby/purple color; a big, ripe, earthy, tar- and roasted black fruit–scented bouquet; deep, full-bodied, muscular flavors; plenty of tannin; and a somewhat clumsy feel on the palate. Although admirably concentrated, it is also coarse. **Anticipated maturity: 1995–2005.** The 1989 Hermitage Les Dionnières exhibits excellent dark ruby/purple color, a big, smoky bouquet of cassis fruit and herbs, and fat, chewy, fleshy flavors. It will not be a long-lived wine by Hermitage standards, but it should drink well for another 7–8 years. Although the 1990 Hermitage Les Dionnières displays some stinky lees character, creating a problem with the bouquet, it is a ripe, rich, round, expansively flavored, supermature, sweet-tasting wine with abundant fruit, superripeness, soft tannins, and low acidity. It will have to be drunk in its first decade of life. The 1989 red Crozes-Hermitage Les Pontaix was overwhelmed by its sulphur, making judgment hopeless. The 1988 Les Pontaix has a good deal of tannin and body, but not much charm or fruit.

EDDIE FÉRAUD* * * *

| 1990 Châteauneuf-du-Pape Cuvée Réservée | C | 90 |

Eddie Féraud produces a natural, unfiltered, personality-filled wine. The saturated deep purple color suggests high extraction, and the impressive fragrant, peppery, gingery, plummy nose is already evolved. Rich and full bodied, this exotic, intense wine is not without a flaw or two (some volatile acidity is present), but for a gutsy, rich, artisanal style of Châteauneuf-du-Pape that delivers tremendous intensity and complexity, Féraud's is a wine to search out. **Anticipated maturity: Now–2005.**

FERRATON PÈRE ET FILS* * *

1990 Crozes-Hermitage La Matière	B	86
1989 Crozes-Hermitage La Matière	B	87
1988 Crozes Hermitage La Matière	B	81
1990 Hermitage Cuvée Les Miaux	D	90
1989 Hermitage Cuvée Les Miaux	D	88
1988 Hermitage Cuvée Les Miaux	D	83

Ferraton has a spotty record, and his two 1988s fall below expectations. Both have annoyingly high acidity and decent concentration but are small-scale wines. The 1989s are much better. The 1989 Crozes-Hermitage La Matière is rich, herbal, and spicy, as well as delicious for drinking over the next 5–8 years. The 1989 Hermitage Cuvée Les Miaux is a powerhouse—full, fat, concentrated, and low in acidity. **Anticipated maturity: 1995–2005.** Ferraton's deeply colored 1990 Crozes-Hermitage La Matière offers a forceful, gamey, spicy, herbal, Syrah nose. Full bodied, rich, and concentrated, with considerable extract, this wine should drink well for 7–8 years. I would keep an eye out for his 1990 Hermitage Cuvée Les Miaux. It is the finest Hermitage

I have tasted from Ferraton. Dark purple-colored, with a fragrant, penetrating bouquet of cassis, meat, and herbs, as well as considerable tannins, this lavishly endowed, full-bodied, superconcentrated wine is loaded. **Anticipated maturity: 1996–2010.**

DES FINES ROCHES* * *

1990 Châteauneuf-du-Pape	C	78
1989 Châteauneuf-du-Pape	C	86
1988 Châteauneuf-du-Pape	C	80
1991 Châteauneuf-du-Pape Blanc	C	77

The Mousset family runs this magnificent vineyard, where the château itself doubles as a luxurious hotel/restaurant known as the Hostellerie des Fines Roches. The wines are commercially styled, with a ripe, heady, alcoholic, exuberant fruitiness. The white wines have consistently disappointed me with their neutral, innocuous style. The 1991 white Châteauneuf-du-Pape is fresh but lacks soul and personality. The 1990 red Châteauneuf-du-Pape is soft, round, and tasty, but straightforward and boring. Drink it over the next 5–6 years. In complete contrast, the 1989 exhibits a ruby/purple color; a big, black cherry, intensely perfumed nose; gobs of soft, luscious fruit; plenty of alcohol; and moderate tannins in the finish. There is reason to believe this wine will evolve nicely over the next 6–8 years. The 1988 is disappointingly light, medium bodied, insipid, and one-dimensional.

FONT DU LOUP* * *

1990 Châteauneuf-du-Pape	C	89
1989 Châteauneuf-du-Pape	C	86
1988 Châteauneuf-du-Pape	C	86

Charles Melia's dark ruby-colored 1990 exhibits plenty of black fruit, herbs, and minerals in its aroma, surprising multidimensional flavors, and an attractive unctuous quality that serves its rich, concentrated, ripe, opulent style. It should drink well for the next 10 years. The 1989 regular *cuvée* is a ripe, powerful, heady wine with plenty of fruit, glycerin, and spice. The 1988 is elegant, with a perfumed bouquet of rich, berry-scented aromas intertwined with the taste of herbs and minerals. In the mouth it is medium to full bodied, ripe, but soft. Drink it over the next 4–5 years. Melia produced 100 cases of a 1989 *cuvée spéciale* that is extraordinary and immense. However, he had not released it for sale as of spring 1993.

FONT DE MICHELLE* * * *

1990 Châteauneuf-du-Pape	C	89
1989 Châteauneuf-du-Pape	C	87
1988 Châteauneuf-du-Pape	C	80
1991 Châteauneuf-du-Pape Blanc	C	84
1989 Châteauneuf-du-Pape Cuvée Étienne Gonnet	D	88

The 1991 Châteauneuf-du-Pape Blanc exhibits a perfumed, floral, melony nose, adequate intensity of fruit, medium body, clean, well-endowed flavors, and a soft, refreshing finish. Drink it before the summer of 1994. The 1988 red Châteauneuf-du-Pape is relatively cooked with raisiny fruit. The wine displays a medium-bodied, herbal, decently concentrated, soft, forward style. In 1989 the Gonnets produced two *cuvées* of Châteauneuf-du-Pape. The regular 1989 Châteauneuf-du-Pape is a tasty wine with a big, herbaceous, peppery nose, rich red and black fruit flavors, full body, and robust tannins in its long finish. It should last for 10–12 or more years. The 1989 Cuvée Étienne Gonnet displays a peppery, cassis- and toasty, vanillin-scented bouquet. It is structured, rich, and ripe as well as full bodied. More closed and less flattering to taste than the 1989 regular *cuvée*, it will drink well over the next 10–12 years. The 1990 Châteauneuf-du-Pape possesses a splendid black/ruby color, a terrific bouquet of crushed, jammy, raspberry fruit, a full-bodied, concentrated palate, and gobs of fruit, glycerin, and spices in its long finish.

DOMAINE DE FONT-SANE* * * * *

1990	Côtes du Ventoux	A	85
1989	Côtes du Ventoux	A	85
1990	Gigondas	C	87
1989	Gigondas	C	89
1988	Gigondas	C	87
1988	Gigondas Cuvée Spéciale Fut Neuf	C	90

Domaine de Font-Sane produces two *cuvées* of Gigondas, a flashy, dramatically flavored regular *cuvée* and a prestige *cuvée* that is aged in new oak. There is also an attractively fruity, tasty, value-priced Côtes du Ventoux, of which both the 1989 and 1990 are good examples. Drink them by the end of 1994. The 1990 Gigondas exhibits an impressive purple color, a pure bouquet of cassis and black raspberries, full-bodied, lusciously fruity, fat flavors, and a long finish. The tender tannins and low acid suggest that the wine should drink well for 6–7 years. The 1989 Gigondas exhibits a black/purple color, a huge bouquet of spring flowers, ripe blackcurrants, herbs, and minerals, a voluptuous texture, low acidity, big, rich, chewy flavors, and a long, intense finish. It should be at its best between now and 2003. The 1988 Gigondas displays a fragrant, roasted, Provençal herb character in the nose, round, generously endowed, full-bodied flavors, and a soft finish. Drink it over the next 5–7 years. The 1988 Gigondas Cuvée Spéciale Fut Neuf is a deeper-colored, more richly extracted Gigondas, exhibiting copious amounts of new oak. With superb underlying richness and fruit, this wine should be marvelous to drink over the next decade.

FORTIA* * *

1990	Châteauneuf-du-Pape	D	82
1989	Châteauneuf-du-Pape	D	86
1988	Châteauneuf-du-Pape	D	86
1986	Châteauneuf-du-Pape	C	85

1985 Châteauneuf-du-Pape	C	84
1991 Châteauneuf-du-Pape Blanc	C	72

Château Fortia, once a phenomenal source of exquisite Châteauneuf-du-Pape, is in serious decline. The 1990 Châteauneuf-du-Pape displays some ripeness, but it is diffuse, lacks concentration, and finishes with a flabby fruitiness and excessive alcohol. Drink it over the next 4–5 years. The 1989 reveals plenty of tannin and glycerin, some richness, and a spicy, jammy, sweet nose. Drink it between now and 2000. The 1988 exhibits a dark ruby color, a dense, alcoholic, spicy taste, some notes of truffles, leather, and ground beef, a soft texture, and a round, gentle finish. Drink it over the next 4–7 years. The 1986 also displays an exotic, Oriental spice, sweet pruny fruit nose, rich, velvety texture, and plenty of smoky, juicy fruit in its finish. It should be consumed. The 1985 reveals a big, spicy, fruitcake sort of nose, very low acidity, a fat, heady fruitiness, and plenty of alcohol and pepper in the finish. It should be consumed over the next 2–4 years. The 1991 white Châteauneuf-du-Pape is thin, sterile, and uninteresting.

RATINGS FOR OLDER VINTAGES OF FORTIA CHÂTEAUNEUF-DU-PAPE: 1983 (86), 1982 (77), 1981 (87), 1979 (82), 1978 (93)

DOMAINE LA FOURMONE—ROGER COMBE* * * *

1990 Gigondas L'Ousteau Fauquet	B	87
1989 Gigondas L'Ousteau Fauquet	B	88
1988 Gigondas L'Ousteau Fauquet	B	75
1990 Vacqueyras Selection du Maître du Chai	A	88
1990 Vacqueyras Tresor du Poet	A	85

Roger Combe produces two *cuvées* of Vacqueyras from his Domaine La Fourmone. The 1990 Vacqueyras Tresor du Poet represents a softer, more up-front style of wine. The peppery, spicy nose is followed by a supple, medium-bodied wine with light tannins. Drink it over the next 4–5 years. The 1990 Vacqueyras Selection du Maître du Chai displays a more opaque color, a roasted, cassis nose, a chewy texture, and a longer finish.

Combe also produces Gigondas. Both his 1989 and 1990 are full-bodied wines with excellent concentration. The 1990 is slightly higher in alcohol, with a more rustic, chewy character. The 1989 is more delineated, although just as ripe and rich. Both wines should continue to drink well for the next 5–6 years. The 1988 was soft, light, and decently fruity, but shallow. It should be consumed over the next 1–2 years.

LOU FRÉJAU* * *

1990 Châteauneuf-du-Pape	C	87
1989 Châteauneuf-du-Pape	C	85
1988 Châteauneuf-du-Pape	C	87
1991 Châteauneuf-du-Pape Blanc	C	86

The 1991 white Châteauneuf-du-Pape is a success in a mediocre to poor year. The flowery, alcoholic nose is backed up by adequate ripeness, excellent fruit, and a medium to full body. It should be consumed before the end of 1994. The 1990 red Châteauneuf-du-Pape offers a big, nicely scented, herbal, jammy nose as well as ripe, unctuous, full-bodied flavors reminiscent of black cherries and fruitcake. The finish is sweet, round, spicy, and alcoholic. Drink it over the next 7–8 years. The 1989 red Châteauneuf-du-Pape is fragrant and soft, with attractive berry fruitiness, medium to full body, and a round finish. There are some elements of apricot and peach jam, suggesting the grapes had reached *sur-maturité*. Drink this charming wine over the next 4–5 years. The 1988 red Châteauneuf exhibits an exuberant, chocolaty, black raspberry, cedary bouquet, deep, rich, full-bodied flavors, and a soft, velvety texture. Drinkable now, it should last for another 3–5 years.

DOMAINE DE GACHON—PASCAL PERRIER* * * * *

1990 St.-Joseph	B	88
1989 St.-Joseph	B	90

The 1990 St.-Joseph has an opaque black/purple color, with a huge, unevolved bouquet of cassis, licorice, and herbs. There is astonishing richness for a St.-Joseph, a full-bodied, almost massive display of fruit, as well as long, supple tannins in the dramatic finish. This is about as big and rich a St.-Joseph as I have ever tasted. The 1989 St.-Joseph is also impressive, with even more richness. The color is opaque black/purple. The bouquet suggests mint, cassis, Provençal herbs, and hickory wood. There is an explosion of fruit, wonderful, chewy, fleshy texture, and a long, superconcentrated finish. It has at least 8–10 more years of aging potential.

PIERRE GAILLARD* * *

1990 Côte Rôtie Côtes Brune et Blonde	D	85
1989 Côte Rôtie Côtes Brune et Blonde	D	86
1988 Côte Rôtie Côtes Brune et Blonde	D	89
1989 St.-Joseph	C	84
1988 St.-Joseph	C	85
1990 St.-Joseph Clos de Cuminaille	C	82

The 1990 St.-Joseph Clos de Cuminaille possesses a closed nose and a chunky, monolithic personality. There is good fruit, but hard tannins in the finish. It should keep for 5–7 years. His 1989 St.-Joseph offers a deep, dark ruby color, a bouquet of black raspberries, soft, ripe flavors, and medium body. **Anticipated maturity: Now–1997.** The 1988 St.-Joseph reveals a black cherry– and plum-scented bouquet, heady, ripe flavors, medium body, and noticeable tannins. It should drink nicely for another 2–3 years.

The 1990 Côte Rôtie possesses good extraction, but the finish is lean and hard. The 1989 Côte Rôtie, which was aged in new oak casks, is a full-bodied, rich, surprisingly tannic wine, with an underlying elegance and purity. It should be at its best between now and 2000. The 1988 looks to be a better wine. It exhibits an intense ruby, black/purple color, a ripe cassis nose intertwined with aromas of vanilla and caramel, excellent richness, an attractive fatness and midpalate depth, and long, alcoholic, rich, tannic flavors. It should continue to drink well for 7–8 years.

DOMAINE DU GALET DES PAPES* * */* * * *

1990 Châteauneuf-du-Pape	C	86
1989 Châteauneuf-du-Pape	C	89
1991 Châteauneuf-du-Pape Blanc	C	73

Jean-Luc Mayard's 1990 Châteauneuf-du-Pape exhibits an attractive dark ruby color and a ripe, sweet, jammy nose of black fruits and herbs. The wine is medium to full bodied, monolithic, dense, and nicely concentrated, with considerable tannin and alcohol. The 1989 offers an inner core of sweet, black fruits and a tight but blossoming bouquet of minerals, licorice, tobacco, fruitcake, and black fruits. The acids in the 1989 were lower than in the 1990 and the alcohol level higher. **Anticipated maturity: Now–2005.** I was disappointed in the stripped, thin, high-acid 1991 white Châteauneuf-du-Pape.

HENRI GALLET* * * */* * * * *

1990 Côte Rôtie Côte Blonde	D	93

Gallet has proven to be an amazing discovery. With vines that average 40 years, all located on the steep slopes of the Côte Blonde (Gallet owns only 6.7 acres), Gallet's first wine, his 1989, sold out before I could taste it. His 1990, from a troublesome year for Côte Rôtie vignerons, is one of the greatest wines of the vintage. It exhibits an opaque, dark ruby/purple color, a sensational nose of black raspberries, minerals, and spices, with spectacular depth, and an unctuous, rich, long finish. It can be drunk now, but will easily last for 15 more years. Interestingly, until 1989, Gallet sold his entire crop to Marcel Guigal. Gallet's wine includes 8% Viognier and is bottled unfiltered.

DE LA GARDINE* * * * *

1990 Châteauneuf-du-Pape	C	88
1989 Châteauneuf-du-Pape	C	90
1988 Châteauneuf-du-Pape	C	89
1991 Châteauneuf-du-Pape Blanc	C	72
1990 Châteauneuf-du-Pape Cuvée des Générations	D	93+

The 1990 Châteauneuf-du-Pape reveals a deeply saturated purple color, a tight but blossoming bouquet of sweet black fruit, and a tannic, well-structured, full-bodied feel. The wine can be drunk now, but it promises to be at its best between 1995 and 2005. The 1989 Châteauneuf-du-Pape exhibits a similar black cherry–, smoke-, herb-, and toasty vanillin-scented bouquet. The dense purple color suggests exceptional ripeness and richness. It is even more tannic and muscular than the 1990. The impressive extract levels clearly stand up to the wine's tannins. **Anticipated maturity: 1995–2008.** The 1988, which is surprisingly backward for the vintage, is extremely rich and full bodied, with a bouquet that reminded me of superripe black plums intertwined with aromas of toasty new oak, licorice, and violets. Drink it between 1995 and 2010. Brunel's top offering is his Cuvée des Générations. The 1990 is black/purple in color, with a closed but promising bouquet of vanillin, smoke, minerals, and blackcurrants. The concentration and length are dazzling in this large-scale, tannic, blockbuster wine that will require 4–5 years of cellaring. It will last for 20–25 years. **Anticipated maturity: 1996–2014.**

VINCENT GASSE* * * *

1990 Côte Rôtie Côte Brune	D	90

Vincent Gasse has only 2.47 acres of Côte Rôtie, but 75% of his vineyard is planted in old vines on the famous Côte Brune vineyard of La Landonne. Twenty-five percent new oak is used, and Gasse bottles his wines unfiltered. A teacher by profession, he has just begun to estate-bottle more of his wines. This is an organically produced wine with no pesticides, herbicides, or fungicides used in the vineyard. The 1990 is a terrific success for the vintage, displaying a huge nose of bacon fat and black raspberry, earthy fruit. Full-bodied and rich, with moderate tannins, this big, intense wine needs another 2–3 years of cellaring but should last through the first decade of the next century.

MARIUS GENTAZ-DERVIEUX* * * * *

1991 Côte Rôtie Côte Brune	D	90
1990 Côte Rôtie Côte Brune	D	89
1989 Côte Rôtie Côte Brune	D	91
1988 Côte Rôtie Côte Brune	D	94
1987 Côte Rôtie Côte Brune	D	88

A trip to Marius Gentaz's small, dingy cellars, where the barrels must all be at least 40 years old, is highly recommended. Here is winemaking in its purest and most artisanal state. Gentaz, who is now in his late sixties (or just slightly older than his barrels), made a fine 1991 Côte Rôtie. It displays medium body and excellent concentration; a deep ruby/purple color; a sweet nose of roasted black raspberry fruit, saddle leather, ground beef, and damp earth; a velvety texture; and a long, sweet, round finish. It is a wine to drink over the next decade. The 1990 is a charming, medium-weight Côte Rôtie with a raspberry, earthy fragrance and a lovely, fat, luscious personality. It should evolve rapidly, so I would recommend drinking it over the next 6–8 years. The 1989 Côte Rôtie Côte Brune is pure finesse and seduction. With black/ruby color and a huge bouquet of smoky, raspberry fruit intertwined with the scent of violets and minerals, it exhibits excellent ripeness, rich, medium- to full-bodied texture, plenty of glycerin, and a long finish. **Anticipated maturity: Now–2006.** The 1988 Côte Rôtie Côte Brune is a spectacularly rich, concentrated wine. Splendidly opaque dark ruby in color, it displays a huge nose of cassis, minerals, licorice, and flowers, astonishing concentration, great flavor delineation, medium to full body, plenty of tannin, and a long, spicy finish. This is a great Côte Rôtie for ringing in the next century, as it should last for at least 20 years. Last, the 1987 Côte Rôtie Côte Brune offers an exotic black fruit character, medium body, and a rich, heady finish. Drink it over the next 3–5 years.

FRANÇOIS GÉRARD* *

1989 Côte Rôtie	D	71
1988 Côte Rôtie	D	78

These two Côte Rôties were disappointing. In addition to displaying a weedy, nearly vegetal, green aroma, the 1989 lacked concentration and exhibited short, angular flavors. The 1988 Côte Rôtie is straightforward, soft, and fruity, but undistinguished.

J. M. GÉRIN* * *

1991	Condrieu Côteau de la Loye	D	84
1990	Côte Rôtie Champin de Seigneur	C	74?
1991	Côte Rôtie Grand Place	C	87
1991	Côtes du Rhône	A	77

Gérin's 1991 Condrieu Côteau de la Loye offers an attractive fragrance, medium body, tasty, underripe, apricotlike fruitiness, and a quick finish. Drink it over the next 1–2 years. The 1991 Côtes du Rhône is light, soft, fruity, and undistinguished. The 1991 Côte Rôtie Grand Place (Gérin's top *cuvée*) exhibits a fragrant, sweet oaky nose, ripe, fleshy, black raspberry flavors, medium to full body, soft tannins, low acidity, and a lush finish. Drink it over the next 7–8 years. The 1990 Côte Rôtie Champin de Seigneur is light, lean, acidic, and lacking fruit.

DOMAINE LES GOUBERTS* * * *

1990	Côtes du Rhône	A	78
1989	Côtes du Rhône	A	83
1988	Côtes du Rhône	A	84
1990	Côtes du Rhône-Villages Beaumes-de-Venise	B	84
1989	Côtes du Rhône-Villages Beaumes-de-Venise	A	85
1988	Côtes du Rhône-Villages Beaumes-de-Venise	A	87
1989	Côtes du Rhône Sablet	A	78
1988	Côtes du Rhône Sablet	A	85
1990	Gigondas	B	85
1989	Gigondas	B	86
1988	Gigondas	B	87
1990	Gigondas Cuvée Florence	D	87
1989	Gigondas Cuvée Florence	D	90
1988	Gigondas Cuvée Florence	D	91

In what was a terrific vintage for ripeness and richness, the 1990 offerings range from a straightforward, soft, pleasant, but compact, monolithic 1990 Côtes du Rhône, to medium-bodied, slightly richer and riper selections from the Côtes du Rhône villages of Sablet and Beaumes-de-Venise. The 1990 Sablet is a bit compact, but solidly built. In the past the Beaumes-de-Venise has been one of Cartier's best wines and top values, but the 1990 appears to have been excessively processed. Although it exhibits fine color, the finish is lean and compact. The 1990 Gigondas regular *cuvée* tastes ripe, soft, and medium bodied, but, again, lacking in concentration. This forward wine will need to be drunk in its first 5–6 years of life. The austere 1990 Gigondas Cuvée Florence reveals toasty new oak aromas combined with an attractive fragrance of black cherry and cassis fruit. **Anticipated maturity: Now–1999.** The basic 1989 Côtes du Rhône displays good dark color, ripe, peppery fruitiness, soft texture, and an easygoing personality. Drink it over the next several years. The 1989 Côtes du Rhône-Villages Beaumes-de-Venise exhibits more muscle, richness, and intensity. The 1988 Côtes du Rhône offers an intense bouquet of ripe raspberry fruit intertwined with the scent of freshly ground black pepper. It is ripe, soft, and supple, providing a delicious, fleshy mouthful of wine. It should be drunk up. The 1988 Côtes du Rhône-Villages Beaumes-de-Venise exhibits plenty of blackberry and peppery fruit scents, concentrated flavors, and a long, intensely rich finish. This full-throttle, impeccably made Côtes du Rhône should be drunk over the next 4–6 years. The 1989 Côtes du Rhône Sablet is surprisingly tough, tannic, and hard textured. The 1988 Sablet reveals a bouquet and flavor that ooze roasted blackberry and raspberry fruit. A full-bodied, lush Côtes du Rhône with a long, heady finish, it should be drunk up. The regular *cuvée* of 1989 Gigondas offers up an open-knit, attractive, spicy, peppery, curranty nose intermingled with the scent of Provençal herbs. Sweet, ripe, and fleshy, with moderate tannins and a chewy, concentrated finish, it should continue to evolve for 4–5 years. The 1988 Gigondas regular *cuvée* is made in a big, rich, impeccably clean, muscular style, with a high alcohol content and a heady, lusty finish. It will drink well for another 4–6 years. The 1989 Gigondas Cuvée Florence exhibits more toasty, spicy, new oak in its nose, but there are also intense smells of herb-scented cassis and overripe plums. This full-bodied, voluptuously textured, opulent wine displays soft tannins, a nice touch of vanillin and smoky new oak, and a long, lusty finish. **Anticipated maturity: Now–2002.** The 1988 Cuvée Florence offers a dark ruby/purple color as well as a huge, highly extracted bouquet of violets, black raspberries, and toasty, smoky oak. Rich, full bodied, and amply endowed, with soft tannins and moderate acidity, it should drink beautifully for 5–8 more years.

DOMAINE DU GOUR DE CHAULE* * * *

1990 Gigondas	C	88
1989 Gigondas	C	88
1988 Gigondas	C	87
1986 Gigondas	C	87

Madame Bonfils's 1990 Gigondas exhibits a bold, peppery, herb- and black raspberry–scented nose, rich, chocolaty, smoky, fruit flavors, and medium to full body. The 1989 is equal in quality, but slightly riper, as well as sweeter on the palate, with less alcohol than the 1990. It is also a full-bodied, opulently styled wine that should drink well for the next decade. The 1988 offers that unmistakable Grenache smell of kirsch, roasted peanuts, and pepper. The wine is spicy, rich, and heady, with excellent concentration, plenty of soft tannins, and a long finish. The 1986 exhibits a sizable tannin level, as well as the requisite fruit to balance the tannins. This rich, full-bodied, more rustic-style wine offers plenty of peppery, blackberry and black cherry fruit flavors, a hint of roasted peanuts in its nose, and a long, spicy finish. It should drink well for the next 3–5 years.

ALAIN GRAILLOT* * * * *

1990 Crozes-Hermitage	B	92
1989 Crozes-Hermitage	B	90
1988 Crozes-Hermitage	B	87
1990 Crozes-Hermitage La Guiraude	C	94
1989 Crozes-Hermitage La Guiraude	C	92
1988 Crozes-Hermitage La Guiraude	C	90
1990 Hermitage	D	89
1990 St.-Joseph	C	89
1989 St.-Joseph	C	84
1988 St.-Joseph	C	78

Graillot's 1990 Crozes-Hermitage tastes like Hermitage. The sensational dark purple color is followed by a huge bouquet of roasted black raspberry fruit, smoky, earthy scents, and a nice touch of toasty new oak. There is mind-boggling richness in this wine, yet the underpinnings of acidity, tannin, and alcohol are there. It should last for 12–15 years. The similarly styled 1989 Crozes-Hermitage is a dazzling wine, with at least 10–15 years of aging potential. Its black/ruby/purple color, huge bouquet of vanillin-scented new oak, roasted fruit (particularly cassis and black plums), sensational extract, rich, full-bodied taste, and good length make for a profound bottle. The 1988 Crozes is a deeply colored wine with an extremely fragrant bouquet that suggests aromas of black raspberries, Provençal herbs, and spicy, toasty oak. It is a solidly built, muscular, rich, concentrated wine with soft tannins, crisp acidity, grip, and length. It should drink well for the next 5–8 years. The 1990 Crozes-Hermitage La Guiraude, Graillot's luxury *cuvée*, reveals a nose of smoke, Oriental spices, black fruits, and oak, a multidimensional personality, phenomenal ripeness and richness, decent acidity, and gobs of glycerin, alcohol, and extraction of flavor. **Anticipated maturity: 1994–2008.** The multidimensional 1989 Crozes-Hermitage La Guiraude possesses a black/ruby/purple color, a sensational bouquet of licorice, Provençal herbs, vanillin, black cherries, and black raspberries, and super concentration. Full bodied, with admirable length and depth, it is a superb expression of the Syrah grape. **Anticipated maturity: Now–2007.** The 1988 La Guiraude offers a sensational bouquet of superripe black plums, black raspberries, minerals, and licorice. The wine exhibits plenty of toasty new oak, which serves to frame its considerable size and concentration. It should drink well for up to a decade. Graillot's Hermitage is, ironically, not as concentrated. The 1990 offers up sweet-smelling aromas of black cherries, toasty new oak, and herbs. It is full bodied, with excellent concentration, a long, moderately tannic, unevolved taste, and a spicy, moderately tannic finish. It needs 4–5 years of cellaring. The purple-colored 1990 St.-Joseph displays a huge nose of licorice, black fruits, and minerals. It is stuffed with unctuous layers of creamy, curranty fruit and has decent acidity and an explosively long, velvety finish. It should continue to drink well for 4–6 years. The 1988 and 1989 St.-Josephs are both relatively light, but soft, fruity, and correct.

DOMAINE GRAMENON* * * * *

1990 Côtes du Rhône	A	88
1990 Côtes du Rhône Cuvée des Laurentides	B	92
1989 Côtes du Rhône Cuvée des Laurentides	B	92

Proprietor Philippe Laurent has become one of the hottest winemakers of France. The 1990 Côtes du Rhône, from his vineyards near Valréas, is an explosively rich wine with a huge nose of black fruits, herbs, and dried pit fruits; sweet, expansive, full-bodied flavors; fine purity and balance; and a gorgeously long, heady finish. The 1989 Cuvée des Laurentides is awesome, exhibiting a smoky, licorice, vintage port–like aroma of intense black fruits, extraordinary richness, a full-bodied texture, superb ripeness, and interesting vanillin, oaky aromas. The 1990 Cuvée des Laurentides reveals a character similar to that of the 1989, with perhaps a bit more vanillin and toasty oakiness and a slightly hotter, more alcoholic finish. Nevertheless it is another intensely concentrated, unctuous, superbly rich wine that should continue to drink well for another 7–10 years.

DOMAINE GRAND JEAN* * * *

1990 Châteauneuf-du-Pape	B	90

This *cuvée* of Châteauneuf-du-Pape, made from 40-year-old vines, reveals an attractively deep, ruby/purple color, a big, spicy, herb-, berry-, roasted nut-, and black fruit–scented nose, and deep, expansive, full-bodied flavors that exhibit considerable glycerin, richness, and sweet, soft tannins. It should drink well for at least another 6–8 years.

DU GRAND MOULAS* * * *

1989 Côtes du Rhône-Villages	A	87

There is a sumptuous quality to this wine's big, cherry- and plumlike fruitiness. It exhibits layers of fruit, a beautifully rich, satisfying texture, and a long, heady, spectacular finish.

DOMAINE GRAND PRÉBOIS* * * *

1990 Côtes du Rhône	A	85

This estate produces a solid, attractively fruity, medium-bodied, structured red wine. The 1990 should drink well for 5–6 years.

DOMAINE LE GRAND ROMANE* * *

1990 Gigondas	C	88
1989 Gigondas	C	87

This 1990 Gigondas will make robust drinking for the next 7–9 years. The opaque ruby/purple color is followed by a huge nose of spicy, herb- and earth-scented black fruit, and a deep, rich, full-bodied wine. Although it is not yet exhibiting much complexity, for pure flavor power and a tremendously full mouth-feel, this Gigondas has considerable appeal. Dark ruby/purple in color, the 1989 displays an enticingly complex bouquet of spicy, toasty new oak, rich, ripe cassis fruit, pepper, and licorice. The wine is full bodied, velvety, and generously endowed, with a long, heady finish. It should age gracefully for 7–8 years.

DOMAINE DU GRAND TINEL* * *

1990 Châteauneuf-du-Pape	C	85
1989 Châteauneuf-du-Pape	C	89
1988 Châteauneuf-du-Pape	C	89
1991 Châteauneuf-du-Pape Blanc	C	76

This vast estate of 185 acres produces huge quantities of Châteauneuf-du-Pape under its primary label, Grand Tinel, as well as under a secondary label, Les Caves St.-Paul. Its best vintages have been the 1981 and 1978. The estate's large production has resulted in the absurd practice of bottling its wines as they are sold. Consumers, unfortunately, have no way of knowing which bottling they are buying, except for the fact that the newest vintage of Grand Tinel usually arrives in the market 2 years after the vintage. The 1991 white Châteauneuf-du-Pape displays a pleasant fragrance of honey and pears, but on the palate the wine reveals little fruit as well as a clipped, short finish. The 1990 red wine displays Grand Tinel's in-your-face, full-throttle, high-alcohol, gaudy style that wine snobs might criticize, but there is no doubting the satisfying personality of this wine. The extroverted bouquet of jammy red berry fruit and Provençal herbs is followed by a fleshy, fat wine with a dizzying level of alcohol, plenty of unctuous, thick fruit flavors, a weighty, chunky texture, and a hot finish. Drink it over the next 5–6 years. The 1989 is a large-scale, concentrated wine with an explosive, jammy, black fruit personality. Opulent, with powerful flavors, but lacking finesse, it should provide rewarding drinking over the next 5–7 years. The 1988 is less overwhelmingly weighty and thick. It has a dense color, big, chocolaty, fruitcake, meaty aromas, and powerful, bold flavors. It will keep for a decade or more.

DOMAINE GRAND VENEUR* * *

1990 Châteauneuf-du-Pape	C	87
1989 Châteauneuf-du-Pape	C	87
1988 Châteauneuf-du-Pape	C	84
1991 Châteauneuf-du-Pape Blanc	C	72

The 1991 white Châteauneuf-du-Pape displays a vague nose of little more than citrusy acidity. Diluted yet clean, high-acid flavors lack body and depth. Although proprietor Alain Jaume's 1990 red Châteauneuf-du-Pape reveals slight overripeness in its pruny, plummy, herb-scented nose, this medium-dark, ruby-colored wine exhibits powerful, concentrated, rich, unctuous, chewy flavors as well as a long, heady, alcoholic finish. Drink it over the next 6–7 years. Jaume's 1989 is an interesting wine, displaying a big, forceful bouquet of raspberries, tobacco, and minerals, abundant fruit, a soft, seductive texture, and low acidity. The finish is heady, alcoholic, and jammy. Drink this style of Châteauneuf over the next 4–5 years. The straightforward 1988 is lighter, less concentrated, and smaller-scaled.

DOMAINE DES GRANDS DEVERS* * * */* * * * *

1989 Côtes du Rhône Enclaves des Papes	A	90
1989 Côtes du Rhône Syrah	A	91

The 1989 Côtes du Rhône Enclaves des Papes is pure opulence and richness. The sumptuous fruit and the gorgeous anise, Provençal herb and cassis nose is followed on the palate by layer upon layer of silky, rich fruit. Drink it over the next 2–3 years. The 1989 Côtes du Rhône Syrah offers a huge peppery, smoky, cassis- and olive-scented nose, voluptuous, stunningly deep, opulent flavors, soft tannins, plenty of alcohol, and a luscious finish. It should drink well for 5–8 years.

DOMAINE DU GRAPILLON D'OR* * *

1990 Gigondas	B	86
1989 Gigondas	B	86
1988 Gigondas	B	85

These offerings represent chunky, rich, full-bodied, precocious-tasting Gigondas with abundant fruit and alcohol. Some slight mustiness quickly blows off in the 1990's otherwise attractive, roasted, chocolaty, herb- and olive-scented nose. Highly extracted, this soft wine should be drunk over the next 5–7 years. The 1990 is the most concentrated, the 1989 the most flattering and jammy, and the 1988 the lightest. Enjoy them for their exuberant, fleshy styles.

GRILLET* * *

1989	E	88
1988	E	87

Château Grillet, the tiny appellation of 7.4 acres all to itself, is the Rhône Valley's most famous white wine–producing estate. Much has been written about its unrealized potential, and undoubtedly the finger of blame for so many indifferent winemaking efforts during the 1980s can be pointed directly at the proprietors. The estate's high percentage of young vines, as well as the tendency to harvest too early, has had predictable results. Nevertheless, the 1988 and 1989 have turned out better than most recent releases. Their big, flowery, peach-, apricot-, and lychee nut–scented bouquets are followed by wines with crisp acidity, an underlying taste of herbs, and rich, medium-bodied, tightly knit flavors backed up by some fascinating mineral, earthy spiciness. The 1988 is a worthy candidate for 5–10 years of cellaring, the 1989 less so.

BERNARD GRIPA* */* * *

1988 St.-Joseph	B	84
1990 St.-Joseph Le Berceau	C	86
1988 St.-Joseph Le Berceau	C	85

Gripa produces both a regular *cuvée* and a *cuvée préstige* aged in new oak casks. The latter, the 1990 St.-Joseph Le Berceau, exhibits plenty of toasty new oak as well as an opaque dark ruby/purple color, attractive, ripe, black raspberry and cassis fruit, an expansive, chewy texture, soft tannins, and a long finish. **Anticipated maturity: Now–2000.** The 1988 red Le Berceau is full bodied and concentrated, with excellent ripeness and length, some structure, and surprising tannin. It should last for 4–6 years. The regular bottling of 1988 St.-Joseph offers an attractive, moderately intense, herbaceous, black raspberry– and black cherry–scented nose, medium body, and fine ripeness and length.

J. L. GRIPPAT* * */* * * *

1990 Hermitage	D	88
1988 Hermitage	D	82
1990 Hermitage Blanc	D	89
1990 St.-Joseph	C	85
1989 St.-Joseph	C	85
1988 St.-Joseph	C	81
1990 St.-Joseph Blanc	C	85
1990 St.-Joseph Cuvée des Hospices	D	90

The lemony, melon-scented, extremely elegant, and fresh 1990 St.-Joseph Blanc is a dry, medium-bodied, delightful wine for drinking over the next 3–4 years. Grippat always produces an exceptionally fresh, pure, white Hermitage. Offering a rich nose of wet stones, peaches, and honey, his 1990 is full bodied, with lavish amounts of glycerin, enough acidity to provide focus, and a long, explosively rich finish. It should last for up to a decade. I do not think I have ever tasted better red wines from Grippat than his two 1990 St.-Joseph offerings. His regular *cuvée* of 1990 St.-Joseph displays an opaque, vibrant ruby color, a rich, black cherry– and herb-scented nose, attractive, spicy flavors, and a medium-bodied, soft finish. The 1990 St.-Joseph Cuvée des Hospices has an awesome bouquet of black fruits, licorice, flowers, and road tar as well as exceptional balance between its power and elegance. This delicious St.-Joseph should last for 10 years. There is no doubting the charm, juicy, ripe raspberry and blackcurrant fruitiness of the medium-bodied, satin-textured 1989 St.-Joseph. The 1988 St.-Joseph is much lighter, but clean, berry scented, and pleasant. Both wines should be drunk before the end of 1995. Grippat's surprisingly forward 1990 Hermitage displays an impressive saturated dark ruby/purple color and a forceful nose of black cherries, minerals, and herbs. It is medium to full bodied and rich, with a generous taste, soft tannins, low acidity, and an authoritative finish. It will last for 10 or more years. The 1988 Hermitage is a straightforward, medium-bodied, light, round, and fruity wine that should be drunk over the next 2–3 years, as it lacks structure and length.

DOMAINE DE LA GUICHARD* * * * *

1990 Côtes du Rhône les Genests	A	89

Here is a blockbuster, incredibly rich and complex Côtes du Rhône that reveals an opaque ruby/purple color, an intense, peppery, cassis- and Provençal herb-scented nose, superb richness, surprisingly good acidity, and a spectacularly long, stunning finish. It should last for 5–6 years.

GUIGAL* * * * *

1990	Châteauneuf-du-Pape	C	88
1989	Châteauneuf-du-Pape	C	90
1988	Châteauneuf-du-Pape	C	89
1986	Châteauneuf-du-Pape	C	86
1991	Condrieu	E	92
1991	Côte Rôtie Côtes Blonde et Brune	D	89
1990	Côte Rôtie Côtes Blonde et Brune	D	88
1989	Côte Rôtie Côtes Blonde et Brune	D	90
1988	Côte Rôtie Côtes Blonde et Brune	D	92
1987	Côte Rôtie Côtes Blonde et Brune	D	89
1986	Côte Rôtie Côtes Blonde et Brune	D	87
1991	Côte Rôtie La Landonne	EEE	96
1990	Côte Rôtie La Landonne	EEE	98
1989	Côte Rôtie La Landonne	EEE	99
1988	Côte Rôtie La Landonne	EEE	100
1987	Côte Rôtie La Landonne	EEE	96
1986	Côte Rôtie La Landonne	EEE	90
1991	Côte Rôtie La Mouline	EEE	94
1990	Côte Rôtie La Mouline	EEE	99
1989	Côte Rôtie La Mouline	EEE	97
1988	Côte Rôtie La Mouline	EEE	100
1987	Côte Rôtie La Mouline	EEE	95
1986	Côte Rôtie La Mouline	EEE	92
1991	Côte Rôtie La Turque	EEE	99
1990	Côte Rôtie La Turque	EEE	93
1989	Côte Rôtie La Turque	EEE	100
1988	Côte Rôtie La Turque	EEE	100
1987	Côte Rôtie La Turque	EEE	97
1986	Côte Rôtie La Turque	EEE	95
1990	Côtes du Rhône	A	88
1989	Côtes du Rhône	A	88
1988	Côtes du Rhône	A	88
1990	Côtes du Rhône Blanc	A	85
1990	Gigondas	C	89

1989	Gigondas	C	90
1988	Gigondas	C	86
1990	Hermitage	D	92
1989	Hermitage	D	90
1988	Hermitage	D	93
1990	Hermitage Blanc	D	89
1989	Hermitage Blanc	D	89
1988	Hermitage Blanc	C	92
1991	Tavel Rosé	C	85
1990	Tavel Rosé	C	88

How does this planet's greatest winemaker continue to turn out profound wines year after year? Guigal, like most of the great wine producers in the world, follows principles that are strikingly basic: a notorious late harvest for Guigal's own vineyards, low yields, plus Guigal's own philosophy that the winemaker's role should be minimal and that intervention in the winemaking should be practiced only when something goes wrong. Like all of the world's finest winemakers, he believes in preventive rather than curative oenology. The 1990 Côtes du Rhône Blanc, which contains some Viognier, reveals a lovely nose of honeysuckle and crisp, citrusy fruit, medium body, fine ripeness and roundness, and a fresh finish. Drink it before the end of 1994. Guigal's 1991 Condrieu possesses sumptuous quantities of fruit, gobs of body and richness, and a smashingly long, intense finish. It is an immensely seductive, fragrant wine, with aromas of apricots, peaches, and flowers leaping from the glass, medium to full body, good acidity, and wonderful freshness. Drink it before the summer of 1994. The 1988 white Hermitage offers up a super bouquet of honey, hazelnuts, and acacia flowers. It is rich, with full body, plenty of glycerin, crisp acidity, powerful, highly extracted, intense fruit flavors, and a long, lusty finish. It should age well for 15–20 or more years. The 1989 white Hermitage is slightly lighter and low in acidity, with a big, fat, fleshy, honeyed style but less complexity. It should drink well for at least 12–15 years. The dense, chewy 1990 white Hermitage appears to be a synthesis in style between the relatively low-acid 1989 and the massive yet highly structured 1988. There is plenty to like about this obviously intense but low-acid wine.

While much of the world wine press focuses on his single-vineyard Côte Rôties, Guigal has built most of his success and popularity among wine consumers with copious quantities of delicious and fairly priced Côtes du Rhône, Gigondas, and Châteauneuf-du-Pape. The 1990 Côtes du Rhône exhibits an opaque black/ruby/purple color, spicy, peppery, cassis aromas, wonderful suppleness, a rich, medium- to full-bodied, chewy texture, sweet tannins, and a long, luscious finish. The 1989 Côtes du Rhône displays a deep ruby/purple color, a big, spicy, blackberry- and herb-scented nose, supple, rich flavors, medium to full body, and a spicy finish. It should drink beautifully for the next 4–5 years. The seductive, rich, attractive 1988 Côtes du Rhône is a full-bodied, peppery, cassis- and black raspberry–scented and –flavored wine. This rich, full, and admirably balanced offering should drink well for 2–3 more years. The 1990 Gigondas is a big, beefy, full-bodied wine, with considerable extraction of flavor but a firm, backward personality. The 1989 Gigondas offers a precocious, evolved nose of black fruits, cedar, Provençal herbs, and damp earth. It is full bodied, with a deep, unctuous, chewy texture and a splendid ripe, heady finish. The 1988 Gigondas is structured, displaying plenty of tannin, without the intense, superripe black fruit character of the 1989 and 1990. The 1990 Châteauneuf-du-Pape displays a deep ruby/purple color, a nose of jammy cassis and herbs, and a full-bodied, long finish. It is capable of aging for 10–15 or more years. The 1989 Châteauneuf-du-Pape is a more opulent, slightly richer wine, with a whopping 14.8% natural alcohol. The color is a splendid deep ruby/purple, and the nose offers up copious scents of flowers, black fruits, and roasted nuts. This big wine enjoys superb concentration, full body, plenty of glycerin, and an exceptionally long, smooth finish. It should continue to drink well for 10–12 years. The 1988 Châteauneuf-du-Pape is almost as good, with its abundant raspberry and black cherry fruit and herbaceousness. It is fully mature now but will drink well for another 10–12 years. The 1986 Châteauneuf-du-Pape is a tannic, tough-textured wine lacking generosity and finishing with some astringency. The 1988 Hermitage is Guigal's best red Hermitage since 1983. It exhibits an opaque, dark ruby/purple color and a huge, relatively undeveloped, but promising perfume of cassis and minerals, sensational concentration, dramatic flavors, and plenty of robust tannins in the long finish. It will keep for 20–30 years. The 1989 red Hermitage is a softer, less concentrated, less powerful style of wine. Since it is more tender, it will have to be drunk earlier. The 1990 red Hermitage displays fatness, low acidity, and softness, with excellent concentration and length. It will drink well for 15 or more years.

Guigal's basic *cuvées* can be prodigious wines, even in lighter years. The 1990 Côte Rôtie promises to be soft and forward, in a style not terribly different from the 1989 and 1987. The acids are low, the tannins smooth, and the fruit superripe, fleshy, and altogether delicious. The 1989 Côte Rôtie is tender, soft, and less structured than the 1988. I also think it is marginally less concentrated, although that may be because the 1988 has more tannin and pure power. Nevertheless, Guigal has made a round, elegant, generously flavored, soft, precocious 1989 Côte Rôtie. I do not think it will ever have the aging potential or complexity of his 1988. His regular *cuvée* of 1988 Côte Rôtie has sensational levels of sweet, voluptuous, smoky, raspberry fruit intermingled with scents of new oak, bacon fat, and flowers. It exhibits up-front, precocious softness and lushness, complexity, structure, and tannin. Although drinkable now, this wine is capable of lasting for at least 15 years. The 1987 Côte Rôtie is a fragrant, satiny-textured wine with a lovely bouquet and smooth-as-silk flavors. Forward and surprisingly concentrated, with a bouquet crammed with black raspberries and smoky, vanillin, toasty oak, this luscious, opulently textured, medium-bodied, elegant wine should be drunk over the next 4–6 years. It will not make old bones. The 1986 Côte Rôtie is a good bottle of wine. Deep ruby/purple in color, with a reticent but emerging bouquet of road tar, licorice, blackcurrants, and smoky oak, it is among the more austere and tannic renditions I have tasted of this wine.

Guigal's single-vineyard Côte Rôties are exceptional. They offer extraordinary flavor intensity, impeccable purity, and awesome length and complexity. The yields from the three vineyards—La Mouline, La Landonne, and La Turque—rarely exceed 2 tons per acre. Moreover, no one harvests any later.

That the wines spend nearly 3½ years in 100% new oak tells you something about the level of extraction Guigal is able to achieve. Although the oak is noticeable for 1–2 years after bottling, anyone who has tasted the 1985s, 1983s, 1982s, 1980s, or 1978s would be hard-pressed to find evidence of new oak. The level of fruit extraction in these wines literally soaks up the oak, making them all the more structured and complex. All three wines share phenomenal concentration and marvelous perfumes, but they could not be more different. I do not think anyone can adequately articulate the multitude of aromas of flavors they possess, but let me try. La Mouline contains the highest percentage of Viognier. The amount can vary, but it is usually between 8 and 12%. This gives La Mouline the most intense perfume of this trio. The color is always a dark ruby/purple, but La Mouline will never be as black as La Landonne, which is made from 100% Syrah, or La Turque, which may include a small percentage of Viognier. La Mouline is the most seductive of the three wines when young, offering a sweet, chewy, multitextured style that is impossible to resist. It is also the least ageworthy. Although vertical tastings have proven that La Mouline will easily keep for 15–20 years, it can be drunk when it is released. La Mouline also comes from Guigal's oldest vineyard, with vines that are over 75 years in age. If La Mouline is Mozart, then La Landonne is Brahms. Made from 100% Syrah from the Côte Brune, it could not be more different from La Mouline. La Landonne's color is nearly black. A true blockbuster, it is a massive, almost impenetrable wine, which, with cellaring, is marked by aromas of smoked game, spicy nuts, saddle leather, and a roasted black fruit character. It is a wine with extraordinary power and forcefulness, as well as more acidity and tannin than La Mouline. La Landonne requires 10–15 years of patience. Most observers who have had a chance to see all the vintages of La Landonne since its debut in 1978 agree that it possesses 30–40 years of longevity. La Turque is the newest of the Guigal single-vineyard wines. Although it is also from the Côte Brune, its character represents a synthesis of La Mouline and La Landonne. La Turque vineyard is on an extremely precipitous slope (a 60-degree gradient), but, unlike La Mouline, it is not old. The vines were planted only in 1981. La Turque may also include 5–7% Viognier. Neither as tannic nor as muscular as La Landonne, La Turque is frequently as concentrated. It can be as compelling as La Mouline. It is a wine of enormous richness and character, but, like La Mouline, it can be drunk young and at the same time support 20–25 years of longevity. It also exhibits smoky, black raspberry aromas, but there is always something more kinky, more expansive, and even sweeter about the taste of La Turque. Like its two siblings, it is an impressively endowed, majestic wine. Based on the vintages produced since its debut in 1985, La Turque may be the most enthralling and complex of these single-vineyard Guigal Côte Rôties. All three single-vineyard Côte Rôties spend 42 months in new small oak casks and are bottled without fining or filtration. Should readers run across any of the 1986 and 1987 single vineyard Côte Rôties, do not pass them up because of the so-so reputation of these two vintages. The 1986 La Landonne is an outstanding wine, even though it lacks the magical perfume of La Mouline and the indescribable, riveting character of La Turque. It is more tannic and amply endowed. The 1986 La Mouline displays its characteristic exotic aroma of smoky oak, bacon fat, and spring flowers, followed by layer upon layer of opulent black fruits. It can be drunk now and should last for 10–15 years. The 1986 La Turque offers a bouquet that takes the best elements of Guigal's La Mouline, combines them with a Richebourg from Lalou Bize-Leroy and the Romanée-Conti of the Domaine de la Romanée-Conti, then fuses in some of the exotic character of Pétrus and Lafleur from Pomerol. There is no wine quite like it, and it saddens me that so few consumers will ever get a chance to taste it. It should drink well for 10–15 years. The 1987 La Mouline is spectacular, with fabulous extract, a profound finish and concentration, and a remarkable, mind-boggling perfume. **Anticipated maturity: Now–2005.** The 1987 La Turque is compelling, deeper in color, more concentrated, and capable of 10–15 years of longevity. The 1987 La Landonne is Guigal's biggest, richest, most splendidly concentrated and structured wine. It will not be ready to drink until the mid-1990s, but it should last for 15–20 years.

I have given a disproportionate number of perfect scores to Guigal's single-vineyard Côte Rôties. And guess what? Guigal's current releases, the 1988s, all merit perfect scores. I thought they were potentially perfect from cask, and now that they are in the bottle I have to believe that they are Guigal's most successful wines since his 1978s. They are richer even than the extraordinary 1985s and more concentrated than the magnificent 1983s. The 1988 La Mouline will have 20–25 years of aging potential, even though it can be drunk now. The 1988 La Landonne should last for 30–40 years. Celebrate the beginning of the new century by pulling the cork on your first bottle. The 1988 La Turque can also be drunk now, but it, too, should last for 25–30 years. Guigal's yields were so low in 1988 that the concentration of these wines is mind-boggling. They come closest to what Guigal achieved in 1978 and 1976. The 1989 single-vineyard Côte Rôties are also magnificent. Now that they are 3 months away from bottling, their taste is reminiscent of Guigal's 1985s and 1982s. All possess fabulous concentration and sweet, expansive personalities. The 1989 La Mouline is an explosively rich wine with its profound perfume of violets, black raspberries, and creamy, toasty new oak. It should drink well for the next 10–15 years. The 1989 La Turque's smoky, licorice, and black raspberry aromas, as well as its phenomenal richness, make for another extraordinary tasting experience. There is almost the essence of black cherries in the 1989, which is already gorgeous to drink. It, too, should be drunk over the next 12–15 years. I suspect the 1989 La Landonne possesses more tannin than it is currently revealing, but there is so much fruit that the tannins are largely concealed. Nevertheless, this is another mammoth-size wine with extraordinary extract and 20–30 years of aging potential. The 1989s will be released during the spring of 1993. In the drought year of 1990, the thicker, heavier soils of the Côte Brune suffered less. As a result, the black-colored, massive 1990 La Landonne looks to be the star. La Mouline is again magnificent, although voluptuous, forward, and destined to be consumed in its first 12–15 years of life. La Turque possesses a meaty, animal, Chambertin-like personality, with a leathery, black cherry–, soy sauce–scented nose, ripe, full-bodied, rich flavors, and outstanding length and richness. I suspect it will be even better once it is in the bottle. I should note that I tasted it on August 30, one month after it had been racked. The 1991 La Turque appears to be another perfect wine in the making. Guigal harvested his tiny vineyard (400 cases produced) on October 15, making these the last grapes to be picked in the northern Rhône. Nearly black in color, with a huge perfume of violets, sweet black fruits, toasty oak, and minerals, the wine possesses an unforgettable level of extract. Not surprisingly, it exhibits layer upon layer of flavor and complexity. As with most 1991 Côte Rôties, the acidity is low and the tannins noticeable but soft. This should be a wine to drink over the next 15 years. The 1991 La Mouline (408 cases produced) includes 8% Viognier in the blend. Sweet, expansive, and forward, it is as captivating and compelling as always. Although not as superconcentrated as the 1988, 1989, and 1990, it is still a voluptuous, opulently textured wine that should drink well in its first 15 years of life. The black-colored 1991 La Landonne offers a grilled meat–, roasted nut–, tar–, and truffle-scented nose, magnificently rich, huge, massive flavors, explosive length, and a gigantic feel and finish. A total of 475 cases were produced, making it the most abundant. These 1991 single-vineyard wines will not be bottled until February 1994. Guigal also produces an excellent Tavel made in a big, deep, strawberry- and cherry-scented style, with full body and a long, heady finish. The 1991, from a difficult year, is pleasant and fruity. The 1990 could easily stand up against the finest dry rosés from the Côtes de Provence and Bandol. The French claim these wines will last for 4–5 years. I drink them younger, but you be the judge.

RATINGS FOR OLDER VINTAGES OF GUIGAL CÔTE RÔTIE CÔTE BLONDE ET BRUNE: 1985 (91), 1983 (88), 1982 (87), 1980 (86), 1979 (86), 1978 (89) 1976 (91), 1971 (89)

RATINGS FOR OLDER VINTAGES OF GUIGAL CÔTE RÔTIE LA LANDONNE: 1985 (100), 1984 (77), 1983 (100), 1982 (95), 1981 (90), 1980 (96), 1979 (91), 1978 (98)

RATINGS FOR OLDER VINTAGES OF GUIGAL CÔTE RÔTIE LA MOULINE: 1985 (100), 1984 (86), 1983 (100), 1982 (95), 1981 (87), 1980 (95), 1979 (89), 1978 (100), 1977 (83), 1976 (100), 1970 (88), 1969 (100), 1966 (86)

RATINGS FOR OLDER VINTAGES OF GUIGAL CÔTE RÔTIE LA TURQUE: 1985 (100)

DOMAINE HAUT DES TERRES BLANCHES* * * *

1990 Châteauneuf-du-Pape	C	88
1989 Châteauneuf-du-Pape	C	88
1988 Châteauneuf-du-Pape	C	88

This is another estate that continues the undesirable practice of bottling its wine at different times, offering older vintages that have been kept, in many cases, far too long in oak. The key for the consumer is to purchase the newest vintage when it is first released. The 1990 is a round, gorgeously perfumed, Burgundy-like wine with a sweet raspberry fruitiness, soft tannins, and low acid. Drink this succulent wine over the next 7–8 years. The 1989 displays an attractive, overripe, sweet, raspberry-scented nose, delicious, richly fruity, round, totally hedonistic flavors, soft tannins, and a velvety texture. Given its stuffing, it should drink beautifully for another 8–9 years. The 1988 possesses a big, chocolaty, roasted black raspberry–scented bouquet, ripe, hedonistic flavors, low acidity, and a velvety texture. It should drink beautifully for the next 5–8 years. Diffonty's wines are also sold under the name of Domaine de la Glacière.

PAUL JABOULET AINÉ* * * * *

1990 Châteauneuf-du-Pape Les Cèdres	C	90
1989 Châteauneuf-du-Pape Les Cèdres	C	87

1991	Cornas	C	87
1990	Cornas	C	86
1989	Cornas	C	79
1989	Côte Rôtie Les Jumelles	D	85
1988	Côte Rôtie Les Jumelles	D	82
1990	Côtes du Rhône Parallel 45	A	85
1989	Côtes du Rhône Parallel 45	A	85
1990	Côtes du Rhône Parallel 45 Blanc	A	85
1990	Côtes du Rhône-Villages	B	87
1989	Côtes du Rhône-Villages	B	86
1990	Côtes du Ventoux	A	86
1989	Côtes du Ventoux	A	84
1990	Crozes-Hermitage Les Jalets	B	87
1989	Crozes-Hermitage Les Jalets	B	84
1991	Crozes-Hermitage La Mule Blanche	B	86
1990	Crozes-Hermitage La Mule Blanche	B	87
1989	Crozes-Hermitage La Mule Blanche	B	85
1991	Crozes-Hermitage Thalabert	C	87
1990	Crozes-Hermitage Thalabert	C	92
1989	Crozes-Hermitage Thalabert	C	90
1988	Crozes-Hermitage Thalabert	B	86
1990	Gigondas	B	89
1989	Gigondas	B	86
1989	Gigondas Cuvée Pierre Aiguille	C	90
1991	Hermitage La Chapelle	E	88
1990	Hermitage La Chapelle	E	100
1989	Hermitage La Chapelle	E	97
1988	Hermitage La Chapelle	E	93
1991	Hermitage Chevalier de Stérimberg	D	89
1990	Hermitage Chevalier de Stérimberg	D	93
1989	Hermitage Chevalier de Stérimberg	D	86
1988	Hermitage Chevalier de Stérimberg	D	87
1990	Muscat de Beaumes-de-Venise	C	91
1990	St.-Joseph Le Grand Pompée	B	89
1989	St.-Joseph Le Grand Pompée	B	86

1988 St.-Joseph Le Grand Pompée	B	85
1990 Vacqueyras	B	87
1989 Vacqueyras	B	86
1988 Vacqueyras	A	79

This firm has made considerable progress with the quality of their white wines. The 1990 Côtes du Rhône Parallel 45 exhibits a honeyed, flowery complexity as well as good crispness, body, and fruit. Drink it over the next 2–3 years. Jaboulet's 1991 Crozes-Hermitage La Mule Blanche displays gobs of honeyed, lemony fruit, excellent definition, rich, medium to full body, crisp acidity, and a fine finish. The 1990 Crozes-Hermitage La Mule Blanche is even bigger and more honeyed. The 1989 Crozes-Hermitage La Mule Blanche is an aromatic, deliciously fruity, fleshy, ripe wine that should be drunk up. The 1991 Hermitage Chevalier de Stérimberg is rich, deep, and full bodied, with excellent ripeness, a honeyed nose and texture, and deep flavors. These wines can last for decades. The 1990 Hermitage Chevalier de Stérimberg is the finest dry white wine I have tasted from Jaboulet. It will evolve effortlessly for 25–30 years. If you are looking for something other than Chardonnay, check out this full-bodied wine. The 1989 Hermitage Chevalier de Stérimberg reveals smoky, nutty aromas, ripe, fruity flavors, medium to full body, and soft acidity in its round, generous finish. It should drink well for 4–8 years. The 1988 Hermitage Chevalier de Stérimberg is more concentrated. It exhibits a great deal of toasty vanillin oakiness, some hazelnut- and flowery-scented fruit, full body, and fine depth and acidity. It should last for 6–12 years. Nectar lovers who are looking for complex sweet wines without an overlay of new oak should make a dash to their local wine shop and try a bottle of Jaboulet's 1990 Muscat de Beaumes-de-Venise. The orange color, the huge nose of tropical fruit and spices, and the medium-sweet, rich, honeyed flavors are the ideal foil for a fruit-based dessert.

 The 1990 red wines are the finest lineup of wines the Jaboulets have produced since their glory years of 1961, 1970, and 1978. Jaboulet's 1990 Côtes du Ventoux offers plenty of flavor and character. It is a deeply colored wine with an excellent, big, jam-scented nose, spicy, medium-bodied flavors, and light tannins in the finish. It may improve for 1–2 years and is capable of 5–6 years of evolution. Jaboulet's 1989 Côtes du Ventoux is an elegantly rendered, ripe, round, supple wine that should provide serviceable drinking for another 2–4 years. The 1990 Côtes du Rhône Parallel 45 reveals a saturated, deep ruby color, a big, peppery, roasted cassis nose, fine extraction of flavor, medium to full body, and tough tannins in the finish. The 1989 Côtes du Rhône Parallel 45 is more peppery and spicy, full bodied, and sturdy. It should last for 4–6 years and provide simple but satisfying drinking. Jaboulet's 1990 Côtes du Rhône-Villages is an immensely seductive wine, with a huge nose of black cherries, kirsch, and peanuts. There is not a hard edge to be found in this voluptuously textured, smooth-as-silk wine. Drink it over the next 4–5 years. The 1989 Côtes du Rhône-Villages is a spicy, richly fruity, attractive wine for drinking over the next 2–3 years. Jaboulet's 1990 Vacqueyras displays a huge, sweet nose of jammy fruit and smoke. The wine is full bodied, with excellent concentration, low acidity, fine depth, and sweet, ripe tannins. Drinkable now, it should last for up to a decade. The 1989 Vacqueyras is a powerful, full-bodied, ripe, heady wine with a fiery alcohol content, gobs of fruit and tannin, soft acidity, and a rich finish. Drink it over the next 2–4 years. Jaboulet's change during the 1980s to a lighter, more wimpish style for his Gigondas and Châteauneuf-du-Pape has apparently been reversed, if my instincts about the firm's 1989s and 1990s are correct. The 1990 Gigondas is a big, lusty, rustic style of wine with a saturated purple color, a tight but promising nose of black fruits, licorice, and herbs, superconcentration, and tons of tannin. It should keep for 12–15 years. I was knocked out by the spectacular 1989 Gigondas Pierre Aiguille. This black/ruby-colored wine makes a super impression, as it is crammed with fruit and exhibits a bouquet of roasted nuts, chocolate, black cherries, raspberries, and minerals. Although drinkable now, it can be cellared for up to 15 years. The regular *cuvée* of 1989 Gigondas offers a mouthful of relatively simple but jammy, rich, concentrated, roasted blackberry fruit, heady, alcoholic flavors, and a lush finish. It will provide immense satisfaction over the next 4–6 years. The 1990 Châteauneuf-du-Pape Les Cèdres reveals an impressive dark ruby/purple color, a big, spicy, earthy, bacon-scented nose, deep, unctuous, full-bodied flavors, and a dense, alcoholic, tannic finish. Unevolved, young, and backward, this wine can last through the first decade of the next century. The 1989 Châteauneuf-du-Pape Les Cèdres is a seductive, rich, generously endowed wine with soft tannins. Unctuous and velvety, it is ideal for drinking over the next decade. The northern Rhône selections are top-notch. The 1990 St.-Joseph Le Grand Pompée is a thick, rich, concentrated wine. The opaque, saturated purple color is followed by a huge nose of blackcurrants and minerals, full-bodied, highly extracted flavors, a significant lashing of tannin, and a long finish. It should last for 10–15 years. The 1989 Le Grand Pompée possesses superripe aromas, medium to full body, and a velvety texture. It should be consumed over the next 7–8 years. The 1988 Le Grand Pompée is medium bodied, revealing good, firm tannins in the finish and an attractive ripeness. It will drink well for the next 4–5 years. Jaboulet is now producing two *cuvées* of Crozes-Hermitage. The Crozes-Hermitage Les Jalets is a lighter, fruitier, softer Crozes. The 1990 Crozes-Hermitage Les Jalets exhibits a nose of black fruits, herbs, smoke, and damp woodsy aromas. Dense, rich, and opulent, with gobs of fruit, it should be drunk over the next 5–7 years. The 1989 Les Jalets is more savage, with a tobacco-, herb-, leaf-, and earth-scented nose, moderately tannic flavors, and a shorter finish. It is a serviceable Crozes-Hermitage. Jaboulet's Crozes-Hermitage Thalabert has long been the standard-bearer for this appellation. The 1991 Crozes-Hermitage Thalabert possesses the sweet perfume of spicy black fruits, round, opulent, full-bodied flavors, surprisingly good concentration, low acidity, and soft tannins. The 1990 Crozes-Hermitage Thalabert is a winner. It exhibits a huge, roasted Syrah nose and the massive power produced by the hot sun and drought. The huge, smoky, superripe nose of herbs, coffee, and cassis is followed by a densely packed, authoritatively rich, nearly massive, surprisingly well-balanced wine. It should evolve gracefully for at least 10–15 years. The 1989 Crozes-Hermitage Thalabert is no weak sibling. A dark ruby/black-colored wine, it offers up an intense bouquet of sweet, cedary spices, herbs, and black fruits. Lusher and less tannic than the 1990, it is rich in fruit and full bodied, with plenty of glycerin and tannin. It should be at its apogee between 1994 and 2005. The 1988 Thalabert is very good, with a big, spicy, plummy, herb-scented bouquet, medium- to full-bodied flavors, and a dense, concentrated, tannic finish. It should last until the turn of the century. The 1991 Cornas offers an attractive perfume of red and black fruits as well as some toasty new oak. It is medium bodied, round, and ideal for drinking over the next 5–7 years. The 1990 Cornas is more tannic and austere, with a forceful, spicy, peppery, herb- and earth-scented nose. Medium to full bodied, this wine needs 5–6 years of cellaring. I have never been that impressed with the Côte Rôties from Jaboulet (although a friend of mine recently sent me a bottle of the 1961 that was fabulous). Soft and lacking concentration, the 1989 Côte Rôtie is no great wine. The 1988 Côte Rôtie Les Jumelles is an elegant, straightforward, fruity wine. The Hermitage La Chapelle is Jaboulet's most famous as well as his most enormously concentrated and massive wine. It has become legendary in vintages such as 1961, 1978, and now 1989 and 1990. The 1991 Hermitage La Chapelle is soft and ripe, revealing an excellent deep purple color, a rich, unformed, but intense nose, medium- to full-bodied flavors, excellent concentration, sweet tannins, and low acidity. It should drink well for 15 years. The 1990 Hermitage La Chapelle is monumental. It should prove to be the finest La Chapelle made since 1961. Black in color, with a huge nose of pepper, underbrush, and black fruits, this wine has awesome concentration, extraordinary balance and power, and a fabulously long finish that lasts for more than a minute. The tannins are considerable, but the lavish quantities of sweet fruit and multidimensional, layered feel to the wine make it one of the most incredible young reds I have ever tasted. **Anticipated maturity: 2005–2040+.** The 1989 Hermitage La Chapelle is also phenomenal. The opaque black/ruby color and the huge bouquet of coffee, hickory wood, jammy cassis, minerals, and spices are the stuff of legends. The wine is massive, with layer upon layer of unctuous, highly extracted, superripe fruit. The finish offers an extraordinary explosion of fruit, glycerin, and tannin. The 1988 La Chapelle continues to evolve beautifully. Powerful and extremely rich, it is a classic expression of the Syrah grape.

RATINGS FOR OLDER VINTAGES OF PAUL JABOULET-AINÉ HERMITAGE LA CHAPELLE: 1987 (83), 1986 (88), 1985 (90), 1984 (78), 1983 (90+), 1982 (90), 1980, (85), 1979 (90), 1978 (100), 1976 (86), 1974 (76), 1973 (87), 1972 (93), 1971 (93), 1970 (95), 1969 (89), 1967 (80), 1966 (94), 1964 (90), 1962 (88), 1961 (100)

PIERRE JACUMIN—CUVÉE DE BOISDAUPHIN* * * *

1990 Châteauneuf-du-Pape	C	88+
1989 Châteauneuf-du-Pape	C	91

Pierre Jacumin's wines are impressive, old-style Châteauneuf-du-Papes with rich, sweet, thick fruit, oodles of peppery, herb, raspberry, and tobacco notes in the bouquet, and huge, muscular, fleshy, chewy textures. Although slightly less profound than the 1989, the 1990 offers a husky mouthful of wine. The earthy, cherry-scented nose, rich, tannin-laden flavors, and full-bodied, alcoholic finish suggest it will be at its best between 1994 and 2005. The 1989 displays more complexity, a dramatically intense, spicy, peppery, licorice nose, sweet, long, opulent flavors, and an explosively rich finish. I would drink the 1989 between now and 2008.

JEAN-PAUL and JEAN-LUC JAMET* * * * *

1991 Côte Rôtie	D	91
1990 Côte Rôtie	D	89

1989 Côte Rôtie	D	92
1988 Côte Rôtie	D	95
1987 Côte Rôtie	D	87

Jamet fashioned a velvet-textured, rich, full 1991 Côte Rôtie. Its opaque purple color is followed by a huge nose of black raspberries, full body, low acidity, and soft tannins. **Anticipated maturity: Now–2003.** The 1990 Côte Rôtie has a splendid opaque ruby/purple color, a peppery, herb- and jam-scented bouquet, and fat, fleshy flavors. Its low acidity and high tannins make it hard to project how this wine will ultimately evolve, but it should last for 10–15 years. The 1989 Côte Rôtie exhibits a dark ruby/purple color as well as a dense, exotic nose of licorice, cassis, herbs, and spicy oak. There is richness, plenty of power, high alcohol, density, a chewy character, and an opulent, even voluptuous quality to the finish. It should be drinkable long before the 1988, and last for at least 15–20 years. As for the 1988 Côte Rôtie, I would cellar it for another 4–5 years in order to give it a chance to shed some of its considerable tannin. It has already thrown a heavy sediment. Opaque black/purple, with an incredible knockout bouquet of cassis, leather, herbs, smoked meats, and Oriental scents (soy), this is a fabulously rich, dense, chewy Côte Rôtie. It should reach maturity by 1996 and last for at least 15–20 years. The bacon fat– and cassis-scented 1987 is smooth, medium bodied, deliciously ripe, and round. It should drink well for another 5–6 years.

DOMAINE DE LA JANASSE* * * *

1990 Châteauneuf-du-Pape	C	85
1989 Châteauneuf-du-Pape	C	90
1988 Châteauneuf-du-Pape	C	86
1991 Châteauneuf-du-Pape Blanc	C	86
1990 Châteauneuf-du-Pape Chaupoins	C	91
1990 Châteauneuf-du-Pape Cuvée Vieilles Vignes	C	91

Proprietor Aimé Sabon has fashioned a tasty 1991 white Châteauneuf-du-Pape that offers fragrant, flowery, pear, and honey scents. Drink it over the next 1–2 years. There are three *cuvées* of 1990 Châteauneuf-du-Pape. The medium-bodied, soft, pleasant 1990 (*cuvée normale*) offers a ruby/garnet color and an attractive and evolved bouquet of black cherries, leather, spices, and smoke. The 1990 Châteauneuf-du-Pape Chaupoins exhibits an opaque, dark ruby/purple color, a huge nose of fiery black raspberries, roasted herbs, and chocolate, sensational concentration, gobs of glycerin and extraction, plenty of alcohol, and a moderately tannic finish. It should last for 15–20 years. Even bigger is the 1990 Cuvée Vieilles Vignes, a massive, highly extracted, densely colored wine that displays excellent aging potential and boasts a whopping 15% natural alcohol. **Anticipated maturity: 1995–2009.** The ruby/purple-colored, full-bodied 1989 Châteauneuf-du-Pape possesses a ripe nose of cassis, herbs, and other black fruits, fine stuffing, and an impressive, chewy, concentrated finish. **Anticipated maturity: 1995–2008.** The 1988 Châteauneuf offers an attractive, plummy, peppery bouquet, ripe, round flavors, and a soft, easy-going finish. It should be drunk over the next 2–3 years.

ROBERT JASMIN* * * *

1989 Côte Rôtie	D	88
1988 Côte Rôtie	D	91
1987 Côte Rôtie	D	86

Robert Jasmin often sells different wines under the same label. The wines can range from his regular, straightforward *cuvée* of so-so Côte Rôtie to his splendid Reserve bottles. Nothing on the label informs the consumer as to which wine is in the bottle. The following notes are from Jasmin's best *cuvées,* which average 5–6 points higher than his regular *cuvée.* The 1989 Côte Rôtie is fat, velvety, heady, and perfumed. Its succulent, soft, velvety texture and long, rich finish make it a seductive wine for drinking within its first decade. The 1988 is a splendidly rich, concentrated, deeply flavored wine with firm tannins and a huge bouquet of black raspberry fruit, spring flowers, and toasty oak. Supple enough to be drunk now, it possesses enough body and tannin to support a decade of aging. The lovely, supple, concentrated, velvety 1987 is ideal for drinking over the next 5–6 years.

MARCEL JUGE* * * *

1988 Cornas	C	79
1988 Cornas Cuvée C (Hillside Vines)	D	84
1987 Cornas Cuvée C (Hillside Vines)	D	84

All of these offerings are light. While the 1988 regular *cuvée* is simple and straightforward, the 1988 Cuvée C has more to it. It possesses a lovely nose of black raspberries, violets, and mushrooms, but there is not much extract or length. The 1987 Cuvée C is softer, more supple, and ready to drink.

JACQUES LEMENCIER* * * *

1990 Cornas	C	88
1989 Cornas	C	87
1988 Cornas	C	90

Of these three vintages, the star is the 1988, a black/purple-colored wine possessing a huge, chocolaty, cassis-scented nose, rich, concentrated flavors, full body, and solid, but soft tannins in the finish. **Anticipated maturity: 1994–2008.** In 1989 Lemencier's Cornas displays an impressive, deep ruby/purple color, a big, spicy, earthy, mineral, and black fruit–scented nose, a sweet, expansive palate, and some noticeable tannins. It is a classic Cornas for drinking over the next 12–15 years. Lemencier's 1990 appears to be fuller bodied and more structured. A raw, tough wine, it is rich in color, with a spicy, stemmy earthiness and gobs of black fruit.

BERNARD LEVET* */* * *

1989 Côte Rôtie Côtes Blonde et Brune	D	86
1988 Côte Rôtie Côtes Blonde et Brune	D	88

The 1989 is medium to full bodied, with a big, peppery, spicy, raspberry-scented bouquet, moderate tannins, relatively low acidity, and fleshy, concentrated flavors with an underlying taste of Provençal herbs. It should be at its best between now and 2003. The 1988 is a more structured wine, with crisp acidity and slightly more aggressive tannins. I liked the openness of the 1989 and the fact that it will be drinkable over a broader range of years. The 1988 will need at least 3–4 years in the cellar to shed its tannic clout, but it is a well-made, concentrated, medium- to full-bodied wine. Drink it between 1994 and 2003. Although I found the 1989 Côte Rôtie to be aggressively herbaceous, there is no doubting its attractive ripeness or spicy, leathery, herbal fruitiness, medium body, and soft tannins. Drink it over the next 7–8 years.

JEAN LIONNET* * *

1991 Cornas Rochepertuis	C	79
1990 Cornas Rochepertuis	C	85
1991 St.-Péray	C	78

The 1991 St.-Péray is fresh and decent, but the nose of glue and the short finish left me unmoved. The compact 1991 Cornas Rochepertuis exhibits an aggressively herbal, animal-scented nose and decent, streamlined flavors. It should be drunk over the next decade. The 1990 Cornas Rochepertuis displays better color, none of the herbaceousness that plagues the 1991, a spicy, earthy, black-fruit character, attractive toastiness, and good, firm, medium- to full-bodied, uncomplex flavors. Drink it over the next decade.

DOMAINE DE MARCOUX* * * * *

1990 Châteauneuf-du-Pape	C	91
1989 Châteauneuf-du-Pape	C	85
1988 Châteauneuf-du-Pape	C	82
1991 Châteauneuf-du-Pape Blanc	C	76
1990 Châteauneuf-du-Pape Cuvée Vieilles Vignes	D	97
1989 Châteauneuf-du-Pape Cuvée Vieilles Vignes	D	97

The 1991 Châteauneuf-du-Pape Blanc offers up a high-acid, citrusy style that has plenty of freshness but not much fruit or character. It should be drunk before the end of 1994. With respect to the two *cuvées* of red Châteauneuf in 1990, the remarkable 1990 regular *cuvée* is bolstered by the inclusion of wine made from 50- to 90-year-old vines. The wine reveals a dark ruby/purple color and a huge nose of jammy, sweet black fruits and herbs. The sweetness, glycerin, high alcohol, and gorgeous extract levels make for a sumptuous drinking experience. The tannins are silky, and the finish is formidable. It should evolve for 10–15 years. The 1990 Châteauneuf-du-Pape Vieilles Vignes is opaque black/purple in color, with a nose of superripe cassis, spring flowers, and licorice. It is awesomely rich and concentrated, with a thick, unctuous texture, plenty of tannin, and some heady alcohol in the finish. It should drink well for at least 15–20 years. The 1989 Châteauneuf-du-Pape is soft, round, and generously endowed, with low acidity and a fleshy, meaty personality. A straightforward, richly fruity Châteauneuf-du-Pape, it should be consumed over the next 5–6 years. The 1989 Châteauneuf-du-Pape Vieilles Vignes exhibits an opaque black/purple color, with a huge, undeveloped bouquet of cassis, black raspberries, and licorice. This smashingly rich, exceptionally concentrated wine possesses awesome extract levels, massive concentration, and amazing length. It is a monument to Châteauneuf-du-Pape. **Anticipated maturity: 1994–2010.** The 1988 regular *cuvée* of Châteauneuf is surprisingly soft, shallow, fruity, and straightforward.

LE MAS DES COLLINES* *

1989 Gigondas	B	72
1988 Gigondas	B	82

The 1989 reveals relatively shallow, soft, watery flavors. It is surprisingly light and weedy to the point of being vegetal. The 1988 is a straightforward, spicy, peppery, herb- and red fruit–scented wine, with medium body, decent concentration, and a pleasant character. It should be drunk over the next 2–3 years.

DOMAINE MATHIEU* * *

1990 Châteauneuf-du-Pape	C	86
1989 Châteauneuf-du-Pape	C	87
1988 Châteauneuf-du-Pape	C	85
1991 Châteauneuf-du-Pape Blanc	C	70

The red wine offerings from proprietor Charles Mathieu are jammy, spicy, fruity wines with soft tannins, good glycerin, high alcohol, low acid, and an element of *sur-maturité*. The 1990 offers explosive cherry aromas and a powerful combination of chewy fruit, alcohol, and tannin. I would opt for drinking this soft, low-acid wine over the next 6–8 years. The round, superripe 1989 exhibits an intense aromatic character, suggesting spicy, herb-scented raspberries and smoky tobacco. Drink it over the next 5–6 years. The 1988 offers an attractive bouquet but it is not as big as the 1989, which should turn out to be a better wine. It exhibits a cedary, cassis-scented bouquet, round, juicy flavors, and a long, elegant finish. Consume it over the next 3–4 years. Domaine Mathieu's 1991 Châteauneuf-du-Pape Blanc has a vague smell of underripe bananas. The absence of fruit, along with the high acid and short, attenuated flavors, makes for a disappointing wine.

DOMAINE DE LA MAVETTE* * *

1990 Gigondas	B	82
1989 Gigondas	B	79
1988 Gigondas	B	76
1990 Gigondas Cuvée Prestige	B	83

All of these wines from the Domaine de la Mavette exhibit ripeness, a soft, straightforward, medium-bodied style, with above-average concentration. What the wines all lacked was intensity, character, and complexity.

DOMAINE DE LA MILLIÈRE* * *

1990 Châteauneuf-du-Pape	C	86
1991 Châteauneuf-du-Pape Blanc	C	70

The 1991 white Châteauneuf-du-Pape is completely neutral, devoid of any bouquet, with hollow, bland flavors. The 1990 red Châteauneuf-du-Pape is a straightforward, robust wine, with moderate tannins, an attractive black cherry–, herb-, and spice-scented nose, and medium- to full-bodied, concentrated flavors. Drink it over the next 5–7 years.

DOMAINE DE MONTEILLET* * * */* * * * *

1991 St.-Joseph	C	90

Monteillet's St.-Joseph is one of the finest of the appellation. It comes from steep hillside vineyards that are conservatively cropped. His 1991, which was a surprisingly good vintage in the northern Rhône, is a spectacular expression of the Syrah grape. The wine has a black/purple color, and a huge nose of sweet cassis, raspberries, and bacon fat. It is long, full bodied, deep, and impeccably well balanced. The wine can be drunk now or over the next decade. Although I have not tasted them, Proprietor Montez also produces a luxury *cuvée* of St.-Joseph called Cuvée Papy, which is aged in new oak, and a tiny quantity of Condrieu.

DOMAINE DE MONTPERTUIS* * * *

1991 Châteauneuf-du-Pape Blanc	B	72
1990 Châteauneuf-du-Pape Cuvée Classique	B	87
1989 Châteauneuf-du-Pape Cuvée Classique	B	86
1988 Châteauneuf-du-Pape Cuvée Classique	B	85
1990 Châteauneuf-du-Pape Cuvée Tradition	D	89
1989 Châteauneuf-du-Pape Cuvée Tradition	D	90

There are two *cuvées* of red wine produced at the Domaine de Montpertuis— the Cuvée Classique, made from 20- to 60-year-old vines and meant to be drunk within its first 10 years of life, and the Cuvée Tradition, made only from 60- to 110-year-old, low-yielding vines and meant to last 10–20 years. The 1990 Cuvée Classique is ready to drink, with a soft, up-front, herbal, berry fragrance, tasty, medium- to full-bodied, well-endowed flavors, low acidity, and plenty of alcoholic punch. Drink it over the next 4–5 years. The 1990 Cuvée Tradition is much deeper in color, with a minty, black raspberry, spicy, peppery nose, medium to full body, and a tannic, hard finish. Although the 1990 lacks the opulence, dazzling richness, and full-throttle power and authority of the 1989 Cuvée Tradition, it should last for 10–15 years. The 1989 will keep for 12–18 years. The ruby/purple-colored 1989 Cuvée Classique possesses a whopping natural alcohol of 14.8%. The rich bouquet of black raspberries, spices, and herbs needs coaxing from the glass. This full-bodied, tannic wine is large-scaled, yet well balanced. **Anticipated maturity: Now–1999.** The 1988 reveals a spicy, black cherry–scented bouquet, peppery, full-bodied flavors, and some astringent tannins in the finish. **Anticipated maturity: Now–1997.**

DOMAINE DE MONT-REDON* * *

1990 Châteauneuf-du-Pape		C	85
1989 Châteauneuf-du-Pape		C	87
1988 Châteauneuf-du-Pape		C	85
1987 Châteauneuf-du-Pape		C	76
1991 Châteauneuf-du-Pape Blanc		C	76
1990 Côtes du Rhône		A	82
1989 Côtes du Rhône		A	84

Mont-Redon has been using some small oak barrels for aging a percentage of their red wine, and this has resulted in an almost Bordeaux-like structure and austerity in certain vintages. The 1990 displays an impressive deep ruby/purple color, a ripe, medium- to full-bodied, highly structured feel on the palate, plenty of tannin, and a closed, firm style. After bottling there was significantly less to the wine than prior to its filtration. Drink it over the next 4–8 years before it dries out. The careful management of the vineyard and the impeccable winemaking practiced in the cellars, not to mention the character of the vineyard and vintage, have all been compromised by a sterile filtration. The 1989 reveals considerable tannin as well as a touch of new oak in its closed bouquet of black fruits and spices. Full bodied, rich, and concentrated, this wine should last for 10–15 or more years, yet it is much less impressive from bottle than it tastes out of cask. The 1988 is a more structured, lean style of Châteauneuf. It is good but restrained. I wonder how much more fruit and perfume it would have had had it not been vigorously fined and filtered prior to bottling. The 1987 is spicy, medium bodied, and lighter than usual, but pleasant for drinking over the next 1–2 years. This estate is making fruity, ripe, round Côtes du Rhônes. The round, soft, juicy 1990 should be consumed over the next 2–3 years. The 1989 Côtes du Rhône is attractive, although lighter in style and less concentrated. The 1991 white Châteauneuf-du-Pape is austere and innocuous.

MONTMIRAIL* * * *

1989 Gigondas		B	76
1990 Gigondas Cuvée Beauchamp		B	89
1988 Gigondas Cuvée Beauchamp		B	83
1989 Vacqueyras Deux Frères		B	87

There is enormous variation in quality at this estate. The 1989 is alcoholic and ripe but essentially one-dimensional, diluted in the midpalate, and short in the finish. It reminded me of some of the 1982 wines from Gigondas. Drink it over the next 3–5 years. The 1990 Cuvée Beauchamp is deeply colored, with a big, jammy nose, full body, and a lusty, alcoholic finish. Full, chewy, and splendidly long, it possesses lavish quantities of fruit that nearly conceal its considerable tannins. Drink it over the next 10–12 years. The richer 1988 Cuvée Beauchamp is medium bodied, soft, and charming, but monolithic. Drink it over the next 2–3 years. Last, the excellent 1989 Vacqueyras Deux Frères offers up a vivid raspberry-scented nose as well as long, deep, yet supple flavors.

Full bodied and lusty, with an alcoholic finish, it should be drunk over the next 1–3 years.

MOULIN DE LA GARDETTE* * * *

1990 Gigondas	B	88
1989 Gigondas	C	87

The 1990's color is an opaque dark ruby/purple, and the nose offers up sweet vanillin aromas as well as copious quantities of black raspberries. This opulent, full-bodied wine exhibits superb concentration, a big, muscular, chewy texture, and an alcoholic finish. It is well constituted enough to last for 10–12 years. The 1989 is backward, tough-textured, tannic, and closed. Wth airing it displays a considerable amount of ripe fruit and ample concentration. It has the potential to last 12–15 or years.

MOULIN-TACUSSEL* * * *

1990 Châteauneuf-du-Pape	C	85
1989 Châteauneuf-du-Pape	C	87
1988 Châteauneuf-du-Pape	C	86

The style of Moulin-Tacussel's Châteauneuf-du-Pape has a similarity to a Napa Valley Cabernet Sauvignon. Its minty, eucalyptus aromas are unusual for a Châteauneuf. The 1990 exhibits a bouquet of mint and cassis, rich, full-bodied, tannic flavors, and a spicy finish. The 1989 possesses more depth but a similar character. Both wines should last for 8–9 years. The 1988 is less concentrated but also bizarrely minty, with fleshy, chewy flavors and light tannins. Drink it over the next 5–7 years.

DOMAINE DE NALYS* * *

1990 Châteauneuf-du-Pape	C	86
1989 Châteauneuf-du-Pape	C	86
1991 Châteauneuf-du-Pape Blanc	C	83

Nalys is a competent source for some fine white Châteauneuf-du-Papes. The 1990 white Châteauneuf offers a tropical fruit–scented nose, lovely, fruity flavors, enough acidity for focus, and a good finish. Drink it over the next 2 years. Nalys's red wines are some of the fruitiest, most exuberant and delicious wines made by the carbonic method of vinification. The 1989 and 1990 red Châteauneuf-du-Papes share similar styles, illustrating one of my criticisms of the carbonic maceration method—it tends to blur vintage differences. Admittedly 1989 and 1990, two hot, dry years, are similar. Both wines are richly fruity, round, nearly sweet, with soft tannins, low acidity, and velvety textures. The colors are dark ruby, and the overall impression is of grapey, richly fruity, exuberant wines that provide a lot of enjoyment. Both vintages should keep well for at least 7–8 years.

NERO-PINCHON* * *

1991 Condrieu	D	87
1990 Côtes du Rhône Ste.-Agathe	B	87

The 1991 is an elegant, lighter style of Condrieu with an attractive floral-, underripe apricot–scented nose, medium body, admirably concentrated flavors, decent acidity, and a good finish. It should be drunk over the next 1–2 years. The terrific 1990 Côtes du Rhône Ste.-Agathe is made from 100% Syrah. It smells like a slightly downsized Côte Rôtie with its bacon fat, black raspberry, and toasty scents. Ripe, well constituted, with soft acids as well as a fleshy, fruity finish, it should be drunk over the next 3–5 years.

DE LA NERTHE* * * *

1990	Châteauneuf-du-Pape	C	85
1989	Châteauneuf-du-Pape	C	90
1988	Châteauneuf-du-Pape	C	87
1991	Châteauneuf-du-Pape Blanc	C	79
1990	Châteauneuf-du-Pape Clos de Beauvenir Blanc	D	86
1990	Châteauneuf-du-Pape Cuvée des Cadettes	D	90+
1989	Châteauneuf-du-Pape Cuvée des Cadettes	D	93
1988	Châteauneuf-du-Pape Cuvée des Cadettes	D	91

La Nerthe is one of the most important properties in Châteauneuf-du-Pape, and the vineyards, gardens, and château make it the showcase property of this area. It produces two *cuvées* of white and two *cuvées* of red wine. The regular *cuvée* of white Châteauneuf-du-Pape is made from 40% Clairette, 20% Bourboulenc, 20% Grenache Blanc, and 20% Roussanne. The prestige *cuvée*, the Clos de Beauvenir, is made from 60% Roussanne and 40% Clairette. It is also vinified and aged for 6 months in new oak casks. The 1991 regular *cuvée* of white Châteauneuf exhibits a reticent floral, pearlike nose, good freshness, crisp acidity, a fruity midpalate, and a soft finish. The 1990 Clos de Beauvenir displays some new oak, good lemony, melony fruit, medium body, and a spicy, long finish. The ruby-colored 1990 Châteauneuf-du-Pape (regular *cuvée*) possesses a tight, backward nose, a tannic, compact palate, high acidity and tannin, and a lean-tasting finish. It should last for 7–10 years. The 1989 has an impressive dense ruby/purple color, a bouquet of black raspberries and minerals, full-bodied, intensely concentrated flavors, noticeable tannins, decent acidity, and a promising finish. **Anticipated maturity: 1994–2006.** The 1988 is lighter, with more of a black cherry, herb, and spicy nose, plus good body and richness. Approachable now, it should keep for another 10–12 years. The luxury wine, Cuvée des Cadettes, consists of a blend of 60% Grenache, 30% Mourvèdre, and 10% Syrah from the estate's oldest vines. It is a bigger, richer wine that should have significantly more aging potential than the regular *cuvée*. The 1990 Cuvée des Cadettes is a deeply colored wine with the scent of ripe fruit and a ton of sweet oak. It possesses admirable richness, an attractive oakiness, medium to full body, and a highly structured, crisp finish. It has an international style and, for me, seems like an atypical Châteauneuf-du-Pape. **Anticipated maturity: 1995–2006.** The highly saturated, black/ruby/purple-colored 1989 Cuvée des Cadettes is sweeter on the palate, with a developed, more penetrating bouquet of jammy cassis, spices, and vanillin from the new oak barrels. It is a large-scale, well-balanced wine, with superb depth of flavor and a surprisingly well-focused personality. **Anticipated maturity: 1995–2007.** The 1988 Cuvée des Cadettes is the most precocious of this trio, with a ripe, sweet bouquet of plums, chocolate, hickory wood, and Provençal herbs. It does not have the weight, muscle, or tannin of the 1989 or 1990, but it is a rich, generously endowed wine. **Anticipated maturity: Now–2002.**

MICHEL OGIER* * * *

1991 Côte Rôtie Côte Blonde		D	93
1990 Côte Rôtie Côte Blonde		D	87
1989 Côte Rôtie Côte Blonde		D	90

Ogier's 1991 offers further evidence that this year was more successful in Côte Rôtie than 1990. The superb nose of Ogier's 1991 soars from the glass, offering aromas of black fruits, peaches, jammy raspberries, and toasty new oak. Long and unctuous, with a velvety texture, superconcentration, and a satiny finish, it is an undeniably seductive wine for drinking over the next 10–12 years. The 1990 is a tasty, medium-bodied, attractive Côte Rôtie for drinking over the next 6–8 years. Ogier's 1989 Côte Rôtie Côte Blonde exhibits exceptional elegance and perfume. This medium-bodied wine's flavors suggest drinking it between 1994 and 2001.

DOMAINE LES PALLIÈRES* * *

1990 Gigondas	C	83
1989 Gigondas	C	87
1988 Gigondas	C	82

I have tasted many classic examples of Gigondas from this producer, so I am perplexed by the austere, rather light wines that have emerged over recent vintages. This estate tends to bottle as the wines are sold, which can result in an enormous variation in quality. I thought the 1990 to be pleasant, essentially soft and fruity, but lacking weight, extract, and body. It will have to be drunk in its first 5–7 years of life. The 1989 offers a big, animal, almost savage, smoked meat smell and powerful, chewy, alcoholic flavors. Full bodied, spicy, but rustic, this broadly flavored Gigondas will drink well for 8–10 years. The 1988, which is the current vintage in the marketplace, reveals amber/orange hues (a sign of age), a peppery, herb-, and berry-scented nose, medium-bodied, soft, spicy, decent flavors, and a short finish. It should be drunk over the next 2–3 years.

DOMAINE DU PAVILLON-MERCUROL* * * *

1991 Crozes-Hermitage	B	85
1990 Crozes-Hermitage	B	88
1991 Crozes-Hermitage Blanc	B	85

The 1991 Crozes-Hermitage Blanc (made from 100% Marsanne) exhibits a fresh, lemony, fruity nose, ripe, medium-bodied flavors, and some power and authority. Drink it over the next 4–5 years. The 1991 red Crozes-Hermitage is spicy and well made, with good fruit, medium body, and soft tannins. The 1990 red Crozes-Hermitage's black color is followed by aromas of cherry fruit, herbs, and spices. The wine exhibits admirable intensity, highly extracted black cherry flavors, medium to full body, soft tannins, and a long finish. It should continue to drink well for 7–8 years.

DOMAINE DU PEGAU* * * * *

1990	Châteauneuf-du-Pape	C	96
1989	Châteauneuf-du-Pape	C	95
1988	Châteauneuf-du-Pape	C	90
1985	Châteauneuf-du-Pape	C	95
1981	Châteauneuf-du-Pape	D	93
1979	Châteauneuf-du-Pape	D	91
1991	Châteauneuf-du-Pape Blanc	C	79
1989	Châteauneuf-du-Pape Blanc	C	84
N.V.	Vin de Pays Rouge Gorge Lot 91	A	85

Proprietor Paul Feraud fashions an old-style, massive, unbelievably rich, rustic Châteauneuf-du-Pape. The 1990 is a superstar. The color is an impenetrable black/purple. The huge nose of truffles, tar, superripe black fruits, licorice, tobacco, and spices is profound. In the mouth there is sweet, expansive fruit, a superconcentrated, powerful, tannic taste, lavish amounts of glycerin and body, and a finish that lasts nearly a minute. With plenty of tannin, this wine is destined to have 20–25 years of evolution. Feraud's 1989 resembles something between a dry red table wine and vintage port. Its dark purple/black color, exceptional concentration, great extract, and huge body loaded with glycerin and tannin make it one of the most immense wines of this superlative vintage. Surprisingly forward (blame the superb ripeness and relatively low acidity of the vintage), it should last for at least 15 more years. The 1988 tastes civilized next to the 1989 and 1990. It is a heady, alcoholic, rich, concentrated wine, but it is much smoother. Consume it over the next decade. The blockbuster 1985 is another large-scale wine that reveals whopping proportions of extract, alcohol, and glycerin. Approachable now, it should continue to drink well for at least another 15–20 years. It is a sensational wine. The 1981 is another exceptional Châteauneuf-du-Pape that has just reached full maturity. The huge bouquet of Provençal herbs, superripe, extracted red fruits, leather, smoked meats, coffee, and Oriental spices is followed by a remarkably concentrated, rich, almost portlike wine with enough alcohol, body, and extract to carry it until the new millennium. The 1979 is also a terrific bottle of old-style Châteauneuf-du-Pape, with a huge bouquet of leather, smoked meats, and cassis as well as thick, high-alcohol, huge flavors that suggest earth, nutmeg, truffle, leather, and black fruits. Although both the 1979 and 1981 are fully mature, they should continue to drink well for at least a decade. The nonvintage Vin de Pays called Rouge Gorge Lot 91 is a velvety-textured, fruity (raspberries and cassis), medium-bodied wine that offers immediate gratification. Drink it over the next 2–3 years. The 1991 white Châteauneuf-du-Pape is spicy and full bodied, but short and simple.

PÈRE ANSELME* * *

1990 Châteauneuf-du-Pape	C	85
1989 Châteauneuf-du-Pape	C	85
1988 Châteauneuf-du-Pape Cuvée Prestige	C	86

Père Anselme, a *négociant*, is one of the biggest producers of Châteauneuf-du-Pape. The 1990 regular *cuvée* is a ripe, attractive wine with plenty of sweet, roasted peanut–, and cassis-scented fruit. The 1989 regular *cuvée* is a round, fruity, solidly made wine with succulent black cherry flavors and soft tannins. Both wines should drink nicely for 3–6 years. The 1988 Cuvée Prestige is powerful, spicy, and rich, with a mineral-scented, roasted bouquet, rich, full-bodied flavors, and moderate tannins.

DOMAINE DU PÈRE CABOCHE* * *

1989 Châteauneuf-du-Pape	C	84
1988 Châteauneuf-du-Pape	C	83

This estate is usually a reliable source for soft, fruity, easy-to-drink red and white wines. In certain vintages a *tête de cuvée* called Elisabeth Chambellan is produced. The 1989 red Châteauneuf exhibits an interesting nose of pine trees, cassis fruit, and roasted peanuts. The 1988 offers a distinct aroma of licorice and cassis. Both wines are soft, medium bodied, and best drunk before 1996.

DOMAINE DU PÈRE PAPE* * *

1990 Châteauneuf-du-Pape Clos du Calvaire	C	87
1989 Châteauneuf-du-Pape Clos du Calvaire	C	89
1988 Châteauneuf-du-Pape Clos du Calvaire	C	83
1991 Châteauneuf-du-Pape Clos du Calvaire Blanc	C	71

The 1991 Châteauneuf-du-Pape Clos du Calvaire Blanc is of little interest. There is medium body and crisp acidity, but no depth or fruit. There are two red wines, a regular *cuvée* and a richer, purportedly more ageworthy wine called Clos du Calvaire. The dark ruby-colored 1990 Clos du Calvaire exhibits spicy, herbaceous, bing cherry fruit, soft, full-bodied, earthy flavors, a velvety texture, and an alcoholic finish. The tannins are present, but they are largely concealed by the jammy fruit. This is a wine to consume over the next 4–5 years. The 1989 is more tannic, with a spicy, herb-, black cherry–, and apricot-scented nose, medium-bodied flavors, superripe fruit, and high alcohol. This big, full-flavored wine should keep for 7–8 years. The 1988 Clos du Calvaire is soft, fruity, medium to full bodied, and concentrated.

ANDRÉ PERRET* * * * *

1991 Condrieu Coteau du Chery	D	89
1990 Condrieu Coteau du Chery	D	93
1990 Condrieu Vendange Tardive	D	93
1990 St.-Joseph	C	88

1990 St.-Joseph Les Grisières	C	90
1989 St.-Joseph Les Grisières	C	86
1988 St.-Joseph Les Grisières	C	85

Many consider Perret to be the star of Condrieu. His 1991 Condrieu Coteau du Chery possesses a big, floral, apricot, peachy nose, fine acidity for a Condrieu, excellent richness, and a long, medium- to full-bodied, honeyed finish. Drink it over the next 2–3 years. The 1990 Condrieu Coteau du Chery offers superb extraction of flavor, exceptional depth and richness, a floral, banana-, and apricot-scented nose, and unctuous flavors. The 1989 Coteau du Chery exhibits a honeyed, apricot- and lychee nut–scented bouquet, gorgeously ripe, long, concentrated flavors, and enough acidity to provide delineation. The slightly sweet 1990 Condrieu Vendange Tardive exhibits a sensational nose of honeyed fruits intertwined with aromas of spring flowers, a chewy, rich, unctuous texture, adequate acidity for definition, and a lavishly rich finish. Perret's 1990 St.-Joseph offers a fragrant bouquet of ripe cherries, spicy vanillin from new oak, and nuts. Velvety and supple, with a medium-bodied texture, sweet, berry flavors, and a silky finish, it should be drunk over the next 4–5 years. The outstanding 1990 St.-Joseph Les Grisières reveals a knockout nose of sweet red and black fruits, flowers, and toast. Drink it over the next 6–7 years. The fine 1989 Les Grisières offers aromas of herbs, black cherries, and cassis that are followed by a superripe, rich, concentrated wine bursting with fruit. I would opt for drinking it over the next 5–6 years. The 1988 Les Grisières is a deliciously fruity, forward, flattering style of St.-Joseph that is meant to be drunk over the next 2–3 years.

ROGER PERRIN* * *

1990 Châteauneuf-du-Pape	C	88
1989 Châteauneuf-du-Pape	C	85
1988 Châteauneuf-du-Pape	C	78
1991 Châteauneuf-du-Pape Blanc	C	62

Perrin's 1991 white Châteauneuf-du-Pape is watery, acidic, and alcoholic. As for the red wine vintages, I have a preference for Perrin's 1990. It possesses a deep, impressive ruby/purple color, a rich, cassis-dominated nose, well-balanced flavors, and a chewy finish. Its tannin levels suggest it should last for 10–12. The 1989 exhibits dry, hard tannins and good concentration, but its backward style made judgment less certain. **Anticipated maturity: Now–2000.** The 1988 red Châteauneuf is light and fruity, but lacks concentration and complexity.

DOMAINE DES PESQUIERS* * * *

1990 Gigondas	B	90
1989 Gigondas	B	86
1988 Gigondas	B	83

This domaine is known for its rustic, traditional, old-style Gigondas. Both the robust, rich, chewy, massive 1990 and the 1989 display dried pit fruit, spicy, peppery, cherry flavors, robust tannins, and high alcohol. The 1990 should prove to have an uncommonly long life, even for a Gigondas, up to 15 years. **Anticipated maturity: 1995–2005.** The 1989 looks to be a wine that can last for 10–15 years, but tasters who are opposed to big wines with dusty, coarse tannins and a slightly oxidized style would be advised to pass up this hefty Gigondas. The 1988 is similarly styled, smooth and fruity, with average concentration and decent length.

DOMAINE DE PIAUGIER* * * *

1990 Côtes du Rhône Les Briguières	A	87
1990 Côtes du Rhône Montmartel	A	86
1990 Gigondas	B	88
1989 Gigondas	B	88
1988 Gigondas	A	86

The 1988 is slightly more tannic and structured, the 1989 more opulent, with lower acidity, and an extremely flattering, impressive, up-front ripeness and richness. The 1990 is expansive, with gobs of sweet fruit, an impressive deep purple color, and a long, chewy, intense finish. These wines can be drunk young or cellared for 10–12 years. Proprietor Autran produces two Côtes du Rhônes. Both are excellent and nearly as tasty as his Gigondas. The attractive, fragrant 1990 Côtes du Rhône Montmartel (from sandy soils) exhibits a spicy, herb, hickory-, and black cherry–scented nose, followed by soft, medium-bodied flavors. It is ideal for drinking over the next 2–3 years. The 1990 Côtes du Rhône Les Briguières (from clay soils) is even richer, a worthy candidate for 5–7 years of fine drinking.

PHILIPPE PICHON* * * * *

1990 Condrieu Moelleux	D	95
1990 Condrieu Sec	D	93

Philippe Pichon's 1990 Condrieu Moelleux offers up a decadent nose of co-conut, peaches, apricots, and spring flowers, a honeyed, voluptuous richness, staggering concentration, and a moderately sweet, long finish. Drink it over the next several years. Readers who want no part of this moderately sweet, explosive style of Condrieu should check out Pichon's 1990 Condrieu Sec. It possesses a fabulous aroma of jammy apricots and honeysuckle, super-concentration, and full body, but the wine is drier and easier to drink than the later-harvested Moelleux. It, too, should be drunk over the next 2–3 years.

DOMAINE LES PIERRELLES—TARDY AND ANGE* *

1989 Crozes-Hermitage	B	75
1988 Crozes-Hermitage	B	77

The 1989 Crozes-Hermitage is soft and light bodied, with decent concentration. It will require immediate drinking when released. The 1988 red Crozes is also soft, simplistic in flavor, with medium body, and a soft, diluted finish.

DOMAINE DE LA PINÈDE* * *

1990 Châteauneuf-du-Pape	C	87
1989 Châteauneuf-du-Pape	C	84
1991 Châteauneuf-du-Pape Blanc	C	74

The 1990 red Châteauneuf-du-Pape's huge bouquet of peppery, spicy, herb, tobacco, chocolate, and salty ocean water is followed by a rich, long, fat, sweet, expansively flavored wine with super extract and an alcoholic, heady finish. Soft enough to be appreciated now, it has the structure, muscle, and concentration to last for 5–7 years. The 1989 is ripe, tasty, and generously endowed, but one-dimensional. Furthermore, it does not have the structure and profound depth found in the 1990. I would opt for drinking it over the next 4–6 years. The 1991 white Châteauneuf-du-Pape is clean, but shallow and boring.

DOMAINE PONTIFICAL—FRANÇOIS LAGET* * * *

1990 Châteauneuf-du-Pape	C	87
1989 Châteauneuf-du-Pape	B	92
1991 Châteauneuf-du-Pape Blanc	C	84

These wines appear under two separate labels, the Domaine Pontifical and the Domaine François Laget. The 1991 white Châteauneuf is good for the vintage. It exhibits a floral, honeyed bouquet and sound, fruity, full-bodied flavors that have not been overly processed. The 1990 red Châteauneuf-du-Pape will not make old bones. It displays a deep ruby color, a seductively fragrant perfume of sweet berry fruit, supple flavors, full body, low acidity, and a fleshy finish. It has neither the depth nor the structure of the superb 1989. The 1989 is magnificent. The opaque, dark ruby/purple color and immensely impressive nose of pepper, herbs, cassis, and tobacco are followed by full-bodied, rich flavors with impressive levels of extract, abundant power, moderate tannins, and a long finish. **Anticipated maturity: Now–2003.**

DOMAINE PRADELLE* *

1989 Crozes-Hermitage Les Hirondelles	C	85
1990 Crozes-Hermitage Les Hirondelles Blanc	C	79

The 1990 white Crozes-Hermitage Les Hirondelles exhibits a crisp, tart, clean, monolithic nose, medium-bodied, pure, elegant flavors, and decent acidity. The bouquet of the 1989 red Crozes-Hermitage Les Hirondelles is reminiscent of spicy, cherry fruit and overripe tomatoes. There is good concentration, spicy, gamelike, medium-bodied flavors, and a soft finish. Drink it over the next 2–3 years.

DOMAINE DE LA PRÉSIDENTE (M. AUBERT)* * */* * * *

1990 Cairanne Côtes du Rhône	A	86
1990 Cairanne Goutillonnage	B	88
1990 Châteauneuf-du-Pape La Nonciature	C	87

The 1990 Cairanne Côtes du Rhône exhibits a rich berry- and herb-scented nose and a soft, round finish. Drink it over the next 1–2 years. The 1990

Cairanne Goutillonnage offers a saturated color, a big, rich nose of bacon and cassis, a dense, unctuous texture, and a satiny-smooth finish. Drink it over the next 4–5 years. The 1990 La Nonciature is a rich, full-bodied Châteauneuf-du-Pape, with low acidity, light tannins, and plenty of gutsy fruit. Drink it over the next 4–5 years.

RASPAIL—GABRIEL MEFFRE* * *

1990 Gigondas	C	84
1989 Gigondas	B	?
1988 Gigondas	B	87

The 1990 is an alcoholic, husky Gigondas with touches of plummy, prune, and herb scents to its bouquet and thick, chewy, soft flavors that reveal an elevated degree of alcohol. **Anticipated maturity: Now–1998.** At times the 1989 has tasted thin and insubstantial, but at other times it has been full and concentrated—perplexing! Was there a competent blending of all the *cuvées* prior to bottling? The 1988 is intense, with gobs of extract and tannin as well as roasted, peppery, black fruit flavors. Drink it between now and 1998.

DOMAINE RASPAIL—DOMINIQUE AY* * * *

1990 Gigondas	C	90
1989 Gigondas	B	86
1988 Gigondas	B	86
1987 Gigondas	B	77

The 1990 has a saturated ruby/purple color; a superripe nose of roasted, mineral, cassis aromas intermingled with the scents of Provençal herbs; full-bodied, deep, concentrated flavors; excellent depth; and moderate tannins in the finish. **Anticipated maturity: 1995–2005.** I thought Raspail's attractive 1988 and 1989 were well made but tight and closed. The 1989 is dark ruby-colored, with a spicy, herb-, and black cherry–scented nose, full body, and gobs of hard tannin in the finish. The 1988 is a spicy, soft, tough-textured wine. The 1987 is soft and weedy.

RAYAS* * * * *

1990 Fonsalette Blanc	C	89
1989 Fonsalette Blanc	C	88
1988 Fonsalette Blanc	C	86
1990 Fonsalette Côtes du Rhône	C	92
1989 Fonsalette Côtes du Rhône	C	92
1988 Fonsalette Côtes du Rhône	C	87
1990 Fonsalette Côtes du Rhône Cuvée Syrah	D	94
1989 Fonsalette Côtes du Rhône Cuvée Syrah	D	93
1988 Fonsalette Côtes du Rhône Cuvée Syrah	D	92
1989 Pignan Châteauneuf-du-Pape	C	90

1990 Rayas Blanc	D	91
1989 Rayas Blanc	D	87
1988 Rayas Blanc	D	85
1990 Rayas Châteauneuf-du-Pape	E	99
1989 Rayas Châteauneuf-du-Pape	E	95
1988 Rayas Chateauneuf-du-Pape	D	95

When you come upon a truly exotic and sumptuous wine, with a huge nose of sweet, overripe, black cherry fruit that envelops the taster and kinky, undeniably thrilling, velvety, creamy-textured flavors, chances are you are tasting Rayas—the most decadently rich and hedonistic wine of the southern Rhône. Jacques Reynaud, who produces his marvels in some of the most cramped and dingy cellars in the winemaking world, is antioenologist, antitechnology, and anticommercialism. But what an example he sets for those of us who love distinctive flavor and personality-filled wines! I was immensely impressed with the massive richness, complexity, and drama offered by the 1990 Fonsalette Blanc. From its huge bouquet of tropical fruit and cantaloupe to its chewy, unctuous flavors, this is a fleshy, deep, intense wine that suggests early drinkability because of low acidity. Reynaud suggested that the more backward 1990 Rayas Blanc, which is not as flattering to taste, needed 10–15 years just to reach full maturity! The wine reveals a huge nose of honey and pears, expansive, unctuous flavors, gorgeous extraction of fruit, and a long, alcoholic finish. It should drink well for 15–20 years. The 1989 Fonsalette Blanc offers a heady, dizzying perfume of honeyed pineapples and rich, alcoholic, concentrated, low-acid flavors. The 1989 Rayas Blanc is more elegant without the blockbuster, fleshy, opulence of the other vintages. The 1990 Fonsalette Côtes du Rhône displays the essence of cherry and kirsch in its nose, followed by corpulent, sweet, expansive, rich flavors that linger on the palate. It is a lavishly rich Côtes du Rhône, with a thick texture and enough alcohol and soft tannins to keep it going for at least 10–15 years. The 1989 Fonsalette is a beautifully made, seductive mouthful of wine. It is all velvet and silk, and there is a whopping degree of alcohol in the finish. It appears to be the best Fonsalette since the late 1970s, although the 1990 is just as superb. The tannins are soft and the acidity is low, yet the wine's concentration and magical flavors are dazzling. Drink it over the next 12–15 years. The 1988 Fonsalette is also a rich, intense, powerful Côtes du Rhône, with plenty of alcohol in its heady finish. It should drink well for another 5–6 years. The Fonsalette Cuvée Syrah is Reynaud's best-kept secret. The 1990 is black in color, with an extraordinary perfume of hickory wood, chocolate, cassis, and black fruits, staggering richness, astonishing opulence, plenty of alcohol, and gobs of tannin. I suspect this massive wine will need at least 10 years of cellaring to reach its zenith. The 1989 Fonsalette Cuvée Syrah is similarly endowed, exhibiting exceptional intensity, a black/ruby/purple color, a huge perfume of black raspberries, and a whoppingly long, moderately tannic finish. The 1988 Cuvée Syrah is a riveting wine, with splendid dark ruby/purple color, a spicy Provençal herb- and superripe cassis-scented bouquet, highly extracted flavors, and a rich, full-bodied, velvety texture; it needs at least 10–15 more years of evolution. The 1990 Rayas is overwhelming in its richness and intensity. I am certain this giant of a wine will turn out to be a masterpiece. From its exquisite bouquet, which is almost the essence of black cherry and black raspberry fruit, to its lavish dimensions, extraordinary precision, and expansive unctuousness on the palate, this phenomenally concentrated wine should prove to have an awesome future. **Anticipated maturity: 1996–2010+.** The 1989 Rayas is also an exceptional wine. It displays a dark ruby color and an intense nose of kirsch, combined with scents of smoke, earth, and roasted nuts. Extremely concentrated, with an almost portlike texture, this is a beautifully made, rich, full, heady wine that is worth a special effort to find. **Anticipated maturity: Now–2008.** The 1988 Rayas is a structured, powerful, backward wine, with a super bouquet of raspberries and cherries. Rich and full bodied, with a natural alcohol content of 14.5%, it exhibits elevated, aggressive tannins. My best guess is that it should be drunk between now and 2005. The 1989 Pignan (the second wine of Rayas) is a decadent, rich, full-throttle wine with a forceful nose of jammy cherry fruit. Thick and portlike, with plenty of fruit and glycerin, this lusty wine will drink well for the next 7–9 years.

RATINGS FOR OLDER VINTAGES OF RAYAS CHÂTEAUNEUF-DU-PAPE: 1986 (87), 1985 (90), 1983 (92), 1981 (94), 1979 (94), 1978 (96), 1976 (74), 1971 (80)

RATINGS FOR OLDER VINTAGES OF RAYAS FONSALETTE CÔTES DU RHÔNE: 1986 (85), 1985 (89), 1983 (96), 1982 (88), 1981 (89), 1979 (90), 1978 (92), 1969 (91), 1966 (89)

RATINGS FOR OLDER VINTAGES OF RAYAS FONSALETTE CÔTES DU RHÔNE CUVÉE SYRAH: 1985 (90), 1983 (92), 1978 (93+)

REDOITIER* * * *

1990 Gigondas	C	87
1989 Gigondas	C	91
1988 Gigondas	C	83

The 1988 displays a spicy, peppery, herb-scented nose, but the color lacks saturation, and the wine is too soft and already fully mature. Drink it over the next 2–3 years. The 1989 exhibits a ruby/purple color and a huge nose of olives, Provençal herbs, cassis, and licorice. It coats the palate with glycerin and concentrated fruit. It should develop for at least 12–15 years. The 1990 is soft, with considerable alcohol, an intense bouquet of herbaceous, overripe black cherries, concentrated, thick flavors, and a long, velvet-textured finish. It should drink well for a decade.

DOMAINE DES RELAGNES—CUVÉE VIGNERONNE* * *

1990 Châteauneuf-du-Pape	C	84
1989 Châteauneuf-du-Pape	C	86
1988 Châteauneuf-du-Pape	C	78
1991 Châteauneuf-du-Pape Blanc	C	73

The light, diluted 1991 Châteauneuf-du-Pape Blanc displays an artificial bubble-gum aroma. The two red wine *cuvées* in both 1989 and 1990 have medium ruby color, pleasant spicy, herb-, and red fruit–scented noses, moderately endowed flavors, good body, soft textures, and the telltale peppery, peanut smell of superripe Grenache. Both should be drunk in their first 4–6 years of life. Already beginning to fade, the 1988 reveals a peppery, spicy, intensely herbaceous bouquet and round, soft, flabby flavors.

DOMAINE DE LA RÉMÉJEANNE* * * *
1990 Côtes du Rhône	A	86

The ripe, solid, muscular, black cherry– and herb-scented 1990 Côtes du Rhône displays medium body, supple flavors, and some heady alcohol. It should be drunk over the next 2–3 years.

DOMAINE DES REMEZIÈRES—DESMEURE* *
1989 Crozes-Hermitage Cuvée Particulière	C	80
1988 Crozes-Hermitage Cuvée Particulière	C	72
1989 Hermitage	D	83
1988 Hermitage	D	75
1989 Hermitage Blanc	C	87
1988 Hermitage Blanc	C	86

Both the 1988 and 1989 Crozes-Hermitage Cuvée Particulières are mediocre. The 1989 exhibits a dullness and lightness. The 1988 is thin, with excessively high acidity and a sourness to its taste. The two Hermitages are surprisingly light and diluted. The simple 1989 offers jammy, ripe fruit and a smooth texture. The 1988 has excessive amounts of oak that obliterate the light, strawberry and cherry fruitiness and give the wine an angular, tart, hollow texture.

DOMAINE RICHARD* * * *
1990 Cairanne Cuvée L'Ebrescade Côtes du Rhône-Villages	B	86
1989 Cairanne Cuvée L'Ebrescade Côtes du Rhône-Villages	B	87
1990 Côtes du Rhône-Villages	A	86
1989 Côtes du Rhône-Villages	A	83

Both the densely colored 1990 and 1989 standard *cuvées* of Côtes du Rhône are plump, chunky, peppery, intense wines with long, gutsy finishes. They are ideal for drinking over the next 3–4 years. Richer and more interesting is the Cuvée L'Ebrescade. The 1990 is spicy and rich, but more angular and tannic than the blockbuster, rich, chewy, concentrated 1989 Cuvée L'Ebrescade. The 1989 is a beautifully made wine, with a huge, peppery, spicy, black cherry–scented nose and surprisingly rich, multidimensional flavors. The 1989 should drink well for 5–7 years, the 1990 for 3–4 years.

DOMAINE DE LA ROQUETTE* * * *
1990 Châteauneuf-du-Pape	C	88
1989 Châteauneuf-du-Pape	C	90
1988 Châteauneuf-du-Pape	C	88

The 1990 La Roquette exhibits an attractive sweet smell of overripe black fruits, spicy herbs, coffee, and tobacco, as well as rich, plump, smooth flavors in a velvet-textured format. It should provide immense pleasure over the next

7–8 years. The 1989 is a more ambitiously styled, bigger, richer, more ageworthy wine. It is less flattering than the 1990, but there is no doubting its intense black cherry–, herb-, licorice-, and earth-scented fruitiness, sweet, exotic, black fruit flavors, gobs of glycerin, and rich, powerful finish. **Anticipated maturity: Now–2024.** The 1988 has a fragrant bouquet of chocolate-covered black cherries, cedar, and spices. Intense and supple, with an alcoholic finish, it should be drunk over the next 4–5 years.

RENÉ ROSTAING * * * * *

1991 Côte Rôtie	D	87
1990 Côte Rôtie	D	87
1991 Côte Rôtie Côte Blonde	E	92
1990 Côte Rôtie Côte Blonde	E	93
1989 Côte Rôtie Côte Blonde	E	89
1988 Côte Rôtie Côte Blonde	E	92
1991 Côte Rôtie Côte Brune La Landonne	E	95
1990 Côte Rôtie Côte Brune La Landonne	E	91
1989 Côte Rôtie Côte Brune La Landonne	E	87
1988 Côte Rôtie Côte Brune La Landonne	E	90
1991 Côte Rôtie Côte Brune La Viaillère	E	93
1989 Côte Rôtie Côte Brune La Viaillère	E	85

René Rostaing, who has become one of the most important producers of estate-bottled Côte Rôtie, produced four *cuvées* in 1991. His 1991 Côte Rôtie (regular *cuvée*) is a rich, full-bodied wine, with soft tannins, low acidity, and plenty of rich Syrah fruit with that telltale smoky, bacon fat–scented nose as well as luscious black fruit character. It is a wine to drink in its first 6–7 years of life. The 1991 Côte Rôtie Côte Brune La Viaillère will prove to be fabulous. This wine exhibits an animal, meaty, earthy side of Côte Rôtie. The nearly black color is followed by huge aromas of soy sauce, smoked game, and black raspberries intertwined with scents of toasty new oak. Full bodied, tannic, and loaded with extract, this forceful Côte Rôtie should drink well for 15 or more years. The 1991 Côte Rôtie Côte Blonde is sweeter, fatter, and more voluptuous. A seductive, generous mouthful of wine, it should drink well for 8–10 years. The black-colored 1991 Côte Rôtie La Landonne offers an exquisite perfume of licorice, violets, blackberries, and toast, staggering concentration, smooth tannins, and low acidity. An exceptionally opulent, multidimensional wine with layers of flavor, it should drink well for 10–15 years. The regular *cuvée* of 1990 Côte Rôtie is a soft, supple, fragrant, delicious wine that should be consumed over the next 5–7 years. It possesses toasty new oak to go along with its black raspberry– and herb-scented nose. The 1990 Côte Rôtie Côte Blonde exhibits a penetrating, smoky, roasted aroma, sweet black raspberry–scented, supple, medium-bodied flavors, and a fleshy finish. I would opt for drinking this wine over the next decade. Rostaing's 1990 Côte Rôtie Côte Brune La Landonne has an earthy, animal, smoky character, superb richness of fruit, gobs of glycerin and extraction, soft tannins, and low acidity. **Anticipated maturity: Now–**

2002. The 1989 Côte Rôties from Rostaing are already delicious. The 1989 Côte Rôtie Côte Blonde reveals a super nose of black fruits, flowers, and smoke, followed by chewy flavors, soft tannins, and crisp acidity. The 1989 Côte Rôtie Côte Brune La Landonne has a pronounced earthy, licorice- and berry-scented bouquet, oak-tinged, medium-bodied, attractive flavors, and moderate tannins. It should age gracefully for at least 10–12 years. Less impressive is the 1989 La Viaillère, a straightforward, fruity, ripe, but one-dimensional wine lacking concentration. The 1988 Côte Rôtie Côte Brune La Landonne has a fabulous bouquet. From its soaring black raspberry, vanillin perfume to its rich, full-bodied flavors, this wine is a tour de force in marrying power with finesse. It can be drunk over the next 10–12 years. The 1988 Côte Blonde is a smooth, velvety-textured wine with glorious reserves of fruit. Extremely intense and ripe, with a similar raspberry- and cassis-dominated bouquet touched judiciously by new oak, this profound, full-flavored wine should be drunk over the next 8–10 years.

DU ROZAY* * *

1991 Condrieu	D	88
1990 Condrieu	D	86
1991 Condrieu J. Multier	C	86
1990 Condrieu J. Multier	C	85

Multier is now producing two *cuvées* of Condrieu. The 1991 regular *cuvée* carries the name Jean Multier rather than du Rozay. Made from young vines, it is stylish and fresh, with some attractive aromas of peaches and underripe apricots. It is ideal for drinking over the next 4–5 years. The 1990 J. Multier is an elegant, clean, lighter-style Condrieu, with aromas and flavors of underripe peaches, bananas, and apricots. There is good, crisp acidity to this restrained style of Condrieu. Drink it over the next two years. Slightly richer, with an underripe apricot- and grapefruit-scented aroma, the 1991 du Rozay Condrieu reveals a chewy texture and medium body. It is a departure in style from the massive Condrieus produced in the 1980s by Multier's late father. The 1990 du Rozay Condrieu exhibits new oak, attractive fruit, ripeness, and a tasty, medium-bodied personality.

DOMAINE ROGER SABON* * * *

1990 Châteauneuf-du-Pape Cuvée Prestige	D	90
1990 Châteauneuf-du-Pape Cuvée Réservée	D	86
1989 Châteauneuf-du-Pape Cuvée Réservée	C	85
1990 Châteauneuf-du-Pape Les Olivets	C	85
1991 Châteauneuf-du-Pape Les Olivets Blanc	C	76

This domaine produces a number of different *cuvées*, the best being its Cuvée Prestige. The 1990 Châteauneuf-du-Pape Cuvée Prestige boasts 14.5% alcohol as well as a cascade of sweet black cherry fruit and interesting bacon fat and roasted-peanut aromas. Dense and full bodied, it has the potential to last for 12–15 years. The 1990 Châteauneuf-du-Pape Les Olivets offers a medium to dark ruby color, aromas of overripe cherries and oranges, solid, straightforward flavors, and soft tannins. I would opt for drinking it over the next 5–6 years. The 1990 Châteauneuf-du-Pape Cuvée Réservée is higher in alcohol as well as richer, with a more fleshy texture and deep red and black fruit scents to its spicy, earthy nose. The 1989 Cuvée Réservée is ready to drink but should last for at least 5–7 more years. It offers a bing cherry–, herb-scented nose and round, full-bodied flavors, and the impression is one of generosity and softness. Sabon's 1991 Les Olivets Blanc offers a neutral nose, crisp, medium-bodied, green apple flavors, and a nonexistent finish. Drink it over the next year.

DOMAINE SAINT-BENÔIT* * * *

1989 Châteauneuf-du-Pape	C	88
1988 Châteauneuf-du-Pape	C	87
1990 Châteauneuf-du-Pape Cuvée de Grand Garde	C	91

The 1990 Cuvée de Grande Garde, a luxury *cuvée*, has a huge nose of black pepper, jammy fruit, tobacco, Provençal herbs, and roasted meats. The wine's balance and muscular, rich finish suggest it should last for 10–12 years. The 1989 regular *cuvée* is excellent. Its dark ruby color is followed by a wine with a spicy, black cherry, and blackberry nose and ripe, opulent, smooth, heady, alcoholic flavors. Drink it over the next 7–8 years. The 1988 offers a chocolaty, cedary, blackberry-dominated bouquet, expansive flavors, and the impression of sweetness because of its rich fruit. It should provide attractive drinking over the next 4–5 years.

DOMAINE SAINT-GAYAN* * * *

1990 Gigondas	C	90
1989 Gigondas	C	91
1988 Gigondas	C	89
1990 Rasteau Côtes du Rhône-Villages	A	86
1989 Rasteau Côtes du Rhône-Villages	A	86

The 1988 Gigondas promises to be the most backward, tannic, and structured of these three offerings, with an intense, herbal, black cherry–scented nose, rich, ripe, well-structured flavors, and serious tannins. This big, old-style, impeccably well-made Gigondas should be at its best between 1994 and 2008. The 1989 Gigondas should develop into a blockbuster wine. The tannins are soft and the acidity is low, but there is also good concentration of fruit, a huge, almost viscous texture, a super perfume of licorice, tar, herbs, and pepper, and layers of black fruit. The wine will last for 12–15 years. The 1990 Gigondas is a flattering, powerful, opulent wine. It has a deep purple/black color, a provocative perfume of exotic spices, admirable concentration, and considerable power and muscle. This classic Gigondas will last for 10–12 years. Proprietor Roger Meffre turns out excellent Côtes du Rhône from the village of Rasteau. The 1990's dark ruby/garnet color, nose of black plums, pepper, and fruitcake, medium to full body, and heady flavors are enticing. Drink it over the next 3–4 years. The 1989 Rasteau offers an opaque black/ruby color; a big, richly fruity, spicy, herb-, and pepper-scented nose; deeply etched, full-bodied flavors; plenty of glycerin; and a long finish. It should continue to drink well for 5–6 years.

DOMAINE SANTA DUC* * * * *

1990 Côtes du Rhône	A	87
1989 Côtes du Rhône	A	87
1990 Gigondas	B	90
1989 Gigondas	B	90
1988 Gigondas	B	88
1990 Gigondas Cuvée Prestige des Hautes Garrigues	C	93
1989 Gigondas Cuvée Prestige des Hautes Garrigues	C	93

The Domaine Santa Duc produces the finest wines of Gigondas as well as excellent Côtes du Rhône. The 1989 Côtes du Rhône is a full-bodied, heady, smashingly rich, complex, fleshy Côtes du Rhône that offers all the seduction these generously endowed wines can possess. The 1990 Côtes du Rhône offers up a huge, plummy, black raspberry–scented bouquet that is followed by a wine crammed with black fruits and scents of minerals and licorice. Drink both these wines over the next 4–5 years. The 1990 regular *cuvée* of Gigondas is an opaque black/purple-colored wine with a pure nose of black raspberries and minerals. This full-bodied, superconcentrated wine is long, opulent, powerful, and well balanced. It will easily last for up to a decade. The 1989 regular Gigondas is a dynamite wine, with an opaque black/ruby/purple color; a super-intense nose of violets, cassis, smoke, and minerals; rich, almost extravagantly intense, ripe flavors; an unctuous texture; and a spectacularly long finish. It promises to drink well for at least 12–15 years. The 1988 Gigondas is an excellent, nearly outstanding wine. Concentrated, with an opaque, dark ruby/purple color, this spicy, peppery, richly fruity wine is full bodied, with some toasty, vanillin, oaky aromas and fine length. It should drink well for the next 6–8 years. Santa Duc's 1990 Cuvée Prestige has a huge nose of cassis, vanillin, smoke, flowers, and minerals. A deeply concentrated, full-bodied wine with soft tannins, considerable complexity, and a voluptuous finish, it can be drunk over the next 10 years. The black/purple-colored 1989 Gigondas Cuvée Prestige displays generous, smoky, vanillin, toasty, cassis-scented aromas, and huge flavors of coffee, chocolate, herbs, and superripe black fruits. It should last for up to 15 years.

DOMAINE SÉNÉCHAUX* * *

1990 Châteauneuf-du-Pape	C	76
1989 Châteauneuf-du-Pape	C	84

The slightly eviscerated, medium ruby-colored 1990 Châteauneuf-du-Pape offers a vague nose of herbs and fruit, medium body, dusty, coarse tannins, and some round, ripe fruit. A fragile wine, it should be consumed over the next 4–5 years. The 1989 is slightly richer, low in acidity, and flabby.

SIMIAN* * *

1990 Châteauneuf-du-Pape	C	85
1989 Châteauneuf-du-Pape	C	88
1988 Châteauneuf-du-Pape	C	87

The 1990 red Châteauneuf exhibits a moderately intense bouquet of cherries and raspberries, with some vague aromas of Provençal herbs. The wine displays a spicy ripeness, medium- to full-bodied flavors, and a soft, up-front, precocious style. Drink it over the next 4–5 years. The 1989 red Châteauneuf-du-Pape possesses a good ruby/purple color and an intense bouquet of hickory smoke, black cherries, and chocolate. Generously endowed, it will drink well for 5–7 years. The 1988 exhibits a fragrant, fruitcake sort of bouquet, chewy, alcoholic flavors, a full-bodied, concentrated feel on the palate, and a spicy, tannic finish. **Anticipated maturity: Now–1998.**

DOMAINE DE LA SOLITUDE* * * *

1990 Châteauneuf-du-Pape	C	90
1989 Châteauneuf-du-Pape	C	87
1988 Châteauneuf-du-Pape	C	85
1991 Châteauneuf-du-Pape Blanc	C	77

The 1990 signals the return of this famous domaine to the forefront of Châteauneuf-du-Pape's finest producers. Displaying an opaque black/ruby/ purple color, an impressive vanillin, black cherry–, and cassis-scented nose, and rich, robust, herblike flavors, this wine was aged in small oak casks, making it an untraditional style of Châteauneuf-du-Pape. It will drink well for 10–15 years. The 1989 exhibits aromas of smoky new oak, rich, tobacco-scented, raspberry fruit, medium to full body, and a spicy finish. **Anticipated maturity: Now–2003.** The attractive 1988 reveals a judicious use of toasty oak, ripe, pleasant, chewy flavors, medium body, and a soft finish. It should be drunk over the next 3–4 years.

HENRI SORREL* * * *

1990 Hermitage	C	88
1989 Hermitage	C	89+
1988 Hermitage	C	88
1990 Hermitage Le Gréal	C	93+
1989 Hermitage Le Gréal	C	95
1988 Hermitage Le Gréal	C	92
1991 Hermitage Les Rocoules	C	88
1990 Hermitage Les Rocoules	C	90
1989 Hermitage Les Rocoules	C	90
1988 Hermitage Les Rocoules	C	93

The 1991 Hermitage Les Rocoules is a honeyed white wine, with an expansive, full-bodied, chewy texture and at least 10–15 years of aging potential. The

1990 Hermitage Les Rocoules is a closed but powerful wine with a floral component to the otherwise muted nose. The big, rich, honeyed flavors exhibit considerable concentration, full body, and a slight touch of oak. A big, thick, chewy wine that needs time in the cellar, it will provide riveting drinking for those with the patience to wait 10–15 years. The 1989 Hermitage Les Rocoules is attractively forward and precocious, with more alcohol, lower acidity, and a chewy texture. The 1988 Les Rocoules has sensational extract and incredible length and richness. It should last for 10–20 or more years. Sorrel's tannic 1990 reds are savage and ferocious in their backwardness and full-bodied, rustic styles. The 1990 red Hermitage (regular *cuvée*) displays a nearly black color and an earthy, leathery, animal-scented nose that is followed by full-bodied, tannic flavors. **Anticipated maturity: 1997–2010.** The blockbuster 1990 Hermitage Le Gréal reveals an opaque black/purple color and a promising nose of licorice, damp earth, leather, and black raspberries. The wine is awesomely concentrated, full bodied, and enormously weighty and massive, and its tough-textured, tannic finish suggests that considerable cellaring is necessary. **Anticipated maturity: 2005–2040.** The 1989 regular *cuvée* of Hermitage displays a backward, closed style, black/ruby color, a reticent bouquet of plums, hickory wood, coffee, chocolate, and cassis, and significant tannins. There can be no doubting its weight, richness, and layers of concentration. It is capable of lasting for 20–25 years. The black/purple-colored 1989 Hermitage Le Gréal has a bouquet of tar, spices (including soy), smoke, coffee, and cassis, a heady, chewy ripeness, extraordinary presence, and massive weight and fruit, all crammed into a well-delineated, backward, tannic wine. **Anticipated maturity: 2000–2035.** The larger-scale 1988 regular Hermitage is ripe, rich, concentrated, and approachable. The 1988 Hermitage Le Gréal is another blockbuster, bursting with smoky, roasted, jammy, cassis fruitiness, some vanillin, oaky components, and highly extracted flavors. It should be at its best between 1995 and 2005.

JEAN-MARC SORREL* * *

1991 Hermitage Blanc	D	87
1990 Hermitage Le Vignon	D	87?
1989 Hermitage Le Vignon	D	86
1988 Hermitage Le Vignon	D	86
1989 Hermitage Le Vignon Blanc	D	87
1988 Hermitage Le Vignon Blanc	D	89

Jean-Marc Sorrel has fashioned a 1991 white Hermitage with a rich, forward nose, excellent ripeness, and a dense, chunky texture. It should be drunk over the next 6–7 years. Both the 1988 and 1989 white Hermitage Le Vignon are rich, deep, full bodied, and muscular and promise to drink well for the next 4–5 years. The 1988 is slightly fuller and more concentrated. The 1990 Hermitage Le Vignon is an opaque black/purple color, with a promising nose of gamey Syrah fruit and some noticeable herbaceousness. Its acids are alarmingly high, even shrill, and the astringent tannins sear the palate. If the fruit does not fade before the tannins, it will turn out to be excellent. The 1989 Hermitage Le Vignon offers a deep ruby color, a complex bouquet of spices, oak, and roasted cassis, and an alcoholic finish. It should last for a decade. The 1988 Hermitage Le Vignon is soft, round, and ripe. It will drink well for 5–7 years.

DOMAINE DE LA SOUCO-PAPALE* * *

1990 Châteauneuf-du-Pape	C	87+

This 1990 Châteauneuf-du-Pape exhibits an impressive dark ruby/purple color, a nose of black cherry, earthy, roasted meat scents, good body, plenty of tannin and glycerin, and a powerful finish. This big wine should keep for 15 years.

DOMAINE LA SOUMADE* * * */* * * * *

1990 Côtes du Rhône-Villages Rasteau Prestige	B	88
1989 Côtes du Rhône-Villages Rasteau Prestige	A	89

The black/purple color and the huge bouquet of rich, superripe black raspberries, spices, and Provençal herbs combine to make both of these wines head turners. Opulently rich, full bodied, and splendidly concentrated, these wines should drink beautifully for up to a decade.

DOMAINE TERRE FERME* * *

1990 Châteauneuf-du-Pape	C	82
1989 Châteauneuf-du-Pape	C	88
1991 Châteauneuf-du-Pape Blanc	C	76

I have never been particularly enamored with the Domaine Terre Ferme's white Châteauneuf-du-Pape. The 1991 exhibits little character or fruit and possesses a tart, short finish. The ruby-colored 1990 Châteauneuf-du-Pape has straightforward, medium- to full-bodied, soft, fruity flavors. I suspect much of this wine's soul and character were left in a filter. The 1989 has begun to close up, although the bouquet does display some elements of overripeness, as suggested by its peach, apricot, and jammy scents. It reveals a streak of herbaceousness, firm tannins, and plenty of ripe fruit. This is a large-scale, yet backward Châteauneuf. **Anticipated maturity: 1995–2005.**

DES TOURS* * * * *

1990 Côtes du Rhône	A	88
1990 Vacqueyras	B	90
1989 Vacqueyras	B	91
1990 Vin de Pays Vaucluse	A	87

Château des Tours is a budding Rhône superstar, so move quickly while these wines are still bargains. The 1990 Vin de Pays Vaucluse is densely colored, with an enticing fragrance of sweet black fruits, spices, olives, and cedar. The wine is flattering to drink, with a luscious texture, fine depth, and a satiny-smooth finish. It should drink well for at least 4–5 years. The 1990 Côtes du Rhône offers the roasted peanut, sweet kirsch nose typical of late-harvested Grenache. The predominant flavor is that of overripe black cherries. Drink it over the next 4–5 years. The 1990 Vacqueyras has a huge, ripe nose of black raspberry fruit and roasted nuts, gobs of chewy, intense flavors, moderate tannins, and an explosively long finish. It will last for 10–20 years. The rich, dense 1989 Vacqueyras is bursting with overripe Grenache fruit. With an explosive richness, superconcentration, and depth, this beauty will last for 12–15 years.

DOMAINE JEAN TRINTIGNANT* * *

1990 Châteauneuf-du-Pape	C	86
1989 Châteauneuf-du-Pape	C	87
1991 Châteauneuf-du-Pape Blanc	C	78
1989 Châteauneuf-du-Pape La Reviscoulado	C	85

The 1991 Châteauneuf-du-Pape Blanc displays open-knit, straightforward flavors, medium body, and decent acidity. Both the 1990 and 1989 red Châteauneuf-du-Papes exhibit aromas of jammy, cherry-, apricot-, and peach-flavored fruit. Both are also long, fat, chewy, luscious, thick wines without much finesse. The 1989 is slightly fuller and richer. I would opt for drinking both wines over the next 5–7 years. The 1989 red La Reviscoulado is forward and supple, somewhat commercial, but well flavored and ideal for drinking over the next 3–4 years.

DOMAINE RAYMOND USSEGLIO* * *

1990 Châteauneuf-du-Pape	C	88
1991 Châteauneuf-du-Pape Blanc	C	75

This 1991 white Châteauneuf-du-Pape reflects the current obsession among most of the *vignerons* in Châteauneuf to sterile filter and make essentially innocuous, modern-style white wines with no character or fruit. I admired Usseglio's 1990 red Châteauneuf-du-Pape for its huge nose of jammy red and black fruits, roasted nuts, and black olives, as well as for its big, opulent, high-alcohol, lusty style. It requires consumption in its first 5–7 years.

L. DE VALLOUIT* * * * *

1990 Châteauneuf-du-Pape	C	88
1988 Châteauneuf-du-Pape	C	87
1990 Cornas	C	82
1989 Cornas	C	75
1988 Cornas	C	76
1990 Côte Rôtie	C	85
1989 Côte Rôtie	C	86
1991 Côte Rôtie Les Roziers	E	90
1990 Côte Rôtie Les Roziers	E	92
1989 Côte Rôtie Les Roziers	E	89
1988 Côte Rôtie Les Roziers	E	93
1991 Côte Rôtie Vagonier	E	92

1990 Côte Rôtie Vagonier	E	89
1990 Crozes-Hermitage	C	75
1989 Crozes-Hermitage	C	82
1990 Crozes-Hermitage L'Arnage	C	86
1990 Gigondas	B	79
1990 Hermitage	C	85
1991 Hermitage Blanc	C	89
1990 Hermitage Blanc	C	87
1990 Hermitage Greffières	E	94
1989 Hermitage Greffières	E	90
1988 Hermitage Greffières	E	92
1990 St.-Joseph	B	79
1988 St.-Joseph	B	76
1990 St.-Joseph Les Anges	C	86
1989 St.-Joseph Les Anges	C	87
1988 St.-Joseph Les Anges	D	89
1990 Syrah Les Sables—Vin de Pays	A	85

Since 1983 the quality has jumped dramatically at the firm of de Vallouit, with the luxury *cuvées* of Côte Rôtie Les Roziers, Hermitage Greffières, and St.-Joseph Les Anges among the finest in the Rhône. The 1991 white Hermitage is a full-bodied, chunky, fleshy wine with obvious glycerin and alcohol. It possesses at least 8–10 years of longevity. The 1990 Condrieu, a dry, intensely rich, flowery, apricot- and peach-scented and -flavored wine, will drink well for the next several years. The 1990 white Hermitage is a big wine that possesses plenty of power and concentration but needs cellar time; it should last for 10–15 years.

This firm also produces wines from the southern Rhône. The 1988 and 1989 Châteauneuf-du-Papes are big, dense, old-style wines with fine color, ripeness, and chunky, coarse, ripe fruit. Both will be drinkable young but age nicely for 10–12 years. De Vallouit's Vin de Pays called Les Sables offers excellent quality/price rapport. This 100% Syrah wine is made in a semicarbonic style, and the result is a richly fruity wine, bursting with herb-scented cassis aromas and flavors. It is a delicious, medium-weight Syrah ideal for consuming over the next 2–3 years.

De Vallouit's luxury *cuvées* of St.-Joseph, Côte Rôtie, and Hermitage are among the finest wines of the northern Rhône. The 1990 St.-Joseph Les Anges is a grapey wine with fabulous black/ruby color, a rich, cassis- and herb-scented, subtly oaky nose, and ripe, opulent, rich flavors as well as some solid tannins. The 1989 St.-Joseph Les Anges exhibits more new oak, excellent superripeness, an elegant berry- and herb-scented bouquet, medium-bodied, concentrated, soft flavors, and an expansive, lush finish. It should be consumed over the next 5–6 years. De Vallouit's 1988 St.-Joseph Les Anges is one of the best St.-Josephs I have tasted. It is powerful and rich, with a lovely combination of toasty new oak, black cherries, and cassis aromas and flavors, deep, medium- to full-bodied flavor extraction, and a spicy, drinkable style. It will drink well for another 7–10 years. The 1990 regular *cuvée* of St.-Joseph is less interesting. Pleasant in a monolithic way, it is meant to be drunk upon release. The regular *cuvée* of 1988 St.-Joseph is similar. De Vallouit produces three *cuvées* of Côte Rôtie. The regular *cuvée* of 1990 Côte Rôtie is a soft, herb-scented, moderately rich, medium-bodied wine that should be drunk over the next 5–7 years. The 1989 Côte Rôtie is made from ripe, more concentrated grapes than the 1990. Possessing less of the herbaceous nose and more of the smoky, bacon fat, raspberry character, it is soft, medium to full bodied, and should be drunk over the next decade. The 1988 Côte Rôtie's raspberry-scented, exotic bouquet of red fruits and flowers is followed by a medium-bodied, tannic, impressively deep wine. The 1991 Côte Rôtie Les Roziers (the top *cuvée*) exhibits a deep color, a spicy, smoky, black raspberry fruitiness, full body, and a lush, succulent texture. The 1990 Côte Rôtie Les Roziers offers a dark ruby/purple color and a nose of raspberry fruit intermingled with smoky aromas. The intense layers of supple fruit are soft and superripe. This Côte Rôtie should be at its best between 1994 and 2005. The big, sexy, oaky, cassis-scented nose, luscious, silky texture, and heady, smooth finish of the 1989 Côte Rôtie Les Roziers make for a charming wine to drink over the next 7 years. The best Les Roziers vintage to date has been the magnificent 1988. Deeply colored, with a huge roasted bouquet of raspberries and creamy fruit and bacon fat and a velvety, voluptuous texture, it is a real turn-on. There is plenty of tannin and spicy new oak in the long but firm finish. Approachable now, this wine should last for at least 10–15 more years. In 1989, de Vallouit began to produce the Cuvée Vagonier of Côte Rôtie. Twenty percent of the blend is Viognier. De Vallouit made striking wines in 1991, 1990, and 1989 that demonstrate just how much the fragrant, highly perfumed Viognier can add to the tannic, intense concentration of Syrah. I was blown away by the sensual qualities of the 1991 Vagonier. It possesses a dark ruby color, Condrieu-like aromas of peach, apricot, honeysuckle, and smoky black raspberries, a lush, velvety texture, and gobs of expansive ripe fruit. The soft and voluptuous 1990 Vagonier exhibits a stunning fragrance. The 1989 Côte Rôtie Vagonier offers a knockout bouquet of spring flowers and raspberries, smooth, honeyed flavors, and a wonderful, open-knit, in-your-face style. For drinking over the next 4–6 years, these wines are stunners. Many believe de Vallouit's best wine is the luxury *cuvée*, Hermitage Greffières. The 1990 Hermitage Greffières is powerful and backward with tremendous intensity. The overall impression is of a massive wine with extraordinary density and extraction. It should be drunk between 2000 and 2015. The 1989 Hermitage Greffières has gone into a shell. The bouquet hints at black cherries, herbs, and new oak. The wine is tight, backward, broodingly deep, and impenetrable, with much of its character nearly obscured by tannins. It is a large-scale, rich wine that will age well for 15–20 years. The 1988 Hermitage Greffières is even more backward. Extremely dense, this powerful, unbelievably rich and concentrated wine has the potential to last 25–35 years. The hard 1990 Hermitage is spicy and well colored, with adequate concentration. Compared to the Hermitage Greffières, it is unimpressive. De Vallouit's Cornas, whether it be the 1988, 1989, or 1990, is light, astringent, and hard.

DOMAINE DE VALORI* *

1990 Châteauneuf-du-Pape	C	74
1989 Châteauneuf-du-Pape	C	77

This domaine produces highly stabilized, clipped, denuded, sterile wines. It is hard to believe a 1990 Châteauneuf-du-Pape could have no bouquet and so little flavor. Drink it over the next 3–4 years. The 1989 is tannic, backward, and richer, but it lacks character.

VAUDIEU* * *

1990 Châteauneuf-du-Pape	C	86
1989 Châteauneuf-du-Pape	C	85
1988 Châteauneuf-du-Pape	C	85

Although this producer has a tendency to process his wines excessively, there is no question that the 1990 red Châteauneuf-du-Pape has come through its manufacturing process with some charm and appeal intact. The color is a brilliant medium ruby, and the nose offers gobs of sweet black raspberry fruit. This full-bodied wine exhibits opulent, chunky, jammy black fruits, low acidity, a chewy texture, and heady levels of alcohol and glycerin. Drink it over the next 5–6 years. Although the 1989 red Châteauneuf is full bodied, rich, and straightforward, with a fat, fleshy character, it lacks complexity and individuality. It should provide pleasurable drinking over the next 3–5 years. The 1988 is similarly styled—robust and medium bodied, with a spicy, peppery, jammy, cassis bouquet, soft tannins, and low acidity. It should be drunk over the next 2–4 years.

GEORGES VERNAY* * * *

1990 Condrieu	D	86
1990 Condrieu Coteaux du Vernon	E	88
1990 Côte Rôtie	C	72
1989 Côte Rôtie	C	77
1991 Viognier Vin de Pays	C	75

The tasty, elegant, medium-bodied 1990 Condrieu offers a nose of melon, roses, and ripe apricot scents. Vernay's best *cuvée* is from the famed Coteaux du Vernon vineyard, which sits on a steep hillside. The 1990 Condrieu Coteaux du Vernon reveals a fragrant nose of honeyed apricots. Rich, full bodied, and viscous, with gobs of fruit, glycerin, and alcohol, this lush wine makes for a hefty mouthful. Drink it before the end of 1994. Vernay has yet to make an interesting Côte Rôtie. The 1989 has more suppleness, as well as more fat and concentration. The 1990 Côte Rôtie is simple and light, with washed-out, meager flavors and an annoying vegetal character. Vernay has begun to offer a Viognier entitled only Vin de Pays. Although reasonably priced, the 1991 merits little interest.

NOËL VERSET* * * * *

1990 Cornas	C	94
1989 Cornas	C	88
1988 Cornas	C	89
1987 Cornas	C	85

For pure, decadently rich, authoritatively flavored Cornas, few wines match those made by Noël Verset. After tasting Verset's 1990 Cornas, I wrote, "The quintessence of Syrah and of Cornas—almost like port." The wine is remarkably rich, thick, and opaque and so phenomenally intense that you could almost stand a spoon in it! The 1990 is a remarkable, even spectacular Cornas that is supple enough to drink now or keep for 12–15 years. The dark purple-colored 1989 Cornas has a sweet, ripe, herbaceous, cassis-scented nose and a round, concentrated taste. It should be drunk over the next 7–8 years. Verset's 1988 Cornas is more structured, tannic, and muscular. It possesses a big, blackberry, jammy bouquet of Oriental spices, licorice, violets, and minerals. **Anticipated maturity: Now–2003.** The 1987 offers low acidity, round, tasty, generously endowed flavors, a supple texture, and at least another 5–7 years of aging potential.

RATINGS FOR OLDER VINTAGES OF NOËL VERSET CORNAS: 1987 (88), 1986 (85), 1985 (93), 1983 (90+)

VIDAL-FLEURY* * * *

1990 Châteauneuf-du-Pape	C	85
1988 Châteauneuf-du-Pape	C	85
1985 Châteauneuf-du-Pape	C	84
1991 Condrieu	D	89
1989 Cornas	C	77
1988 Cornas	C	84
1989 Côte Rôtie Côtes Blonde et Brune	D	86
1988 Côte Rôtie Côtes Blonde et Brune	D	89
1987 Côte Rôtie Côtes Blonde et Brune	D	87
1991 Côte Rôtie La Chatillonne Côte Blonde	D	92
1990 Côte Rôtie La Chatillonne Côte Blonde	D	90
1989 Côte Rôtie La Chatillonne Côte Blonde	D	90
1988 Côte Rôtie La Chatillonne Côte Blonde	D	90
1987 Côte Rôtie La Chatillonne Côte Blonde	D	92
1990 Côtes du Rhône	A	80
1989 Côtes du Rhône	A	85
1988 Côtes du Rhône	A	86
1990 Côtes du Ventoux	A	86

1989 Côtes du Ventoux	A	85
1990 Crozes-Hermitage	B	79
1989 Crozes-Hermitage	B	86
1990 Crozes-Hermitage Blanc	B	77
1989 Gigondas	B	76
1988 Gigondas	B	82
1989 Hermitage	D	76
1990 Hermitage Blanc	D	78
1987 Hermitage Blanc	D	78
1990 Muscat de Beaumes-de-Venise	B	92
1989 St.-Joseph	C	87
1988 St.-Joseph	C	85
1991 St.-Joseph Blanc	C	86
1990 St.-Joseph Blanc	C	75
1990 Vacqueyras	A	86
1989 Vacqueyras	A	86

Vidal-Fleury's red wines tend to be superior to the quality of the whites, which are one-dimensional and straightforward. Most of the white wines are light, one-dimensional, and acidic. The best include an enjoyable 1991 Condrieu that offers peach, apricot, and floral aromas, ripe, broad flavors, and an unctuous texture. Vidal-Fleury's 1991 St.-Joseph Blanc has a lemony, citrusy fruitiness, some fleshy, chewy flavors, and an attractive mineral undertone. It should be drunk over the next several years. Vidal-Fleury also does a consistently good job with some of the less prestigious appellations of the Rhône Valley. The traditionally styled 1990 Côtes du Ventoux reveals gobs of spicy, peppery, cassis fruit, excellent concentration, medium to full body, and a soft, opulent finish. Drink it over the next 4–5 years. The 1989 Côtes du Ventoux, which is made in a quasi-carbonic style, is a vibrantly fruity, round, delicious wine for restaurants and consumers looking for immediate gratification. The 1990 Côtes du Rhône is too tannic. The 1989 Côtes du Rhône has a deep ruby color, a robust, rich, peppery, black cherry–scented nose, chunky, medium- to full-bodied flavors, and soft tannins. It should last for 2–3 more years. The 1988 Côtes du Rhône is a surprisingly full-bodied wine with rich, roasted black cherry flavors, a lusciously soft texture, good depth, and plenty of fruit to hide the sizable alcohol level in its finish. It should drink nicely for another 1–3 years. I was also impressed with the 1990 Vacqueyras, a full-bodied, pepper-scented wine bursting with rich fruit. Drink it over the next 4–5 years. The 1989 Vacqueyras is intriguing, with a roasted, tar-scented, smoky nose and medium-bodied, chewy flavors. The 1988 Vacqueyras smells of roasted peanuts, black plums, and pepper. The wine is rich and soft, with plenty of alcohol in the fiery finish. It should drink nicely for another 2–3 years. The 1990 Crozes-Hermitage offers rustic aromas of damp earth, wild berries, and herbs. The tannins are noticeable, but the wine is powerful. The plum-, herb-, and cassis-scented 1989 Crozes-Hermitage is capable of 4–6 years of aging. The 1988 Crozes-Hermitage tastes like a downsized Hermitage. The big bouquet of herbs and rich, superripe cassis fruit is followed by a medium- to full-bodied wine with good acidity and a velvety finish. It should drink nicely for another 4–5 years. The supple, tasty, medium-bodied 1989 St.-Joseph is ideal for drinking over the next 3–4 years. I also enjoyed the 1988 St.-Joseph, a medium-bodied, elegant, spicy, cassis-scented wine. Vidal-Fleury's 1990 Gigondas is disappointingly lean, tough, and tannic. The 1988 Gigondas is one-dimensional. The same thing can be said about the 1989 Cornas, a hard, tough, severe style of wine. The 1988 Cornas offers up a mushroomlike bouquet and spicy, ripe flavors that are dominated by nasty tannins. The 1989 Hermitage is also mediocre. The 1990 Châteauneuf-du-Pape is richly fruity, soft, and ready to drink. Vidal-Fleury's 1988 Châteauneuf-du-Pape exhibits plenty of ripe black cherry and raspberry fruit, a nice, spicy, peppery nose, and a full-bodied, alcoholic finish. Vidal-Fleury's finest wines are its Côte Rôties. The 1989 Côte Rôtie has a rich, smoky, raspberry-and-oak-scented nose, rich, medium-bodied flavors, moderate tannins, and a good finish. Drink it over the next 10–12 years. The 1988 Côte Rôtie has the classic bacon fat, smoky, roasted, raspberry fruitiness, rich, full-bodied, expansive flavors, and considerable length. It should evolve nicely over the next 10–15 years. The rarest offering from Vidal-Fleury is the Côte Rôtie La Chatillonne. The 1991 Côte Rôtie La Chatillonne is stunning. Its plummy color is followed by a huge nose of black fruits, bacon fat, and violets. The succulent, rich, multidimensional, full-bodied flavors are buttressed by soft tannins and low acidity. This will be a wine for drinking in its first 10–12 years of life. The 1990 Côte Rôtie La Chatillonne is superb, with a penetrating fragrance of flowers, black fruits, and roasted nuts. Sweet, expansive, and charming, it will drink beautifully young but last a decade or more. The 1989 Côte Rôtie La Chatillonne exhibits a toasty, vanillin-scented nose, plenty of red and black fruit scents in its bouquet, but less opulence and concentration. The 1988, typical of many northern Rhônes from this vintage, is a structured, muscular, tannic wine, with gobs of black raspberry and cassis fruit wrapped in smoky oak with intriguing aromas of roasted nuts and herbs. It has 10–15 years of aging potential. The 1987 La Chatillonne offers a profound bouquet of smoky, roasted plums and new oak. It is a gorgeously rich, smoky, concentrated wine with oodles of velvety black fruits, judiciously framed by toasty new oak. Full bodied, with soft tannins and moderate acidity, it should be drunk over the next 6–7 years. Vidal-Fleury produces a tasty, sweet dessert wine from Beaumes-de-Venise. The apricot-scented, honeyed, lavishly rich 1990 Muscat de Beaumes-de-Venise should not be missed! Drink it over the next 2–3 years.

LA VIEILLE FERME* * * *

1990	Côtes du Lubéron Blanc	A	85
1990	Côtes du Rhône Blanc Gold Label	A	86
1990	Côtes du Rhône Gold Label	A	86
1990	Côtes du Ventoux	A	86

The 1990 Côtes du Lubéron Blanc offers attractive crisp, floral scents, dry, medium-bodied flavors, and refreshing zestiness. The 1990 Côtes du Rhône

Gold Label Blanc is a richer, fuller, fleshier wine, with a floral- (roses?) and honey-scented nose, full-bodied flavors, good acidity, and excellent purity. Both of these wines should be drunk now. The 1990 Côtes du Ventoux is fruity and supple, with great color, an excellent bouquet of cassis and herbs, and a long, tasty, round finish. The 1990 Côtes du Rhône Gold Label is a big, bold, dramatically flavored, spicy, berry-scented wine, with admirable intensity, soft tannins, a heady alcohol and glycerin content, and a robust, spicy finish. Drink these red wines over the next 2–4 years.

DOMAINE DE LA VIEILLE JULIENNE* * * *

1990 Châteauneuf-du-Pape	C	89+
1989 Châteauneuf-du-Pape	C	85?
1988 Châteauneuf-du-Pape	C	?

This domaine bottles its wines as they are sold, resulting in *cuvées* of the same vintage spending anywhere from 18 months to 10 years in large wood *foudres*. The result is troublesome bottle variation, as the wine tends to oxidize and lose its fruit after 2–4 years in wood. The 1990 displays a chocolaty, smoky, cassis-scented nose and peppery, rich, powerful, full-bodied flavors oozing with extract, glycerin, and tannins. It is impressive for its size and potential longevity. The 1989 tasted terrific from barrel, but from bottle it is a grapey, muscular, fruity wine, with some tannins in the finish. The 1988 has plenty of extract, but something was wrong with its nose.

VIEUX DONJON* * * *

1990 Châteauneuf-du-Pape	C	92
1989 Châteauneuf-du-Pape	C	91
1988 Châteauneuf-du-Pape	C	88

The opaque purple-colored 1990 is the finest wine I have yet tasted from this estate. It displays an intense bouquet of olives, black plums, and truffles. Rich, with a gorgeous purity, it boasts superb intensity, a sweet midpalate, and an admirable balance of power and elegance. There are tons of highly extracted fruit, but it is all wrapped together in a full-bodied, graceful package. It should keep for at least 15 years. The 1989 also boasts an opaque dark ruby/purple color, a ripe nose of cassis, black cherries, herbs, and licorice, and a moderately tannic finish. **Anticipated maturity: 1994–2008.** The 1988 is lighter, with a lovely berry-scented bouquet intertwined with aromas of herbs and coffee. In the mouth it is medium to full bodied and richly fruity. RATINGS FOR OLDER VINTAGES OF VIEUX DONJON CHÂTEAUNEUF-DU-PAPE: 1985 (88), 1983 (89), 1981 (90)

VIEUX LAZARET* * *

1990 Châteauneuf-du-Pape	C	85
1989 Châteauneuf-du-Pape	C	86
1990 Châteauneuf-du-Pape Blanc	C	70

I found the crisp, simple 1990 Châteauneuf-du-Pape Blanc to be undistinguished. In contrast, the 1990 red Châteauneuf exhibits a deep ruby/purple color, an attractive nose of black raspberry fruit, flowers, and herbs, an unctuous texture, low acidity, and moderate tannins. It will keep for 7–8 years. The 1989 has an intense perfume of black fruits, hefty alcohol, and a long finish. Drink this charming yet concentrated Châteauneuf-du-Pape over the next 10 years.

DOMAINE DU VIEUX TÉLÉGRAPHE* * * *

1990 Châteauneuf-du-Pape	C	89
1989 Châteauneuf-du-Pape	C	85
1988 Châteauneuf-du-Pape	C	86
1987 Châteauneuf-du-Pape	C	75
1991 Châteauneuf-du-Pape Blanc	C	70
1990 Vin de Pays Vaucluse le Pigeoulet	A	84

Vieux Télégraphe's white Châteauneuf-du-Pape has been disappointing over recent vintages. The 1991 is light and watery. The 1990 red Châteauneuf-du-Pape displays a deep ruby/garnet color, intense tobacco-, herb-, black fruit-, and sea salt–like aromas, gobs of sweet, jammy fruit, sweet tannins, and low acidity. The finish is heady but lush. I would opt for drinking this beefy, full-bodied Vieux Télégraphe over the next 7–8 years. The 1989 Châteauneuf-du-Pape tasted superb in France but was less impressive stateside. It reveals a dark ruby/purple color, a sweet bouquet of black fruits, herbs, olives, and pepper, more structure and muscle than the 1988, and some tannin in the finish. It will last for up to a decade. The 1988 was also profound in France but merely good on America's shores. It displays a deep ruby color and a perfume of roasted cassis fruit, spices, and damp wood. The wine is full bodied, but not that concentrated or long. Drink it over the next 6–7 years. The 1987 comes across as skinny, even anorexic. Consumers looking for a super value made by the Brunier family should seek out 1990 Le Pigeoulet, a tasty, low-priced wine made just outside the appellation of Châteauneuf-du-Pape. The herb-, olive-, and black fruit–scented nose is attractive. Soft and fruity, with surprising length, it should continue to drink well for 1–2 years.

RATINGS FOR OLDER VINTAGES OF DOMAINE DU VIEUX TÉLÉGRAPHE CHÂTEAUNEUF-DU-PAPE: 1986 (85), 1985 (89), 1983 (89), 1982 (86), 1981 (87), 1980 (83), 1979 (87), 1978 (96), 1976 (87), 1972 (88)

ALAIN VOGE* * * * *

1990 Cornas Cuvée Barriques	C	87
1990 Cornas Cuvée Vieilles Vignes	C	90

Voge produces two *cuvées* of Cornas—his Cuvée Barriques, from a wine aged in small new oak casks, and his Cuvée Vieilles Vignes, a wine made from 75- to 80-year-old vines. The 1990 Cornas Cuvée Barriques is surprisingly refined and soft for a Cornas, as the new oak has tamed some of the rusticity and harsh tannins. It offers aromas of smoky, roasted black fruit combined with scents of toasty new oak. The wine is medium to full bodied and generous, with excellent ripeness, a supple, smooth texture, and a moderately long finish. Drink it over the next 5–7 years. The superb 1990 Cornas Vieilles Vignes exhibits an opaque dark ruby/garnet color and a rich, sweet nose of roasted nuts, herbs, and black fruits. It boasts the expansive, full-bodied, chewy richness that comes from old vines, plenty of soft tannins, low acidity, and a fat, heady, spicy, superconcentrated finish. Approachable now, this wine should age effortlessly for another 10–15 years.

BERGERAC AND THE SOUTHWEST

Something to Talk About

The Basics

TYPES OF WINE

This remote corner of France, although close to Bordeaux, remains an unexplored territory when it comes to wine. Some appellations have recognizable names such as Madiran, Bergerac, Cahors, and Monbazillac, but how many consumers can name one producer, good or bad, from the Côtes du Frontonnais, Gaillac, Pacherenc du Vic Bilh, Côtes de Duras, or Pécharmant? The best wines are serious, broodingly deep red from Madiran, Pécharmant, and Cahors; lighter, effusively fruity reds from Bergerac and the Côtes du Frontonnais; and some fine sweet whites from Monbazillac and Jurançon. Remarkable dry white wine values are plentiful in the Côtes de Gascogne.

GRAPE VARIETIES

In addition to the well-known varieties such as Cabernet Sauvignon, Merlot, and Syrah, this vast area is home to a number of grape varieties that are little known and mysterious to the average consumer. In Madiran there is the Tannat; in the Côtes du Frontonnais, the Mauzac and Négrette. For the white wines of Pacherenc du Vic Bilh and Jurançon, rare varieties such as the Gros Manseng, Petit Manseng, Courbu, and Arrufiac are planted.

FLAVORS

The red wines of Bergerac are light and fruity; those of Madiran and Cahors are dense, dark, rich, and often quite tannic. The red wines from the Côtes de Buzet, Côtes de Duras, and Côtes du Frontonnais, often vinified by the carbonic maceration method, are light, soft, and fruity. The best dry white wines are crisp, light, and zesty. Some surprisingly rich, sweet wines that resemble a fine Sauternes can emerge from Monbazillac and Jurançon.

AGING POTENTIAL

Except for the top red wines of Madiran, Pécharmant, and Cahors, all of the wines from France's southwest corner must be drunk very young.

Bergerac: 2–5 years
Cahors: 4–12 years
Côtes de Buzet: 1–5 years
Côtes de Duras: 1–4 years
Gaillac: 1–4 years
Jurançon: 3–8 years
Madiran: 6–15 years
Monbazillac: 3–8 years
Pécharmant: 3–10 years

OVERALL QUALITY

The overall quality is extremely irregular. Improvements have been made, but most wines sell for very low prices, so many producers have little incentive to increase quality. For the top estates listed below, the quality is good to excellent.

FRANCE'S GREATEST WHITE WINE VALUE?

Just about every shrewd importer has been making a trek to the area of Armagnac in search of crisp, fruity, deliciously light, dry white wines from a region not entitled to either *appellation* or VDQS status: the Côtes de Gascogne. Grapes such as Ugni Blanc, Colombard, Gros Manseng, and Sauvignon produce dry wines with crisp acidity, fragrant, lemony, fruity bouquets, zesty, lively flavors, and light- to medium-bodied, crisp finishes. Almost all sell for under $6 a bottle. They have proven exceptionally successful in the American marketplace. These are wines to buy by the case and drink within 18–20 months of the vintage. For example, the 1992s (released in summer 1993) should be consumed by June 1994! If you are not already eagerly gulping these light, fruity wines, you are missing one of the most unlikely success stories in the wine world. The most successful, palate- and purse-pleasing dry white wines are from Domaine de Pouy, Domaine de Pomès, Domaine de Tariquet, Domaine de Rieux, Domaine de Tuilerie, Domaine Varet, Domaine Lasalle, Domaine de Joy, Domaine de Puits, Domaine du Bergerayre, and Domaine de Puts.

MOST IMPORTANT INFORMATION TO KNOW

Learn the top two or three estates for each of the better-known appellations and their styles of wine.

1993–1994 BUYING STRATEGY

These wines are for the shrewd and adventurous consumer who wants to experience different aromas and flavors at a bargain-basement price. For white wines, stick to recent vintages such as 1992. Approach 1991 with considerable caution. Although some good wines were produced, the dry white wines from this area require consumption within 2 years of the vintage, so the 1991s may already be too old. The red wines, particularly those of Madiran and Cahors, can easily be drunk back to the early 1980s, as long as the wines have been well stored by retailers. However, the recent top vintages for Madiran and Cahors are 1990 (exceptional), followed by 1989 (very good), 1988 (good), and 1986 (very good).

DRY RED WINES

* * * * * (OUTSTANDING PRODUCERS)

Château d'Aydie-Laplace (Madiran)
Château Montus (Madiran)

Domaine Pichard Cuvée Vigneau
(Madiran)

* * * * (EXCELLENT PRODUCERS)

Domaine de l'Antenet (Cahors)
Domaine de Barréjat (Madiran)
Domaine Bibian (Madiran)
Domaine Bouscassé (Madiran)
Château Champerel (Pécharmant)
Clos la Coutale (Cahors)

Clos de Gamot (Cahors)
Clos de Triguedina Prince Phobus
(Cahors)
Domaine Pichard (Madiran)
Château Pineraie (Cahors)

* * * (GOOD PRODUCERS)

Château de Belingard (Bergerac)
Château de Cayrou (Cahors)
Château de Chambert (Cahors)
Clos de Triguedina (Cahors)
Château Court-les-Mûts (Bergerac)
Domaine Jean Cros (Gaillac)
Domaine de Durand (Côtes de Duras)
Domaine du Haut-Pécharmant
  (Pécharmant)
Domaine de Haute-Serre (Cahors)
Château de la Jaubertie (Bergerac)
Château Michel de Montague
  (Bergerac)
Château de Padére (Buzet)

Château de Panisseau (Bergerac)
Château Le Payssel (Cahors)
Château Pech de Jammes (Cahors)
Château du Perron (Madiran)
Château de Peyros (Cahors)
Château Poulvère (Bergerac)
Château St.-Didier Parnac (Cahors)
Domaine des Savarines
  (Cahors)* * */* * * *
Château Thénac (Cahors)
Domaine Theulet et Marsalet
  (Bergerac)
Château de Tiregand (Pécharmant)

* * (AVERAGE PRODUCERS)

Domaine de Boliva (Cahors)
Château La Borderie (Bergerac)
Château Le Caillou (Bergerac)
Domaine Constant
  (Bergerac)* */* * *
Les Côtes d'Oit (Cahors)

Duron (Cahors)
Château Le Fage (Bergerac)
Domaine de Paillas (Cahors)
Château Peyrat (Cahors)
Domaine de Quattre (Cahors)

DRY WHITE WINES

* * * * (EXCELLENT PRODUCERS)

Château de Bachen (Tursan)
Château Court-les-Mûts (Bergerac)
Château Grinou (Bergerac)
Domaine de la Jaubertie (Bergerac)

Château de Panisseau (Bergerac)
Château Tiregand–Les Galinux
  (Bergerac)

* * * (GOOD PRODUCERS)

Château Belingard (Bergerac)
Château Haut-Peygonthier (Bergerac)
Domaine de Joy (Côtes de Gascogne)
Domaine Lasalle (Côtes de Gascogne)
Domaine de Pomès
  (Côtes de Gascogne)
Domaine de Pouy
  (Côtes de Gascogne)
Domaine de Puits
  (Côtes de Gascogne)

Domaine de Puts
  (Côtes de Gascogne)
Domaine de Rieux
  (Côtes de Gascogne)
Domaine Tariquet
  (Côtes de Gascogne)
Domaine de Tuilerie
  (Côtes de Gascogne)
Domaine Varet (Côtes de Gascogne)

SWEET WHITE WINES

* * * * * (OUTSTANDING PRODUCERS)

Domaine Cauhaupe Cuvée
  Quintessance (Jurançon)

* * * * (EXCELLENT PRODUCERS)

Domaine Cauhaupe (Jurançon)
Domaine Guirouilh Cuvée Petit
  Cuyalaa (Jurançon)

* * * (GOOD PRODUCERS)

Domaine Bellegarde Sélection de
  Petit Marseng (Jurançon)
Clos Uroulat (Jurançon)
Cru Lamouroux (Jurançon)

Château Le Fage (Monbazillac)
Château du Treuil-de-Nailhac
  (Monbazillac)

* * (AVERAGE PRODUCERS)

Domaine Bru-Baché (Jurançon)
Henri Burgue (Jurançon)

Clos Lapeyré (Jurançon)
Château de Rousse (Jurançon)

2. ITALY

The Basics

TYPES OF WINE

The glories of Piedmont (aside from the scenery and white truffles) are the robust, rich, multidimensional red wines made from the Nebbiolo grape. The top wines made from the Nebbiolo—Barbaresco, Barolo, Gattinara, and Spanna—are at their best between 6 and 15 years of age but can last up to 25 years. At the opposite extreme are the wines called Dolcetto d'Alba, which are wonderfully supple, rich, and fruity but are meant to be drunk within their first 4–5 years of life. Then there is Barbera. A new generation of winemakers has begun to turn out splendid and expensive examples of this grape that historically has been too acidic for non-Italian palates. Last, there is Cabernet Sauvignon and a host of insipid, usually inferior red wines that are less likely to be seen in the international marketplace. I am referring to Freisa, Grignolino, and Brachetto. Piedmont's white wine production is growing, and although most of the wines are overpriced and bland, some potential is evident with the indigenous Arneis grape and Cortese di Gavi. Chardonnay is making its ubiquitous presence felt, Erbaluce di Caluso is underrated, and Moscato, the low-alcohol, fizzy, slightly sweet wine, is perhaps Piedmont's best value in white wine. Finally, there is the ocean of sweet, industrially produced Asti Spumante.

GRAPE VARIETIES

Nebbiolo, Barbera, and Dolcetto are the top red wine grapes in Piedmont, producing the finest wines. For the white wines, the Muscat, Arneis, Cortese di Gavi, and Erbaluce di Caluso are the most successful. Of course, there are many other grapes, but the wines made from these varietals are generally of little interest.

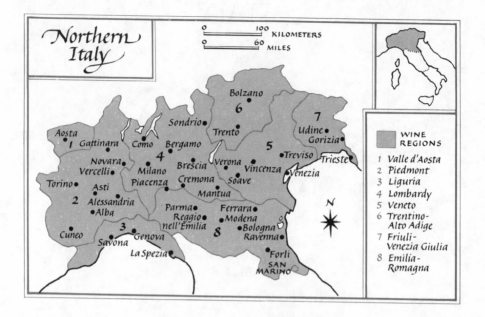

Northern Italy

0 — 100 KILOMETERS
0 — 60 MILES

Aosta
1 Gattinara
Novara
Vercelli
Torino
Asti
Alessandria
Alba
2
Cuneo
3
Savona
Genova
La Spezia

Como
Sondrio
Bergamo
Milano
Brescia
Piacenza
Cremona
Mantua
Parma
Reggio
nell'Emilia
Modena
8
Ferrara
Bologna
Ravenna
Forlì
SAN
MARINO

Bolzano
6
Trento
Verona
Vincenza
Soave
5

7
Udine
Gorizia
Treviso
Trieste
Venezia

N

WINE REGIONS

1 Valle d'Aosta
2 Piedmont
3 Liguria
4 Lombardy
5 Veneto
6 Trentino-
Alto Adige
7 Friuli-
Venezia Giulia
8 Emilia-
Romagna

Southern Italy

WINE REGIONS

1 Campania
2 Puglia
3 Basilicata
4 Calabria
5 Sicily

TYRRHENIAN
SEA

San Severo
Manfredonia
Benevento
Foggia
Napoli
Bari
Salerno
2
1
Rionero
Matera
Ostuni
Potenza
Brindisi
Metaponto
Taranto
3
Gallipoli

Cetraro
Ciro
Paola
Cosenza
4
Catanzaro
Caraffa

Palermo
Messina
Reggio di
Calabria
Trapani
Taormina
Marsala
5
Catania
Agrigento
Siracusa
Ragusa

N
W   E
S

0 — 60 MILES
0 — 100 KILOMETERS

Central Italy

ADRIATIC SEA

LIGURIAN SEA

Lucca
Pisa
Livorno
Firenze
Arrezo
Siena

1

Grosseto

3
Perugia
Spoleto
Terni

Viterbo

5

Roma

Latina

Pesaro
Ancona
Macerata

2

Ascoli Piceno

L'Aquila
Pescara
Chieti

4

Isernia
6

8

CORSICA

TYRRHENIAN SEA

Olbia
Sassari
Alghero
Nuoro
Bosa **7**
Tortoli
Oristano

Cagliari

MILES
KILOMETERS

0 60
0 50 100

N
W E
S

WINE REGIONS

1 Tuscany   5 Lazio
2 Marche   6 Molise
3 Umbria   7 Sardinia
4 Abruzzo   8 San Marino

FLAVORS

RED WINES

Barolo   Barolo is one of the world's most stern, tannic, austere yet full-flavored wines, dominated by aromas of road tar, leather, bing cherries, tobacco, and dried herbs. This is a massive yet intensely fragrant wine.

Barbaresco   Often better balanced as well as lighter than Barolo (less tannin, more fruit), with the same aromas and flavors, Barbaresco often has more intense jammy fruit and sometimes more cedar and chocolate; it can be sublime.

Dolcetto   Purple in color and not at all sweet (as the name incorrectly implies), this dry, exuberant, effusively fruity and grapey wine tastes of blackberries, almonds, chocolate, and spices and is very soft and supple. It is a joyful wine.

Barbera   In the old days it was too acidic, harsh, oxidized, and dirt cheap. The new-style Barberas, often aged in 100% new French oak, exhibit saturated purple color, great fruit, and super richness that serve to balance out the naturally high acidity. Most of the best will set consumers back $25–$50, so their potential market is microscopic.

Gattinara/Spanna   These wines come from Nebbiolo grown in the hills north of Barolo and Barbaresco. Intense tar and earthy aromas dominate, and there is a pronounced Oriental spice-box character to the bouquet. The wines tend to be softer and fruitier than Barolo, but no less ageworthy.

Carema   The lightest of the Nebbiolo-based wines, Carema, made in a marginally mountainous climate near Valle d'Aosta, can be quite smooth, fruity, and elegant, but adequate ripeness is often a problem.

WHITE WINES

Arneis   The ancient wine of Piedmont, Arneis is a rich, gloriously fruity, mouth-filling wine that is soft, even unctuous. This may seem to imply a certain heaviness, but the best examples are light and a joy to drink.

Gavi or Cortese di Gavi   Often outrageously overpriced and frightfully bland, this supposedly prestigious wine is high in acidity, has a lemony, flinty, stony character, and, in the best examples, possesses good body.

Moscato d'Alba   One of the world's most seductive wines to smell and drink, Moscato d'Alba when well made and drunk within 18 months of the vintage is a gorgeously fragrant, apricot- and floral-scented, slightly sweet, crisp, vibrant wine that is ideal as an aperitif. It should not be confused with the cloyingly sweet Asti Spumante.

AGING POTENTIAL

Barbera: 5–15 years
Barbaresco: 8–25 years
Barolo: 8–25 years
Carema: 6–12 years
Dolcetto: 3–5 years

Gattinara/Spanna: 8–20 years
Arneis: 2–3 years
Gavi: 2–4 years
Moscato: 12–18 months

OVERALL QUALITY LEVEL

The best Piedmont wines are impeccably made, brilliant wines. Producers such as Bruno Giacosa, Angelo Gaja, Elio Altare, and Luciano Sandrone, to name just a few, fashion wines of great individuality and uncompromising quality. But despite the number of compelling Barolos, Barbarescos, and some barrique-aged Barberas, a considerable quantity of wine made in Piedmont is still technically defective, with shrill levels of acidity and a flawed, musty taste. Some of this is the result of inferior grapes, but most is due to indifferent as well as careless and primitive winemaking methods. In short, Piedmont offers the best and worst in wine quality. If you are going to shop with confidence, you must know the finest producers.

MOST IMPORTANT INFORMATION TO KNOW

Learning the top producers for Barbaresco, Barolo, Nebbiolo, Barbera, and Dolcetto is of utmost importance. However, since the early 1980s, more and more of the best producers have begun to make single-vineyard wines, so it is necessary to have some understanding of the finest vineyards and who is exploiting them successfully. Below is a list of the major Piedmontese vineyards that consistently stand out in my tastings and the producer(s) making the finest red wine from these vineyards.

Piedmont's Best Red Wines

VINEYARD	WINE	BEST PRODUCER(S)
Annunziata	Barolo	Lorenzo Accomasso, Silvio Grasso, the late Renato Ratti
Arborina	Barolo	Elio Altare
Arionda or Vigna Rionda	Barolo	Bruno Giacosa
Asili	Barbaresco	Bruno Ceretto, Produttori di Barbaresco
Basarin	Barbaresco	Castello di Neive
Batasiolo	Barolo	F. Ili Dogliani
Bernadotti	Barbaresco	Giuseppe Mascarello
Bianca	Barolo	Fontanafredda
Boscaretto	Barolo	F. Ili Dogliani, Scarpa
Boschis	Barolo	Cavalotto
Briacca	Barolo	Vietti
Bric del Fiasc	Barolo	Paolo Scavino
Bric in Pugnane	Barolo	Giuseppe Mascarello
Bricco Asili	Barbaresco	Bruno Ceretto
Bricco Cicala	Barolo	Aldo Conterno
Bricco Colonello	Barolo	Aldo Conterno
Bricco Faset	Barbaresco	La Spinona
Bricco Fiasco	Barolo	Azelia
Bricco Punta	Barolo	Azelia
Bricco Rocche	Barolo	Bruno Ceretto
Bricco Viole	Barolo	G. D. Vajra

VINEYARD	WINE	BEST PRODUCER(S)
Brunate	Barolo	Giuseppe Rinaldi, Elvio Cogno, Ceretto, Luigi Copo, Robert Voerzio, Vietti, Sebaste
Bussia	Barolo	Bruno Giacosa, Clerico, Fenocchio, Giuseppe Mascarello, Michele Chiarlo, Sebaste
Camp Gros	Barbaresco	Marchese di Gresy
Cannubi	Barolo	L. Sandrone, Luciano Rinaldi, Bartolo Mascarello, Paolo Scavino, Enrico Scavino, E. Pora, Carretta
Cannubi Boschis	Barolo	L. Sandrone, Francesco Rinaldi
Cascina Alberta	Barbaresco	Contratto
Cascina Francia	Barolo, Dolcetto, Barbera	Giacomo Conterno
Cascina Nuova	Barolo	Elio Altare
Cascina Palazzo	Barolo	Francesco Rinaldi
Cascina Rocca	Barbaresco	Ricardo Cortese
Cerequio	Barolo	Michele Chiarlo, Cogno-Marcarini, Oddero, Roberto Voerzio
Ciabot Mentin Genestra	Barolo	Clerico
Codana	Barolo	Paolo Scavino, Vietti
Conca	Barolo	Renato Ratti
Costa Russi	Barbaresco	Angelo Gaja
Crichet Paje	Barbaresco	Roagna
Darmagi	Cabernet Sauvignon	Angelo Gaja
Delizia	Barolo	Fontanafredda
Enrico VI	Barolo	Cordero di Montezemolo
Falletto	Barolo	Bruno Giacosa
Faset	Barbaresco	Oddero, Luigi Bianco, Ceretto
Gaiun	Barbaresco	Marchese di Gresy
Gallina	Barbaresco	Bruno Giacosa
Ginestra	Barolo	Clerico, Prunotto, Renzo Seghesio, Conterno Fantino
La Ghiga	Barbaresco	La Spinona
Gran Bussia	Barolo	Aldo Conterno
Lazzarito	Barolo	Fontanafredda
Marcenasco	Barolo	Renato Ratti
Marenca e Ribetti	Barolo	Angelo Gaja
Margaria	Barolo	Michele Chiarlo
Martinenga	Barbaresco	Marchese di Gresy

VINEYARD	WINE	BEST PRODUCER(S)
Messoirano	Barbaresco, Barbera, Dolcetto	Castello di Neive
Moccagatta	Barbaresco	Produttori di Barbaresco
Monfalletto	Barolo	Cordero di Montezemolo
Monfortino	Barolo	Giacomo Conterno
Monprivato	Barolo	Giuseppe Mascarello
Montanello	Barolo	Tenuta Montanello
Montefico	Barbaresco	Produttori di Barbaresco
Monte Stefano	Barbaresco	Produttori di Barbaresco
Ornato	Nebbiolo, Barbera, Barolo	Pio Cesare
Otinasso	Barolo	F. Ili Brovia
Ovello	Barbaresco	Produttori di Barbaresco
Pian della Polvere	Barolo	R. Fenocchio
Pora	Barbaresco	Produttori di Barbaresco
Prapo	Barolo	Bruno Ceretto
Rabaja	Barbaresco	Produttori di Barbaresco
Rabera	Barolo	G. E. Vajra, Giuseppe Rinaldi
Rio Sordo	Barbaresco	Brovia, Produttori di Barbaresco
Rionda (same as Arionda)	Barolo	Bruno Giacosa, Michele Chiarlo, Giuseppe Mascarello
La Rosa	Barolo	Fontanafredda
Rocche di Bussia	Barolo	Oddero, Parusso
Rocche di Castiglione Falletto	Barolo	Bruno Giacosa, Vietti, Parusso
San Pietro	Barolo	Fontanafredda
San Rocco	Barolo	Eredi Virginia Ferrero
Santo Stefano	Barbaresco	Bruno Giacosa, Castello di Neive
La Serra	Barolo	Cogno-Marcarini, Roberto Voerzio
Serra Boella	Barbaresco	Cigliuti
Sori d'Paytin	Barbaresco	Pasquero-Secondo
Sori San Lorenzo	Barbaresco	Angelo Gaja
Sori Tilden	Barbaresco	Angelo Gaja
Villero	Barolo	Giuseppe Mascarello, Bruno Giacosa, Cordero di Montezemolo
Zonchetta	Barolo	Bruno Ceretto

Piedmont's Best White Wines

For what one gets in the bottle, the top white wines of Piedmont are vastly overpriced (Gavi continues to be a rip-off although prices were plunging in

1993). The exception is the lovely flower blossom– and apricot-scented Moscato and the dry version of Erbaluce. The former wine has low alcohol (usually 5%–9%), is slightly sweet and effervescent, and overall is a gorgeous wine to drink as an aperitif or with fresh fruit for dessert. Arneis, a perfumed dry white wine with loads of character, is my favorite white from Piedmont. However, at prices of $18–$30, it is too expensive. Chardonnay and Sauvignon have arrived in Piedmont; Angelo Gaja produces the finest, but also the most expensive.

The best Piedmont white wines are listed below. Readers should look for the 1992s, 1991s, and 1990s—nothing older!

WINE	PRODUCER
Arneis	Bruno Giacosa
Arneis	Castello di Neive
Arneis	Ceretto
Brut Spumante	Bruno Giacosa
Chardonnay Rossij-Bass	Angelo Gaja
Chardonnay Bussiador	Aldo Conterno
Chardonnay Gaia and Rey	Angelo Gaja
Chardonnay Giarone	Poderi Bertelli
Cortese di Gavi	Pio Cesare
Cortese di Gavi	Broglia Fasciola
Gavi	La Scolca
Gavi	La Chiara
Erbaluce di Caluso	Carretta
Erbaluce di Caluso	Boratto
Erbaluce di Caluso	Ferrando
Moscato d'Asti	Rivetti
Moscato d'Asti	Giorgio Carnevale
Moscato d'Asti	Ceretto
Moscato d'Asti	Coppo
Moscato d'Asti	Bruno Giacosa
Moscato d'Asti	Berra
Moscato d'Asti	Giorgio Carnevale
Roero Arneis	Carretta
Sauvignon Alteni di Brassica	Angelo Gaja
Traminer	Poderi Bertelli

1993–1994 BUYING STRATEGY

Recently there have been two great Piedmontese vintages, 1990 and 1989, and one excellent vintage, 1988, all now coming on the market. Readers who love Nebbiolo, Barbera, Barbaresco, and Barolo are well advised to take a serious look at the 1990s, 1989s, and 1988s. The top wines will be very expensive, as quantities are small and most of the production is sold in Europe. Avoid vintages such as 1981, 1983 (grossly overrated by the wine press), 1984, and 1986. If you can still find any of the superb 1985s or great 1982s, buy them. The 1982s are just beginning to drink beautifully, and the 1985s can be drunk or cellared. Both vintages have the potential to last at least another 10–15 years. When buying Dolcetto, stick to the 1990s and 1989s, unless you are lucky enough to find a good 1991 or 1992, which are both problematic vintages.

For older vintages of Barolo, Barbaresco, or the less well-known Gattinara/Spanna, look for the 1979s, which are delicious as well as underrated; the great 1978s, one of the finest long-term vintages; and 1971, a spectacular Piedmont vintage that is just now reaching its full potential.

VINTAGE GUIDE

1992—Rain hit Piedmont during the harvest, causing sugars to drop, acidity to fall, and ripeness to be uneven. For the second year in a row Piedmont will turn out lighter-style wines. Certainly 1992 was a bigger crop than 1991, but many serious producers reported low sugar readings and were hoping 1992 would turn out to be as pleasant and charming as 1987. This may be optimistic given that the harvest was only a week old when 3 straight weeks of rain inundated most of the vineyards.

1991—A relatively small crop was harvested of lightweight Barolos, Barbarescos, Dolcettos, and Nebbiolo d'Albas. This is an average-quality vintage, believed to be on a par with 1987 and 1986. The wines will be drinkable early, with a maximum of 10 years of aging potential. In a year such as this, the growers who were more selective will produce more interesting wines.

1990—This is a magnificent vintage, with aromatic wines of extraordinary richness, high glycerin and alcohol, and spectacular intensity. The colors are deeply saturated ruby/purple. Most producers claim these wines are richer, fuller, and potentially greater than the exceptional 1989s. Producers such as Gaja, Giacosa, and Altare believe that the 1990 Piedmontese wines will have to be considered along with the 1971 and 1947 as one of the three finest vintages for Piedmont following World War II. High praise indeed.

1989—A vintage of abundant quantity, superhigh quality, and great ripeness and richness. The wines possess surprisingly sound acidity given their dizzying level of alcohol and dense, rich, chewy flavors. Wealthy Italian wine collectors will have fun for decades comparing the merits of their favorite producers in years such as 1989 and 1990.

1988—This overly hyped year has turned out to be very good, but it is not a great vintage. In fact, I do not think it is as good as 1982 or 1985. The wines are austere and lack the great ripeness that was achieved in 1989 and 1990. They exhibit considerable tannin, which is not always balanced out by deep, rich fruit. Given the fact that the 1989s and 1990s are unlikely to be priced any higher than the 1988s, I would skip this vintage and concentrate your resources on its two younger siblings.

1987—Pessimism was the word of the day during the growing season of 1987, but the wines have turned out surprisingly well, and comparisons with the underrated vintage of 1980 are not invalid. The wines are lighter than usual but do show excellent fruit, ripeness, and a forward, charming personality. This will be a good commercial vintage to drink early on.

1986—A fair year—not better and not worse, despite some perennial Italian wine cheerleaders who are calling it another "great" year. The red wines are well colored and balanced, have some depth and tannin to shed. They lack drama and boldness, but this is a good, useful vintage as the quantity of wine produced was high.

1985—Gaja, Ceretto, and their peers call this one of the greatest vintages of the century. I believe they said the same thing about 1990, 1989, 1988, 1982, 1978, and 1971. Nevertheless, broker Neil Empson claims it is better than either 1982 or 1978, which is difficult to imagine given the superlative quality of the latter two years. However, one taste of these wines reveals a flamboyant, rich, intense, velvety fruitiness not unlike the opulence of 1982. There are many rich, lush, sensational wines that will drink well over the next 10 years.

1984—Justifiably maligned by the press corps (as was the case everywhere in Europe), this vintage in Piedmont is average to below average in quality, with the wines light and forward but deficient in fruit.

1983—A vintage of rather tannic, stern wines. The 1983s may turn out to be similar to the unyielding 1974s; most wines have a hollow, dry, astringent taste and lack fruit.

1982—A very great vintage. The wines are loaded with ripe, rich fruit and have plenty of tannins, full body, and a real alcoholic punch to them. They are tasting surprisingly forward, but given the fact that most great vintages of Barolo and Barbaresco can last 15–25 years, the 1982s offer an opportunity to enjoy a rich, dense, ripe, full, and fruity Barolo or Barbaresco during its entire life in the bottle. Despite the accessible nature of this vintage, the top wines should keep 25 years. A year to buy, but most of the finest wines disappeared long ago.

1981—Rain during September ruined what could have been a very good year. Many of the best growers declassified their entire crop. My tastings have revealed compact, short wines that are of little interest.

1980—Somewhat of a sleeper vintage, the 1980s are medium-bodied, rather light wines, but the good growers have produced wines with plenty of fruit, soft tannins, and charm. It is a vintage to drink up.

1979—One of the best vintages for current drinking is 1979. Elegant, ripe, fruity wines were produced. They may lack the muscle, power, and great concentration of a vintage such as 1978 or 1982, but they offer plenty of finesse and complexity. Not to be overlooked.

1978—This is a great vintage of very long-lived wines, huge in structure, very tannic, and very concentrated, and the best of them are still a good 5 years away from maturity. The crop size was small, the style of the wines aggressive, rich, and tough. They have developed very slowly, causing impatient critics to downgrade them, but this is a great vintage that just needs more time.

1977—A horrendous year of rain and cold weather. Most good growers declassified their entire crops.

1976—Another bad year; the wines lacked ripeness, had excessive tannins, and are now drying out.

1975—The first of a trio of consecutive poor vintages, the 1975s I have tasted have had aromas of tea, light-intensity flavors, and shallow personalities.

1974—This is a highly rated vintage, but one I find overrated. After 18 years the wines remain rather hard and tannic and continue to reveal a lack of ripeness and richness. Perhaps time will prove me wrong, but most of the Piedmont wines from 1974 lack length, grace, and charm.

1973—Relatively easy-to-drink, soft, pleasant, light wines were produced in 1973. All should have been drunk by now.

1972—As in most of Europe's viticultural regions, rain was the ruination of this vintage.

1971—Until the advent of the remarkably promising 1982s, 1985s, 1989s, and 1990s, the 1971s were, and may remain, the reference point for Piedmont. Rich, perfumed, and deeply concentrated, these wines have entered their plateau of maturity. They are all fully mature, so only the best examples should be kept another 10–15 years.

OLDER VINTAGES

The 1970s are very good, eclipsed in stature by the admittedly greater 1971s; the 1969s are average in quality and best drunk up. The 1968s are disastrous; the 1967s very good, but now beginning to slip; the 1966s and 1965s below average to poor; and the 1964 another great vintage. Well-stored bottles of 1964 Piedmontese wines are gloriously rich and scented.

RATING PIEDMONT'S BEST PRODUCERS

* * * * * (OUTSTANDING PRODUCERS)

Elio Altare Barbera Vigna Larigi
Elio Altare Barolo Vigna Arborina
Giacomo Bologna Barbera
  Bricco della Figotta
Giacomo Bologna Barbera
  dell'Uccellone
Clerico Barolo Bricoto Bussia
Clerico Barolo Ciabot Mentin
  Ginestra
Giacomo Conterno Barolo Monfortino
Renato Corino Barolo la Mora
Renato Corino Barolo Vigna Giachini
Angelo Gaja Barbaresco Sori San
  Lorenzo

Angelo Gaja Barbaresco Sori Tilden
Angelo Gaja Barolo Sperss
Bruno Giacosa Barbaresco
  Santo Stefano
Bruno Giacosa Barolo Rionda
Bruno Giacosa Barolo le Rocche
Giuseppe Mascarello Barolo
  Monprivato
Luciano Sandrone Barolo Cannubi
  Boschis
Filippo Sobrero Barolo†
Vietti Barolo Villero

* * * * (EXCELLENT PRODUCERS)

Elio Altare Barolo
Elio Altare Dolcetto
Antoniolo Gattinari Osso S. Grato
Azelia Dolcetto d'Alba Bricco
  dell'Orido
Azelia Dolcetto d'Alba Vigneto
  Azelra
Poderi Bertelli Barbera Giarone
Poderi Bertelli Barbera Montetusa
Borgogno Barolo

Bruno Ceretto Barbaresco Bricco
  Asili
Bruno Ceretto Barolo Bricco Rocche
  Bricco Rocche
Bruno Ceretto Barolo Bricco Rocche
  Prapo
Bruno Ceretto Barolo Brunate
Bruno Ceretto Barolo Zonchetta
Cigliuti Barbaresco
  Serraboella****/*****

---

†Sobrero sold all of his vineyards in 1985 and is no longer producing wine under his name.

Cigliuti Barbera d'Alba Serraboella
Clerico Arté
Clerico Dolcetto
Le Colline-Cascina Bordino
  Barbaresco
Elvio Cogno Barolo Brunate
Elvio Cogno Barolo Brunate
  Canon****/*****
Elvio Cogno Barolo La Serra
Elvio Cogno Dolcetto Boschi-di-Berri
Elvio Cogno Nebbiolo Lasarin
Cogno-Marcarini Barolo Brunate
Aldo Conterno Barolo Bussia
  Soprano****/*****
Aldo Conterno Barolo Bussia
  Soprano Vigna Cicala****/*****
Aldo Conterno Barolo Bussia
  Soprano Vigna
  Colonnello****/*****
Aldo Conterno Barolo Gran
  Bussia****/*****
Aldo Conterno Dolcetto d'Alba
Giacomo Conterno Barolo Cascina
  Francia Riserva
Renato Corino Dolcetto
Renato Corino Barbera Vigna Pozzo
Giuseppe Cortesi Barbaresco Rabaja
Damonte Barbera San Guglielmo
Drago Dolcetto d'Alba
Ricardo Fenocchio Barbera d'Alba
  Pianpolvere
Ricardo Fenocchio Barolo
  Pianpolvere Soprano
Luigi Ferrando Carema
Angelo Gaja Barbaresco
Angelo Gaja Barbaresco Costa Russi
Angelo Gaja Barbera d'Alba Vignarey
Bruno Giacosa Barbaresco Gallina
Bruno Giacosa Barolo Falletto
Bruno Giacosa Barolo Villero
Elio Grasso Barolo Gavarini
Elio Grasso Barolo Ginestra
Manzone Barbera d'Alba
Manzone Barolo Le
  Gramolere****/*****
Marcarini Barolo Brunate
Marchesi di Gresy Barbaresco
  Martinenga
Marchesi di Gresy Barbaresco
  Martinenga Camp Gros

Marchesi di Gresy Barbaresco
  Martinenga Gaiun
Marchesi di Gresy Dolcetto Monte
  Aribaldo
Bartolo Mascarello
  Barolo****/*****
Bartolo Mascarello Dolcetto d'Alba
Mauro Mascarello Barbaresco
  Marcarini
Mauro Mascarello Barolo Bricco
Matteo-Correggia Barbera d'Alba
  Bricco Marun****/*****
Matteo-Correggia Nebbiolo d'Alba
  Val Preti
Moccagatta Barbaresco Basarin
Moccagatta Barbaresco Bric Balin
Moccagatta Barbaresco Cole
Monsecco Gattinara
Castello di Neive Barbaresco Santo
  Stefano
Armando Parusso Barolo Bussia
  Rocche
Armando Parusso Barolo Rocche
Armando Parusso Dolcetto d'Alba
  Mariondino
Elia Pasquero Secondo Barbaresco
  Sori d'Paytin
Pio Cesare Dolcetto d'Alba
Produttori di Barbaresco Barbaresco
  Asili
Produttori di Barbaresco Barbaresco
  Moccagatta
Produttori di Barbaresco Barbaresco
  Monte Stefano
Produttori di Barbaresco Barbaresco
  Ovello
Produttori di Barbaresco Barbaresco
  Rabaja
Alfredo Prunotto Barbaresco Monte
  Stefano
Alfredo Prunotto Barolo Bussia
Alfredo Prunotto Barolo Cannubi
Renato Ratti Barolo Marcenasco
Renato Ratti Barolo Marcenasco
  Conca
Renato Ratti Barolo Marcenasco
  Rocche
Francesco Rinaldi Barolo
Giuseppe Rinaldi Barolo
  Brunate****/*****

Rocca Barbaresco Ronchi
Rocche dei Manzoni Barolo Vigna Big
Rocche dei Manzoni Barolo Vigna
  Mesdi
Rocche dei Manzoni Barolo Vigna
  d'la Roul
Rocche dei Manzoni Bricco Manzoni
  (Nebbiolo/Barbera)
Luciano Sandrone Barolo
Luciano Sandrone
  Dolcetto****/*****
Enrico Scavino Barbera Carati
Enrico Scavino Barolo
Enrico Scavino Barolo Bric del
  Fiasc****/*****
Enrico Scavino Barolo
  Cannubi****/*****
Aldo & Ricardo Seghesio Barolo La
  Villa

Antonio Vallana Gattinara
Antonio Vallana Spanna
Vietti Barbaresco Masseria
Vietti Barolo Lazzarito
Vietti Barolo Rocche
Roberto Voerzio Barbera d'Alba
  Vignasse****/*****
Roberto Voerzio Barolo
  Brunate****/*****
Roberto Voerzio Barolo
  Cerequio****/*****
Roberto Voerzio Barolo La
  Serra****/*****
Roberto Voerzio Dolcetto d'Alba
  Privino
Roberto Voerzio Vigna La Serra
  (Nebbiolo/Barbera blend)

* * * (GOOD PRODUCERS)

Giacomo Accomasso
Mario Antoniolo Gattinara***/****
Associati di Rodello Dolcetto d'Alba
Azelia Barolo Bricco Fiasco***/****
Azelia Barolo Bricco Punta***/****
F. Ili Barale Barbaresco
  Rabaja***/****
F. Ile Barale Barolo
  Castellero***/****
Bel Colle Barolo
  Monvigliero***/**** (since 1989)
Boccadigabbia Cabernet Sauvignon
  Akronte
Borgogno Barbaresco
Brovia Barbaresco Rio Sordo
Brovia Barolo Rocche
Cantina del Glicine Barbaresco Cura
Cantina del Glicine Barbaresco
  Marcorino
Cappellano Barolo Chinato***/****
Cappellano Barolo Gabutti***/****
Carretta Barolo Cannubi***/****
Carretta Nebbiolo d'Alba Bric
  Paradiso***/****
Carretta Nebbiolo d'Alba Bric
  Tavoleto***/****
F. Ili Cavallotto Barolo Bricco
F. Ili Cavallotto Barolo Punta Eignolo

F. Ili Cavallotto Barolo Punta
  Martello***/****
F. Ili Cavallotto Barolo San
  Giuseppi***/****
Cerequio Barolo
Bruno Ceretto Barbaresco Asij
Bruno Ceretto Barbaresco
  Faset***/****
Bruno Ceretto Barbera d'Alba Piana
Bruno Ceretto Dolcetto d'Alba
  Rossana
Bruno Ceretto Nebbiolo d'Alba
  Lantasco
Cogno-Marcarini Barolo La Serra
Aldo Conterno Il Favot
Cordero di Montezemolo Barolo
  Enrico VI***/****
Cordero di Montezemolo Barolo
  Monfalletto
Cordero di Montezemolo Dolcetto
  Monfalletto
Giuseppe Cortesi Barbaresco
  Rabaja
Giuseppe Cortesi Dolcetto d'Alba
Defurville Barbaresco Rabaja
Dessilani Gattinara***/****
Dessilani Ghemme***/****
Luigi Einaudi Dolcetto

Eredi Virginia Ferrero Barolo San
  Rocco***/****
Fontanafredda Barolo Bianca
Fontanafredda Barolo Delizia
Fontanafredda Barolo
  Lazzarito***/****
Fontanafredda Barolo La
  Rosa***/****
Angelo Gaja Dolcetto d'Alba
  Vignaveja
Angelo Gaja Nebbiolo d'Alba
  Vignaveja***/****
Manzone Dolcetto
Manzone Nebbiolo
Giuseppe Mascarello Barbera d'Alba
  Fasana
Giuseppe Mascarello Barolo
  Dardi***/****
Giuseppe Mascarello Dolcetto
  Gagliassi
Mauro Mascarello Barolo Santo
  Stefano
Moccagatta Barbera Basarin
Monsecco Gheme
Castello di Neive Dolcetto d'Alba
  Basarin
Castello di Neive Dolcetto d'Alba
  Messoriano

Armando Parusso Barbera
  Pugnane***/****
Pio Cesare Barolo
E. Pira
Produttori di Barbaresco Barbaresco
Produttori di Barbaresco Barbaresco
  Pora
Alfredo Prunotto Barbera d'Alba
Alfredo Prunotto Barbera d'Alba
  Pian Romulado
Franceso Rinaldi Barbaresco
Scarpa Barbaresco
Scarpa Barbaresco Payore Barberis
  di Treiso
Scarpa Barolo Boscaretti di
  Serralunga d'Alba***/****
Scarpa Barolo I Tetti di Neive
Enrico Scavino Dolcetto d'Alba
Aldo & Ricardo Seghesio Barbera
Aldo & Ricardo Seghesio Dolcetto
  d'Alba
Spinona Barbaresco Bricco Faset
Spinona Barbaresco Podere Albina
Travaglini Gattinara
G. D. Vajra Barolo

* * (AVERAGE PRODUCERS)

Orlando Abrigo Barbaresco
Orlando Abrigo Barolo
Orlando Abrigo Barolo della
  Rocca**/***
Flavio Acconero Barbaresco
Flavio Acconero Barolo
Marchesi di Barolo Barbaresco
Marchesi di Barolo Barolo
Marchesi di Barolo Barolo Brunate
Marchesi di Barolo Barolo Cannubi
Batasiolo Barbera d'Alba
Batasiolo Barolo Castiglione
  Falleto**/***
Batasiolo Barolo La Morra**/***
Batasiolo Barolo Serralunga
  d'Alba**/***
Bersano Barbaresco
Bersano Barolo
Poderi Bertelli Cabernet I Fossaretti

Luigi Bianco Barbaresco
  Faset**/***
Luigi Bianco Barbaresco
  Rabaja**/***
Luigi Bianco Barbaresco Ronchi
Ca Rome Barbaresco
Ca Rome Barolo
Luigi Caldi Barbera d'Alba
Luigi Caldi Barolo
Luigi Caldi Gattinara
Luigi Calissano Barbaresco Bricco
  Malaspina
Luigi Calissano Barolo Bricco
  Mira Langa
Luigi Calissano Barolo Castelletto
Luigi Calissano Dolcetto d'Alba
  Bricco d'Altavilla
Aldo Canale Barolo
Cappellano Barbaresco

Michele Chiarlo Barbaresco
Michele Chiarlo Barbera d'Asti Valle
  del Sole
Michele Chiarlo Barilot
Michele Chiarlo Barolo
Cogno-Marcarini Dolcetto d'Alba
Fantino Conterno Barolo Sori Ginestra
Fantino Conterno Barolo Vigna del
  Gris
Giuseppe Contratto Barbaresco
Giuseppe Contratto Barolo
Luigi Coppo Barbaresco
Luigi Coppo Barolo
Deforville Barbaresco
Deforville Barbera d'Alba
Deforville Nebbiolo d'Alba
Dosio Barbera d'Alba
Dosio Barolo Vigna Fossati
Dosio Dolcetto d'Alba
Luigi Einaudi Barolo**/***
Franco-Fiorina Barbaresco
Franco-Fiorina Barolo
Angelo Gaja Cabernet Sauvignon
  Darmagi**/***
Bruno Giacosa Dolcetto d'Alba Plinet
  di Trezzo**/***

Bruno Giacosa Nebbiolo d'Alba
  Valmaggiore
Mauro Molino Acanzio
Montanello Barolo
Luigi Nervi Gattinari
Oddero Barbaresco
Oddero Barbera d'Alba
Oddero Barolo
Oddero Dolcetto d'Alba
Pio Cesare Barbaresco
Pio Cesare Ornato
Punset Barbaresco
Punset Barolo
Roagna Barbaresco
Roagna Crichet Pajè
Sebaste Barolo Brunate
Sebaste Barolo Bussia
Sebaste Dolcetto d'Alba
Renzo Seghesio Barolo
Terre del Barolo Barolo
  Brunate**/***
Terre del Barolo Barolo Rocche di
  Castiglione Fallatto
G. D. Vajra Barbera d'Alba
G. D. Vajra Dolcetto d'Alba

Selected Tasting Notes

GIOVANNI ACCOMASSO
Barolo Rocchette* * *

1985 Barolo Rocchette	D	88

A tightly structured, old-style Barolo, this 1985 offering from Giovanni Accomasso displays a wonderful inner core of sweet, earthy, herbal, leathery fruit,
gobs of tannin, a fragrant yet tightly strung bouquet of ripe fruit and spices,
and a long, robust, muscular finish. Even though it is 7 years old, this wine is
still young and will benefit from another 2–4 years of cellaring. It should last
through the first decade of the next century.

ELIO ALTARE
Barbera Vigna Larigi* * * * *, Barolo* * * *,
Barolo Vigna Arborina* * * * *, Dolcetto* * * *

1989 Barbera d'Alba	B	89
1989 Barolo	D	92
1988 Barolo	D	90
1989 Barolo Arborina	E	94

1988 Barolo Arborina	D	96
1989 Dolcetto d'Alba Cascina Nuova	B	87
1989 Nebbiolo della Langhe	B	88
1990 Vigna Arborina (100% Nebbiolo)	E	97
1989 Vigna Arborina (100% Nebbiolo)	D	90
1990 Vigna Larigi (100% Barbera)	D	92
1989 Vigna Larigi (100% Barbera)	D	93
1990 La Villa (50% Nebbiolo/50% Barbera)	D	89

Altare is making some of the most magnificent wines in Italy. His two 1988 Barolos are both stunning wines. The 1988 regular Barolo offers an attractive floral, tarlike nose, dense, hugely tannic, massive flavors, and a backward, highly concentrated finish. It easily needs 3–4 years in the cellar, but it should last for up to 2 decades. The 1988 Barolo Arborina is a brilliant example of Nebbiolo. The deep black/ruby color and huge nose of black fruits, tar, and spices are followed by a wine with explosive richness, layer upon layer of dense, chewy Nebbiolo fruit, and a blockbuster, moderately tannic, phenomenally long finish. If you are able, defer your gratification until the mid-1990s, then be prepared to experience the magic over the following 12–15 years. The 1989 Vigna Arborina Nebbiolo and 1989 Vigna Larigi Barbera, both aged in small oak casks, were made in extremely limited quantities. The 1989 Vigna Arborina Nebbiolo reveals an intense, opaque ruby/purple color, a big, oaky, intensely fruity nose, great richness, and a full-bodied, luscious, opulent finish. The moderate tannin levels are concealed by the wealth of fruit. The finish lasts for nearly a minute. This gorgeous, voluptuous wine can be drunk now or held for up to a decade. The 1989 Vigna Larigi Barbera is a compelling example of what this grape can attain. The color is an opaque purple, and the nose offers up sweet aromas of vanillin, smoke, and black fruits. In the mouth there is exceptional richness, a thrilling midpalate with considerable expansion and sweetness of fruit, and a long finish. This pure, rich, medium- to full-bodied wine should continue to provide dazzling drinking over the next 7–10 years. Altare's 1989 Dolcetto d'Alba Cascina Nuova is crammed with raspberry-, chocolate-, and almond-flavored fruit. It is medium bodied and wonderfully rich, with enough acidity and tannin to hold up to 3–4 years of cellaring, although there is no doubt that this wine's appeal is its current explosive fruitiness. Finishing long and smooth, this wine would be delightful with antipasto. No one makes better Barbera than Altare, so keep in mind that the 1989 Barbera d'Alba is his bottom-of-the-line *cuvée* of this varietal. Since this regular *cuvée* is so super, one wonders just how spectacular his single-vineyard Barbera and luxury *cuvée* aged in new oak will turn out to be. The dark purple, almost black color of the Barbera d'Alba is saturated to the edge. The first impression is one of black cherries combined with tar and licorice scents that zoom from the glass. Exceptionally rich and supple, with an opulent, nearly unctuous texture, this full-bodied, wonderfully ripe, concentrated Barbera has none of the annoyingly high acidity that often plagues wines made from this varietal. This gorgeous, lavishly appointed wine should be drunk over the next 5–7 years. The 1989 Nebbiolo Della Langhe is more marked by new oak, with its sweet, vanillin, spicy, black fruit–scented nose and long, deep, full-bodied, black cherry flavors. It makes for a succulent, gorgeous mouthful of wine. What is so admirable about Altare's winemaking is the purity, richness, and overall balance he manages to obtain. Furthermore, he has that rare talent of producing wines that are drinkable young yet give every indication of lasting for extended periods when well cellared.

Altare's newest releases continue to confirm his role as one of Italy's superstars. His regular *cuvée* of 1989 Barolo is stunning, with a deep color and a huge, perfumed nose of roses, black fruits, and smoke. It offers great richness, full body, and a superb, well-defined finish. With the precociousness and softness of the 1989 vintage, it can be drunk now, although it promises to last for at least 15 more years. The 1989 Barolo Arborina is even more expansive and complex. Its huge, jammy nose of black cherries, smoke, licorice, and roasted nuts is followed by spectacular concentration, a dense, chewy texture with gobs of glycerin and extract, and a smashingly long, luscious finish. Like so many of these stunning 1989s, it can already be enjoyed for its voluptuous qualities, but it should last for 2 decades. Altare makes some of the most interesting Piedmontese wines from Nebbiolo and Barbera. His 100% Nebbiolo, the 1990 Vigna Arborina, is more profound than his Barolo. Aged in small oak casks, this awesome wine has a density and extraction of flavor that must be tasted to be believed. The huge nose of black fruits, tar, and spices soars from the glass. Superrich, extraordinarily well balanced, and long and intense, it is the essence of wine. Drinkable now, it should evolve for 12–15 or more years. If you can find any, it is a must purchase! Altare's 1990 La Villa, a blend of equal parts of Nebbiolo and Barbera, offers a big, smoky, toasty, fruity nose; sweet, ripe, medium- to full-bodied flavors; excellent richness; and a soft, moderately long finish. Drink it over the next 7–8 years. The 1990 Vigna Larigi, made from 100% Barbera, exhibits attractive subtle toasty oaky components married nicely to stunning aromas of sweet black fruits. The wine is deep, full bodied, spicy, and opulent. Drink it over the next decade.

AZELIA
Barolo Bricco Fiasco* * */* * * *,
Barolo Bricco Punta* * */* * * *, Dolcetto d'Alba Bricco dell'Oriolo* * * *,
Dolcetto d'Alba Vigneto Azelia* * * *

1990 Dolcetto d'Alba Bricco dell'Oriolo	B	86
1990 Dolcetto d'Alba Vigneto Azelia	B	86

These two tasty Dolcettos differ slightly in style. Both enjoy excellent ruby color and fragrant, fruity noses, but the Vigneto Azelia is softer and not as high in acidity. Their wonderful purity of flavor, medium body, and crunchy, delicious fruit are deliciously displayed in this ripe vintage. Drink both wines over the next 1–3 years.

PODERI BERTELLI
Barbera Giarone* * * *, Barbera Montetusa* * * *, Cabernet I Fossaretti* *

1988 Barbera Giarone	D	86
1989 Barbera Montetusa	E	90

1989 Cabernet I Fossaretti	D	85

1988 Cabernet I Fossaretti	D	83

Bertelli is an interesting winemaker who has gone from strength to strength during the 1980s. His best wines continue to be his Barberas. The 1988 Barbera Giarone is a light, herbaceous, meaty wine with pronounced aromas of truffles and damp earth. Soft, oaky, and enticing in its complexity and individuality, it should drink well for 5–6 years. The exceptional 1989 Barbera Montetusa exhibits a saturated, deep purple color and a spectacular nose of sweet, toasty new oak, ripe black fruits, and flowers. Deep, rich, and full bodied, this wine is crammed with fruit and glycerin. Its finish must last nearly a minute. Drink it over the next 10–15 years. Bertelli was one of the first Italian producers to make a Cabernet. To date, they have been irregular. For example, the 1988 is pleasant, but light, spicy, earthy, and a bit short to merit high marks. The 1989 is sweeter and riper, with plenty of new oak. However, it is good rather than exciting. Their prices make them frightfully bad values. Bertelli has made a breakthrough with Traminer and Chardonnay. Readers who can find any of the microscopic quantities of his 1990 Chardonnay Giarone or 1991 Traminer should definitely give them a look. They are two of the finest white wines being made in Piedmont. The Traminer possesses as much of the Gewürztraminer character as I have ever tasted in an Italian wine. The 1990 Chardonnay Giarone is a worthy rival to the spectacular Chardonnays being made by Angelo Gaja.

GIACOMO BOLOGNA
Barbera Bricco della Figotta* * * * *, Barbera dell'Uccellone* * * * *

1989 Barbera Bricco della Figotta	D	90

1989 Barbera dell'Uccellone	D	92

The late Giacomo Bologna made some of Italy's most flamboyant and dramatic Barberas. These two offerings, from an opulent, dramatically rich vintage, are examples of what viscosity and depth can be obtained from this grape. Both wines display dark, nearly black/purple colors and huge perfumes of smoke, toast, herbs, and black fruits, as well as evidence of aging in new oak casks. I thought the 1989 Barbera dell'Uccellone possessed slightly more flesh, a longer finish, and more aromatic dimension. However, that is splitting hairs, as both are terrific Barberas. Delicious to drink now, they should last for at least a decade.

CARRETTA
Barolo Cannubi* * */* * * *, Nebbiolo d'Alba Bric Paradiso* * */* * * *,
Nebbiolo d'Alba Bric Tavoleto* * */* * * *

1985 Barolo Cannubi	D	87

A traditional producer, Carretta offers a 1985 Barolo that possesses mouth-searing tannins, plenty of body and alcohol, and a dusty, rustic texture. Because of the 1985 vintage, the wine evidences more sweet fruit, with an attractive scent of almonds and black cherries. This spicy, full-bodied wine can be drunk now, but it promises to be even better with several more years of cellaring. It should last through the first decade of the next century.

BRUNO CERETTO

Barbaresco Asij* * *, Barbaresco Bricco Asili* * * *,
Barbaresco Faset* * */* * * *, Barbera d'Alba Piana* * *, Barolo Bricco
Rocche Prapo* * * *, Barolo Brunate* * * *, Barolo Zonchetta* * * *,
Dolcetto d'Alba Rossana* * *, Nebbiolo d'Alba Lantasco* * *

1988 Barbaresco Asij	D	86
1988 Barbaresco Bricco Asili	D	87
1987 Barbaresco Bricco Asili	D	86
1988 Barbaresco Faset	D	87
1989 Barbera d'Alba Piana	C	86
1986 Barolo Bricco Rocche	EE	87
1986 Barolo Prapo	E	86
1989 Dolcetto d'Alba Rossana	C	86
1989 Nebbiolo d'Alba Lantasco	C	85

These wines confirm Ceretto's elegant, understated, restrained style of wine-making. The 1989 Barbera d'Alba Piana is the densest-colored wine among these offerings, with a big, spicy, herbal, rich nose, medium- to full-bodied flavors, and a youthful, fresh finish. Drink it over the next 5–7 years. Much more evolved, lighter in color, and sweeter and more supple on the palate is the 1989 Nebbiolo d'Alba Lantasco. Fully mature, round and fruity, with a soft finish, it should be drunk over the next 5–6 years. All three 1988 Barbarescos would benefit from more cellaring. Although the Bricco Asili and Faset were closed, both are elegant wines with bouquets that suggest bing cherry, cedar, and leather. On the palate they are medium bodied and tannic. Although similar in weight and personality, I thought the Bricco Asili was a more classic Nebbiolo with its sweet, dusty, cherry fruit. The Faset is jammier, perhaps because it was made from riper grapes. Both wines should evolve gracefully for at least 8–10 years. The Barbaresco Asij is a medium-bodied, stylish Barbaresco that can be drunk now or cellared for 7–8 years. I should note that all three Barbarescos were tight when they were first opened and needed a minimum of 1 hour's breathing. Even the following day the wines were considerably more flattering to taste than immediately after opening. The 1989 Dolcetto d'Alba Rossana has a medium ruby/purple color, with a fresh, lively bouquet of red and black fruits and spring flowers. It is supple and medium bodied, with plenty of fruit in reserve. It finishes with just enough grip and acidity to give the wine zest and focus. Drink it over the next 1–2 years. The 1987 Barbaresco Bricco Asili is medium ruby/garnet in color, with an intense bouquet of leather, truffles, spices, and dried fruits; this soft, round, adequately concentrated wine offers delicious drinking at present and should be given consideration by restaurants and consumers looking for serious Italian wines for immediate consumption. It will last for at least another 3–4 years. I liked the spicy, mushroom- and truffle-scented 1986 Barolo Prapo. No one would suggest that this is a great vintage in Piedmont, but the good producers have made forward, spicy, generously endowed wines that are full of fruit and ready to drink. The Prapo is a wonderful choice for drinking with risotto topped with grated Parmesan. The superexpensive 1986 Barolo Bricco Rocche—a medium- to full-bodied, smoky, saddle leather–scented wine, with flavors of dried red fruits, roses, and herbs—was only slightly deeper, with perhaps an extra 5–7 years of aging potential. Should you want to splurge, this 1986 is a spicy, well-constructed, surprisingly rich wine.

MICHELE CHIARLO

Barbaresco* *, Barbera d'Asti Valle del Sole* *, Barilot* *, Barolo Cuvées* *

1988 Barbaresco	C	70
1988 Barbaresco Rabaja	D	78
1988 Barbera d'Asti Valle del Sole	C	82
1988 Barilot	D	86
1988 Barolo	C	71
1988 Barolo Cerequio	D	73
1988 Barolo Rionda	D	78
1988 Barolo Rocche di Castiglione	D	76

"If you enjoy kissing your sister, eating frozen food prepared in the microwave, and listening to Muzak while strolling in suburban shopping centers, these bland, tame, eviscerated, characterless wines are for you. Don't misunderstand me—there is nothing wrong with these wines. They are remarkably clean, straightforward, and inoffensive. But, don't you deserve more—especially when they are priced in the near-luxury class?" The above quote was the text that appeared in the 1989 edition of this book for the 1983, 1982, and 1978 offerings from this firm. Since then, this firm, which was then known as Gran Duca, has changed its name, upgraded its label, and begun to bottle its wines in expensive designer bottles. Despite doubling the price, despite the effort to go to single vineyards, and despite the upgrading of cosmetic appearances, the wines are no better than they were when they appeared under the name Gran Duca. Given how fragrant Nebbiolo is, it is hard to believe that wines with virtually no bouquets can be made. The only explanation possible is that they are either pasteurized or sterilized at bottling, thus insuring their longevity and stability at the expense of the wines' character. Additionally, every one of these wines is tart and lean. If I did not know otherwise, I would assume they were made by an overzealous California oenologist who never drank a bottle of wine. Don't be fooled by the luxury packaging, high prices, and attractive labels; these are mediocre wines that represent the quintessence of blandness.

CIGLIUTI

Barbaresco Serraboella* * * */* * * * *, Barbera d'Alba Serraboella* * * *

1990 Barbaresco Serraboella	D	94+
1988 Barbaresco Serraboella	D	88
1990 Barbera d'Alba Serraboella	C	88
1989 Barbera d'Alba Serraboella	C	85

Cigliuti has a well-deserved reputation for turning out some of Piedmont's most stylish and elegant wines. The 1990 Barbera d'Alba Serraboella reveals a saturated deep purple color, a sweet, fragrant nose of spices, ripe tomatoes, and plummy fruit. In the mouth there is superb density and flavor without the searing, abrasive acidity that can be Barbera's principal defect. This big, rich, lusty Barbera may lack complexity, but it does deliver copious quantities of fruit. Drink it over the next decade. This highly reliable winery has not managed to tame Barbera's frightfully high acidity, but in the case of the 1989, they have counterbalanced the high acidity with superextraction of fruit. Dark ruby/purple, medium bodied and spicy, with its wonderful purity of raspberry fruit and high acidity, it is an ideal accompaniment to any tomato-based sauce. Drink it over the next 5–7 years. The 1990 Barbaresco Serraboella has nearly unmatched elegance and finesse combined with extraordinary richness of fruit, a stunning bouquet, and superb, well-delineated black cherry, flowery aromas and flavors. Medium to full bodied, it possesses perfect balance as well as admirable intensity and complexity. Barbaresco rarely gets more compelling than this. Drink it over the next 6–15 years. The 1988 Barbaresco Serraboella offers a complex nose of dried pit fruit, spicy wood, and an earthy herbaceousness. There is excellent ripeness, moderate tannins, medium to full body, and a moderately tannic, spicy finish. Although more evolved than many 1988s, it will benefit from 1–2 years in the cellar and should last for a decade or more.

CLERICO
Arté* * * *, Barolo Bricotto Bussia* * * * *,
Barolo Ciabot Mentin Ginestra* * * * *, Dolcetto* * * *

1990 Arté	D	90
1989 Barolo Bricotto Bussia	E	93
1988 Barolo Bricotto Bussia	D	88
1989 Barolo Ciabot Mentin Ginestra	E	95
1988 Barolo Ciabot Mentin Ginestra	D	92
1990 Dolcetto	C	88

The 1990 Dolcetto reveals a brilliant, dark purple color, a big, exuberant nose of ripe fruit and flowers, lusciously rich, fleshy fruit, and a clean, velvety finish with just enough acidity to provide grip. The 1988 Barolo Bussia is closed. With airing, aromas of gamelike smoked meat, tar, and dusty fruit emerge. In the mouth there is excellent richness, a beautiful black cherry fruitiness, and an elegant, pure, stylish finish. This is not blockbuster Barolo, but a medium-weight wine that should drink well for 12–15 years. Clerico's 1988 Barolo Ginestra is a super wine, with a dense, dark ruby color and a big, ripe nose of tar, spices, and earthy red fruit. In the mouth the wine displays superconcentration, as well as a ripe, full-bodied, glycerin-dominated, tannic finish. The wine has terrific potential and extremely high tannins, but it is still backward and unevolved. **Anticipated maturity: 1995–2007.** Clerico's newest releases include his proprietary wine, the 1990 Arté. The best Arté since the 1985, it reveals a huge, sweet, oaky, curranty nose; long, luscious, voluptuously textured flavors; and a heady, expansive finish. Drink it over the next 7–8 years. Clerico's 1989 Barolo Bricotto Bussia has one of the purest, sweet cherry–like bouquets I have ever encountered. The spectacular perfume is followed by an opulent, unctuously textured, thick, rich Barolo that is bursting with fruit and personality. Its low acidity and high alcohol and glycerin make for a hedonistic mouthful of wine. Drink it over the next 15–20 years. As impressive as the Barolo Bricotto Bussia is, the 1989 Barolo Ciabot Mentin Ginestra is even more compelling. It combines magnificent power and massiveness with exceptional elegance and finesse—a rare and difficult combination to achieve. The color is dense, dark ruby/purple. Although reticent at first, with airing the nose offers huge aromas of smoked nuts, flowers, minerals, and black and red fruits. Spectacularly rich and deep, this staggeringly proportioned Barolo should be at its best between 1997 and 2012.

LE COLLINE-CASCINA BORDINO
Barbaresco* * * *

1985 Barbaresco	C	87

This late-released 1985 (proprietor Bruno Cervi tends to hold his wines 7–10 years before releasing them, à la Giacomo Conterno) is a delicious, old-style, rich, lusty Barbaresco with a wonderful perfume of cedar, red fruits, herbs, and smoked nuts. There is noticeable tannin, and a rich, full-bodied fruitiness that has taken on an attractive mellowness and satiny texture. The finish is admirably long. Fully mature, this wine should easily hold for 5–8 years.

ALDO CONTERNO
Barolo Cuvées* * * */* * * * *, Il Favot* * *

1989 Barolo Bussia Soprano Vigna Cicala	D	92+
1989 Barolo Bussia Soprano Vigna Colonnello	D	93
1989 Barolo Gran Bussia	D	95

As a longtime fan of Aldo Conterno's Barolos, I must admit these are potentially the best he has yet made. No well-funded Nebbiolo lover will be able to resist them. The 1989 Barolo Gran Bussia reveals a saturated, deep ruby/purple color and a huge nose of smoky tobacco, black cherries, herbs, and truffles. Although the wine is tannic, it exhibits stellar concentration, fine acidity, and spectacular length. This massive Barolo will require considerable cellaring. **Anticipated maturity: 1998–2020.** Conterno's most flattering Barolo is the 1989 Vigna Cicala. Slightly less saturated in color, with a huge nose of smoke, jammy red berries and blackberries, licorice, herbs, and tobacco, this opulent, voluptuously textured Barolo has significant tannin, but the tannin is nearly buried under lavish quantities of sweet, expansive fruit. This hedonistic Barolo should continue to evolve for 15 or more years. Of these three wines, the Vigna Cicala is the one to pull the cork on first. Although the 1989 Barolo Vigna Colonnello is deeply colored, tannic, and backward, it displays tremendous potential for future evolution. There is more of an herb-and-tobacco character to the Vigna Colonnello. It will not be at its best until the late 1990s, but it should evolve gracefully through the first 2 decades of the next century.

GIACOMO CONTERNO
Barolo Cascina Francia Riserva* * * *, Barolo Monfortino* * * * *

1988 Barolo Cascina Francia	D	92
1985 Barolo Cascina Francia	D	94
1985 Barolo Monfortino	EE	96

While there will be a Barolo Monfortino in both 1988 and 1990 (but not in 1989), the 1985 is the most recent release. A typical Monfortino, with a deep ruby color, and a saturated bouquet of saddle leather, spices, smoked meats, herbs, and truffles, this rich, ferociously tannic, massive, backward, nearly impenetrable wine should be cellared for at least another 10–15 years. Drink it between 2001 and 2025. If you can't stomach the frightfully high price of the 1985 Monfortino, don't despair. Giovanni Conterno made a fabulous 1985 Barolo Cascina Francia that is one-half the price. Even more than the Monfortino, it possesses the classic Nebbiolo nose of roses and tar, as well as masses of rich red and black fruits. Unctuous and intense, with spectacular fruit, it has great fragrance and massive body to go along with its high extract and huge tannins. The most recent Barolo release, the 1988 Barolo Cascina Francia, shares a similar rose-and-tarlike nose as the 1985. It possesses deep, full-bodied flavors with aggressive tannins, plenty of ripeness and glycerin, and a heady, spicy, cherry, leather, and herb-flavored finish. Drink this huge, large-scaled, full-throttle Barolo over the next 20 years. The Monfortino will last for another 25–35 years, and the Cascina Francia for another 20.

CORDERO DI MONTEZEMOLO

Barolo Enrico VI* * */* * * *, Barolo Monfalletto* * *, Dolcetto Monfalletto* * *

1988 Barolo Enrico VI	D	89
1988 Barolo Monfalletto	D	86+

The 1988 Barolo Monfalletto displays a medium ruby color, a sweet, cherry-scented nose, and alcoholic, heady flavors dominated by significant acidity and tannin. It will either dry out before the tannins melt away or develop more richness. My score may be optimistic. The deep color and persistent classic perfume of roasted nuts, roses, and black truffles make the 1988 Barolo Enrico VI a sure bet. Round, rich, and thick in the mouth, with plenty of tannin, this full-bodied wine needs several more years of cellaring. Drink it between 1996 and 2005.

RENATO CORINO

Barbera Vigna Pozzo* * * *, Barolo La Mora* * * * *,
Barolo Vigna Giachini* * * * *, Dolcetto* * * *

1990 Barbera Vigna Pozzo	C	89
1988 Barolo la Mora	D	93
1989 Barolo Vigna Giachini	D	96
1991 Dolcetto	B	86

Corino produces the blackest-colored Piedmontese wines I have seen. The 1988 Barolo La Mora exhibits a superjammy nose of black fruits, licorice, minerals, and melted road tar. In the mouth there is spectacular depth, layer upon layer of chewy, thick, glycerin-endowed fruit, and a moderately tannic, robust finish. The wine is immensely impressive but needs at least 5–6 years to develop more complexity and shed some of its toughness. This powerful, monstrous-size 1988 Barolo possesses the requisite extraction of fruit to stand up to its ferocious tannins. Corino fashioned a gorgeous, perfumed, round, intensely fruity 1991 Dolcetto that should be drunk over the next 3 years. It offers extraordinary purity of fruit. The 1990 Barbera Vigna Pozzo reveals a purple/black color, a huge nose of wild black fruits and spices, a rich, medium- to full-bodied, succulent texture, and an explosively rich finish. If it had more complexity, it would have merited an outstanding score. Nevertheless, it is a superrich Barbera. Corino's 1989 Barolo Vigna Giachini is a blockbuster. If Pétrus were made from Nebbiolo, would it taste like this? Dark in color, with a huge, sweet, spicy, exotic nose of black fruits and minerals, this young, unevolved wine exhibits spectacular depth, a multilayered feel, and persistence and richness that last for well over a minute. Although soft enough to be drunk now, it has just begun its evolution, which should continue gracefully over the next 15–20 years. Absolutely magnificent!

DEFORVILLE
Barbaresco* *, Barbaresco Rabaja* * *, Barbera d'Alba* *, Nebbiolo d'Alba* *

| 1988 Barbaresco Rabaja | D | 89 |

As disappointed as I was with Deforville's 1990 Dolcetto, which reeked of stinky lees, their Barbaresco from the highly renowned Rabaja vineyard is an excellent wine that has been made in a classic, old style. The rustic nose of dried cherries, herbs, leather, and cedar is a real turn on. In the mouth the wine is concentrated, full bodied and rich, with spicy, earthy, tannic flavors. Forward enough to be drinkable now, this wine has the potential to evolve for 7–10 years.

DESSILANI
Gattinara* * */* * * *, Ghemme* * */* * * *

| 1985 Gattinara Riserva | C | 86 |

When I first opened a bottle of this wine, it had such a funky, unattractive aroma that I was ready to dismiss it. But past experience with Dessilani's releases have proven that a good 2 hours of breathing can do wonders for these kinky-scented wines. In fact, 3 hours later the wine had blown off its barnyard aromas to reveal a relatively rich, spicy, meaty, animal-scented wine with a great deal of fruit and a smoky, roasted character. In the mouth it is round, generous, and exotic. This is not a wine for everybody, but if you decide to take the plunge and try a distinctive Gattinara, be sure to decant it for at least 2 hours or open it 3 or 4 hours in advance.

DRAGO
Dolcetto d'Alba* * * *

| 1990 Dolcetto d'Alba | C | 90 |

This is as delicious, seductive, and satisfying as Dolcetto can be. The color is a vibrant deep ruby, and the nose explodes from the glass, offering up intense, jammy, berry aromas. In the mouth this gorgeously made wine is packed with pure, vibrant fruit, exhibits medium body, a satiny texture, and enough acidity to give focus and frame the lavish amounts of fruit this wine possesses. Drink it over the next 2–3 years.

LUIGI EINAUDI
Barolo* */* * *, Dolcetto* * *

1988 Barolo	D	92
1985 Barolo	D	90
1988 Dolcetto di Dogliani	C	85
1990 Nebiolo della Langhe	C	87

The 1988 Barolo is an intensely concentrated wine that possesses a sweet, cedary, earthy, cigar-box aroma and great concentration. The superb inner core of fruit suggests low yields and/or old vines. The finish is explosively long, moderately tannic, and intense. It is soft enough to be drunk now but promises to be even better with 5–7 years of aging; it should keep for 12–15 years. Absolutely gorgeous! The 1985 Barolo is superb. When it was first poured it seemed closed, making it difficult to penetrate, but it swells in the glass, offering up those unmistakable aromas of hot road tar, roses, almonds, sweet tobacco, and black fruits. It is full bodied, admirably concentrated and long, and buttressed beautifully by crisp acidity and moderate levels of soft tannins. This is a big, yet graceful Barolo that exhibits wonderful purity to its flavors. Accessible now, it should continue to age gracefully for at least 10–15 years. According to the importer, Einaudi declassified his 1990 Barolo crop into his Nebiolo (which he spells with only one b). Rich, thick, and chewy, the wine has not yet developed much complexity, but who can ignore the abundant glycerin, fruit, and alcohol that make for a lusty, heady glass of Nebbiolo? The wine should age nicely for at least 6 years and will no doubt develop more aromatic dimension. Einaudi's 1988 Dolcetto dropped off slightly on the palate yet it is an exuberant wine that should be consumed over the next 2–4 years.

ANGELO GAJA
Barbaresco* * * *, Barbaresco Costa Russi* * * *,
Barbaresco Sori San Lorenzo* * * * *, Barbaresco Sori Tilden* * * * *,
Barbera d'Alba Vignarey* * * *, Barolo Sperss* * * * *,
Cabernet Sauvignon Darmagi* */* * *, Dolcetto d'Alba Vignaveja* * *,
Nebbiolo d'Alba Vignaveja* * */* * * *

1989 Barbaresco	E	91
1988 Barbaresco	E	87
1989 Barbaresco Costa Russi	EEE	90
1988 Barbaresco Costa Russi	EE	90
1987 Barbaresco Costa Russi	EE	88
1989 Barbaresco Sori San Lorenzo	EEE	96+
1988 Barbaresco Sori San Lorenzo	EE	96
1987 Barbaresco Sori San Lorenzo	EE	90
1989 Barbaresco Sori Tilden	EEE	96+
1988 Barbaresco Sori Tilden	EE	94
1987 Barbaresco Sori Tilden	EE	92

1990 Barbera d'Alba Vignarey	D	90
1989 Barolo Sperss	E	93
1988 Barolo Sperss	E	92
1990 Chardonnay Gaia and Rey	E	93
1991 Chardonnay Rossj Bass	D	88
1991 Dolcetto d'Alba Vignabajla	C	89
1989 Nebbiolo d'Alba Vignaveja	D	87

Consistently one of the reference points for Italian wines, Angelo Gaja has fashioned some spectacular new releases. His 1991 Rossj Bass Chardonnay is a more delicately styled, floral, richly fruity, medium-bodied wine with admirable depth and richness, adequate acidity, and a spicy touch of subtle new oak. It should drink well for 2–3 years. In contrast, the 1990 Gaia and Rey Chardonnay is a blockbuster by any standards. A huge, buttery, floral, smoky nose is followed by a viscous, superrich, multilayered Chardonnay that has more in common with a Grand Cru from Burgundy's Chassagne-Montrachet than an Italian Chardonnay. Although delicious now, it should last for another 2–3 years. The red wine offerings include an excellent 1991 Dolcetto d'Alba Vignabajla, which reveals abundant chocolatey, cherry fruit, light to medium body, and a spicy finish. The 1991 Barbera d'Alba Vignarey (a small barrique-aged Barbera) is rich with scents of smoky new oak, surprisingly soft, opulent, fleshy flavors, and a long finish. It is drinkable now and should last for 7–10 years. Although Gaja's 1989 Nebbiolo d'Alba Vignaveja is lighter than I would expect, it is attractively fruity, with a moderately intense, spicy aroma, and soft, medium- to full-bodied, supple flavors. It should drink well for another 5–6 years. The glories of this estate are the Barbarescos, and the 1989s promise to be the best since 1985 and 1982. Only time will tell if they are better, but they are wonderfully expansive, superrich, concentrated wines. You are not likely to find a better Barbaresco regular *cuvée* than Gaja's 1989. Sweet, rich, tobacco, black-cherry, spicy fruit touched gently by new oak is offered in a full-bodied, powerful style, with admirable depth. Approachable now, this wine should only improve over the next 10–12 years; it will last for 2 decades. The three single-vineyard Barbarescos include the 1989 Costa Russi, the most monolithic and "new world–like" wine of this trio. The deep ruby/purple color is followed by scents of new oak. There is less of a Nebbiolo character than I would like to see. One has to admire the wine's terrific concentration and overall sense of balance, but I found it interesting that in several tastings, lovers of Nebbiolo (including me) thought it to be the least impressive of these Barbarescos. Those who tend to like a more international style preferred it. Nevertheless, it is a large-scale wine for drinking between 1997–2009. Both the 1989 Sori San Lorenzo and 1989 Sori Tilden are monuments to the Nebbiolo grape, as well as to Barbaresco. The 1989 Sori San Lorenzo is the most concentrated wine I have tasted from this vineyard. There is a sweeetness and unctuosity to the fruit that I did not detect in either the great 1985 or 1982. Still tannic, backward, and unevolved, this huge, rich, spice, tobacco, black-cherry-scented wine is massive on the palate. It should be at its best between 1998–2015. It is a remarkable winemaking effort! Not surprisingly, the 1989 Sori Tilden is even more massive, as well as the most backward, tannic, muscular, and masculine of these Gaja Barbarescos. With tons of tannin, and a broad, rich, fleshy, expansive personality, it is the least flattering. Do not touch a bottle for at least 6–7 years. It should last until 2015. Gaja's longtime dream of owning vineyards in Barolo has finally been realized. No one who loves his wines will be disappointed with his first two Barolo releases. Moreover, by Gaja's standards, even the price is nearly palatable. The 1988 Barolo Sperss exhibits a deep color, tremendous extraction of fruit, and soft acids and tannins. It is a backward, unevolved, potentially exceptional wine. Tightly packed, full bodied, and muscular, its wonderful tar, rose, and black-cherry-scented nose is just beginning to emerge. Drink it between 1995–2010. The 1989 Barolo Sperss gives the impression of being more evolved, softer and fatter. Although there appears to be more depth of fruit, and the nose is more expressive, sweeter, and flamboyant, a thorough examination of the wine reveals considerable tannin, probably more than in the 1988. Nevertheless, the rich, sweet, broad, expansive fruit, full-bodied, chewy texture, and soft acids make for a decadently rich, complex, compelling bottle of Barolo. Drink it between 1995–2012. All of Gaja's 1988 Barbarescos are backward, reserved wines. Even after sitting 4 days with the corks pulled, they exhibited no signs of oxidation. Although they should be uncommonly long-lived, I did not see quite the flesh and richness possessed by such vintages as 1985 and 1982. The 1988 Barbaresco offers the classic nose of dried cherries, herbs, cedar, and toasty oak. It is medium to full bodied, with considerable tannic clout. The long finish is dominated by the wine's tannins. It should benefit from 3–4 years of cellaring and keep for 10–15. Among the three single-vineyard Barbarescos, the most aromatic and complex is the 1988 Sori San Lorenzo. This intense wine offers up a bouquet of spices, vanillin, herbs, cedar, and red and black fruits. Although perfumed, the wine is once again dominated by tannins. There is freshness, full body, and plenty of length. Despite the precocious bouquet, this wine will not be at its best for 5–6 years; it should keep for 20 years. The full-bodied 1988 Costa Russi reveals a purple tinge to its color as well as a straightforward, rich nose of black fruits and new oak. At present it is more monolithic than the other single-vineyard Barbarescos. My favorite of these offerings is Gaja's 1988 Barbaresco San Lorenzo. This compelling wine exhibits sweet scents of tobacco, black fruits, coffee, and herbs. There is more body, richness, and weight than in the other Barbarescos, as well as a rich, long, tannic finish. Its size and tannic ferocity suggest that 7–8 years of cellaring are warranted. The wine will last for up to 3 decades. For a so-called mediocre vintage, Angelo Gaja turned out three astonishing Barbarescos in 1987. They will be ready to drink within the next decade yet will still have an aging potential of 20 or more years. As is usual when tasting these three vineyard-designated Barbarescos, the 1987 Sori San Lorenzo (3,450 bottles produced) is the most fragrant, perfumed, and, in terms of elegance, compelling. The huge, smoky, toasty new oak– and vanillin-scented nose is followed by a wine with wonderful richness and sweet, round, expansive flavors that are buttressed by considerable soft tannins. The wine is full bodied, with a long, luscious finish. Forward by the standards of Angelo Gaja, it still needs at least 3–4 years of bottle age and should last for at least 15 years. It is an immensely seductive, complex, profound Barbaresco that ranks as one of the best wines made from this vintage. The 1987 Costa Russi (3,600 bottles produced) is always less complex and more New-Worldish than the Sori San Lorenzo. I say this because of its pronounced and intense, somewhat straightforward bouquet of new oak and black fruits. Muscular and full, with plenty of oak-tinged flavors, it is closed and needs at least 4–5 years of bottle age. It should last for up to 2 decades, but I do not find the underlying profundity or individuality that is possessed by the Sori San Lorenzo or Sori Tilden. As for the 1987 Sori Tilden (3,100 bottles produced), this is usually the most concentrated and backward of the Gaja Barbarescos. The wine is amazing in the 1987 vintage, because it has a concentration level that is superior to many producers' 1985s. Gaja is a perfectionist, and he knows his wines have to be brilliant given the prices they fetch. The Sori Tilden has a huge, smoky, truffle- and black fruit–scented, exotic bouquet. In the mouth there are forceful, sweet, powerful flavors that beg for at least 5–6 years of cellaring. An immensely impressive Barbaresco, it is less complex at the moment than the Sori San Lorenzo, but more concentrated and potentially the longest-lived. It is an extraordinary success in a so-called off year. If you have the discretionary income necessary to purchase these Barbarescos, it would be a mistake to ignore the 1987 vintage from Angelo Gaja.

BRUNO GIACOSA

Barbaresco Gallina* * * *, Barbaresco Santo Stefano* * * * *, Barolo Falletto* * * *,
Barolo Rionda* * * * *, Barolo Le Rocche* * * * *, Barolo Villero* * * *,
Dolcetto d'Alba Plinet di Trezzo* */* * *, Nebbiolo d'Alba Valmaggiore* *

1987 Barbaresco Gallina	D	88
1988 Barbaresco Santo Stefano	E	94
1987 Barbaresco Santo Stefano	E	87
1986 Barolo Falletto di Serralunga	E	90
1986 Barolo Le Rocche	E	89
1986 Barolo Villero	E	87

The 1987 vintage in Piedmont has turned out to be a mixed bag, but the best wines I have tasted, from the likes of Bruno Giacosa, Angelo Gaja, and Elio Altare, have been texturally not unlike their 1987 counterparts in Bordeaux. The wines are obviously lighter than a vintage such as 1985 or 1988 but are forward, round, supple, and, in the best examples, amply endowed, with surprisingly good concentration. Despite the fact that Giacosa often releases his wines late, they still need significant time in the bottle to strut their impressive personalities. The advantages of both the 1987 Barbaresco Gallina and the 1987 Barbaresco Santo Stefano is that these wines can be drunk now. However, both have the potential to last for 6–8 years. I just finished some of my 1980 Giacosa Barbaresco Santo Stefano, another light vintage. Not only was it delicious, but it could easily have been held for another 4–5 years. As for the 1987 Barbaresco Gallina, it had a gorgeous bouquet of dried fruits, leather, and spices, as well as round, expansive, sweet flavors that come closest in texture to that of a top-notch burgundy. The long, lush finish is captivating. It is an ideal wine for restaurants looking for ready-to-drink, high-quality Piedmontese wine from a great producer. For the first time in memory, I marginally preferred the 1987 Gallina to the 1987 Barbaresco Santo Stefano. The Santo Stefano is delicious, with a more spicy, earthy, leathery nose, less of a floral, dried fruit character than the Gallina, a soft, full-bodied texture, and a long, round finish. It is delicious, seductive, and ideal for consuming over the next 5–6 years. As I have said so many times, 1986 was a good rather than great vintage in both Piedmont and Tuscany. However, Giacosa has managed to produce a big, full-bodied, forward 1986 Barolo Le Rocche. The huge bouquet of roses, tar, and spicy fruit is followed by a generously endowed, surprisingly rich, soft-edged wine that should drink well for the next decade. Those looking to cellar any of the current Giacosa offerings would be best advised to do so with the 1986 Barolo Villero. This is a much tougher, harder, more structured style of wine. It is concentrated, deeper in color than the Barolo Le Rocche, but much less charming and drinkable at present; it needs at least 2–3 years of bottle age to shed some of its tannins. The 1985 Barolo Falletto di Serralunga is the richest of these offerings. This dark ruby/garnet-colored wine has a huge bouquet of nuts, smoke, flowers, tar, and dried fruits. Rich, full bodied, and expansive in the mouth, it offers a long, alcoholic, and substantial finish. Like many 1985s, this wine is precocious enough to be consumed with great pleasure today, but its glory days should be between 1995 and 2005. This great master of the traditional style of Nebbiolo has produced a deep ruby-colored, fragrant 1988 Barbaresco Santo Stefano (intense aromas of cedar, cherry jam, tobacco, and herbs) that coats the palate. Full bodied and expansive, with layers of sweet fruit, this wine offers immense appeal, but it promises to evolve gracefully for another 10–20 years. The fruit is so rich and thick that the tannins are nearly obscured. This is another monument to the heights Nebbiolo can achieve!

MARCHESE DI GRESY
Barbaresco Martinenga* * * *, Barbaresco Martinenga Camp Gros* * * *,
Barbaresco Martinenga Gaiun* * * *, Dolcetto Monte Aribaldo* * * *

1988 Barbaresco Martinenga	E	86
1988 Barbaresco Martinenga Camp Gros	E	87
1988 Barbaresco Martinenga Gaiun	E	88

This estate has exquisite potential, but the wines often turn out slightly light. They are made in a forward, fragrant, medium-weight style that I feel compromises their full potential. Nevertheless, for drinking within 8–10 years of the vintage, they are very appealing. All three of the 1988s possess the classic Nebbiolo nose of roses, cherries, and tar. All exhibit light to moderate tannins, moderate concentration, and soft, supple finishes. The most expansive and richest on the palate is the Martinenga Gaiun; the lightest and shortest is the Martinenga.

MANZONE
Barbera d'Alba* * * *, Barolo Le Gramolere* * * */* * * * *,
Dolcetto* * *, Nebbiolo* * *

1990 Barbera d'Alba	C	88
1989 Barolo Le Gramolere	D	92+
1988 Barolo Le Gramolere	D	90?

1991 Dolcetto	B	86
1991 Nebbiolo	B	80

The extremely saturated, opaque, dark ruby color of the 1988 Barolo Le Gramolere is atypical for Barolo. The nose offers up funky, kinky, tar, mineral, and sweaty saddle leather aromas intertwined with superripe black fruit notes. In the mouth there is great ripeness but a disjointed feel to this big wine. With such impressive extraction of flavor, this Barolo should prove to be outstanding provided one has the patience to wait 5–7 years. It is a controversial style of Barolo. The 1989 Barolo Le Gramolere is an intensely spicy, long, thick wine with gobs of glycerin, alcohol, and tannin. It is not as forward as many 1989s, but it is huge in the mouth, with exceptional extraction of fruit as well as a sensational finish. **Anticipated maturity: 1997–2015.** Manzone made a gorgeous 1990 Barbera d'Alba. Exhibiting a dark ruby/purple color and a huge nose of mint and black cherry cough syrup, it is rich and full bodied, with superlative ripeness and a long, lusty finish. It should drink well for at least 10 years. Manzone's 1991 is a light yet fruity, clean, pleasant wine that should be consumed before the end of 1994. I preferred his 1991 Dolcetto, one of the better examples I have tasted from that vintage. It offers a perfumed nose of cherries and roses (that sounds like a Barolo rather than Dolcetto) and a rich, exuberant, fruity personality with a soft finish. It should be consumed before the summer of 1995.

MARCARINI
Barolo Brunate* * * *

1985 Barolo Brunate	D	90

This deceptively charming Barolo has a bouquet that jumps from the glass with smells of spicy, cedary, tobacco-tinged, red and black fruits. Seemingly soft, opulent flavors disarm the taster until one notices the elevated tannin levels and crisp acidity in the finish. Rich, concentrated, opulent, and satiny textured enough for current drinking, Marcarini's 1985 Barolo Brunate will continue to age well for 10–12 years.

BARTOLO MASCARELLO
Barolo* * * */* * * * *, Dolcetto d'Alba* * * *

1988 Barolo	D	93

This is one of the traditionalists who continues to make Barolo for drinking after 10–12 years of cellaring. Mascarello's wines remind me of the great vintages of Filippo Sobrero, such as the 1978 and 1982. No new oak is used, and consumers will have to accept some minor flaws, such as some volatile acidity and rough tannins, to fully appreciate what Bartolo Mascarello does. The 1988 Barolo displays the classic bouquet of old saddle leather, black truffles, roses, and huge quantities of sweet, jammy cherry fruit. Full bodied, with huge tannins and spectacular concentration, this wine will not be at its best until the end of this decade; it should last for 10–15 years into the next century. I can only imagine how stunning Bartolo Mascarello's 1989 and 1990 must be.

GIUSEPPE MASCARELLO

Barbera d'Alba Fasana* * *, Barolo Dardi* * */* * * *,
Barolo Monprivato* * * * *, Dolcetto Gagliassi* * *

1989 Barolo Monprivato	D	95
1988 Barolo Monprivato	D	90+

Anyone who has tasted Mascarello's wines knows they are never cheated on extraction of flavor, power, or tannin. These are wines that require significant patience. The 1988 Barolo Monprivato is lighter than I had expected, but the 1988 vintage is good rather than exceptional. Nevertheless, this wine displays a telltale tar, earthy, herbal, cherry-scented nose, huge tannins, high acidity, and fine fruit and richness. It needs 4–5 more years of cellaring. **Anticipated maturity: 1996–2006.** Mascarello's 1989 Monprivato should prove to be the finest wine made by this great producer since 1982 and 1978. Dark ruby colored, with a huge nose of black truffles, herbs, tobacco, and highly extracted red and black fruits, it is a full, chewy, thick, authoritatively flavored, tannic wine that needs at least 7–10 years of cellaring. **Anticipated maturity: 1999–2015.**

MATTEO-CORREGGIA

Barbera d'Alba Bricco Marun* * * */* * * * *, Nebbiolo d'Alba Val Preti* * * *

1990 Barbera d'Alba Bricco Marun	94
1990 Nebbiolo d'Alba Val Preti	90

Correggia's single-vineyard Barbera is one of the greatest Barberas I have ever tasted. The dark purple color and intense bouquet—which screams from the glass, offering aromas of plums, blackcurrants, licorice, and spices—are amazing. Rich and full bodied, with awesome extract levels, this unbelievably rich, complex wine can be drunk now or cellared for another 10–12 years. Amazing! The 1990 Nebbiolo d'Alba Val Preti was made from yields of 2 tons per acre and aged in 100% new oak. The wine's 14% alcohol is buried under a cascade of lavishly rich, sweet-tasting (the wine is totally dry) black cherry and plum fruit. Combined with the sexy aromas of toast and vanillin, it makes for an exceptionally well-delineated, rich, full-bodied, spectacularly well-endowed wine that should drink well for another 10–15 years.

MOCCAGATTA

Barbaresco Basarin* * * *, Barbaresco Bric Balin* * * *,
Barbaresco Cole* * * *, Barbera Basarin* * *

1990 Barbaresco Basarin	D	90
1990 Barbaresco Bric Balin	C	92+
1990 Barbaresco Cole	D	92+
1990 Barbera Basarin	C	88

The 1989 and 1990 were such great vintages that producers who generally make good wines often made sensational ones. Moccagatta's 1990s are the best I have ever tasted from this small producer. For starters there is the 1990 Barbera Basarin, a gorgeously assembled, rich, authoritatively flavored, spicy, fruity wine that cuts a deep impression on the palate. Drink it over the next decade. The three 1990 Barbarescos offer slightly different styles. The most developed and opulent, as well as the best for near-term drinking (over the next 10–12 years), is the 1990 Barbaresco Basarin. It is rich, with a spicy, smoky, black cherry–scented nose, lavish quantities of fruit, full body, and a lovely, velvety-textured finish. The most tannic of this trio, the 1990 Barbaresco Cole, is also the biggest and densest. Although rich, superintense, large-scale, and tannic, it needs at least 3–4 years in the cellar. The wine's purity and its finish are both impressive. Drink it between 1997 and 2015. The 1990 Barbaresco Bric Balin also needs a few years, although it is currently more voluptuously rich and succulent than the 1990 Barbaresco Cole. Full bodied and rich, with stunning length, this is another great Barbaresco from an exceptional vintage. Drink it between 1995 and 2010.

CASTELLO DI NEIVE

Barbaresco Santo Stefano* * * *, Dolcetto d'Alba Basarin* * *,
Dolcetto d'Alba Messoriano* * *

1989 Barbaresco Santo Stefano	D	90
1985 Barbaresco Santo Stefano	D	90

The 1989 Barbaresco Santo Stefano is clearly the best example of this wine made by the Castello di Neive since 1985. The big, leathery, meaty, herb- and tobacco-scented bouquet is followed by a rich, concentrated, medium- to full-bodied wine. It has already shed some of its tannin and can be drunk now or over the next 12–15 years. The dark ruby/garnet color of the 1985 Santo Stefano is just beginning to display some amber/orange at the edge, and the explosive bouquet of dried red fruits, mushrooms, and, I believe, white truffles soars from the glass. In the mouth this full-bodied, massively concentrated, yet surprisingly forward Barbaresco is beautifully endowed with layer upon layer of sweet, expansive fruit. The finish is long, alcoholic, and impressive. Drinkable now, this great Barbaresco should continue to evolve for another 5–10 years.

ARMANDO PARUSSO

Barbera Pugnane* * */* * * *, Barolo Bussia Rocche* * * *, Barolo Rocche* * * *,
Dolcetto d'Alba Mariondino* * * *

1990 Barbera Pugnane	C	85
1989 Barolo Bussia Rocche	D	92
1988 Barolo Bussia Rocche	D	87
1989 Barolo Mariondino Ealletta	D	89
1988 Barolo Mariondino Ealletta	D	89
1991 Dolcetto	B	85

Parusso's style of Barolo is lighter than that of many other producers. His 1988 Barolo Bussia Rocche displays a medium ruby color, a sweet, fruity nose, medium- to full-bodied flavors, moderate tannins, and a spicy, moderately endowed finish. The modern style makes it more approachable and easier to understand. Parusso's 1988 Barolo Mariondino Ealletta is more intense, with a pronounced nose of bing cherries, smoked almonds, and earth. In the mouth there is considerable tannin as well as full body and excellent concentration. It possesses a supple texture, particularly for a young Barolo. Drink it over the next 10–12 years. Parusso's newest releases are the strongest wines he has yet made. The 1991 Dolcetto is another good example from this maligned vintage. Soft and fruity, with excellent ripeness and an attractive suppleness, it should be drunk before the end of 1994. The 1990 Barbera Pugnane reveals good ripeness and chewiness, a dense texture, plenty of perfume, and a spicy, crisp, zesty finish. It should drink well for another 5–7 years. Parusso's two best wines among his newest releases are the 1989 Barolo Mariondino and 1989 Barolo Bussia. The Mariondino exhibits tons of sweet, spicy new oak in the nose, as well as abundant quantities of ripe red and black fruits, such as cherries. The wine has a deep, velvety texture with a lingering, super finish. Drink it over the next 10–15 years. Parusso's fabulous 1989 Barolo Bussia displays an opaque deep ruby color and a sweet, spicy, stunning nose with the telltale Nebbiolo aromas of tar and roses. There is super richness and extraction of fruit, a multidimensional, medium- to full-bodied texture, and moderately high tannins in the long finish. Drink it between 1996 and 2010.

PIO CESARE
Barbaresco* *, Barolo* * *, Dolcetto d'Alba* * * *, Ornato* *

1985 Barolo Riserva	D	84
1991 Dolcetto d'Alba	B	82
1985 Ornato	C	82

This old, well-respected firm does not appear to know the direction it wishes to take. The firm has always been traditionalist, but the lighter-style wines that have recently emerged appear to be making excessive concessions to the commercialization of Barolo and Barbaresco. These offerings are distinctly lighter than what Pio Cesare has produced in the past, and, yes, I found them disappointing. The pleasant, straightforward, fruity 1991 Dolcetto d'Alba should be drunk before the summer of 1995. The 1985 Barolo Riserva is already exhibiting significant orange and rust at the edge. It possesses a spicy, leathery, sweat-scented nose, with the fruit already beginning to take on that faded, leafy character. There is still good body, glycerin, and alcohol, and the wine clearly was made from fully ripe grapes, but it must be drunk up before it deteriorates further. The Ornato has been consistently mediocre. The 1985 is slightly above average because of its deep color and good ripeness, but it is a monolithic, one-dimensional, vastly overpriced wine. This firm needs to take a look at what it, as well as other Piedmont producers, are now accomplishing.

PRODUTTORI DI BARBARESCO
Barbaresco* * *, Barbaresco Asili* * * *, Barbaresco Moccagatta* * * *,
Barbaresco Monte Stefano* * * *, Barbaresco Ovello* * * *,
Barbaresco Pora* * *, Barbaresco Rabaja* * * *

1989 Barbaresco	D	88
1989 Barbaresco Asili	D	93
1989 Barbaresco Moccagatta	D	89+
1989 Barbaresco Monte Stefano	D	90

1989 Barbaresco Ovello	D	90
1989 Barbaresco Rabaja	D	90

In top years I have consistently recommended the wines of this cooperative, which may be the best-run growers cooperative in the world. I have followed the evolution of the 1978s and 1982s and have never been disappointed with the way these wines mature. They are exceptionally clean and rich, as well as different from cru to cru. Moreover, their prices are 30% less expensive than the single-vineyard Barbarescos from any other Piedmontese producer. The 1989s are the finest wines I have tasted from the Produttori di Barbaresco since their 1978s. I liked them even better than the 1982s because they are richer, with deeper fruit. The most forward and elegant include the regular *cuvée* of 1989 Barbaresco, the 1989 Asili, and the 1989 Ovello. These wines can be drunk now, but they possess the richness and structure to age for 12 or more years. The most backward wines include the 1989 Rabaja, 1989 Mocca-gatta, and 1989 Monte Stefano. Rich and full bodied, these wines all exhibit a sweet tobacco, black cherry, jammy fruitiness, huge body, and plenty of glyc-erin, alcohol, and tannin in the finish. Although approachable now, they should be cellared until 1996 and drunk over the following 15 years.

ALFREDO PRUNOTTO
Barbaresco Monte Stefano* * * *, Barbera d'Alba* * *,
Barbera d'Alba Pian Romulado* * *, Barolo Bussia* * * *, Barolo Cannubi* * * *

1989 Barbaresco Monte Stefano	D	93
1988 Barbaresco Monte Stefano	D	90
1989 Barbera d'Alba	C	85
1988 Barbera d'Alba Pian Romulado	C	87
1989 Barolo Bussia	D	94
1988 Barolo Bussia	D	90
1989 Barolo Cannubi	D	91
1988 Barolo Cannubi	D	87+

This firm has been making spectacular wines recently. Their 1988s are excel-lent and their 1989s potentially superb. The most forward and flattering of these offerings is Prunotto's Barbaresco from the Monte Stefano vineyard. The 1988 Monte Stefano, which is evolving quickly, is delicious to drink. The medium ruby color is already showing some amber at the edge. The nose re-veals earthy, sweet berry, spicy aromas that are followed by a smooth, velvety-textured wine with gorgeous fruit and a soft, luscious finish. Drink it over the next 7–8 years. The 1989 Monte Stefano is deeper in color, much richer, and overall a larger-scale, thicker, riper, more concentrated wine. There is plenty of tannin, but this is a voluptuous, sexy Barbaresco to drink over the next 10–15 years. The same differences in vintages are well displayed in Prunotto's Barolos. Both the 1988 Barolos are more tannic than the Barbarescos, as well as surprisingly forward and developed, with classic aromas of tar, tobacco, and sweet cherry fruit. They can be drunk now or cellared for another 12–15 years. The 1989 Barolo Cannubi and 1989 Barolo Bussia are deeper in color, with greater concentration as well as rich, expansive, sweet, superconcentrated flavors. The 1989 Cannubi is more elegant and not as powerful as the 1989 Bussia, which is a huge, well-endowed, glycerin-infused, giant Barolo that should drink well for 15 or more years. These two Barberas offer ripe, spicy fruit, an enticing perfume of tomatoes and herbs, and excellent fat and glycerin to balance out their naturally high acidity. The 1989 displays the superripeness that was easily attained in this vintage, but it does not yet boast the complexity of the 1988 Barbera d'Alba Pian Romulado. The latter wine is a big, opulent, deep Barbera with surprising length and complexity. Both wines should drink well for the next 4–5 years, possibly longer.

GIUSEPPE RINALDI
Barolo Brunate* * * */* * * * *

1988 Barolo Brunate Riserva	D	93

This old-style Barolo will be adored by consumers who love the style of Giacomo Conterno and Bartolo Mascarello. It possesses the huge, earthy, truffle-, smoked nut–, black fruit–scented nose that one either adores or finds slightly dirty. A huge wine, it has mouth-filling, glycerin-dominated, rich, chewy, sweet flavors, surprising suppleness, and a massive finish with gobs of fruit and equally impressive tannin levels. It is likely to be a controversial Barolo, but I thought it spectacular. Drink it over the next 15–20 years.

ROCCA
Barbaresco Ronchi* * * *

1990 Barbaresco Ronchi		89

I have had little experience with this producer, but this 1990 Barbaresco Ronchi had a huge nose of sweet saddle leather, black cherry fruit, and herbs. Soft, voluptuous, and rich, as well as elegant and stylish, this full-bodied, suave, velvety-textured Barbaresco can be drunk now and over the next 10 years.

LUCIANO SANDRONE
Barolo* * * *, Barolo Cannubi Boschis* * * * *, Dolcetto* * * */* * * * *

1989 Barolo Cannubi Boschis	E	97
1988 Barolo Cannubi Boschis	E	93
1990 Dolcetto	B	90

Sandrone is one of the finest producers of Barolo. Fortunately I have some bottles of his spectacular 1982 and 1985 in my cellar. The 1988 Cannubi Boschis promises to rival his 1985, but will it be as stunning as his 1982? Styled traditionally, the 1988 is unbelievably intense, with a super nose of damp earth and black fruits. In the mouth there is sensational chewy, ripe, opulent fruit, softer tannins than many producers appear to have obtained, and a massively long, heady finish. Approachable now, this wine should hit its peak of maturity in 3–4 years and last for up to 15. Wow! The 1989 Barolo Cannubi Boschis is another treasure to be added to Sandrone's impressive résumé. Backward for a 1989, it exhibits a dense purple color; a blossoming nose of smoky new oak, black fruits, and tar; rich, full-bodied, multilayered flavors; and awesome dimension and persistence in the mouth. **Anticipated maturity: 1996–2010.** Sandrone has turned in a magnificent effort with his 1990 Dolcetto. The ruby/purple color suggests superripeness and extraction. The nose of spring flowers, superripe black plums, and minerals is stunning. There is an expansive, full-bodied sweetness to this muscular, juicy, and succulent Dolcetto. It should be drunk over the next 2–4 years.

SCARPA
Barbaresco* * *, Barbaresco Payore Barberis di Treiso* * *,
Barolo Boscaretti di Serralunga d'Alba* * */* * * *,
Barolo I Tetti di Neive* * *, Rouchet* * *

1990 Rouchet Vino da Tavola	C	87

Scarpa usually makes impossibly backward, tough-textured red wines, so what a delight it was to find his 1990 Rouchet so enjoyable. It is bursting with sweet red and black fruits and has a supple texture, plenty of body, and moderate alcohol levels. This delicious, exuberantly fruity, medium- to full-bodied wine should drink well for 4–6 years.

ENRICO SCAVINO
Barbera Carati* * * *, Barolo* * * *, Barolo Bric del Fiasc* * * */* * * * *,
Barolo Cannubi* * * */* * * * *, Dolcetto d'Alba* * *

1990 Barbera Carati	C	88
1989 Barolo	D	90
1989 Barolo Bric del Fiasc	E	93+
1988 Barolo Bric del Fiasc	D	90
1989 Barolo Cannubi	E	96
1988 Barolo Cannubi	D	87
1991 Dolcetto	B	85

Enrico Scavino's newest releases include an attractive, elegant, stylish 1991 Dolcetto that should be drunk before the end of 1994. He has also turned out a stunning single-vineyard 1990 Barbera Carati. It exhibits a dense purple color; a fragrant nose of red and black fruits, spices, and herbs; a gorgeously rich, medium- to full-bodied, chewy texture; superlative fruit extraction; and a spicy, rich finish. Drink it between 1994 and 2002. Scavino's three 1989 Barolos are spectacular. The 1989 Barolo has an earthy, meaty, gamelike nose with tremendous fruit, long, rich, supple, dense flavors, plenty of alcohol and glycerin, and a lusty, yet supple finish. It should drink well for 12–15 years. The 1989 Barolo Cannubi is a legend in the making. Its spectacular nose of sweet black fruits, licorice, grilled meats, and smoky new oak is followed by a wine with immense richness, stunning opulence, a multidimensional personality, and a spectacularly long, well-delineated finish. Approachable now, it promises to drink well and even improve for another 15–20 years. The 1989 Barolo Bric del Fiasc is also rich and full, but more backward, revealing more tannin than the other two 1989 offerings. After 5–6 years of cellaring, it should rival the 1989 Barolo Cannubi. These are the finest Barolos I have tasted from Scavino. Scavino's 1988 Barolo Bric del Fiasc exhibits an intense ruby color that is followed by an elegant, spicy, herbal, cherry-scented nose intermingled with aromas of earth and roasted nuts. A full-bodied, extremely tannic feel accompanies ripe, superbly extracted flavors. The wine is tight but promising.

Anticipated maturity: 1994–2005. Given its huge overlay of tannin, the 1988 Barolo Cannubi reveals a traditional style of winemaking. It is less flattering, and the wine is even tighter and more austere than the Barolo Bric del Fiasc. Nevertheless, aromas of almonds, cherries, and tar are present in this classic Barolo. **Anticipated maturity: 1995–2005.**

ALDO & RICARDO SEGHESIO
Barbera* * *, Barolo La Villa* * * *, Dolcetto d'Alba* * *

1991 Barbera	C	86
1989 Barolo La Villa	D	93+
1988 Barolo La Villa	D	93

This tiny producer in Monforte has turned out two deeply colored, magnificent examples of Barolo. The 1988 La Villa exhibits a telltale Barolo nose of jammy bing cherries, dried pit fruit, almonds, and tar. In the mouth there is superlative richness, a full-bodied, moderately tannic, chewy texture, and an intense, robust finish. Drinkable now, it should be at its best between 1994 and 2008. The 1989 La Villa is a spectacular example of this terrific vintage. With a deep ruby color and a bouquet that soars from the glass, offering scents of sweet, jammy, cherry fruit, almonds, smoke, and truffles, this wine displays fabulous fruit, full body, and a tremendously powerful, rich, moderately tannic finish. As impressive as it is now, it will be at its best between 1995 and 2012. Seghesio's 1991 Barbera is a smoky, herb, almost tomato-scented wine with tasty, rich, soft, supple fruit and a moderately long finish. Drink it over the next 4–5 years.

FILIPPO SOBRERO
Barolo* * * *

1982 Barolo	D	95

This is an old-style, classic Barolo, the likes of which are rarely seen today. Telltale Barolo aromas of tar, roses, and superripe Nebbiolo fruit are present, as well as a trace of volatile acidity. In the mouth there is spectacular concentration, an unbelievably rich, chewy, glycerin-infused texture, and a spectacularly sweet, expansive, explosive finish. Despite considerable tannin, the wine is characterized by its extraordinary voluptuousness and viscous, rich, astonishingly long finish. Readers who want straightforward, sterile, monolithic aromas of fruit and wood are going to be put off by the noticeable volatile acidity and the size of this massive Barolo. Those who do not mind a little excitement with their wine should be checking out the better Italian wine retailers to see if they can latch on to a few bottles of this individualistic Barolo. I would opt for drinking this wine over the next decade. It is stunning stuff! Sadly, Sobrero has sold his vineyards and is no longer making wine.

VIETTI
Barbaresco Masseria* * * *, Barolo Lazzarito* * * *, Barolo Rocche* * * *,
Barolo Villero* * * * *

1988 Barbaresco Masseria	D	90
1988 Barolo Rocche	D	90+

Vietti's 1988s are classic wines from this traditional Piedmontese winemaker. Both are big, forceful, tannic wines that are meant to be cellared. The 1988 Barbaresco Masseria exhibits a dusty, dark ruby color; a jammy, black cherry–, roasted nut–scented nose; rich, powerful, full-bodied flavors; and tons of tannin in the relatively hard, tough finish. **Anticipated maturity: 1997– 2012.** The 1988 Barolo Rocche has a similar color, as well as a classic Barolo nose of roses, tar, and black cherry fruit. Rich and full bodied, with considerable tannins and crisp acidity, this wine finishes with a wallop, with most of its richness perceived at the end of the palate. Do not touch a bottle until 1998; it should keep for 15–20 years thereafter.

ROBERTO VOERZIO
Barbera d'Alba Vignasse* * * */* * * * *, Barolo Cuvées* * * */* * * * *, Dolcetto d'Alba Privino* * * *, Vigna La Serra* * * *

1989	Barbera d'Alba Vignasse	C	90
1988	Barolo Brunate	D	91
1988	Barolo Cerequio	D	91
1988	Barolo La Serra	D	90
1987	Barolo La Serra	D	89
1990	Dolcetto d'Alba Privino	B	88
1990	Nebbiolo della Langhe Croera Fossati	B	86
1988	Vigna La Serra (Nebbiolo/Barbera)	C	88

It has been a number of years since I have tasted this producer's wines, but I was immensely impressed with his current offerings. His 1990 Dolcetto d'Alba Privino is all that a Dolcetto should be. The big, fragrant nose of black fruits is followed by a ripe, unctuous, opulent wine bursting with fresh jammy fruit. The finish is long and well balanced. It is one of the more gorgeous efforts in a terrific vintage for most Piedmontese red wines. Drink it over the next 2–3 years. The 1990 Nebbiolo della Langhe Croera Fossati resembles a downsize Barolo. It offers elegance, medium to full body, attractive ripe fruit, moderate extract levels, and a spicy, tannic finish. It should drink nicely for 5–6 years. Voerzio's flamboyant 1990 Barbera d'Alba Vignasse could easily compete with the terrific Barberas produced by Elio Altare. Almost opaque dark ruby/purple in color, the wine reveals a huge smoky, oaky, richly fruity nose, gobs of lusty, voluptuous fruit, and a long, spicy, rich finish. There is good acidity as well as wonderful sweetness and length that suggest this wine should continue to drink beautifully for 5–10 years. Voerzio's innovative blend of Barbera and Nebbiolo, the 1988 Vigna La Serra, is an uncommonly seductive wine, with a wonderful fragrance of red fruits, spices, herbs, and tar. The wine exhibits gorgeous ripeness, a round, generously endowed, supple texture, and a long, rich, concentrated finish. Precocious enough to be drunk now, this wine should easily last for 5–7 years. Impressive! As for Voerzio's Barolos, his 1987 Barolo La Serra is one of the best I have tasted from the vintage. It is much more developed and softer than most 5-year-old Barolos, but copious levels of fruit are present, as well as the classic aromas of tar, roses, and sweet red fruit. On the palate this seductive wine is generous, round, full bodied, and supple. Fully mature and unlikely to improve, this wine should be drunk over the next 4–5 years. All three 1988 Barolos were outstanding examples. It is hard to pick a favorite since they are young and unevolved. The 1988 Barolo La Serra appears to have the most elegance and forward, sweet fruit, but also less intensity, glycerin, and tannin. The 1988 Barolo Cerequio is rich and tight, with a beautiful inner core of sweet fruit as well as a fragrant, tar-scented Nebbiolo nose. The 1988 Barolo Brunate is the biggest, most masculine and full bodied of this trio; it is also the most concentrated and tannic. If all the tannins melt away, it will have the highest potential for longevity. If you can afford them, purchase several bottles of each. These immensely impressive wines are the finest I have yet tasted from Roberto Voerzio.

TUSCANY

Italian Roulette

The Basics

TYPES OF WINES

Beautiful Tuscany is the home of Italy's most famous wine region, Chianti, and one of Italy's most celebrated wines, Brunello di Montalcino. Both wines can be either horrendous or splendid. Quality is shockingly irregular. Yet it is in Tuscany that Italy's wine revolution is being fought, with adventurous and innovative producers cavalierly turning their backs on the archaic regulations that govern wine production. They are making wines, often based on Cabernet Sauvignon, Merlot, and Sangiovese, aged in small oak casks, filled with flavor and personality, and put in designer bottles. I disagree completely with critics who have called them French look-alikes, and though entitled to be called only Vino da Tavola, they represent some of the most exciting red wines made in the world. The same cannot be said for Tuscany's white wines. Except for the light, tasty whites called Vernaccia from the medieval hill fortress of San Gimignano, Tuscan whites are ultraneutral, boring wines. Shame on those producers who package these wines in lavish-looking bottles that are appallingly overpriced.

GRAPE VARIETIES

The principal and greatest red wine grape of Tuscany is Sangiovese. The highest-yielding, most insipid wine from Sangiovese comes from the most widely planted clone called Sangiovese Romano. The better producers are using clones of Sangiovese with names such as Sangioveto, Prugnolo, and Brunello. All produce a richer, deeper, more complex wine. Of course, Cabernet Sauvignon, Merlot, Cabernet Franc, and even Pinot Noir and Syrah are making their presence felt in Tuscany.

As for the white wines, there is the sharp, uninteresting Trebbiano, produced in ocean-size quantities. Trebbiano is an inferior grape that produces distressingly innocuous wines. Vernaccia has potential, and of course there are such international blue bloods as Chardonnay and Sauvignon Blanc. Tuscany, in my mind, means red not white wine, but if you are inclined to try a white wine, take a look at my list of recommended producers for Vernaccia di San Gimignano.

FLAVORS

Chianti Classico   It is virtually impossible to provide specific information given the extraordinary range in quality—from wines that are musty, poorly vinified, and washed out to wines with soft, supple, raspberry, chestnut, and tobacco flavors, crisp acidity, medium body, and a fine finish. Stick to the recommended producers listed subsequently. Remember, at least 50% of wines called Chianti, despite tighter regulations governing quality, are thin, acidic, and unpleasant.

Brunello di Montalcino   Wines should be rich, powerful, tannic, superbly concentrated, and heady, with a huge, spicy bouquet of smoky tobacco, meat, and dried red fruits. Only a few are. Most close encounters offer an alarming degree of tannin and musty old oak to the detriment of fruit. Selection is critical. Rosso di Montalcino, often much less expensive and considerably fresher, is red wine made from the Brunello clone of Sangiovese that is not aged long enough to qualify as Brunello di Montalcino.

Carmignano   This is an underrated viticultural area whose wines show good fruit, balance, and character. The best of them behave like Chiantis with more character and structure. Not surprisingly, Carmignano is made from Sangiovese, with 10%–15% Cabernet added.

Vernaccia di San Gimignano   Tuscany's best dry white table wine, this nutty, zesty, dry, fruity white is meant to be drunk within 2–3 years of the vintage. A satisfying rather than thrilling wine.

Vino Nobile di Montepulciano   A neighbor of Chianti with identical characteristics (the grape is the same), Vino Nobile di Montepulciano costs more but rarely provides more flavor or pleasure.

Other Tuscan whites   The names Bianco di Pitigliano, Bianco Vergine della Valdichiana, Galestro, Montecarlo, Pomino, and any Tuscan producer's name plus the word *bianco* translates into wines that taste wretchedly neutral and bland and provide no more flavor than a glass of water. Sadly, most cost $12–$25, so the operative phrase is "Caveat emptor"!

Vino da Tavolas   The most thrilling red wines of Tuscany are the designer show wines that are being made by Tuscany's most innovative growers. They can be 100% Cabernet Sauvignon, 100% Sangiovese, or a blend of the two plus Cabernet Franc. Even some Merlot, Syrah, and Pinot Noir can now be found. The wines are usually aged in mostly new French oak casks. Top Tuscan vintages, such as 1982, 1985, 1988, and 1990, can offer sensational aromatic dimension and remarkable flavor breadth. Following are the best-known Vino da Tavolas, their top vintages, and the grapes used.

NAME	PRODUCER	TOP VINTAGES	PRIMARY GRAPE	RATING
Acciaiolo	Fattoria di Albola	1990, 1988	Sangiovese	***
Alte d'Altesi	Altesino	1990, 1988	Sangiovese	****
Anagallis	Lilliano	1988	Sangiovese	***
Ania	Gabbiano	1990, 1988	Cab. Sauvignon	***
Armonia	Querciavalle	1990, 1988	Sang./Canaiolo	***
Balifico	Castello di Volpaia	1990, 1988	Sangiovese	***
Barco Reale	Capezzana	1990, 1988	Cab. Sauvignon	***
Bel Convento	Del Roseti	1988	Sangiovese	**
Bianchi V. Scanni	Monsanto	1990, 1988	Sangiovese	***/****
Predicatodi Biturica	Agricoltoria del Geografico	1990, 1988	Sangiovese	***
Boro Cepparello	Isole e Olena	1990, 1988	Sangiovese	***
Brusco di Barbi	Barbi	1990, 1988	Sangiovese	**
Ca del Pazzo	Caparzo	1990, 1988	Sangiovese	****
Cab. Sauvignon	Altesino	1990, 1988	Cab. Sauvignon	***
Cab. Sauvignon	Avignonesi	1990, 1988	Cab. Sauvignon	****
Cabreo Il Borgo	Ruffino	1988	Cab. Sauv./Sang.	***
Cabreo Vigneto	Ruffino	1990, 1988	Sangiovese	***
Campaccio Barrique	Temabianca	1988	Sangiovese	**
Capannelle Barrique	Rossetti	1990, 1988	Sangiovese	***
Capannelle Rosso	Capannelle	1990, 1988	Sangiovese	***
Capannelle Rosso	Rossetti	1990, 1988	Sangiovese	***
Carmartina	Querciabella	1990, 1988	Sangiovese	***
Carmerlengo	Pagliarese	1990, 1988	Sangiovese	**/***
Cerviolo	Villa Calcinara	1988	Sangiovese	***/****
Cetinaia	San Polo	1990, 1988	Sangiovese	**
Colle Picchioni-Vassallo	Paola di Mauro	1990, 1988	Sangiovese	**
Collezione de Marchi l'Ermo	Isole e Olena	1988	Syrah	****
Coltassala	Castello di Volpaia	1990, 1988	Sangiovese	****
Coltibuono Rosso	Badia a Coltibuono	1990, 1988	Sangiovese	***
I Coltri Rosso	Melini	1990, 1988	Sangiovese	**
Concerto	Fonterutoli	1990, 1988	Sangiovese	**/***
Coniale di Castellare	Castellare di Castellina	1990, 1988	Cab. Sauv./Sang.	****/****
Cortaccio	Villa Cafaggio	1990, 1988	Cab. Sauvignon	***
La Corte	Castello di Querceto	1990, 1988	Sangiovese	****
Donna Marzia	Giuseppe Zecca	1990, 1988	Sangiovese	**
Elegia	Poliziano	1990, 1988	Prugnolo	****/*****
Flaccianello	Fontodi	1990, 1988	Sangiovese	****
Fontalloro	Felsina Berardenga	1990, 1988	Sangiovese	****
Geremia	Castello di Cacchiano	1990, 1988	Sangiovese	***
Ghiaie della Furba	Cappezzana	1990, 1988	Cab. Sauvignon	***
Granchiaia	Le Macie	1990, 1988	Sangiovese	**
Grattamacco	Podere Grattamacco	1990, 1988	Sangiovese	**
Grifi	Avignonesi	1990, 1988	Sangiovese	****
Grosso Sanese	Il Palazzino	1990, 1988	Sangiovese	****/*****
Isole e Olena Rosso	Isole e Olena	1990, 1988	Sangiovese	**
Liano	Umberto Cesari	1990, 1988	Sangiovese	**
Logaiolo	Fattoria dell'Aiola	1990, 1988	Sangiovese	**
Marzeno di Marzeno	Zerbina	1990, 1988	Sangiovese	**
Masso Tondo	Le Corti	1990, 1988	Sangiovese	****
Merlot	Avignonesi	1990, 1988	Merlot	****/*****
Monte Antico	Monte Antico	1990, 1988	Sangiovese	****
Monte Vertine	Monte Vertine	1990, 1988	Sangiovese	***
Mormoreto	Frescobaldi	1990, 1988	Sangiovese	***
Nemo	Monsanto	1990, 1988	Cab. Sauvignon	****
Nero del Tondo	Ruffino	1988	Pinot Noir	**
Niccolo da Uzzano	Castello di Uzzano	1990, 1988	Sangiovese	**
Ornellaia	L. Antinori	1990, 1988	Cab. Sauvignon	*****

NAME	PRODUCER	TOP VINTAGES	PRIMARY GRAPE	RATING
Ornellaia Masseto	L. Antinori	1988	Merlot	*****
Palazzo Altesi	Altesino	1990, 1988	Sangiovese	****/*****
Il Pareto	Nozzole	1990, 1988	Cab. Sauvignon	***
Parrina	DOC	1990, 1988	Sangiovese	**
Percarlo	San Giusto	1990, 1988	Sangiovese	*****
Le Pergole Torte	Monte Vertine	1990, 1988	Sangiovese	****
Piano del Cipresso	Temabianca	1988	Sangiovese	**
Poggio Brandi	Fattoria Baggiolino	1990, 1988	Sangiovese	*****
Porta della Pietra	John Matta	1988	Sangiovese	****
Prunaio	Viticcio	1990, 1988	Sangiovese	****
Il Querciolaia	Castello di Querceto	1990, 1988	Cab. Sauv./Sang.	*****
R & R	Castello di Gabbiano	1990, 1988	Cab. Sauv./Sang.	****
Ripa della More	Vicchiomaggio	1990, 1988	Cab. Sauv./Sang.	****
Rocca di Montegrossi	Castello di Cacchiano	1990, 1988	Sangiovese	**
Rosso dell'Oca	Fattoria di Petriolo	1990, 1988	Merlot	****
Rosso di Altesino	Altesino	1990	Cab. Sauv./Sang.	****
Sammarco	Castello di Rampolla	1990, 1988	Cab. Sauvignon	*****
San Felice	Predicato di Biturica	1990, 1988	Sangiovese	**
San Martino	Villa Cafaggio	1990, 1988	Sangiovese	****
Sangioveto di Coltibuono	Badia a Coltibuono	1990, 1988	Sangiovese	****
Sangioveto Grosso	Monsanto	1990, 1988	Sangiovese	****
Santa Cristina	P. Antinori	1990, 1988	Sangiovese	**
Sassello	Castello di Verrazzano	1990, 1988	Sangiovese	**
Sassicaia	San Guido	1990, 1988	Cab. Sauvignon	*****
Secentenario	Antinori	nonvintage	Cab. Sauv./Sang.	****
Ser Niccolo	Conti Serristori	1990, 1988	Sangiovese	**
Il Sodaccio	Monte Vertine	1990, 1988	Sangiovese	***
I Sodi di San Niccolo	Castellare	1990, 1988	Sangiovese	***
Sodole	Guicciardini Strozzi	1990, 1988	Sangiovese	****/*****
Solaia	P. Antinori	1990, 1988	Cab. Sauvignon	*****
Solatia Basilica	Villa Cafaggio	1990, 1988	Sangiovese	****
Soldera Intistieri	Soldera	1988	Sangiovese	***/****
Spargolo	Cecchi	1990	Sangiovese	**
Le Stanze	Poliziano	1990, 1988	Cab. Sauvignon	****/*****
Tavernelle	Villa Banfi	1988	Cab. Sauvignon	**
Tignanello	P. Antinori	1990, 1988	Sangiovese	****
Tinscvil	Castello di Monsanto	1990, 1988	Sangiovese	****
Tremalvo	Barone Ricasoli	1988	Cab. Sauvignon	**
L'Unico	Petroio	1990	Cab. Sauvignon	***
Vigna l'Apparita	Castello di Ama	1990, 1988	Merlot	****/*****
Vigna di Bugialla	Poggerino	1990, 1988	Cab. Sauv./Sang.	****
Vigna il Chiuso	Fattoria di Ama	1990, 1988	Pinot Noir	***
Vigna di Fontevecchia	Agricola Camigliano	1990, 1988	Sangiovese	**
Vigna Pianacci	Castello di Luiano	1990, 1988	Sangiovese	**
Le Vignacce	Villa Cilnia	1990, 1988	Sangiovese	***/****
Vigneto La Gavine	Villa Cerna	1990	Cab. Sauvignon	****
Vigorello	San Felice	1988	Cab. Sauv./Sang.	***
Villa di Bagnolo	Marchesi Pancrazi	1990	Pinot Noir	***
Vinattieri Rosso II	M. Castelli	1990, 1988	Sangiovese	***
Vocato	Villa Cilnia	1988	Cab. Sauvignon	***

AGING POTENTIAL

Brunello di Montalcino: 8–25 years
Carmignano: 5–8 years
Chianti Classico: 3–15 years*
Rosso di Montalcino: 5–8 years
Tuscan Whites: 1–2 years

Vino Nobile di Montepulciano: 5–10 years
Vino da Tavolas (red wine blends): 5–15 years

* Only a handful of Chianti producers make wines that age and last this long.

OVERALL QUALITY LEVEL

For one of the world's most famous wine regions, the quality, although on the upswing, is depressingly variable. Some famous estates in Brunello continue to live off their historic reputations while making poor wine, and there is an ocean of mediocre Chianti producers. The exciting new breed of Sangiovese/Cabernet, Cabernet Franc, and Merlot wines can be superb, but they are expensive. As for the white wines, the situation is intolerable, and the Italians need to wake up to the fact that high-tech, computerized, stainless-steel tanks, centrifuges, sterile bottling, and obsessive reliance on micropore filter machines offer a fail-safe policy for making pleasureless wines.

MOST IMPORTANT INFORMATION TO KNOW

Forget Italian wine regulations that are supposed to promote a better product. Many disgustingly poor wines carry the government's highest guarantee of quality, the DOCG, or Denominazione di Origine Controllata e Garantita. Many of the Vino de Tavolas—supposedly Italy's lowest-level, generic wines—are vastly superior. Only if you know the top producers will you be able to make your way through the perilous selection process for Italian wines.

1993–1994 BUYING STRATEGY

For Tuscany, a buying strategy is simple. The spectacular 1985s are long gone from the marketplace, but consumers should be able to find some of the excellent 1986 Chianti Classico Riservas. That vintage has turned out far better than expected, and prices are relatively modest for such delicious wines so close to full maturity. The 1987 vintage is a washout, the 1988 very good to excellent (although not the "vintage of the decade," as some pundits declared). The wines are tannic and structured, with good richness, but they lack the extra aromatic and flavor dimensions that characterize top years. The 1989 is a hit-or-miss vintage, with most wines mediocre. The 1990 is a terrific vintage, the best overall year since 1985. The acid levels are slightly higher in 1990 than they were in 1985, so the wines should be longer-lived, but perhaps less flattering than the voluptuous 1985s. Unfortunately, 1991 and 1992 are difficult years, so concentrate your buying forays on the 1990s.

VINTAGE GUIDE

1992—First reports were ominous, but growers seemed more enthusiastic after the wines had finished malolactic fermentation in spring 1993. Rain interrupted the harvest, but most of the white wine grapes were in, and many producers were not far from finishing the red wine harvest. Look for the wines to be soft and fruity, with relatively low acidity. Because of the rains there will be frightful irregularity. This is not a vintage that can be summarized in a general fashion, but the successful wines will be drinkable young, and short-lived.

1991—A very difficult year throughout Tuscany; it may turn out like 1987. If so, the vintage will produce some light, agreeable, correct wines that need to be drunk in the first 3–5 years. On paper, this is a below average–quality vintage.

1990—This is the best year for Tuscany since the fabulous 1985 vintage. The wines exhibit terrific color, superripe aromas, wonderful richness, and surprisingly crisp acidity, something difficult to achieve in years of great ripeness. Even the lower-level Chiantis, many of which can be found for under $10 a bottle, are drinking deliciously and should last until 1995–1996. The bigger Chiantis and Chianti Classico Riservas will last for 10–15 years, and the Cabernet Sauvignon/Sangiovese–based Vino da Tavolas should last for 15 or more years. A stunning vintage!

1989—Tuscany was inundated by rain in 1989. Consequently the wines exhibit a certain hollowness and lightness. Some competent examples have emerged, but this is a below average–quality vintage.

1988—Touted as a great year in Tuscany, 1988 is certainly a very good one. The wines display pronounced tannins and considerable structure. In some cases the green, astringent tannins suggest that not all the grapes reached full physiological maturity. Nevertheless, there are enough good wines to rate this vintage as one of the best of the decade, eclipsed in quality by 1985, 1982, and 1990.

1987—Light, agreeable, pleasantly fruity wines were made, but most are now fading. Avoid.

1986—A good vintage that at present is lost in the hype surrounding 1985, but the wines are well balanced and round. The Chianti Classico Riservas are especially recommended.

1985—A smashing, no-holds-barred, incredible year; the wines burst at the seams with a superripe, velvety, opulent, plummy fruitiness, full body, and a lushness and precociousness not seen since 1971. The wines are seductive, glamorous, voluptuous, and fabulously tasty. The lighter-style Chiantis should have been drunk up; the serious Chiantis and Vino da Tavolas will drink well until 2000–2005; the Brunellos will keep for another 20 years. The wines from the top producers are not to be missed.

1984—A dreadful year, much worse in Tuscany than in Piedmont to the north. Rain and a paucity of sunshine were the culprits. No doubt the trade will say the wines are light and commercial, but at this point this looks to be a vintage to pass up.

1983—Quite highly regarded. Tuscany had weather similar to that experienced in Bordeaux hundreds of miles to the west. A drought year of intense heat caused sugars and the consequent alcohol level to skyrocket in the grapes. The wines are ripe, alcoholic, fat, low in acidity, and jammy, with deep layers of fruit. Drink them between now and 1999.

1982—Considered more "classic" than 1983, which I suppose means less powerful and less opulently fruity and rich wines. Certainly this is a good vintage with firm tannins and fine depth and ripeness. The second-best year between 1975 and 1990, and one year to be taken seriously. For Brunello di Montalcino, it is the best vintage since 1970.

OLDER VINTAGES

Avoid 1978, 1977, 1976, 1974, 1973, and 1972. If the wines have been well stored, 1971 and 1970 are superb years.

RATING TUSCANY'S BEST PRODUCERS OF CHIANTI, BRUNELLO, VINO NOBILE DI MONTEPULCIANO

NOTE: Most producers make both a Chianti Classico and a Chianti Classico Riserva. On the following chart, for purposes of simplification, the star rating shown for each producer's Chianti Classico or Burnello di Montalcino also pertains to their Chianti Classico Riserva or Brunello di Montalcino Riserva. Single-vineyard Chiantis are treated as a separate qualitative item.

* * * * * (OUTSTANDING PRODUCERS)

Ambra (Carmignano Riserva
  Vigna Alta)
Felsina Berardenga (Chianti Classico
  Riserva Rancia)
Costanti (Brunello di Montalcino)

Pertimali (Brunello di Montalcino)
Ciacci Piccolomini d'Aragona
  (Brunello di Montalcino)
Salvioni-Cerbaiola
  (Brunello di Montalcino)

* * * * (EXCELLENT PRODUCERS)

Altesino (Brunello di
  Montalcino)****/*****
Ambra (Carmignano)
Anfiteapo Vecchie Terre di Montefili
  (Chianti Classico Riserva)
P. Antinori (Chianti Classico Riserva
  Marchese)
P. Antinori (Chianti Classico Riserva
  Villa Antinori)
Avignonesi (Vino Nobile di
  Montepulciano)
Badia a Coltibuono (Chianti
  Classico)
Felsina Berardenga (Chianti
  Classico)
Biondi Santi (Brunello di Montalcino
  Il Greppo Riserva)
Bologna Buonisignoir (Brunello di
  Montalcino)
Bologna Buonisignoir (Vino Nobile di
  Montepulciano)
Boscarelli (Vino Nobile di
  Montepulciano)
Castello di Cacchiano (Rocca di
  Montegrossi Chianti Classico
  Riserva)

Campogiovanni San Felice (Brunello
  di Montalcino)****
Canalicchio (Brunello di Montalcino)
Canalicchio di Sopra (Brunello di
  Montalcino)
Canalicchio di Sopra Pacenti Franco
  e Rosildo (Brunello di
  Montalcino)****/*****
Podere Capacci (Chianti Classico)
Caparzo (Brunello di Montalcino La
  Casa)
Caprili (Brunello di
  Montalcino)****/*****
Carletti della Giovampaola (Vino
  Nobile di Montepulciano)
Case Base Soldera (Brunello di
  Montalcino)
Castell'in Villa (Chianti Classico)
Castell'in Villa (Chianti Classico
  Riserva)****
Cerbaiona (Brunello di
  Montalcino)****/*****
Dei (Vino Nobile di Montepulciano)
Fanetti (Vino Nobile di
  Montepulciano)
Fontodi (Chianti Classico)

Fontodi (Chianti Classico Riserva Vigna del Sorbo)

Gracciano (Vino Nobile di Montepulciano)

Castelli del Grevepesa (Chianti Classico San' Angiolo Vico Labate)

Lisini (Brunello di Montalcino)

Monsanto (Chianti Classico Riserva Il Poggio)****/*****

Il Palazzino (Chianti Classico)

Il Palazzino (Chianti Classico Riserva)

Pertimali (Rosso di Montalcino)

Cracci Piccolomini d'Aragona (Rosso di Montalcino)

Poggio Antico (Brunello di Montalcino)****/*****

Poggio Salvi (Brunello di Montalcino)

Poggio Salvi (Brunello di Montalcino Riserva)

Il Poggiolo–Roberto Cosimi (Brunello di Montalcino)

Il Poggione–R. Franceschi (Brunello di Montalcino)

Il Poggione–R. Franceschi (Brunello di Montalcino Riserva)

Poliziano (Vino Nobile di Montepulciano)

Castello di Querceto (Chianti Classico)

Castello di Querceto (Chianti Classico Riserva)

Quercetorto (Chianti Classico Riserva)

Querciabella (Chianti Classico)

Castello di Rampolla (Chianti Classico)

Rocca di Montegrossi (Chianti Classico)

Ruffino (Chianti Classico Riserva Ducale)

Salvioni-Cerbaiola (Rosso di Montalcino)

San Giusto a Rententano (Chianti Classico)

Selvapiana (Chianti Classico)

Selvapiana (Chianti Rufina Bucerchiale)

Soldera (Brunello di Montalcino)

Talenti (Brunello di Montalcino)

Tenuta Il Poggione (Brunello di Montalcino)

Val di Suga (Brunello di Montalcino)

Vecchie Terre di Montefili (Chianti Classico)

Castello Vicchiomaggio (Chianti Classico Paola Matta)

Castello Vicchiomaggio (Chianti Classico Riserva Petri)

Castello Vicchiomaggio (Chianti Classico San Jacopo)

Vignamaggio (Chianti Classico)

Vignamaggio (Chianti Classico Riserva)

Villa Selvapiana (Chianti Rufina Riserva)

* * * (GOOD PRODUCERS)

Castello d'Albola (Chianti Classico)

Castello d'Albola (Chianti Classico Riserva)

Altesino (Rosso di Montalcino)

Castello di Ama (Chianti Classico)

Castello di Ama (Chianti Classico Vigneto Bellavista)***/****

Castello di Ama (Chianti Classico Vigneto Bertinga)***/****

Castello di Ama (Chianti Classico Vigneto La Casuccia)***/****

Castello di Ama (Chianti Classico Vigneto San Lorenzo)***/****

Ancilli (Vino Nobile di Montepulciano)

Antinori (Chianti Classico Peppoli)

Argiano (Brunello di Montalcino)***/****

Biondi Santi (Brunello di Montalcino)

Bonacossi (Carmignano Riserva)***/****

Boscarelli (Chianti Colli Senesi)

Brolio (Chianti Classico Riserva del Barone)

Cabreo di Ruffino (Vigneto Il Borgo)

Castello di Cacchiano (Chianti Classico)

Cantine Baiocchi (Vino Nobile di Montepulciano)

Caparzo (Brunello di Montalcino)

Cappelli (Chianti Classico Riserva)***/****

Cappelli (Chianti Classico Riserva Vigna Casaloste)***/****

Castellare (Chianti Classico)

Colognole (Chianti Ruffina)

Colombini Fattoria dei Barbi (Brunello di Montalcino)

Le Corti (Chianti Classico)

Dievole (Chianti Classico Vigna Dieuele)

Dievole (Chianti Classico Vigna Sessina)

Castello di Farnetella (Chianti Colli Senesi)

S. Filippo (Brunello di Montalcino)

Fonterutoli (Chianti Classico)***/****

Fossi (Chianti)

Frescobaldi (Chianti Rufina Riserva Montesodi)

Castello di Gabbiano (Chianti Classico Riserva)***/****

Cantina Gattavecchi (Chianti Colli Senesi)

Geografico (Chianti Classico)

Geografico (Chianti Classico Castello di Fagnano)

Geografico (Chianti Classico Contessa di Radda)

Isole e Olena (Chianti Classico)

Lamole di Lamole (Chianti Classico)

Lilliano (Chianti Classico)

Monsanto (Chianti Classico)***/****

Monte Vertine (Chianti Classico)

Castello di Nipozzano di Frescobaldi (Chianti Rufina Riserva)

Nittardi (Chianti Classico)

Nozzole (Chianti Classico)

Paneretta (Chianti Classico)

Petroio (Chianti Classico Montetondo)

Quercia al Poggio (Chianti Classico)

S. Quirico (Chianti Classico)

Riecine (Chianti Classico)

Rocca di Castagnoli (Chianti Classico Riserva)

Rocca delle Macie-Tenuta Sant'Alfonso (Chianti Classico)

Roccadoro (Chianti Classico)

Ruffino (Chianti Classico)

Ruffino (Chianti Classico Aziano)

Ruffino (Chianti Classico Nozzole)

Castello di San Polo in Rosso (Chianti Classico)

Talosa (Chianti)

Talosa (Rossodi Montalcino)

Talosa (Vino Nobile di Montepulciano)

Toscolo (Chianti Classico)

Toscolo (Chianti Classico Riserva)

Trerose (Vino Nobile di Montepulciano)

Fattoria Valtellina (Chianti Classico Giorgio Regni)

Villa Cafaggio (Chianti Classico)

Villa Cerna (Chianti Classico)

Villa Cilnia (Chianti Colli Aretini)

Vistarenni (Chianti Classico)

Vistarenni (Chianti Classico Assolo)

Viticcio (Chianti Classico)

Castello di Volpaia (Chianti Classico)

Castello di Volpaia (Chianti Classico Riserva)

* * (AVERAGE PRODUCERS)

Castello Banfi (Brunello di Montalcino)

Castello Banfi (Brunello di Montalcino Poggio all'Oro)

Barbi (Chianti Colli Senesi)

F. Bonfio (Chianti Le Poggiolo)

Brolio (Chianti Classico)

Buracchi (Vino Nobile di Montepulciano)**/***

Cantina Biaocchi (Vino Nobile di Montepulciano)

S. Carlo (Brunello di Montalcino)

Carpineto Casa Vinicola (Chianti Classico)

Castelgiocondo (Brunello di Montalcino)

Castelgiocondo (Rosso di Montalcino)

Castiglion del Bosco (Brunello di
   Montalcino)**/***
Cecchi Luigi (Chianti Classico)
Cecchi Luigi (Vino Nobile di Mon-
   tepulciano)
La Chiesa di S. Restituta (Brunello di
   Montalcino)
Col d'Orcia (Brunello di Montalcino)
Col d'Orcia (Brunello di Montalcino
   Poggio al Vento)
Costanti (Chianti Colli Senesi)
Dei Roseti (Brunello di Montalcino)
La Fortuna (Brunello di Montalcino)
Fattoria Illuminati di Dino Illuminati
   (Montepulciano d'Abruzzo Vecchio
   Zanna)
Frescobaldi-Montesodi (Chianti
   Rufina)
Il Marroneto (Brunello di Montalcino)
Mastrojanni (Brunello di Montalcino)
Melini (Chianti Classico Riserva
   Granaio)
Melini (Chianti Classico Riserva
   Laborel)
Melini (Chianti Classico Riserva
   Rossa)

Melini (Chianti Classico Riserva La
   Selvanella)
Pagliarese (Chianti Classico)
Pian di Conte (Brunello di
   Montalcino)**
Podere Lo Locco (Carmignano)
Poggio al Sorbo (Chianti Classico)
Il Poggiolo (Chianti Colli Senesi)
San Felice (Chianti Classico)
San Felice (Chianti Classico Riserva
   Il Grigio)
San Leonino (Chianti Classico)
Savignola Paolina (Chianti Classico)
Fattoria di Selvole (Chianti Classico)
Castello di Tizzano (Chianti Classico)
Castello di Uzzano (Chianti Classico)
Fattoria di Vetrice (Chianti Rufina)
Villa Banfi (Brunello di Montalcino)
Villa Francesca (Chianti Classico)
Villa de Monte (Chianti Rufina)
Villa Nicole (Brunello di Montal-
   cino)**/***
Villa La Selva (Chianti Colli
   Aretini)

RATING TUSCANY'S BEST PRODUCERS OF VINO DA TAVOLA

* * * * * (OUTSTANDING PRODUCERS)

Antinori (Ornellaia)
Antinori (Solaia)
Ornellaia (Tuscan Red Wine)

Castello di Rampolla (Sammarco)
San Giusto a Rententano (Percarlo)
San Guido (Sassicaia)

* * * * (EXCELLENT PRODUCERS)

Altesino (Alte d'Altesi)
Altesino (Palazzo Altesi)****/*****
Altesino (Rosso di Altesino)
Castello di Ama (Vigna
   l'Apparita)****/*****
P. Antinori (Secentenario)
P. Antinori (Tignanello)
Avignonesi (Cabernet Sauvignon)
Avignonesi (Grifi)
Avignonesi (Merlot)****/*****
Badia a Coltibuono (Sangioveto di
   Coltibuono)
Fattoria Baggiolino (Poggio Brandi)

Felsina Berardenga (Fontalloro)
Castello di Cacchiana (Geremia)
Caparzo (Ca del Pazzo)
Castellare di Castellina (Coniale di
   Castellare)****/*****
Castell'in Villa (Santa Croche)
Castelnuovo Berardenga (Santa
   Croche)
Le Corti (Masso Tondo)
Fontodi (Flaccianello)
Castello di Gabbiano (R & R)
Isole e Olena (Collezione de Marchi
   l'Ermo)

Castello di Monsanto (Tinscvil)

Monsanto (Nemo)

Monsanto (Sangioveto Grosso)

Monte Antico (Monte Antico)

Monte Vertine (Le Pergole Torte)

Il Palazzino (Grosso
  Senese)****/*****

Fattoria di Petriolo (Rosso dell'Oca)

Poggerino (Vigna di Bugialla)

Poggio Antico (Altero)

Poliziano (Elegia)****/*****

Poliziano (Le Stanze)

Castello di Querceto (La Corte)

Castello di Querceto (Il Querciolaia)

Guicciardini Strozzi
  (Sodole)****/*****

Vicchiomaggio (Ripa della More)

Villa Cafaggio (San Martino)

Villa Cafaggio (Solatia Basilica)

Villa Cerna (Vigneto La Gavine)

Viticcio (Prunaio)

Castello di Volpaia (Coltassala)

* * * (GOOD PRODUCERS)

Castello d'Albola (Acciaolo)

Altesino (Cabernet Sauvignon)

Altesino (Rosso di Montalcino)

Fattoria di Ama (Vigna il Chiuso)

Badia a Coltibuono (Coltibuono
  Rosso)

Castello di Cacchiano (Geremia)

Capezzana (Barco Reale)

Capezzana (Ghiaie Della Furba)

Castellare (I Sodi di San Niccolo)

M. Castelli (Vinattieri Rosso II)

Frescobaldi (Mormoreto)

Castello di Gabbiano (Ania)

Castello di Gabbiano (Agricoltori del
  Geographico)

La Gioia di Riecine (Tuscan Red
  Wine)

Isole e Olena (Boro Cepparello)

Lilliano (Anagallis)

Monsanto (Bianchi V.
  Scanni)***/****

Monte Vertine (Monte Vertine)

Monte Vertine (Il Sodaccio)

Nozzole (Il Pareto)

Marchesi Pancrazi (Villa di Bagnolo)

Petroio (L'Unico)

Querciabella (Carmartina)

Querciavalle (Armonia)

Rossetti (Capannelle Barrique)

Rossetti (Capannelle Rosso)

Ruffino (Cabreo Il Borgo)

Ruffino (Cabreo Vigneto)

San Felice (Vigorello)

Soldera (Soldera Intistieri)***/****

Villa Cafaggio (Cortaccio)

Villa Calcinara (Cerviolo)***/****

Villa Cilnia (Le Vignacce)***/****

Villa Cilnia (Vocato)

Castello di Volpaia (Balifico)

* * (AVERAGE PRODUCERS)

Agricola Camigliano (Vigna di
  Fontevecchia)

Fattoria dell'Aiola (Logaiolo)

Antinori (Santa Cristina)

Barbi (Brusco di Barbi)

Cecchi (Spargolo)

Umberto Cesari (Liano)

Conti Serristori (Ser Niccolo)

Dei Roseti (Bel Convento)

Fonterutoli (Concerto)**/***

Podere Grattamacco (Grattamacco)

Isole e Olena (Isole e Olena Rosso)

Castello di Luiano (Vigna Pianacci)

Le Macie (Granchiaia)

Melini (I Coltri Rosso)

Pagliarese (Carmerlengo)**/***

Paola di Mauro (Colle Picchioni
  Vassallo)

Parrina (Parrina)

Barone Ricasoli (Tremalvo)

Rocca delle Macie-Tenuta
  Sant'Alfonso (Granchiaia)

Ruffino (Nero del Tondo)

San Felice (San Felice)

San Polo in Rosso (Cetinaia)

Temabianca (Campaccio
  Barrique)

Temabianca (Piano del Cipresso)

Castello di Uzzano (Niccolo da   Villa Banfi (Tavernelle)
   Uzzano)   Giuseppe Zecca (Donna Marzia)
Castello di Verrazzano (Sassello)   Zerbina (Marzeno di Marzeno)

Selected Tasting Notes

CASTELLO D'ALBOLA

Acciaolo Vino da Tavola* * *, Chianti Classico* * *, Chianti Classico Riserva* * *

1988 Acciaolo	C	86
1988 Chianti Classico	A	86
1985 Chianti Classico Riserva	B	87

All three of these wines are modern-style Tuscan reds that are impeccably clean, soft, and deliciously fruity. Of the three, I preferred the 1985 Chianti Classico Riserva because it was most faithful not only to Chianti, but to Tuscany. It was the only one of the three wines that could actually be identified in a blind tasting as a Sangiovese-based Tuscan wine. It is lusciously full and fleshy, with a big, leathery, dried fruit, spicy bouquet; its flavors have shed all their tannins and are now opulent and accessible. It should be drunk over the next 3–4 years. The 1988 Chianti Classico is a medium-bodied, more straightforward, deliciously fruity, slightly more compact style than the 1985, but it is a well-made and spicy wine, with more acidity and a more narrow framework. Castello d'Albola's proprietary red table wine, the 1988 Acciaolo, exhibits a great deal of new oak and represents an interesting blend of 65% Sangioveto and 35% Cabernet Sauvignon. It is an impeccably clean, oenologist's wine that has a lot of new oak, a straightforward red and black fruit character, and good body, but just not enough excitement or individuality to merit higher marks. Nevertheless, it is soft, supple, and ideal for consumers and restaurants looking for a tasty, velvety-textured, concentrated, nicely packaged Tuscan red wine.

ALTESINO

Alte d'Altesi Vino da Tavola* * * *, Brunello di Montalcino* * * */* * * * *,
Cabernet Sauvignon Vino da Tavola* * *,
Palazzo Altesi Vino da Tavola* * * */* * * * *,
Rosso di Altesino, Rosso di Montalcino* * *

1988 Alte d'Altesi	D	90
1985 Brunello di Montalcino Vigna Altesino	D	92
1988 Palazzo Altesi	D	90
1990 Rosso di Altesino	C	90
1990 Rosso di Montalcino	C	90

Altesino has always been a reference point for Brunello di Montalcino. This superb 1985 Vigna Altesino has enough opulence and richness to be consumed now, although it would be a shame not to lay away a few bottles for drinking around the turn of the century. Dark ruby/garnet, with a huge, smoked, black fruit–, cocoa–, and herb-scented bouquet, this impressively endowed, full-bodied wine is highly extracted but has slightly lower acidity than many other 1985 Brunellos. No doubt the wine was made from superripe grapes. Long, opulent, and dramatic, this is a beautifully made Brunello for drinking over the next 15 or more years. The 1988 Alte d'Altesi (a blend of Sangiovese Grosso and Cabernet Sauvignon aged in new oak casks) is a stunning wine. The huge nose of cedar, tobacco, black fruits, and spices is intensely fragrant. In the mouth this full-bodied wine is bursting with glycerin and reveals impressive extraction of fruit, moderate tannins, and a spicy, long, rich finish. Drinkable now, this wine should continue to evolve beautifully over the next decade. Altesino's 1988 Palazzo Altesi (made completely from the Sangiovese Grosso grape grown in their Montosoli vineyard) is a more evolved, sweet-scented wine, with huge aromas of jammy, earthy, red and black fruits intermingled with herbs and toasty new oak. In the mouth it is expansive, full bodied, even voluptuous, with soft tannins and an opulent, long finish. This is a seductive red wine to drink over the next 7–8 years. Altesino has scored successfully with both the 1990 Rosso di Montalcino and 1990 Rosso di Altesino. The former wine exhibits great density of fruit, super richness, a perfumed nose of cassis, spices, and herbs, and a lush finish. Drink it between 1994 and 2002. The softer Rosso di Altesino is equally stunning, with a sweet nose of jammy berry fruit, leather, vanillin, and smoke as well as a rich, medium- to full-bodied texture. Drink this juicy, exciting Vino da Tavola between 1994 and 2001.

CASTELLO DI AMA
Chianti Classico* * *, Chianti Classico Single Vineyards* * */* * * *,
Merlot Vigna l'Apparita* * * */* * * * *

1990 Chianti Classico	C	87
1988 Chianti Classico Vigneto Bellavista	D	88+
1988 Chianti Classico Vigneto Bertinga	D	89
1988 Chianti Classico Vigneto La Casuccia	D	86
1988 Chianti Classico Vigneto San Lorenzo	D	87
1988 Merlot Vigna l'Apparita	E	93

This producer turns out a relatively austere, tannic, tight-fisted style of Chianti that is not my favorite, but one has to admire the wines' purity and structure. They are more architectural than hedonistic. The 1990 Chianti Classico is an elegant wine, with a pure, ripe cherry-scented nose, supple, medium-bodied flavors, fine ripeness, and a tasty, spicy, long finish. Drink it over the next 4–5 years. My favorite of the single-vineyard Chiantis is the 1988 Vigneto Bertinga. Dark colored, with an intriguing nose of tar, roasted pine nuts, and cherries, it is firm and tannic, with medium body, and fine extraction of flavor in the long finish. Drink it between now and 2003. The 1988 Chianti Classico San Lorenzo exhibits tougher tannins and more firmness and tightness. While the color is deep ruby and there is excellent underlying fruit and ripeness, this wine requires 2–3 years of patience. If the tannins do not fully melt away, my rating will look too generous. The 1988 Vigneto Bellavista reveals an impressive, deep ruby/purple color, a big, spicy, tobacco, herb, and leather-scented nose, spicy, ripe, rich flavors, and plenty of underlying depth to back up the tannins. It appears to be the best candidate for an outstanding score after another 1–2 years of cellaring. It should drink well for 12–15 years. The 1988 La Casuccia has 15% Merlot blended in, but you would never know that by its tightness, hardness, tough tannins, and astringent finish. The color is impressive and there is good underlying fruit, but again, this is a closed, austere style of Chianti that some readers may enjoy more than I did.

I have never had any doubts about Castello di Ama's magnificent Merlot. The 1988 Vigna l'Apparita is a spectacular wine, with black/purple color, and a huge nose of cassis, black cherries, licorice, and vanillin. It offers staggering concentration, great definition, and a medium- to full-bodied, terrific finish. Although there is plenty of tannin, the copious quantities of fruit overwhelm it. While approachable now, this Merlot should age beautifully for 10–15 years. Made in frightfully tiny quantities, it will require "insider" contacts to find a bottle or two.

AMBRA
Carmignano* * * *, Carmignano Riserva Alta* * * * *

1990 Carmignano	C	92
1990 Carmignano Riserva Vigna Alta	D	90+

Ambra has become my favorite producer of Carmignano. I am a sucker for their superrich, expansive, creamy-textured style of red wine. Ambra's wines are the Pomerols of Tuscan viticulture. The 1990 Carmignano is the best regular *cuvée* I have tasted from this producer. It reveals sensational richness, a terrific nose of black fruits and spices, low acidity, a luscious, fleshy, chewy texture, and whoppingly long finish. Although impossible to resist now, it should continue to drink well for at least a decade. The 1990 Riserva Vigna Alta will probably merit an even higher score in 3–4 years. Even more concentrated than the regular *cuvée*, it is buttressed by more noticeable spicy new oak, has a higher tannin level, and is more structured and backward. It does not sing quite as loudly as the regular *cuvée*, but it is an impressively endowed, rich, multidimensional wine for drinking between 1996 and 2008.

ANFITEAPO VECCHIE TERRE DI MONTEFILI* * * *

1986 Chianti Classico Riserva	B	89

This terrific Chianti possesses a wonderfully sweet, expansive, perfumed nose of black cherries, oak, damp earth, and spices. In the mouth this generously endowed, deep, concentrated wine exhibits fine richness of fruit, an attractively endowed, silky texture, and a long, spicy, rich finish with so much fruit that the tannins, acid, and alcohol are beautifully concealed. Drink this seductive, full-flavored Chianti over the next 5–6 years.

L. ANTINORI
Ornellaia Tuscan Red Wine Vino da Tavola* * * * *

1988 Merlot Masseto	E	93
1988 Ornellaia Tuscan Red Wine	D	93

This brilliant wine is one of the best new-breed Tuscan reds I have tasted. The color is a sensational black/purple, and the nose offers gorgeously intense aromas of black plums, cassis, licorice, and spicy new oak. In the mouth there is extraordinary opulence and richness, enough acidity to provide grip, and plenty of tannin lurking behind the cascade of fruit. The explosive finish goes on and on. Approachable, even delicious now, this splendid wine promises to get even better over the next 4–6 years and possibly last through the first decade of the next century. Impressive! Unfortunately, the availability of this spectacular single-vineyard Merlot is limited. Made by Marchese Lodovico, it rivals the superb Tuscan Merlots produced by Avignonesi and Castello di Ama. Its rarity and price make it a collector's item. Stunningly rich and densely concentrated, it exhibits saturated color, a big, rich, black-cherry and toasty oak–scented nose, opulent, superconcentrated flavors, adequate acidity, and a blockbuster finish. It should drink well for 10–12 more years.

P. ANTINORI

Chianti Classico Peppoli* * *, Chianti Classico Riserva Marchese* * * *,
Santa Cristina Vino da Tavola* *, Secentenario Vino da Tavola* * * *,
Solaia Vino da Tavola* * * * *, Tignanello Vino da Tavola* * * *

1988 Solaia	EE	90
1988 Tignanello	D	90

The Antinori name on a bottle of Italian wine is about as close to a guarantee of quality as one is likely to find. Just about everything he does, in all price ranges, is good. Even his white wines offer more pleasure than the run-of-the-mill, innocuous character most Italian whites seem to share. His Tignanello, one of the first proprietary red Tuscan table wines, is gorgeous in 1988. The color is deep ruby/purple, and the nose offers up penetrating aromas of sweet red and black fruits and toasty new oak. In the mouth this medium- to full-bodied wine offers wonderfully precise flavors, excellent richness, good acidity, soft tannins, and a spicy, long, rich finish. Drinkable now, this wine should continue to evolve for at least 10–12 years. I would have to rank this vintage of Tignanello alongside the glorious 1985. The 1988 Solaia is outstanding. Deep in color, with a rich bouquet of olives, cassis, and vanillin, the wine is full bodied, deep, very rich, and tannic. **Anticipated maturity: 1995–2008.** RATINGS FOR OLDER VINTAGES OF ANTINORI SOLAIA: 1986(87), 1985(96), 1982(93), 1979(89).

AVIGNONESI

Cabernet Sauvignon Vino da Tavola* * * *, Grifi Vino da Tavola* * * *,
Merlot Vino da Tavola* * * */* * * * *, Vino Nobile di Montepulciano* * * *

1988 Grifi	D	87
1988 Merlot	D	90

An impeccably run Tuscan winery, Avignonesi is known for making one of the best Vin Santos in Italy (check out their 1983 if you like this sweet, nutty-flavored, sherrylike style). They also produce some excellent red wines. I have been a consistent admirer of their Cabernet Sauvignon–based wine called Grifi, which has been delicious in vintages such as 1982, 1983, and 1985. The 1988 Grifi (a blend of 50% Cabernet Sauvignon and 50% Prugnolo Gentile) offers up a moderately intense bouquet of cherries, oak, and herbs. In the mouth there is good structure, a sense of firmness and tightness, excellent ripeness, a medium-bodied, rich palate, and fine length. The wine will benefit from another several years of cellaring and should last for at least a decade. The 1988 Merlot reveals a dark ruby/purple color and a huge nose of jammy plums and cassis intermingled with scents of toast and smoke. It is a beautifully etched, well-delineated, medium- to full-bodied Merlot, bursting with fruit yet with surprising structure and firmness for its ripe aroma and taste. Delicious now, it should continue to drink well for 7–8 years.

BADIA A COLTIBUONO
Chianti Cetamura* * *, Chianti Classico* * * *,
Coltibuono Rosso Vino da Tavola* * *,
Sangioveto di Coltibuono Vino da Tavola* * * *

1990 Chianti Cetamura	A	87
1990 Chianti Classico	B	89
1988 Chianti Classico	B	87

This superlative Chianti producer continues to offer one spectacular bargain that consumers would be foolish to ignore. The Chianti Cetamura was delicious in 1988 and is even better in 1990. The wine offers a terrific purity and richness of fruit, a medium- to full-bodied, soft texture, and a fragrant berry-, spice-, tobacco-, and herb-scented nose. Already delicious, it will keep until 1997–98. What a joy it is to find a wine of this quality level priced at $8 a bottle. The nearly outstanding 1990 Chianti Classico displays a beautifully complex, smoky, berry-scented nose; rich, full-bodied flavors that exhibit excellent concentration and ripeness; low acidity; and an opulent, fleshy, heady finish. It, too, is delicious now but promises to last longer than the Cetamura. Drink it between 1994 and 2002. The 1988 Chianti Classico is an uncommonly deep ruby/purple color, a large-scale Chianti possessing gobs of sweet black raspberry, black cherry fruit, medium to full body, and impressive power and length. Perhaps I have underrated this wine, which is supple enough to be drunk now yet holds the potential to last for 5–8 years.

FELSINA BERARDENGA
Chianti Classico* * * *, Chianti Classico Riserva Rancia* * * * *,
Fontalloro Vino da Tavola* * * *

1990 Chianti Classico	B	88
1988 Chianti Classico	B	86
1986 Chianti Classico Rancia	C	88
1988 Chianti Classico Riserva	C	88
1986 Chianti Classico Riserva	C	88
1988 Chianti Classico Riserva Rancia	D	90
1986 Chianti Classico Riserva Rancia	C	91
1988 Fontalloro	D	89
1987 Fontalloro	D	86

This producer consistently turns out some of Tuscany's finest Chiantis. Both the 1988 and 1990 Chianti Classicos offer sweet, ripe black fruit aromas inter-

mingled with hints of damp earth, wood, and leather. In the mouth they are elegant and round, with lovely fruit, soft tannins, and adequate acidity. Drink the
1988 over the next 4–5 years. The richer 1990 will keep 6–10 years. The 1988
Chianti Classico Riserva has a rich, licorice-, earth- (truffles?), black
cherry–scented nose; rich, full-bodied, expansive flavors; good tannin; adequate acidity; and a long finish. Drink it between 1994 and 2005. The 1986
Chianti Classico Riserva is a potentially outstanding wine. The big nose of
leather and plummy, cherry fruit is followed by a superconcentrated, rich,
well-balanced wine with heaps of sweet, expansive fruit. In the finish there is
enough tannin to warrant another 5–7 years of cellaring. It should last for 7–12
years. The backward 1988 Riserva Rancia exhibits superb richness and
tremendous density to go along with its saturated dark ruby color. It is a large-
scale, superrich Chianti that can be drunk now but should evolve gracefully
between 1994 and 2008. The 1986 Riserva Rancia is profound. A dense,
nearly opaque ruby/purple color is followed by intense, multidimensional aromas of herbs, leather, and black cherries. In the mouth there is gorgeous extraction of fruit, fine balance, and a sensationally long finish. Drink this terrific
Chianti over the next 7–8 years. The 1986 Chianti Classico Rancia offers a
substantial mouthful of wine. The dark ruby color and big, black fruit–,
licorice-, and spicy, oak-scented bouquet is followed by a round, chewy, full-
bodied Chianti with a great deal of extract, low acidity, and soft tannins in the
finish. Drink this heady, succulent Chianti over the next 5–6 years. Although
1987 was a dreadful vintage for Tuscany, Felsina Berardenga managed to produce a good Fontalloro, their proprietary red table wine made from 100% Sangiovese and aged in 60% new oak casks. The 1987 is a surprisingly
concentrated, round, supple, medium-bodied wine, with a long, silky-textured
finish. This notable success from a tough Tuscan year is delicious to drink
now. Consume it over the next 2–3 years. The 1988 Fontalloro is a bigger,
more structured wine, with an enthrallingly sweet, smoky, cassis, almost Bordeaux-like bouquet. In the mouth the wine is expansive, round, and generously
endowed, with none of the high acidity and tough tannins so noticeable in
many 1988 Tuscan wines. In fact, it is surprisingly soft and luscious for a
1988. It should be drunk over the next 5–7 years.

BIONDI SANTI
Brunello di Montalcino* * *, Brunello di Montalcino Riserva* * * *

1982 Brunello di Montalcino	EE	90
1982 Brunello di Montalcino Riserva Il Grepo	EE	92
1977 Brunello di Montalcino Riserva Il Greppo	EE	80

While I have maligned this estate for its rather hard, overly tannic, austere, inconsistent wines, it would appear it has made two top wines. Their 1982 regular and Riserva bottlings are superb. However, this hardly excuses some of the
mediocre wines from 1978 and 1979, as well as the 1977 Brunello di Montalcino Riserva, which is deficient in fruit and not concentrated enough to warrant the outrageous price tag it carries. Of course the winery will tell you these
wines need a good 24–48 hours of predrinking breathing, but my experience
suggests they decline rather than improve with airing. Certainly those consumers who want to invest in a famous label should make their reservations
now for the 1982s, the best Biondi Santi Brunellos in decades. Their great in-

tensity, high acidity, and wonderful length and richness on the palate suggest both will last 20–30 years.

BOSCARELLI
Chianti Colli Senesi* * *, Vino Nobile di Montepulciano* * * *

1988 Vino Nobile di Montepulciano Riserva	C	89

This is a beautifully made Vino Nobile, with a sweet, spicy, ripe nose of red and black fruits. In the mouth the impression is one of expansive, rich fruit, good grip, and a long, flowing finish that must last 40–45 seconds. Delicious now, this Vino Nobile should continue to evolve gracefully for another 5–7 years.

CASTELLO DI CACCHIANO
Chianti Classico* * *, Rocca di Montegrossi Rosso Vino da Tavola* *,
Rocco di Montegrossi Chianti Classico Riserva* * * *

(Note: For more information on this estate, please refer to the entry for Rocca di Montegrossi on page 677.)

1988 Chianti Classico	A	87
1986 Chianti Classico Riserva Millennio	B	86

The 1988 Chianti Classico offers a super nose of black cherries, herbs, and smoked meat. The palate confirms the fine initial impression, as this wine possesses great fruit and ripeness, wonderful intensity, a medium-bodied, supple texture, and a long, luscious finish. This is a delicious and fairly priced Chianti for drinking over the next 3–4 years. The 1986 Chianti Classico Riserva offers intense leathery, cherry, spicy aromas. In the mouth there is good sweetness of fruit and an elegant, soft, lush finish with considerable personality. Drink it over the next 4–5 years.

CAPARZO
Brunello di Montalcino* * *, Brunello di Montalcino La Casa* * * *,
Ca del Pazzo Vino da Tavola* * * *

1985 Brunello di Montalcino	D	86
1985 Brunello di Montalcino La Casa	E	89

The 1985 Brunello di Montalcino has the telltale saddle leather, sweet, cedary, spicy, earthy, berry-scented nose and expansive, round, generous flavors, with moderate tannins in the finish. It has been made in a forward, accessible style. The only problem with shorter maceration periods is that some of the concentration is sacrificed. Drinking well now, it should continue to evolve nicely for at least another 5–6 years. Caparzo's single-vineyard 1985 Brunello di Montalcino La Casa is a deeper-colored, more substantial wine with excellent concentration and, once again, a big, sweet, saddle leather, spicy, herbaceous, cedary nose. In the mouth it is fuller bodied than the regular *cuvée*, more extracted, but relatively supple and smooth for such a young Brunello di Montalcino. Despite its obvious appeal at present, it should age nicely for another 6–7 years.

CAPEZZANA
Barco Reale Vino da Tavola* * *, Ghiaie Della Furba* * *

1988 Ghiaie Della Furba	C	87

This elegant wine possesses an almost Margaux-like fragrance. Its penetrating mineral, floral, black fruit character offers considerable complexity for such a young wine. The finesse continues in the mouth, with smooth, velvety, medium-bodied flavors that exhibit good ripeness, a nice touch of toasty oak, and a long, flowing, easygoing finish. It is hard to believe this wine could get much better, as it is already evolved, graceful, and seductive. Drink it over the next 4–6 years.

CASTELL'IN VILLA
Chianti Classico* * * *, Chianti Classico Riserva* * * *,
Santa Croche Vino da Tavola* *

1985 Chianti Classico Riserva	C	88
1986 Santa Croche Vino da Tavola	D	87

At first the 1985 Chianti Classico Riserva was completely closed, revealing little character. But with 10–15 minutes of airing, a huge, herbal, leathery, cedary, earthy nose emerged. In the mouth there is medium to full body, considerable richness, and a rustic, old style. This immensely satisfying, mouth-filling Chianti is just beginning to open up; it can easily keep for another decade. The backward, densely concentrated Santa Croche needs another 2–3 years of cellaring. It boasts impressive concentration, a spicy, earthy, black fruit–scented nose intermingled with aromas of minerals and herbs. In the mouth it is full bodied, moderately tannic, but closed. A promising wine, it should be cellared until 1994–1995.

COLOGNOLE
Chianti Ruffina* * *

1990 Chianti Ruffina	A	86

A fleshy, opulently styled Chianti, this 1990 offering from Colognole is bursting with gobs of red and black fruits, displays plenty of glycerin, medium to full body, and a satiny-smooth texture. Even though it is undeniably delicious at present, it should continue to evolve for at least 2–3 years.

LE CORTI
Chianti Classico* * *, Masso Tondo Vino da Tavola* * * *

1988 Chianti Classico	B	86

Aside from being a notable value, this is a delicious, round, spicy Chianti, with gobs of fruit, a lush, supple texture, and a fine finish. There is also an underlying cherry, smoky component that adds complexity. All in all, this is a delicious, reasonably priced Chianti Classico for drinking over the next 2–3 years.

COSTANTI
Brunello di Montalcino* * * * *, Chianti Colli Senesi* *

1985 Brunello di Montalcino	D	89

This wine may very well prove to be outstanding with another 4–5 years of bottle age. It is backward and reserved, but there is no doubting its high quality. The dark ruby/garnet color suggests excellent ripeness. After an hour of breathing, the bouquet stubbornly emerges to reveal aromas of smoked meats, new saddle leather, almonds, vanilla, and red and black fruits. On the palate the wine is powerful, but tannic and closed; yet it is impressive for its strength and structure. I would not touch this wine until after another 4–5 years of bottle age. **Anticipated maturity: 1995–2010.**

DEI
Vino Nobile di Montepulciano* * * *

1990 Vino Nobile di Montepulciano	C	92

Dei's 1990 Vino Nobile di Montepulciano reveals how terrific this vintage was for Tuscany. Dei always makes good wines, but this offering has a level of richness and a headiness and length that one only sees in the greatest vintages. The stunning nose of sweet, jammy, black cherry fruit, herbs, and spices is followed by an expansive, superconcentrated wine that is full bodied and heady, with relatively high alcohol and a long, satiny, decadent finish. Drink this delicious wine now and over the next 8–10 years.

DIEVOLE
Chianti Classico Vigna Dieuele* * *, Chianti Classico Vigna Sessina* * *

1988 Chianti Classico Vigna Dieuele	85
1988 Chianti Classico Vigna Sessina	87

Both of these single-vineyard Chiantis offer attractive perfumes of ripe berry fruit, fine medium-bodied textures, excellent ripeness, good balance, and moderately soft tannins. The 1988 Vigna Sessina possesses more depth and intensity. Both wines should be consumed over the next 4–5 years.

CASTELLO DI FARNETELLA
Chianti Colli Senesi* * *

1990 Chianti Colli Senesi	B	86

This firm, earthy, intensely spicy Chianti reveals the superripeness achieved in the 1990 vintage. Deep ruby, full, and spicy, with some tannins to shed, this robust, tasty Chianti can be drunk now or cellared for 4–6 years.

FONTERUTOLI
Chianti Classico* * */* * * *, Concerto Vino da Tavola* */* * *

1990 Chianti Classico	B	86
1986 Chianti Classico Riserva Ser Lapo	C	87

Fonterutoli's 1990 Chianti Classico does not yet display much aromatic complexity. The wine reveals excellent deep ruby color, a spicy, leathery, woodsy nose, medium body, moderate tannins, and a firm, attractively full finish. It should last for 7–8 years. The attractive deep ruby/garnet color of the 1986 Chianti Riserva Ser Lapo suggests fine extraction of fruit. The nose of sweet leather, herbs, and cherries is both fragrant and persistent. In the mouth there is fine ripeness, a rich, medium-bodied texture, and attractive fruit levels in the soft, moderately long finish. Drink it over the next 4–5 years.

FONTODI

Chianti Classico* * * *, Chianti Classico Riserva Vigna del Sorbo* * * *,
Flaccianello Vino da Tavola* * * *

1990 Chianti Classico	B	87
1988 Chianti Classico Riserva Vigna del Sorbo	C	87
1986 Chianti Classico Riserva Vigna del Sorbo	C	87
1988 Flaccianello	D	89

Flaccianello, a Sangiovese-based wine, has been aged in small oak casks and is fashioned by the excellent Chianti producer Fontodi. The color is a deep ruby, and the nose offers up attractive aromas of spicy new oak, red fruits, and a whiff of herbs. In the mouth there is excellent richness, medium body, a sense of elegance, and good length in its moderately tannic, well-endowed finish. Approachable now, it should continue to age well for another 6–8 years. The 1990 Chianti Classico is an excellent wine, displaying pure, rich, spicy fruit, medium body, soft tannins, and a long, chewy finish. Delicious now, it will last for 5–7 years. The 1988 Chianti Classico Riserva is still tightly knit but exhibits beautifully pure black cherry and curranty fruit, crisp acidity, solid tannins, and a structured, well-delineated feel. Concentrated and long, it will benefit from another 1–2 years of bottle age; it has the potential to last until 2005. The 1986 Chianti Classico Riserva, aged in 30% new oak barrels, offers a moderately intense, wonderfully pure, spicy, black fruit–scented nose and soft, round, exceptionally graceful and elegant flavors. It can be drunk now or cellared for another 3–5 years.

CASTELLO DI GABBIANO

Agricoltori del Geografico Vino da Tavola* * *, Ania Vino da Tavola* * *,
Chianti Classico Riserva* * */* * * *, R & R Vino da Tavola* * *

1988 Chianti Classico Riserva Titolato	C	86
1986 R & R Vino da Tavola	D	88

This well-run estate has turned out a spicy, leathery, earthy, medium-bodied 1988 Chianti Classico Riserva Titolato. Although drinking well now, it should last until 1998–99. Even more interesting is the 1986 R & R, a Vino da Tavola made from 60% Cabernet Sauvignon and Cabernet Franc, 30% Sangiovese, and 10% Merlot. The wine is rich, with an herbaceous, cassis-scented nose, medium- to full-bodied flavors, soft tannins and acidity, and a spicy, opulent finish. It is reminiscent of a classy St.-Émilion. It should drink well until the beginning of the next century.

CANTINA GATTAVECCHI

Chianti Colli Senesi* * *

1988 Chianti Colli Senesi	B	85

This is a lighter-style Chianti, but its moderately intense, pure raspberry-scented bouquet and soft, medium-bodied flavors caress the palate, making it an ideal wine, provided one consumes it over the next 1–2 years.

GEOGRAFICO
Chianti Classico* * *, Chianti Classico Castello di Fagnano* * *,
Chianti Classico Contessa di Radda* * *

1990 Chianti Classico	A	87
1990 Chianti Classico Castello di Fagnano	A	87

This firm deserves more recognition for its delicious, reasonably priced wines. Given their quality, these two 1990 Chianti Classicos will not linger on retailers' shelves. The single-vineyard 1990 from the Castello di Fagnano offers a spicy, earthy, black cherry– and licorice-scented nose; a deep, velvety texture; medium-bodied flavors; excellent ripeness; and a spicy finish. Drink it between 1994 and 1999. The 1990 Chianti Classico also exhibits a deep ruby color; a big, spicy, smoky, roasted nut–like bouquet; ripe, medium-bodied, low-acid flavors; and plenty of glycerin and alcohol in the lusty finish. Drink it before the end of the century.

LA GIOIA DI RIECINE
Tuscan Red Wine* * *

1988 Tuscan Red Wine	C	86

This 1988 is surprisingly up-front and soft for the vintage. It offers good, spicy, leathery, berry fruitiness, medium body, and soft tannins in the highly satisfying, long finish. Drink it over the next 4–5 years.

GRACCIANO
Vino Nobile di Montepulciano* * * *

1990 Vino Nobile di Montepulciano	C	90

This is the finest wine I have tasted from Gracciano, raising hopes that this producer has moved to a new quality level. This 1990 offers a huge fragrance of flowers, roasted nuts, and sweet cherry fruit. Chewy and full bodied, with noticeably high alcohol, this forward, plump, opulently styled wine offers tons of fleshy, dramatic, black fruits. Already delicious, it should be consumed between now and 2000.

ISOLE E OLENA
Boro Cepparello Vino da Tavola* * *, Chianti Classico* * *,
Collezione de Marchi l'Ermo Vino da Tavola* * * *

1990 Chianti Classico	B	87
1988 Chianti Classico	B	86

Isole e Olena's juicy, richly fruity, densely colored 1990 Chianti Classico offers additional evidence of how fine this Tuscan vintage has turned out. The color is very deep, and the nose offers up spicy, raspberry- and cherrylike flavors. The fruit is crammed into a medium-bodied, tightly knit package with crisp acidity and light tannins in the finish. It is a vibrant, exuberant Chianti that should be drunk between 1994 and 2001. The 1988 Chianti offers a fragrant perfume of black raspberries, oak, and toast. In the mouth there is a lovely, medium-bodied, supple texture, with excellent fruit, decent acidity, and a velvety-smooth, impressively long finish. Neither large-scale nor wimpishly light, this is a tasty wine for drinking over the next 5–6 years.

LAMOLE DI LAMOLE
Chianti Classico* * *

1988 Chianti Classico	B	87
1986 Chianti Classico Riserva	C	87

A moderately dark-colored wine, the 1988 Chianti Classico offers solid aromas of black fruits and woodsy notes intermingled with the smell of herbs. In the mouth it displays a chewy, medium- to full-bodied, robust constitution, considerable tannin, and a deep, long, intensely concentrated finish. Drinkable now, it should improve and possibly merit a higher score. The 1986 Chianti Riserva displays excellent ripeness, deep color, and a wonderful herb-scented, black cherry fruitiness complemented by aromas of new saddle leather. The wine possesses an excellent spicy finish. Drink it over the next 5–6 years.

LILLIANO
Anagallis Vino da Tavola* * *, Chianti Classico* * *,
Chianti Classico Riserva Eleanora* * *

1986 Anagallis	C	89
1990 Chianti Classico	A	87
1988 Chianti Classico	A	86
1988 Chianti Classico Riserva	C	90

The 1990 Chianti Classico is the type of Chianti restaurants should be buying by the boatload. It is exuberant, rich, and fruity, with a good Chianti's classic bing cherry–, leathery–, tobacco–, and herb-scented nose; wonderfully pure, ripe, medium- to full-bodied flavors; soft tannins; and a luscious finish. It was drinking gorgeously in 1993, but there is so much fruit and body, it will easily last another 5–8 years. The chunky, deeply colored, backward 1988 Chianti Classico is densely concentrated, with spicy cedar and tobacco aromas, chocolatey, black cherry flavors, and a tough, tannic finish. It should be cellared for several years. Lilliano's terrific 1988 Chianti Classico Riserva exhibits a smoky, tobacco, curranty bouquet; full-bodied, densely concentrated flavors; impeccable balance; crisp acidity; and moderate tannins in the long finish. Once again, it was delicious and complex when tasted in spring 1993, and it promises to evolve gracefully for at least a decade.

The 1986 Anagallis is one of the most impressive proprietary red table wines I tasted from Tuscany's 1986 vintage. The big, smoky, meaty, powerful bouquet is followed by full-bodied, concentrated, rich flavors that exhibit good, soft tannins, adequate acidity, as well as plenty of intensity and length. I have to admit that when I tasted it, I was sure it was from the 1985 vintage, given its opulence, and great ripeness and depth. Drink it over the next 10 years.

LISINI
Brunello di Montalcino* * * *

1988 Brunello di Montalcino	D	90

I remember having some wonderful Lisini Brunellos in the mid-seventies, after which the quality dropped. Since the mid-eighties, this firm has been making a strong comeback. The 1988 Brunello di Montalcino offers a complex nose of roasted nuts, earth, and copious quantities of black fruits. Full bodied yet rich and concentrated, with decent acidity, moderate tannins, and a terrific finish, this precocious wine can be drunk now, but it has the requisite depth to last until 2010+.

MONSANTO

Chianti Classico Il Poggio* * * */* * * * *, Chianti Classico Riserva* * */* * * *,
Nemo Vino da Tavola* * * *, Sangioveto Grosso Vino da Tavola* * * *,
Tinscvil Vino da Tavola* * * *

1985　Chianti Classico Il Poggio	D	94
1988　Chianti Classico Riserva	C	87
1988　Nemo Vino da Tavola	D	90
1988　Tinscvil Vino da Tavola	D	90

One of the most renowned Tuscan estates, Monsanto is especially prized for its extraordinary Chianti Classicos from the Il Poggio vineyard. I have wonderful memories of the 1964, 1969, 1970, and 1971 (bottles of the latter two vintages tasted in 1993 were still holding their fruit). The 1985 Chianti Classico Il Poggio (a late-release 1985 Tuscan) is the best wine Monsanto has produced since the glorious duo of 1970 and 1971. The quality makes the wait worthwhile. Although expensive, it is exemplary juice! A huge nose of cedar, roasted berries, herbs, and tobacco leaps from the glass with remarkable intensity. The mouthfeel is one of voluptuous, superconcentrated, multidimensional fruit, glycerin, and hefty alcohol. This full-bodied, spectacular Chianti is already drinking magnificently. It can be expected to improve for at least another 7–8 years, based on past vintages, and last through most of the first decade of the next century. An exceptional wine, it serves as a benchmark for the heights Chianti can attain. The 1988 Chianti Classico Riserva is excellent. Unlike many of the 1988 Chiantis, it needs several years in the cellar to shed its considerable tannins. A deep ruby/garnet–colored wine, it boasts good concentration; a long, spicy, cedary, leathery bouquet; firm, rich, full-bodied flavors; and at least 10–12 years of aging potential. The 1988 Tinscvil Vino da Tavola is a stunning wine. Made from 70% Sangioveto/30% Cabernet Sauvignon and aged in small French oak casks, it exhibits an excellent brilliant-ruby color, and an intense bouquet of plums and other black fruits, toasty new oak, and licorice. Full bodied yet surprisingly soft, even opulent and voluptuous on the palate, this delicious, captivating wine should be drunk over the next 4–5 years. I also liked the 1988 Nemo (which in Italian means "second to none"). I would not have guessed from the taste, but as the back label indicated the wine was made from 100% Cabernet Sauvignon from a vineyard first planted in 1976. This wine, too, was aged in new, small oak casks. It was less oaky than the Tinscvil and, perhaps because it had an extra 2 years of age, it dislayed an enthrallingly complex bouquet of spices, black fruits, minerals, and Provençal herbs. Soft, plump, and succulent on the palate, with excellent concentration and length, this is another top example of what the innovative and highly motivated Italian wine producers are capable of achieving outside the existing Italian wine regulations.

CASTELLO DI NIPOZZANO DI FRESCOBALDI
Chianti Rufina Riserva* * *

1988 Chianti Rufina Riserva	C	86

Castello di Nipozzano's Chianti is made by one of the most ancient and noble Florentine families, the Frescobaldis. Their expensive wine is usually good, but rarely dazzling. This 1988 Riserva displays an attractive cherry, leathery, spicy, oaky nose suggesting the use of new wood barrels. In the mouth there is appealing ripeness and plenty of tannin, as well as an austere finish. The wine is certainly good, but I cannot see it ever evolving into anything special. Drinkable now, it should keep for at least a decade.

PODERIE IL PALAZZINO
Chianti Classico* * * *, Chianti Classico Riserva* * * *,
Grosso Senese* * * */* * * * *

1988 Chianti Classico	C	86
1988 Chianti Classico Riserva	C	90
1986 Chianti Classico Riserva	D	87
1990 Grosso Senese	D	93+
1988 Grosso Senese	D	87

During the 1980s, the Il Palazzino winery has proven to be one of the leaders in the field, not only for their beautifully crafted, concentrated, elegant Chiantis, but also for their proprietary red wine made from 100% Sangiovese, Grosso Senese. The 1988 is shaping up as the best vintage for Chianti since 1985. Despite pronouncements from the trade that it is better than 1985, I do not believe that to be the case. The wines are a bit more narrowly constructed, with higher acidity and less ripeness and lusciousness. They have more tannin and structure but lack the forward, opulent joys of the 1985s, which to me is the benchmark Tuscan vintage. Il Palazzino's 1988 Chianti Classico has a saturated deep ruby/purple color; a spicy, vanillin- and red currant–scented nose; medium-bodied flavors exhibiting fine flavor extraction; good, crisp acidity; moderate tannins; and an overall sense of tightness and good structure. It is a Chianti that has been built to last for at least 5–7 years. Although drinkable now, it ideally needs another year or 2 in the bottle. The 1988 Chianti Classico Riserva is one of the stars of the vintage. An exquisite nose of raspberries and spices is followed by a deep, rich, generously endowed wine with soft acidity, huge masses of fruit buttressed by oak and glycerin. Drink this rich, medium- to full-bodied, dramatic Chianti between now and 2002. The 1986 Chianti Classico Riserva is one of the best examples I have tasted from a good rather than excellent vintage. The wines tend to be much more forward than the 1988s, and the best examples have enough fruit to cover their frames. Il Palazzino's Chianti Classico Riserva, with its intense, sweet, plummy, oaky nose and rich, round, amply endowed, medium-bodied flavors, exhibits fine winemaking. There is plenty of supple, lush fruit in the finish, and this wine should continue to drink well for another 5–6 years. The best Grosso Senese I have tasted from Il Palazzino is the 1985. I do not think the 1988 will turn out to be that good. It is not nearly as concentrated, and at present it is extremely hard, tightly knit, and exhibiting a great deal of tannin. However, as it sits in the glass, a big oaky, cassis nose emerges, and in the mouth, once past the tannin and crisp acidity, there is plenty of ripeness, extraction, and a relatively long, medium-bodied finish. Much like the Chianti Classico, the Grosso Senese could benefit from 1–2 years of bottle age. It should last up to 10 years. By the way, purchasers of the glorious 1985 Grosso Senese can begin drinking it. The last bottle I had was stunning. The 1990 Grosso Senese exhibits more promise than flattering aromas and flavors. It displays an impressively saturated dark ruby/purple color and a reticent but emerging bouquet of smoky oak, leafy tobacco, and copious quantities of black raspberry fruit. The tannins and surprisingly high acidity give the wine a toughness and backward feel, but this is one case where there is more than enough fruit to carry it for 10–15 years. Impressive—but, patience is essential! **Anticipated maturity: 1998–2010.**

CASTELLO DELLA PANERETTA
Chianti Classico* * *

1988 Chianti Classico	C	87

Paneretta has turned out a cleanly made, modern-style red wine. The color is an admirably deep ruby, and the nose offers up pure scents of black cherries, spicy oak, and a touch of earth. In the mouth the wine is medium bodied, with fine concentration and elegance, as well as a long, crisp, moderately tannic finish. Enjoyable now, it should easily last for 5–6 years.

PERTIMALI
Brunello di Montalcino* * * * *, Rosso di Montalcino* * * *

1988 Brunello di Montalcino	D	95+
1987 Brunello di Montalcino	D	89
1985 Brunello di Montalcino	D	92
1991 Rosso di Montalcino	B	82
1990 Rosso di Montalcino	C	87
1988 Rosso di Montalcino	C	88

This tiny estate makes some of the finest red wines in Tuscany. The 1991 Rosso di Montalcino underscores what a tough vintage this was. It is tart and lean, but there is some pleasant, clean fruit and enough richness to carry it until 1997. The 1990 Rosso di Montalcino is a much richer, fuller wine, with a huge, earthy, leathery, black cherry–scented nose; round, generous, succulent flavors; plenty of body; and plenty of glycerin and soft tannins in the finish. Drink it between 1994 and 2002. The 1988 Rosso di Montalcino offers a fragrant, broad nose of damp earth, rich, plummy, black cherry fruit, leather, and licorice. In the mouth there is sweet, expansive fruit, full body, plenty of glycerin, soft tannins, and an impressively long finish. Drinking beautifully now, it should continue to provide exciting tasting for at least 5–7 more years.

I am beginning to think that if I had only one Brunello di Montalcino to drink, it would have to be Pertimali. This producer has been making spectacular wines since 1982. Unfortunately quantities are microscopic, making availability a major headache. The awesome and inspirational 1988 Brunello di Montalcino is superextracted, with an opaque, deep ruby/purple color and a highly promising nose of roasted nuts, black fruits, herbs, and Asian spices. The wine is massively rich yet impeccably well balanced, with fabulous purity and a multidimensional feel to it. If you can find any, it is a must purchase. **Anticipated maturity: 1997–2010.** The 1987 Brunello di Montalcino is unquestionably a top success for this vintage. It exhibits a superb nose of truffles and earthy, black, plum and cherry fruit. Spicy, with surprising richness, medium to full body, and an expansive, soft, velvety finish, it should drink well through 2003. The 1985 Brunello di Montalcino is a worthy successor to Pertimali's superb 1982 and 1983 Brunellos. With a deep opaque color and a huge nose of grilled meats, saddle leather, and roasted black fruits, this opulent, sensationally rich wine exhibits brilliant delineation to its intense, full-bodied flavors. Surprisingly soft for an 8-year-old Brunello, it can be drunk now or cellared for 10–15 years.

PETROIO
Chianti Classico Montetondo* * *, L'Unico Vino da Tavola* * *

1990 Chianti Classico Montetondo	B	85
1990 L'Unico	D	86

Petroio's 1990 Chianti Classico Montetondo is an elegant, stylish, fruity wine with soft tannins, an attractive berry fruitiness, and a smooth finish. It should be drunk before the end of 1987. Petroio's Vino da Tavola, a Cabernet Sauvignon/Merlot/Sangiovese blend, is aged in new oak casks. Despite its rich, jammy, cassis-scented nose, wonderful ripeness, and medium- to full-bodied character, it lacks the complexity and length to merit a higher rating. Perhaps that will emerge, but my advice is to drink it between 1994 and 2000.

CIACCI PICCOLOMINI D'ARAGONA
Rosso di Montalcino* * * *, Brunello di Montalcino* * * * *

1990 Rosso di Montalcino	B	90
1988 Rosso di Montalcino	B	89

These wines, two of the most stunning Rosso di Montalcinos I have ever tasted, sell for one-third to one-fourth the price of the winery's Brunello di Montalcino. The 1990 reveals a dense, highly saturated, deep ruby/purple color. The nose offers up sweet smells of black fruits, minerals, herbs, and spices. In the mouth there is massive concentration, full body, and moderate tannins in the long finish. Given the ripeness, glycerin, and richness, this wine can be drunk now, but it promises to improve for at least 7–10 years. I should also note that the label indicates this wine was produced from a single vineyard called Vigna della Fonte. Can you imagine how profound this producer's Brunello di Montalcino must be in 1990? The 1988 offering is deeply colored, with an intense nose of jammy black cherries, cedar, and Provençal herbs. In the mouth there is exceptional richness, a big, full-bodied, brawny texture, and an explosively fruity, luscious, voluptuous finish. Drink this terrific wine over the next 6–7 years.

POGGIO AL SORBO
Chianti Classico* *

1990 Chianti Classico	B	85

This Chianti Classico reveals what appear to be the virtues of the 1990 vintage—super ripeness, low acidity, soft tannins, and plenty of fruit. Displaying an excellent medium to dark ruby color, a straightforward, immensely enjoyable berry-scented nose, medium body, and a fleshy, velvety-textured finish, this is a Chianti meant for drinking over the next 3–4 years.

POGGIO ANTICO
Altero Vino da Tavola* * * *, Brunello di Montalcino* * * */* * * * *

1986 Altero Tuscan Red Wine	D	88

Readers may remember that I extolled Poggio Antico's 1985 Brunello di Montalcino as one of the best Brunellos of that vintage. This winery appears to have the magic touch when it comes to obtaining complexity and rich, ripe fruit in their wines. They have released a 1986 new-breed Tuscan wine called Altero, which displays a ruby/garnet color, a fully mature nose of sweet saddle leather, and jammy, herb-scented red and black fruits. On the palate the wine is admirably endowed with ripe tannins, low acidity, and a fleshy, long, delicious finish.

POGGIO SALVI
Brunello di Montalcino* * * *, Brunello di Montalcino Riserva* * * *

1985 Brunello di Montalcino	D	88
1982 Brunello di Montalcino Riserva	E	90

These two well-made, traditionally styled Brunellos are clearly from the old school of winemaking, where aromas such as smoke, mushrooms, and dried pit fruits dominate the style of the wine. The 1985 is not ready to drink, but one has to admire its high concentration levels, mouth-watering acidity, huge body, and long, intense, tannic finish. There is plenty of aging potential, but I would not touch a bottle for another 2–3 years. It is the type of wine that can last for 15–20 years. Given how good the regular *cuvée* of 1985 is, one would expect the 1982 Riserva to be awesome. The 1982 Riserva has reached full maturity and displays a sensational bouquet of tobacco, smoke, earthy blackcurrants, truffles, and aged beef. In the mouth the wine is round, generous, and full bodied, with gobs of fruit and a long, intense, supple finish. Drinkable now, it should continue to evolve for at least 5–10 years, perhaps much longer.

IL POGGIOLO–ROBERTO COSIMI
Brunello di Montalcino* * * *, Chianti Colli Senesi* *

1985 Brunello di Montalcino	D	90

Here is another excellent example of a young, promising, full-bodied, muscular Brunello di Montalcino that should be laid away for at least 4–5 years. Dark ruby/garnet, with a big, spicy, leathery, mushroomy, smoky, animal-scented aroma, this intense, full-bodied, tannic wine is jammed with fruit and has an impressively long finish. Ideally I would cellar this Brunello for at least 4–5 years and drink it between 1995 and 2010.

IL POGGIONE–R. FRANCESCHI

Brunello di Montalcino* * * *, Brunello di Montalcino Riserva* * * *

1985 Brunello di Montalcino Riserva	D	88

I would not be surprised to see this wine prove to be outstanding with another 4–5 years of cellaring. The color is a dense, dark ruby, and the backward nose is extremely promising with its scents of smoked meats, nuts, black fruits, and leather. In the mouth this austere, full-bodied, impressively concentrated wine appears to have the requisite depth needed to balance out the high level of tannins. Do not touch this wine for at least 3–4 years; it should last for 15–20 years.

POLIZIANO

Elegia Vino da Tavola* * * */* * * * *, Le Stanze Vino da Tavola* * * *,
Vino Nobile di Montepulciano* * * *

1988 Elegia	D	90
1988 Le Stanze	D	90
1988 Vino Nobile di Montepulciano	C	88

My first look at these wines left a memorable impression. The 1988 Vino Nobile di Montepulciano possesses an opaque, dark ruby/garnet color and a spicy, oaky nose filled with aromas of saddle leather, ripe red and black fruits, and smoked nuts. In the mouth it is rich, medium to full bodied, with good underlying structure and acidity, as well as plenty of tannin, glycerin, and extraction of fruit in the finish. Because of the soft tannins, the wine is approachable now, but it should only get better as it ages over the next 10–12 years. Poliziano's 1988 Elegia, made from 100% Cabernet Sauvignon, was aged in new oak casks. This dark ruby/purple-colored wine is immensely impressive. It is made in a Bordeaux style, with its fragrant vanillin, toasty, cassis-scented aromas, medium- to full-bodied flavors, superb extraction of fruit, moderate tannins, and long, intense finish. This world-class Cabernet Sauvignon should age extremely well for at least a decade. Last, the 1988 Le Stanze, a wine made from 100% Sangiovese, was also immensely impressive. The dark ruby/purple color is followed by a big, earthy, leathery, curranty nose that exhibits fine intensity and admirable purity. In the mouth this medium- to full-bodied wine displays considerable flavor extraction, soft tannins, adequate acidity, and a long, rich finish. Approachable now, it should improve with another 4–6 years of age and last for at least 10–12.

CASTELLO DI QUERCETO

Chianti Classico* * * *, Chianti Classico Riserva* * * *,
La Corte Vino da Tavola* * * *, Il Querciolaia Vino da Tavola* * * *

1988 Chianti Classico	B	86
1986 Chianti Classico Riserva	B	88

Deep ruby in color, with a fragrant, spicy nose of cedar, herbs, and dried cherry fruit, this ripe, medium-bodied, tasty 1988 Chianti Classico exhibits good fruit, adequate acidity, and soft tannins in the finish. Drink it over the next 4–5 years. The 1986 Riserva has been a popular wine among some of my friends who consume considerable quantities of Chianti. The excellent nose of spicy, earthy, black fruits and minerals is followed by a deeply concentrated, intense, expansively flavored wine that displays excellent sweetness of fruit. The velvety finish should please hedonists. Drink it over the next 5–6 years.

QUERCETORTO
Chianti Classico Riserva* * * *

1985 Chianti Classico Riserva	A	88

This small estate has a considerable cult following for its rich, lusty, complex Chiantis. The 1985 is a worthy successor to the fine 1981 and 1983. A huge, smoky, tobacco-, leather-, and ripe fruit–scented bouquet is impressive. Velvety, generous, full-bodied flavors linger and linger. This is a top-flight, immensely enjoyable Chianti for a super price.

QUERCIABELLA
Carmartina Vino da Tavola* * *, Chianti Classico* * * *

1988 Chianti Classico	B	87

The seductively fragrant, rich nose of black cherries, herbs, leather, and smoked duck is followed by a concentrated, medium-bodied wine with excellent extract levels, zesty acidity, and ripe, soft tannins in the supple finish. This is a beautiful Chianti for drinking over the next 5–6 years.

S. QUIRICO
Chianti* * *

1990 Chianti	A	87

This is a controversial style of Chianti, with a bouquet that offers rich, earthy, berry scents combined with aromas of grilled sausage. The wine reveals an expansive, soft texture, excellent ripeness and depth, fine length, and an overall round, generous personality. Drink it between 1994 and 1998.

CASTELLO DI RAMPOLLA
Chianti Classico* * * *, Sammarco Vino da Tavola* * * * *

1988 Chianti Classico	C	86

The Castello di Rampolla is one of my favorite Tuscan producers. Their 1988 Chianti Classico is closed and surprisingly tannic, but the deep, dark color and the weighty, ripe fruit are more than sufficient to stand up to the wine's tannin level. I would not want to drink this Chianti without another year of cellaring. It has the potential to last up to 10 years.

ROCCA DELLE MACIE-TENUTA SANT'ALFONSO
Chianti Classico* * *, Granchiaia Vino da Tavola* *

1988 Chianti Classico	B	86

A spicy, almost mushroomy, woodsy, black fruit–scented nose is followed by surprisingly deep, chunky flavors that exhibit excellent concentration and considerable tannins and toughness. Not yet ready for drinking, this wine will benefit from 1–2 years of cellaring.

ROCCA DI MONTEGROSSI
Chianti Classico* * * *, Chianti Classico Riserva* * * *,
Geremia Vino da Tavola* * * *

(Note: For more information on this estate, please refer to the entry for Castello di Cacchiano on page 664.)

1990 Chianti Classico	C	89
1988 Chianti Classico Riserva	C	86
1988 Geremia	D	92

One can easily see the difference between the 1988 and 1990 Chianti vintages in these two offerings. The excellent 1988 Chianti Classico Riserva is crisp, tight, with relatively hard tannins but fine underlying ripeness and rich fruit. Its firmness and structure suggest to me that the tannins will probably outlive the fruit. Drink it over the next 7–8 years. On the other hand, the 1990 Chianti Classico exhibits a gorgeously perfumed, sensual nose of black fruits, wonderful purity, a voluptuous texture, medium to full body, and a satiny-textured finish. It is gorgeous for drinking over the next 6–7 years. The 1988 Geremia, which is aged in small new oak casks, offers a huge, sweet, vanillin, toasty, black fruit–scented nose, rich, full-bodied flavors, stunning balance and focus, and an explosively long, rich finish. The new oak has tamed some of the tannins, resulting in a wine that should be drunk between now and 2002.

ROCCADORO
Chianti Classico* * *

1990 Chianti Classico	86

This wine possesses an attractive ruby color and a nose that consists mostly of cherry fruit, smoke, and earth. Although not the most complex 1990 Chianti Classico, it offers an exuberance and purity to its medium-bodied, ripe, fruity personality.

RUFFINO
Cabreo Il Borgo Vino da Tavola* * *, Chianti Classico* * *,
Chianti Classico Aziano* * *, Chianti Classico Nozzole* * *,
Chianti Classico Riserva Ducale* * * *, Nero del Tondo Vino da Tavola* *

1988 Chianti Classico Aziano	A	85
1988 Chianti Classico Nozzole	A	86
1985 Chianti Classico Riserva Ducale	C	89

Ruffino's 1988 offerings are made in an up-front, jammy, richly fruity style that offers considerable attraction and charm. I would opt for drinking the medium-bodied, vividly pure, fragrant, soft 1988 Aziano over the next 1–3 years. There is no question that the 1988 Nozzole is deeper, with more evidence of toasty wood in the background. In addition, it is riper, with more tannin, and the finish is bigger and slightly more persuasive. This fuller, bigger wine can hold up to 5–7 years of cellaring. One of the later-released 1985s, the Chianti Classico Riserva Ducale, which has been on the market for nearly a year, is typical of that sensational vintage. Although the color is beginning to take on some garnet at the edge, it is saturated and impressive. The big, spicy nose of black cherries, herbs, leather, and earth is followed by a full-bodied, rich, concentrated wine with huge reserves of fruit, glycerin, and soft tannins. The authoritative finish is stunning. This wine will not reach its peak for several years, at which time it may merit an outstanding rating. Drink it over the next decade.

SALVIONI-CERBAIOLA

Brunello di Montalcino* * * * *, Rosso di Montalcino* * * *

1986 Brunello di Montalcino	E	89
1985 Brunello di Montalcino	E	92
1988 Rosso di Montalcino	C	87

My first look at this producer's wines left a favorable impression. The attractive characteristic of a good Rosso di Montalcino is that it possesses all the leathery, berry, earthy, spicy fruitiness of a Brunello without the tannin and weight. This 1988 Rosso di Montalcino displays a supple texture, a fragrant perfume of dried red fruits, herbs, and saddle leather, a luscious texture, and plenty of heady alcohol in the finish. Drink it over the next 5–6 years. Salvioni made a relatively firm, tannic, structured 1986 Brunello di Montalcino that is already revealing some attractive spicy, fruitcake aromas intertwined with scents of damp earth and leather. In the mouth there is medium to full body, moderate tannins, and a long finish. The 1985 Brunello di Montalcino enjoys a more saturated color as well as a more intense, riper perfume. The aromas of gorgeously rich black fruits and Oriental spices are followed by a full-bodied, magnificently rich wine that still has considerable tannin to shed. This superb Brunello can be drunk now, but it promises to be even better with another 3–4 years of cellaring. It should last for 10–15 years or more.

SAN FELICE

Chianti Classico* *, Chianti Classico Riserva Il Grigio* *,
San Felice Vino da Tavola* *, Vigorello Vino da Tavola* * *

1990 Chianti Classico	A	85
1988 Chianti Classico Riserva Il Grigio	B	86

These two somewhat commercially oriented Chiantis have been made in a clean, fruity, soft style ideal for drinking between now and 1995. The 1990 Chianti Classico possesses vibrant fruit, light to medium body, soft tannins, and low acidity. The 1988 Il Grigio Riserva exhibits more substance but is soft, round, and charming. It should be drunk by the end of 1996.

SAN GIUSTO A RENTENTANO

Chianti Classico* * * *, Percarlo Vino da Tavola* * * * *

1990 Chianti Classico	B	86
1988 Chianti Classico	B	88
1988 Chianti Classico Riserva	C	88+
1986 Chianti Classico Riserva	C	88
1990 Percarlo	E	93

This producer has released some thrilling wines over the last few years, particularly their 1985 proprietary red table wine called Percarlo (rated 96 in June

1993). Their dense 1988 Chianti Classico offers beautiful, pure, spicy, smoked cherry- and nutlike aromas that are followed by superripe, rich, concentrated flavors, medium to full body, and a long, lusty finish. This terrific Chianti may merit a higher score once all the tannins have melted away. The 1986 Chianti Riserva reveals some evidence of spicy, toasty new oak to go along with its big, black and red fruit–scented nose. In the mouth there is sweet, ripe fruit, medium body, and a long, moderately tannic finish. Although drinkable now, it has the potential to last for another 7–8 years. The most recent San Giusto releases include their 1990 Chianti Classico, a surprisingly light wine for this producer, made in an up-front, fruity, medium-bodied style with spicy, cherry fruit, soft tannins, and enough richness to carry it until 1998. The 1988 Chianti Classico Riserva is a more complete and complex wine, exhibiting a deep ruby color and an excellent nose of saddle leather, black fruits, herbs, tobacco, and spice. Rich and dense, with layer upon layer of richly extracted fruit, this youthful, bigger-style Chianti should reach its peak by 1995 and last for 10 years. The seductive 1990 Percarlo is a worthy rival to the otherworldly 1985 Percarlo. The deep ruby/purple color is followed by a nose that offers abundant amounts of smoky, toasty new oak and cassis. Voluptuous, medium to full bodied, with exceptional concentration and delineation, this rich Vino da Tavola has consistently been one of the stars of Tuscany. **Anticipated maturity: 1995–2010.**

SAN GUIDO
Sassicaia* * * * *

1988 Sassicaia	E 90

This firmly structured, medium-weight, restrained example of Sassicaia exhibits an impressive deep, dark ruby color and a perfumed, superripe nose of black fruits and toasty vanillin from aging in new oak casks. In the mouth there is excellent concentration, crisp acidity, and plenty of tannin, glycerin, and alcohol in the admirable finish. Though it is not as multidimensional or as concentrated as the otherworldly 1985, nor as opulent as the 1982, it is nevertheless another brilliant example of the heights Cabernet Sauvignon can achieve in the soils of Tuscany.

RATINGS FOR OLDER VINTAGES OF SAN GUIDO SASSICAIA: 1986(86), 1985(100), 1983(87), 1982(94), 1981(90), 1980(84), 1979(84)

SOLDERA
Brunello di Montalcino* * * *, Soldera Intistieri Vino da Tavola* * */* * * *

1986 Brunello di Montalcino	E 89

Made in an elegant style, this precocious Brunello already provides delicious drinking. The color is dark ruby, and the nose offers up classy aromas of sweet currant fruit and spices. The wine is medium to full bodied, with surprisingly soft tannins, a sure-handed sense of elegance and style, and a long, rich, extremely well-balanced finish. I suspect this impressive Brunello—unburdened by excessive earthiness or astringent tannins—should continue to drink well for at least a decade.

GUICCIARDINI STROZZI
Sodole Vino da Tavola* * * */* * * * *

1988 Sodole	D	87

I remember awarding wildly enthusiastic notes to this producer's 1985 Sodole. Although the 1988 is neither as concentrated nor as potentially profound, it is still a delicious, generously endowed, complex wine that is already offering aromas of herbs, berry fruit, and earth. In the mouth there is medium to full body, soft tannins, low acidity, and a gentle, supple texture. Drink it over the next 5–6 years.

TALOSA
Chianti* * *, Rosso di Montalcino* * *, Vino Nobile di Montepulciano* * *

1990 Chianti	A	86
1990 Rosso di Montalcino	C	88

Talosa's bargain-priced 1990 Chianti offers wonderfully ripe fruit, a lovely chewy texture, vivid purity, and a tasty, medium-bodied, heady finish. It is all a Chianti should be—satisfying and a joy to drink. Consume it between 1994 and 1998. The 1990 Rosso di Montalcino is even deeper, with a superb nose of black fruits and spices. Unctuous, thick, and soft, this low-acid, hedonistic Rosso di Montalcino will provide considerable pleasure if drunk between 1994 and 2000.

TOSCOLO
Chianti Classico* * *, Chianti Classico Riserva* * *

1990 Chianti Classico	A	85
1985 Chianti Classico Riserva	B	85

The 1990 Chianti Classico exhibits a straightforward but intense red fruit character, medium body, soft tannins, and a velvety, lusciously fruity finish. Drink it over the next 2–3 years. The spicy, ripe, leathery, almond-, and black cherry–scented and -flavored 1985 Chianti Classico Riserva is medium bodied, with soft, well-endowed flavors and a good, spicy, heady finish. It is an ideal Chianti for drinking over the next 3–4 years.

TREROSE
Vino Nobile di Montepulciano* * *

1985 Vino Nobile di Montepulciano Riserva	C	86

This spicy, full-bodied, sweet, ready-to-drink wine offers considerable flavor complexity and lusciousness on the palate. The tannins have melted away, and the result is an expansive, nicely extracted, round wine with good grip and a long, heady finish. Despite its current drinkability, given its balance, extract levels, and general harmony, it should continue to age well for at least another 5–6 years.

VAL DI SUGA
Brunello di Montalcino* * * *

1985 Brunello di Montalcino	D	90

Purists might quibble over the fact that this excellent Brunello is drinking so well at such a young age, but there is no doubting the beautiful fragrance of red and black fruits, spices, cedar, coffee, and smoked meats. In the mouth this expansive, full-bodied wine has excellent flavor concentration; ripe, soft, moderate tannins; decent acidity; and a long, heady, nearly explosive finish. This is undeniably a great Brunello di Montalcino for drinking over the next 8–12 years.

VIGNAMAGGIO
Chianti Classico* * * *, Chianti Classico Riserva* * * *

1988 Chianti Classico	B	87
1985 Chianti Classico Riserva	C	86

The big, earthy, spicy, woodsy aromas of the 1988 Chianti Classico are followed by a wine with gobs of rich bing cherry fruit, fine extraction and balance, and a long, spicy, moderately tannic finish. Drinkable now, it should last for 5–6 years. Evidence continues to mount that 1985 is the finest vintage Tuscany has enjoyed in at least 15 years. This rich, concentrated 1985 Chianti Classico Riserva has a big, bold, mushroomy, spicy, black fruit–scented nose, medium- to full-bodied flavors, and a long, spicy, meaty finish. Drinkable now, it should continue to shed some of its tannins and evolve gracefully over the next 4–6 years.

VILLA CILNIA
Chianti Colli Aretini* * *, Le Vignacce Vino da Tavola* * */* * * *,
Vocato Vino da Tavola* * *

1990 Chianti Colli Aretini	A	85
1988 Vocato	C	86

It appears that 1990 will be an exciting Tuscan vintage. This 1990 Chianti Colli Aretini is light to medium bodied, wonderfully fruity, soft, and round, with an easygoing, velvety finish. Drink it over the next 2–3 years. Villa Cilnia's 1988 Vocato, their proprietary wine, offers considerable elegance, soft, cherry fruitiness, medium body, low acidity, and a round, smooth finish. It should be consumed over the next 2–4 years.

VITICCIO
Chianti Classico* * *, Prunaio Vino da Tavola* * * *

1988 Chianti Classico	B	87

This supple, fruity Chianti is not likely to improve, but I admired it for the superripe aromas of black and red fruits and supple, medium-bodied fruit flavors. The finish is long and satiny. Drink it over the next several years.

CASTELLO DI VOLPAIA
Chianti Classico* * *, Chianti Classico Riserva* * *

1986 Chianti Classico Riserva	C	87

It is not surprising that this consistently fine producer's 1986 Chianti Riserva reveals a sweet nose of ripe raspberry fruit, spicy wood, and a touch of vanillin intermingled with scents of flowers. There is excellent concentration, a round, long, medium-bodied texture that exhibits fine extraction of fruit, and a soft, gentle finish. Drink it over the next 4–5 years.

TUSCANY'S WHITE WINES

Improvements are certainly noticeable, but the overall situation with respect to Tuscany's white wines remains deplorable. Although much has been made of the modern style of white winemaking, Tuscany continues to rely on high-tech processing to fashion too many white wines that are (1) bland and fruitless, (2) packaged in designer bottles, and (3) sold at $20 and up a bottle. Wines such as Frescobaldi's Pomino, Antinori's Galestro, and the wave of luxury-priced, designer-packaged Chardonnays (such as Castello d'Albola's Le Fagge, Castellare's Canonico, Felsina Berardenga's I Sistri, Castello di Ama's Vigna al Poggio, Caparzo's Le Grance, Banfi's Fontanelle, Montellori's Castelrapiti, and Ruffino's Cabreo la Pietra and Libaio, a Chardonnay/Sauvignon blend, are frightfully overpriced and usually too oaky. I find it hard to believe that consumers are gullible enough to buy these slick products.

The only Tuscan white wine that I can recommend consistently is the Vernaccia di San Gimignano from the best producers. It is not made from overoaked Chardonnay or from the bland, neutral, tart Trebbiano, but from the Vernaccia grape that comes from the amazing, medieval, fortified hill town of San Gimignano. At its best, it is refreshingly crisp, light, nutty flavored, and dry, and it is a wonderful match with fish or chicken. The best recent vintage is 1990, but many of the 1990s may be tiring. The 1991s are correct wines, and the early released 1992s are light, fruity, and good, but not as rich and complete as the 1990s once were.

VERNACCIA DI SAN GIMIGNANO RECOMMENDED PRODUCERS

For the last 15 years the finest Vernaccias have come from the following producers:
Falchini
di Pancole
Pietraserena Vigna del Sol
Guiccardini Strozzi
Guiccardini Strozzi San Biagio Riserva
Teruzzi & Puthod
Teruzzi & Puthod Terre di Tufo

OTHER TUSCAN WHITE WINES OF MERIT

Avignonesi Bianco Vergine Valdichiana
Avignonesi Il Vignola (Sauvignon Blanc)
Fontodi Meriggio (Traminer/Pinot Bianco/Sauvignon blend)
Poliziano Bianco Vergine Valdichiana
La Stella Lunaia Bianco di Pitigliano

OTHER SIGNIFICANT WHITE WINES OF ITALY

Below are some other attractive dry white wines produced in Italy. They represent a balanced approach to winemaking. Some may have benefited from new oak, but the fruit, not the wood, dominates the wine's character. Moreover, these wines are a class above the bulk of Italy's eviscerated, neutral, and innocuous white wines.

Note: Vintages vary in quality, but these producers consistently perform better than their peers in good and bad years.

PRODUCER	BEST WINES	VINTAGES TO BUY	PRICE CODE	RATING
Abbazia di Rosazzo	Pinot Bianco	(1990, 1991)	C	***
Abbazia di Rosazzo	Ronco Acacie	(1990, 1991)	C	***
Abbazia di Rosazzo	Sauvignon	(1990, 1991)	C	**
Abbazia di Rosazzo	Tocai	(1990, 1991)	C	***
Anselmi	Soave	(1990, 1991)	C	***
Anselmi	Soave Capitel Foscarino	(1990, 1991)	B	****
Bellavista	N. V. Brut Sparkling	(nonvintage)	C	***
Bellavista	Franciacorta Brut	(1990, 1991)	C	***
Bellavista	Gran Cuvée Pas Opere	(1990, 1991)	C	***
Berlucchi	Cuvée Imperiale Brut	(nonvintage)	C	***
Berlucchi	Cuvée Rose Imperiale Brut	(nonvintage)	C	***
Bigi	Orvieto Classico	(1990, 1991)	B	**
Bisci	Verdicchio	(1991)	B	***
Bisci	Verdicchio Fogliano	(1991)	B	***
Bisci	Verdicchio Matelica	(1991)	B	***
Borgo Conventi	Chardonnay	(1990, 1991)	C	***
Borgo Conventi	Pinot Bianco	(1990, 1991)	C	***
Borgo Conventi	Pinot Grigio	(1990, 1991)	C	***
Borgo Conventi	Tocai	(1990, 1991)	C	***
Bortoluzzi	Chardonnay	(1990, 1991)	C	***
Bortoluzzi	Foian Blanc	(1990, 1991)	C	***
Bortoluzzi	Pinot Grigio	(1990, 1991)	C	***
Boscaini	Soave	(1990, 1991)	B	***
Bucci	Verdicchio	(1990, 1991)	C	***
Ca' del Bosco	Brut Méthode Champenoise	(nonvintage)	D	**/***
Ca' del Bosco	Chardonnay	(1990, 1991)	D	**/***
Ca' del Bosco	Dosage Zéro	(nonvintage)	D	**/***
Ca' del Bosca	Rosé Brut Sparkling	(nonvintage)	D	**/***
La Cadalora	Chardonnay	(1991)	B	***
La Cadalora	Pinot Bianco	(1991)	B	***
La Cadalora	Pinot Grigio	(1991)	B	***
La Cadalora	Sauvignon	(1991)	B	***
La Castellada	Chardonnay	(1991)	B	**
La Castellada	Pinot Grigio	(1991)	B	**
La Castellada	Ribolla Gialla	(1991)	B	**
La Castellada	Sauvignon	(1991)	B	**
La Castellada	Tocai	(1991)	B	**
Enofriulia	Müller-Thurgau	(1990, 1991)	B	***/****
Enofriulia	Pinot Grigio	(1990, 1991)	B	***/****
Enofriulia	Tocai	(1990, 1991)	B	***/****

PRODUCER	BEST WINES	VINTAGES TO BUY	PRICE CODE	RATING
Foss Marai	Prosecco Sparkling	(1991)	C	***
F. Furlan	Pinot Grigio	(1990, 1991)	B	***
F. Furlan	Ribolla Gialla	(1990, 1991)	B	***
F. Furlan	Tocai	(1990, 1991)	B	***
Alois Lageder	Chardonnay	(1991)	B	**
Alois Lageder	Pinot Bianco	(1991)	B	**
Alois Lageder	Pinot Grigio	(1991)	B	**
Alois Lageder	Sauvignon	(1991)	B	**
Maculan	Breganze di Breganze	(1990, 1991)	C	****
Maculan	Chardonnay	(1990, 1991)	C	****
Maculan	Prato di Canzio	(1990, 1991)	C	****
Marini (Trevi)	Chardonnay	(1990, 1991)	A	**
Marini (Trevi)	Pinot Grigio	(1990, 1991)	A	**
Mastroberardino	Fiano di Avellino Vignadora	(1990, 1991)	D	**
Mastroberardino	Greco di Tufo Vigna d'Angelo	(1990, 1991)	D	**
Mastroberardino	Plinius	(1990, 1991)	C	**
Maso Poli	Chardonnay	(1990, 1991)	B	***
Maso Poli	Pinot Grigio	(1990, 1991)	B	***
Mirafiore	Soave	(1990, 1991)	B	***
Il Palazzone	Orvieto Terre Vineate	(1991)	B	***
Il Palazzone	Orvieto Campo Del Guardino	(1991)	B	***
Puiatti	Chardonnay	(1991)	C	****
Puiatti	Pinot Bianco	(1991)	C	****
Puiatti	Pinot Grigio	(1991)	C	****
Puiatti	Riesling	(1991)	C	****
Puiatti	Sauvignon	(1991)	C	****
Guerrieri Rizzardi	Dogoli	(1990, 1991)	B	***
Guerrieri Rizzardi	Soave Costeggiola	(1990, 1991)	B	***
Ronchi di Fornaz	Pinot Bianco	(1990, 1991)	B	***
Ronchi di Fornaz	Tocai	(1990, 1991)	B	***
Roncho del Gnemiz	Chardonnay	(1990, 1991)	B	****
Roncho del Gnemiz	Müller-Thurgau	(1990, 1991)	B	****
Roncho del Gnemiz	Pinot Grigio	(1990, 1991)	B	****
Roncho del Gnemiz	Tocai Fiulano	(1990, 1991)	B	****
Ruffino	Monte Rossa Rosé Sparkling	(nonvintage)	C	**
Santa Margherita	Chardonnay	(1991)	C	***/****
Santa Margherita	Luna dei Feldi	(1991)	C	***/****
Santa Margherita	Pinot Grigio	(1991)	C	***/****
Mario Schiopetto	Blanc des Roses	(1991)	C	****
Mario Schiopetto	Ribolla	(1991)	C	****
Mario Schiopetto	Riesling Renano	(1991)	C	****
Castel Schwanburg	Chardonnay	(1990, 1991)	C	**
Castel Schwanburg	Pinot Grigio	(1990, 1991)	B	**
Tedeschi	Bianco di Custoza	(1990, 1991)	B	***

PRODUCER	BEST WINES	VINTAGES TO BUY	PRICE CODE	RATING
J. Tiefenbrunner	Chardonnay	(1990, 1991)	B	***/****
J. Tiefenbrunner	Pinot Grigio	(1990, 1991)	B	***/****
Valentini	Trebbiano d'Abruzzi	(1990, 1991)	D	****
Vie di Romans	Chardonnay	(1991)	C	****
Vie di Romans	Flor d'Uis	(1991)	C	****
Vie di Romans	Pinot Grigio	(1991)	C	****
Vie di Romans	Sauvignon Piere	(1991)	C	****
Vie di Romans	Sauvignon Vieris	(1991)	C	****
Vie di Romans	Tocai Friulano	(1991)	C	****
Villanova	Chardonnay	(1991)	C	***
Villanova	Pinot Bianco	(1991)	C	***
Villanova	Pinot Grigio	(1991)	C	***
Zardetto	Brut Prosecco di Conegliano	(nonvintage)	C	**
Zeni	Chardonnay	(1991)	B	**/***
Zeni	Müller-Thurgau	(1991)	B	**/***
Zeni	Pinot Bianco	(1991)	B	**/***

In summary, Italy is making *some* improvements in fashioning white wines with more character and flavor, but most of these wines remain frightfully overpriced for what the consumer actually gets in the bottle. Prices aside, my personal favorites (in alphabetical order) are

Anselmi—superlative dry wines from Soave

Maculan—delicious wines from Veneto

Puiatti—textbook, classic dry whites from Collio

Roncho de Gnemiz—intense, pure, exuberant, and richly fruity wines

Mario Schiopetto—the godfather of Friuli-Venezia-Giulia whites still makes lovely wines

Vie di Romans—Italy's most flavorful whites from Isonzo

OTHER SIGNIFICANT RED WINES OF ITALY

An enormous quantity of red wine is made outside of the Piedmont and Tuscany regions of Italy. Lamentably, much of it remains poor to mediocre. There are exceptions—especially the after-dinner, superrich, heavy Amarones and Reciotos. The finest producers of these thick, rich wines include Quintarelli, whose Amarone and Recioto from the Monte Ca Paletta vineyards are spectacular and capable of lasting for 20 or more years. Another producer of stunning Amarone and Recioto is Roberto Mazzi. Mazzi's Amarone is called Punta di Villa, and his Recioto is called Le Calcarole. Mazzi's style is pure finesse allied to considerable richness. His wines are not as thick and heavy as those of Quintarelli, but they may be more brilliant. Allegrini also makes a top Amarone called Fieramonte and a fine Recioto called Gardane. Anselmi makes exceptionally limited quantities of a highly renowned Recioto called Recioto de Capitelli.

Other top producers of Amarone and Recioto include the Fratelli Tedeschi and Serego Alighieri. Tedeschi makes several Amarones called Fabriseria, Capitel Monte Olmi, and a Recioto called Capitel Mont Fontana. Serego

Alighieri's Amarone is called Vaio Armoron, and his Recioto is Casal dei Ronchi.

Numerous other producers are making Amarone and Recioto, including Bolla, Bertani, Righetti, Tommasi, and Zeni. Although larger production ensures an international reputation of sorts, none of their products match those from the top producers indicated above.

Below are selected tasting notes for some of the best-known, and in some cases the best, dry red wines from other Italian viticultural areas. Most reds from Emilia-Romagna, Friuli-Venezia-Giulia, and Veneto are washed-out, vegetal, thin wines that have little redeeming social value.

CONTE TASCA D'ALMERITA (SICILY)* * *

1989 Regaleali	A	86

This producer is renowned for making Sicily's best red wine. The 1989 Regaleali displays a deep ruby color, a spicy, richly fruity, chocolatey, roasted fruit nose, excellent richness and definition, and a deep, full-bodied, lusty finish. It should drink well between 1994 and 2001.

D'ANGELO (BASILICATA)* * *

1985 Aglianco del Vulture Riserva	C	89

This producer, the best in Basilicata, has vineyards planted in volcanic soil. His wines can be stunning. The 1985 Aglianco del Vulture Riserva is one of the best examples I have tasted from d'Angelo. The wine reveals a huge, roasted coffee–, herb-, chocolate-, and black fruit (plums)–scented bouquet, great power and massiveness, and an explosively long, rich, glycerin-dominated finish. This is a wine for drinking with intensely flavored dishes such as stews and cassoulets.

DAL FORMA ROMANO (VENETO)* * * *

1988 Valpolicella Superiore	C	91

My reference point for Valpolicella has always been those produced by Quintarelli, but this wine is unquestionably the greatest Valpolicella I have ever tasted. One does not expect a Valpolicella to be this complex, rich, and potentially ageworthy. The nose offers up huge aromas of ripe plums, spices, and sweet cedary scents. Unctuously textured, with lavish quantities of fruit, this medium- to full-bodied wine is undeniably seductive, as well as thoroughly delicious. Although the price seems high for a Valpolicella, this is a great red wine! This decadent Valpolicella should drink well for at least 5–7 years.

BONCOMPAGNI LUDOVISI PRINCIPE DI VENOSA (LAZIO)* * * * *

1988 Fiorano	C	88
1985 Fiorano	C	89
1983 Fiorano	C	88
1982 Fiorano	C	90

Perhaps the best-kept secret of Italy is the tiny quantities of Fiorano, based on Merlot and Cabernet Sauvignon, made south of Rome along the ancient Appian Way. International winebroker Neil Empson represents this estate, which ages its wines 2 years in oak before releasing them. The result is a wine with the decadent richness and succulence of a great Pomerol of France. This serious wine is probably one of Italy's top ten red wines and certainly the best wine made from Cabernet Sauvignon and Merlot, yet it has received little publicity. The tiny quantities produced are no doubt the reason it lacks celebrity status. A 1970 tasted in 1987 showed just how extraordinary this wine can be when it reaches maturity, but the softness of the Merlot in the blend gives the wine an accessibility while young. This rare, fabulous wine is well worth searching out.

LUNGAROTTI (UMBRIA)* *

1988 Rubesco	B	76
1980 Rubesco Riserva Monticchio	D	74
1982 San Giorgio	D	76

Lungarotti's wines have continued to disappoint me, which is sad given the many bottles I enjoyed during the 1970s and early 1980s. Lungarotti is one of the great pioneers of the wines of Umbria, but consumers would not know that today. The 1988 Rubesco is a spicy, lightweight, excessively austere wine that exhibits little charm. The 1980 Rubesco Riserva Monticchio (the 1975 was a classic) is diluted and dull, with cooked-fruit flavors, too much tannin, and a dusty texture. The 1982 San Giorgio, a Cabernet Sauvignon–based wine, is overwhelmingly vegetal, disjointed, too acidic, and lacking ripe fruit. Although it has enormous potential, this firm could use a wake-up call.

MASTROBERARDINO (CAMPANIA)* *

1991 Lacryma Christi	B	84
1988 Radice	B	88
1987 Radice	B	85
1986 Taurasi	C	87
1985 Taurasi Riserva	C	88

More than a few knowledgeable observers have long believed that Taurasi Riserva is one of Italy's half dozen best red wines. Certainly the winery, which dates from 1580 and is working from probably the most ancient vineyards in all of Italy, is of great historical significance. Furthermore, the wines can be good and sometimes even outstanding, as was the case with the famous 1968 Taurasi Riserva. Over recent years the quality has been a bit spotty, the wines lacking fruit in vintages such as 1982, 1981, and 1978. In addition, the smell and taste of Taurasi is quite different; its earthy, almost cheesy nose seems unusual and at first off-putting. But the wines age extremely well, in fact seem to fill out and show much more intensity after 7–8 years than they do when tasted young. Recent vintages seem to be getting better. It is interesting to note that Mastroberardino considers 1985, 1987, 1988, and 1990 to be among his finest vintages in the last 30 years. Consumers who like these wines are advised to stock up. The 1991 Lacryma Christi is a soft, fruity wine with an attractive suppleness, smooth tannins, and 4–5 years of longevity. The 1987 and 1988 Radices are far more interesting, fuller, and more complete wines. The big, earthy, black truffle– and cherry-scented noses are enthralling. The deeper-colored 1988 is fuller, richer, and exhibits greater extraction of flavor and structure. It will be at its best between 1996 and 2005. The 1987 is more drinkable, but some rough tannins in the finish cause concern for its balance. The rustic 1986 Taurasi offers a cherry, peppery nose, rough tannins, and good fruit and body, but a tough, hard finish. The 1985 Taurasi Riserva may rival the 1977 Riserva and the legendary 1968 Riserva. Deeply colored, with a big, spicy, rich, sweet nose of roasted nuts, tar, and black cherry fruit, the wine is full bodied, with excellent concentration and length. It can be drunk now but promises to last through the first 15 years of the next century.

ELIO MONTI (ABRUZZI)* * */* * * *

1990 Montepulciano d'Abruzzo	A	87

Consumers looking for one of the finest red wine values of Italy should check out the wines of Elio Monti. His unfined and unfiltered style of red winemaking results in a saturated purple/black-colored wine bursting with raspberry and cherry fruit. This 1990 exhibits tremendous depth, an unctuous, thick texture, and fine purity and length. Although not complex, for under $10 a bottle it is a terrific bargain. Moreover, it will last for up to a decade.

EMILIO PEPE (ABRUZZI)* */* * * *

1987 Montepulciano d'Abruzzo	C	86

This producer's wines are hard to fathom. I remember an interesting 1974 with a spicy, cigar-box bouquet and a deep, full-bodied, rustic feel on the palate. However, the 1978 was flawed by excessive volatile acidity. This is a good producer making interesting, unmanipulated wines, but consistency is certainly a problem. Two bottles of this 1987 were consistent in their heavy, thick style, spicy, earthy fruitiness, and long, rich finish. Although Pepe's wines are not complex, and a bit dusty and tannic, they do not lack for personality.

QUINTARELLI (VENETO)* * * *

1985 Valpolicella	B	87
1986 Valpolicella	B	88

This 1985 Valpolicella is bursting with deliriously enjoyable, succulent red fruit; it is supple, fat, even crunchy on the palate and makes for a totally hedonistic but enjoyable drink. The 1986 is similarly styled but even more full bodied and ripe. Drink it over the next 6–7 years.

DR. COSIMO TAURINO (APULIA)* * * *

1985 Notarpanaro	A	89
1983 Notarpanaro	A	90
1985 Patriglione	C	89
1983 Patriglione	C	86
1988 Salice Salentino Riserva	A	89
1986 Salice Salentino Riserva	A	87

If you are looking for a great value from Italy for under $8 a bottle, there are no better wines than the full-bodied, robust, black cherry– and tar-scented, richly flavored, exuberant, fleshy 1986 and 1988 Salice Salentino Riservas. These are among the greatest red wine values in the world. These big, rich, pure, well-balanced wines are perfect for bistro cooking. If you have not yet discovered the thrills these wines provide, don't hesitate. Virtually any vintage of Salice Salentino will age well for 10–12 years. The Riserva, which is the same wine but has been aged longer at the winery, has a slightly more mellow, softer style. The 1985 and 1983 Notarpanaros are even richer wines, with darker, more saturated colors, licorice-, truffle-, blackcurrant-, and black cherry–scented noses, huge masses of fruit and glycerin, full body, and super length and ripeness. The 1983 is slightly more drinkable, but it has at least another decade of life in it. The younger, more backward 1985 should last through the first decade of the next century. Last, Taurino's Patriglione tastes like a blend of a late-harvest California Zinfandel and an Italian Recioto. The 1983, for me, is too raisiny, thick, and heavy to receive high marks, but I admire its individuality. If it is paired with the right cheese or food, it might merit a higher mark. Nevertheless, it is a heady wine with an alcohol content that must be over 15%. In contrast, the 1985 Patriglione is well balanced, very rich, full bodied and long, but avoids the heaviness and prunelike aspects of the 1983. It should drink well for at least a decade.

EDOARDO VALENTINI (ABRUZZI)* * * *

1988 Montepulciano d'Abruzzo   C 90

Valentini is considered by most authorities to be the finest producer of Montepulciano d'Abruzzo. I have enjoyed tremendous luck with his unfiltered, fascinating wines, and his 1988 may be the best I have tasted. All his wines share that huge, cedary, spicy aroma allied with viscous, alcoholic, thick fruit that is not only juicy, but superconcentrated. One bottle of Valentini's Montepulciano d'Abruzzo can easily serve 6–8 people. Be careful what food you serve with it, as it can easily overwhelm delicate dishes. The 1988 should last through the first 15 years of the next century.

3. GERMANY

The Basics

TYPES OF WINE

Germany's winedom is controlled by the 1971 law that divided German wines into seven grades, all based on ascending levels of ripeness and sweetness, as well as price. These seven levels are

1. Tafelwein
2. Qualitätswein (QbA)
3. Kabinett
4. Spätlese
5. Auslese
6. Beerenauslese
7. Trockenbeerenauslese

In addition to these there are other categories of German wines. The Trocken and Halbtrocken wines are the two generic types of dry German wine. The Trockens tend to be drier, but they are also boring, thin wines with little body or flavor. Halbtrockens also taste dry but are permitted to have slightly more residual sugar and are marginally more interesting. I rarely recommend either because, as commercial creations made to take advantage of the public's demand for "dry" wine, they are not very good. A third type, called Eiswein, is Germany's rarest and most expensive wine, made from frozen grapes generally picked in December or January, or even February. It is quite rare, and very, very sweet, but it has remarkably high acidity and can last and improve in the bottle for decades. It does have great character, but one must usually pay an unbelievably steep price to experience it.

There are also the sparkling wines of Germany called Deutscher Sekt, which should be drunk only by certified masochists, as they are a ghastly lot of overly sulphured wines. Last, there is the German wine that everyone knows about, the ubiquitous Liebfraumilch. This sugary, grapey drink is to quality German wine what California wine coolers are to that state's serious wine producers.

GRAPE VARIETIES

Müller-Thurgau   Representing 25% of Germany's vineyards, Müller-Thurgau has become the most widely planted grape because of its predilection to give prolific yields of juice (90–100 hectoliters a hectare is not uncommon). Ignore all of the self-serving promotion from German wine importers about Müller-Thurgau because it is not a great wine grape, and the Germans have planted it for quantity not quality.

Riesling   Although Riesling accounts for only 20% of the vineyards in Germany, it produces about 95% of that country's finest wines. If the bottle does not say "Riesling" on it, chances are you are not getting Germany's best wine. Riesling achieves its greatest success in Germany, whether with a dry, crisp, tangy Kabinett or decadently sweet, nectarlike Trockenbeerenauslese.

Sylvaner   This unimpressive grape accounts for 10% of Germany's vineyards and rarely results in anything interesting. Most Sylvaners have either a nasty vegetal streak to them or are simply dull and flat.

Other grape varieties   Much of Germany's problem today is that such a large proportion of its vineyards are planted with mediocre grape varieties. The remaining 45% of the vineyards generally consists of grapes that have little personality and names such as Kerner, Gutedel (Chasselas), Morio-Muskat, Bacchus, Faberrebe, Huxelrebe, Optima, and Elbling. The only other grapes that can do something special are Gewürztraminer, Rulander (Pinot Gris), Scheurebe, and Germany's answer to Pinot Noir, Spatburgunder.

FLAVORS

Müller-Thurgau   At its best it resembles a can of fruit salad, obvious but pleasant in an open-knit, uncomplicated manner. At its worst it tastes washed out, acidic, green, and reminiscent of a watered down, mediocre Riesling.

Riesling   The most exciting flavors in German wines come from Riesling. In the drier and slightly sweet versions there is a lovely concoction of apple, lime, wet stone, citric flavors, and scents. As the Riesling becomes sweeter, the flavors move in the direction of tropical fruits such as mangoes, pineapples, and honeyed apples, peaches, and apricots. Behind all the flavor (in the top Rieslings) is a steely, zesty, vibrant natural fruit acidity that gives those wines an exceptional degree of clarity and focus.

Rulander   From some of the best vineyards in Baden and the Rheinpfalz, this grape—also known as Grauburgunder—produces oily, rich, honeyed, intense wines that are probably the most underrated great white wines of Germany.

Spatburgunder   German Pinot Noir is a grotesque and ghastly wine that tastes like a defective, sweet, faded, and diluted red burgundy from an incompetent producer. Need I say more?

Sylvaner   On occasion, Sylvaner from selected vineyards in Franken and the Rheinhessen can be a rich, muscular, deep wine, but more often it is vegetal, thin, and dull.

AGING POTENTIAL

Auslese: 3–15 years
Qualitätswein (QbA): 2–4 years

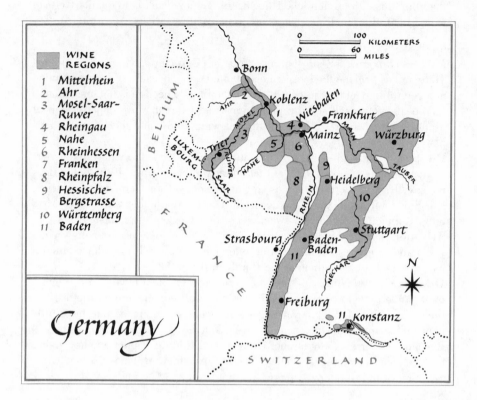

Germany

WINE REGIONS

1 Mittelrhein
2 Ahr
3 Mosel-Saar-Ruwer
4 Rheingau
5 Nahe
6 Rheinhessen
7 Franken
8 Rheinpfalz
9 Hessische-Bergstrasse
10 Württemberg
11 Baden

Bonn
Koblenz
Wiesbaden
Frankfurt
Würzburg
Mainz
Heidelberg
Strasbourg
Baden-Baden
Stuttgart
Freiburg
Konstanz

BELGIUM
LUXEMBOURG
FRANCE
SWITZERLAND

AHR
MOSEL
RUWER
SAAR
NAHE
RHEIN
MAIN
TAUBER
NECKAR

Trier

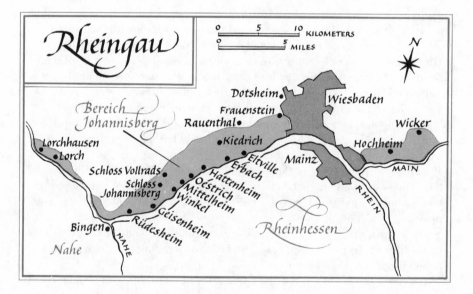

Rheingau

Bereich Johannisberg

Lorchhausen
Lorch
Schloss Vollrads
Schloss Johannisberg
Bingen
Rüdesheim
Geisenheim
Winkel
Mittelheim
Oestrich
Hattenheim
Erbach
Eltville
Kiedrich
Rauenthal
Frauenstein
Dotsheim
Wiesbaden
Wicker
Hochheim
Mainz

Nahe
NAHE
Rheinhessen
RHEIN
MAIN

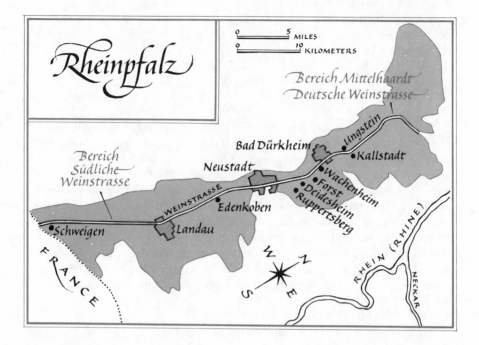

Rheinpfalz

0 — 5 MILES
0 — 10 KILOMETERS

Bereich Mittelhaardt
Deutsche Weinstrasse

Bereich
Südliche
Weinstrasse

Bad Dürkheim
Neustadt
Ungstein
•Kallstadt
•Wachenheim
•Forst
•Deidesheim
Ruppertsberg

WEINSTRASSE
Edenkoben

•Schweigen
Landau

F R A N C E

RHEIN (RHINE)

NECKAR

N
W E
S

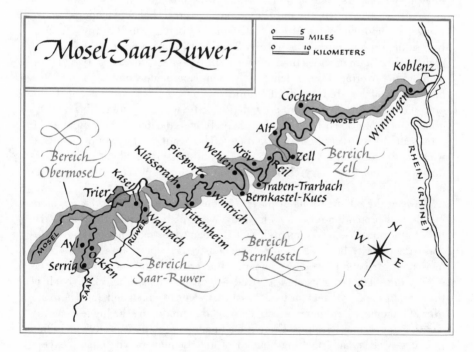

Mosel-Saar-Ruwer

0 — 5 MILES
0 — 10 KILOMETERS

Koblenz

Cochem

MOSEL

Winningen

Alf

Kröv
Wehlen
Zell
Reil

Bereich
Zell

Bereich
Obermosel

Klüsserath
Piesport

Trier
Kasel
Traben-Trarbach
Bernkastel-Kues

Ayl
Waldrach
Wintrich
Trittenheim

RUWER

Serrig
Ockfen

SAAR

Bereich
Saar-Ruwer

Bereich
Bernkastel

MOSEL

RHEIN (RHINE)

N
W E
S

Beerenauslese: 10–40+ years
Spätlese: 3–10 years
Kabinett: 3–6 years
Tafelwein: 8–16 months
Liebfraumilch: 8–16 months
Trockenbeerenauslese: 10–40+ years

OVERALL QUALITY LEVEL

The top level of quality is impeccably high and dominated by small estates that usually produce Riesling. However, the German government has been inexcusably remiss over recent decades in allowing too many high-yielding, low-quality grapes to be planted (the 1987 average yield per hectare was an incredible 97 hectolitres) and has allowed consumers to become increasingly skeptical about the seriousness of German wine quality. For example, in the mediocre year of 1987, 77% of the wine produced was allowed to be called QbA and only 2% was declassified as simple table wine (Tafelwein). That's ridiculous. A campaign to promote the top-quality German estates that are making the finest German wines is long overdue. Until the consumer begins to believe that Germany is serious about quality, sales of these wines will remain difficult.

THE MOST IMPORTANT INFORMATION TO KNOW

Although a number of U.S. importers have small portfolios of German wines, three major players dominate the German wine business in America. From a consumer's perspective, the most important is Terry Theise Selections, whose wines are imported by the Milton S. Kronheim Company in Washington, D.C. In less than a half dozen years Terry Theise has done more for the image of high-quality German wines than anyone in the previous 9 decades. By ignoring many of the overrated, more famous German wine names, and by beating the back roads of less-renowned viticultural regions, Theise has put together a portfolio of producers who turn out individualistic wines of astonishing quality, often at modest prices. Theise keeps his profit margins low so the wines can be represented effectively in the marketplace. The result is a bevy of phenomenal wines and extraordinary wine bargains. If you are serious about buying German wines, look for "Terry Theise Selection" on the label. You will not be disappointed.

Between the other two major players in the German wine market, the more visible and promotion-conscious is Rudy Weist of ILNA Selections in Carlsbad, California. Weist has long felt that German wines have not enjoyed widespread popularity because they are inexpensive. His portfolio focuses on the more renowned and prestigious domaines that are all members of an elite association of winemaking estates referred to collectively as the VDP. Each of these estates sports a neck or back label that identifies its members. There are over 200 members. In theory all are dedicated to producing the highest-quality wines, usually from Riesling. There are a number of fabulous producers in this group, as well as an appalling number of underachievers who charge exceptionally high prices because their wines are produced from renowned vineyards. Moreover, a premium is charged for the wines represented by Weist because of his belief that higher prices translate into higher prestige. As my tasting notes often attest, Theise's wines, from the same vineyards but from less well-known producers, often outperform those from Weist.

The third major importer of German wines is Bob Rice of Chapin Cellars in Virginia Beach, Virginia. Rice is a low-profile importer who is content to have most of his German producers represented regionally, so you are not likely to see him promoting his name as much as that of his producers. His reasonably priced portfolio includes numerous excellent wines.

In addition to becoming familiar with these German wine importers, there are other facts to keep in mind when buying German wines:

1. There are eleven major wine-producing zones in Germany. Within these zones there are three subdistricts, the most general of which is called a Bereich. This is used to describe a wine from anywhere within the boundaries of that particular Bereich. An analogy that may help facilitate this distinction would be the closest French equivalent, a wine entitled to Appellation Bordeaux Contrôlée or Appellation Bourgogne Contrôlée. Within the Bereich are more specific boundaries called Grosslagen, to which the closest French equivalent would be the generic Appellation St.-Julien Contrôlée or Appellation Morey-St.-Denis Contrôlée. These would be wines that are not from a specific château or vineyard, but from a particular region or collection of sites for vineyards. There are 152 different Grosslagen in Germany. The most specific zone in Germany is called an Einzellage, which is a particular site or vineyard. There are 2,600 of them in Germany, and again, by analogy, the closest French equivalent would be a single St.-Julien château such as Ducru-Beaucaillou, or a specific Premier Cru or Grand Cru Burgundy vineyard in Morey-St.-Denis such as Clos des Lambrays. Perhaps this will help to understand the breakdown of the German wine zones. However, few people have the patience to memorize the best Einzellagens or Grosslagens, so it is much more important to remember the names of some of the best producers.

2. The majority of the best producers in Germany are located in nine wine zones.

OVERALL CHARACTERISTICS OF THE MAJOR GERMAN WINE ZONES

Middle Mosel   For German wine lovers, as well as for tourists to Germany's wine regions, the Middle Mosel is the most beloved and scenic. The frightfully steep, slate-based slopes are so forbidding that it seems impossible vineyards could be planted on such dangerously precipitous hills. With its plethora of high-profile producers, such as J. J. Prüm, Willi Haag, Dr. Loosen, and Dr. Thanisch, this region has no shortage of admirers and potential buyers. The fact is that although Riesling grown on these slopes has unlimited potential, this is also an area filled with overpriced, underachieving producers who have long lived off their reputations. Nevertheless, anybody who has tasted a great Wehlener Sonnenuhr, Brauneberger Juffer, Erdener Treppchen, Zeltinger Sonnenuhr, or Graacher Himmelreich knows that this area's soils can produce magical Rieslings. By analogy, the Middle Mosel is to Germany what Puligny-Montrachet is to Burgundy. There are a number of great producers, but prices are high and the quality is frightfully irregular.

Lower Mosel   This obscure vineyard area with supersteep slopes is located at the junction of the Mosel and the Rhine. The wines from the Lower Mosel are underestimated, a fact that consumers should put to good use. Try some recent vintages from two of this area's most spectacular producers, von Schleinitz and von Heddesdorff, and experience the high quality available at reasonable prices. Although the vineyard sites are not considered to be as ideal as those in the Middle Mosel, top Lower Mosel producers can produce wines equal in quality to those from the Middle Mosel.

Saar   This cool region is able to maintain the steely, razor-blade sharpness of the Riesling grape. Many authorities consider the Saar vineyards to be among the greatest in Germany, but as in the Middle Mosel, fame has its price. Some fabulous producers are located in this area. However, some well-known Saar producers have a tendency to overcrop, making relatively hollow, flabby wines that lack definition. Superlative producers include the likes of Egon Müller, Dr. Wagner, von Kesselstatt, and, from time to time, Zilliken.

Ruwer   Trier is the spiritual and commercial center for the Ruwer wines. Textbook, quintessential Rieslings emerge from this area from producers such as Friedrich-Wilhelm-Gymnasium, Geltz-Zilliken, Karthäuserhof, von Kesselstatt, Karlsmuhle, and von Schubert's Maximin Grunhaus.

Rheingau   Many of the most famous producers of German winedom are located in this highly renowned region. However, it is not unusual for many of the unknown overachievers to outperform their more celebrated neighbors. Three of the most prominent underachievers are Schloss Groenesteyn, Schloss Vollrads, and Schloss Johannisberg. If you want to taste what many consider to be some of the finest Rieslings made in Germany, check out producers such as H. H. Eser, Freiherr zu Knyphausen, Deinhard's Konigin Victoria Berg, Dr. Heinrich Nagler, and the best *cuvées* of Schloss Schonborn.

Rheinhessen   All the German wine zones offer considerable diversity in quality but none more than the Rheinhessen, which has Nierstein as its commercial center. Müller-Thurgau and Sylvaner are the two most popular grape varieties of this region. Additionally, such odd grapes as Scheurebe, Huxelrebe, and Kerner have found an enthusiastic reception among this region's producers. This is also the region where most of Germany's Liebfraumilch is produced. Consumers often make major errors in buying wines from this region. Over recent years, some of the best producers have included Freiherr Heyl zu Herrnsheim, J.u.H.A. Strub, and Merz.

Rheinpfalz   The Rheinpfalz is the warmest of the major German wine zones. Although Müller-Thurgau is widely planted, Riesling, Rulander, and Scheurebe produce the most stunning wines. If you think German wines are too understated, light, and wimpish, check out the powerful, meaty, fleshy, supergenerous wines from the Rheinpfalz. The quality level appears to be hitting new heights with every vintage. This is the home of the producer Müller-Catoir, who is making the most riveting wines of Germany. It is also the base for supertalented producers such as K. and H. Lingenfelder, Kurt Darting, Klaus Neckerauer, Koehler-Ruprecht, Kimich, Werle, and perhaps one of the best-known Rheinpfalz estates, Dr. Burklin-Wolf.

Nahe   This is another underrated source of high-class Riesling, as well as a wine zone with a competitive group of producers who, for now, lack the one superstar needed to draw worldwide attention to the region's virtues. A Nahe wine is considered to possess some of the character of a Saar wine and the spice, meatiness, and flesh of a Rheingau. The curranty, smoky aromas of a Nahe are reminiscent of those found in a red wine, making them among the most distinctive of all German wines. None of the Nahe producers are well known, so prices tend to be low, except for those producers who are members of the prestigious VDP group (like Hans Crusius). Top producers include von Plettenberg, Hehner-Kiltz, Kruger-Rumpf, Adolph Lotzbeyer, and perhaps the finest, Hermann Donnhoff and Prinz zu Salm.

Franken With the wonderful city of Würzburg as its commercial center, the wines of Franken have developed a considerable cult following. Although these wines fetch high prices and are put in unattractive squat bottles that are impossible to bin, Franken wines can be bold, dramatic, and heady. Moreover, they enjoy remarkable loyalty from their admirers. This is one region where the Sylvaner grape hits heights that exist nowhere else on earth. The two best estates are Burgerspital and Hans Wirsching. I have also been increasingly impressed (especially by the 1990s) with wines from Schloss Sommerhausen. Once past the quality of these superlative producers it is caveat emptor.

3. The best German wines are those produced at the Kabinett, Spätlese, Auslese, Beerenauslese, and Trockenbeerenauslese levels of ripeness and sweetness. Most consumers tasting a Kabinett wine would not find it particularly sweet, although there is residual sugar in the wine. Because of a high natural acidity found in German wines, a Kabinett generally tastes fresh, fruity, but not sweet to most palates. However, most tasters will detect a small amount of sweetness in a Spätlese, and even more with an Auslese. All three are ideal as aperitifs or with food, whereas Beerenauslese and Trockenbeerenauslese are clearly dessert wines, very rich and quite sweet. One should keep in mind that the alcohol level in most German wines averages between 7% and 9%, so one can drink much more without feeling the effects. One of the naive criticisms of German wines is that they do not go well with food. However, anyone who has tried a fine Kabinett, Spätlese, or Auslese with Oriental cuisine, with roast pork, or even with certain types of fowl such as pheasant or turkey can tell you that these wines work particularly well, especially Spätlese and Auslese.

4. The best German wines age like fine Bordeaux. In great vintages, such as 1990 or 1971, one can expect a Kabinett, Spätlese, or Auslese from a top producer to evolve and improve in the bottle for 5–10 years. A Beerenauslese or Trockenbeerenauslese has the ability in a great vintage to improve for 2 or 3 decades. This is a fact, not a myth, to which those who have recently tasted some of the great Ausleses from 1959 can easily attest. German wines at the top levels, from the top producers, do indeed improve remarkably in the bottle, although the trend among consumers is to drink them when they are young, fresh, and crisp.

VINTAGE GUIDE

1992—This looks to be a promising vintage with some superlative, drier-style wines coming from the Ruwer and Middle Mosel. Most estates reported it was very difficult to produce sweet wines in these areas. Therefore this will be a vintage of mostly Kabinetts and Spätleses—a good sign for consumers looking for wines from the drier end of the German wine spectrum. All things considered, 1992 should be a very fine year throughout the Mosel, Saar, and Ruwer regions, with fewer superrich dessert wines than in years such as 1990 and 1989. In the Rheingau, Rheinpfalz, and Rheinhessen, the vintage looks to be excellent, with plenty of rich wines as well as sweet late-harvest wines, particularly in the Rheinhessen. Many of the top producers are superenthusiastic about the prospects of this vintage given the superb ripeness and relatively small yields achieved. Producers in the Rheinhessen and Rheinpfalz have already begun to compare 1992 with 1990, so this may turn out to be one of the most successful viticultural regions in Europe.

1991—This has turned out to be a surprisingly good vintage, far better than many of the doom-and-gloom reports suggested. The 1991 is not of the level of 1990 or 1989 in terms of rich, intense, sweet Spätlese and Auslese wines, but it is still a very appealing vintage, particularly for the top estates in the drier Kabinett styles. The down side of the 1991 vintage is that some wines have shrill levels of acidity, raising questions as to whether their fruit will hold up. Most German wine specialists suggest this was a year of the winemaker rather than of Mother Nature, and producers who were able to keep yields down and picked physiologically ripe fruit made wines with crisp acidity and good depth and character. Those who didn't made hollow, high-acid wines that merit little attention.

1990—This is an outstanding vintage. The wines have fabulous ripeness, surprisingly crisp acidity, and an intense perfume and midpalate. In addition to many outstanding Kabinetts and Spätleses, this is another vintage, much like 1989, that produced spectacular sweet Ausleses and even more decadently rich Beerenauslese and Trockenbeerenauslese wines. If you are a German wine enthusiast, this vintage warrants a serious look.

1989—This is another top-notch vintage that has been compared with 1976, 1971, and 1959. The late harvest and the extraordinary amount of sweet wine made at the Auslese, Beerenauslese, and Trockenbeerenauslese levels garner considerable enthusiasm. Unlike 1990, where every wine zone enjoyed success, or 1991, where it was a question of the winemaker's ability, 1989 saw top wines produced in the Saar, Rheinpfalz, Ruwer, and Rheinhessen regions. This was not a rain-free harvest, production yields were high, and acidity levels in many cases remain suspiciously low, suggesting most consumers would be well advised to drink wines below the Auslese level over the next 3–4 years. One of the good but somewhat disappointing wines in the context of the vintage is the Middle Mosel, where a number of the most famous domaines overcropped and have produced somewhat fluid, loosely knit, fragile wines.

1988—The strength of this vintage is the Middle Mosel. Based on my tastings, the drier Kabinetts and Spätlese offerings look to be the best wines made. This vintage has now been largely forgotten in all the hype over 1989 and 1990, so bargains can be found.

1987—A mediocre vintage followed an unusual growing season that was characterized by a poor, wet, cold summer but glorious September and mixed bag of weather in October. The quality is expected to be better than either 1980 or 1984, and many growers reported harvests close in size to those in 1986. The average production was a whopping 96 hectolitres per hectare, which is excessive. Interestingly, this appears to be a good year for the rare nectarlike Eisweins. Consumers should be drinking their wines below the Auslese level over the next several years.

1986—A copious crop of grapes has resulted in pleasant, agreeable, soft, fruity wines that will have broad commercial appeal. Because of the size of the crop, prices dropped after the smaller than normal crop in 1985. All in all this vintage will be regarded by the trade as a useful, practical year of good rather than great wines. Wines below the Auslese level should be drunk up over the next several years.

1985—The German wine trade has touted this year rather highly, but except for a handful of areas it is not comparable with the outstanding 1983 vintage. Nevertheless, it is a very good year, with a moderate production of wines with good acidity and more typical textures and characteristics than the opulent, richly fruity 1983s. Like 1983, the dryness during the summer and fall prevented the formation of *Botrytis cinerea*. The Rieslings in many cases can be very good but will be firmer, slower to evolve, and less open than the more precocious, overt, fruity 1983s. Overall, the 1985s should be at their best between now and 1998. The top successes are in the Middle Mosel, with potentially great wines from villages such as Urzig and Erden. Wines below the Auslese level should be drunk over the next 1–2 years.

1984—Fresh, light, very pleasant, straightforward wines that are neither green nor too acidic were produced in this vintage of average quality and below average quantity. They will not keep, so drink the 1984s over the next 3–4 years.

1983—This vintage has received the most publicity since the 1976. Most growers seem to feel that it is certainly the best since the 1976. It was a very large crop throughout all viticultural areas of Germany, but it was especially large and exceptional in quality in the Mosel-Saar-Ruwer region. The wines have excellent concentration, very fine levels of tartaric rather than green malic acidity, and a degree of precocious ripeness and harmonious roundness that gives the wines wonderful appeal now. However, because of their depth and overall balance, they should age well for at least 10 or more years. The vintage seemed strongest at the Spätlese level, as very few Auslese, Beerenauslese, and Trockenbeerenauslese wines were produced. Also, 1983 was a great year for Eiswein, where, as a result of an early freeze, above normal quantities of this nectarlike, opulent wine were produced. However, despite larger quantities than normal, prices are outrageously high for the Eisweins, although very realistic and reasonable for the rest of the wines.

OLDER VINTAGES

The great sweet wine vintage that can still be found in the marketplace is 1976. By German standards, this vintage produced incredibly ripe, intense, opulent wines, with a significant amount produced at the Auslese and Beerenauslese levels. The top wines should continue to last for another 5–15 years. Some critics have disputed the greatness of this vintage, saying that the 1976s are low in acidity, but that is a minority point of view. The wines remain reasonably priced at the Auslese level, but the Beerenausleses and Trockenbeerenausleses from this vintage are absurdly expensive. The 1977 vintage should be avoided, and 1978, unlike in France, was not a particularly successful year in Germany. Well-kept 1975s can provide great enjoyment, as can the wines from another great vintage, 1971. I would avoid the wines from 1972, and the once good 1973s are now in serious decline!

RATING GERMANY'S BEST PRODUCERS

* * * * * (OUTSTANDING PRODUCERS)

Kurt Darting (Rheinpfalz)

Fritz Haag (Mosel)

Heribert Kerpen (Mosel)

J. F. Kimich (Rheinpfalz)

K. & H. Lingenfelder (Rheinpfalz)

Monchhof (Mosel)

Egon Müller (Saar)

Müller-Catoir (Rheinpfalz)

Klaus Neckerauer (Rheinpfalz)

J. J. Prüm (Middle Mosel)

Willi Schaefer (Mosel)

Schloss Schonborn (Rheingau)

von Schubert–Maximin Grunhaus
   (Ruwer)

* * * * (EXCELLENT PRODUCERS)

Christian-Wilhelm Bernhard
   (Rheinhessen)

von Brentano (Rheingau)

Burgerspital (Franken)

Dr. Burklin-Wolf (Rheinpfalz)

J. J. Christoffel (Mosel)

Hermann Donnhoff (Nahe)

August Eser (Rheingau)

H. H. Eser-Johannishof (Rheingau)

F. W. Gymnasium (Mosel)

Willi Haag (Mosel)

Freiherr von Heddesdorff (Mosel)

Hehner-Kiltz (Nahe)

Heyl zu Herrnsheim (Rheinhessen)

von Hövel (Saar)

Immich-Batterieberg (Mosel)

E. Jacoby-Mathy (Mosel)

Karlsmuhle (Mosel-Ruwer)

Karp-Schreiber (Mosel)

von Kesselstatt (Mosel-Saar)

Freiherr du Knyphausen (Rheingau)

Koehler-Ruprecht (Rheinpfalz)

Konigin Victoria Berg-Deinhard
   (Rheingau)

Kruger-Rumpf (Nahe)

Kuhling-Gillot (Rheinhessen)

Kunstler (Rheingau)

Dr. Loosen-St.-Johannishof (Mosel)

Adolf Lotzbeyer (Nahe)

Alfred Merkelbach (Mosel)

Meulenhof-Justen (Mosel)

Nahe Staatsdomaine (Nahe)

Pfeffingen (Rheinpfalz)

von Plettenberg (Nahe)

Jakob Schneider (Nahe)

Selbach-Oster (Mosel)

von Simmern (Rheingau)

J.U.H.A. Strub (Rheinhessen)

Dr. Heinz Wagner (Saar)

Werle (Rheinpfalz)

* * * (GOOD PRODUCERS)

Paul Anheuser (Nahe)

Conrad-Bartz (Mosel)

Basserman-Jordan (Rheinpfalz)

Josef Biffar (Rheinpfalz)

Bischoflisch Weinguter (Mosel)

Bruder Dr. Becker (Rheinhessen)

Christoffel-Berres (Mosel)

Hans Crusius (Nahe)

Josef Dienhart (Mosel-Saar)

Epenschild (Rheinhessen)

Dr. Fischer (Saar)

Four Seasons Coop (Rheinpfalz)

Hans Ganz (Nahe)

Gebruder Grimm (Rheingau)

Gernot Gysler (Rheinhessen)

Grans-Fassian (Mosel)

Gunderloch-Usinger (Rheinhessen)

Dr. Heger (Baden)

von Hövel (Mosel)

Toni Jost (Mittelrhein)

Klaus Kemmer (Mittelrhein)

Johann Koch (Mosel-Saar)

Gebruder Kramp (Mosel)

Lehnert-Matteus (Mosel)

Licht-Bergweiler (Mosel)
Weingut Benedict Loosen Erben (Mosel)
Merz (Rheinhessen)
Herbert Messmer (Rheinpfalz)
Dr. Nagler (Rheingau)
Peter Nicolay (Middle Mosel)
Claus Odernheimer/Abteihof St.-Nicolaus (Rheingau)
von Ohler'sches (Rheinhessen)
Dr. Pauly-Bergweiler (Mosel)
Petri-Essling (Nahe)
Okonomierat Piedmont (Mosel-Saar-Ruwer)
S. A. Prüm (Mosel)
S. A. Prüm-Erben (Mosel)
Erich Wilhelm Rapp (Nahe)
Max Ferdinand Richter (Mosel)
Salm (Nahe)
Prinz zu Salm (Nahe)
Peter Scherf (Ruwer)

von Schleinitz (Mosel)
Schmitt-Wagner (Mosel)
Georg Albrecht Schneider (Rheinhessen)
Schumann-Nagler (Rheingau)
Wolfgang Schwaab (Mosel)
Seidel-Dudenhofer (Rheinhessen)
Bert Simon (Saar)
Schloss Sommerhausen (Franken)
Sturm (Rheinhessen)
Dr. Thanisch (Middle Mosel)
Tyrell-Karthauserhof (Ruwer)
Vereinigte Hospitien (Mosel)
Wegeler-Deinhard (Mosel, Rheinpfalz, Rheingau)
Adolf Weingart (Mittelrhein)
Dr. F. Weins-Prüm (Mosel)
Domdechant Werner (Rheingau)
Conrad Wittman (Rheinhessen)
Wolff-Metternich (Rheinhessen)
G. Zilliken (Mosel)

* * (AVERAGE PRODUCERS)

von Buhl (Rheinpfalz)
Stephan Ehlen (Mosel)
Alexandre Freimuth (Rheingau)
Le Gallais (Mosel)
Siegfried Gerhard (Rheingau)
Martin Gobel (Franken)
Schloss Groenesteyn (Rheingau)
Louis Guntrum (Rheinhessen)
Schloss Johannisberg (Rheingau)

Burgermeister Carl Koch (Rheinhessen)
Lucashof (Rheinpfalz)
Milz-Laurentiushof (Middle Mosel)
Schloss Reinhartshausen (Rheingau)
Schloss Saarstein (Saar)
Staatsweingüter Eltville (Rheingau)
Studert-Prüm/Maximinhof (Mosel)
Schloss Vollrads (Rheingau)

Selected Tasting Notes

DR. BURKLIN-WOLF (RHEINPFALZ)* * * *

1988 Deidesheimer Hohenmorgen Riesling Kabinett	B	87
1989 Deidesheimer Hohenmorgen Riesling Spätlese	B	90
1988 Forster Kirchenstuck Riesling Kabinett	B	85
1989 Forster Kirchenstuck Riesling Spätlese	B	88
1989 Ruppertsberger Gaisbohl Riesling Auslese	C	90
1990 Ruppertsberger Gaisbohl Riesling Spätlese	C	80
1988 Ruppertsberger Gaisbohl Riesling Spätlese	B	89
1989 Ruppertsberger Gaisbohl Riesling Beerenauslese	E	90
1990 Wachenheimer Rechbachel Riesling Auslese	D	81

1989 Wachenheimer Rechbachel Riesling Beerenauslese	E	98
1990 Wachenheimer Rechbachel Riesling Spätlese	C	78
1988 Wachenheimer Rechbachel Riesling Spätlese	C	87
1990 Wachenheimer Rechbachel Riesling Trockenbeerenauslese	EE	?

This famed Rheinpfalz producer made extremely lean, backward, high-acid 1990s that tasted closed and unforthcoming when I saw them in late October. The 1990 Wachenheimer Rechbachel Riesling Spätlese exhibited a difficult-to-penetrate, vaguely spicy, mineral nose; dry, crisp, high tension; zesty flavors; and an uninspiring yet pretty finish. The 1990 Ruppertsberger Gaisbohl Riesling Spätlese displayed a pronounced green-apple, stony nose and backward yet well-delineated flavors buttressed by high acids. The state of evolution of both of these Spätlese selections suggest that cellaring of several years is warranted, because today neither wine is that enjoyable. Far more interesting is Burklin-Wolf's 1990 Wachenheimer Rechbachel Riesling Auslese. The elegant, floral, crisp, mineral-scented nose is followed by taut, high-strung, dry, concentrated fruit flavors that exhibited high acidity as well as structure and length. Much of the wine comes forward at the end of the palate, suggesting that 3–4 years of cellaring would be wise. Last, the 1990 Wachenheimer Rechbachel Riesling Trockenbeerenauslese is stern, backward, and unforthcoming. There are some attractive whiffs of superripe fruit, but for now the acidity tends to obscure much of the wine's personality. Burklin-Wolf enjoyed very fine vintages in both 1988 and 1989. The 1988 Deidesheimer Hohenmorgen Riesling Kabinett is a beautifully made dry wine with a big, spicy, cinnamon, earth-scented bouquet, gobs of ripe fruit, crisp acidity, medium body, and a long, fresh, exuberant finish. It should last for at least 3–4 years. In comparison, the 1988 Forster Kirchenstuck Riesling Kabinett tastes more reserved but is also more marked by a spicy, earthy character. This is a well-delineated yet angular wine at the moment, but it should age for 4–5 years. There is no doubt that Burklin-Wolf excelled in both 1988 and 1989 with his Spätlese selections. They are all wonderfully extracted, essentially dry wines, with brilliant clarity to their flavors. For example, the 1988 Ruppertsberger Gaisbohl Riesling Spätlese is gloriously extracted, rich, medium bodied, and dry, with a huge, spicy, citrusy, juicy, pineapple fruitiness. This intensely flavored, well-balanced wine should drink well for 4–5 years. By comparison, the 1988 Wachenheimer Rechbachel Riesling Spätlese is a much more flamboyant, exotic, lychee nut–scented wine that is slightly off-dry, but rich, opulent, and very forward and tasty. One will have to be more careful in serving it with food given its flashy personality. Both of the 1989 Spätlese offerings are gorgeous. The 1989 Forster Kirchenstuck Riesling Spätlese displays a huge, flowery, citrusy nose; long, deep, intense, ripe flavors; medium body; and a dry, long finish. Outstanding yet more backward is the 1989 Deidesheimer Hohenmorgen Riesling Spätlese. This impeccably pure wine exhibits an expansive bouquet that displays flavors of ripe apples, pineapples, and minerals. In the mouth the wine is tightly knit but has exhilarating flavor depth as well as definition. Spicy, lean, dry, and muscular, this excellent wine should last for at least 5–6 years. Although the 1989 Ruppertsberger Gaisbohl Riesling Auslese is expensive, its vivid definition, exceptional richness, and exotic, almost Condrieu-like nose make it worth the price. Amazingly, this wine, because of its high acidity, does not taste as sweet as one would expect for an Auslese. It is off-dry and is probably best served with creamy fish dishes rather than as a dessert wine. It should last for 5–6 years. The two 1989 Beerenauslese offerings are frightfully expensive, but both are wine titans. The 1989 Ruppertsberger Gaisbohl Riesling Beerenauslese is more backward, with extraordinarily high acidity and fabulous richness. But for now it remains a tightly knit, almost steely style of Beerenauslese that should unfold slowly over the next 10–20 years. For those who are unable to defer their gratification, there is the monumental 1989 Wachenheimer Rechbachel Riesling Beerenauslese. It, too, displays very fine acidity, but it is so spectacularly perfumed and sensationally concentrated, it is nearly perfect. In the mouth it exhibits layer upon layer of rich fruit that avoids the sticky, gooey heaviness of some wines because of its great acidity. The extract levels must have been phenomenal for this wine. Although the price may seem high, this is one of the finest sweet wines I have ever tasted from Germany. It should drink well for 20 or more years.

FREIHERR VON HEDDESDORFF (MOSEL)* * * *

1990 Winninger Rottgen Riesling Auslese	C	90
1989 Winninger Rottgen Riesling Auslese	C	92
1989 Winninger Uhlen Riesling Kabinett	A	87
1990 Winninger Uhlen Riesling Spätlese	B	87

Superlative winemaking is exhibited in every one of these offerings from Freiherr von Heddesdorff. In today's wine world, $10 rarely buys anything with extra-special dimensions, but Heddesdorff's 1989 Winninger Uhlen Riesling Kabinett is a distinctive bottle of wine with evidence of superrich, botrytised peach and apricot flavors and gobs of opulent fruit barely brought into focus by crisp acids. If you think I am describing a succulent, lavishly rich Kabinett, you are right on the money. This nearly dry wine is a knockout, and the price makes it a steal! In total contrast is the 1990 Winninger Uhlen Riesling Spätlese. Here opulence takes a backseat to a medium-bodied, tart, mineralscented, extremely elegant, high-strung style of Riesling that exhibits excellent definition and concentration, as well as a long, stony, dry finish. The contrast between the more reserved, steely, austere, beautifully structured 1990 vintage and the more obvious, opulent gushingly fruity 1989 vintage is again perfectly exemplified by the 1990 and 1989 Winninger Rottgen Riesling Ausleses from Heddesdorff. The 1990 offers high acidity, a steely backbone, and gobs of fruit in its medium-bodied, dry, spicy, powerful style. This super wine should be drunk over the next 10 years or more. The 1989 could not be more different, offering up a mammoth nose of botrytised fruit, minerals, and spices. In the mouth it is rich, with that element of overripe tropical fruit that makes many 1989s so tantalizing to drink now. The gorgeous richness and decent acidity in this authoritative wine make a statement of individuality. I loved it, although I would want to drink it within the next 7–8 years.

KARLSMUHLE (MOSEL-RUWER)* * * *

1990 Kaseler Nies'chen Riesling Auslese	C	93
1989 Kaseler Nies'chen Riesling Auslese	C	90

1989 Lorenzhofer Felslay Riesling Auslese Halbtrocken	C	90
1990 Lorenzhofer Felslay Riesling Auslese Long Gold Cap	D	95
1990 Lorenzhofer Felslay Riesling Kabinett Halbtrocken	B	87
1989 Lorenzhofer Felslay Riesling Spätlese Halbtrocken	B	89
1990 Lorenzhofer Mauerchen Riesling Auslese	C	92
1989 Lorenzhofer Mauerchen Riesling Auslese	C	90
1990 Lorenzhofer Mauerchen Riesling Kabinett	B	87
1989 Lorenzhofer Mauerchen Riesling Kabinett	B	88
1989 Lorenzhofer Riesling Beerenauslese	E	96
1989 Lorenzhofer Riesling Eiswein	E	98

Karlsmuhle's 1990s are sensational wines, with some offerings qualifying as candidates for the wine of the vintage. The 1990 Lorenzhofer Felslay Riesling Kabinett Halbtrocken offers an absolutely sensational nose of fruit and minerals, followed by highly extracted yet delicately poised, spicy, cinnamon-flavored fruit. The acidity is high, but so is the ripeness and extract. There is a fascinating inner core of strength and finesse in this fresh, lively, beautifully made wine. My rating may be conservative. Drink it over the next 4–5 years. The backward yet delicate style of Karlsmuhle's 1990 Lorenzhofer Mauerchen Riesling Kabinett has appeal. Although it may be difficult to articulate, one taste of this wine suggests someone knows what fine winemaking is all about. Dry and unevolved, it has an alluring texture, as well as depth and delineation. Drink it over the next 5–6 years. At the Auslese level, Karlsmuhle's wines are not only exciting, they are compelling. The 1990 Lorenzhofer Mauerchen Riesling Auslese possesses staggering extraction of fruit and a huge, flowery nose that is followed by off-dry to dry, impeccably well-balanced, vivid flavors. On the palate it goes on and on with cleanliness and gracefulness. It is hard to imagine an Auslese of this richness that does not taste heavy-handed. This beauty should last for up to a decade. The 1990 Kaseler Nies'chen Riesling Auslese exhibits a penetrating nose of flowers, berry fruit, and steel. In the mouth there is once again that astonishing concentration allied with zinging acidity. It is drier than the Lorenzhofer Mauerchen, and even more highly extracted, and the texture titillates the taster. This magnificent Auslese should have extraordinary flexibility with food given its dry style. Absolutely brilliant! The 1990 Lorenzhofer Felslay Riesling Auslese Long Gold Cap blew me away. Made in a sweeter style than the other two Ausleses, it exhibits an extraordinary nose of cherry fruit, minerals, and flowers. Exceptionally ripe, rich flavors linger on the palate. The acidity is terrific, and the length is something rarely encountered. It truly is a wine of extraordinary magnitude and beauty. Drink it over the next 5–10 years. As a postscript, it is available only in the new 500-ml size. I have stated before how difficult it is to judge Eisweins, Beerenausleses, and Trockenbeerenausleses when they are so young and unevolved. However, there is no question that the 1990 Lorenzhofer Riesling Eiswein is one of the most magnificently sweet, young wines I have ever tasted. There is evidence of botrytis in the nose, and the honeyed richness is something to appreciate. All of this is magnified as the acidity gives zest, refreshment, and razor-like sharpness to every component of this huge, unbelievably extracted, magnificently pure Eiswein. How long will it last? Twenty-five years should pose no problem, and perhaps even 50 years is within the reach of this monumental wine. The price is remarkably fair, not only in view of the quality, but also considering the sad fact that less than 25 cases of this nectar were produced. The 1989 Lorenzhofer Riesling Beerenauslese is a minor let-down after tasting the Eiswein. No doubt about it, the wine is extraordinary. It possesses surprisingly high acidity, extraordinary richness and opulence, and a spectacularly long, zesty, clean, uplifting finish. This should prove to be "only" a 25- to 30-year wine. There are two sensational dry wines from the 1989 vintage. The 1989 Lorenzhofer Felslay Riesling Spätlese Halbtrocken exhibits high acidity, but the acids are neutralized by the extraordinary opulence of lemony, mineral, and apple fruit. Elegant, yet rich, spicy, deep, and highly extracted, this wine has a razor's edge of clarity and great precision. Drink this bone-dry wine over the next 2–3 years. Karlsmuhle's 1989 Lorenzhofer Felslay Riesling Auslese Halbtrocken possesses even greater flavor dimension. It is one of the finest Halbtrockens I have ever tasted. Of course, the whole theory behind an Auslese Halbtrocken is to pick the grapes at superripe Auslese levels and then vinify the wine dry. What one gets here is something that texturally resembles a great white burgundy rather than what most readers would perceive as a German Riesling. Spectacular depth and richness unfold as the wine sits in the glass. I could not make up my mind whether there was more apple- or peach-like fruit, but I kept thinking of any number of shrimp, scallop, and trout courses that would serve as an ideal foil for this gorgeously built, rich, yet dry Riesling. Don't miss it! I would opt for drinking this wine, like the Spätlese Halbtrocken, over the next 2–3 years, although some of my German wine enthusiast friends tell me that in a decade this wine will be even more fascinating. Karlsmuhle's 1989 Lorenzhofer Mauerchen Riesling Kabinett is an exceptionally clean and vivid wine with gobs of extract yet extremely high acidity, giving it a closed-in, tightly knit character. There is no doubting its extraction. Those who favor intellectual expressions of Riesling might well rate this wine higher. It should easily last for a decade. The two 1989 Auslese selections blew me away. The 1989 Lorenzhofer Mauerchen Riesling Auslese is like drinking liquid slate. Very backward, the wine has an inner core of depth that tastes as if it were the essence of slate-, apple-, and peachlike Riesling fruit. Beautifully structured, with crisp acidity and a huge, fragrant perfume, this deep, surprisingly dry, impeccably made Auslese is a tour de force. For a few additional dollars, you can buy an even more titanic expression of Riesling. Karlsmuhle's 1989 Kaseler Nies'chen Riesling Auslese is one of the most sensational Rieslings I have ever tasted. In fact, its incredible bouquet and flavors almost suggest eau-de-vie of apricots. High acidity makes the wine taste drier than it is, but this superbly extracted, profoundly concentrated wine offers a dazzling interplay of mineral, slate, and honeyed peach- and applelike fruitiness. It is rich, full, long, and, more important, impeccably focused. Drink this phenomenal Riesling over the next 2–4 years.

HERIBERT KERPEN (MOSEL)* * * * *

1990 Bernkasteler Badstube Riesling Auslese	C	95
1989 Bernkasteler Badstube Riesling Spätlese	B	89
1990 Graacher Himmelreich Riesling Auslese	C	90

1989 Graacher Himmelreich Riesling Beerenauslese	E	93
1989 Graacher Himmelreich Riesling Eiswein	E	90
1989 Graacher Himmelreich Riesling Spätlese	B	91
1990 Wehlener Sonnenuhr Riesling Auslese (1-star)	C	91
1989 Wehlener Sonnenuhr Riesling Auslese (1-star)	C	90
1990 Wehlener Sonnenuhr Riesling Auslese (2-star)	C	94
1989 Wehlener Sonnenuhr Riesling Auslese (2-star)	C	94
1990 Wehlener Sonnenuhr Riesling Auslese (3-star)	D	98
1989 Wehlener Sonnenuhr Riesling Auslese (3-star)	D	97
1990 Wehlener Sonnenuhr Riesling Beerenauslese	E	95
1989 Wehlener Sonnenuhr Riesling Beerenauslese	E	94
1990 Wehlener Sonnenuhr Riesling Eiswein	E	93
1989 Wehlener Sonnenuhr Riesling Kabinett	B	89
1989 Wehlener Sonnenuhr Riesling Spätlese	B	92
1989 Wehlener Sonnenuhr Riesling Trockenbeerenauslese	EE	98

The wines of Kerpen are unquestionably challenging the exceptional wines that emerge from the steep slopes of Graacher Himmelreich and Wehlener Sonnenuhr made by renowned producers such as J. J. Prüm and Dr. Ernst Loosen. Kerpen's 1988s were stunning, as were his 1989s. It is worth noting that many Mosel producers, particularly Fritz Haag and J. J. Prüm, did not excel in the latter vintage. The 1990s, not surprisingly, are wines of extraordinary depth of flavor, delicacy, and precision. The 1990 Graacher Himmelreich Riesling Auslese is phenomenal, if only because of its remarkable freshness, lemony, floral, slatelike nose, and superb richness of fruit buttressed by zinging acidity. A wonderful wine to smell and taste, it should last for at least 4–6 years. The 1990 Wehlener Sonnenuhr Riesling Auslese (1-star) exhibits an explosive nose of floral-scented fruit, rich, admirably concentrated flavors, crisp acidity, and a refreshingly long, clean, off-dry finish. The balance is nearly perfect. It seems redundant to say, but the 1990 Bernkasteler Badstube Riesling Auslese is another profound, rich, yet remarkably well-balanced wine. With an acidic tension etched throughout its personality, the wine possesses an extraordinary presence on the palate, along with an unbelievable length and intensity; yet it is delicate, lively, and refreshing. The finish must last for nearly a minute. Drink this staggering Riesling over the next 5–10 or more years. There is not much difference between the 2-star and 3-star 1990 Wehlener Sonnenuhr Riesling Auslese offerings. Both are great Rieslings that are still relatively unevolved, yet they reveal striking concentration and balance. The 2-star displays gobs of extract, is more closed than any of the other Kerpen wines, and is seemingly more unevolved. Yet the rich, slate, apple, floral character of the Riesling sings from the glass in this medium-sweet, brilliantly balanced wine. The 3-star must be tasted to be believed. It is hard to imagine Riesling can be so staggeringly rich, lavish, and intense, yet so well delineated, with enough acidity to provide uplift and exceptional clarity. The huge nose suggests some botrytis in the honeyed, leather, apricot, peach, and multitude of other fruit and mineral smells that emanate from the glass. In the mouth there is layer upon layer of fruit, yet the finish pulls everything into focus, resulting in a moving drinking experience. This is a monumental Riesling for drinking over the next decade. Kerpen's 1990 Wehlener Sonnenuhr Riesling Eiswein is also outstanding, with its unctuous, hugely concentrated, deep, cherry, apple, and floral flavors buttressed with just enough acidity. Again, its exceptional purity of flavor is memorable. These wines can last 40–50 years, and although the price is justifiable, given the microscopic quantities produced, it is intimidating. Kerpen's 1990 Wehlener Sonnenuhr Riesling Beerenauslese also has awesome length and extraordinary clarity and purity, all characteristics of wines made by this prodigious producer. It is not unlikely that 20–40 or more years of aging potential is possible. Among Kerpen's 1989 selections, the Wehlener Sonnenuhr Riesling Kabinett is an impeccably delineated, rich, full wine bursting with dry, honeyed, apple, peach, and floral flavors. It is gorgeously fruity yet has retained its sense of elegance and precision and finishes in a dry, highly satisfying manner. Drink it over the next 1–2 years. Kerpen produced three Spätlese wines that all provide a remarkable degree of ecstasy, particularly when one considers their amazingly modest prices (at a time when the American dollar buys almost nothing against the European currencies, especially the German mark). The 1989 Graacher Himmelreich Riesling Spätlese is a superconcentrated, beautifully made wine that is slightly off-dry but rich and deep, with that haunting apple blossom, flowery component that can be found in both the wine's bouquet and flavors. This is a smashingly good Spätlese with a remarkable finish. It should drink well for the next 3–4 years. Kerpen's 1989 Bernkasteler Badstube Riesling Spätlese is a bit drier but gloriously fruity, with that superb flinty, minerallike character intertwined with intense flavors of apples and peaches. This medium-bodied, highly extracted wine has just enough acidity to provide balance and grip. Drink it over the next 2–3 years. As good as the Bernkasteler Badstube Riesling is, the 1989 Wehlener Sonnenuhr Riesling Spätlese offers a smorgasbord of opulent fruit that is terrific to smell, terrific to taste, and terrific to ponder over after swallowing. All of these wines are unbelievably crystal clear in their presentations and boggle the taster with their ripeness and opulence while maintaining a pinpoint precision. They should offer profound drinking for at least 2–4 years. In top vintages, Kerpen produces three separate *cuvées* of Auslese. They are easy to distinguish, as either 1, 2, or 3 stars are marked on the label. All of these Wehlener Sonnenuhr Auslese offerings in 1989 are outstanding wines, but there is no doubting that the 2- and 3-star Ausleses are ravishing, with extraordinary extract to go along with their exquisite balance and clarity. The 1989 Wehlener Sonnenuhr Riesling Auslese (1-star) has a delicate yet persistent and intense, flowery bouquet, followed by crisp, lovely, graceful flavors exhibiting intense concentration of fruit, an off-dry taste, and a long, impeccably pure, well-delineated finish. The wine is softer than the 1988 but capable of lasting for at least 4–5 years. The 1989 Wehlener Sonnenuhr Riesling Auslese (2-star) is sensational, with its ultrarefined yet pristine flavors, gobs of apple- and slatelike fruit, medium body, and an inner core of depth and richness that is almost frightening. I cannot imagine a greater Auslese, even from the master of Wehlener Sonnenuhr— J. J. Prüm. Given its slightly sweet style, it should be drunk as either an aperi-

tif or following the meal. The 3-star 1989 Wehlener Sonnenuhr Riesling
Auslese is an unbelievably profound, honeyed, sweet wine with extraordinary
depth and enough liquid slate– and eau de vie–like apple fruit to please any
Mosel fanatic. The sad news is that only 30 cases of this wine were produced—
for the world! The importer tells me that 20 cases were shipped to the United
States. It is phenomenal, but I recognize few readers will ever have a chance to
taste a bottle. It should drink well for at least 4–7 years. Kerpen made a
plethora of big, sweet, extremely late-harvest wines in 1989. There is no doubting that the 1989 Graacher Himmelreich Riesling Eiswein is outstanding, but
frankly, when compared with what Kerpen did at the Auslese, Spätlese, and
Kabinett levels, I was less enthralled by the Eiswein. It is intense, firmly structured, and stylish, possessing as well that crystal-clear focus that Kerpen manages to get in these rich, highly extracted wines. However, it did not sing, and I
wondered whether the wine was just closed and suffering from bottling. It is
undoubtedly outstanding, but just how good this wine will turn out vis-à-vis
Kerpen's other extraordinary successes remains to be seen. There can be no
questions concerning the success of the two Beerenauslese offerings from Kerpen in 1989. The 1989 Graacher Himmelreich Riesling Beerenauslese has a
huge aroma of cherries, apples, superripe peaches, as well as spectacularly
rich, thick, unctuous flavors that are buoyed by just enough acidity. It is a
decadently ripe, opulent, supersweet wine for drinking by itself or with fruit
tarts. In comparison, the 1989 Wehlener Sonnenuhr Riesling Beerenauslese
has higher acidity and residual sugar yet comes across as less sweet and more
elegant and riveting. It is restrained but should last for at least 10–20 years.
Last, there is Kerpen's 1989 Wehlener Sonnenuhr Riesling Trockenbeerenauslese. This fabulous wine is incredibly sweet yet awesomely balanced by
crisp acidity. What is amazing is the level of extraction that gives this wine the
taste of essence of apples and slate. Irrefutably exquisite! The only sobering
aspect is its price. **Anticipated maturity: Now–2010.**

J. F. KIMICH (RHEINPFALZ)* * * * *

1989 Deidesheimer Grainhubel Riesling Beerenauslese	D	93
1989 Deidesheimer Herrgottsacker Riesling Kabinett	A	90
1989 Deidesheimer Herrgottsacker Riesling Spätlese	B	90
1990 Deidesheimer Kalkofen Riesling Auslese Trocken	B	87
1989 Deidesheimer Kieselberg Riesling Spätlese Halbtrocken	B	88
1989 Deidesheimer Langenmorgen Scheurebe Auslese	B	90
1989 Deidesheimer Leinhohle Riesling Auslese	C	92
1989 Deidesheimer Leinhohle Riesling Kabinett	B	88
1989 Deidesheimer Nonnenstuck Grauburgunder Spätlese Trocken	B	72
1990 Forster Elster Riesling Kabinett	A	88
1989 Forster Mariengarten Riesling Beerenauslese	D	97
1990 Forster Pechstein Riesling Spätlese Halbtrocken	B	89
1990 Forster Pechstein Riesling Spätlese Trocken	B	86

1989 Forster Stift Gewürztraminer Auslese	C	85
1989 Forster Stift Gewürztraminer Spätlese Trocken	B	88
1989 Forster Ungeheuer Riesling Auslese	C	92
1989 Forster Ungeheuer Riesling Spätlese Trocken	B	90
1990 Ruppertsburger Nussbien Riesling Kabinett	A	87
1989 Ruppertsburger Nussbien Riesling Kabinett	A	90
1990 Ruppertsburger Reiterpfad Riesling Auslese	C	86
1989 Ruppertsburger Reiterpfad Riesling Kabinett Halbtrocken	A	86
1990 Ruppertsburger Reiterpfad Riesling Kabinett Trocken	A	85

The wines of J. F. Kimich offer excellent quality/price rapport. The Kimich style offers an intense bouquet and well-balanced, concentrated, explosively fruity flavors. The 1990 Ruppertsburger Reiterpfad Riesling Kabinett Trocken was bone dry, with loads of dried peach fruit. Although there is a degree of austerity to the wine, the elegance, high acidity, and underlying concentration suggest it will last for another 4–5 years. Quite tasty! The 1990 Forster Pechstein Riesling Spätlese Trocken displayed the telltale Kimich perfume of flowery scents combined with a degree of earthiness and the smell of ripe peaches. In the mouth there is a good inner core of nicely concentrated fruit, crisp acidity, and good structure. The finish is admirably long. Drink it over the next 5–6 years. The 1990 Deidesheimer Kalkofen Riesling Auslese Trocken was floral, rich, and dry, with gorgeous ripeness and intensity. I even detected an enthralling vanillin character in the wine's taste. Drink it over the next 5 or more years. Even richer, but still dry, was the 1990 Forster Pechstein Riesling Spätlese Halbtrocken. The nose of dried fruits, vanillin, and mineral scents is followed by a rich, deep, medium-bodied wine with a distinctive spicy character. With its good acidity and extraction, this wine should easily last for up to a decade. The more flamboyantly styled and intensely fragrant 1989 Deidesheimer Langenmorgen Scheurebe Auslese not only represents an exceptional bargain, it offers big, chewy, lusty fruit in a dry, medium-bodied style. The fragrance could almost fill the room, and the long finish suggests even greater evolution over the next 4–6 years. This is a super wine from the consistently underrated Scheurebe grape. The 1989 Deidesheimer Leinhohle Riesling Kabinett exhibited an attractive flowery perfume, followed by long, admirably concentrated, spicy, crisp flavors, and a dry finish. Although not as ostentatious as some of Kimich's wines, it is more classically oriented in its restrained personality. The 1990 Forster Elster Riesling Kabinett displayed the distinctive smell of petrol that is much more commonly encountered with Rieslings from Alsace. It is medium bodied and dry, with excellent concentration, fine clarity to its flavors, and a long finish. For $10, it is a super bargain. The 1990 Ruppertsburger Nussbien Riesling Kabinett, which was more backward, exhibited a dried pit fruit character, elegance, and Kimich's fragrant bouquet, followed by pure, impressively delineated flavors. The finish is long and dry. Drink it over the next 5–6 years. For some reason Kimich's 1990 Ruppertsburger Reiterpfad Riesling Auslese was more closed and less fragrant than his other wines. My rating may be conservative, but I did not see the underlying depth or personality that most of Kimich's other wines exhibited. Last, the

1989 Deidesheimer Grainhubel Riesling Beerenauslese, with its huge, smoky, pineapple, exotic-scented nose, was a beautifully made, unctuous, sweet wine. In the mouth it possessed a stony, earthy, petrollike essence of fruit, excellent acidity, and a long, unctuous finish. Drink this beauty over the next 15–20 years. With the exception of Kimich's misconceived 1989 Deidesheimer Non-nenstuck Grauburgunder Spätlese Trocken—a lean, acidic, insipid wine—this Rheinpfalz producer has enjoyed as great a success as any other producer in the region. For authoritative, intense, dry, full-bodied wines, there is no one who makes better Trockens than Kimich. The 1989 Forster Ungeheuer Riesling Spätlese Trocken is a big, rich, full-bodied, explosively fruity, flowery wine, with dry, intensely concentrated flavors and a long, beautifully balanced finish. It would be an ideal wine for fish and poultry. Drink it over the next 3–4 years. The 1989 Ruppertsburger Reiterpfad Riesling Kabinett Halbtrocken exhibits a great spring flower garden nose, broad-shouldered, long, ripe, succulent flavors, and a dry, surprisingly intense finish. In comparison, the 1989 Deidesheimer Kieselberg Riesling Spätlese Halbtrocken is even more perfumed, with medium to full body, excellent extract, and a long, dry, crisp, impeccably pure finish. Both of these Halbtrockens should be consumed over the next 2–3 years. The 1989 Ruppertsburger Nussbien Riesling Kabinett and the 1989 Deidesheimer Herrgottsacker Riesling Kabinett are sensational values. The Ruppertsberger Nussbien offers an exotic cinnamon and baked apple–scented bouquet, full body, and gorgeously rich, intense, dry, medium-to full-bodied flavors. The Deidesheimer Herrgottsacker is also exotic, with a full-bodied, highly extracted, rich, intense character and a dry, spicy finish. These two wines could easily be inserted in a tasting of white burgundies. What one gets is sensational levels of dry fruit extract, without any weakness being masked by new oak or faulty winemaking. These are wines to buy by the case and drink over the next 2–3 years. The powerful, authoritative style of Kimich is also evident in his 1989 Deidesheimer Herrgottsacker Riesling Spätlese. Michael Broadbent's expression, "an iron fist in a velvet glove," comes to mind when tasting this well-focused, surprisingly dry Spätlese with immense body and a long, muscular finish. This is a big, drier-style Spätlese that is meant to be served with intensely flavored food. If tasted blindfolded, the 1989 Forster Ungeheuer Riesling Auslese could almost be mistaken for a red wine, perhaps even a Côte Rôtie. The huge aroma of bacon fat and the explosively rich, awesomely concentrated palate give this slightly off-dry wine a fabulous presence. In the mouth it is deep, exotic, opulent, and tasty. Given the fact that it is an Auslese, I would have expected it to be even sweeter, but there is only a slight degree of residual sweetness. It should drink well for at least 5–8 years. The 1989 Deidesheimer Leinhohle Riesling Auslese has better acidity than the Forster Ungeheuer, as well as stupendous concentration, a fabulously deep, opulent palate, and that aggressively fragrant, intense perfume that Kimich seems to have gotten in most of his 1989s. It, too, should drink well for the next 5–7 years. Kimich does as fine a job with Gewürztraminer as does the famous German winery of Müller-Catoir. The 1989 Forster Stift Gewürztraminer Spätlese Trocken is an extremely dry, finesse-filled wine, with that intense lychee nut, spicy, tangy, smoky character that Gewürztraminer produces. It is a bone-dry, austere, yet amazingly lively, medium-bodied Gewürztraminer that could give some of the competition from Alsace a run for its money. Drink it over the next 2–3 years. The 1989 Forster

Stift Gewürztraminer Auslese exhibits extremely high acidity and is a much fuller, richer wine than the Gewürztraminer Spätlese Trocken, but it is still relatively dry and very intense. What impressed me the most was the correct Gewürztraminer nose of lychee nuts and roses. However, its finish is a bit short compared with the Gewürztraminer Spätlese Trocken. A number of great sweet wines were produced in Germany in the 1989 vintage, but the Forster Mariengarten Riesling Beerenauslese, a declassified Trockenbeerenauslese, has staggering concentration and is very sweet, with persistently long yet wonderfully well-focused, apricot, cinnamon, and honeyed melon flavors and a finish that must last for over a minute. It should drink well for 10–15 years.

ADOLF LOTZBEYER (NAHE)* * * *

1990	Feilbingerter Konigsgarten Riesling Eiswein	D	98
1989	Feilbingerter Konigsgarten Riesling Trockenbeerenauslese	E	94
1989	Feilbingerter Konigsgarten Rulander Eiswein	D	92
1990	Feilbingerter Konigsgarten Scheurebe Auslese	B	93
1989	Feilbingerter Konigsgarten Scheurebe Beerenauslese	D	90
1989	Niederhauser Stollenberg Scheurebe Beerenauslese	D	91
1990	Niederhauser Stollenberg Scheurebe Spätlese	B	91
1990	Norheimer Dellchen Riesling Auslese	C	88

If there was ever a case where the unadulterated expression of vividly pure fruit can turn wines into something majestic, it is here. Based on aroma, Lotzbeyer's 1990 Niederhauser Stollenberg Scheurebe Spätlese is a dead ringer for a Côte Rôtie. The huge, smoky, bacon fat, exotic nose of this wine has more in common with a single-vineyard Guigal Côte Rôtie—a red wine—than anyone can imagine. In the mouth this dry, rich, exotic, kinky wine is loaded with decadent levels of fruit. Everything comes together in a sensationally concentrated, hedonistic package. Drink this wine of almost unbearable richness, purity, and fruit over the next 4–5 years. The 1990 Norheimer Dellchen Riesling Auslese is, by Lotzbeyer's standards, a tightly knit, more high-strung style of wine where the acidity holds everything in check. It is off-dry and extremely intense, so that one can sense the impressive extraction of fruit in the mouth and finish. This could turn into an exciting wine in another year or so. One does not have to wait that long for the 1990 Feilbingerter Konigsgarten Scheurebe Auslese (available only in the new 500-ml packaging). This explosively rich, dazzling wine displays plenty of acidity to keep its powerful flavors in check. There is layer upon layer of fruit in this monster, off-dry Auslese. Wow! Drink this knockout wine over the next 5–6 years. The 1990 Feilbingerter Konigsgarten Riesling Eiswein is one of the titans of the vintage. Moreover, the price is not that intimidating for an Eiswein. Some botrytis is present in the nose. In the mouth the honeyed richness goes on and on. Tantalizing acids give the huge fruit and weight of this wine a degree of precision and clarity that makes for a spellbinding drinking experience. It is intense, decadent, rich, and fun, as well as a pleasure, even a privilege, to taste. It will last for 20 or more years.

ALFRED MERKELBACH (MOSEL)* * * *

1990 Erdener Treppchen Riesling Auslese Fuder #3	B	88
1990 Erdener Treppchen Riesling Auslese Fuder #4	C	92
1990 Erdener Treppchen Riesling Spätlese	B	89
1989 Erdener Treppchen Riesling Spätlese #8	B	90
1989 Erdener Treppchen Riesling Spätlese #9	B	89
1989 Erdener Treppchen Riesling Spätlese #16	B	89
1990 Kinheimer Rosenberg Riesling Auslese	B	90
1989 Kinheimer Rosenberg Riesling Kabinett	A	86
1990 Kinheimer Rosenberg Riesling Spätlese	B	87
1990 Urziger Wurzgarten Riesling Auslese Fuder #9	C	94
1990 Urziger Wurzgarten Riesling Auslese Fuder #10	C	90
1990 Urziger Wurzgarten Riesling Auslese Fuder #11	C	93
1990 Urziger Wurzgarten Riesling Auslese Fuder #13	C	90
1989 Urziger Wurzgarten Riesling Auslese #17	C	91
1989 Urziger Wurzgarten Riesling Kabinett	A	88
1990 Urziger Wurzgarten Riesling Spätlese Fuder #6	B	89
1990 Urziger Wurzgarten Riesling Spätlese Fuder #7	B	92
1989 Urziger Wurzgarten Riesling Spätlese #13	B	86
1989 Urziger Wurzgarten Riesling Spätelse #14	B	85
1989 Urziger Wurzgarten Riesling Spätelse #10	B	90

Considering the popularity of wines from the Mosel, and the quality and astonishingly modest prices of the 1990s from Alfred Merkelbach, these offerings should be runaway hits. I did not think Merkelbach could improve on his splendid performance in 1989, but as my palate and pen suggest, he has done just that. Merkelbach appears to ignore all the drier wines in the German spectrum and goes right for the taster with a Spätlese palate. The 1990 Kinheimer Rosenberg Riesling Spätlese exhibits vividly ripe aromas of apples and minerals. In the mouth its crisp acidity provides uplift and a refreshing zest to the tasty gobs of ripe fruit that are present. This off-dry, beautifully rendered Spätlese should be drunk over the next 4–5 years. The 1990 Erdener Treppchen Riesling Spätlese possesses even more depth and is also more tightly knit and higher strung. Plenty of classy minerals, flowers, and apples are present in its bouquet and flavors. The finish is drier than in the Kinheimer Rosenberg. Drink it over the next 5–7 or more years. The same elegance, clarity, super-ripeness, and liquid essence of minerals, currants, and berries can be found in Merkelbach's 1990 Urziger Wurzgarten Riesling Spätlese Fuder #6. It is borderline great stuff, as well as a great deal at $13 a bottle. It, too, should have at least 5–7 years of graceful evolution. I was really turned on by the 1990 Urziger Wurzgarten Riesling Spätlese Fuder #7. The huge, soaring aromas of freshly squeezed lemons and other citrus fruits, combined with the vivid scents of steel, slate, strawberries, and apples, offer a dramatic introduction to this drier-style, phenomenally concentrated, astonishingly well-balanced Spätlese. This reasonably priced beauty should be gobbled up by consumers—even in tough economic times. The extraordinary values continue with the 1990 Kinheimer Rosenberg Riesling Auslese. The decadence level is raised a notch with the penetrating, powerful nose of slate, minerals, citrus, spring flowers, and ripe fruit. In the mouth there is excellent depth, penetrating acidity, and a sense that no one element dominates the wine's character. The wine's harmony is nearly perfect. This off-dry Auslese should last for at least a decade. Though it may appear redundant to discuss the different fuder (separate *cuvée*) offerings from Merkelbach, they are all slightly different. For example, the 1990 Erdener Treppchen Riesling Auslese Fuder #3 is a more direct, open-knit style of wine than the 1990 Erdener Treppchen Riesling Auslese Fuder #4, which is somewhat reserved and steely and at the same time more concentrated, with extraordinary focus and precision to its flavors of oranges, minerals, flowers, and apples. It exhibits a super backbone of acidity, as well as a finish that goes on and on. Fuder #4 should drink well for at least a decade or more. If you prefer pure elegance, Fuder #3 should get your nod. If you want balance and elegance accompanied by greater depth and authoritative flavors, Fuder #4 is the likely choice. The 1990 Urziger Wurzgarten Riesling Auslese Fuder #13 is an intense, strawberry-scented, off-dry wine that makes a wonderfully pure impact on the palate. Gobs of streamlined fruit caress the palate, and there is enough acidity to provide zest and self-expression. It is a real winner. Fuder #11 of this wine was awesome. Its extraordinary display of ripeness, high acid levels, and aromatic purity and complexity offer everything I could want in an off-dry, brilliantly balanced, rich Riesling. Both the Fuder #13 and #11 should last for up to a decade or more. The 1990 Urziger Wurzgarten Riesling Auslese Fuder #10 was relatively closed. In 4–5 years it may prove to be the best of this group of wines, but at present it is less evolved and sweeter than the other Auslese offerings from Merkelbach. Although the wine possesses considerable concentration, it does not sing. Nevertheless, you cannot ignore the liquid stone character in its baked pear and apple fruitiness. Undoubtedly a terrific wine, it will require several years in the cellar. Merkelbach's Fuder #9 (only 110 cases were produced) is a breathtaking wine of extraordinary precision, richness, and opulence. The sweetest of all of these wines, it tastes as if it were a downgraded Beerenauslese. The wine exhibits not only an almost perfect sense of balance because of the high acids achieved in the 1990 vintage, but also extraordinary flavor concentration and persistence. The finish lasts well over a minute. Although it would be a pleasure to drink now, German wine enthusiasts tell me that it will evolve gracefully for at least a decade. The best wines from Merkelbach tend to be those from the Erdener Treppchen vineyard, and that again is the case in 1989. There are two beguiling Kabinetts. The 1989 Kinheimer Rosenberg Riesling Kabinett is fresh and delicate, with a powerful slate-scented and -flavored character. It is dry and has a good crisp finish. Drink it over the next 1–2 years. The 1989 Urziger Wurzgarten Riesling Kabinett has a more flowery, mineral-scented bouquet, beautiful, nicely extracted fruit flavors, medium body, and good acidity in its moderately long, dry finish. It is a classic example of just how tasty, and how reasonably priced, a fine Kabinett can be. There is a range of six Spätlese wines from both Erdener Treppchen and Urziger Wurzgarten, all of

which are designated by special cask numbers. I gave my highest marks to the
Erdeners, because they tasted more mouth-filling, forward, and interesting.
The 1989 Erdener Treppchen Riesling Spätlese #16 has a gorgeous applelike,
floral-scented bouquet; dry, rich, fresh, slaty flavors; and a clear-as-crystal,
dry, zippy finish. Even more impressive was the 1989 Erdener Treppchen
Riesling Spätlese #8. Riper, with an even more steely, liquid slate character,
this rich, spicy, yet amazingly delicate wine tasted slightly off-dry but fuller
and longer in the mouth. The Erdener Treppchen Riesling Spätlese #9 was
dominated by a linear structure, tasted leaner than the #8, but had a powerful
bouquet of liquid slate and cold metal. Light, lovely, perfumed, and spicy, this
was the most backward of the Erdener Treppchen Spätlese offerings from
Merkelbach. I would opt for drinking all three of these wines over the near
term, given their soft, forward fruitiness. As for the three offerings from Urziger
Wurzgarten, the 1989 Urziger Wurzgarten Riesling Spätlese #14 was tightly
knit, as well as the lightest and least ripe of all the Spätlese offerings. There
was a certain bluntness present, but it possessed enough fruit to merit a respectable rating. I had a similar impression of the off-dry 1989 Urziger
Wurzgarten Riesling Spätlese #13. However, in the mouth it tasted more concentrated, with plenty of spicy, apple- and mineral-flavored fruit, medium
body, and a slightly sweet, soft, and concentrated finish. The star, however, is
the 1989 Urziger Wurzgarten Riesling Spätlese #20. Sumptuously fruity, with
a rich, creamy, almost burgundian texture, this highly extracted, opulent, gorgeously perfumed wine was the most concentrated and richest of all the
Merkelbach Spätlese offerings from both Urziger and Erdener. I would drink
this wine over the next 5–6 years. Last, take all of the characteristics of the
Urziger Wurzgarten Riesling Spätlese #10 and intensify them, then add more
spice and an intriguing smoky element. What you then will get is the 1989
Urziger Wurzgarten Riesling Auslese #17. It is sweeter yet remains a sleekly
built, concentrated, decadently fruity Auslese that would make an ideal aperitif wine or one to have at the conclusion of a meal. It should drink well for 4–6
years.

MÜLLER-CATOIR (RHEINPFALZ)* * * * *

1989 Gewürztraminer Trocken	C	94
1989 Gimmeldinger Meerspinne Gewürztraminer Auslese	C	97
1990 Haardter Burgergarten Muskateller Spätlese Halbtrocken	C	93
1989 Haardter Burgergarten Riesling Kabinett	B	88
1990 Haardter Burgergarten Riesling Kabinett Halbtrocken	B	91
1990 Haardter Burgergarten Riesling Kabinett Trocken	B	89
1989 Haardter Burgergarten Riesling Spätlese	B	92
1989 Haardter Burgergarten Riesling Spätlese Halbtrocken	B	88
1989 Haardter Herrenletten Grauburgunder Beerenauslese	D	94
1990 Haardter Herrenletten Riesling Spätlese	C	93
1990 Haardter Mandelring Scheurebe Auslese	C	95
1988 Haardter Mandelring Scheurebe Kabinett	B	88

1990 Haardter Mandelring Scheurebe Spätlese	C	94
1989 Haardter Mandelring Scheurebe Spätlese Halbtrocken	C	93
1990 Mussbacher Eselshaut Rieslaner Auslese	C	90
1989 Mussbacher Eselshaut Rieslaner Auslese	C	91
1990 Mussbacher Eselshaut Rieslaner Beerenauslese	D	98.
1990 Mussbacher Eselshaut Rieslaner Trockenbeerenauslese	E	100
1986 Mussbacher Eselshaut Rieslaner Trockenbeerenauslese	E	98
1990 Mussbacher Eselshaut Riesling Auslese	D	94
1989 Mussbacher Eselshaut Riesling Kabinett Halbtrocken	B	85
1988 Mussbacher Eselshaut Riesling Spätlese Trocken	C	86
1988 Mussbacher Eselshaut Scheurebe Auslese	C	96
1989 Mussbacher Eselshaut Scheurebe Auslese Trocken	C	95

Müller-Catoir's 1990s confirm that this is one of the world's greatest wineries, producing from such unfashionable grapes as Rieslaner, Scheurebe, and Muskateller some of the most profound white wines I have ever had the pleasure to taste. Interestingly, Hans-Günter Schwarz is another minimal interventionist winemaker, letting the grapes do the talking and interfering as little as possible oenologically. Isn't it ironic that so many of the world's most pleasurable wines are the result of producers who tend to keep the oenologists out of the winemaking process? Although it is easy to forget Müller-Catoir's success with Riesling because of the winery's fascination with other varietals, they do turn out some remarkable wines from this classic grape. The 1990 is a showcase vintage for Müller-Catoir and Riesling. For starters there is the 1990 Haardter Burgergarten Riesling Kabinett Trocken, a wine that smells like a zesty gin and tonic. It exhibits a quinine-lime-like nose; dry, intensely flavored, orange and mineral fruit; and a long, full-bodied, vividly pure finish. Drink this beauty over the next 5–6 years. The 1990 Haardter Burgergarten Riesling Kabinett Halbtrocken is a fantastic bargain. If this were a Grand Cru white burgundy selling at $14 a bottle, consumers would be standing in line for a bottle or two. This beautiful, ripe, intensely rich wine displays sensational extraction of flavor, a dry, impeccably well-balanced finish, and an astonishing inner core of fruit and spice. It should evolve beautifully given its good acidic spine. Drink it over the next decade. For a more exotic, flamboyant, decadent style of wine, check out the 1990 Haardter Burgergarten Muskateller Spätlese Halbtrocken. Although it possesses exceptionally high acidity, there is no doubting its tropical fruit–scented, exotic nose. In the mouth it is terrific, with layer upon layer of fruit (oranges, grapefruit, and lemons), as well as a smashingly pure, dazzlingly well-defined finish. Again, the length and extraction noticeable at the end of the palate is something to behold. Drink it over the next 5–6 years.

This winery tends to turn out mind-boggling efforts from the Scheurebe grape, and the 1990 Haardter Mandelring Scheurebe Spätlese is no exception. The spectacular nose offers a smorgasbord of tropical fruit aromas intertwined with scents of minerals and spices. In the mouth there is phenomenal extraction of fruit, a dry, chewy texture, and a ripe, awesome finish. This is an exciting wine, the likes of which cannot be found from any other winemaker or vineyard in the world. Drink it over the next 5–6 years. The 1990 Haardter Herrenletten Riesling Spätlese exhibits the telltale Müller-Catoir immense bouquet of spices, minerals, and applelike fruit. To say that it is penetrating is an understatement. In the mouth it is full bodied, with explosive power and richness, impeccable balance, and an overall sense of elegance and harmony. The high acidity of the 1990 vintage has made it a more ageworthy prospect than most of Müller-Catoir's previous efforts. Drink it over the next decade.

With respect to the three Auslese offerings, the 1990 Mussbacher Eselshaut Riesling Auslese displays extraordinary precision to its off-dry, ripe, superextracted, explosive flavors. The overwhelming sensation to this wine, which has an enthralling texture, is the essence of stones, citrus, apples, and flowers. It exhibits remarkable length and frighteningly perfect balance for its size. The 1990 Haardter Mandelring Scheurebe Auslese offers a fiery nose of brandy-soaked cake, followed by flavors that are fabulously rich, intense, and buttressed by good acidity. Despite its significant size and intensity, the wine is restrained because of sound acids. There is drama at almost every turn with this profoundly exotic and massively rich, slightly off-dry Auslese. Drink it over the next 4–7 years. By Müller-Catoir's standards, the 1990 Mussbacher Eselshaut Rieslaner Auslese is nearly a disappointment. Even though it is an outstanding wine, tasted alongside its peers the wine is less impressive. Perhaps it is more closed, or perhaps I caught it at a time when much of its slumbering personality had yet to awaken. Although the wine possesses impressive stuffing, the nose appears reticent. Overall it did not turn me on as much as the wines that preceded it.

With the extraordinary concentration and intensity Müller-Catoir obtains at almost all levels, readers can imagine just what decadence is offered by the 1990 Mussbacher Eselshaut Rieslaner Beerenauslese (60 cases produced) and the 1990 Mussbacher Eselshaut Rieslaner Trockenbeerenauslese (70 cases produced). Both are virtually perfect wines. Honeyed, with mind-blowing richness, they have a sizzling, electrifying, crisp acidity that cuts through all the fat to give them a surreal feel of perfection on the palate. Interestingly, I noticed that both wines had an intense cherry component to their multidimensional, honeyed flavors. Knockouts in every sense of the word, both should continue to evolve, developing further nuances and complexities, for at least another 15–25 years. Should you be so lucky as to come across a bottle of either of these beauties, they are well worth their prices. Müller-Catoir's 1989 Mussbacher Eselshaut Scheurebe Auslese Trocken tastes like a blend of Guigal's La Mouline, Mongeard-Mugneret's Grands-Echézeaux, and Château Le Pin, even though it is a white rather than a red wine. Light golden in color, with an explosive bouquet of smoky bacon fat, cassis, and honeyed fruit, this rich, full-bodied, staggeringly concentrated, dry wine is about as remarkable and distinctive a bottle of white wine as I have ever tasted. This mind-boggling wine should drink well for another 1–2 years. Müller-Catoir produced two Halbtrockens in 1989. The 1989 Mussbacher Eselshaut Riesling Kabinett Halbtrocken is good rather than exhilarating. It is an austere, spicy, dry, medium-bodied wine with fine extract and nicely delineated flavors, but in the company of Müller-Catoir's other wines, it tastes shy and less well endowed. It should drink nicely for another 4–5 years. In contrast, the 1989 Haardter Burgergarten Riesling Spätlese Halbtrocken is a wine with excellent intensity, rich, almost blockbuster flavors, a deep, chewy texture, an exotic, honeyed, almost banana-, peach-, and other tropical fruit–scented bouquet, and a long, heady finish. It is a smashing dry Riesling for pairing with intensely flavored dishes. It should drink well for the next 3–5 years. The 1989 Haardter Burgergarten Riesling Kabinett has a spicy, baked apple pie–, cinnamon-scented bouquet, wonderful delineating, relatively high acidity for a Müller-Catoir wine, and the concentration, weight, and richness that are a signature of his winemaking style. It is very dry and should last for another 4–5 years. In contrast, the 1989 Haardter Burgergarten Riesling Spätlese is, for $3 more, a profoundly rich, fabulously intense wine that most consumers would consider dry, although it is technically an off-dry style of wine. Its huge nose of spices, minerals, and applelike fruit is penetrating and persistent. In the mouth it is deep and full bodied, with gobs of tropical fruit and the lush, highly extracted inner core Müller-Catoir achieves consistently in his wines. The finish is amazingly long. It should drink well for another 3–5 years.

Müller-Catoir has produced one of the greatest Gewürztraminers I have ever tasted. The 1989 Gimmeldinger Meerspinne Gewürztraminer Auslese has an explosively potent, aromatic bouquet of bacon fat, lychee nuts, and dried rose petals. In the mouth its concentration is stupendous. The wine is off-dry. Because of its weight and low acidity, it is so overwhelmingly rich and intense that it must be served alone or paired only with the spiciest and most extreme styles of cooking. Drink this beauty over the next 4–5 years. By the standards of this winery, the 1989 Mussbacher Eselshaut Rieslaner Auslese is a restrained wine. Nevertheless one would be hard-pressed to find more depth of fruit extract and precision and intensity than in this exceptional wine that finishes dry and could easily match the greatest white burgundies and pre-1982 Chalone Chardonnays for power and muscle. Its huge bouquet of bananas and other tropical fruits nearly disguises its massive power and intensity. This extraordinary effort should provide terrific drinking over the next 3–5 years.

Only 50 cases of the 1989 Haardter Herrenletten Grauburgunder Beerenauslese were produced. This decadently rich, honeyed, sweet wine must be served at the end of a meal. One can extrapolate from the drier style of Müller-Catoir wines the concentration this man is capable of achieving in his sweet wines. Its huge, ripe nose of superripe peach fruit assaults the palate with persuasive power and does not let loose. It has it all from start to finish. My best guess is that this superbly balanced, rich Beerenauslese will drink well over the next 5–10 years. The 1988 Mussbacher Eselshaut Scheurebe Auslese left me groping for appropriate superlatives. It offers a gloriously fragrant bouquet suggestive of mint, cassis, and rum-soaked fruitcake. In the mouth the concentration level is thrilling. This is the essence of a wine, fabulously deep, profoundly tasty and exotic, with a finish that explodes. This superb, off-dry wine should be drunk over the next 3–4 years. One can hardly find a better Kabinett than the 1988 Haardter Mandelring Scheurebe Kabinett. By Müller-Catoir's standards this is a relatively shy, understated wine, but it is still bursting with complexity and flavor. The intense bouquet suggests limes, apples, and melons. With rich, full-bodied, yet exceptionally polished and elegant flavors, this wine has a surprisingly long, even astonishing finish. It is a beauty, with higher extract than one finds in many of France's top burgundies. I would opt for drinking it over the next 2–3 years. Müller-Catoir's 1988 Mussbacher Eselshaut Riesling Spätlese Trocken has an intriguing grapefruit-, herblike bouquet, leaner flavors than the Kabinett, and a spritziness that I never before noticed in Müller-Catoir's wines. It is very good rather than exceptional. Ironically, it seems that Müller-Catoir excels with grapes such as Grauburgunder, Rieslaner, Scheurebe, and Gewürztraminer more frequently than it does with Riesling, normally the classic white wine grape of Germany. The 1989 Gewürztraminer Trocken can rival the finest wines I have ever tasted from such superlative Alsatian producers as Domaine Weinbach and Zind-Humbrecht. I do not say that lightly, being an unequivocal Gewürztraminer fanatic. The huge bouquet of smoky bacon fat and barbecued fowl soars from the glass. In the mouth this superripe, incredibly spicy, rich, decadently intense wine is dry, with extraordinary precision, extract, and concentration to its flavors. This is the kind of Gewürztraminer that one dreams about. Drink it over the next 3–4 years. Another great 1989 wine just released by Müller-Catoir is the Haardter Mandelring Scheurebe Spätlese Halbtrocken. Vinified dry, this full-bodied, intensely concentrated wine offers a kaleidoscope of aromas and intense, exotic, fruit flavors combined with an opulent, chewy texture and a dry, explosive finish. If one were to be supercritical, I suppose the relatively low acidity makes this wine's aging potential suspect. But who cares? These dry wines are among the most pleasurable and dramatic offerings from Germany I have had the good fortune to taste in the last year. For readers who have a craving for nectar, Müller-Catoir offers a 1986 Mussbacher Eselshaut Rieslaner Trockenbeerenauslese. I doubt there is any other sweet wine in the world selling for $60 that has such remarkable intensity yet riveting precision to its massive, unbelievably extracted fruit flavors. This amazing wine gets my nomination for the most exotic wine I have recently tasted. At 5 years of age the wine is young and unevolved, so I suspect this monumental sweet wine will last for at least another decade.

J. J. PRÜM (MIDDLE MOSEL)* * * * *

1990	Graacher Himmelreich Riesling Auslese	D	94
1989	Graacher Himmelreich Riesling Kabinett	B	82
1990	Wehlener Sonnenuhr Riesling Auslese	D	93
1989	Wehlener Sonnenuhr Riesling Auslese	D	89
1989	Wehlener Sonnenuhr Riesling Auslese Long Gold Capsule	EEE	92
1989	Wehlener Sonnenuhr Riesling Kabinett	C	83
1990	Wehlener Sonnenuhr Riesling Spätlese	D	91
1989	Wehlener Sonnenuhr Riesling Spätlese	C	85

Prüm is unquestionably the most renowned producer in Germany, and often his wines are candidates for best of the vintage. He made great 1988s that are largely superior to his sound but somewhat indifferent 1989s. The 1990s look to be a return to the exceptional quality one expects from J. J. Prüm. I should point out that his top 1989 was not reviewed last year, but I did finally have a chance to taste it, and it is overwhelmingly Prüm's most interesting wine in 1989. The 1989 Wehlener Sonnenuhr Riesling Auslese Long Gold Capsule is a moderately sweet, superbly concentrated, ripe wine with a beautiful perfume of wet stones, flowers, and supermature fruit. As outstanding as it is, however, it is dwarfed by some of the younger, more concentrated and compelling 1990s that J. J. Prüm has released. The price is as obscene as it is absurd.

The 1990 looks to be J. J. Prüm's greatest vintage since 1983. For starters, there is the 1990 Wehlener Sonnenuhr Riesling Spätlese, with its bouquet of vanilla, apples, and minerals. In the mouth there is great fruit, beautifully etched flavors, and a long, crisp, highly extracted finish. Drink this dry Spätlese over the next 7–10 years. The 1990 Wehlener Sonnenuhr Riesling Auslese displayed riveting aromas of cold steel, minerals, and flowers. Sensationally rich and off-dry, with astonishing concentration, this represents a phenomenal glass of Riesling. Drink it over the next decade. Last, the 1990 Graacher Himmelreich Riesling Auslese smelled and tasted like eau-de-vie of pears. There was a honeyed richness to this superbly concentrated, blazingly well-delineated wine. This absolutely staggering, off-dry Riesling should evolve even more nuances and subtleties over the next 10–12 or more years.

Both the 1989 Wehlener Sonnenuhr Riesling Kabinett and 1989 Graacher Himmelreich Riesling Kabinett were dry, lean, tart, pleasant, but uninspiring wines that lacked concentration and finished surprisingly short. I was also unimpressed with the 1989 Wehlener Sonnenuhr Riesling Spätlese. Although it clearly had more fruit, ripeness, and concentration than either of the Kabinetts, it was made in a relatively dry style. The best wine I tasted from Prüm in the 1989 vintage was his Wehlener Sonnenuhr Riesling Auslese, a honeyed, rich, medium-bodied wine with an excellent creamy, apple- and apricotlike fruitiness married beautifully with well-integrated ripe acidity. This lovely, intense wine should drink well for at least 5–7 years. All things considered, however, I would buy J. J. Prüm's 1988s rather than his 1989s.

VON SCHUBERT–MAXIMIN GRUNHAUS (RUWER)* * * * *

1989	Abtsberg Riesling Auslese	D	96
1990	Abtsberg Riesling Auslese Fuder #96	E	95
1989	Abtsberg Riesling Auslese Fuder #98	C	96
1990	Abtsberg Riesling Auslese Fuder #101	D	93
1989	Abtsberg Riesling Auslese #133	E	98
1989	Abtsberg Riesling Beerenauslese	EEE	99
1990	Abtsberg Riesling Eiswein	EEE	92
1990	Abtsberg Riesling Kabinett	C	86
1989	Abtsberg Riesling Kabinett	C	90
1990	Abtsberg Riesling Spätlese	C	90
1989	Abtsberg Riesling Spätlese	C	96
1990	Abtsberg Riesling Spätlese Trocken	C	87
1989	Bruderberg Riesling Kabinett	B	87
1990	Herrenberg Riesling Auslese	D	91
1989	Herrenberg Riesling Auslese	D	94

1990 Herrenberg Riesling Auslese Fuder #92	E	94
1989 Herrenberg Riesling Auslese #93	E	98
1989 Herrenberg Riesling Auslese Trocken	D	89
1990 Herrenberg Riesling Kabinett	C	86
1989 Herrenberg Riesling Kabinett	B	88
1989 Herrenberg Riesling Kabinett Trocken	B	86
1990 Herrenberg Riesling Spätlese	C	90
1989 Herrenberg Riesling Spätlese	C	92
1990 Herrenberg Riesling Trocken	B	85

These are among the most expensive German wines, but the 1989s from von Schubert were some of the vintage's most compelling wines, and the 1990s are among the stars of the year. Readers unfamiliar with Dr. Carl von Schubert may be interested to learn that the wines from his *monopole* vineyards Bruder-berg, Herrenberg, and Abtsberg are made in a highly concentrated, backward, high-acid style that requires years of patience. I recently participated in a ver-tical tasting with vintages going back over 20 years. Von Schubert's wines re-tain their freshness for at least 2 decades in the top years, with even the drier-style Kabinetts from years such as 1964 and 1967 fresh and glorious. The 1990s will require a considerable up-front investment in both money and patience. They will need at least 5–10 years to begin to display their true pedi-grees. The least expensive introduction to the style of von Schubert's wines is the 1990 Herrenberg Riesling Trocken. Tightly buttoned up, with bracingly high acidity, it is lean, hard, nearly impenetrable, and dry. Yet it contains an extra dimension of complexity and fragrance that tells you something more in-teresting will emerge with several more years of aging. The 1990 Abtsberg Riesling Spätlese Trocken exhibits more character, offering up more intense, floral, stony aromas, with more weight and depth on the palate. It finishes in a dry and austere manner. Lay it away for at least 2 years. Both the 1990 Her-renberg Riesling Kabinett and 1990 Abtsberg Riesling Kabinett are struc-tured, austere wines. The Herrenberg appears to be even more backward, needing at least 5–6 years of cellaring, whereas the Abtsberg is already ex-hibiting more complexity in its stony, mineral-, floral-scented nose and ripe, impressively extracted flavors. Both are drier-style Kabinetts that will hand-somely repay 10 years of cellaring. The difference between the 1990 Herren-berg Riesling Spätlese and 1990 Abtsberg Riesling Spätlese is nearly identical with that noticed between the two Kabinetts from these *monopole* vineyards. The Herrenberg is clearly outstanding, with its rich, stony, cherry-, floral-scented nose and highly extracted, rich, off-dry flavors. But the Abtsberg is even more concentrated, with an extraordinary combination of power, finesse, depth, and elegance on the palate. These two wines will be magnificent in 15–20 years; both possess that wonderful balance between intensity and fi-nesse, as well as the essence of minerallike flavors that make these wines so brilliantly well delineated in the mouth. The other five Riesling Ausleses I tasted from Maximin Grunhaus were all outstanding, off-dry wines with extra-ordinary high acidity as well as impressive extract levels. They were a shade behind the level of von Schubert's 1989s, but that might just be because the acid levels are higher. All of these wines should be given at least 5 years of cellaring, and they have the potential to last for at least 20–25 more years. The 1990 Herrenberg Riesling Auslese exhibited a superb, earthy, flinty nose intertwined with scents of lemons and flowers. In the mouth there was crisp acidity, superextraction, and a long, off-dry finish. The 1990 Abtsberg Riesling Auslese possessed searing acidity, and was tight (more backward than the Herrenberg), with exceptional length and wonderful purity and clarity. The 1990 Herrenberg Riesling Auslese Fuder #92 displayed a nervous tension between the acidity and the wine's fruit. Exceptionally long, it is oh, so backward. Here is an example of a great Riesling that should be cellared for 10 years before opening a bottle. Can you believe that? The 1990 Abtsberg Riesling Auslese Fuder #96 was similarly styled, although even more rich, with more of the liquefied mineral character that makes these wines so provocative. The 1990 Abtsberg Riesling Auslese Fuder #101 was riper, with more emphasis on pure, lemony-, apple-, mineral-scented and -flavored fruit. Determining the length of the finish is a hard call given how unevolved and young these exceptional wines now taste. The 1990 Abtsberg Riesling Eiswein (60 cases for the world) is, I am told, in need of at least 20 years of cellaring before it can be judged properly. That being said, I am a little leery of scoring it only a 92. Although it was frightfully high in acidity, it clearly possessed superrichness and potential. But, wow, what an investment in money and time is required in waiting for the magic! The 1989 Abtsberg Riesling Auslese Fuder #98, which is available only in half bottles, demonstrates that 1989 was a vintage of legendary proportions, at least for Maximin Grunhaus. The huge nose of liquefied minerals, earth, lemons, and flowers is something to relish. In the mouth there is dazzling concentration, extraordinary clarity of flavors, and a long, dry, superextracted finish. This is sensational Riesling from a great producer. When will it be ready to drink? No doubt the 1989s will mature before the 1990s, so this offering should be ready in another 3–4 years, although it will keep for at least 2 decades.

The 1989 Herrenberg Riesling Kabinett Trocken had a very intriguing lemon-lime-like, chalky, mineral, flowery-scented nose, light body, but wonderful precision and a fresh, exuberant finish. It is dry and should age nicely for another 3–4 years. The 1989 Herrenberg Riesling Auslese Trocken had fresh lemon-lime-like acidity and great focus to its flowery, apple blossom–like flavors. It is a tightly knit wine that is already bursting at the seams. This ripe, very dry, rich Auslese Trocken can be drunk over the next 5–7 years. The three Kabinett offerings from von Schubert ranged from excellent to sensational. The 1989 Bruderberg Riesling Kabinett had zipping acidity, a liquid mineral–like taste, very fine, ripe, yet delicate flavors, and a crisp finish. Very backward, it barely reveals its promising potential. The 1989 Herrenberg Riesling Kabinett displayed an intense apple, minerallike fruit bouquet, gobs of rich, fresh, intensely concentrated fruit, and a tart acidity that suggests the wine needs 3–4 years before it will reach its plateau of maturity. This is a Kabinett with enough ripeness, balance, and precision to last for a decade. The most impressive of this trio was the 1989 Abtsberg Riesling Kabinett. It displayed a huge bouquet of green apples, minerals, oranges, and peaches that was followed by a long, rich, ripe, dry, superextracted, perfectly balanced wine. It is hard to believe a Kabinett could have such impeccable balance, particularly in view of the amazing concentration. It is a glorious expression of a dry Riesling Kabinett from one of Germany's greatest producers. Drink it over the next 12–14 years. To put it mildly, the two Spätlese offerings are among the greatest Spätlese wines I have ever tasted. Perhaps it is a combination of three factors: (1) von Schubert uses wild yeasts; (2) only old oak *foudres* are employed for aging the wine; and (3) von Schubert is one of only a handful of German winemakers who refuse to filter. All three contribute to making remarkably intense wines loaded with aging potential. The 1989 Herrenberg Riesling Spätlese is an awesomely concentrated yet backward, profoundly flavored wine displaying remarkable depth (no doubt the result of low yields) and a superabundance of vanillin, peachlike fruit combined with scents of minerals and almonds. In the mouth the wine is amazingly deep, yet so crystal clear and defined that it gives the impression of dryness, although the overall acidity must be masking abundant quantities of sweetness. This wine should be at its best between 1993 and 2005. As stunning as the Herrenberg Spätlese is, the 1989 Abtsberg Riesling Spätlese is even greater and probably the most extraordinary Spätlese I have ever tasted. Full, rich, and splendidly extracted, this wine has intriguing honeyed, peach, herbal, vanillin, and tropical fruit scents that dance across the palate with purity and militarylike precision. Frankly, this wine, which tastes dry, is awesome. When did $21 buy such potential greatness and joy? It should drink well for another 12–15 years. There is a plethora of Auslese offerings from Maximin Grunhaus in 1989. The most expensive bottlings have a number indicated on the neck label, but one does not have to indulge in $50 Ausleses to find phenomenal richness and high quality. For example, the 1989 Herrenberg Riesling Auslese has a honeyed, tropical fruit, liquid mineral character and sensational depth, is off-dry, and has an amazingly long, intense finish. Drinking the 1989 Abtsberg Riesling Auslese is like drinking honeyed stones, an unusual description, I know, but all I could think of when the wine was in my mouth. It is a terrific, spectacularly deep, rich, off-dry Auslese that has layer upon layer of fruit and a dazzling finish. The problem is that the 1989 Herrenberg Riesling Auslese #93 and the 1989 Abtsberg Riesling Auslese #133 have even greater extraction and more precision and are as spectacular as any Riesling money can buy. They are massive, yet at the same time elegant and impeccably balanced wines. I suppose that is what makes them so hauntingly close to perfection. Last, there is the monumental 1989 Abtsberg Riesling Beerenauslese priced at $164 for a half bottle. This declassified Trockenbeerenauslese gushes with peach, apple, apricot, and mineral scents and flavors; it is extraordinarily rich and unctuous but never heavy or cloyingly sweet because of its sensational definition and acidity. I may have been unkind in not awarding it another point. Drink this fabulous dessert wine over the next 20–25 years. The wines from von Schubert's Maximin Grunhaus vineyards are true reference points in 1989.

4. PORTUGAL

PORT

Americans have finally begun to realize the great pleasures of a mature vintage port after a meal. For years this sumptuous and mellow fortified red wine was seriously undervalued; most of it was drunk in the private homes and clubs of the United Kingdom. Prices, which soared in the early and mid-1980s, collapsed in the early 1990s. Although not much vintage port is produced (there are rarely more than four declared vintages a decade), the international recession and bloated marketplace have caused prices to tumble.

WHAT TO BUY IN 1994

1. The port market has taken an enormous beating over the last several years, with prices tumbling for virtually every vintage, even such illustrious years as 1977, 1970, and 1963. Port, one of the greatest and most pleasurable red wines in the world, may be perceived by many as out of place in modern-day life. The high alcohol, the residual sweetness, and the fact that it is drunk after a meal (when guests are inclined to refuse more alcohol as they contemplate the drive home), have combined to impact negatively on port. Moreover port, more than any other wine, is fattening. Of course, one does not usually drink more than a small glass or two, but it is this perception, plus the international recession, that has caused port prices to fall. As a result, consumers now have an exceptional opportunity to stock up on recent vintages.

2. The vintages that have suffered the most precipitous drops in price are 1985 (a super year) and 1983 (another fine year). Major port houses that declared 1982 and 1980 vintages have seen little interest in their wines. Even the magnificent 1977s and 1970s have dropped in price. However, the market has remained stable with respect to such classic mature vintages as 1963, 1955, and 1948.

3. If you are going to purchase vintage port, are you prepared to wait a *minimum* of 10 years after the vintage to permit the port to develop that lush, mellow complexity that makes it so seductive? Some of the great 1963s are

just beginning to reach full maturity. Most of the massive 1970s, although spectacular, are still relatively young vintage ports. If you are not willing to invest the necessary time, consider some intelligent alternatives, such as tawny ports.

VARIOUS PORT STYLES

Crusted Port   Rarely seen today, crusted port is usually a blend of several vintages that is bottled early and handled in the same manner as a vintage port. Significant sediment will form in the bottle, and a crusted port will have to be decanted prior to drinking.

Tawny Port   One of the least expensive ways of securing a mature port is to buy the best shippers' tawny ports. Tawny ports are aged in wood by the top houses for 10, 20, 30, 40, or even 50 years. Tawny port represents a blend of vintages. Tawnys can have exceptional complexity and refinement. I highly recommend some of the best tawnys from firms such as Taylor Fladgate, Fonseca, and Graham.

Ruby and Branded Ports   Ruby ports are relatively straightforward, deeply colored young ports that are cherished for their sweet, grapey aromas and supple, exuberant, yet monolithic taste. Most are meant to be drunk when released. Each house has its own style, and four of the most popular are Fonseca's Bin No. 27, Taylor's 4XX, Cockburn's Special Reserve, and Graham's Six Grapes. Stylistically, all four of these ruby or branded ports are different. The richest and fullest is the Fonseca Bin No. 27; the most complex is usually the Taylor 4XX; the sweetest and fruitiest is the Graham Six Grapes; and the most mature and evolved, as well as the least distinguished, is the Cockburn Special Reserve.

White Port   I have never understood the purpose of white port, but the French find it appealing. However, the market for these eccentricities is dead.

Late-Bottled Vintage Port (L.B.V.P.)   Certain vintages are held in cask longer than 2 years (the time required for vintage port) and bottled 5–7 years following the vintage. These ports tend to throw less sediment, as much of it has been already deposited in cask. In general, late-bottled ports are ready to drink when released. I often find them less interesting and complex than the best tawnys and vintage ports.

Single-Quinta Vintage Port   This has become an increasingly important area, especially since the late 1980s, when a number of vintages, particularly 1987 and 1990, could have been declared vintage years but were not because of the saturated marketplace. Many of the best single-quintas, or vineyards, have been offered as vintage-dated single-quinta ports. These are vintage ports from a single vineyard. Most port authorities feel it is the blending from various vineyards that gives vintage port its greatest character. Others will argue that in a top year the finest single-quinta ports can be as good as a top vintage port. I tend to believe that a great vintage port is better than a single-quinta port, yet the finest single-quintas from 1987 and 1990 are stunning. Readers should refer to the star ratings of the different single-quinta ports.

Vintage Port   Potentially the finest and most complex, and the subject of most of this chapter, are the vintage ports. Vintage ports are declared by the port shippers the second spring after the harvest. At the time of this writing, it was believed that 1991 would be declared a vintage year by most of the top port shippers. For example, Graham, Dow, and Warre have already declared it a vintage, and other major shippers are expected to follow. Vintage port, which is a blend of the very best *cuvées* from various vineyards, is bottled unfiltered 2 years after the harvest. It can improve and last for 50 or more years. To be a vintage port there must be exceptional ripeness, a great deal of tannin, and plenty of rich fruit and body. In fact, the quality of a shipper's vintage port is the benchmark by which a shipper is evaluated in the international market-place. Each top house has a distinctive style, which I have tried to capture in the tasting notes.

VINTAGE GUIDE

The greatest port vintages in this century have been 1912, 1927, 1931, 1935, 1945, 1948, 1955, 1963, 1970, 1977, 1983, 1985, and possibly 1991, which at the time of this writing had just been declared by all the Symington estates (Graham, Dow, Warre, and so on). Barrel samples tasted of these 1991s in June 1993 revealed ports that appear to resemble a hypothetical blend of 1983 and 1985, although British port authorities have said the 1991s are rem-iniscent of the 1970s. Great vintages often require a significant amount of time before they are ready to drink because of their richness, extract, and tannin. Thus consumers often neglect very fine to excellent vintages, such as 1960, 1966, and 1980, which can provide great pleasure in their first 10–20 years of life because they are softer and evolve more quickly.

VINTAGE YEARS FOR MAJOR FIRMS

Cockburn   1947, 1950, 1955, 1960, 1963, 1967, 1970, 1975, 1983, 1985
Croft   1945, 1950, 1955, 1960, 1963, 1966, 1970, 1975, 1977, 1982, 1985
Dow   1945, 1947, 1950, 1955, 1960, 1963, 1966, 1970, 1972, 1975, 1977, 1980, 1983, 1985, 1991
Fonseca   1945, 1948, 1955, 1960, 1963, 1966, 1970, 1975, 1977, 1980, 1983, 1985
Graham   1945, 1948, 1955, 1960, 1963, 1966, 1970, 1975, 1977, 1980, 1983, 1985, 1991
Quinta do Noval   1945, 1947, 1950, 1955, 1958, 1960, 1963, 1966, 1967, 1970, 1975, 1978, 1982, 1985
Quinta do Noval Nacional   1931, 1950, 1960, 1962, 1963, 1964, 1966, 1967, 1970, 1975, 1978, 1980, 1982, 1985, 1987
Sandeman   1945, 1947, 1950, 1955, 1957, 1958, 1960, 1962, 1963, 1966, 1967, 1970, 1975, 1977, 1980, 1982, 1985
Taylor Fladgate   1945, 1948, 1955, 1960, 1963, 1966, 1970, 1975, 1977, 1980, 1983, 1985
Warre   1945, 1947, 1950, 1955, 1958, 1960, 1963, 1966, 1970, 1975, 1977, 1980, 1983, 1985, 1991

RATING PORTUGAL'S BEST PRODUCERS OF PORT

***** (OUTSTANDING PRODUCERS)

Dow	Quinta do Noval Nacional
Fonseca	Taylor Fladgate
Graham	

* * * * (EXCELLENT PRODUCERS)

Calem Quinta da Foz	Ferreira Quinta do Seixo
Churchill	Graham Malvedos Centenary
Churchill Quinta Agua Alta	Quinta do Noval
Cockburn	Symington Quinta do Vesuvio
Croft	Warre
Dow Quinta do Bomfim	

* * * (GOOD PRODUCERS)

Calem	Martinez
Croft Quinta do Roed	Offley Forrester
Delaforce	Poças Junior
Delaforce Quinta da Corte	Ramos-Pinto
Ferreira	Sandeman
Gould Campbell	Smith-Woodhouse
Quarles Harris	Taylor Quinta do Vargellas
Hooper	Warre Quinta do Cavadinha

* * (AVERAGE PRODUCERS)

Almeida Barros	Pintos dos Santos
Borges & Irmao	Quinta do Crasto
J. W. Burmester	Quinta do Infantado
C. da Silva	Quinta do Panascal
H. & C. J. Feist	Quinta do Romaneira
Feuerheerd	Quinta de la Rosa
C. N. Kopke	Vasconcellos
Messias	Wiese & Krohn
Niepoort	Van Zellers
Osborne	

Selected Tasting Notes

CALEM* * *

1985	C	84

Deep ruby/purple in color, the 1985 Calem is a soft, medium-bodied, relatively lightweight style of wine with a good deal of juicy fruit, soft tannins, and an alcoholic finish.

CHURCHILL* * * *

1985	C	88

Churchill's 1985 showed extremely well in my tastings. Dark ruby/purple with a projected full-intensity bouquet of ripe plums, licorice, and fruitcake, full bodied, seductively soft, rich, and concentrated, this overtly fruity wine seems precocious and only 5–7 years away from maturity. It is deep, delectable, and delicious.

COCKBURN* * * *

1963	E	86
1970	E	87

1975	D	82
1983	D	95
1985	D	90

This house tends to produce quite full-bodied, rich, alcoholic, spirity vintage ports that never quite have a great deal of complexity or finesse but offer meaty, chocolatey, spicy, full-bodied, alcoholic flavors at the expense of elegance. The 1985 was placed in a tasting where I also inserted the 1983 Cockburn as a ringer. I was surprised to find out upon revealing the wines that the massive blockbuster of the tasting was the 1983, and the soft, intensely fruity, forward wine was the 1985. Although the 1983 Cockburn is superior to the 1985, the latter wine should offer rich, opulent, multidimensional flavors in 6–8 years. Like the other 1985s, Cockburn's is low in acidity, but the loosely knit character it displayed in its youth appears to have taken on greater delineation as it has aged in the bottle. The result is a powerful, heady wine with an amazing level of black cherry fruit, glycerin, and intensity. The 1975 is light, a little alcoholic, and not terribly distinguished. The 1970 is big and powerful and just now reaching maturity. The 1963 is fully mature, spicy, with a chocolatey, meaty texture and a somewhat hot, short finish.
RATINGS FOR OLDER VINTAGES OF COCKBURN PORT: 1960 (78), 1950 (73), 1947 (85)

CROFT* * * *

1963	E	86
1966	E	89
1970	E	85
1975	D	86
1977	D	88
1982	D	88
1985	D	87

Croft never seems to get much publicity since the wines, though always very good, sometimes even excellent, never quite reach the superb level of the top houses in Oporto. However, Croft seems to do surprisingly well, often rivaling the top ports in the less glamorous vintages such as 1975 and 1966. The 1975 is almost as good as Croft's 1977. Both are rich, creamy, intense ports that should be fully mature within 10–12 years, relatively soon for a vintage port. The 1970 is quite good but, in the context of the vintage, marginally disappointing. The 1966 is a sleeper—complex, rich, and very aromatic with long, deep flavors. The 1963, one of the great vintages for port, is good but unexciting. However, the 1982 is superb, a powerful, broadly flavored wine with exhilarating depth and richness on the palate and at least 25 years of life ahead of it. I prefer it to the 1985, which will be an early-developing port. The 1985 shows aromas that border on overripeness and offers scents of plums and black cherries. Full bodied and rich, yet lush and soft, this husky wine has loads of concentration, a very sweet, long finish, and light tannins.
RATINGS FOR OLDER VINTAGES OF CROFT PORT: 1963 (88), 1960 (90), 1955 (78), 1945 (92)

DELAFORCE* * *

Eminence's Choice 16-year-old Tawny	B	85
1966	E	86
1970	E	84
1975	D	82
1978 Quinta da Corte	D	85
1982	D	85
1985	D	82

This house tends to make good port and sell it at rather reasonable prices. The 16-year-old tawny is soft and pleasant but lacks a bit of character. The 1978 single-vineyard port, Quinta da Corte, is straightforward and chunky, with good length but not much complexity; the same can be said for the 1975 and 1970, both of which are fully mature. It has been several years since I have tasted a 1966, but my recollection is that it is the best Delaforce port I have had. The 1985 has a heady perfume of sugary fruit, sweet, soft, medium-bodied flavors, good concentration, and an adequate finish. It suffers in comparison with the major ports of 1985 but is not at all bad.

DOW* * * * *

Boardroom 15-year-old Tawny	B	87
Gold Label 30-year-old Tawny	D	90
1963	E	92
1966	D	91
1970	E	86
1975	D	85
1977	E	95
1980	D	88
1983	D	93
1985	D	87
1990 Quinta do Bomfim	D	96

This is an extraordinary house that seems to have been particularly successful with its vintage ports since 1977. Of course, the 1963 is a classic, a monumental, rich, still tannic wine that will last at least another 30 years. The 1966 is also a top success for that vintage; in fact, it would be hard to find a better port that year. The 1970 is good but for some reason has never blossomed and developed any complexity, and the same can be said for the fully mature, fruity, soft 1975. However, starting with the 1977, Dow has hit its stride. The 1977, still a baby, is fabulously scented, very rich and concentrated and has a potential longevity of at least another 30–50 years. The 1980 is very, very good and certainly better than what this house produced in 1975 and 1970. It should mature relatively fast and be ready to drink by 1992. The 1983 is rich, concentrated, very fruity, and magnificently perfumed, suggesting that it is going to mature early, long before the 1977. The 1985 is dark ruby/purple with a rather closed, one-dimensional aroma. On the palate the Dow is restrained but rich, tannic, and full bodied, although not nearly as concentrated as one would expect. Have I missed something? As for the tawny ports from Dow, they can also be superb. The 30-year-old tawny has a scent of sweet saddle leather, hazelnuts, and rich fruit. The 15-year-old tawny, for one-third the price, is a somewhat lighter but no less interesting version. The black/purple-colored 1990 single-vineyard Quinta do Bomfim reveals a huge, powerful, intense palate, with gobs of flesh and viscous fruit. It is a massive port with considerable tannin and no indication of excessive alcohol in the finish. A magnificent young, dry-style vintage port that just goes on and on in the mouth, it should last for 20–30 years.

RATINGS OF OLDER VINTAGES OF DOW PORT: 1947 (81), 1945 (93)

FERREIRA* * *

Duque de Bragança 20-year-old Tawny	B	88
1970	D	85
1975	D	86
1977	D	87
1980	D	85
1983	D	88
1985	D	86

This house is terribly underrated when top ports are mentioned. Their vintage ports tend to lack a bit in complexity and sheer majesty of aromas but do offer rich, robust, concentrated flavors of chocolate, spices, and deep, plummy fruit. However, their 20-year-old tawny, Duque de Bragança, must certainly be one of the top tawny ports made in Portugal and is well worth seeking out for those who want something to drink immediately. Their most recent vintage port, the 1985, is deep ruby/purple and among the more tannic and backward ports of the vintage. Quite robust and brawny, this concentrated, relatively intense wine needs 5–7 years of cellaring to shed its cloak of tannin. Will the style change under new owners Sogrape, the huge firm that produces Mateus Rosé?

FONSECA* * * * *

Bin 27	B	86
Fonseca 10-year-old Tawny	B	87
1963	E	96
1966	E	94
1970	E	95
1975	D	89
1977	D	93
1980	D	87
1983	D	92
1985	D	95

Fonseca is clearly one of the great port lodges. It produces the most exotic and most complex port. If Fonseca lacks the sheer weight and power of a Taylor, Dow, or Warre, or the sheer opulent sweetness and intensity of a Graham, it excels in its magnificently complex, intense bouquet of plummy, cedary, spicy fruit and long, broad, expansive flavors. One might call it the Pomerol of vintage ports with its lush, seductive character. When it is young, it often loses out in blind tastings to the heavier, weightier, more tannic wines, but I always find myself upgrading my opinion of Fonseca after it has had 7–10 years of age. However, for vintage ports, the newly released 1985 looks to be one of the top successes of the vintage, eclipsing in richness and complexity the superb 1983 and otherworldly 1977. Dense ruby/purple with the Oriental spice-box aroma, this expansive, sweet, broadly flavored wine has outstanding depth, concentration, and balance. It finishes with a solid lashing of alcohol and tannin. The 1983 is magnificently scented, full bodied, creamy, and rather forward, but it shows great length and character. The 1980 is very good, possibly excellent, but it tasted lighter than some of the best ports from that vintage. The 1977 has developed magnificently in the bottle, and although it clearly needs another decade to reach its summit, it is the best Fonseca since the 1970 and 1963. Fonseca's 1975, which is fully mature, shows just how good this house can be; it is a port to seek out since the vintage does not have the reputation or the price tag that the 1977 and 1970 do. It should drink magnificently for another decade or more. The 1970, of course, is a powerful Fonseca with an exotic bouquet and lush, creamy, multidimensional flavors. The 1966, one of the stars of the vintage, is fully mature but will hold for 15 or more years, and the 1963, one of the great modern-day classics of vintage port, is an incredibly aromatic, sublime, majestic port that simply defines Fonseca's style perfectly.

RATINGS FOR OLDER VINTAGES OF FONSECA PORT: 1960 (84), 1955 (96), 1948 (99), 1945 (94)

GOULD CAMPBELL* * *

1977	C	84
1980	C	85
1983	C	82
1985	C	89

My experience with this house is limited, but I have found the 1980 and 1983 rich, full bodied, well colored, and complex. The 1985 from Gould Campbell is one of the surprises of this vintage. It has an intense nose of chocolate, berry fruit, and tar. On the palate the wine is very concentrated, powerful, and full bodied, with layers of fruit. It finishes sweeter than some of the other ports, with a great deal of tannin. One rarely sees this brand stateside.

GRAHAM* * * * *

Emperor Tawny 20-year-old	C	85
Prince Regent's 10-year-old Tawny	B	88
1963	E	93
1966	E	88
1970	E	97

1975	D	82
1977	D	98
1980	D	88
1983	D	95
1985	D	98
1990 Malvedos Centenary	D	92

Graham is another one of the great port houses, producing one of the deepest-colored and sweetest styles in vintage port. Along with Taylor and Fonseca, Graham has probably been the most consistent producer of great port in the post–World War II era. Their tawnys are quite good rather than exceptional, but their vintage ports are truly sublime and sumptuous. Graham is the undisputed star and kingpin of the 1985 vintage ports. Yes, it is made in a sweeter style than the other ports, but it is a fabulous wine because of a dazzling level of black cherry fruit, an enormous structure, and staggering depth, dimension, and length. It is forward, as are all the 1985s, and I would speculate that this port will be approaching maturity by 2000 and will keep 15–20 years thereafter. The 1983, like most vintage ports, seems more forward than normal but has a great depth of very ripe, viscous, unctuous, plummy, tarry fruit and significant tannin in its very long finish. It is black/purple in color. I doubt that it will either be as profound or as long-lived as the great 1977, but it is certainly one of the top two or three ports of this vintage and better than the excellent 1980 that Graham produced. The 1970 is a monumental vintage port and one of the great ports of that vintage. It begs to be drunk now, although it will last for at least another 2 decades. The 1966, which I initially thought rather mediocre, has developed beautifully in the bottle and is a much finer vintage port than I originally suspected. Owners of it should proceed to drink it, as it is not likely to get any better. The 1975 is the only recent vintage of Graham that I find disappointing. It is rather light in color, finishes very short on the palate, and obviously lacks depth and ripeness. The 1990 Malvedos Centenary is sweet, fragrant, and highly extracted. Its flamboyant, up-front fat and decadence provide more initial appeal than the monstrous but restrained Dow. It also reveals extraordinary richness and a fabulous finish.

RATINGS FOR OLDER VINTAGES OF GRAHAM MALVEDOS: 1987 (92+), 1986 (92), 1979 (82), 1976 (90), 1964 (90), 1962 (83), 1958 (91)
RATINGS FOR OLDER VINTAGES OF GRAHAM PORT: 1955 (98), 1948 (98), 1945 (95)

QUARLES HARRIS* * *

1985	B	84

This robust, densely colored port has plenty of muscle, power, and alcohol yet is short on finesse. Slightly disjointed, with the alcohol quite noticeable, this port needs 4–5 years to find its balance, but all the component parts are there. It may prove to merit a higher rating in the future.

HOOPER* * *

1985	B	83

Surprisingly opaque and purple, this port has a tightly knit but compact structure, fine depth of fruit, and full body, yet it seems to tail off in the finish. It is one of the more tannic and closed ports of this otherwise charming, precocious vintage.

MARTINEZ* * *

1963	D	78
1967	D	85
1975	C	86
1982	B	84
1985	B	86

This house is rarely seen in the United States, and I was unimpressed with the example of the 1963 that I had in a comparative tasting. However, the recent notes I have for the 1967 and 1975 show that both were good, medium-weight, tarry, plummy ports without a lot of character but with good ripeness and clean winemaking. The 1982 is light and mature. The 1985 has a deep, juicy fruitiness, excellent color, full body, and firm tannins in the finish. It is not as complex as some ports but offers robust, fruity drinking.

OFFLEY FORRESTER* * *

1970	C	86
1972	C	83
1977	C	86
1980	B	83
1983	B	85

Offley Forrester produces medium-weight ports that, given their reasonable price, offer value rather than great complexity and richness. Curiously, the 1972, a vintage not declared by most port shippers, produced a very good wine, and I have good notes on the 1970, 1977, and 1983.

QUINTA DO NOVAL* * * *

1963	E	82
1970	E	84
1975	D	85
1978	D	79
1982	D	85
1985	D	87

The beautiful Quinta do Noval is undoubtedly the most famous port producer, largely because its 1931 and 1927 were to vintage port what the 1947 Cheval Blanc and 1945 Mouton-Rothschild were to the Bordeaux trade—divine, monumental wines of extraordinary depth of flavor. Also, the Quinta do Noval produces a rare vintage port from a small vineyard of ungrafted, prephylloxera vines called Nacional. It is so rare that I have never seen, much less tasted, a bottle of what is supposedly a great port. However, the truth of the matter is that recent vintages of Quinta do Noval have not been nearly as impressive as they should be. Commentators have described the wines as light, elegant, and charming, when in fact they lack richness and depth of flavor. The 1963 and 1970, two great vintages for port, are disappointing. The 1975 has turned out charming, fruity, and actually better than the 1970 or 1963, which is inexplicable. The most recent vintages, 1978, 1982, and 1985, have shown more richness of flavor and character in bouquet and aroma. The 1985 is quite concentrated, seductive, and amazingly delicious now and should mature quite quickly. The finish is long and flavorful, but I wonder about the lack of tannic structure to this wine.

RAMOS-PINTO* * *

Quinta da Bom Retiro Tawny 20-year-old	B	86
Quinta de Ervamoira Tawny 10-year-old	C	85
1970	C	86
1980	C	84
1983	C	85
1985	C	79

I know little about this firm other than that both their tawnys are excellent and offer considerable value, and that the two vintage ports currently on the market show a style not unlike that of Fonseca, a lush mellowness and complex, plummy, chocolatey bouquet. Their 20-year-old tawny, the Quinta da Bom Retiro, is really quite sumptuous.

SANDEMAN* * *

Founder's Reserve	B	80
N. V. Royal Tawny	B	83
1970	D	84
1975	D	84
1977	D	87
1980	C	82
1982	C	87
1985	C	86

Sandeman is one of the biggest and most conspicuous of the port houses with extensive interests in the sherry business as well. They advertise significantly, and their products are well represented in virtually every American marketplace. The quality is quite good given the quantity of wine produced, but rarely does a Sandeman tawny or vintage port hit the heights of a Dow, Fonseca, Taylor, or Graham. Their Royal Tawny has an attractive, nutty, ripe black cherry character. Their Founder's Reserve, which is highly publicized, is a good, inexpensive, straightforward port without much complexity but with plenty of mellow, savory, sweet flavors. Their vintage ports have been a bit light, but the 1977 and 1982 show considerable strength and richness. The newest release, the 1985, has less of a deep ruby/purple color but does offer a spice-box, fruitcake sort of aroma, mildly sweet, medium- to full-bodied flavors, and a ripe, tasty finish. Not a heavyweight, this wine represents a lighter style of vintage port. The 1980, 1975, and 1970 are good rather than exciting in quality.

SMITH-WOODHOUSE* * *

1980	C	85
1985	C	90

My experience with Smith-Woodhouse is limited, but I was impressed with the 1980, which showed a lovely, supple, ripe, rich, fruity character in an early-maturing style. Is the 1985 the sleeper of the vintage? An astonishing amount of creamy, black cherry– and chocolate-scented fruit fills the olfactory senses. On the palate this full-bodied wine is loaded with extract, possesses great length, and has a super finish with plenty of fruit and tannin in proper balance.

SYMINGTON* * *

1990 Quinta do Vesuvio	D	93

This port possesses an opaque black/purple color, a sweet, rich nose with a whiff of licorice, and powerfully ripe fruit. In the mouth it is full bodied, with superb concentration as well as a rich, opulent, deep finish. Although drinkable now, it has at least 20 years of evolution.

TAYLOR FLADGATE* * * * *

N. V. Tawny	B	87
10-year-old Tawny	C	89
20-year-old Tawny	D	90
30-year-old Tawny	D	87
1963	E	95
1966	E	88
1970	E	96
1975	D	87
1977	D	96
1980	D	89
1983	D	94
1985	D	89

This house must certainly be the Latour of Portugal. Their ports are remarkably backward yet still impressive when young. Of all the vintage ports, those of Taylor need the longest time to mature and even when fully mature seem to have an inner strength and firmness that keep them going for decades. Their tawnys are also among the very best, though somewhat expensive. For current drinking, the 20-year-old tawny is a wonderfully fragrant, nutty-scented wine with great character and complexity. Among their vintage ports there has not been an unsuccessful year since 1963. The 1963 is quite fabulous yet still seemingly capable of developing for another decade or more. The 1966 is drinking well now and is a very good rather than exceptional Taylor. The 1970 is fabulous, a broodingly dense-colored, backward port that has all the signs of future greatness, provided one is willing to cellar it until 2000 or later. The 1975 has turned out richly fruity and supple and offers delicious drinking for the near future. The 1977 has consistently been at the top of my list of vintage ports in this great vintage, although the Dow, Graham, and Fonseca are equally splendid. It is a mammoth, opaque, statuesque vintage port of remarkable depth and power but should not be touched before 2000. The 1980 is probably the best port of the vintage, and the 1983 is wonderfully aromatic and so perfumed (a characteristic of this charming vintage), yet powerful, long, and deep on the palate. It gives every indication of being an early-maturing Taylor, but I wouldn't want to drink it before 1995. As for the 1985, readers may remember that in the last *Wine Buyer's Guide* I had reserved judgment. I have had the port on three additional occasions, and it is hard for me to believe it is going to be one of Taylor's top efforts. Very dark in color, it is less expressive than most 1985s and appears to be less concentrated, although there are harsh tannins and considerable body in the relatively austere finish. My instincts suggest that it is in a dumb, nearly mute stage that makes evaluation difficult. Certainly there is good length, and the color is relatively saturated, although by no means is it among the darkest ports of the vintage. I suspect it needs at least another 10 years of cellaring. One hopes it will turn out to be exceptional.

RATINGS OF OLDER VINTAGES OF TAYLOR PORT: 1960 (87), 1955 (98), 1948 (100), 1945 (98), 1935 (89)

WARRE* * * *

Nimrod Tawny	B	85
1963	E	87
1966	E	86
1970	E	87
1975	D	86
1977	D	92
1980	D	88
1983	D	90
1985	D	90

This house makes rather restrained yet rich, flavorful vintage port and a very good tawny called Nimrod. Their vintage ports seem slow to develop, and although they never quite have the voluptuous richness of a Dow, Graham, or Fonseca, they have a unique mineral-scented character that gives them their own complexity and style. Warre has been making exceptionally fine ports of late, and their 1985 is the sweetest and richest of their recent vintages. Extremely concentrated, rich, even luscious, this full-bodied, intense, opulent wine has layers of fruit, a full-blown bouquet, and impeccable balance. The soft tannins and precocious appeal of the 1985 suggest rapid maturation. The 1983 is richly perfumed and fragrant, which is so typical of the ports from this vintage, and is seemingly more forward than normal. The 1980 is backward and firm and has yet to reveal its true personality; the 1977 is quite powerful, very deep, and intense, particularly for Warre; and the 1975 is soft, supple, and clearly mature. Of the older vintages, the 1970 remains rather unyielding but still impressive; the 1966 fully mature and good but not exciting, and the 1963 very, very good and now fully mature.

RATINGS OF OLDER VINTAGES OF WARRE PORT: 1955 (87), 1945 (90)

TABLE WINES

Except for the unctuous, rich, almost decadent joys of vintage port and Madeira, one of the greatest nectars of all is Muscatel de Setubal. The Setubal from J. M. da Fonseca is legendary. In 1993 they released in 500-ml bottles a 1966 (rated 91) and a 1962 Roxo (rated 98) from a 5-acre vineyard that are sensational wines with which to conclude a meal. The potential for fine wine from Portugal has yet to be discovered by most wine enthusiasts. Of course, the ubiquitous, spritzy, rather sweet Portuguese rosés are known the world over and are what many consumers first drink when they deem themselves too old or too sophisticated for soda pop. But Portugal produces some good red wines (that could even be superb if winemaking was not still adhering to nineteenth-century practices), as well as a few lively, crisp, tart white wines, the best of which are the *vinho verdes*. The best of the dry red wines are from such regions as Dão, Bairrada, and the Douro; the most reliable whites are from Palacio de Brejoeira, Antonio de Pires da Silva, and Casal Mendes.

VINTAGE GUIDE

Vintages in Portugal seem to have relevance only to the port trade. For the dry red table wines, none of the wineries seem to think vintages matter, but the Fonseca family, irrefutably Portugal's leading producer of dry red table wine, claims the finest recent years include 1991, 1990, 1988, 1986, and 1980.

RATING PORTUGAL'S BEST PRODUCERS OF TABLE WINES

* * * * *(OUTSTANDING PRODUCERS)
None

* * * * (EXCELLENT PRODUCERS)

Quinta do Carmo (Alentejo)
Ferreira (Barca Velha)
J. M. da Fonseca (Dão Terras Altas)
J. M. da Fonseca (Garrafeira TE)
J. M. da Fonseca (Morgado do
  Reguengo-Portalegre)

J. M. da Fonseca
  (Quinta da Camarate)
J. M. da Fonseca
  (Rosado Fernandes)

* * * (GOOD PRODUCERS)

Carvalho, Ribeiro, Ferreira
  (Garrafeira)
Carvalho, Ribeiro, Ferreira
  (Serradayres)
Caves do Barrocas (Garrafeira)

Caves Dom Teodosio (Garrafeira)
Caves San João (Bairrada)
Caves Velhas
Conde de Santar (Dão)
Falcoaria

J. M. da Fonseca (Pasmados)
J. M. da Fonseca (Periquita)
J. M. da Fonseca (Periquita Reserva)
Luis Pato (Bairrada)
João Pires (Quinta da Bacalhoa)
João Pires (Tinta de Anfora)

Porta dos Cavalheiros (Dão)
Quinta do Cotto (Grande Escolha)
Quinta da Lagoalva de Cima
Quinta de la Rosa
Sogrape (Grao Vasco)
Vasconcellos

* * (AVERAGE PRODUCERS)

Arruda Cooperative
Borges
Caves Alianca (Vinho Verde)
Caves St.-Jão (Garrafeira)
Quinta da Aveleda (Vinho Verde)

Quinta da Carmo
Quinta da Pacheca
Reguengos (Garrafeira)
Santa Marta Penaguiao (Douro)
J. Serra (Serra Vidiqueira)

Selected Tasting Notes

QUINTA DO CARMO* * * *

1987 Alentejo	C	88

The owners of Lafite-Rothschild acquired this vast estate (2,500 acres) in 1992, and have the laudable goal of producing the finest red wine in Portugal. The 1987 was released in 1993 and is an excellent wine. Dense and plum colored, it has a rustic bouquet of sweet black fruits, pepper, and leather. Full bodied and very rich, this impressively endowed wine will drink well for at least the balance of this century.

FERREIRA* * * *

1983 Barca Velha	D	90

Barca Velha is widely renowned as Portugal's finest dry red table wine. It has become increasingly rare given a resurgence of interest in Portugal's wines. I have had a half-dozen vintages, all of which have been big, chewy, thick wines with earthy, licorice, black fruit–scented aromas; hard, intensely concentrated flavors; and whopping levels of tannin and acidity in the blockbuster finish. None of the wines I have tasted have been close to maturity, so I do not know if this wine will fully resolve all of its tannins and develop into something harmonious. Nevertheless, for sheer richness and extraction levels, Barca Velha is an impressive wine. Readers may still be able to find some of the stunning 1981, which is every bit as good as well as slightly softer. This firm was purchased by Sogrape (makers of Mateus) in 1988.

J. M. DA FONSECA* * * *

1988 Dão Terras Altas	A	87
1985 Garrafeira TE	B	91
1989 Morgado do Reguengo-Portalegre	A	88
1988 Morgado do Reguengo-Portalegre	A	86
1986 Pasmados	A	84
1990 Periquita	A	86

1986 Periquita Reserva	A	87
1986 Quinta da Camarate	A	90
1988 Tinto Velho Rosado Fernandes	A	90
1986 Tinto Velho Rosado Fernandes	A	90

This winery, not to be confused with the port lodge also named Fonseca, consistently produces Portugal's finest dry red table wine. For starters, the 1988 Dão Terras Altas tastes like a blend of an excellent California Zinfandel and a solid southern Rhône Valley wine. It is a substantial wine with a deep ruby/garnet color; a big, spicy, meaty, cedary nose; rich, chunky, complex flavors, and soft tannins in the finish. The price is ridiculous given such a delicious wine. Drink this sensational bargain over the next 5–6 years. The 1986 Quinta da Camarate offers a fragrant, spicy, cedary, Médoc-like nose of berries, spices, and herbs. In the mouth it exhibits rich, medium-bodied flavors, boasts considerable elegance and length, and finishes with soft tannins and alcohol. The blend for this wine is 50% Cabernet Sauvignon and 50% Portuguese varietals such as Castelao, Frances, and Espadeiro. It should continue to drink well for at least 5–7 years. If I had this wine in a blind tasting, I might mistake it for a super second St.-Julien such as Ducru-Beaucaillou or Léoville-Las Cases. The 1986 Pasmados reveals sweet, chocolatey, cedary fruit in the nose and flavors, medium to full body, a soft texture, some amber color that suggests full maturity, and a long, heady, totally satisfying finish. Although fully mature now, it will last for another 4–5 years. The 1988 Morgado do Reguengo-Portalegre exhibits a deep purple color, a spicy new oak–scented nose, and gobs of rich berry fruit. Long, sweet, expansive, and rich in the mouth, this relatively young, less evolved wine can be drunk now or aged for 5–7 years. The 1989 Morgado do Reguengo-Portalegre is even richer. Aged in 100% new limousin oak, this rich, full-bodied wine exhibits tremendous extraction of fruit, excellent purity, and a gutsy finish. It reminded me of a top California Zinfandel. Looking for something that reminds you of great Chambertin from Domaine Rousseau or one of the earthy, meaty, smoky, top Premier Crus from Gevrey-Chambertin's Philippe Leclerc? Do not be surprised if the 1986 Tinto Velho from Rosado Fernandes reminds you of these wines. The huge, meaty, smoky, coffee- and chocolate-scented nose is followed by a wine of remarkable concentration and richness, plenty of spices, and the earthy, Oriental spice character that resembles a great burgundy. None of the grapes that went into this wine remotely resemble Pinot Noir, but the wine is spectacular. Wow, did I enjoy this wine! Curiously, it is packaged in a Burgundy-shaped bottle. Drink it over the next 5–8 years. The similarly styled 1988 is made from riper fruit and is lower in acidity. The 1985 Garrafeira TE is in a Bordeaux-shaped bottle. Could that be because it smells like a first-growth 1966 Pauillac? This remarkable wine is made from 35% Cabernet Sauvignon and the remainder an obscure Portuguese varietal. The color is deep ruby/garnet, and the nose exhibits classic Pauillac scents of cedar, minerals, and oak. There is an austere, almost gravelly flavor and a rich, chocolatey, cedary finish. I am convinced this remarkable wine could be inserted in a tasting of first-growth Bordeaux and not be identified as something from Portugal. Although it is close to full maturity, it should continue to drink well for another 10 years. The 1990 Periquita is also a success. Somewhat overwhelmed by many of the other offerings, it reminds me of a hypothetical blend of a California Zinfandel and a French Pinot Noir. Spicy, with lovely berry fruit and a robust character, it should be drunk over the next 4–8 years. The 1986 Periquita Reserva is deep, chewy, and bursting with ripe fruit. Drink this full-bodied wine over the next 4–6 years. These are wines of extremely high quality that are available at prices that boggle the mind. I should also note that as I went to press I tasted the 1987 Quinta da Camarate and the 1986 Casa da Insua. I was somewhat disappointed by these offerings, which seemed to be a drop in quality from the vintages reviewed above.

5. SPAIN

The Basics

Aside from the glories of sherry, which is synonymous with Spain, this beautiful sun-drenched country is best known as a treasure trove for red wine values. Forget the white wines, which once tasted musty and oxidized. Now, thanks to high technology, they taste like lemon water. And while the booming Spanish sparkling wine business stays in the headlines, as my producer's chart indicates, few makers of sparkling wine actually merit serious interest from those who enjoy good wine. Red wine is king in Spain, but regrettably this country is still one of unrealized potential rather than existing achievement. The best red wines all come from northern Spain. The areas that stand out for quality are the famous Rioja region, the generally well-known Penedès viticultural area in Catalonia near the Mediterranean coast, the Ribera del Duero region, and several emerging areas such as Navarra and Toro. To understand Spanish red wines one must first realize that the Spanish want their red wines supple, with an aged taste of maturity as well as a healthy (many would say excessive) dosage of oak. Once you realize this, you will understand why many Spanish wineries, called *bodegas*, age their wines in huge oak or concrete vats for 7 or 8 years before they are released. The Spanish are not fond of grapey, tannic, young wines, so expect the wineries to mature the wines for the Spanish consumer. Consequently most Spanish wines have a more advanced color and are smooth and supple, with the sweet vanillin taste of strong oak (usually American) well displayed. Many wineries actually hold back their best lots for a decade or more before releasing them, enabling the consumer to purchase a mature, fully drinkable wine.

GRAPE VARIETIES

RED WINES

Cabernet Sauvignon An important part of Spain's most expensive and prestigious red wine, Vega Sicilia, Cabernet Sauvignon has flourished where it has been planted in Spain.

Carinena   In France this is the Carignan grape, and in Spain this workhorse grape offers the muscle of Arnold Schwarzenegger. Big and brawny, the tannic, densely colored wine made from this grape varietal is frequently used as a blending agent, particularly with Grenache.

Fogoneu   This varietal is believed to be related to the French Gamay. It produces light, fruity wines that are meant to be drunk young. Most Fogoneu is planted on the island of Majorca.

Garnacha   Garnacha, which is the Spanish spelling of Grenache, is widely planted in Spain. Three types of Garnacha are used. The Garnacha Blanc, which produces white wines, is relatively limited, although it is especially noticeable in Tarragona. The Garnacha Tinto, which is similar to the Grenache known in France, is one of the most widely planted red wine grapes in Spain. There is also the Garnacha Tintorera, which is actually Alicante, a grape that produces black-colored, tannic, dense wines. It is used primarily for blending.

Merlot   This relatively new varietal for Spain has performed well. It is planted primarily in the Ribera del Duero.

Monastrell   This varietal produces sweet, alcoholic wines. Although planted widely, it is found most frequently in hotter microclimates.

Tempranillo   The finest indigenous red wine grape of Spain, Tempranillo travels under a number of names. In Penedès it is called Ull de Llebre and in the Ribera del Duero, Tinto. It provides rich, well-structured wines with good acidity and plenty of tannin and color. The bouquet often exhibits an intense black raspberry character. It makes an ideal blending mate with Garnacha but is complex enough to stand on its own.

WHITE WINES

The white wine grapes parade under names such as Albarino, Chardonnay, Macallo, Malvasia, Palomina (used for sherry), Parellada (the principal component of most sparkling wine *cuvées*), Pedro Ximenez, Riesling, Sauvignon, Torrontes, Verdejo, Xarello, and Moscatel. None of these varietals has proven to be capable of making anything more than neutral-tasting wines, but several appear to have potential if yields are kept low and the wine is impeccably vinified. Perhaps the best is the Albarino, which, when produced by a top winery in Galicia, has a stunning perfume similar to that of a French Condrieu. However, in the mouth the wine is much lighter, with less body and intensity. At its best it is light, refreshing, and fragrant.

Other white wines that have shown potential include some of the Chardonnays and the Torrontes, which, when made in Galicia, has a perfumed personality, lovely fruit salad–like flavors, and a pleasant finish.

FLAVORS

Penedès   The dominant winery here is Torres, which produces a bevy of excellent red wines from the typical Spanish varietals. Yet the top wine is the 100% Cabernet Sauvignon Black Label Gran Coronas, which has a rich, open-knit bouquet of plums, sweet oak, and often licorice and violets. Its chief rival is the Cabernet Sauvignon from Jean León, another concentrated, blackberry-scented and -flavored, full-throttle wine with a whopping influence from sweet, toasty oak. The best vintages are 1990, 1989, 1987, 1984, 1981, and 1978.

Ribera del Duero   Two of Spain's greatest red wines are produced in this

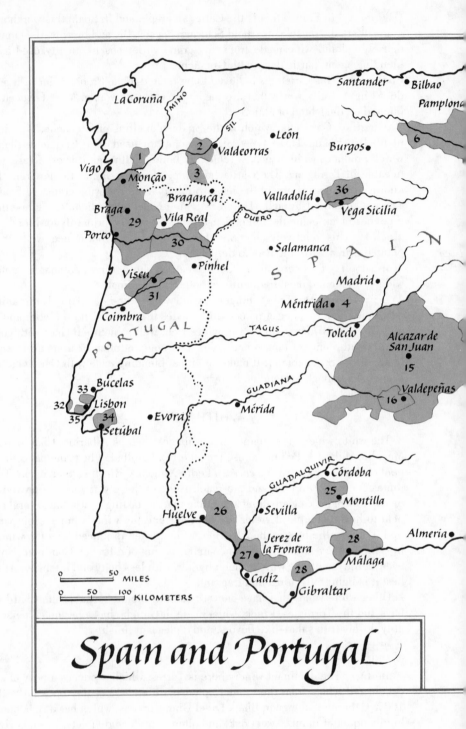

La Coruña

Santander • Bilbao
Pamplona

MIÑO

SIL

• León

Burgos •

Valdeorras

2 • Valdeorras

Vigo •

Monção

3

Bragança

Valladolid •

36

Braga •

29

Vila Real

DUERO

Vega Sicilia

Porto •

30

S   P   A   I   N

• Salamanca

Viseu •

• Pinhel

31

Madrid •

Coimbra

Méntrida • 4

PORTUGAL

TAGUS

Toledo •

Alcazar de
San Juan

15

Bucelas

33

GUADIANA

Valdepeñas

32

Lisbon

16 •

35

34

Évora •

Mérida •

Setúbal

GUADALQUIVIR

Córdoba •

25

Montilla •

26

• Sevilla

28

Almeria •

Huelve •

Jerez de
la Frontera

27

28

Málaga •

Cadiz •

Gibraltar •

0 ___ 50 ___ MILES
0 ___ 50 ___ 100 ___ KILOMETERS

Spain and Portugal

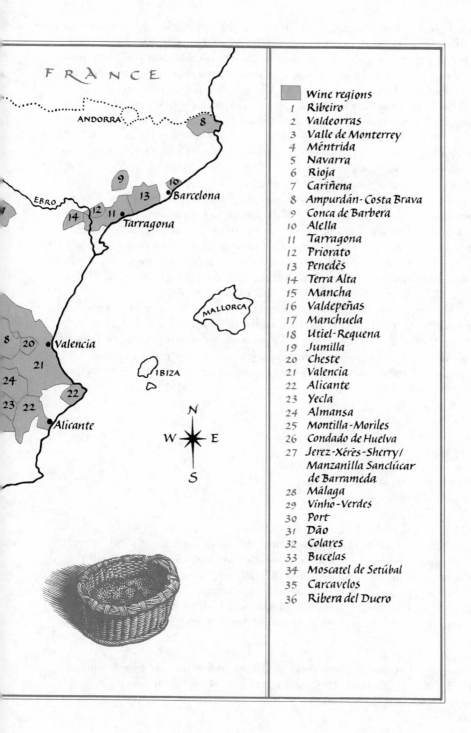

F R A N C E

ANDORRA

8

9

10 ● Barcelona

13

EBRO

14 12 11

● Tarragona

MALLORCA

8 20 ● Valencia

21

24

22

23 22

● Alicante

IBIZA

N

W ━✴━ E

S

◼ Wine regions
1 Ribeiro
2 Valdeorras
3 Valle de Monterrey
4 Méntrida
5 Navarra
6 Rioja
7 Cariñena
8 Ampurdán-Costa Brava
9 Conca de Barbera
10 Alella
11 Tarragona
12 Priorato
13 Penedès
14 Terra Alta
15 Mancha
16 Valdepeñas
17 Manchuela
18 Utiel-Requena
19 Jumilla
20 Cheste
21 Valencia
22 Alicante
23 Yecla
24 Almansa
25 Montilla-Moriles
26 Condado de Huelva
27 Jerez-Xérès-Sherry/
   Manzanilla Sanclúcar
   de Barrameda
28 Málaga
29 Vinho-Verdes
30 Port
31 Dão
32 Colares
33 Bucelas
34 Moscatel de Setúbal
35 Carcavelos
36 Ribera del Duero

broad river valley: Pesquera, which comes primarily from the Tempranillo grape; and Vega Sicilia, primarily a Cabernet Sauvignon/Merlot/Malbec wine. What is noticeable about these wines is the remarkable purity of berry fruit that can be found in the top vintages. Take superripe fruit and combine it with a minimum of 3 years (in the case of Vega Sicilia, 8–12 years) in oak casks, and you have powerfully heady, rich, supple, explosively rich wines that offer a great deal of spicy, sweet, toasty, vanillin-scented oak. The best vintages have been 1990, 1989, 1986, 1983, 1982, 1976, 1975, 1968, and 1962.

Rioja　When made by the best producers, such as La Rioja Alta or Muga, Rioja will be a mature wine having a medium-ruby color (often with a touch of orange or brown, normal for an older wine) and a huge, fragrant bouquet of to-bacco, cedar, smoky oak, and sweet, ripe fruit. On the palate there will be no coarseness or astringency because of the long aging of the wine in cask and/or tank prior to bottling. Despite its suppleness, the wine will keep for 5–10 years after its release. Even a young Rioja released after just 3–4 years, such as a Marqués de Cáceres, will show a ripe, fat, rich, supple fruitiness and a soft, sweet, oaky character. The best vintages include 1990, 1989, 1987, 1982, 1981, 1978, 1973, 1970, 1968, 1964, and 1958.

Toro　Once known for overwhelmingly alcoholic, heavy wines, Toro has adopted modern technology, and the results have been some rich, full-bodied, deeply flavored, southern Rhône–like wines from wineries such as Farina. They taste similar to the big, lush, peppery wines of France's Châteauneuf-du-Pape and Gigondas, and they represent astonishing values. The best vintages are 1990 and 1989.

AGING POTENTIAL

Navarra: 5–7 years
Rioja: 6–25 years*
Penedès: 6–15 years
Sparkling White Wines: 3–6 years
Ribera del Duero: 6–30 years†

OVERALL QUALITY LEVEL

Although it may be fashionable to tout the quality and value of all Spanish wines, only the red wines merit serious attention and sadly, only a small per-centage can hold up to the best international competition. The whites are atro-ciously boring; and although the sparkling wines are inexpensive, only a few offer value. Despite the fabulous climate and high percentage of old vines, most of Spain's wines have not yet realized their potential, which is formidable.

MOST IMPORTANT INFORMATION TO KNOW

Knowing the names of the best producers and a few top recent vintages (1982, 1985, 1986, 1987, 1990, and 1991) will get you a long way if you avoid the white wines from this country.

---

*Only a handful of Rioja wines, principally the Gran Reservas from La Rioja Alta, Marqués de Murrieta, and CVNE, can age this long.
†Only the wines of Pesquera and Vega Sicilia will keep 25–30 years.

In practice, vintages are less important in Spain than in France or Italy. As in many hot areas, ripeness is not usually a problem, but Spain's most famous viticultural region, Rioja, can experience heavy rains at an inopportune time, as they did in years such as 1984, 1979, 1977, and 1972. Most of the best Riojas have become pricey and no longer represent the values they once did. The best recent vintages include 1985, 1986, 1989, and 1990. Of the luxury-priced Gran Reservas, the 1982s and 1981s from the best *bodegas* can be stunning. For the inexpensive red wines, my buying strategy is to stay within 5–7 years of the vintage, although there are exceptions.

Although I buy and taste Spanish white wine, I rarely drink it. I have not found any reason to change this practice, although some of the tasty Albarinos from Galicia offer persuasive evidence that improvements have been made. Yet these wines are priced at $15–$20, which is far too expensive for what is in the bottle.

VINTAGE GUIDE

1992—This should be a mixed vintage given the heavy rains that hit most of northern Spain. In Rioja producers talked about a great vintage until the harvest was picked in a soaking downpour.

1991—This was a better vintage for most of Spain than it was in France. Many top viticultural areas, such as Ribera del Duero and Rioja, report a generally high-quality crop. Spain could be one of Europe's surprising success stories in this vintage.

1990—Overall an abundant, high-quality crop was produced throughout Spain.

1989—Another generous, abundant crop of good-quality wine was produced.

1988—A cooler but certainly good year for Spain, with most areas reporting good rather than excellent or outstanding quality.

1987—Rioja is considered to be of very high quality and not far off the mark of wines produced in Rioja's two best vintages of the 1980s, 1981 and 1982. Elsewhere the vintage is mixed, although it is generally considered to be above average in quality.

1986—Considered to be spectacular in the Duero, but the crop size was down from 1985. In Rioja it is a good year.

1985—Virtually every wine-producing region of Spain reported 1985 to be a very successful, high-quality vintage. In Rioja it was a record-setting crop in size.

1984—This vintage has a terrible reputation because of a poor, cool European summer, but while the better red wines of Spain have turned out to be among the best made in Europe they are still mediocre.

1983—A hot, dry year caused some problems, but the wines range from good to very good.

1982—For Rioja and Ribera del Duero, the finest vintage since 1970 and largely regarded as a great year, superior to 1985 and equal to 1986 in the Duero.

1981—Spain enjoyed a very good vintage in 1981, but as time has passed it has become apparent that Rioja had an exceptional year, in many cases equal to 1982.

1980—An average-quality year.

1979—A good year in the Penedès area, but only average in Rioja.

1978—For Rioja, Penedès, and the Ribera del Duero, the best overall vintage between 1970 and 1981.

OLDER VINTAGES

For most of northern Spain, 1970 was a great vintage. Prior to that, 1964 was another superb vintage. Well-kept bottles of 1970 and 1964 red wines from Rioja and the Ribera del Duero are still excellent.

RATING SPAIN'S BEST PRODUCERS OF DRY TABLE WINES

(Wines are red unless specified)

* * * * * (OUTSTANDING PRODUCERS)

CVNE Contino (Rioja)

Muga Prado Enea Reserva (Rioja)

Marqués de Murrieta Castillo de Ygay Gran Reserva (Rioja)

Pesquera Ribero del Duero (Castilla-León)

La Rioja Alta Reserva 890 (Rioja)

La Rioja Alta Reserva 904 (Rioja)

Scala dei Priorato Cartoixa Priorat (Cataluna)

Scala dei Priorato Clos Mogador (Cataluna)

Vega Sicilia N. V. Gran Reserva Especial (Castilla-León)

Vega Sicila Unico Reserva (Castilla-León)

* * * * (EXCELLENT PRODUCERS)

Can Rafols dels Caus Penedès (Cataluna)

Julian Chivite 125 Anniversario Reserva (Navarra)

CVNE Imperial (Rioja)

CVNE Viña Real (Rioja)

Domecq-Marqués de Arienzo Reserva (Rioja)

Farina Colegiata Toro (Castilla-León)

Farina Gran Colegiata Toro (Castilla-León)

Faustino Martinez Faustino I (Rioja)

Marqués de Griñon (Castillo-La Mancha)

Inviosa Lar de Barros (Extremadura)

Lan Viña Lanciano Reserva (Rioja)

Jean León Penedès (Cataluna)

Lopez de Heredia Bosconia Reserva (Rioja)

Lopez de Heredia Tondonia Reserva (Rioja)

Martinez Bujanda Conde de Valdemar (Rioja)

Martinez Bujanda Conde de Valdemar Gran Reserva (Rioja)

De Muller Tarragona (Cataluna)

Marqués de Murrieta Reserva (Rioja)

Perez Pasqua Viña Pedrosa Ribero del Duero (Castilla-León)

La Granja Remelluri (Rioja)

La Rioja Alta Viña Alberdi (Rioja)

La Rioja Alta Viña Araña (Rioja)

La Rioja Alta Viña Ardanza (Rioja)

Marqués de Riscal Baron de Chirel (Rioja)

Bodegas de Sarria Gran Vino del Señorío Reserva (Navarra)

Torres Gran Sangre de Toro Penedès (Cataluna)

* * *(GOOD PRODUCERS)

Señorío de Almansa (Castillo-La
  Mancha)
Amezola de la Mora (Rioja)
Palacio de Arganza Bierzo
  (Castilla-León)
René Barbier Penedès (Cataluna)
Pablo Barrigon Tovar (Castilla-León)
Pablo Barrigon Tovar San Pablo
  (Castilla-León)
Pablo Barrigon Tovar Viña Cigalena
  Reserva (Castilla-León)
Pablo Barrigon Tovar Viña Solona
  (Castilla-León)
Masia Barril Priorato (Cataluna)
Bilbainas Viña Pomal (Rioja)
Marqués de Cáceres (Rioja)
Marqués de Cáceres Reserva (Rioja)
Campo Viejo (Rioja)
Julian Chivite Gran Feudo (Navarra)
Martin Codax Albarino white wine
  (Galicia)
CVNE Cune (Rioja)
Estola (Castillo-La Mancha)
Faustino Martinez Faustino V (Rioja)
Faustino Martinez Faustino VII
  (Rioja)
Franco Españolas Bordon (Rioja)
Baron de Ley El Coto (Rioja)
Los Llanos Valdepenas (Castillo-La
  Mancha)
Martinez Bujanda Conde Valdemar
  Vino Tinto (Rioja)
Mauro Ribero del Duero
  (Castilla-León)
Montecillo Viña Monty Reserva
  (Rioja)
Muga (Rioja)

Ochoa Reserva (Navarra)
Parxet-Alella white wine (Cataluna)
Pazo de Senorans Rias Baixas white
  wine (Galicia)
Piqueras Castilla de Almansa
  (Castillo-La Mancha)
Salvador Poveda (Alicante)
Raimat Costers del Segre (Cataluna)
Rioja Santiago Gran Condal (Rioja)
Riojanas Monte Real Reserva (Rioja)
Santiago Ruiz Rias Baixas Albarino
  white wine (Galicia)
Bodegas de Sarria Viña del Perdon
  (Navarra)
Scala dei Priorato Negro (Cataluna)
Taja proprietary red wine (Monastrel)
Miguel Torres Coronas Penedès
  (Cataluna)
Miguel Torres Gran Coronas Penedès
  (Cataluna)
Miguel Torres Gran Coronas Black
  Label Penedès (Cataluna); since
  1981, for vintages prior to and
  including 1981*****
Migues Torres Gran Viña Sol Green
  Label Penedès (white wine)
  (Cataluna)
Miguel Torres Viña Sol Penedès
  (white wine) (Cataluna)
Vega Sicilia Valbuena Ribero del
  Duero (Castilla-León)
Viñas del Vero Compania Somontano
  (Aragon)
Castilla de Vinicole Gran Verdad
  (Castillo-La Mancha)
Castilla de Vinicole Señorio de
  Duadianeja (Castillo-La Mancha)

* * (AVERAGE PRODUCERS)

Alavesas Solar de Samaniego (Rioja)
Los Arcos Bierzo (Castilla-León)
Masia Bach Penedès (Cataluna)
Berberana Berberana Reserva (Rioja)
Berberana Carta de Plata (Rioja)
Berceo (Rioja)
Beronia (Rioja)
Bilbainas Viña Paceta (Rioja)
Bilbainas Viña Zaco (Rioja)

Bleda Jumilla (Murcia)
Bordejé (Aragon)
Borruel (Aragon)
Campo Viejo (Rioja)
Carricas (Navarra)
Casa de la Viña (Castillo-La
  Mancha)
Castano Yecla (Murcia)
Corral Don Jacobo (Rioja)

Cueva del Granero (Castillo-La
  Mancha)
Augusto Egli (Valencia)
Eval (Alicante)
Freixenet Penedès (Cataluna)
Frutos Villar Cigales (Castilla-
  León)
Poveda Garcia (Alicante)
Irache Gran Irache (Navarra)
Lagunilla Viña Herminia (Rioja)
Lan Lander (Rioja)
Lopez de Heredia Cubillo (Rioja)
Louis Megia Duque de Estrada
  (Castillo-La Mancha)
Marqués de Monistrol Penedès
  (Cataluna)
Montecillo Cumbrero (Rioja)
Olarra Anares (Rioja)
Olarra Anares Gran Reserva (Rioja)
Olarra Cerro Añon Gran Reserva
  (Rioja)
Olarra Cerro Añon Reserva (Rioja)
Frederico Paternina Banda Azul
  (Rioja)

Frederico Paternina Conde de los
  Andes Gran Reserva (Rioja)
Frederico Paternina Viña Vial
  (Rioja)
Raimat (Costers del Segre)
Penalba Lopez Ribero del Duero
  (Castilla-León)
Pulido Romero (Medellin)
Castell del Remei (Cataluna)
Ribero Duero Ribero del Duero
  (Castilla-León)
Marqués de Riscal Gran Reserva
  (Rioja)
Marqués de Riscal Reserva (Rioja)
Ruiz (Canamero)
Miguel Torres Pinot Noir Penedès
  (Cataluna)
Unidas Age Marqués de Romeral
  (Rioja)
Unidas Age Siglo (Rioja)
Vinos de León (Castilla-León)

RATING SPAIN'S BEST PRODUCERS OF SPARKLING WINE

* * * * * (OUTSTANDING PRODUCERS)

None

* * * * (EXCELLENT PRODUCERS)

None

* * * (GOOD PRODUCERS)

Bilbainas
Cadiz
Cavas Ferret
Chandon
Gran Codorniu Brut
Freixenet Cuvée DS
Freixenet Reserva Real
Juvé y Champs Gran Cru

Juvé y Champs Gran Reserva
Juvé y Champs Reserva de la
  Familia
Mont Marcal Brut
Josep-Maria Raventos Blanc Brut
Segura Viudas Aria
Segura Viudas Brut Vintage
Segura Viudas Reserva Heredad

* * (AVERAGE PRODUCERS)

Castellblanch
Conde de Caralt
Paul Cheneau
Codorniu Extra Dry
Codorniu Non-Plus-Ultra

Codorniu Rosé Brut
Freixenet Brut Nature
Freixenet Carta Nevada
Freixenet Cordon Negro
Lembey

Marqués de Monistrol   Segura Viudas Brut
Muga Conde de Haro   Segura Viudas Rosé
Castello de Perelada

Selected Tasting Notes

BODEGAS FARINA (TORO)* * *

1989 Peromato	A	85
1988 Gran Colegiata	A	87
1988 Tierra del Vino	A	87
1989 Toro Colegiata	A	86

I have written about previous releases from this winery numerous times, and they continue to represent some of the finest values coming out of Spain. The 1989 Peromato is a soft, generously endowed wine with excellent fruit, a fine spiciness, and a full-bodied, lush finish. Drink it over the next several years. The differences between the 1989 Toro Colegiata and the 1988 Gran Colegiata are marginal. Both exhibit copious amounts of rich, luscious fruit as well as plenty of alcohol and glycerin. The Gran Colegiata is slightly deeper and more defined and intense. Both are super bargains. The oak-aged 1988 Tierra del Vino, a 50% Cabernet Sauvignon, 50% Tempranillo blend, is a dark ruby-colored wine with a black cherry–, herb-, cassis-, and oak-scented nose, rich, full-bodied flavors, good tannins, adequate acidity, and a spicy, long finish. All of these wines should continue to drink well for at least 3–4 years.

BODEGAS INVIOSA (BARROS)* * * *

1986 Lar de Barros	A	87

This wine's deep ruby color, intense bouquet of chocolate-covered black cherries, and lush, fleshy flavors are more reminiscent of a fine Pomerol than a red wine from the backwoods of Spain. A more expensive offering called Lar de Larros is also made.

MARQUÉS DE MURRIETA (RIOJA)* * * */* * * * *

1968 Castillo de Ygay	EE	90
1985 Rioja Tinto	B	88
1983 Rioja Tinto	B	87

No one doubts that this winery produces exceptional Rioja. These offerings are more alike than different. Both the 1983 and 1985 Rioja Tintos are full-bodied, wonderfully aromatic, soft, opulently fruity wines that are delicious to drink. Both will last for another 4–8 years. What makes Murrieta's Riojas among the best of the region is their concentrated, intense, highly extracted fruit character. The 1983 has slightly more evolved aromas, but both are fleshy, hedonistic Riojas for near-term drinking. Those who want to indulge in one of the great rarities of Spain should check out the superexpensive, only marginally better 1968 Castillo de Ygay. In the last 50 years less than half a dozen vintages of this wine have been declared. The 1968 is an outstanding wine, full bodied, rich, sweet, luscious, and fragrant, with that aged woody complexity that the Spanish routinely obtain and admire in their wines.

BODEGAS PESQUERA RIBERA DEL DUERO
(CASTILLA-LEÓN)* * * * *

1990 Ribera del Duero	D 91
1989 Ribera del Duero	D 90
1986 Ribera del Duero	D 93

Owner/proprietor Alejandro Fernandez has become one of the superstars of Spain. His wine is made from the Tempranillo grape and is aged 2–2½ years in casks, which produces remarkable depth and richness, and a texture not unlike a top-notch Pomerol. The rich fruit combined with the sweet oaky smells of Spanish oak (although Fernandez has also begun to use some new French oak casks) has resulted in some opulent and voluptuous wines that are real head turners. The 1986 Pesquera Ribera del Duero rivals the 1990 as the finest wine Fernandez has made yet, and comparisons to a top Bordeaux are not unjustified. Very deep in fruit, quite tannic, and well structured, this wine should last 20 or more years in a good cool cellar. It looks to be even superior to some of his great wines produced in 1982 and 1975. Aromatic, fat, and fleshy, the flattering 1989 should continue to improve for another 5–10 years. The 1990 may equal the compelling 1986. It is deep and opaque in color, with a huge nose of sweet vanillin oak, jammy black fruits, and spices, followed by a flashy, flamboyant wine oozing with massive levels of fruit, chewy quantities of glycerin, and sweet tannins. The wine is full and packed with flavor, although relatively unevolved. Approachable now, it is capable of lasting for another 12–20 years. When compared to top Riojas, Pesquera's prices have remained remarkably fair, even down to earth, which bodes well for this wine's popularity among consumers.

BODEGAS LA GRANJA REMELLURI (RIOJA)* * * *

1988 Rioja Unfiltered	C 89

Founded in 1970 by Jaime Rodriguez Salis, this tiny *bodega* is dedicated to producing only one red wine from its 90 acres of vines planted with 80% Tempranillo, 10% Mazuel, and 10% Viura. This is consistently one of my favorite Riojas among the most complex and fragrant wines produced in that area of Spain. The wines have a burgundylike lushness and richness, with that wonderful expansion on the palate of sweet, ripe berry flavors intertwined with gobs of toasty oak. Every vintage I have tried from this winery has been good enough to recommend, and that's saying something. The newly released 1988 reveals layers of rich berry fruit, plenty of spicy oak, and a smooth, harmonious, velvety texture. It is hard to believe it can get better, but my experience is that it should evolve even further with 4–7 more years in the bottle.

LA RIOJA ALTA (RIOJA)* * * */* * * * *

1988 Alberdi	A 86
1982 Reserva 904	C 90
1976 Reserva 904	C 90

1978 Reserva 890	E	92
1973 Reserva 890	E	91

This *bodega* consistently produces what I consider to be the finest example of a Rioja wine. The 1982 Reserva 904 is a classic expression of Rioja, with its superintense fragrance of smoky oak, cedar, tobacco, and minerals. Rich, medium bodied, and multidimensional, this complex, impeccably made, elegant wine lingers on the palate. The color is already showing some amber, but that is typical of these wines, which are not usually released by the winery until they are at least ten years old. The 1976 Reserva 904 offers a compelling bouquet of tobacco, plums, spice, leather, and black fruits. It is rich, concentrated, round, and amply endowed, with no hard edges. Fully mature, yet capable of lasting for another decade or more, this excellent Rioja is about as complex as these wines can be. The 1978 Reserva 890 is a spectacular Rioja, with a profound nose of sweet cedar, curranty fruit, smoke, minerals, and herbs. Rich, with layer upon layer of glycerin-imbued, deep, chewy fruit, this stunningly rich, complex Rioja should continue to drink well for at least 10 more years. Awesome! The 1973 Reserva 890 shares some of the leafy tobacco character of the Reserva 904 but has more of a cedary, mineral character added for complexity. Though slightly lighter in the mouth, it is rich, with excellent concentration and a deep, full-bodied finish. Although fully mature, it is capable of lasting for another 7–10 years. La Rioja Alta's Alberdi is always a rich, soft, succulent style of Rioja with plenty of cedary, fleshy fruit, medium body and an overall sense of elegance. Drink the 1988 over the next 3–4 years.

SCALA DEI PRIORATO (CATALUNA)* * */* * * * *

1987 Cartoixa Priorat	B	90
1990 Clos Mogador	B	90
1989 Negra	A	86

Cartoixa Priorato, the top *cuvée* for Scala dei Priorato, is consistently a rich, powerful, multidimensional wine, with a chocolatey, black cherry, herbal, cedary nose and deep, full-bodied flavors. The 1987 possesses enough extraction of fruit and tannin to continue to evolve for another decade. The 1989 Negra, made from 100% Garnacha, has a character not unlike a southern Rhône. Reminiscent of a Châteauneuf-du-Pape, this 1989 Negra possesses a roasted, herb- and berry-scented nose; rich, glycerin-infused, deep, full-bodied flavors; and a lusciously intense, heady, alcoholic finish. Drinkable now, it should age nicely for 5–7 more years. Made from 100% Garnacha from exceptionally old vines, the 1990 Clos Mogador is a stunning example of what Spain can produce but so rarely does. A superrich nose of kirsch, blackcurrants, and roasted herbs is followed by a deep wine with an opulent, even voluptuous texture, great length and extraction of fruit, and a rich, succulent finish. Drink it over the next 7–8 years.

VEGA SICILIA (RIBERA DEL DUERO)* * * * *

1982 Unico Reserva	EE	93
1975 Unico Reserva	EE	96
1974 Unico Reserva	EE	87

| 1968 Unico Reserva | EEE | 96 |
| 1988 Valbuena | D | 90 |

It is irrefutable that Vega Sicilia produces Spain's greatest red wine. The black/purple-colored 1968 Unico Reserva is still amazingly young. The bouquet offers up lavish quantities of cassis, new oak, earth, and cedar. In the mouth there is spectacular concentration, a rich, multidimensional, full-bodied texture, and gobs of glycerin, extract, and tannin in its smashingly long finish. It possesses the potential to continue to evolve, and perhaps even improve, for at least another 15–20 years! Of all the great Unicos produced recently, the 1974 is the least flattering and most austere and tannic. In fact, one might second-guess the decision to declare this a Unico. It is young enough to last another 15 years, but I wonder if the fruit will dry up before the tannins melt away. The 1975 Unico is an amazingly young wine with a purple hue to its deep ruby color. The young, backward bouquet offers up sweet aromas of ripe plums, licorice, and plenty of toasty new oak. There is phenomenal concentration, unbelievable extract, and a fabulously long, ripe, voluptuous finish with gobs of tannin. After decanting for several hours, the wine can be drunk with great pleasure. It promises to continue to evolve for at least another 20–25 years. As with most Unicos, the 1982's color is deep, dark ruby, and the nose offers up generous aromas of sweet toasty new oak and black raspberry fruit. There is almost a burgundian fragrance to the wine if you can divorce the strong oaky aromas. This phenomenally concentrated, full-bodied, rich, chewy wine is bursting with extraction. Still remarkably young and unevolved, it finishes with considerable tannic clout. Soft enough to be drunk, this potentially profound wine should be at its best between 1996 and 2010. Vega Sicilia will not produce a Unico in 1988. The 1988 Valbuena is produced from declassified Unico juice. It exhibits an excellent, rich, deep ruby color; a big, oaky, spicy, black raspberry–scented nose; ripe, full-bodied, powerful flavors; soft tannins; and a lush finish. Drink it over the next 10–15 years. It is the finest Valbuena I have tasted.

RATINGS FOR OLDER VINTAGES OF VEGA SICILIA UNICO: 1979 (92), 1976 (94), 1962 (92), 1960 (87)

Some Thoughts on Sherry

Most Americans think of sherry as that cloyingly sweet, gooey stuff called cream sherry. In fact, great sherry, along with the great Madeiras of Portugal, are probably the two most underrated and misunderstood hedonistic pleasures in winedom.

Sherries come in different styles. The lightest and driest are called fino. Finos are straw-colored, bone-dry sherries with no residual sugar. Manzanilla, which is even lighter, is among the most remarkable sherries when served fresh and well chilled as an aperitif. Other types of sherries include amontillado, which is essentially an older, rarer fino that has taken on some amber color and developed a more spicy, forceful aroma, usually of nuts and spices. Oloroso sherries are the most full bodied. They are much darker than other sherries and can vary from completely dry to slightly sweet.

Palo cortado is a relatively full-bodied sherry with a bouquet reminiscent of an amontillado but the full body and alcoholic headiness (20%–22% is not unusual) of an oloroso. Truly authentic palo cortados are rare and hard to find. For that reason Lustau's palo cortados are in a class by themselves in terms of complexity and richness.

There is such a thing as cream sherry. In the hands of a great producer such as Lustau, it can be vintage-dated as well as dry. Other cream sherries, particularly the commercial brands encountered in most liquor stores, are heavy and sweet, even flabby.

There are a number of exceptionally high-quality sherry houses, including some of the giants of the industry.

Alvear   An obscure but superlative house that produces very delicate and dry sherries. Their terrific amontillados are elegant, dry, and flavorful. Alvear also produces a rich but not heavy Pedro Ximenez.

Diez-Merito   Highly regarded, this firm produces an entire range of sherries, with the finest being its Fino Imperial and exquisite Oloroso Victoria Regina.

Domecq   This sherry house is widely represented. Look for the freshest examples of its top sherries, which include the renowned fino sherry called La Ina, the dry oloroso called Rio Viejo, and the extraordinary sibarita, which is a relatively old Palo Cortado.

Gonzalez Byass   This huge company can make very good sherry. One can find little wrong with its dry, fresh, lively Tio Pepe fino, its La Concha amontillado, its Amontillado de Duque, or its limited-production, rich, sweet, expensive Matusalem oloroso and Solera 1847 oloroso.

Hidalgo y Cia   This house makes one of the finest manzanillas. The La Gitana is a splendid, full-bodied, exceptionally fresh, delicate, and elegant manzanilla.

Emilio Lustau   For my tastes, this house produces the very finest range of sherries. High-quality sherry, particularly the drier style, needs to be cellared just like wine and, upon opening, consumed within several days. Lustau's sherries are vividly alive, and so much of their appeal is their extraordinary range of aromatic and flavor nuances, all of which become muted with prolonged exposure to air.

Many of the Lustau sherries are called almacenista. This word is used to refer to stockholders of old sherries that are sold on demand to the big sherry houses to fortify or improve their blends. The almacenista sherries are pure, unblended sherries held 20, 30, or more years as investments. Lustau, an almacenista until 1950, has released an entire line of these single-cask sherries. They are Spain's purest and most authentic sherries, with each one completely different from the other. Their quality is stupendous. Moreover, their prices remain surprisingly low for such splendid products.

Perez Marin   This is another top-quality firm noted for its superdry, crisp, remarkably perfumed, vineyard-designated manzanilla called Le Guita.

Sanchez Romate Hermanos   Another small producer in Jerez, this house is the official supplier of sherry to the Spanish royal family. Its NPU amontillado is considered by connoisseurs to be one of the greatest sherries produced.

Sandeman   This is a large firm with considerable interest in the port trade. Although its ports can be good, its finest products are the spectacular and expensive palo cortado called Royal Ambrosante and the stunning olorosos called Imperial Corregidor (dry) and Royal Corregidor (sweet).

Selected Tasting Notes

EMILIO LUSTAU

Almacenista Amontillado Borrego ½   A   90

Great, pungent, nutty nose, rich flavors; amazing length.

Almacenista Cayetano Palo Cortado ¼₀   A   90

Very rich, long, dry, great fragrance and palate persistence.

Almacenista Covenas Amontillado ½₂   A   87

Dry, nutty, spicy.

Almacenista Fino del Puerto el Puerto de Santa Maria ⅟₁₁₄   B   93

Exceptionally dry, superb, nutty, fresh nose; tasty, ripe, rich, extraordinary intensity; and a sense of lightness.

Almacenista Light Manzanilla Argueso San Lucas ⅟₁₇   B   90

Pale, bone-dry, gorgeous, delicate nose; perfect aperitif.

Almacenista Manzanilla Argueso San Lucas ⅟₁₇   A   90

For pure lightness and freshness, a superb sherry.

Almacenista Oloroso Borrego ⅛   B   96

Pale, bone-dry, gorgeous, delicate nose; perfect aperitif; unbelievable.

Almacenista Oloroso Borrego ¼₄   B   96

Totally dry, powerful, rich; great length; absolutely superb.

Almacenista Oloroso Borrego ⅟₁₇   B   88

Very subtle, understated, dry, less opulent and deep, but with great elegance.

Almacenista Oloroso Pata de Gallina J. G. Jaranda   B   94

Deep golden color; super nose of nuts; great flavor definition; quite dry, but spectacular richness and amazing finish.

Amontillado Miguel Florida Dry Sherry   B   94

Amber-colored, profound bouquet of nuts and raisins; extraordinary concentration and intensity; fabulous balance; dry, crisp, long finish.

Cream Sherry Vendimia 1986   B   94

Exactly like vintage port: dark gold, staggering nose; rich, dry, spectacular, long flavors; overall impression of lightness; and razor-sharp focus.

Dry Oloroso Don Nuno Dry Sherry   A   92

Brown/amber color; penetrating dry, nutty aromas; wondrously precise, pleasant flavors.

Light Fino Jarana   A   86

Alcohol content 15.5%; light, nutty, pale, great finesse.

Light Manzanilla   A   88

Light, dry, very fresh and vivacious, tangy.

| Moscatel Superior Emilin Sweet Sherry | A | 90 |

Heavy, blockbuster dessert wine; works splendidly when spooned over vanilla ice cream.

| Muscat Superior Emilin | A | 94 |

Dark brown, 50 years old, great perfume, very sweet.

| Old East India Sherry | A | 88 |

Nutty, sweet, crème brûlée smell.

| Oloroso Vieja Vin da Antonio Borrego Dry Sherry | A | 96 |

One of the most riveting dry sherries I have ever tasted: dry, intense, with a smoky, nutlike bouquet; dazzling, penetrating flavors; zesty, dry finish.

| Palo Cortado Peninsula | A | 88 |

Dry, full-bodied, great fragrance and richness.

| Palo Cortado Peninsula Dry Sherry | A | 92 |

Deep amber color; rich, spicy nose; superb intensity and fabulous length; quite dry, with an overall impression of remarkable freshness and lightness; sensationally extracted flavors.

| Pedro Ximenez San Emilio | A | 94 |

Superb, amazingly long and deep; golden brown; very sweet; 50 years old.

| Rare Amontillado Escuradrilla | A | 92 |

Great power and richness; ripe, long; super fruit.

| Rare Cream Solera Sweet Sherry | A | 96 |

Slightly sweet, or off-dry sherry, with fabulously rich bouquet; intense, concentrated flavors; and long finish.

| Rare Cream Superior | A | 90 |

Sweet, creamy, velvety; quite complex.

| Rare Fino Reserva Balbaina | A | ? |

Bottle corky and impossible to judge.

| Very Rare Oloroso Emperatriz Eugenia | B | 93 |

Incredible perfume and finish; dry, very rich, great complexity.

| Very Rare Oloroso Principe Rio | B | 94 |

Dry, full-bodied, fabulous nose and length.

Any Hope for Spanish White Wines?

Despite efforts by the Spanish government and a number of its supporters to encourage consumers to try them, as a group Spanish white wines remain appallingly devoid of flavor and character. Some decent white wines have emerged from Miguel Torres in Penedès, but they are correct rather than exciting.

One grape that has the potential to produce interesting and delicious white wines is the fruity, fragrant Albarino, which flourishes in the northwestern sector of Spain known as Galicia. A good Albarino is not inexpensive (most sell for $15.00–$20.00), but at its best it offers a big, flowery, apple-, pear-, and peach-scented nose that is reminiscent of Riesling and Viognier. In the mouth the wine is lighter than a Condrieu but possesses more body than most Rieslings. The problem is, only a handful of producers have done well with this varietal. The best is the Bodegas de Vilarino-Cambados, which markets its Albarino under the name Martin Codax. Consumers should look for its most recent vintages, 1992 and 1991.

THE WINES OF NORTH AMERICA

California
Oregon
Other American
Viticultural Regions

6. CALIFORNIA

Is it Genuine, or Straight Off the Assembly Line?

The Basics

Virtually every type of wine seen elsewhere in the wine world is made in California. Fortified port-style wines, decadently sweet, late-harvest Rieslings, sparkling wines, and major red and white dry table wines from such super grapes as Chardonnay and Cabernet Sauvignon—all are to be found in California.

The fine wines of California are dominated by Cabernet Sauvignon and Chardonnay, as much of the attention of that state's winemakers is directed at these two grapes. However, California makes wonderful red Zinfandel and increasing amounts of world-class Merlot and Syrah, plus some Petite Sirah. Despite improved quality, Pinot Noir is still a questionable wine in the hands of all but a dozen or so California wine producers (especially in the Santa Barbara region). Two notable trends in the late 1980s have proven popular with consumers: the proliferation of proprietary red wine blends (usually Cabernet Sauvignon–dominated and quite expensive) and the development of authoritatively flavored, robust, supple red wines made from blends of Syrah, Carignane, Grenache, Mourvèdre, and Alicante, collectively referred to as the "Rhône Rangers." As for the white wines, Sauvignon Blanc and Semillon, and blends thereof, can be wonderfully complex and fragrant, but the great majority are nondescript wines. It is a shame that Chenin Blanc has so little sex appeal among consumers, but it can be a very inexpensive, delicious drink. Colombard and Muscat suffer from the same image problems as Chenin Blanc, but shrewd consumers know the good ones and seek them out. Gewürztraminer and dry Rieslings have been dismal wines, although a handful of wineries have broken through the wall of mediocrity. For years California has made it simple for the consumer, naming each wine after the varietal from which it is made. By law a Chardonnay or Cabernet Sauvignon must contain 75% of that grape in the wine. The recent trend, accompanied by very high prices, has been to produce luxury-priced proprietary wines with awe-inspiring, often silly names such as Dominus, Opus, Rubicon, Trilogy, and Insignia. These are supposed to

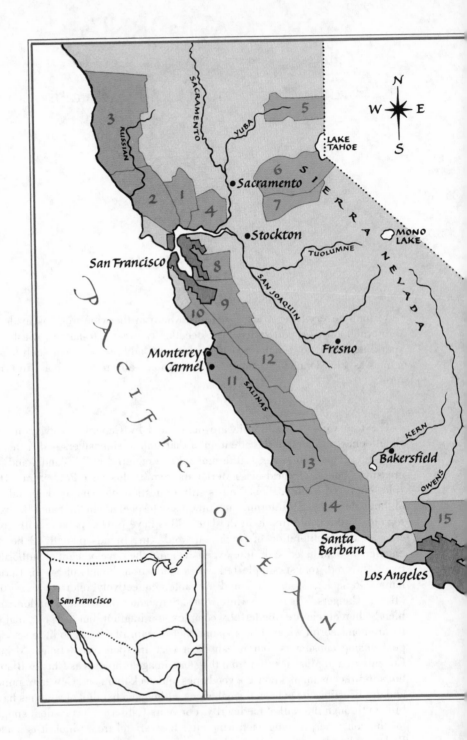

California

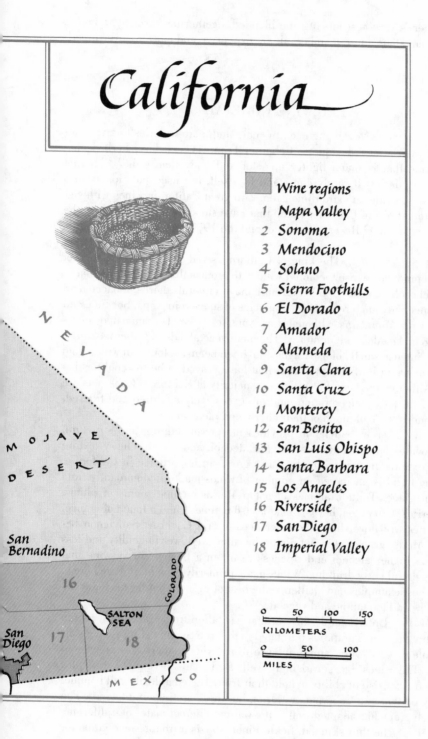

Wine regions

1. Napa Valley
2. Sonoma
3. Mendocino
4. Solano
5. Sierra Foothills
6. El Dorado
7. Amador
8. Alameda
9. Santa Clara
10. Santa Cruz
11. Monterey
12. San Benito
13. San Luis Obispo
14. Santa Barbara
15. Los Angeles
16. Riverside
17. San Diego
18. Imperial Valley

NEVADA

MOJAVE DESERT

San Bernadino

COLORADO

San Diego

SALTON SEA

16

17

18

MEXICO

```
0        50      100      150
KILOMETERS

0        50      100
MILES
```

be the winery's very best lots of wine blended together for harmony. Some of them are marvelous, but remember, all are expensive and most are overpriced.

FLAVORS

RED WINE VARIETALS

Cabernet Franc   Now being used by more and more wineries to give complexity to their wines' bouquets, Cabernet Franc is a cedary, herbaceous-scented wine that is much lighter in color and body than either Cabernet Sauvignon or Merlot. It rarely can stand by itself, but used judiciously in a blend, it can provide an extra dimension. Two great California wines with significant proportions of Cabernet Franc that have stood the test of time are the 1971 Robert Mondavi Reserve Cabernet and the 1977 Joseph Phelps Insignia red wine.

Cabernet Sauvignon   The king of California's red wine grapes, Cabernet Sauvignon produces densely colored wine with aromas that can include blackcurrants, chocolate, cedar, leather, ground meat, minerals, herbs, tobacco, and tar. Cabernet Sauvignon reaches its pinnacles of success in Napa, Sonoma, and the Santa Cruz Mountains, although top examples have also emanated, infrequently, from Amador and Monterey. The more vegetal side of Cabernet Sauvignon, with intense smells of asparagus and green beans, is found in wines from Monterey or Santa Barbara, two areas that have proved to be too cool for this varietal. Although they can be superb the majority of California Cabernets are too astringent, lack concentration, and are excessively acidified and filtered, which denudes them of much of their charm and pleasure.

Merlot   If Cabernet Sauvignon provides the power, tannin, and structure, Merlot provides opulence, fatness, higher alcohol, and a lush, chewy texture when crop yields are not too high. It has grown in importance in California. One strong trend is an increased number of wines made predominantly from the Merlot grape. Telltale aromas of a top Merlot include scents of plums, black cherries, toffee, tea, herbs, tomatoes (sometimes), and a touch of orange. Merlot wines will never have the color density of a Cabernet Sauvignon because the Merlot grape's skin is thinner, but they are lower in acidity and less tannic. The higher alcohol and ripeness result in a fleshy, chewy wine that makes wonderful early drinking. Wines made primarily from Merlot are here to stay. The best examples can challenge the best of France, but far too many remain hollow and too tannic and vegetal.

Petite Sirah   Unfortunately this varietal has fallen from grace. Petite Sirah (in actuality the Duriff grape) is unrelated to the true Syrah, yet it produces almost purple-colored, very tannic, intense wines with peppery, cassis-scented bouquets. The wines age surprisingly well, as 15- to 20-year-old examples have shown a consistent ability to hold their fruit. The complexity and bouquet will rarely be that of a Cabernet or Merlot, but these are important wines. The Petite Sirah grape has adapted well to the warmer microclimates of California.

Pinot Noir   The thin-skinned, fickle Pinot Noir is a troublesome grape for everybody. While California continues to produce too many mediocre, washed-out, pruny, vegetal wines from this varietal, no American region has demonstrated more progress with this varietal than California. Major breakthroughs have been made. While good Pinot Noirs are increasingly noticeable from the

North Coast areas of Mendocino, Napa, and Sonoma, the really stunning Pinot Noirs appear to be emanating from farther south—the Santa Cruz Mountains, the Monterey area, and the most promising region of all, Santa Barbara. A good Pinot Noir will exhibit medium to dark ruby color and an intense explosion of aromatics, including red and black fruits, herbs, earth, and floral scents. Pinot Noir tends to drop what tannin it possesses quickly, so acidity is important to give it focus and depth. Most Pinot Noirs are drinkable when released. Consumers should be particularly apprehensive of those that taste too tannic.

Syrah   Syrah is the great red grape varietal of France's Rhône Valley. An increasing number of California wineries have begun to bottle 100% Syrah wines, and some have been exquisite. The style ranges from light, fruity, almost Beaujolais-like wines to black/purple-colored, thick, rich, ageworthy, highly extracted wines bursting with potential. A great Syrah will possess a hickory-, smoky-, tar-, and cassis-scented nose; rich, full-bodied, occasionally massive flavors; and considerable tannin. Like Cabernet Sauvignon, a Syrah-based wine can be a thoroughbred when it comes to aging, easily lasting for 10–20 or more years.

Zinfandel   Seemingly against all odds, Zinfandel, the red, full-bodied type, is making a fashion comeback. Its reasonable price, combined with its gorgeous, up-front, peppery, berry (cherries, blackberries, and raspberries) nose, spicy fruit, and lush, supple texture has helped to boost its image. Additionally, Zinfandel's burgeoning popularity might be explained by a growing and, may I say, healthy trend away from excessively priced glamour wines, particularly the chocolate and vanilla flavors of California's Chardonnay and Cabernet Sauvignon. Zinfandel is grown throughout California, but the best clearly comes from relatively old vines grown on hillside vineyards. Selected vineyards from the hillsides of Napa, the Dry Creek Valley, Sonoma, Alexander Valley, Sierra Foothills, Paso Robles, and Amador have consistently produced the most interesting Zinfandels. Although soil certainly plays an important role (gravelly loam is probably the best), low yields, old vines, and harvesting fully mature, physiologically rather than analytically ripe fruit are even more important. Today most Zinfandels are made in a medium- to full-bodied, spicy, richly fruity style, somewhat in the image of Cabernet Sauvignon. Although there is some backbone and structure, Zinfandel is usually a wine that consumers can take immediate advantage of for its luscious, rich fruit and drink during the first decade of its life. My experience suggests that Zinfandel rarely improves after 7–8 years and is best drunk within that time, although many can last longer.

Carignane   A somewhat lowly-regarded grape that deserves more attention; some of California's oldest vineyards are planted with Carignane. As wineries such as Trentadue and Cline have proven, where there are old vines, low yields, and full ripeness, the wines can have surprising intensity and richness in a Rhône-like style. There is a dusty earthiness to most Carignane-based wines that goes along with its big, rich, black fruit and spicy flavors.

Alicante Bouschet   Another grape that has fallen out of favor because of its low prestige, it is still revered by those who know it well. It yields a black/purple-colored wine with considerable body and richness. With time in the bottle, it sheds its hardness, and when treated respectfully, as the two Sonoma wineries Trentadue and Topolos do, this can be an overachieving grape that handsomely repays cellaring. When mature, the wine offers a

Châteauneuf-du-Pape–like array of spicy, earthy flavors, significant body, and alcohol.

Mourvèdre/Mataro   This variety is making a comeback. Some wineries, such as Edmunds St. John, Cline Cellars, Ridge, and Sean Thackrey, have turned out fascinating wines from this varietal. Mataro produces a moderately dark-colored wine with a mushroomy, earthy, raspberry-scented nose, surprising acidity and tannin, and considerable aging potential.

FLAVORS

WHITE WINE VARIETALS

Chardonnay   The great superstar of the white wines, Chardonnay at its best can produce majestically rich, buttery wines with, seemingly, layers of flavors suggesting tropical fruits (pineapples and tangerines), apples, peaches, and even buttered popcorn when the wine has been barrel-fermented. It flourishes in all of California's viticultural districts, with no area having superiority over another. Great examples can be found from Mendocino, Sonoma, Napa, Carneros, Monterey, Santa Cruz, and Santa Barbara. The problem is that of the 600-plus California wineries producing Chardonnay, less than 4 dozen make an interesting wine. Crop yields are too high, the wines are manufactured rather than made and are excessively acidified, making them technically flawless but lacking in bouquet, flavor intensity, and character. The resulting tart, vapid wines are of no interest. Moreover they have to be drunk within 12 months of the vintage. Another popular trend has been intentionally to leave sizable amounts of residual sugar in the wine while trying to hide part of it with additions of acidity. This gives a superficial feel of more richness and roundness, but these wines, too, crack up within a year of the vintage. Most Chardonnays are mediocre and overpriced, with very dubious aging potential, yet they remain the most popular "dry" white wines produced in California.

Chenin Blanc   This maligned, generally misunderstood grape can produce lovely aperitif wines that are both dry and slightly sweet. Most wineries lean toward a fruity, delicate, perfumed, light- to medium-bodied style that pleases increasing numbers of consumers looking for delicious wines at reasonable prices. This varietal deserves more attention from consumers.

French Colombard   Like Chenin Blanc, Colombard is rarely accorded much respect. Its charm lies in its aromatic character and crisp, light-bodied style.

Gewürztraminer   Anyone who has tasted a fine French Gewürztraminer must be appalled by what is sold under this name in California. A handful of wineries, such as Navarro, Z. Moore, and Babcock, have produced some attractive, although subdued, Gewürztraminers. The bald truth remains that most California Gewürztraminers are made in a slightly sweet, watery, shallow, washed-out style.

Muscat   Several Muscat grapes are used in California. This is an underrated and underappreciated group of varietals that produce remarkably fragrant and perfumed wines loaded with tropical fruit flavors. They are ideal as an aperitif or with desserts.

Pinot Blanc   Pinot Blanc is a more steely, crisper, firmer wine than Chardonnay. In the hands of the best producers it can have considerable richness and intensity. Because it often receives less exposure to aging in new oak casks, the wine possesses more vibrancy and fruit than most Chardonnays.

Sauvignon Blanc California winemaking has failed miserably to take advantage of this grape. Overcropping, excessive acidification, and a philosophy of manufacturing the wines have resulted in hundreds of neutral, bland, empty wines with no bouquet or flavor. This is unfortunate, because Sauvignon is one of the most food-friendly and flexible wines produced in the world. It can also adapt itself to many different styles of fermentation and upbringing. At its best, the non-oaked examples of this wine possess vivid, perfumed noses of figs, melons, herbs, and minerals, crisp fruit, wonderful zesty flavors, and a dry finish. More ambitious barrel-fermented styles that often have some Semillon added can have a honeyed, melony character and rich, medium- to full-bodied, grassy, melon- and figlike flavors that offer considerable authority. Unfortunately, too few examples of either type are found in California. No viticultural region can claim a monopoly on either the successes or the failures.

Semillon One of the up-and-coming California varietals, on its own, Semillon produces wines with considerable body and creamy richness. It can often be left on the vine and has a tendency to develop botrytis, which lends itself to the making of sweet, honeyed, dessert wines. But Semillon is best when added to Sauvignon, where the two make the perfect marriage, producing wines with considerable richness and complexity.

Riesling or Johannisberg Riesling Occasionally some great late-harvest Rieslings have been made in California, but attempts at making a dry Kabinett- or Trocken-style Riesling as produced in Germany most frequently result in dull, lifeless, empty wines with no personality or flavor. Most Riesling is planted in soils that are too rich and in climates that are too hot. This is a shame. Riesling is another varietal that could prove immensely popular to the masses.

AGING POTENTIAL

Cabernet Franc: 5–10 years
Cabernet Sauvignon: 5–25 years
Chardonnay: 1–3 years
Chenin Blanc: 1–2 years
Colombard: 1–2 years
Gamay: 2–4 years
Merlot: 5–10 years
Muscat: 1–3 years
Petite Sirah: 5–15 years

Pinot Blanc: 1–3 years
Pinot Noir: 4–7 years
Riesling (dry): 1–2 years
Riesling (sweet): 2–8 years
Sauvignon Blanc: 1–2 years
Semillon: 1–4 years
Sparkling Wines: 2–7 years
Syrah: 5–20 years
Zinfandel: 3–10 years

OVERALL QUALITY LEVEL

The top 3 or 4 dozen producers of Cabernet Sauvignon, Merlot, or proprietary red wines, as well as the 2 dozen or so who produce Chardonnay, make wines that are as fine and as multidimensional as anywhere in the world. However, for well over 15 years my tastings have consistently revealed far too many California wines that are not made, but manufactured. Excessively acidified by cautious oenologists, and sterile filtered to the point where there is no perceptible aroma, many wines possess little flavor except for the textural abrasiveness caused by shrill levels of acidity and high alcohol and, in the case of the red wines, excessive levels of green, astringent tannins. Producers have tried to hide their excessive crop yields by leaving residual sugar in the finished wine, hoping to give the impression of more body. This practice is only a quick fix, as the white wines tend to fall apart 6–9 months after bottling and the red wines taste cloying.

The prevailing philosophy of California winemaking remains problematic, given the finished product. The obsession with the vineyard as a manufacturing plant, and the industrial winemaking encouraged in the cellars, result in monolithic, simplistic, squeaky-clean wines that suffer from such strictly controlled technical parameters. This encourages apathy among wine enthusiasts, who are turning their backs on what potentially could be some of the most delicious wines made in the world.* It is no secret that the principal objective of most California wineries is to produce sediment-free, spit-polished, stable wines. The means used to attain this goal too frequently eviscerate the wines of their flavor, aromas, and personality- and pleasure-giving qualities. It is even more unsettling that this same philosophy encourages an appalling lack of respect for the integrity of a vintage's personality, the vineyard's character, the varietal's identity, and, most important, the consumer's desire to maximize his pleasure. An industry willing to ignore these issues—along with wine writers who are often unwilling to offend those with whom they are on cozy terms—has resulted in a level of mediocrity that betrays the entire notion of wine enthusiasm.

1993–1994 BUYING STRATEGY

After erratic, so-so years in 1988 and 1989, California is on a roll, with a terrific white wine vintage in 1990, a great red wine vintage in 1990, a good white wine vintage in 1991, and another terrific red wine vintage in 1991. Moreover, 1992 is both abundant and of high quality, with the white wines richly fruity and fat, and the red wines already being compared with the outstanding 1984s. There are 3 years in a row where most of the state's producers have turned out wines that should be made from ripe fruit. Only the top producers who keep crop yields to a minimum and refuse to excessively manipulate and process their wines will turn out the best wines, but this is clearly a time to be buying California wines. The pipeline is filled with 3 top vintages— 1990, 1991, and 1992.

The best California buys continue to be the "Rhône ranger" blends and Zinfandels for red wines and, when you can find them, the good Chenin Blancs, Sauvignon Blancs, and Colombards for white wines.

VINTAGE GUIDE

1992—An abundant crop was harvested that should be of very good quality. When Mother Nature is as generous as she was in most viticultural regions in 1992, the potential high quality can be diluted by excessive crop yields and by harvesting grapes that are not physiologically mature. It is too soon to make any conclusive statements, other than that the materials are there for some very fine wines.

*In all fairness, many oenologists are following the commands of the owners who too frequently see wine as an innocuous industrialized product.

1991—A cool, surprisingly long growing season resulted in potentially excessive crop yields. However, producers who had the patience to wait out the cool weather and harvest fully mature fruit, as well as keep their yields down, made some superb red wines that will compete with the finest 1990s, 1987s, 1986s, 1985s, and 1984s. For the red wine varietals of Zinfandel, Petite Sirah, and so on, 1991 is a top year, with many producers expressing a preference for their 1991s because of the incredibly long hang time on the vine. This year also produced an enormous crop of good white wines. Although many Chardonnays are significantly better than their 1989 counterparts, only a few reveal as much concentration as the finest 1990 Chardonnays, except in Santa Barbara where the Chardonnays are superb.

1990—For Cabernet Sauvignon, Zinfandel, and other major red wine varietals, 1990 was a mild growing season. The crop was moderate in size, particularly when compared with 1991 and 1992. The wines are very concentrated, rich, and well made. It has all the markings for a banner year for California's top red wines. For Chardonnay, 1990 is the best year since 1986, but most of these wines should be consumed by mid-1994. For Cabernet Sauvignon, 1990 may ultimately eclipse 1985, the most recent reference point for top Cabernet.

1989—What started off as a promising vintage was spoiled by significant September rains that arrived before most producers were able to harvest. There is no question that the better-drained hillside vineyards suffered less dilution than the vineyards on the valley floors. In addition, producers who had the foresight to wait out the bad weather were rewarded with some beautifully hot, Indian summer weather that lasted through much of October. Virtually everything, both white and red, was harvested during or immediately after the rains, resulting in diluted and problematic wines. The best wines were made (1) from well-drained hillside vineyards, (2) by producers who waited for the rains to stop, (3) by producers who gave their vineyards a chance to throw off the excess moisture, and (4) by producers who gave the grapes sufficient time to replenish their acids and sugars. These fine wines will suffer only because of the general mediocre reputation of this vintage. Certainly all of the white wines from 1989 should have been consumed by now. Some excellent to outstanding red wines were produced, but selection is critical. An irony of the vintage is that Paso Robles and Santa Barbara had very good vintages, but this year's reputation was established by Napa and Sonoma.

1988—A cooler than normal summer had an impact on the concentration levels of most of the red wines. However, the top Cabernet Sauvignons and Zinfandels, as well as other red wine varietals, are not without some charm and pleasure; they are soft, up-front, consistent wines that lack depth and aging potential. Most California 1988 red wines should be drunk by 1998. Chardonnay and Sauvignon fared better in 1988, but if you have any stocks languishing in your wine cellar, their time may already have passed.

1987—This vintage has turned out to be more mixed than I initially believed, but there is no question that even at the bottom level of the quality hierarchy, the wines are at least good. At the top level there are many outstanding red wines, particularly Zinfandel- and Cabernet-based wines that show superb color, wonderful richness, and considerable aromatic dimension. Some wines resemble the soft, forward, precocious 1984s; others have the structure and depth of the finest 1985s. The best producers have made wines with considerable richness and the potential for 10–15 more years of aging. Along with 1990 and 1991, 1987 is one of the finest Zinfandel vintages in the last 2 decades.

1986—Although overshadowed by the resounding acclaim for 1985, 1986 has produced rich, buttery, opulent Chardonnays that have lower acidities than the 1985s but frequently more fruit and plumpness. The best examples should have been drunk up (Mount Eden, Chalone, and Stony Hill are three exceptions). The red wines follow a similar pattern, exhibiting a rich, ripe, full-bodied character with generally lower acids than the nearly perfect 1985s, but also more tannins and body. It appears to be an excellent year for red wines that should age quite well.

1985—On balance, this is the finest vintage for California Cabernet Sauvignon since 1974. A perfect growing season preceded near perfect conditions for harvesting. Napa and Sonoma look to be the best, with Santa Cruz and Mendocino just behind in quality. Less extroverted and opulent in their youth than the 1984s, the Cabernets should be both rich and longer lived. Most authorities continue to argue that 1985 should prove to be the best overall vintage since 1970 for California Cabernets, but many revisionists have begun to question their relatively high acidity and the lean, compact, evolutionary stage through which many of the wines are now going. This should be temporary. The best top wines are superrich but less showy and dramatic than most people expect from California Cabernet.

1984—Somewhat overshadowed by 1985, 1984 was excellent, as well as one of the hottest years on record, with temperatures frequently soaring over 100° F during the summer. An early flowering and early harvest did create problems, as many grape varietals ripened at the same time. The Chardonnays and Cabernets generally exhibit very good to excellent concentration, an engaging, opulent, forward fruitiness that gives the wines appeal in their infancy, but good overall balance. Mendocino is less successful than elsewhere, but the ripe, rich, forward character of the wines of this vintage gives them undeniable charm and character. The majority of winemakers call 1985 a more classic year, 1984 a more hedonistic and obvious year. Recent tastings of the top 1984 Cabernets reveal wines that are all drinking gloriously now and should continue to hold their fruit for at least another decade. The top red wines are splendidly rich and dramatic, but only a handful of the white wines will still retain their fruit.

1983—An average year for most of California's viticultural regions, and although the Chardonnays from Napa were very good, most are now too old. The Cabernets are medium bodied, rather austere, and lack the flesh and richness found in top years. Nevertheless, some stars are to be found (such as the Hess Collection Reserve, Château Montelena, and Dunn). The red wines will keep for at least another 4–6 years.

1982—The growing season was plagued by heavy rains followed by high temperatures. The press seemed to take a cautionary approach to the vintage and, as it turns out, justifiably so. Sonoma is more consistent than Napa, and Santa Cruz is surprisingly weak in 1982. The Sonoma red wines are ripe, rich, very forward, and much more interesting than those of Napa, which range in quality from outstanding to out of balance. Chardonnays were mediocre, diluted, and lacking depth and acidity. They should have been drunk up long ago.

1981—Like 1984, 1981 was a torridly hot growing season that had all varietals ripening at once. The harvest commenced early. Many fine, ripe, rich, dramatic Chardonnays were produced, but they should have been drunk up by 1987. The Cabernets are good rather than exciting, with the best of them having another 4–6 years of life. Most 1981 Cabernets, because of their forward character, should be drunk before 1997.

1980—A relatively long, cool growing season had wineries predicting a classic, great vintage. The Cabernets are very good, but hardly great. The Cabernets do, however, have good acidity levels and seem by California standards to be evolving rather slowly. This is a vintage that has a top-notch reputation but in reality appears to be a very fine rather than a monumental year.

OLDER VINTAGES

Since I fervently believe California's Chardonnays and Sauvignon Blancs rarely hold their fruit or improve after 3 years, older vintages are of interest only with respect to California red wines, principally Cabernet Sauvignon.

1979—This year produced a good vintage of tannic, well-endowed wines that are now fully mature.

1978—An outstanding vintage (and a very hot year) that produced concentrated, rich, plummy, dense wines that have aged well. The best examples should continue to offer splendid drinking for at least another 10–15 years. This has turned out to be a great year for California Cabernet.

1977—An above-average vintage that rendered elegant, fruity, supple wines that are now just beginning to tire a bit.

1976—A hot drought year in which production yields per acre were very small. The wines are very concentrated and tannic, sometimes out of balance. Nevertheless, the best examples (where the level of fruit extract matches the ferocity of the tannins) should prove to be among the longest-lived Cabernets of this generation. Despite irregularity here, there are some truly splendid Cabernets.

1975—This was a cool year, and most authorities consider the wines rather hollow and short-lived. However, some magnificent examples have emerged from this vintage that should last for another 10–15 years. As a general rule, most 1975 California Cabernets should be consumed over the next 4–5 years.

1974—One of the great blockbuster years for California Cabernet, 1974 introduced many American consumers to the potential for full-bodied, rich, complex wines from the best wineries. Many have criticized the wines for aging erratically and quickly, but the best 1974s exhibit a richness, voluptuousness, and intensity that recalls such vintages as 1984, 1987, and 1990. Some of the top 1974s are not yet ready for prime-time drinking. However, this vintage must be approached with caution on the auction market because of the potential for badly stored, abused bottles. Additionally, there are some major disappointments from big names.

1973—A large crop was harvested after a moderately warm summer. The quality is uneven, but the wines are well balanced, with many having the potential for long aging.

1972—A rain-plagued vintage, much like 1989; it is almost impossible to find any successes that have survived 20 years of cellaring.

1970, 1969, 1968, 1958, 1951—All great vintages.

WHERE TO FIND CALIFORNIA'S BEST WINE VALUES
(WINERIES THAT CAN BE COUNTED ON FOR VALUE)

Alderbrook (Sauvignon Blanc, Chardonnay)
Amador Foothill (white Zinfandel)
Bel Arbors–Fetzer (Zinfandel, Sauvignon Blanc, Merlot)
Belvedere (Chardonnay *cuvées*)
Beringer (Knight's Valley Chardonnay, Sauvignon Blanc, Meritage white,
    Gamay Beaujolais)
Bonny Doon (Clos de Gilroy)
Carmenet (Colombard)
Cline (Côtes d'Oakley)
Duxoup (Gamay, Charbono)
Edmunds St.-John (New World and Port O' Call reds)
Estancia (Chardonnay *cuvées*, Meritage red)
Fetzer (Sundial Chardonnay)
Franciscan (Merlot, Chardonnay)
Daniel Gehrs (all white wines)
Guenoc (Petite-Sirah, Zinfandel)
Hacienda (Chenin Blanc)
Hess Collection (Hess Select Chardonnay)
Kendall-Jackson (Vintner's Reserve Chardonnay, Fumé Blanc, Vintner's
    Reserve Zinfandel)
Kenwood (Sauvignon Blanc)
Konocti (Fumé Blanc)
Laurel Glen (Counterpoint and Terra Rosa proprietary red wines)
Liberty School–Caymus (Cabernet Sauvignon, Sauvignon Blanc, Chardonnay)
J. Lohr (Gamay, Cypress Chardonnay)
Marietta (Old Vine Red)
Mirassou (white burgundy—Pinot Blanc)
Robert Mondavi (Chenin Blanc)
Monterey (Classic *cuvées* of Merlot, Cabernet Sauvignon, Chardonnay,
    Sauvignon Blanc, Zinfandel; generic Classic White and Classic Red)
Murphy-Goode (Fumé Blanc)
Napa Ridge–Beringer (Chardonnay)
Newton (Claret Proprietary Red Wine)
Parducci (Sauvignon Blanc)
Robert Pecota (Gamay)
J. Pedroncelli (Sauvignon Blanc, Zinfandel, Cabernet Sauvignon)
R. H. Phillips (Night Harvest *cuvées* of Chardonnay and Sauvignon Blanc)
Preston (Cuvée de Fumé)
Ravenswood (Zinfandel and Merlot Vintner's blends)
Stratford (the Chardonnay and Canterbury line of wines, particularly Chardon-
    nay and Sauvignon Blanc)
Evan Tamas (Trebbiano, Fumé Blanc, Chardonnay)
Topolos (Grand Noir Proprietary Red Wine, Zinfandel, Alicante Bouschet)
Trentadue (Old Patch Red, Zinfandel, Carignan, Sangiovese, Petite Sirah,
    Merlot, N. V. Alexander Valley red, Salute Proprietary Red Wine)
Westwood (Barbera)

RATING CALIFORNIA'S BEST PRODUCERS OF CABERNET SAUVIGNON, MERLOT, OR BLENDS THEREOF

* * * * * (OUTSTANDING PRODUCERS)

Beringer Private Reserve (Napa)
Caymus Special Selection (Napa)
Dalla Valle Maya (Napa)
Dominus (Napa)
Dunn (Napa)
Dunn Howell Mt. (Napa)
Girard Reserve (Napa)
Grace Family (Napa)
Heitz Martha's Vineyard (Napa)
Hess Collection Reserve (Napa)

La Jota Howell Mt. (Napa)
Laurel Glen Sonoma Mt. (Sonoma)
Robert Mondavi Reserve (Napa)
Château Montelena Estate (Napa)
Newton Merlot (Napa)
Ravenswood Pickberry Proprietary
  Red Wine (Sonoma)
Ridge Monte Bello (Santa Cruz Mt.)
Stag's Leap Cask 23 Proprietary Red
  Wine (Napa)

* * * * (EXCELLENT PRODUCERS)

Beaulieu Private Reserve
  (Napa)****/*****
Bellerose Merlot (Sonoma)
Beringer Merlot Bancroft Vineyard
  (Napa)
Cain Cellars Merlot (Napa)
Cain Five Proprietary Red Wine
  (Napa), since 1987
Carmenet Proprietary Red Wine
  (Sonoma)
B. R. Cohn Olive Hill Vineyard
  (Sonoma)
Conn Valley (Napa)
H. Coturri and Sons Remick Vine-
  yard (Sonoma)
Dalla Valle (Napa)
Duckhorn (Napa)
Duckhorn Merlot (Napa)
Duckhorn Merlot 3 Palms Vineyard
  (Napa)****/*****
Durney Reserve
  (Monterey)****/*****
Gary Farrell Cabernet Sauvignon
  Ladi's Vineyard (Sonoma)
Gary Farrell Merlot Ladi's Vineyard
  (Sonoma)
Forman (Napa)
Foxen (Santa Barbara)
Franciscan Meritage Oakville Estate
  (Napa)
Geyser Peak Reserve Alexandre
  Proprietary Red Wine (Sonoma)
Girard (Napa)

Grgich Hills (Napa)
Groth Reserve (Napa)****/*****
Harrison (Napa)
Havens Merlot Truchard Vineyard
  (Napa)
Heitz Bella Oaks (Napa)
Hess Collection (Napa)
Jaeger-Inglewood Merlot Inglewood
  Vineyard (Napa)
Justin (San Luis Obispo)
Justin Isosceles Proprietary Red
  Wine (San Luis Obispo)
Justin Merlot (San Luis Obispo)
Katherine Kennedy (Santa Cruz)
Kenwood Artist Series (Sonoma)
Kenwood Jack London Vineyard
  (Sonoma)
Laurel Glen Terra Rosa (Sonoma)
Marietta (Sonoma)
Matanzas Creek Merlot
  (Sonoma)****/*****
Peter Michael Les Pavots Proprietary
  Red Wine (California)
Monticello Corley Reserve (Napa)
Nelson Estate Cabernet Franc (Napa)
Newton Cabernet Sauvignon
  (Napa)****/*****
Newton Claret (Napa)
Opus One (Napa)
Page Mill Volker Eisele Vineyard
  (Napa)
Palhmeyer Caldwell Vineyard
  (Napa)

Joseph Phelps Backus Vineyard
(Napa)

Joseph Phelps Insignia Proprietary
Red Wine (Napa)****/*****

Rancho Sisquoc Cellar Select
Red Estate (Santa Barbara)

Ravenswood Merlot Sangiacomo
(Sonoma)

Rubicon Proprietary Red Wine
(Napa)

St. Francis Merlot Reserve
(Sonoma)

Shafer Hillside Select
(Napa)****/***** since 1986

Shafer Merlot (Napa)

Signorello Founder's Reserve (Napa)

Silver Oak (Napa)****/*****

Silver Oak Alexander Valley
(Sonoma)****/*****

Silver Oak Bonny's Vineyard
(Napa)****/*****

Simi Reserve (Sonoma)****/*****
since 1986

Spottswoode (Napa)

Staglin (Napa)

Terra Rosa Proprietary Red Wine
(Laurel Glen—Sonoma)

Philip Togni (Napa)****/*****

Tudal (Napa)

Tulocay (Napa)

Viader Propietary Red Wine (Napa)

Vichon Stag's Leap District (Napa)

Von Strasser (Napa)

Whitehall Lane Cabernet Sauvignon
Morisoli (Napa)

Whitehall Lane Merlot Summer's
Ranch (Alexander Valley)

ZD Estate (Napa)

* * * *(GOOD PRODUCERS)*

Ahlgren Bates Ranch (Santa
Cruz)***/****

Ahlgren Besson Vineyard (Santa
Cruz)***/****

Alexander Valley (Sonoma)

Amizetta (Napa)

Arrowood (Sonoma)

Bellerose Cuvée Bellerose
(Sonoma)

Benziger Tribute (Glen Ellen)

Beringer Knight's Valley (Napa)

Boeger (El Dorado)

Boeger Merlot (El Dorado)

Buehler (Napa)***/****

Burgess Vintage Selection
(Napa)***/****

Caymus (Napa)

Chalk Hill (Sonoma)***/**** since
1990

Chalk Hill (Sonoma)***/**** since
1991

Château Chevre Merlot
(Napa)***/****

Clos du Bois (Sonoma)

Clos du Bois Briarcrest (Sonoma)

Clos du Bois Marlstone (Sonoma)

Clos du Bois Merlot (Sonoma)

Clos du Val Merlot (Napa)

Clos du Val Reserve (Napa)***/****

Corison (Napa)

Cosentino (Napa)

Cosentino Reserve (Napa)

Cuvaison (Napa)

Dehlinger (Sonoma)

Dehlinger Merlot (Sonoma)

Dry Creek Meritage (Sonoma)

Durney (Monterey)

Eberle (Paso Robles)

Estancia Merlot (Alexander Valley)

Étude (Napa)***/****

Fetzer Barrel Select (California)

Field Stone Alexander Valley
(Sonoma)

Field Stone Reserve (Sonoma)

Firestone (Santa Barbara)

Firestone Reserve (Santa
Barbara)***/****

Fisher Coach Insignia (Sonoma)

Louis Foppiano Fox Mt. Reserve
(Sonoma)

Franciscan Merlot (Napa)

Franciscan Oakville Estate (Napa)

Frog's Leap (Napa)

Frog's Leap Merlot (Napa)

Gainey Merlot Limited Selection
(Santa Barbara)***/****

E. & J. Gallo Private Reserve
(Sonoma)

Geyser Peak Estate Reserve
(Sonoma)
Groth (Napa)***/****
Gundlach-Bundschu Rhine Farm
Vineyard (Sonoma)
Hacienda (Sonoma)
Hallcrest (Santa Cruz)
Hanna (Sonoma)
Harbor (Sacramento)***/****
Havens Merlot (Napa)
Heitz (Napa)
William Hill Gold Label Reserve
(Napa)
Husch (Mendocino)
Iron Horse Cabernets Proprietary
Red Wine (Sonoma)
Johnson-Turnbull (Napa)
Johnson-Turnbull Vineyard
Selection 67 (Napa)***/****
Jordan (Sonoma)
Judd's Hill (Napa)***/****
Kalin Reserve (Marin)
Robert Keenan (Napa)
Robert Keenan Merlot (Napa)
Katherine Kennedy Lateral (Santa
Clara)***/****
Kenwood (Sonoma)
Kistler (Sonoma)
Klein (Santa Cruz)
Liberty School (California)
Livingston Moffett Vineyard
(Napa)***/****
Long (Napa)
Robert Mondavi Napa Cuvée (Napa)
Monterey Classic Cabernet
Sauvignon (Monterey)
Monterey Classic Merlot (Monterey)
Monterey Classic Red (Monterey)
Monticello Jefferson Cuvée
(Napa)***/****
Monticello Merlot (Napa)
Murphy-Goode Merlot (Sonoma)
Nevada City (Nevada County)
Niebaum-Coppola Estates Rubicon
(Napa)***/****
Peachy Canyon (Paso Robles)
J. Pedroncelli Reserve
(Sonoma)***/****

Robert Pepi Vine Hill Ranch (Napa)
Joseph Phelps Eisele Vineyard
(Napa)***** before 1987
Pine Ridge Andrus Reserve (Napa)
A. Rafanelli (Sonoma)
Rancho Sisquoc Merlot Estate (Santa
Barbara)
Rancho Sisquoc Cabernet Sauvignon
Estate (Santa Barbara)
Rancho Sisquoc Cabernet Franc
(Santa Barbara)
Raymond Private Reserve (Napa)
Renaissance (Yuba)***/****
Ridge Santa Cruz (Santa Clara)
Ritchie Creek (Napa)
J. Rochioli (Sonoma)
Rocking Horse (Napa)
St. Francis Merlot (Sonoma)
Santa Cruz Mt. Bates Ranch (Santa
Cruz)***/****
Sebastiani single-vineyard *cuvées*
(Sonoma)
Sequoia Grove (Napa)
Sequoia Grove Estate (Napa)
Shafer Stag's Leap (Napa)
Simi (Sonoma)
Château Souverain (Sonoma), since
1990
Stag's Leap Fay Vineyard (Napa)
Stag's Leap Stag's Leap Vineyard
(Napa)***/****
Stratford Merlot (California)
Swanson (Napa)
The Terraces (Napa)***/****
Trefethen Eschol Red (Napa)
Trefethen Reserve (Napa)
Trentadue (Sonoma)
Trentadue Merlot (Sonoma)***/****
Truchard Merlot (Napa)
Vichon (Napa)
Vichon Merlot (Napa)***/****
Whitehall Lane (Napa)
Whitehall Lane Reserve
(Napa)***/****
Whiterock Claret Proprietary Red
Wine (Napa)
ZD (Napa)

* * *(AVERAGE PRODUCERS)*

Alexander Valley Vineyard Merlot
  (Sonoma)**/***
S. Anderson (Napa)
Arrowood Merlot (Sonoma)**/***
Bargetto (Santa Cruz)
Beaulieu Beau Tour (Napa)**/***
Beaulieu Rutherford (Napa)**/***
Bel Arbors (California)
Bel Arbors Merlot (California)
Belvedere Wine Company
  (Sonoma)
Belvedere Wine Company Merlot
  (Sonoma)
Benziger (Sonoma)
Benziger Merlot (Glen Ellen)
Brander Bouchet Proprietary Red
  Wine (Santa Ynez)
Buena Vista Carneros (Sonoma)
Buena Vista Private Reserve
  (Sonoma)**/***
Cafaro (Napa)**/***
Cafaro Merlot (Napa)
Cakebread (Napa)
Carey Arabesque Proprietary Red
  Wine (Santa Ynez)
Chappellet (Napa)
Chappellet Merlot (Napa)
Chimney Rock (Napa)
Cinnabar (Santa Cruz)**/***
Clos Pegase (Napa)
Clos Pegase Clos Pegaso Proprietary
  Red Wine (Napa)
Clos Pegase Merlot (Napa)
Clos Ste.-Nicole (California)
Clos du Val (Napa)
B. R. Cohn Merlot (Napa)
Congress Springs (Santa Clara)
Conn Creek (Napa)
Creston Manor (San Luis Obispo)
Cronin (Santa Cruz)
Cutler Cellar (Sonoma)
De Loach (Sonoma)
De Moor (Napa)
Diamond Creek Gravelly Meadow
  (Napa)**/***; before 1987*****
Diamond Creek Lake (Napa)**/***;
  before 1987*****
Diamond Creek Red Rock Terrace
  (Napa)**/***; before 1987*****

Diamond Creek Volcanic Hill
  (Napa)**/***; before 1987*****
Dry Creek (Sonoma)**/***
Estancia (Alexander Valley)
Far Niente (Napa)**/***
Ferrari-Carano Merlot (Sonoma)
Flora Springs (Napa)
Flora Springs Trilogy Proprietary
  Red Wine (Napa)
Folie À Deux (Napa)
Louis Foppiano (Sonoma)
Freemark Abbey Boché (Napa)
Freemark Abbey Sycamore
  (Napa)**/***
Gan Eden (Sonoma)
Georis (Monterey)**/***
Glen Ellen (California)
Grand Cru (Sonoma)
Greenwood Ridge (Sonoma)
Groth (Napa)**** before 1987
Guenoc Beckstoffer Vineyard
  (Carneros)
Gundlach-Bundschu (Sonoma)**/***
Hacienda Antares Proprietary Red
  Wine (Sonoma)
Hagafen (Napa)
Hanzell (Sonoma)**/***
Haywood (Sonoma)
William Hill Silver Label (Napa)
Houltz (Santa Ynez)
Indian Springs Merlot (Sierra
  Foothills)
Inglenook (Napa)
Inglenook Reserve Cask
  (Napa)**/***
Inglenook Reunion Proprietary Red
  Wine (Napa)**/***
Jekel Home Vineyard (Monterey)
Jekel Symmetry Proprietary Red
  Wine (Monterey)**/***
Château Julien (Monterey)
Château Julien Merlot (Monterey)
Kendall-Jackson Cardinale Meritage
  Proprietary Red Wine
  (California)**/***
Kendall-Jackson Vintner's Reserve
  (California)
Konocti (Lake)**/***
Konocti Merlot (Lake)

Charles Krug Vintage Selection
(Napa)**/****
Lakespring (Napa)
Lakespring Reserve (Napa)
Leeward (Ventura)
J. Lohr Reserve (Santa Clara)
Markham (Napa)
Markham Merlot (Napa)
Louis Martini (Sonoma)
Louis Martini Monte Rosso
(Sonoma)**/***
Mayacamas (Napa)**/***; before
1979*****
McDowell Valley (California)
Meridian (San Luis Obispo)
Merryvale Proprietary Red Wine
(Napa)
Domaine Michel (Napa)
Mirassou (Santa Clara)
Montevina (Amador)
Morgan (Monterey)
J. W. Morris Fat Cat (Sonoma)
Mt. Eden (Santa Cruz)
Mt. Veeder (Napa)
Mt. Veeder Meritage Proprietary Red
Wine (Napa)
Mountain View (Santa Clara)
Murphy-Goode (Sonoma)**/***
Domaine Napa (Napa)
Napa Ridge (Napa)
Newlan (Napa)
Neyers (Napa)
Gustave Niebaum Collection
(Napa)**/***
Parducci (Mendocino)
Parducci Merlot (Mendocino)
Robert Pecota (Napa)
J. Pedroncelli (Sonoma)
Peju Province (Napa)
Joseph Phelps (Napa)
R. H. Phillips (Yolo)
Pine Ridge Diamond Mt.
(Napa)**/***
Pine Ridge Merlot (Napa)
Pine Ridge Rutherford Cuvée
(Napa)**/***
Pine Ridge Stag's Leap District
(Napa)**/***
Château Potelle (Napa)
Preston (Sonoma)

Quail Ridge (Napa)
Rabbit Ridge (Sonoma)
Raymond Napa Cuvée (Napa)
Richardson (Sonoma)
Rocking Horse Claret (Napa)
Rombauer (Napa)
Roudon-Smith (Santa Cruz)
Round Hill (Napa)
Round Hill Reserve (Napa)**/***
Rubissow-Sargent (Napa)
Rubissow-Sargent Merlot (Napa)
Rutherford Hill (Napa)
Rutherford Hill Merlot (Napa)****
until 1985
St. Andrews (Napa)
St. Clement (Napa)
Château St. Jean (Sonoma)
St. Supery (Napa)
Santa Barbara (Santa Barbara)
V. Sattui cuvées (Napa)
Sebastiani regular cuvées (Sonoma)
Seghesio (Sonoma)
Shenandoah Amador
(Amador)**/***
Sierra Vista (El Dorado)
Silverado (Napa)
Robert Sinskey Claret (Sonoma)
Château Souverain Merlot (Sonoma)
Spring Mountain (Napa)
Stag's Leap Napa (Napa)**/***
Steltzner (Napa)
Steltzner Merlot (Napa)
Sterling Merlot (Napa)
Sterling Napa (Napa)
Sterling Diamond Mtn. Ranch
(Napa)**/***
Sterling Reserve (Napa)**/***
Stevenot (Calaveras)
Stone Creek (Napa)
Stonegate (Napa)
Stonegate Merlot (Napa)
Stratford (California)
Straus Merlot (Napa)
Rodney Strong Alexander's Crown
(Sonoma)**/***
Rodney Strong Reserve
(Sonoma)**/***
Rodney Strong (Sonoma)
Sullivan (Napa)**/*****
Sullivan Merlot (Napa)**/*****

Sutter Home (Napa)
Swanson Merlot (Napa)
Evan Tamas (Livermore)
Tobin James (Paso Robles)
Trefethen Napa Cuvée (Napa)**/***

Vichon Coastal Selection (Napa)
Villa Zapu (Napa)
Weinstock (Sonoma)
Wellington (Sonoma)
J. Wile and Sons (California)

RATING CALIFORNIA'S BEST PRODUCERS OF CHARDONNAY

* * * * * *(OUTSTANDING PRODUCERS)*

Au Bon Climat Bien Nacido (Santa
   Barbara)
Au Bon Climat Sanford & Benedict
   Vineyard (Santa Barbara)
Calera Mt. Harlan (San Benito)
Chalone Estate (Monterey)
Chalone Reserve (Monterey)
Ferrari-Carano Reserve (Sonoma)
Foxen (Santa Barbara)
Hanzell (Sonoma)
Kalin Cuvée W (Livermore)
Kistler Durrell Vineyard (Sonoma)
Kistler Dutton Ranch (Sonoma)
Kistler Kistler Estate (Sonoma)
Marcassin (Sonoma)
Peter Michael Howell Mountain
   (Napa)
Peter Michael Monplaisir (Sonoma)

Mt. Eden Santa Cruz Estate (Santa
   Cruz)
Newton Unfiltered (Napa)
Sanford Barrel Select (Santa Barbara)
Sanford Sanford & Benedict (Santa
   Barbara)
Silverado Limited Reserve (Napa)
Steele Du Pratt Vineyard
   (Mendocino)
Steele Lolonis Vineyard (Mendocino)
Steele Sangiacomo Vineyard
   (Sonoma)
Robert Talbott Estate (Monterey)
Robert Talbott Diamond T Estate
   (Monterey)
Williams-Selyem Allen Vineyard
   (Sonoma)

* * * * *(EXCELLENT PRODUCERS)*

Acacia Marina Vineyard (Napa)
Alderbrook Reserve (Sonoma)
Au Bon Climat (Santa Barbara)
Au Bon Climat Talley Vineyard
   (Santa Barbara)****/*****
Bancroft (Napa)
Beringer Private Reserve
   (Napa)****/*****
Cain Cellars (Napa)
Calera Central Coast (California)
Cambria Katherine's Vineyard
   (Santa Maria)
Cambria Reserve (Santa Maria)
La Chimiere (Santa Barbara)
Cinnabar (Santa Clara)
Crichton Hall (Napa)
Cronin *cuvées* (San Mateo)
De Loach O.F.S. (Sonoma)
Dehlinger (Sonoma)

Durney Estate (Monterey)
Edna Valley (San Luis Obispo)
El Molino (Napa)
Ferrari-Carano (Sonoma)
Fisher Whitney's Vineyard
   (Sonoma)
Flora Springs Barrel Fermented
   (Napa)
Forest Hill (Sonoma)
Forman (Napa)
Franciscan (Napa)
Daniel Gehrs (Monterey)
Girard (Napa)
Girard Reserve (Napa)
Grgich Hills (Napa)
Hacienda Clair de Lune (Sonoma)
Harrison (Napa)
Hess Collection (Napa)
Kalin Cuvée DD (Marin)

Kalin Cuvée LD (Sonoma)

Kendall-Jackson Camelot Vineyard
  (Lake)

Kistler McCrea Vineyard
  (Sonoma)****/*****

Kistler Vine Hill Road Vineyard
  (Sonoma)****/*****

Logan (Robert Talbott—Monterey)

Long (Napa)

Matanzas Creek
  (Sonoma)****/*****

Peter McCoy Clos des Pierres
  Vineyard (Sonoma)****/*****

Robert Mondavi Reserve
  (Napa)****/*****

Château Montelena
  (Napa)****/*****

Mt. Eden MacGregor Vineyard (Edna
  Valley)

Napa Ridge Reserve (Napa)

Newton (Napa)****/*****

Pahlmeyer Unfiltered (Napa)

Patz and Hall (Napa)****/*****

Pinnacles (Franciscan—Monterey)

Rabbit Ridge (Sonoma)

Rabbit Ridge Russian River Valley
  (Sonoma)

Rancho Sisquoc Estate (Santa
  Barbara)

Kent Rasmussen (Carneros)

Ravenswood Sangiacomo
  (Sonoma)****/*****

Raymond Private Reserve (Napa)

Ridge Howell Mt. (Napa)

Ridge Santa Cruz (Santa Cruz)

J. Rochioli (Sonoma)

Salmon Creek (Napa)

Sanford (Santa Barbara)

Shafer (Napa)

Signorello (Napa)

Signorello Founder's Reserve
  (Napa)****/*****

Steele California (Sonoma)

Steele Durell Vineyard (Sonoma)

Stony Hill (Napa)****/*****

Robert Talbott Logan (Monterey)

Talley (Arroyo Grande)

Marimar Torres (Sonoma)

Trefethen (Napa)

Château Woltner St. Thomas
  Vineyard (Napa)

Château Woltner Titus Vineyard
  (Napa)

ZD (Napa)

* * * (GOOD PRODUCERS)

Acacia (Napa)

Alderbrook (Sonoma)

S. Anderson (Napa)

Arrowood (Sonoma)

Babcock (Santa Barbara)

Bargetto Cyprus (Central Coast)

Belvedere Wine Company (Sonoma)

Benziger (Sonoma)

Beringer (Napa)

Bernardus (Monterey)

Burgess Triere Vineyard
  (Napa)***/****

Byron (Santa Barbara)

Byron Reserve (Santa
  Barbara)***/****

Chalk Hill (Sonoma)***/**** since
  1991

Christophe (Napa)

Domaine de Clarck (Monterey)

Clos du Bois Barrel-Fermented
  (Sonoma)

Clos du Bois Calcaire
  (Sonoma)***/****

Clos du Bois Flintwood
  (Sonoma)***/****

B. R. Cohn Olive Hill Vineyard
  (Sonoma)

De Loach (Sonoma)

Elliston (Central Coast)

Estancia (Franciscan—Napa)

Far Niente (Napa)***/****

Gary Farrell (Sonoma)

Fetzer Barrel Select (Mendocino)

Fetzer Sundial (California)

Fisher Coach Insignia (Sonoma)

Flora Springs (Napa)

Thomas Fogarty (Monterey)

Folie À Deux (Napa)

Frog's Leap (Napa)

Gainey (Santa Barbara)

Gan Eden (Sonoma)

Gan Eden Reserve (Sonoma)

Gauer Estate (Sonoma)
Geyser Peak (Sonoma)
Guenoc Estate (Lake County)
Guenoc Reserve (Lake County)***/****
Hacienda Clair de Lune (Sonoma)***/****
Handley (Dry Creek)***/****
Hanna (Sonoma)
Harbor (Napa)
Hess Collection Hess Select (Napa)
Hidden Cellars (Mendocino)
Husch (Mendocino)
Iron Horse (Sonoma)
Jekel (Monterey)
Château Julien Sur-Lie (Monterey)
Kendall-Jackson Proprietor's Grand Reserve (Lake)
Kendall-Jackson Vintner's Reserve (Lake)
Kenwood Beltane Ranch (Sonoma)
Konocti (Lake)
Charles Krug Carneros Reserve (Napa), since 1990
Kunde Estate Reserve (Sonoma)
Landmark cuvées (Sonoma)
Liparita (Napa)***/****
J. Lohr Riverstone (Monterey)
Lolonis (Mendocino)
MacRostie (Carneros)
Meridian (San Luis Obispo)
Robert Mondavi (Napa)
Monterey Classic Chardonnay (Monterey)
Monticello Corley Reserve (Napa)
Monticello Jefferson Cuvée (Napa)
Morgan (Monterey)
Mount Eden (Santa Barbara)***/****
Murphy-Goode (Sonoma)
Murphy-Goode Reserve (Sonoma)
Napa Ridge (Napa)
Navarro (Mendocino)
Pahlmeyer (Napa)
Fess Parker (Santa Barbara)
Philippe-Lorraine (Napa)
R. H. Phillips (Yolo)
Pine Ridge Knollside Cuvée (Napa)

Pine Ridge Stag's Leap District (Napa)
Rutherford Hill XVS Reserve (Napa)
St. Francis Barrel-Fermented (Sonoma)
Saintsbury (Napa)
Saintsbury Reserve (Napa)
Santa Barbara Lafond Vineyard (Santa Barbara)***/****
Sarah's Estate (Santa Clara)
Sarah's Ventana Vineyard (Santa Clara)
Sausal (Sonoma)
Sebastiani single-vineyard cuvées (Sonoma)
Silverado (Napa)
Simi (Sonoma)
Simi Reserve (Sonoma)***/****
Robert Sinskey (Sonoma)
Sonoma-Cutrer Cutrer Vineyard (Sonoma)***/****
Sonoma-Cutrer Les Pierres (Sonoma)***/****
Sonoma-Cutrer Russian River Ranches (Sonoma)
Château Souverain (Sonoma), since 1990
Stag's Leap Reserve (Napa)
Sterling Diamond Mountain Ranch (Napa)
Sterling Winery Lake (Napa)
Storrs (Santa Cruz)
Stratford (Napa)
Stratford Partner's Reserve (Napa)
Rodney Strong Chalk Hill Vineyard (Sonoma)
Swanson (Napa)
Evan Tamas (Livermore)
Thomas-Hsi (Napa)***/****
Tiffany Hill (San Luis Obispo)***/****
Vichon (Napa)***/****
Vita Nova (Santa Barbara)
Wente Brothers Reserve (Alameda), since 1988
Wente Brothers Wente Vineyard (Alameda), since 1988
William Wheeler (Sonoma)
Whitehall Lane Reserve (Napa)

Wild Horse (Central Coast)
Château Woltner Estate Reserve
(Napa)

Château Woltner Frederique
Vineyard (Napa)

* * (AVERAGE PRODUCERS)

Adler Fels (Sonoma)
Alexander Valley (Sonoma)
David Arthur (Napa)
Beaulieu Carneros Reserve
(Napa)**/***
Beaulieu Napa Beaufort
(Napa)**/***
Bel Arbors (California)
Boeger (El Dorado)
Bon Marché (Napa)
Bonny Doon (Santa Cruz)
Bouchaine (Los Carneros)
Bouchaine (Napa)
David Bruce (Santa Cruz)
Buena Vista Carneros (Sonoma)
Buena Vista Private Reserve
(Sonoma)
Davis Bynum (Sonoma)
Cakebread (Napa)
Callaway Calla-lees (Temecula)
Chalone Gavilan (Monterey)**/***
Chamisal (San Luis Obispo)
Chappellet (Napa)
Chimney Rock (Napa)
Clos Pegase (Napa)
Clos du Val (Napa)
Congress Springs (Santa Clara)
Conn Creek (Napa)
Cosentino (Napa)
Cottonwood Canyon (San Luis
Obispo)
Creston Manor (San Luis Obispo)
Cuvaison (Napa)
De Moor (Napa)
Dry Creek (Sonoma)
Eberle (Paso Robles)**/***
Firestone (Santa Barbara)
Louis Foppiano (Sonoma)
Fox Mountain Reserve (Sonoma)
Freemark Abbey (Napa)
Freemont Creek (California)
Glen Ellen (Sonoma)
Grand Cru (Sonoma)
Groth (Napa)

Gundlach-Bundschu (Sonoma)
Hagafen (Napa)**/***
Hagafen Reserve (Napa)
Havens (Napa)
Haywood (Sonoma)
William Hill Gold Label Reserve
(Napa)**/***
William Hill Silver Label (Napa)
Indian Springs (Sierra Foothills)
Inglenook (Napa)
Inglenook Reserve (Napa)
Jordan (Sonoma)
Château Julien Barrel Fermented
(Monterey)**/***
Karly (Amador)
Robert Keenan (Napa)
Lakespring (Napa)
Leeward (Central Coast)**/***
J. Lohr Cypress (Santa Clara)**/***
Markham (Napa)
Louis Martini (Napa)**/***
Mayacamas (Napa)
McDowell Valley (Mendocino)
Meeker (Sonoma)
Melim (Sonoma)
Merry Vintners (Sonoma)**/***
Merryvale (Napa)
Mirassou (Monterey)
Morgan Reserve (Monterey)**/***
J. W. Morris Douglas Hill
(Sonoma)**/***
J. W. Morris Gravel Bar
(Sonoma)**/***
Mt. Veeder (Napa)
Mountain View (California)
Napa Creek Winery (Napa)
Newlan (Napa)
Gustave Niebaum Collection Bayview
Vineyard (Napa)**/***
Gustave Niebaum Collection Laird
Vineyard (Napa)**/***
Noble Hill (Santa Cruz)**/***
Obester Winery Barrel Fermented
(Mendocino)**/***

Ojai (Ventura County)
Parducci (Mendocino)
J. Pedroncelli (Sonoma)**/***
Robert Pepi (Napa)
Joseph Phelps (Napa)
Joseph Phelps Sangiacomo (Napa)
Château Potelle (Napa)
Quail Ridge (Napa)
Qupé (Santa Barbara)**/***
Richardson (Sonoma)
Rombauer (Napa)
Round Hill (Napa)
Rutherford Hill Jaeger Vineyard
  (Napa)
St. Andrews (Napa)
St. Clement (Napa)
Château St. Jean (all cuvées)
  (Sonoma)
St. Supery (Napa)
Santa Barbara Reserve (Santa
  Barbara)**/***
Schug Beckstoffer Vineyard
  (Carneros)
Sea Ridge (Sonoma)
Sebastiani regular cuvées (Sonoma)

Seghesio (Sonoma)
Sequoia Grove Carneros (Napa)
Sequoia Grove Estate (Napa)
Sierra Vista (El Dorado)
Spring Mountain (Napa)
Stag's Leap (Napa)
Sterling (Napa)
Stevenot (Calaveras)
Stone Creek (all cuvées) (Napa)
Taft Street (Sonoma)
Tulocay (Napa)
Vichon Coastal Selection (California)
Villa Mt. Eden Grand Reserve
  (Napa)
Villa Zapu (Napa)
Weinstock (Sonoma)**/***
Mark West (Sonoma)
Westwood (El Dorado)
William Wheeler (Sonoma)
White Oak (Sonoma)
White Oak Limited Reserve
  (Sonoma)
Whitehall Lane Le Petit (Napa)
Windemere (Sonoma)
Zaca Mesa (Santa Barbara)

RATING CALIFORNIA'S BEST PRODUCERS OF PINOT NOIR

* * * * * (OUTSTANDING PRODUCERS)

Au Bon Climat La Bauge Au Dessus
  Bien Nacido Vineyard
  (Santa Barbara)
Au Bon Climat Sanford & Benedict
  Vineyard (Santa Barbara)
Calera Jensen Vineyard (San Benito)
Calera Mills Vineyard (San Benito)
Calera Reed Vineyard (San Benito)

Calera Selleck Vineyard (San Benito)
Robert Mondavi Reserve (Napa)
Sanford Barrel Select (Santa Barbara)
Williams-Selyem Allen Vineyard
  (Sonoma)
Williams-Selyem Rochioli Vineyard
  (Sonoma)

* * * * (EXCELLENT PRODUCERS)

Au Bon Climat (Santa Maria)
Au Bon Climat Talley Vineyard
  (Arroyo Grande)
Cambria Julia's Vineyard (Santa
  Maria), since 1991
La Chimière (Santa Maria)
El Molino (Napa)
Gary Farrell Bien Nacido Vineyard
  (Santa Barbara)

Gary Farrell Howard Allen Vineyard
  (Sonoma)
Foxen Vineyard Sanford & Benedict
  Vineyard (Santa Barbara)
Gainey Sanford & Benedict Vineyard
  (Santa Barbara)
Kalin Cuvée DD (Sonoma)
Kalin Cuvée LW (Sonoma)
Mt. Eden Estate (Santa Cruz)

Kent Rasmussen (Carneros)
Saintsbury Carneros (Napa)
Saintsbury Reserve (Napa)
Sanford (Santa Barbara)
Signorello (Napa)

Talley (San Luis Obispo)
Lane Tanner (Santa Barbara)
Lane Tanner Sanford & Benedict
    Vineyard (Santa Barbara)

* * * (GOOD PRODUCERS)

Byron (Santa Barbara)
Carneros Creek (Napa)
Chalone Estate (Monterey)
Domaine de Clarck
    (Monterey)***/****
Edna Valley (San Luis Obispo)
Étude (Napa)***/****
Ferrari-Carano (Napa)
Robert Mondavi (Napa)
Monticello Estate (Napa)
Morgan (Monterey)
Navarro (Mendocino)***/****
Page Mill Bien Nacido
    Vineyard (Santa Barbara)
Pepperwood Springs
    (Mendocino)***/****
J. Rochioli (Sonoma)

Saintsbury Garnet (Napa)
Santa Barbara (Santa Barbara) since
    1989
Santa Barbara Reserve (Santa
    Barbara)***/**** since 1989
Santa Cruz Mountain (Santa
    Cruz)***/****
Robert Sinskey (Sonoma)***/****
Steele Pinot Noir Carneros (Sonoma)
Steele Sangiacomo Vineyard
    (Sonoma)***/****
Robert Stemmler (Sonoma)
Westwood (El Dorado)
Whitcraft Bien Nacido Vineyard
    (Santa Barbara)
Wild Horse (Santa Barbara)***/****

* * (AVERAGE PRODUCERS)

Acacia Iund Vineyard
    (Napa)**/***
Acacia St. Clair (Napa)**/***
Adler Fels (Sonoma)
Alexander Valley (Sonoma)
Beaulieu Carneros Reserve (Napa)
Bon Marché (Napa)
Bouchaine (Napa)
David Bruce (Santa Cruz)**/***
Buena Vista (Sonoma)
Davis Bynum (Sonoma)
Calera (Central Coast)**/***
Cambria (Santa Maria)
Caymus Special Selection (Napa)
Clos du Val (Napa)
Cottonwood Canyon (Santa
    Barbara)**/***
Cronin (Santa Cruz)
De Loach (Sonoma)
Dehlinger (Sonoma)**/***
Thomas Fogarty (Santa Cruz)
Gainey (Santa Barbara)
Gundlach-Bundschu (Sonoma)
Hacienda (Sonoma)

Hanzell (Sonoma)
Husch (Mendocino)
Kistler (Sonoma)
Charles Krug Carneros Reserve
    (Napa)
Meridian (Santa Barbara)
Mountain View Vintners
    (California)**/***
Parducci (Mendocino)
Fess Parker (Santa Barbara)
Richardson (Sonoma)**/***
Roudin-Smith (Santa Cruz)
Schug Beckstoffer Vineyard
    (Carneros)
Schug Heinemann Vineyard
    (Napa)
Sea Ridge (Sonoma)
Sterling (Napa)
Rodney Strong River East Vineyard
    (Sonoma)
Joseph Swan**/***
Truchard (Napa)
Tulocay (Napa)
Tulocay Haynes Vineyard (Napa)

Mark West (Sonoma)   ZD (Napa)
Whitehall Lane (Napa)

RATING CALIFORNIA'S RHÔNE RANGERS

* * * * * (OUTSTANDING PRODUCERS)

Calera Viognier   Ridge York Creek Petite Sirah
Edmunds St. John Syrah   Sean Thackrey Orion (Syrah)
Qupé Syrah Bien Nacido Vineyard   Sean Thackrey Sirius (Petite Sirah)
Qupé Viognier Los Olivos Vineyard   Sean Thackrey Taurus (Mourvèdre)

* * * * (EXCELLENT PRODUCERS)

Bonny Doon Clos de Gilroy   Frey (Syrah)
  (Grenache)   Hop Kiln Petite Sirah
Bonny Doon Le Sophiste (Blend)   Jade Mountain Les Jumeaux (Blend)
Bonny Doon Vin Gris de Cigare Rosé   Jade Mountain La Provençale (Blend)
Cambria Syrah   Jade Mountain Syrah
Cline Côtes d'Oakley (Blend)   Fess Parker Syrah
Cline Mourvèdre   Preston Syrah
Edmunds St. John Les Côtes   Qupé Marsanne
  Sauvages (Blend)   Qupé Syrah
Edmunds St. John Mourvèdre   Ridge Mataro Evangelo Vineyard
Edmunds St. John Port o'Call (Blend)   Trentadue Carignane
Edmunds St. John La Rosé Sauvage   Trentadue Old Patch Red (Blend)
Field Stone Petite Sirah   Trentadue Petite Sirah
Forman La Grande Roche (Grenache)

* * * (GOOD PRODUCERS)

Arrowood Viognier   Marietta Petite Sirah
Bonny Doon Le Cigare Volant   McDowell Valley Les Vieux
  (Blend)   Cépages
Bonny Doon Old Telegram   Ojai Syrah
  (Mourvèdre)   Joseph Phelps Vin du Mistral *cuvées*
Bonny Doon Syrah   R. H. Phillips Mourvèdre EXP
David Bruce Petite Sirah   Preston Sirah-Syrah
Edmunds St. John Viognier   Preston Marsanne (Sonoma)
Fetzer Petite Sirah Reserve   Preston Syrah (Sonoma)
Field Stone Viognier Staten Family   Ritchie Creek Viognier
  Reserve   Santino Satyricon (Blend)
Louis Foppiano Petite Sirah   Shenandoah Serene (Blend)
Guenoc Petite Sirah   Stags' Leap Petite Sirah
Jade Mountain Mourvèdre   Topolos Alicante Bouschet***/****
Karly Petite Sirah   Topolos Petite Sirah***/****
Kendall-Jackson Durell Vineyard   William Wheeler RS Reserve (Blend)
  Syrah***/****   Zaca Mesa Syrah/Malbec

** *(AVERAGE PRODUCERS)*

Alban Viognier
Duxoup Syrah (Sonoma)
La Jota Viognier
Meridian Syrah**/***
J. W. Morris Petite Sirah Bosun Crest
Parducci Bono Syrah **/***
Parducci Petite Sirah**/***
Joseph Phelps Syrah

R. H. Phillips Viognier EXP
Preston Viognier
Roudon-Smith Petite Sirah
Sierra Vista Syrah
Domaine de la Terre Rouge**/***
William Wheeler Quintet (Blend)
Zaca Mesa Mourvèdre
Zaca Mesa Syrah

RATING CALIFORNIA'S BEST PRODUCERS OF SAUVIGNON BLANC AND SEMILLON AND BLENDS THEREOF

***** *(OUTSTANDING PRODUCERS)*

Kalin Sauvignon Blanc Reserve
  (Potter Valley)

Peter Michael Sauvignon Blanc
  l'Après-Midi (California)

**** *(EXCELLENT PRODUCERS)*

Babcock Sauvignon Blanc 11 Oaks
  Ranch (Santa Barbara)
Babcock Sauvignon Blanc (Santa
  Barbara)
Caymus Conundrum Proprietary
  White Wine (Napa)
Chalk Hill Sauvignon Blanc
  (Sonoma), since 1991
Clos du Bois Sauvignon Blanc
  (Alexander Valley)
Cronin Sauvignon Blanc/Chardonnay
  (Napa)
Dry Creek Fumé Blanc (Sonoma)
Flora Springs Soliloquy Proprietary
  White Wine (Napa)
Gainey Limited Selection (Santa
  Ynez)****
Grgich Hills Fumé Blanc (Napa)
Handley Sauvignon Blanc
  (Dry Creek)
Hidden Cellars Alchemy Proprietary
  White Wine (Mendocino)
Hidden Cellars Sauvignon Blanc
  (Mendocino)

Kalin Sauvignon Blanc (Potter
  Valley)
Kalin Semillon (Livermore)
Karly Sauvignon Blanc (Amador)
Kenwood Sauvignon Blanc (Sonoma)
Matanzas Creek Sauvignon Blanc
  (Sonoma)
Robert Mondavi Fumé Blanc Reserve
  (Napa)****/*****
Murphy-Goode Fumé Blanc Reserve
  (Sonoma)
Navarro Sauvignon Blanc
  (Mendocino)
Preston Cuvée de Fumé (Sonoma)
Rancho Sisquoc Sauvignon Blanc
  (Santa Barbara)
Sanford Sauvignon Blanc (Santa
  Barbara)
Signorello Sauvignon Blanc (Napa)
Signorello Semillon Founder's
  Reserve (Napa)****
Simi Sendal Proprietary White Wine
  (Sonoma)
Philip Togni Sauvignon Blanc (Napa)

*** *(GOOD PRODUCERS)*

Ahlgren Semillon (Santa Cruz)
Alderbrook Sauvignon Blanc
  (Sonoma)
Babcock Fathom Proprietary White
  Wine (Santa Barbara)

Beaulieu Fumé Blanc (Napa)
Bel Arbors Sauvignon Blanc
  (California)
Bellerose Sauvignon Blanc
  (Sonoma)

Benziger Tribute Proprietary White
   Wine (Glen Ellen)***/****
Beringer Meritage (Napa)
Beringer Sauvignon Blanc (Napa)
Brander (Santa Ynez)
Buena Vista Fumé Blanc (Lake)
Byron Sauvignon Blanc (Santa
   Barbara)***/****
Cain Cellars Sauvignon Musqué
   (Napa)***/****
Carmenet Meritage Proprietary White
   Wine (Sonoma)***/****
Caymus Sauvignon Blanc (Napa)
Chappellet Chenin Blanc (Napa)
De Loach Fumé Blanc (Sonoma)
Duckhorn Sauvignon Blanc (Napa)
Ferrari-Carano Fumé Blanc (Sonoma)
Field Stone Sauvignon Blanc (Sonoma)
Geyser Peak Sauvignon Blanc
   (Sonoma)
Geyser Peak Semchard
   (Sonoma)***/****
Louis Honig Sauvignon Blanc (Napa)
Husch Sauvignon Blanc (Mendocino)

Iron Horse Fumé Blanc (Sonoma)
Konocti Fumé Blanc (Lake)
Lolonis Fumé Blanc (Mendocino)
Robert Mondavi Fumé Blanc (Napa)
Monterey Classic Sauvignon Blanc
   (Monterey)
Morgan Sauvignon Blanc (Monterey)
Murphy-Goode Fumé Blanc (Sonoma)
Ojai Cuvée Spéciale St. Helene
   (California)
Ojai Sauvignon Blanc (California)
R. H. Phillips Sauvignon Blanc (Yolo)
Rabbit Ridge Sauvignon Blanc
   (Sonoma)
Spottswoode Sauvignon Blanc (Napa)
Stag's Leap Sauvignon Blanc Rancho
   Chimiles (Napa)
Rodney Strong Sauvignon Blanc
   Charlotte's Home Vineyard
   (Sonoma)
Evan Tamas Fumé Blanc
   (Livermore)***/****
William Wheeler Fumé Blanc
   (Sonoma)

* * (AVERAGE PRODUCERS)

Adler Fels Fumé Blanc (Sonoma)
Davis Bynum Fumé Blanc (Sonoma)
Callaway Fumé Blanc/Sauvignon
   Blanc (Temecula)
Christophe Sauvignon Blanc (Napa)
Clos Pegase Sauvignon Blanc (Napa)
Clos du Val Semillon (Napa)
Louis Foppiano Sauvignon Blanc
   (Sonoma)
E. & J. Gallo Sauvignon Blanc
   (California)
Glen Ellen Sauvignon Blanc
   (Sonoma)
Grand Cru Sauvignon Blanc
   (Sonoma)
Groth Sauvignon Blanc (Napa)
Guenoc Langtry Meritage Proprietary
   White Wine (Lake)
Hanna Sauvignon Blanc (Sonoma)
Inglenook Gravion Proprietary White
   Wine (Napa)
Innisfree Sauvignon Blanc (Napa)
Jekel Scepter Proprietary White
   Wine (Monterey)

Château Julien Sauvignon Blanc
   (Monterey)
Lakespring Sauvignon Blanc (Napa)
Liberty School Sauvignon Blanc
   (California)
Louis Martini Sauvignon Blanc
   (Napa)
Mayacamas Sauvignon Blanc
   (Napa)
Napa Ridge Sauvignon Blanc
   (Napa)
Obester Sauvignon Blanc
   (Mendocino)
Joseph Phelps Sauvignon Blanc
   (Napa)
Château Potelle Sauvignon Blanc
   (Napa)
J. Rochioli Sauvignon Blanc
   (Sonoma)
St. Clement Sauvignon Blanc (Napa)
Château St. Jean Fumé Blanc (all
   cuvées) (Sonoma)
St. Supery Sauvignon Blanc (Napa)
Seghesio Sauvignon Blanc (Sonoma)

Shenandoah Sauvignon Blanc
(Amador)
Silverado Sauvignon Blanc (Napa)
Simi Semillon (Napa)
Sterling Sauvignon Blanc (Napa)

Stratford Sauvignon Blanc
(California)
Weinstock Sauvignon Blanc
(Sonoma)

RATING CALIFORNIA'S BEST PRODUCERS OF ZINFANDEL

* * * * * (OUTSTANDING PRODUCERS)

Au Bon Climat Sauret Vineyard
(Paso Robles)
Edmunds St. John Mt. Veeder (Napa)
Lytton Springs Reserve (Sonoma)
Peachy Canyon West Side (Paso
Robles)
Ravenswood Belloni Vineyard
(Sonoma)
Ravenswood Cooke Vineyard
(Sonoma)
Ravenswood Dickerson Vineyard
(Napa)
Ravenswood Old Hill Vineyard
(Sonoma)

Ridge Geyserville Proprietary Red
Wine (mostly Zinfandel)
(Sonoma)
Ridge Lytton Springs (Sonoma)
Rosenblum Cellars Michael Marston
Vineyard (Napa)
Rosenblum Cellars Samsel Vineyard
(Sonoma)
Teldeschi (Sonoma)
Topolos Rossi Ranch (Sonoma)
Williams-Selyem Martinelli Vineyard
(Sonoma)

* * * * (EXCELLENT PRODUCERS)

Amador Foothill Grand-Père
Vineyard (Amador)
Bial Aldo's Vineyard (Napa)
Caymus (Napa)
Cline Reserve (Contra Costa)
Cline (Contra Costa)
H. Coturri and Sons Chauvet
Vineyard (Sonoma)
De Loach single-vineyard cuvées
(Sonoma)
De Loach O.F.S. (Sonoma)
Deer Park (Napa)
Dry Creek Old Vines
(Sonoma)****/*****
Deux Amis (Sonoma)
Eberle (Paso Robles)
Elyse Morisoli Vineyard (Napa)
Elyse Howell Mountain (Napa)
Ferrari-Carano (Sonoma)
Franciscan (Napa)
Frey (Mendocino)
Green and Red Chiles Mill Vineyard
(Napa)
Grgich Hills Cellars (Sonoma)

Hidden Cellars (Mendocino)
Hop Kiln Primativo (Sonoma)
Kendall-Jackson Ciapusci Vineyard
(Mendocino)
Kendall-Jackson Dupratt Vineyard
(Lake)
Kendall-Jackson Proprietor's Grand
Reserve (California)
Lamborn Family Howell Mt.
(Napa)
Limerick Lane (Sonoma)
Lytton Springs (Sonoma)
Marietta (Sonoma)
Meeker (Sonoma)
Château Montelena (Napa)
Monterey Peninsula Ferrero Ranch
(Amador)
Nalle (Sonoma)
Peachy Canyon Reserve (Paso
Robles)
Preston (Sonoma)
Quivera (Sonoma)
Rabbit Ridge (Sonoma)
A. Rafanelli (Sonoma)****/*****

Ravenswood Old Vines (Sonoma)
Ridge Paso Robles (San Luis
  Obispo)
Rosenblum Cellars (Contra Costa)
Rosenblum Cellars (Paso Robles)
Rosenblum Cellars (Sonoma)
Rosenblum Cellars Richard Sauret
  Vineyard (Paso Robles)
Rosenblum Cellars George Henry
  Vineyard (Napa)
Rosenblum Cellars Brandlin Ranch
  (Napa)
Ross Valley (Sonoma)
Saucelito Canyon (Arroyo Grande)
Sausal (Sonoma)
Sausal Private Reserve
  (Sonoma)****/*****

Scherrer Old Vines (Alexander
  Valley)
Storybook Mountain (Napa)
Storybook Mountain Reserve
  (Napa)****/*****
Storybook Mountain Howell
  Mountain (Napa)
Joseph Swan Frati Ranch (Russian
  River)
Joseph Swan Zeigler
  Vineyard (Russian River)
Joseph Swan Stellwagen Vineyard
  (Sonoma)
Topolos Ultimo (Sonoma)
Trentadue (Sonoma)
Whaler Estate Flagship
  (Mendocino)

* * * (GOOD PRODUCERS)

D'Annco Old Vines***/****
Bel Arbors (California)
Benziger (Sonoma)
Beringer (Napa)
Boeger (El Dorado)
David Bruce (Santa Cruz)
Buehler (Napa)
Burgess (Napa)
Clos du Bois (Sonoma)
Clos du Val (Napa)
De Loach Estate (Sonoma)
De Moor (Napa)
Fetzer Reserve (Mendocino)
Louis Foppiano Reserve (Sonoma)
Frick (Santa Cruz)
Fritz (Sonoma), since 1988
Frog's Leap (Napa)
Greenwood Ridge (Sonoma)
Guenoc (Lake)
Gundlach-Bundschu Rhine Farm
  Vineyard (Sonoma)
Haywood (Sonoma)
Hop Kiln (Sonoma)
Karly (Amador)
Kenwood Jack London Vineyard
  (Sonoma)***/****

Mountain View (Amador)
J. Pedroncelli (Sonoma)
Joseph Phelps (Alexander Valley)
Ravenswood Vintner's Blend
  (Sonoma)
Ridge Howell Mountain (Napa)
Ridge Sonoma (Santa Clara)
Rocking Horse Lamborn Vineyard
  (Napa)
St. Francis (Sonoma)
Santino Wines (Amador)
V. Sattui Suzanne's Vineyard (Napa)
Seghesio (Sonoma)
Seghesio Reserve (Sonoma)
Shenandoah Sobon Estate (Amador)
Sierra Vista (El Dorado)
Signorello (Napa)
Sky (Napa)
Summit Lake (Napa)***/****
Sutter Home Reserve (Amador)
The Terraces (Napa)***/*****
Twin Hills (Paso Robles)
Wellington (Sonoma)***/****
Mark West Robert Rue Vineyard
  (Sonoma)
Whaler Estate (Mendocino)

* * (AVERAGE PRODUCERS)

Duxoup Wineworks (Sonoma)
Eagle Ridge (Amador)
Harbor (Sacramento)**/****

Charles Krug (Napa)
Lolonis (Mendocino)
Louis Martini (Sonoma)

Mazzocco (Sonoma)
Robert Mondavi (Napa)
Montevina (Amador)****/*****
  before 1979
J. W. Morris Kramer Ridge (Sonoma)
Parducci (Mendocino)
Roudon-Smith (Santa Cruz)
St. Supery (Napa)
Sebastiani (Sonoma)

Shenandoah Special Reserve
  (Amador)
Château Souverain (Sonoma)**/***
Stevenot (Calaveras)**/***
Rodney Strong Old Vines River West
  Vineyard (Sonoma)**/***
Sutter Home (Cailfornia)
Tobin James (Paso Robles)**/***

RATING CALIFORNIA'S BEST SPARKLING WINE PRODUCERS

* * * * * (OUTSTANDING PRODUCERS)

None

* * * * (EXCELLENT PRODUCERS)

Domaine Chandon Reserve Brut
  (Napa)
Maison Deutz Blanc de Noir (San
  Luis Obispo)
Iron Horse (all *cuvées*) (Sonoma)

Kalin Cuvée Rosé (Potter Valley)
Domaine Mumm Blanc de Noir Rosé
  (Napa)
Roederer Estate (all *cuvées*)
  (Mendocino)

* * * (GOOD PRODUCERS)

Domaine Carneros (Napa)
Domaine Chandon Blanc de Noir
  (Napa)
Domaine Chandon Brut (Napa)
Domaine Chandon Étoile (Napa)
Maison Deutz (San Luis Obispo)
Handley (Mendocino)
Robert Mondavi Brut (Napa)
Monticello Domaine Montreaux
  (Napa)

Domaine Mumm Brut Prestige Cuvée
  (Napa)***/****
Domaine Mumm Brut Winery Lake
  Cuvée (Napa)***/****
Schramsberg J. Schram (Napa)
Tribault Brut (Monterey)
Tribault Brut Rosé (Monterey)

* * (AVERAGE PRODUCERS)

S. Anderson *cuvées* (Napa)**/***
Beaulieu Brut (Napa)
Culbertson Blanc de Noir (Riverside)
Culbertson Brut (Riverside)
Culbertson Brut Rosé (Riverside)
Domaine Carneros (Napa)
Richard Cuneo (Sonoma)
Gloria Ferrer *cuvées* (Sonoma)**/***

Jordan J Cuvée (Sonoma)
Mirassou (Monterey)
Piper Sonoma (Sonoma)**/***
Scharffenberger *cuvées* (Mendocino)
Schramsberg *cuvées* (Napa)
Shadow Creek Champagne Cellars
  Brut (San Luis Obispo)

ACACIA (NAPA)

Chardonnay* * *, Chardonnay Marina Vineyard * * * *, Pinot Noir Cuvées* */* * *

1990	Chardonnay Carneros	Napa	C	80
1990	Chardonnay Marina Vineyard	Napa	C	78
1989	Pinot Noir Carneros	Napa	C	73

Acacia started off strongly in the early 1980s, but over the last 5 or 6 years has settled into a middle-of-the-road quality level. The Chardonnays are crisp, lean, and supposedly elegant, but to my taste they have consistently lacked flavor authority over recent vintages. The Pinot Noir is clean and fruity, but one-dimensional and seemingly made within those well-defined technical parameters that are designed to offend no one. Given the moderately high prices, consumers should expect more.

ADLER FELS (SONOMA)

Chardonnay* *, Fumé Blanc* *, Gewürztraminer* *, Pinot Noir* *

1989	Chardonnay Sangiacomo	Sonoma	B	77
1989	Gewürztraminer	Sonoma	B	73
1988	Pinot Noir	Sonoma	C	68

This winery has been in business for over a decade, and the quality of its wines has been inconsistent. Although its Fumé Blancs are generally admired on the West Coast, I find them intensely vegetal. The 1989 Chardonnay from Sangiacomo has an advanced color and is already beginning to drop its fruit, suggesting it should be consumed immediately. The 1989 Gewürztraminer is an off-dry wine with little of the varietal character I have come to expect from the best examples found in France. The clones used in California must be different, as I see none of the spicy, lychee nut–, rose-scented Gewürztraminer character in this wine.

AHLGREN VINEYARD (SANTA CRUZ)

Cabernet Sauvignon* * */* * * *, Semillon* * *

1988	Cabernet Sauvignon Bates Ranch	Santa Cruz	C	79
1987	Cabernet Sauvignon Bates Ranch	Santa Cruz	C	93
1986	Cabernet Sauvignon Bates Ranch	Santa Cruz	C	88
1985	Cabernet Sauvignon Bates Ranch	Santa Cruz	C	90
1988	Cabernet Sauvignon Besson Vineyard	Santa Cruz	B	72
1987	Cabernet Sauvignon Besson Vineyard	Santa Cruz	B	87

Ahlgren is an underrated producer of long-lived Cabernet Sauvignons. These wines, which are unfined and unfiltered, are available in limited quantities, making them difficult to find outside California. However, I was taken by the elegant, smooth, satiny-textured, rich, curranty 1987 Cabernet Sauvignon Besson Vineyard. Drink it over the next 5–7 years. In complete contrast was the formidable 1987 Cabernet Sauvignon Bates Ranch (260 cases produced). The latter wine exhibits an opaque purple/black color, a huge nose of un-evolved black raspberries, minerals, and smoke, and exceptional concentration and expansiveness on the palate. One of the most concentrated, well-balanced Cabernets I have recently tasted, it has the potential to last for at least 2 decades. The minty yet full-bodied, rich, backward 1986 Bates Ranch is loaded with fruit and has enough suppleness to be drunk in 1–2 years, but it promises to last for 10–12. It is an impressive, full-bodied wine from a vintage in which a number of more famous Santa Cruz producers (such as Ridge) did not do terribly well with their Cabernet. The 1985 Bates Ranch is stunningly deep and concentrated, but closed. With one hour of breathing it seems to open enough to be drinkable. However, its best years are likely to be between now and 2005. Its deep ruby/purple color and highly extracted yet well-balanced palate impression suggest low yields and talented winemaking. Unfortunately 1988 was a troublesome vintage in California, and even Ahlgren turned out relatively thin wines that lack substance. The 1988 Cabernet Sauvignon Besson Vineyard is underripe and vegetal, and the 1988 Bates Ranch is entirely too tannic and lean. Ahlgren also fashions a big, fleshy, substantially sized Semillon that, although admirable and interesting, is not complex. I have consistently rated it in the low to middle 80s. If you like a full-throttle style of Semillon, check it out.

ALDERBROOK (SONOMA)

Chardonnay* * *, Chardonnay Reserve* * * *, Sauvignon Blanc* * *

1990	Chardonnay	Dry Creek	B	85
1990	Chardonnay Reserve	Dry Creek	C	87
1990	Duet	Dry Creek	B	87
1991	Sauvignon Blanc	Dry Creek	A	84

The 1990 Chardonnay is a pleasant, medium-bodied, popcorn-scented, fleshy Chardonnay with good depth, adequate acidity, and a long, luscious finish. Drink it before the end of 1994. The 1990 Chardonnay Reserve is a richer, more oaky wine, with more glycerin, body, and length. It should be drunk over the next 1–2 years. Alderbrook produced a proprietary white wine in 1990 called Duet. Made from 50% Sauvignon Blanc and 50% Semillon, it is an excellent, tasty wine with a lovely concoction of herbs, figs, melons, and fruit presented in a medium-bodied, crisp, flavorful format. This winery continues to offer good quality at reasonable prices, thus meriting attention from consumers.

ALEXANDER VALLEY VINEYARD (SONOMA)

Cabernet Sauvignon* * *, Chardonnay* *, Merlot* */* * *, Pinot Noir* *

1990	Cabernet Sauvignon Estate	Alexander Valley	B	86
1987	Cabernet Sauvignon Estate	Alexander Valley	B	87
1990	Merlot	Alexander Valley	B	85

Alexander Valley's 1990 Merlot is a plump, tasty, soft-textured wine with some appealing, fat, herb and berry flavors, low acidity, and a smooth finish. Drink it over the next 5–6 years. The 1990 Cabernet Sauvignon is also a near-term wine, with spicy, herb, and curranty flavors, medium body, adequate acidity, ripe tannins, and an attractive, lush, ripe finish. Drink it over the next decade. The big, curranty-, herbaceous-scented bouquet of the 1987 Cabernet Sauvignon is followed by a ripe, smoothly textured, supple wine with plenty of concentration and a luscious, velvety finish. Drink this hedonistic Cabernet over the next 5–7 years. Occasionally Alexander Valley turns out super Cabernet Sauvignon, as readers who run across any bottles of their flamboyant and dramatic 1984 would attest. The winery's Chardonnays are generally mediocre, even disappointing, and too frequently lacking fruit and substance. Their Pinot Noir, a vegetal, herbal wine with sour tannins, is clearly in need of reevaluation.

ALMADEN (SAN JOSE)
Cabernet Sauvignon*/* *, Chardonnay*/* *, Fumé Blanc*/* *,
Other Wines*

This huge winery began to get more serious about its top wines in the early 1980s, but after releasing some surprisingly good Chardonnays and Cabernets, the quality has again reverted to a straightforward, one-dimensional style that offers little interest. The wines are low priced, but . . .

AMADOR FOOTHILL WINERY (AMADOR)
White Zinfandel* * *, Zinfandel* * * *

1990	Zinfandel Ferrero Vineyard	Amador	B	85
1989	Zinfandel Ferrero Vineyard	Amador	B	87
1988	Zinfandel Fiddletown Eschen Vineyard	Amador	B	86
1987	Zinfandel Fiddletown Eschen Vineyard	Amador	B	86
1990	Zinfandel Grand-Père Vineyard	Amador	B	86

In a low-profile manner, this winery continues to turn out tasty and rich Zinfandels. Gobs of smooth, velvety, raspberry and black cherry fruit is the prominent characteristic of the tasty, medium-bodied, heady 1987 Zinfandel Fiddletown Eschen Vineyard. Drink it over the next 4–5 years. The 1988 Zinfandel from the Eschen Vineyard exhibits a big, spicy, raspberry-scented nose; surprisingly elegant, generously endowed, supple flavors; and a smooth finish. Drink it over the next 4–5 years. The 1989 Zinfandel from the Ferrero Vineyard is a bigger wine, with a superripe nose of black cherries and herbs. In the mouth the wine is full bodied and rich, finishing with a lusty, heady, alcoholic clout. Drink this larger-scale Zinfandel with strongly flavored cheese or meat dishes. The fact that both of the 1990 Zinfandels are surprisingly light in color is deceiving. Both possess big, perfumed noses of sweet berry fruit and spices. In the mouth the 1990 Ferrero Vineyard Zinfandel (1,039 cases produced) displays lusty, full-bodied, satiny-smooth, berry flavors, copious amounts of alcohol, and a spicy, long finish. It lacks grip and structure, but who cannot admire its pure, vibrant fruitiness? The 1990 Zinfandel from the Grand-Père Vineyard (680 cases produced from 125-year-old vines) offers a huge aroma of sweet berry fruit. In the mouth the wine is far more expansive and richer than its light to medium ruby color would suggest. The finish is heady, but, amazingly, the 15.8% alcohol level is hidden under a cascade of luscious berry fruit. I find it intriguing that neither of these wines exhibits any of the pruny, raisiny, late-harvest character one would expect given their whopping alcohol levels. Last, this winery turns out one of the more tasty, aromatic white Zinfandels. The vintage of choice is the most recent, as these wines must be drunk within a year of the vintage. If your tastes lean toward these light, fresh wines, Amador Foothill is one of the best.

AMIZETTA (NAPA)
Cabernet Sauvignon* * *

| 1986 | Cabernet Sauvignon Estate | Napa | C | 87 |

This is an excellent Cabernet Sauvignon, with a deep, dark ruby color and a classic Napa Valley nose of rich, minty blackcurrants and spicy oak. On the palate the wine shows excellent definition, very fine depth, medium to full body, and plenty of length and balance. **Anticipated maturity: Now–2000.**

S. ANDERSON (NAPA)

Cabernet Sauvignon* *, Chardonnay* * *, Sparkling Wines* */* * *

1989	Cabernet Sauvignon Richard Chambers Vineyard	Stag's Leap	C	83
1990	Chardonnay	Stag's Leap	C	84
1989	Chardonnay	Stag's Leap	C	78

This winery is capable of turning out good Chardonnays from their vineyard in the Stag's Leap district. They have also begun producing numerous *cuvées* of sparkling wines that are straightforward and pleasant but unexciting. The only Cabernet Sauvignon I have tasted is their single-vineyard offering in 1989. It exhibits deep color, a compact, cassis character, plenty of tannin and acidity, and just enough fruit to give the wine interest. It should be drunk over the next 5–7 years.

ARROWOOD (SONOMA)

Cabernet Sauvignon* * *, Chardonnay* * *, Merlot* */* * *, Viognier* * *

1989	Cabernet Sauvignon	Sonoma	C	77
1988	Cabernet Sauvignon	Sonoma	C	84
1986	Cabernet Sauvignon	Sonoma	C	87
1990	Chardonnay	Sonoma	C	84
1989	Chardonnay	Sonoma	C	79
1990	Viognier	Sonoma	C	85

Dick Arrowood, the renowned winemaker at Château St. Jean between 1974 and 1990, now has his own operation. The Chardonnays have been crisp, light, and clean, but lacking in intensity. More promising are the microscopic quantities of Viognier that Arrowood is producing. The debut vintage, the 1990, offers a floral, honeysuckle nose and excellent fruit and varietal character. This could prove to be a promising wine, but quantities are extremely limited. Although some Merlot is made (the 1989 is tart and lean), Arrowood's best wine is its stylish Cabernet Sauvignon. The 1986 displays a creamier texture and much more interesting fruit flavors than the narrowly constructed, compact 1985. It is not a blockbuster style of Cabernet, but it offers gracious, elegant, curranty fruit wrapped nicely in toasty new oak. On the palate it has a medium-bodied, lush personality with a good finish. Drinkable now, this wine should age nicely for another 5–7 years. The 1988 and 1989 are less well endowed, with less fruit, substance, and depth. Both should be consumed over the next 3–5 years.

ATLAS PEAK VINEYARDS (NAPA)

Sangiovese* *

1990	Consenso	Napa	C	78
1990	Sangiovese	Napa	C	77
1989	Sangiovese	Napa	C	72

There are high hopes for this well-funded operation owned by an international conglomerate whose two most notable partners are Piero Antinori of Italy and France's Bollinger firm. The two Sangiovese releases to date have been lean, light, fluid wines with high acidity, harsh tannins, and little concentration. Despite the ambitious marketing program, bold label, and heavy glass bottle, the quality needs to improve if this producer is to succeed. The 1990 proprietary red wine called Consenso (a blend of 80% Cabernet Sauvignon and 20% Sangiovese) is a medium-bodied wine with decent concentration but no focal point for interest and not much length.

AU BON CLIMAT (SANTA BARBARA)

Chardonnay* * * *, Chardonnay Bien Nacido* * * * *, Chardonnay Sanford
& Benedict Vineyard* * * * *, Chardonnay Talley
Vineyard* * * */* * * * *, Pinot Noir* * * *, Pinot Noir
La Bauge Au Dessus Bien Nacido Vineyard* * * * *, Pinot Noir Sanford
& Benedict Vineyard* * * * *, Pinot Noir Talley Vineyard* * * *,
Zinfandel Sauret Vineyard* * * * *

1992	Barbera	Santa Barbara	B	90
1991	Chardonnay	Santa Barbara	C	89
1991	Chardonnay Reserve Bien Nacido Vineyard	Santa Barbara	D	92
1991	Chardonnay Reserve Sanford & Benedict Vineyard	Santa Barbara	D	90+
1991	Chardonnay Reserve Talley Vineyard	Arroyo Grande	D	89
1992	Chardonnay Talley Vineyard	Arroyo Grande	C	90
1992	Pinot Blanc	Santa Barbara	B	86
1991	Pinot Noir	Santa Maria	C	85
1992	Pinot Noir La Bauge Au Dessus Bien Nacido Vineyard	Santa Barbara	C	92
1991	Pinot Noir La Bauge Au Dessus Bien Nacido Vineyard	Santa Barbara	C	90
1990	Pinot Noir La Bauge Au Dessus Bien Nacido Vineyard	Santa Barbara	D	93
1991	Pinot Noir Sanford & Benedict Vineyard	Santa Barbara	D	92
1990	Pinot Noir Talley Vineyard	Arroyo Grande	C	89
1991	Zinfandel Sauret Vineyard	Paso Robles	B	92

There is something about winemaker Jim Clendenen that inspires confidence. This fast-talking, superenthusiastic Pinot Noir fanatic is fashioning some of the most dazzling wines in California. Readers may remember I selected Au Bon Climat (or ABC as it is affectionately known in Santa Barbara) as the winery of the year several years ago. Since then, ABC has gone from strength to strength. Its current and upcoming releases offer a remarkable array of gorgeously fragrant, authoritatively flavored wines that combine complexity with decadence. Although Au Bon Climat's reputation was founded on its stunning Chardonnays and Pinot Noirs, Jim Clendenen has the Midas touch, as evidenced by his other offerings—ranging from Pinot Blanc to Barbera, to even microquantities of a sumptuous Zinfandel. The 1992 Pinot Blanc exhibits a light bouquet of oranges, and lovely, clean, rich, fruity flavors. There is good underlying acidity and an overall sense of balance in this medium-bodied, delightful wine. Drink it over the next year. The Chardonnays are all special, even the regular bottling of the 1991 from Santa Barbara. An opulent, chewy, fleshy wine, it displays superb fruit and purity, an enticing perfume, and a lusty, long finish. Although it is not as well defined as the other Chardonnays, it offers plenty of rich Chardonnay fruit. The unreleased 1992 Chardonnay Talley Vineyard from the Arroyo Grande Valley possesses copious amounts of honeyed, lemony, buttery fruit, and rich, apple/pineapple like flavors intertwined with smoky new oak. It is a rich, powerful, impeccably well-made and well-delineated Chardonnay that will be released in spring 1994. Don't miss it! The 1991 Chardonnay Reserve Talley Vineyard reveals a light golden color; an exotic, buttery, honeyed, pineapple-scented nose; rich, opulent, voluptuously textured, intense fruit flavors; and tremendous density and length in the long finish. Loaded with character, it should drink well for another 1–3 years. The above-mentioned Chardonnay offerings may even have scored higher if they had not had the misfortune to be tasted alongside the 1991 Reserve Chardonnay from the Bien Nacido Vineyard and the 1991 Reserve Chardonnay from the Sanford & Benedict Vineyard—two extraordinary Chardonnays that are among the best California has produced. These two Chardonnays are not only richer than the other ABC Chardonnays, they offer more complexity in addition to exceptional personalities. The more flattering at present is the 1991 Bien Nacido Chardonnay. This spectacular unfiltered wine offers a huge nose of vanillin, ripe apples, and tropical fruits, as well as a full-bodied, multilayered, multidimensional richness and character. All of this has plenty of zesty acidity for support. The wine is exceptionally dense and concentrated, yet brilliantly well balanced. I was told that the yields were less than 2 tons per acre, which is about one-third the yields of most Sonoma and Napa Valley Chardonnay vineyards. This wine is just beginning to evolve. Although I could not resist it now, readers may want to lay down a few bottles for 2–3 years. One Chardonnay that should evolve and last for 7–10 years is Au Bon Climat's 1991 Reserve Chardonnay from the Sanford & Benedict Vineyard. Potentially, this may turn out to be the finest of all these Chardonnays, but at present it is the most backward. A nose of cinnamon, minerals, and spices is just beginning to emerge. Tightly knit, with huge reserves of fruit and a mouthfilling, viscous texture, this large-framed, chewy Chardonnay should improve for at least 3–5 years and last for up to a decade— a rarity! However, you will not be able to find it at your local liquor store as only 250 cases were produced.

The upcoming and current releases of Pinot Noir from Au Bon Climat are equally stunning in terms of their complexity and richness. Barrel samples of the 1992 Pinot Noir La Bauge Au Dessus Bien Nacido Vineyard reveal a sweet, raspberry, smoky bouquet, opulent, full-throttle, rich flavor, and a meaty, fleshy, exceptionally rich, chewy finish. It will not be released for another year. At present, consumers will have to be content with the spectacular 1991 and 1990 Pinot Noir La Bauge Au Dessus Bien Nacido Vineyard. The

1991 exhibits a dark, plummy color, a rich, fragrant, smoky, raspberry-scented nose, voluptuous richness, medium to full body, soft tannins, and a spicy, luscious finish. Drink it over the next 5–6 years. The 1990, along with Sanford's 1990 Pinot Noir from the Sanford & Benedict Vineyard, ranks as one of the two greatest American Pinot Noirs I have tasted. Like the Sanford single-vineyard Pinot, it could blow away 90% of the red burgundies that sell for twice the price. The 1990 La Bauge Au Dessus enjoys a more saturated color than the 1991, as well as a terrific nose of ripe plums, smoke, meats, and flowers. There is staggering concentration, impeccable delineation and focus, and a ripe, heady, superconcentrated finish. The tannins are soft enough to enjoy this smashingly intense Pinot Noir now, but it promises to last for 6–10 years. The 1991 Pinot Noir Sanford & Benedict Vineyard is the more classic wine in the sense that there is more structure, a Michel Lafarge–Volney *premier cru*–like elegance and finesse, a beautifully pure black raspberry, vanillin bouquet, and silky, wonderfully textured, rich, graceful flavors that flow across the palate with no hard or acidic edges. It reveals the high glycerin content and sweetness of fruit that comes from low-yielding vines, as well as an exceptionally long finish. Drink this beauty over the next 7–8 years. The 1991 Pinot Noir Talley Vineyard displays a woodsy, herbaceous, cinnamon, and black cherry–scented nose, supple, fat, luscious flavors, excellent length, and a long, soft, spicy finish. Drink it over the next 5–6 years.

If you are lucky enough to come across a few bottles of ABC's 1991 Zinfandel Sauret Vineyard, don't hesitate to latch on to them. I lament the fact that only 25 cases (1 barrel) of this great Zinfandel were produced. The combination of black raspberry and jammy black cherry fruit along with smoky, toasty, new oak gives the wine a Côte Rôtie–like bouquet. The thrills do not stop with the bouquet. This Zinfandel possesses unctuous, full-bodied richness, low acidity, and enough tannin to provide support. Drink it over the next decade.

Lastly, readers should be on the lookout for Au Bon Climat's 1992 Barbera, a superrich, flamboyant wine that must be Jim Clendenen's homage to the great Piedmontese Barbera winemaker Elio Altare. While this wine will not be released until late fall or early next spring, it has the potential to be the best Barbera ever made in America!

BABCOCK VINEYARDS (SANTA BARBARA)

Chardonnay* * *, Fathom Proprietary White Wine* * *,
Sauvignon Blanc* * * *, Sauvignon Blanc 11 Oaks Ranch* * * *

1990	Chardonnay	Santa Barbara	B	84
1990	Chardonnay Grand Cuvée	Santa Barbara	C	87
1990	Fathom Proprietary White Wine	California	B	82
1991	Gewürztraminer	Santa Barbara	B	85
1990	Pinot Noir Estate	Santa Barbara	C	84
1991	Sauvignon Blanc	Santa Ynez	A	86
1991	Sauvignon Blanc 11 Oaks Ranch	Santa Ynez	C	87

Babcock's 1991 tasty Sauvignon Blanc has spicy, lemony, melonlike flavors, a touch of vanillin, medium body, and a long, zesty finish. The 1991 Sauvignon Blanc 11 Oaks Ranch possesses a knockout bouquet that leaps from the glass, offering up scents of toasty oak, figs, melons, and tropical fruits. For a wine from this varietal, it is rich and concentrated, and its oak aging has nicely framed its components as well as given it a sense of precision and lift. Both wines should be drunk over the next several years. California wineries that are turning out sterile, insipid Sauvignon Blancs should take a look at what Babcock has achieved with these two offerings. As for Babcock's Chardonnay, the 1990 has a relatively heavy overlay of oak, as well as spicy fruit, medium body, and personality. The 1990 Grand Cuvée is richer, with a more honeyed personality and well-integrated acidity. The Pinot Noir is light, a trifle oaky, but pleasant for consuming over the next 1–3 years. This winery also occasionally produces a Gewürztraminer and a Riesling, but I have not seen any recent vintages. The Fathom Proprietary White Wine is a fruity, soft, simple white for drinking within 1–2 years of the vintage.

BANCROFT (NAPA)
Chardonnay* * * *

1991	Chardonnay Howell Mountain	Napa	C	90
1990	Chardonnay Howell Mountain	Napa	C	89

At first seemingly backward and withdrawn, the 1990 Chardonnay Howell Mountain opens up handsomely in the glass to reveal scents of lemon, apples, toast, and butter. In the mouth the wine is medium to full bodied, ripe, and rich, with good acidity, weight, power, and elegance. Drink it over the next 1–3 years. The 1991 is more seductive and open, with lavish quantities of fruit. Readers should note that Bancroft is also the source for Beringer's excellent Bancroft Merlot.

BARGETTO (SANTA CRUZ)
Cabernet Sauvignon* *, Chardonnay Cyprus* * *, Pinot Noir*

1985	Cabernet Sauvignon Bates Ranch	Santa Cruz	C	83
1991	Chardonnay Cyprus	Central Coast	A	83
1990	Chardonnay Cyprus	Central Coast	A	80
1987	Pinot Noir	Santa Maria	C	72

The Bargetto winery fashions a pleasant, straightforward, inexpensive Chardonnay called Cyprus. The 1990 and 1991 are citrusy, floral-scented, cleanly made wines that offer good value. Bargetto's Pinot Noir has been harsh, hollow, and excessively herbaceous. The winery also produces some white Zinfandel and Gewürztraminer, which I have not tasted. The most recent Cabernet Sauvignon I have tasted is the 1985 Bates Ranch. The Bates Ranch in the Santa Cruz Mountains has long been a source of excellent and long-lived Cabernets. This offering shows a deep ruby color, very good body, and good depth, but very high tannin levels, which make me worry about its future evolution. Nevertheless, there are some good qualities to this wine, and if the tannins subside without the fruit drying out first, this wine will certainly merit a higher score in 4 or 5 years.

BEAULIEU (NAPA)
Brut* *, Cabernet Sauvignon Beau Tour* */* * *, Cabernet Sauvignon Private Reserve* * * */* * * * *, Cabernet Sauvignon Rutherford* */* * *,

PARKER'S WINE BUYER'S GUIDE

Chardonnay Carneros Reserve* */* * *, Chardonnay Napa Beaufort* */* * *,
Fumé Blanc* * *, Pinot Noir Carneros Reserve* *

1989	Cabernet Sauvignon Beau Tour	Napa	A	75
1987	Cabernet Sauvignon Beau Tour	Napa	A	84
1988	Cabernet Sauvignon Private Reserve	Napa	D	84
1987	Cabernet Sauvignon Private Reserve	Napa	D	88
1986	Cabernet Sauvignon Private Reserve	Napa	D	90
1985	Cabernet Sauvignon Private Reserve	Napa	D	91
1984	Cabernet Sauvignon Private Reserve	Napa	D	85
1990	Cabernet Sauvignon Rutherford	Napa	B	84
1989	Cabernet Sauvignon Rutherford	Napa	B	76
1988	Cabernet Sauvignon Rutherford	Napa	B	84
1985	Cabernet Sauvignon Rutherford	Napa	B	86
1990	Chardonnay Beaufort	Napa	A	75
1990	Chardonnay Reserve	Carneros	C	80
1989	Chardonnay Reserve	Carneros	C	75
1990	Fumé Blanc	Napa	A	85
1989	Pinot Noir Reserve	Carneros	C	79
1988	Pinot Noir Reserve	Carneros	C	81

This fabled, historic Napa Valley winery had a surprisingly mixed record over the last decade. Even their flagship wine, the Private Reserve Georges de Latour Cabernet Sauvignon, seems to be less exciting. This is a shame, given some of the legendary Cabernets produced (1951, 1958, 1966, 1968, 1970, and 1976). Recent vintages have been noticeably lighter, which makes the oak dominate the wine's personality. The 1988 is light to medium bodied, with no more than a decade of aging potential. The 1987 Cabernet Sauvignon Private Reserve displayed a good, deep ruby/purple color. Although closed, the wine was clearly made in an elegant, austere, medium-bodied style that has become popular with so many California wineries. There is excellent ripeness, but the wine now tastes short. **Anticipated maturity: 1995–2005.** More opaque than the 1987, with a developed and intense nose of jammy cassis, new oak, herbs, and earth, the 1986 is medium bodied, with excellent concentration, fine acidity, plenty of tannin, and a firm yet positive finish. **Anticipated maturity: 1996–2010.** The dense, dark ruby/purple color of the 1985 exhibited more saturation than either the 1986 or 1987. The wine is closed, yet with coaxing its nose revealed aromas of black fruits, spices, and vanillin. In the mouth the 1985 is rich, medium to full bodied, with excellent texture and a long, powerful, stylish finish. **Anticipated maturity: 1996–2010.** The 1984's simple nose of black fruits and herbs is followed by a monolithic, medium-bodied, compactly built wine that lacks the opulence and chewiness of so many top 1984 Cabernets. The finish was surprisingly short. Overall, this wine lacked the power and richness of its three successors. **Anticipated maturity: Now–2003.** Beaulieu has never made particularly impressive

Chardonnays, preferring to offer a one-dimensional, straightforward style of Chardonnay. There appeared to be an improved level of quality beginning in the mid-1980s with the Carneros Reserve, as well as the less expensive Beaufort, but that has been negated by those wines released in the late 1980s. Beaulieu's Pinot Noir is a strange wine that tastes more like a Gamay that has been generously oaked. It has its admirers, but I am not one. If there is a wine in the Beaulieu portfolio that is underrated, it is the excellent Fumé Blanc. It is a vibrant, deliciously fruity wine, with an expressive bouquet of herbs, melons, and honeyed fruit. It is also a notable value. The Fumé Blanc, which sometimes has as much as 10% Semillon added to provide more body, is best if drunk within 2–3 years of the vintage.

The 1987 Cabernet Sauvignon Beau Tour, which is meant to be a lighter-style Cabernet designed for drinking in the first 4–5 years after its release, is a soft, medium-bodied, well-made, straightforward Cabernet with good fruit, a certain degree of elegance, and, most important, a degree of pleasure that is rarely found in a wine of this class. The 1985 Rutherford Cabernet shows wonderfully smooth, ripe blackcurrant flavors, medium to full body, a somewhat opulent texture, and a good finish. It's not a blockbuster, but it's certainly one of the best Rutherford Cabernets made this decade.

RATINGS FOR OLDER VINTAGES OF BEAULIEU CABERNET SAUVIGNON PRIVATE RESERVE: 1983 (84), 1982 (90), 1981 (85), 1980 (90), 1979 (88), 1978 (79), 1977 (88), 1976 (96), 1975 (85), 1974 (87), 1973 (88), 1972 (59), 1971 (75), 1970 (92), 1969 (88), 1968 (95), 1967 (85), 1966 (90), 1965 (84), 1964 (85), 1963 (52), 1962 (57), 1961 (74), 1960 (89), 1959 (78), 1958 (93), 1951 (96)

BEL ARBORS (MENDOCINO)
Cabernet Sauvignon* *, Chardonnay* *, Merlot* *,
Sauvignon Blanc* * *, White Zinfandel* *, Zinfandel* * *

1990	Zinfandel Founder's Reserve	California	A	85

This huge operation is run by Fetzer Vineyards and tends to produce inexpensive wines (generally under $7 a bottle) that can be drunk immediately and offer a good quality/price rapport. I have yet to taste a bad wine from Bel Arbors. Although some of their wines, such as the Merlot and Chardonnay, tend to be light and fluid, there is enough varietal character to justify the low price. From time to time they make delicious Zinfandel, such as the 1990, which is made in a Beaujolais-like style. It is difficult to resist the 1990's big, spicy, aromatic nose; richly fruity, berrylike flavors; medium-bodied, fleshy texture; and elegant, heady finish. It is amazing to find a wine of this quality selling at such a low price. Drink it over the next year. As for Bel Arbors' other offerings, the most consistently good wine is its Sauvignon. If you like a somewhat sweet-style rosé, the white Zinfandel is also good. All in all, this is a reliable source of attractively priced wines.

BELLEROSE VINEYARD (SONOMA)
Cabernet Sauvignon Cuvée Bellerose* * *, Merlot* * * *, Sauvignon Blanc* * *

1988	Cabernet Sauvignon Reserve	Dry Creek	C	86+
1986	Cuvée Bellerose Proprietary Red Table Wine	Sonoma	C	86
1986	Merlot	Sonoma	C	86

1988	Merlot Reserve	Dry Creek	C	88
1990	Sauvignon Blanc Reserve	Dry Creek	B	85

This small Sonoma operation has demonstrated potential in its brief history. Certainly the wines have significant flavor and are made in a distinctively rich, full-bodied, powerfully tannic style. Its Sauvignon Blanc leans toward the overtly herbaceous style, but there is some new oak to tame it, as well as more flavor than most wines made from this grape. Bellerose's red wines all appear to need considerable time when they are released. Even the Merlot, which is often blended with generous quantities of Cabernet Franc and small amounts of Cabernet Sauvignon, is a big, deep, chewy wine. The 1988s were among the stars of this rather so-so vintage, with the Merlot offering an explosively rich, coffee-, cassis-, and mocha-scented nose, medium to full body, excellent depth and richness, and a long, gutsy finish. It can be drunk now but should last and improve for up to a decade. The 1988 Cabernet Sauvignon Reserve is exceptionally tannic and dense, as well as surprisingly full bodied and powerful for the vintage. It is a wine to lay away for 2–3 years and hope all the tannins melt away. If they do, there is plenty of underlying material, and the wine may come close to being outstanding. The 1986 Merlot was tough to taste when young, but it has thrown off what appeared to be excessive amounts of sulphur and now exhibits ripe fruit, full body, a rich, deep, powerful personality, and plenty of length. The 1986 Cuvée Bellerose (made from a blend of 80% Cabernet Sauvignon, 11% Cabernet Franc, 5% Merlot, 3% Petit Verdot, and 1% Malbec) is a deep, rich, full-bodied wine, but the level and type of tannins make the wine difficult to penetrate and have caused me to be conservative in my judgment. If the wine comes into better balance and there is good fruit, it could prove to be intense, rich, and full bodied. This winery also made excellent 1984 and 1985 Merlots. If Bellerose was able to keep the concentration and extract levels as high as it does, and cut down on the astringency of the tannins, it could become one of California's more interesting producers of top-quality wines.

BELVEDERE WINE COMPANY (SONOMA)
Cabernet Sauvignon* *, Chardonnay* * *, Merlot* *

1990	Chardonnay	Alexander Valley	A	86
1990	Chardonnay	Russian River	B	87
1986	Merlot Robert Young Vineyard	Alexander Valley	C	78

Since its inception in 1979, Belvedere's wines have gone through numerous stylistic changes. The winery appears to be settling into a good groove with reasonably priced Chardonnays from both the Russian River Valley and the Alexander Valley. The 1990 Chardonnay Russian River offers a big, toasty, smoky, buttery nose that is followed by a wine with excellent richness, medium body, good glycerin, and an opulent, rich, lusty finish. It will not be long-lived, yet for drinking over the next 12–18 months it is a classic expression of California Chardonnay. The 1990 Chardonnay Alexander Valley is a delicious, buttery, herb-, and toasty-scented wine, with surprisingly bold, rich flavors, good acidity, and a wonderful freshness and purity. Drink it over the next year. However, Belvedere's red wines continue to be excessively vegetal, short, thick, and generally uninteresting, narrowly constructed offerings. For example, the 1986 Merlot from the Robert Young Vineyard has light to medium body and a pleasant berry fruitiness, but it is, in essence, a narrowly focused, compact wine that finishes a bit short. Drink it over the next 2–3 years. Recent Cabernet Sauvignons from the York Creek Vineyard and Robert Young Vineyard have proven similarly acidic and overwhelmingly herbaceous.

BENZIGER (SONOMA)

Cabernet Sauvignon* *, Cabernet Sauvignon Tribute* * *,
Chardonnay* * *, Merlot* *, Proprietary White Wine* * */* * * *, Zinfandel* * *

1987	Cabernet Sauvignon	Sonoma	B	86
1988	Cabernet Sauvignon Tribute	Sonoma	D	86
1987	Cabernet Sauvignon Tribute	Sonoma	C	85
1990	Chardonnay	Sonoma	B	87
1990	Chardonnay Premiere Vineyard	Carneros	D	87
1990	Tribute (50% Semillon/50% Sauvignon Blanc)	Sonoma	C	87
1989	Zinfandel	Sonoma	A	86

These are the more expensive and higher-quality wines from Glen Ellen. The quality has gradually moved up over recent vintages. The Chardonnays and occasionally the Meritage white and Fumé Blanc are the pick of Benziger's portfolio. Recent attempts to seduce wine enthusiasts with wines that possess plenty of up-front fruit and appeal have been successful. Even critics are taking notice of these drinkable, often elegant wines. The Cabernets, too, have shown improvement over some of the earlier vintages. The 1988 Cabernet Sauvignon Tribute offers an enticing cassis, spicy, cedary nose, medium-bodied, ripe fruit, soft tannins, and a lush finish. Drink it over the next 3–4 years. The 1987 Cabernet Sauvignon Tribute exhibits a deep, dark color, a big, rich, spicy nose, medium to full body, and fine fruit. There is not a lot of complexity, but the wine offers soft acidity and a long, generous, round finish. The 1987 regular bottling is an elegant, supple, delicious Cabernet. Medium-dark ruby, with a moderately intense, expansive bouquet of blackcurrants, Provençal herbs, and a touch of cedar and wood, this wine is medium bodied and soft, with round, charming flavors. Altogether it is a delicious Cabernet for drinking over the next 2–4 years. An excellent example of a top-notch vintage for California Chardonnay, the 1990 Benziger Chardonnay displays a popcorn- and fruit-scented nose, medium- to full-bodied flavors, good richness, adequate acidity, and a smooth, fresh finish. Drink it up. The 1989 vintage was not the easiest in which to produce concentrated, high-quality wines. Yet Benziger has turned out a tasty, even elegant, generously endowed, expansively flavored Zinfandel without any hard edges. It offers plenty of soft, ripe berry fruit, herbs, and peppers. Drink it over the next 3–4 years. The 1990 Tribute, a high-quality, concentrated, complex blend of Sauvignon and Semillon, has been admirably made by the Benziger family. The moderately intense bouquet of melons, figs, and herbs is reminiscent of a top-quality Pouilly Fumé. In the mouth there is surprising richness, a medium- to full-bodied, opulent texture, and a long, spicy, crisp finish. This excellent wine, which would be ideal with salmon and richer fish dishes, should be drunk over the next year. All things considered, this is a winery that continues to improve its level of quality, producing wines that are designed to be drunk in their youth.

BERINGER (NAPA)

Cabernet Sauvignon Knight's Valley* * *, Cabernet Sauvignon Private Reserve* * * * *, Chardonnay* * *, Chardonnay Private Reserve* * * */* * * * *, Chenin Blanc* * *, Gamay* * *, Meritage White* * *, Merlot Bancroft Vineyard* * * *, Sauvignon Blanc* * *, Zinfandel* * *

1986	Cabernet Sauvignon	Knight's Valley	B	85
1985	Cabernet Sauvignon	Knight's Valley	B	85
1986	Cabernet Sauvignon Estate	Napa	B	85
1988	Cabernet Sauvignon Private Reserve	Napa	D	85
1987	Cabernet Sauvignon Private Reserve	Napa	D	93
1986	Cabernet Sauvignon Private Reserve	Napa	D	92
1985	Cabernet Sauvignon Private Reserve	Napa	D	91
1991	Chardonnay	Knight's Valley	A	87
1991	Chardonnay Private Reserve Ed Sbragia	Napa	D	92
1991	Chardonnay Private Reserve	Napa	C	87
1990	Chardonnay Private Reserve	Napa	C	89
1990	Chardonnay Proprietor Grown	Napa	C	87
1991	Chenin Blanc Proprietor Grown	Napa	A	85
1992	Gamay Beaujolais Premier Nouveau	North Coast	A	84
1991	Meritage White	Napa	A	87
1989	Merlot Bancroft Vineyard	Howell Mountain	D	89
1988	Merlot Bancroft Vineyard	Howell Mountain	D	85
1987	Merlot Bancroft Vineyard	Howell Mountain	D	90
1990	Zinfandel	Napa	B	81

This winery continues to do many things right. Since 1984 their Private Reserve Cabernets have been among the top dozen Cabernets produced in California. The 1988 Reserve is much lighter than usual, soft, and already mature, and the 1987 is a worthy competitor to the terrific 1986. The 1987's dark ruby/garnet color is followed by a super bouquet. There are huge aromas of chocolate, spicy new oak, herbs, cassis, and tobacco in this beautifully scented wine. In the mouth it is full-bodied, voluptuous, spicy, and crammed with fruit, glycerin, and enough tannin to support 15–16 years of cellaring. Like the 1986, the tannins are soft, and fortunately the acids are not shrill enough to prevent immediate drinkability. This is a skillfully made, complex Cabernet Sauvignon that will not linger long on retailers' shelves. My gut feeling is that Beringer's superb 1986 Cabernet Sauvignon has turned out even better than the 1985. Perhaps it is just that the 1986 tastes more forward, but I also thought the super bouquet of this wine and the creamy, expansive, rich, full-bodied flavors had even more dimension than the wonderful 1985. It has a stunning bouquet of ripe, smoky, oaky, berry-scented fruit, extravagantly rich, luscious flavors, and great length. It would appear to have a more multidimensional character and a richer, fuller personality than the 1985. Pleasurable now, this gorgeously made Cabernet Sauvignon should continue to offer superlative drinking for another 10–12 years. The 1985 Private Reserve is a deep, well-structured, highly concentrated wine exhibiting layers of superripe blackcurrant fruit backed up by gobs of tannins, plenty of toasty oak, and good acidity. It is a wine that can be drunk now, although my preference would be to cellar it for at least several years; it has the potential to last through the first decade of the next century. The only disappointment in recent Private Reserves is the 1988, but then the vintage has a lot to do with Beringer's performance. The light 1988 exhibits good color but not much substance, and it has a short finish. Nevertheless, its softness and fruity, supple character should appeal if the wine is drunk over the next 2–4 years. For those who do not have the patience or financial well-being to afford the Private Reserve, don't miss Beringer's 1986 Estate Cabernet Sauvignon. Made to be consumed over the next 3–4 years, it has a moderately intense bouquet of herbs, blackcurrants, and licorice. In the mouth it is wonderfully supple, smooth, and altogether a seductive wine for drinking over the near term. This winery has clearly upgraded the quality of their Knight's Valley Cabernet, as both the 1985 and 1986 are very good and offer surprising value. The 1985 showed excellent ripeness, a rich, blackcurrant-scented bouquet, medium body, plenty of suppleness, and an attractive bouquet. It's a bit more structured and tannic than the full, plump, round, deliciously soft and fat 1986. Both wines can be drunk now or over the next 5–6 years. The 1987 Merlot from the Bancroft Vineyard is powerful, rich, concentrated, and surprisingly full, with at least a decade's worth of aging potential. Although drinkable now, it is clearly not as soft as many wines made from this varietal. There is plenty of punch and tannin in the finish, but the tannins are neither astringent nor coarse. Deep ruby in color, full and impressive, this is a highly meritorious effort from Beringer. The 1988 Bancroft Vineyard Merlot is lighter and less powerful, but still a good example from this vintage. The real surprise is the nearly outstanding 1989 Merlot from the Bancroft Vineyard, a big, rich, chocolatey, toffee-scented wine that displays considerable evidence of aging in toasty new oak. This rich, full-bodied, fleshy wine is a terrific example from such an irregular vintage. There is less difference between the regular and Reserve Chardonnays than the prices might suggest. Those who love out-and-out rich, buttery, vividly pure Chardonnay fruit will enjoy the regular 1990 Chardonnay Proprietor Grown Napa. It should provide sumptuous drinking over the next several years. The 1990 Chardonnay Private Reserve Napa is a more oaky, smoky, delicately balanced wine. Although bigger and richer, it is only marginally better than the excellent regular bottling. In 1991 I thought the wines were qualitative equals, but the Reserve is decidedly oakier. Be sure not to miss (assuming you can find any of the microscopic quantities produced) the blockbuster 1991 Reserve Ed Sbragia Chardonnay, a gloriously rich wine. The 1991 Chenin Blanc is a brilliantly focused, vibrant, fresh, delicious, off-dry wine that is bursting with fruit and seductive, flowery aromas. This crisp, fragrant wine is what Chenin Blanc is all about—juicy, delicious, and inexpensive. It is hard to think of a better aperitif than a wine such as this, particularly when value is important. Drink it over the next year. Beringer has consistently made fine Sauvignon Blancs, but in 1991 the wine is officially a Meritage since an important component of this juicy, succulent, tasty wine is Semillon. Beringer's 1992 Gamay Beaujolais Premier Nouveau, a soft, uncomplicated, exuberantly fruity, supple, smoothly textured wine, reveals what can result from impeccable winemaking. There is a lot of pleasure to be found in this easygoing, deliciously fruity wine. Drink it over the next year. A soft, pleasant wine, the 1990 Zinfandel from Beringer lacks stuffing and complexity. Nevertheless, for a commercially correct Zinfandel designed to please the masses, it suffices. Drink it over the next 3–4 years.

BERNARDUS (MONTEREY)
Chardonnay* * *

| 1991 | Chardonnay | California | C | 86 |

The debut release from this Carmel Valley winery reveals a kinship with a French white burgundy. This medium-bodied wine displays a judicious use of toasty, vanillin-scented new oak, good purity, a honeyed, ripe apple component, and buttery, rich fruit. The finish is too short to merit a higher score, but there is plenty to like in this Chardonnay; drink it over the next 1–2 years.

BOEGER WINERY (EL DORADO)
Cabernet Sauvignon* * *, Chardonnay* *, Merlot* * *, Zinfandel* * *

1989	Cabernet Sauvignon	El Dorado	B	85
1985	Cabernet Sauvignon Estate	El Dorado	B	73
1990	Chardonnay	El Dorado	B	84
1987	Merlot Estate	El Dorado	B	85
1986	Merlot Estate	El Dorado	B	67
1990	Zinfandel	El Dorado	A	87

Boeger's track record has been mixed, but recent vintages have shown more consistency. Boeger is always a good source for Zinfandel. For example, the 1990 is the best Zinfandel I have tasted from the Boeger winery. Made in a succulent, medium- to full-bodied, soft-as-silk style, it offers immediate gratification. The deep, fleshy flavors suggest plums, earth, and black cherries. The fragrant nose has not been destroyed by sterile filtration. This delicious, upfront style of Zinfandel should drink well for 5–6 years. I have also enjoyed this winery's Merlots, which offer smooth coffee- and chocolate-scented fruit. The 1987 Merlot from Boeger offers textbook Merlot fruit in a lush, round, amply endowed, medium-bodied format with no hard edges. There is little tannin, and the overall impression is one of soft, luscious, plump fruit. Drink this wine, which has considerable charm, over the next 2–3 years. Readers are advised to avoid the 1986 Merlot Estate, which is watery, thin, and disappointing. Although the 1985 Cabernet Sauvignon Estate displays some ripeness and length, an annoying bitterness in the finish detracts from its overall appeal. The 1989 Cabernet Sauvignon is a fleshy, round, medium- to full-bodied wine with fine fruit, spice, and appeal. It should be drunk over the next 4–5 years. The winery has also produced a competent Sauvignon Blanc, and for consumers looking a decent value, Hangtown Red and Hangtown Gold are light, pleasant, fresh blended wines that sell for under $6 a bottle.

BON MARCHÉ (NAPA)
Chardonnay* *, Pinot Noir* *

1990	Chardonnay	Sonoma	A	85
1990	Pinot Noir	Sonoma	A	85

Bon Marché is the secondary label of the Buehler winery. The 1990 Chardonnay displays excellent ripeness. There is plenty of round, apple/butter-like fruit flavors, good crisp acidity for freshness, and a pleasant, fleshy, satisfying finish. Drink it over the next year. Although the 1990 Pinot Noir is not a profound example of this varietal, there is no doubting its correct varietal character or the soft, herb, berry-scented nose and round, gentle, expansive flavors. Easy to drink and appreciate, this wine should also appeal to restaurants.

BONNY DOON VINEYARD (SANTA CRUZ)
Chardonnay* *, Cigare Volant* * *, Clos de Gilroy Grenache* * * *,
Old Telegram Mourvèdre* * *, Le Sophiste* * * *, Syrah* * *,
Vin Gris de Cigare (Rosé)* * * *

N. V.	Ca del Solo Il Pescatore	California	A	85
1991	Ca del Solo Moscato	California	A	86
1990	Le Cigare Volant	California	C	85
1992	Clos de Gilroy California Grenache	California	A	85
1990	del Solo California	California	B	88
1990	Old Telegram (Mourvèdre)	California	C	84
1991	Pacific Rim Riesling	California	A	83
1990	Pinot Meunier	California	C	77
1990	Le Sophiste (Marsanne/Roussanne)	California	C	86
1989	Syrah Estate	Santa Cruz	C	78
1988	Syrah Estate	Santa Cruz	C	86
1992	Vin Gris de Cigare Rosé	California	A	85

Bonny Doon continues to be one of the leaders in offering an innovative group of Rhône Valley–inspired wines. I have been an unabashed admirer of their Clos de Gilroy since Randall Grahm began producing it. It has been a gloriously exuberant, deliciously hedonistic wine that would satisfy the masses if it were available in enormous quantities. The 1992 is gushing with berry fruit and exhibits a soft underbody and a generally elegant, medium-bodied texture. Drink it before the summer of 1994. The 1992 Vin Gris de Cigare Rosé (70% Grenache, 26% Mourvèdre, 4% Pinot Noir) is a fragrantly scented strawberry- and raspberry-flavored, relatively dry, luscious rosé. Grahm's charming non-vintage Il Pescatore, a deliciously made, cunningly packaged wine with an intensely floral, fruity nose, and dry, crisp flavors, will make enjoyable drinking over the next year. Even more impressive was his 7% alcohol 1991 del Solo California, a slightly effervescent Muscat-based wine made from grapes grown in Monterey. I have been a big advocate of the Italian version of these wines for years, and if ever there were a perfect breakfast wine, these light-alcohol, overwhelmingly fruity, apricot-, peach-, pineapple-, floral-scented and slightly sweet-tasting Muscats would be a unanimous choice. These wines should be consumed immediately. Certainly Randall Grahm has lost none of his eccentricities with respect to the packaging of his 52% Marsanne/48% Roussanne blend called Le Sophiste. This is a wine with a bouquet that would merit a score in the middle 90s (it lacks the follow-through and finish necessary to get a higher score). The fabulous nose zooms out of the glass, offering up aromas of honeyed oranges and scents of flowers, making for a wonderful first impression. The wine is not nearly as impressive as the bouquet suggests. It is relatively high in acidity and has good ripeness, but its tendency to tail off may suggest young vines. Those who purchase this wine will love Grahm's label and its plastic-top hat, used instead of a conventional capsule. The Cigare Volant has gotten progressively lighter since the debut vintage, 1985. Like the 1989 and 1988, the 1990 is missing the profound color, bouquet, and flavor extraction that I have come to expect from previous editions, particularly the 1984, 1985, and 1986. What a shame the price has gone up and the quality has come down! Drink it over the next 2–3 years. The 1990 Old Telegram offers a bouquet of red fruits and earth, medium body, and crisp, well-delineated flavors. Although I would have loved to taste more depth, as well as a longer finish, I found it an interesting red wine for drinking over the next 4–5 years. The 1988 Syrah had a sensational smoky, coconut-, cassis-, peppery-scented bouquet and an impressive, dark ruby color, but in the mouth the acidity was annoyingly shrill, and the wine lacked depth and fell off in the finish. Though a good Syrah, it is eclipsed by the Syrahs now being produced by Sean Thackrey and Edmunds St. John. The Syrah should last at least 5–7 years. The thin, uninteresting 1989 Syrah is a disappointment. The irrepressible Grahm is also producing a Riesling called Pacific Rim. The 1991 is a pleasant, off-dry wine that could use more complexity but makes for a tasty drink. Another new wine for Grahm is the 1991 Pinot Meunier. Although it exhibits an excellent nose of pure raspberries, it is short and thin on the palate. Bonny Doon also makes a Chardonnay, which I have found rather chunky and one-dimensional, without any personality. Although Randall Grahm continues to be a leader in innovative labeling, marketing, and originality, I cannot help noticing that the overall quality of his wines has become less exciting than it was 5 years ago. One would hate to think success has encouraged higher yields, but there appears to be no other explanation for the lighter, less concentrated style of many of Bonny Doon's new releases.

DAVID BRUCE WINERY (SANTA CRUZ)

Chardonnay* *, Petite Sirah* * *, Pinot Noir* */* * *, Zinfandel* * *

1990	Chardonnay Meyley Vineyard	Santa Cruz	D	68
1990	Chardonnay Vineyard Selection	Santa Cruz	C	71
1990	Petite Sirah	California	B	88
1989	Pinot Noir	Santa Cruz	C	76
1988	Pinot Noir	Santa Cruz	C	80
1990	Zinfandel	San Luis Obispo	B	85

The David Bruce Winery has moved 180 degrees with respect to the style of its wines. In the late 1960s and early 1970s, these wines were known largely for their individualistic, frequently excessive style. Recently they have tended to be conventional and straightforward, lacking the personality and richness boasted by the earlier releases. They now taste too polite and subdued. Bruce is most widely known for Chardonnay and Pinot Noir, but it is these two wines that I often find musty and mediocre. Far better is the Zinfandel: the attractive 1990 boasts a nice scent of fragrant raspberry fruit, followed by a ripe, medium-bodied texture that reveals good concentration, fine acidity, and moderate tannins in the finish. Approachable now, it should continue to drink well for another 4–5 years. The finest wine I have tasted recently from David Bruce is his 1990 Petite Sirah, peppery, big, and rich, with considerable depth and fine balance among all of its components. Drinkable now, it should age nicely for another 7–8 years. The winery also makes an interesting proprietary red wine called Côte de Chandon, which is a blend of Cabernet Pfeffer, Carignane, and Syrah. I have not had this reasonably priced red since the 1987, but it is one of the more intriguing wines David Bruce now produces—peppery and spicy, with a kinship to a medium-weight Rhône. I wish Bruce would go back to the style of wine that made this winery famous 20 years ago.

BUEHLER VINEYARDS (NAPA)
Cabernet Sauvignon* * */* * * *, Pinot Blanc* *,
White Zinfandel* * *, Zinfandel* * *

1989	Cabernet Sauvignon	Napa	C	76
1988	Cabernet Sauvignon	Napa	C	78
1987	Cabernet Sauvignon	Napa	C	88
1986	Cabernet Sauvignon	Napa	B	87
1984	Cabernet Sauvignon	Napa	C	89
1982	Cabernet Sauvignon	Napa	C	90
1978	Cabernet Sauvignon	Napa	C	89
1990	Zinfandel	Napa	B	77
1989	Zinfandel	Napa	A	87

This winery developed a following for its blockbuster, opaquely colored, thick, tannic Cabernet Sauvignons, of which the 1978, 1982, 1984, and 1986 have been the best to date. In fact, the 1978 has still not reached maturity. Buehler may be moving toward a lighter, more accessible style if the 1988 and 1989 are any indication. These two vintages did not produce that many concentrated, husky Cabernets, but Buehler's wines were surprisingly soft, light, and shallow. The winery has also made fine, ripe, tannic Zinfandel. However, recent vintages have been somewhat lighter, especially the 1990. Given the blockbuster style of so many of Buehler's red wines, I was shocked to see such a light, somewhat diluted 1990 Zinfandel emerge. Although this is a pleasant, slightly jammy, soft Zinfandel, it lacks grip, concentration, and character. Drink it over the next several years. Buehler has fashioned a gorgeously ripe, opulent 1989 Zinfandel that is bursting with spicy, berry fruit, has a full-bodied, smooth-as-silk texture, and offers a long, heady finish. The fruit dances over the palate. Although it is not a Zinfandel for making "old bones," it will drink well for the next 4–5 years. The 1987 Cabernet Sauvignon is a typical effort from Buehler, which can never be accused of cheating the consumer on the flavor or aging potential of its Cabernet Sauvignons, save for the 1988 amd 1989. Full bodied, with a rich, toasty, licorice-, and blackcurrant-scented aroma, this deep, chunky, muscular style of Cabernet Sauvignon should last for 10–15 years. Although it has the precociousness of the vintage, I would not drink it for at least another 2–3 years. The 1986 is another very typically proportioned Buehler Cabernet Sauvignon—robust, chewy, and muscular, with great individual style, plenty of richness and depth, and the potential to age well in the bottle for 10–12 years. It certainly is as good as the 1985, but not as rich and deep as the 1984. The 1982 Cabernet Sauvignon is still opaque black/purple-colored, with a vividly rich, spicy, earthy, animal, cassis-scented nose and long, opulent, highly extracted flavors. This big, full-throttled wine needs at least another 4–5 years to resolve its considerable tannic clout. **Anticipated maturity: 1997–2010.** Amazingly young and backward, the 1978 Buehler Cabernet Sauvignon exhibits an opaque garnet/purple color that is followed by a huge nose of licorice, Oriental spices, leather, and ground beef. In the mouth there is stunning concentration, high, astringent tannins, and a massive, amazingly youthful finish. **Anticipated maturity: 1995–2005.** Buehler also makes a straightforward, fruity, light Pinot Blanc and an attractive, off-dry white Zinfandel. Prices have remained fair in view of the high quality, but I cannot help wondering if Buehler is moving away from the rich style that made it so many friends.

BUENA VISTA (SONOMA)

Cabernet Sauvignon Carneros* *, Cabernet Sauvignon Private
Reserve* */* * *, Chardonnay Carneros* *, Chardonnay Private
Reserve* *, Fumé Blanc* * *, Pinot Noir* *

1990	Chardonnay	Carneros	B	80
1989	Chardonnay	Carneros	B	74
1989	Pinot Noir	Carneros	C	72
1988	Pinot Noir	Carneros	C	73

This large Sonoma winery was founded in the middle of the nineteenth century, making it one of California's most historically significant producers. It has grown into a large operation, with a production in excess of 250,000 cases. Across the board the wines lack richness, are products of a food-processing, manufacturing mentality that appears to put a premium on tart, high-acid, spit-polished, clean, and innocuous wines. In accomplishing that, the numerous filtrations and other clarification procedures strip the wines of much of their charm and fruit. Too often the results are simple, hard, eviscerated wines that are hollow and entirely too acidic. For value, the best wine is the Fumé Blanc, which despite all of the processing it must endure still retains some of its herbal, melony fruitiness. The Chardonnays tend to be lean, with the Reserve displaying more oak but no depth or character. The same can be said for the often overtly herbaceous and tart Cabernet Sauvignons. Even the Special Selection, an expensive wine, is one-dimensional and occasionally insipid. The overtly herbaceous Pinot Noirs are hard, compact, lean wines that are the antithesis of charm. This is a wealthy winery with considerable vineyard holdings. Although it has the potential to make wines with greater flavor dimension and interest, it apparently prefers to spend lavish amounts advertising rather than address the issue of its high-tech, high-acid, usually charmless wines.

BURGESS CELLARS (NAPA)
Cabernet Sauvignon Vintage Selection* * */* * * *,
Chardonnay Triere Vineyard* * */* * * *, Zinfandel* * *

1987	Cabernet Sauvignon Vintage Selection	Napa	C	79
1986	Cabernet Sauvignon Vintage Selection	Napa	C	82
1985	Cabernet Sauvignon Vintage Selection	Napa	C	85
1991	Chardonnay Triere Vineyard	Napa	C	89
1990	Chardonnay Triere Vineyard	Napa	C	88
1989	Chardonnay Triere Vineyard	Napa	C	76
1990	Zinfandel	Napa	B	87
1989	Zinfandel	Napa	B	86
1988	Zinfandel	Napa	B	79

The 1990 Zinfandel is a richly extracted, berry-scented wine with a touch of spice, medium to full body, lovely black raspberry flavors, and a long, heady finish. It is slightly richer and more complex than the 1989 Zinfandel. The 1989 offers good purity, rich berry fruit, a touch of oak and earth, and a long, heady, moderately tannic finish. Drink it over the next 4–6 years. The 1988 Zinfandel is a narrowly constructed, medium-weight Zinfandel with a reticent but adequate nose of peppery, berry fruit. In the mouth there is decent body, pleasant fruit, and an austere, moderately tannic finish. I do not see much more developing with cellaring, so drink it over the near term. Lamentably, the 1988, 1987, 1986, and 1985 Burgess Cabernet Sauvignon Vintage Selections are considerably lighter than their predecessors. In fact, the last truly concentrated, rich, intense Cabernet Sauvignon made by Burgess was the 1984 Vintage Selection. Given the outstanding raw materials offered by such years as 1985, 1986, and 1987, it appears Burgess Cellars is moving toward a lighter, more polished, yet far less interesting style of wine. How could a winery, particularly one that built a fine reputation for big, bold all-American Cabernets, begin to sacrifice the considerable richness and flavor authority that its vineyards provide for less interesting, lighter-weight, compact wines? All of these Cabernets remain hard and tannic, yet I do not see the depth that existed in prior years. As for the Chardonnays, the big, oaky (sometimes excessively woody) Chardonnays of the 1970s have given way to a rich but more fruity wine that balances its extraction of flavor with spicy wood. The best recent vintages have included the 1988, 1990, and 1991, yet even the 1989 was surprisingly successful for that difficult vintage.

RATINGS FOR OLDER VINTAGES OF BURGESS CELLARS CABERNET SAUVIGNON VINTAGE SELECTION: 1982 (87), 1980 (90), 1979 (86), 1978 (91), 1977 (90), 1976 (86), 1975 (87), 1974 (88)

DAVIS BYNUM WINERY (SONOMA)
Chardonnay* *, Fumé Blanc* *, Pinot Noir* *

1990	Chardonnay	Russian River Valley	B	84
1989	Chardonnay Limited Release	Russian River Valley	B	76
1990	Pinot Noir Limited Release	Russian River Valley	C	82

To date, the wines from Davis Bynum have been relatively straightforward and uninspiring. There appears to be slightly more consistency since the late 1980s, but the wines continue to display one-dimensional fruit and a compact, lean, hard style. The Chardonnays are light but fresh. The Pinot Noirs, with which the winery claims to be a specialist, are dull and light.

BYRON (SANTA BARBARA)
Chardonnay* * *, Chardonnay Reserve* * */* * * *, Pinot Noir* * *,
Sauvignon Blanc* * */* * * *

1992	Chardonnay Estate	Santa Maria	B	85
1991	Chardonnay Reserve	Santa Barbara	C	88
1991	Pinot Noir	Santa Barbara	C	74
1992	Pinot Noir Reserve	Santa Barbara	C	81
1992	Sauvignon Blanc	Santa Barbara	A	84
1991	Sauvignon Blanc	Santa Barbara	A	86

The Byron winery, which was acquired by Robert Mondavi in 1990, continues to turn out attractive Sauvignon Blanc and Chardonnay. Improvements are warranted with respect to the Pinot Noir program. Both the Chardonnay offerings are rich, lavishly oaked wines with copious quantities of buttery, honeyed, apple-, and pineapplelike fruit. The spicy 1992 Chardonnay Estate is neither as rich nor as thick as the 1991 Reserve. Both wines are best drunk over the next several years. Both Sauvignon Blancs are attractive. The 1992 is pleasant in a straightforward manner, crisp, delicious, and light to medium bodied. The 1991 is slightly softer, as well as richer and more expansive on the palate, with attractive honeyed-fig, melon, and herb scents and flavors. Both should be drunk over the next 12–18 months. Byron's Pinot Noirs lack aromatic and flavor dimension. The 1992 Pinot Noir Reserve, which has not yet been released, displays some elegance and a spicy, red-fruit character, but comes across on the palate as simple, light, short, and compact. The 1991 Pinot Noir reveals some earthy, funky lees aromas that dissipate with airing. However, the wine offers little excitement, with medium-bodied, straightforward, cherry fruitiness and crisp acidity.

CAFARO (NAPA)
Cabernet Sauvignon* */* * *, Merlot* *

1991	Cabernet Sauvignon	Napa	C	83
1991	Merlot	Napa	C	81
1989	Merlot	Napa	C	78
1988	Merlot	Napa	C	83
1987	Merlot	Napa	C	84

This microscopic operation (under 500 cases) is dedicated to the production of Merlot and Cabernet Sauvignon. The wines clearly possess character, but based on the 1987 and 1988, much of the potential appears to be buried under an abrasive wall of unripe tannin. Even in richer, riper years such as 1991, Cafaro managed to tame the tannins but produced light, rather one-dimensional wines.

CAIN CELLARS (NAPA)

Cain Five Proprietary Red Wine* * * *, Chardonnay* * * *,
Merlot* * * *, Sauvignon Musqué* * */* * * *

1991	Cain Five Proprietary Red Wine	Napa	D	91
1990	Cain Five Proprietary Red Wine	Napa	D	90
1987	Cain Five Proprietary Red Wine	Napa	D	89
1985	Cain Five Proprietary Red Wine	Napa	D	85
1990	Chardonnay Napa/Carneros	California	C	89
1990	Merlot	Napa	C	88
1990	Sauvignon Musqué	Napa	B	86

Cain Cellars has been making increasingly fine wines since 1987, and the 1991 and 1990 Cain Five proprietary red wine offerings would be worthy additions to any Cabernet enthusiast's cellar. The 1991 gets my nod as being slightly better. Fleshier and more deeply extracted, as well as possessing a superb sense of balance, it offers an attractive herbal, cassis, and chocolatey nose, sweet, curranty, expansive flavors, decent acidity, and a long, fleshy, spicy finish. It will be flattering to drink early on, but it should keep for at least 12 years. The 1990 is fashioned from a similar mold, although it is more evolved, with tobacco, coffee, and cassis aromas, ripe, rich fruit flavors, excellent concentration, and a medium- to full-bodied, lush finish. Drink it over the next 10 or more years. Deep ruby/purple-colored, the 1985 exhibits a super bouquet of black and red fruits, spicy oak, allspice, and vanillin. Rich and full bodied, with an opulent texture, adequate acidity, and a long, heady, admirably extracted finish, this is an enthralling proprietary wine that should make delicious drinking over the next 10–12 years. From the rich, cedary, olive- and cassis-scented bouquet to the full-bodied, fleshy, impeccably balanced, deep, ripe flavors, the full-size 1987 Cain Five is loaded with those qualities that define both character and pleasure. Soft enough to be consumed now, it will only get better with another 4–5 years of bottle age. It has the potential to last for 10–12 years. Cain's 1990 Merlot is an impressively endowed, supple, rich, medium- to full-bodied wine with plenty of herbal, chocolatey, berry fruit, a nice touch of oak, and a succulent, chewy texture. Drink it over the next 5–6 years. Cain Cellars's 1990 Chardonnay exhibits a gorgeously ripe, buttery, honeyed apple–scented nose. On the palate there is full body, with plenty of rich fruit buttressed by crisp acidity and framed by vanilla-tasting, smoky new oak. The finish is long and opulent. Do not defer your pleasure, as this delicious Chardonnay will probably begin its decline in less than a year. The intensely perfumed bouquet of the 1990 Sauvignon Musqué offers up aromas of herbs, sweet, creamy fruit, and toasty oak. In the mouth this round, generously endowed, ripe Sauvignon Musqué has gobs of fruit. Interesting as well as innovative, this wine should drink well for the next year.

CAKEBREAD CELLARS (NAPA)
Cabernet Sauvignon* *, Chardonnay* *

1988	Cabernet Sauvignon	Napa	D	82
1987	Cabernet Sauvignon	Napa	D	83
1986	Cabernet Sauvignon	Napa	C	77
1990	Chardonnay	Napa	C	84
1989	Chardonnay	Napa	C	74

I am unable to muster much enthusiasm for these wines, which all tend to be relatively tart, lean, technically correct but essentially indifferent and one dimensional. In short, there is a severe character and charm deficit. The Chardonnays taste too tart and austere, and the Cabernets are too tannic and acidic. The latter wines lean toward the pungently herbaceous side of this varietal. I should note that my position on these wines seems to be in the minority, at least when compared with the praise this winery receives from the West Coast press.

CALERA WINE COMPANY (SAN BENITO)
Chardonnay Central Coast* * * *, Chardonnay Mount Harlan* * * * *,
Pinot Noir Jensen Vineyard* * * * *, Pinot Noir Mills Vineyard* * * * *,
Pinot Noir Reed Vineyard* * * * *, Pinot Noir Selleck Vineyard* * * * *,
Viognier* * * * *

1991	Chardonnay Central Coast	California	C	90
1990	Chardonnay Central Coast	California	C	89
1990	Chardonnay Mount Harlan	San Benito	C	94
1989	Chardonnay Mount Harlan	San Benito	C	93
1988	Chardonnay Mount Harlan	San Benito	C	92
1989	Pinot Noir Jensen Vineyard	California	D	90
1988	Pinot Noir Jensen Vineyard	California	D	93
1989	Pinot Noir Mills Vineyard	Mt. Harlan	D	88
1988	Pinot Noir Mills Vineyard	Mt. Harlan	D	88
1989	Pinot Noir Reed Vineyard	California	D	90
1988	Pinot Noir Reed Vineyard	California	D	90
1988	Pinot Noir Selleck Vineyard	California	D	92
1991	Viognier	Mt. Harlan	D	93
1989	Viognier	Mt. Harlan	D	93

Calera continues to produce the best Viognier in the New World, and one that competes with the finest offerings from Condrieu. Although the price is high and quantities are minuscule, do not hesitate to buy this wine should you be lucky enough to find any. It exhibits a huge, honeyed, flowery fragrance of tropical fruits, rich, gorgeously ripe, opulent flavors, and a blockbuster finish. Any wine made from the Viognier grape should be drunk in its first 1–2 years of life. The 1990 and 1991 Central Coast Chardonnays are terrific bottles of unbelievably unctuous, rich, expansively flavored, dramatic Chardonnay. Both ooze with buttery, tropical fruit, exhibit plenty of glycerin and alcohol, and offer lusty, heady finishes. They represent authoritative examples of what California can do with Chardonnay but so rarely does. For drinking over the next 1–2 years, this is Chardonnay at its most decadent. The 1988 Chardonnay Mount Harlan is a dead ringer for a great Bâtard or Chevalier-Montrachet from the likes of Domaine Ramonet. I have not seen such incredible concentration and opulence, as well as complexity in a California Chardonnay since the profound 1980 Chalone. The wine seems actually to grow in the glass. I've had the wine on three occasions; on the last two, I decanted the bottle and left it open for 30 minutes before drinking. This extraordinary winemaking effort proves what low yields and talented winemaking can do in selected viticultural areas of California. Remarkably, the 1989 is even richer than the 1988 Mount Harlan Chardonnay, and the 1990 is richer still. The consistently high quality of this Mount Harlan Chardonnay suggests it may be the finest Chardonnay now being made in California. The wine is stunningly rich, with a degree of complexity and concentration that is rare, even from the greatest French white burgundies. Although drinkable, each wine has the requisite depth and structure to last for another 3–5 years. Josh Jensen's Calera Wine Company has turned in a number of formidable performances with respect to American Pinot Noir. The 1988s are every bit as sensational as his striking 1987s; in fact, they are probably richer and more concentrated, as well as potentially longer-lived, than the 1987s. The 1988 Pinot Noir Mills Vineyard is made from a relatively young 12-acre vineyard. It displays a beautiful dark ruby color, a big, aromatic bouquet of black fruits, medium-bodied, long, rich flavors, and more compactness than Jensen's other Pinots yet wonderful spice and purity. Drink it over the next 7–8 years. The 1988 Pinot Noir Selleck Vineyard is made from a tiny 5-acre vineyard. An animal, cinnamon, spicy, Côte de Nuits–like style emerges from this wine. The color is sensational, as are the rich, medium- to full-bodied, intense flavors. There is plenty of extraction and moderate tannins in this wine, which clearly begs for another 2 years of cellaring. This impressive wine can easily stand up against some of the finest French burgundies from Morey St.-Denis and Gevrey-Chambertin. The 1988 Pinot Noir Reed Vineyard is the softest of this quartet, and more herbaceous, with a creamy texture. It is the most seductive and forward of these wines for current drinking. Although it lacks the concentration of the Selleck, and is also more weedy and stemmy, I loved its big, forward bouquet, and rich, supple, satiny-smooth flavors. Drink it over the next 5–7 years. Perhaps the finest of all Calera's 1988 Pinot Noirs is the 1988 Pinot Noir Jensen Vineyard. Made from a 14-acre vineyard, this is the richest, darkest-colored, longest, most profound of Calera's newest offerings. It is also backward, very deeply concentrated, with profound Pinot Noir flavors and extraordinary presence and aromatic dimension. These are compelling Pinot Noirs by any standard. Don't miss them! The 1989 Pinot Noir Reed Vineyard displays a surprisingly deep, nearly opaque, dark ruby color, a big, intense, earthy, spicy, herb-, smoke-scented nose, and rich, black cherry flavors intermingled with the suggestion of Provençal herbs, spicy new oak, and chocolate. This complete, rich, moderately tannic wine is approachable now but is capable of lasting for a decade. The 1989 Pinot Noir Jensen Vineyard is as rich, slightly less earthy, but more herbaceous, with sweeter fruit on the palate, less noticeable tannins, and a superbly rich, opulent, long finish. The 1989 Pinot Noir from the Mills Vineyard offers a beautiful herb-, berry-, earthy-scented nose, rich, ripe, deep, spicy flavors, and moderate tannins, as well as good body and length. Although more approachable than are many Calera Pinot Noirs when released, it should continue to drink well for 5–7 years. This winery continues to solidify its position as America's top producer of Pinot Noir. Calera also produces a Vin Gris of Pinot Noir, a remarkably intense, deeply colored, very Pinot Noir–scented rosé, with aromas of herbs, berries, and spices. It is a full-bodied, fleshy rosé that should always be drunk within 1 year of the vintage.

CALLAWAY VINEYARDS (TEMECULA)
Chardonnay Calla-lees* *, Fumé Blanc/Sauvignon Blanc* *, White Riesling*

1990	Cabernet Sauvignon	California	B	55
1990	Chardonnay Calla-lees	Temecula	A	78
1989	Chardonnay Calla-lees	Temecula	A	68

Well intended, the Chardonnay Calla-lees (the name derived from the lees on which this Chardonnay is aged) is designed to be a fresh, lively, floral, fruity wine. However, the quality level is, at best, average. The 1990 and 1989 are both hollow and stale tasting. Callaway's 1990 Cabernet Sauvignon is an appallingly bad wine, with no recognizable varietal character, a vegetal taste, and a stripped, lean, hard finish. Other wines, including a cloyingly sweet Sauvignon Blanc and a bizarre Chenin Blanc, have also proved to be disappointing. Given the realistic prices, this is sad.

CAMBRIA WINERY AND VINEYARD (SANTA MARIA)
Chardonnay Cuvées* * * *, Pinot Noir Julia's Vineyard* * * * (since 1991)

1992	Chardonnay Katherine's Vineyard	Santa Maria	C	87
1991	Chardonnay Katherine's Vineyard	Santa Maria	C	88
1992	Chardonnay Reserve	Santa Maria	C	89
1990	Chardonnay Reserve	Santa Maria	C	89
1991	Pinot Noir Julia's Vineyard Estate	Santa Maria	C	87

This winery, which is owned by Kendall-Jackson, has established a good track record for lavishly oaked, lusty, rich Chardonnays. Their Pinot Noir program began with some difficulty, but appears to have improved significantly over the last few vintages. Upcoming releases include a 1992 Chardonnay Katherine's Vineyard and a 1992 Chardonnay Reserve (not yet released). Both are rich, toasty, honeyed, buttery Chardonnays with admirable intensity and up-front appeal. They will need to be consumed in their first 2–3 years of life. Current releases include the 1991 Chardonnay Katherine's Vineyard, a lush, richly fruity, boldy flavored wine that offers abundant honeyed, pineapple fruit allied to smoky, toasty new oak. Drink this hedonistic Chardonnay over the next year. The 1990 Chardonnay Reserve exhibits a more honeyed character, as well as more definition and complexity. Explosive richness, great intensity, and a huge, luscious finish make for a flamboyant mouthful of Chardonnay fruit. Cambria's 1991 Pinot Noir Julia's Vineyard Estate is their best Pinot to date. Medium to dark ruby in color, it offers up aromas of nearly overripe plums, underbrush, and flowers. It has a succulence bordering on fatness, a fleshy, voluptuous texture, and a lusty, heady finish. Drink this decadent Pinot Noir over the next 2–4 years. Readers may also want to keep an eye out for Cambria's 1992 Syrah, which will not be released until at least 1994. From the barrel, it had spectacular extraction of flavor, and a huge, bacon fat, cassis-scented nose that reminded me of top-notch Hermitage. Its texture was softer than a classic Hermitage, but the tannins were ripe and the purity of fruit was admirable. It is potentially, a 90+ wine.

CARMENET VINEYARD (SONOMA)
Colombard Old Vines* * * *, Proprietary Red Wines* * * *,
Meritage Proprietary White* * */* * * *

1991	Cabernet Franc	Sonoma	C	82
1990	Colombard Old Vines	Napa	A	87
1991	Colombard Old Vines	Napa	A	86
1991	Dynamite Cabernet	Sonoma	C	84
1991	Meritage Proprietary White Wine (70% Sauvignon/30% Semillon)	Edna Valley	B	85
1991	Moon Mountain Estate	Sonoma	C	87
1990	Proprietary Red Wine	Sonoma	C	89
1989	Proprietary Red Wine	Sonoma	C	84
1990	Proprietary Red Wine Reserve	Sonoma	C	91
1988	Proprietary Red Wine	Sonoma	C	87
1987	Proprietary Red Wine	Sonoma	C	88
1986	Proprietary Red Wine	Sonoma	C	92
1985	Proprietary Red Wine	Sonoma	C	90
1991	Vin de Garde Reserve	Sonoma	D	92

Since Carmenet's first vintage in 1982, their wines have been at least very good, often quite special, with a degree of complexity and elegance that is often missing from many of Sonoma's other Cabernet-based wines. While imbibers wanting a blockbuster heavyweight Cabernet from California might be disappointed with Carmenet, those who prefer deeply aromatic, spicy, perfumed, complex wines should find considerable merit in these offerings. The 1990, produced from 64% Cabernet Sauvignon, 22% Cabernet Franc, and 14% Merlot, displays a big, spicy, oaky, olive- and cherry-scented nose, elegant, medium-bodied, rich flavors, a chewy texture, soft tannins, adequate acidity, and a fleshy finish. There is a pronounced leafy (bell pepper?) quality to both of the 1990 proprietary red wine offerings. The 1990 Reserve, made from 84% Cabernet Sauvignon, 13% Cabernet Franc, and 3% Merlot, is a fuller-bodied, richer wine, with an attractive, surprisingly complex nose of cinnamon, clove, olive, and berry fruit intermingled with aromas of toasty new oak. In the mouth there is elegance, a wonderful chewy, rich texture supported by fine acidity, plenty of glycerin, and a moderately tannic finish. Both of these wines should be immensely impressive young and easily evolve for more than a decade. While the 1989 is light, tannic, and lacking depth, the successful

1988 proprietary red wine is made from a blend of 85% Cabernet Sauvignon, 9% Cabernet Franc, and 6% Merlot. The nose offers sweet, smoky aromas of herbs and black cherry fruit. In the mouth there is an evolved, cedary, earthy, herbal component, rich, medium- to full-bodied flavors, and soft tannins, as well as a heady, spicy finish. Drink this charmer over the next 7–10 years. Most consumers will be enthralled by the big, leafy, cedary, surprisingly oaky and flamboyant bouquet of the 1987 Proprietary Red Wine. The color is medium to dark ruby. The wine displays relatively sculptured, medium-bodied, smooth, herbaceous, curranty flavors that reflect the use of extremely toasty new oak barrels. This wine could have been outstanding with a bit more stuffing and a less heavy hand with the oak, yet there is no doubting its forward appeal and distinctive style. I would drink it over the next 7–8 years. I found that both the 1985 and 1986 Carmenet Proprietary Red Wines improve with a good 30 minutes of breathing or decantation prior to drinking. The 1985 has a slightly deeper, richer color than the 1986 and seems a bit more tightly knit. However, the levels of concentration in both wines are approximately the same, although the 1986 does seem to have a more developed and interesting bouquet. In a way, both wines are somewhat exotic by California's rather strait-laced standards. The 1985 reveals a gorgeous bouquet of mineral-scented, smoky blackcurrants and herbs, followed by a wine with medium to full body, excellent depth and length, and a complexity that is rare in California red wines. The 1986 has even more complexity, a wonderful, supple, expansive richness on the palate, and superb length. For those who have been weaned on the highly sculptured, high-acid, emasculated style of California Cabernet, the wines of Carmenet will present a sort of culture shock. In 1991 Carmenet produced four *cuvées* of red wine and renamed its basic Carmenet red Moon Mountain Estate and the Carmenet Reserve Vin de Garde Reserve. The 1991 Cabernet Franc is light, weedy, medium bodied, and compact. Drink it over the next 4–8 years. The 1991 Dynamite Cabernet is straightforward, pleasant, and ideal for consuming over the next 5–7 years. There is nothing explosive about it. The 1991 Moon Mountain Estate exhibits an olive, cassis, spicy nose; soft, moderately endowed flavors; and an easygoing, user-friendly finish. It should drink well for 8–9 years. The 1991 Vin de Garde Reserve is a much more serious wine. Supple and forward with complexity and richness, great extract, and considerably more personality, it should evolve gracefully for 12–18 years. I hope Carmenet, for purposes of commercial greed, is not saving all the best *cuvée* of juice for the Reserve and producing three slightly above-average *cuvées* of red wine from the balance. From the all-important perspective of pleasure, I doubt there is a dry white table wine from California that I enjoy more than the Colombard Old Vines offerings from Carmenet. What does that say about such a lowly grape as the Colombard? Well, I suppose if the vines are old enough, the yields low enough, and the wine treated as if it were from a more renowned varietal, then many consumers could be drinking rich, tasty, personality-filled white table wines for under $10. These two offerings are both beauties, with the 1991 slightly lighter, although no less interesting. Both possess gorgeous levels of fruit, an attractive perfume, medium body, crisp acid, and plenty of midpalate fruit, as well as length. These two wines are never tiring or boring to drink. The 1991 proprietary white wine, Meritage, is an excellent, full-flavored white Graves-style blend of Sauvignon Blanc and Semillon. A nice touch of smoky, vanillin-scented, new oak gives framework to the wine's honeyed, melonlike, fig and herbaceous, smoky flavors. Drink it over the next several years. Although I did not taste the 1991, in 1990 Carmenet excelled with a herbaceous but richly flavored Edna Valley Sauvignon Blanc and a fruitier, more mineral-, melon-, and fig-scented and -flavored Sonoma Sauvignon Blanc. Whether the winery intends to go forward with these wines now that the Meritage White is in place remains to be seen.

DOMAINE CARNEROS (NAPA)
Sparkling Wine* * *

This new sparkling wine estate, owned by the famous Champagne firm of Taittinger and their American importer, the Kobrand Corporation, has gotten off to a reasonably good start with an attractive nonvintage Brut sparkling wine. Although light bodied, it offers flavor and finesse. Prices are reasonable, so it will be interesting to see how this wine's style emerges throughout the 1990s.

CAYMUS VINEYARD (NAPA)
Cabernet Sauvignon* * *, Cabernet Sauvignon Estate (before 1987)* * * *, Cabernet Sauvignon Special Selection* * * * *, Conundrum Proprietary White Wine* * * *, Pinot Noir* *, Sauvignon Blanc* * *, Zinfandel* * * *

1989	Cabernet Sauvignon	Napa	C	85
1988	Cabernet Sauvignon	Napa	C	83
1987	Cabernet Sauvignon	Napa	C	90
1986	Cabernet Sauvignon Estate	Napa	C	90
1988	Cabernet Sauvignon Special Selection	Napa	E	85
1987	Cabernet Sauvignon Special Selection	Napa	E	89
1986	Cabernet Sauvignon Special Selection	Napa	E	94
1985	Cabernet Sauvignon Special Selection	Napa	D	95
1991	Conundrum Proprietary White Wine	California	C	88
1988	Pinot Noir Special Selection	Napa	C	78
1990	Zinfandel	Napa	B	88

Few wineries in the world can boast such an enviable record of consistent excellence as can Caymus. The 1991 Conundrum Proprietary White Wine possesses a gorgeously fragrant nose of tropical fruits with a subtle touch of toasty oak. In the mouth there is voluptuous fruit, a dry, succulent, juicy texture, and a long, crisp finish. A delightful wine made from an innovative blend of Chardonnay, Muscat, Semillon, and Sauvignon Blanc, it can be drunk either as an aperitif or with seafood or chicken. Be sure to consume it over the next 1–2 years. To eliminate the confusion that previously existed, the highly successful Caymus Vineyard has decided to merge its Napa Valley *cuvée* and Estate Cabernet Sauvignons into one bottling. The 18,000 cases of this beautiful 1987 Cabernet Sauvignon should be gobbled up by consumers looking for outstanding wine at a reasonable price. The dark ruby/purple color suggests ripeness and depth, confirmed by the intensely fragrant, vanillin-scented, cedary, rich, curranty, almost sweet nose that is enticing as well as penetrating. The wine is expansively flavored, rich, medium to full bodied, with soft tannins, admirable length, and an impeccable sense of balance. The style of this deliciously forward, round, tasty Cabernet might be fairly compared with Bordeaux's Pichon-Lalande. Drink it over the next 5–6 years. Both the 1988 and 1989 Caymus Cabernet Sauvignons are significantly less rich and structured, without the concentration of the 1987. The 1988, in particular, is light, although the 1989 exhibits slightly better depth and ripeness. Both wines should be drunk over the next 5–6 years. The 1986 Estate Cabernet has a huge, smoky, blackcurrant bouquet with just a touch of cedar and herbs but plenty of new oak and jammy currant fruit. The wine is rich, full bodied, and chewy, with extra layers of extract and plenty of soft tannins in the finish. Overall, it presents gorgeous flavors wrapped in a lush framework. This wine is all seduction, although I have no doubt it will continue to improve for another 3–5 years. No Cabernet Sauvignon is more esteemed or in greater demand than the exceptional Special Selection Cabernet made by Caymus. Both the 1988 and 1987 Special Selection Cabernet Sauvignons are noticeably lighter and less intense than previous vintages. The 1988 reveals a dark color, plenty of oak in the nose, medium body, very good concentration, and a short, soft finish. The 1987, from a top vintage, is also much lighter. Nevertheless it is still an excellent wine with its rich, oaky, cassis and spicy nose, creamy-textured, medium- to full-bodied flavors, and moderately long finish. I would drink the 1988 over the next 7–8 years and the 1987 over the next 7–10 years. The 1986 Special Selection is a beautifully rendered wine. Dark ruby in color (although not as intensely colored as the 1985, 1984, 1980, or 1978 were at a similar stage), this is one of the more elegant Special Selections Caymus has produced. The bouquet of ripe blackcurrants, toast, and oak, with some scents of cocoa and vanilla, is truly world class. The wine is full bodied, admirably concentrated, and soft enough to be approachable now. It possesses the requisite overall harmony and length necessary to last for at least another 10–12 years. It is a beautifully made Cabernet, less muscular than many previous vintages but still profoundly perfumed and undeniably delicious. The 1985 Special Selection is a monumental effort from this winery. The predominant characteristic of any wine that spends 3 years or more in small casks would normally be oak, but it is a tribute to the concentration of Caymus's Special Selection that, although the oak is there, it plays a supporting rather than overwhelming role. This dark ruby/purple–colored wine is closed and less flattering than other recent Special Selections. The intriguing bouquet of minerals, licorice, road tar, blackcurrants, and smoky oak is fabulously enticing. The wine seems to ooze with a jammy concentration of fruit, yet it is admirably supported by good acidity and plenty of tannin in the finish. Like most of Caymus's Special Selections, it will be hard to resist, but having cellared many of these wines since the 1975, I can say they age magnificently. **Anticipated maturity: Now–2010.** Nearly every red wine that emerges from this fashionable winery displays wonderful flavor as well as an appealing up-front richness and fruitiness. Not surprisingly, the dark ruby/purple-colored 1990 Zinfandel offers a fine nose of superripe cherry fruit and herbs. In the mouth there is excellent ripeness, good intensity, enough acidity to provide delineation, and soft tannins in the finish. Clearly meant to be consumed over the near term, Caymus's 1990 Zinfandel should continue to drink well for at least 5–6 years. If there is one red wine that I find unexciting, it is the overly oaked, herbal, chunky Pinot Noir Special Selection.

The wine lacks complexity and comes across as nothing more than a sound, fleshy, medium-bodied red wine. Although it holds up in the bottle, it does not develop complexity.

RATINGS FOR OLDER VINTAGES OF CAYMUS VINEYARD SPECIAL SELECTION CABERNET SAUVIGNON: 1984 (96), 1983 (89), 1982 (88), 1981 (91), 1980 (93), 1979 (92), 1978 (98), 1976 (99), 1975 (98)

CHALK HILL WINERY (SONOMA)

Cabernet Sauvignon* * */* * * * (since 1990), Chardonnay* * */* * * * (since 1991), Sauvignon Blanc* * * * (since 1991)

1990	Cabernet Sauvignon	Sonoma	C	88
1991	Chardonnay	Sonoma	C	88
1991	Sauvignon Blanc	Sonoma	B	87

This winery was a perennial underachiever during its first decade of existence. In 1990 the proprietor hired the gifted David Ramey as the winemaker. Ramey excelled when working at Matanzas Creek, as well as for the Jean-Pierre Moueix firm in Pomerol. Ramey's influence was immediately noticeable: the two 1991s are the best wines Chalk Hill has made. The complex 1991 Sauvignon Blanc offers surprising richness, a bold, dramatic bouquet of melons, spicy oak, herbs, and rich fruit, medium to full body, and layers of concentration. Drink this rich, dry, impressive Sauvignon over the next 2–3 years. The powerful 1991 Chardonnay is admirably endowed, with a lusty nose of toasty oak, honeyed fruit, and butter. Rich, full bodied, and heady, this impressive Chardonnay should drink well for several more years. One hopes the mediocre Cabernet Sauvignons that were made by Chalk Hill during the 1980s will also soar in quality. For example, the 1990 Cabernet Sauvignon may turn out to be one of the sleepers of this exceptional vintage. It is densely colored, with a rich blackcurrant-scented nose, spicy, full-bodied, concentrated flavors, decent acidity, admirable soft tannins, and a rich, authoritative finish. The wine is relatively unevolved, but its copious quantities of sweet fruit make it accessible now. Drink it over the next 10–12 or more years.

CHALONE VINEYARDS (MONTEREY)

Chardonnay Estate* * * * *, Chardonnay Gavilan* */* * *, Chardonnay Reserve Estate* * * * *, Pinot Blanc* * * * *, Pinot Noir Estate* * *

1990	Chardonnay Reserve Estate	California	E	93
1991	Chardonnay Estate	California	D	91
1990	Chardonnay Estate	California	D	87
1991	Chardonnay Gavilan	California	C	81
1990	Chardonnay Gavilan	California	C	86
1990	Pinot Blanc Estate	California	C	90
1991	Pinot Blanc Estate	California	C	90
1990	Pinot Noir Gavilan	California	C	83
1989	Pinot Noir Estate	California	C	84

Chalone makes California's longest-lived Chardonnays and Pinot Blancs. Chalone's Pinot Blanc has been consistently excellent, and not surprisingly, both the 1990 and 1991 are exceptional. With stony, crisp, apple/orange-like noses, deep, elegant, well-balanced, tightly focused flavors, good concentration, and plenty of length, both wines should drink well for the next 6–10 years. The aging potential of Chalone's Pinot Blanc is amazing as evidenced by the glorious 1979, 1980, and 1981 drunk in May 1993. The 1990 Gavilan Chardonnay (Chalone's second label) exhibits a husky personality and adequate fruit and ripeness. It represents straightforward, chunky Chardonnay for drinking over the next 2–3 years. The 1991 Gavilan has good fruit but an earthy, somewhat cardboardlike bouquet. Chalone's 1990 and 1991 Chardonnays are their finest efforts since 1982. These wines remain tightly knit, but explosively rich and powerful, reluctantly exuding aromas of butter, oak, and spices. In the mouth there is superb depth and richness, fine acidity, and an overall sense of tightness and extreme youthfulness. I would not be surprised to see these take 5–6 years to reach full maturity. The 1990 Chardonnay Estate has a nice buttery, popcorn aroma, medium- to full-bodied fruit flavors, a soft, opulent texture, and a decent finish. It is delicious, but I suspect the Reserve bottlings made available only to stockholders are now receiving the benefit of the highly extracted fruit from the oldest vines. Drink the 1989 Chardonnay Estate over the next 2–3 years. Over the years I have had some immensely impressive Pinot Noirs from Chalone. The 1978 and 1980 are now complex, beautifully rich, earthy wines with considerable character. Certainly the 1990 Pinot Noir Gavilan is a pleasant wine, but the excessively leafy, grassy nose is off-putting. In the mouth there is good ripeness, medium body, and an attractive berry fruit. Drink it over the next 3–4 years. Chalone's 1989 Pinot Noir Estate offers a medium-deep ruby color, a spicy, oaky, barnyardlike nose, decent concentration, good ripeness, and a soft, pleasant finish. It is not nearly as concentrated as some older vintages, so it is best consumed over the next 5–6 years.

Note: An inducement to purchase stock in Chalone Inc., is the fact that their Reserve wines are sold only to stockholders. The Reserve Chardonnay can be brilliant—a 5-star wine in vintages such as 1980, 1981, 1983, and 1990, and the Reserve Pinot Blanc, astonishing in years such as 1980, 1981, and 1990.

RATINGS FOR OLDER VINTAGES OF CHALONE VINEYARDS ESTATE CHARDONNAY: 1988 (82), 1987 (87), 1986 (86), 1985 (86), 1984 (87), 1983 (85), 1982 (88), 1981 (93), 1980 (96), 1979 (86)

RATINGS FOR OLDER VINTAGES OF CHALONE VINEYARDS RESERVE ESTATE CHARDONNAY: 1990 (93), 1988 (84), 1986 (90), 1984 (78), 1983 (90), 1981 (92), 1980 (96)

RATINGS FOR OLDER VINTAGES OF CHALONE VINEYARDS PINOT BLANC: 1988 (88), 1987 (87), 1986 (86), 1985 (86), 1984 (87), 1983 (87), 1982 (88), 1981 (90), 1980 (91), 1979 (86)

RATINGS FOR OLDER VINTAGES OF CHALONE VINEYARDS RESERVE PINOT BLANC: 1990 (91+), 1988 (81), 1986 (84), 1983 (90), 1981 (91), 1980 (93)

CHAMISAL VINEYARD (SAN LUIS OBISPO)
Chardonnay* *

1991 Chardonnay	Edna Valley	C	86
1990 Chardonnay	Edna Valley	C	79

1989	Chardonnay	Edna Valley	B	87
1988	Chardonnay	Edna Valley	B	72

Excessive oak often dominates these wines. To date the quality has been irregular and the fruit has tended to dry out at a rapid pace because the wines are too woody. The 1991, the finest wine yet produced, is rich, boldly flavored, and not excessively oaky.

DOMAINE CHANDON (NAPA)
Blanc de Noir* * *, Brut* * * Étoile* * *, Reserve Brut* * * *

The Domaine Chandon is one of Napa Valley's must-see tourist attractions, with an excellent restaurant and informative, well-run tours of the facility. They have just celebrated their twentieth anniversary and their production has grown to over one-half million cases of reliable sparkling wine. In fact, the limited-release Reserve Brut reveals excellent flavor depth and character. It is especially delicious if drunk from magnum. Prices are reasonable, but the question remains as to whether the rich soils on Napa's valley floor and the area's hot climate can produce grapes that will ever achieve the elegance, complexity, and flavor intensity that Domaine Chandon's parent company, Moet and Hennessy, are able to routinely produce in France from the Champagne firms they own, Moët & Chandon, Ruinart, Mercier, Veuve Clicquot, Canard-Duchêne, and Henriot.

CHAPPELLET VINEYARD (NAPA)
Cabernet Sauvignon* *, Chardonnay* *, Chenin Blanc* * *, Merlot* *

1988	Cabernet Sauvignon Reserve	Napa	C	79
1987	Cabernet Sauvignon Reserve	Napa	C	81
1990	Chardonnay	Napa	C	78
1989	Chardonnay	Napa	C	74
1989	Merlot	Napa	C	64

Two of the greatest Napa Cabernet Sauvignons produced 20 or more years ago must have been the Chappellet 1969 and 1973. Since that time, despite 2 decades of mediocrity, this winery continues to produce a bevy of uninteresting, indifferent wines. The Chardonnays are too acidic and hollow, without charm or fruit. It is hard to understand their objective. The Cabernet Sauvignons have been light-bodied, excessively tannic, tart wines that suffer from a lack of fruit, concentration, and depth, not to mention elevated levels of green tannin. The winery began to produce Merlot under its own designation, and if the 1989 is typical, consumers can anticipate another disappointment, as it is an overtly vegetal effort that should never have been released. If there is a bright side to what this perennial underachiever produces, it is the bone-dry Chenin Blanc, which is ironically Chappellet's best and least expensive wine. It is consistently vivacious, exuberant, and tasty—a beverage of joy.

CHÂTEAU CHEVRE WINERY (NAPA)
Cabernet Franc* * *, Merlot* * */* * * *

1986	Cabernet Franc	Napa	C	87
1986	Chevre Reserve	Napa	C	86
1986	Merlot	Napa	C	79
1986	Merlot Reserve	Napa	C	87

This small Napa winery has shown a consistently fine touch with the Merlot grape and has now added Cabernet Franc to its portfolio. The 1986s are all very good, except for the 1986 Merlot, which seems rather light, simple, and just too straightforward to merit a higher rating. However, the 1986 Merlot Reserve shows a great deal of complexity; has a wonderfully round, plump, lush texture, delicious plummy fruit, and plenty of stuffing and length; and is drinking extremely well now. It should continue to age well for another 5–6 years. The 1986 Cabernet Franc is an extremely stylish, graceful wine with excellent fruit, deep ruby color, an aromatic mineral-, curranty-, cedary-scented bouquet, and good length on the palate. It's forward enough to drink now and should only get better with another 3–4 years of cellaring. Last, their proprietary red wine, the Chevre Reserve, shows excellent ripeness, a spicy, medium-bodied, fruity texture, and an elegant, stylish finish. Drink it over the next 4–5 years.

CHIMNEY ROCK (NAPA)
Cabernet Sauvignon* *, Chardonnay* *

1980	Cabernet Sauvignon	Stag's Leap	C	76
1990	Chardonnay	Stag's Leap	C	73
1989	Chardonnay	Stag's Leap	C	70

Chimney Rock's winemaker, Doug Fletcher, has an impressive résumé, so it is perplexing why these wines are so one-dimensional and innocuous. The Chardonnays are too acidic and lack flavor authority and character. The Cabernet Sauvignons are small-scale wines with a leafy, vegetal side and excessive acidity for their frail personalities. Chimney Rock also produces a Fumé Blanc and a Reserve Proprietary Red Wine, neither of which have I tasted. In a highly competitive marketplace, this winery needs to lower its prices and improve its quality.

CHRISTIAN BROTHERS WINERY (NAPA)
Cabernet Sauvignon*/* *, Chardonnay*/* *, Johannisberg Riesling*,
Merlot*, Zinfandel*

1988	Cabernet Sauvignon	Napa	A	65
1989	Chardonnay	Napa	A	72

This historic winery dates from the late nineteenth century. In 1989 it was sold to the huge British syndicate called Grand Metropolitan. It is too early to know whether the new owners will be able to improve the quality of what is a line of terribly dull, unexciting, generally disappointing offerings. Although inexpensive, the wines tend to be diluted, with only a vague notion of their varietal character and place of origin.

CHRISTOPHE VINEYARDS (NAPA)
Cabernet Sauvignon*, Chardonnay* * *, Sauvignon Blanc* *

This *négociant* firm owned by Burgundy's Jean-Claude Boisset can make good, reasonably priced, tasty Chardonnay. Both a regular *cuvée* and reserve are offered. Their Sauvignon Blanc has also been pleasant. The most disappointing wine from Christophe has been a rather vegetal, lean Cabernet Sauvignon. Readers searching out fine values should look for the proprietary red and white blends that Christophe Vineyards offers under the name Joliesse; these normally sell for well under $10 a bottle.

CINNABAR VINEYARD AND WINERY (SANTA CLARA)
Cabernet Sauvignon* */* * *, Chardonnay* * * *

1988	Cabernet Sauvignon	Santa Cruz	C	78
1987	Cabernet Sauvignon	Santa Cruz	C	79
1986	Cabernet Sauvignon	Santa Cruz	C	91
1990	Chardonnay	Santa Cruz	D	89

Although this winery has had an erratic track record over the 7 years it has been in business, one has to be impressed with the ambitious style of its wines. The Chardonnays tend to be full-throttle, oaky, creamy, lusty wines with honeyed textures and plenty of ripe, sweet fruit. The 1990 is a lusty Chardonnay that takes its oak to the limit. Readers are advised to drink it within the first 3–4 years of its life. The Cabernet Sauvignons have been a mixed bag. More recent vintages, such as 1987 and 1988, are too vegetal and oaky. However, the 1986 is a ruby/purple-colored wine, with a blossoming bouquet of minerals, licorice, and blackcurrants. In the mouth it exhibits an expansive richness that suggests tiny yields and/or old vines. Concentrated, with layers of extract but soft tannins and an overall sense of harmony, this well-knit, beautifully rendered Cabernet Sauvignon should ideally not be drunk for several more years. It has the potential to last for 10–15 years.

DOMAINE DE CLARCK (MONTEREY)
Chardonnay* * *, Pinot Noir* * */* * * *

1991	Chardonnay	Monterey	C	84
1991	Chardonnay Premier Release Unfiltered	Carneros	C	85
1990	Pinot Noir Unfiltered	Monterey	C	87
1991	Pinot Noir Villages	Monterey	C	85
1990	Pinot Noir Villages	Sonoma	C	86

This ambitious producer is clearly aiming for a French style of wine. The wines have fallen just short of outstanding, and if Domaine de Clarck can find a way to get more concentration in its wines, this will be one of California's most interesting sources of Pinot Noir and Chardonnay. The Pinot Noirs possess very burgundian noses of earth, herbs, spicy oak, and plummy, cherrylike fruit. The 1991 Pinot Noir Villages from Monterey displays a streak of herbaceousness that kept it from getting higher marks. Nevertheless, I liked the wine's texture and style. Although light in color, there is plenty of flavor, and the wine should drink well for another 4–5 years. The 1990 Pinot Noir Villages from Sonoma also exhibits considerable character; a fine cherry, berry, earthy, smoky nose; rich, medium-bodied, fleshy flavors; and good overall balance. The strong herbal element in the nose kept the 1990 Unfiltered Pinot Noir Monterey from getting an outstanding score. However, this is a rich, expansive, multidimensional wine with a gorgeous texture. My instincts suggest this winery is close to making some riveting Pinot Noirs. The 1991 Chardonnay from Monterey offers a super nose of lemons and honeyed, citrusy fruit. But in the mouth it tails off quickly to reveal a leanness and high acidity. The 1991 Premier Release, a rare, unfiltered Chardonnay, could have been outstanding, but a heavy hand with the oak resulted in a wine that was too woody. The wood dominates what appears to be attractive fruit. There is no question that this winery appears to be headed in the right direction to produce complex, elegant, flavorful wines with considerable character. Let's hope they can find a way to increase the depth of fruit.

CLINE CELLARS (SONOMA)
Côtes d'Oakley* * * *, Mourvèdre* * * *, Zinfandel* * * *

1990	Côtes d'Oakley	Contra Costa	A	87
1988	Mourvèdre	Contra Costa	C	87
1990	Oakley Cuvée (Mourvèdre)	California	B	88
1989	Oakley Cuvée	Contra Costa	B	86
1988	Oakley Cuvée	Contra Costa	B	87
1990	Zinfandel	Contra Costa	A	87
1989	Zinfandel	Contra Costa	B	87
1987	Zinfandel	Contra Costa	B	88
1990	Zinfandel Reserve	Contra Costa	B	89
1989	Zinfandel Reserve	Contra Costa	A	87

One of California's most successful "Rhône Rangers," Cline has consistently impressed me with their attractive wines. The 1990 Côtes d'Oakley succeeds in emulating a Côtes du Rhône. Juicy, succulent, robust, peppery fruitiness, with attractive weight and balance on the palate, the wine offers a soft, fleshy finish. It should be consumed over the next 3–4 years. The 1989 Oakley Cuvée, a blend of 53% Mourvèdre, 29% Carignane, and 18% Zinfandel, has a very chunky, solid, rich, full-bodied, Rhône-like personality. The big, spicy, black raspberry–, herb-scented nose is attractive, and in the mouth the full, expansive, hefty flavors offer plenty of satisfaction as well as a boatload of glycerin. Drink this full-bodied red wine over the next 3–4 years. The 1988 Oakley Cuvée, an innovative blend of 51% Mourvèdre, 30% Zinfandel, and 19% Carignane, offers a round, lusciously rich, full-bodied, gutsy wine with a great deal of extract and character. It could easily hold its own against some of the very top Côtes du Rhônes such as the Cru de Coudoulet and Fonsalette. It should continue to drink well for another 5–6 years. The 1990 is similar to both the 1988 and 1989, but even richer and more perfumed. The winery also fashions a fine Mourvèdre and enticing blends of Carignane and Zinfandel. The impressive 1988 Mourvèdre, with its French Bandollike tree-bark aroma, exhibits a spicy, ripe, black fruit character, rich, full-bodied, deep, chewy flavors, and a long, moderately tannic finish. Low yields and impeccable wine-making are all present in this impressive effort that should age nicely for 6–7 years. The 1990 Zinfandel possesses a big, briary, earthy, plumlike nose; deep, rich, full-bodied flavors; dusty tannins; and an excellent, powerful, au-thoritative finish. Not a shy Zinfandel, it offers plenty of flavor in a rustic style. Drink it over the next 6–8 years. The 1990 Zinfandel Reserve offers similar flavors, but they are more intense. It is brawny wine, not to mention chewy, fleshy, and slightly higher in alcohol, with considerable density and richness. Fortunately none of the raisiny, pruny, late-harvest character is evident. This impressive Zinfandel may ultimately merit an outstanding score. Drink it over the next decade. The 1989 Zinfandel displayed a big, berry-scented, spicy nose; ripe, very full-bodied flavors; excellent concentration; and intense, berry fruit. The 1989 Zinfandel Reserve is a full-bodied, robust, hefty wine with im-pressive color, a pungent, peppery, black raspberry–scented nose, and spicy, chewy flavors. It possesses enough tannin, glycerin, and overall depth to pro-vide delicious drinking for at least another decade. Cline Cellars also pro-duced a gorgeously pure, velvet-textured, rich, impressive 1987 Zinfandel that should drink beautifully for another 5–6 years.

CLOS DU BOIS WINERY (SONOMA)

Cabernet Sauvignon* * *, Chardonnay Barrel-Fermented* * *,
Chardonnay Calcaire* * */* * * *, Chardonnay Flintwood* * */* * * *,
Briarcrest* * *, Marlstone* * *, Merlot* * *, Sauvignon Blanc* * * *

1991	Chardonnay Calcaire	Alexander Valley	D	90
1990	Chardonnay Calcaire	Alexander Valley	D	88
1991	Chardonnay Flintwood	Dry Creek	D	90
1990	Chardonnay Flintwood	Dry Creek	D	88
1990	Merlot	Sonoma	C	86
1992	Sauvignon Blanc Barrel-Fermented	Alexander Valley	A	87

After some indifferent performances in the late eighties, it is good to see this Sonoma winery get back on track with these excellent vineyard-designated Chardonnays. Both the 1990 and 1991 Flintwood *cuvées* possess excellent focus, a rich, toasty, smoky, mineral, applelike fruitiness, medium to full body, and admirable ripeness and length. The 1991 is slightly richer, with a longer finish. Both wines should be drunk within 4 years of the vintage. In contrast, the 1991 and 1990 Calcaire Chardonnays are bigger, more obvious, tropical fruit–dominated wines. The fully mature 1990 is rich and supple, with luscious fruit. It is ideal for drinking over the next year. The 1991 combines richness with elegance, but the toasty, tropical fruit character is quite evident. Drink the 1991 over the next 2 years. The 1992 Sauvignon Blanc is a gorgeously up-front, effusively fruity, seductive wine that is bursting with melony fruit. The overall impression is one of freshness, liveliness, and lusty, heady fruit. Drink it over the next year. This is a hedonistic Sauvignon. It is a shame that the sen-sational 1990 Marlstone and 1990 Briarcrest Cabernet-based wines will not be released until the end of 1994. In the meantime, readers should try the deli-cious, somewhat commercial yet richly fruity, fleshy, in-your-face 1990 Mer-lot. There is 20% Cabernet Sauvignon in the blend to give the wine more definition. This is a juicy, succulent, richly fruity Merlot that is fun to drink. It should be consumed over the next 2–3 years. Clos du Bois also produces a cloying, flabby, uninteresting Gewürztraminer, a delicious, inexpensive, herbal, fruity Sauvignon Blanc, and a good, soft berry-flavored Zinfandel. There are also small quantities of Pinot Noir, but the vintages I have tasted (1986, 1987, 1988, and 1989) were blatantly vegetal, thin, and simple.

CLOS PEGASE (NAPA)
Cabernet Sauvignon* *, Chardonnay* *, Clos Pegase Proprietary Red Wine* *, Merlot* *, Sauvignon Blanc* *

1986	Cabernet Franc	California	C	70
1987	Cabernet Sauvignon	Napa	C	76
1990	Chardonnay	Napa	B	82
1989	Chardonnay	Napa	B	81
1988	Clos Pegaso Proprietary Red Wine	Napa	C	78
1988	Hommage Proprietary Red Wine	Napa	C	67
1989	Merlot	Napa	C	65
1986	Merlot	Napa	C	79

Perhaps it is symptomatic of winemaking in the New World, but I am sure I am not the only one who questions the priorities of this producer, who first built an ostentatious winery/art museum and *then* began to think about making wine. To date, virtually everything coming out of Clos Pegase has ranged in quality from below average to average. Once again the obsession with making technically perfect but excessively acidic, neutral-tasting wines that only a non-wine-consuming oenologist could like has dominated the winemaking philosophy. Caveat emptor.

CLOS DU VAL WINE CO. (NAPA)
Cabernet Sauvignon* *, Cabernet Sauvignon Reserve* * */* * * *, Chardonnay* *, Merlot* * *, Pinot Noir* *, Semillon* *, Zinfandel* * *

1989	Cabernet Sauvignon	Stag's Leap	C	79
1988	Cabernet Sauvignon	Stag's Leap	C	80
1986	Cabernet Sauvignon	Napa	C	87
1990	Chardonnay	Carneros	C	70
1989	Chardonnay	Carneros	C	68
1987	Merlot	Napa	C	85
1988	Zinfandel	Napa	B	82
1987	Zinfandel	Napa	B	87

This Franco-American operation burst on the scene 20 years ago with some highly successful wines. Early vintages of Clos du Val's Cabernet Sauvignon, particularly 1973 and 1974, were rich, complex wines that have gracefully stood the taste of time. The winery added a blockbuster Zinfandel to its portfolio, as well as Chardonnay, Semillon, and Pinot Noir. Frenchman Bernard

Portet obviously has considerable talent, but apparently a decision was made in the late 1970s and early 1980s to go to a safer, more restrained and polite style of wines. That decision is hard to justify given the success Clos du Val enjoyed in the early 1970s. Clos du Val may be returning to a richer style, if some of the ripe vintages of the mid-1980s are any indication. Although more delicate, the Cabernet Sauvignon can be good. The Zinfandel may be the winery's most underrated offering. The Chardonnays have continued to be disappointingly thin, acidic, and flavorless. Despite raves from the West Coast press, the Pinot Noir is an innocuous wine with no bouquet (a shame for a wine made from this varietal) and straightforward, clipped flavors. I suspect the 1988 Clos du Val Zinfandel could have been a terrific wine, given the fact that there is still plenty of body, glycerin, and alcohol left in the mouth. But, lamentably, the wine has only a faint aroma, having been stripped by multiple filtrations. The color is a brilliant, polished, medium ruby/garnet. In the mouth the wine is broad shouldered and full bodied, but monolithic and straightforward. I suspect this wine was terrific before it was sterile filtered at bottling. Now it is barely above average. Drink it over the next 4–5 years. The big, rich, curranty, smooth-as-silk 1987 Zinfandel offers a full-intensity, black fruit–scented bouquet and a lush, heady finish. Precocious in taste, with gobs of Zinfandel fruit, it should be drunk over the next 4–5 years. An excellent Cabernet Sauvignon, the 1986 should continue to drink well for at least a decade. It displays a deep ruby color, a moderately intense, spicy, toasty, blackcurrant-scented bouquet, excellent concentration, fine balance, extract, and a smooth finish. Here is another very good 1987 Merlot from a highly regarded vintage. The nose offers up rich, plummy, berry fruit flavors. On the palate the wine is silky, medium bodied, and delicious to drink. Restaurants should stock up on this wine, which is ideal for consuming over the next 5–6 years.

B. R. COHN (SONOMA)
Cabernet Sauvignon Olive Hill Vineyard* * * *,
Chardonnay Olive Hill Vineyard* * *, Merlot* *

1989	Cabernet Sauvignon Olive Hill Vineyard	Sonoma	C	89
1988	Cabernet Sauvignon Olive Hill Vineyard	Sonoma	C	88
1987	Cabernet Sauvignon Olive Hill Vineyard	Sonoma	C	88
1986	Cabernet Sauvignon Olive Hill Vineyard	Sonoma	C	90
1988	Cabernet Sauvignon Silver Label	Sonoma	D	75
1991	Chardonnay	Sonoma	C	87
1990	Chardonnay Olive Hill Vineyard	Sonoma	B	86
1989	Chardonnay Olive Hill Vineyard	Sonoma	B	72
1989	Merlot	Napa	B	68

This winery burst on the scene in the mid-1980s with a spectacular 1984 Cabernet Sauvignon from the Olive Hill Vineyard. That was followed by terrific Cabernets in 1985. Since then this vineyard has produced a succession of top-flight Cabernets, so it is apparent that B. R. Cohn is one of Sonoma's, as well as one of California's, finest Cabernet Sauvignon producers. The winery tends to gussy up its Cabernet Sauvignons with gobs of sexy, toasty, smoky new oak, which gives the wines remarkable up-front appeal. Of course, they would not have that appeal unless there was enough underlying rich cassis fruit to stand up to all the wood. The 1987 is a flashy, dramatic, but very oaky, ripe style of Cabernet that should drink well for the next 7–8 years. I do not think, however, that the wine is up to the splendid quality of the 1984 (the best wine the winery has produced) or the 1985. The 1986 exhibits wonderfully rich, opulent fruit, full body, a lovely toasty oakiness, and a deep, long finish. **Anticipated maturity: Now–2000.** The top-notch 1989 falls just short of being profound. The color is an opaque, deep ruby/purple, and the nose offers up a classic combination of cassis, spices, herbs, and toasty new oak. In the mouth there is wonderful intensity, medium- to full-bodied richness, soft tannins, fine depth, and excellent length. Approachable now, this wine should easily age for a decade. The fleshy, seductive 1988 gets my nod as one of the best Cabernet Sauvignons I have tasted from that vintage. It is dark ruby/purple, with an intense, roasted bouquet of herbs, blackcurrants, leather, and cedar; in the mouth there is a deep core of richly extracted fruit, full body, gobs of spicy new oak, and a long, very flattering, silky-textured, smooth finish. Delicious at present, this wine should continue to drink well for the next 7–8 years. B. R. Cohn's Chardonnay has been more irregular, with a disappointing 1989, a very good 1990, and a 1991 that is plump, rich, and tasty, with good varietal fruit. I have never tasted any of the tiny quantity of Pinot Noir made by B. R. Cohn, nor its sparkling wine called Platinum.

RATINGS FOR OLDER VINTAGES OF B. R. COHN CABERNET SAUVIGNON OLIVE HILL VINEYARD: 1985 (91), 1984 (92)

CONGRESS SPRINGS WINERY (SANTA CLARA)
Chardonnay* *

Congress Springs Winery is in a state of flux. Dan Gehrs, the winemaker responsible for making Congress Springs competitive and producing a number of top-notch Chardonnays, including a Reserve *cuvée* and a single-vineyard *cuvée* from the Monmartre vineyard, left to start his own enterprise. Financial difficulties caused many grape growers to take a controlling interest in Congress Springs in the late 1980s. That group, collectively called Anglo-American Agriculture, is now completely revamping the line of wines, with an emphasis on inexpensive Chardonnay. The first releases, 1990 and 1991, were pleasant, but dull and unexciting. Additionally, other wines, such as Pinot Blanc and Pinot Noir, have been unsuccessful. Time will tell. There appears to be plenty of potential given the access to some excellent grape sources.

CONN CREEK WINERY (NAPA)
Cabernet Sauvignon* *, Chardonnay* *

Other than barrel samples of the 1989 and 1990 vintages, I have not seen any Cabernet Sauvignons or Chardonnays from Conn Creek since 1988. This winery's track record during the 1980s was poor. The original owners, the Collins family, marketed one of the all-time great Cabernet Sauvignons, the 1974 Cabernet from Milton Eisele's vineyard in Calistoga. They also made top-notch Cabernets and Zinfandels in 1976 and 1978. However, the 1980s produced a string of fluid, disjointed wines that ended up undermining the financial stability of the winery, which was sold to the huge Washington State conglomerate called Stimson Lane (owners of Château Ste.-Michelle and Napa Valley's Villa

Mt. Eden). Reports continue to circulate that better wines will emanate from Conn Creek. Certainly the barrel samples I have tasted suggest that the quality has at least moved from below average to average. Nevertheless, whether it is the Barrel-Select Cabernet Sauvignon or the Private Reserve Cabernet Sauvignon, the wines leave a great deal to be desired. The Chardonnays have been marked by too much acidity and oak and insufficient fruit and concentration. I have not seen a Zinfandel from Conn Creek in years, which is a shame because their Zinfandel came from a magnificent vineyard near Calistoga with exceptionally old vines (it was planted during the 1930s).

CORISON (NAPA)
Cabernet Sauvignon* * *

1991	Cabernet Sauvignon	Napa	C	87
1990	Cabernet Sauvignon	Napa	C	87
1989	Cabernet Sauvignon	Napa	C	83
1988	Cabernet Sauvignon	Napa	C	84
1987	Cabernet Sauvignon	Napa	C	85

I suspect I am in a minority with respect to the wines of Corison, which have played to good reviews in many quarters. What I have noticed is an excessive stylization resulting in streamlined wines that appear to be relatively straightforward and too acidic and lean, with high, relatively abrasive tannins in the finish. Although the quality of the fruit is impressive (there is certainly good ripeness), my instincts suggest the wines are too processed and manipulated. The best wines to date are the 1991 and 1990. Less opaquely colored than many other 1990s, the restrained, medium-bodied 1990 Cabernet offers pure cassis flavors allied with toasty oak, fine ripeness and body, and moderate alcohol and tannin in the finish. Rich and straightforward, it is slightly less intense and complex than several of its peers. The 1991 has medium body, excellent deep ruby color, deep, rich, ripe cassis flavors, and moderately high acidity. It should be at its best between 1995 and 2005.

COSENTINO WINE COMPANY (NAPA)
Cabernet Sauvignon* * *, Chardonnay* *, The Poet* * *

1989	Cabernet Sauvignon	Napa	C	82
1988	Cabernet Sauvignon	North Coast	C	80
1987	Cabernet Sauvignon	North Coast	C	77
1985	Cabernet Sauvignon Reserve	North Coast	C	88
1991	Chardonnay	California	B	79
1990	Chardonnay The Sculptor	Napa	C	78
1989	Chardonnay The Sculptor	Napa	C	76
1989	The Poet	California	C	82
1988	The Poet	California	C	77
1987	The Poet	California	C	83
1986	The Poet	California	C	88

The red wines are hardly classics, yet one has to admire the fact that Mitch Cosentino is not afraid to give the wine consumer some serious flavor. In addition, he throws in a hefty amount of spicy new oak. These are clearly wines to drink young, preferably within the first 6–8 years of the vintage. The 1985 Cabernet Sauvignon Reserve offers a plentiful mouthful of plump, chewy, lush blackcurrant fruit backed up by lavish amounts of toasty, spicy oak. Elegant . . . no, but hedonistic, yes. This full-bodied, juicy, succulent wine will drink well for the next 4–5 years. The 1986 The Poet, a blend of 58% Cabernet Sauvignon, 22% Cabernet Franc, and 20% Merlot, is similarly bold, flashy, chewy, and immensely enjoyable for drinking over the next 5–6 years. Its deep ruby/purple color, big, sweet, oaky, plummy bouquet, long, luxurious flavors, and layers of fruit and oak are sure to make this wine a big hit with consumers. As good as the 1986 The Poet and the 1985 Reserve Cabernet are, Cosentino's efforts with this varietal in 1987, 1988, and 1989 have generally resulted in excessively oaked, mediocre wines. Why they do not possess the fruit and substance to balance out the wood as 1986 and 1985 did is difficult to fathom. Certainly the 1988 and 1989 vintages were far more troublesome. Also, Cosentino relies on purchased grapes to make his wines. The Chardonnays, which are blatantly overoaked, are hollow in the middle, with the fruit tending to dry out at an accelerated pace. Cosentino also produced a proprietary red wine called Cos, but litigation from Bordeaux's famed Château Cos d'Estournel torpedoed the use of this name. From time to time a medium-bodied, pleasant Merlot is produced, the last vintage of merit being 1986. This winery, which started off with such promise, seems to be in a slump at present.

COTTONWOOD CANYON (SAN LUIS OBISPO)
Chardonnay* *, Pinot Noir* */* * *

1989	Chardonnay	Central Coast	B 85
1989	Chardonnay Barrel Select	Santa Barbara	C 87
1989	Pinot Noir	Santa Barbara	D 84

The only releases I have tasted from Cottonwood Canyon were two *cuvées* of 1989 Chardonnay, one from the central coast and one called Barrel Select. Both wines had a lot of fruit and ripeness, as well as big, honeyed, bold flavors. This could be a promising source for Chardonnay. Cottonwood Canyon is believed to be an up-and-coming specialist in Pinot Noir. The only vintage I have tasted, 1989, displayed good fruit, attractive, jammy, cherry fruit flavors, spicy oak, and hard tannins in the compact finish.

H. COTURRI AND SONS (SONOMA)
Alicante Bouchet Ubaldi Vineyard* * *,
Cabernet Sauvignon Remick Vineyard* * * *, Zinfandel Chauvet Vineyard* * * *

1992	Alicante Bouschet Ubaldi Vineyard	Sonoma	B 87
1990	Cabernet Sauvignon Remick Vineyard	Sonoma	B 90
1991	Zinfandel Chauvet Vineyard	Sonoma	B 87
1990	Zinfandel Chauvet Vineyard	Sonoma	B 91

Warning: Lovers of Velveeta cheese, Muzak, and sterile wines with no bouquet or personality should avoid this! California's league of wine writers/technocrats who look only for the technical faults in a wine rather than its pleasure-giving qualities should have a field day ripping these wines apart. But if wine is meant to be appreciated for its individuality, as well as for pleasure, then who can fail to admire what this winery has achieved? Coturri believes in organically farmed vineyards, and their wines can, from time to time, be eccentric, if not bizarre. This 1990 Zinfandel is neither, but its 15.1% alcohol and slight whiff of volatile acidity will unnerve puritanical technocrats incapable of understanding wines that have more to their bouquets than wood and simplistic black or red fruits. This is a Zinfandel with a profound peppery, hickory-, mineral-, licorice-scented nose, clearly a winter-weight offering that should be served with intensely aromatic and flavored stews or dishes. Amazingly, the high alcohol is concealed by the extraordinary richness of fruit, which, along with the wine's expansive palate, makes for an extraordinary tasting and drinking experience. I suggest decanting this wine for at least an hour before drinking. A heavy sediment is likely to emerge in the bottle with several more years of cellaring. I would not be surprised to see this wine drink well for at least 10–12 years. The more civilized 1991 Zinfandel Chauvet Vineyard is softer, more flattering, and less opaquely colored, as well as less powerful and concentrated when compared with the blockbuster 1990. Coturri's 1990 Cabernet Sauvignon Remick Vineyard is closer to the modern-day image of a California Cabernet than its other wines. It reveals an opaque, thick plum/purple color, a spicy, black cherry–, earthy-scented nose, and unctuous, viscous, rich flavors that offer spicy, clove, truffle, and cherry/black-raspberry fruit. There is superb density, fine balance, and a long finish covering what appears to be high but ripe tannin. The wine will need to be decanted as it will no doubt deposit considerable sediment. If you do not like an intense perfume of earthy, olive, cedary scents in Cabernet Sauvignon, try another producer's more straightforward, politically correct example. Coturri's 1990 Cabernet should last for 10–15 years. The 1992 Alicante Bouschet Ubaldi Vineyard is one of the most concentrated red wines I have ever tasted. Although not particularly complex, it boasts an opulent texture and enormous richness of fruit and depth. It is not so much unusual as just overwhelmingly rich, thick, and big. This wine will make a great complement to a winter-weight stew, soup, or aromatic cheeses. Coturri also produces a dense but heavy Pinot Noir and, occasionally, Chardonnay. I have not seen any of these wines for a number of years, but my notes suggest that the stars of their portfolio are their exotic Zinfandel and Cabernet Sauvignon.

CRICHTON HALL VINEYARD (NAPA)
Chardonnay* * * *

| 1991 Chardonnay | Napa | C | 89 |

This powerful, authoritatively flavored 1991 Chardonnay exhibits a nice touch of toasty new oak, rich, full-bodied, buttery, applelike flavors, considerable depth and richness, zesty underlying acidity, and a solid inner core of extraction and flavor. The finish is deep and spicy. This is an admirable wine that should age well for 1–2 years.

CRONIN VINEYARDS (SAN MATEO)
Cabernet Sauvignon* *, Chardonnay Cuvées* * * *, Pinot Noir* *,
Sauvignon Blanc* * * *

1988	Cabernet Sauvignon	Santa Cruz Mountains	C	52
1989	Cabernet Sauvignon	Robinson Vineyard	C	62
1989	Chardonnay	Alexander Valley	C	86
1988	Chardonnay	Napa	C	88
1990	Chardonnay	Napa	C	87
1990	Chardonnay	Santa Cruz Mountains	C	78
1990	Chardonnay	Stuhlmuller Vineyard	C	87
1990	Chardonnay Joe's Cuvée	California	C	75
1990	Chardonnay Ventana Vineyards	Monterey	C	86
1988	Chardonnay Ventana Vineyards	Monterey	C	90
1987	Chardonnay Ventana Vineyards	Monterey	C	91
1988	Pinot Noir Martinrue Vineyard	Santa Cruz	C	74
1990	Sauvignon Blanc	Napa	B	89

This winery made many terrific Chardonnays during the 1980s. In 1984, 1985, 1986, 1987, and 1988 a succession of Chardonnays from Alexander Valley, Napa Valley, and Ventana Vineyards were exciting examples of the barrel-fermented, *sur-lie* style of Chardonnay. For that reason I am perplexed by the quality of the 1989s and the inconsistent 1990s. Certainly 1989 was a difficult vintage for Chardonnay producers, but 1990 was one of the best Chardonnay vintages in the last 10 years, and Cronin's performance is disheartening. The lack of fruit, rather muted character of the wines, and the shortness and deficiencies in several of their 1990 Chardonnays must be a shock to all who have enjoyed the many wonderful Chardonnays made by Cronin in the 1980s. The winery has always had a problem with its red wines. The Cabernet Sauvignons are frightfully acidic, empty, and astringently tannic. There is no pleasure to be found in these lean, high-acid, charmless wines. Although somewhat better, the Pinot Noir is vegetal, with plenty of smoky oak and entirely too much acidity and tannin for its feeble fruitiness.

CUTLER CELLAR (SONOMA)
Cabernet Sauvignon* *

1987	Cabernet Sauvignon Batto Ranch	Sonoma	C	85
1986	Cabernet Sauvignon Batto Ranch	Sonoma	C	84

This small operation, run by the winemaker for Sonoma's Gundlach-Bundschu Winery, has turned out compact but deeply colored wines with a pronounced herbal, oaky, cassis character. They are stylistic and elegant but lack richness and intensity. Both the 1986 and 1987 Batto Ranch Cabernets exhibit plenty of herbal, chocolatey fruit, tannin, and acidity. Both are candidates for drinking over the next 7–8 years.

CUVAISON (NAPA)
Cabernet Sauvignon* * *, Chardonnay* *

1988	Cabernet Sauvignon	Napa	C	75
1987	Cabernet Sauvignon	Napa	C	86
1985	Cabernet Sauvignon	Napa	C	86
1990	Chardonnay	Carneros	C	80
1989	Chardonnay	Napa	C	77
1989	Merlot	Napa	C	82

Cuvaison, which owns significant vineyard holdings in the Carneros region and is well funded, appears poised to turn out better wines than what has emerged to date. The winery's Chardonnays have become lighter, presumably more elegant and less woody, but the depth of fruit is often questionable. Although pleasant, the 1990 is tart and understated to the point of being bland. The 1989 reveals the dilution caused by the significant rainfall that occurred during the harvest. Cuvaison's Cabernet Sauvignons have moved from a rich, thick, tannic style in the 1970s to a lighter format that emphasizes near-term drinking. To date the wines have been straightfoward, fruity, and supple, but they give no signs of being either complex or long-lived. For the price, consumers should expect more.

DALLA VALLE VINEYARDS (NAPA)
Cabernet Sauvignon* * * *, Maya Proprietary Red Wine* * * * *

1990	Cabernet Sauvignon	Napa	D	93
1989	Cabernet Sauvignon	Napa	D	85
1988	Cabernet Sauvignon Estate	Napa	D	90
1987	Cabernet Sauvignon Estate	Napa	D	89
1990	Maya Proprietary Red Table Wine	Napa	D	94
1989	Maya Proprietary Red Table Wine	Napa	D	87
1988	Maya Proprietary Red Table Wine	Napa	D	93

This tiny producer has burst on the scene with some extraordinary wines. The 1990 Cabernet Sauvignon reveals an astonishingly deep color, as well as a huge aroma of smoky cassis, chocolate, and licorice. In the mouth it is a powerful wine, with great stuffing, wonderful structure, enough acid and tannin to frame the wine's immense size, and a formidable finish. I was told the yields were a minuscule 2 tons per acre. Although it should not be drunk before the mid- to late- 1990s, it has the potential easily to last for 20 years. The 1987 Cabernet Sauvignon Estate, a black/ruby/purple-colored wine, exhibits a touch of oak, but the overall impression is one of rich, full-bodied, intensely concentrated fruit wrapped in toasty French oak, with decent acidity as well as a long, moderately tannic, youthful finish. This very impressive wine needs 3–4 years to develop; it will last for 10–15 or more years. Even more impressive is the 1988, a vintage in which few California wineries made profound Cabernet Sauvignon. The 1988 Cabernet Sauvignon Estate is black/ruby/purple, has exceptional concentration, a huge bouquet of superripe cassis and minerals, and a long, full-bodied, concentrated palate and finish. Still amazingly young, with none of the precocious, supple, light-bodied, soft fruit of so many other wines from the 1988 vintage, this standout should be at its best between 1994 and 2010. The 1990 Maya, a proprietary red wine (named after the proprietor's daughter) of almost equal proportions of Cabernet Franc and Cabernet Sauvignon, is a monster in the making. Its supersaturated, opaque black/ruby color is followed by a tight but promising nose of earth, cassis, smoke, and gobs of sweet fruit. In the mouth it is even richer, as well as more tannic, than the regular Cabernet. The finish is long, sweet, and compelling. The 1988 Maya, made from a blend of 55% Cabernet Sauvignon and 45% Cabernet Franc, has a dense, very opaque black/purple color and a huge bouquet of superripe cassis, licorice, and vanillin aromas, followed by astonishingly intense, highly extracted, impeccably well-balanced, full-bodied flavors. The bad news is that only 200 cases were produced, so latching on to a bottle or two will not be easy. It should drink well over the next 20–25 years, probably longer. Dalla Valle's only Cabernets that are less than stellar, but still very good, are their two 1989s. Given the vintage, they are powerful and tannic, but not as concentrated in extract or fruit. It remains to be seen how they will age. If the fruit holds up and the tannins melt away, my ratings will look conservative. This new winery appears to be making super wines that merit significant interest by connoisseurs of Cabernet Sauvignon. They are not easygoing, forward, commercial wines meant to be drunk upon release, but, rather, deeply extracted, individualistic wines for long-term cellaring. Bravo to proprietor Gustave Dalla Valle for this super expression of California, and particularly Napa Valley Cabernet Sauvignon.

THE JOHN DANIEL SOCIETY (NAPA)
Dominus Proprietary Red Wine* * * * *

1991	Dominus	Napa	D	99
1990	Dominus	Napa	D	97
1989	Dominus	Napa	D	94
1988	Dominus	Napa	D	92
1987	Dominus	Napa	D	96
1986	Dominus	Napa	D	91

The John Daniel Society, a partnership of Californians Robin Lail and Marcia Smith and Frenchman Christian Moueix, was founded in 1982. Their wine, called Dominus, is produced from a renowned Napa Valley vineyard called Napanook, just to the west of Yountville.

Christian Moueix, who oversees the winemaking of such Bordeaux superstars as Pétrus, Trotanoy, Latour à Pomerol, and Magdelaine, has used traditional Bordeaux techniques to produce a world-class Cabernet-based wine. His winemaking philosophy calls for minimal intervention. The reaction to Dominus has been surprisingly controversial. Moueix has had the courage to employ traditional French winemaking techniques with Napa Valley grapes. During a trip to California, one well-known Cabernet Sauvignon producer said, "Who does he think he is to believe French techniques can be made to work with Napa Cabernet?" A wine writer for the *Los Angeles Times* went so far as to suggest that Dominus is a flawed wine. Other writers have been less foolish, but criticisms that the wines are "too tannic" and "different" are widespread, particularly among the West Coast wine press. There is no question that in a tasting of California Cabernets, Dominus offers a distinctively different aromatic and flavor profile. I believe that anyone who has had experience tasting world-class wines would consider the wine prodigious. Dominus tastes as if it were made in France, which is no small accomplishment. That Moueix and his two California assistant winemakers, Daniel Baron and Christopher Phelps, have refused to employ a formula to manufacture their wine must be unsettling to oenologists who rely on centrifuges, acid additions, and sterile filters to sculpture a wine. Moueix follows such traditional practices as (1) severe crop thinning to ensure conservative yields, (2) a late harvest to obtain physiologically ripe grapes, (3) minimal or no acid adjustments, (4) the avoidance of sterile filtration that can eviscerate and denude a wine, and (5) the refusal to rely on a heavy cosmetic overlay of toasty new oak to flatter provincial wine journalists. This renowned Frenchman and his Bordeaux-trained assistants have done something few others have managed to achieve in California—they have fashioned an immensely complex, compellingly rich and elegant wine with profound aromatic and flavor dimension. Moueix has broken the standard operating rules of California viticultural management and winemaking and has produced a wine of historic significance that is simply more majestic than most others. His contribution to Napa Valley's prestige merits accolades, not envy and jealousy. If Dominus is to be considered controversial, it is, I suppose, because of the portraits of Moueix that appear on the labels (a different artist, a different visage). They are, to my knowledge, unprecedented in label design.

May I boldly suggest that the 1991 is reminiscent of the 1982, 1989, and 1990 Pétrus? There is no Merlot in the blend, yet the wine possesses extraordinary intensity and a portlike viscosity and richness, phenomenal fruit extraction, a huge aroma of roasted cassis fruit, an unctuous, rich, full-bodied palate, and a spectacularly long, superrich finish. The tannins remain concealed behind the wine's wealth of fruit. This wine exhibits enormous potential; one of the greatest red wines produced anywhere in the world, it should last for 15–20 or more years. Interestingly, because of the tiny crop in Pomerol, Moueix shipped some of his unused new casks to California for Dominus. Consequently, 50% new oak barrels were used in 1991. Total production is not yet certain, as barrels deemed not worthy will be eliminated, but should approximate 5,000–7,000 cases. The 1990 Dominus nose offers thrilling aromas of ripe cassis, spices, and minerals. In the mouth there is gorgeous richness, a full-bodied, stunningly extracted midpalate, and a dazzlingly long, moderately tannic finish. Again, the sweet, rich fruit is lavishly displayed. I do not think the 1990 has quite the weight of the 1991, but it is still a brilliantly made, complex wine with extraordinary aromatic and flavor dimension. Again, it tastes more like an opulent Pomerol than a California Cabernet. **Anticipated maturity: Now–2008.** The 1989 is undoubtedly the Cabernet Sauvignon of the vintage. The color is a dark ruby/purple, and the nose offers up sweet, fragrant scents of black fruits, cedar, herbs, and spicy wood. In the mouth there is extraordinary concentration, medium to full body, and an authoritatively rich, lingering finish. *Terroir*ists will have a difficult time explaining why the wine tastes more like a Pomerol than Napa Cabernet. Interestingly, Moueix said the key to his success in 1989 was to wait 6 to 7 days after the rains had stopped before harvesting so the vines could shed their excess moisture. The 7,000

cases of this wine that were produced will be released in the fall of 1993. The 1988 has to be among the top two or three Cabernets of the vintage. Other than 1983, the 3,300 cases produced in 1988 is the smallest production of Dominus to date, as over half the crop was deemed unsatisfactory. The wine, released in October 1992, was made with 25% new oak. The dense, opaque ruby/purple color exhibits great saturation and intensity, and the nose is beginning to offer up smoked herb and ripe cassis aromas. In the mouth the wine is deep, medium to full bodied, with excellent concentration and one of the longest, richest finishes I have found in a Cabernet Sauvignon from 1988. The tannins are noticeable but softer than in the 1989 or 1987. Of all the current Dominus offerings, I suspect the 1988 and 1984 are the most flattering to drink at present. Nevertheless, this wine should easily evolve for another 10–15 years or more. There were 6,500 cases produced of the 1987 Dominus, one of the great wines of the vintage in a year when a handful of California producers made profound Cabernets (including the Robert Mondavi Reserve, Dunn Howell Mountain, and Château Montelena). The wine is beginning to shut down, but it still displays a rich ruby color and an intensely spicy, fragrant nose of toasty vanillin oak, cassis, and cedar. In the mouth this medium- to full-bodied wine displays considerable tannins, fine integrated acidity, and an opulent, rich, spicy finish. I would suggest cellaring it for another 3–4 years; it should easily keep through the first decade of the next century. Along with the 1988 and 1984, the 1986, of which 6,500 cases were produced, is one of the more precocious and flattering vintages of Dominus. The wine offers a nose of black fruits (black cherries in particular), spices, cedar, and Provençal herbs. In the mouth the wine exhibits excellent opulence, is slightly lighter and less concentrated than either the 1987 or 1985, and finishes with a clean, satiny mouth-feel. Approachable now, this wine should continue to evolve for another 12–15 years.
RATINGS FOR OLDER VINTAGES OF THE JOHN DANIEL SOCIETY DOMINUS: 1985 (96), 1984 (90), 1983 (90)

DE LOACH VINEYARDS (SONOMA)

Cabernet Sauvignon* *, Chardonnay* * *, Chardonnay O.F.S.* * * *,
Fumé Blanc* * *, Gewürztraminer* *, Zinfandel Estate* * *,
Zinfandel O.F.S.* * * *, Zinfandel Single-Vineyard Cuvées* * * *

Year	Wine	Region		
1989	Cabernet Sauvignon	Russian River	C	80
1991	Chardonnay	Russian River	B	83
1990	Chardonnay	Russian River	C	87
1991	Chardonnay O.F.S.	Russian River	D	90
1990	Chardonnay O.F.S.	Russian River	C	90
1991	Fumé Blanc	Russian River	A	83
1990	Gewürztraminer Early Harvest	Russian River	A	70
1991	Zinfandel Barbieri Ranch	Sonoma	B	86
1990	Zinfandel Estate Russian River Valley	Sonoma	B	86
1991	Zinfandel Estate Papera Ranch	Sonoma	B	87
1990	Zinfandel Estate Papera Ranch	Sonoma	B	86

1991	Zinfandel Estate Pelletti Ranch	Sonoma	B	85
1990	Zinfandel Estate Pelletti Ranch	Sonoma	B	88

De Loach produces a bevy of tasty wines, the most successful of which are their slightly sweet but rich, voluptuous Chardonnays and classy, spicy, richly fruity Zinfandels. The disappointments include an insipid Gewürztraminer, and although I have not seen a vintage in more than 4 years, the Pinot Noirs have been excessively herbaceous and thin. Additionally, De Loach's Cabernet Sauvignon could possess more character and richness. The Chardonnay O.F.S from De Loach has consistently been a rich, opulent, slightly sweet style of Chardonnay with gobs of fruit. Although the 1990 is no exception, I sense more structure in this vintage than in previous renditions. The unctuous, opulent fruit, chewy texture, and buttery, tropical fruit flavors are abundantly displayed. Take advantage of all the pleasure-giving qualities of this Chardonnay and consume it over the next year. The 1991 O.F.S. is also a lavish, rich wine, with crisper acids than the 1990. Most consumers are familiar with the slightly sweet, richly fruity style of De Loach Chardonnays, but their high-quality 1990 Zinfandels should put this winery on the map. The 1990 Russian River Valley Estate reveals a textbook Zinfandel nose of black pepper and berry fruit, medium to full body, a sense of elegance, and an attractive, smooth finish. It will not make old bones, but it should drink well for 4–5 years. The best of this trio is the 1990 Zinfandel Pelletti Ranch. The color is a saturated, deep ruby/purple, and the nose offers up a ripe, intense perfume of black raspberries, vanilla, herbs, and crushed black peppers. Rich and full bodied, with gobs of luscious black fruit, this is a lavishly rich yet well-balanced Zinfandel for drinking over the next 7–8 years. The 1990 Papera Ranch does not possess quite the intensity of the Pelletti Ranch. It appears to more closely resemble the Russian River Valley Estate Zinfandel. Displaying fine ripeness, a good berry, spicy, peppery nose, excellent purity and cleanliness, as well as a medium-bodied finish, it should drink well for 5–6 years. The 1991 releases are also very good. The best of the three I tasted is the 1991 Papera Ranch Zinfandel, which exhibits more rich, briary fruit and length. The lightest *cuvée* is the tasty but tart, medium-bodied 1991 Pelletti Ranch Zinfandel. Last is an attractively priced, light-style Fumé Blanc, of which the 1991 is a crisp, herbaceous, fruity example. De Loach is to be commended for the reasonable prices and generally fine quality of its wines.

DEER PARK WINERY (NAPA)
Zinfandel* * * *

1990	Zinfandel Reserve Beatty Ranch	Howell Mountain	C	86

I would not be surprised to see this 1990 Zinfandel merit a higher rating in 4–5 years. Typical of many of the Howell Mountain wines, there are gobs of tannin, resulting in an overall impression of tightness and a muscular, backward style. Airing and introspection reveal the ripe black raspberry fruit intermingled with scents and flavors of minerals. Though there is fine balance, at present this wine tastes as if much of its charm and fruit has been harnessed by the wine's structure. Do not be surprised to see a much more flattering and supple wine in 5–6 years.

DEHLINGER WINERY (SONOMA)

Cabernet Sauvignon* * *, Chardonnay* * * *, Merlot* * *, Pinot Noir* */* * *

1988	Cabernet Sauvignon	Russian River	C	78
1985	Cabernet Sauvignon	Russian River	C	83
1986	Cabernet Sauvignon Estate	Russian River	C	86
1990	Chardonnay	Russian River	C	86
1990	Chardonnay Montrachet Cuvée	Russian River	C	87
1985	Merlot	Sonoma	C	85
1990	Pinot Noir	Russian River	C	84

The two 1990 Chardonnay offerings differ considerably in style. The 1990 Russian River is more up front, with tasty, tropical fruit, a touch of oak, spicy acidity, and excellent definition and depth. Drink it over the next 1–2 years. The 1990 Montrachet Cuvée is a more ambitious effort—richer in the nose, much more structured on the palate, with more intensity and a backward feel. Although it is slightly better, the difference in price is not totally justified. The 1985 Merlot is a very good, perhaps excellent, wine showing a fine, dark ruby color, spicy, plummy, oaky fruitiness, medium to full body, very good concentration, and immediate accessibility. It should also last 4–6 years, perhaps even improving as it ages. The 1985 Cabernet Sauvignon is a leaner wine than the Merlot and shows perhaps a bit too much oak for the amount of fruit, but I liked its elegance and style. It could have used more depth and length. It should be at its best now. The full-intensity, relatively evolved bouquet of herbs, tar, and chocolatey, currant fruit of the 1986 Cabernet Sauvignon Estate is followed by a wine that exhibits excellent ripeness, fleshy texture, full body, and at least 5–7 more years of drinkability. More recent Cabernet Sauvignons have not displayed the fruit and intensity of earlier vintages. That may be due to the fact that 1988 and 1989 were irregular, if not disappointing, years. Dehlinger also produces a variable Pinot Noir that can often be ripe, spicy, and interesting. However, like many Pinots, it has a tendency to be a trifle too vegetal. I continue to wonder why this winery does not get more good press given the consistently fine winemaking efforts it turns out.

MAISON DEUTZ WINERY (SAN LUIS OBISPO)

Sparkling Wine Cuvées* * *

N.V.	Blanc de Noir	San Luis Obispo/Santa Barbara	B	88

The nonvintage *cuvées* released by Maison Deutz, a brut and a rosé, have been crisp, pleasant, and cleanly made, although somewhat short on the palate. A real breakthrough in quality was the Blanc de Noir released in spring 1993. I have been an outspoken critic of most California sparkling wines. But Deutz's Blanc de Noir lifted my spirits—both figuratively and literally. This delicate rosé sparkling wine offers an excellent floral and berry-scented nose, fine tiny uniform-sized bubbles, a long effervescence, and medium-bodied, surprisingly rich, graceful, and elegant flavors. An excellent sparkling wine, it can easily compete with French Champagnes—something I have rarely said about California sparklers. Drink it over the next several years.

DIAMOND CREEK VINEYARDS (NAPA)

Single-Vineyard Cabernet Sauvignons produced before 1987* * * * *,
Single-Vineyard Cabernet Sauvignons produced after 1987* */* * *

1991	Cabernet Sauvignon Gravelly Meadow	Napa	84
1990	Cabernet Sauvignon Gravelly Meadow	Napa	78
1989	Cabernet Sauvignon Gravelly Meadow	Napa	76
1987	Cabernet Sauvignon Gravelly Meadow	Napa	88
1991	Cabernet Sauvignon Red Rock Terrace	Napa	79
1990	Cabernet Sauvignon Red Rock Terrace	Napa	70
1989	Cabernet Sauvignon Red Rock Terrace	Napa	82
1987	Cabernet Sauvignon Red Rock Terrace	Napa	90
1991	Cabernet Sauvignon Volcanic Hill	Napa	82
1990	Cabernet Sauvignon Volcanic Hill	Napa	73
1989	Cabernet Sauvignon Volcanic Hill	Napa	83
1987	Cabernet Sauvignon Volcanic Hill	Napa	88
1991	Cabernet Sauvignon Three Vineyard Blend	Napa	78

Since 1988 the three vineyard-designated Cabernets from Diamond Creek have been noticeably less concentrated, too tannic, very acidic, and lacking depth. What is wrong? The most recent offerings are embarrassingly light and diluted when compared with the estate's rich, intense wines from the 1970s to the mid-1980s. Could the wines be going through a temporarily awkward stage, or are they being made in a lighter, more easily accessible style? The answer is obvious—they have changed gears to produce something shamefully one-dimensional! The 1991 Red Rock Terrace reveals sweet, leathery, smoky aromas, an austere, Bordeaux-like palate, and a medium-bodied, short finish. The somewhat cheesy, locker-room scents are surprising. Although the 1990 Red Rock Terrace offers an interesting, spicy, smoky, sweet nose, fine ripe fruit, and considerable tannins in the finish, it displays neither the midpalate nor the extraction of flavor I have come to expect from this winery. The 1989 Red Rock Terrace is extremely tannic and high in acidity, and it lacks depth and fruit. Disjointed, it is unlikely to come into balance. The 1987 Red Rock Terrace has an extra dimension of huge, cedary, weedy, blackcurrant flavors intertwined with the smell of tar and smoke. In the mouth it is deep, full bodied, and easily the most concentrated of all the 1987 Diamond Creek Cabernets. It should also prove to be extremely long-lived. **Anticipated maturity: 1997–2015.** The 1991 Volcanic Hill exhibits a stewed, leathery, spicy, herbaceous-scented nose and diffuse, watery, medium-bodied flavors. Again, some annoying off smells are present. The 1990 Volcanic Hill is also light, with an oaky, spicy nose; simple, straightforward, medium-bodied flavors; and a surprisingly short finish. I would opt for drinking it over the next 7–8 years. The 1989 Volcanic Hill is another surprisingly light, malnourished wine exhibiting little of the intensity one has come to expect from this vineyard and producer. The 1987 Volcanic Hill is a rich, tannic, muscular wine, with a smoky, broad-shouldered character, intense, full-bodied flavors, and gobs of tannin, but not the complexity one might expect from one of the leading producers of hand-crafted California Cabernet Sauvignon. The 1991 Gravelly Meadow is the most backward of the 1991s, with less evolution in its attractive, spicy, earthy, elegant nose. Its medium-bodied flavors exhibit moderate tannins and some vague earthy, ripe, sweet fruit. It should be at its best in 2–3 years and last for 10–12. The 1990 Gravelly Meadow is less endowed, with a straightforward, simple nose, disjointed flavors, high acidity, and dry, hard, nearly astringent tannins. I could not find the fruit and flesh needed to cover its framework. If the 1990 Gravelly Meadow is disappointing, so is the 1989. It is vegetal, with little depth, and its short finish suggests a lack of physiological maturity in the grapes as well as a lack of fruit. The lightest of the 1987 Diamond Creek Cabernets is the Gravelly Meadow, a stylish, earthy, medium- to full-bodied wine with some hard, raw tannins in the finish. It needs 4–5 years in the cellar to shed its tannic clout. The overall impression is one of hard-edged fruit, a lean, more restrained style, and a distinctive earthy, minerallike quality. **Anticipated maturity: 1995–2005.** The 1991 Three Vineyard Blend is also a compact, short, emaciated wine. After tasting barrel samples of the 1992s, I am convinced that Diamond Creek is in serious decline, as the 1992s were also thin, acidic, and hollow. It is sad that proprietor Al Brounstein, who did so much in the 1970s and early 1980s to produce wines of extraordinary individuality and distinction, has permitted the quality to slide so dramatically.

RATINGS FOR OLDER VINTAGES OF DIAMOND CREEK VINEYARDS CABERNET SAUVIGNONS: GRAVELLY MEADOW: 1986 (90), 1985 (90), 1984 (92), 1983 (87), 1982 (87), 1981 (89), 1980 (93), 1979 (89), 1978 (93)

RED ROCK TERRACE: 1986 (92), 1985 (90), 1984 (94), 1983 (87), 1982 (87), 1981 (90), 1979 (90), 1978 (95) 1976 (94)

VOLCANIC HILL: 1986 (92), 1985 (90), 1984 (95), 1983 (86), 1982 (87), 1981 (89), 1980 (92), 1978 (99) 1976 (95)

LAKE: 1984 (94), 1978 (98)

DRY CREEK VINEYARD (SONOMA)
Cabernet Sauvignon* */* * *, Chardonnay* *, Fumé Blanc* * * *,
Meritage* * *, Zinfandel Old Vines* * * */* * * * *

1989	Cabernet Sauvignon	Sonoma	B	80
1986	Cabernet Sauvignon	Sonoma	B	86
1990	Chardonnay Reserve	Sonoma	C	77
1991	Chenin Blanc	Dry Creek	A	84
1991	Fumé Blanc	Sonoma	A	86
1986	Meritage Red Table Wine	Sonoma	C	87
1991	Zinfandel Old Vines	Dry Creek	B	91
1990	Zinfandel Old Vines	Dry Creek	B	87
1988	Zinfandel Old Vines	Dry Creek	B	86

Dry Creek Vineyard has long been one of California's standard-bearers for crisp, elegant, and satisfying, dry Sauvignon-based wines. The 1991 Fumé Blanc continues its success with this varietal. The subtle herb-, fig-, and flint-like nose is followed by dry, medium-bodied flavors that possess remarkable clarity as well as a disarming vivaciousness. Drink this delicious wine over the next year. The immensely satisfying 1990 Zinfandel displays a dark ruby color and a big bouquet of superripe, peppery, black cherry, black raspberry, and herbal fruit. In the mouth there is excellent concentration, soft tannins, a lovely supple texture, and a smooth, velvety finish. Delicious now, it should continue to drink well for 7–8 years. The 1991 is similarly styled, but even richer and more unctuous on the palate. Although the 1988 is not as concentrated and compelling as this winery's wonderful 1987, I doubt readers will be able to resist the bright, plummy, intensely fragrant bouquet, soft, velvety-textured flavors, and exuberant, robust style of this easily gulped Zinfandel. It will not make old bones, but it will provide enjoyable drinking over the next 3–4 years. The 1986 Meritage is a significant improvement over Dry Creek's mediocre 1985. A big, flashy bouquet of blackcurrants, minerals, and spicy oak is followed by a fleshy, ripe, oaky wine with considerable body and a heady, smooth, alcoholic finish. This wine is a pure joy to drink now but should last in the bottle for at least 5–6 years. While David Stare, Dry Creek's owner, has always had a large following for his excellent Fumé Blancs and crisp, delicate Chenin Blancs, he has quietly and without a great deal of fanfare begun to fashion some delicious Cabernets. The 1986 is typical of his style. It has a precocious, forward, highly satisfying, rich, berry, spicy bouquet; supple, round, fleshy flavors; no hard edges or excessive acidity; and a long, lush, richly fruity finish. This is the kind of Cabernet one can drink with a great deal of pleasure now, yet it should age well for another 4–5 years. The 1988 and 1989 were less successful. One varietal over which Dry Creek continues to stumble is Chardonnay. The wines, whether the Reserve or regular *cuvée*, are bland, too acidic, and, in the case of the Reserve, excessively oaked. Last, do not overlook Dry Creek's delicate, floral-scented, dry Chenin Blanc. It is a super bargain as well as a tasty wine that has considerable flexibility with food.

DUCKHORN VINEYARDS (NAPA)

Cabernet Sauvignon* * * *, Merlot* * * *,
Merlot Three Palms Vineyard* * * */* * * * *, Sauvignon Blanc* * *

1986	Cabernet Sauvignon	Napa	C	89
1990	Merlot	Napa	C	90
1989	Merlot	Napa	C	82
1987	Merlot	Napa	C	89
1990	Merlot Three Palms Vineyard	Napa	D	88
1989	Merlot Three Palms Vineyard	Napa	D	84
1986	Merlot Three Palms Vineyard	Napa	C	90
1986	Merlot Vine Hill Vineyard	Napa	C	86
1991	Sauvignon Blanc	Napa	B	85

Duckhorn Vineyards was one of the first California wineries to recognize the potential for high-quality Merlot. Their first vintage in 1978 set the standard for this grape and has rarely been eclipsed by any other California winery. Even in lighter years Duckhorn's Merlots are consistently good, and in top vintages, such as 1978, 1984, 1985, 1986, and 1990, they can be splendidly rich, chocolatey, full-bodied wines with tremendous intensity of fruit. In 1990 both the regular *cuvée* of Merlot, a large-scale, rich wine that should drink well for 10–15 years, and the Three Palms Vineyard Merlot, which is slightly less rich yet more elegant, are delicious examples of this varietal. Although they can be drunk now, they will benefit from 5–12 or more years of cellaring. The 1989s are significantly less concentrated. Nevertheless they are still attractive, lighter-weight wines from this difficult vintage. The 1987 Merlot from Duckhorn is an exceptionally intense, opulent, concentrated wine that rivals the finest Merlots made in California by the likes of Matanzas Creek and Ravenswood. It exhibits splendidly rich, concentrated, dazzling coffee-, berry-, and herb-scented, chocolatey fruit, full body, and a lushness in its satiny-smooth finish. It should drink beautifully for the next 5–7 years. The 1986 Merlot Vine Hill Vineyard has excellent richness and depth, but I lowered the score somewhat because of an earthy, fertilizer smell in the bouquet. Nevertheless this is a wine that should last for 7–10 years. It shows overall excellent balance and depth. The outstanding 1986 Merlot Three Palms Vineyard has a wonderfully elegant, complex bouquet of plumlike fruit, mint, spicy new oak, and raspberries. On the palate it's rich, well structured, and deep, and although drinkable now, it will no doubt benefit from another 2–3 years in the bottle. It will certainly last for up to a decade. The 1986 Cabernet Sauvignon is even better than the lovely 1985. Full bodied, rich, and deep, it possesses excellent color and ripeness, good spicy oak to frame its flavors, and nicely integrated acidity. I would ideally give it 2–3 years in the bottle, but it should drink beautifully throughout the rest of this century. Duckhorn also fashions a handsome Sauvignon Blanc that usually includes 25% Semillon. It offers an attractive flinty, mineral, melony nose, and crisp, lively, medium-bodied flavors. The 1991 continues the success Duckhorn has enjoyed with this varietal. A second label, Decoy, is being used for vats of wine not considered rich and complex enough to be sold under the Duckhorn name. Reports also indicate that a proprietary red wine is to be produced, but I have not seen or tasted it. Year in and year out, Duckhorn is one of the top performers in Napa Valley.

DUNN VINEYARDS (NAPA)

Cabernet Sauvignon Howell Mountain* * * * *, Cabernet Sauvignon Napa* * * * *

1991	Cabernet Sauvignon	Napa	D	88
1990	Cabernet Sauvignon	Napa	D	90
1989	Cabernet Sauvignon	Napa	D	87
1988	Cabernet Sauvignon	Napa	D	84
1987	Cabernet Sauvignon	Napa	D	91
1986	Cabernet Sauvignon	Napa	D	92
1991	Cabernet Sauvignon Howell Mountain	Napa	D	90
1990	Cabernet Sauvignon Howell Mountain	Napa	D	91
1989	Cabernet Sauvignon Howell Mountain	Napa	D	86
1988	Cabernet Sauvignon Howell Mountain	Napa	D	84

| 1987 | Cabernet Sauvignon Howell Mountain | Napa | D | 94 |
| 1986 | Cabernet Sauvignon Howell Mountain | Napa | D | 94 |

Dunn produces dense, nearly opaque Cabernets that are very backward and filled with gorgeously rich, blackcurranty, mineral, and licorice scents and flavors. However, consumers looking for a soft style of Cabernet should beware. These wines are brutally tannic and nearly impenetrable in their youth. Although Dunn's Cabernets slumped in quality in the difficult vintages of 1988 and 1989, the 1990s exhibit enough richness, depth, power, and ferocious tannins to suggest they will be the best wines produced since the 1987s. At this early stage they do not look as superconcentrated as Dunn's wines from the early and mid-1980s. Perhaps more depth will emerge from these outstanding wines. The Howell Mountain is slightly more tannic and the Napa more open. Both possess a telltale mineral, cassis, flowery nose and rich, full-bodied, dense, tannic personalities. Similar commentary applies to the 1991s. Although lighter than Dunn's 1990s, they are among the richest wines of the 1991 vintage. Both 1991s should age well for 10–15 years. The 1987 Napa Cabernet reveals an opaque, dark purple color and a strong yet unevolved bouquet of cassis, minerals, and toasty oak. Rich, but very tannic and full, this wine should be at its best between 1998 and 2010. The massive 1987 Cabernet Sauvignon Howell Mountain is superrich, extremely tannic, and very long. It needs at least 7–8 years to soften and should last for up to 20. The 1986 Napa bottling is bursting with mineral-, tar-, licorice-, and blackcurrant-scented fruit; exhibits full body, stunning concentration, and moderate tannins in its finish; and presents an overall sense of balance—all of which is admirable given its broad-shouldered, muscular, immense size. It is California Cabernet at its best. Although drinkable now, it will come into its own in another 2–3 years and last for 10–12 years. The 1986 Howell Mountain is close in quality; it has a longer finish, but that may be offset by the higher tannin levels and its impenetrable personality. It is a profound Cabernet Sauvignon. Stuffed with blackcurrant fruit and exhibiting remarkable depth and length, it seems to be at least 5–6 years away from drinkability. It should last 15 or more years. Consumers who have trouble deferring their gratification would be well advised to seek out the less expensive Napa bottling, rather than the larger-scale, closed, backward Howell Mountain.

RATINGS FOR OLDER VINTAGES OF DUNN CABERNET SAUVIGNONS: NAPA CUVÉE: 1985 (92), 1984 (90), 1983 (88), 1982 (87), 1980 (92)
HOWELL MOUNTAIN: 1985 (95), 1984 (95), 1983 (88), 1982 (95), 1981 (90), 1979 (90)

DUNNEWOOD (MENDOCINO)
Cabernet Sauvignon*, Chardonnay*, Sauvignon Blanc*

This winery produces indifferent wines regardless of the varietal. The wines are acidic, lean, compact, and short and generally offer little charm.

DURNEY VINEYARD (MONTEREY)
Cabernet Sauvignon* * *, Cabernet Sauvignon Reserve* * * */* * * * *,
Chardonnay Estate* * * *

1990	Cabernet Sauvignon	Carmel Valley	C	82
1989	Cabernet Sauvignon	Carmel Valley	C	86
1985	Cabernet Sauvignon Reserve	Carmel Valley	D	92
1990	Chardonnay Estate	Carmel Valley	C	90
1989	Chardonnay Estate	Carmel Valley	C	81
1988	Chardonnay Estate	Carmel Valley	C	90

There is no doubt that Monterey is a top-notch source for Chardonnay. Durney continues to produce full-throttle, rich, exceptionally ageworthy Chardonnays that can easily last for 5–7 years, an uncommonly long time for California Chardonnay. Its style emphasizes plenty of oak, a big, honeyed, rich, bold fruitiness, and a tight structure that unfolds with 3–4 years in the bottle. The 1988 Chardonnay is just now coming into full bloom. The 1990 may not hit its pace for another year, but it, too, is a dramatic, blockbuster wine that reminds me of the Chalone Chardonnays made prior to 1982. The 1989 is light and compact, clearly not up to the quality of the 1988 and 1990. Even more significant, in an area known for exceptionally vegetal Cabernet Sauvignons, Durney has frequently managed to make terrific Cabernet Sauvignon that can last for 12–20 years and is not overtly herbaceous. The wines are superrich, with plenty of toasty, sweet oak, a lot of tannin, yet an alluring chewy texture, wonderful purity and focus, and explosively long, rich finishes. The 1990 Cabernet is a baby in terms of its development. It has the potential to develop into a good wine, but at present it is tart, lean, and closed. The 1989 is slightly more forward. The 1985 Reserve is Durney's finest Cabernet Sauvignon since the great 1978. The blockbuster 1985 Reserve shows clearly what heights this winery can achieve in an area not known for this varietal. Nearly black in color, this massive wine is still youthful and in need of cellaring. The earthy, cassis nose opens with airing. Exceptionally rich, full bodied, and multidimensional, this tightly knit wine will last for another 20 or more years.
RATINGS FOR OLDER VINTAGES OF DURNEY CABERNET SAUVIGNON: 1983 (88), 1980 (89), 1978 (90)

DUXOUP WINEWORKS (SONOMA)
Charbono* * * *, Gamay* * * *, Syrah* *, Zinfandel* *

1990	Charbono	Napa	A	87
1988	Charbono	Napa	A	86
1990	Gamay	Napa	A	85
1988	Syrah	Napa	B	78

This winery excels with its inexpensive yet exuberantly fruity, rich wines made from Charbono and Gamay. One could argue that no one makes a better Charbono or Gamay than Duxoup. Both wines are loaded with a huge, grapey, black fruit character and admirable intensity and concentration. They are wines to drink within their first 5–6 years of life. Duxoup's Syrah has been less successful. The Syrah offers a fine nose of bacon fat–scented, smoky, cassis aromas, but in the mouth the wine is disappointingly light and acidic. Duxoup also produces a Zinfandel. It has been irregular in quality, which is surprising given how well this winery does with Gamay and Charbono. If you are looking for tasty wines at reasonable prices, do not miss Duxoup's Charbono or Gamay.

EBERLE WINERY (SAN LUIS OBISPO)
Cabernet Sauvignon* * *, Chardonnay* */* * *, Zinfandel* * * *

1990	Cabernet Sauvignon	Paso Robles	C	86
1988	Cabernet Sauvignon	Paso Robles	C	77
1990	Chardonnay	Paso Robles	B	82
1989	Chardonnay	Paso Robles	B	79
1990	Zinfandel Sauret Vineyard	Paso Robles	B	87

This is a reliable winery turning out good, chunky, mouth-filling Cabernets with dusty, blackcurrant fruit, medium to full body, soft tannins, and the potential to last for 7–8 years. The Chardonnays have been a mixed bag—sometimes excessively oaked and other times ripe, with loads of tropical fruit and spicy oak. The 1990 is a pleasant wine; the 1989 is slightly less concentrated and already beginning to dry out. Among recent Zinfandel vintages, my favorite is the 1990 Sauret Vineyard. Although it needs time in the bottle to shed some of its tannins, it has considerable potential. A deep purple color suggests excellent concentration, which is exactly what one finds in the mouth. Spicy, briery, blackberry and black raspberry fruit exhibit superb ripeness, fine concentration, and moderate tannins and acidity in the relatively long finish. I would recommend cellaring this wine for 1–2 years and then enjoying it over the next decade.

EDMUNDS ST. JOHN (ALAMEDA)
Les Côtes Sauvages* * * *, Mourvèdre* * * *, Port o'Call* * * *, Syrah* * * * *,
Viognier* * *, Zinfandel* * * * *

N. V.	Les Côtes Sauvages Cuvée Wahluke	America	B	88
1991	Les Côtes Sauvages	California	B	90
1989	Les Côtes Sauvages	California	C	87
1988	Les Côtes Sauvages	California	C	90
1991	Marchini Bianco (Grenache Blanc)	El Dorado	B	72
1988	Mourvèdre	California	B	90
N. V.	New World Red	America	A	86
1992	Pinot Grigio	El Dorado	B	87
1989	Port o'Call	America	B	87
N. V.	Port o'Call New World Red	America	B	88
1992	La Rosé Sauvage	El Dorado	A	87
1990	Syrah	Sonoma	C	93
1988	Syrah	Sonoma	C	92

1991	Syrah Durell Vineyard	Sonoma	C	91
1990	Syrah Durell Vineyard	Sonoma	C	94
1992	Viognier	Knight's Valley	C	87
1988	Zinfandel Amarone	Napa	C	88
1990	Zinfandel Mount Veeder	Napa	B	91

Within the group of California wineries dedicated to producing wines from grapes made famous by France's Rhône Valley, Edmunds St. John may be the finest practitioner. The wines exhibit exceptional winemaking talent, a sense of balance and grace, and considerable pleasure and character. The 1990 Zinfandel from Napa Valley's Mt. Veeder is a stunning example of this varietal. The intensely fragrant nose of spices, pepper, and cassis fruit offers convincing evidence of just how fascinating Zinfandel's aromatic profile can be. In the mouth this saturated, dark ruby/purple-colored wine exhibits splendid opulence of fruit, plenty of grip and structure, wonderful jammy fruit intensity, and a long, moderately tannic finish. Although the tannins are soft enough to make the wine appealing now, this Zinfandel should age gracefully for 7–8 years. The 1989 Port o'Call is a knockout, chunky, robust, fleshy wine, oozing with scents of herbs, black cherry, and black raspberry fruit. Full bodied and opulent, and providing a mouthful of delicious red wine, it is the perfect foil for the substantial, hearty fare served at your local bistro. The 1989 Les Côtes Sauvages (a blend of 53% Mourvèdre, 24% Grenache, 17% Syrah, and 6% Carignan) exhibits a big, spicy, herbaceous, black cherry and black raspberry–scented nose; intense, ripe, elegant flavors; and a medium-bodied, attractive finish. Lighter than the 1988, it is a graceful, tasty wine for drinking over the next 4–8 years. Edmunds has ventured far and wide to track down Syrah from the Durell Vineyard in Sonoma, Zinfandel from Napa, Mourvèdre from Mt. Veeder and Livermore, and Grenache from the McDowell Valley and the Columbia River area of Washington State. If you are a Rhône wine enthusiast, do not miss the opportunity to try this wine. It also represents a great value. The 1988 Les Côtes Sauvages offers a huge, opaque, dark ruby/purple color, followed by an intriguing bouquet of herbs, roasted peanuts, violets, smoke, black plums, and tree bark. The wine is sensationally rich, with fabulous concentration and hefty quantities of glycerin that provide a generous mouthfilling texture. In fact, the richness and huge glycerin content conceal what are some surprisingly bountiful yet soft tannins. Along with the 1988 Taurus from Sean Thackrey, the 1988 Mourvèdre from Edmunds St. John is among the most impressive wines from this varietal I have ever tasted. The deep, intense, leafy, tree bark–scented bouquet suggests a roasted black cherry character intermingled with aromas of coffee and chocolate. The wine has a fascinating satiny texture, full body, extraordinary concentration, and enough tannin and acidity to give it delineation and aging potential. It should be even better with another 2–3 years of cellaring but should last for 12–15 years. The 1990 and 1988 Syrahs are dead ringers for a great Hermitage. How Steve Edmunds pulled this off is amazing, for these are historic wines with a remarkable complexity and personality more akin to the massive Hermitage Hill in the Rhône Valley than the Durell Vineyard in Sonoma. The huge smoky, bacon fat–scented nose also delivers aromas of ground beef, leather, and massive black fruit. These wines are extraordinarily concentrated, yet the tannins are soft. The richness, high extract levels, and impeccable balance suggest that the 1990 and 1988 will last for 10–15 years. If you are a lover of Syrah or Hermitage, I recommend you latch on to every bottle you can find of these spectacularly made, sensational Syrahs. Edmunds has turned out a 1988 Zinfandel he knows will be controversial. The Amarone Zinfandel, made from raisined grapes, is a massive, large-scale wine that is best drunk with cheeses or by itself following a meal. It is an innovative concept and reminds me of the great 1970 Ridge Jimsomare that has always been the most compelling late-harvest Zinfandel I have ever tasted. It should easily keep for 10–20 years. It is hard to find Pinot Grigio this good from Italy, so you know how special this wine is. Today most Pinot Grigios are innocuous, sterile wines that are devoid of any bouquet, offering meager flavors dominated by acidity and alcohol. This offering from Edmunds St. John is bursting with soft, buttery, nutty, fruit flavors that are medium bodied and lively, and a fragrant perfume. This delicious Pinot Grigio begs to be drunk with grilled salmon over the next 8–12 months. Edmunds St. John's rich 1992 Viognier comes close to rivaling the superb Viogniers being made at Calera and Qupé. It offers an ostentatious, honeysuckle-, peach-, and apricot-scented nose, gobs of unctuous, rich fruit, and a lush, fat finish. It is a big white wine oozing with fruit. Serve it with full-flavored poultry or fish dishes within 12 months of its release. Americans are beginning to realize how much pleasure a good rosé can provide. The 1992 La Rosé Sauvage, a 97% Grenache/3% Viognier blend, is loaded with flavor, personality, and, most important, pleasure. The big, berry-scented nose jumps from the glass. Even more impressive is the cascade of luscious fruit that flows over the palate. It is a terrific rosé for drinking now! Get your orders in before this wine sells out! As a postscript, kudos go to winemaker Steve Edmunds for taking a risk and preserving all of his grapes' flavor by bottling these wines with no filtration!

EDNA VALLEY VINEYARDS (SAN LUIS OBISPO)
Chardonnay* * * *, Pinot Noir* * *

1991	Chardonnay	Edna Valley	C	90
1990	Chardonnay	Edna Valley	C	90
1990	Pinot Noir	Edna Valley	C	83

Both the 1991 and 1990 are terrific bottles of opulent, superripe, expansive, powerful Chardonnay oozing with lavish, buttery fruit. A treat to drink, both wines should easily last for another 2–3 years. The 1990 Pinot Noir exhibits a murky, medium ruby color, a big, earthy, herbaceous, plum-scented nose, medium body, fine ripeness, and relatively hard tannins in the compact finish. Drink it over the next 4–5 years.

EL MOLINO (NAPA)
Chardonnay* * * *, Pinot Noir* * * *

1990	Chardonnay	Napa	C	90
1989	Chardonnay	Napa	C	86
1988	Chardonnay	Napa	D	90
1990	Pinot Noir	Napa	D	87
1989	Pinot Noir	Napa	D	85

El Molino continues to produce impressive wines with excellent richness, texture, and complexity. The 1990 Chardonnay, which could easily be mistaken for a top Meursault or Chassagne-Montrachet, displays a smoky, nutty, buttered popcorn nose; rich, fleshy, well-balanced flavors that possess enough acidity for focus; and a heady, toasty, long finish. Drink it over the next 1–2 years. The 1988 Chardonnay, although frightfully expensive, has a very burgundian, smoky, hazelnut, buttery bouquet and rich, deep, expansive, slightly sweet flavors. It has obviously been produced from fully ripe Chardonnay grapes. This is a beautifully made Chardonnay for drinking over the next year. The 1990 Pinot Noir is also surprisingly complex and interesting. Its medium ruby/garnet color suggests it might be aging rapidly, but in the nose there is plenty of spicy new oak and rich, sweet, jammy fruit intermingled with aromas of herbs. On the palate the wine is velvety, full bodied, very round, and soft, with a fine, heady finish. I would opt for drinking it over the next 2–3 years. Because of the difficulties of the vintage, the 1989 Chardonnay and 1989 Pinot Noir are less concentrated and intense than the 1988s and 1990s. The 1989 Chardonnay should be drunk up; the Pinot Noir should last for 2–3 more years. One has to be impressed with the complexity and flavor authority El Molino is obtaining in its wines.

ELLISTON VINEYARDS (ALAMEDA)
Chardonnay* * *, Pinot Blanc* *

1990	Chardonnay Elliston Vineyard	Central Coast	C	87
1990	Chardonnay Sunol Valley Vineyard	Central Coast	B	87
1989	Pinot Blanc Sunol Valley Vineyard	Central Coast	B	69

Here are two impressive Chardonnays from a small, relatively obscure California winery. Both exhibit fine winemaking and plenty of flavor. The rich 1990 Chardonnay Sunol Valley Vineyard exhibits a generous, full-bodied texture, excellent length, and fine ripeness and character. The similarly styled 1990 Chardonnay Elliston Vineyard is more alcoholic and heady, as well as fatter and more concentrated. Both wines offer excellent flavor richness for a reasonable price. They should be consumed over the next 1–2 years. The 1989 Pinot Blanc is the second vintage that I have found to be thin, tart, and uninteresting.

ELYSE (NAPA)
Nero Misto Proprietary Red Wine* * */* * * *,
Zinfandel Howell Mountain* * * *, Zinfandel Morisoli Vineyard* * * *

N.V.	Nero Misto	Napa	C	89
1990	Nero Misto	Napa	C	86
1991	Zinfandel Howell Mountain	Napa	C	91
1991	Zinfandel Morisoli Vineyard	Napa	C	88
1990	Zinfandel Morisoli Vineyard	Napa	B	89

I have been impressed by the wines that emerge from this tiny winery, which produces microscopic quantities of high-class Zinfandel from a vineyard near Rutherford. Its 1990 displays a deep, saturated, dark ruby/purple color, with a restrained but promising bouquet of cassis, spicy oak, herbs, and earth. In the mouth there is wonderful purity of flavor, a medium- to full-bodied texture, and a long, crisp, moderately tannic finish. Approachable now, this wine should blossom in 1–2 years and last for up to a decade. The 1990 Nero Misto, a blend of 60% Petite Sirah, 20% Zinfandel, and the rest an assorted field blend, offers a spicy, earthy, peppery, black fruit–scented nose, tasty, medium- to full-bodied flavors, considerable tannin, plenty of depth, and a fine sense of balance. It is tough at the moment, but another 1–2 years of aging should cause the tannins to melt away. It will last for a decade. The newest release (in 1993) of the Nero is a nonvintage wine. It is an interesting blend of 46% Petite Sirah, 28% Zinfandel, and 26% unfashionable red-wine varietals—whatever that means. This black/purple–colored wine offers a super nose of pepper, black fruits, licorice, and minerals; tremendous depth of fruit; ripe, medium- to full-bodied, rich flavors; a chewy texture; and a long finish. It reveals this winery's predilection to produce pure, well-delineated wines. Elyse has produced 350 cases of a 1991 Zinfandel from Howell Mountain that might have been crafted by Randy Dunn if he were making Zinfandel. It is a blockbuster, broodingly backward, dense wine with a saturated black/purple color, and a closed but promising nose of minerals and black raspberries. Deep and full bodied, with tremendous extraction of fruit, as well as high tannins, it should prove to be an uncommonly long-lived Zinfandel. It needs at least 2–3 years of cellaring. Zinfandel has a tendency to drop its tannins more quickly than Cabernet Sauvignon, so it may come around even sooner. This massive, large-scaled Zinfandel, which has such terrific focus and wonderful richness, should be drunk between 1996 and 2005+. Although the 1991 Zinfandel Morisoli Vineyard does not enjoy the saturated black/purple color of the Howell Mountain offering, it is still a deep ruby/purple-colored wine. The nose offers an elegant concoction of red and black fruits, pepper, and spices. Long, rich, and medium to full bodied, with fine balance and harmony, this stylish wine is about as graceful as Zinfandel can be. Drink it over the next decade.

ESTANCIA (FRANCISCAN VINEYARDS, NAPA)

Cabernet Sauvignon* *, Chardonnay* * *, Merlot* * *, Proprietary Red Wine* * *

1988	Cabernet Sauvignon	Alexander Valley	A	78
1991	Chardonnay	Monterey	A	85
1990	Chardonnay	Monterey	A	86
1988	Meritage Red Table Wine	Alexander Valley	A	86

Estancia is the inexpensive line of wines from the fine Franciscan winery. Its 1990 Chardonnay is a richly fleshy, ripe, tasty wine with plenty of fruit, glycerin, and body, as well as a long, crisp, refreshing finish. The 1991 is similar but slightly lighter. Drink both wines within 3–4 years of the vintage. The 1988 Meritage offers an evolved, spicy, cedary-scented nose, smooth, medium-bodied, ripe, fruity flavors, soft acids, and light tannins. It is ideal for drinking over the next 2–3 years. The 1988 Cabernet Sauvignon is herbaceous, fruity, and simple. Based on the wines to date, Estancia appears to be a label to search out for reasonably good values. The Chardonnays and Meritage wines are consumers' best bets.

ÉTUDE (NAPA)
Cabernet Sauvignon* * */* * * *, Pinot Noir* * */* * * *

1991	Cabernet Sauvignon	Napa	D	91
1990	Cabernet Sauvignon	Napa	D	89
1988	Cabernet Sauvignon	Napa	D	84
1987	Cabernet Sauvignon	Napa	D	88
1990	Pinot Noir	Napa	C	85
1988	Pinot Noir	Napa	C	86

Winemaker Tony Soter (of Spottswoode fame) has demonstrated that his touch with Cabernet Sauvignon can also extend to the fickle Pinot Noir. The 1988 Pinot Noir has a lovely, toasty, black cherry–scented bouquet; soft, fleshy flavors; decent acidity; and a heady, alcoholic finish. It is a delicious Pinot for drinking over the next 2–3 years. In comparison, the 1990 Pinot Noir exhibits more structure and tannin and slightly less supple fruit. It should last longer than the 1988, but I do not see the same seductive style. The 1987 Cabernet Sauvignon is dark ruby in color, with a big, minty-, cassis-scented bouquet. The wine is medium bodied, with excellent ripeness and a good, spicy, long finish. It needs another year or so to shed some tannins, but this wine is a good candidate for drinking over the next decade. The light 1988 is drinking well, with soft cassis fruit and a nice touch of oak. The 1990 is a boldly styled, rich, deep wine with excellent definition and length. **Anticipated maturity: Now–2003.** The terrific 1991 is one of the stars of the vintage. Purple colored, full, rich, multi-dimensional, and long, it should reach full maturity between 1995 and 2006.

EVENSON VINEYARDS AND WINERY (NAPA)
Gewürztraminer* * *

This has been one of California's few wineries capable of producing an authentic, dry, medium- to full-bodied Gewürztraminer with good varietal character. Production is tiny, and the wines are available only in California.

FAR NIENTE (NAPA)
Cabernet Sauvignon* */* * *, Chardonnay* * */* * * *

1988	Cabernet Sauvignon	Napa	D	79
1987	Cabernet Sauvignon	Napa	D	82
1990	Chardonnay	Napa	D	86
1989	Chardonnay	Napa	D	85

Although Far Niente's bold pricing policy has justifiably drawn some criticism, the fact remains that their Chardonnays have been consistently good. Made in a rich, medium- to full-bodied style, they exhibit plenty of toasty oak and ripe fruit. The 1989 is unquestionably a success in a year that produced mostly thin, watery white wines. The 1990, although more tightly structured, displays greater depth, richness, and length. It is a candidate for 4–5 years of cellaring. The Cabernet Sauvignons have been irregular, often too tannic, too oaky, and not rich enough in fruit and extract. The impression on the palate is one of astringency and hollowness. A vertical tasting done in 1992 of all Far Niente's

Cabernets since their debut release in 1982 revealed that, although still alive, they were generally hard, unyielding wines that may, in years such as 1984 and 1987, attain harmony among all their elements. The winery has begun to make a superexpensive, sweet, botrytised 80% Semillon/20% Sauvignon Blanc blend that is obviously meant to resemble the famed Château d'Yquem. The first vintage was impressive, although frightfully expensive.

RATINGS FOR OLDER VINTAGES OF FAR NIENTE CABERNET SAUVIGNON: 1987 (86), 1986 (85), 1985 (85), 1984 (89), 1983 (79), 1982 (78)

GARY FARRELL (SONOMA)
Cabernet Sauvignon* *, Cabernet Sauvignon Ladi's Vineyard* * * *,
Chardonnay* * *, Merlot Ladi's Vineyard* * * *, Pinot Noir Cuvées* * * *

Year	Wine	Region		
1987	Cabernet Sauvignon	Sonoma	C	77
1990	Cabernet Sauvignon Ladi's Vineyard	Sonoma	C	88
1989	Chardonnay	Sonoma	C	82
1990	Merlot Ladi's Vineyard	Sonoma	C	88
1990	Pinot Noir	Russian River	C	85
1991	Pinot Noir Howard Allen Vineyard	Sonoma	D	88
1990	Pinot Noir Howard Allen Vineyard	Sonoma	D	89
1990	Pinot Noir Bien Nacido Vineyard	Santa Barbara	D	87

After some uneven performances in the early 1980s, this producer is starting to make waves with some interesting, rich, complex Pinot Noirs. Numerous small batches of wine are made. The best to date have been from the Howard Allen Vineyard in Sonoma and the Bien Nacido Vineyard in Santa Barbara. The wines are completely different, with the Santa Barbara *cuvée* exhibiting a more leafy, herbaceous, peppery character to go with its sweet, expansive fruit. The Sonoma *cuvée* has more dusty, black fruit and an expansive, seductive style. Both 1990s are textbook California Pinot Noirs that are about as good as I have tasted from that state. The 1990 Russian River Pinot Noir is also attractive, smooth, richly fruity, and spicy. Farrell's increasingly magic touch with Pinot Noir has not, however, extended to his Chardonnays. His 1989 Chardonnay is better than many of the wines from that disappointing vintage while the 1987 Cabernet Sauvignon is overtly vegetal, lean, hard, tannic, and bitter in the finish. The superexpensive 1991 Pinot Noir from the excellent Howard Allen Vineyard exhibits a deep ruby color, a big, spicy, minty, berry-scented nose, lovely rich, full-bodied flavors, outstanding flavor extract, and a spicy, long finish. The mint component is unusually pronounced for Pinot Noir, but, overall, this is a rich, complex Pinot for drinking over the next 7–8 years. The 1990 Merlot Ladi's Vineyard is a deep-ruby-colored, richly extracted, black cherry–, chocolate-, herb-, and vanillin-scented and -flavored wine with fine ripe fruit. It is also well structured for a Merlot, with slightly higher acidity than usually found in this varietal. Drink this appealing wine over the next 5–7 years. Farrell's 1990 Cabernet Sauvignon Ladi's Vineyard displays a moderately intense, wonderfully pure, rich, cassis-scented nose intertwined with aromas of new oak and herbs. Deep and rich, with a pronounced spiciness, this medium- to full-bodied, generously endowed wine possesses moderate tannins and crisp acidity. Drink it over the next 10–12 years.

FERRARI-CARANO WINERY (SONOMA)
Chardonnay* * * *, Chardonnay Reserve* * * * *,
Fumé Blanc* * */* * * *, Merlot* *, Pinot Noir* * *, Zinfandel* * * *

1990	Chardonnay	Alexander Valley	C	88
1990	Chardonnay Reserve	Alexander Valley	C	90
1991	Fumé Blanc	Alexander Valley	A	82
1987	Merlot	Alexander Valley	B	85
1986	Merlot	Alexander Valley	B	78
1990	Pinot Noir Rhonda Reserve	Napa/Sonoma	C	85
1990	Zinfandel	Dry Creek	C	91

This winery, which had its first release only a decade ago, has leaped on the scene as one of California's finest producers of Chardonnay. For example, both 1990s are bursting with fruit and exhibit a nice touch of oak and lush perfumes. Altogether they are fun to consume. Although they will not be long-lived, they are filled with pleasure, the Reserve displaying a more noticeable oaky overlay as well as greater depth, glycerin, and intensity. Ferrari-Carano also makes an herbaceous, Loire Valley style of Fumé Blanc that is normally one of the most delicious made in California. The 1991 is a bit lighter and less concentrated than previous vintages. The red wines have been more of a mixed bag, but certainly the 1990 Zinfandel from Dry Creek is a spectacular effort, with stunning richness, a huge nose of black raspberries and pepper, awesome richness, full body, and an explosively long finish. It should drink well for another decade. Even the 1990 Pinot Noir Rhonda Reserve is a good effort. Although not complex, it exhibits plenty of juicy red fruits, a nice herbaceous touch, and a round, expansive finish. It should be drunk over the next 4–5 years. The Cabernet Sauvignons have been weedy and vegetal. The 1987 Merlot was delicious, but the 1986 was lean and herbal. Nevertheless this is a winery dedicated to high quality and making individualistic, fun-filled wines.

GLORIA FERRER (SONOMA)
Sparkling Wine Cuvées* */* * *

This is another European/American venture. The Spanish sparkling wine giant, Freixenet, is the European connection. Like most California sparkling wines, the offerings to date have been crisp and clean but essentially one-dimensional, without the ampleness and richness of fruit one finds in the finest French champagnes. It may not be totally fair to compare these sparkling wines with the world's reference point, Champagne, but questions must be raised about the short growing season and the necessity of having to harvest unripe grapes in order to preserve enough acidity to make sparkling wine. Several *cuvées* are offered, including a green, lean nonvintage Brut and a vintage wine called Rural Cuvée that possesses more body and power. The difference in quality is negligible.

FETZER VINEYARD (MENDOCINO)
Cabernet Sauvignon Barrel Select* * *, Chardonnay Barrel Select* * *,
Chardonnay Sundial* * *, Chenin Blanc* *, Gewürztraminer *,
Petite Sirah Reserve* * *, Riesling *, Zinfandel Reserve* * *

1989	Cabernet Sauvignon Barrel Select	California	B	75
1988	Cabernet Sauvignon Barrel Select	California	B	85
1986	Cabernet Sauvignon Barrel Select	Mendocino	A	85
1985	Cabernet Sauvignon Reserve	Sonoma	C	85
1989	Cabernet Sauvignon Valley Oaks	Lake	A	70
1990	Chardonnay Barrel Select	Mendocino	B	85
1991	Chardonnay Sundial	California	A	85
1991	Fumé Blanc Valley Oaks	Lake	A	83
1991	Gewürztraminer	California	A	72
1987	Petite Sirah Reserve	California	B	87
1991	Riesling	California	A	73
1989	Zinfandel Barrel Select	California	B	86
1986	Zinfandel Reserve	Mendocino	B	85

For 25 years Fetzer has been a reliable winery that continues to win over the masses with reasonably priced, generally good-quality wines. None of these selections is likely to dazzle the taster, but they are capable of providing immensely satisfying drinking at a modest price. The 1988 Cabernet Sauvignon Barrel Select reveals deep, black cherry–, herb-scented cassis flavors, good body, low acidity, nice flavor extraction, and a clean, round finish. It should drink well for the next 3–4 years. The deliciously fruity, smoky, toasty, robust, satiny-smooth 1986 Cabernet Sauvignon Barrel Select lacked some complexity, but for a nice, plump, tasty mouthful of soft Cabernet, it is hard to beat. Drink it over the next 5–6 years. The 1985 Cabernet Sauvignon Reserve is a competently made, attractive, crowd-pleasing wine with lavish amounts of new oak, gobs of blackcurrants, medium body, and considerable tannin in the finish. Drinkable now despite the tannins, this wine should improve and age nicely for another 7–8 years. The 1990 Chardonnay possesses tart acidity, but there is plenty of apple and buttery fruit, some obvious toasty, oaky notes, and a medium-bodied, clean finish. Drink it over the next year. A black/ruby-colored, admirably concentrated, large-scale wine, the 1987 Reserve Petite Sirah from Fetzer possesses a big, blackberry-, raspberry-, tar-, and peppery-scented bouquet, powerful, ripe, full-bodied flavors, gobs of extract, and moderately soft tannins in its substantial finish. Quite mouth-filling with a purity of fruit that is impressive, this wine should age nicely for another 7–10 years. As for the 1986 Zinfandel Reserve, a big, peppery, robust, intense, almost Rhône-like bouquet is followed by a wine with a smooth, velvety texture, heady, alcoholic flavors, and a long, rustic finish. Drink this precocious-tasting, full-bodied Zinfandel over the next 3–4 years. The 1989 Zinfandel is an aromatic, spicy, richly fruity wine with medium-bodied flavors, silky texture, and a long, heady finish. Drink it over the next 3–4 years. I found the 1989 Cabernet Sauvignon Barrel Select to be excessively oaky without enough fruit and the 1989 Valley Oaks Cabernet Sauvignon hollow and thin. Fetzer's two best values continue to be its nonoaked Sundial Chardonnay, of which the 1991 is bursting with lemony, applelike fruit. Crisp and medium bodied, it is a total pleasure to drink. It is what Chardonnay should be but so rarely is. Moreover, it is a terrific bargain. The 1991 Valley Oaks Fumé Blanc is also pleasant, slightly herbaceous, fruity, soft, and ideal for drinking within several years of the vintage. This winery produces less expensive wines under the Bel Arbors label that can be very good. Additionally, there is a lineup of Riesling, Chenin Blanc, and Gewürztraminer, which, although light and fresh, have lacked varietal character and fruit. In 1993 Fetzer also launched a line of organic wines.

FIELD STONE (SONOMA)

Cabernet Sauvignon Alexander Valley* * *, Cabernet Sauvignon Reserve* * *, Petite Sirah* * * *, Sauvignon Blanc* * *, Viognier Staten Family Reserve* * *

1990	Cabernet Sauvignon	Alexander Valley	C	85
1989	Cabernet Sauvignon	Alexander Valley	C	82
1988	Cabernet Sauvignon	Alexander Valley	C	82
1990	Cabernet Sauvignon Estate Reserve	Alexander Valley	C	86
1989	Cabernet Sauvignon Staten Family Reserve	Alexander Valley	C	85
1988	Cabernet Sauvignon Staten Family Reserve	Alexander Valley	C	78
1990	Petite Sirah Estate	Alexander Valley	C	85
1989	Petite Sirah Estate	Alexander Valley	C	84
1988	Petite Sirah Estate	Alexander Valley	C	83
1987	Petite Sirah Estate	Alexander Valley	C	90
1991	Sauvignon Blanc	Sonoma	A	85

This winery continues to produce interesting wines, yet, surprisingly, it receives little press coverage. The 1991 Sauvignon Blanc offers a stony, herb-scented bouquet that is followed by a wine with a juicy, fleshy texture, medium body, excellent purity and cleanliness, and a dry, concentrated finish. Field Stone has consistently produced excellent Petite Sirah (made from a vineyard planted in 1894), and the dark ruby-colored, fragrant, intensely concentrated 1987 offers further evidence of such high quality. Though much more supple than their excellent 1986, the wine should last for 10–12 years. It is deep and full bodied, with a bouquet of black raspberries, currants, spices, and pepper. In the mouth the extraction of fruit suggests very old vines and low yields. This full-bodied, nearly massive Petite Sirah should be at its best between now and 2002. The 1988, 1989, and 1990 Petite Sirahs are less concentrated than the 1987 but are still deeply colored. The 1988 needs 10 years of aging, the 1989 is considerably lighter, and the 1990 is closed but full of potential. My ratings may be conservative, especially for the 1990, given its youthfulness and backward state. A bevy of Cabernet Sauvignons are produced, including an Estate Reserve, an Alexander Valley, a Staten Family Reserve, and, in vintages from the early to mid-1980s, single-vineyard Cabernets from the Home Ranch and Turkey Hill vineyards. Although erratic in quality, Field Stone certainly does not cheat the consumer on flavor. These are big, tannic, backward wines that frequently fail to develop the finesse and charm suggested by their style. The stylish 1990s lean toward a more elegant, less ripe style of Cabernet than previous vintages. The 1989 Staten Family Reserve and Alexander Valley *cuvées* were tannic, austere, lean wines. Although both are interesting, I wonder if the fruit in them will fade before the tannins melt away. The 1988s are tannic and herbal, as well as less impressive.

RATINGS FOR OLDER VINTAGES OF FIELD STONE CABERNET SAUVIGNONS: ALEXANDER VALLEY: 1987 (87), 1986 (86), 1979 (86), 1978 (65), 1977 (87)
ESTATE: 1983 (79), 1980 (74)
HOME RANCH: 1985 (86+), 1985 (84)
TURKEY HILL VINEYARD: 1985 (89), 1984 (85), 1982 (78)
STATEN FAMILY RESERVE: 1987 (88)

FIRESTONE VINEYARDS (SANTA BARBARA)

Cabernet Sauvignon* * *, Cabernet Sauvignon Reserve* * */* * * *,
Chardonnay* *, Gewürztraminer* * *, Merlot* *, Johannisberg Riesling* * *

1990	Cabernet Sauvignon	Santa Ynez	B	85
1990	Cabernet Sauvignon Reserve	Santa Ynez	C	87
1991	Chardonnay Barrel Fermented	Santa Ynez	B	85
1991	Gewürztraminer	Santa Ynez	A	84
1991	Johannisberg Riesling	Santa Ynez	A	77
1991	Vintage Reserve Proprietary Red Wine	Santa Ynez	C	89

For 20 years, this beautifully designed winery, perched on a mesa in the Santa Ynez Valley north of Los Olivos, has been producing wines with mixed results. Recent vintages suggest that the quality of the Chardonnays and Cabernets is moving upward. Firestone has long been known for its fine Johannisberg Riesling, but I found the 1991 to be tart, with only vague whiffs of apple fruitiness. Although competently made for uncritical quaffing, it lacks excitement. The 1991 Gewürztraminer displays a subtle rose-petal fragrance, good body, and enough fruit and character to warrant attention. I am an unabashed admirer of Alsatian Gewürztraminer and have been openly critical of the insipid efforts emanating from California, but this wine has merit. A bit more intensity could have put Firestone's Gewürztraminer near the top of the microscopic hierarchy of good Gewürztraminer producers in California. The 1991 Chardonnay Barrel Fermented is an attractive, subtle, elegant wine with a graceful, apple blossom– and orange-scented bouquet, medium-bodied flavors, admirable acidity, and a fine finish. It is one of the best Chardonnays Firestone has made in years. The real surprises were the three red wines. The most striking characteristics of the subtly herbaceous 1990 Cabernet Sauvignon are its attractive, spicy, chocolatey, berry-scented nose, fleshy, supple, medium- to full-bodied flavors, and its round, generous, satiny finish. Drink this delicious Cabernet over the next 6–7 years. Restaurants would be smart to consider it as a house wine. On a more serious level, and unquestionably the best Cabernet Sauvignon Firestone has yet produced, is the 1990 Cabernet Sauvignon Reserve. It offers all the suppleness of the 1990 regular bottling, as well as more generous quantities of cassis, vanillin, and spice in the bouquet. The wine has excellent depth, a chewy, layered texture, and a long, rich, well-balanced finish. The moderate tannins are nearly submerged beneath the considerable extraction of fruit. This Cabernet can be drunk now or cellared for a decade or more. The

1990 Vintage Reserve Proprietary Red Wine may turn out to be Firestone's finest red wine to date. Though still in barrel, there will be 675 cases made of this 60% Cabernet Franc, 28% Merlot, 12% Cabernet Sauvignon blend. It reveals a huge, seductive nose of black cherries, herbs, and spices. Rich, deep, and full bodied, with superb color saturation and purity, this is unquestionably the best red wine I have tasted from Firestone. Let's hope it does not get overly processed at bottling because it is an enticing wine with considerable style and personality. It will drink well for 10–12 years. Readers should not overlook the "best buy" Prosperity White wine Firestone produces. It is a delicious, aromatic, fruity, and inexpensive wine.

FISHER VINEYARDS (SONOMA)

Cabernet Sauvignon Coach Insignia* * *, Chardonnay Coach Insignia* * *, Chardonnay Whitney's Vineyard* * * *

1991	Cabernet Sauvignon Coach Insignia	Sonoma	C	90
1990	Cabernet Sauvignon Coach Insignia	Sonoma	C	87+
1989	Cabernet Sauvignon Coach Insignia	Sonoma	C	78
1986	Cabernet Sauvignon Coach Insignia	Sonoma	C	88
1990	Chardonnay Coach Insignia	California	C	86
1990	Chardonnay Whitney's Vineyard	California	C	90

Fisher has produced two fine Chardonnays from the outstanding 1990 vintage. The Coach Insignia boasts a floral, lemony, applelike aroma, more restrained flavors, crisp acidity, and an attractive, medium-bodied, well-balanced taste. It should drink well for 1–2 years. The superb Whitney's Vineyard reveals a penetrating fragrance of flowers and fruit; a judicious use of new oak; medium- to full-bodied, crisp, pure, multilayered flavors; and fine length. Drink it over the next 2–3 years. With respect to Fisher's Cabernet Sauvignons, the 1990 may ultimately eclipse the fine 1986. The stylish 1990 Coach Insignia offers considerable richness and plenty of tannins in the finish. Deeply colored and long, it needs at least 4–5 years of cellaring and should last for 10–15 years. Fisher's finest Cabernet to date is the 1991, a gorgeously rich, pure wine that is bursting with cassis fruit. Powerful yet elegant, this full-bodied wine exhibits fabulous extraction and terrific length. It should drink well for 12–15 years. The 1989 Coach Insignia is a hollow, lean, austere wine without enough fruit to balance out the hard tannins. The 1986 Coach Insignia is among the finest wines I have tasted from Fisher. The intense bouquet of cassis, herbs, and oak is enthralling. In the mouth the wine displays medium- to full-bodied flavors, an opulent texture, an expansive, long finish, excellent depth and overall harmony. Drinkable now, it should continue to last for another 6–10 years. This winery has always made good wines, but recent releases appear to have hit a new quality level.

FLORA SPRINGS WINE CO. (NAPA)

Cabernet Sauvignon* *, Chardonnay* * *, Chardonnay Barrel Fermented* * * *, Soliloquy Proprietary White Wine* * * *, Trilogy Proprietary Red Wine* *

| 1988 | Cabernet Sauvignon Cellar Select | Napa | C | 82 |
| 1990 | Cabernet Sauvignon Flora Springs | Napa | C | 85 |

1989	Cabernet Sauvignón Flora Springs	Napa	C	75
1991	Cabernet Sauvignon Reserve	Napa	C	88
1990	Cabernet Sauvignon Reserve	Napa	C	85
1990	Chardonnay	Napa	C	86
1990	Chardonnay Barrel Fermented	Napa	B	88
1991	Soliloquy Proprietary White Wine	Napa	C	89
1991	Trilogy Proprietary Red Wine	Napa	D	86
1990	Trilogy Proprietary Red Wine	Napa	D	85
1989	Trilogy Proprietary Red Wine	Napa	D	81
1988	Trilogy Proprietary Red Wine	Napa	D	78
1987	Trilogy Proprietary Red Wine	Napa	D	79

This is a perplexing winery to handicap. For example, the white wines, especially the Chardonnays and the Sauvignon Blanc called Soliloquy, are consistently delicious and in some vintages exceptional. The barrel-fermented Chardonnay exhibits more oak, spice, and depth than the crisper, more floral, fruity nonreserve. However, Flora Springs' red wines, including the stylized but beautifully packaged Trilogy, are reminiscent of an excessively contrived, gimicky, superexpensive nouvelle cuisine that offers less for more. Much of what emerges from Flora Springs' red wine portfolio places aesthetics over substance. The wines are usually acidic and made within clearly defined technical parameters, where safety, security, and sterility are prized over personality and joy. The 1990 Cabernet Sauvignon Reserve possesses some subtle aromas of cassis, herbs, and oak, but it lacks grip and extraction of flavor and reveals an abrupt finish. The 1987, 1988, and 1989 Trilogy offerings continue to be nearly vapid wines with little personality, a shallow fruit intensity, and a frightfully quick finish. Although it reveals some pretty, herb-flavored black fruits in the nose and on the palate, the wine lacks substance and length. There is a tendency by many writers to call such wines "elegant" and "graceful," when in fact they are lacking personality and character. If you think I am being too tough, go back and taste any of the Trilogy offerings to date; these wines have not lived up to either the prices asked or their enthusiastic press. The 1985 Cabernet Sauvignon offers light to moderately intense, spicy, cedary aromas, medium body, and a soft, pleasant finish. But there is no great character or complexity in this wine. The overpriced 1985 Trilogy is an elegantly wrought wine with tightly knit, spicy, curranty flavors, a judicious use of new oak casks, and an austere finish. If it fills out, it may well merit a higher score, but my guess is that it will always remain a rather narrowly constructed wine. As the 1990s began, some signs suggested that the proprietors might be budging slightly from this empty doctrine of winemaking. Let's hope so. Flora Springs has also launched an inexpensive line of wines under the Floreal label. If the 1990 Chardonnay, 1990 Merlot, 1990 Sauvignon Blanc, and 1989 Cabernet Sauvignon are indicative of Floreal's quality, at $9–$12 a bottle, these wines are disappointments.

THOMAS FOGARTY WINERY (SAN MATEO)
Chardonnay* * *, Pinot Noir* *

1988	Chardonnay Ventana Vineyard	Monterey	C	82
1987	Chardonnay Ventana Vineyard	Monterey	C	86
1990	Pinot Noir	Santa Cruz	C	79
1989	Pinot Noir	Santa Cruz	C	82
1987	Pinot Noir	Santa Cruz	C	84

This winery has made some surprisingly complex, earthy, spicy Pinot Noirs and Chardonnays from the Ventana Vineyard. I do not see enough of these wines to follow them on a regular basis. In addition to the Pinot Noir and Chardonnay Ventana Vineyard, the winery releases other Chardonnay *cuvées*, as well as a cloyingly sweet Gewürztraminer. However, the schizophrenic track record makes loyalty to this winery a painful endeavor. Some of the Pinot Noirs can be too vegetal and hollow, and others are fruity and ripe. The same is true with the Chardonnays. The last tasty Chardonnay was the 1987. The Thomas Fogarty Winery appears to have high aspirations to make individualistic wines and therefore bears watching.

FOLIE À DEUX WINERY (NAPA)
Cabernet Sauvignon* *, Chardonnay* * *, Chenin Blanc* * *

1989	Cabernet Sauvignon	Napa	C	75
1990	Chardonnay	Napa	C	86
1991	Dry Chenin Blanc	Napa	A	85

This winery has been in existence for nearly a decade. Its best wine is the least expensive, a dry, oak-aged Chenin Blanc that is bursting with floral, melony aromas. It is wonderfully pure, crisp, and altogether a delight to drink. The Chardonnay, which is made in a lighter style, is pleasant in a lemony, appley, medium-bodied style that is good but unexciting. The consistently disappointing Cabernet Sauvignon has been too tannic, herbal, austere, and compact.

LOUIS FOPPIANO WINE CO. (SONOMA)
Cabernet Sauvignon* *, Cabernet Sauvignon Fox Mountain Reserve* * *,
Chardonnay* *, Petite Sirah* * *, Sauvignon Blanc* *, Zinfandel Reserve* * *

1990	Cabernet Sauvignon	Sonoma	A	75
1985	Cabernet Sauvignon Fox Mountain Reserve	Sonoma	C	86
1989	Chardonnay	Sonoma	A	76
1989	Petite Sirah	Sonoma	A	82
1987	Zinfandel Reserve	Dry Creek	B	86

Foppiano produces inexpensive wines, but the general quality level is mediocre. The major exception tends to be the fine Petite Sirah, of which the 1989, although lighter than normal because of the vintage, is a deep-colored, spicy wine with a lot of body but not much complexity. The gushingly fruity, grapey 1987 Zinfandel Reserve lacks complexity, but who can ignore its soft, velvety, fleshpot style, round, creamy texture, and long, heady finish? It is a

Zinfandel to enjoy over the next 4–5 years. Foppiano's other offerings are simple, one-dimensional, and uninteresting.

FOREST HILL (SONOMA)
Chardonnay* * * *

1991	Chardonnay Private Reserve	Sonoma	C	90
1990	Chardonnay Private Reserve	Sonoma	C	90

Forest Hill has burst on the California wine scene with an excellent—and beautifully packaged—Chardonnay. The 1990 exhibits a huge nose of buttery, apple fruit touched gently by toasty new oak. It is followed by a superbly structured, rich, concentrated wine with excellent definition, a natural acidity, and a honeyed, long, powerful finish. This classically rendered Chardonnay should evolve for 2–4 years. The similarly styled 1991 is slightly more tightly knit, but rich, beautifully pure, and well balanced. It is capable of 3–4 years of aging.

FORMAN WINERY (NAPA)
Cabernet Sauvignon* * * *, Chardonnay* * * *

1990	Cabernet Sauvignon	Napa	D	92
1989	Cabernet Sauvignon	Napa	D	87
1988	Cabernet Sauvignon	Napa	D	84
1987	Cabernet Sauvignon	Napa	D	83
1986	Cabernet Sauvignon	Napa	D	90
1991	Chardonnay	Napa	C	87
1990	Chardonnay	Napa	C	88
1990	Château La Grande Roche Grenache	Napa	B	87

Owner/winemaker Ric Forman is undeniably talented. He burst onto the scene with his own operation in the early 1980s with some terrific Cabernet Sauvignons in vintages such as 1983, 1984, 1985, and 1986. Between 1987 and 1989, the quality of his Cabernets, although good, was less dramatic, and the wines appeared to have lightened up and displayed less richness and complexity. Perhaps the vintages account for some of these changes. Forman's 1990 Cabernet Sauvignon may be this winery's best effort to date. This deep purple–colored wine displays a superexpressive nose of blackcurrants, licorice, and vanillin. With a beautifully etched, medium- to full-bodied feel, exquisite concentration, decent acidity, and firm but soft, sweet tannins, this is a graceful, authoritatively flavored Cabernet for drinking over the next 12–15 years. The 1989 Cabernet Sauvignon is an improvement over the disappointingly light, hollow 1988 and relatively lean, sterile 1987. The 1989 is dark ruby/purple, with a rich nose of cassis and spicy oak. In the mouth there is excellent concentration, good weight and elegance, and soft tannins in the finish. It should drink well for at least 8–10 years. Forman continues to turn out high-quality, rich, tightly knit, full-bodied, concentrated, multidimensional Chardonnays. The 1991 reveals crisp acidity, a restrained but promising bouquet of lemons, butter, and ripe apples, a judicious use of new oak, and full body. Well delineated, as well as pure, it should drink well for another 3–4 years. The 1990 Chardonnay is also extremely tightly knit, offering backward and subtle aromas of lemons, wood, and apples. There is plenty of fruit, excellent richness, and fine acidity, but the wine is just beginning to open up. It should drink well for 1–3 years. Only 300 cases were produced of Forman's least expensive wine, a Beaujolais-style wine made from Grenache. The label, Château La Grande Roche, may be used for other inexpensive wines. This is a wine to search out, not only for its price, but for its glorious nose of red fruits and spices, supple texture, wonderful freshness and vivacity, and medium ruby color. It is not meant to last, so readers lucky enough to latch on to a few bottles should drink it before the spring of 1994. Incidentally, I also tasted Forman's 1990 Pinot Noir, of which only 100 cases were made. I must admit that the big, gamey, earthy, Oriental spice–scented nose reveals more than a casual resemblance to the profound bouquets offered by the Pinot Noir made by some of Burgundy's finest domaines. In the mouth the wine is medium bodied. Although not quite as profound as the nose suggested, it is still excellent Pinot Noir. Bravo!

FOXEN VINEYARD (SANTA BARBARA)
Cabernet Sauvignon* * * *, Chardonnay* * * * *, Chenin Blanc* * * *,
Pinot Noir Sanford & Benedict Vineyard* * * *

1990	Cabernet Sauvignon	Santa Barbara	C	89+
1992	Chardonnay	Santa Maria	C	90
1991	Chardonnay	Santa Maria	C	91
1992	Chenin Blanc Barrel Fermented	Santa Barbara	C	87
1991	Chenin Blanc Barrel Fermented	Santa Barbara	C	86
1991	Pinot Noir	Santa Maria	C	86
1991	Pinot Noir Sanford & Benedict Vineyard	Santa Barbara	D	90

Foxen is another idiosyncratic Santa Barbara winery marching to a different beat. This small winery offers distinctive, original, and frequently outstanding wines that possess a character completely different from anything you are likely to taste from north coast viticultural regions such as Napa, Mendocino, and Sonoma. It is fashioning some noteworthy barrel-fermented dry Chenin Blanc. If you prefer light, floral, crisp, delicate Chenin Blancs, Foxen's Chenin will require some adjustment. It is likely to be controversial because it is so rich and dry. It offers lovely honeyed, floral, tropical fruit, wonderful precision, and a surprisingly well-integrated, subtle oakiness. The 1992 displays slightly deeper fruit flavors, but both the 1991 and 1992 are large-scaled Chenin Blancs that should drink nicely for 2–3 years. Foxen produces intensely concentrated Chardonnays from the Santa Maria Valley. The 1992 Chardonnay, which should prove to have outstanding potential, is still in barrel. It displays a bold, rich, full-bodied style. The super 1991 Chardonnay is light- to medium-straw-colored, with a flamboyant, even audacious nose of butter, honey, oak, and ripe oranges and apples. This superrich, densely packed, full-bodied Chardonnay possesses excellent underlying acidity to support its considerable weight and intensity. Drink it over the next 2–3 years. Readers fortunate enough to have access to the outstanding 1991 Pinot Noir Sanford & Benedict Vineyard should not hesitate to buy it. One of the deepest-colored Pinot Noirs

I have seen, this undeveloped Pinot offers a beautiful nose of black fruits (plums and raspberries), vanillin, and earth. Rich, with plenty of glycerin and sweet, ripe fruit, this deep, profound, full-bodied, heady Pinot Noir exhibits intense black-raspberry and black-cherry flavors that are well knit and offer considerable length in the explosive finish. The overall impression is one of a young, but voluptuous, luxuriously rich Pinot Noir for drinking over the next 6–7 years. The 1991 Pinot Noir from the Santa Maria Valley displays a deep ruby color, a spicy, herbal, black cherry–scented nose, tasty, round, generous flavors, but not the complexity, definition, or mind-boggling depth of the 1991 Sanford & Benedict Vineyard. Foxen makes Santa Barbara's finest Cabernet Sauvignon. Impressively colored and tightly knit, it suffers from none of the vegetal character that plagued Santa Barbara Cabernets and Merlots until the late eighties. The 1990 Cabernet Sauvignon may merit an outstanding score in 2–3 years. It possesses a black/purple, saturated color, a tight yet blossoming bouquet of cassis, herbs, and spices, big, rich, full-bodied flavors buttressed by considerable acidity, moderate tannin, and a long, crisp, powerful finish. Drink it between 1995 and 2003.

FRANCISCAN VINEYARDS (NAPA)

Cabernet Sauvignon Oakville Estate* * *, Chardonnay* * * *,
Meritage Oakville Estate* * * *, Merlot* * *, Zinfandel* * * *

1989	Cabernet Sauvignon Oakville Estate	Napa	B	74
1988	Cabernet Sauvignon Oakville Estate	Napa	B	86
1985	Cabernet Sauvignon Oakville Estate	Napa	A	86
1990	Chardonnay Cuvée Sauvage	Napa	C	87
1988	Meritage Red Table Wine Oakville Estate	Napa	C	87
1987	Meritage Red Table Wine Oakville Estate	Napa	C	90
1986	Meritage Red Table Wine Oakville Estate	Napa	C	90
1987	Merlot	Napa	B	87
1989	Merlot Oakville Estate	Napa	B	85
1990	Zinfandel Oakville Estate	Napa	B	89
1988	Zinfandel Oakville Estate	Napa	B	87

This well-placed winery has soared in quality under the inspired leadership of its current owner, Augustus Huneeus. The top Franciscan wines all carry the Oakville Estate designation. The less expensive line of wines appears under the Estancia label, which offers excellent value. Since the mid-1980s the Franciscan wines have taken on greater richness and more complexity and are consistent across the field of play. There is delicious, ripe, full-bodied, complex Chardonnay; explosively rich, raspberry-scented Zinfandels; a fine proprietary red wine, Meritage, that has been excellent over recent years; and delicious Cabernet Sauvignons and Merlots. In fact, this winery is on a hot streak, and to its credit, it has kept prices more reasonable than many of its neighbors. In short, consumers should beat a path to Franciscan's door, particularly with respect to its less expensive line of wines, Estancia. Although the 1989 is a major disappointment, with green-tea aromas and washed-out flavors, the 1988 Cabernet Sauvignon Oakville Estate exhibits an herbal, cassis-scented nose; excellent, rich, medium- to full-bodied flavors; soft tannins; and a fleshy, clean finish. Drink it over the next 5–6 years. The 1985 Cabernet Sauvignon Oakville Estate possesses fine structure and balance. This dark ruby–colored wine has a bouquet of herbaceous blackcurrants and spicy oak, is ample and generous on the palate, and is medium to full bodied. It can be drunk now or cellared for 5–6 years. The 1988 Meritage reveals an herb-, berry-, chocolatey-, spicy-scented nose; big, rich, velvety flavors; soft tannins; low acidity; and a fine, lush finish. It should be drunk over the next 5–6 years. The 1987 Meritage has a fragrant black cherry, chocolatey, oaky aroma; expansive, full-bodied flavors; excellent intensity; and a long, smooth, heady finish. Drinkable now, it should continue to improve for at least another 5–7 years. The 1986 Meritage is a wonderfully concentrated, splendidly perfumed Cabernet-based wine that combines both power and elegance into a rich, full-bodied, lusciously flavored, smoothly textured wine bursting with smells of toasty new oak, cedar, and black fruits. Since it is forward and delicious, I would have no objections to consuming it over the next 5–6 years. However, I think this wine should last for at least a decade despite its precociousness. The 1989 Merlot reveals excellent fruit; a soft, generous texture; attractive herb, mocha, and berry flavors; and a clean, medium-bodied finish. Drink it over the next 2–3 years. The 1987 Merlot is a textbook offering, exhibiting rich, plummy fruit, a judicious touch of new oak, a round supple texture, and enough acidity and tannin to guarantee a longevity of at least 5–6 years. The acidity is in balance, and the wine has excellent clarity. The 1990 Zinfandel is a powerful, deeply scented wine, exhibiting plenty of toasty new oak; rich, luscious, berry fruit; gobs of glycerin and alcohol; and a generously endowed, velvety-textured finish. The words *seductive, voluptuous,* and *opulent* come to mind when tasting this up-front, full, broad-shouldered Zinfandel. It should be drunk over the next 4–6 years. The 1988 Zinfandel Oakville Estate is a round, gloriously fruity, velvety-textured wine with medium to full body, admirable ripeness, and plenty of succulent, peppery, black raspberry fruit. Given its precocious style, this wine should be drunk over the next 3–4 years. I suspect the 1990 Chardonnay Cuvée Sauvage is Franciscan's example of a reserve *cuvée.* This intense Chardonnay exhibits dramatic oak, a lot of smoky toast behind its rich, luscious fruit, and relatively low acidity. Drink it over the next year. My experience has been that wines made in this style tend to fade quickly.

FREEMARK ABBEY (NAPA)

Cabernet Sauvignon*, Cabernet Sauvignon Bosché* *, Cabernet Sauvignon Sycamore Vineyard* */* * *, Chardonnay* *, Edelwein Sweet Riesling* * * *

1989	Cabernet Sauvignon	Napa	C	78
1988	Cabernet Sauvignon	Napa	C	74
1987	Cabernet Sauvignon Bosché	Napa	D	79
1986	Cabernet Sauvignon Bosché	Napa	D	71
1986	Cabernet Sauvignon Sycamore Vineyard	Napa	D	84
1990	Chardonnay	Napa	C	78

1989	Chardonnay	Napa	C	72
1991	Edelwein Late-Harvest Riesling	Napa	D	88

For more than 2 decades this renowned Napa Valley winery has produced indifferent wines, apparently content to live off the excellent reputation it established in the late 1960s and early 1970s. The sad results range from excessively green and acidified, lean, sterile Chardonnays to harsh, bitterly astringent, vegetal, hollow Cabernet Sauvignons. Even the great Bosché Vineyard (located in the heart of Napa's Rutherford Bench) has not produced a top Cabernet since 1970. A single-vineyard Sycamore Vineyard wine was launched in 1985. It appeared to have more intensity and richness. The winery has also added a single-vineyard Chardonnay called Carpi Ranch, of which the 1990 and 1989 were rated in the high 70s. The only wine that still merits attention is Freemark Abbey's decadently rich, honeyed, late-harvest Riesling. It is still a thrilling dessert wine, as evidenced by the 1991. This is a winery in desperate need of a wake-up call.

FREY VINEYARDS (MENDOCINO)
Zinfandel* * * *

1990	Zinfandel	Mendocino	A	89

I have had limited experience with the wines from this producer, but the more I went back to their 1990 Zinfandel, the more charmed I was. The color is a healthy, deep ruby/purple. At first tight, the nose opens beautifully in the glass to reveal gorgeous black raspberry, spicy, mineral scents that could easily pass for a high-class, rich Volnay Premier Cru from Burgundy. In the mouth the wine is generously concentrated, with high acidity that tastes completely natural and gives the superripe fruit zest and lift. The finish is long, impressively pure, and satisfying. This delicious Zinfandel should continue to drink well for 4–7 years. Frey Vineyards, one of California's leaders in producing organic wines with no sulphites, pesticides, or fungicides used in the vineyard, also produces Pinot Noir, Carignane, Gewürztraminer, Sauvignon Blanc, Syrah, and Cabernet Sauvignon. The only recent vintages I have seen of any of these wines is the 1989 Cabernet Sauvignon, which is lean and skinny.

FRITZ CELLARS (SONOMA)
Zinfandel* * * (since 1988)

1990	Zinfandel	Sonoma	A	85

Made from 80-year-old vines, the 1990 Zinfandel offers up a spicy, earthy, peppery, berry-scented nose; soft, fleshy, full-bodied flavors; and an excellent finish. It should be drunk over the next 5–6 years.

FROG'S LEAP WINERY (NAPA)
Cabernet Sauvignon* * *, Chardonnay* * *, Merlot* * *, Zinfandel* * *

1989	Cabernet Sauvignon	Napa	C	78
1987	Cabernet Sauvignon	Napa	C	86
1991	Chardonnay	Carneros	C	87
1990	Merlot	Napa	C	85

1990	Zinfandel	Napa	B	87
1987	Zinfandel	Napa	B	86

Although this winery turns out decent Cabernet Sauvignons and Chardonnays, it is their Zinfandels I find most interesting. Medium-weight, emphasizing the black cherry/black raspberry character of the varietal, they offer a balanced glass of wine. The 1990, nicely married with spicy, toasty oak, reveals fine ripeness, excellent richness, a medium-bodied feel on the palate, and a crisp, clean, delicious finish. Hop to it and drink this wine over the next 5–6 years. Lush, lusty black fruit and black cherry flavors dominate the 1987's bouquet. In the mouth the impression of ripe and vibrantly pure fruit continues. This soft, medium- to full-bodied Zinfandel should be consumed over the next 3–4 years. Frog's Leap's 1989 Cabernet Sauvignon is somewhat malnourished and short. If the 1987 Cabernet Sauvignon had a little more complexity, it would be outstanding. What it does offer are layers of rich, curranty fruit nicely buttressed by fresh, crisp acidity and a touch of oak. The overall impression is one of crunchy, grapey fruit in a medium-bodied format. Delicious today, it should age well for another 5–6 years. In 1990 Frog's Leap added a tasty, fleshy, richly fruity Merlot to its portfolio. Although it can lack flavor dimension, it offers plenty of fruit in a medium-bodied, soft, lush style. Drink the 1990 over the next 5–6 years. This winery has lagged behind in its Chardonnays, but both the 1990 and 1991 exhibit more fruit and depth than previous offerings. The 1991 possesses crisp acidity; plenty of apple, buttery fruit; medium body; and a smooth, rich finish. It should drink well for another 2–3 years.

GAINEY VINEYARDS (SANTA BARBARA)

Cabernet Franc Limited Selection* * * *, Chardonnay * * *, Merlot* *,
Merlot Limited Selection* * */* * * *, Pinot Noir* *, Pinot Noir Sanford &
Benedict Vineyard* * * *, Sauvignon Blanc Limited Selection* * * *

1990	Cabernet Franc Limited Selection	Santa Barbara	D	87
1991	Chardonnay	Santa Barbara	C	82
1990	Merlot	Santa Ynez	C	83
1990	Merlot Limited Selection	Santa Ynez	D	86
1991	Pinot Noir Sanford & Benedict Vineyard	Santa Barbara	D	89
1991	Pinot Noir	Santa Maria	C	86
1990	Pinot Noir	Santa Barbara	C	82
1991	Sauvignon Blanc	Santa Ynez	A	87
1991	Sauvignon Blanc Limited Selection	Santa Ynez	C	90

Located in the Santa Ynez Valley, this attractive winery has had a mixed track record since its debut vintage in the mid-1980s. However, under the increasingly inspired winemaking hand of Rich Longoria, Gainey has begun to exploit its considerable potential. Vintages in the 1990s, including unreleased barrel samples of their 1992s, should make Gainey Vineyard a more noteworthy competitor at the top end of the fine-wine market. Significant improvement is noticeable with the winery's Sauvignon Blanc. There are now two offerings. The 1991

Sauvignon Blanc (regular bottling) displays a moderately intense melon- and fruit-scented nose, and ripe, tasty flavors with crisp acidity and excellent length and definition. The 1991 Sauvignon Blanc Limited Selection, which has been 100% barrel fermented, is superb. A spicy, vanillin, mineral, and herb-scented nose is followed by deep, rich, beautifully ripe, well-focused flavors, medium body, excellent depth, and a crisp, luscious finish. It is a dead ringer for a top white Graves. Both Sauvignons should be drunk over the next several years. While Gainey also produces two *cuvées* of Chardonnay, in 1991 they did not make a Limited Selection. The 1991 Chardonnay (regular bottling) is closed, although it does reveal some toasty, spicy oak in the nose. Lean, with medium body and an austere personality, this is a straightforward Chardonnay for drinking over the next several years. Readers may want to make a note to check out Gainey's 1992 Chardonnay Limited Selection, which should prove to be outstanding. It was still in barrel when I tasted it, but with gorgeous levels of extract and Meursault-like nutty richness, it should prove to be a knock-out wine. I remember well the vegetal red wines produced by Gainey in the 1980s, but this problem has been rectified. Although their 1990 Merlot is austere, lean, and herbaceous, the 1990 Merlot Limited Selection offers plenty of black cherry fruit; a subtle, herbaceous component; rich, spicy, medium-bodied flavors; and more opulence and chewiness than the regular *cuvée*. Both Merlots should be consumed over the next 4–5 years. The 1990 Cabernet Franc Limited Selection is even more enticing, with a spicy, black fruit–, vanillin-scented bouquet, excellent richness and definition, as well as a long, silky finish. Deliciously forward, it promises to last for 5–7 years. Gainey has made its best Pinot Noirs to date with the 1991s and the unreleased 1992s. The only unexciting Pinot I tasted is the 1990 Pinot Noir Santa Barbara, a straightforward, ripe, tasty, spicy wine with good fruit, but not much aromatic or flavor complexity. It is ideal for uncritical quaffing over the next several years. The two *cuvées* of 1991 Pinot Noir are more serious wines, and I am delighted to report that they were bottled unfiltered—a first for this winery. The 1991 Pinot Noir Santa Maria exhibits a moderately intense, spicy, herb-, and berry-scented nose; round, fleshy flavors; a sense of elegance; and a succulent, soft finish. It should be consumed over the next 4–5 years. The 1991 Pinot Noir from Santa Barbara's superb Sanford & Benedict Vineyard displays a deeper color, with a rich, spicy, vanillin, plum, and raspberry-scented nose. There is gorgeous richness, a multidimensional flavor profile, plenty of power, yet a wonderful velvety texture and layered feel. Drink this sumptuous Pinot Noir over the next 5–6 years. Readers will also be glad to note that barrel samples of the 1992 Pinot Noir from the Bien Nacido Vineyard and the 1992 Pinot Noir from the Sanford & Benedict Vineyard are exceptionally promising. The Bien Nacido *cuvée* is potentially outstanding, and the Sanford & Benedict Pinot is a worthy rival to the superlative 1991.

E. & J. GALLO WINERY (MODESTO)

Cabernet Sauvignon*/* *, Cabernet Sauvignon Private Reserve* * *,
Chardonnay*/* *, Sauvignon Blanc* *, Other Wines*

1978	Cabernet Sauvignon Private Reserve	Sonoma	C	89
1991	Chardonnay Estate	Sonoma	D	88

Gallo is one of the great American success stories. Consider the fact that nearly 30% of American wine sold in this country is a product of Gallo or one of its subsidiary operations—Carlo Rossi, Bartles and James, and the Totts sparkling wines. Gallo produces an enormous array of wines. Many of their varietal-named wines are not only old tasting when released, but also thin and disappointing. As hard as it may be to believe, some of their least expensive wines, such as their nonvintage Chablis Blanc and Hearty Burgundy, both made in a slightly sweet, grapey style and selling for under $4 a bottle, offer more character and pleasure than the varietal-named wines. Even though they have residual sugar left in them to give them roundness and fullness, they are surprisingly pleasant and agreeable. From time to time interesting wines are released in the marketplace, including the 1978 Cabernet Sauvignon Private Reserve from Sonoma (this should not be confused with the Gallo regular 1978 Cabernet Sauvignon, a nondescript, simple wine). Only 1,000 cases of this wine were produced, and the bottling was aged 12 years by Gallo prior to release. The wine is excellent, dark ruby/garnet, with a rich, cedary, cassis, and spicy bouquet. Full bodied, rich, intense, well balanced, complex, and long, this is a top-flight Cabernet that should continue to drink well for at least another 5–8 years. Gallo has nearly 2,000 acres of vines in Sonoma, so I hope this is the first of many Private Reserves to be released. A special estate Chardonnay from Gallo's vineyard holdings in Sonoma marked a new campaign aimed at the luxury-priced category. The 1991 is an excellent, richly fruity, luscious wine that should drink well for 1–3 years.

GAN EDEN WINERY (SONOMA)
Cabernet Sauvignon* *, Chardonnay* * *, Chardonnay Reserve* * *,
Chenin Blanc* * *, Gamay Beaujolais* *, Gewürztraminer *

1988	Cabernet Sauvignon	Alexander Valley	C	72
1990	Chardonnay Reserve	Sonoma	C	86

This Sonoma winery produces kosher wines that can be surprisingly good, especially the Chenin Blanc and Chardonnay. The wines are simple, fruity, clean, and reasonably priced. To Gan Eden's credit, although the quality of the wines may not be superb, neither is it disappointing.

GAUER ESTATE VINEYARD (SONOMA)
Chardonnay* * *

1988	Chardonnay	Alexander Valley	C	86
1987	Chardonnay	Alexander Valley	C	82

These beautifully packaged Chardonnays are made in a tight, backward style that suggests consumer patience is required. Whether the fruit blossoms remains to be seen. The 1988 is a promising if restrained style of Chardonnay, and the 1987 is quite acidic. Both wines possess a good lashing of oak. If they were rated by packaging alone, they would be among the finest made in California. This is a property to keep an eye on.

DANIEL GEHRS (MONTEREY)
Chardonnay* * * *, Le Chenay Proprietary White Wine* * * *,
La Chenière Chenin Blanc* * * *, Red Wines* *

1991	Chardonnay	Monterey	B	88
1991	Le Chenay	Monterey	A	87
1991	La Chenière (Chenin Blanc)	Monterey	A	89

Daniel Gehrs, formerly the winemaker at Congress Springs, has started his own operation, and the first results are impressive, delicious white wines that are budget-priced and filled with personality and charm. Gehrs's 1991 La Chenière, a dry Chenin Blanc that has been barrel-fermented, may be one of the greatest white wine values in the world at $8 a bottle. It reminds me of a big, medium- to full-bodied, dry Loire Valley Chenin Blanc. It boasts super fruit, a huge, honeyed, floral-scented nose, rich, lingering flavors, excellent acidity for crispness, and an overall sense of grace and charm. It's one heckuva delicious wine for drinking over the next several years. The 1991 Chardonnay is another excellent bargain. Few Chardonnays under $20 possess such richness. The wine exhibits a lemony, apple and buttery nose, great purity, ripeness, and richness of fruit, medium to full body, and deep, long, lingering flavors. Drink it over the next 1–2 years. Last, Gehrs produced a 1991 Le Chenay, which is a barrel-fermented blend of Chardonnay and Chenin Blanc. This excellent, dry wine offers a floral, buttery, honeyed nose, chewy, rich flavors, a lively feel in the mouth, and a long finish. It, too, should be drunk over the next 1–2 years.

GEYSER PEAK WINERY (SONOMA)

Cabernet Sauvignon Estate Reserve* * *, Chardonnay* * *, Reserve Alexandre
Proprietary Red Wine * * * *, Sauvignon Blanc* * *, Semchard* * *

1989	Cabernet Sauvignon Estate Reserve	Alexander Valley	C	79
1987	Cabernet Sauvignon Estate Reserve	Alexander Valley	C	85
1985	Cabernet Sauvignon Estate Reserve	Alexander Valley	B	84
1990	Chardonnay	Sonoma	A	87
1987	Reserve Alexandre	Alexander Valley	C	89
1984	Reserve Alexandre	Alexander Valley	C	86
1991	Sauvignon Blanc	Sonoma	A	86
1990	Sauvignon Blanc	Sonoma	A	86
1991	Semchard (75% Semillon/25% Chardonnay)	California	A	85
1990	Semchard (75% Semillon/25% Chardonnay)	California	A	89
1989	Semchard (75% Semillon/25% Chardonnay)	California	A	86

Although quality is soaring at the up-and-coming Geyser Peak, prices have yet to keep pace with what is in the bottle. Consumers take note of Geyser Peak's delicious white wines. The 1990 and 1991 Sauvignon Blancs exhibit a super bouquet of melons, figs, and herbs. In the mouth they are medium to full bodied, with gobs of fruit, plenty of freshness, and a long, crisp, zesty, dry finish. The same can be said for the 1990 Chardonnay. Geyser Peak is to be commended for offering a full-bodied, flavorful, ripe style of Chardonnay that has not been overly oaked or excessively acidified. Someone who obviously understands consumers' tastes provided plenty of flavor. This excellent, richly fruity, creamy-textured Chardonnay will make delicious drinking over the next year. The real star of this trio is the sensational 1990 Semchard, an innovative as well as stunning blend of 75% Semillon from the Livermore Valley and 25% Chardonnay. This wine possesses a striking nose of honeyed fruit, melons, and figs; a buttery, opulent palate; great flavor depth and definition; and wonderful length and precision to its flavors. Despite its size and bold personality, the overall impression is one of freshness and personality. Drink this riveting wine over the next several years. Bravo! Is my rating too low? The 1989 Semchard is a spicy, intensely ripe, complex wine with gobs of delicious ripe fruit, a luscious texture, surprising concentration, and a fascinating character. I would opt for drinking it with chicken and fish over the next year. The 1991 Semchard is much lighter but still delicious. The 1987 Cabernet Sauvignon Estate Reserve has excellent jammy, rich, black cherry fruit, medium to full body, a chunky, somewhat monolithic character, but plenty of richness and intensity. If more complexity develops, my rating will look stingy. This robust Cabernet is drinkable now but promises to last for at least a decade. The 1985 Cabernet Sauvignon Estate Reserve reveals a supple, ripe, curranty fruitiness, an intelligent use of spicy new oak, a smooth texture, and a good finish. It should be drunk over the next 2–3 years. I was disappointed with the lean, compact, tart, tannic 1989 Cabernet Sauvignon. The 1987 Reserve Alexandre, a proprietary blend of 41% Cabernet Sauvignon, 34% Merlot, 15% Cabernet Franc, 7% Malbec, and 3% Petit Verdot, is an impressively wrought, rich, powerful Cabernet that should easily last for 10–15 years. Opaque dark ruby/purple, with a pronounced bouquet of spicy new oak, herbs, currants, and coffee, this full-bodied, solidly knit, highly extracted wine is bursting with superripe fruit, has plenty of glycerin, and offers a long, deep, moderately tannic finish. I would drink it between now and 2007. The 1984 Reserve Alexandre, made from 41% Cabernet Sauvignon, 40% Merlot, 16% Cabernet Franc, and 3% Malbec, is a plump, fleshy, full-bodied wine with excellent color, plenty of depth, and a roundness that gives it its precocious appeal. It could be more complex, but it certainly offers plenty of mouth-filling flavors. Drink it over the next 4–6 years.

GIRARD WINERY (NAPA)
Cabernet Sauvignon* * * *, Cabernet Sauvignon Reserve* * * * *,
Chardonnay* * * *, Chardonnay Reserve* * * *,
Chenin Blanc* * */* * * *, Pinot Noir* *

1989	Cabernet Sauvignon	Napa	C	79
1988	Cabernet Sauvignon	Napa	C	76
1986	Cabernet Sauvignon	Napa	C	87
1985	Cabernet Sauvignon	Napa	C	87
1991	Cabernet Sauvignon Estate	Napa	D	89
1990	Cabernet Sauvignon Estate	Napa	D	89
1991	Cabernet Sauvignon Reserve	Napa	D	91

1990	Cabernet Sauvignon Reserve	Napa	D	93
1985	Cabernet Sauvignon Reserve	Napa	D	88+
1984	Cabernet Sauvignon Reserve	Napa	D	92
1990	Chardonnay	Napa	C	86
1990	Chardonnay Reserve	Napa	C	90
1989	Chardonnay Reserve	Napa	C	84
1989	Pinot Noir	Oregon	C	74

Girard's style of Cabernet Sauvignon continues to reveal tightly knit, firm, full-bodied, highly concentrated yet structured wines that are built for the long haul. Even its regular bottlings seem surprisingly backward, and the Reserves need 2–3 years of aging when first released by the winery. The 1986 regular bottling exhibits a moderately intense, spicy, pure, blackcurrant nose; full-bodied, tightly knit, highly structured flavors; and at least 9–15 years of aging potential. I do not find it as flattering to drink young as many of the other 1986s and would suggest cellaring it for a minimum of 3–4 years. It should prove to be one of the longer-lived wines of the 1986 vintage. The 1985 regular bottling reveals plenty of fleshy, harmonious, blackcurrant fruit backed up by medium to full body, good tannins, and moderate amounts of spicy oak. It should last for at least a decade. The 1991 and 1990 Girard Cabernet Sauvignon Reserves performed extremely well. Among the two estate bottlings, the 1990 reveals sweeter fruit and more length, as well as some vivid purity. The impressive 1991 Estate bottling is similar, although higher in acidity, without the weight present in the 1990. Perhaps those characteristics will emerge with further barrel aging. Both Reserve offerings were outstanding, with a slight edge going to the more tannic 1990. It exhibits sensational richness of fruit, a wonderfully pure aroma of cassis and toasty new oak, and a long, generously endowed, moderately tannic finish. The 1991 Reserve, which is softer and not as full bodied, is intensely rich, with a beautiful black cherry and cassis nose intermingled with aromas of smoky new oak. The Estate wines should have at least a decade's worth of aging, the Reserves 12–15 or more years. The 1985 Reserve is backward, tight, and reserved at the moment yet impressively colored. A close examination of the wine reveals superb extract, plenty of weight and concentration, crisp acidity, a hefty dosage of toasty new oak, and layer upon layer of superpure blackcurrant fruit. It is a beautifully made wine for drinking at the end of the decade. **Anticipated maturity: 1996–2015.** The 1984 Reserve Cabernet is a deep, rich, profound wine in every sense. It carries the opulence and fleshy fruit that is such a characteristic of this vintage, yet it also displays a wonderful balance as a result of good, crisp acidity and a hefty dose of toasty new oak. It should be at its best between now and 2005. Girard's Chardonnays are among the best made in California. The consistently fine regular bottling displays plenty of oak as well as enough rich, honeyed apple fruit to stand up to the wood. The Reserve bottling is richer, fuller, and supposedly more ageworthy, although I am not sure that is the case. Nevertheless it is a dramatic, rich Chardonnay that gives exceptional pleasure if drunk within 3–4 years of the vintage. The 1990 and 1988 are the best two Reserves among recent bottlings. This winery also owns an Oregon Pinot Noir vineyard. The 1989 offering is a mediocre, thin, light wine that is well below the quality level of this stellar producer's other products. They also make a pleasant, inexpensive dry Chenin Blanc. The last vintage I tasted was the flowery 1990.

GLEN ELLEN (SONOMA)
Cabernet Sauvignon* *, Chardonnay* *, Sauvignon Blanc* *

These inexpensive offerings are all labeled Proprietor's Reserve and sell for under $7 a bottle. Not surprisingly, they are one-dimensional, fruity wines designed to be drunk within 1–3 years of the vintage. Although not thrilling, they are serviceable, cleanly made wines.

GRACE FAMILY VINEYARDS (NAPA)
Cabernet Sauvignon* * * * *

1990	Cabernet Sauvignon	Napa	E	93
1989	Cabernet Sauvignon	Napa	E	83
1988	Cabernet Sauvignon	Napa	E	87

Although this winery, like most other North Coast California wineries, stumbled in the tough vintages of 1988 and 1989, proprietor Dick Grace continues to fashion microscopic quantities (less than 300 cases) of superrich, lavishly oaked Cabernet Sauvignon that resembles the famed Special Selection Cabernet Sauvignon from Caymus. In fact, the wine was made by Caymus until 1983. The Grace Family Cabernet is now a cult item, and the price (over $50) reflects that. The wine is almost impossible to find, but it is worth the effort if you have plenty of patience and money. The 1989 is much lighter and leaner than previous vintages, no doubt because of this problematic year. The soft, luscious 1988 does not exhibit the structure or depth of other top vintages. If you have the riches of a superstar athlete, as well as connections in the wine world, look for the 1990 Cabernet Sauvignon, an explosively rich, expansive, full-bodied wine with great depth, extraction of fruit, and potential. **Anticipated maturity: 1995–2008.**

RATINGS FOR OLDER VINTAGES OF GRACE FAMILY VINEYARD CABERNET SAUVIGNON: 1987 (93), 1986 (92), 1985 (94), 1984 (94), 1983 (88), 1982 (86), 1981 (85), 1980 (92), 1979 (89), 1978 (90)

GRAND CRU VINEYARDS (SONOMA)
Cabernet Sauvignon* *, Chardonnay* *, Gewürztraminer*, Sauvignon Blanc* *

| 1985 | Cabernet Sauvignon Collector's Reserve | Alexander Valley | C | 86 |
| 1989 | Chardonnay Premium Selection | Sonoma | C | 78 |

This winery produces straightforward, crisp, simple Chardonnays, a pleasant and fruity Chenin Blanc that has wide appeal, and an increasingly attractive Sauvignon Blanc. The Cabernet Sauvignons have been erratic, but the 1985 Collector's Reserve must be the best Cabernet the Grand Cru winery has yet made. Its appeal is its rather obvious, fleshy, plump, blackcurrant fruit; supple texture; rich, full-bodied finish; and immediate accessibility and charm. It is a big, fleshy, fruity wine that should be drunk over the next 6 years.

GREEN AND RED VINEYARD (NAPA)
Zinfandel Chiles Mill Vineyard* * * *

1990	Zinfandel Chiles Mill Vineyard	Napa	B	86
1991	Zinfandel Chiles Mill Vineyard	Napa	C	88

This soft, charming, seductive 1990 Zinfandel lacks the power and intensity of some of the larger-scale examples, but there is no doubting its fine balance, round, herb, black cherry, and earthy flavors, velvety tannins, and satiny finish. Drink it over the next 5–6 years. The label indicates the wine was bottled unfiltered. The 1991 is slightly richer and more powerful but it remains an exceptionally graceful wine.

GREENWOOD RIDGE VINEYARDS (SONOMA)
Cabernet Sauvignon* *, Zinfandel* * *

1990	Cabernet Sauvignon Reserve	Alexander Valley	C	77
1990	Zinfandel	Sonoma	B	85
1990	Zinfandel Scherer Vineyard	Sonoma	B	86

I am not familiar with other wines from Greenwood Ridge, but the 1990 Zinfandel exhibits medium to dark ruby color, a spicy, peppery, raspberry-scented nose, excellent purity of fruit, medium body, a generous palate impression, and a spicy, moderately well-endowed finish. Drinkable now, it should last for another 5–6 years. Technocrats will no doubt object to the intense nose of berry fruit and saddle leather (suggestive of the brett yeast) that can be detected in the 1990 Zinfandel Scherer Vineyard. But this full-bodied, black cherry–scented and –flavored wine exhibits expansive, sweet, ripe fruit and light tannins in the finish. With another year of cellaring, some of the tannins should melt away to reveal even more opulence and intensity. Except for the musty, damp wood–scented nose, the 1990 Cabernet Sauvignon Reserve is an admirable effort. Although rich and well endowed, the wine retained its odd off smell even after 2 hours of airing.

GRGICH HILLS CELLARS (NAPA)
Cabernet Sauvignon* * * *, Chardonnay* * * *, Fumé Blanc* * * *, Zinfandel* * * *

1987	Cabernet Sauvignon	Napa	C	87
1986	Cabernet Sauvignon	Napa	C	87
1985	Cabernet Sauvignon	Napa	C	91
1984	Cabernet Sauvignon	Napa	C	88
1990	Chardonnay	Napa	D	88
1989	Chardonnay	Napa	D	84
1991	Fumé Blanc	Napa	B	89
1990	Fumé Blanc	Napa	B	88
1990	Zinfandel	Sonoma	B	88
1989	Zinfandel	Sonoma	B	82
1988	Zinfandel	Sonoma	B	87
1987	Zinfandel	Sonoma	B	88

If you thought Grgich Hills made only superb Chardonnay, you clearly have not tried their Fumé Blanc, Cabernet Sauvignon, or Zinfandel. The 1984 Cabernet is a deep, brawny, intense wine, loaded with fruit and presented in a very forward, supple, fleshy style that should have many admirers. It seems very typical of the 1984 vintage in its precociously rich, ripe fruit and fat, chewy flavors. Drink this beauty over the next 7–8 years. The 1985 should prove to be one of the best red wines this high-quality producer has ever made. It is much more structured than the 1984, with outstanding depth and richness, classic mineral- and blackcurrant-scented fruit, medium to full body, and an impressively long finish. It should prove to be one of the top 1985s. **Anticipated maturity: Now–2005.** More recent Cabernets, such as the 1986 and 1987, have been slightly less concentrated, more firmly tannic, and less flattering wines to taste. Perhaps they will equal the 1984 and 1985, but at present there is a toughness and backwardness to the wines that requires 3–4 more years of cellaring. They should prove to be capable of lasting 12–15 years. Grgich Hills has consistently made one of California's finest Zinfandels, using fruit from relatively old vineyards located on nonirrigated hillsides. The wine has traditionally been made in an intense, ripe, full-bodied style that can support 7–10 years of cellaring. The 1990 offers a deep ruby color, an intense nose of black raspberries and spices, a rich, medium- to full-bodied palate-feel, and a moderately tannic, excellent finish. The peppery, raspberry fruitiness is reminiscent of a fine Rhône Valley red wine. Despite the obvious richness and power, this is a wine with a sense of elegance. The 1988 Zinfandel offers surprisingly deep color, a rich, berry-, herb-, black raspberry–scented nose, and oaky, full-bodied, concentrated flavors. The copious quantities of fruit are buttressed by soft tannins, thus the overall impression is one of authentic varietal character made in a bright, rich, full-bodied style. It is hard to believe this much intensity could have been achieved in this vintage. Drink this beauty over the next 10 years. The 1987 Zinfandel offers at least a decade's worth of aging potential, although there is no need to defer your gratification. The intense bouquet of black raspberry fruit is followed by a rich, extracted, full-bodied, velvety-textured wine that gushes over the palate, creating no sense of imbalance or harshness. This concentrated, beautifully pure Zinfandel should drink well for at least a decade. Both the 1991 and 1990 Fumé Blancs are gorgeous white wines. Their big, melony, herbal, fruity noses display the subtle influence of toasty oak. The wines exhibit surprisingly rich, opulent flavors, good acidity, and plenty of body, glycerin, and alcohol in their luscious finishes. Drink them over the next 2 years. I thought the 1991 Fumé to be the finest I have yet tasted from Grgich, with a superfragrant nose of herbs, melons, and smoke followed by a medium- to full-bodied richness. The 1989 Chardonnay is more subdued and lighter than usual. The 1990 promises to be as good as the fine 1988; it is a rich, ripe, tasty wine with a nice touch of oak, good acidity, and a long, heady finish. If you have not yet realized it, Grgich Hills is one of California's finest wineries, performing at a high level with all varietals.

GROTH VINEYARDS AND WINERY (NAPA)

Cabernet Sauvignon* * */* * * *, Cabernet Sauvignon Reserve* * * */* * * * *
Sauvignon Blanc* *

1991	Cabernet Sauvignon	Napa	C	86
1990	Cabernet Sauvignon	Napa	C	88
1988	Cabernet Sauvignon Reserve	Napa	E	77
1987	Cabernet Sauvignon Reserve	Napa	E	86
1986	Cabernet Sauvignon Reserve	Napa	E	90
1985	Cabernet Sauvignon Reserve	Napa	EE	100
1984	Cabernet Sauvignon Reserve	Napa	E	93

Both the 1991 and 1990 regular *cuvées* of Cabernet Sauvignon offer the classic Groth style—sweet, almost intensely opulent fruit flavors, silky tannins, and hedonistic mouthfuls of ripe, herb-, coffee-, and cassis-flavored Cabernet fruit. The slightly less concentrated 1991 offers copious quantities of fruit in an up-front, precocious style. Although it will probably not make old bones, it should provide gorgeous drinking in its first 7–8 years of life. The expansive 1990, which has had 15% Merlot added, is another near-termer, with low acidity, satiny-smooth, rich flavors, and gobs of toffee, mocha, and cassis in its bouquet. Cabernet lovers should find this flattering wine immensely appealing. One can only imagine how impressive Groth's 1990 and 1991 Reserves will be in light of how tasty these regular *cuvées* have turned out. I was disappointed with the regular 1987, 1988, and 1989 Groth Cabernets, which I found excessively vegetal. The 1987 Reserve, however, is a better wine, with an impressively opaque dark ruby/purple color. The nose offers up aromas of sweet new oak, bell peppers, and weedy Cabernet fruit. Although the wine is concentrated and rich on the palate, it does not possess the stature or profound qualities of the 1984, 1985, or 1986. I am shocked by the vegetal character of the 1988 Groth Reserve. Drink it over the next 7–8 years, and let's hope the wine develops more dimension. For long-term aging, the 1986 Reserve may outlive the 1985. Impressive dark ruby/purple, with a saturated opaqueness to its color, it offers a somewhat reluctant bouquet of new oak, herbs, and superripe blackcurrants. In the mouth the wine is powerful, full, very tannic, and closed, needing at least 2–3 years of bottle age. Significantly less flattering than the 1985 Reserve, this big, muscular Cabernet Sauvignon should age gracefully for at least 10–15 years. It was inevitable that an American Cabernet would eventually merit a perfect rating. The utterly compelling and magical 1985 Cabernet Sauvignon Reserve from Groth offers the splendid opulence of the 1985 Cask 23, the power and depth of the 1985 Heitz Martha's Vineyard, and the unsurpassed perfume and lavish richness of the 1982 and 1986 bottlings of Mouton-Rothschild. The opaque ruby/purple color suggests awesome extract and low yields. The extraordinary bouquet of superripe and pure blackcurrants is enhanced by scents of toasty new oak, subtle mint, and violets. Sumptuous on the palate, with mind-boggling richness and brilliantly precise, well-focused, multidimensional flavors, this full-bodied wine is crammed with blackcurrant fruit that lingers on the palate for more than several minutes. This breathtaking wine should be at its apogee between now and 2005. It is a tour de force in winemaking! Bravo! Unfortunately only 500 cases were produced.

Given how splendid the regular bottling of 1984 Cabernet Sauvignon was, one might have expected the 1984 Reserve to be astonishing. It is. Dense black/ruby/purple, with a big bouquet of roasted coffee, chocolate, plums, and spicy oak, this gorgeously rich, velvety, intense, full-bodied wine can be drunk now and over the next 3–10 years. I hope Groth's inexplicable slump in 1987, 1988, and 1989 has been reversed in 1990 and 1991. Nevertheless, the winery still has problems with its Chardonnay and Sauvignon Blanc, which tend to be neutral, bland wines with too much acidity and not enough fruit and depth.

GUENOC WINERY (LAKE COUNTY)

Cabernet Sauvignon Beckstoffer Vineyard* *, Chardonnay Estate* * *,
Chardonnay Reserve* * */* * * *, Langtry Meritage White Wine* *, Petite Sirah* * *

1991	Chardonnay Estate	Guenoc Valley	B	82
1990	Chardonnay Estate	Guenoc Valley	B	86
1990	Chardonnay Reserve Genevieve Magoon Vineyard	California	C	87
1989	Langtry Meritage	Guenoc Valley	C	79
1990	Langtry Meritage	Guenoc Valley	C	82
1989	Petite Sirah	Lake	A	76
1987	Petite Sirah	Lake	B	87
1990	Sauvignon Blanc	Lake	A	80

Guenoc continues to experiment with different offerings and labels. At present there appear to be four quality levels. The top-of-the-line wines are Guenoc's vineyard-designated reserves, such as the Genevieve Magoon Vineyard Chardonnay and a Cabernet Sauvignon from the Beckstoffer Vineyard that I find disappointing. The next level are the so-called Estate wines, which sell for $10–$12 a bottle. They include a good Petite Sirah in the better vintages. A less expensive group of wines are the Guenoc Selections. The winery has recently added a low-priced group of wines under the Le Breton label. These offerings are extremely light, fluid, simple, and innocuous. The 1990 Chardonnay Reserve from the Genevieve Magoon Vineyard offers an outstanding nose of butterscotch, toasted nuts, and superripe fruit that is followed by a wine with excellent concentration. There is plenty of richness, a full-bodied, honeyed character, and a fine, spicy, fresh finish. If the finish had been just a bit longer, the score would have risen by several points. Drink it over the next year. Both the 1991 and 1990 Chardonnay Estates are medium-bodied wines with some attractive, buttery, apple-flavored fruit and good crisp acidity. The 1990 displays more opulence and a chewier texture; the 1991 is lighter and shorter in the finish. Both should be drunk before the end of 1994. Although the 1989 Petite Sirah is lean and tannic, the 1987 Petite Sirah exhibits an opaque deep ruby/purple color; a big, peppery, blackberry-, licorice-scented nose; massive, full-bodied flavors; and considerable tannins that need to be shed. Nevertheless, after some airing, the fruit was still impressively rich and pure. I would lay this wine away for 1–2 years. It should last for at least a decade. Guenoc has also begun to produce a Meritage white wine. Although heavily oaked, it is still attractive. From time to time there is also a good Zinfandel, but I have not seen a recent vintage. All in all, the quality is variable, but some good values frequently emanate from this producer.

GUNDLACH-BUNDSCHU WINERY (SONOMA)

Cabernet Franc* * *, Cabernet Sauvignon* */* * *, Cabernet Sauvignon Rhine Farm Vineyard* * *, Chardonnay* *, Gewürztraminer*, Pinot Noir* *, Zinfandel Rhine Farm* * *

1990	Bearitage	Sonoma	A	68
1988	Cabernet Franc Estate Rhine Farm Vineyard	Sonoma	C	86
1987	Cabernet Sauvignon Estate Rhine Farm Vineyard	Sonoma	C	86
1985	Cabernet Sauvignon Rhine Farm Vineyard	Sonoma	B	88
1991	Chardonnay	Sonoma	B	75
1990	Chardonnay	Sonoma	B	76
1991	Gewürztraminer	Sonoma	A	70
1989	Merlot	Sonoma	C	79
1990	Pinot Noir	Sonoma	B	73
1990	Pinot Noir Rhine Farm Vineyard	Sonoma	B	60
1990	Zinfandel Estate Rhine Farm Vineyard	Sonoma	B	87

This is a consistently reliable producer of red wine that rarely gets the media attention it deserves. The winery has moved from a thick, blockbuster style to a slightly lighter wine in the 1980s. The 1985 Cabernet Sauvignon Rhine Farm Vineyard is a deliciously plump, hedonistic wine with supple, lush, even opulent, full-bodied, ripe, blackcurrant and plummy fruit, plenty of length, and good structure, tannin, and acidity. It should continue to drink well for at least 5–7 more years. There is plenty of guts and character to the 1987 Cabernet Sauvignon. The chocolatey, ripe, herbaceous, berry-scented bouquet will please the masses, as will the relatively rich, medium- to full-bodied, supple flavors that exhibit a nice touch of oak and finish with a spicy, herbaceous note. This delicious Cabernet Sauvignon will not make old bones, but for drinking over the next 5–6 years, it offers considerable value. The 1988 Cabernet Franc from the Rhine Farm Vineyard is the first wine I have tasted from this winery that is dedicated exclusively to this varietal. It was soft, with a smooth, velvety texture, a fragrant, herbaceous, berry-scented bouquet, good ripeness, and a lush, velvety finish. It is a fine example of Cabernet Franc, resembling a midlevel St.-Émilion from France. Drink it over the next 5 years. The sumptuously styled 1990 Zinfandel will not be long-lived. But who can deny its appeal? The superintense nose of black fruits, herbs, berries, and chocolate is followed by a wine that exhibits super ripeness, a lush, velvety-textured palate, and heady fruit, glycerin, and alcohol in the finish. Drink it over the next 5–6 years for its exuberant, in-your-face style. The winery's other offerings are significantly less impressive. They include acidic, dull, light-intensity Chardonnays; a Gewürztraminer that exhibits none of the varietal character I associate with this exotic wine; and a vegetal, stripped, out-of-balance Pinot Noir. At the low-priced end of the Gundlach-Bundschu line are two pleasant generic white and red wines that are priced under $6. Last, Gundlach-Bundschu has come up with the hilarious idea of mocking all the Meritage wines that are frequently, and arrogantly, priced sky high. Their 1990 offering, called Bearitage, is a blend of 60% Cabernet Sauvignon, 30% Merlot, and 10% Zinfandel. The price is appealing, and the label is a howl; however, the wine is insipid, green, and excessively acidified, with a vegetal character in both the bouquet and skimpy flavors—in short, a grizzly effort.

HACIENDA WINE CELLARS (SONOMA)

Antares Proprietary Red Wine* *, Cabernet Sauvignon Sonoma* * *,
Chardonnay Clair de Lune* * * *, Chenin Blanc* * * *, Pinot Noir* *

1987	Antares Proprietary Red Wine	Sonoma	D	76
1986	Antares Proprietary Red Wine	Sonoma	D	72
1986	Cabernet Sauvignon	Sonoma	B	85
1985	Cabernet Sauvignon	Sonoma	B	86
1991	Chardonnay Clair de Lune	Sonoma	C	87
1991	Chenin Blanc	Sonoma	A	84

Like so many wineries, Hacienda offers a mixed bag of quality. It makes one of California's better dry Chenin Blancs, wonderfully pure, vivid, crisp, and delightful. The Clair de Lune Chardonnay is another example of a beautiful, well-knit, subtle, yet authoritatively flavored wine that offers subtle oak aromas as well as wonderful ripe, lemony, apple, buttery flavors. The 1991 is the best Chardonnay Hacienda has made in at least 3–4 years. The red wines are inconsistent, with the Sonoma Cabernet Sauvignon usually the best. Both the 1986 and 1985 are good examples of the vintage. The 1986 is more tannic. The 1985, which needs several more years in the cellar, offers a big, chocolatey, coffee- and berry-scented bouquet that is reminiscent of those aromas often found in the Cabernets of Stag's Leap Wine Cellars. In the mouth this wine exhibits very good richness, medium to full body, and a velvety, smooth texture. Drink it over the next 3–4 years. In 1986 Hacienda launched an expensive proprietary red wine called Antares. If the 1986 and 1987 are valid barometers of this wine's style, it is too acidic, austere, lean, excessively tannic, and uninteresting.

HAGAFEN WINERY (NAPA)

Cabernet Sauvignon* *, Chardonnay* */* * *, Chardonnay Reserve* *, Pinot Noir*

1988	Cabernet Sauvignon	Napa	C	76
1987	Cabernet Sauvignon	Napa	C	86
1991	Chardonnay	Napa	B	84
1990	Chardonnay Reserve	Napa	C	73
1991	Pinot Noir	Napa	B	73

This Napa Valley winery is one of the leading kosher wine specialists in the United States. The wines can be very good, even excellent. Current releases include an already drying out, faded 1990 Reserve Chardonnay; a tasty, richly fruity, medium-bodied 1991 Chardonnay; a disappointingly jammy, soft, diluted 1991 Pinot Noir; and a medium-bodied, straightforward, one-dimensional 1988 Cabernet Sauvignon. In contrast, the 1987 Cabernet is one of the finest kosher Cabernet Sauvignons I have tasted. Rich and full bodied, with a big, blossoming, smoky, oaky, blackcurrant-scented bouquet, this wine displays excellent extract, medium to full body, a smooth, supple texture, and a long finish. Whether purchased specifically for religious occasions or enjoyed for itself alone, this is a fine Cabernet Sauvignon selling at a realistic price.

HALLCREST VINEYARDS (SANTA CRUZ)
Cabernet Sauvignon* * *

1986	Cabernet Sauvignon de Cascabel Vineyard	El Dorado	B	86

Surprises abound, both positive and negative, when tasting California Cabernets. This example from the Hallcrest winery, a Cabernet Sauvignon from the backwoods of El Dorado County, exhibited a classic spicy, blackcurrant-scented bouquet, rich, full-bodied, lush and supple flavors, and a long finish. Drinkable now, it should last for another 5–6 years. Although I have not tasted any, this winery also produces a Gewürztraminer and Riesling.

HANDLEY (MENDOCINO)
Chardonnay* * * *, Gewürztraminer* *, Sauvignon Blanc* * * *,
Sparkling Wine* * *

1987	Brut Rosé	Anderson Valley	C	85
1988	Brut Sparkling Wine	Anderson Valley	C	85
1990	Chardonnay	Dry Creek	C	86
1991	Sauvignon Blanc	Dry Creek	B	86

Handley continues to display a sure touch with all of its offerings, save for the straightforward Gewürztraminer. The Sauvignon Blancs, made in an elegant, medium-bodied, complex style, have consistently possessed personality and copious quantities of fruit. The Chardonnays are lovely wines with fine flavor as well as a sense of restraint and charm. The sparkling wine production is small, but *cuvées* released to date have shown more fruit and depth than many of the more publicized California sparkling wine producers. Prices are fair.

HANNA WINERY (SONOMA)
Cabernet Sauvignon* * *, Chardonnay* * *, Sauvignon Blanc* *

1988	Cabernet Sauvignon	Sonoma	C	78
1987	Cabernet Sauvignon	Sonoma	C	85
1986	Cabernet Sauvignon	Sonoma	B	85
1990	Chardonnay	Sonoma	C	88
1990	Merlot	Sonoma	B	72
1990	Sauvignon Blanc	Sonoma	A	83

The 1990 Chardonnay from Hanna displays bold, nearly dramatic, buttery, apple-, popcornlike flavors and an expansive, broad-shouldered, rich palate impression. The finish is clean, crisp, and well balanced. Drink it over the next 1–2 years. Typical of the vintage, the 1988 Cabernet Sauvignon is hollow although pleasant, with a nose of ripe black fruit flavors, medium body, and a compact, angular, tannic finish. The deep ruby–colored 1987 Cabernet Sauvignon has a ripe, spicy, curranty bouquet, chunky, fleshy flavors, not a great deal of concentration, but gobs of fruit crammed into a medium- to full-bodied format. Drink this appealing Cabernet over the next 5–7 years. The 1986 Cabernet Sauvignon, with its opaque ruby/purple color and ripe, rich, black-currant- and licorice-scented bouquet, is well made. The rich, chewy, supple flavors show excellent intensity and have plenty of pleasure-giving qualities. This is a relatively forward, soft style of Cabernet that can be drunk now and over the next 6–7 years. The 1990 Sauvignon Blanc is crisp, fruity, light to medium bodied, and pleasant.

HANZELL WINERY (SONOMA)

Cabernet Sauvignon* */* * *, Chardonnay* * * * *, Pinot Noir* *

1988	Cabernet Sauvignon	Sonoma	D	73
1987	Cabernet Sauvignon	Sonoma	D	79
1990	Chardonnay	Sonoma	D	88
1988	Chardonnay	Sonoma	D	91
1988	Pinot Noir	Sonoma	C	72
1987	Pinot Noir	Sonoma	C	75

For many years Hanzell was one of California's most revered names, as it produced a number of blockbuster Chardonnays and occasionally a full-throttle Pinot Noir. The Chardonnays continue to be among the finest made in California, with the 1990 an impressively endowed, spicy, herb-, and apple-scented wine with full body, excellent acidity, and a long finish. Much of the wine's flavor is at the end of the palate, which suggests to me it may possess more aging potential than most California Chardonnays. Drink it over the next 3–4 years. If you can still find any, the 1988 is an even richer, fuller wine. Along with the 1991, it is one of only a handful of California Chardonnays that is likely to age for 5 or more years. On the other hand, Hanzell's recent Pinot Noirs have been excessively tannic and hard, with almost a chalky astringency to their taste. Additionally, they are completely lacking in fruit. Perhaps more fruit and charm will emerge, but I am skeptical. The Cabernet Sauvignons were disappointing in both 1988 and 1987, with entirely too much tannin for the amount of concentration. My advice: If you have deep pockets, search out Hanzell's top-flight Chardonnay, but avoid the other wines.

HARBOR WINERY (SACRAMENTO)

Cabernet Sauvignon* * */* * * *, Chardonnay* * *, Zinfandel* */* * * *

1984	Cabernet Sauvignon	Napa	B	86
1987	Chardonnay	Napa	B	85

The old-fashioned, thick, exotic, kinky style of Harbor's wines is controversial by any standards. I have had both oxidized and superb bottles, so it is hard to say what consumers are likely to find. Nevertheless, no one will feel cheated with the Chardonnay, Cabernet Sauvignon, or the Zinfandel from Amado when proprietor Charles Meyers produces it. The style here is for huge, unctuous, chewy wines, which, if not oxidized or marred by a strange off character, can be stunning. This winery also makes one of California's most interesting after-dinner drinks, the Mission del Sol, produced from late-harvested Amador grapes. It contains a whopping degree of alcohol and is best reserved for sipping after a meal. Harbor has a policy of releasing wines with 4–6 years of bottle age—an admirable although unconventional marketing policy. Despite the inconsistencies and occasional oxidized bottle, this is a winery worth searching out.

HARRISON WINERY (NAPA)

Cabernet Sauvignon* * * *, Chardonnay* * * *

1991	Cabernet Sauvignon	Napa	C	91
1990	Cabernet Sauvignon	Napa	C	90
1989	Cabernet Sauvignon	Napa	C	87
1991	Chardonnay	Napa	C	88
1990	Chardonnay	Napa	D	89

In the problematic 1989 vintage, this small winery produced one of the finest California Cabernet Sauvignons; it was clearly made from undiluted, ripe fruit. The big nose of spicy vanillin, ripe cassis, and herbs is followed by a rich, full-bodied wine with plenty of glycerin, extraction of flavor, and purity. The moderately soft tannins in the long finish suggest this wine will age for 10–15 years, although it can be drunk now. Harrison has followed the successful 1989 with two outstanding wines in 1990 and 1991. Both are boldly styled Cabernets with intense aromas of oak, cassis, chocolate, and black cherries. The 1991 is opulent, even fat, with great purity and extraction of fruit. It should drink well for 10–15 years. The 1990 is slightly more perfumed, as well as more structured, exhibiting huge chocolate-, cassislike flavors. **Anticipated maturity: 1995–2007.** The 1991 Chardonnay is forward and precocious, with a sweet, perfumed nose, supple, velvety texture, low acidity, and a good finish. Drink it over the next 1–2 years. The 1990 Chardonnay was also made in a full-throttle, almost French style, with a huge nose of toasty, smoky new oak, honeyed apples, and ripe peaches. Rich and full bodied, with enough acidity to provide lift and focus, this large-scale Chardonnay is bursting with flavor and personality. Drink it over the next 4–5 years.

HAVENS (NAPA)

Chardonnay* *, Merlot* * *, Merlot Truchard Vineyard* * * *

1989	Chardonnay Carneros	Napa	B	79
1989	Merlot	Napa	B	75
1988	Merlot	Napa	B	78
1989	Merlot Reserve Truchard Vineyard	Napa	C	80
1988	Merlot Reserve Truchard Vineyard	Napa	C	72
1987	Merlot Reserve Truchard Vineyard	Napa	C	88

It is probably because of the two difficult vintages, but certainly Havens's Merlot offerings in 1988 and 1989 are disappointing. These hard, lean, light-bodied wines offer neither depth nor fruit, and are well below the quality of the wines produced by this winery in the mid-1980s. For example, the 1987 Merlot Reserve will satisfy even the most demanding palates. For a Merlot it is surprisingly well knit and built for the long haul. Yet it can be enjoyed now for its full-bodied, chewy, fleshy, plummy flavors that are backed up nicely with a touch of toasty oak. The bouquet exhibits scents of plums, toast, and a whiff of herbs. Some tart acidity in the finish should keep the wine fresh and give it at least 6–10 years of aging potential. Considering the performance of Havens's wines in 1985 and 1986, my instincts suggest that the 1987, rather than the 1988 or 1989, is more indicative of what this winery is capable of. Consumers should be on the lookout for the 1990s and 1991s, two excellent vintages. The winery also produces a small amount of Chardonnay, of which the 1989 is light and fluid. It is already losing its fruit.

HAYWOOD WINERY (SONOMA)
Cabernet Sauvignon Sonoma* *, Cabernet Sauvignon California*,
Chardonnay* *, Zinfandel* * *

| 1989 | Zinfandel Chamizal Vineyard | Sonoma | B | 77 |
| 1988 | Zinfandel Chamizal Vineyard | Sonoma | B | 86 |

Haywood has a tendency to exaggerate a wine's structure to the detriment of its fruit and charm. However, the 1988 Zinfandel Chamizal Vineyard is a wine with the right balance. Plenty of juicy, black raspberry fruit makes this a seductive Zinfandel. This medium- to full-bodied, attractively made Zinfandel should drink well for the next 5–6 years. The nonexistent bouquet of the 1989 Zinfandel Chamizal Vineyard suggests a sterile-filtered wine. Although the color is medium-dark ruby and the flavors offer a peppery, berry fruitiness, this wine has been manufactured, not made. The finish exhibits moderate tannins. Drink this squeaky-clean wine over the next 3–4 years. I have been disappointed by the lean, austere, herbal Cabernet Sauvignons produced by Haywood from its holdings in Sonoma Valley and, more recently, by its inexpensive offering under a California designation. The Chardonnays have also proved to be malnourished wines with more structure than charm or fruit. A controlling interest in this winery was purchased by Buena Vista in 1991—not, in my mind, a sign that improvements are likely to be forthcoming.

HEITZ CELLARS (NAPA)
Cabernet Sauvignon Napa* * *, Cabernet Sauvignon Bella Oaks* * * *, Cabernet
Sauvignon Martha's Vineyard* * * * *, Chardonnay *, Grignolino*, Zinfandel*

1988	Cabernet Sauvignon	Napa	C	78
1987	Cabernet Sauvignon	Napa	C	76
1986	Cabernet Sauvignon	Napa	C	87
1985	Cabernet Sauvignon	Napa	C	91
1984	Cabernet Sauvignon	Napa	B	87
1988	Cabernet Sauvignon Bella Oaks	Napa	D	82
1987	Cabernet Sauvignon Bella Oaks	Napa	D	86
1986	Cabernet Sauvignon Bella Oaks	Napa	D	89
1985	Cabernet Sauvignon Bella Oaks	Napa	D	88
1984	Cabernet Sauvignon Bella Oaks	Napa	C	89
1988	Cabernet Sauvignon Martha's Vineyard	Napa	E	85

1987	Cabernet Sauvignon Martha's Vineyard	Napa	E	90
1986	Cabernet Sauvignon Martha's Vineyard	Napa	E	92
1985	Cabernet Sauvignon Martha's Vineyard	Napa	E	98
1984	Cabernet Sauvignon Martha's Vineyard	Napa	D	94

It is fashionable to criticize Joe Heitz. He takes no quarter, and wine writers are hardly his favorite species. Nevertheless there has been a noticeable drop in the quality of the Heitz Cabernets. It began with the 1987 Napa bottling and has continued with the 1988s. Much of this may be the result of the 1988 vintage, which produced a plethora of mediocre wines. The 1988 Cabernet Sauvignon Napa bottling is a short, compact, earthy wine with plenty of tannin but not much fruit or depth. The 1988 Bella Oaks is light and elegant, with some style and charm, but the finish is quick. The 1988 Martha's Vineyard is surprisingly light, even considering the vintage. It possesses less tannin, so one can get to the fruit more easily, but the nose appears to be sterile and the finish short. Nevertheless some of the famed mint notes are present in the moderate cassis aromas. For drinking over the next 10 years, the 1988 Martha's Vineyard is a straightforward, medium-bodied Cabernet. All three of the 1987 offerings are extremely tight, closed in, tannic, and hard. The 1987 Cabernet Sauvignon Napa bottling also displays a cardboardlike component in its otherwise reticent nose. The color is deep, and there is plenty of glycerin, richness, and concentration on the palate, but the tannins are extremely high. When first opened, the 1987 Bella Oaks offered no aroma at all, but after 3 days it reluctantly gave up smells of earth and cassis. It is one of the fullest-bodied, most tannic and astringent offerings from the Bella Oaks Vineyard that I have tasted. There is plenty of concentration, so if it comes into complete harmony and the tannins melt away, my rating may look conservative. The 1987 Martha's Vineyard possesses an opaque, dense ruby/purple color and a shockingly subdued, almost nonexistent nose. Only after 5 days of breathing did the famed mint and eucalyptus nose of the Martha's Vineyard Cabernet emerge! The wine is rich, burly, and full bodied, but also tannic and unflattering to taste. To say the wine needs significant time in the cellar is an understatement. **Anticipated maturity: 1997–2010.** The 1986s from Joe Heitz and family are worthy successors to his splendid 1985s. The Napa has a deep, dark ruby color and a spicy, tarry, herb-, plum-, and cassislike bouquet. Medium to full-bodied, with very fine concentration and moderate levels of soft tannins, this wine can be drunk now or cellared for 8–12 plus years. The Bella Oaks is more fragrant (scents of spicy oak, leaves, cassis, and cedar), round, precocious, and expansive on the palate, with softer tannins than the Napa and a long, silky finish. Elegant, as well as drinkable now, this attractive wine should evolve nicely for at least another 8–10 years. The Martha's Vineyard is the most broodingly dark-colored wine of this trio. The bouquet, at first reserved, opens with airing to reveal the telltale aromas of mint, blackcurrants, and smoky, tar-scented, spicy oak. Full bodied, rich, and more tannic and structured than the 1985, but not as deeply extracted, this is another beautifully rendered wine that at this stage is reminiscent of the 1979 and 1973. **Anticipated maturity: 1992–2008.** These three brilliant 1985s should have Cabernet enthusiasts drooling for at least the next 15–20 years. The feisty Joe Heitz has turned out wines that will ultimately rival the legendary Cabernets he made in 1974,

1973, 1970, 1969, and 1968. Do not make the mistake of overlooking the regular bottling of 1985 Napa Cabernet. This powerful, rich, full-bodied blockbuster is stuffed with rich, curranty fruit, has gobs of tannin, and yields a savory, mouth-filling texture. It should be at its best between now and 2005. The 1985 Bella Oaks is a lighter wine than the regular bottling and is more evolved and elegant. It is, however, no wimp. A velvety texture of earthy, blackcurrant fruit is admirably balanced by soft acids and satiny tannins. Medium bodied, lush, and easily the most precocious tasting of the 1985 Heitz Cabernets, this charming wine should drink well for 8–12 years. The 1985 Martha's Vineyard is sure to register high on anyone's pleasure meter. This opulent, splendidly rich, highly concentrated wine has so much power and fruit that its sizable levels of ripe tannins are beautifully concealed. The huge bouquet of lavish red and black fruits, subtle mint, and vanillin oakiness is only the opening act to a thrilling drinking experience. Layers of rich fruit, soft tannins, and a fleshy, harmonious, fabulous finish are what makes bottles such as this close to perfection. It is a dazzling effort that should drink well (and improve) for 12–20 or more years. The 1984 regular Napa Cabernet Sauvignon is an ideal wine for drinking over the next 5–7 years. Medium to full bodied and opulently fruity, with broad, velvety, curranty flavors, this is a delicious wine for the near term. The 1984 Bella Oaks raises the level of intensity and is more tannic, with plenty of spicy oak, full body, and good tannins. It is the finest Bella Oaks made by Heitz since 1977. As for the famed Martha's Vineyard, the 1984 is an extraspecial wine of explosive richness, plenty of power, layers of spicy oak, blackcurrant notes, subtle mint, and a fabulous finish. It is an exceptionally deep wine that can be drunk between now and 2010. Although Joe Heitz would vehemently argue otherwise, the Chardonnays made here are earthy to the point of being dirty. Occasionally a good bottle can be found, but generally this is a one-dimensional, heavy-handed wine with no finesse or elegance. The Zinfandels I have tasted have also been disappointing. The rosé-style Grignolino can be a lot of fun to drink, but its herbal streak is entirely too pronounced, and the wine often tastes awkward, if not funky.

RATINGS FOR OLDER VINTAGES OF HEITZ CELLARS CABERNET SAUVIGNONS:

MARTHA'S VINEYARD: 1983 (88), 1982 (86), 1981 (88), 1980 (89), 1979 (90), 1978 (89), 1977 (89), 1976 (93), 1975 (91), 1974 (96), 1973 (92), 1970 (94), 1969 (90), 1968 (96)

BELLA OAKS VINEYARD: 1983 (82), 1980 (86), 1978 (78), 1977 (84)

HESS COLLECTION WINERY (NAPA)

Cabernet Sauvignon* * * *, Cabernet Sauvignon Reserve* * * * *,
Chardonnay* * * *, Hess Select Chardonnay* * *

1989	Cabernet Sauvignon	Napa	C	87
1988	Cabernet Sauvignon	Napa	C	86
1987	Cabernet Sauvignon	Napa	C	89
1986	Cabernet Sauvignon	Napa	C	87
1987	Cabernet Sauvignon Reserve	Napa	D	91
1986	Cabernet Sauvignon Reserve	Napa	D	89
1990	Chardonnay	Mount Veeder	C	86

1991	Chardonnay	Napa	C	87
1990	Chardonnay	Napa	C	88
1991	Chardonnay Hess Select	Napa	A	85
1989	Merlot	Napa	B	78

This winery has a young but superlative track record for its first 10 years of life. The Swiss proprietor, Donald Hess, can be lauded for the fact that there is not a disappointing wine to be found in his entire portfolio. The regular *cuvées* of Cabernet Sauvignon, which were delicious in the top Cabernet vintages of the 1980s, are surprisingly good and among the stars of the so-so vintages of 1988 and 1989. The Chardonnays have consistently been excellent wines, with plenty of fruit, personality, richness, and length. They exhibit the judicious use of oak and have proven to last for 3–5 years. Hess recently added an inexpensive line of $10 Cabernets and Chardonnays called Hess Select. The Hess Select Cabernet is a competent example of a low-priced Cabernet, and the Hess Select Chardonnay is one of the best values of Chardonnay for under $10 a bottle. The 1989 Cabernet Sauvignon Napa exhibits excellent richness as well as surprising breadth and depth for a wine of this vintage; it should drink well for at least 10 years. Although not as dramatic, the 1988 Napa is a competent, tasty, cassis-, herb-, mineral-, and toasty-scented and -flavored wine for drinking over the next 7–8 years. The 1987 Cabernet Sauvignon Napa is a strong effort from the Hess Collection. Although it may not have the massiveness of the 1984 Reserve, it is nevertheless a beautifully rendered, spicy, oaky, cassis-scented wine with medium to full body, supple, ripe flavors, and a long, graceful, moderately tannic finish. Drinkable now, it should easily evolve for another 10–15 years. The 1986 regular Cabernet exhibits excellent ripeness, a great deal of tannin, plenty of depth and body, and a good finish. It should last for at least a decade. I remember tasting the 1987 Cabernet Sauvignon Reserve in its infancy, and now that it is in the bottle, it clearly justifies the high praise I gave it several years ago when I issued my barrel-tasting notes on the 1987 vintage. The color is an impressive dark ruby/purple, and the nose, although somewhat closed, can be coaxed from the glass to reveal scents of minerals, black cherries, licorice, and spices. In the mouth it is full bodied, intense, tannic, and backward. The acidity is sound and the finish long and powerful. Although everything is in balance, this wine is not recommended for near-term drinking. It should be cellared for at least 4–5 years and should easily last for 15–20 years. The 1986 Cabernet Sauvignon Reserve is not quite as concentrated or as opulent as the superb 1984. However, although drinkable at present, it should continue to evolve for at least a decade. It is deep, dark ruby with a classic as well as pure bouquet of blackcurrants and cassis interspersed with nuances of vanilla and smoky oak. In the mouth the wine is full bodied and tannic, with excellent concentration and a long, deep finish. If it sheds some of its tannin and develops a more expansive palate, it may well merit an outstanding rating in several years. Although both the 1991 and 1990 Hess Collection Chardonnays are excellent wines, the 1991 is slightly lighter. However, both are rich and authoritatively flavored. The delicious 1991 Hess Select Chardonnay offers attractive floral, pineapple, and buttery fruit aromas, opulent, rich flavors, crisp acidity, and a fleshy, zesty finish. In 1990 Hess added a third Chardonnay to his portfolio, this offering with a Mount Veeder

designation. The Hess Collection is one of California's most reliable producers
of high-quality Cabernet Sauvignon and Chardonnay.

HIDDEN CELLARS (MENDOCINO)
Alchemy Proprietary White Wine* * * *, Chardonnay* * *,
Sauvignon Blanc* * * *, Zinfandel* * * *

1991	Alchemy	Mendocino	C	90
1990	Alchemy	Mendocino	C	90
1991	Chardonnay	Mendocino	B	86
1990	Chardonnay Reserve Barrel Fermented	Mendocino	C	87
1989	Chardonnay Reserve Barrel Fermented	Mendocino	C	86
1990	Sauvignon Blanc	Mendocino	A	86
1990	Zinfandel	Mendocino	B	87

Hidden Cellars is another of those California wineries that turn out interesting,
delicious wines that do not get as much publicity as they deserve. The superb
1991 and 1990 Alchemy offerings from Hidden Cellars could easily pass for a
white Graves. Both wines offer rich aromas of melons, figs, and toast; an unctuous, deep, chewy texture; a gorgeous inner core of ripe fruit; and a long, nicely
extracted, well-balanced, rich, dry finish. Both should last 3–4 years. The
1989 vintage did not produce many top Chardonnays, but Hidden Cellars'
Chardonnay Reserve Barrel Fermented is a competent effort. Spicy, oaky,
vanillin, apple, and lemony flavors are present in quantities abundant enough
to give this wine plenty of appeal; drink it over the next year. The 1990
Chardonnay Mendocino is a fruity, crisp wine that will make for delicious
drinking over the next 2–3 years. Hidden Cellars also does a top-notch job
with Sauvignon Blanc. The delicious 1990 is bursting with fruit and character
and exhibits plenty of herbaceousness, which is meshed with considerable
richness and character. The Zinfandel also remains underrated, much like the
winery itself. The 1990 Zinfandel displays an explosive nose of black raspberry fruit, a soft, voluptuous texture, good purity and balance, and a long,
lusty, medium- to full-bodied finish. Drink it over the next 5–6 years. Although
I have not tasted the most recent release, Hidden Cellars also produces a potentially outstanding sweet, late-harvest, botrytised Semillon and Sauvignon
Blanc blend called Chanson d'Or.

THE WILLIAM HILL WINERY (NAPA)
Cabernet Sauvignon Gold Label Reserve* * *, Cabernet Sauvignon Silver Label* *,
Chardonnay Gold Label Reserve* */* * *, Chardonnay Silver Label* *

1989	Cabernet Sauvignon Reserve	Napa	C	55
1988	Cabernet Sauvignon Reserve	Napa	C	76
1990	Chardonnay Reserve	Napa	C	82
1991	Chardonnay Silver Label	Napa	B	79

This winery began with considerable promise, particularly in its Cabernet
Sauvignons. A strong argument can be made that the 1978 William Hill Cabernet Sauvignon (the debut release) remains Hill's finest wine. Since 1978 there
has been a procession of high-acid, tart wines that have increasingly become

sterile and narrowly constructed, with dubious flavor extraction. Even the initially impressive 1984, 1985, and 1986 Reserve Cabernets now taste compact, angular, and shrill from the bottle. They can age well, but unless one has a fetish for copious quantities of acidity, tannin, and sharpness, there will be little joy to be found. This is a shame, as William Hill's vineyards are capable of producing outstanding grapes. The less expensive Silver Label Cabernet is a straightforward, one-dimensional wine. The Chardonnays have gone from overblown, oaky monsters to crisp, tart, medium-bodied wines that offer a restrained bouquet of oak and citric acidity. The Silver Label, which in the past has offered fine value, is now a light, washed-out wine. The Reserve exhibits plenty of oak as well as frightfully high acid levels. Sadly, Hill's wines are monuments to the abuses of California technology and oenology.

LOUIS HONIG (NAPA)
Sauvignon Blanc* * *

| 1991 | Sauvignon Blanc | | B | 84 |

The only wines I have ever tasted from this relatively small producer are the Sauvignon Blancs, although Chardonnay, Cabernet Sauvignon, and Merlot are also produced. The good 1991 Sauvignon Blanc offers a moderately intense, herbaceous, fruity nose, medium body, good cleanliness, crisp acidity, and a pleasant finish. This wine requires consumption within 2–3 years of the vintage.

HOP KILN WINERY (SONOMA)
Petite Sirah* * * *, Zinfandel Primativo* * * *, Zinfandel Sonoma* * *

1987	Petite Sirah Marty Griffin's Vineyard	Sonoma	B	87
1990	Zinfandel	Sonoma	B	87
1987	Zinfandel	Sonoma	A	86
1990	Zinfandel Primativo Old Vines	Sonoma	B	89

This Russian River Valley winery produces brawny, full-bodied Zinfandels that admirably stand the test of time. No doubt both of the 1990s will provide sumptuous drinking for another 6–7 years, perhaps longer where well stored. The 1990 Sonoma offers up an opulently rich, peppery, spicy, black raspberry–scented nose, medium- to full-bodied, soft, luscious flavors, fine glycerin, and a mouth-filling feel. Too tasty to resist drinking now, it should age well for 6–7 years. The 1990 Primativo, made from an old hillside vineyard, could prove to be outstanding. Slightly darker in color, with more tannin, alcohol, glycerin, and extract, it is not as seductive as the regular bottling, but it is loaded with the gorgeous berry fruit that Zinfandel can provide when the yields are kept low and the vines are old. Approachable now, this wine should hit its peak by 1994 and last for 7–10 years. The 1987 Zinfandel could easily go unnoticed in a blind tasting of some of the better wines from Gigondas and Châteauneuf-du-Pape in the Rhône Valley. Its big, spicy, peppery, earthy bouquet displays abundant ripeness and concentration. The lush, heady, alcoholic, full-bodied flavors are packed with fruit and glycerin. This multidimensional, big, mouth-coating Zinfandel should drink beautifully for another 5–6 years. The good Petite Sirahs from California rarely get the accolades they deserve, which actually works to the advantage of the shrewd consumer who can pick up some potentially long-lived, rich, full-bodied wines for a song. Hop Kiln's 1987 Petite Sirah has a gorgeous bouquet of spicy black pepper and ripe black fruits. It is dense, intense, and full bodied, with great persistence and excellent richness and extract. Drinkable now, this muscular, fleshy Petite Sirah should age well for 10–12 years.

HUSCH VINEYARDS (MENDOCINO)

Cabernet Sauvignon* * *, Chardonnay* * *, Chenin Blanc* * * *, Gewürztraminer* *, Pinot Noir* *, Sauvignon Blanc* * *

1989	Cabernet Sauvignon	Mendocino	B	83
1988	Cabernet Sauvignon La Ribera Vineyard	Mendocino	B	85
1987	Cabernet Sauvignon La Ribera Vineyard	Mendocino	B	86
1987 -	Cabernet Sauvignon North Field Select	Mendocino	C	86
1991	Chardonnay	Mendocino	B	86
1990	Chardonnay	Mendocino	B	85
1992	Chenin Blanc	Mendocino	A	88
1990	Gewürztraminer	Mendocino	A	76
1990	Pinot Noir	Anderson Valley	B	84
1991	Sauvignon Blanc	Mendocino	A	86

The Husch winery continues to turn out highly satisfying, pleasurable, unpretentious wines. The floral, exuberant, fresh, relatively dry, light-bodied 1992 Chenin Blanc is a classic example of how tasty wines from this varietal can be. Drink it before the summer of 1994. The soft, ripe 1988 Cabernet Sauvignon from the La Ribera Vineyard has a bouquet that jumps from the glass with aromas of herbs and red fruits. There are round, graceful flavors touched by some oak, but the overall impression is of delicious, unadorned Cabernet fruit picked when it was ripe and not excessively processed or overly acidified. It has more depth than the light but fruity 1989 Cabernet Sauvignon. Drink this charmer over the next 3–5 years. I would have loved to upgrade the 1987 Cabernet Sauvignon La Ribera Vineyard, but in all fairness its aging potential is limited and it is not as stunningly concentrated, nor will it be as profound as some of the higher-rated Cabernets. That being said, this is one of the most totally delicious Cabernets from my tastings, and if more California wineries produced wines like this, perhaps wine consumption in America would become more popular. What is so appealing is that the winery has captured the vibrant, effusive fruitiness of the Cabernet Sauvignon grape yet has not betrayed its varietal character. This wine gushes with soft, hedonistic, blackcurrant fruit, is round and opulent on the palate, and has a satiny finish. It is a totally captivating, delicious Cabernet Sauvignon for drinking over the next 2–3 years. If I were in the restaurant business, I would be stockpiling such wines. Don't miss it! The beautifully made, velvety-textured 1987 Cabernet Sauvignon North Field Select offers up aromas of herbs and blackcurrants, has delicious, ripe fruit, and delivers a gentle finish. How nice it is to drink a Cabernet without having to brush your teeth after being overdosed on massive quantities of acidity and tannin. This stylish, elegant Cabernet should be drunk over the next 2–4 years. Husch's philosophy of making up-front, fruity, tasty red wines is equally evident in the winery's portfolio of white wines. Never dazzling, but always delicious and satisfying, Husch produces a floral, light-bodied, exuberantly fruity and zesty Sauvignon Blanc and a tasty Chardonnay that gushes with lemony, buttery, apple fruit. These wines are meant to be drunk within 3 years of the vintage. If this winery has a weakness, it is its straightforward Gewürztraminer and washed-out Pinot Noir. Although there is enough of an earthy, weedy, plum and cherry nose in the Pinot Noir to create some interest, the wine usually lacks concentration and a finish. I thought the 1990 Anderson Valley Pinot Noir was an improvement over other efforts. It is a light, fruity, almost Gamay-tasting wine that should be drunk over the next 2 years.

INDIAN SPRINGS (SIERRA FOOTHILLS)
Chardonnay* *, Merlot* *

1991	Chardonnay Reserve	Sierra Foothills	B	83
1990	Merlot	Sierra Foothills	B	78

I found the 1991 Chardonnay to be soft, plump, woody, and ideal for drinking over the next 1–2 years. Although the 1990 Merlot has an impressive color, the depth of fruit is not sufficient for the strong, herbal, earthy notes and excessive tannin.

INGLENOOK VINEYARDS (NAPA)
Cabernet Sauvignon Napa* *, Cabernet Sauvignon Reserve Cask* */* * *,
Chardonnay* *, Chardonnay Reserve* *, Gravion Proprietary White Wine* *,
Niebaum Claret*, Reunion Proprietary Red Wine* */* * *

1988	Cabernet Sauvignon	Napa	B	74
1987	Cabernet Sauvignon	Napa	B	78
1987	Cabernet Sauvignon Reserve Cask	Napa	D	83
1986	Cabernet Sauvignon Reserve Cask	Napa	D	84
1990	Chardonnay	Napa	B	81
1989	Chardonnay	Napa	B	76
1990	Gravion Proprietary White Wine	Napa	C	84
1986	Niebaum Claret	Napa	A	70
1985	Reunion Proprietary Red Wine	Napa	D	78

This winery, a perennial underachiever, was once one of Napa's finest, especially under the legendary John Daniel, who was renowned for the extraordinary special-cask Cabernet Sauvignons he made during the 1950s and 1960s (many of them still in marvelous condition). In the 1980s, Inglenook exhibited signs that it was cognizant the future rested in quality, not in a historic reputation. Some proprietary wines were introduced: the Reunion in 1983 and, more recently, the Gravion (a Semillon/Sauvignon Blanc blend). Despite the positive signs, and improved quality when compared with what was produced in the

1970s, the sad fact is that Inglenook's top wines are highly processed and bland. Excessively acidified and sterile filtered by overly cautious oenologists, the resulting wines, predictably, are lean, austere, hard, and tough, undermining the notion that wine is a beverage of pleasure. The most tasty, delicious wine may be Inglenook's proprietary white Gravion, an intriguing, subtle, flavorful offering with a kinship to a top white French Graves. The Reserve Cask reds are designed to last for 15–20 years, but they are deficient in bouquet, fruit, and depth. Inglenook could use a wake-up call. Its less expensive wines, including the jug wines under the Navalle label, are straightforward and uninteresting.

INNISFREE (NAPA)
Cabernet Sauvignon*, Chardonnay*, Sauvignon Blanc* *

1989	Cabernet Sauvignon	Napa	B	69
1990	Chardonnay	Napa	A	72
1991	Sauvignon Blanc	Napa	A	80

The only good news to report about this winery is that the Sauvignon Blanc is pleasant. However, the excessively acidified, tart, austere, almost fruitless Chardonnays and Cabernet Sauvignons are just what the wine consumer does not need—another innocuous, empty style of wine that discourages consumption.

IRON HORSE RANCH AND VINEYARDS (SONOMA)
Cabernets Proprietary Red Wine* * *, Chardonnay* * *, Fumé Blanc* * *,
Sparkling Wine Cuvées* * * *

1989	Cabernets	Alexander Valley	C	82
1988	Cabernets	Alexander Valley	C	84
1990	Chardonnay	Green Valley	C	85
1990	Fumé Blanc	Alexander Valley	B	84
1987	Sparkling Wine Blanc de Blancs	Sonoma	C	89
1988	Sparkling Wine Brut	Sonoma	C	85
1987	Sparkling Wine Brut Late-Disgorged	Sonoma	C	88
1989	Sparkling Wine Brut Rosé	Sonoma	D	90
1987	Vrais Amis	Sonoma	C	87

The two finest sparkling wine producers in California are Iron Horse and the French-owned Roederer. These offerings from Iron Horse are distinctive and totally different in style. The 1988 Brut is the lightest wine, with a great deal of tart, fresh acidity, good fruit, a "Wheat Thins," green apple–like taste, liveliness, and a clean, pure finish. The 1987 Blanc de Blancs has a slightly deeper straw color and is fresh, with persistent pinpoint, well-defined bubbles. The spring flower garden bouquet is followed by the tastes of ripe apples and a rich, creamy finish. It is a gorgeous, clean, impeccably made sparkling wine for drinking over the next several years. My favorite, the 1989 Brut Rosé, is probably the most controversial sparkling wine Iron Horse produces. It is the closest any California winery comes to the style achieved by the famous Dom

Pérignon rosé. This medium salmon-colored wine offers up a bouquet of rich raspberry fruit intermingled with the aroma of freshly picked tomatoes. Fuller bodied than the other offerings from Iron Horse, this rich, wonderfully textured, yet fresh sparkling wine impresses on the palate because of its depth and fullness. I was also pleased by the stamina of its tiny, well-formed bubbles. It clearly must be served with food given its size and flamboyant personality. Iron Horse's other sparkling wine *cuvées* include a relatively yeasty, full bodied, classy 1987 Late-Disgorged Brut. It makes more of an impact on the palate and is not as delicate as their Blanc de Blancs. The 1987 Vrais Amis offers tart, applelike aromas, a nice touch of toasty oak, plenty of ripe fruit, and fine length. It should improve for another 2–3 years and last for 5–6. The still wines are all made in a delicate, subtle style. The proprietary red wine called Cabernets exhibits an herbaceous streak that recalls a medium-weight St.-Émilion. The 1988 has attractive cherry fruit, not much intensity or length, but considerable style. The tasty 1990 Fumé Blanc offers a subtle touch of oak, plenty of melony, fig-, herblike fruit, and a crisp, zesty finish. The Chardonnay is also an understated, subtle, lemony-, apple-tasting wine with good acidity and wonderful purity. All things considered, this is a top-notch winery that is making some of the best sparkling wines in the new world.

JADE MOUNTAIN (NAPA)
Mourvèdre* * *, Rhône Ranger Cuvées* * * *

1990	Les Jumeaux Unfiltered	California	B	89
1990	Mourvèdre Unfiltered	California	C	86
1990	La Provençale	California	B	87
1990	Syrah	Sonoma	C	89

This is an impressive portfolio of Rhône Valley–inspired wines. They all exhibit wonderfully ripe fruit, fine richness, and a great deal of personality. Made in a forward style, the 1990 Mourvèdre is the only wine that does not express its varietal character as strongly as it might have. Nevertheless, it possesses a deep ruby/purple color, a spicy, earthy-scented nose, rich, intense, black-fruit flavors, good viscosity and glycerin, and a spicy, lush finish. Drink it over the next 4–5 years. The 1990 La Provençale, a Mourvèdre/Syrah blend, reveals a big, dramatic nose of black pepper and spices. It is voluptuous, with gobs of black cherry and raspberry fruit, plenty of glycerin, and a heady, rich, medium- to full-bodied finish. It should drink well for 5–7 years. Jade Mountain's 1990 Les Jumeaux (the twins), a Cabernet Sauvignon/Mourvèdre blend, tastes akin to a California rendition of a top-notch Bandol. It offers an excellent saturated deep ruby/purple color; a spicy, peppery, cassis, earth, and herb-scented nose; layer upon layer of velvety-textured, jammy–black fruit flavors; an unctuous texture; and a rich, long, satisfying finish. It will last for at least 7–8 years. Last, the 1990 Syrah reveals more evidence of toasty, smoky, vanillin new oak in the nose, as well as rich, bacon fat, meaty, cassis flavors, massive quantities of fruit, and a full-bodied, moderately tannic finish. This should prove to be the longest-lived wine of this quartet, yet it can be drunk now given its superb ripeness and relatively low acidity. I am impressed!

JAEGER-INGLEWOOD VINEYARD (NAPA)

Merlot Inglewood Vineyard* * * *

1987	Merlot Inglewood Vineyard	Napa C	88
1985	Merlot Inglewood Vineyard	Napa C	87

The 1987 Merlot from the Inglewood Vineyard appears to be the best effort yet from the Jaeger-Inglewood winery. With an impressively opaque, dark ruby/purple color, an enticing coffee-, chocolate-, and berry-scented nose, intense, full-bodied, opulent flavors, a multidimensional texture, and a long, chewy, ripe finish, this beautiful Merlot will drink well for 8–10 years. The intense yet forward, cedary, herbaceous yet richly fruity bouquet of the 1985 soars from the glass. In the mouth this generously stuffed, concentrated, satin-textured Merlot is bursting with plummy fruit, is full bodied, and finishes with a heady, alcoholic kick. It is a lush, lavishly rich Merlot for drinking over the next 5–6 years—all that Merlot can and should be!

JEKEL VINEYARD (MONTEREY)

Cabernet Sauvignon Home Vineyard* *, Chardonnay* * *, Riesling* * *,
Scepter Proprietary White Wine* *, Symmetry Proprietary Red Wine* */* * *

1989	Cabernet Sauvignon Arroyo Seco	Monterey C	77
1986	Cabernet Sauvignon Arroyo Seco	Monterey B	73
1990	Chardonnay Arroyo Seco	Monterey B	84
1989	Chardonnay Arroyo Seco	Monterey B	76
1988	Scepter Proprietary White Wine Jekel Vineyard	Monterey C	70
1987	Symmetry Proprietary Red Wine	Monterey C	78

This is an interesting yet perplexing winery to evaluate. Unquestionably the reds have a profound green pepper, vegetal side. However, after seeing how some of Jekel's older vintages have aged (particularly 1978 and 1980), it appears that the bell pepper quality can evolve into a lovely, sweet, cedary character. I have often felt my initial reviews were not only unfair but unreliable. That being said, one has to evaluate these wines based on what is in the bottle when it is tasted and not on unfounded optimism. The 1987 Symmetry exhibits plenty of depth and may well turn out to be far superior to what I have indicated. But the annoying vegetal element is off-putting—at least for now. The 1986 Cabernet Sauvignon Arroyo Seco is much less concentrated and leaner. I do not see it ever developing into anything of interest. Jekel has also made some relatively long-lived, rich Chardonnays, but the 1989 is not one of them. It is short, compact, and malnourished. In the past this winery has also made some fine Rieslings that displayed excellent freshness and a Kabinett-style fruitiness and personality. I have not seen any recent vintages of the Riesling. The 1988 Scepter, a proprietary white wine made from Chardonnay, has already lost all of its fruit, which makes for a hollow, neutral taste.

JOHNSON-TURNBULL VINEYARDS (NAPA)

Cabernet Sauvignon* * *, Cabernet Sauvignon Vineyard Selection 67* * */* * * *

1990	Cabernet Sauvignon Vineyard Selection 67	Napa	C	88
1988	Cabernet Sauvignon Vineyard Selection 67	Napa	C	79
1986	Cabernet Sauvignon Vineyard Selection 67	Napa	C	87

Johnson-Turnbull consistently produces a distinctive style of Cabernet, always emphasizing smoky, overtly minty, cassis aromas. The style sought also places importance on restraint and elegance. Excellent ripeness, a medium-bodied texture, and a long, graceful finish are all evident in the attractive, stylish 1990 Cabernet. It should age nicely for 10–12 years. Johnson-Turnbull's 1986 Cabernet Sauvignon Vineyard Selection 67 shares with its Cabernets an intense bouquet of mint and eucalyptus to go along with its moderately full-bodied flavors, tart, high acidity, and concentrated, berry, plummy fruitiness. The wine promises to blossom and emerge after another 1–2 years in the cellar. The 1988 Cabernet, short, lean, and lacking depth, is not up to the quality of either the 1986 or 1990.

JORDAN VINEYARD AND WINERY (SONOMA)

Cabernet Sauvignon* * *, Chardonnay* *, J Sparkling Wine* *

1988	Cabernet Sauvignon	Alexander Valley	C	80
1987	Cabernet Sauvignon	Alexander Valley	C	87
1986	Cabernet Sauvignon	Alexander Valley	C	87
1985	Cabernet Sauvignon	Alexander Valley	C	87
N. V.	Cuvée J Sparkling Wine	Sonoma	C	81

This winery has been frequently criticized, but its forward, herbaceous, cassis, sweetly oaked Cabernet Sauvignon is loved by most consumers for its up-front, luscious style. When it debuted in 1976 it was boldly priced, but prices have held steady over recent years. Although it is not made to be long-lived, I have been surprised by how well many vintages have held up. Even though the wines are released 4 years after the vintage and taste fully mature, the top years have a 6- to 8-year window of drinkability. Of recent vintages, the 1988 is short and light, which is typical of most California Cabernets in this rain-plagued vintage. The 1987, 1986, and 1985 are all very good, emphasizing medium- to full-bodied, forward, precocious, herb-scented fruit that appeals to both neophytes and connoisseurs. The 1985 is more structured and less herbaceous than the 1987. All of the wines are concentrated and delicious, with immediate drinkability and moderately intense, spicy, curranty, herb-tinged flavors. They consistently combine fine ripeness, medium to full body, and plenty of blackcurrant fruitiness, with a heady, soft finish. The 1985 and 1986 should prove to have another 5–6 years of life, and the 1987, perhaps 7–8 more years. To date, Jordan's Chardonnays have been aggressively oaky, light, and earthy. The designer-bottled sparkling wine called "J" is adequate but, like so many California sparkling wines, narrowly constructed, with noticeable residual sweetness that tries but fails to hide a deficiency in fruit, body, and length.

RATINGS OF OLDER VINTAGES OF JORDAN CABERNET SAUVIGNON: 1983 (74), 1982 (70), 1981 (73), 1980 (75), 1979 (76), 1976 (86)

JORY WINES (SANTA CLARA)
Chardonnay *, Pinot Noir *

It is a shame, but I have never met a Jory wine that I have enjoyed. Recent vintages of the Chardonnay, such as 1989 and 1990, were excessively woody, hollow, and poor examples. The Pinot Noir has been consistently washed out and weedy. Other wines, including the gimicky-packaged generic wines and blends made from grapes such as Mourvèdre, have been anorexic, virtually charmless offerings devoid of pleasure.

LA JOTA VINEYARD (NAPA)
Cabernet Sauvignon* * * * *, Viognier* *

1991	Cabernet Sauvignon	Howell Mountain	D 93
1990	Cabernet Sauvignon	Howell Mountain	D 92
1989	Cabernet Sauvignon	Howell Mountain	D 90
1988	Cabernet Sauvignon	Howell Mountain	D 88
1987	Cabernet Sauvignon	Howell Mountain	D 90
1986	Cabernet Sauvignon	Howell Mountain	D 93
1991	Viognier	Howell Mountain	D 79

This small boutique producer on Howell Mountain remains one of California's premier producers of world-class, complex red wine. Every time I taste a La Jota I lament the fact that I do not own more bottles of its wine. The beautiful 1991 Cabernet Sauvignon manages to marry considerable power and intensity with a gorgeously scented nose of black cherries, herbs, coffee, and toast. Gushing with richness, the wine offers a multidimensional taste as well as a super texture that leads into a long, intense finish with moderate tannins and decent acidity. This is a stunning bottle of Cabernet. In comparison, the 1990 Cabernet is slightly tougher in texture, with more noticeable tannins. Profoundly rich, it exhibits the wonderfully expansive, broad texture this producer routinely achieves because of low yields and impeccable winemaking. The big cassis-, mineral-, and spice-scented nose is backed up by a rich, intense wine with considerable tannin, leathery, smoky, tobaccolike flavors that add complexity, and an authoritative finish. Though it is a tough call, I suspect the 1991 will be more flattering to drink young. Both wines will easily last for 15–20 years. For wines of such rarity and quality, the prices are a steal—even in today's buyer's market. The 1989, another stunning success from that vintage, continues to suggest that shrewd buyers will take a closer look at this generally maligned vintage. Although there are plenty of disappointing wines, particularly among the whites, some of the reds are a match in quality and complexity for other top vintages from Napa Valley during the 1980s. La Jota's 1989 Cabernet Sauvignon is more evolved and forward than usual. The huge, earthy, weedy, tobacco-, and blackcurrant-scented nose is followed by a rich, generously endowed, satiny-textured wine that coats the palate and finishes with impressive quantities of fruit, glycerin, and alcohol. Most Howell Mountain Cabernets start life with a hard, firm, tannic edge, but this offering is pure suppleness and pleasure. Drink it over the next 10–12 years. The impressively dark ruby/purple-colored 1988 offers aromas of black cherries, spices, herbs, and toasty oak. In the mouth there is excellent richness, full body, moderate tannins, and the potential for at least 10–12 years of aging. The 1987 Cabernet Sauvignon is another tannic behemoth that has been intentionally constructed to last 15–20 years. In fact, I would venture to say it probably will not have softened enough to drink before 1997–1998. Dense ruby/purple in color, with a rich yet backward bouquet of cassis, cedar, and spices, this full-bodied, tough-textured, yet splendidly deep and concentrated wine should be purchased only by those who have the patience to wait. **Anticipated maturity: 1998–2015.** The 1986 Cabernet Sauvignon is a truly extraordinary wine with great extract, a fabulously intense, multidimensional personality with layers of blackcurrant- and mineral-scented fruit, a good use of spicy new oak, fabulous depth and length, and at least 10–15 years of further aging potential. If you haven't realized it yet, this is one of California's up-and-coming superstar wineries, and the 1986 Cabernet Sauvignon should be in any conscientiously stocked wine cellar. La Jota has begun to produce Viognier from relatively young vines. The 1991's bouquet is reminiscent of a lightweight Condrieu. The wine tails off to reveal relatively shallow, greenish flavors. Perhaps as the vineyard gets older this wine will offer flavors to match its bouquet.

JUDD'S HILL (NAPA)
Cabernet Sauvignon* * */* * * *

1991	Cabernet Sauvignon	Napa	C	88

The former winemaker of Napa's Whitehall Lane Winery has started this operation. Made from a blend of 86% Cabernet Sauvignon, 11% Merlot, and 3% Cabernet Franc, the 1991 Cabernet Sauvignon possesses the potential to be outstanding. The color is deep dark ruby/purple, and the nose offers up attractive black cherry, herb, and sweet, oaky aromas. There is fine ripeness, high flavor extraction, gobs of tannin, and a deep, rich, tannic finish. A more backward style of a 1991, the Judd's Hill Cabernet will require 4–5 years of patience before consumption. It is an impressive, reasonably priced wine.

CHÂTEAU JULIEN (MONTEREY)
Cabernet Sauvignon* *, Chardonnay Barrel Fermented* */* * *, Chardonnay Sur-Lie* * *, Gewürztraminer*, Merlot* *, Riesling* *, Sauvignon Blanc* *

1989	Cabernet Sauvignon Private Reserve	Monterey	C	75
1991	Chardonnay Barrel Fermented	Monterey	B	78
1991	Chardonnay Sur-Lie Private Reserve	Monterey	B	83
1990	Chardonnay Sur-Lie Private Reserve	Monterey	B	84
1991	Merlot	Monterey	B	73
1989	Merlot	Monterey	B	79

This winery produces correct, occasionally good wines that fall short in terms of excitement. The Chardonnays, especially the barrel-fermented *cuvée*, are all lavishly oaked. If more fruit and concentration were present, they could merit 4 stars. The Merlots and Cabernet Sauvignons have been erratic—sometimes light, fruity, and pleasant, other times green, tart, and astringent. Occasionally a Riesling, Gewürztraminer, and Sauvignon Blanc are also made. These wines are average in quality. Château Julien also produces two inexpensive lines of wine called Emerald Bay and Garland Ranch.

JUSTIN WINERY AND VINEYARD (SAN LUIS OBISPO)
Cabernet Sauvignon* * * *, Isosceles Proprietary Red Wine* * * *, Merlot* * * *

1989	Cabernet Franc	Paso Robles	C 87
1989	Cabernet Sauvignon	Paso Robles	C 89
1989	Isosceles Reserve Proprietary Red	Paso Robles	D 90
1988	Isosceles Reserve Proprietary Red	Paso Robles	D 90
1987	Isosceles Reserve Proprietary Red	Paso Robles	C 86
1989	Merlot	Paso Robles	C 89
1988	Merlot	Paso Robles	C 88

This relative newcomer (6 years old), which owns a 72-acre vineyard just west of Paso Robles, is producing a bevy of red wines that may be California's best-kept secret—at least for now. One taste of a Justin red wine will reveal that these folks know how to make fine wine. All of the wines display the complex-ity and elegance of a top-notch Bordeaux, combined with the richness and chewy texture of a fine California red. The 1989 Cabernet Franc reminds me of a classic St.-Émilion, with its suave, graceful style, rich midpalate, and ele-gant, soft finish. There is a touch of herbs, but the overwhelming aromas are those of red and black fruits and spicy oak. It should drink well over the next 5–7 years. The 1989 Cabernet Sauvignon exhibits a spicy, cedary, black fruit–scented nose, rich, medium- to full-bodied flavors, and fine elegance, depth, and length. The 1989 Merlot is a terrific example of this varietal. Chocolatey, black cherry, and mocha aromas and flavors dominate this full-bodied, opulent wine, which makes for quite a mouthful of succulent fruit. De-licious, complex, and exceptionally well balanced, it should be drunk over the next 7–8 years. The 1988 Merlot, which can stand up to the best wines of that vintage, possesses a huge bouquet of chocolate and cassis fruit, followed by jammy, rich, opulent, even sumptuous flavors exhibiting low acidity but plenty of intensity. This is a gorgeously decadent Merlot for drinking over the next 5–7 years. The 1989 Isosceles Reserve Proprietary Red, a blend of 59% Cabernet Sauvignon, 24% Merlot, and 17% Cabernet Franc, is a dead ringer for a top-class Bordeaux. It displays wonderful richness and opulence, a com-plex nose, and rich, multidimensional flavors. It, too, should drink well for the next decade. The 1988 Isosceles, made from a blend of 58% Cabernet Sauvi-gnon, 30% Merlot, and 12% Cabernet Franc, is an outstanding wine, with super concentration; a big, herbaceous, blackcurrant-, coffee-, and smoky-scented bouquet; lush, full-bodied, highly extracted flavors that display soft tannins; and just enough acidity to provide balance and delineation. Ap-proachable now, this impressively constituted wine should easily last for 10–15 years. The 1987 Isosceles, made from 59% Cabernet Sauvignon, 30% Merlot, and 11% Cabernet Franc, is lighter and less well endowed, but it is round, with a velvety texture and rich, green pepper, black raspberry, and oaky flavors. It should be drunk over the next 4–5 years. Justin also produces Chardonnay, but I have not seen a vintage since the rather boldly styled, toasty, buttery 1988. This impressive newcomer merits significant consumer attention.

KALIN CELLARS (MARIN)

Cabernet Sauvignon Reserve* * *, Chardonnay Cuvée DD* * * *,
Chardonnay Cuvée LD* * * *, Chardonnay Cuvée W* * * * *,
Cuvée d'Or Sweet Dessert Wine* * * */* * * * *, Cuvée Rosé Sparkling Wine* * * *,
Pinot Noir Cuvée DD* * * *, Sauvignon Blanc* * * *, Sauvignon
Blanc Reserve* * * * *, Semillon* * * *

1988	Cabernet Sauvignon Reserve	Sonoma	C	87+
1989	Chardonnay Cuvée LD	Sonoma	C	88
1988	Chardonnay Cuvée LD	Sonoma	C	87
1989	Chardonnay Cuvée W	Livermore	C	90
1990	Cuvée d'Or	California	C	95
1987	Cuvée Rosé Sparkling Wine	Potter Valley	D	92
1986	Cuvée Rosé Sparkling Wine	Potter Valley	D	90
1988	Pinot Noir Cuvée DD	Sonoma	C	90
1987	Pinot Noir Cuvée DD	Sonoma	C	92
1990	Sauvignon Blanc Reserve	Potter Valley	B	92
1988	Sauvignon Blanc Reserve	Potter Valley	C	90
1989	Semillon	Livermore	C	90

It would seem illogical that a full-time microbiologist, working part-time out of a warehouse in Novato, can produce some of California's most profound and long-lived wines. But that is what winemaker Terry Leighton has achieved. Leighton's reference points are French wines, and he stands nearly alone in the Golden State when it comes to producing Chardonnays that require considerable cellaring. Most California Chardonnays drop their fruit by the time they are 3 years of age. Kalin's Chardonnays do not begin to open until they are 4 or 5. What is also admirable about Leighton's winemaking philosophy is that he has exploited little-known, low-yielding old vineyards in backwater viticultural areas such as Potter Valley, Livermore, and Marin County. Virtually all his wines are bottled without filtration, which undoubtedly causes panic attacks among restaurateurs and jittery retailers loath to explain to their clients that the particles deposited in the bottom of a bottle of wine are a positive sign of a handcrafted, unprocessed wine. Kalin's new releases include what is certainly its best sparkling wine to date. Only 500 cases were made of the barrel-fermented 1987 Potter Valley Cuvée Rosé. The color is deep, similar to a Krug or Dom Pérignon Rosé, and the nose offers a huge fragrance of red berry fruit. The palate impression is one of richness, full body, and considerable flavor authority and individuality. Those weaned on California's relatively green, flavorless sparkling wines will find this to be a superb rosé sparkling wine. The wine was aged 3 years *sur-lies* before bottling. The 1986 Rosé Cuvée Sparkling Wine has a wonderful strawberry, raspberry, spicy bouquet, excellent pinpoint, uniform bubbles, medium body, plenty of lingering effervescence, and a real mid-palate and length. Kalin makes what is unquestionably the finest

Sauvignon Blanc in California. I have had it in blind tastings against such Bordeaux thoroughbreds as Fieuzal, Haut-Brion Blanc, and Laville Haut-Brion, and it inevitably places first or second as one of the most complex and richest wines. I still have bottles of this winery's sumptuous 1984 Reserve Sauvignon, which is magnificent, and the 1985 Reserve Sauvignon, which remains an infant in terms of development. The 1990 Sauvignon Blanc is made from an old Potter Valley Vineyard that yielded only 2.5 tons of grapes per acre. Compare that with the average production of 5–8 tons per acre of other Sauvignon vineyards, and you will appreciate why this wine has such concentration and personality. The 1989 Sauvignon Blanc Reserve offers a huge nose of honeyed, waxy, melony, and fig-like fruit intertwined with floral aromas. It is followed by a medium-bodied, gorgeously rich, well-delineated wine that lingers on the palate. Leighton blended in 10% Semillon to give the wine more weight and fatness. Only 500 cases were made. A good friend of mine told me that his local wine retailer was already complaining that the wine had thrown some sediment, making it "look suspicious." That sediment suggests to me many wonderful things, but most important that the flavors and integrity of the vineyard's fruit have not been compromised. The 1988 Sauvignon Blanc Reserve offers up aromas of pure honeyed melons intermixed with rich, highly extracted fruit. Medium to full bodied, with layer upon layer of concentrated fruit, this is a rich, splendidly dry, impeccably made, complex Sauvignon. Based on previous renditions, it can be expected to last for 7–8 years, an astonishingly long time for a California Sauvignon Blanc. Kalin also makes California's finest Semillon. I have been buying this wine since the early 1980s, and unlike most California white wines, it actually benefits from cellaring. Kalin's 1989 Semillon does not taste as if it emerged from a rain-plagued vintage. The wine displays an intense, buttery, waxy, richly fruity nose; concentrated, well-delineated flavors that offer considerable body and glycerin; and a long, crisp finish. Those who have never tried Semillon with salmon should check it out; the fatness of the fish works marvelously with the character of Semillon, creating a magical combination. The 1989 Chardonnay Cuvée LD reveals a tight, almost Meursault-like, hazelnut, smoky fruitiness, extremely high natural acidity, and a long, ripe, crisp, concentrated finish. Like so many of Kalin's Chardonnays, it is tightly wound and needs at least 2 years of cellaring to fully express itself. Even richer and more profound is the 1989 Chardonnay Cuvée W. Made from 60-year-old vines that yielded only 1.5 tons per acre, the wine is tightly knit with a gravelly, mineral character that reminds me of a Grand Cru Chablis. Although there is superintensity of fruit and whopping length, the wine is amazingly young and unevolved. I do not expect this wine to reach full maturity for another 4–5 years; it should last for a decade or more. The 1988 Chardonnay Cuvée LD is more developed and precocious than most Kalin Chardonnays tend to be. It possesses an attractive toasty, lemony, apple-scented nose; ripe, tasty, medium-bodied flavors with a nice inner core of fruit; and a long, crisp, natural-tasting finish. Drinkable now, it should easily last for 4–5 years. On a disturbing note, since 1987 I have noticed that Kalin's Chardonnays have become more and more acidic, making them nearly impossible to enjoy when released. The two Pinot Noir offerings are among the most distinctive and original expressions of American-made Pinot Noir I have ever tasted. Although I have only a vague notion of what great Chambertin from Burgundy is supposed to taste like (because so much of it is watery and thin), both of these wines approximate what Chambertin tastes like when made by the likes of Lalou Bize-Leroy. The 1987 Pinot Noir Cuvée DD will be a stunning wine with another 3–4 years of bottle age. Given its unbelievable richness, intensity, and tannic clout, it is a Pinot Noir that can easily last for 12–15 years. Presently it exhibits a stunning concoction of aromas—hickory, chocolate, cloves, and herbs, as well as unbelievably earthy, sweet black fruit flavors with an exotic personality. This blockbuster Pinot Noir is rich, spicy, and altogether a knockout, but cellaring is suggested. The 1988 Pinot Noir Cuvée DD displays a similar character, with its sweaty, smoky, animal-, duck meat–, and earth-scented nose. In the mouth it is rich, full bodied, and deep, not as tannic as the 1987, but gorgeously rich and exotic. Both wines are already throwing considerable sediment; thus I recommend immediate decanting and serving. These are formidable efforts! I have never been a fan of Leighton's Cabernet Sauvignons. However, I recently had his 1979 Cabernet Sauvignon from Santa Barbara, which was overwhelmingly vegetal when first released. Today it is a cedary, sweet, cigar box–scented wine that could easily pass for a top Bordeaux. Still youthful at age 13, it has developed tremendous character and complexity. The 1988 Cabernet Sauvignon Reserve Sonoma is the best young Cabernet I have tasted from Kalin. It possesses a deep, dark ruby/purple color, sweet, ripe aromas of cassis and herbs, medium to full body, soft tannins, and excellent clarity and definition. Although approachable now, it ideally needs 4–5 years of aging. Based on the fact that Kalin's previous Cabernets have evolved far more gracefully than I predicted, this wine should last for 12–15 or more years. Last, Leighton's sweet wine, Cuvée d'Or, has always been delicious, but he has engineered a major breakthrough with the 1990 Cuvée d'Or. Light gold in color and made from 80% Semillon and 20% Sauvignon Blanc (the same percentage as used at Château d'Yquem), this wine exhibits a sensational fragrance of honeyed tropical fruits, flowers, and spicy, toasty oak. The bouquet clearly could be mistaken for that from a great vintage of Château Coutet's Cuvée Madame. In the mouth the breathtakingly rich, well-delineated, botrytised flavors offer lavish, even unctuous, richness buttressed by crisp, zesty acidity. It will be fascinating to follow the development of this wine—the finest young sweet wine I have ever tasted from California.

KARLY WINERY (AMADOR)
Chardonnay* *, Sauvignon Blanc* * * *, Zinfandel* * *

1991	Zinfandel	Amador	B	84
1990	Zinfandel	Amador	B	85
1990	Zinfandel Pokerville	Amador	A	85

No one can deny that Karly's Zinfandels offer considerable bang for your buck. The 1990 exhibits opulent fruit; a thick, glycerin-dominated, chewy texture; and a lush, heady, spicy finish. The 1991 possesses less berry fruit and has an earthy, straightforward, medium-bodied personality. Both wines should drink well for another 3–4 years. Last, Karly has turned out a super value with an offering called Pokerville—a straightforward, richly fruity, full-bodied Zinfandel bursting with fruit, glycerin, and heady alcohol. Although there is not much complexity, the wine is immensely satisfying as well as mouth-filling. Drink it over the next several years. Karly also produces a woody, somewhat inconsistent Chardonnay that is not up to the quality of its other wines. The Sauvignon Blanc is one of the more boldly flavored, attractive wines made in California. It has been excellent in vintages such as 1990. Consumers should seek out this reasonably priced wine.

ROBERT KEENAN WINERY (NAPA)
Cabernet Sauvignon* * *, Chardonnay* *, Merlot* * *

1987	Cabernet Sauvignon	Napa	C	87
1990	Chardonnay	Napa	C	85
1989	Chardonnay	Napa	C	78
1989	Merlot	Napa	C	86

In many Robert Keenan wines the tannins have a tendency to obliterate the fruit. However, the 1989 Merlot offers a rich, full-bodied, coffee-, herb-, and berry-scented wine that is not weighed down by excessive tannin. The palate exhibits ripe, luscious flavors, low acidity, and a generously endowed, chewy finish. I would opt for drinking this textbook Merlot over the next 5–6 years. The 1987 Cabernet Sauvignon displays significantly richer fruit, more body, and enthralling ripeness and intensity to its big blackcurrant flavors and full body. It should drink well for another 5–6 years. Recent improvements in getting more charm and fruit in the Cabernets and Merlots have not been as apparent with respect to the Chardonnays, which remain angular and compact. Although the 1990 is certainly good, the 1989 is deficient and beginning to dry out.

KENDALL-JACKSON VINEYARD (LAKE)
Cabernet Sauvignon Vintner's Reserve* *, Cardinale Meritage Proprietary Red Wine* */* * *, Chardonnay Camelot Vineyard* * * *, Chardonnay Proprietor's Grand Reserve* * *, Chardonnay Vintner's Reserve* * *, Syrah Durell Vineyard* * */* * * *, Zinfandel Ciapusci Vineyard* * * *, Zinfandel Dupratt Vineyard* * * *, Zinfandel Proprietor's Grand Reserve* * * *

1988	Cabernet Sauvignon Proprietor's Grand Reserve	California	C	75
1985	Cabernet Sauvignon Proprietor's Grand Reserve	California	C	87
1990	Cabernet Sauvignon Vintner's Reserve	California	B	75
1986	Cabernet Sauvignon Vintner's Reserve	California	B	76
1987	Cardinale Meritage Proprietary Red Wine	California	E	81
1986	Cardinale Meritage Proprietary Red Wine	California	E	80
1985	Cardinale Meritage Proprietary Red Wine	California	E	78
1991	Chardonnay Camelot Vineyard	Santa Maria	C	89

1991	Chardonnay Proprietor's Grand Reserve	California	C	86
1991	Chardonnay Vintner's Reserve	California	A	87
1989	Grand Finale Select Late-Harvest	California	B	88
1985	Merlot	Alexander Valley	B	72
1990	Merlot Vintner's Reserve	California	A	76
1990	Pinot Noir Vintner's Reserve	California	B	58
1990	Syrah Durell Vineyard	Sonoma	C	84
1988	Syrah Durell Vineyard	Sonoma	C	87
1988	Zinfandel Ciapusci Vineyard	Mendocino	C	85
1987	Zinfandel Dupratt Vineyard	Anderson Valley	B	89
1990	Zinfandel Proprietor's Grand Reserve	California	C	90

This winery can be criticized for sugaring its wines, it can be criticized for adding non-Chardonnay varietals to the blend, if in fact that is what it does, but the bottom line is that its 1991 Chardonnay Vintner's Reserve is one heck of a generously endowed, richly textured, satisfying white wine with enough Chardonnay character to make it a top seller. If more wines like this were available, perhaps Americans would be spending more time in wine shops than in video stores. Drink it over the next year. On the other hand, the 1991 Chardonnay from the Camelot Vineyard obtains its richness from extraction of flavor rather than from residual sugar. It is a rich, oily, tropical fruit–scented and –flavored wine with an opulent texture. Because of its low acidity, it too should be drunk over the next 12 months. The 1991 Chardonnay Proprietor's Grand Reserve is a big, lusty, toasty, creamy-textured wine with plenty of fruit, not much complexity, excellent richness, and a soft, attractive finish. Drink it before the end of 1994. Kendall-Jackson has also released a compelling, deca-dently rich, sweet wine, Grand Finale, made from 80% Semillon and 20% Sauvignon Blanc—the same percentages used at Château d'Yquem. This unc-tuous, viscous wine has a great many things going for it. The acidity is just right to give it balance and character, the flavors are massively rich, full, and sweet, and the wine exhibits plenty of botrytis in its honeyed, apricot, *crème brûlée* flavors. Drink it over the next 7–8 years. Impressive! As a longtime ad-mirer of the white wines from this winery, I could never muster much enthusi-asm for the often vegetal, compact, tart, and excessively acidified Cabernets and Merlots. The 1986 Merlot runs true to form, as it is disturbingly green, compact, and short, with absolutely no finish and a highly acidic, charmless personality. However, a surprise in a recent blind tasting was the 1985 Propri-etor's Cabernet Sauvignon from Kendall-Jackson. A subtle bouquet of herbs, blackcurrants, and oak creates an attractive initial impression. On the palate the wine exhibits surprising richness, a long, supple texture, and 2–6 more years of drinkability. The 1986 Cabernet Sauvignon Vintner's Reserve has an attractive, cedary, berry-scented bouquet intertwined with some nice toasty oak. However, its downfall is a lean, highly acidic, narrowly constructed palate that offers little charm and meager amounts of fruit. Acidification would appear to be the culprit. The 1988 Cabernet Sauvignon Grand Reserve displays the problems with excess acidification that often plague the red wines. Moreover, the grotesquely overpriced proprietary red wine, Cardinale Meritage, is an example of what is wrong with California oenology: fabulous raw materials have been subverted into a narrowly constructed, tart, very acidic wine with little in the nose other than oak and a finish that is hard and tannic. Although they have received rave reviews from the West Coast press, I find the Cardinale Meritage wines to be charmless. For all the problems Kendall-Jackson seems to have with its tart Cabernets, its Zinfandels can be superb. However, the 1988 Zinfandel Ciapusci Vineyard is so excessively oaked it is impossible to find either the Zinfandel varietal character or much fruit. That plus a somewhat cardboard-tasting finish (filter pads?) made for an unpleasant tasting experience. Perhaps it was just a bad bottle, but the wine tasted overwhelmingly woody and hollow. Kendall-Jackson has always made fine Zinfandels from the Dupratt Vineyard, and the 1987 may well be its best. Dark ruby/purple, with a big, black cherry and black raspberry bouquet intermingled with scents of spicy oak and vanillin, this full-bodied wine has excellent depth in the mouth, a concentrated, full-bodied, rich texture, good ripe acidity, and firm but soft tannins. It can be drunk now or cellared for up to a decade. The 1990 Zinfandel Proprietor's Grand Reserve is a stunningly proportioned, opulent Zinfandel bursting with black fruit aromas. Full bodied and luscious, it will provide exciting drinking for another 5–6 years. The 1988 Syrah from Sonoma's Durell Vineyard is also a noteworthy effort. The exotic bouquet of fried bacon, smoked herbs, and cassis is top class. In the mouth the wine is full bodied and rich, with an amply endowed, nearly opulent texture. Drinkable now, it should continue to age gracefully for at least 7–8 years. The 1990 Syrah Durell Vineyard offers a provocative bouquet of bacon fat, toasty new oak, smoke, and black fruits. However, in the mouth the wine is entirely too acidic (too much added acidity). The result is some wonderful rich fruit dominated totally by a coat of armor. Thus, this wine, which could have been something special, is too lean and tart. It's a shame.

KATHERINE KENNEDY WINERY (SANTA CLARA)
Cabernet Sauvignon* * * *, Lateral* * */* * * *

1989	Cabernet Sauvignon	Santa Cruz	E	86?
1988	Cabernet Sauvignon	Santa Cruz	D	86
1987	Cabernet Sauvignon	Santa Cruz	D	90
1986	Cabernet Sauvignon	Santa Cruz	C	88
1985	Cabernet Sauvignon	Santa Cruz	C	87
1989	Lateral Red Table Wine	Santa Cruz	C	87
1988	Lateral Red Table Wine	Santa Cruz	C	86

I found Katherine Kennedy's 1989 Lateral (an interesting blend of 60% Merlot, 33% Cabernet Franc, and 7% Cabernet Sauvignon) to be a graceful, stylish wine that is obviously meant to be drunk in the first 7–8 years of its life. Its herb, berry, and earthy fruitiness continues to remind me of a fine St.-Émilion. With not a hard edge to be found in the mouth, this interesting and complex proprietary red table wine offers plenty of soft, opulent fruit. The 1988 Lateral is a delicious wine for drinking over the next 3–5 years. The big, bold, complex bouquet of herbs and red fruits, backed up gently by toasty oak, is alluring. The attraction continues with smooth, velvety, spicy, ripe berry flavors that display no hard edges and finish gently on the palate. It is a lovely wine for drinking over the near term. This small winery continues to excel in producing ageworthy, rich, full-bodied, concentrated Cabernet Sauvignon. The 1989 is a successful wine for the vintage. The bouquet remains unevolved, but on the palate there is a rich, multilayered feel, crisp acidity, moderate tannins, and excellent depth. It should be drinkable young but will last for 8–10 years. If the acidity were not so tart, this wine would merit a higher score. I should also note that the first bottle tasted had a flawed "lees smell." The 1988 Cabernet Sauvignon is less powerful than usual but is still an ageworthy, tannic wine that one hopes will develop more balance after 2–3 years in the bottle. Although the 1987 Cabernet Sauvignon Santa Cruz is backward and tannic, it is a marvelously concentrated and rich Cabernet for drinking in about 7–8 years. It should last for up to 3 decades. Dark ruby/purple-colored, with a tight but promising bouquet of cassis, minerals, licorice, and toast, it displays full, dry, austere, yet loaded flavors. Do not touch it before the end of this century. The 1986 exhibits a moderately intense bouquet of sweet, vanillin-scented new oak, blackcurrants, and a subtle whiff of herbs. It displays full-bodied yet supple, fleshy, black fruit flavors that are precise, clean, well balanced, and velvety enough to appreciate now. This relatively large-scale yet harmonious Cabernet Sauvignon should drink well for another 8–10 years. The 1985 is a very backward yet impressively deep, classically structured, full-bodied Cabernet that should last 10–15 years. This is a well-made wine that clearly shows what an excellent area the Santa Cruz mountain region is for Cabernet Sauvignon.

KENWOOD VINEYARDS (SONOMA)

Cabernet Sauvignon Artist Series* * * *, Cabernet Sauvignon Jack London Vineyard* * * *, Chardonnay Beltane Ranch* * *, Sauvignon Blanc* * * *, Zinfandel Jack London Vineyard* * */* * * *

1988	Cabernet Sauvignon Artist Series	Sonoma	D	82
1987	Cabernet Sauvignon Artist Series	Sonoma	D	90
1986	Cabernet Sauvignon Artist Series	Sonoma	D	88
1985	Cabernet Sauvignon Artist Series	Sonoma	D	87
1989	Cabernet Sauvignon Jack London Vineyard	Sonoma	C	82
1986	Cabernet Sauvignon Jack London Vineyard	Sonoma	C	89
1990	Chardonnay Beltane Ranch	Sonoma	C	87
1991	Sauvignon Blanc	Sonoma	B	86
1990	Zinfandel Jack London Vineyard	Sonoma	B	84
1987	Zinfandel Jack London Vineyard	Sonoma	A	87

Kenwood quietly and solidly continues to turn out highly extracted, dense, concentrated, broodingly big, powerful Cabernets meant to endure over a 10- to 20-year period. This licorice, blackcurrant, smoky, earthy 1987 Cabernet

Sauvignon Artist Series is bursting at the seams with layer upon layer of fruit, body, and power. Long and rich, it is an altogether impressive wine. **Anticipated maturity: 1994–2010.** The full-throttle, rich, opulent 1986 Cabernet Sauvignon Artist Series has a huge bouquet of roasted blackcurrant fruit, herbs, oak, and spices. Extremely concentrated and intense, with layers of powerful fruit flavors and soft tannins in the finish, this muscular, broad-shouldered Cabernet Sauvignon is drinkable now but should continue to age gracefully for another 10–12 years. It is not for the shy! The 1985 Cabernet Sauvignon Artist Series possesses an austere character but offers a wonderful harmony of oak, spicy, herbaceous, blackcurrant fruit, and minerals. On the palate it is medium to full bodied, has crisp acids and a very elegant, graceful personality. **Anticipated maturity: Now–2002.** The 1986 Cabernet Sauvignon Jack London Vineyard is deep black/ruby in color with a promising yet still young, unevolved bouquet of black fruits, toast, licorice, and herbs. This tannic, muscular, deep, chewy, full-bodied wine boasts intensely concentrated flavors, and plenty of aging potential. **Anticipated maturity: Now–2003.** As one might expect given the vintage, the 1988 Cabernet Sauvignon from the Jack London Vineyard is less well endowed, with a medium-bodied, softer personality and less richness and length than Kenwood's other Cabernets. Kenwood has been one of the earliest and most consistent advocates of Zinfandel. Its first Zinfandel was produced over 20 years ago, and it has consistently made an attractive wine from this varietal. Given the robust style favored by this winery, I expected the 1990 Jack London Vineyard to be considerably richer and more powerful than it is currently showing. The color, which is only medium ruby, did not reveal the saturation I expected. The nose is also somewhat backward. Although there is good glycerin and extract, as well as a spicy, berry fruitiness, the wine lacks the intensity, extraction of flavor, and length that some Kenwood Zinfandels have exhibited in the past. The 1990 should be drunk over the next 5–7 years. Loaded with spicy new oak and raspberry-scented and -flavored fruit, the supple, rich, full-bodied 1987 Zinfandel Jack London Vineyard offers a wonderful purity of flavors, plenty of body, soft tannins, and a long, velvety finish. Drink it over the next 5–6 years. With excellent concentration, a clean, fruity, citrusy, floral-scented nose, and ripe, medium- to full-bodied flavors, Kenwood's fine 1990 Chardonnay Beltane Ranch should be drunk over the next year. The wine that has given Kenwood its biggest commercial success is its Sauvignon Blanc, one of the best made in California. It offers authoritative flavors that possess a sense of elegance, crispness, and exuberance. The vegetal character has been toned down to a subtle herbaceousness, and the wine offers vividly pure, melony, herb-, and figlike fruit in a medium-bodied, zesty format. It is a wine to drink in its first several years of life.

KISTLER VINEYARDS (SONOMA)

Cabernet Sauvignon* * *, Chardonnay Durell Vineyard* * * * *,
Chardonnay Dutton Ranch* * * * *, Chardonnay Kistler Estate* * * * *,
Chardonnay McCrea Vineyard* * * */* * * * *, Chardonnay Vine Hill Road
Vineyard* * * */* * * * *, Pinot Noir* *

1988	Cabernet Sauvignon Kistler Estate	Sonoma	C	90
1990	Chardonnay Durell Vineyard	Sonoma	D	92

1991	Chardonnay Durell Vineyard Sand Hill	Sonoma	D	90
1991	Chardonnay Dutton Ranch	Sonoma	D	87
1990	Chardonnay Dutton Ranch	Sonoma	C	90
1990	Chardonnay Kistler Estate	Sonoma	D	95
1991	Chardonnay McCrea Vineyard	Sonoma	D	90
1990	Chardonnay McCrea Vineyard	Sonoma	D	91
1991	Chardonnay Vine Hill Road Vineyard	Russian River	D	87
1990	Chardonnay Vine Hill Road Vineyard	Sonoma	C	91

Kistler's 1991 Chardonnays are not as opulent and explosively rich as their 1990s. Nevertheless, they are delicious, complex, and concentrated. One of the stars is the 1991 McCrea Vineyard, a light, golden-colored, tightly knit, rich wine, with a spicy, vanillin, honey, buttery, apple-scented nose and flavors that display impressive acid, integration, and balance. This wine should blossom with several more months of bottle age and last for 2–3 years. The 1991 Durell Vineyard Sand Hill is more elegant, with more mineral scents, and leaner, more austere flavors, as well as plenty of underlying depth to merit its lofty score. Ripe and rich, with a spicy finish, this wine needs several more months of bottle age, and should last for 3–4 years. The slightly deeper-colored 1991 Vinehill Road Vineyard exhibits more alcohol and plenty of richness. Slightly chunkier, it offers a big, fleshy mouthful of interesting Chardonnay fruit. Drink it over the next several years. The 1991 Dutton Ranch does not possess the depth or dimension of the 1990 or 1988, but it is an excellent Chardonnay, with a subdued, attractive bouquet of buttery fruit and subtle oak, lively ripeness, medium to full body, and admirable chewiness. The finish lacks the persistence of some of Kistler's more noteworthy efforts. Drink it over the next 4–5 years. The 1990 Chardonnays represent the pinnacle of what this grape is capable of achieving in California. The 1990 Durell Vineyard Chardonnay revealed a nose that was reminiscent of Louis Latour's 1989 Batard-Montrachet. The scents of vanillin oak, nuts, butter, tropical fruits, and minerals are riveting. In the mouth it is expansive, with superb richness, a multidimensional personality, layer upon layer of fruit, and a long, zesty finish. This is a beautifully made, complex Chardonnay for drinking over the next 4–5 years. I would not be surprised to see the 1990 Chardonnay McCrea Vineyard approach, and possibly eclipse, the quality of the Durell. A more austere wine at the moment, it is dominated by scents of minerals, lemons, and subtle, buttery fruit. Although it is lighter in the mouth, there is a super inner core of richness, and the finish is as graceful as it is stylish. It possesses a polite personality, but there is plenty of underlying depth, so this wine should evolve effortlessly over the next 4–5 years. For pure decadent richness, as well as a formidable combination of power and elegance, Kistler's fantastic 1990 Chardonnay Kistler Estate is unsurpassed. A superb nose of smoky bacon fat, buttery fruit, and toast is dazzling. There is exceptional concentration, extraordinary richness and presence on the palate, and a long, intense, full-bodied finish. About as profound as Chardonnay gets in the New World, this wine could easily be mistaken for a top Batard- or Chevalier-Montrachet from

France. The 1990 Dutton Ranch Chardonnay may potentially be a better wine in several years than the Vine Hill Road Vineyard Chardonnay. Although much more closed and structured, it exhibits a powerful, tightly knit nose of vanillin, smoke, buttery fruit, and wet stones. In the mouth it evinces ample extraction of fruit as well as fine acidity, good richness, and impressive length. I would not be surprised to see this wine drink beautifully for at least 6–7 years. In contrast, the 1990 Vine Hill Road Vineyard Chardonnay is more open and forward, with an intense, buttery, apple blossom–, toasty-scented nose and opulent, rich, and powerful flavors that possess enough acidity to provide delineation to the wine's personality. Drink this intense, concentrated, stylish, French-like Chardonnay over the next 3–4 years. Kistler's 1988 Cabernet Sauvignon should turn out to be one of the best wines from this average-quality vintage. Unfortunately, just over 100 cases were made, so availability is a problem. The opaque, dark ruby/purple color and the big nose of cloves, spices, vanillin, and cassis are followed by a rich, full-bodied, surprisingly concentrated wine. Also evident are soft tannins, good acidity, and a long finish. Drinkable now, this wine should easily evolve for another 10–15 years. I have not seen a Kistler Pinot Noir in several years; in the past I have found it to be concentrated but too vegetal for my taste.

KLEIN VINEYARDS (SANTA CRUZ)
Cabernet Sauvignon* * *

1988	Cabernet Sauvignon	Santa Cruz	C	88

Another star from the 1988 vintage, this big, oaky, spicy, black cherry–, and black raspberry–scented wine displays excellent concentration of flavor, full body, a generously endowed palate, and a long, smooth finish. Delicious at present, it should continue to drink well and perhaps evolve into something even more special over the next 10–12 years.

KONOCTI WINERY (LAKE)
Cabernet Sauvignon* */* * *, Cabernet Franc* * *, Chardonnay* * *,
Fumé Blanc* * *, Merlot* *

1988	Cabernet Franc	Lake	A	85
1991	Chardonnay	Lake	A	85
1991	Fumé Blanc	Lake	A	84
1988	Merlot	Lake	A	84

Looking for a Chardonnay with fruit and character for under $10? This generously endowed, round, exuberantly fruity 1991 is cleanly made, has admirable extract for its price range, and possesses an honest varietal character. Drink it over the next year. Cabernet Franc can be too vegetal if it does not ripen fully, but in a not-so-easy vintage, Konocti has managed to produce a tasty, round, herb- and currant-scented Cabernet Franc that offers gobs of up-front fruit, a silky texture, and a soft, surprisingly long finish. It is a wine for drinking over the next 2–3 years. The same comments can be applied to the Merlot, only it is more noticeably herbaceous. Its appeal is in its round, soft texture and perfumed character. It should be drunk over the next 1–2 years. Not surprisingly, Konocti turns out a very likable, fruity, herbaceous Fumé Blanc that is fresh, lively, and dry. This winery, while not aiming to hit the highest-quality levels, does an admirable job in producing fresh, fruity wines that consumers can both enjoy and afford.

CHARLES KRUG (NAPA)
Cabernet Sauvignon*, Cabernet Sauvignon Vintage Selection* */* * * *,
Chardonnay*, Chardonnay Carneros Reserve* * * (since 1990),
Pinot Noir Carneros Reserve* *, Zinfandel* *

1989	Cabernet Sauvignon	Napa	B	68
1988	Cabernet Sauvignon	Napa	B	70
1984	Cabernet Sauvignon Vintage Selection	Napa	C	87
1990	Chardonnay	Napa	B	75
1990	Chardonnay Carneros Reserve	Napa	C	88
1990	Pinot Noir Carneros Reserve	Napa	C	82
1989	Zinfandel	Napa	A	73

The excellent 1990 Chardonnay Carneros Reserve suggests that the winemaking at this perennial underachiever has taken a turn for the better. A big, spicy, buttery, oaky nose is a joy to smell. And how about the deep, full-bodied flavors that exhibit fine definition? The finish is spicy, rich, and immensely satisfying. Drink it over the next year. Although it is not good enough to merit a recommendation, the deceptively pale-colored 1990 Pinot Noir Carneros Reserve offers tasty, authentic Pinot flavors in a light- to medium-bodied format. However, if you can still find a bottle, the 1984 Cabernet Sauvignon Vintage Selection is a promising wine. From its rich, ripe, broad, intense bouquet of blackcurrants, spicy oak, and herbs to its deep, full-bodied, concentrated, expansive flavors, this is classic Napa Valley Cabernet at its best. Drink this beauty over the next 5–8 years. I hope wines such as the 1990 Chardonnay Reserve are indicative of an improvement in winemaking at Charles Krug.

LAKESPRING WINERY (NAPA)
Cabernet Sauvignon* *, Cabernet Sauvignon Reserve* *, Chardonnay* *,
Sauvignon Blanc* *

1982	Cabernet Sauvignon Vintage Selection	Napa	D	76
1990	Chardonnay	Napa	B	74
1989	Chardonnay	Napa	B	71

The wines from Lakespring Winery, made consistently in a straightforward, dull style, have yet to be impressive. The Chardonnays tend to be bland and oaky, the Sauvignon Blancs are often too herbaceous, and the regular *cuvée* of Cabernet Sauvignon is indifferent. From time to time the winery releases a Reserve Cabernet from their library stock. The 1982 Cabernet Sauvignon Vintage Selection was just released at $40 a bottle. It is a tart, lean, nearly fruitless wine.

LAMBORN FAMILY VINEYARD (NAPA)
Zinfandel* * * *

1990	Zinfandel Howell Mountain	Napa	C	87
1989	Zinfandel Howell Mountain	Napa	C	87
1988	Zinfandel Howell Mountain	Napa	C	87
1987	Zinfandel Howell Mountain	Napa	B	88

The 1990 Zinfandel is a typical Howell Mountain wine, with its considerable structure and large-boned, austere, concentrated style. The high tannins make the wine nearly impenetrable; nevertheless, the saturated color and ripe, rich fruit suggest that ultimately fine things will emerge from behind the muscular facade. What can be detected in this full-bodied Zinfandel are copious quantities of black raspberries and minerallike fruit. I would cellar it for at least 4–5 years and would be surprised if my rating does not appear conservative by the turn of the century. With nowhere near the weight, power, or muscle of the 1990, the 1989 is still a successful wine, particularly when considering the weather problems most North Coast vintners endured. The wine displays a dark ruby/garnet color and an attractive, moderately intense bouquet of plummy fruit intertwined with the scent of minerals and flowers. In the mouth there is medium to full body, as well as fine concentration, crisp acidity, and moderate tannins in the finish. This will not be a blockbuster wine but, rather, an attractive, elegant example of Zinfandel. Not quite ready for prime-time drinking, it should be at its best in 1–2 years and drink well for 7–10 years. There is admirable power, fruit, tannin, extract, and body in the backstrapping, ageworthy, tannic 1988 Zinfandel, from a tasty but light, soft, forward vintage. I would put away this blockbuster for at least 5 years and then drink it over the next 15 or so. This would be an extremely impressive Zinfandel in a top vintage, so the fact that it has emerged from a less renowned year is amazing. Bravo! Many Zinfandels from Howell Mountain have a tendency to be exceedingly tannic in their youth, but this winery has produced not only an ageworthy 1987 Zinfandel, but one that can be drunk at present. From its bouquet, which gushes with the scent of ripe raspberries and subtle hints of spice, pepper, and minerals, to its rich, seriously extracted, deep, black fruit flavors, this large-scale yet well-balanced Zinfandel should drink extremely well through the end of this century.

LANDMARK VINEYARDS (SONOMA)
Chardonnay Cuvées* * *

1990	Chardonnay	California	B	80
1991	Chardonnay Damaris Reserve	Alexander Valley	B	87
1991	Chardonnay Overlook	Sonoma	C	87
1991	Chardonnay Two Williams Vineyard	Sonoma	C	86

For years I have been unable to muster much enthusiasm for this producer's Chardonnays, so I am delighted to see how well they performed in a recent tasting. They are all high-quality wines, with the Overlook *cuvée* possessing the most up-front tropical fruit, opulence, and richness. Although the Damaris Reserve displays more obvious new oak and is more austere, it is just as concentrated and may turn out to be a longer-lived wine. The 1991 Two Williams is very good, but with slightly less personality and richness than the Overlook and Damaris Reserve. I would opt for drinking all of these Chardonnays over the next 2 years.

LAUREL GLEN (SONOMA)

Cabernet Sauvignon* * * * *, Counterpoint* * *, Terra Rosa* * * *

1991	Cabernet Sauvignon	Sonoma Mountain	D	93
1990	Cabernet Sauvignon	Sonoma Mountain	D	95
1988	Cabernet Sauvignon	Sonoma Mountain	D	90
1987	Cabernet Sauvignon	Sonoma Mountain	D	91
1990	Counterpoint	Sonoma	B	86
1990	Terra Rosa	Sonoma	B	88

Proprietor Patrick Campbell's superb Cabernet Sauvignon vineyard on the slopes overlooking the Sonoma Valley has proven to be one of the finest sources for Cabernet in California. The use of traditional winemaking techniques, designed not to strip the wine, results in a wine that is full of character. Even the secondary wines, Terra Rosa and Counterpoint, are delicious, as the 1990s so convincingly attest. Terra Rosa offers a huge nose of cedar, olives, and dusty blackcurrant fruit; a rich, sweet, expansive palate; and a long, lush finish. It should drink well for the next 5–6 years. The glories are the spectacular Cabernet Sauvignons. The 1991 reveals an opaque dark ruby color as well as a huge nose with aromas reminiscent of leg of lamb cooked over a wood fire and doused with Provençal herbs. The gorgeous, big, meaty, herbaceous, sweet, black fruit aromas and flavors are followed by superripe, rich, luxurious flavors. There is plenty of tannin to provide the framework, and the result is one of the most impressive wines I have yet to taste from this superb estate. The 1990 offers an even more spectacular nose, largely because it has enjoyed an additional year of evolution. Smoky, cassis, herb, sweet, leathery, meaty aromas are as equally profound as in the 1991. The wine is even more unctuous and flattering. This full-bodied, gorgeously put together wine should be approachable young but will last for up to 15–20 years. The 1988 is one of the leading candidates for "Cabernet of the Vintage." Dark ruby/purple, with a moderately intense, licorice-, herb-, and cassis-scented bouquet, this opulently styled, full-bodied, intense Cabernet Sauvignon coats the palate with viscous, rich flavors and has a finish that must last for nearly 40 seconds. Laurel Glen made a strict selection in 1988, and the commitment to excellence by proprietor Patrick Campbell is evident in this generously constituted, impressive, albeit expensive Cabernet. **Anticipated maturity: Now–2003.** The 1987 is another rich, intense, well-made wine. It is very dark ruby, with a full intensity bouquet of tobacco, herbs, cassis, and blackcurrants. On the palate, this wine is very concentrated, with a beautiful texture, firm but soft tannins, full body, and outstanding depth and length. **Anticipated maturity: Now–2000.**

RATINGS FOR OLDER VINTAGES OF LAUREL GLEN SONOMA MOUNTAIN CABERNET SAUVIGNON: 1986 (90), 1985 (92), 1984 (90), 1982 (73), 1981 (90)

LEEWARD WINERY (VENTURA)
Cabernet Sauvignon* *, Chardonnay* */* * *

1988	Cabernet Sauvignon	Alexander Valley	B	79
1991	Chardonnay	Central Coast	B	80
1990	Chardonnay	Central Coast	B	85
1990	Chardonnay	Edna Valley	C	76

I have generally given Leeward's Chardonnays from the Central Coast and Edna Valley better ratings than the scores from these vintages would suggest. The wines are usually made in a lusty, oaky, lavishly fruity style and provide immense satisfaction if consumed within several years of the vintage. Both of these Chardonnays were much lighter in style, with the 1991 straightforward and fruity and the 1990 already drying out, with the wood dominating the remaining fruit. Leeward's red wines have been erratic, with annoyingly high herbaceous and vegetal aromas, chalky, harsh tannins, and little charm.

LIBERTY SCHOOL (CAYMUS—NAPA)
Cabernet Sauvignon* * *, California White Wine* * *, Sauvignon Blanc * *

N. V.	Cabernet Sauvignon Series 2	California	A	86
1990	California White Wine 3 Valley Select	California	A	85

Liberty School is the secondary label of the excellent Caymus winery. The vintages and *cuvées* change quickly, so these two offerings may not still be in the marketplace. However, they will give readers an idea of the Liberty School wines, which generally offer excellent value, whether it be Chardonnay, Cabernet Sauvignon, or Sauvignon Blanc. Caymus does a good job with these everyday wines, and the prices can't be beat. There is not a hard edge to be found in the chunky, surprisingly dense and concentrated, powerful N. V. Cabernet Sauvignon Series 2, which offers gobs of rich cassis fruit in a robust, hefty format. One has to applaud those responsible for putting together such a flavorful and attractive blend. Drink it over the next 2–4 years. The 1990 California White Wine 3 Valley Select is a terrific everyday white wine that displays a huge, flowery, intensely perfumed aroma (do they use Muscat in the blend?), a richly fruity, medium-bodied, opulent palate, and a gorgeously fresh, lively finish. Drink this beauty over the next year for its undeniable charm.

LIMERICK LANE CELLARS (SONOMA)
Zinfandel* * * *

1991	Zinfandel	Russian River Valley	B	90
1990	Zinfandel	Russian River Valley	B	89
1989	Zinfandel	Russian River Valley	B	87

I know little about this producer, but these impressive Zinfandels leave no question about their quality. These are wines to be taken seriously. The 1990 offers up a full-blown nose of black cherry fruit, herbs, and even a touch of chocolate and earth, a boatload of glycerin, excellent concentration, and good structure, yet it provides plenty of up-front appeal. This full-bodied, vividly pure, and expressive Zinfandel should drink well for another 7–8 years. The 1991 is richer and more expansive than even the 1990. In the problematic vintage of 1989, Limerick Lane Cellars produced an excellent Zinfandel, with deep color; an intense, black cherry, herb, and earthy nose; wonderfully extracted, full-bodied flavors; soft tannins; and enough acidity to provide grip and focus. It is unquestionably a top success for the vintage. This is a winery worth learning more about.

LIPARITA CELLARS (NAPA)
Chardonnay* * */* * * *

| 1990 | Chardonnay Howell Mountain | Napa | C | 75 |
| 1989 | Chardonnay Howell Mountain | Napa | C | 88 |

This could be an interesting Chardonnay producer. Liparita has been selling Chardonnay to such superlative producers as Château Montelena and Grgich Hills. The 1989 is one of the better efforts from that disappointing vintage for California's North Coast. This wine is tightly knit, with a stony, minerallike richness, firm acidity, and plenty of structure, body, and length. It should improve over the next 6–12 months and last for 4–5 years. As good as the 1989 is, the 1990, from an excellent, perhaps even outstanding, year for California Chardonnay, is a disappointment. It is lean, short, underripe, and lacking depth.

LIVINGSTON VINEYARDS (NAPA)
Cabernet Sauvignon* * */* * * *

1991	Cabernet Sauvignon Moffett Vineyard	Napa	D	86
1990	Cabernet Sauvignon Moffett Vineyard	Napa	D	88
1989	Cabernet Sauvignon Moffett Vineyard	Napa	D	81
1988	Cabernet Sauvignon Moffett Vineyard	Napa	D	85
1987	Cabernet Sauvignon Moffett Vineyard	Napa	D	87
1986	Cabernet Sauvignon Moffett Vineyard	Napa	D	87

I have a preference for the herb-, cassis-, and coffee-scented 1990 Cabernet Sauvignon over the attractive, medium-weight, somewhat uninspiring 1991. The 1990 offers more richness, as well as a deeper, more interesting midpalate and a classic, moderately tannic finish. Exhibiting soft tannins, this wine should easily last for 10–15 years. The lighter-style 1991 is pure and well made but lacks the intensity of many of its peers. Perhaps more character and richness will emerge with barrel aging. Livingston's 1989 Cabernet Sauvignon, an austere, compact, and lean wine, lacks the richness achieved in other vintages. It should be drunk over the next 5–6 years. I am concerned about the balance between fruit extraction and tannins. Although more charming than the 1989, the 1988 is noticeably lighter than other vintages. It exhibits fine dark ruby color, plenty of round, lush cassis fruit, medium body, noticeable hard tannins, and a quick finish. Drink it over the next 5–7 years. Despite my sense that the 1987 is a bit too sculptured and acidified, I still admire its wonderfully pure and streamlined character. The pure bouquet of cassis fruit and some smoky oak is followed by a medium-bodied, slightly acidic, but rich, concentrated, ripe wine that should age handsomely for 7–8 years. Patience is most definitely required with respect to the broodingly deep, rich, full-bodied yet powerfully tannic, muscular 1986 Cabernet Sauvignon Moffett Vineyard.

Although impressively concentrated, it needs 2–3 more years in the cellar to shed its toughness. The wine has plenty of extract, a wonderfully clean, mineral-scented, blackcurrant fruitiness, good, zesty acidity, and plenty of tannin. **Anticipated maturity: Now–2005.**

J. LOHR WINERY (SANTA CLARA)

Cabernet Sauvignon Cypress*, Cabernet Sauvignon Reserve* *, Chardonnay
Cypress* */* * *, Chardonnay Riverstone* * *, Gamay* * *, Merlot Cypress*

1991	Cabernet Sauvignon Cypress	California	A	73
1985	Cabernet Sauvignon Reserve Carol's Vineyard Lot 2	Napa	C	86
1989	Cabernet Sauvignon Seven Oaks	Paso Robles	B	82
1991	Chardonnay Cypress	Monterey	A	84
1990	Chardonnay Riverstone	Monterey	D	86
1991	Gamay Wild Flower	Monterey	A	84
1991	Merlot Cypress	California	A	72

If you have not yet noticed, J. Lohr is making better and better wines, and prices have not yet caught up with their renaissance in quality. I have tasted a number of fine Gamays, but the 1991 Gamay Wild Flower from J. Lohr is one of the best. You will find none of the vegetal smell that often afflicts red wine varietals grown in the soils of Monterey. It is a wine with a big, bright, vividly intense, cherry-scented nose; excellent, rich, medium-bodied, fruity flavors; a sense of style; and admirable purity. Moreover, I like the wine's exuberance. Drink this delicious wine over the next 1–2 years. The attractive spicy, blackcurrant bouquet of the 1985 Cabernet Sauvignon Reserve Carol's Vineyard Lot 2 suggests that this wine is far more approachable than the taste actually reveals. There is plenty of concentration, high tannins, borderline high acidity, excellent depth, and a finish that suggests 10–15 years of potential longevity. The 1991 Merlot Cypress and 1989 Cabernet Sauvignon Cypress are disappointingly light, vegetal wines. Among J. Lohr's other offerings is a fruity 1991 Cypress Chardonnay (bargain priced) and a very good 1990 Chardonnay Riverstone from its vineyard in Monterey. The latter wine offers an attractive package, as well as a floral, buttery, lemony nose, medium- to full-bodied flavors, good purity, and plenty of depth. The 1991 Chardonnay Cypress is soft, ripe, and delightfully fruity and tasty. The 1989 Cabernet Sauvignon Seven Oaks is surprisingly competent for the vintage, revealing a deep color, an herbaceous, peppery, spicy, curranty nose, medium body, and enough depth to age for 3–4 more years.

LOLONIS WINERY (MENDOCINO)

Cabernet Sauvignon*, Chardonnay* * *, Fumé Blanc* * *, Zinfandel* *

1990	Cabernet Sauvignon	Mendocino	C	72
1991	Chardonnay Private Reserve	Mendocino	C	87
1991	Fumé Blanc Reserve	Mendocino	A	85

After a shaky beginning, Lolonis has made significant progress with its white wines. The reds, particularly the Cabernet Sauvignon and Zinfandel, are lean, nasty, high-acid, astringent wines that lack charm and fruit and have been consistently out of balance. However, the white wines show remarkable improvement. They include a terrific value, the 1991 Fumé Blanc Reserve, which reveals a big, bold nose of herbaceous, melony fruit, medium body, plenty of depth and charm, and a crisp, zesty finish. The 1991 Chardonnay Private Reserve is also an impressively endowed, rich, voluptuously styled Chardonnay that is supported by subtle, toasty new oak. Full and fleshy, it (as well as the Fumé Blanc) should be consumed before the summer of 1994.

LONG VINEYARDS (NAPA)
Cabernet Sauvignon* * *, Chardonnay* * * *

1991	Cabernet Sauvignon	Napa	D	87
1990	Chardonnay	Napa	D	89
1989	Chardonnay	Napa	D	85

This small operation has a significant following for its structured, backward, rich style of Chardonnay and tannic, hard Cabernet Sauvignons. I can understand the excitement with the Chardonnays, as some vintages are capable of lasting 5 or more years. The 1990 is an excellent wine, with an attractive, citrusy, oaky, ripe apple–scented nose and buttery, crisp, structured flavors. Drink it before the end of 1995. The lighter 1989, from a vintage that produced many washed-out Chardonnays, exhibits fruit, character, and a tasty, medium-bodied style. Long's Cabernet Sauvignons are frequently too hard and tannic. Vintages that I have purchased and cellared, such as 1984, 1985, and 1986, are still young, unevolved wines. I see little aromatic development and a growing tendency for the wines to become more compact and leaner as they age. Long did not make a 1990 Cabernet Sauvignon but did produce a more forward-style 1991. It is deep in color and pure, with a moderately intense bouquet of cassis and medium-bodied, tasty, moderately tannic flavors. It appears to have less astringent tannins than previous releases, so perhaps there is a movement to more charm and elegance. It should last for 10–15 years.

LYTTON SPRINGS (SONOMA)
Zinfandel* * * *, Zinfandel Reserve* * * * *

1989	Zinfandel	Sonoma	B	86

Although the vintage no doubt accounts for the fact that the 1989 is not the typical blockbuster Zinfandel routinely produced by this winery, the wine still has fine concentration, a robust, tarry, peppery, earthy, berry-scented nose, and medium- to full-bodied flavors. The tannins are lower than normal, as is the extract level. Because of that, this wine may be more charming in its youth than some of the monster efforts this winery has produced in the past. Drink it over the next 6–7 years. Readers who come across older vintages of Lytton Springs Zinfandel should not hesitate to take a gamble. A number of splendidly rich, unfined, unfiltered wines have been made by this producer. Vintages such as 1987, 1985, 1984, 1983, and 1982 are staggeringly rich, muscular Zinfandels that have not only stood the test of time, but have, in many cases, years of life left.

MACROSTIE (SONOMA)
Chardonnay* * *

1991	Chardonnay	Carneros	B	78
1990	Chardonnay	Carneros	B	86

This is a creamy-textured, round, generously endowed Chardonnay. The honeyed, apple- and orange-scented bouquet offers a judicious touch of new oak. Drink this graceful and delicious, medium-weight wine before the end of 1994.

MARCASSIN (SONOMA)
Chardonnay* * * * *

1990	Chardonnay Hyde Vineyard	Carneros	D	92
1990	Chardonnay Lorenzo Vineyard	Sonoma Coast	D	94
1991	Chardonnay Gauer Ranch	Sonoma	D	96

I am sorry to say that there are only 100 cases of each of these marvelous Chardonnays, both of which were bottled unfiltered. The 1990 Chardonnay Hyde Vineyard is tightly knit. With some coaxing, huge, buttery, herb-, and ripe apple–like aromas begin to drift upward. In the mouth there is exceptional depth, a multidimensional richness, good acidity, and a spicy, opulent, brilliantly delineated finish. This superb Chardonnay should age well for 4–5 years. The 1990 Chardonnay Lorenzo Vineyard has a remarkable resemblance to a great white burgundy from Ramonet. The nose is subtle, although intense in its own delicate way. Aromas of oranges, toast, buttery apples, and even popcorn waft from the glass. In the mouth there is stunning concentration, an unctuous richness, crisp acidity to provide grip and focus, and a phenomenally long, intense finish. Impressive! Bring on the 1991s! The 1991 Gauer Ranch Chardonnay is another exquisite wine that combines power and richness with considerable complexity.

MARIETTA CELLARS (SONOMA)
Cabernet Sauvignon* * * *, Old Vine Red* * *, Petite Sirah* * *, Zinfandel* * * *

1990	Cabernet Sauvignon	Sonoma	B	92
1988	Cabernet Sauvignon	Sonoma	A	84
N. V.	Old Vine Red Lot 12	Sonoma	A	88
1988	Petite Sirah	Sonoma	B	86
1990	Zinfandel Reserve	Sonoma	B	86

This winery produces good wines at reasonable prices. For lovers of gutsy, rich, massive Petite Sirah, the 1988 offers considerable up-front enjoyment—a rarity for a young wine made from this grape. The color is nearly black, the nose intensely peppery, and in the mouth there is an expansive, sweet, jammy character. Although the wine may lack complexity, there is fine depth, body, glycerin, and tannin. Drink it over the next 8–10 years. The medium- to full-bodied 1990 Zinfandel Reserve offers a spicy, berry fragrance, sweet, soft, jammy flavors, and supple, ripe tannins. Drink it over the next 4–5 years. The nonvintage Old Vine Red Lot 12, a robust, richly fruity wine, includes a good amount of Zinfandel in its blend. There is plenty of raspberry fruit in evidence, as well as an attractive spiciness and smooth, medium-bodied, lush flavors.

Drink this mouth-filling charmer over the next 2–3 years. To my mind, Marietta's 1990 Cabernet Sauvignon from Sonoma is the finest Cabernet bargain California has produced since those marvelous 1974 Souverains. It exhibits a saturated black/purple color, as well as a huge nose of jammy cassis, flowers, and spices. Full bodied, with nearly viscous, superpure, gorgeously rich flavors that are well endowed with glycerin, and a lusty, impressive finish, this great California Cabernet Sauvignon merits buying by the case. It should drink well for another 10–15 years. Unfortunately, just under 1,400 cases were produced, so availability is limited. An exceptional value!

MARILYN MERLOT (NAPA)
Merlot*

My vote for the most repugnant idea and tasteless exploitation of the late actress Marilyn Monroe goes to this winery. If the label were not appalling enough, the wine, which is an international blend, is tart, acidified, and sadly deficient in flesh and taste.

MARKHAM WINERY (NAPA)
Cabernet Sauvignon* *, Chardonnay* *, Merlot* *

1988	Cabernet Sauvignon	Napa	B	78
1987	Cabernet Sauvignon	Napa	C	80
1991	Chardonnay	California	B	83
1990	Chardonnay Barrel Fermented	Napa	B	79
1989	Merlot	Napa	B	77
1988	Merlot	Napa	B	86

This is not a source of exciting wines, although the 1988 Merlot is a plump, soft, coffee- and black fruit–flavored wine that exhibits round, gentle flavors and a tasty, supple, lush finish. It is ideal for drinking over the next 2–4 years. The other wines, too compact, acidified, stripped, and one-dimensional, suffer from malnutrition. There has been talk that significant improvements will be made since this winery was sold in 1988 to a Japanese firm. Perhaps it is too soon to see any noticeable changes. Even the 1990 Chardonnay is one-dimensional and simple.

MARTIN BROTHERS WINERY (SAN LUIS OBISPO)
Chardonnay*, Nebbiolo*, Zinfandel*

1989	Chardonnay	Paso Robles	A	73
1990	Nebbiolo	Paso Robles	A	70
1990	Zinfandel Primativo	Paso Robles	A	68

Thin, often musty, and hollow wines routinely emerge from this producer. The only positive thing to say is that the prices are low.

LOUIS M. MARTINI (NAPA)
Cabernet Sauvignon* *, Cabernet Sauvignon Monte Rosso* */* * *,
Chardonnay* */* * *, Pinot Noir *, Sauvignon Blanc* *, Zinfandel* *

1988	Cabernet Sauvignon	Sonoma	B	75
1989	Cabernet Sauvignon Monte Rosso	Sonoma	C	83

1988	Cabernet Sauvignon Monte Rosso	Sonoma	D	75
1987	Cabernet Sauvignon Reserve	Napa	C	82
1991	Chardonnay	Napa	A	77
1990	Chardonnay	Napa/Sonoma	A	83
1989	Chardonnay	Napa/Sonoma	A	68
1989	Chardonnay Las Amigas Vineyard	Napa	C	77
1990	Chardonnay Reserve	Napa	B	78
1988	Pinot Noir	Napa	B	65
1990	Sauvignon Blanc	Napa	A	75
1987	Zinfandel	Sonoma	A	73

One of California's most historic wineries continues to offer indifferent wines. Although I thought things had begun to improve in the mid-1980s, recent tastings suggest otherwise. Some of the faces might change, but this winery is largely content to offer feeble, washed-out wines. Although many of them are reasonably priced, few offer interest or pleasure. The Chardonnays can be more interesting, but the Reserve wines seem less endowed. There is no excuse for wines such as its Zinfandel, Pinot Noir, and the once attractive Barbera to lack fruit, concentration, and character. The Cabernet Sauvignons are average in quality, and even the single-vineyard flagship wine from Monte Rosso, the winery's excellent Sonoma vineyard, lacks intensity and is too acidified and processed. I find all of this sad and depressing.

PAUL MASSON VINEYARDS (MONTEREY)
All wines*

This huge winery, with sales in excess of 5 million cases of wine a year, makes relatively sweet, innocuous, inexpensive wines that are always simple, cloyingly fruity, sometimes heavy, and made to attract those who have been weaned on sweet soda pop. There is nothing I can recommend, even from such inexpensive offerings as its Emerald Dry Riesling. All are made to capture the lowest end of the wine market, where quantity, not quality, is the prerequisite.

MATANZAS CREEK WINERY (SONOMA)
Chardonnay* * * */* * * * *, Merlot* * * */* * * * *, Sauvignon Blanc* * * *

1990	Chardonnay	Sonoma	C	90
1991	Merlot	Sonoma	C	92
1990	Merlot	Sonoma	C	93
1991	Sauvignon Blanc	Sonoma	B	86
1990	Sauvignon Blanc	Sonoma	B	89

Both the 1991 and 1990 Merlots should turn out to be knockout wines. Moreover, both wines should offer up to a decade's worth of hedonistic drinking. The 1991 reveals that telltale smoky, coffee, mocha nose that reminds me of one of my favorite flavors of ice cream from Baskin-Robbins—jamocha almond fudge. In the mouth the creamy texture, sweet ripe fruit, and lusciousness make for a delicious glass of wine. The 1990, which is essentially identical, although more evolved, shares the same luscious palate, and wonderfully rich, toffee, coffee, and berry fruit flavors married brilliantly with sweet, toasty new oak. The finish is explosively rich. These top-class Merlots remain the benchmark for this varietal in California. Not surprisingly, Matanzas Creek has turned out a personality-filled, rich, mineral-, herb-, melon-, and oaky-scented 1990 Sauvignon Blanc, with plenty of ripe flavors, medium to full body, good acidity and focus, and a deliciously long finish. This is consistently one of the best Sauvignons made in California. The 1990 promises to provide immense satisfaction for at least another year. The 1991 Sauvignon is slightly less intense, crisper and zestier, but less flavorful, as well as more limited aromatically. The 1990 Chardonnay is one of the best Matanzas Creek has made in recent years. It offers generous, opulent buttery, peach-, applelike scents, medium to full body, and excellent definition to go along with its deep concentration, crisp acidity, and long finish. Drink it over the next 3–4 years.

MAYACAMAS VINEYARDS (NAPA)
Cabernet Sauvignon* */* * * (since 1979),* * * * * (before 1979)
Chardonnay* *, Sauvignon Blanc* *

1987	Cabernet Sauvignon	Napa	E	81
1986	Cabernet Sauvignon	Napa	E	77
1988	Chardonnay	Napa	D	82
1987	Chardonnay	Napa	D	81
1989	Sauvignon Blanc	Napa	C	77

Anyone who has tasted the 1975 Mayacamas Chardonnay or the 1968, 1970, 1973, 1974, 1976, 1978, or 1979 Cabernet Sauvignons knows they were tasting some of the finest wines made from these two varietals. In fact, the 1970 and 1974 Cabernets are monumental wines that are still remarkably young and unevolved. Certainly this backward style needs time, but I remember tasting both of those wines when they were released, and they were overwhelming in their depth, richness, concentration, and thick, chewy textures. That can no longer be said about current offerings. Recent Cabernets have possessed an annoying vegetal streak, exceptionally high tannins and acidity, and a pronounced deficiency in rich fruit and flesh, and their textures come across as skeletal. The tannins and acidity are still evident, but the concentration is no longer present. The 1986 Cabernet Sauvignon is still hard and appears to be less impressive than when first released. It has also taken on a pronounced, earthy, vegetal character. The 1987 Cabernet is extremely high in acidity, very lean and austere, with no sense of richness or depth to the short, astringent, tart finish. The Chardonnays are similarly styled. Although there is a bit more fruit, they appear to be made in an old, slightly oxidized style. That would be acceptable if there were also depth and richness, which is not the case. The Sauvignon Blanc is monolithic, muted, relatively high in alcohol, and essentially uninteresting. This winery occasionally releases a Pinot Noir and late-harvest Zinfandel, but I have not seen either in over a decade. What a shame!

PETER MCCOY (SONOMA)
Chardonnay* * * */* * * * *

1991	Chardonnay Clos des Pierres Vineyard	Knight's Valley	C	90
1990	Chardonnay Clos des Pierres	Knight's Valley	C	90

The Clos des Pierres Chardonnays from Peter McCoy consistently possess a stony, mineral component in their bouquet and flavors. They are also made from what must be extremely low yields given their layers of rich Chardonnay fruit, nicely integrated with crisp acidity and subtle oak. Both the 1990 and 1991 are complex, elegant, persuasively flavored Chardonnays for drinking over the next 4–5 years.

MCDOWELL VALLEY VINEYARDS (MENDOCINO)
Cabernet Sauvignon* *, Chardonnay* *, Les Vieux Cépages* * *

1988	Cabernet Sauvignon	California	A	74
1991	Chardonnay	Mendocino	A	75
1989	Chardonnay	California	A	69
1991	Fumé Blanc	Mendocino	A	85
1991	Les Vieux Cépages Grenache Rosé	California	B	84
1989	Les Vieux Cépages Grenache	California	A	86
1988	Les Vieux Cépages Syrah	California	C	84
1987	Les Vieux Cépages Syrah	California	C	89
1988	Les Vieux Cépages le Trésor	California	B	83
1990	Zinfandel	Mendocino	B	85

This winery is one of the leading Rhône Ranger specialists, offering some innovative wines under the Les Vieux Cépages name. Their 1991 Grenache Rosé is a delicious, fragrant, full-flavored wine with more character than most California white Zinfandels. The Syrah does not possess the weight and richness of the best California examples, but it is an attractive wine that has remained fairly priced. The 1988 is significantly less impressive than the 1987. The saturated, dark purple color of the 1987 Les Vieux Cépages Syrah gives evidence of considerable extract levels. The bouquet is not disappointing. Young but enticingly pure and intense scents of cassis, licorice, and subtle herbs emerge with airing. Powerful, authoritative, full-bodied flavors are packed with an opulent, chewy fruitiness. If additional complexity develops, this wine will prove to be outstanding. A beauty! The 1989 Les Vieux Cépages Grenache is bursting with strawberry- and cherry-scented fruit. It has a pleasant texture in the mouth and finishes with excellent fruit and body. It is also dry. Drink it for its remarkable balance, freshness, and flavor. The only other wine that recalls the Rhône Valley is the Viognier; unfortunately the 1991 is disappointingly light and diluted. McDowell has also begun to produce a line of wines called LVC Bistro. Both the LVC Bistro blended red wine and the LVC Bistro Syrah sell for under $10 a bottle and are light, clean, fruity, and serviceable. The other wines in McDowell's portfolio are from more conventional varietals such as Cabernet Sauvignon, Chardonnay, Zinfandel, and Sauvignon. Mediocre to above average, they can lack fruit and character, something that cannot be said for the Rhône Ranger offerings.

MEEKER VINEYARD (SONOMA)
Zinfandel* * * *

| 1990 | Zinfandel | | Dry Creek | B | 89 |

This winery continues to impress me with its opaquely colored, rich, full-bodied, expansively flavored, superripe, broad-shouldered Zinfandels. The 1990 is made in a backward style that needs 2–3 years to shed its tannins but is capable of lasting for a decade or more. Once the tannins begin to fall away, the huge, black raspberry, spicy fruit and unctuous glycerin-laden texture will provide an enthralling glass of Zinfandel. Excellent value! Impressive!

MERIDIAN VINEYARDS (SAN LUIS OBISPO)
Cabernet Sauvignon* *, Chardonnay* * *, Pinot Noir* *, Syrah* */* * *

1989	Cabernet Sauvignon	Paso Robles	B	80
1991	Chardonnay	Edna Valley	C	84
1991	Chardonnay	Santa Barbara	B	82
1990	Pinot Noir	Santa Barbara	C	76
1988	Pinot Noir	Santa Barbara	C	72
1990	Syrah	Paso Robles	C	77
1988	Syrah	Paso Robles	C	86

Both 1991 Chardonnays display fine ripe fruit. Unfortunately, the tendency of this winery to go overboard on acid additions gives them a relatively tart, lean, almost shrill side that negates much of their richness. Nevertheless, they are still pleasant, above-average quality Chardonnays. The red wines appear to have been made from excessively acidified grapes that were picked before physiological ripeness was attained. The results are shallow wines that come across on the palate as acidic, hard edged, underripe, and charmless. The Pinot Noir also reveals a vegetal streak. The only red wine I enjoyed was the 1988 Syrah. This fine effort from Meridian Vineyards is a softer, lighter, more elegant style than other Syrahs, but there is no doubting its charming, rich, oaky, berry-scented nose, soft, smoky, expansive, bacony, cassislike flavors, and smooth finish. Given its style, it should be consumed over the next 2–3 years. High hopes continue to abound for Meridian since it has the vast resources of the Nestlé company behind it. To date, the wines have been similar to many run-of-the-mill California wines—too processed, too high-tech, too acidified, too innocuous, and too flavorless.

MERRYVALE VINEYARDS (NAPA)
Chardonnay* *, Proprietary Red Wine* *

| 1989 | Chardonnay | Napa | C | 75 |
| 1986 | Proprietary Red Wine | Napa | D | 72 |

Things are changing at Merryvale. Readers who have followed the extraordinary success and magical talents of France's famed oenologist Michel Rolland will be happy to know that he has been consulting at Merryvale since 1992.

This is great news, so look for the quality to soar. The Chardonnays are mono-lithic, simple, muted, highly stylized, and acidic, wholly lacking in charm. The same can be said for the oaky, acidic, excessively tannic, and green propri-etary red table wine. Rolland will keep acidification to a minimum and pre-serve the wine's personality, accentuate its fruit and richness, and encourage Merryvale (also the owners of the fabulous Meadowood Country Club in St. He-lena) to harvest later, picking only physiologically mature fruit. Look for some major improvements at this winery.

PETER MICHAEL WINERY (SONOMA)

Chardonnay Howell Mountain* * * * *, Chardonnay Sonoma Monplaisir* * * * *,
Les Pavots Proprietary Red Wine* * * *, Sauvignon Blanc l'Après-Midi* * * * *

1990	Chardonnay	Howell Mountain	C	90
1989	Chardonnay Monplaisir	Sonoma	C	90
1990	Les Pavots Proprietary Red Wine	California	D	87
1989	Les Pavots Proprietary Red Wine	California	D	88
1988	Les Pavots Proprietary Red Wine	California	D	87
1991	Sauvignon Blanc l'Après-Midi	California	C	90

This is clearly one of the up-and-coming stars of California. The emphasis is on making natural and unmanipulated wines that express the vineyard, the va-rietal, and the vintage. To date, everything has been at least exciting, and some of the wines are compelling. Only a fortunate few consumers have been able to find these Chardonnays, which are expensive and limited in production. Both the 1990 Howell Mountain and 1989 Monplaisir are superrich, buttery, hon-eyed wines bursting with fruit, voluptuous textures, plenty of toasty oak, and an overall sense of balance. They are a far cry from the excessively processed, neutral, innocuous, hollow, overacidified California Chardonnays that domi-nate that state's production. The 1989 is especially strong when one considers the difficulties most Chardonnay winemakers confronted in that vintage. The 1990 is tighter. Both wines should drink well for another 3–4 years. To the portfolio of dazzling Chardonnays has been added one of California's two or three finest Sauvignon Blancs, called l'Après-Midi. The 1991 exhibits a text-book aroma of mineral, spices, herb, and melony fruit, is rich and authoritative on the palate, yet still graceful and elegant. Drink this stunning Sauvignon Blanc before the end of 1994. The Cabernet-based proprietary red wine is called Les Pavots. As anyone who has tasted through the 1988 and 1989 red wines from California's North Coast knows, not too many wines merit ratings above the low to middle 80s. In 1988 Peter Michael has made an exceptionally elegant, classy wine that displays a cedary, cassis, plummy nose, rich, medium- to full-bodied flavors, fine depth, a wonderful sense of harmony, and a long finish. This wine clearly draws its inspiration from a top classified growth from Bordeaux. It should drink well for up to a decade. The 1989 Les Pavots is even better—a worthy candidate, along with Christian Moueix's Dominus, for the best Cabernet-based wine of the vintage. Its deep color is fol-lowed by a huge nose of vanillin, cassis, and spices, superb richness, great bal-ance, well-integrated, soft acidity, and a long, graceful finish. Approachable now, it should last through most of the first decade of the next century. The

1990 Les Pavots, exhibiting good complexity and overall harmony, continues the trend toward a stylized, elegant, well-balanced wine.

MIRASSOU VINEYARDS (SANTA CLARA)

Cabernet Sauvignon* *, Chardonnay* *, Pinot Blanc White Burgundy* * * *,
Pinot Noir*, Sparkling Wine Cuvées* *

Year	Wine	Region	Class	Score
1989	Blanc de Noir Sparkling Wine	Monterey	B	72
1988	Brut Sparkling Wine	Monterey	B	73
1988	Cabernet Sauvignon Harvest Reserve	Monterey	B	77
1990	Chardonnay Family Selection	Monterey	A	78
1989	Chardonnay Family Selection	Monterey	A	69
1990	Harvest Chardonnay	Monterey	B	84
1989	Pinot Noir Harvest Reserve	Monterey	B	70
1990	Sauvignon Blanc	Monterey	B	77
1990	White Burgundy (Pinot Blanc)	Monterey	A	85

The Mirassou family has done much to establish viticulture in Monterey. Despite a restrained reception from critics, this winery has had to increase its production to nearly 400,000 cases to meet popular demand. The best wine is its Pinot Blanc, called "white burgundy." The 1990 White Burgundy from Mirassou is a vividly pure, medium-bodied, dry wine loaded with fruit. It displays surprising character and more richness and individuality than most California Chardonnays. The price is a steal! The other wines are variable in quality. From the herbaceous Cabernet Sauvignons to a stemmy Pinot Noir and, from time to time, a big, dense, rich Petite Sirah, all of these offerings are plagued by the vegetal character so often found in Monterey County reds. Having bought and cellared some of Mirassou's Petite Sirah and Harvest Cabernets from the late 1970s, I can confirm that the vegetal character does not dissipate with aging. The sparkling wine *cuvées* can often be found discounted for under $10. Although these wines are light-bodied, vaguely fruity, crisp, and tart, I have never found much flavor complexity. The other wine that Mirassou can do a good job with is the Harvest Chardonnay. Much like the white burgundy, it has a pronounced herbaceous nose, but honeyed, rich, tropical fruit flavors, decent acidity, and fine body. It represents a considerable value—when it is good. Although the so-called Family Selection was a good wine in 1990, the 1989 is disappointing.

ROBERT MONDAVI WINERY (NAPA)

Cabernet Sauvignon* * *, Cabernet Sauvignon Reserve* * * * *
(since 1987),* * * (between 1975 and 1985),* * * * * (between 1971 and 1974),
Chardonnay* * *, Chardonnay Reserve* * * */* * * * *, Chenin Blanc* * * *,
Fumé Blanc* * *, Fumé Blanc Reserve* * * */* * * * *, Pinot Noir* * *,
Pinot Noir Reserve* * * * *

Year	Wine	Region	Class	Score
1990	Cabernet Sauvignon	Napa	C	86
1989	Cabernet Sauvignon	Napa	C	77
1988	Cabernet Sauvignon	Napa	C	80

1987	Cabernet Sauvignon	Napa	C	85
1992	Cabernet Sauvignon Reserve	Napa	D	88
1991	Cabernet Sauvignon Reserve	Napa	D	92
1990	Cabernet Sauvignon Reserve	Napa	D	96
1989	Cabernet Sauvignon Reserve	Napa	D	81
1988	Cabernet Sauvignon Reserve	Napa	D	84
1987	Cabernet Sauvignon Reserve	Napa	D	98
1991	Chardonnay	Napa	C	79
1991	Chardonnay Reserve	Napa	D	89
1990	Chardonnay Reserve	Napa	D	90
1991	Chenin Blanc	Napa	A	85
1991	Fumé Blanc	Napa	B	85
1991	Fumé Blanc Reserve	Napa	C	89
1990	Pinot Noir	Napa	C	85
1991	Pinot Noir Reserve Unfiltered	Napa	D	89
1990	Pinot Noir Reserve Unfiltered	Napa	D	88

Robert Mondavi and his family have brought more attention to the potential for world-class Napa Valley wines than any other California wine producer. Their search for quality has been never-ending. After a slump between 1976 and 1985, Mondavi's wines, especially the Reserves, are now among the best in the world. This winery cultivates its image based on its top-of-the-line Reserve and Estate wines, but it also produces hundreds of thousands of cases of inexpensive (under $10 a bottle) wines from its operation in Woodbridge. Although they are not complex, the Sauvignon Blanc, Chenin Blanc, Chardonnay, and Cabernet Sauvignon from Woodbridge are pleasant, fruity, and well made. Of the wines that emerge from Mondavi's architecturally stunning winery in Oakville (Napa Valley), there is a good, fruity, round, generous, regular *cuvée* of Chardonnay that needs to be drunk within its first 3–4 years and a ripe, toasty, honeyed, richly oaky, big Reserve Chardonnay, of which the 1991 and 1990 are typical. Although I have been disappointed with how some of the Reserve Chardonnays have aged, the 1990 should last for at least 3–4 years, the 1991 for 2–3 years. Although expensive, it is one of the best California Chardonnays produced. It was Mondavi who proved to the rest of California that great wines could be made from Sauvignon. Called Fumé Blanc by Mondavi, both the regular, fruity, melony, medium-bodied Fumé and the more oaky, honeyed, lavishly rich Reserve are wines to search out. Superflexible with food, they are at least very good, and the Reserve is often stunning. If you are looking for pure fruit and flowers, check out the Chenin Blanc, an intensely floral, slightly sweet, richly fruity wine with undeniable charm. The great breakthrough at Mondavi over recent years was with its Reserve Pinot Noir. After going high-tech in the mid-1970s and 1980s with sterile-filtered, one-dimensional wines, Mondavi has become a leader in the movement toward an unmanipulated, natural style of winemaking that stresses the importance of the vineyard, the varietal, and the vintage. The results are most evident in its Pinot Noir program. The regular *cuvée* of Pinot Noir—the 1990, for example—is a delicious, jammy, fruity wine; the real glories, however, are the Reserves, which are virtually indistinguishable from a top-notch red burgundy. The only disappointing aspect is that they have not aged well. Nevertheless, for drinking in their first 4–6 years of life, Mondavi's Reserve Pinot Noirs are among the finest made in the New World. The 1990, which is unfined and unfiltered, offers a superb bouquet of spicy oak, herbs, rich red and black fruits, and flowers. Lush, expansive, and generously endowed, this is Pinot Noir at its most seductive. Mondavi is a Cabernet Sauvignon specialist. Although the quality of the Reserve Cabernets between 1975 and 1985 was not what it should have been (excessive acidification and sterile filtration eviscerated the wines), since 1987 (save for a relatively lean, malnourished 1989 Reserve) the wines have been exceptional. Although it will not be released until 1995, the 1992 Reserve is a supple, richly fruity wine with considerable class and charm. The 1991 Cabernet Sauvignon Reserve is a rich, full-bodied wine with plenty of toasty oak and cassis in the bouquet; expansive, chewy, moderately tannic flavors; and superb definition and purity. It is not quite as concentrated and aromatically complex as the 1990, nor is it as massive or rich as the 1987, but it comes close to these two stunners. Approachable now, it should drink well for at least 15 or more years. The 1990 Cabernet Sauvignon Reserve looks to be a worthy rival of the great 1987 Mondavi Reserve. Although slightly less powerful than that magnificent wine, the 1990 exhibits an opaque, dark ruby/purple color and a huge nose that offers up abundant aromas of sweet, toasty, new oak, cassis, roasted nuts, and animal scents. In the mouth the wine reveals a gorgeous concentration of cassis fruit welded to gobs of sweet, soft tannins. There is a wonderful inner core of richness and concentration, as well as a finish that is disarmingly velvety until some tannins emerge as the wine sits in the glass. This superconcentrated, beautifully made wine should age magnificently for 15–20 years. Mondavi has turned in a strong effort in the good but generally unexciting 1988 Cabernet Sauvignon vintage. In contrast with his compelling 1987 Reserve, the 1988 is much softer and not nearly as concentrated. It has a gorgeously smoky, cassis-, and vanillin-scented bouquet; ripe, round, generously endowed flavors; soft acids; and moderate tannins in its smooth-as-silk finish. Much more advanced and approachable than the 1987 Reserve, the 1988 is ideal for both restaurants and consumers looking for near-term gratification. Drink it over the next 7–10 years. The celestial 1987 Reserve will require a great deal of patience. Black/ruby in color, with an intense but unevolved bouquet of superripe cassis enhanced by scents of mint and toasty new oak, this exceptionally concentrated, full-bodied wine behaves as if it wants to be a 1986 Mouton-Rothschild. It is a dazzling wine that the Mondavis, justifiably, feel is the greatest Cabernet Sauvignon they have ever made. It should certainly prove to be uncommonly long-lived. The embossed, engraved, colorful label and monster-size cork are also special. This is a sensational and profound winemaking effort. **Anticipated maturity: 1996–2015.**

RATINGS OF OLDER VINTAGES OF ROBERT MONDAVI CABERNET SAUVIGNON RESERVE: 1986 (88), 1985 (84), 1984 (80), 1983 (75), 1982 (78), 1981 (76), 1980 (79), 1979 (72), 1978 (89), 1977 (76), 1976 (84), 1975 (87), 1974 (95), 1973 (87), 1971 (94), 1970 (not Reserve, but an unfiltered wine) (88)

CHÂTEAU MONTELENA (NAPA)
Cabernet Sauvignon Estate* * * * *, Chardonnay* * * */* * * * *, Zinfandel* * * *

1988	Cabernet Sauvignon Estate	Napa	D	86
1987	Cabernet Sauvignon Estate	Napa	D	98
1986	Cabernet Sauvignon Estate	Napa	D	92
1985	Cabernet Sauvignon Estate	Napa	D	96
1990	Chardonnay	Napa	D	90
1990	Zinfandel Estate	Napa	C	89

There is something reassuring about seeing a bottle of Château Montelena. This classic, old Napa Valley winery is best known for its Cabernet Sauvignon, but it can also fashion wonderful Chardonnay from the Alexander and Napa valleys. Moreover, the winery has never deviated from the decision to make all American wine. Château Montelena has never yielded to the temptation to sugar its wines or do malolactic fermentation for the Chardonnay and gussy them up with lavish quantities of new oak. The result is the quintessential California style of Chardonnay that has remained unchanged after nearly 2 decades. Their Chardonnays drink well young, yet certain vintages can improve for 5–10 years. The 1990 Chardonnay has a textbook Montelena lemon/apple bouquet, a vague scent of buttery popcorn, crisp acidity, and rich, multidimensional, layered flavors. It should drink well for at least 4–5 years. Montelena's 1988 Cabernet Sauvignon is one of the most tannic, densest wines of the vintage, and I am somewhat alarmed by the high level of tannins. This bruiser is boldly flavored, but the tannins are hard and astringent, making one wonder if everything will come into balance. I remember having similar reservations about the 1983, which is now beginning to drink well. Château Montelena has made so many sensational Cabernets that it seems almost impossible to believe its 1987 Cabernet Sauvignon Napa Valley Estate could be even more profound than any of the exceptional wines made previously at this property. The black/purple color, extraordinary bouquet (rich cassis, violets, and licorice), massive extraction of flavors, sensational depth, super ripeness, and length (certainly over a minute) all suggest that this is easily the most concentrated and potentially longest-lived Cabernet Sauvignon Château Montelena has ever made. The extract level is incredible, yet the balance is there. **Anticipated maturity: 1997–2025.** Much of Château Montelena's production goes to restaurants, but this wine clearly belongs in any Cabernet enthusiast's cellar. A winemaking tour de force! The 1986 Cabernet Sauvignon Estate is another great success from this winery. Those who missed the otherworldly 1985 must get in line immediately for this sumptuous 1986. It is actually performing better than the 1985 at the moment, but in the long run I do not think it will approach the heights the 1985 is capable of achieving. However, it is more forward and more flattering to taste than the 1985 was at a similar stage. This is an example of Château Montelena at its best. The big, cassis- and chocolate-scented bouquet has a whiff of toast but relies primarily on powerfully rich, ripe aromas that explode upward from the glass. There is no letting up in the mouth, as the wine is exceptionally concentrated and full bodied, with softer tannins and a bit lower acidity than the 1985. It is gloriously rich and full and, although approachable now, should be at its best between 1993 and 2008. Bravo! Renowned for its fine Chardonnays and superb Cabernet Sauvignon, Château Montelena also produces high-quality Zinfandel that tends to be ignored because of all the hoopla over its other wines. Not surprisingly, the 1990 Estate Zinfandel is a large-scale, spicy, fleshy wine with gobs of fruit, plenty of alcohol, and fine underlying depth. Drinking lusciously now, it should be at its best between now and 2000. There are soft tannins, an unctuous, chewy mouth-feel and gobs of berry, peppery fruit.

RATINGS FOR OLDER VINTAGES OF CHÂTEAU MONTELENA CABERNET SAUVIGNON: 1984 (90), 1983 (87), 1982 (90), 1981 (82), 1980 (91), 1979 (88), 1978 (93), 1977 (92), 1976 (87), 1975 (84), 1974 (Sonoma) (84)

MONTEREY VINEYARDS (MONTEREY)

Classic Cabernet Sauvignon* * *, Classic Chardonnay* * *, Classic Merlot* * *,
Classic Red* * *, Classic Sauvignon Blanc* * *, Classic White* * *

1991	Classic Cabernet Sauvignon	Monterey	A	85
1991	Classic Chardonnay	Monterey	A	85
1991	Classic Gamay Beaujolais	Monterey	A	85
1990	Classic Merlot	Monterey	A	85
1990	Classic Red	California	A	85
1991	Classic Sauvignon Blanc	California	A	84
1991	Classic White	Monterey	A	86

Most consumers looking for "fine" wine probably bypass this prolific producer since its products are often stacked in unattractive piles at liquor stores. That is a shame, because the quality of these wines is appealing. The competently made, inexpensive offerings from Monterey Vineyards are delicious and should have broad appeal to both neophytes and more finicky connoisseurs. Given the overwhelming number of vapid California-produced Sauvignon Blancs, I was surprised by the amount of personality and character present in this estate's 1991 Classic Sauvignon Blanc. There are melon and herbs to be found in its moderately intense bouquet. Crisp, pure, and fresh, it is a delight to drink. Rather than challenge its aging potential, I would recommend consumption over the next year. I was even fond of the 1991 Classic Chardonnay, which displays elegant, floral, applelike fruit flavors; good, crisp acidity; a stylish, graceful personality; and true varietal character. Drink it over the next year. Amazingly, the 1991 Classic White, a generic blend, is even better. It gets my nod as one of the finest white wine values in the world. The 1990 Classic Red offers a Côtes du Rhône–like, peppery, berry fruitiness; a chunky, medium-bodied, soft texture; and a spicy, ripe, nearly fat finish. It makes for a tasty mouthful of dry red wine. The 1990 Classic Cabernet Sauvignon displays a spicy, herbaceous, berry-scented nose, medium-bodied flavors, good structure, some tannin, and a clean, surprisingly long finish. It should drink well for at least 2–3 years. The 1990 Classic Merlot is rounder and tastes sweeter and more expansive, with low acidity and a ripe, chocolatey, coffee-, berry-scented personality. Like the Cabernet and Classic Red, it is ideal for drinking over the next 2–3 years. If you are tired of tasting too many tannic, overly oaked, processed, acidified "boutique" wines at $15–$30 or more a bottle, try one of these modestly priced gems from Monterey Vineyards. Restaurants looking for an exuberantly fruity, crunchy, fresh, delicious-tasting red should make the 1991 Classic Gamay Beaujolais their house wine. Clean and vibrant, with depth and balance, this wine also provides joy to go along with its remarkable value. It should be drunk over the next year.

MONTEVINA (AMADOR)

Barbera* * *, Cabernet Sauvignon* *, Chardonnay*, Sangiovese* *,
Zinfandel* * (since 1979), * * * */* * * * * (before 1979)

1987	Barbera Reserve Selection	Amador	A	87
1989	Cabernet Sauvignon	Amador	A	74
1990	Chardonnay	Amador	A	69
1989	Zinfandel	Amador	A	72
1990	Zinfandel	Shenandoah	A	75
1989	Zinfandel Reserve	Amador	A	74

Dark ruby/purple-colored, with a tar- and berry-scented nose, the unctuous, spicy 1987 Barbera Reserve Selection exhibits low acidity (amazing for a Barbera) and a robust, heavy finish. Drink it with pizza and grilled foods. Montevina's current-day Zinfandels are not even vaguely reminiscent of the profound Zinfandels the winery made in the mid-1970s. The Zinfandels made at Montevina in such vintages as 1975 and 1976 have aged superbly, making one wonder why they are now producing such one-dimensional, commercial, simple wines. This watery 1990 offering is obviously made for someone who wants to drink a slightly sweet red wine without any personality. It is a shame to witness one of California's finest Zinfandel producers turning out such an innocuous product. The other wines in Montevina's portfolio are equally mediocre. They lack fruit, are excessively acidified, and come across on the palate as empty and soulless.

MONTICELLO CELLARS (NAPA)

Cabernet Sauvignon Corley Reserve* * * *, Cabernet Sauvignon Jefferson
Cuvée* * */* * * *, Chardonnay Corley Reserve* * *, Chardonnay
Jefferson Cuvée* * *, Domaine Montreaux Sparkling Wine* * *,
Merlot* * *, Pinot Noir Estate* * *

1991	Cabernet Sauvignon Corley Reserve	Napa	C	88
1990	Cabernet Sauvignon Corley Reserve	Napa	C	87
1989	Cabernet Sauvignon Corley Reserve	Napa	C	84
1987	Cabernet Sauvignon Corley Reserve	Napa	C	87
1990	Chardonnay Corley Reserve	Napa	C	87
1991	Merlot Estate	Napa	C	87
1990	Pinot Noir Estate	Napa	C	85

Monticello's two 1991 offerings reveal some of the telltale characteristics of that vintage. The cool weather that year produced wines with intensely saturated colors, but they are lower in alcohol and lighter bodied than the 1990s. Although the 1991 Merlot possesses fleshy fruit, it does not have the weight or alcoholic clout of many other Merlots. Pure and well balanced, it is an attractively made wine for drinking over the next 7–8 years. Between the two Corley Reserve Cabernets, I prefer the 1990. The 1991 is a graceful wine, with attractive blackcurrant fruit, a touch of oak, a sleek texture, and a medium-bodied, elegant style. The 1990 offers a deeper color, a more evolved, spicy, blackcurrant, oaky nose, rich, medium- to full-bodied flavors, and more length, concentration, and depth. It also possesses lower acidity than the 1991. Both wines should easily last for 10–12 years. Monticello's 1989 Corley Reserve Cabernet Sauvignon is leaner and lacks the fatness and richness of the 1990 and 1991. The finish is austere; however, given numerous disappointments from this vintage, this wine is a modest success. The 1987 Corley Reserve Cabernet is extremely tannic and powerful, with full body and plenty of depth and richness, but it exhibits a closed, firm personality. It should be at its best between 1997 and 2008. Monticello Cellars also produces a softer, less tannic, fruitier Cabernet called Jefferson Cuvée. I have not seen this wine since the excellent 1987. There are also two *cuvées* of Chardonnay. The Corley Reserve Chardonnay is a big, bold, oaky, rich wine. The Jefferson Cuvée Chardonnay is lighter, more fruity, and less intense. The Corley Reserve can be aggressively woody, and the Jefferson Cuvée can lack fruit. Both offerings are reliably good Chardonnays, with the 1990 Corley Reserve a dramatic, rich wine for drinking over the next several years. Personal taste will dictate which wine is preferred. Monticello also makes a sparkling wine under the label Domaine Montreaux. A fuller-bodied, more toasty style of sparkling wine than other California sparkling wines, it has generally been an attractive wine that relies more on its size and toasty character than on crisp, delicate fruit. Last, Monticello has produced small amounts of Pinot Noir that occasionally exhibit considerable potential. The promising 1990 offers medium ruby color, an attractive, pure nose of red and black fruits, and spicy oak. It is a soft, round, generous wine for drinking over the next several years.

Z. MOORE WINERY (SONOMA)
Gewürztraminer* * * *

1988	Gewürztraminer	Sonoma	B	88
1990	Gewürztraminer Barrel Fermented Dry	California	B	85
1989	Gewürztraminer Barrel Fermented Dry	California	B	85
1990	Gewürztraminer Vineyard Designated Cuvée	California	B	88

As an unabashed lover of Gewürztraminer from Alsace, I have found California's Gewürztraminers to be insipid, with an artificial bubble-gum, tutti-frutti quality and a shameful deficiency of depth and character. However, the Z. Moore Winery stands out for consistently producing dry, spicy, rose- and lychee nut–scented Gewürztraminers that boast an amazing resemblance to the finest examples from France. Both of these barrel-fermented, completely dry wines have considerable merit. The 1990 regular *cuvée* is leaner and crisper, with excellent fruit and a dry, medium- to full-bodied finish. The 1990 Vineyard Designated Cuvée (60% made from the McElroy Vineyard and 40% from the Martinelli Vineyard) displays a big, spicy, perfumed nose; excellent, rich, dry, medium- to full-bodied flavors; and a crisp, long finish. Why is it that no other California producers appear to be able to get this much character in their Gewürztraminer? Both the 1988 and 1989 offerings lean toward the spicy, flamboyantly fragrant style of Gewürztraminer so frequently found in Alsace. The 1989 Gewürztraminer Barrel Fermented Dry possesses an excellent, intense bouquet, good body, and solid depth in the finish. The 1988 Gewürztraminer is better—and a dead ringer for an Alsatian Gewürztraminer. It has more body and is less dry than the 1989. Both are provocative examples of this exotic varietal, and it is a delight to see a California winery finally capture the character of this fascinating grape.

MORGAN WINERY (MONTEREY)

Cabernet Sauvignon* *, Chardonnay* * *, Chardonnay Reserve* */* * *,
Pinot Noir* * *, Sauvignon Blanc* * *

1988	Cabernet Sauvignon	California	C	65
1991	Chardonnay	California	C	86
1990	Chardonnay Reserve	California	C	79
1991	Pinot Noir	California	C	78
1990	Pinot Noir	California	C	87
1989	Pinot Noir	California	C	79
1988	Pinot Noir	California	C	85
1990	Pinot Noir Carneros Reserve	Carneros	C	87
1990	Pinot Noir Monterey Reserve	Monterey	C	88
1991	Sauvignon Blanc	California	A	85

More and more California wineries seem to be closer to capturing the mystique of the elusive Pinot Noir grape. These attractive as well as elegant Pinots are made in a style reminiscent of a good Côte de Beaune. The attractively spicy, herb-, cherry-, and strawberry-scented bouquet of this 1988 Pinot Noir is followed by a wine with soft, velvety, medium-bodied flavors, a nice touch of vanillin oak, the underlying Pinot weedy character, and good, heady finishes. Drink them over the next 2–3 years. This winery also produces one of California's better Sauvignon Blancs, always vibrant and fruity, with subtle herbaceous notes, good body, and freshness. The excellent 1991 should drink well over the next several years. Several Chardonnays are produced, including a regular cuvée, and a reserve. The regular cuvée tends to be richly fruity, with a lot of tropical fruit aromas and flavors, good body, crispness, and excellent purity. The Reserve Chardonnay is generally too oaky, with quickly fading fruit that leaves only a harsh skeleton of acidity, alcohol, and wood. Given the much higher price, I would opt for the less expensive bottlings. Last, like so many Monterey County producers, this winery has problems with its Cabernet Sauvignons. The herbaceous 1988 Cabernet Sauvignon displays exceptionally astringent tannins, tart acidity, and a big hole in the middle.

J. W. MORRIS WINERY (SONOMA)

Cabernet Sauvignon Fat Cat* *, Chardonnay Douglas Hill* */* * *, Chardonnay
Gravel Bar* */* * *, Petite Sirah Bosun Crest* *, Zinfandel Kramer Ridge* *

1990	Black Mountain Vineyard Cabernet Sauvignon Fat Cat	Alexander Valley	C	86
1991	Black Mountain Vineyard Chardonnay Douglas Hill	Alexander Valley	B	87
1990	Black Mountain Vineyard Chardonnay Gravel Bar	Alexander Valley	C	85
1990	Black Mountain Vineyard Petite Sirah Bosun Crest	Alexander Valley	A	72
1990	Black Mountain Vineyard Zinfandel Kramer Ridge	Alexander Valley	A	74

These offerings from the J. W. Morris Winery include a richly fruity, medium-
to full-bodied, luscious 1991 Douglas Hill Chardonnay. Readers will love the
pineapple fruitiness and purity of this wine, which should be drunk before the
end of 1994. The 1990 Chardonnay Gravel Bar is a bigger, fuller-bodied wine
with copious quantities of sweet fruit and glycerin as well as a lusty finish. It,
too, should be drunk before the end of 1994. The red wines are a mixed bag.
The 1990 Cabernet Sauvignon Fat Cat displays a dense, saturated, dark ruby
color, a big, chocolatey, earthy, spicy nose, and plenty of depth and richness,
but not a lot of complexity. Drink it over the next 5–8 years. I was disappointed
by both the 1990 Petite Sirah Bosun Crest, a light, insipid example from this
varietal, and the barely adequate, washed-out, simple 1990 Zinfandel Kramer
Ridge.

MT. EDEN VINEYARDS (SANTA CLARA)

Cabernet Sauvignon* *, Chardonnay MacGregor Vineyard* * * *, Chardonnay Santa
Barbara* * */* * * *, Chardonnay Santa Cruz Estate* * * * *

1988	Cabernet Sauvignon Estate	Santa Cruz	C	85
1990	Chardonnay MacGregor Vineyard	Edna Valley	C	88
1990	Chardonnay	Santa Barbara	C	86
1990	Chardonnay Estate	Santa Cruz	D	90

Mt. Eden is unquestionably one of the two or three finest producers of
Chardonnay in California. Its less expensive 1990 Santa Barbara offering exhibits attractive viscosity, plenty of superripe tropical fruit, full body, and a
long, plump finish. Drink it over the next year. The 1990 Estate Chardonnay is
much tighter as well as more compelling. The nose of toasty new oak, earthy,
buttery fruit, and minerals is followed by a tightly knit, rich, full-bodied, concentrated wine that is a dead ringer for a top Premier Cru or Grand Cru white
burgundy. Based on past efforts, this wine should last for 4–8 years. Mt. Eden's
1990 MacGregor Vineyard Chardonnay offers a veritable fruit salad concoction of honeyed pineapples, mangoes, and overripe apples. Lush, richly fruity,
and medium to full bodied, this obvious, wonderfully fleshy, in-your-face
Chardonnay should provide ideal drinking over the next year. While Mt. Eden
made some stunningly rich, backward, almost impenetrable monster Cabernet

Sauvignons in the early 1970s (check out the 1973 for an example of how great these Cabernets were), recent vintages have been lean and overtly herbaceous, without much underlying depth or concentration. Among recent vintages, barrel samples of the 1990 and 1991 appeared to possess more cassis, richness, and suppleness, with 12–15 or more years of aging potential.

RATINGS FOR OLDER VINTAGES OF MOUNT EDEN CHARDONNAY SANTA CRUZ ESTATE: 1989 (87), 1988 (92), 1987 (94), 1986 (93), 1985 (86), 1984 (90)

Note: This is one of a handful of California Chardonnays that can easily stand up to nearly a decade of cellaring. In fact, 2 years ago I had the 1973, which was still a marvel of rich fruit and complexity.

MT. VEEDER WINERY (NAPA)

Cabernet Sauvignon* *, Chardonnay* *, Meritage Proprietary Red Wine* *

1990	Cabernet Sauvignon	Napa	C	88
1990	Chardonnay	Napa	B	82
1990	Meritage Proprietary Red Wine	Napa	C	87
1988	Meritage Proprietary Red Wine	Napa	C	74

After a succession of listless performances (for example, the lean 1988 Meritage and the fruity but one-dimensional 1990 Chardonnay), Mt. Veeder has produced two 1990 red wine offerings that strongly suggest things may have gotten back on track. The 1990 Meritage exhibits plenty of fruit and fine ripeness. It has not been excessively acidified, and spicy, ripe, cassis flavors reveal fine purity and complexity. This beauty should drink well young but keep for a decade or more. The 1990 Cabernet Sauvignon is a more spicy, leafy, herb- and blackcurrant-scented wine, with excellent definition, medium to full body, and fine acidity, as well as a long, rich, concentrated finish. Drink it over the next 10–12 years. If the 1990s are typical of the new level of quality from Mt. Veeder, look for ratings to move up a notch.

MOUNTAIN VIEW WINERY (SANTA CLARA)

Cabernet Sauvignon* *, Chardonnay* *, Pinot Noir* */* * *, Zinfandel* * *

1990	Cabernet Sauvignon	Mendocino	A	78
1991	Chardonnay	California	A	75
1990	Pinot Noir	Monterey/Napa	A	85
N. V.	Zinfandel	Amador	A	84

This winery makes a bevy of inexpensive wines, all of which are of at least sound quality. The surprisingly generous, opulent, luscious 1990 Pinot Noir lacks complexity but does offer gobs of rich fruit, silky-smooth texture, and authentic Pinot varietal character. It is hard to believe one could find a Pinot Noir of this caliber for such a price. I also admired the spicy, robust, chunky nonvintage Zinfandel from Amador. I suspect this blend changes from time to time, but it has displayed remarkable consistency in style over the last 4–5 years. Although it is a bigger wine than the Pinot Noir, it is true to its Zinfandel heritage. Both wines should be drunk over the next 2–3 years. The 1990 Cabernet Sauvignon and 1991 Chardonnay are both one-dimensional, diluted, and uninteresting. But keep in mind that with any *négociant* brand such as

Mountain View Winery, blends change quickly. What could be a super buy in the market one year can be much lighter the next. This winery has been a generally reliable source, particularly for its Pinot Noir and nonvintage Zinfandel. The Chardonnays, Sauvignon Blancs, and Cabernet Sauvignons have been more erratic.

DOMAINE MUMM (NAPA)
Blanc de Noir Rosé* * * *, Brut Prestige Cuvée* * */* * * *,
Brut Winery Lake Cuvée* * */* * * *

N. V.	Blanc de Noir Rosé	Napa	C	87
N. V.	Brut Prestige Cuvée	Napa	C	85
1989	Brut Winery Lake Cuvée	Napa	C	86

The first wines to be released from this French-American syndicate have shown encouraging signs. Long-term questions remain concerning whether the climate is too hot and the soil too rich to produce sparkling wines with great flavor depth. The three best *cuvées* of Mumm sparkling wine are the N. V. Brut Prestige, the vintage-dated Winery Lake Cuvée, and an enthralling delicate rosé, the nonvintage Blanc de Noir. These products display complexity, richness, and length, which places Mumm among the top three or four producers of quality California sparkling wines.

MURPHY-GOODE (SONOMA)
Cabernet Sauvignon* */* * *, Chardonnay* * *, Chardonnay Reserve* * *, Fumé
Blanc* * *, Fumé Blanc Reserve* * * *, Merlot* * *, Pinot Blanc* * */* * * *

1990	Cabernet Sauvignon	Alexander Valley	C	84
1988	Cabernet Sauvignon	Alexander Valley	B	82
1991	Chardonnay	Alexander Valley	B	85
1990	Chardonnay Reserve	Alexander Valley	C	86
1991	Fumé Blanc	Alexander Valley	A	85
1990	Fumé Blanc	Alexander Valley	A	87
1991	Fumé Blanc Reserve	Alexander Valley	B	87
1991	Merlot	Alexander Valley	C	84
1990	Merlot	Alexander Valley	C	83
1987	Merlot Premier Vineyard	Alexander Valley	C	87
1991	Pinot Blanc G.M.S.	Alexander Valley	B	87

This relatively new winery (founded in 1986) has demonstrated an intelligent pricing approach as well as a sure touch when it comes to fashioning wines that have considerable character and complexity and provide copious quantities of up-front fruit. Its wines to date have included excellent Fumé Blancs, with the Reserve often one of the best wines of the vintage; competent Chardonnays; fruity, reliable Merlots; and inconsistent Cabernets. Prices remain exceptionally fair, so consumers take note. Murphy-Goode's red wines are not designed for long-term cellaring, so drink them within 4–6 years of the vintage.

NALLE (SONOMA)
Cabernet Sauvignon* *, Zinfandel* * * *

1988	Cabernet Sauvignon	Dry Creek	C	69
1991	Zinfandel	Dry Creek	B	89
1990	Zinfandel	Dry Creek	B	88

The deep, thick-looking, ruby/purple-colored 1990 Zinfandel is enticing, and the cascade of berry fruit that soars from the glass is enough to make Zinfandel fanatics jump with joy. This medium- to full-bodied wine exhibits exceptional ripeness, a beautifully etched personality, plenty of intensity, but no sense of heaviness or excessively high alcohol. Moreover, I admire its purity of flavor. Drink this beauty over the next 7–8 years. Nalle's 1991 Zinfandel is just terrific. The dark ruby/purple color, classic Zinfandel nose of black raspberries and spices, graceful, medium- to full-bodied texture, and amply endowed flavors bursting with ripe fruit make for a gorgeously seductive wine. It is not likely to make old bones, but 7–8 years of life are within reach. The 1988 Cabernet Sauvignon was relatively hollow, astringent, and lean, without the charm or intensity of this winery's excellent Zinfandel.

NAPA RIDGE (NAPA)
Cabernet Sauvignon* *, Chardonnay* * *, Chardonnay Reserve* * * *,
Chenin Blanc* *, Sauvignon Blanc* *, White Zinfandel* *

This inexpensive line of wines is part of the Beringer/Wine World, Inc., empire. Thus far the emphasis has been on producing nearly 800,000 cases of wines that retail for around $6 a bottle. The best wines to date have been the tasty, light-bodied, well-made Chardonnay and the soft, round, herbaceous Cabernet Sauvignon. The Sauvignon Blanc is generally diluted and thin, the white Zinfandel cloying, and the Chenin Blanc heavy-handed and sweet. In Summer 1993, a Chardonnay Reserve (the 1991) was released. It is a gorgeously rich, honeyed, concentrated wine that represented a super bargain.

NAVARRO VINEYARDS (MENDOCINO)
Chardonnay* * *, Pinot Noir* * */* * * *, Sauvignon Blanc* * * *

1990	Chardonnay	Anderson Valley	B	86
1989	Pinot Noir Deep End Blend	Anderson Valley	C	86
1989	Pinot Noir Méthode l'Ancienne	Anderson Valley	C	86
1990	Sauvignon Blanc Cuvée 128	Anderson Valley	A	86

This is a winery that elicits my interest because each wine makes an individual statement. One is likely to find a product that not only provides pleasure, but also offers a distinctive character and respect for the varietal, the vintage, and the vineyard. Much of Navarro's early acclaim derived from its Riesling and Gewürztraminer. I have not tasted recent vintages of these wines, but I never found them to be nearly as interesting as did other writers. I find the winery's Chardonnays especially promising. They exhibit plenty of fruit and are made in a medium-bodied style with just enough toasty oak to add interest and structure. The Pinot Noirs are also intriguing, possessed of expressive, rich, smoky, berry, spicy noses; rich, ripe, pure fruit; medium body; and firm finishes. If they exhibited slightly more depth, they could rank among the finest made in

California. The most underrated wine from Navarro is the Sauvignon Blanc. The 1990 offers a fragrant, powerful nose of spices, herbs, and melons, rich fruit, crisp acidity, and a long, zesty finish—all that a Sauvignon should be. It possesses considerable character, something often missing from this varietal.

NELSON ESTATE (SONOMA)
Cabernet Franc* * * *

1988	Cabernet Franc	Napa	C	87

It may be too soon to give this winery a four-star rating, but the impressive 1988 Cabernet Franc exhibits a wonderfully expressive bouquet of cedar, black fruits, minerals, and herbs. Medium bodied, with a multidimensional personality, this rich, soft wine can be drunk now or cellared for 7–8 years.

NEVADA CITY WINERY (NEVADA COUNTY)
Cabernet Sauvignon* * *, Douce Noir (Charbono)* * *

1987	Cabernet Sauvignon	Sierra Foothils	B	86
1986	Douce Noir (Charbono)	Nevada County	A	87

An excellent bargain for a drinkable, medium- to full-bodied, supple style of Cabernet Sauvignon, this 1987 exhibits attractive ripeness, authentic varietal character, and a serious finish. Drink it over the next 4–5 years. Looking for a seriously rich, full-bodied, robust red wine for under $10? This is one of the best Charbonos I have tasted from California. The big, spicy, smoky, vanillin-scented bouquet exhibits abundant oak but has enough intense blackcurrant fruit behind it to balance out the wood. In the mouth the wine is full bodied and deep, with a gorgeous level of fruit extract, no hard edges, and plenty of power and alcohol in the finish. This is a hefty yet impressively constructed wine that is also a splendid bargain. Drink it over the next 7–8 years.

NEWLAN VINEYARDS (NAPA)
Cabernet Sauvignon* *, Chardonnay* *

1987	Cabernet Sauvignon	Napa	C	72
1990	Chardonnay	Napa	C	78

Although 1987 and 1990 are fine vintages, I have been disappointed with the recent releases from this winery. They lack fruit and seem overly structured and tannic, with too much acidity. The 1987 Cabernet Sauvignon has a nonexistent bouquet, as well as hard, tough, astringent, out-of-balance flavors. The woody 1990 Chardonnay is already displaying fatigue, with inadequate fruit for its size.

NEWTON VINEYARDS (NAPA)
Cabernet Sauvignon* * * */* * * * *, Chardonnay* * * * *,
Claret* * * *, Merlot* * * * *

1990	Cabernet Sauvignon	Napa	D	94
1991	Chardonnay Unfiltered	Napa	D	95
1990	Chardonnay Unfiltered	Napa	C	92

1990	Claret	Napa	B	88
1990	Merlot	Napa	C	93

After an erratic performance in the 1980s, Newton appears to have turned over a new leaf with some spectacular 1990s. Interestingly, the famed Bordeaux oenologist Michel Rolland has been consulting with proprietor Hugh Newton and his wife, Sue Hua, and their excellent winemaker, John Kongsgaard. It appears Rolland has had a positive influence on the wines. Even the 1990 Claret, the least expensive, is delicious. An inexpensive proprietary red wine made from a blend of 64% Merlot, 33% Cabernet Franc, and 3% Cabernet Sauvignon, the 1990 offers gorgeous drinking. The sweet, black cherry–, herb-, and vanillin-scented nose is enticing as well as complex. On the palate the wine displays smooth, beautifully crafted, ripe, rich, cassis flavors nicely supported by wood and soft tannins. The finish is velvety and delicious. Drink this stylish wine over the next 7–8 years. The 1991 Unfiltered Chardonnay is worth fighting over. It is one of the greatest new-world Chardonnays I have tasted. It possesses a Montrachet-like nose of minerals, opulent fruit, vanillin, and floral aromas that soar from the glass. Sensationally extracted, with viscous, opulent, highly concentrated flavors, this full-bodied, unctuous Chardonnay has much in common with a DRC Montrachet or Niellon Bâtard-Montrachet. The only other California Chardonnays that have been this profound have been some of the Mount Harlan offerings from Calera, and the Chalone Chardonnays from vintages such as 1981, 1980, 1979, and 1978. Newton's 1991 Chardonnay should drink well for at least 3–4 years. A must buy! In addition to the stunning white wines, Newton is making one of the two best Merlots in California. The 1990 Merlot rivals the best wines of Pomerol. It possesses an exotic, Asian-spice, chocolate, mocha, sweet, black cherry–scented bouquet, thick, succulent, voluptuous flavors that reveal admirable fruit, glycerin, and body, and a whoppingly long finish. This superrich, intense, spectacular Merlot is more exotic and flamboyant than the terrific 1990 Matanzas Creek. It should also prove to be long-lived. Drink it over the next 10–14 years. Readers should also keep an eye out for the 1991, which will be released December 1993. It is just as dramatically flavored and stunning. For more structure, massiveness, and chocolatey cassis, check out Newton's 1990 Cabernet Sauvignon. With a huge nose of chocolate, cedar, and cassis, this rich, full-bodied, spectacular wine offers unbelievably concentrated flavors, firm, sweet tannins, and enough acidity to give it grip and delineation. All three of these Newton offerings were bottled unfiltered. Newton is making some of the most riveting wines in America.

NEYERS WINERY (NAPA)
Cabernet Sauvignon* *, Chardonnay*

1988	Cabernet Sauvignon	Napa	B	74
1989	Chardonnay	Napa	B	70

Bruce Neyers, formerly the national marketing agent for the Joseph Phelps Vineyards and now the national rep for the excellent French wine importer Kermit Lynch, has his own operation producing Chardonnay and Cabernet Sauvignon. Vintages to date have been marked by dull, straightforward wines with too much acidity and not enough depth, fruit, or personality. Prices are realistic, but quality needs to improve significantly for these wines to compete in the marketplace.

GUSTAVE NIEBAUM COLLECTION (NAPA)

Cabernet Sauvignon Mast Vineyard* */* * *, Cabernet Sauvignon Reference
Vineyard* */* * *, Cabernet Sauvignon Tench Vineyard* */* * *,
Chardonnay Bayview Vineyard* */* * *, Chardonnay Laird Vineyard* */* * *

This operation, a branch of Inglenook Vineyards, was designed to produce relatively expensive, single-vineyard, limited-production wines aimed at the high end of the marketplace. The first vintages have proven to be mediocre wines. Once again, the problems afflicting these wines are the same as those found in many California wines—they are made in a safe, highly processed, sterile style that offers little bouquet; simple, monolithic, excessively acidic flavors; too much hard tannin in the red wines; and too much wood in the whites. Someone should tell the winemaker that wine is first and foremost a beverage of pleasure. Excessive acidification, which prevents the consumer from enjoying the wine's fruit, and obsession with sterile filtration, which renders the wine stable but denuded and one-dimensional, may be all right for jug wines selling at $5–$6 a bottle but will not do for wines meant to represent top vineyards (and are priced accordingly). Some concern must be shown for the consumer's desire to maximize his pleasure!

NIEBAUM-COPPOLA ESTATES (NAPA)
Rubicon* * */* * * *

1987	Rubicon	Napa	D	82
1986	Rubicon	Napa	D	90

The renowned movie producer Francis Ford Coppola owns this vineyard, one of the most historic in Napa. From it he makes a proprietary red wine called Rubicon, a blend of primarily Cabernet Sauvignon with some Cabernet Franc and Merlot. From the first vintage, 1978, through the 1986, the wines were made in a big, rich, rustic style, with considerable aging potential. The 1987 suggests a change to a more accessible, modern style. For that reason the wine appears less concentrated and more one-dimensional. Let's hope this is not a sign of things to come. Despite its critics, Rubicon is a distinctive wine with considerable personality. For example, the 1986 Rubicon, although still an outstanding wine, is not as robust and rustic as some of its predecessors. However, it is concentrated and full bodied, with a big, spicy, earthy, cassis-scented nose and rich, full-bodied flavors that reveal considerable extraction of fruit and tannins. The wine is just beginning to open up, and after 60 minutes in a decanter there was perceptible evolution and softening. I have often thought that Coppola has wanted to make Cabernet in the image of an Italian Barolo, but the 1986 leans more toward a classic expression of traditional, age-worthy, concentrated Napa Valley Cabernet. It should last for 15–20 years.
RATINGS OF OLDER VINTAGES OF NIEBAUM-COPPOLA RUBICON: 1984 (87), 1982 (92), 1981 (90), 1980 (88), 1979 (90), 1978 (87)

OBESTER WINERY (SAN MATEO)
Chardonnay* */* * *, Sauvignon Blanc* *

1991	Chardonnay Barrel Fermented	Mendocino	B	86
1991	Sauvignon Blanc	Mendocino	A	74

Although correctly made, these wines lack character and concentration. The neutral-tasting, insipid Sauvignon Blanc has nothing to it other than acidity and alcohol. However, the Chardonnay is soft, precocious, and richly fruity, with medium body, gobs of fruit, and a nice touch of subtle oak. Drink it before the summer of 1994.

OJAI VINEYARD (VENTURA COUNTY)
Chardonnay* *, Cuvée Spéciale St.-Helene * * */* * * *,
Sauvignon Blanc* * *, Syrah* * *

1991	Chardonnay	Santa Barbara	C	86
1991	Chardonnay	Arroyo Grande	C	86
1991	Cuvée Speciale St.-Helene White Wine	Arroyo Grande	B	87
1991	Sauvignon Blanc	California	B	84
1990	Syrah	California	C	86
1989	Syrah	California	C	86

The tasty 1991 Sauvignon Blanc (it also has 15% Semillon blended in) offers up a melony, citrusy nose, excellent ripeness, medium body, and a crisp finish. Even better is the 1991 Cuvée Spéciale, a 67% Sauvignon Blanc/33% Semillon blend, which exhibits more richness in the nose and a discernible scent of melon. In the mouth there is a honeyed texture, as well as spicy, fruity, figlike, elegant flavors. The finish is long, crisp, and clean. Both the 1989 and 1990 Syrah, although not blockbusters, display excellent deep ruby color, a spicy, peppery, herb-, and black fruit–scented nose, medium body, good flavor depth, soft tannins, and crisp acidity. They should drink well for at least 4–6 years.

OPUS ONE (NAPA)
Proprietary Red Wine* * * *

1989	Proprietary Red Wine	Napa	E	84
1988	Proprietary Red Wine	Napa	E	88
1987	Proprietary Red Wine	Napa	E	93
1986	Proprietary Red Wine	Napa	E	88

At first sniff, I thought the 1986 might turn out to be even better than the outstanding 1985 Opus One. The wonderfully smoky, curranty, mineral, and oaky bouquet is intriguing and enjoyable. Once past the nose, the wine does not seem to have nearly the flavor depth or concentration suggested by its bouquet. It is elegant, medium bodied, moderately concentrated, and very soft, but close inspection reveals a slight deficiency in depth as well as a tendency to fall off in the finish. This is an excellent wine, but I would suggest drinking it over the next 4–7 years. Those who want more concentration, and perhaps more aging potential, should consider the 1985. The gloriously fragrant, concentrated 1987 Opus One is clearly superior to any wine this high-profile producer has yet turned out. Although the wine now offers profound fragrance, concentration, and character, it will also prove rewarding for consumers willing to lay it away for another 5–6 years. Fortunately, gratification need not be deferred, given the sumptuously rich, mineral- and vanillin-scented, cassis-dominated bouquet. I even detected hints of violets and licorice aromas. In the mouth the wine is fleshy, admirably concentrated, and medium to full bodied. It has the rare quality of being a complete wine from start to finish. **Anticipated maturity: Now–2002.** Although the best Opus One to date is the 1987, the 1988 is certainly one of the finest red wines I have tasted from this uninspiring vintage. Impressively dark ruby colored, it reveals an attractive nose of currants and smoky new oak. In the mouth the wine is medium bodied, with excellent concentration, a velvety texture, soft tannins, low acidity, and a smooth, attractive finish. Although hard to resist now, it should age gracefully for 7–8 years. The 1989 Opus One is one of the lightest wines released by this joint venture between the Rothschild family in France and the Mondavi family in Napa Valley. The 1989 exhibits deep color and spicy oak aromas and flavors, but it is hollow and austere on the palate, with sharp tannins in the finish. It should be drunk over the next 7–8 years, as I suspect it will become more attenuated with age.

RATINGS FOR OLDER VINTAGES OF OPUS ONE: 1985 (90), 1984 (88), 1983 (86), 1982 (86), 1981 (78), 1980 (82), 1979 (75)

Note: Sadly, none of these older wines are showing as well as they did in their youth. I would like to think this is just because the wine has closed up, but vintages before 1984 have generally lost their fruit much faster than one would have hoped, given the talent and enormous wealth behind this operation. In short, the frightfully high price is at odds with the performance of these wines over time. Perhaps vintages from 1986 on will fare better at an older age.

PAGE MILL (SANTA CLARA)
Cabernet Sauvignon Volker Eisele Vineyard* * * *, Pinot Noir* * *

1989	Cabernet Sauvignon Volker Eisele Vineyard	Napa	C	75
1988	Cabernet Sauvignon Volker Eisele Vineyard	Napa	C	82
1987	Cabernet Sauvignon Volker Eisele Vineyard	Napa	C	87
1986	Cabernet Sauvignon Volker Eisele Vineyard	Napa	C	87
1985	Cabernet Sauvignon Volker Eisele Vineyard	Napa	C	89
1984	Cabernet Sauvignon Volker Eisele Vineyard	Napa	C	88
1990	Pinot Noir Bien Nacido Vineyard	Santa Barbara	C	85

Except for the 1989, all of the wines in this minivertical of Cabernets from the underrated Page Mill winery performed well. The 1989 is light and washed out, with simple, one-dimensional fruit flavors that lack depth and richness. A modest success for the vintage, the 1988 reveals herbal, fruity, oaky notes; soft, medium-bodied flavors; and a short yet supple finish. The 1987 has a ripe, deep, black cherry-and-cassis-scented bouquet, excellent concentration and intensity, and an overall sense of balance and elegance. It is soft enough to be drunk now, yet its moderate tannin content and overall level of extract suggest that a decade's worth of cellaring is possible. The aromatic and elegant

character of many of the 1987 California Cabernets is admirably expressed in
this wine. The 1986 is a rich, medium- to full-bodied, classy Cabernet Sauvignon displaying abundant quantities of berry fruit. It is not as well built as the
1987—I thought it to be very good rather than outstanding. My two favorite
Cabernets from Page Mill are the 1985 and 1984. My preference for the 1985
should come as no surprise, as this is probably the top vintage among a quartet
of fine years for Cabernet Sauvignon. It is the richest and most powerful wine
of the four offerings, with full-bodied, intensely concentrated, cassis-flavored
fruit; long, dense, opulent flavors; a pure, classic bouquet of cassis, black
cherries, and herbs; and moderate tannins in the finish. Drinkable now, it
should age beautifully for another 10–12 years. Last, the 1984 displays that
vintage's more opulent and generous style with its soft tannins, unctuous texture, and heady, alcoholic finish. It is much softer than either the 1985 or
1987. Although stunningly delicious, the 1984 is capable of at least a decade's
aging potential. These are classic Cabernets from one of California's most underrated producers. Page Mill's success is not limited to Cabernet Sauvignon.
Its 1990 Pinot Noir from Santa Barbara's well-known Bien Nacido Vineyard is
an intensely fruity, herbaceous wine that manages to avoid the pronounced
vegetal character possessed by so many Pinot Noirs from this area. It is a rich,
expansively flavored, medium-bodied wine with a big bouquet and soft flavors.
Drink it over the next 2–4 years.

PAHLMEYER (NAPA)
Cabernet Sauvignon Caldwell Vineyard* * * *, Chardonnay* * * *

1991	Cabernet Sauvignon Caldwell Vineyard	Napa	D	85
1990	Cabernet Sauvignon Caldwell Vineyard	Napa	D	89
1989	Cabernet Sauvignon Caldwell Vineyard	Napa	D	84
1988	Cabernet Sauvignon Caldwell Vineyard	Napa	D	86
1987	Cabernet Sauvignon Caldwell Vineyard	Napa	D	88
1991	Chardonnay Unfiltered	Napa	C	92

The 1991 Cabernet Sauvignon is atypically hard and tannic for this vintage.
But behind the toughness is good fruit, medium body, and fine length. Will the
fruit dry out before the tannin? The 1990 Pahlmeyer Cabernet Sauvignon
Caldwell Vineyard looks to be another excellent example from this relatively
new producer. The nose offers vividly pure, dramatic aromas of smoke, cassis,
and cinnamon. In the mouth there is an intense, spicy element complemented
by deep, ripe, rich, curranty flavors and firm, elevated tannins. I suspect this
will not be one of the more flattering 1990s to taste young, but it should be
drinking well by the mid-1990s and evolve nicely for 10–15 years. Because of
the vintages, neither the 1989 nor 1988 Pahlmeyer Cabernet Sauvignon is as
impressive as the 1990. They are good wines given the trying vintage conditions, but they do not possess the depth, structure, or fatness of the 1990 or the
1987. The 1987 displays a mineral, blackcurrant, smoky character, good acidity, a medium- to full-bodied feel, and enough depth and richness to last for
10–15 years. The 1991 Chardonnay is rich, creamy textured, and oozing with
nutty, buttery, baked-apple fruit. It also has the multilayered feel one finds in
minimally processed wines, with wonderful purity, and a soft, rich, well-

focused finish. This is Pahlmeyer's finest Chardonnay to date. Drink it over the next 1–3 years. Accolades to Pahlmeyer for taking the risk of bottling this Chardonnay unfined and unfiltered, giving the consumer all the flavor inherent in the grapes!

PARDUCCI WINE CELLARS (MENDOCINO)
Bono Syrah* */* * *, Cabernet Sauvignon* *, Chardonnay* *,
French Colombard* * *, Merlot* *, Petite Sirah* */* * *, Pinot Noir* *, Zinfandel* *

1990	Bono Syrah	Mendocino	A	82
1989	Cabernet Franc	Mendocino	A	73
1988	Cabernet Sauvignon	North Coast	A	74
1987	Cabernet Sauvignon	North Coast	A	85
1991	Chardonnay	North Coast	A	75
1991	Chenin Blanc	North Coast	A	80
1991	French Colombard	North Coast	A	82
1990	Merlot	North Coast	A	78
1989	Merlot	North Coast	A	85
1990	Petite Sirah	Mendocino	A	78

This winery has always produced sound, clean, reliable wines at fair prices. The wines are made to be drunk young, but some vintages of Cabernet have aged well. Parducci does not make as rich a Cabernet Sauvignon or Petite Sirah as he did in the 1970s. I remember buying a case of the 1970 Cabernet Sauvignon and drinking it until the mid-1980s. At that time it was still an excellent wine, deeper and more intense than anything the winery is now producing. Today Parducci's wines are not likely to win any tastings, but from time to time the French Colombard, Chenin Blanc, Petite Sirah, and Cabernet Sauvignon can be charming, light- to medium-bodied wines with plenty of fruit. The French Colombard and Chenin Blanc are made in a slightly sweet style. The Cabernet Sauvignon, Merlot, and Petite Sirah are soft, richly fruity wines with good concentration.

FESS PARKER (SANTA BARBARA)
Chardonnay* * *, Pinot Noir* *, Riesling* * * *, Syrah* * * *

1992	Johannisberg Riesling	Santa Barbara	A	87
1990	Merlot	Santa Barbara	B	75
1992	Syrah	Santa Barbara	C	89

I have to admit that as a child I had no bigger heroes than Davy Crockett and Daniel Boone, both played by the well-known actor, Fess Parker. Parker is even bigger in real life than the immense image he projected on television. Six and a half feet tall, with a big frame and a flowing mane of silver-gray hair, he is a remarkable physical specimen, not to mention one of the nicest people anyone could hope to meet. Since he got into the wine business a few years ago, he has consistently turned out one of California's most delicious and reasonably priced Johannisberg Rieslings. His 1992 continues this success. This off-dry, peach-and-apricot-scented wine exhibits wonderful fruit, excellent purity, and a luscious, ripe finish. It is a real crowd pleaser. Although spicy, the 1990 Merlot is short and compact, without enough flesh or texture. However, the cask sample of 1992 Syrah reveals a potentially outstanding wine. The saturated black/purple color and huge, meaty, smoky, cassis-scented nose will cause even the most fanatical Rhône Valley–Syrah purist to think of Hermitage. This highly extracted, rich, dense wine possesses awesome potential. Let's hope it is not too processed before it goes into the bottle. Interestingly, Fess Parker told me that Jed Steele, the winemaking wizard who is fashioning such marvelous wines under his own label, has been hired as a consultant and will be overlooking the winemaking at Parker's estate. This can only have positive results.

PATZ AND HALL (NAPA)
Chardonnay* * * */* * * * *

1991	Chardonnay	Napa	C	88
1990	Chardonnay	Napa	C	92

The 1990 Patz and Hall Chardonnay Napa is a brilliantly made wine with a light straw color, a big, juicy nose of subtle oak, buttery tropical fruit, and ripe apples, voluptuous texture, and layer upon layer of fruit. All of this is nicely supported by just enough acidity to provide freshness and focus. The wine is complex, even compelling. The 1991 Chardonnay, which is more noticeably oaky and not as concentrated as the 1990, is an excellent, medium- to full-bodied Chardonnay for drinking over the next 3–4 years. Production from this winery is extremely limited.

PEACHY CANYON WINERY (PASO ROBLES)
Cabernet Sauvignon* * *, Zinfandel Reserve* * * *, Zinfandel West Side* * * * *

1990	Cabernet Sauvignon	Paso Robles	C	85
1990	Zinfandel	Paso Robles	B	90
1991	Zinfandel Especiale	Paso Robles	C	90
1989	Zinfandel Especiale Reserve	Paso Robles	B	88
1990	Zinfandel West Side	Paso Robles	B	92
1991	Zinfandel West Side	Paso Robles	B	88

After having tasted two vintages of this winery's Zinfandel, I am a believer! Unfortunately, only tiny quantities are produced. The 1990 Zinfandel Especial Reserve exhibits a deep, opaque ruby/purple color; a big, Rhône-like, peppery, spicy, black raspberry–scented nose; and rich, jammy, impressively constituted and structured flavors. Those lucky enough to run across a bottle should drink this large-scale, well-balanced Zinfandel over the next 7–8 years. The 1990 is even more profound than the fine 1989. The dense ruby/purple color offers up an intense nose of black fruits, minerals, and spices. In the mouth the wine has a fascinating texture that provides a full-bodied impact crammed with opulent levels of berry fruit, glycerin, and alcohol. The wine explodes in the finish, suggesting there will be considerable development in the immediate future. This splendidly rich, multidimensional, stunning Zinfandel is worth a special search. The best Zinfandel of this trio is the 1990 Zinfandel West Side. The gorgeous, smoky, black raspberry–scented nose, deep, chewy, superripe flavors, succulent texture, and a stupendously long finish make this a great Zinfandel for drinking over the next 7–8 years. Peachy Canyon has fashioned impressive Zinfandels in 1991. The dark ruby–colored 1991 Westside Zinfandel possesses a spicy, peppery, ripe fruit–scented nose, and tasty, rich, seductive flavors that reveal fine concentration as well as a sense of elegance and style. This excellent, rich, velvety-textured Zinfandel will make delicious drinking over the next 5–6 years. The 1991 Zinfandel Especiale reveals a denser, more saturated, dark ruby/purple color. The bouquet explodes from the glass, offering intensely ripe aromas of raspberries, spicy black pepper, and minerals. There is superb extraction of fruit, a deep, chewy, unctuous texture, and a long, spicy, rich, briery finish. Drink this classic, large-scaled wine over the next decade. Peachy Canyon's 1990 Cabernet Sauvignon is soft, supple, fruity, and pure, with soft tannins and a moderately long finish. Drink it over the next 5–6 years.

ROBERT PECOTA WINERY (NAPA)

Cabernet Sauvignon* *, Gamay Beaujolais* * * *, Merlot* * *, Muscato di Andrea* * * *

1988	Cabernet Sauvignon Kara's Vineyard	Napa	C	77
1992	Gamay Beaujolais	Napa	A	86
1991	Merlot Steven André Vineyard	Napa	C	81
1990	Merlot André	Napa	C	82
1989	Merlot André	Napa	C	72
1992	Muscato di Andrea	Napa	B	87
1991	Sauvignon Blanc	Napa	A	73

The 1992 Gamay Beaujolais is a delicious, richly fruity, vividly pure and well-focused, medium-bodied red wine that successfully demonstrates what intelligent winemaking can do with a less renowned grape varietal. With gobs of fruit and surprisingly deep color, the wine gives an overall impression of opulence and an exuberant, vivacious fruitiness. Drink it over the next year. The other consistently successful Robert Pecota wine is the superfragrant, delicious, moderately sweet, yet light Muscato di Andrea. One of the best of its type in California, it is gorgeous to drink as an aperitif or by itself following a meal. The other offerings, of average quality, include a lean, hard, tannic Cabernet Sauvignon from Kara's Vineyard; a tough-textured, undernourished, charmless Merlot; a crisp but one-dimensional Sauvignon Blanc; and a straightforward, neutral Chardonnay.

J. PEDRONCELLI WINERY (SONOMA)

Cabernet Sauvignon* *, Cabernet Sauvignon Reserve* * */* * * *,
Chardonnay* */* * *, Chenin Blanc* * *, Gamay Beaujolais* *, Pinot Noir*,
Zinfandel* * *, Zinfandel Rosé* * *

1988	Cabernet Sauvignon	Sonoma	A	84
1990	Chardonnay	Dry Creek	A	85
1990	Fumé Blanc	Dry Creek	A	85

1991	White Zinfandel	Sonoma	A	84
1990	Zinfandel	Sonoma	A	86
1989	Zinfandel	Sonoma	A	86

Would you like a sound rule for buying well-made, inexpensive California wines? Just about any California winery with an Italian name that has been in existence for more than 20 years produces good wine. Although keeping a low profile, Pedroncelli continues to turn out well-made, tasty wines. Even its 1991 White Zinfandel, from a category of wines that are often too cloyingly sugary, heavy, and designed to take advantage of America's sweet tooth, is a stylish, slightly off-dry, richly fruity, crisp, strawberry-scented and -flavored wine that makes an ideal aperitif. Pedroncelli's 1990 Fumé Blanc is surprisingly full flavored, with a pungent nose of herbs and melons. In the mouth it is rich, medium bodied, with lush fruitiness and plenty of length. The 1990 Chardonnay, one of the best efforts I have ever tasted from this winery, offers a citrusy, apple-scented nose and subtly oaky, glycerin-endowed, rich, fruity flavors. All three white wines should be drunk over the next year. The 1988 Cabernet Sauvignon displays a weedy, curranty nose, straightforward cassislike flavors, a more firmly structured texture, and some tannin in the finish. Given its overall fine balance, this wine will drink well for at least 4–6 years. The 1990 Zinfandel is medium ruby colored, with an attractively pure, sweet berry–scented nose, medium to full body, a velvety texture, and a soft, satiny finish. Drink it over the next 5–6 years. The 1989 Zinfandel exhibits a big, berry-scented nose, ripe, full-bodied flavors, a smooth, silky texture, and a long, robust finish. It should continue to evolve gracefully for at least 4–5 years.

PEJU PROVINCE (NAPA)
Cabernet Sauvignon* *

1988	Cabernet Sauvignon HB Vineyard	Napa	D	78
1987	Cabernet Sauvignon HB Vineyard	Napa	C	81
1986	Cabernet Sauvignon HB Vineyard	Napa	D	80

This type of Cabernet—overly tannic, extremely tart, forbiddingly hard, and lacking fruit, charm, and character—is definitely not my style. Unquestionably these wines will age well, but the result, once the tannins melt away, is likely to be a firm, hard skeleton of wood, acid, and alcohol.

ROBERT PEPI (NAPA)
Cabernet Sauvignon Vine Hill Ranch* * *, Chardonnay* *

1987	Cabernet Sauvignon Vine Hill Ranch	Napa	C	83
1986	Cabernet Sauvignon Vine Hill Ranch	Napa	C	86
1990	Chardonnay Puncheon Fermented	Napa	C	83
1989	Colline di Sassi (Sangiovese)	Napa	C	74

I found Robert Pepi's 1990 Chardonnay to be straightforward but lively, with decent fruit and a crisp finish. Although vibrant, it is lacking in substance and character. With respect to the Cabernet Sauvignons from the Vine Hill Ranch (a potentially superb vineyard in Yountville situated next to the more renowned Martha's Vineyard exploited by Heitz Cellars), the 1987 has a pronounced minty, nearly vegetal nose, deep color, and tart, tannic, black cherry, cassis, and earthy flavors. If the acidity and tannins were less objectionable and the fruit deeper, this could have been a much better wine. The classic blackcurrant, herbaceous-scented bouquet of the 1986 Cabernet Sauvignon Vine Hill Ranch displays a judicious use of new oak. In the mouth there are ripe, plummy flavors, medium to full body, good extract levels, and a long, ripe finish. Drink this well-made Cabernet over the next 6–7 years. Pepi has also begun to make wines from the Sangiovese grape, a varietal that produces some of the finest reds made in Tuscany. His first vintage, 1988, produced a disappointingly light wine. The 1989 is even worse. Although there is some fruit in the nose, the wine is entirely too acidified and hollow. The price is ridiculous for such quality, so consumers beware!

PEPPERWOOD SPRINGS (MENDOCINO)
Pinot Noir* * */* * * *

I have not seen a Pinot Noir from Pepperwood Springs in more than 3 years, but the vintages I have tasted revealed a good big, spicy, peppery, black cherry–scented nose, good flavor definition, fine fruit, and a long finish. The tiny quantities of wine produced here are sold largely in California.

JOSEPH PHELPS VINEYARDS (NAPA)
Cabernet Sauvignon Napa* *, Cabernet Sauvignon Backus Vineyard* * * *,
Cabernet Sauvignon Eisele Vineyard* * * (since 1987), * * * * * (before 1987),
Chardonnay* *, Chardonnay Sangiacomo* *, Gewürztraminer* *,
Insignia Proprietary Red Wine* * * */* * * * *, Sauvignon Blanc* *, Syrah* *,
Vin du Mistral Selections* * *, Zinfandel* * *

1989	Cabernet Sauvignon	Napa	C	76
1988	Cabernet Sauvignon	Napa	C	72
1991	Cabernet Sauvignon Backus Vineyard	Napa	D	90
1990	Cabernet Sauvignon Backus Vineyard	Napa	D	90
1989	Cabernet Sauvignon Backus Vineyard	Napa	D	82
1988	Cabernet Sauvignon Backus Vineyard	Napa	D	78
1991	Cabernet Sauvignon Eisele Vineyard	Napa	D	84
1989	Cabernet Sauvignon Eisele Vineyard	Napa	D	84
1988	Cabernet Sauvignon Eisele Vineyard	Napa	D	80
1991	Chardonnay	Napa	C	77
1991	Chardonnay Sangiacomo	Sonoma	C	82

1991	Insignia Proprietary Red Wine	Napa	D	90
1990	Insignia Proprietary Red Wine	Napa	D	93
1989	Insignia Proprietary Red Wine	Napa	D	83
1988	Insignia Proprietary Red Wine	Napa	D	82
1989	Merlot	Napa	B	72
1990	Le Mistral	Napa	C	?
1991	Sauvignon Blanc	Napa	A	76
1988	Syrah	Napa	A	88
1991	Vin du Mistral Grenache Rosé	Napa	A	85
1991	Vin du Mistral Syrah	Napa	C	84
1991	Vin du Mistral Viognier	Napa	D	85
1990	Zinfandel	Alexander Valley	B	85
1989	Zinfandel	Alexander Valley	B	75

As a longtime follower and admirer of Joseph Phelps Cabernets, I have been extremely disappointed by the 1987, 1988, and 1989 vintages. In fact, the 1987s, which were so promising from the barrel, had absolutely no bouquets when they were released. They appeared to have been sterile-filtered and/or excessively processed at bottling, which removed much of the richness they had possessed in the barrel. Neither the 1988s nor 1989s are exciting. All of the Cabernets in the Phelps portfolio in these 2 vintages are lean, excessively tannic, and hollow, without sufficient fruit, flesh, or charm. Even more alarming is their lack of bouquet, something first evident in the 1987s. Except for the 1991 Eisele, the 1990s and 1991s appear to be the best efforts from Phelps since the 1986s. The 1991 Eisele lacks the depth and complexity that wines from this great Napa Valley vineyard have possessed in the past. Although a well-made, ripe-tasting wine, its deficiencies—a one-dimensional taste and a short finish—are obvious. The 1991 Backus Vineyard exhibits an intensely minty, chocolatey, cassis-scented nose as well as dense, ripe, potentially outstanding flavors. Let's hope it is not excessively tampered with at bottling. It should reach full maturity by the mid-1990s and last through the first decade of the next century. Of the three 1991 offerings, the 1991 Insignia displays the most depth and complexity. The color is opaque ruby/purple, and the nose offers up forcefully intense Provençal herb and cassis scents that are followed by dense, thick, chewy, black fruit flavors infused with considerable amounts of glycerin, alcohol, and tannin. This big, solidly built, muscular Insignia could ultimately rival the superb 1985 and 1986. There is no separate 1990 Eisele Cabernet bottling, but the 1990 Backus Vineyard possesses the big, minty, chocolatey nose typical of this vineyard; full-bodied, ripe, unctuous, chewy flavors; plenty of tannin; and a spicy, lush finish. This potentially outstanding wine should be drinkable several years before the 1991. Although dominated by a streak of herbaceousness, the 1990 Insignia is an extremely strong wine. It offers rich cassis fruit, less body and density than the 1991, and spicy flavors. It should drink well for 10–14 years. The soft, somewhat flabby 1990 Zinfandel Alexander Valley is light to medium ruby in color, with a big, jammy nose of superripe fruit; although tasty, I would not gamble on its holding together for more than another 1–2 years. There is plenty of sweet, lush fruit, but not much structure. I would put this Zinfandel in an ice bucket for 10 minutes and enjoy it for its uncomplicated fruit and charm. The 1989 Zinfandel Alexander Valley suffers from considerable bottle variation. Several bottles were dull, light bodied, diluted, and beginning to lose their fruit; others were round, fruity, and pleasant. These wines are a far cry from some of the terrific Alexander Valley Zinfandels this winery produced in years such as 1975, 1976, and 1980. The 1990 Zinfandel from Napa Valley is a ripe, tasty, deliciously fruity, exuberant wine that is a total delight to smell and taste. Moreover, it is reasonably priced. Drink it over the next several years. The 1988 Syrah has to be one of the great red wine values in today's marketplace of bloated prices. It is certainly the best Syrah that Joseph Phelps has yet produced. The deep ruby/purple color is impressive, but even more so is the seductively rich, exotic bouquet of black raspberries and sweet, vanillin-scented, spicy oak that soars from the glass. In the mouth this rich, full-bodied wine offers up plenty of extract and a wonderful multidimensional and highly textured finish that must linger for at least a minute. Surprisingly forward and soft, with tannins kept well in check, this beautifully made, intense Syrah should drink admirably for another 5–6 years—good news, as other Syrahs produced by Phelps have been average in quality. Although Phelps continues to struggle with its Chardonnays, there have been encouraging signs that more fruit, character, and complexity are being sought by winemaker Craig Williams. However, the 1991s are relatively light, straightforward, and one-dimensional. Even the Sauvignon Blanc, once one of the better wines from that varietal in California, is diluted and bland in comparison with some older vintages. The new Rhône Ranger offerings called Vin du Mistral are generally good wines meant to be consumed within their first several years of life. Prices are fair, and the wines should continue to receive favorable acceptance from consumers. Joseph Phelps makes superlative sweet dessert wines from Riesling and a Sauternes look-alike blend of botrytised Semillon called Delice de Semillon.

This winery, which has always been one of my favorites, may be making too many wines, which might explain why there are more disappointments than there should be. Nevertheless, the high quality of so many Joseph Phelps Cabernets, particularly the Insignia and Eisele, from the mid-1970s on has clearly established this winery as one of the best in the New World for Cabernet Sauvignon. The decline in the quality of its Zinfandel, its regular *cuvée* of Cabernet Sauvignon, and its Sauvignon Blanc needs to be addressed.

RATINGS FOR OLDER VINTAGES OF JOSEPH PHELPS VINEYARDS INSIGNIA PROPRIETARY RED WINE: 1986 (92), 1985 (93), 1984 (92), 1983 (86), 1982 (84), 1981 (90), 1979 (87), 1978 (85), 1977 (90), 1976 (99), 1975 (78), 1974 (93)

RATINGS FOR OLDER VINTAGES OF JOSEPH PHELPS VINEYARDS CABERNET SAUVIGNON EISELE VINEYARD: 1986 (90), 1985 (92), 1984 (90), 1983 (85), 1982 (86), 1981 (88), 1979 (90), 1978 (98), 1977 (89), 1975 (99)

R. H. PHILLIPS VINEYARD (YOLO)
Cabernet Sauvignon* *, Chardonnay* * *, Mourvèdre* * *,
Sauvignon Blanc* * *, Viognier* *

1990	Cabernet Sauvignon	Yolo	A	73
1992	Chardonnay Barrel Cuvée	Yolo	A	86
1990	Mourvèdre EXP	Yolo	B	84
1988	Mourvèdre EXP	Yolo	B	88
1992	Sauvignon Blanc Night Harvest Cuvée	Yolo	A	85
1991	Viognier EXP	Yolo	A	78

The attractively packaged 1992 Sauvignon Blanc Night Harvest Cuvée (in the
new 500-ml bottle) is an elegant, spicy, melony, crisp Sauvignon. Cleanly
made, medium bodied, soft and effusively fruity, and faithful to its varietal
character, it should be drunk over the next year. For the price, it's a steal.
Once again this winery has turned out one of the most successful and reasonably priced Chardonnays of the vintage. Phillips's 1991 Chardonnay Barrel
Cuvée exhibits a perfume of apple blossoms, oranges, and buttery fruit; fine
texture and depth; and a juicy, fleshy, well-focused finish. Drink this delicious
Chardonnay over the next year. I am delighted to see that R. H. Phillips is ex-
perimenting with Rhône varietals, in this case a Mourvèdre. It has been packaged in a designer bottle that I had thought was reserved for expensive
Balsamic vinegars and luxury-priced olive oils. Brilliant packaging aside,
the 1988 and 1990 are surprisingly good. Both offer an excellent truffle,
black fruit, woodsy nose, and soft yet rich, ripe flavors that marry well with
the Mourvèdre's underlying acidity and tannic structure. The 1988 should
evolve gracefully over the next 4–6 years, the 1990 for 3–5 years. Phillips's
other wines, particularly the Cabernet Sauvignon, have been mediocre and
disappointing. The Syrah has been light and vegetal. Nevertheless this winery
generally offers fine products at excellent prices, and the packaging is top-
notch.

PINE RIDGE WINERY (NAPA)
Cabernet Sauvignon Andrus Reserve* * *, Cabernet Sauvignon Diamond
Mountain* */* * *, Cabernet Sauvignon Rutherford Cuvée* */* * *, Cabernet
Sauvignon Stag's Leap District* */* * *, Chardonnay Knollside Cuvée* * *,
Chardonnay Stag's Leap District* * *, Chenin Blanc* * *, Merlot* *

1987	Cabernet Sauvignon Andrus Reserve	Napa	E	84
1986	Cabernet Sauvignon Andrus Reserve	Napa	E	80
1987	Cabernet Sauvignon Rutherford Cuvée	Napa	C	74
1989	Cabernet Sauvignon Stag's Leap District	Napa	C	75
1988	Cabernet Sauvignon Stag's Leap District	Napa	C	74
1987	Cabernet Sauvignon Stag's Leap District	Napa	C	72
1990	Chardonnay Knollside Cuvée	Napa	C	85
1990	Chardonnay Stag's Leap District	Napa	C	86

| 1991 | Chenin Blanc Yountville | Napa | A | 81 |
| 1989 | Merlot Select Cuvée | Napa | C | 76 |

This winery produces multiple wines that have often been impressive from cask, but in the bottle the reds are frequently hard, tough, high in acid, restrained, and austere. Certainly proprietor Gary Andrus, who had training in Bordeaux, has been influenced by the more subtle style of French wines, but that does not excuse a lack of flesh and charm. Of course the 1988 and 1989 vintages were problematic for many California producers, but I wonder why these wines come across as too skinny, even anorectic, and in need of more fruit and depth. Elegance is a worthy goal, but I continue to have reservations about the level of fruit extraction versus the level of acidity and tannin. On potential, the Andrus Reserve Cabernet Sauvignon is the most backward and complete, but even recent vintages of that wine have seemed less dense than some earlier ones. The Chardonnays are made in a similar restrained, elegant, subtle style. For some reason more fruit comes across, and the balance among acidity, alcohol, wood, and extraction is more complete. The 1990s are attractive, lighter-style, polite Chardonnays that require some introspection. Although Pine Ridge has made some good Merlots in the past, recent vintages have been less impressive. The 1989 is a compact, austere, clipped wine that left me asking, "Where's the fruit?" In many vintages the Chenin Blanc is delicious, but the 1991 is diluted and muted. All things considered, one senses considerable talent at Pine Ridge. But are too many different *cuvées* and too excessive a reliance on acidification, fining, and filtration resulting in too many compact, attenuated, indifferent wines?

PINNACLES (FRANCISCAN—MONTEREY)
Chardonnay* * * *

| 1990 | Chardonnay | Monterey | B | 89 |

The first release from Franciscan's Pinnacles Vineyard in Monterey, the 1990 Chardonnay, is an impressive wine with a big, melony, buttery, honeyed nose; deep, rich, full-bodied flavors; decent acidity; and a spicy, oaky, long finish. Although delicious now, this Chardonnay can last for several years.

PIPER SONOMA (SONOMA)
Sparkling Wines* */* * *

I continue to be unimpressed by the relatively tart, lean, simple sparkling wines released by Piper Sonoma. Nevertheless, its production now exceeds 150,000 cases, so someone is obviously enjoying them. Selections include a lean Brut; a superpolite, innocuous Blanc de Noir; and two supposedly richer, more yeasty styles, the Reserve Brut and the Tête de Cuvée. The latter wine, which spends up to 7 years on its lees, should have more flavor.

CHÂTEAU POTELLE (NAPA)
Cabernet Sauvignon* *, Chardonnay* *, Sauvignon Blanc* *

1988	Cabernet Sauvignon	Alexander Valley	C	77
1989	Chardonnay	Napa	C	74
1991	Sauvignon Blanc	Napa	B	75

To date the wines from Château Potelle, owned by a French family from Bordeaux, have been neutral, excessively acidified, and diluted.

PRESTON VINEYARDS (SONOMA)
Barbera* * */* * * *, Cabernet Sauvignon* *, Chenin Blanc* * * *,
Cuvée de Fumé* * * *, Faux Castel Rouge* * *, Marsanne* * *, Syrah* * * *,
Viognier* *, Zinfandel* * * *

1990	Barbera	Dry Creek	C	86
1991	Cuvée de Fumé	Dry Creek	A	86
1991	Dry Chenin Blanc	Dry Creek	A	86
1991	Faux Castel Rouge	Dry Creek	A	85
1991	Marsanne	Dry Creek	B	86
1990	Syrah	Dry Creek	C	86
1991	Viognier	Dry Creek	C	78
1990	Zinfandel Estate	Dry Creek	B	87

This Dry Creek Valley winery continues to turn out delicious white wines priced to please the masses. Preston's 1991 Dry Chenin Blanc, bursting with delicate floral scents, is dry, vibrantly fruity, medium bodied, and a total treat to drink. Drink it over the next year. I adore the 1991 Cuvée de Fumé. I dare anyone to find a more tasty Sauvignon Blanc/Semillon blend in the world for this price. The intense bouquet of melons, figs, and honey is a real turn-on. In the mouth the wine is crisp, richly fruity, complex, and dry. This is a wine of unmistakable class and character. Preston's success with such white wine varietals as Sauvignon and Chenin Blanc has been extended to the Marsanne grape. The rich 1991 is not the most complex wine, but it is loaded with gobs of fruit, has excellent focus, and is a delight to drink. The 1991 Viognier offers a superperfumed nose of flowers and peachy fruit, but in the mouth it tails off and reveals a diluted character, probably because of the young vines. Preston has turned out a medium-weight 1990 Zinfandel Estate with excellent color; a spicy, deep, herb-, peppery- and black cherry–scented nose; soft, ripe fruit; plenty of focus and delineation; and moderate tannins and acidity in the finish. Although unlikely to improve significantly, it will certainly last for the next 4–5 years. Preston also produces a fine Syrah. The 1990 exhibits a big, peppery, spicy nose, rich, deep, soft flavors, and a long finish. Drink it over the next 7–8 years. Their other red wine *cuvées* include a so-so Cabernet Sauvignon and a delicious Barbera. The Barbera's acidity has been tamed, resulting in a wine with tremendous exuberance, a vivid personality, and loads of berry fruit in a medium-bodied format. Preston occasionally makes a Sirah-Syrah, a blend of Petite Sirah and Syrah. I have not seen a recent vintage, but the wine is usually well made. Preston is a fine, consistent producer that charges reasonable prices.

QUIVIRA (SONOMA)
Zinfandel* * * *

1989	Cabernet Cuvée	Dry Creek	C	76
1991	Zinfandel	Dry Creek	B	89
1990	Zinfandel	Dry Creek	B	88
1989	Zinfandel	Dry Creek	B	85

If one is striving to make a Zinfandel for consuming in its first 6–7 years of life yet yielding plenty of intensity and wonderful purity and fragrance, Quivira has the right formula. I have had all its Zinfandels since its debut release in the early 1980s, and all have offered vivid bouquets of penetrating raspberry fruit intermingled with scents of spicy new oak. These Zinfandels are both authoritatively flavored and elegant. What really turns me on about these wines is their wonderful balance, great ripeness, purity of fruit, and luscious, smooth finishes. The 1990 offering is as good as any of its previous vintages, all of which were successful. It is hard to ignore the vividly expressive black cherry and raspberry fruit of the ripe, medium-bodied, supple 1989. Excellent purity is evident, as well as a sense that the winemaker knows how to deliver pleasure. Drink this fun wine over the next 4–5 years. The 1991 Zinfandel is an unequivocal success, combining the ripe, lush berry fruit with toasty, smoky new oak. This medium- to full-bodied wine exhibits fine definition and heady alcohol in the lusty finish. Drink it over the next 5–7 years. As much as I love Quivira's Zinfandels, the 1989 Cabernet Cuvée is a straightforward wine of no particular distinction.

QUPÉ WINERY (SANTA BARBARA)
Chardonnay* */* * *, Marsanne* * * *, Syrah Bien Nacido* * * * *,
Syrah* * *, Viognier* * * *

1992	Bien Nacido Cuvée	Santa Barbara	C	90
1991	Chardonnay Sierra Madre Reserve	Santa Barbara	C	78?
1991	Los Olivos Cuvée	Santa Barbara	C	90
1992	Marsanne Los Olivos Vineyard	Santa Barbara	R	87
1991	Syrah	Central Coast	B	88
1991	Syrah Bien Nacido Reserve	Santa Barbara	C	90
1992	Viognier Los Olivos Vineyard	Santa Barbara	C	89

The wines of Bob Lindquist, the owner/winemaker of Qupé Winery, continue to go from strength to strength. His current offerings are the best he has yet produced. This is a winery dedicated to the rich, bold personalities of Rhône Valley varietals. In fact, other than Calera, no California winery makes a better Viognier. The 1992 Viognier Los Olivos Vineyard displays a huge, honeysuckle, apricot/peach-scented nose, superabundant, unctuous fruit flavors, and a dry, rich finish. Only 120 cases of this luscious Viognier were produced. If you are lucky enough to find any bottles, serve them with crab cakes or grilled salmon. Qupé's 1992 Bien Nacido Cuvée, an innovative blend of 50% Viognier and 50% Chardonnay, is similarly styled, although slightly more defined, as well as richer and longer on the palate. It shares with the 1992 Viognier a compelling fragrance of spring flowers, peaches, and apricots, but there is more definition and body because of the Chardonnay's influence. It is a great dry white wine that may last for up to 2 years. Wonderful juice! I preferred the 1992 Marsanne/Los Olivos Vineyard to the winery's 1991 Chardonnay Sierra Madre Reserve. The latter wine comes across as aggressively oaky, with the wood dominating the fruit. I also detected some greenness to the wood. Readers whose thirst for vanillin oak knows no limit will enjoy it more than I did. The Marsanne, one of the finest I have tasted from California, has more fruit, charm, and personality than many produced in the Rhône Valley. There is excellent depth, an attractive bouquet, and lovely, long, rich, medium-bodied flavors. It should drink well for another 2 years. The three red wine *cuvées* I tasted all possess saturated, deep ruby/purple colors. Velvety-textured, rich, full-bodied wines, they reveal exceptional winemaking. The 1991 Syrah Central Coast exhibits a dark ruby/purple color, a sweet nose of cassis, herbs, and pepper, a rich, gorgeously fruity, viscous midpalate, and a soft finish. Delicious now, it should continue to evolve nicely for another 6–8 years. The 1991 Los Olivos Cuvée, a 60% Syrah/40% Mourvèdre blend, offers more aromatic complexity in its spicy, earthy, black raspberry–, and cherry-scented nose. With marvelous concentration, and a gamey, meaty side to its long, full-bodied, superconcentrated flavors, it is reminiscent of a top Bandol. It is a stunning example of what can be produced from Rhône varietals planted in this area of California. Drink it over the next 6–7 years. Another explosively rich, superconcentrated, black/purple-colored wine is the 1991 Syrah Bien Nacido Reserve. A huge nose of tobacco, pepper, cassis, and herbs is followed by a wine with surprisingly soft tannins, penetrating richness, and a long, tannic, spicy finish. It is a terrific Syrah for drinking over the next decade.

RABBIT RIDGE VINEYARDS WINERY (SONOMA)
Cabernet Sauvignon* *, Chardonnay Sonoma* * * *, Chardonnay Russian River Valley* * * *, Proprietary Red and White Wines* * */* * * *, Sauvignon Blanc* * *, Zinfandel* * * *

1989	Allure Proprietary Red Wine	Sonoma	A	85
1991	Chardonnay	Sonoma	B	86
1990	Chardonnay Rabbit Ridge Ranch	Sonoma	C	88
1991	Mystique Proprietary White Wine	Sonoma	A	84
1990	Oddux Reserve Proprietary Red Wine	Sonoma	C	83
1990	Petite Sirah	Sonoma	B	85
1991	Sauvignon Blanc	Sonoma	B	84
1990	Zinfandel	Sonoma	B	87

This winery continues to impress me with its rich, pure, tasty wines that admirably express the varietal characteristics and offer considerable pleasure. It is hard to find a disappointing wine from Rabbit Ridge. The delicious, inexpensive Allure, a Rhône Ranger blend, offers fleshy, rich, peppery, berry fruit in a medium-bodied, velvety-textured format. Let's hope subsequent vintages are as good as this terrific value. The 1991 Mystique, its barrel-fermented proprietary white wine, is also a crisp, clean, tasty, fruity wine that offers considerable value. My praise extends to the crisp, medium-bodied, fragrant 1991 Sauvignon Blanc and the chunky, muscular, dense, tannic 1990 Petite Sirah. There is also a more expensive proprietary red wine called Oddux Reserve. The 1990, although good, is less impressive than the other Rabbit Ridge wines. The excellent 1991 Chardonnay Rabbit Ridge Ranch offers a nose that gushes from the glass with aromas of tropical fruit, smoky oak, and buttery apples. Ripe and full bodied, with decent acidity, this mouth-filling wine should continue to drink well for another year. The 1991 Sonoma Chardonnay is a more obviously fruity, up-front style of wine. Loaded with fruit, soft, clean, and exuberant, it requires consumption over the next year. The 1990 Zinfandel exhibits a big, peppery, black fruit–scented nose, lush, medium- to full-bodied flavors, soft tannins, adequate acidity, and a well-endowed, chewy finish. It offers considerable appeal. This winery is also beginning to produce a Tuscan-style wine from Sangiovese called Montepiano. I have not yet tasted it, but the price of $12 a bottle is more appealing than the prices of some of the disappointing Sangiovese-based wines coming out of California. Consumers are also advised to look for the wines produced under Rabbit Ridge's second label, Meadow Glen. To date these offerings have been super bargains at about $6 a bottle. In particular, the Zinfandel and Sauvignon Blanc have been delicious in recent vintages.

A. RAFANELLI WINERY (SONOMA)
Cabernet Sauvignon* * *, Zinfandel* * * */* * * * *

1989	Cabernet Sauvignon Dry Creek Unfiltered	Dry Creek	B	86
1991	Zinfandel Unfiltered	Dry Creek	B	91
1990	Zinfandel Unfiltered	Dry Creek	B	90
1988	Zinfandel Unfiltered	Dry Creek	B	88

Although Rafanelli's 1989 Cabernet is not as voluptuous as its 1990 Zinfandel, it is an attractively fruity, supple-textured, deep, generously endowed wine bursting with cassis fruit. The complexity has yet to emerge, but once it does, my rating may look conservative. Drink it over the next 5–6 years. Not surprisingly, Rafanelli produces Zinfandel from old, low-yielding vineyards and bottles it unfiltered so nothing is removed from what is in the barrel. The 1990 is gloriously opulent and deeply colored, with an intensely expressive and penetrating nose of earthy black fruits. In the mouth it is full bodied and rich, even sumptuous, with gobs of fruit, an expansive palate, and a stunningly long finish. Since the tannins are soft, this wine can easily be gulped down now; but given past examples of Rafanelli Zinfandel, it should stand up to a decade's worth of aging. The 1991 Zinfandel is also a blockbuster, but the acidity is slightly higher than in the 1990, and the wine is presently more reserved. Its deep opaque purple color, superrich taste, and chewy texture suggest it may become even better than my score suggests. Drink it between 1995 and 2005. I was totally charmed by the rich, ripe, deliciously smooth 1988 Zinfandel and reminded of the great Châteauneuf-du-Pape produced by Château Beaucastel. Why? Who else makes wines with such a big, rich, leathery, ground beef–scented bouquet, intermingled with intensely ripe aromas of plums and black raspberries? In the mouth Rafanelli's 1988 is expansively flavored, round, deliciously smooth, and ideal for drinking over the next 4–5 years. This wonderful Zinfandel, from a mediocre vintage, is about as tasty as one can find. Bravo!

RANCHO SISQUOC WINERY (SANTA BARBARA)

Cabernet Franc* * *, Cabernet Sauvignon Estate* * *, Cellar Select Red Estate* * * *, Chardonnay Estate* * * *, Franken Riesling (Sylvaner)* * * *, Merlot Estate* * *, Sauvignon Blanc* * * *

1991	Cabernet Franc	Santa Maria	B	86
1989	Cabernet Sauvignon Estate	Santa Maria	B	87
1989	Cellar Select Red Estate	Santa Maria	C	88
1991	Chardonnay Estate	Santa Maria	B	88
1991	Franken Riesling (Sylvaner)	Santa Maria	A	86
1991	Johannisberg Riesling Estate	Santa Maria	A	87
1990	Merlot Estate	Santa Maria	B	86
1991	Sauvignon Blanc	Santa Maria	A	90

Virtually all of the 4,000+ cases of Rancho Sisquoc's wines are sold via a mailing list or directly from the winery, so subscribers are not likely to see much of this producer's wines on retailers' shelves. That is the case with many of Santa Barbara's highest-quality wineries. This vast ranch includes over 200 acres, but most of the grapes are sold to wineries such as Robert Mondavi, Foxen, and Gainey. The wines that are bottled under the Rancho Sisquoc label are a distinctive group that includes a Sylvaner made from exceptionally old vines, which is a rarity in California. The 1991 Franken Riesling (Sylvaner) possesses more character, fruit, and charm than most Sylvaners from Alsace. Its fruit is accompanied by a delicacy, as well as excellent definition of crispness. Consume this tasty wine as an aperitif or with Asian to Mexican cooking. The 1991 Johannisberg Riesling is one of the best dry American Rieslings I have tasted. Floral scented, with considerable body and length, as well as an inner core of mineral, applelike fruit, and broad, expansive flavors, this classy, complex, impeccably made wine is delicious. The exceptional 1991 Sauvignon Blanc reminds me of the white Graves made at Château Fieuzal. A big nose of toasty, smoky new oak, honeyed melon, and sweet figs is followed by a wine that is loaded with rich fruit, medium body, crisp acidity, and a long, opulent finish. It is a sensational Sauvignon. Rancho Sisquoc's 1991 Chardonnay offers a medium golden color, a big, buttery, honeyed apple, tangerine-scented nose, opulent, deep fruit, fine acidity, and a luscious, long finish. Like the Sauvignon, it should be consumed over the next 2–3 years. Rancho Sisquoc's Cabernet Sauvignon and Cabernet Franc vineyards are considered to be among the best in Santa Barbara. All their red wines possess crisp, high, natural acidity, dense, almost purple saturated colors, and leafy, black-fruit characters. The acidity makes them taste austere and crisp, but there is fine underlying flesh and richness. The dense, purple-colored 1991 Cabernet Franc exhibits wonderful purity. The 1990 Merlot Estate is a lush, fleshy, densely concentrated wine with plenty of cherry fruit. Drink it over the next 6–8 years. Even better is the 1989 Cellar Select Proprietary Wine, a blend of Cabernet Sauvignon, Cabernet Franc, and Merlot. It exhibits that full, natural, unmanipulated, unprocessed taste that so many Santa Barbara wines share. The acidity is all natural, and the wine possesses a wonderful color, a great mouth-feel, a chewy texture, and copious quantities of red and black fruits nicely touched by subtle new oak. Drink this long, attractive wine over the next 6–7 years. The 1989 Cabernet Sauvignon Estate offers a huge, herbaceous, black cherry, chocolatey, vanillin-scented nose; full-bodied, concentrated flavors that offer power allied with surprising elegance and finesse; crisp acidity; and impressive length. It can be drunk now or cellared for up to a decade.

KENT RASMUSSEN WINERY (NAPA)
Chardonnay* * * *, Dolcetto* * * *, Pinot Noir* * * *

1991	Chardonnay	Carneros	C	87
1990	Chardonnay	Carneros	C	87
1990	Dolcetto	Napa	B	86
1990	Pinot Noir	Carneros	D	86

I have enjoyed everything this winery has produced. The Chardonnays display an attractive, almost burgundian, smoked, nutty, buttery component; rich, honeyed, applelike fruit; enough acidity for focus; and long, concentrated finishes. These are delicious wines with a lot of personality. Although they may not age well, they can be kept for 3–4 years after the vintage. Kent Rasmussen has also begun to turn out a super Dolcetto, with a gorgeously ripe, fragrant nose, and vivacious, fruity flavors. It is packaged in a blue bottle, making for an interesting presentation. How thrilling it is to see offbeat wines of such high quality coming out of California! Drink this charmer over the next several years. California producers continue to offer more and more persuasive evidence that they have begun, albeit on a limited scale, to capture the elusive yet fascinating qualities of Pinot Noir. This richly fruity, lush, ripe, succulent 1990 Pinot is ideal for drinking over the next 4–5 years. The earthy, flowery, raspberry fruitiness is irresistible, as is the silky, velvety texture and opulent length. It is a beauty!

RAVENSWOOD WINERY (SONOMA)
Chardonnay Sangiacomo* * * */* * * * *, Merlot Sangiacomo* * * *, Pickberry
Proprietary Red Wine* * * * *, Zinfandel Belloni* * * * *, Zinfandel Cooke
Vineyard* * * * *, Zinfandel Dickerson Vineyard* * * * *, Zinfandel Old Hill
Vineyard* * * * *, Zinfandel Sonoma* * * *, Zinfandel Vintner's Blend* * *

1991	Chardonnay Sangiacomo	Sonoma	C	89+
1990	Chardonnay Sangiacomo	Sonoma	C	93
1991	Merlot Sangiacomo	Sonoma	C	86
1990	Merlot Sangiacomo	Sonoma	C	90
1989	Merlot Sangiacomo	Sonoma	C	89
1990	Merlot Vintner's Select	Sonoma	C	85
1991	Pickberry Proprietary Red Wine	Sonoma	D	92
1990	Pickberry Proprietary Red Wine	Sonoma	D	92

1987	Pickberry Proprietary Red Wine	Sonoma	D	90
1990	Zinfandel	Sonoma	B	88
1991	Zinfandel Belloni Vineyard	Sonoma	C	92+
1991	Zinfandel Cooke Vineyard	Sonoma	C	93
1990	Zinfandel Cooke Vineyard	Sonoma	C	94
1991	Zinfandel Dickerson Vineyard	Napa	C	92+
1990	Zinfandel Dickerson Vineyard	Napa	C	95
1991	Zinfandel Old Hill Vineyard	Sonoma	C	95
1990	Zinfandel Old Hill Vineyard	Sonoma	C	92
1991	Zinfandel Old Vines	Sonoma	B	89
1990	Zinfandel Vintner's Blend	Sonoma	B	86

If California is ever going to realize its potential for producing compelling wines, there will have to be more people with Joel Peterson's vision of wine. His philosophy of winemaking is no different from that of many of the world's greatest winemakers. Everything starts in the vineyard—preferably in an old vineyard that produces no more than 2½–3 tons of grapes per acre. Second, the aim of the actual winemaking is to extract the most from the fruit by prolonging the fermentation and by avoiding commercial yeasts in favor of the vineyard's wild yeasts. A noninterventionist approach to the product is also essential. The wine that goes in the barrel is touched only if racking is required. There is no fast-food/processing wine approach at Ravenswood. All of the Zinfandels go into the bottle unfiltered unless Peterson believes there may be a stability problem. The results are among the most individualistic, splendidly rich, and delicious wines made on earth. The University of California at Davis would be smart to invite Joel Peterson as guest lecturer on making profound wines that provide immense pleasure. I doubt that will ever happen since exploiting the vineyard's maximum production level and ensuring a wine's stability rather than its quality and joy are the university's overriding objectives. Ravenswood's 1990 Zinfandels are dazzling. Zinfandel fanatics should have considerable fun comparing the 1990s with the successes Ravenswood enjoyed in 1984, 1985, 1986, and 1987. Moreover, winemaker Joel Peterson claims his 1991 Zinfandels are slightly better than his 1990s. For starters there is the inexpensive, expansively flavored, supple, richly fruity 1990 Vintner's Blend. Although this is an attractive introduction to the Ravenswood style, it has nowhere near the stature, richness, or complexity of the three-vineyard-designated 1990 Zinfandels. There are 700 cases of the 1990 Cooke Vineyard Zinfandel. Opaque ruby/purple in color, the wine offers up an intense fragrance, with penetrating aromas of minerals, black fruits, spices, and pepper. Believe me, it is a real turn-on. Once past the bouquet, this voluptuously styled, full-bodied Zinfandel is bursting with fruit and displays wonderful extraction of flavor, soft tannins, and an explosively long, heady finish. This sensational Zinfandel can easily be drunk now but promises to last for at least 8–10 years. Just 550 cases of the 1990 Zinfandel Old Hill Vineyard were produced (from 99-year-old vines). Although it does not have the color saturation of the Cooke Vineyard Zinfandel, and appears slightly less massive on the palate, it is not shy. A huge nose of black cherries, earth, and spices is followed by a wine with a sensational midpalate and great length. With wonderful balance, as well as grip and structure, the wine is impossible to resist drinking but should last for at least a decade. Ravenswood's 1990 Zinfandel from the Dickerson Vineyard in Napa Valley continues to be the Mouton-Rothschild of Zinfandel. Its huge nose of cassis, mint (perhaps eucalyptus), and spicy oak is stunning. In the mouth there is terrific extract, great focus and delineation to the wine's flamboyant character, and an overall sense of drama. It is a mouth-filling, broad-shouldered, extraordinary wine that, like its siblings, proves what phenomenal heights Zinfandel can achieve when made by someone who believes in the varietal and uses traditional techniques for making wine. The problem with the single-vineyard Zinfandels is that there are more customers than wine. More available is Ravenswood's tasty, inexpensive, yet wonderfully fruity, full-bodied 1990 Zinfandel Vintner's Blend and the opulent, rich, explosively big, deep, dramatic 1990 Zinfandel Sonoma. The 1991 Sonoma Old Vines Zinfandel is a big, expansive wine bursting with smoky, peppery, berry fruit. There is significant tannin (which is more noticeable in the 1991 than in the 1990), as well as a big, spicy, sweet nose, and broad, audacious flavors. The purity of fruit is super, and the finish long, lusty, and heady. This wine will benefit from another 6–12 months of bottle age and should last for 7–9 years. As in 1990, the most sexy and flattering wine is the 1991 Cooke Vineyard Zinfandel. The deep ruby/purple color is followed by a smoky, earthy, plummy nose. There is a Pomerol-like velvety texture and lushness with tremendous quantities of succulent, rich fruit. Fragrant, lusty, and voluptuous—altogether a real turn-on—it is presently the most complex and satisfying of the Ravenswood Zinfandels. Drink it over the next decade. A new offering in the Ravenswood portfolio, the 1991 Zinfandel Belloni Vineyards displays an opaque, saturated black/purple color, and an unevolved nose of soaring scents of black raspberries, earth, and pepper. There is exceptional density of fruit, spectacular intensity and structure, as well as a full-bodied, moderately tannic, well-delineated finish. Along with the 1991 Zinfandel Old Hill, the Belloni Vineyard offerings gets my nod as potentially one of the two finest Zinfandels Ravenswood has produced. But be forewarned, the Belloni needs at least 3–4 years of cellaring. It should last through most of the first decade of the next century. The 1991 Zinfandel Old Hill is the quintessential Zinfandel. It exhibits an opaque purple color, and a huge, peppery, black raspberry–scented nose with subtle oak in the background. In the mouth it is pure decadence—rich, fabulously concentrated, expressive, and chewy. Layer upon layer of black raspberry fruit coats the palate with glycerin and alcohol. This is a fabulous Zinfandel for drinking now and over the next 12–15 years. True to form, the 1991 Zinfandel from the Dickerson Vineyard in Napa reveals a Mouton-Rothschild–like minty and cassis-scented nose. Although deeply colored, it is not as saturated as either the Old Hill or the Belloni Vineyard Zinfandels. The Dickerson Vineyard *cuvée* is a classic Zinfandel marked by its Napa heritage. There is not quite the richness of the Belloni, or the seductive powers of the Cooke or Old Hill offerings. Nevertheless, it is a blockbuster, full-bodied, superconcentrated, well-structured Zinfandel that needs another 1–2 years of cellaring. It will keep for 10–12 or more years. Winemaker Joel Peterson has done it again!

The potentially fabulous 1991 Pickberry is nearly opaque in color. A huge nose of cassis, herbs, and damp earth is followed by a multidimensional, rich wine with a chewy texture and plenty of soft tannins. This is a complete wine from start to finish. The 1990 Pickberry is more oaky, no doubt because of the additional year of aging in cask. It has a minty nose intermingled with aromas of sweet cassis. Opulent and rich, with seemingly less tannin, this superconcentrated, expansively rich wine should be drinkable at an earlier age than the 1991. The 1987 Pickberry will ultimately turn out to be one of the best and longest-lived red table wines Ravenswood has produced. It is more forward, perfumed, and elegant than the muscular, brawny 1986. However, do not think for a moment that it is anywhere close to maturity. The wine needs at least 4–5 years in the bottle. It displays impeccably pure, rich, herb-tinged red and black fruit flavors, a whiff of spicy oak, and splendid depth and balance. Readers who taste it alongside the 1986 will probably think it forward. It should be at its best between now and 2008. Peterson has considerable enthusiasm for Merlot. The quality of his Merlots places them in the top league, rivaling those of Matanzas Creek, Duckhorn, and Havens. The 1990 Merlot may prove to be outstanding. The nose is already revealing relatively evolved aromas of tobacco, coffee, mocha, and spices. In the mouth it is round, seductive, and exotic, with just enough backbone to provide focus and grip. This tasty, lusciously rich, smooth-textured Merlot should drink well for at least a decade. By comparison, the 1991 Merlot is leaner and not as concentrated. The best 1989 I tasted from Ravenswood was the 1989 Merlot Sangiacomo. With a super nose of mocha, herb-scented berry fruit and spices, it reveals excellent richness and ripeness in the mouth, as well as good length, moderate tannins, and a fine, well-balanced, concentrated finish. Drink it over the next 10–12 years. The 1987 Merlot is more structured and initially less flattering and dramatic than the plump, precocious, profound 1986. In fact, the 1987 Merlot reminds me more of the tightly knit 1985 than any other vintage of Merlot from Ravenswood. The wine is concentrated, with a rich, plummy, berry-scented bouquet judiciously enhanced by the use of toasty new oak. In the mouth it is full bodied, possesses good, crisp acidity, and gives one the impression that it may need another several years to reach its plateau of maturity. This beautifully crafted, stylish, yet hedonistic Merlot should last for at least a decade. The 1990 Chardonnay from the Sangiacomo Vineyard is the finest Chardonnay Joel Peterson has ever produced. This explosively rich wine is profound, with tightly knit, powerful, concentrated, spicy, richly fruity flavors, zesty acidity, and whopping length. This super bottle of Chardonnay should prove to be uncommonly long-lived by California's standards. In a blind tasting, most people would think it to be a Grand Cru from Burgundy's Côte d'Or. The 1991 Chardonnay Sangiacomo is less flamboyant and concentrated, as well as more tightly knit, than the 1990. With coaxing, the reluctant bouquet reveals scents of waxy fruit and earth (the latter characteristic is sure to offend the technocrats). The wine's richness and complexity are even more obvious in the mouth, where layer upon layer of flavor may be savored. The overall impression is one of tightness and restraint, as the acidity is crisp, and the wine has yet to blossom and open. This impressively endowed, full-bodied Chardonnay, clearly molded in a different style, should last for 4–5 years.

RAYMOND VINEYARD AND CELLAR (NAPA)
Cabernet Sauvignon Napa* *, Cabernet Sauvignon Private Reserve* * *,
Chardonnay Private Reserve* * * *

1989	Cabernet Sauvignon	Napa	B	74
1988	Cabernet Sauvignon	Napa	B	73
1985	Cabernet Sauvignon Private Reserve	Napa	C	86
1990	Chardonnay Private Reserve	Napa	C	86
1989	Chardonnay Private Reserve	Napa	C	87
1988	Chardonnay Private Reserve	Napa	C	87

The 1990 Chardonnay Private Reserve is rich, but less boldly styled than previous editions. One of the most successful 1989s, this Chardonnay Private Reserve offers ripe, buttery apple fruit, an opulent texture, and surprising
midrange and length for a 1989. Drink it over the next year. The 1988
Chardonnay, a chunky, toasty, tropical fruit–flavored wine, performed well in
my peer-group tastings. In addition to good intensity, it offers a long, luscious
finish and a hefty dose of new oak. Drink it over the next 12 months. Gobs of
toasty new oak compete with abundant quantities of blackcurrant and blackberry fruit in this medium- to full-bodied, soft, lushly styled 1985 Cabernet
Sauvignon Private Reserve. It should drink well for another 5–6 years. No, it
will not make old bones, but this is a delicious, forward-style Cabernet Sauvignon that should have popular appeal. Recent regular bottlings of Cabernet
Sauvignon, particularly the 1988 and 1989, are disappointing, hollow, stripped
wines with no bouquet and little flavor.

RENAISSANCE VINEYARD (YUBA)
Cabernet Sauvignon* * */* * * *

I have been remiss in not tasting any of the Renaissance wines recently. The
handful of Cabernets I have tasted, including those that appear under their
second label, Da Vinci, have been rich, full bodied, and interesting, with considerable flavor authority. The winery also produces a Sauvignon Blanc and
both a dry Riesling and a late-harvest Riesling, which I have never had the
pleasure of tasting. Renaissance has a policy of not releasing wines until they
have significant bottle age.

REVERE WINERY (NAPA)
Chardonnay *

1989	Chardonnay	Napa	B	70
1988	Chardonnay	Napa	B	68

It is hard to know what the winemaking objective is at this small Napa Valley
Chardonnay specialist. The wines are excessively woody, entirely too acidic,
and lacking in fruit, depth, charm, and pleasure. Older vintages, such as the
1985 and 1986, which started life so oaky and acidic, have completely lost
their fruit and are undrinkable.

RICHARDSON VINEYARDS (SONOMA)
Cabernet Sauvignon* *, Chardonnay* *, Pinot Noir* */* * *

1990	Merlot Sangiacomo	Sonoma	B	59
1990	Pinot Noir Sangiacomo	Sonoma	C	72

I had the opportunity to taste through Richardson's portfolio for three separate vintages and found the wines to be monolithic, straightforward, and heavy, without soul or personality.

RIDGE VINEYARDS (SANTA CLARA)
Cabernet Sauvignon Monte Bello* * * * *, Cabernet Sauvignon Santa Cruz* * *,
Chardonnay Howell Mountain* * * *, Chardonnay Santa Cruz Mountains* * * *,
Geyserville Proprietary Red Wine* * * * *, Mataro Evangelo* * * *, Petite Sirah York
Creek* * * * *, Zinfandel Howell Mountain* * *, Zinfandel Lytton Springs* * * * *,
Zinfandel Paso Robles* * * *, Zinfandel Sonoma* * *

1992	Cabernet Sauvignon Monte Bello	Santa Cruz	D	90
1991	Cabernet Sauvignon Monte Bello	Santa Cruz	D	92
1990	Cabernet Sauvignon Monte Bello	Santa Cruz	D	90
1989	Cabernet Sauvignon Monte Bello	Santa Cruz	D	75
1988	Cabernet Sauvignon Monte Bello	Santa Cruz	D	77
1987	Cabernet Sauvignon Monte Bello	Santa Cruz	D	90
1990	Chardonnay	Santa Cruz	C	90
1990	Chardonnay Howell Mountain	Napa	C	88
1991	Geyserville Proprietary Red Wine	Sonoma	C	90
1990	Geyserville Proprietary Red Wine	Sonoma	C	90
1991	Mataro Evangelo Vineyard	Contra Costa	B	87
1990	Mataro Evangelo Vineyard	Contra Costa	B	88
1989	Merlot Bradford Mountain	Sonoma	C	75
1988	Petite Sirah York Creek	Napa	C	88
1991	Zinfandel Lytton Springs	Sonoma	C	92
1990	Zinfandel Lytton Springs	Sonoma	C	93
1991	Zinfandel	Paso Robles	B	92
1990	Zinfandel	Paso Robles	C	88

The 1992 Cabernet Sauvignon Monte Bello is atypically soft and forward for a wine from this producer. The cassis-, smoke-, and mineral-scented bouquet is followed by a wine that is deep, expansive, supple, and elegant. The velvety-textured finish confirms the wine's precocious style. **Anticipated maturity: 1995–2008.** The 1991 Ridge Monte Bello tastes similar to a classic Bordeaux in the sense that the lead pencil–, cassis-, licorice-scented nose is reminiscent of a high-class Pauillac. One would never guess it was aged in American oak because the wood character is so subtle and well balanced. A rich, yet restrained wine, it exhibits a formidable inner core of intensity as well as great balance and superb style. Given the glacial pace at which the Monte Bello Cabernets evolve, I suspect owners will still be extolling this wine's virtues in 25–30 years. I would not touch a bottle before the turn of the century. The 1991 should prove to be a classic Monte Bello and probably the best wine produced by Ridge since its exquisite 1984 and 1985. The 1990 Monte Bello should prove to be nearly as good as the 1991. Backward, tannic, and rich, it offers a sensational cassis-, mineral-, and oak-scented nose, medium- to full-bodied flavors, good acidity, and a long, tight, closed finish. This is another wine that will require considerable patience. Both the 1989 and 1988 Monte Bellos are mediocre. The 1989 exhibits adequate fruit and a spicy nose, but a relatively green, underripe, tannic, hard texture and a compact, austere, short finish. The 1988 has a more vegetal streak and is quite tannic and angular, with excessive acidity for the amount of fruit present. It will only become more attenuated and gets my nod as one of the most disappointing Monte Bellos ever made. The 1987 Monte Bello is exceptionally backward, even by Ridge's standards, and I would not dare contemplate drinking a bottle prior to 1997–1998. However, this is one of those profound mountain Cabernets that should last for 20–25 years. Not much is available, as quantities produced in 1987 from the Monte Bello Vineyard were tiny. However, should you have the requisite patience to wait up to a decade for this wine to shed its considerable tannic clout, then move quickly, as this will be one of the rarest of the Ridge Monte Bellos. Dark black/ruby, with a rich, ripe, yet reticent bouquet of minerals, blackcurrants, and toasted oak, this wine is exceptionally concentrated, full bodied, and extremely firm and closed. With airing, some blossoming flavors of licorice, blackcurrants, and vanillin emerge. The finish is long but forbiddingly tannic. This is a large-scale yet impeccably balanced wine for drinking during the first 2 decades of the next century. I enjoyed Ridge's 1991 and 1990 Mataro Evangelos (Mourvèdre), both of which exhibited a fragrant, woody, spicy, earthy, berry-scented nose; luscious, round, smooth-as-silk flavors; and plenty of up-front, sexy appeal. Displaying good flavor and character, these charming wines should be drunk over the next 7–8 years. Admirers of Ridge's classic Petite Sirah from York Creek will not be disappointed with the black-colored, concentrated, full-bodied 1988. Although it does not possess the richness of the 1987, 1986, 1985, or 1984, it is a top-notch effort from what is generally a mediocre vintage. The nose reluctantly offers up aromas of licorice, pepper, and black raspberries. In the mouth it is spicy, full bodied, and moderately tannic. Drink it between 1995 and 2010. It should not come as a surprise that Ridge has again produced three terrific Zinfandels in 1990. If you are not convinced that this is the most underrated varietal made in California, try one of these offerings. Although all three are rich and full bodied, the most elegant is the 1990 Paso Robles (made from 95% Zinfandel and 5% Carignane). Fat and sumptuous, with gobs of berry fruit and excellent color, this is a forward, mouth-filling, amply endowed wine bursting with glycerin and ripe fruit—a hedonistic Zinfandel that should make super drinking over the next 5–7 years. The 1990 Geyserville (which does not have Zinfandel on the label, as it is produced from 64% Zinfandel, 18% Petite Sirah, and 18% Carignane) is a blockbuster wine. Once past the huge perfume of black raspberries, spices, and minerals, you will find a supple texture with oodles of rich berry fruit. It offers layer upon layer of supple, decadently rich fruit, with enough acidity and tannin to hold everything together. The overall impression is of a gorgeously rich, complete, and complex wine that should drink well for at least 7–8 years. Last, the 1990 Zinfandel Lytton Springs may be one of the finest I have ever tasted from Ridge (which is saying something given its extraordinary track record). Made from 80% Zinfandel, 10% Petite Sirah, 6% Carignane, and 4% Grenache, this phenomenal wine reminded me of the 1989 Rayas Châteauneuf-du-Pape. It exhibits a roasted, black fruit character, sensational concentration, gobs of glycerin, and a heady, spicy, nearly mind-boggling finish. This truly profound Zinfandel should make superb drinking over the next 10–12 years. Ridge is now using a Geyserville designation for its proprietary red wine. It is still composed largely of Zinfandel. However, in 1991, the Zinfandel component is less significant than in 1990, representing only 50% of the blend. The balance is 30% Carignane and 20% Petite Sirah. The big 1991 Geyserville has 14.3% alcohol, but there is so much fruit that the wine's power and alcohol are marked. The color is deep ruby/purple, and the nose offers up fragrant ripe aromas of black fruits, minerals, and oak. There is surprising elegance allied with superconcentrated, rich fruit. The finish is all fruit, glycerin, and lushness. This seductive, spicy, mouth-filling wine should drink well for 8–10 years. The 1991 Zinfandel Lytton Springs (80% Zinfandel, 12% Petite Sirah, 6% Grenache, 2% Carignane) also has over 14% alcohol, but like its sibling, the superconcentration of fruit covers any alcoholic heat. The deep ruby/purple color is followed by gobs of jammy blackcurrant and black raspberry fruit. This big, heady, spicy, chewy, fleshy wine is soft and succulent, with a velvety finish. Drink it over the next 7–8 years. I thought Ridge's 1991 Zinfandel from Paso Robles was the best I have tasted from this impeccably run winery. Gushing with black cherry and black raspberry fruit, it is a soft, nearly corpulent wine because of its lush, chewy, fleshy style, with superb ripeness and richness, as well as a long, unctuous, rich finish. It is one of the most seductive 1991 Zinfandels, and readers should not buy more than they will drink over the next 5–6 years. Ridge's 1990 Chardonnay from Howell Mountain is the finest Chardonnay I have tasted from this property. Displaying impressive richness, a burgundylike, buttery, baked apple–, toasty-scented nose and flavors, high acidity, and a tightly knit structure, it should age for 5–10 years. Several disappointing wines include a 1989 Merlot from Bradford Mountain. This hollow, empty wine offers none of the charm or flesh one expects in a Merlot. The same can be said for the 1989 Cabernet Sauvignon Santa Cruz, a dull, lifeless product that Ridge should never have released. Virtually everyone who has taken the time to taste it agrees that Ridge's York Creek Petite Sirah is a heckuva wine. However, today's glamour red wine grapes are Cabernet Sauvignon, Merlot, Cabernet Franc, Pinot Noir, and, of late, true Syrah. Petite Sirah is generally considered a "lesser varietal" as well as harder to sell, or so say the wizards of wine marketing. Petite Sirah's less than sexy image and sales strength can be put to good use by consumers, especially if they are savvy enough to try a few bottles of Ridge Petite Sirah, my nominee for California's most underrated (and underpriced) great red table wine. Ridge has been making Petite Sirah from Napa's York Creek vineyard for over 20 years. Between 1971 and 1980 it split the production with Freemark Abbey. In 1980 Freemark Abbey, unwisely so in my view, chose to discontinue Petite Sirah. Paul Draper, the immensely talented architect of Ridge's wines, jumped at the opportunity to take the entire crop, and since 1980 the production of Ridge Petite Sirah has ranged from 1,500 to 3,600 cases, all of it broodingly dark, powerfully scented, concentrated, and ageworthy. This is probably California's only high-quality, dry red table wine that can age for 20 or more years and yet be purchased for $10–$13 a bottle.

RATINGS FOR OLDER VINTAGES OF RIDGE VINEYARDS CABERNET SAUVIGNON MONTE BELLO: 1986 (85), 1985 (92), 1984 (94), 1982 (74), 1981 (90), 1980 (78), 1978 (92), 1977 (92), 1976 (69), 1975 (89), 1974 (90), 1973 (83), 1972 (90), 1971 (93) (there is also a 1971 Ridge Eisele Vineyard Cabernet Sauvignon that I have rated as high as 94), 1970 (94), 1964 (90)

RATINGS FOR OLDER VINTAGES OF RIDGE VINEYARDS YORK CREEK PETITE SIRAH: 1987 (90), 1986 (90), 1985 (92), 1984 (86), 1982 (90), 1979 (93), 1976 (91), 1975 (89), 1974 (82), 1973 (83), 1972 (83), 1971 (92)

J. ROCHIOLI (SONOMA)
Cabernet Sauvignon* * *, Chardonnay* * * *, Gewürztraminer*,
Pinot Noir* * *, Sauvignon Blanc* *

1989	Cabernet Sauvignon Reserve	Russian River	C	86
1990	Chardonnay	Russian River	C	87
1990	Chardonnay Reserve	Russian River	D	89
1990	Pinot Noir	Sonoma	C	82
1990	Pinot Noir Reserve	Russian River	C	87
1991	Sauvignon Blanc	Russian River	B	80

This winery continues to move up the quality ladder, offering a lineup of wines that are all worth trying. Rochioli has achieved success with a medium-weight, fragrant, spicy, berry-scented Pinot Noir. The Reserve Pinot is richer and slightly more oaked than the regular *cuvée*. The Chardonnays have gone from strength to strength. The 1990s are both super wines. The regular *cuvée* is bursting with opulent quantities of fruit buttressed by just enough toasty oak. The acidity is well integrated, and the finish is crisp and long. The Reserve bottling offers more of everything, with a bigger, richer bouquet and a larger impact on the palate. In the so-so 1989 vintage, Rochioli has made one of the better Cabernets. With a deep color, an attractive spicy, cassis nose, and a wonderfully sweet, expansive palate, it is one of the few 1989s that actually possesses gobs of fruit and richness. Although not complex, it is a delicious Cabernet for drinking over the next 3–4 years. If you have not yet noticed, the wines from Rochioli are worth a try.

ROCKING HORSE (NAPA)
Cabernet Sauvignon* * *, Claret* *, Zinfandel* * *

1989	Cabernet Sauvignon Hillside Cuvée	Napa	B	84
1990	Cabernet Sauvignon Robinson Vineyard	Napa	B	86
1990	Claret	Napa	B	75
1990	Zinfandel Lamborn Vineyard	Howell Mountain	C	87
1989	Zinfandel Lamborn Vineyard	Howell Mountain	C	84

It is too early to get a feeling for the direction this winery is heading in, but these offerings, save for the innocuous Claret, are unquestionably well made.

The impressive 1990 Zinfandel from the Lamborn Vineyard is a huge, monstrous wine with great fruit and sweet enough tannins to make it approachable now, although it will last for up to 10 years. The 1990 Claret (a blend of 58% Cabernet Sauvignon and 42% Cabernet Franc) is narrowly constructed and herbaceous, but behind the vegetal streak is a sweet black fruit character. Perhaps more charm will emerge with aging. The 1989 Hillside Cuvée of Cabernet Sauvignon is a supple, round, tasty wine without much complexity but with good fruit, medium body, and an attractive personality.

ROEDERER ESTATE (MENDOCINO)
Sparkling Wine Cuvées* * * *

1988	Sparkling Wine	Anderson Valley	C	88
N. V.	Sparkling Wine	Anderson Valley	C	89

Roederer has succeeded in producing the best sparkling wine of all the French/American joint ventures in California. The newest nonvintage release has a brilliant bouquet of "Wheat Thins" and ripe apples; crisp, brilliantly focused, ripe, medium-bodied flavors; a long, fresh aftertaste; and good acidity. There is beautiful fruit in this wine, and who would not admire the impeccable winemaking that has resulted in such uniform pinpoint bubbles that persist in the glass? Drink this beauty over the next 1–2 years. Roederer's first vintage offering, the 1988, reveals excellent definition and richness, medium to full body, and significantly more fruit, depth, and style than the majority of California sparkling wines.

ROMBAUER VINEYARDS (NAPA)
Cabernet Sauvignon* *, Chardonnay* *, Merlot* *

1987	Cabernet Sauvignon	Napa	B	75
1989	Chardonnay	Napa	A	72
1989	Merlot	Napa	B	73

This winery has consistently turned out lean, austere, malnourished wines that lack fruit and depth. From time to time there has also been a proprietary red wine called Le Meilleur de Chai, which has typified the uninspiring, even indifferent efforts that routinely emerge from this producer.

ROSENBLUM CELLARS (ALAMEDA)
Zinfandel Michael Marston Vineyard* * * * *, Zinfandel Other Cuvées* * * *,
Zinfandel Samsel Vineyard* * * * *

1991	Zinfandel	Contra Costa	B	87
1990	Zinfandel	Paso Robles	B	87
1990	Zinfandel	Sonoma	B	86
1991	Zinfandel Brandlin Ranch Mount Veeder	Napa	C	90
1990	Zinfandel George Henry Vineyard	Napa	B	89
1991	Zinfandel George Henry Vineyard Reserve	Napa	C	88

1991	Zinfandel Maggie's Reserve Samsel Vineyard	Sonoma	C	90
1990	Zinfandel Maggie's Reserve Samsel Vineyard	Sonoma	B	90
1991	Zinfandel Michael Marston Vineyard	Napa	C	90
1990	Zinfandel Michael Marston Vineyard	Napa	B	90
1991	Zinfandel Richard Sauret Vineyard	Paso Robles	B	87
N.V.	Zinfandel Vintner's Cuvée	California	A	87
N.V.	Zinfandel Vintner's Cuvée VI	California	A	87

Rosenblum Cellars continues to rank among California's leading Zinfandel producers. In 1991 they increased the size of their Zinfandel portfolio without any diminution of quality. The 1991s are all marvelous wines. Readers should especially take note of the N.V. Vintner's Cuvée VI, which is a super bargain. Its soft, fleshy, peppery, raspberry-scented nose and flavors offer wonderful ripeness in a lush, opulent, heady style. It should drink well for 3–4 years. The spicy, rich, medium- to full-bodied, soft, chewy 1991 Zinfandel Richard Sauret Vineyard in Paso Robles should be drunk over the next 5–6 years. Rosenblum's 1991 Zinfandel Maggie's Reserve Samsel Vineyard from Sonoma Valley is a more backward, ageworthy Zinfandel. The saturated purple color, spicy, peppery, black fruit–scented nose, and rich, intense, medium- to full-bodied flavors are buttressed by surprisingly crisp acidity and moderate tannins. The finish is long and persuasive. Drink this wine over the next decade. The 1991 Zinfandel from the George Henry Vineyard on Napa's Mount Veeder is made in a completely different style. A flowery, fragrant, penetrating, evolved bouquet is followed by a wine with crisp, rich, wonderfully pure fruit, excellent definition, medium body, and a spicy, well-endowed style. Drinkable now, this wine promises to last for up to a decade. Rosenblum Cellar's 1991 Zinfandel from the Michael Marston Vineyard exhibits a sensational nose of black cherries, black raspberries, minerals, and vague scents of chocolate and pepper. It is a blockbuster wine, with massive quantities of fruit, glycerin, and alcohol. This large-scale, full-throttle Zinfandel is the biggest of the Rosenblum offerings. Drink it over the next 10–12 years. The 1991 Zinfandel from Contra Costa reveals a plummy color; a big, spicy, cinnamon-and-pepper-scented nose; dense, chewy, full-bodied flavors; and plenty of extract and glycerin. With its husky mouth-feel, it is ideal for drinking over the next 5–6 years. The 1991 Zinfandel Brandlin Ranch (from a vineyard on Mount Veeder) possesses fabulous purity and richness to its black raspberry fruitiness. Full bodied, with spicy, moderate tannins, and a multilayered feel, this big yet gracefully made, well-balanced Zinfandel should last for 7–10 years. The fragrant, spicy, berry-flavored, medium- to full-bodied 1990 Zinfandel from Paso Robles should be delicious to drink over the next 3–4 years. The tannins are soft, the acidity provides lift and focus, and the overall impression is of gorgeous up-front fruit and fragrance. The 1990 Zinfandel from Sonoma is much more earthy, with a denser texture, more blackberry than raspberry or cherry flavors, and a good medium-bodied, spicy finish. It, too, should drink well for the next 3–4 years. The 1990 Zinfandel George Henry Vineyard displays a saturated, deep dark ruby/purple color; an intense nose of ripe berries and spicy oak; long, medium- to full-bodied, black cherry and black raspberry flavors; and a dramatic, lusty finish. It should drink well for 6–7 years. Slightly more concentrated, tannic, and fuller bodied is Rosenblum's 1990 Zinfandel Michael Marston Vineyard. This wine is tighter and appears to need several years of cellaring given the fact that the tannins are not only more evident, but are tougher in character. It is an exceptionally concentrated, full-bodied, classic Zinfandel that should handsomely repay 2–3 years of cellaring and last for up to a decade. Similarly styled, but a bit more earthy, opulent, and alcoholic, is Rosenblum's 1990 Zinfandel Maggie's Reserve Samsel Vineyard. Though a powerful Zinfandel, everything is in balance and the wine exhibits tremendously pure fruit, gorgeous intensity, and a long finish. More approachable than the Michael Marston Vineyard Zinfandel, the Samsel can be drunk now or cellared for up to a decade. Finally, shrewd consumers looking for a great bargain should check out the N.V. Vintner's Cuvée. It is loaded with delicious superripe berry fruit, displaying a soft texture and a mouth-filling, generous finish. Drink it over the next 1–2 years. Rosenblum Cellars appears intent on challenging Ravenswood and Ridge as one of California's leading Zinfandel producers.

ROSS VALLEY (SONOMA)
Zinfandel* * * *

1990	Zinfandel	Sonoma	B	88
1989	Zinfandel	Sonoma	B	73
1988	Zinfandel Hillside Vineyard	Alexander Valley	B	87
1990	Zinfandel Parson's Vineyard	Sonoma	C	78
1988	Zinfandel Parson's Vineyard	Sonoma	B	87

The first releases I tasted from this winery, both 1988 Zinfandels from a not-so-easy vintage, displayed fine intensity and good structure and are made to withstand a decade's worth of aging. The 1988 Zinfandel Hillside Vineyard is slightly lighter than its sibling but exhibits very ripe berry fruit, a big, aromatic bouquet, a chewy, dense texture, and enough tannin and body to support 10–12 years of cellaring. It can be drunk now, but I would recommend pairing it with equally robust foods. The 1988 Zinfandel Parson's Vineyard is even more extracted, but accompanying such intensity are intimidating tannin levels and a slight rustic quality. I liked it just as much as the Hillside *cuvée*, but it is a richer, more masculine and muscular wine. Although the Hillside can be drunk now, the Parson's Vineyard needs to be cellared for 2–3 years but should last for 12–15 years. Both 1988 Zinfandels are impressive wines. In the super 1990 vintage, the Parson's Vineyard Zinfandel tasted too rustic, with astringent tannins and a lack of richness. The 1989 Sonoma Zinfandel was disappointingly thin, astringent, and austere. The 1990 is a return to the promising form this winery exhibited in 1988. It is a rich, full-bodied Zinfandel bursting with aromas of black fruits, minerals, spicy oak, and earth. Rich and powerful, this large-scale Zinfandel can be drunk now or cellared for up to a decade.

ROUDIN-SMITH VINEYARDS (SANTA CRUZ)
Cabernet Sauvignon* *, Chardonnay*, Petite Sirah* *, Pinot Noir* *, Zinfandel* *

1988	Chardonnay	Mendocino	B 74
1986	Pinot Noir	Santa Cruz	B 72

This winery has had an inconsistent track record over the last 20 years, but occasionally some blockbuster Cabernet Sauvignons, Zinfandels, and Petite Sirahs have emerged. The two current releases are light-bodied, restrained, dull wines of little interest.

ROUND HILL (NAPA)
Cabernet Sauvignon* *, Cabernet Sauvignon Reserve* */* * *, Chardonnay* *

1989	Cabernet Sauvignon	Napa	B 76
1988	Cabernet Sauvignon	Napa	B 73
1990	Chardonnay	California	A 75

Round Hill can be a source of good values, but its recent releases have been mediocre. There are Reserve wines for both Chardonnay and Cabernet, but I have found them to be excessively oaky and out of balance. The three recent releases include two washed-out, hollow Cabernets and a light, acidic, lean Chardonnay.

RUBISSOW-SARGENT (NAPA)
Cabernet Sauvignon* *, Merlot* *

1988	Cabernet Sauvignon Mt. Veeder	Napa	C 72
1989	Merlot Mt. Veeder	Napa	C 75
1988	Merlot Mt. Veeder	Napa	C 73

The first releases I tasted from this winery were unimpressive, but perhaps that is partially the fault of the vintages. One can hardly be impressed with tannic wines that lack concentration, fruit, and complexity.

RUTHERFORD HILL WINERY (NAPA)
Cabernet Sauvignon* *, Chardonnay Jaeger* * Chardonnay XVS Reserve* * *,
Merlot* * (since 1985) * * * * (before 1985), Sauvignon Blanc*

1989	Chardonnay Jaeger Vineyard	Napa	C 74
1988	Chardonnay XVS Reserve	Napa	C 72
1989	Merlot	Napa	C 69
1990	Sauvignon Blanc	Napa	A 68

From time to time a good Chardonnay, as well as a splendid Merlot, has emerged from Rutherford Hill. In particular, the 1984 and 1980 Merlots were terrific when released and are still wonderful wines. I had a magnum of the 1980 Merlot in early 1993 that was sensational. However, the winery has a frightfully erratic record since the mid-1980s, and my instincts, as well as recent tastings, suggest a weak portfolio of wines. For example, the 1990 Sauvignon Blanc has no bouquet, washed-out, thin, diluted flavors, and too much acidity. The 1989 Chardonnay Jaeger Vineyard is already losing its fruit; what is left is a skeleton of acidity, oak, and alcohol. The 1988 Chardonnay XVS

Reserve (supposedly the top *cuvée*) has taken on a medium-golden color and exhibits a pronounced oaky, almost oxidized nose with quickly fading fruit. The 1989 Merlot is an embarrassment. Thin, clipped, short, and diluted, it possesses no character.

ST. ANDREWS WINERY (NAPA)
Cabernet Sauvignon* *, Chardonnay* *

1988	Cabernet Sauvignon	Napa	C	72
1990	Chardonnay	Napa	B	78

The St. Andrews winery was sold several years ago to the group that also owns Napa's nearby Clos du Val winery. One hopes this means St. Andrews's quality will improve. At present the straightforward Chardonnay offers some oak, plenty of acidity, and not much fruit or character. The Cabernet Sauvignon has been a hollow, tannic wine.

ST. CLEMENT VINEYARDS (NAPA)
Cabernet Sauvignon* *, Chardonnay* *, Sauvignon Blanc* *

1989	Cabernet Sauvignon	Napa	C	76
1988	Cabernet Sauvignon	Napa	C	71
1990	Chardonnay Abbot's Vineyard	Carneros	C	85
1991	Sauvignon Blanc	Napa	B	86

After a string of innocuous, hollow wines, St. Clement has released two meritorious efforts. The 1990 Chardonnay Abbot's Vineyard exhibits good fruit, crisp acidity, and far more bouquet, flavor, and character than anything St. Clement has produced over the last 6 years. The 1991 Sauvignon Blanc is slightly more enticing, with well-integrated acidity; a melony, fruity nose backed up by subtle, toasty oak; and medium-bodied, crisp, richly fruity flavors that will continue to provide enjoyment for another year. Perhaps the showing of these two white wines from recent vintages is an encouraging sign that St. Clement is intent on increasing its qualitative profile.

ST. FRANCIS VINEYARD (SONOMA)
Chardonnay Barrel Fermented* * *, Merlot* * *, Merlot Reserve* * * *,
Muscat Canelli* * * *, Zinfandel* * *

1991	Chardonnay	Sonoma	B	83
1990	Chardonnay Estate Barrel Fermented	Sonoma	B	89
1990	Merlot Reserve	Sonoma	C	88
1989	Zinfandel Old Vines	Sonoma	B	87

In the mid-1980s St. Francis was one of the hottest California wineries, turning out splendid wines across the board. For whatever reason, it went into a slump, and the once explosively rich, fragrant Merlots and intense Cabernet Sauvignons lighten up considerably in vintages such as 1985, 1986, 1987, and 1988. However, barrel tastings of the 1990s and the in-the-bottle 1989 Merlot and Zinfandel suggest the slump was short-lived. St. Francis's Chardonnay from the 1990 vintage is terrific, a big, nutty, smoky, buttery-scented wine that bears an uncanny resemblance to a top Meursault from France. In the mouth there are chewy, viscous flavors, enough acidity to provide focus and lift, and a rich, lusty finish. Drink this beauty over the next year. Some readers may find the 1989 Merlot too herbaceous, yet I enjoyed the coffee, herbal, and concentrated berry fruitiness, presented in a smooth-as-silk, medium- to full-bodied format. Drink this tasty Merlot over the next 4–5 years. The 1990 Merlot Reserve has a huge nose of rich, chocolatey, herb, and plummy fruit that is followed by a wine with lovely coffee, berrylike flavors, an opulent texture, low acidity, and plenty of lush fruit in the finish. Drink it over the next 5–6 years. The delicious yet exotic 1987 Merlot, with its bouquet dominated by aromas of mint, smoke, and Oriental spices, displays considerable lush fruit, medium to full body, and enough acidity for focus. There are also sufficient tannins to support cellaring for 6–8 years. This is an excellent wine from one of California's premier Merlot specialists. I was enthralled by St Francis's delicious, upfront 1989 Zinfandel, which knocked me over with its blast of superripe berry fruit, sexy new oak, and velvety, luscious flavors. The finish is long, lusty, and altogether decadent. Drink this beauty over the next 2–3 years. St. Francis also produces a straightforward, simple Riesling and Gewürztraminer in an off-dry style. Perhaps the best of its other wines is the delightfully fragrant, medium-sweet, richly fruity Muscat Canelli, a wine that should be drunk in its first year of life for its vivaciousness and perfume, which disintegrates quickly. Readers should be looking for the 1992.

CHÂTEAU ST. JEAN (SONOMA)
Brut Cuvées* , Cabernet Sauvignon* *, Chardonnay* *, Fumé Blanc* *

1987	Brut Blanc de Blancs	Sonoma	C	76
1987	Brut Sparkling Wine	Sonoma	B	77
1987	Cabernet Sauvignon Reserve	Alexander Valley	C	65
1990	Chardonnay	Sonoma	C	68
1989	Chardonnay Belle Terre	Alexander Valley	C	74
1990	Chardonnay Estate Select	Sonoma	C	72
1990	Chardonnay Robert Young	Alexander Valley	D	75
1990	Fumé Blanc La Petite Étoile	Russian River Valley	B	78
1990	Fumé Blanc	Sonoma	B	72

It is ironic that most winery acquisitions by Japanese companies have resulted in higher quality; but this is not the case at Château St. Jean. Here the wines have become increasingly leaner, less concentrated, and, sadly, less enjoyable. The Fumé Blancs and Chardonnays, once reference points for California, are now appallingly neutral and dull. Can anyone believe that a Chardonnay made from the Robert Young Vineyard could taste so innocuous, compact, and short? The other wines are all monuments to the school of modern-day oenology, which values technical perfection over flavorful, character-filled wines. The Fumé Blancs and Chardonnays are a sad group of innocuous, sterile wines. The 1987 Cabernet Sauvignon Reserve actually had a bouquet, but it was so unusual in its stewed, vegetal component, so poorly made, with its disjointed, unpleasant, astringent tannins, that it is hard to believe it came from a well-financed, seemingly well-run winery. I have never been a fan of the sparkling wines from Château St. Jean. Although they have not gotten worse, neither have they improved. They are green, with shrill acid and no noticeable flavor depth or length.

ST. SUPERY (NAPA)
Cabernet Sauvignon* *, Chardonnay* *, Sauvignon Blanc* *

1988	Cabernet Sauvignon Dollar Hide Ranch	Napa	B	78
1990	Chardonnay Dollar Hide Ranch	Napa	B	83
1990	Sauvignon Blanc Dollar Hide Ranch	Napa	A	78

It appeared at first that St. Supery's ambition was to produce squeaky clean wines with no flavor or personality, albeit at fair prices; but after that indifferent beginning the quality seems to be moving slowly upward. The white wines are still light, acidic, and lacking fruit. But the 1990 Chardonnay from its Dollar Hide Ranch Vineyard in Polk Valley possesses more fruit than any wine I have tasted to date from St. Supery. Unfortunately the Cabernet Sauvignons are still lean and vegetal, with too much tart acidity and astringent tannins.

SAINTSBURY WINERY (NAPA)
Chardonnay* * *, Chardonnay Reserve* * *, Pinot Noir Carneros* * * *,
Pinot Noir Garnet* * *, Pinot Noir Reserve* * * *

1991	Chardonnay	Carneros	B	85
1990	Chardonnay Reserve	Carneros	C	86
1990	Pinot Noir	Carneros	C	87
1991	Pinot Noir Garnet	Carneros	B	86
1990	Pinot Noir Reserve	Carneros	C	92
1992	Vin Gris	Carneros	A	85

The Saintsbury operation began on a strong note in the early 1980s and has since built on that foundation of success. There are now two *cuvées* of Chardonnay and three of Pinot Noir. The Reserve was launched only with the 1990 vintage. There is also a delicious, very gulpable rosé made from Pinot Noir called Vin Gris. The 1992 goes down the throat all too easily. The Chardonnays are made in a medium-weight style, with good fruit and, in the case of the Reserve, plenty of lavish oak. In fact, I often like the regular *cuvée* just as much because the oak sometimes interferes with the wine's expression of its varietal character. Nevertheless, the Chardonnays are always at least good and in some cases excellent. Both the regular *cuvée* and the Reserve are wines to consume within their first 2–3 years of life. Until 1990, proprietors David Graves and Dick Ward produced a very light, delicate Pinot Noir Garnet that was reminiscent of a good Côte de Beaune from France. Soft, expansive, and perfumed, the wine offered immediate appeal. It should have been a huge success with restaurants wanting to offer their clients tasty Pinot Noir at a reasonable price. Along with the Garnet *cuvée*, they produced a more ambitious, richer Carneros bottling that emphasized more black fruits, body, glycerin, and slightly higher alcohol; it was also framed by more noticeable use of oak. This has always been a very good wine, with its personality defined by rich, juicy, succulent black cherry fruitiness. In 1990 Saintsbury offered a limited-production Pinot Noir Reserve, which is unquestionably the best Pinot Noir made in its short existence. A stunning wine, it offers a huge perfume of toasty new oak and red and black fruits. Opulent and voluptuous, with copious quantities of sweet, expansive Pinot fruit, this wine is impossible to resist now but promises to last another 4–6 years. This winery is a model for making wines with broad appeal to neophytes and connoisseurs. It has also kept its pricing structure reasonable.

SALMON CREEK VINEYARDS (NAPA)
Chardonnay* * * *

1990	Chardonnay		Napa C	88

Has anyone ever heard of this 1,000-case producer of Chardonnay? The articulate, highly talented Daniel Baron, the French-trained American winemaker who spends most of his time working at the Dominus estate, is making crisp, classic Chardonnay that has more in common with a top Premier Cru or Grand Cru Chablis than just about anybody else's California Chardonnay. His wines need several years to reveal their character. Just when most consumers think California Chardonnay should be fading, Salmon Creek's is beginning to blossom. The 1990 exhibits a crisp, lemony, mineral component, plenty of fruit, good body, and zesty acidity. It should last for 4–7 years.

SANFORD WINERY (SANTA BARBARA)
Chardonnay* * * *, Chardonnay Barrel Select* * * * *,
Chardonnay Sanford & Benedict Vineyard* * * * *, Pinot Noir* * * *,
Pinot Noir Barrel Select* * * * *, Pinot Noir Sanford & Benedict Vineyard* * * * *,
Sauvignon Blanc* * * *

Year	Wine	Region		Score
1991	Chardonnay	Santa Barbara	C	89
1990	Chardonnay Barrel Select Unfiltered	Santa Barbara	D	90
1992	Chardonnay Sanford & Benedict Vineyard	Santa Barbara	D	90
1991	Pinot Noir	Santa Barbara	C	90
1992	Pinot Noir Barrel Select Sanford & Benedict Vineyard	Santa Barbara	D	92
1991	Pinot Noir Barrel Select Sanford & Benedict Vineyard	Santa Barbara	D	92
1990	Pinot Noir Barrel Select Sanford & Benedict Vineyard	Santa Barbara	D	93
1991	Pinot Noir Vin Gris	Santa Barbara	A	87
1991	Sauvignon Blanc	Santa Barbara	A	86?

As the scores attest, Sanford is one of California's highest-achieving wineries. Consumers are demanding more flavor and complexity, and Sanford's wines deliver the goods. While these wines may be criticized for lacking subtlety, they are exciting wines that can dazzle the palate. One of the finest rosés made from Pinot Noir is Sanford's 1991 Pinot Noir Vin Gris. Crisp, fragrant, and bursting with fruit, it exhibits fine body and a juicy, lusty finish. Drink it before the end of 1993. Sanford is long known for its brilliant, dramatic, oaky Chardonnays. Lovers of this lusty, no-holds-barred style of Chardonnay will be thrilled with Sanford's current releases. The 1991 Chardonnay Santa Barbara possesses a big, expressive nose of honeyed tropical fruits and toasty oak. Fleshy, rich, and concentrated, it is all a Chardonnay should be. Moreover, it is nicely held together with crisp acidity, essential in a wine of these proportions. The 1991 Chardonnay Barrel Select Unfiltered makes for a huge mouthful of buttery tropical fruit. Full bodied and loaded, this full-throttle Chardonnay's richness and fruit nearly buries the abundant quantities of toasty new oak. The crisp acidity puts everything in focus in this blockbuster Chardonnay. My experience with the aging of California Chardonnay has been one disappointment after another, so don't tempt fate! Drink this beauty over the next 12–18 months. The 1992 Chardonnay from the Sanford & Benedict Vineyard is a compelling example of its type. Although not as fleshy and powerful as the 1991 Barrel Select, it is persuasively rich and full bodied, with a multilayered personality, a subtle use of toasty new oak, and gobs of flavor all buttressed by excellent acidity. It may actually improve over the next 2–3 years. I find Sanford's Sauvignon Blanc to be its most controversial wine. Among the richest and most concentrated of the California Sauvignons, its intense, honeyed and herbaceous character borders on being vegetal. Readers who do not care for too much green in their Sauvignon may want to avoid it. Made in a no-holds-barred style, it is an authoritative example of this varietal. While Sanford's Chardonnays can be stunning, its Pinot Noirs have become increasingly exquisite and are now among the four or five best Pinot Noirs in the United States. The 1992 and 1991 Pinot Noir Sanford & Benedict Vineyard Barrel Select should prove to be exceptional Pinot Noirs of uncommon richness, complexity, and flavor authority. They will be must buys for Pinot Noir enthusiasts. Other offerings include the 1991 Pinot Noir Santa Barbara, a superrich wine with a ravishing nose of raspberries, plums, pepper, and spicy new oak. There is a silky, voluptuous texture, gobs of rich fruit, soft tannins, and wonderful length. A superb example of the heights Pinot Noir can reach in Santa Barbara, it should drink well for another 4–5 years. Remarkably, the 1990 Pinot Noir Sanford & Benedict Vineyard Barrel Select is richer and more profound. In fact, it is one of the greatest American Pinot Noirs I have ever tasted. The dense, deep color is followed by dazzling aromas of Oriental spices, black cherries, toast, and flowers. There is stunning concentration, full body, magnificent richness, and a chewy, succulent, heady finish. This is Pinot Noir at its most decadent and sumptuous! Drink it over the next 7–8 years.

SANTA BARBARA WINERY (SANTA BARBARA)
Cabernet Sauvignon* *, Chardonnay Lafond Vineyard* * */* * * *,
Chardonnay Reserve* */* * *, Pinot Noir* * * (since 1989),
Pinot Noir Reserve* * */* * * * (since 1989)

1988	Cabernet Sauvignon	Santa Ynez	C	72
1990	Chardonnay Lafond Vineyard	Santa Barbara	C	88
1990	Chardonnay Reserve	Santa Barbara	C	84
1989	Chardonnay Reserve	Santa Barbara	C	79
1990	Pinot Noir	Santa Barbara	B	84
1989	Pinot Noir	Santa Barbara	B	76

1990	Pinot Noir Reserve	Santa Barbara	C	86
1989	Pinot Noir Reserve	Santa Barbara	C	83

I cannot think of any winery that has made as much progress with the quality of its wines as the Santa Barbara Winery. Grotesquely vegetal, excessively oaked, high-acid, empty wines were routinely produced in the mid-1980s. Since the late 1980s, however, the quality has soared. Although there is still room for improvement, Santa Barbara is now making some distinctive Chardonnays, with the Reserves displaying good fruit and the single-vineyard Lafond Chardonnay offering classic, nutty, smoky aromas to go along with copious quantities of rich Chardonnay fruit. This is a complex, authoritatively flavored Chardonnay. Santa Barbara's Pinot Noirs have also improved immensely. The vegetal character that plagued them for much of the 1980s has been toned down to a spicy herbaceousness, and the level of concentration has increased, resulting in expansively flavored, juicy, spicy, herbaceous Pinot Noirs for drinking in their first 4–5 years of life. The Reserve exhibits more oak and slightly deeper, richer fruit extraction. The winery continues to suffer with its Cabernet Sauvignon, Zinfandel, and bizarre Beaujour, a fruity but often overtly vegetal wine made in a Beaujolais style from the Zinfandel grape. I have not seen recent vintages, so perhaps this wine has also improved.

SANTA CRUZ MOUNTAIN VINEYARD (SANTA CRUZ)
Cabernet Sauvignon Bates Ranch* * */* * * *, Pinot Noir* * */* * * *

1989	Pinot Noir	Santa Cruz	C	86
1990	Pinot Noir Matteson Vineyard	Santa Cruz	C	85
1989	Pinot Noir Matteson Vineyard	Santa Cruz	C	86

The wines of Santa Cruz Mountain Vineyard are always interesting. Proprietor Ken Burnap has made some huge Cabernet Sauvignons from the Bates Ranch Vineyard and some equally massive Pinot Noirs that may be the biggest and richest wines made from this varietal in California. I still have the 1978, which is becoming more civilized as the Pinot Noir character emerges. It is often hard to give Burnap's wines ecstatic reviews when young, as they are so intense, almost savage in character. It will be interesting to see what he has done in top vintages such as 1990 and 1991 with his Bates Ranch Cabernet Sauvignon. The 1989 and 1988 are relatively light wines. The last two excellent Bates Ranch Cabernets were the 1985 and 1986, and the last really superb Bates Ranch was the 1978. The Pinot Noirs are characterized by untamed aromas of smoky oak, coffee, chocolate, superripe berry fruit, herbs, and pepper. Rich and sometimes intimidating in size, they always stand out in a blind tasting of Pinot Noirs as distinctively different. Nevertheless, my experience suggests that they generally pull themselves together and outage just about anything produced from this grape in California. Current releases feature some excellent 1989s and 1990s, including the new single-vineyard offerings from the Matteson Vineyard. Santa Cruz Mountain Vineyard also produces a Merlot, which can be very good but rarely hits the heights of Burnap's finest Cabernets. Although it is a huge improvement over the mediocre 1987, the 1988 is good rather than dazzling.

SANTINO WINES (AMADOR)

Zinfandel Fiddletown Vineyard* * *, Zinfandel Grand-Père Vineyard* * *

I have not seen any recent vintages of this winery's Zinfandels, but based on past experiences they are often extremely high in alcohol and surprisingly light in color, although richly fruity and clearly of interest for those who like the vivid, exuberant berry fruit of Zinfandel. To me the best wine has always been the Zinfandel from the Grand-Père Vineyard, which is planted with exceptionally old vines. This winery is noted for its white Zinfandel and has also joined the Rhône Rangers with Satyricon, a wine made from a blend of Mourvèdre, Syrah, and Grenache. I have not tasted this offering.

SARAH'S VINEYARD (SANTA CLARA)

Chardonnay Estate* * *, Chardonnay Ventana Vineyard* * *

1988	Chardonnay Estate	Santa Clara	D	87
1989	Chardonnay Ventana Vineyard	Monterey	C	78

This small Chardonnay specialist has raised eyebrows with a pricing policy that borders on the absurd, particularly for wines that, although good, lack the excitement and dramatic richness that would justify a cost of more than $25 a bottle. The 1988 Chardonnay Estate is a boldly oaked, medium- to full-bodied wine, which, although mouth-filling and pleasant, is preposterously overpriced. The 1989 Ventana Vineyard Chardonnay is straightforward and pleasant, but the fruit is not able to stand up to all the wood. In a time when consumers are more leery than ever of pretentiously priced wines that do not deliver quality proportional to their cost, Sarah's Vineyards needs to either produce California's greatest Chardonnay or lower its prices by half.

V. SATTUI WINERY (NAPA)

Cabernet Franc Rosenbrand Vineyard *, Cabernet Sauvignon Cuvées* *,
Zinfandel Suzanne's Vineyard* * *

1990	Cabernet Franc Rosenbrand Vineyard	Napa	C	70
1988	Cabernet Sauvignon Preston Vineyard	Napa	C	82
1989	Cabernet Sauvignon Suzanne's Vineyard	Napa	C	65
1990	Zinfandel Suzanne's Vineyard	Napa	B	73
1987	Zinfandel Suzanne's Vineyard	Napa	B	86

Both the 1990 Cabernet Franc Rosenbrand Vineyard and 1990 Zinfandel Suzanne's Vineyard are so sterile, acidified, and harsh in tannins that there is a shield surrounding what little fruit is present. Since 1990 is unquestionably a top year, one can only wonder how huge the crop size and how harsh the manufacturing process must have been to strip this wine so efficiently. On the other hand, the 1987 Suzanne's Vineyard is a textbook Zinfandel, displaying an abundant use of spicy new oak, rich, raspberry and curranty flavors, medium to full body, and a long, somewhat aggressive finish. One to 2 years of cellaring will round out the wine's tough edges. The aging potential of this wine may well be 8–10 years. Among the most disappointing of these offerings from Sattui is the thin, undernourished, acidic, harsh 1989 Cabernet Sauvignon Suzanne's Vineyard. This angular, hard wine is seriously deficient in fruit—all in all, a pleasureless experience. The 1988 Cabernet Sauvignon Preston Vineyard is typical of many of the Sattui Cabernets—astringent, tough, and hard, without sufficient fruit and ripeness. This winery also produces Sauvignon Blanc and several *cuvées* of Riesling that I have not tasted.

SAUCELITO CANYON VINEYARD (ARROYO GRANDE)
Zinfandel* * * *

1991	Zinfandel	Arroyo Grande	B	89
1990	Zinfandel	Arroyo Grande	B	90

The 1990 Zinfandel has a gorgeous deep purple color and a huge fragrance of intense black cherries, black raspberries, herbs, and minerals; a wonderful, full-bodied, expansive texture; and a spicy, deep, well-delineated, moderately tannic finish. This is a stunning Zinfandel that should continue to drink splendidly for another 7–8 years. The 1991 Saucelito Canyon is a classic Zinfandel that nearly jumps from the glass with peppery, raspberry, and black cherry aromas. Deep, broad, and expansive, this velvety-textured, full-bodied wine is already delicious. Drink it over the next 4–6 years.

SAUSAL (SONOMA)
Chardonnay* * *, Zinfandel* * * *, Zinfandel Private Reserve* * * */* * * * *

1991	Chardonnay	Alexander Valley	B	82
1990	Chardonnay	Alexander Valley	B	83
1990	Zinfandel	Alexander Valley	B	87

Although Sausal's Chardonnays are competent, fresh, lively wines, they are just too straightforward and unexciting. However, the Zinfandel is another matter. Sausal produces a Private Reserve Zinfandel in top vintages, so I would not be surprised to see a special *cuvée* emerge from the 1990 vintage. The regular 1990 offering exhibits a lovely, oaky, tar-, and berry-scented nose; rich, chewy, expansive flavors; plenty of glycerin, extract, and soft tannins; and a long, heady finish. This is a full-bodied, brawny Zinfandel that should age nicely for 7–8 years.

SCHARFFENBERGER CELLARS (MENDOCINO)
Sparkling Wine Cuvées* *

Scharffenberger was sold to the French Champagne producer Pommery several years ago, so it will be interesting to see what direction the wines take. To date, all the Scharffenberger *cuvées* of sparkling wine have been typical of so many California sparkling wines: relatively austere and lean; lacking in fruit, charm, and body; and finishing short. If cleanliness and innocuousness were virtues, these wines would have their place.

SCHRAMSBERG VINEYARDS (NAPA)
Blanc de Blancs Sparkling Wine* *, Brut Rosé* *, Brut Vintage Reserve* *

Schramsberg is a pioneer in the making of *méthode champenoise* California wines. Perhaps because it was one of the first, there was a certain mystique about its product. However, consistent tastings have revealed wines that are often green, short in character, and mediocre. Occasionally one of the Reserve wines will perform slightly above average, but like so many other California sparkling wines, once past the glimmering bubbles there is a noticeable deficiency in fruit, character, and charm. It should be obvious, although few will acknowledge it, that the growing season in most of Napa Valley is entirely too short, the soils too rich, the climate too hot, and the crop yields too abundant to produce rich, complex sparkling wines. I hope the future proves me wrong. Certainly outside Napa there is room for optimism given the performances of the Roederer Estate, the Domaine Mumm, Sonoma Valley's Iron Horse sparkling wine operation and the Central Coast's Deutz bubbly offerings.

SCHUG CELLARS (SONOMA)
Chardonnay Beckstoffer Vineyard* *, Pinot Noir Beckstoffer Vineyard* *,
Pinot Noir Heinemann Vineyard* *

1990	Chardonnay Beckstoffer Vineyard	Carneros	C	82
1988	Chardonnay Beckstoffer Vineyard	Carneros	C	72
1989	Pinot Noir Beckstoffer Vineyard	Carneros	C	70
1988	Pinot Noir Beckstoffer Vineyard	Carneros	C	74

It is impossible to understand what might be wrong at this winery. Walter Schug was responsible for many of the greatest wines Joseph Phelps produced during the 1970s. His philosophy of winemaking, which emphasizes minimal intervention, seems totally appropriate for the production of high-quality Chardonnay and Pinot Noir. Yet to date the wines have lacked fruit and concentration, with the Chardonnay too tart, crisp, and austere, with no charm or character. The Pinot Noirs have been plagued consistently by a pervasive, earthy, vegetal character that dominates what little fruit is present. The wines are either simple and fruity or too vegetal and hollow, with excessive acidity and bitter tannins in the finish. Schug has proven the enormous talent he possesses, so what is wrong?

SEA RIDGE WINERY (SONOMA)
Chardonnay* *, Pinot Noir* *

1989	Chardonnay Mill Station	Sonoma	C	74
1990	Pinot Noir Hirsch Vineyard	Sonoma	C	83
1989	Pinot Noir Hirsch Vineyard	Sonoma	C	78
N. V.	Rustic Red	North Coast	A	85

Looking for a wine that suggests Pinot Noir and can be purchased for $6? This one, inappropriately named Rustic Red (it is elegant rather than rustic), exhibits a moderately intense, raspberry-scented bouquet; ripe, tasty, soft Pinot Noir flavors; enough acidity for focus; and a clean, fresh, fruity finish. Drink it over the next 1–2 years. Oddly enough, I prefer Sea Ridge's nonvintage red wine blend to its Pinot Noir and Chardonnay. At one time this winery showed considerable promise with its Pinot Noir, but the wines have become lighter, with a simple, berry fruitiness and a lack of complexity and depth. The 1989 Chardonnay is already losing its fruit, revealing signs of oxidation.

SEBASTIANI WINERY (SONOMA)
Barbera* */* * *, Cabernet Sauvignon Regular Cuvées* *, Cabernet Sauvignon
Single-Vineyard Cuvées* * *, Chardonnay Regular Cuvées* *,
Chardonnay Single-Vineyard Cuvées* * *, Other Wines* *

1988	Barbera	Sonoma	A	60
1987	Barbera	Sonoma	A	86
1989	Cabernet Sauvignon	Sonoma	B	77
1991	Chardonnay	Sonoma	A	85
1989	Zinfandel	Sonoma	A	74

The 1987 Barbera exhibits that intense, tomato-scented, smoky, almost gamey aroma of Barbera, a rich, robust, full-bodied texture, good rather than excessive acidity, and a spicy, intense finish. Wines such as this are the perfect foil for lasagna and other pasta dishes. The 1988 is disappointingly thin and light. The 1991 Chardonnay is a dramatic improvement over the regular *cuvées* of Chardonnay that have recently emerged from this winery. Fruity, with good depth and ripeness, it provides considerable character for a modest price. Sebastiani Winery went through considerable turmoil during the 1980s, at the height of which Sam Sebastiani was replaced by his brother Donn. Many changes have taken place since, but essentially the hierarchy of Sebastiani wines starts with its so-called Country wines, which are simple, pleasant jug wines that are often a better value than some of their more expensive offerings. Of course the blends often change with each vintage, but the Zinfandel Country can be a pleasant, one-dimensional wine that sells for under $10 for a 1.5-liter bottle. It rarely has a vintage designation. Sebastiani also has Sonoma varietals, of which the best current offerings are the 1991 Chardonnay and the 1987 Barbera. The Merlot and Cabernet Sauvignon have been mediocre at best. There are also estate bottlings, all of which sell for $15–$20 a bottle. The wines released have all been vineyard-designated and include Chardonnays from the Clark Ranch, Kinneybrook, Wildwood, and Wilson Ranch vineyards. There are also Cabernet Sauvignons from the Bell Ranch and Cherry Block vineyards. These wines have been at least above average in quality, with point ratings consistently in the 83–86 range. However, the most recent vintages I have seen were the 1988 Chardonnay, which could already be starting to fade, and the 1986 and 1987 Cherry Block and Bell Ranch Cabernet Sauvignons, which are good but not exciting. Perhaps as we move into the 1990s, the identity of Sebastiani will become more delineated under the leadership of Donn Sebastiani. Certainly Sebastiani has enormous resources and potentially excellent vineyards.

SEGHESIO WINERY (SONOMA)
Cabernet Sauvignon* *, Chardonnay* *, Pinot Noir*, Sauvignon Blanc* *,
Zinfandel* * *, Zinfandel Reserve* * *

1990	Cabernet Sauvignon	Sonoma	A	75
1991	Chardonnay	Sonoma	A	81
1990	Pinot Noir	Sonoma	A	73
1990	Zinfandel	Sonoma	A	84
1990	Zinfandel Reserve	Sonoma	C	85

This winery is a reliable source for reasonably priced wines that are serviceable and tasty. The Chardonnay is light but pleasant. The two Zinfandels, probably Seghesio's best wines, are richly fruity, with the Reserve being a more tannic, bigger wine. The 1990 Reserve is one of the best Zinfandels I have tasted from Seghesio. The Sauvignon Blanc tends to be fruity, light, and refreshing. If there are any disappointments, they are the herbaceous, light Pinot Noir and the one-dimensional Cabernet Sauvignon. This winery has also begun to experiment with Italian varietals. In 1991 it released a pleasant but unexciting Sangiovese. There are also generic wines that sell for about $6 a bottle; notables include a straightforward, pleasant white wine called Strata and a similarly named red wine that exhibits fine berry fruit and a soft texture. This underrated producer is turning out light- to medium-bodied wines with round, fresh red fruit, good ripeness, soft tannins, and an up-front, easy to appreciate and consume style. The 1990 Zinfandel should be drunk over the next 2–4 years.

SEQUOIA GROVE WINERY (NAPA)

Cabernet Sauvignon Estate* * *, Cabernet Sauvignon Napa* * *,
Chardonnay Carneros* *, Chardonnay Estate* *

1988	Cabernet Sauvignon	Napa	C	78
1987	Cabernet Sauvignon	Napa	C	85
1988	Cabernet Sauvignon Estate	Napa	C	83
1987	Cabernet Sauvignon Estate	Napa	C	86
1990	Chardonnay Estate	Napa	C	86

This winery consistently turns out reliable, solid wines that are neither exciting nor disappointing. One can expect a flavorful, medium- to full-bodied, straightforward, chunky style. Of the two Cabernet Sauvignons, the best is usually the Estate bottling. The wine emphasizes plenty of sweet oak and herbaceous, cassis fruit, light to moderate tannins, medium body, and a soft, round finish. Although it is not meant for long-term cellaring, it can easily last for 10 years. The two 1987 *cuvées* are richer than the light, lean 1988s. The 1990 Chardonnay Estate is a big, rich wine that suffers from a lack of complexity. I enjoyed its purity, chewy, fleshy flavors, and long finish.

SHAFER VINEYARDS (NAPA)

Cabernet Sauvignon Hillside Select* * * */* * * * * (since 1986), Cabernet Sauvignon
Stag's Leap* * *, Chardonnay* * * *, Merlot* * * *

1991	Cabernet Sauvignon Hillside Select	Napa	D	89
1990	Cabernet Sauvignon Hillside Select	Napa	D	89
1988	Cabernet Sauvignon Hillside Select	Napa	D	85
1987	Cabernet Sauvignon Hillside Select	Napa	D	91
1988	Cabernet Sauvignon Stag's Leap	Napa	C	85
1991	Chardonnay	Napa	D	87
1990	Chardonnay	Napa	C	90
1990	Merlot	Napa	C	87
1987	Merlot	Napa	C	87

Shafer's style of Cabernet results in one of the more graceful, subtle, and supple wines produced in Napa Valley. It bears a kinship in texture and weight to Cabernets from Stag's Leap Winery, without its exotic eccentricities. Shafer's 1991 is a classic example of an elegant, gracefully put together Cabernet, with a spicy, toasty, cherry-scented nose and wonderfully ripe, velvety flavors that exhibit a broad, expansive texture and excellent ripeness. The finish is long, stylish, and altogether satisfying. **Anticipated maturity: 1995–2005.** The 1990 is medium-weight and oaky, with a suave, berry fragrance, and rich, ripe berry flavors touched by herbaceous scents. My instincts suggest this wine may be going through an awkward stage, so my rating may be conservative. The 1988 Hillside Select is supple, fruity, and charming, but significantly less well endowed than the 1987, 1990, and 1991. Drink it between 1994 and 2000. The 1987 Cabernet Sauvignon Hillside Select displays an attractive dark ruby color; a big, spicy, vanillin-, chocolate-, herb-, and blackcurrant-scented nose; ripe, deep, full-bodied flavors; velvety texture; and a long, graceful finish. There is not a tough edge to be found in this meticulously crafted wine. Given its balance and extract levels, it should age well for at least 10–12 years. The 1988 Stag's Leap Cabernet Sauvignon is lighter and relatively straightforward, with an herbal, chocolatey character that is also found in the 1987 Hillside Select. The Stag's Leap *cuvée* does not possess the great richness and length of the Hillside Select. Drink it over the next 4–5 years. The 1990 Merlot offers up copious quantities of herbs, coffee, and plummy fruit and a luscious, medium- to full-bodied, soft texture. It is ideal for drinking now and over the next 5–6 years. Merlot enthusiasts will enjoy the 1987 Merlot's big, open bouquet of herbs, ripe plummy fruit, and spices. In the mouth it manifests more structure than many 1987 Merlots but still continues to provide charm as a result of its unabashed fruitiness and plump, round, generous texture. Delicious for drinking now, it should age well for another 4–5 years. As good as it is, the 1991 Chardonnay does not have the richness or impact on the palate that the 1990 possesses. Nevertheless it is a fine, elegant, richly fruity wine with a smoky, buttery, apple-scented nose, good acidity, and an overall sense of grace and balance. Drink it over the next 1–2 years. Shafer's 1990 Chardonnay gets my nod as the best this winery has yet produced. There is almost a Meursault-like nuttiness to its honeyed, tropical fruit–scented nose. In the mouth there is superb fruit, deep, concentrated flavors, good acidity, and a full-bodied, luscious finish. It should drink well for 1–2 years.

RATINGS FOR OLDER VINTAGES OF SHAFER VINEYARDS CABERNET SAUVIGNON HILLSIDE SELECT: 1986 (90), 1985 (88), 1984 (87), 1983 (83), 1982 (87)

SHENANDOAH VINEYARDS (AMADOR)

Cabernet Sauvignon Amador* */* * *, Sauvignon Blanc* *, Zinfandel Special
Reserve* *, Zinfandel Sobon Estate* * *

1991	Sauvignon Blanc	Amador	B	75
1991	Zinfandel	Amador	A	60
1990	Zinfandel Sobon Estate	Amador	B	85
1991	Zinfandel Special Reserve	Amador	B	70
1990	Zinfandel Special Reserve	Amador	B	78?

Proprietor/winemaker Leon Sobon has long enjoyed a fine reputation for his Amador County Zinfandels. However, the 1990 Special Reserve is completely dominated by wood, extremely acidic, and so closed, backward, and tight, I had a difficult time finding any fruit. I suspect there is more to the wine, but when I tasted it, it was closed. The 1990 Sobon Estate is a more conventional, textbook Zinfandel, with the classic, briery, blackberry-scented nose intermingled with aromas of pepper. On the palate the wine displays fine character, spicy new oak, medium to full body, and a gutsy fruitiness. Drink it over the next 4–5 years.

SIERRA VISTA (EL DORADO)
Cabernet Sauvignon* *, Chardonnay* *, Syrah* *, Zinfandel* * *

1988	Cabernet Sauvignon	El Dorado	B	85
1989	Syrah	El Dorado	B	73
1990	Zinfandel	El Dorado	B	86
1989	Zinfandel	El Dorado	B	83

Reasonably priced, underrated wines frequently emerge from this El Dorado winery. The 1990 Zinfandel possesses a vividly pure nose of black raspberries, followed by rich, medium- to full-bodied, ripe, concentrated flavors that offer up soft tannins, heady alcohol and glycerin, and a moderately endowed, rich finish. Drink it over the next 5–6 years. The 1989 Zinfandel does not share the intensity or length of the 1990, but it does offer elegant, spicy, berry, earthy fruit flavors, medium body, and tough tannins in the finish. I doubt that all the tannins will melt away, so I would opt for drinking this rustic wine over the next 3–4 years.

SIGNORELLO VINEYARDS (NAPA)
Cabernet Sauvignon Founder's Reserve* * * *, Chardonnay* * * *, Chardonnay Founder's Reserve* * * */* * * * *, Pinot Noir* * * *, Sauvignon Blanc* * * *, Semillon Founder's Reserve* * * *, Zinfandel* * *

1989	Cabernet Sauvignon Founder's Reserve	Napa	C	90
1988	Cabernet Sauvignon	Napa	C	86
1991	Chardonnay	Napa	B	86
1990	Chardonnay	Napa	B	89
1990	Chardonnay Founder's Reserve Unfiltered	Napa	C	93
1991	Il Taglio Proprietary White Wine	Napa	B	78
1988	Pinot Noir	Napa	C	88
1991	Sauvignon Blanc	Napa	B	84
1989	Sauvignon Blanc	Napa	B	87
1990	Semillon Barrel Fermented	Napa	C	90
1988	Semillon Founder's Reserve	Napa	C	87
1990	Zinfandel	Napa	C	88

This winery is making some of the most exciting wines in Napa Valley. Unfortunately, less than 100 cases of the 1990 Zinfandel were produced. The wine's label notes it was bottled unfined and unfiltered, which to me signifies Signorello's willingness to accept some risk by bottling a wine that has not been eviscerated or sterilized. The gorgeously ripe, rich berry fruit is married gently with attractive smoky, toasty new oak. In the mouth there is an attractive opulence, medium to full body, and a silky, long finish. According to the winery, the grapes came from a 100-year old hillside vineyard near Calistoga, which seems likely given the intensity and length of this wine. Drink it over the next 7–10 years. The 1989 Cabernet Sauvignon Founder's Reserve clearly demonstrates the high points that were occasionally reached in this inconsistent vintage. This wine, which was bottled unfined and unfiltered, boasts an opaque, deep ruby/purple color, and the nose offers up classic Cabernet odors of weedy cassis, tobacco, cedar, and sweet new oak. In the mouth the wine is rich and full bodied, with ripe tannins and a beautifully balanced, long, generously endowed finish. Because of its softness this wine is approachable now, but it should continue to make outstanding drinking for at least a decade. In what was a difficult vintage, Signorello has turned out an expansively flavored, plummy, toasty, oaky, rich, generously endowed 1988 Cabernet Sauvignon with low acidity and a forward, captivating personality. The rich aromas of cassis and sweet oak offer plenty of appeal. Drink this charmer over the next 4–7 years. Look out, Burgundy! The progress some California wineries have made with Pinot Noir over the last few years is striking. Here is another example of a luscious, complex, rich, nearly compelling Pinot Noir that could embarrass a great majority of France's red burgundies that sell for 3–4 times the price. This 1988 Pinot comes close to resembling 1988 Robert Mondavi's Reserve. It is crammed with hedonistic levels of sumptuous strawberry and black cherry fruit, has a nice touch of oak, sustains that fleshy, velvety texture in the mouth that makes burgundy so enthralling. The finish is sweet and expansive, almost like eating candy, another characteristic reminiscent of great burgundy. This is an extremely impressive effort from a new winery. I am also delighted to report that the wine was bottled unfined and unfiltered, much like the 1988 Robert Mondavi Reserve. Drink this sexy Pinot over the next 4–5 years. The spectacular 1990 Semillon Barrel Fermented exhibits a huge, waxy, honeyed, lemony, almost Thai lemon grass sort of nose; superb rich, chewy, multidimensional flavors; a texture that suggests high extraction of flavor and/or low yields; and a long, heady finish. It would be excellent with grilled fish. The 1988 Semillon Founder's Reserve is a rich, full wine and one of the best Semillons I have tasted from Napa Valley. The waxy, leafy, exotic bouquet is followed by a relatively dense, concentrated, chewy wine that is meant to be served with fish dishes such as salmon, bluefish, lobster, or scallops. In the mouth there are gobs of fruit, medium to full body, and enough acidity and toasty oak to provide the proper parameters for definition and focus. After tasting Signorello's 1989 Sauvignon Blanc, you would not believe that 1989 was actually a difficult vintage for California's white wines. The melony, herb-, floral-scented bouquet jumps from the glass. In the mouth there is a touch of toasty new oak to give the wine some structure and add a degree of flavor dimension. Surprisingly rich and concentrated, this well-balanced, impeccably made wine should drink nicely for at least another 12–18 months. The two 1990 Chardonnays are also undeniable successes. The regular *cuvée* of Chardonnay is a reasonably priced, rich, full-bodied, buttery wine with loads of apple-, pineapple-, and popcorn-flavored fruit that has been judiciously touched with sweet new oak. This wine, which has freshness allied with considerable power and flavor authority, should drink well for at least a year. The 1991 is lighter, yet juicy and tasty. Speaking of taking the ultimate risk, the Signorellos bottled their 1990 Founder's Reserve Chardonnay unfiltered in order to give the consumer all the flavor the vineyard produced. They should be commended. Other than the Domaine de la Romanée-Conti, Domaine Coche-Dury, and Domaine Comte Lafon in France, and American wineries such as Kalin, Newton, Pahlmeyer, Patz and Hall, Basignani, Evesham Wood, and Sanford, I cannot think of another top producer willing to take such a gamble. Anyone fortunate enough to run across a bottle of this compelling Chardonnay (only 250 cases were produced) must give in to temptation: the huge nose of buttered popcorn, tropical fruits, and toasty new oak is followed by a wine with exquisite flavor richness, brilliant definition to its flavor profile, and a splendidly opulent, long, clean finish. No doubt this is a magnificent Chardonnay that proves what amazing heights this grape can achieve when made without compromise. Drink it over the next 2–3 years. Move quickly, as this winery is becoming a reference point for quality in the Napa Valley. At the time of this printing, Signorello had just released its 1991 Sauvignon Blanc, which was much lighter than the 1990, and a white proprietary wine, the 1991 Il Taglio. The latter offering is a charming but essentially light-bodied, fresh, fruity wine for drinking over the next several years.

SILVER OAK CELLARS (NAPA)

Cabernet Sauvignon Alexander Valley* * * */* * * * *, Cabernet Sauvignon Napa* * * */* * * * *, Cabernet Sauvignon Bonny's Vineyard* * * */* * * * *

1988	Cabernet Sauvignon	Alexander Valley	D	82
1987	Cabernet Sauvignon	Alexander Valley	D	89
1988	Cabernet Sauvignon	Napa	D	84
1987	Cabernet Sauvignon	Napa	D	90
1987	Cabernet Sauvignon Bonny's Vineyard	Napa	E	86
1986	Cabernet Sauvignon Bonny's Vineyard	Napa	E	92

Napa Valley's leading hedonist, winemaker/proprietor Justin Meyer, has again made top-notch Cabernets in 1987. However, they do not have quite the weight, richness, and multidimensional character of his 1984s, 1985s, and 1986s. The 1988s are barely above average. The 1987 Alexander Valley has a big, dramatic, spicy, oaky, smoky nose that is also intermingled with aromas of herbs and black fruits. In the mouth it offers a big, generous, supple mouthful of Cabernet fruit bolstered by adequate acidity. The wine is framed nicely by the vanillin notes of American oak—another elegant, very smooth and forward Cabernet for drinking over the next 7–8 years. The 1987 Napa Valley Cabernet offers more of a black fruit character in the nose and less of the herbaceous, spicy component found in the Alexander Valley. It is also a bit denser, more tannic, and slightly deeper and more ageworthy than the Alexander Valley. Irresistibly precocious, it can be guzzled now with great pleasure, but it could also be cellared for at least a decade. The 1987 Bonny's Vineyard is a controversial wine. The almost pickle-barrel smell in the nose will be as much loved as it is detested, yet the wine exhibits huge amounts of fruit and depth. This could potentially turn out to be an outstanding Cabernet, but the pickly, vegetal qualities in the nose have kept my rating conservative. I must say in defense that that character, often present in other Bonny's Vineyard Cabernets in their youth, does age into a sweet, almost cedary component with cellaring. If that happens here, the 1987 will merit a much higher score. The 1986 Bonny's Vineyard is another exotic, rich, distinctive, individualistic wine that should have Cabernet enthusiasts drooling. The huge bouquet of coffee, herbs, Oriental spices, black fruits, tobacco, and new oak has about everything one could want in a top Cabernet. In the mouth it exhibits rich, full-bodied, smooth, spicy flavors and a long, dazzling finish. Although it does not have the size of the 1985 or 1984, it is still a big, chewy, classic expression of Cabernet Sauvignon from one of California's very finest wineries. Drink it over the next 10–12 years. Both the 1988 Alexander Valley and Napa Valley Cabernets from Silver Oak are barely above average in quality. They possess adequate color, but both suffer from intensely herbaceous, even vegetal noses. The new oak is more aggressive because the underlying richness and extraction of fruit is missing, and the finish is relatively short. The wines have some up-front appeal, but if you were weaned on the Silver Oak 1984s, 1985, 1986, and 1987s, you are going to be disappointed with these lightweight, aggressively oaky, vegetal wines.

RATINGS FOR OLDER VINTAGES OF SILVER OAK CELLARS CABERNET SAUVIGNONS:
ALEXANDER VALLEY: 1986 (90), 1985 (92), 1984 (92), 1983 (85)
NAPA VALLEY: 1986 (91), 1985 (96), 1984 (95), 1983 (78)
BONNY'S VINEYARD: 1985 (96), 1984 (97), 1983 (87), 1982 (83), 1981 (86), 1980 (87)

SILVERADO VINEYARDS (NAPA)
Cabernet Sauvignon* *, Chardonnay* * *, Chardonnay Limited Reserve* * * * *,
Sauvignon Blanc* *

1988	Cabernet Sauvignon Stag's Leap	Napa	C	84
1987	Cabernet Sauvignon Stag's Leap	Napa	C	86
1990	Chardonnay	Napa	B	84
1990	Chardonnay Limited Reserve	Napa	D	93
1991	Sauvignon Blanc	Napa	A	82

This winery, owned by the widow of the late Walt Disney, is making Cabernet Sauvignons that are one-dimensional and too acidified. However, I enjoy its attractive cassis fruit even if it is packaged in a compact, angular style. The one wine that will send you to the Magic Kingdom is the Limited Reserve Chardonnay. The 1990's explosive bouquet offers enticing aromas of vanillin, smoke, coconuts, and honeyed fruit. There is great structure, superb richness, multidimensional flavors, a chewy texture, and high acidity. The overall impression is of a sensationally concentrated, well-knit Chardonnay with tremendous richness and impeccable balance. All the components are present for 2–3 years of compelling drinking. This is the first time Silverado has made this wine since its stunning 1987. The crisp, light, fruity Sauvignon Blanc, although not exciting, is competently made and refreshing. The winery also produces a Merlot. If the 1986, 1987, and 1988 vintages are any indication, this is a fruity, medium-bodied wine made within well-defined technical parameters—just the right acidity, just the right body, and too heavy a reliance on the filter at bottling.

SIMI WINERY (SONOMA)

Cabernet Sauvignon* * *, Cabernet Sauvignon Reserve* * * */* * * * * (since 1986), Chardonnay* * *, Chardonnay Reserve* * */* * * *, Chenin Blanc* *, Rosé of Cabernet Sauvignon* * *, Semillon* *, Sendal Proprietary White Wine* * * *

1988	Cabernet Sauvignon	Alexander Valley	B	78
1989	Cabernet Sauvignon	Alexander Valley	B	82
1988	Cabernet Sauvignon	Alexander Valley	C	82
1987	Cabernet Sauvignon	Alexander Valley	C	87
1986	Cabernet Sauvignon	Alexander Valley	C	87
1985	Cabernet Sauvignon	Sonoma	C	85
1988	Cabernet Sauvignon Reserve	Sonoma	D	86
1987	Cabernet Sauvignon Reserve	Sonoma	D	94
1986	Cabernet Sauvignon Reserve	Sonoma	D	91
1985	Cabernet Sauvignon Reserve	Sonoma	D	88
1988	Chardonnay Reserve	Sonoma	D	89
1990	Semillon	Napa	B	86
1990	Sendal Proprietary White Wine	Sonoma	C	88

The 1988 Cabernet Sauvignon Reserve, although not bad for the vintage, is much more narrowly constructed and not nearly as rich as the three previous vintages. The 1987 Cabernet Sauvignon Reserve is Simi's finest Cabernet to date. The opaque color suggests considerable richness and intensity. The complex nose offers aromas of licorice, toast, cassis, herbs, and berry fruits. In the mouth there is spectacular concentration, medium to full body, ripe tannins, and adequate acidity. This is a classic Cabernet that balances power and richness with elegance and finesse; it is one of the stars of this vintage, and it belongs in the cellar of any admirer of California Cabernet Sauvignon. Although somewhat closed, the 1986 Cabernet Sauvignon Reserve is nevertheless a stunningly rich, complex wine with aromas of herbs, mocha, blackcurrants, licorice, and toasty oak. In the mouth it exhibits elegance and power (not an easy thing to achieve), layer upon layer of fruit, a fine structure, good but not excessive acidity, and soft tannins in its rich, admirably extracted finish. This beauty can be drunk now or cellared for 15–20 years. Based on the barrel samples I tasted, I had hoped the 1985 Cabernet Sauvignon Reserve would turn out to be outstanding. It has not. But it is still a classic, elegantly rendered, beautifully made Cabernet Sauvignon that has soft, delicious, blackcurrant fruitiness buttressed intelligently by spicy new oak. In the mouth it is medium to full bodied, long, rich, and gracefully built for drinking both now and over the next 8–10 years. The 1988 Cabernet Sauvignon is light, pleasant, soft, and ideal for drinking over the next 3–4 years. The 1987 Cabernet Sauvignon is Simi's finest regular bottling in my memory. Possessing a deep ruby/purple color, a rich, spicy, herbaceous, cassis-scented bouquet, full-bodied, firmly structured flavors, and excellent concentration, this relatively backward 1987 displays considerable palate presence. Although approachable now, it should not be fully mature for at least 3–4 years. Moreover, it has the potential to last until at least 2005. Impressive! For the difference in price, smart buyers might well be advised to opt for Simi's 1986 regular bottling rather than the Reserve. Of course, Libourne's famed oenologist, Michel Rolland, helped consult on the making of this wine, and one can see the positive influence his remarkable talents have had. The wine is initially closed, so decanting 35–40 minutes prior to drinking is recommended. Dark ruby in color, with a classy and ever-expanding bouquet of blackcurrants, plums, toasty new oak, and minerals, this rich yet restrained, medium- to full-bodied Cabernet Sauvignon has crisp, integrated acidity and a long finish with gentle tannins—an excellent example of this varietal, and the most complete and complex regular Cabernet Simi has made in many years. Drink the regular 1986 *cuvée* over the next 10–12 years. The elegantly crafted, curranty, medium-bodied 1985 Cabernet Sauvignon has a moderately intense, herb-tinged, black fruit–scented bouquet, good acidity, soft tannins, and an overall impression of gracefulness and charm. It should be drunk over the next 5–6 years. The 1988 Chardonnay Reserve offers an intriguing nose of oak, butter, and tropical fruits. In the mouth the overall impression is one of elegance and ripeness. Full bodied, but also restrained, this wine exhibits a spicy, clean, graceful finish. Moreover, the oak is subtle rather than aggressive, which cannot be said of previous offerings. The wine should continue to drink well for 1–2 years. Understated, citrusy, and elegant, the interesting 1990 Semillon exhibits abundant fruit and fine crispness. The herbal, waxy, honeyed character of the Semillon grape is nicely displayed in a lighter style. The winery's new proprietary white wine, Sendal, has a French Graves–like melony, rich, discreet nose, medium-bodied, lovely flavors, and an authoritative, fruity, dry finish. I thought it to be impressive! Simi's regular *cuvée* of Chardonnay is quite delicious. It should be sought out by those who like a lovely, rich, fruity Chardonnay made in a medium- to full-bodied format. In some vintages it is actually more enjoyable than the Reserve, which has a tendency to be released late and, consequently, can be too oaky and already dropping some of its fruit. Simi also does a superlative job with its rosé, which is made from Cabernet Sauvignon. This is one of the better off-dry styles of rosé made in California; it has a pronounced herbal quality, which may not work well in a red wine but in a chilled rosé adds an interesting component. Normally it must be drunk within a year of the vintage. If there is a disappointing wine in Simi's portfolio, it is the dull, medium- sweet Chenin Blanc. I was particularly disappointed with the 1990.

ROBERT SINSKEY (NAPA)

Chardonnay* * *, Claret* *, Pinot Noir* * */* * * *

1988	Claret Proprietary Red Wine	Carneros	B	86
1990	Pinot Noir Signature Reserve	Russian River Valley	C	87

Sinskey fashions attractive wines. The 1988 Carneros Claret, an innovative blend of 59% Merlot, 22% Cabernet Sauvignon, and 19% Cabernet Franc, exhibits tasty, spicy, berry flavors, crisp acidity, fine texture, and soft tannins in the finish. If it had possessed more of a bouquet, I would have given it a higher score. The 1990 Pinot Noir is also an attractive, medium-bodied wine with spicy, berry, herbaceous fruit, a touch of toasty oak, medium body, fine glycerin, and a soft, velvety finish.

SKY VINEYARDS (NAPA)
Zinfandel* * *

1990	Zinfandel Estate	Napa	B	87

This producer of microscopic quantities of Zinfandel has a cult following. Although the quality of its wines appears to be consistently inconsistent, the 1990 Zinfandel is a fine example of this varietal. Dark ruby, with a fragrant nose of black raspberries and black cherries, this spicy, medium-bodied wine displays zesty acidity, excellent purity and crispness to its fruit, and a medium-bodied, stylish, elegant finish. The purity and overall balance of this streamlined version of Zinfandel are impeccable. Drink it over the next 7–8 years.

SONOMA-CUTRER (SONOMA)
Chardonnay Cutrer Vineyard* * */* * * *, Chardonnay Les Pierres* * */* * * *, Chardonnay Russian River Ranches* * *

1990	Chardonnay Cutrer Vineyard	Sonoma	C	86
1990	Chardonnay Les Pierres	Sonoma	C	89
1990	Chardonnay Russian River Ranches	Sonoma	C	84

This winery, which is one of the showcase operations in California and worth a visit, may be stretching its production to accommodate the massive demand, resulting in the lighter wines that have emerged over recent vintages. Nevertheless, it has become one of the most popular California Chardonnay producers, with three distinctive styles of Chardonnay. The Russian River Ranches offering is the fruitiest, with wonderful purity and freshness. This offering seems to tail off in quality in vintages after 1986. Although no longer as concentrated, it is still a good Chardonnay that emphasizes plenty of fruit, good acidity, and just enough wood. In the early and middle 1980s, the Cutrer Vineyard *cuvée* was loaded with tropical fruit balanced nicely by toasty, smoky oak. Like the Russian River Ranches offering, the Cutrer Vineyard wine has lightened up over recent vintages. Even in the outstanding 1990 vintage the wine is not as full or deep as I would have expected. Les Pierres is potentially the finest of the Sonoma-Cutrer Chardonnays. It is also the most backward and has a distinctive personality. With a mineral, stony component intertwined with aromas of lemons, oranges, and apples, this wine offers copious quantities of buttery, honeyed fruit buttressed by toasty oak. It, too, has lightened up over recent vintages, with the last superb Les Pierres made in the mid-1980s. On the positive side, the 1990 is the best Les Pierres since the 1985. In summary, what we have is a state-of-the-art winemaking facility, unimpeachable vinification techniques, and an intelligent policy toward aging the wine prior to release. All of this should be synonymous with consistently brilliant wines. Yet after a strong start, and despite every conceivable caution to avoid hazards (particularly exposure to oxidation), Sonoma-Cutrer's offerings are no different from most other California Chardonnays when it comes to aging. In short, consumers must drink them within 2–4 years of the vintage.

CHÂTEAU SOUVERAIN (SONOMA)

Cabernet Sauvignon* * * (since 1990), Chardonnay Sonoma* * * (since 1990),
Merlot* *, Sonoma Single-Vineyard Cuvées* * *, Zinfandel* */* * *

1990	Chardonnay Allen Vineyard Reserve	Russian River	B	83
1990	Chardonnay Barrel Fermented	Sonoma	A	85
1990	Chardonnay Durell Vineyard	Sonoma	B	86
1990	Chardonnay Sangiacomo Vineyard Reserve	Carneros	B	84
1990	Merlot	Sonoma	B	72
1990	Zinfandel	Dry Creek	A	86
1989	Zinfandel	Dry Creek	A	79

Long in the qualitative doldrums, this winery appears to have benefited from considerable infusion of capital by its new owners. The new releases exhibit more fruit and style than anything Souverain has produced in more than 15 years. For example, the 1990 Zinfandel, significantly richer and more interesting than the 1989, reveals an excellent nose of peppery, berry fruit, ripe, medium- to full-bodied flavors, good density, and soft tannins in the smooth finish. Drink it over the next 4–5 years. The 1989 Zinfandel, which is noticeably lighter in color, is pleasant but essentially light-bodied and one-dimensional. It requires immediate consumption. For the price, Château Souverain's 1990 barrel-fermented Chardonnay is an ambitiously styled wine. There is plenty of buttery fruit and smoky toast in its moderately intense bouquet. In the mouth the wine exhibits fine richness, good focus and purity, and a concentrated finish. I would opt for consuming it over the next year. All the other wines from the 1990 vintage on appear to be much improved, particularly the single-vineyard Chardonnays and Cabernets. However, the 1990 Merlot was disappointingly light and vegetal. With a new label and obviously higher ambitions, as well as a realistic pricing policy, Château Souverain may deserve more notice during the 1990s.

SPOTTSWOODE VINEYARD AND WINERY (NAPA)

Cabernet Sauvignon* * * *, Sauvignon Blanc* * *

1991	Cabernet Sauvignon	Napa	D	88
1990	Cabernet Sauvignon	Napa	D	89
1989	Cabernet Sauvignon	Napa	D	84
1988	Cabernet Sauvignon	Napa	D	83
1987	Cabernet Sauvignon	Napa	D	87

Spottswoode's 1991 Cabernet Sauvignon exhibits a deep ruby color, a perfumed nose of cassis and new oak, soft, moderately concentrated flavors, and a smooth finish. **Anticipated maturity: 1994–2003.** The deep ruby/purple color of Spottswoode's 1990 Cabernet Sauvignon is followed by a wine with moderately intense aromas of cassis, vanillin, and licorice. In the mouth the wine is medium bodied, with surprisingly high acidity for a 1990, firm tannins, and excellent length and richness. This attractive, elegant wine should be at its best between 1995 and 2005. Spottswoode's flavorful 1989 Cabernet has a good deep ruby color, a relatively subdued bouquet, and medium-bodied, tart, compact flavors wrapped in an elegant and medium-bodied, although one-dimensional, package. It should drink well for the next 5–7 years. The 1988 Cabernet Sauvignon is slightly softer and again light, without the depth, richness, or concentration of Spottswoode's finest vintages. Drink it over the next 7–8 years. The deep ruby-colored 1987 Cabernet Sauvignon has a moderately intense bouquet of pure cassis fruit intertwined with scents of minerals, toast, and licorice. In the mouth the wine is medium bodied, slightly and surprisingly tart and angular, but ripe, concentrated, and gracefully rendered. The tannins are astringent and noticeably aggressive. At present this wine appears to have less depth and power than the outstanding 1984, 1985, and 1986.

RATINGS FOR OLDER VINTAGES OF SPOTTSWOODE CABERNET SAUVIGNON: 1986 (92), 1985 (93), 1984 (89), 1983 (85), 1982 (88)

SPRING MOUNTAIN VINEYARDS (NAPA)
Cabernet Sauvignon* *

| 1988 | Cabernet Sauvignon | Napa | C | 79 |

This is the only recent tasting note I have from Spring Mountain, which has fallen on tough times. The winery appears content to make technically correct, mediocre wines, whether Cabernet Sauvignon or Chardonnay. This 1988 Cabernet is light, with a lot of green tannins in the finish. Drink it over the next 3–4 years.

STAGLIN (NAPA)
Cabernet Sauvignon* * * *

| 1990 | Cabernet Sauvignon | Napa | C | 90 |

An exceptionally elegant, stylistic Cabernet Sauvignon, this wine appears to be trying to imitate a graceful Bordeaux. Its purity, sense of style, and deep, rich, spicy, cassis flavors, intertwined with well-integrated new oak, make for an impressive performance. There is good underlying acidity as well as an impeccable sense of balance. This restrained yet successful wine brilliantly juxtaposes richness and finesse. It should last for at least a decade.

STAG'S LEAP WINE CELLARS (NAPA)
Cabernet Sauvignon Fay Vineyard* * *, Cabernet Sauvignon Napa* */* * *,
Cabernet Sauvignon Stag's Leap Vineyard* * */* * * *, Cask 23 Proprietary Red
Wine* * * * *, Chardonnay Napa* *, Chardonnay Reserve* * *, Sauvignon Blanc* * *

1989	Cabernet Sauvignon	Napa	C	84
1989	Cabernet Sauvignon Fay Vineyard	Napa	C	85
1989	Cabernet Sauvignon Stag's Leap Vineyard	Napa	C	86
1987	Cabernet Sauvignon Stag's Leap Vineyard	Napa	D	87
1986	Cabernet Sauvignon Stag's Leap Vineyard	Napa	D	87
1987	Cask 23 Proprietary Red Wine	Napa	D	91
1986	Cask 23 Proprietary Red Wine	Napa	D	91

1985	Cask 23 Proprietary Red Wine	Napa	E	98
1990	Chardonnay	Napa	C	82
1990	Chardonnay Reserve	Napa	D	86
1990	Merlot	Napa	C	84
1991	Sauvignon Blanc Rancho Chimiles	Napa	B	85

The quality of Stag's Leap's white wines has lagged behind that of its red wine offerings, but things appear to be improving. The 1991 Sauvignon Blanc Rancho Chimiles is a very subtle, restrained style of Sauvignon that is admirable for its freshness, purity, and light intensity; it offers a fig, melon, herbaceous nose touched with spicy oak. Drink it over the next year. The two Chardonnays are also made in an understated, elegant, polite style. The regular Napa *cuvée* is straightforward, delicate, and attractive. Although the 1990 Chardonnay Reserve reveals a more nutty, buttery component, it is still extremely restrained and delicate. Neither Chardonnay is likely to make old bones, so I suggest drinking them before the end of 1994. The real excitement from Stag's Leap is its red wines. Proprietor Warren Winiarski has done reasonably well in the difficult vintages of 1988 and 1989. Stag's Leap's style of Cabernet offers very complex, chocolatey, coffee, herb, and fruitcake aromas in a medium-bodied, supple format. Both the 1989 Napa bottling and the 1989 Fay Vineyard bottling are soft, elegant wines that are already drinking well. They will last another 4–5 years. The flagship wine of Stag's Leap is the Cask 23, now officially a proprietary red wine with the words *Cabernet Sauvignon* dropped from the label. This wine is not made every year, and it is unlikely one will be offered in either 1988 or 1989. The Cabernet Sauvignon Cask 23 continues to display one of the most distinctive and exotic bouquets of any California Cabernet-based wine. The 1987 Cask 23 offers a huge, profound aroma of coffee, fruitcake, cassis, Oriental spices, toasty new oak, herbs, and black fruits. In the mouth there is an almost endless sensation of voluptuous, velvety fruit, as well as an opulence that borders on decadence. Rich and medium bodied, but soft and supple (almost deceptively so), this distinctive, original expression of winemaking should provide immense pleasure for at least the next 12–15 years. There is no reason to defer your gratification. The 1986 Cask 23 is not nearly as concentrated, dramatic, or flamboyant as the phenomenal 1985, but neither is it subdued nor restrained. It is an exceptional wine displaying the telltale, exotic, Oriental spice, superripe, berry-scented nose, intermingled with aromas of chocolate, herbs, coffee, and mocha. In the mouth the wine has excellent ripeness, a rich, expansive, almost sweet, concentrated palate, and a long, heady finish. The wine's opulent texture conceals considerable soft tannins. Drink this beautiful wine over the next 10–12 years. The 1985 Cask 23 may well attain a perfect score in the years to come, as it is one of the most amazing and individualistic wines I have ever tasted from California. The dense, impressive, dark ruby/garnet color has the appearance of a highly extracted wine. The nose creates an olfactory overload. An extraordinary bouquet of coffee, chocolate, black fruits, cedar, hickory smoke, and superripe Damson plums roars from the glass. The wine has a voluptuous texture as well as extraordinary concentration and depth. These attributes only partially hide the considerable tannins in the finish. The overall impression is one of profound flavors with awesome extract and flavor dimension. This wine will continue to

age remarkably well for at least a decade. I do not think it will retain its exotic
fruit character when it is 20–30 years old, but given its depth and overall balance, that could be possible. My guess is that it will be at full maturity between
now and 2008. If you cannot find any Cask 23 in the marketplace, look for
some of the Stag's Leap Vineyard Cabernet Sauvignon. The two best recent
vintages are 1987 and 1986. The 1987 Stag's Leap Vineyard Cabernet Sauvignon typifies the style sought by this winery. The huge bouquet of coffee,
chocolate, herbs, and fruitcake is followed by a round, rich, velvety-textured
wine that offers admirable concentration, soft tannins, and a fleshy, opulent
finish. It is delicious to drink today, but it should age gracefully for 7–8 years
if well stored. The 1986 Stag's Leap Vineyard is well developed, with an intense bouquet of coffee, herbs, chocolate, and sweet red and black fruit flavors.
In the mouth the wine continues to exhibit an underlying herbaceous, tobacco
flavor intertwined with rich, concentrated, satiny, full-bodied fruit flavors. The
tannins are soft, the acidity is sound, and the overall impression is of a voluptuous, hedonistic, complex bottle of wine. If the finish were a bit longer, this
wine would merit an outstanding score. It should be drunk over the next 5–6
years.
RATINGS FOR OLDER VINTAGES OF STAG'S LEAP WINE CELLARS CASK 23: 1984 (93),
1983 (79), 1978 (93), 1977 (87), 1974 (90)

STEELE (LAKE COUNTY)

Chardonnay* * * *, Chardonnay Durell Vineyard* * * *, Chardonnay Lolonis
Vineyard* * * * *, Chardonnay Du Pratt Vineyard* * * * *, Chardonnay Sangiacomo
Vineyard* * * * *, Pinot Noir* * *, Pinot Noir Sangiacomo Vineyard* * */* * * *

1991	Chardonnay	California	C	89
1991	Chardonnay Durell Vineyard	Sonoma	C	88
1991	Chardonnay Lolonis Vineyard	Mendocino	C	90
1991	Chardonnay Du Pratt Vineyard	Mendocino	C	90
1991	Chardonnay Sangiacomo Vineyard	Carneros	C	91
1991	Pinot Noir	Carneros	C	85
1991	Pinot Noir Sangiacomo Vineyard	Carneros	C	87

Jed Steele (formerly the winemaker at Kendall-Jackson) is to be highly commended for his debut releases. All five of these Chardonnays merit considerable consumer interest. If Mr. Steele is able to follow up on quality such as this
in California's better vintages for Chardonnay, he will quickly establish himself as one of the superstars of his profession. All of these wines possess great
fruit, excellent to outstanding richness, and superb purity and focus. The California Chardonnay offering is rich and opulent, with gobs of fruit and just
enough acidity for balance. The elegant Durell Vineyard Chardonnay exhibits
higher acidity and is more restrained. Attractive peachlike aromas add to the
overall complexity and character of the wine, yet this is the most tightly knit
and highest in acidity. It may even improve over the next 6–12 months. The Du
Pratt Vineyard Chardonnay also reveals high, crisp acidity, as well as wonderful levels of fruit, a medium- to full-bodied texture, and that enticing orange-,
ripe apple-and-tangerinelike character that is often found in top white burgundies. The oak also appears more restrained, although none of these wines is

excessively woody. For my palate, the two best examples include the Lolonis Vineyard Chardonnay—a full-throttle, rich, smoky, buttery wine, with wonderful extraction of flavor, less acidity than the Du Pratt and Durell, a chewy, fleshy texture, and stunning length. The other blockbuster is the deep, rich Sangiacomo Vineyard Chardonnay—an exquisite wine with huge reserves of fruit, an intense, floral, buttery, apple, spicy bouquet, rich, medium- to full-bodied flavors, and an admirably long finish. I doubt that any of these wines are meant to make old bones, but they should continue to drink well for the next 2 years. Don't miss them! Steele's masterful touch is also evident in his two offerings of Pinot Noir. The 1991 Pinot Noir is light ruby in color, with a richly fruity nose of berries, soft tannins, a round, gentle texture, and a pleasant finish. It should be consumed over the next 1–2 years. Slightly more ambitious and richer is the 1991 Pinot Noir Sangiacomo Vineyard. Somewhat deeper in color, this wine displays more smoky, toasty oak, earth, and black fruit aromas in the nose and flavors and is longer and richer in the finish. A fine Pinot Noir with a lot of complexity, it should be drunk over the next 3–4 years.

STELTZNER VINEYARDS (NAPA)
Cabernet Sauvignon* *, Merlot* *

1991	Cabernet Sauvignon	Napa	B	79
1990	Cabernet Sauvignon	Napa	B	86
1991	Merlot	Napa	B	82
1990	Merlot	Napa	B	81

Although the extremely light 1991 and 1990 Merlots exhibit clean winemaking and some attractively pure, ripe flavors, both lack intensity and possess short finishes. Drink them over the next 5–6 years. The 1990 Cabernet Sauvignon offers a light-intensity, stylish, berry- and herb-scented nose, medium-bodied, crisp, fruity flavors, zesty acidity, and moderate tannins in its adequate finish. The 1991 is lean, austere, compact, and short.

STERLING VINEYARDS (NAPA)
Cabernet Sauvignon Diamond Mountain Ranch* */* * *, Cabernet Sauvignon Napa* *, Chardonnay Diamond Mountain Ranch* * *, Chardonnay Napa* *, Chardonnay Winery Lake* * *, Merlot* *, Pinot Noir* *, Reserve Proprietary Red Wine* */* * *, Sauvignon Blanc* *

1989	Cabernet Sauvignon	Napa	C	74
1988	Cabernet Sauvignon	Napa	C	77
1989	Cabernet Sauvignon Diamond Mountain Ranch	Napa	C	85
1988	Cabernet Sauvignon Diamond Mountain Ranch	Napa	C	82
1990	Chardonnay	Napa	B	76
1989	Chardonnay Diamond Mountain Ranch	Napa	B	77
1990	Chardonnay Estate	Napa	C	82

1989	Chardonnay Winery Lake	Carneros/Napa	C	86
1990	Pinot Noir Winery Lake	Carneros/Napa	C	75
1988	Proprietary Red Wine Three Palms Vineyard	Napa	C	65
1988	Reserve Red Table Wine	Napa	D	78
1991	Sauvignon Blanc	Napa	B	83
1990	Semillon	Napa	B	82

Considering the resources this producer enjoys, considering the financial backing this producer enjoys, considering the superlative vineyard sources Sterling either owns or buys grapes from, considering the talent of its winemaker, Sterling gets my nod as the biggest underachiever in California. The potential for extraordinary quality is obvious, but the winery's high-tech philosophy—relying on heavy-handed additions of acidity and striving for a sparkling clear, sediment-free, multiple-filtered product—results in competent, technically flawless, and utterly joyless wines. Somewhere in the corporate boardroom the idea that wine is a beverage of pleasure must have gotten lost. No matter what the varietal—Chardonnay, Sauvignon Blanc, Cabernet Sauvignon, Merlot, or Pinot Noir—there is an absence of personality, a paucity of flesh, fruit, and richness, and a sterile, one-dimensional, bland style that short-changes the wine consumer. The talented Bill Dyer has been the head of winemaking since 1985, and I had hoped there would be a move backward from Sterling's doomed policy of making soulless, characterless, and nearly pleasureless wines. All one has to do is taste through the Diamond Mountain Ranch Cabernets in vintages such as 1982, 1983, 1984, and 1985, and the Reserve Cabernets between 1978 and 1986, to recognize that these wines, although still alive and well, lack bouquets, have hard, green tannins, display hollow, sterile flavors, and are devoid of joy. Sterling need only look south down Route 29 in the direction of two other major players, the Robert Mondavi Winery and the Beringer winery, to realize that a large operation can maintain quality at a high level while providing the consumer with wines that possess significant character and style.

STEVENOT VINEYARDS (CALAVERAS)
Cabernet Sauvignon* *, Chardonnay* *, Zinfandel* */* * *

1990	Cabernet Sauvignon	California	B	72
1990	Chardonnay Grand Reserve	Calaveras	A	80
1989	Zinfandel	California	A	75
1988	Zinfandel Grand Reserve	Calaveras	A	85
1990	Zinfandel Reserve	Calaveras	A	75

This 1988 Zinfandel Grand Reserve Calaveras exhibits a big, ripe, spicy, berry-scented nose, medium- to full-bodied flavors, and moderate tannin in its robust finish. Somewhat backward, this Zinfandel will repay 1–3 years of cellaring, yet it should drink nicely for 5–7 years. The vaguely fruity 1990 Chardonnay Grand Reserve should be drunk before the summer of 1994 for its simple, straightforward style.

STONE CREEK (NAPA)

Cabernet Sauvignon California*, Cabernet Sauvignon Napa* *, Chardonnay* *,
Chardonnay Reserve* *, Chardonnay Special Selection* *, Fumé Blanc*, Merlot*

1989	Cabernet Sauvignon	California	A	70
1986	Cabernet Sauvignon	Napa	A	74
1991	Chardonnay	California	A	75
1989	Chardonnay Reserve	Alexander Valley	B	83
1990	Chardonnay Special Selection	Napa	B	76
1991	Fumé Blanc	Napa	A	72
1991	Merlot	California	B	76

The only thing that can be said for these wines is that they are fresh and light bodied, with no defects. Some of them possess more oak, especially the Reserve and Special Selection offerings. The wines appear to be made from vineyards that produce prolific yields, as there is virtually no flavor definition or intensity. These inexpensive wines should be drunk within 3 years of the vintage.

STONEGATE WINERY (NAPA)

Cabernet Sauvignon* *, Chardonnay*/* *, Merlot* *, Sauvignon Blanc*

1989	Cabernet Sauvignon	Napa	B	70
1988	Cabernet Sauvignon	Napa	B	72
1987	Cabernet Sauvignon	Napa	B	55
1989	Chardonnay	Napa	C	70
1988	Chardonnay	Napa	C	78
1988	Chardonnay Reserve	Napa	C	68
1988	Chardonnay Spaulding Vineyard	Napa	C	77

If ever a winery needed to practice less acidification and junk all its sterile filters, that winery is Stonegate. Some new direction needs to be infused here, since Stonegate appears content to produce thin, monolithic wines that provide little interest or pleasure. Both the Chardonnay and Cabernet Sauvignon offer shrill acidity and hollow, stripped flavors. If squeaky clean wines with no soul or flavor ever come into vogue, these wines will win gold medals.

STONY HILL VINEYARDS (NAPA)

Chardonnay* * * */* * * * *

1990	Chardonnay	Napa	C	89+
1989	Chardonnay	Napa	C	82
1988	Chardonnay	Napa	C	90

Stony Hill is one of the historic names, and longtime reference point for California Chardonnay. The founding proprietors, Eleanor and Frederick McCrea, have passed away, but the quality and style of their wines is likely to remain the same. These long-lived, often compelling Chardonnays generally need time in the bottle. The 1990 exhibits a nearly impenetrable, backward style, with high acidity and considerable weight and richness on the palate. The subtle aromas of lemon butter, apples, minerals, and oak make for an elegant first impression. Beautifully pure and tightly strung, yet rich and medium to full bodied, this wine will benefit from 1–2 years of cellaring; it should last for 5–6 years. The 1989 is pleasant but light bodied, crisp, and short. Drink it over the next 2–3 years. The rich 1988 is still very youthful and could last for another 7–8 years.

STORYBOOK MOUNTAIN VINEYARDS (NAPA)
Zinfandel Howell Mountain* * * *, Zinfandel* * * *,
Zinfandel Reserve* * * */* * * * *

1991	Zinfandel	Napa	B	90
1990	Zinfandel	Napa	B	88
1991	Zinfandel Howell Mountain	Napa	C	88+
1991	Zinfandel Reserve	Napa	C	90+
1990	Zinfandel Reserve	Napa	C	90

Proprietor Jerry Seps has a vineyard dedicated completely to Zinfandel in the northern section of Napa Valley, not far from Calistoga. A strong argument can be made that his Zinfandel is potentially the longest-lived wine from this varietal. Storybook Mountain Vineyards Zinfandels, particularly the Reserves, appear to need at least 5–6 years of cellaring and really do not begin to blossom until they are nearly a decade old. With that in mind, consumers should consider buying the regular 1990 and 1991 Napa bottlings for drinking within the next 10–12 years. The Reserves should be cellared for at least 5 years, perhaps longer in top vintages such as 1990 and 1991. Storybook Mountain Zinfandels offer considerable structure, somewhat higher acidity than other Napa Zinfandels, and a deep, rich, profound, spicy, raspberry fruitiness intermingled with the scent of minerals and pepper. The 1990 regular bottling offers all of this, along with wonderful sweetness and ripeness of fruit, gorgeous structure, a medium- to full-bodied style, and a long finish. The 1990 Reserve is an even richer wine. Full bodied and loaded with extract, it is oh so backward. It could be a Zinfandel that lasts for 2 decades. The 1991 Napa is the easiest to drink and most flattering of the 1991 offerings. It boasts a deep ruby/purple color, a big sweet, peppery, raspberry-scented nose; rich, medium- to full-bodied flavors; fine underlying acidity to bring everything into focus; and a lovely, rich, long finish. Storybook Mountain's Zinfandels generally need considerable bottle age to strut their stuff, but this 1991 Zinfandel is among the more precocious wines that I have tasted from this winery. Drinkable now, it will easily last for 10–12 years. In 1991, there is a new Zinfandel in this winery's portfolio. Made from a vineyard on Howell Mountain, it is an ageworthy, tannic, backward, spicy Zinfandel that is completely closed yet loaded with potential. It needs at least 4–5 years in the cellar and should last for 12–15 years. It is big, brawny, and concentrated; patience is most definitely required. Storybook Mountain's 1991 Zinfandel Reserve will not be released for at least a year, but it promises to rival the quality of the wonderful 1990 and 1987. It reveals a deep ruby/purple color; a broodingly backward, intriguing nose of minerals, black fruits, spices, and pepper; superlative extraction of fruit; full body, high tannin levels, and crisp acidity. There is a layered, multidimensional feel to the wine. As with the Howell Mountain, patience is essential. **Anticipated maturity: 1997–2010.**

STRATFORD (NAPA)

Cabernet Sauvignon* *, Chardonnay Napa* * *, Chardonnay Partner's
Reserve* * *, Merlot* * *, Sauvignon Blanc* *

1990	Chardonnay Partner's Reserve	California	C	87
1987	Merlot	California	B	86

During its first decade of life, this *négociant* has consistently proven that tasty, concentrated blends can be put together by purchasing juice in bulk from other producers. The wines have always been at least above average in quality, in some cases excellent. The best offerings are usually the Merlot and Reserve Chardonnay. Other wines include Cabernet Sauvignon and Sauvignon Blanc. This firm produces a second, even less expensive line of wines that are sold under the Canterbury label. Some of these wines, particularly the Chardonnay, can be terrific values in certain vintages. Big, rich, and ripe, the medium- to full-bodied 1990 Chardonnay Partner's Reserve exhibits tasty tropical fruit, a subtle touch of oak, and a luscious finish. Drink it over the next year. With skyrocketing wine prices, consumers are well-advised to look for a few bottles of this robust, fleshy, delicious 1987 Merlot for drinking over the next 4–5 years. With an impressively deep ruby color as well as a bouquet redolent with red fruit, this medium-bodied, surprisingly full, silky-smooth Merlot has just enough tannin and acidity to warrant investment in a case.

STRAUS VINEYARDS (NAPA)

Merlot* *

1989	Merlot	Napa	C	83
1988	Merlot	Napa	C	80
1987	Merlot	Napa	C	84
1986	Merlot	Napa	C	86
1985	Merlot	Napa	C	86
1984	Merlot	Napa	C	85

This small Merlot specialist is fashioning wines with higher tannins than is usually associated with this grape variety. Moreoever, the tannins possess a bitterness and astringency. Otherwise the wines exhibit deep color and plenty of body and intensity. Unfortunately the harsh tannins make me wonder how these wines will ultimately evolve.

RODNEY STRONG (SONOMA)

Cabernet Sauvignon Alexander's Crown* */* * *, Cabernet Sauvignon
Reserve* */* * *, Cabernet Sauvignon Sonoma* *, Chardonnay Chalk Hill
Vineyard* * *, Pinot Noir River East Vineyard* *, Sauvignon Blanc Charlotte's
Home Vineyard* * */* * * *, Zinfandel Old Vines River West Vineyard * */* * *

1987	Cabernet Sauvignon Alexander's Crown	Sonoma	C	85
1988	Cabernet Sauvignon Reserve	Sonoma	C	83

1991	Chardonnay Chalk Hill Vineyard	Sonoma	B	87
1990	Chardonnay Chalk Hill Vineyard	Sonoma	B	84
1990	Pinot Noir River East Vineyard	Sonoma	C	84
1990	Sauvignon Blanc Charlotte's Home Vineyard	Sonoma	B	85
1988	Zinfandel Old Vines River West Vineyard	Sonoma	B	75

There have been many changes in this well-known Sonoma winery. Over recent vintages the quality of the Rodney Strong wines has increased. There is still considerable distance to cover, but recent vintages have exhibited more fruit, richness, and complexity than the rather insipid, monochromatic, hollow wines produced in the early and middle 1980s. The best of these offerings include a 1991 Chardonnay from the Chalk Hill Vineyard. It is even richer and fuller than the tasty, elegant 1990. Rodney Strong has turned out a good 1990 Sauvignon Blanc from Charlotte's Home Vineyard. It displays more depth than most, a fragrant, melon- and fig-scented nose, medium body, and a dry finish. The 1990 Pinot Noir, which is a relatively soft, commercial wine, is user-friendly, round, tasty, and pleasant. Drink it over the next several years. I remember some great Zinfandels Rodney Strong produced in the mid-1970s (1976, for example) from the Old Vines River West Vineyard, but the 1988 lacks fruit, has entirely too much tannin, and is tough and hard. Another famed wine that Rodney Strong created is his Cabernet Sauvignon from the Alexander's Crown Vineyard. The 1974 caused quite a stir among California Cabernet producers because of its extraordinary richness and power. There has not been a top wine since, but things are beginning to improve. The 1987 Alexander's Crown Cabernet Sauvignon is a medium-bodied, attractive, moderately rich wine with big, spicy, cedary, cassis aromas and attractive depth. Already delicious, it should continue to drink well for 5–7 years. All things considered, this winery is clearly on the rebound. Prices are reasonable for the quality.

SULLIVAN VINEYARDS WINERY (NAPA)

Cabernet Sauvignon* */* * * * *, Chenin Blanc*, Merlot* */* * * * *

1987	Merlot	Napa	C	90

Sullivan has been a schizophrenic winery to follow. In certain vintages its Cabernet Sauvignon is awesome (1982 and 1984). Yet in vintages such as 1985 and 1986, two top-notch years for Napa Cabernet, Sullivan's Cabernets were flawed by excessive quantities of volatile acidity and musty, fecal aromas. When this winery hits the mark, its Cabernet Sauvignon is one of the richest and most interesting made in Napa. But when it fails, which happens with equal frequency, it produces a grotesquely out-of-balance wine that I find nearly undrinkable. So what do you do? Well, if it is the 1987 Merlot, you buy it. Totally clean, with a gigantic bouquet of plummy, chocolatey, tarry fruit, incredibly intense, explosive, full-bodied flavors, and at least 10–15 years of further drinking potential, this spectacular wine sustains a luscious texture that makes it appealing enough to drink now. Sullivan has made one of the most concentrated yet impeccably well-balanced Merlots I have ever tasted from California.

SUMMIT LAKE VINEYARDS AND WINERY (NAPA)
Zinfandel* * */* * * *

1990	Zinfandel	Howell Mountain	B	89
1989	Zinfandel	Howell Mountain	B	85
1988	Zinfandel	Howell Mountain	B	87
1986	Zinfandel	Howell Mountain	B	87

It is a shame only 2,000 cases of this Howell Mountain Zinfandel are produced, because it deserves more attention than it receives. The 1986, although backward and powerful, possesses enough rich fruit to stand up to the tannin. It needs some cellaring, but the wine's depth, intensity, and ripeness persuade me that it will make a strikingly fine Zinfandel between 1992 and 2000. Most of this property's Zinfandel vineyard is relatively young, but you would never know that from tasting the 1988. It enjoys a deep ruby/purple color, a big, briary, spicy, peppery, mineral-scented nose, medium to full body, gobs of clean berry fruit, and a crisp, moderately tannic finish. Based on previous examples I tasted, such as the 1987 and 1986, the tannins appear less elevated, making the wine more supple and flattering to drink. They should continue to offer delicious drinking for 6–8 years. The 1989, which has not been released, appears to have the same weight as the 1988 but less up-front fruit. It may just need more time in the bottle to come out of its shell. There is good color, plenty of peppery, berry fruit, and a moderately long finish. Potentially the best of this trio is Summit Lake's 1990. It displays explosive ripe fruit, a seductive, penetrating fragrance of black fruits, spices, and wood, and a long finish. This beautifully made Zinfandel has more to it than the 1988 and 1989, which is not surprising since 1990 tends to be a riper, fuller vintage for most producers. The 1990 will not be released for several years, but shrewd consumers might want to make a mental note.

SUTTER HOME WINERY (NAPA)
Cabernet Sauvignon* *, White Zinfandel* *, Zinfandel* *, Zinfandel Reserve* * *

1989	Cabernet Sauvignon	California	A	75
1990	Zinfandel Reserve	Amador	A	86

What a pleasure it is to see this producer of industrial-size quantities of sweet, pink-colored "white" Zinfandel produce a fleshy, ripe, generously endowed, tasty, "real" Zinfandel. The wine exhibits plenty of up-front charm, a good, expansive, jammy palate, and a long, lusty finish. Its flavors reminded me of black cherries, herbs, and chocolate. Drink it over the next 3–4 years. This winery's regular Zinfandel is much lighter, but still fruity and clean. Sutter Home's greatest success is with its medium-sweet, fruity, tasty white Zinfandel. You won't hear any carping from me about America's love affair with this wine, because it is *wine*, which cannot be said about wine coolers.

JOSEPH SWAN VINEYARDS (SONOMA)
Single-Vineyard Zinfandels* * * *

1991	Zinfandel Frati Ranch	Russian River	C	90+
1991	Zinfandel Stellwagen Vineyard	Sonoma	C	92
1991	Zinfandel Zeigler Vineyard	Russian River	C	90+

These are the most reassuringly rich, complex wines I have tasted in years from this historic winery. Made for cellaring, they are enormously endowed, tannic, backward wines with considerable body and concentration. All three promise to be thrilling wines, provided buyers exercise some patience. If you do not mind some tannin bite, they can be enjoyed now. The 1991 Zinfandel Frati Ranch exhibits a Barolo-like nose of melted road tar and black fruits. Exceptionally tannic in the mouth, it boasts impressive extraction of flavor, full body, and a deep, long, superrich finish. Most of the depth can be sensed at the back of the mouth. **Anticipated maturity: 1996–2005.** With its garnet color, the 1991 Zinfandel Stellwagen Vineyard even looks different. More developed, it is the easiest of this trio to drink. The big, smoky, cedary, black fruit–scented nose soars from the glass. This spectacularly rich, unctuous, remarkably concentrated Zinfandel offers admirable body and glycerin, as well as softer tannins than its two siblings. Drink this gloriously rich, full-throttle wine over the next decade. The 1991 Zinfandel Zeigler Vineyard reveals an earthy, licorice, black truffle–scented nose intertwined with aromas of peppery black raspberries. The color is nearly opaque. The wine possesses wonderful richness, tremendous extraction of sweet Zinfandel fruit, and a layered, spicy but forbiddingly tannic, blockbuster finish. This dark purple–colored Zinfandel should be at its best between 1996 and 2006. How delighted I am to see such quality emerge from Joseph Swan!

SWANSON VINEYARDS AND WINERY (NAPA)
Cabernet Sauvignon* * * *, Chardonnay* * *, Merlot* *

1991	Cabernet Sauvignon	Napa	C	89
1990	Cabernet Sauvignon	Napa	C	85
1987	Cabernet Sauvignon	Napa	D	90
1990	Chardonnay	Napa	C	86
1989	Chardonnay	Napa	C	79
1990	Merlot	Napa	D	82

This winery, founded only in 1986 and located in the old Cassayre-Forni winery, owns 100 acres of prime vineyard in the Oakville area of Napa Valley. Followers of the Napa Valley scene have been waiting for several years for Swanson's initial releases, which were predicted to be of high quality given the financial resources behind this operation. The superbly endowed, black/ruby/purple 1987 Cabernet Sauvignon exhibits tremendous extraction of flavor and a tight yet promising bouquet of ripe cassis, oak, and spicy, earthy notes. There is exceptional intensity, gobs of tannin, glycerin, and fruit, but the wine remains closed and in need of at least 5–7 years of cellaring. When it reaches its peak toward the end of this decade, my score may look conservative. **Anticipated maturity: 1998–2015.** Although I have not tasted Swanson's 1988 and 1989 Cabernet Sauvignons, from two dubious vintages, there is no question that this winery produced outstanding Cabernets in 1990 and 1991. The forward 1990 offers tarry, chocolatey, cassis-scented aromas, rich, medium- to full-bodied flavors, soft acids, and an excellent finish. Already delicious, it should age well for another 10–15 years. The 1991 Cabernet Sauvignon exhibits an impressive dark ruby/purple color; a dramatic, sweet, black cherry–, cassis-, and toasty oak–scented nose; opulent, rich, multidimensional flavors; and an expansive, decadent, succulent finish. Loaded with fruit, it is made in a more up-front, precocious style than the 1987. Drink it over the next 12–15 years. I was unmoved by the light, narrowly constructed 1990 Merlot and 1989 Chardonnay, which was already beginning to drop its fruit. The 1990 Chardonnay is a good to very good wine with a nice touch of spicy oak and fine ripeness. Drink it over the next 1–2 years.

ROBERT TALBOTT VINEYARDS (MONTEREY)
Chardonnay Diamond T Estate* * * * *, Chardonnay Estate* * * * *,
Logan Chardonnay* * * *

1990	Chardonnay Estate	Monterey	D	93
1989	Chardonnay Diamond T Estate	Monterey	D	89
1990	Chardonnay Diamond T Estate	Monterey	D	93
1989	Chardonnay Estate	Monterey	D	87
1990	Logan Chardonnay	Monterey	C	89

I am not about to argue with anyone who claims this winery is making the finest Chardonnays in California. Logan, its secondary label, has produced a 1990 Chardonnay with wonderful richness; an enthralling, spicy, buttery, mineral-, and ripe apple–scented nose; and lovely, deep, nicely extracted flavors. One can see the strength of the 1990 vintage given the fact that this second label is slightly richer and fuller than Talbott's 1989 estate bottling of Chardonnay! The 1989 Chardonnay Diamond T Estate is beautifully made, but it falls just short of outstanding. Rich, full bodied, and tightly knit, it presents an intriguing smell of buttered apples, minerals, and subtle new oak. Medium to full bodied, nicely concentrated (particularly for a 1989), and long in the finish, it should evolve slowly by the standards of California Chardonnay and drink well for at least 3–4 years. The 1990 Chardonnay reveals a huge bouquet filled with aromas of oranges, butter, minerals, and spicy oak. The wine is full bodied yet brilliantly well balanced by crisp acidity. Rich and deep, this compelling example of California Chardonnay is capable of lasting another 3–4 years, although its charms are impossible to resist now. The 1990 Chardonnay Diamond T Estate is exceptional. It is similar to the regular 1990 but even richer and more mineral infused. It should drink until the turn of the century.

TALLEY VINEYARDS (SAN LUIS OBISPO)
Chardonnay* * * *, Pinot Noir* * * *

1990	Chardonnay	Arroyo Grande Valley	C	87
1990	Pinot Noir	Arroyo Grande Valley	C	87
1988	Pinot Noir	Arroyo Grande Valley	C	87

Both the 1988 and 1990 Pinot Noirs are impressively made wines, exhibiting moderately dark ruby colors; big, rich, minty, ripe berry–scented bouquets; long, round, generously endowed flavors; and soft, lush finishes. From a purely varietal perspective, the 1988 did not remind me so much of Pinot Noir, but I loved the wine and its seductive qualities. Drink it over the next 2–3 years. The 1990 Pinot Noir possesses more of the black cherry, earthy, herbal Pinot

character married with sweet oak in the background. It is no better than the
1988 but may ultimately live longer, perhaps 4–6 years. The 1990 Chardonnay
offers a lovely nose of tropical fruits, toast, and butter that is followed by a honeyed, creamy texture and enough acidity for focus and delineation. This rich,
full-bodied wine should be drunk over the next several years. This winery also
produces small quantities of Riesling and Sauvignon Blanc, which I have
never tasted.

IVAN TAMAS (SANTA CLARA)

Cabernet Sauvignon* *, Chardonnay* * *, Fumé Blanc* * */* * * *,
Trebbiano * * * *

1989	Cabernet Sauvignon	Livermore	B	75
1991	Chardonnay	Livermore	A	86
1991	Fumé Blanc	Livermore	A	87
1991	Trebbiano	Livermore	A	88

These wines, from the underrated but potentially outstanding Livermore Valley, are remarkably full flavored. Readers tired of so many insipid and watery
California wines will not want to miss these terrific bargains. Wine from the
Trebbiano grape is rarely found in California, but this is a strong effort. Although the nose is subdued in Tamas's 1991 Trebbiano, in the mouth this wine
is bursting with rich fruit, displays gobs of glycerin, and is more flavorful and
fuller bodied than most Italian Trebbianos. It would be an ideal white wine to
serve with grilled seafood or poultry. I enjoyed it immensely, as evidenced by
the fact that I finished the bottle with my dinner. Even more impressive is the
1991 Fumé Blanc. Concentrated and intense, it offers a big nose of honey,
melon, figs, and herbs, full body, luscious fruit, and excellent richness. Again,
it should do wonders with full-flavored poultry and seafood dishes. The 1991
Chardonnay from Livermore Valley is a big, full-bodied, concentrated, rich
wine. Exuberant and fleshy, with plenty of buttery, applelike, honeyed fruit, as
well as a subtle touch of oak, this excellent Chardonnay (at a bargain-basement
price) should make highly enjoyable drinking for at least another year. The
white wines continue to go from strength to strength, and proprietors Ivan
Tamas and Steve Mirassou, who founded this operation in 1984, deserve to be
commended. As exciting and inexpensive as the white wines are, the Cabernet
Sauvignon, although reasonably priced, is relatively one-dimensional and
uninteresting. The compact, austere 1989 Cabernet lacks fruit and has harsh
tannins.

LANE TANNER (SANTA BARBARA)

Pinot Noir* * * *, Pinot Noir Sanford & Benedict Vineyard* * * *

| 1991 | Pinot Noir | Santa Barbara | C | 87 |
| 1991 | Pinot Noir Sanford & Benedict Vineyard | Santa Barbara | D | 90 |

This small operation specializes in uncommonly bold, dark-colored, spicy
Pinot Noir. The 1991 Pinot Noir Santa Barbara offers deep color, a ripe,
herbal, black cherry–scented nose, medium-bodied, nicely extracted flavors,
and admirable spice and flesh in the crisp finish. Drink it over the next 5–6

years. The deeper-colored 1991 Pinot Noir Sanford & Benedict Vineyard exhibits a herbaceous, black cherry, mineral, spicy nose, superrich, medium- to full-bodied flavors, a multidimensional, layered texture, and plenty of sweet, ripe fruit in the well-delineated, long finish. It will benefit from another 1–2 years of cellaring and should last for 10 years.

TELDESCHI (SONOMA)
Zinfandel* * * * *

1987	Zinfandel	Dry Creek	B	90
1986	Zinfandel	Sonoma	B	90
1985	Zinfandel	Sonoma	B	92

The opaque black/purple color of the 1985 Zinfandel is followed by a nose that offers up sensationally rich aromas of black raspberries, licorice, and minerals. In the mouth there is exceptional concentration, and this rich, full-bodied wine from a little-known Sonoma producer is bursting with fruit and character. Drink this profound Zinfandel over the next 10–15 years. Teldeschi's 1986 is another blockbuster Zinfandel, with an opaque purple color and an intense, heady perfume of chocolate, cedar, and black raspberry. There is great richness, voluptuous texture, plenty of tannin, and a lingering finish. Although drinkable now, it should continue to age well for another 7–8 years. The 1987 is super Zinfandel selling at a terrific price. From its opaque dark ruby/purple color to its huge nose of black raspberry fruit and spice, this intense, rich, full-bodied wine exhibits velvety tannins, plenty of glycerin and concentration, and a long finish. Although drinkable now, this wine should easily last for 10–15 years. This is a dazzling Zinfandel from what must be the best vintage for that varietal in the last 20 years. Amazingly, this Zinfandel held up 6 days in an open bottle without showing a trace of oxidation! Only 600 cases of the 1987 were produced from 75-year-old vines. All of these wines were bottled unfined and unfiltered. Teldeschi may be California's best-kept secret when it comes to great Zinfandel. I hope consumers put this information to good use.

THE TERRACES (NAPA)
Cabernet Sauvignon* * */* * * *, Zinfandel* * */* * * * *

1988	Cabernet Sauvignon	Napa	D	84
1987	Cabernet Sauvignon	Napa	D	91
1989	Zinfandel	Napa	C	79
1988	Zinfandel	Napa	C	85
1987	Zinfandel	Napa	C	90

The price is high, but there are only 200 cases of this Caymus Special Selection look-alike 1987 Cabernet Sauvignon. Copious amounts of toasty, vanillin, and smoky new oak aromas accompany lavish amounts of rich cassis fruit. The wine exhibits a multidimensional texture, with layers of black cherry and curranty fruit wrapped in generous quantities of new oak. This full-bodied, impeccably well-made Cabernet Sauvignon should drink well in 2–3 years and last for 15 or more. The weakness of the 1988 Napa Cabernet Sauvignon vintage is revealed in The Terraces' 1988 Cabernet. Although it exhibits more richness than many wines, it is extremely tight, with elevated tannins, and tastes tough, astringent, and out of balance. I doubt if it will ever come into harmony. It should be drunk now for its rough-and-tumble coarse style. The intense, toasty new oak bouquet, intermingled with aromas of plums, smoke, and minerals, is followed by a rich, fleshy, gloriously extracted 1987 Zinfandel that offers up sumptuous levels of fruit framed nicely by oak and soft tannins. This classy yet authoritative-tasting Zinfandel comes across on the palate almost as a rich St.-Émilion. It is long and deliciously drinkable now, although its harmony, depth, and soft tannins suggest it should last for at least 7–8 years. Although it pales in comparison with the great 1987, the 1988 Zinfandel displays a smoky, ripe berry–scented nose, medium-bodied flavors, soft tannins, and a pleasing finish. It should be drunk over the next 4–5 years. I was disappointed in the 1989 Zinfandel, which was tart, hard, and skinny, with no underlying depth or richness.

DOMAINE DE LA TERRE ROUGE (AMADOR)
Rhône Ranger Blend* */* * *

1990	Proprietary Red Wine	California	A	82
1989	Proprietary Red Wine	California	A	78
1988	Proprietary Red Wine	California	A	75

I had high hopes when I tasted the first bottling of the nonvintage blend of Domaine de la Terre Rouge in 1987. However, two of these three vintage-designated wines all proved to be average in quality. The 1990 and 1989 are blends of Grenache, Syrah, Mourvèdre, and Cinsault; the 1988 contains no Cinsault and slightly more Syrah than the other *cuvées*. The flawed 1988 offers a bizarre vegetal aroma combined with a lees smell that is off-putting. In the mouth it is light, sharp, and simple. The 1989 reveals slightly more fruit but again appears to be a simple wine with little depth or intensity. The 1990, the best of this trio, exhibits more ripeness and fruit, as well as an attractive, smoky, herbaceous, earthy, black fruit character, medium body, decent acidity, and a moderate finish. There is a lot to admire in this property's winemaking philosophy, which rejects fining and filtering, but I suspect the raw materials lack depth.

SEAN THACKREY & CO. (MARIN)
Orion Syrah* * * * *, Pleiades* * * *, Sirius Petite Sirah* * * * *,
Taurus Mourvèdre* * * *

1990	Orion Syrah	Napa	D	92
1989	Orion Syrah	Napa	D	91
1988	Orion Syrah	Napa	D	93
N. V.	Pleiades	California	C	87
1990	Sirius Petite Sirah Marston Vineyard	California	D	93
1989	Sirius Petite Sirah Old Vines Marston Vineyard	Napa	D	90
1990	Taurus Mourvèdre	California	D	90

1989	Taurus Mourvèdre	California	D	90
1988	Taurus Mourvèdre	California	D	90

As I have stated so many times before, Sean Thackrey's limited-production gems are among the most original expressions of winemaking in California. He has added a new star to his galaxy, a nonvintage blend of Grenache, Syrah, Mourvèdre, and Nebbiolo called Pleiades. I found the recent release (it bears no vintage) to be an interesting, minty, spicy berry–scented wine with soft yet deep, multidimensional flavors, lovely texture, and a moderately long, supple finish. I would opt for drinking it over the next 5–6 years. The 1990 Taurus (Mourvèdre) shares a similar minty character. Although I do not see the same varietal character in French wines made from this grape, there is plenty to admire in this deep, dark-colored wine. It offers a big, forceful perfume of mint and black raspberries with a touch of minerals and earth. The overall impression is of impeccable winemaking and graceful, superconcentrated fruit wrapped in a medium- to full-bodied format. It should age admirably for at least a decade. The 1989 Taurus, made from Mourvèdre, did not exhibit as much of a tree bark, truffle, earthy character as I am used to seeing from Bandols, the French wines from Provence, and the Mourvèdre-dominated Beaucastel from Châteauneuf-du-Pape. In fact, if I had had this wine in a blind tasting, I might have suspected it to be a Pinot Noir, as odd as that may sound. I say that because of the gorgeously rich, spicy, raspberry flavors, although there was a strong scent of mint in the nose that might have made me think of something other than Pinot. In any event, this is a wonderfully pure, beautifully made wine with deliciously rich, well-balanced, and well-delineated flavors. Again, the lighter style of the 1989 vintage has produced a wine with uncommon elegance, yet one that is not lacking in intensity. Given the fact that Mourvèdre evolves slowly in the bottle, this wine should last as well as the Petite Sirah and Syrah. The 1988 Taurus is an impressive wine made from 100% Mourvèdre. In contrast with the rich, spicy, black fruit character of the Orion, the Taurus is a more earthy wine, with aromas of mushrooms, spices, and damp earth. It is sure to be controversial, but one has to admire its impeccable balance, layers of concentrated fruit, and smooth, moderately tannic finish. The 1990 Sirius (Petite Sirah) is a real blockbuster, so viscous it resembles purple 10W-40 motor oil when poured from the bottle. The color is black/purple; the intensity and fruit extraction are amazing. This is a phenomenal example of just how rich, concentrated, and unctuous Petite Sirah can be when made in a traditional manner from extremely old vines. I would not be surprised to see this wine reach its peak by the turn of the century and last through the first decade or more of the twenty-first century. Just phenomenal! The 1989 Sirius, made from old vines of Petite Sirah in the Marston Vineyard of Napa Valley, is a black-colored, dense wine. In addition to the impressive color, this wine gives up a huge bouquet of black raspberries, spices, licorice, and even some fragrant floral scents. It is opulently rich in the mouth, with gobs of fruit, and has avoided the astringency and tannin that one often gets with such intensely flavored Petite Sirah. This beauty can be drunk now for its youthful exuberance, but it should evolve for 10–15 years or more in a cool cellar. Thackrey hit the jackpot with the 1990 Orion, another impressively endowed wine with a gorgeous fragrance of smoke, blackberries, toast, minerals, and pepper. Rich, with layers of fruit, this multidimensional wine reveals gobs of tannin that are nearly concealed by the wine's superb extraction. Full bodied and impressive, this great Syrah should age effortlessly for 12–15 or more years. The 1989 Orion, from the Syrah grape, is a more elegantly stated wine, with an impressive dark ruby color; the telltale cassis, bacon fat, roasted aroma; rich, graceful, medium- to full-bodied flavors; surprisingly soft tannins; and a velvety finish. This beautifully made Syrah may not be as powerful and intense as some of Thackrey's predecessors, but it's probably the most elegant, authoritatively flavored Syrah he has yet produced. It should drink beautifully for 12–15 years. The 1988 Orion builds on the great promise exhibited by earlier efforts. Sensationally rich, but soft enough to be drunk now, this full-bodied, raspberry-, herb-, peppery-scented wine has layers of fruit, excellent extraction, and an inner core of surprising depth. The tannins are fine and soft rather than aggressive and astringent. Although it still seems essentially unevolved and in its infancy, this wine is drinkable now and could well last beyond a decade.

THOMAS-HSI (NAPA)
Chardonnay* * */* * * *

1988	Chardonnay	Napa	C	89

Lamentably, only 240 cases were made of this aromatic, nearly profound Chardonnay. With so many innocuous and insipid California Chardonnays being produced, what a pleasure it is to find one with an intense bouquet of nuts, buttery tropical fruit, and smoke. In the mouth there is an opulent richness that one rarely finds in New World Chardonnay. The acidity provides adequate grip and focus, and the finish is long and lush. This beautifully made, complex, French-style California Chardonnay should be drunk over the next year. My star rating may be conservative based on only one vintage tasted of this producer's wines. If the 1990 and 1991 turn out to be as good as the 1988, this will be a producer to follow closely if you love rich, complex Chardonnays.

TOBIN JAMES (SAN LUIS OBISPO)
Cabernet Sauvignon* *, Zinfandel* */* * *

1990	Cabernet Sauvignon Private Stock	Paso Robles	B	78
1990	Zinfandel Big Shot	Paso Robles	B	83
1990	Zinfandel Blue Moon Reserve	Paso Robles	B	80
N. V.	Zinfandel Ch Le Cacheflo	Paso Robles	A	75
1989	Zinfandel Inspiration	Paso Robles	B	84
N. V.	Zinfandel Ol Blue Jay	Paso Robles	A	78

These innovatively packaged and named wines would have more appeal if they possessed more fruit and flesh. They are straightforward, angular, and tannic, without the requisite depth of fruit to balance out the acids and tannins, or to age. Nevertheless, one has to like the shrewd marketing philosophy of their names.

PHILIP TOGNI VINEYARDS (NAPA)

Cabernet Sauvignon* * * */* * * * *, Cabernet Sauvignon Tanbark Hill* * * *,
Sauvignon Blanc* * * *

1991	Cabernet Sauvignon	Napa	D	92
1990	Cabernet Sauvignon	Napa	D	93
1989	Cabernet Sauvignon	Napa	D	87
1988	Cabernet Sauvignon	Napa	D	90
1987	Cabernet Sauvignon	Napa	C	89
1988	Cabernet Sauvignon Tanbark Hill	Napa	C	87
1991	Sauvignon Blanc	Napa	B	87

The superrich, massive, inky-colored 1991 and 1990 Cabernet Sauvignons are reminiscent of such young vintages of Mayacamas as the 1973 and 1974. Cabernet enthusiasts who have not yet discovered Philip Togni should be on a crusade for his wines, which will handsomely repay extended cellaring. The 1991 is extremely backward in terms of its evolution, and as a consequence it is not as easy to judge as the 1990. But without question it is a stunningly proportioned, massive wine, with extraordinary intensity, gobs of smoky, anise- and cassislike flavors, and a touch of herbaceousness. The multidimensional, thick, rich midpalate is something to behold, as are the glycerin-rich, highly extracted flavors. The alcohol is lower and the acidity higher in the 1991 than in the absolutely sensational 1990. The latter wine exhibits an unctuosity and intensity that was, I suspect, common with some of Bordeaux's Right Bank 1947s. Black in color, with a huge, berry, coffee, chocolate, jammy nose, this powerful, assertive wine displays layer upon layer of richness, a sweet, expansive palate, and a blockbuster finish. This wine should prove to be a knockout Cabernet with 20–25 years of aging potential. I do not think richer, more intense 1989 and 1988 Cabernets can be found than these from Philip Togni. Togni's 1989 Cabernet Sauvignon is one of the most controversial wines he has made under his own name. The flamboyant, herbaceous nose offers aromas of smoky wood and flowers intertwined with scents of damp earth and black fruits. Viscous, thick, and amazingly rich, it is one of the most concentrated wines from this generally disappointing vintage; but an underlying vegetal element becomes noticeable as the wine sits in the glass. The wine is still extremely young; if it pulls itself together, it could merit an even higher score. The 1988 Tanbark Hill (250 cases produced) is an opulently rich, supple, expansively flavored wine bursting with aromas and flavors of licorice and blackcurrants. Deliciously rich and velvety, it should be consumed over the next 7–8 years. For an even more massive and concentrated wine, check out the 1988 Cabernet Sauvignon (386 cases produced). The huge bouquet of melted road tar, chocolate-covered raisins, plums, prunes, and vanillin is knockout stuff. In the mouth the huge, rich, concentrated flavors seem to have more in common with a great California Cabernet year such as 1985 than the lighter 1988. Spectacularly long and rich, with soft tannins, this massive but surprisingly well-balanced wine should be at its best between 1993 and 2010. Wow! This guy can sure make super Cabernet! Philip Togni's 1987 will also be a controversial Cabernet Sauvignon. Black/ruby in color, this exceptionally concentrated, full-bodied wine has an intense bouquet of blackcurrants, Provençal herbs, and toasty oak. Dense and chewy in the mouth, with fabulous ripeness and concentration yet a significantly high level of tannin, this large-scale, authoritative Cabernet may ultimately merit a higher rating when it reaches full maturity. My best guess is that this wine will be at its peak between now and 2005. This is dramatic and individualistic California Cabernet at its best. Togni also makes an assertive, rich, Loire Valley style of Sauvignon Blanc that resembles a big, herbaceous, rich Pouilly-Fumé. The 1991 is one of the most impressive Sauvignons I have tasted from California. Its huge, mineral, herb, and melony nose is followed by a full-bodied wine with excellent purity and richness, as well as plenty of crisp acidity. From my perspective, Togni is making some of California's most authoritatively flavored, distinctive, and pleasure-filled wines.

TOPOLOS AT RUSSIAN RIVER (SONOMA)
Alicante Bouschet* * */* * * *, Grand Noir* * *, Petite Sirah* * */* * * *,
Zinfandel Rossi Ranch* * * * *, Zinfandel Ultimo* * * */* * * * *

1990	Alicante Bouschet	Russian River Valley	A	86
1989	Alicante Bouschet	Russian River Valley	A	85
1988	Grand Noir	Sonoma	A	86
1987	Petite Sirah Rossi Ranch	Russian River Valley	B	90
1991	Zinfandel Rossi Ranch Old Vines	Russian River Valley	B	90
1990	Zinfandel Rossi Ranch Old Vines	Russian River Valley	B	94
1989	Zinfandel Rossi Ranch Old Vines	Russian River Valley	B	88
1988	Zinfandel Rossi Ranch Old Vines	Russian River Valley	B	83
1988	Zinfandel Ultimo	Sonoma	B	88
1986	Zinfandel Ultimo	Sonoma	B	86

This Sonoma winery located near the town of Forestville has proven to be quite a discovery. All the wines are made from organically cultivated vineyards, meaning no pesticides, herbicides, or fungicides are used. The Topolos family primarily produce extraordinary Zinfandel, blockbuster, black-colored Petite Sirah, and, of all things, Alicante Bouschet (an underrated varietal that produces controversial wines). The best wines are the Zinfandels, which age magnificently. Should you be lucky enough to taste some of the vintages from the early 1980s, you will see they are among the most classic expressions of California Zinfandel. Topolos neither fines nor filters, and since he is getting incredibly tiny yields from exceptionally old vineyards (75–100 years old), the wines possess mind-boggling extraction. For example, the 1991 Zinfandel from Rossi Ranch (an 80-year-old vineyard) is almost black in color, with a huge, pure nose of blackcurrants, raspberries, and minerals. In the mouth it is huge, with some of the minty character so evident in 1990. Spectacularly rich and full bodied, it will benefit from 5–6 years of cellaring. It should drink well from 1997 to 2010+. The 1990 Zinfandel is also spectacular. With its inky black/purple color and huge nose of blackcurrants, plums, and eucalyptus, one might think this to be a Martha's Vineyard Cabernet rather than a Zinfandel. In the mouth there is exceptional density and richness and a phenomenally concentrated mouth-feel that must have come from microscopic yields. This is one of the most concentrated wines I have ever tasted from California, yet its balance is nearly perfect. This mammoth Zinfandel needs 3–5 years to shed some of its considerable tannin, but the quality of the fruit and the phenomenal extraction of flavor suggest it will provide memorable drinking for the next 10–15 or more years. Topolos's Ultimo is another superlative *cuvée* of Zinfandel that appears to be more approachable than the Zinfandel Rossi Ranch. The 1988 and 1986 Ultimos offer fragrant, earthy, black fruit; spicy, peppery, raspberry-scented noses; a lot of body and glycerin; expansive, rich textures; and long, intense finishes. The 1988 is a super success for the vintage; the 1986 is surprisingly mature for a Topolos wine. The Alicante Bouschet is undoubtedly a controversial wine. Frankly, I do not know how to rate them because they are impenetrable when young. They exhibit saturated black/purple colors and a thickness and richness that I have never experienced in a young, dry red wine. Alicante Bouschet does not generally develop into a terribly complex wine, so I have some reservations, but the 1990 and 1989 vintages produced superconcentrated wines with none of the late-harvest, pruny, raisiny character that one would expect from such rich wines. It seems to me that Topolos might be better off blending some Grenache, Syrah, or even Zinfandel with its Alicante Bouschet, something the French do to tame the rustic, savage qualities of this varietal. However, should you want to experience one of the richest wines made in the world, and you find the wines from the Rhône Valley Cornas appellation not rustic or concentrated enough, take a look at these Alicante Bouschets. Their prices make them a steal, even if they never turn into harmonious wines. Last, the winery produces a blockbuster, dense, purple-colored Petite Sirah. The 1987 offers aromas of pepper, cassis, and damp earth. Again, you are going to have to brush your teeth after drinking this wine, given its saturation and intensity. It is admirable that a winery that has gotten little national publicity makes wines of such force and individuality. Moreover, its pricing policy is fair. Readers would be foolish not to explore the wines of Topolos; whether you like them or not, they must be admired for their sheer drama and intensity.

MARIMAR TORRES (SONOMA)
Chardonnay* * * *

1991	Chardonnay Don Miguel Vineyard	Sonoma	C	87
1990	Chardonnay Don Miguel Vineyard	Sonoma	C	88

The 1990 Chardonnay's rich, intensely fragrant nose of ripe tropical fruits, toasty new oak, and butter is followed by a wine with a honeyed texture, deep, concentrated flavors, and a spicy, long finish. Everything is in balance in this serious Chardonnay, giving it an overall impression of both elegance and power. Drink it over the next 1–2 years. The 1991 is also a suave, graceful wine, with slightly less flesh and opulence than the 1990. Drink it over the next 3 years. Keep an eye out for the Torres Estate Pinot Noir that will be released in the mid-1990s.

TREFETHEN VINEYARDS WINERY (NAPA)
Cabernet Sauvignon Napa* */* * *, Cabernet Sauvignon Reserve* * *,
Chardonnay* * * * , Eshcol Red* * *, Eschol White* * *

1987	Cabernet Sauvignon	Napa	C	79
1986	Cabernet Sauvignon	Napa	C	85
1986	Cabernet Sauvignon Estate Reserve	Napa	D	88
1990	Chardonnay	Napa	C	82
N. V.	Eshcol Red	Napa	A	84
N. V.	Eshcol White	Napa	A	84
1991	White Riesling	Napa	A	72

Undoubtedly the best Cabernet I have tasted from Trefethen, the 1986 Estate Reserve offers an intense, big, ripe nose of cassis fruit and herbs. In the mouth there is velvety richness as well as enough structure (consisting of acid, tannin, and alcohol) to give the wine at least a decade's worth of drinkability. I admire it for its generously endowed, soft personality. Delicious! The tasty, elegantly styled, soft, supple, herb- and currant-flavored 1986 Cabernet Sauvignon will make ideal drinking over the next 5–6 years. No, it is not a blockbuster, but at least you do not have to fight through a wall of tannins and acidity to get to the charming fruit. As good as the two *cuvées* of 1986 were, I was disappointed with the tart, excessively acidified, hard, graceless 1987 Cabernet. For a Trefethen wine, it is remarkably devoid of personality and charm. Trefethen's Eshcol Red is an attractive berry- and herb-scented wine with fine, fleshy flavors. It exhibits good clean winemaking, as well as a soft, silky finish. Made from 43% Cabernet Sauvignon, 31% Pinot Noir, 18% Zinfandel, and 8% Merlot, it should be drunk over the next several years. The N. V. Eshcol White, made from 90% Chardonnay and 10% white Riesling, has a lovely floral, apple-scented bouquet and light- to medium-bodied flavors, altogether a refreshing, zesty, graceful bottle of Chardonnay-based wine that provides mass appeal. Drink it over the next year. Trefethen has consistently made some of the most elegant, flavorful California Chardonnays. However, its 1990, a superlative vintage for Chardonnay, is a disappointment. Although good, a heavy hand with acid additions has resulted in a supercrisp wine that approaches a level of shrillness. The fruit is masked by the acidity, and the finish is short and sharp. Trefethen's 1991 white Riesling is also a major flop, with its harsh acidity and lack of fruit.

TRENTADUE WINERY (SONOMA)
Cabernet Sauvignon* * *, Carignane* * * *, Merlot* * */* * * *, Old Patch Red
Proprietary Red Wine* * * *, Petite Sirah* * * *, Salute* * * *, Sangiovese* * * *,
Zinfandel* * * *

1989	Cabernet Sauvignon	Sonoma	A	78
1987	Cabernet Sauvignon	Sonoma	A	86
1991	Carignane	Alexander Valley	A	87
1988	Carignane	Alexander Valley	A	87
1987	Merlot	Sonoma	A	87

1991	Old Patch Red	Alexander Valley	A	89
1990	Old Patch Red	Alexander Valley	A	87
1988	Old Patch Red	Alexander Valley	A	90
1985	Old Patch Red	Alexander Valley	A	90
1991	Petite Sirah	Sonoma	B	90
1987	Petite Sirah	Alexander Valley	B	90
N. V.	Red Table Wine	California	A	87
1992	Salute	California	A	88
1991	Sangiovese	Alexander Valley	B	86
1990	Sangiovese	Alexander Valley	B	88
1991	Zinfandel	Sonoma	A	88
1990	Zinfandel	Sonoma	A	87

For much of its existence, Trentadue had a reputation for producing burly, often funky wines that were consistently inconsistent. However, since the mid-1980s Trentadue has eliminated the funkiness in its wines and proven to be a reliable, sometimes brilliant producer of rich, flavorful, full-bodied red wines that sell at some of the most reasonable prices in all of winedom. Recent releases from vintages such as 1987, 1988, 1990, and 1991 have all been fragrant, smashingly rich wines that can be drunk young or cellared. This is clearly a superlative source for terrific red wines at bargain prices. To the winery's credit, most of its wines are bottled unfiltered, so expect some hefty sediment to form if you can keep your hands off them for 3–4 years. Few California wineries produce good Carignane, but Trentadue does. The 1991 exhibits a big, black cherry, spicy nose, rich, elegant, medium- to full-bodied flavors, and a lush finish. Drinkable now, it should mature gracefully for another 7–8 years. The 1988 Carignane is reminiscent of both an Italian Amarone and a California late-harvest Zinfandel. Although it is not a sweet wine, this hefty, robust effort oozes with peppery, spicy, chunky fruit, has gobs of body, and produces a lusty, nearly thick finish. If served with full-flavored cuisine, or with powerful cheeses, this personality-filled wine will make a favorable impression. It should easily drink well for another decade. Perhaps the most amazing red wine made in California is Trentadue's proprietary red called Old Patch Red, a field blend of Carignane, Petite Sirah, Zinfandel, and Alicante from vines planted in the nineteenth century. In 1993 the average age of these vines was 107 years. The 1988, 1990, and 1991 Old Patch Reds all possess a superb southern Rhône-like nose of Oriental spices, superripe red and black fruits, pepper, and new saddle leather. There is gorgeous richness, an expansive, full-bodied, chewy lusciousness, and considerable depth, focus, and length. It is hard to pick a favorite, as they are relatively similar. The 1991 is slightly richer and deeper. Only the 1985 Old Patch Red stands out, displaying a late-harvest Zinfandel character. In a blind tasting it could be mistaken for a huge, chewy Amarone. It should continue to drink well for another 5–6 years. These are amazing wines for the price. Unfortunately, less than 2,000 cases are produced, so move quickly.

Looking for a smoky, chocolatey, black cherry–scented and –flavored Merlot at a reasonable price? Trentadue's 1987 Merlot offers the superripeness, admirable concentration, and chewy texture expected from a top vintage. It also possesses lavish amounts of fruit and flavor. Deep, yet already impressive and evolved, this is a full-flavored, personality-filled Merlot. Drink it over the next 5–7 years. What about Trentadue's Petite Sirah? As one might expect, given the house style of this winery, both the 1987 and 1991 display an impenetrable, black/purple, broodingly deep color. The noses offer up aromas of superripe black raspberries, peppery spices, and loads of fruit. In the mouth it is an enormously concentrated, rich, chewy wine, with soft tannins, and layers of fruit and extract. The tannins are undoubtedly higher than one might suspect, but there is so much richness, the structure of these wines is nearly obscured. These bargain-priced, blockbuster Petite Sirahs are for drinking over the next 10–15 years.

Trentadue's 1987 Cabernet Sauvignon conjures up memories of old-style California Cabernets that were heavily extracted, chunky, and coarse, but wow, what fruit and intensity. Although this wine will never win any awards for finesse or elegance, I would not be surprised to see it embarrass many of its more prestigious siblings in a blind tasting in 10 or so years. Rich, with a nose of black fruits, smoke, and herbs, this full-bodied wine displays soft tannins and an unmistakable voluptuous, intense style. The 1989 Cabernet Sauvignon is too earthy and somewhat disjointed and unusual. It is not nearly as enjoyable as the 1987.

The smooth-as-silk 1990 Zinfandel exhibits generous black cherry aromas and flavors. It is full bodied, supple, and ideal for drinking over the next 5–6 years. The 1991 Zinfandel is another husky wine with nearly opaque black/ruby color, a huge, full-bodied, velvety textured taste, and rich, heady, spicy, long flavors. Again, it is a Zinfandel to drink in its youth—preferably over the next 7–8 years. Trentadue has begun to offer another proprietary red wine called Salute. It is the winery's least expensive wine, selling for around $7 a bottle. The 1992 should be snapped up by any consumer looking for an authoritatively flavored, graceful red wine with smooth tannins, a huge bouquet of red and black fruits, deep, cherry- and raspberrylike flavors, and a ripe, luscious, long finish. Drink it over the next 5–6 years. Another inexpensive wine, a blend of Carignane and Zinfandel, is Trentadue's nonvintage red table wine. The wine's overall impression of raspberries appears in the bouquet and flavors of this soft, superbly fruity, full-bodied wine. It, too, should be consumed over the next 3–5 years.

It should be apparent that this winery is making a bevy of terrific red wines at bargain-basement prices. The wines all sell for between $6 and $12 a bottle. Given their quality/price rapport, these wines will not linger on retailers' shelves.

TRUCHARD VINEYARDS (NAPA)
Merlot* * *, Pinot Noir* *

1990	Merlot	Napa	C	86
1991	Pinot Noir	Napa	C	75

Smoky, toffee, berry, and herb aromas soar from the glass of the 1990 Merlot. Drink this round, soft, generously endowed, richly fruity wine over the next

4–5 years. As tasty as the Merlot is, the 1991 Pinot Noir is a light ruby-colored, spicy, simple wine with little depth or length.

TUDAL WINERY (NAPA)
Cabernet Sauvignon* * * *

1987	Cabernet Sauvignon	Napa	C	86

1986	Cabernet Sauvignon	Napa	C	87

This small Cabernet Sauvignon specialist fashions spicy, herbaceous, rich, tannic, medium- to full-bodied wines that often require 4–5 years of cellaring to reveal their character. Wines such as the 1986 and 1987 Cabernet Sauvignons have the potential to last for 15 years. This is an underrated, high-quality source for Napa Valley Cabernet Sauvignon.

TULOCAY VINEYARDS (NAPA)
Cabernet Sauvignon* * * *, Chardonnay* *, Pinot Noir* *,
Pinot Noir Haynes Vineyard* *

1986	Cabernet Sauvignon	Napa	C	89
1987	Cabernet Sauvignon Egan Vineyard	Napa	C	89
1989	Pinot Noir Haynes Vineyard	Napa	C	73

In the mouth the very dark ruby/purple-colored 1987 Cabernet Sauvignon Egan Vineyard has an emerging bouquet of cedar, spices, black fruits, and a touch of mint. It exhibits excellent concentration, a firm structure, a solid inner core of fruit, and fine depth. Although it is not ready to drink, needing a good 2–4 years to shed its tannins, it should evolve gracefully over a period of 10–15 years. The highly extracted, full-bodied 1986 Cabernet Sauvignon has an explosive bouquet of rich berry fruit and intense mint. In the mouth there is superb ripeness and plenty of tannin. This is a powerful, large-scale wine. Built for cellaring, the 1986 Tulocay should be at its best between now and 2005. I mentioned in my tasting notes that this wine improved significantly with 15 minutes of airing, so decantation is probably recommended if you intend to drink it over the next several years. I cannot muster enthusiasm for the winery's vegetal, funky Pinot Noir.

VIADER (NAPA)
Propietary Red Wine* * * *

1990	Proprietary Red Wine		D	89

A blend of 68% Cabernet Sauvignon and 32% Cabernet Franc, this beautifully packaged, elegant wine offers a complex, fragrant bouquet of spices, herbs, black fruits, and spring flowers. The wine is medium bodied, with admirable definition, excellent richness, crisp underlying acidity, no obvious new oak, but a subtle, cassis, vanillin component to its flavors, and a stylish, medium-bodied finish. Several additional years in the bottle should result in more aromatic development. If the flavors broaden, this will clearly be an outstanding effort. It is already an impressive wine made with a delicate, restrained style.

VICHON WINERY (NAPA)

Cabernet Sauvignon Coastal Selection* *, Cabernet Sauvignon Napa* * *,
Cabernet Sauvignon Stag's Leap District* * * *, Chardonnay* * */* * * *,
Chardonnay Coastal Selection* *, Chevrignon* * *, Merlot* * */* * * *

1988	Cabernet Sauvignon	Napa	C	86
1989	Cabernet Sauvignon Coastal Selection	California	A	74
1987	Cabernet Sauvignon Stag's Leap District	Napa	C	87
1986	Cabernet Sauvignon Stag's Leap District	Napa	C	87
1990	Chardonnay	Napa	B	86
1991	Chardonnay Coastal Selection	California	A	75
1990	Chevrignon	Napa	B	86
1987	Merlot	Napa	C	88

Since the omnipotent firm of Robert Mondavi took over the production at Vichon, the quality has improved. The deliciously forward, soft, pleasant 1988 Cabernet Sauvignon offers a captivating mixture of toasty new oak, creamy, curranty, herbaceous-tinged fruit, and a satiny-smooth texture. It is ideal for drinking over the next 4–5 years. The 1990 Chevrignon, a blend of 50% Semillon and 50% Sauvignon, has a big, spicy, melony, herbaceous bouquet; ripe, opulent, medium-bodied flavors; excellent extract; and a long, luscious texture. It is an ideal wine for drinking with fish and shellfish. I suggest consuming it over the next year. The 1987 Cabernet Sauvignon from the Stag's Leap District is the best Vichon Cabernet to date. Dark ruby/purple in color, it boasts a moderately intense, pure bouquet of blackcurrants, smoky oak, and herbs. In the mouth it is medium bodied and has excellent concentration, good acidity, and moderate tannins. Vichon has admirably succeeded in producing a graceful, middleweight Cabernet of undeniable elegance. Although approachable now, it should be at its best between 1993 and 1999. The 1986 Cabernet Sauvignon has a pronounced, intense bouquet of herbs, cedar, blackcurrants, and oak. In the mouth it is concentrated, medium to full bodied, long, and impressive. Drinkable now, it should last for another 5–7 years. The 1987 Merlot presents further convincing evidence that when all the dust settles about the quality of the remarkable string of California red wine vintages (1984, 1985, 1986, 1987), it eventually may be 1987, not 1985, that takes top marks. For now, this beautifully made Merlot has deep ruby/purple color and exhibits a smooth, velvety, full-bodied texture with layers of seductive black and red fruits wrapped judiciously in a glove of toasty oak. The overall impression is one of lusciousness and silky smoothness. Restaurants should be beating a path to their distributors to get this wine on their lists. It should drink beautifully for another 5–6 years. The quality of Vichon's Chardonnay has also improved. The 1990 is the best wine Vichon has yet produced. The attractive apple, buttery, subtle, toasty aromas are followed by a medium- to full-bodied wine with ripe, round, zesty flavors and fine length. Drink it over the next 1–2 years. In 1989 Vichon began producing an inexpensive line of wines called Coastal Selection. Based on the 1991 Chardonnay and 1990 Cabernet Sauvignon, these are mediocre, thin, malnourished wines that do not represent good value despite their low prices.

VILLA MT. EDEN WINERY (NAPA)

Cabernet Sauvignon California*, Cabernet Sauvignon Cellar Select*, Chardonnay
Grand Reserve* *, Pinot Noir*, Zinfandel Cellar Select*

1990	Cabernet Sauvignon Cellar Select	California	C	59
1988	Cabernet Sauvignon Grand Reserve	Napa	C	75
1988	Cabernet Sauvignon	California	B	75
1990	Chardonnay Grand Reserve	Napa	B	77
1990	Zinfandel Cellar Select	California	B	72

Anyone who has recently tasted the Villa Mt. Eden 1974 or 1978 Cabernet Sauvignons made by Nils Venge, the present-day winemaker at Groth, must be tormented by the insipid, bland, denuded, and diluted wines now emerging from Villa Mt. Eden. Virtually all of these wines are sterile, thin, stripped, and astringent, with nonexistent bouquets, no character or charm, and no fruit. In short, Villa Mt. Eden boasts one of the most distressingly disappointing portfolios of California wines. Given the huge resources of Washington State's Stimson Lane, the owners of Villa Mt. Eden, how much longer can we expect such efforts?

VILLA ZAPU (NAPA)

Cabernet Sauvignon* *, Chardonnay* *

1989	Cabernet Sauvignon	Napa	B	74
1989	Chardonnay	Napa	B	74

Nothing to emerge from this relatively new winery has possessed much fruit. The wines are plagued by excessive acidity and tannin.

VITA NOVA (SANTA BARBARA)

Cabernet Franc* * *, Chardonnay* * *, Reservatum* */* * *

1990	Cabernet Franc	Santa Barbara	B	88
1991	Chardonnay	Santa Barbara	C	79
1989	Reservatum Red Table Wine	Santa Barbara	C	79
1988	Reservatum Red Table Wine	Arroyo Grande	C	87
1991	Reservatum Semillon	Santa Barbara	C	87

Vita Nova is the creation of Au Bon Climat's Jim Clendenen and Qupé's Bob Lindquist. The wines are made from grapes purchased from different sources. The quality is generally high, although I was struck by the fact that the 1991 Chardonnay went over the edge in terms of excessive use of oak. It exhibits a light golden color, and the fruit is already taking a back seat to the wood component. More interesting is the 1991 Reservatum Semillon, made from grapes purchased from Santa Barbara's excellent Buttonwood Farm. It offers a waxy, melony, perfumed nose; ripe, gorgeous, richly textured flavors that display considerable body and glycerin; and a crisp, husky finish. This big, dry white wine requires intensely flavored fish or fowl dishes to be at its best. The red wine offerings include a lean, tart, austere, high-acid 1989 Reservatum. Although well made, it is far too compact and malnourished to merit high marks. More interesting is the 1990 Cabernet Franc, which has 25% Cabernet Sauvignon in the blend. It offers a sweet, spicy, herbaceous, cherry-scented nose, opulent, richly fruity, velvety-textured flavors, and a lush, heady finish. Drink it over the next 5–6 years for its exuberant richness and chewy flavors. The 1988 Reservatum, made from grapes grown in the Arroyo Grande Valley, reveals a dark ruby color, a herbaceous, black fruit–scented nose, rich, medium-bodied flavors, and a generous finish. It lacks the complexity and length of the 1990 Cabernet Franc, but it is an attractive wine for drinking over the next 5–6 years.

VON STRASSER (NAPA)
Cabernet Sauvignon* * * *

1991	Cabernet Sauvignon	Napa	C	90

This new Diamond Mtn. producer has burst on the Cabernet scene with a terrific 1991. It reveals a deep black/purple color and a perfumed nose of ripe cassis, wood, licorice, and spices. Full bodied, with layer upon layer of densely extracted, chewy fruit buttressed by adequate acidity and soft tannins, this impressive Cabernet Sauvignon should drink well through much of the first decade of the next century.

WEINSTOCK CELLARS (SONOMA)
Cabernet Sauvignon* *, Chardonnay* */* * *, Gamay Beaujolais* * *, Sauvignon Blanc* *

I have not seen recent vintages from Weinstock Cellars, but this has been a consistently good producer of kosher wines that emphasize pure fruity aromas and flavors, medium body, and soft tannins. The wines are usually priced under $12 a bottle and represent good values. My favorites to date include the Sauvignon Blanc, Chardonnay, and Gamay Beaujolais.

WELLINGTON VINEYARDS (SONOMA)
Cabernet Franc*, Cabernet Sauvignon* *, Côte de Sonoma* * *, Proprietary Red Wine* * *, Zinfandel* * */* * * *

1990	Cabernet Franc Mt. Veeder	Napa	C	68
1989	Cabernet Sauvignon Mohrhardt and Ridge Vineyards	Sonoma	C	76
1991	Côtes de Sonoma Old Vines	Sonoma	A	86
1989	Random Ridge Proprietary Red Wine	Sonoma	C	82
1990	Zinfandel Old Vines	Sonoma	B	87

This is an intriguing, albeit erratic group of wines. Certainly the 1991 Côtes de Sonoma is a big, bold, hearty, husky red wine with chunky flavors, excellent ripeness, and a mouth-filling, luscious texture. Succulent and velvety enough to be drunk now, it promises to last for 5–6 years. The best wine is the 1990 Zinfandel Old Vines from the Sonoma Valley. It exhibits excellent color; a rich, peppery, black raspberry, briery nose; tasty, medium- to full-bodied flavors; excellent depth and definition; and a long, lusty finish. Drink it over the next 7–8 years. The other Wellington Vineyards offerings include a 1990 proprietary red wine (72% Cabernet Sauvignon and 28% Cabernet Franc) that reveals a good, spicy, St.-Émilion–like nose, but narrow, high-acid, angular flavors that tail off in the mouth. The 1989 Cabernet Sauvignon from the Mohrhardt and Ridge vineyards is viciously tannic to the point of obscuring most of the fruit. This wine will never come into balance given the level of these harsh, astringent tannins. The 1990 Cabernet Franc from Mt. Veeder looks impressive, but it displays a stinky lees smell, suggesting the wine should have been racked. Otherwise, the wine possesses plenty of intensity and richness. It is a shame that the unpleasant lees smell can ruin the other fine raw materials.

WENTE BROTHERS WINERY (ALAMEDA)

Chardonnay Herman Wente Vineyard* * * (since 1988), Chardonnay Reserve* * * (since 1988), Gewürztraminer*, Riesling*, Sparkling Wine Cuvées*/**

1991	Chardonnay Estate	Central Coast	A	86
1990	Chardonnay Herman Wente Vineyard	Livermore	C	88

Wente Brothers, established in the late nineteenth century, is one of California's historic pioneers. Many authorities have remarked that Wente's vineyards are situated in the heart of Livermore Valley and are potentially as superb as any in the state. Perhaps Wente has begun to exploit them, as these two offerings reveal wonderful purity, excellent richness of fruit, plenty of extraction, and an overall sense of balance. Even more important, these wines are clearly made to provide pleasure. Other offerings in the Wente portfolio include a vapid Gewürztraminer and Riesling and a hollow Brut sparkling wine *cuvée*.

MARK WEST VINEYARDS (SONOMA)

Chardonnay* *, Pinot Noir* *, Zinfandel Robert Rue Vineyard* * *

1989	Zinfandel Robert Rue Vineyard	Sonoma	B	86

I rarely understand the wines from this Sonoma winery, but in the problematic 1989 vintage, Mark West has turned out a jammy, spicy, large-scale Zinfandel with considerable tannin and flavor. Not yet revealing any complexity, the wine may benefit from cellaring. It has plenty of stuffing and should easily stand up to 7–8 years of bottle age. The Pinot Noirs and Chardonnays have often been bizarrely flavored wines with the wood outbalancing the skinny fruitiness.

WESTWOOD WINERY (EL DORADO)

Barbera* * */* * * *, Charbono* * */* * * *, Chardonnay* *, Pinot Noir* * *

1990	Barbera Riserva Danna	El Dorado	B	87
1990	Charbono Riserva Danna Arrastra Vyd.	El Dorado	B	86
1990	Pinot Noir	California	B	86

This small winery in El Dorado has turned out some interesting wines. Even its Pinot Noir, which can cause so many problems for California producers, is surprisingly flavorful. Deep in color, with a big, sweet, expansive nose of black cherries, herbs, and earth, the 1990 Pinot Noir exhibits excellent ripeness, decent acidity, and a soft, lush finish. Drink it over the next 2–4 years. The rarely encountered 1990 Charbono from the Arrastra Vineyards also reveals excellent winemaking. Deeply colored, with a thick texture, this chunky, robust, spicy wine offers copious amounts of fruit, some complexity, and plenty of depth and mouth-filling glycerin. It would be ideal with grilled foods and pizza. My favorite wine is the excellent Barbera. Barbera can be bitterly acidic, but Westwood's 1990 is deeply colored, with a big, sweet nose of briery fruit, almonds, and spices. In the mouth there is excellent concentration, abundant quantities of black cherry fruit, moderate acidity, and a long, heady finish. This beautifully made Barbera will offer immensely satisfying drinking for the next 4–6 years.

WHALER VINEYARD WINERY (MENDOCINO)
Pinot Noir*, Zinfandel Estate* * *, Zinfandel Estate Flagship* * * *

1990	Zinfandel Estate	Mendocino	B	88
1990	Zinfandel Estate Flagship	Mendocino	C	87

This small Mendocino property produces just under 2,500 cases of Zinfandel. The two 1990 offerings are excellent. For now, the higher rating goes to the 1990 Estate, which is more forward and luscious than the 1990 Estate Flagship. The 1990 Estate bottling exhibits a huge bouquet of crushed black raspberries and pepper; soft, opulent, medium- to full-bodied flavors; an expansive texture; and a seductively long, lush finish. It is all silk and velvety fruit, so I suspect this is a Zinfandel to drink over the next 5–6 years. The 1990 Estate Flagship (only 250 cases produced) is less expressive, more tightly structured, and rich and full, with most of its intensity coming at the back of the mouth. Although it possesses at least 10–12 years of aging potential, it is currently closed, albeit promisingly intense, ripe, and full bodied. It should be cellared for several years. I have tasted only a few vintages of Pinot Noir from Whaler, all of which left me unimpressed. They all possessed shallow, thin, uninteresting flavors.

WILLIAM WHEELER WINERY (SONOMA)
Cabernet Sauvignon* *, Chardonnay* *, Fumé Blanc* * *,
Quintet Proprietary Red Wine* *

1989	Cabernet Sauvignon	Sonoma	B	70
1991	Chardonnay	Sonoma	B	78
1991	Fumé Blanc	Sonoma	A	84
1990	Quintet Proprietary Red Wine	Sonoma	B	76

This winery has undergone some changes recently, with a new label and a new owner, Paribas Domaines, a French enterprise that also owns the renowned Château La Lagune in Bordeaux and the Champagne firm of Ayala. The Wheeler Winery has had a checkered history since its inception in 1981, and the new releases continue to display the winery's inconsistency. The 1991 Fumé Blanc is a soft, delicious, fruity wine, with good varietal character and a smooth finish. It should be drunk before the summer of 1994. The 1991 Chardonnay is made in a straightforward, pleasant, correct style that will offend no one. More intensity and complexity would have been an added virtue. William Wheeler's Rhône-style blend, the 1990 Quintet (27% Mourvèdre, 25% Zinfandel, 23% Carignane, 18% Gamay, and 7% Syrah), is a soft, light-bodied, fruity wine with no complexity and not much depth or character. In essence, it is equivalent to a decent generic jug wine. The 1989 Cabernet Sauvignon should have been declassified, as it is excessively vegetal, thin, tart, and unpleasant.

WHITCRAFT WINERY (SANTA BARBARA)
Pinot Noir Bien Nacido Vineyard* * *

1991	Pinot Noir Bien Nacido Vineyard	Santa Barbara		87
1990	Pinot Noir Bien Nacido Vineyard	Santa Barbara		?
1991	Pinot Noir Olivet Lane Vineyard	Russian River Valley		84

I immensely enjoyed Whitcraft's 1991 Pinot Noir from the Bien Nacido Vineyard. It exhibits deep, highly saturated color; a ripe, herb, black cherry, meaty nose; deep, rich, concentrated flavors; and a spicy finish. It offers a chewy mouthful of well-made Pinot Noir. Drink it over the next 5–6 years. The 1990 Pinot Noir Bien Nacido Vineyard displays admirable concentration and fine texture, but a musty, funky lees aroma marred the wine's bouquet. This is a wine with considerable raw material, but if the sample I tasted is typical of other bottles, the nose is not clean. Given the handcrafted feel to these wines and the fine raw materials, I would prefer to reserve judgment until this wine can be retasted. Finally, the Whitcraft Winery has ventured outside Santa Barbara County and has traveled to the Russian River Valley to buy grapes from one of that region's finest Pinot Noir sources, Olivet Lane. The 1991 Pinot Noir Olivet Lane Vineyard reveals a less interesting nose than the 1991 Bien Nacido, but it offers a good, rich, spicy, herbaceous, meaty mouthful of wine with relatively high acidity. The acids are sharp, which kept my score lower. This wine offers good Pinot Noir character in a medium-bodied format. Acid freaks will enjoy it more than I did.

WHITE OAK VINEYARDS (SONOMA)
Chardonnay Meyers Limited Reserve* *, Chardonnay Sonoma* *

1990	Chardonnay	Sonoma	B	75
1990	Chardonnay Meyers Limited Reserve	Sonoma	C	80

The problem with every White Oak Chardonnay I have tasted to date has been an excessive amount of oak for the amount of fruit the wines possess. They tend to have high acidity levels, blatant, oaky flavors, and a lack of fruit and depth. Sometimes the Sonoma bottling can be more flattering and pleasant than the Meyers Limited Reserve. Although these are ambitiously styled Chardonnays, they lack the depth necessary to balance out the wood.

WHITEHALL LANE WINERY (NAPA)
Cabernet Sauvignon Morisoli Vineyard* * * *, Cabernet Sauvignon Napa* * *,
Cabernet Sauvignon Reserve* * */* * * *, Chardonnay Le Petit* *,
Chardonnay Reserve* * *, Pinot Noir* *

1990	Cabernet Franc	Napa	C	87
1990	Cabernet Sauvignon Morisoli Vineyard	Napa	D	91
1989	Cabernet Sauvignon Reserve	Napa	D	87
1990	Merlot Summer's Ranch	Alexander Valley	C	90

This is an impressive group of wines. For starters there is a sumptuous, super-concentrated 1990 Merlot Summer's Ranch that offers a big, chocolatey, black cherry–scented nose, spicy, deep, fleshy, authoritatively rich flavors, and a finish that goes on and on. With good underlying acidity and some tannin, this is a flamboyant, rich Merlot for drinking over the next 7–8 years. High quality California Cabernet Francs are few and far between, although more wineries appear to be obtaining the elusive fragrance and finesse that top-notch Cabernet Franc can provide. Whitehall Lane's 1990 Cabernet Franc exhibits a delicious, spice, menthol, herb, and cherry-scented nose, ripe, luscious, expansive, rich flavors that avoid any sense of heaviness. In fact, the wine tastes elegant, medium bodied, and stylish. This is a wonderfully supple, complex Cabernet Franc for drinking over the next 6–7 years. The 1989 Cabernet Sauvignon Reserve, which is scheduled for release in September, is one of the better efforts from this irregular vintage. The saturated deep ruby/purple color is followed by moderately intense aromas of mint and cassis. Medium bodied, with admirable richness, firm tannins, adequate acidity, and a graceful personality, this stylish Cabernet will drink well for another decade.

Whitehall Lane continues to display a talent for turning out high-quality Cabernet Sauvignons. The two 1990 Cabernet Sauvignon cuvées from Whitehall Lane have excellent potential. The single-vineyard Morisoli Cabernet may merit an outstanding rating in a few years. It is dense, with a telltale, minty, cassis aroma and fine richness; its gobs of tannin suggest the wine needs 3–4 years of cellaring. It should keep for at least 12–15 years. Although more approachable, the 1990 regular cuvée again exhibits Whitehall Lane's minty, black fruit–dominated bouquet and pure, rich, medium- to full-bodied flavors. Drink it over the next 7–8 years. The 1987 regular bottling has a moderately intense bouquet of mint and cassis fruit; ripe, long, attractive flavors; medium to full body; and a well-balanced, smooth finish. It should drink nicely for another 5–7 years. Although the dark ruby-colored 1985 Cabernet Sauvignon Reserve seems subdued and restrained, with a bit of introspection the wine reveals considerable character, depth, and quality. The bouquet fairly blossoms with the scents of mint, blackcurrants, and oak. In the mouth, once past the crisp acidity and wall of tannins, there is a full-bodied, highly extracted, ripe, concentrated, tightly knit wine waiting to break loose. Patience is most definitely required, and I would not be surprised if this wine merited an outstanding rating with another 3–5 years of cellaring. It is very impressive, but so, so backward. **Anticipated maturity: 1995–2010.** The light-bodied 1990 Chardonnay Reserve is attractive, with medium depth, zesty peach- and apple-like fruit, a touch of oak, and a crisp finish. Drink it over the next 1–2 years. Should readers run across any of Whitehall Lane's regular bottlings or Reserve cuvées made in 1984 or 1985, do not hesitate to give them a try. All are excellent wines.

WHITEROCK VINEYARDS (NAPA)
Proprietary Red Wine* * *

1986   Claret   Napa   C   87

I suppose this wine is meant to imitate a classic Bordeaux, and if that is the idea, the winery has succeeded admirably. Deep ruby/purple in color, with a stylish bouquet of herbs, cassis, and toasty oak, this interesting, complex wine has considerable power and concentration, as well as plenty of tannin in the

finish. In fact, my only question was whether the tannins might be a bit too elevated for the wine's depth. I do not think they are, but if they fall away and
even more fruit emerges, this wine may turn out to be better than my score indicates. It should drink extremely well for the next 5–8 years, possibly longer.

WILD HORSE WINERY (SAN LUIS OBISPO)

Chardonnay* * *, Pinot Noir* * */* * * *

1990	Chardonnay	Central Coast	B	87
1989	Chardonnay	Central Coast	B	84
1990	Pinot Noir	Santa Barbara	B	86

Every time I have the wines of Wild Horse, I find them pleasing. The 1990
Chardonnay promises to be one of the richer, fuller wines made by propri-
etor/winemaker Ken Volk. A big nose of toasty oak and tropical fruits is followed by a medium- to full-bodied wine with plenty of extract, an opulent
texture, and a spicy, clean finish. Drink it over the next 1–2 years. Wild
Horse's specialty is Pinot Noir, full of spicy, oaky, black cherry fruit offered in
an up-front, lush, medium-bodied style. Both the 1986 and 1987 are very
good, and the 1990 looks to be a worthy rival. There is plenty of oak, but it
does not overwhelm the black cherry, herb-tinged fruit that gushes from the
glass. The wine boasts decent acidity and enough tannin to hold it together for
another 5–6 years, but it clearly requires consumption over the next 3–4 years.

J. WILE AND SONS (CALIFORNIA)

Cabernet Sauvignon*, Chardonnay*, Sauvignon Blanc*

This *négociant* brand, launched by a well-known importer, has consistently
produced light-bodied, diluted, uninteresting, sterile wines that offer only
vague suggestions of their varietal characters. Although inexpensive, the wines
must improve if they are going to capture the interest of consumers looking for
pleasure and value.

WILLIAMS-SELYEM (SONOMA)

Chardonnay Allen Vineyard* * * * *, Pinot Noir* * * *, Pinot Noir
Allen Vineyard* * * * *, Pinot Noir Olivet Lane Vineyard* * * *, Pinot Noir Rochioli
Vineyard* * * * *, Zinfandel Martinelli Vineyard* * * * *

1990	Chardonnay Allen Vineyard	Russian River Valley	D	90
1990	Pinot Noir	Russian River Valley	D	90
1990	Pinot Noir Allen Vineyard	Sonoma	D	91
1991	Pinot Noir Olivet Lane	Russian River Valley	D	93
1990	Pinot Noir Olivet Lane	Russian River Valley	D	89
1990	Zinfandel Martinelli Vineyard	Sonoma	C	94
1989	Zinfandel Martinelli Vineyard	Sonoma	C	90

The wines from this superb producer must be among the hardest to find in the
world. Virtually all of the production is sold via the winery's mailing list, so do
not expect to run across a case or two at your local wine merchant's. The 1990
Chardonnay is the first I have tasted from Williams-Selyem. It will undoubtedly be controversial in high-tech circles. Made in a burgundian, full-bodied,

rich, lavishly oaked, buttery style, it first appears closed and woody, but after 10 minutes in the glass a multitude of honeyed, buttery, apple, and floral aromas emerge and the oak begins to take a back seat to the wine's other characteristics. Deep, unctuous, thick, and chewy, it will prove to be a superrich, complex, nearly decadent style of Chardonnay for drinking over the next 3–5 years. It is becoming increasingly apparent when talking about California Pinot Noir that the two best producers are William-Selyem and Santa Barbara's Au Bon Climat. Over recent vintages they have narrowly surpassed Calera in terms of the complexity and seductive textural aspects of their wines. Williams-Selyem's 1991 Pinot Noir Olivet Lane exhibits abundant quantities of smoky, toasty, bacon fat–scented new oak in the nose; rich, creamy, black cherry flavors that go on and on; a voluptuous texture; and a knock-out finish. This is Pinot Noir at its most seductive and opulent. It should drink well for at least 5–6 years. Good luck finding any! The light to medium ruby color of the 1990 Olivet Lane is somewhat deceiving given the amount of richness offered by the bouquet and flavors. The nose, which displays an intriguing earthy, berry, spicy component, reminds me of a high-class Premier Cru from Beaune. In the mouth the wine is soft, round, and gentle, with delicious berry fruit, toasty oak, and an attractive complexity. I would opt for drinking this lovely Pinot Noir over the next 3–4 years. The other Pinot Noirs are just as exciting. The 1990 Pinot Noir Allen Vineyard displays a huge, black cherry–, spicy oak– and floral-scented nose; rich, medium-bodied flavors that exhibit more structure and tannin than the Olivet *cuvée;* and a luscious finish. The least expensive Pinot Noir is the Russian River Valley *cuvée*, which has lavish quantities of toasty new oak, plenty of succulent cherry fruit, a velvety texture, medium body, and a smooth, silky finish. Drink it over the next 3–4 years. If Williams-Selyem has proven the ability to produce potentially prodigious Pinot Noirs, it has shown an equal talent with Zinfandel. Unfortunately, production is limited. Both the 1989 and 1990 Zinfandels are impressive efforts, displaying huge black raspberry, peppery aromas along with gobs of smoky oak. Both are medium to full bodied (the 1990 shows slightly more glycerin and ripeness), have considerable alcoholic clout, chewy textures, and explosively rich, highly extracted finishes. Both can be drunk now, although the 1989 will last for 5–6 years and the 1990 for up to a decade.

CHÂTEAU WOLTNER (NAPA)

Chardonnay Estate Reserve* * *, Chardonnay Frederique Vineyard* * *, Chardonnay
St. Thomas Vineyard* * * *, Chardonnay Titus Vineyard* * * *

1990	Chardonnay Estate Reserve	Howell Mountain	D	84
1990	Chardonnay Frederique Vineyard	Howell Mountain	E	85
1990	Chardonnay St. Thomas Vineyard	Howell Mountain	D	93
1990	Chardonnay Titus Vineyard	Howell Mountain	E	90

Bold prices aside, this producer, dedicated to making long-lived, French-like Chardonnay from its vineyards on Howell Mountain, has turned out some interesting 1990s. Although the 1990 Chardonnay Frederique Vineyard does not merit its high price, it is good, made in an acidic, medium-bodied, austere, minerallike style. Comparable to good Chablis, it could have benefited from more depth and a longer finish. That is not a problem with the 1990 Chardonnay Titus Vineyard. In spite of its tightness and backward style, this is a wine with plenty of depth, a rich, full-bodied, elegant personality, a nice touch of subtle oak, and a huge, rich finish. Much of the wine's current appeal is in its finish, which indicates to me that the wine will age nicely for up to 5 years or more. The marvelous 1990 Chardonnay St. Thomas Vineyard displays a huge nose of wet stones, buttery fruit, and toast, followed by a wine with exceptional ripeness, dazzling length, and an impeccable sense of balance. The wine is still young but promises to last for at least 4–5 years. Last, the 1990 Estate Reserve is an elegant, lean, unevolved wine with some spicy oak in the nose and dry, one-dimensional fruit flavors. It should display more character and complexity with another 6–12 months of age. Although the quality has been generally very good, and one has to be encouraged by the French style of the Woltner Chardonnays, its pricing policy makes these Chardonnays a tough sell. These days consumers are justifiably demanding that price be linked proportionately to quality, and just how well these wines will age, no one knows. Certainly, California Chardonnays are not known for improving in the bottle, so what can we expect from these offerings?

ZACA MESA (SANTA BARBARA)
Chardonnay* *, Mourvèdre* *, Syrah/Malbec* * *, Syrah* *

1992	Alamo Cuvée	Santa Barbara	B	78
1991	Chardonnay	Santa Barbara	B	85
1990	Chardonnay Reserve	Santa Barbara	C	74
1991	Malbec	Santa Barbara	B	82
1991	Mourvèdre	Santa Barbara	B	73
1991	Syrah	Santa Barbara	B	76
1991	Syrah/Malbec	Santa Barbara	D	86

It is ironic that Zaca Mesa, which produced some of Santa Barbara's finest winemakers (Ken Brown of Byron, Jim Clendenen and Adam Tolmach of Au Bon Climat, and Bob Lindquist of Qupé), has had such an irregular quality record. As the following tasting notes demonstrate, there is not much about which to get excited. However, there is good news. The highly talented Daniel Gehrs, who has fashioned some marvelous white wines under his own label, has been hired as the full-time winemaker at Zaca Mesa. If he is given the independence he deserves, I predict the quality of Zaca Mesa's wines will soar. Gehrs's first true vintage will be 1993, as he arrived following the 1992 harvest. The two best wines at present include the 1991 Chardonnay, which offers good fruit in a straightforward, medium- to full-bodied style, delicious wine. The dark ruby color is followed by a spicy, floral, cassis-scented nose, fleshy, ripe, opulent flavors, excellent richness, and good depth. Drink it over the next 4–5 years. The other wines include a lean, excessively acidic and oaky 1990 Chardonnay Reserve, and a soft, light, one-dimensional 1992 Alamo Cuvée (a red wine made from 50% Grenache, 35% Mourvèdre, and 15% Syrah). I like the idea behind the blend, but this offering is one-dimensional and simple. The 1991 Malbec is a good but not exciting wine that possesses straightforward flavors and little complexity or personality. The disappointing 1991 Mourvèdre is light colored, with musty, tree bark–like flavors, and a thin, hollow personality. The 1991 Syrah is a light example of this varietal, but slightly fruity, with little depth or personality. Although most of these wines are indifferent examples, look for things to dramatically improve under Daniel Gehrs.

ZD WINERY (NAPA)

Cabernet Sauvignon* * *, Cabernet Sauvignon Estate* * * *, Chardonnay* * * *, Pinot Noir* *

1991	Cabernet Sauvignon	Napa	C	86
1991	Cabernet Sauvignon Estate	Napa	C	88
1990	Cabernet Sauvignon Estate	Napa	C	90
1990	Chardonnay	California	C	89

ZD's Cabernets are not for the shy. They are among the most densely colored, powerful, concentrated wines made in Napa Valley. All of the wines spend a minimum of 3 years in small oak barrels, in an attempt, I suppose, to tame their extraordinary richness and tannic ferocity. Moreover, I believe wines such as these must be cellared for at least a decade to realize their maximum potential. That requires a considerable investment in patience. Yet I have to admire a winery that is putting this much effort into making a long-lived, potentially profound Cabernet. The 1991 Napa offering displays a deep ruby/purple color; a sweet, ripe nose; expansive, supple, intense flavors without any hard edges; soft tannins; decent acidity; and an admirable finish. In contrast, the somewhat closed 1991 Estate (from a 3.2-acre vineyard in Rutherford) has an opaque black/purple color and a nose of toasty, smoky new oak, cassis fruit, and licorice. There is excellent concentration, as well as gobs of tannin and glycerin. This big yet shapely wine should evolve gracefully for 10–15 years. The 1990 Estate is similar to the 1991—a super wine with an explosive nose of jammy black fruits and spicy oak. Ripe, deep, and rich, it offers an unctuous texture with just enough acidity and tannin to support its enormous weight. This blockbuster Cabernet should be drinkable slightly before the 1991 but exhibits the potential to last for 10, even 20 years. Impressive! ZD has usually made one of California's most opulent and hedonistic Chardonnays. The wines rarely age well and often need to be drunk within 1–3 years of the vintage. The 1990 should prove to be as good as previous efforts, with its honeyed, oaky, spicy, apple-scented nose and rich, full-bodied, fleshy, chewy texture. Drink this delicious Chardonnay before the summer of 1994. The winery also produces a Pinot Noir that I find odd and offensive.

7. OREGON

Heroes Are Hard to Find

The Basics

TYPES OF WINE

Oregon makes wine from most of the same grapes as California, although the cooler, more marginal climate in Oregon's best viticultural area, the Willamette Valley, has meant more success with cool-climate varietals such as Pinot Noir than with hotter-climate varietals such as Cabernet Sauvignon, Merlot, Syrah, and Grenache. Chardonnay, Riesling, and Sauvignon Blanc have done well in Oregon, but the great white hope here is Pinot Gris, which has shown fine potential and a knack for being the perfect partner for the salmon of the Pacific Northwest. There is also believed to be good potential for high-quality sparkling wine in Oregon, but efforts to date have been insipid. Oregon's wines are distinctive, with a kinship to European wines. The higher natural acidities, lower alcohol content, and more subtle nature of Oregon's wines bode well for this area's future.

GRAPE VARIETIES

Chardonnay I don't doubt for a minute that Oregon can make some wonderful Chardonnay, but far too many winemakers have let it spend too much time in oak and have not chosen the best clones for their vineyards. It is naturally high in acidity in Oregon, and therein lies the principal difference between Chardonnay grown in Oregon and that grown in California. In California the majority of Chardonnays must have tartaric acidity added to them for balance. In Oregon the wines must be put through a secondary or malolactic fermentation, à la Burgundy, in order to lower their acids.
Pinot Gris This is the hardest wine to find, as virtually all of it is sold and drunk before it has a chance to leave Oregon. However, winery owners, knowing a hot item, are planting as much of it as they can get their hands on.

Note: Robert Parker has a one-third interest in an Oregon vineyard that was commercially bonded in 1992 and has begun selling wine in 1993. Because of a potential conflict of interest, this wine will never be mentioned or reviewed in anything written by Robert M. Parker, Jr.

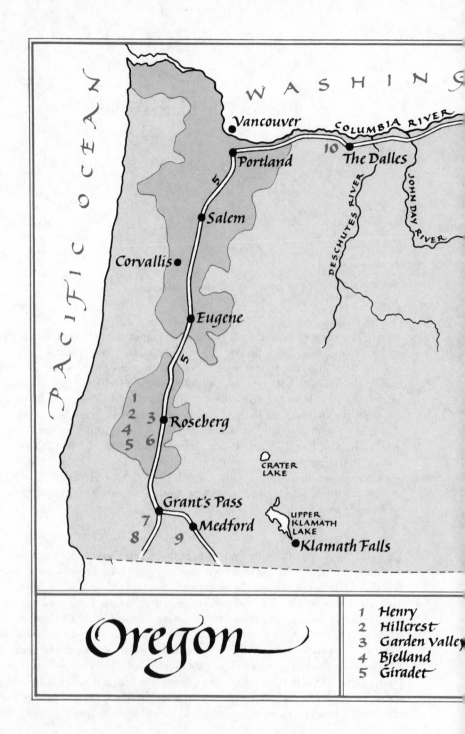

WASHINGTON

PACIFIC OCEAN

Vancouver

COLUMBIA RIVER

Portland

10 The Dalles

5

Salem

DESCHUTES RIVER

JOHN DAY RIVER

Corvallis

Eugene

5

1
2   3 Roseberg
4
5   6

CRATER
LAKE

Grant's Pass

UPPER
KLAMATH
LAKE

7   Medford
8   9

Klamath Falls

Oregon

1 Henry
2 Hillcrest
3 Garden Valley
4 Bjelland
5 Giradet

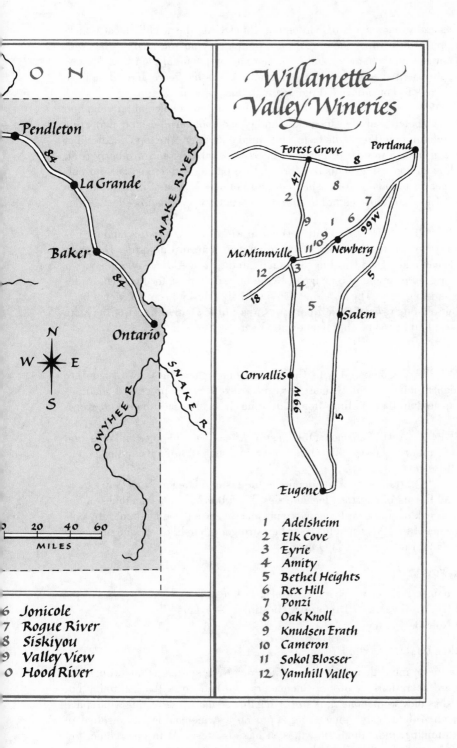

Willamette Valley Wineries

ON

Pendleton
La Grande
Baker
Ontario

N
W E
S

SNAKE RIVER
OWYHEE R.
SNAKE R.

84
84

0   20   40   60
MILES

Forest Grove   Portland
47
2
9
McMinnville   Newberg
12   3
18   4
5

Corvallis

99W
99W
5
5
8
8
7
1   6
11 10 9

Salem

Eugene

6 Jonicole
7 Rogue River
8 Siskiyou
9 Valley View
0 Hood River

1   Adelsheim
2   Elk Cove
3   Eyrie
4   Amity
5   Bethel Heights
6   Rex Hill
7   Ponzi
8   Oak Knoll
9   Knudsen Erath
10 Cameron
11 Sokol Blosser
12 Yamhill Valley

Fruitier and creamier than Chardonnay, Pinot Gris, the world's most under-rated great white wine grape, can be a delicious, opulent, smoky wine with every bit as much character and even more aging potential than Chardonnay. Although it is a specialty of Oregon, much of it is mediocre and diluted. To date, Eyrie and Ponzi have led the way with this grape.

Pinot Noir   As in Burgundy, the soil, yield per acre, choice of fermentation yeasts, competence of the winemaker, and type of oak barrel used in aging this wine profoundly influence its taste, style, and character. The top Oregon Pinot Noirs can have a wonderful purity of cherry, loganberry, and raspberry fruit, revealing an expansive, seductive, broad, lush palate, with crisp acids for balance. Yet far too many are washed out and hollow because of the tendency to harvest less than fully mature fruit and to permit crop yields to exceed 3 tons per acre.

Other Grape Varieties   With respect to white wines, Gewürztraminer has generally proven no more successful in Oregon than in California. However, Oregon can make good Riesling, especially in the drier Alsace style. I have yet to see a good example of Sauvignon Blanc or Semillon or, for that matter, decent sparkling wine. The Cabernet Sauvignon and Merlot to date have not been special, although some made from vineyards in the southern part of the state have resulted in good rather than exciting wines.

FLAVORS

Chardonnay   Compared with California Chardonnay, those of Oregon are noticeably higher in acidity, more oaky, and have less of a processed, manipulated taste than their siblings from California. In many cases the oak is excessive.

Pinot Gris   A whiff of smoke, the creamy taste of baked apples and nuts, and gobs of fruit characterize this white wine, which has shown outstanding potential in Oregon.

Pinot Noir   Red berry fruits dominate the taste of Oregon Pinot Noirs. Aromas and flavors of cherries, loganberries, blackberries, and sometimes plums with a streak of spicy, herbaceous scents characterize these medium ruby-colored wines. Pinot Noir should never be astringent, harsh, or opaque purple in color, and it rarely ever is in Oregon.

AGING POTENTIAL

Chardonnay: 2–5 years   Sparkling wines: 1–4 years
Pinot Gris: 1–3 years   Dry/off-dry Rieslings: 2–4 years
Pinot Noir: 3–8 years

OVERALL QUALITY LEVEL

Bearing in mind that most Oregon wineries were started as underfinanced, backyard operations by owner/winemakers who had no textbook training but learned as they went along, it is surprising that so many interesting wines have emerged. Although this pioneering approach to winemaking has resulted in some stunning, individualistic wines, it has also resulted in poor choices of grape clones and poorly planted vineyards, as well as some questionable wine-making decisions. In short, Oregon as a viticultural region is where California was in the late 1960s. Although Oregon producers are just beginning to realize the potential for Pinot Noir and Pinot Gris, they must be wondering why they planted Riesling, Sauvignon Blanc, and Chardonnay in many of the places they did. This, plus the amazing number of new, meagerly capitalized winery operations, has resulted in a pattern of quality that ranges from poor to excellent.

MOST IMPORTANT INFORMATION TO KNOW

To purchase good wine, know the best wineries and their best wines. However, some additional information worth knowing is that the finest Pinot Noirs generally come from a stretch of vineyards in the Willamette Valley southwest of Portland. For Cabernet Sauvignon and Merlot, the warmer Umpqua Valley to the south and the Grant Pass area farther south are better regions for those varietals.

1993–1994 BUYING STRATEGY

The three most recent Oregon vintages, 1992, 1991, and 1990, are all excellent years.

VINTAGE GUIDE

1992— In the short history of the Oregon wine business, this looks to be the finest vintage yet for Pinot Noir. It was almost too hot and too dry, but some beneficial rain arrived toward the end of the growing season and alleviated stress in the vineyards. Those producers who kept their yields low should make superrich, concentrated wines with relatively low acidity but superb flavor intensity and character. It is a vintage where the climate will shape the personality of the wines more than clones, soils, or winemaking techniques.

1991— This is a very good, potentially excellent vintage of wines that do not have the power or drama of the 1992s or the intensity of the 1990s. Nevertheless, rain at the end of the harvest caught those growers who had excessive crop yields and were waiting for further maturity. For that reason this is a tricky vintage to handicap, but certainly the Pinot Noirs look richly fruity, although softer and less structured than the 1992s and less tannic than the 1990s. It has good potential for high-quality wine—both red and white.

1990— A top vintage if yields were kept to a minimum, 1990 had plenty of heat and adequate rain, and the harvest occurred under ideal conditions. In fact, were it not for 1992, this would be the best Oregon vintage to date. From the top producers, the Pinot Noirs are rich and full, as are some of the Chardonnays. If there is a disappointment, it is that many of the Pinot Gris wines lack concentration because yields were too high.

1989— This is a good vintage for Pinot Noir, Chardonnay, and Pinot Gris. The wines may not have the intensity of the 1990s, but they are generally rich, soft, and elegant. In many respects this is a more typical, classic vintage for Oregon's best producers than 1990 or 1992.

1988— The first of an amazing succession of good years for the Oregon wine business. Fine weather, an abundant crop, and a trouble-free harvest have resulted in a number of excellent Pinot Noirs and Chardonnays.

1987— It was an excessively hot year, and most growers harvested too soon because they were afraid of losing acidity in their grapes. However, because of the summer's heat, many vineyards never reached physiological maturity; as a consequence, many 1987s are lean, too acidic, and disappointing. Six years after the vintage the best wines still have a hard edge, and it is unlikely they will ever fully blossom. If only the growers had waited!

OLDER VINTAGES

As a general rule, most Oregon Pinot Noirs must be consumed within 7–8 years of the vintage. There are always a few exceptions, as anyone who has tasted the 1975 Eyrie or 1975 Knudsen Erath Pinot Noirs can attest, but in general, aging Oregon Pinot Noir for longer than 7–8 years is dangerous.

Oregon's white wines should be drunk within several years of the vintage, even though they tend to have better natural acidity than their California counterparts. Yields are frequently too high and the extract levels questionable, so whether it is Pinot Gris, Chardonnay, or dry Riesling, if you are not drinking these wines within 3–4 years of the vintage, you are more likely to be disappointed than pleasantly surprised.

RATING OREGON'S BEST PRODUCERS OF PINOT NOIR

* * * * * (OUTSTANDING PRODUCERS)

Evesham Wood (Cuvée J)
Panther Creek's single-vineyard
    offerings

Ponzi Reserve
Domaine Serene Evenstad Reserve
Sokol Blosser Redland Vineyard

* * * * (EXCELLENT PRODUCERS)

Adelsheim Elizabeth's Reserve
Amity Winemaker's Reserve
Arterberry Winemaker's Reserve
Bethel Heights Reserve
Cameron Reserve
Domaine Drouhin
Elk Cove La Bohème
Elk Cove Wind Hill Vineyard
Evesham Wood (regular *cuvée*)

Oak Knoll Vintage Select
Panther Creek Late Release Reserve
Ponzi Vineyards (regular *cuvée*)
Redhawk Reserve
Redhawk Stangeland Reserve
St. Innocent O'Connor Vineyard
St. Innocent Seven Springs Vineyard
Domaine Serene Reserve

* * * (GOOD PRODUCERS)

Adams Reserve
Adelsheim Eola Hills Vineyard
Amity Estate
Château Benoit Reserve
Bethel Heights Estate
Bridgeview Winemaker's Reserve
Eyrie Reserve
Knudsen Erath
Lange

Laurel Ridge Vineyard
McKinley
Oak Knoll
Panther Creek First Release
Rex Hill Archibald Vineyard
Rex Hill Dundee Hills Vineyard
Sokol Blosser
Witness Tree Vineyard

* * *(AVERAGE PRODUCERS)*

Adelsheim Oregon Cuvée
Alpine
Alpine Reserve
Ashland
Autumn Wind
Château Benoit
Broadley Vineyard
Cooper Mountain
Davidson Winery
Elk Cove (regular *cuvée*)
Eola Hills
Eyrie (regular *cuvée*)
Flynn Vineyards
Forgeron Vineyard
Foris Vineyards
Girardet Cellars
Henry Estate Winery
Hinman Vineyards
Hood River Vineyards
Rex Hill Vineyards (regular *cuvée*)
Rex Hill Medici Vineyard
Shafer Vineyard Cellars
Springhill Cellars
Tualatin Vineyards
Tyee Cellars
Veritas Vineyard
Willamette Valley
Yamhill Valley Vineyards

RATING OREGON'S BEST PRODUCERS OF PINOT GRIS

* * * * *(OUTSTANDING PRODUCERS)*

None

* * * *(EXCELLENT PRODUCERS)*

Eyrie
Ponzi Vineyards

* * *(GOOD PRODUCERS)*

Adelsheim
Lange Reserve

RATING OREGON'S BEST PRODUCERS OF CHARDONNAY

* * * * *(OUTSTANDING PRODUCERS)*

None

* * * *(EXCELLENT PRODUCERS)*

Evesham Wood (unfiltered)
Eyrie Reserve
Montimore Winemaker's Reserve
Panther Creek
Redhawk Reserve
Redhawk Stangeland Vineyard

* * *(GOOD PRODUCERS)*

Adams
Adams Reserve
Adelsheim Reserve
Argyle
Arterberry
Bridgeview Vineyard
Cameron Reserve
Elk Cove La Bohème
Evesham Wood
Eyrie
Girardet Cellars
Kramer Vineyards
Lange
Lange Reserve
McKinley Special Selection
Montimore
Ponzi Reserve
St.-Innocent Seven Springs Vineyard

Shafer Vineyard Cellars   Valley View Anna Maria Reserve
Sokol Blosser Redland   Veritas Vineyard
Sokol Blosser Yamhill   Witness Tree Vineyard
Tualatin Vineyards

* * (AVERAGE PRODUCERS)

Adelsheim (regular *cuvée*)   Hinman
Alpine   King's Ridge
Amity   Marquam Hill
Autumn Wind   Oak Knoll
Château Benoit   Ponzi Vineyards
Bethel Heights   Rex Hill Vineyards
Cameron Vineyard   Springhill Cellars
Cooper Mountain   Stangeland Winery
Davidson Winery   Tyee Cellars
Flynn Vineyards   Willamette Valley
Henry Estate Winery   Yamhill Valley Vineyards

Selected Tasting Notes

ADAMS VINEYARD AND WINERY* * *

1990 Chardonnay	B	86
1991 Chardonnay	B	87
1991 Chardonnay Reserve	B	88
1991 Pinot Noir	B	84
1990 Pinot Noir	B	84
1990 Pinot Noir Reserve	B	85
1990 Sauvignon Blanc	B	82

The 1990 Sauvignon Blanc offers a spicy, herbal nose, decent ripeness, and a monolithic, straightforward character. Drink this dry, crisp wine over the next year. The three Chardonnays are attractively made in a burgundian style. The 1990 Chardonnay exhibits a nutty bouquet, good richness, medium body, crisp acidity, and the potential to last another 2–3 years. The slightly sweeter 1991 Chardonnay displays more ripeness, good definition, and spicy, buttery, oak- and apple-scented nose and flavors. It should last for 1–2 years. The best of this trio is the 1991 Chardonnay Reserve, which boasts more intensity and spicy new oak, a thicker viscosity, a chewy texture, and a deep, long, excellent finish. Drink this attractive Chardonnay over the next 3–4 years. The three Pinot Noir offerings were less impressive than other vintages of Adams. The 1991 Pinot Noir displays a soft, berry-scented nose, pleasant, round, elegant, but unsubstantial flavors, and a short, narrow finish. Drink it over the next several years. The grapey 1990 Pinot Noir is tasty, with good ripeness and a spicy finish, but it is essentially simple, one-dimensional, and destined to be short-lived. Consume it over the next 3–5 years. Although the 1990 Pinot Noir Reserve is less flattering than either of the regular bottlings, it offers more depth and tannin and finishes with power and spice. But I wonder if the tannins will outlive the wine's fruit. If not, my rating may look conservative. Drink it between 1995 and 1998.

AMITY VINEYARDS* */* * * *

1990 Chardonnay	B	77
1991 Dry Gewürztraminer	A	88
1991 Dry Riesling	A	74
1991 Gamay Noir	A	85
1989 Pinot Noir	B	85
1988 Pinot Noir	B	86
1988 Pinot Noir Winemaker's Reserve	C	88

I found it hard to get turned on by Amity's woody, malnourished 1990 Chardonnay and hollow 1991 dry Riesling. However, winemaker Myron Redford hit the jackpot with a super 1991 dry Gewürztraminer. This is not only the best Gewürztraminer I have tasted from Oregon, but one of the finest I have had from any producer outside Alsace. It boasts a telltale, lychee nut– and grapefruit-scented nose, excellent richness, spicy, multidimensional flavors, and a rich, opulent, dry finish. This gorgeous Gewürztraminer is a breakthrough for this varietal in Oregon. Amity has a policy of releasing the Pinot Noirs after they have had sufficient bottle age. Sometimes this works, but other times the fruit is muted and faded by the time the wines arrive on the market. If you are looking for up-front, delicious, sweet fruit in a medium-bodied, exuberant format, check out Amity's 1991 Gamay Noir. A Beaujolais look-alike made from Pinot Noir, it is a terrific wine for casual drinking or picnics. Serve it chilled and enjoy it for its freshness and purity over the next year. The 1989 Pinot Noir reveals an attractive herbal, earthy, smoky aroma, round, deep flavors, medium body, and a long, soft finish. It is an attractive, smoky, earthy style of Pinot Noir that should drink nicely for another 5–6 years. The 1988 Pinot Noir offers a smoked game–like aroma, tasty, elegant flavors, fine definition and depth, and a moderately tannic finish. Drink it over the next 4–5 years. The recently released 1988 Pinot Noir Winemaker's Reserve represents Amity's finest *cuvée* of Pinot Noir. This offering often has enormous potential, but I sometimes wonder if it is not released too late, after some of its exuberance has begun to fade. The excellent 1988 boasts a deep garnet color and a big, smoky, gamey, Pinot nose with aromas of leafy fruit and earth. Dense, spicy, and rich, with medium to full body and firm, ripe tannins in the finish, this Pinot Noir should continue to drink well for 5–7 years. It bears a resemblance to a rustic wine from Burgundy's Côte de Nuits.

ARGYLE* * *

1989 Chardonnay	B	85
1988 Chardonnay Barrel Fermented	B	85
1990 Dry Riesling Reserve	A	87
1991 Pinot Gris	B	76

This winery tends to hold back its production to give the wines more bottle age. The gem in this portfolio of new releases is the 1990 Dry Riesling Reserve, a rich, full-bodied, concentrated, dry Riesling with a remarkable resemblance to a top dry Riesling from Alsace. The penetrating fragrance of apricots, peaches, and flowers is super. The wine is rich and full, but oh so dry, crisp, and well delineated. It is an immensely flexible dry white wine that can be drunk with numerous dishes, ranging from fish and poultry to Asian food. Drink it over the next 3–4 years. Argyle's two Chardonnays may look old, but both are still tasty and elegant, with good freshness and fruit. I rated them equally, although the 1989 has a lighter color and more up-front fruit. The 1988, which displays a slightly deeper color and more body, is a rich, full wine. Both wines would benefit from more length and drama, but they are solidly made, competent Chardonnays for drinking over the next several years. The only unexciting wine I tasted from Argyle is its 1991 Pinot Gris. It is light, watery, and short.

ARTERBERRY* * */* * * *

1991 Chardonnay	B	87
1990 Pinot Noir	B	85
1990 Pinot Noir Winemaker's Reserve	B	87

Not only are these wines delicious and well made, their prices make them look especially attractive. Many Oregon wineries stumble when it comes to Chardonnay, but Arterberry got it right with its 1991. A medium straw color is followed by a wine with a rich, oaky, buttery nose, ripe, full-bodied flavors, excellent intensity, soft acids, and a smooth finish. Drink it over the next 1–2 years. Also ready for prime-time drinking is the 1990 Pinot Noir. Soft, with a moderately intense leafy, berry-scented nose, elegant, supple flavors, and a decent finish, this Pinot Noir should be consumed over the next 2–3 years. The 1990 Pinot Noir Winemaker's Reserve reveals more fruit, depth, and tannin. The rich, plum- and black raspberry–scented nose exhibits evidence of toasty new oak. Deep and velvety, this medium-bodied wine enjoys admirable richness, soft tannins, and a round, generous, expansive finish. Drink it over the next 5–6 years.

CHÂTEAU BENOIT* */* * *

1991 Chardonnay	B	71
1991 Pinot Noir	B	82
1991 Pinot Noir Reserve	B	86
1991 Sauvignon Blanc	A	69

Both the 1991 Chardonnay and 1991 Sauvignon Blanc are light-bodied, lean, thin wines that offer little value even at an attractive price. The Pinot Noirs are more noteworthy. The 1991 Pinot Noir reveals a light ruby color, a spicy nose of cherry fruit and herbs, and tasty, soft, fruity flavors that fall off in the finish. Drink it over the next 1–2 years. The deeper-colored 1991 Pinot Noir Reserve exhibits an excellent nose of earthy, smoky, red fruits, and herbs. Supple and fat, with excellent ripeness of fruit, this medium-bodied, velvety-textured wine will make ideal drinking over the next 4–5 years.

BETHEL HEIGHTS VINEYARD* */* * * *

1990 Chardonnay Estate	B	80
1990 Pinot Noir Estate	B	87
1991 Pinot Noir Estate First Release	B	85
1990 Pinot Noir Reserve	C	88

This 1990 Chardonnay Estate is light, fruity, and soft, lacking grip, character, and interest. The 1991 Pinot Noir Estate First Release (presumably other *cuvées* will be released later) succeeds in its effort to be a round, supple, fruity Pinot for drinking over the near term. Medium ruby-colored, with an attractive berry-scented nose, succulent fruit flavors, soft tannins, and low acidity, it makes for a delicious and inexpensive glass of Pinot Noir. The 1990 Pinot Noir Estate offers up a cherry, earthy, herblike nose reminiscent of a good *Premier Cru* from France's Côte de Beaune. With admirable elegance, ripeness, medium body, and a rich, crisp finish, it should be drunk over the next 5–6 years. Although the 1990 Pinot Noir Reserve is slightly better, it is nearly $10 a bottle more. The additional sweetness of fruit, increased flavor dimension, and spicy new oak may not justify the price differential. Nevertheless it is a generously endowed, seductive Pinot Noir for drinking over the next 5–6 years.

BRIDGEVIEW VINEYARDS* * *

1990 Chardonnay	A	84
1990 Chardonnay Barrel Select	B	86
1991 Dry Gewürztraminer Vintage Select	A	87
1990 Dry Gewürztraminer Vintage Select	A	84
1991 Pinot Gris	B	80
1990 Pinot Gris	B	75
1990 Pinot Noir Winemaker's Reserve	B	77
1989 Pinot Noir Winemaker's Reserve	B	73
1991 Riesling Vintage Select	A	84

I applaud the reasonable prices Bridgeview charges for its wines. The current and upcoming releases include a green, spritzy, yet tasty, elegant, dry 1991 Riesling Vintage Select and two alluring Gewürztraminers that are made in a dry, full, rich style. The 1990 is good, and the 1991 is an excellent example of this varietal that rarely shows its personality when made outside of Alsace, France. The 1991 from Bridgeview is a textbook Gewürztraminer, with a rose petal– and lychee nut–scented nose, excellent ripeness, and a spicy, long, dry finish. Drink both of these Gewürztraminers over the next several years. Bridgeview enjoyed less success with its two offerings of Pinot Gris. The refreshing 1991 Pinot Gris is too acidic and short, whereas the 1990 Pinot Gris is thin, watery, light bodied, and of little interest. The 1990 Chardonnay regular *cuvée* offers considerable value. It exhibits a lemony/apple- and floral-scented nose, tart, fresh, light- to medium-bodied flavors, good purity and freshness, and a crisp finish. It is not often you find Chardonnay of this quality at such a low price. The 1990 Chardonnay Barrel Select reveals some oak, lively, zesty fruit, a sweet ripeness to its personality, and a long, crisp finish. Drink both of these Chardonnays over the next 1–2 years. I have reservations about both of Bridgeview's Pinot Noirs. The 1989 Pinot Noir Winemaker's Reserve is malnourished, excessively acidic, and short in the finish. Although pleasantly scented, it appears already to be losing its fruit and drying out. On the other hand, the 1990 Pinot Noir Winemaker's Reserve is at the limit of being too pruny and raisiny. The overripe fruit character has some attraction in the jammy fruit flavors, but the overall impression is of diffuseness and a muddled character. It should be consumed over the next 1–3 years.

CAMERON WINERY* */* * * *

1991 Chardonnay	B	86
1990 Chardonnay Reserve	C	84
1990 Pinot Noir Unfiltered	B	86
1989 Pinot Noir Abbey Ridge Unfiltered	C	88

I prefer Cameron's 1991 Chardonnay regular bottling to its 1991 Chardonnay Reserve. Why? Too many wineries use excessive quantities of new oak for the amount of concentration the wines possess and/or keep the wines too long in barrel. That appears to be the problem with the 1990 Reserve vis-à-vis the 1991 regular bottling. The 1991 Chardonnay possesses excellent fruit, a lively and exuberant personality, a subtle touch of oak, and fleshy, buttery, applelike fruit in its finish. Drink it over the next 1–2 years. The 1990 Chardonnay Reserve is a more ambitiously styled Chardonnay, but it comes across as too oaky for the amount of fruit. It was probably a tastier wine 6 to 9 months ago. The wood has now taken the upper hand, and the wine should continue to dry out rather than display more charm. Drink it up. Cameron's two unfiltered Pinot Noirs include a 1990 regular *cuvée* that exhibits plenty of oak as well as gobs of spicy, earthy, leafy Pinot fruit with a meaty, smoky quality. Deep, round, and attractive, it is ideal for consuming over the next 3–4 years. The 1989 Pinot Noir from Oregon's excellent Abbey Ridge Vineyard displays light color but an intensely aromatic bouquet of smoked meats, black and red fruits, leafy vegetables, and spicy oak. Medium bodied and round, with considerable fatness and glycerin, this wine improved with airing. Although drinkable now, it should last for another 3–5 years.

DAVIDSON WINERY* *

1989 Cabin Creek Cabernet Sauvignon	A	74
1991 Cabin Creek Chardonnay	A	77
1990 Pinot Noir Artists Series	B	76
1989 Pinot Noir Artists Series	B	82

Davidson's Chardonnay and Cabernet Sauvignon appear under the Cabin Creek label. The 1991 Chardonnay exhibits adequate fruit, a spicy yet vague and reticent bouquet, light body, and a narrow, compact finish. What was present was clean and amiable. Drink it over the next 6–12 months. The lean, tart 1989 Cabernet Sauvignon displays good color but lacks flesh, depth, and charm. I cannot see it developing any additional character. The 1990 Pinot Noir Artists Series is an unusual wine; in its youthful grapiness and soft, almost flabby fruitiness, it reminds me more of Gamay than Pinot Noir. It has decent concentration and adequate length, but there is no complexity or character. Drink it over the next several years. The 1989 Pinot Noir Artists Series is a dead ringer for Gallo's Hearty Burgundy. Slightly sweet and intensely fruity, but simple and monolithic, this jammy wine should be drunk over the next 2–3 years.

DOMAINE DROUHIN* * * *

1991 Pinot Noir	D	90
1990 Pinot Noir	D	87

Domaine Drouhin's 1990 Pinot Noir is a soft, elegant wine with an attractive black cherry– and toasty new oak–scented nose. Well-structured flavors exhibit fine ripeness and texture as well as moderate length and noticeable tannins. Drink it over the next 4–5 years. It bears more than a casual resemblance to a top Côte de Beaune. The 1991 Pinot Noir, the first wine made from Drouhin's own vineyard and completely vinified by his daughter, Veronique, is a major breakthrough for Drouhin's Oregon operation. I would boldly suggest that this wine is better than most of Drouhin's French Pinot Noir offerings. The color is nearly opaque dark ruby. The nose offers up splendidly ripe scents of black fruits, smoke, toasty oak, and minerals. Rich and medium to full bodied, with layer upon layer of sweet fruit, this voluptuous, rich wine possesses the component parts to drink well young but will last for 7–8 years. Impressive!

ELK COVE VINEYARDS* */* * * *

1990 Chardonnay La Bohème	C	86
1990 Pinot Noir Dundee Hills Vineyard	C	86
1990 Pinot Noir Elk Cove Vineyard	C	84
1990 Pinot Noir Estate Reserve	C	87
1990 Pinot Noir La Bohème Vineyard	C	88
1990 Pinot Noir Wind Hill Vineyard	C	88
1991 Riesling Dry	A	74

The dry, thin, spritzy 1991 Riesling is a disappointment, but Elk Cove's other new releases are all worthy of serious attention. Oregon frequently has problems with Chardonnay, but that is not the case with Elk Cove's 1991 La Bohème, an elegant, stylish wine with good ripeness, medium body, and some attractive apple and tropical fruit aromas and flavors. The crisp acidity brings everything into focus. Drink it over the next several years. With the exception of the Elk Cove Vineyard offering, the 1990 Pinot Noirs are very good to excellent. The pleasant, spicy 1990 Pinot Noir Elk Cove Vineyard is a one-dimensional, straightforward wine that should be consumed over the next several years. I like the big, upfront, gamey, smoked meat-, cinnamon-, and berry-scented nose of the 1990 Pinot Noir Dundee Hills. Since it is already revealing considerable evolution in the nose as well as some amber at the edge, I would drink this medium-bodied, lush Pinot over the next 3–4 years. It is full of charm and character. The 1990 Pinot Noir Estate Reserve offers a similar gamey, clove-, and cinnamon-scented nose, but richer, riper flavors with more tannin, glycerin, and body. It is already delicious, and my instincts suggest it will last 5–7 years. The two best Pinot Noirs from Elk Cove in 1990 are the La Bohème Vineyard and the Wind Hill Vineyard. The 1990 La Bohème Pinot Noir is less spicy, with more cherry, herb, and floral components in its bouquet. Elegant, succulent, and juicy, this luscious Pinot exhibits soft tannins, low acidity, and copious amounts of fruit. It should continue to offer seductive drinking for 4–5 years. The deep ruby-colored 1990 Pinot Noir Wind Hill reveals a sweet, fragrant nose of black fruits, herbs, and smoke. Fat and delicious, it possesses a succulent texture, gobs of glycerin, soft tannins, and a heady finish. It is all that an up-front, lusty Pinot Noir should be. Drink it over the next 4–5 years.

EVESHAM WOOD* * */* * * * *

1991 Chardonnay	B	86
1990 Chardonnay Tête de Cuvée Unfiltered	C	90
1990 Pinot Noir Cuvée J Unfiltered	C	90
1991 Pinot Noir Unfiltered	C	88

Winemaker/proprietor Russ Raney continues to exhibit considerable talent with both Chardonnay and Pinot Noir. Virtually all of his wines go in the bottle unfiltered, which explains in part the rich, chewy texture and length Raney achieves. The two Chardonnay releases include a spicy, rich, buttery, hazelnut-scented 1991 with good ripeness and a moderate finish. Even better is the stunning 1990 Chardonnay Tête de Cuvée. It boasts fabulous richness and depth, great presence in the mouth, and a long, well-delineated, buttery, crisp finish. Delicious now, it should last for another 3–5 years. It is unquestionably the finest Chardonnay in my peer group tastings of new releases from Oregon. Unfortunately quantities are limited. Somewhat closed, the 1991 Pinot Noir Unfiltered exhibits a deep ruby color and a promising nose of spicy oak, jammy red and black fruits, and meat. The chewy texture, deep, concentrated feel, medium to full body, and firm tannins suggest waiting for 6–8 months to pull the cork. This is an impressively endowed Pinot Noir that may garner a higher score when some of the tannins melt away. The 1990 Pinot Noir Cuvée J (made from a yeast cultured from the sediment in a bottle of Henri Jayer's red burgundy; hence the name) is another stunning wine. At present it is not as dramatic or flamboyant as the great 1989 Cuvée J, but it may turn out to be just as compelling. It reveals a deep color and a tight but intense bouquet of sweet red and black fruits, spicy oak, minerals, and a floral component. The wine is dense, rich, and full bodied, with good acidity, soft, abundant tannins, and a lusty, rich finish. I cannot help wondering if the Henri Jayer yeast is the cause for the extra aromatic and flavor dimensions in this impressive Pinot Noir.

THE EYRIE VINEYARDS* * */* * * *

1990 Chardonnay	C	87
1991 Pinot Gris	C	87
1990 Pinot Noir	C	78

David Lett, grandfather of the Oregon wine industry, is capable of producing fine Pinot Gris and rich, opulent Chardonnay. The 1991 Pinot Gris displays a spicy, smoky bouquet, creamy flavors, decent acidity, and a crisp, rich finish.

It should drink well for another 3–4 years. The 1990 Chardonnay is tightly knit, with good depth, an attractive apple/butter/lemon bouquet, crisp acidity, and a medium-bodied finish. It should evolve nicely for at least 4–5 years. Lett's Pinot Noirs continue to be among the lightest colored in Oregon. It is hardly a secret that he has been surpassed in quality by a number of other Oregon producers, most notably Ponzi, Panther Creek, Domaine Drouhin, Evesham Wood, and Domaine Serene. Lett's reaction to his critics has been to question the competence of anyone who claims his Pinot Noirs too frequently lack richness, elegance, charm, and character. His 1990 Pinot Noir, which I tasted twice, reveals an unimpressive light ruby color, a vague yet pleasant diluted cherry- and herb-scented nose, light to medium body, excessive acidity, and a dry, austere, herbaceous finish. Although the wine's shrill levels of acidity will keep it alive for years to come, its hollowness and lack of fruit are troublesome.

FORIS VINEYARDS* *

1990 Cabernet Sauvignon Reserve	B	85
1991 Gewürztraminer	A	84
1990 Gewürztraminer	A	84
1989 Pinot Noir	B	75

Oregon continues to display signs of making more progress with Gewürztraminer than its neighbor to the south, California. Foris has turned out two inexpensive dry Gewürztraminers that offer fine varietal character, good fruit, freshness, and an overall sense of drama and personality. Both should be consumed over the next several years. It is rare to find Gewürztraminers this good selling for such low prices. I also enjoyed Foris's 1990 Cabernet Sauvignon Reserve. It is a thick, rich, medium-bodied wine with good color and fruit, but not excessive tannin or acidity. Drink it over the next 7–8 years. The only disappointment is the 1989 Pinot Noir. It is light bodied and shallow, with a short, watery finish.

FLYNN VINEYARDS* *

1990 Pinot Noir	B	77
1991 Pinot Noir Estate Bottled	B	84

The 1990 Pinot Noir is short and lean, with a hollowness on the midpalate and not enough fruit in the finish. The 1991 Pinot Noir Estate Bottled exhibits a spicy, raspberry-scented nose, elegant, ripe flavors, and a straightforward finish. It should be drunk over the next several years.

HENRY ESTATE WINERY* *

1988 Cabernet Sauvignon	B	71
1991 Chardonnay Umpqua Cuvée	A	77
1990 Gewürztraminer Estate	A	82
1990 Gewürztraminer Estate	A	78
1989 Pinot Noir Umpqua Cuvée	A	78

1991 White Riesling Estate	A	75
1990 White Riesling Estate	A	70

The 1990 White Riesling is odd, the 1991 pleasant but simple. The two Gewürztraminers are more typical of their varietal with their spice and rich fruit. The 1991 is slightly fresher, but both are made in an off-dry style. The Henry Estate 1991 Chardonnay Umpqua Cuvée is straightforward, fruity, and one-dimensional. I found the 1988 Cabernet Sauvignon to be excessively vegetal and short and tannic in the finish—not a very likable personality characteristic. The 1989 Pinot Noir Umpqua Cuvée exhibits a medium ruby color with some amber at the edge, soft, light-bodied flavors, and a short finish.

HOOD RIVER VINEYARDS* *

1989 Cabernet Sauvignon	B	70
1990 Chardonnay	B	83
1990 Pinot Noir	B	83

I found little redeeming value in the acidic, astringently tannic, light-bodied, hard, overtly herbaceous 1989 Cabernet Sauvignon. On the other hand, Hood River Vineyards' 1990 Chardonnay, although light bodied and somewhat superficial, is a pleasant, fruity wine for drinking over the next year. The same can be said of the soft, supple, ripe, tasty 1990 Pinot Noir. Its finish is short, but there is enough varietal character to please purists. Drink it over the next 1–2 years.

KNUDSEN ERATH* * *

1991 Dundee Village Vin Gris Pinot Noir Rosé	A	81
1990 Pinot Noir	B	84
1991 Pinot Noir Reserve	C	86+
1990 Pinot Noir Reserve	C	86
1991 Pinot Noir Vintage Select	B	86

Knudsen Erath produces several *cuvées* of Pinot Noir. The 1991 rosé of Pinot Noir, the Dundee Village Vin Gris, is a soft, fruity wine for drinking over the next 6–12 months. For the price, it is a decent value. The medium garnet-colored 1991 Pinot Noir Vintage Select exhibits fine Pinot character, offering a spicy, earthy, berry-scented nose, good flavor depth, and hard, astringent tannins in the finish. It can be drunk now, but I wonder if all the tannins will melt away. The 1991 Pinot Noir Reserve is slightly more expansive on the palate, with a big, gamey, spicy, berry- and herb-scented nose, excellent richness, and a softer, lusher, but shorter finish. Both of these wines should be consumed over the next 5–6 years. The 1990 Pinot Noir exhibits a soft, herb- and berry-scented nose, ripe, round, medium-bodied flavors, and a smooth finish. Drink it over the next 2–3 years. The 1990 Pinot Noir Reserve is a medium-bodied wine, with a leafy, raspberry- and cherry-scented nose, firm, moderately tannic flavors, good body and cleanliness, and a compact finish. Although it is not likely to improve, it should hold at its present quality level for another 3–4 years.

KRAMER VINEYARDS* * *

1990 Chardonnay Estate	B	87
1990 Pinot Noir Estate	B	86
1991 Pinot Noir Estate	B	87
1991 Riesling Estate	A	85

All of Kramer's wines performed well in my tastings. For starters there is a fresh, elegant, clean Kabinett-style 1991 Riesling Estate that exhibits fine fruit, an attractive floral, applelike component, and zesty acidity. Drink it over the next several years. Kramer's 1990 Chardonnay Estate bordered on being too woody, but there is enough ripe, opulent fruit to stand up to the spicy oak. It is a medium- to full-bodied, tasty wine that should be consumed over the next 1–2 years. Both Pinot Noirs enjoy deep ruby colors, spicy, cherry-scented noses, and an elegant use of toasty oak. The 1990 Estate is as concentrated as the 1991 but tastes slightly less complex and multidimensional. Delicious, round, and supple, it is ideal for drinking over the next 3–4 years. The 1991 Estate offers a more interesting bouquet of spice, black cherries, herbs, and smoked meats. Ripe, velvety textured, and already delicious, it can be drunk over the next 3–5 years.

LANGE* * *

1990 Chardonnay Reserve Canary Hill Vineyard	C	86
1991 Pinot Gris	B	75
1991 Pinot Gris Reserve	C	85
1990 Pinot Noir	C	87

I enjoyed three of these offerings from Lange winery. The only disappointment was the standard *cuvée* of 1991 Pinot Gris, a bland, one-dimensional wine with no character. The same cannot be said for the 1991 Pinot Gris Reserve, a ripe, rich, creamy-textured wine with gobs of fruit, fine purity, and a zesty, lush finish. It would work wonders with grilled salmon from the Pacific Northwest. Lange also produced a fine 1990 Chardonnay Reserve from the Canary Hill Vineyard in the Dundee Hills. It reveals moderate oak in its bouquet to go along with the ripe, orange, pineapple, buttery fruit. Medium body, with admirable richness, enough acidity for focus, and a crisp finish make for a well-proportioned glass of Chardonnay. Drink it over the next 1–2 years. Lange's most impressive wine is its 1990 Pinot Noir. At first I was worried the oak might be excessive, but with airing, some superrich, jammy, black cherry fruit takes over the wine's bouquet, assigning the oak a secondary, more subtle role. The wine displays excellent ripeness and richness, medium to full body, and moderate tannins. It offers a generous mouthful of well-structured Pinot Noir that can be drunk now or cellared for 5 or more years.

LAUREL RIDGE VINEYARD* * *

1991 Dry Gewürztraminer Laurel Ridge Vineyard	B	82
1991 Pinot Blanc Select Harvest	B	86
1990 Pinot Noir	B	85
1990 Sauvignon Blanc Finn Hill Vineyard Reserve	B	85

Although none of these wines is dazzling, all are attractive. Even the 1991 Dry Gewürztraminer Laurel Ridge Vineyard exhibits some of that varietal's personality traits in its spicy, ripe nose and medium-bodied, dry flavors. I liked Laurel Ridge's tasty, excellent 1991 Pinot Blanc Select Harvest even more. It offers the scent of oranges and apples, a honeyed, dry, medium-bodied texture, and excellent definition and richness in the finish. It is a delicious wine for drinking with poultry and fish. The 1990 Sauvignon Blanc Finn Hill Vineyard Reserve is also one of the best examples of this varietal I have tasted from Oregon. The nose of figs, melons, and herbs displays excellent varietal character. The wine is light bodied, with good definition, fine fruit, and a spicy, lean finish. Drink it over the next several years. The only red wine I tasted was the 1990 Pinot Noir. It may have excessive tannins, but I enjoyed the ripe, herbaceous, black cherry fruit, spicy fruit flavors, and the medium-bodied, firm, tannic finish. If the tannins melt away before the fruit fades, this wine could merit a higher rating.

McKINLEY* * *

1990 Chardonnay	B	80?
1990 Pinot Noir	B	86
1990 Pinot Noir Eola Springs Vineyard	C	87+

McKinley's 1990 Chardonnay is certainly controversial. It is too oaky, but behind the lavish quantities of wood can be found enticing flavors of baked apples, butter, and tropical fruits. Although ripe and tasty, it sustains a fragile balance. My instincts say the oak will soon dominate the fruit. Drink it up. The Pinot Noirs offer more interest. The 1990 Pinot Noir regular *cuvée* exhibits a deep ruby color; a big, spicy, black cherry, chocolaty, herb-scented nose; dense, chewy, rich flavors; medium to full body; adequate ripeness; and a long, soft finish. Drink it over the next 5–6 years. The 1990 Pinot Noir Eola Springs Vineyard boasts an impressively saturated color, a chocolate-, cherry-, and candylike nose, rich, full-bodied flavors, soft tannins, adequate acidity, and a powerful, authoritatively rich finish. It should improve over the next 1–2 years and last for 7–8.

MONTIMORE* * */* * * *

1990 Chardonnay Estate	B	86
1990 Chardonnay Winemaker's Reserve	B	86+
1989 Chardonnay Winemaker's Reserve	B	87
1990 Chenin Blanc	A	85
1991 Pinot Gris Estate	A	75
1990 Pinot Noir Estate	B	80
1990 Pinot Noir Winemaker's Reserve	C	86
1989 Pinot Noir Winemaker's Reserve	C	86

With the exception of a clean, hollow, diluted 1991 Pinot Gris, this is a successful portfolio. The best buy among these offerings is Montimore's 1990 Chenin Blanc, which is a dead ringer for a drier-style Vouvray from France's Loire Valley. A honeyed, melon- and floral-scented nose is followed by a tasty, ripe, crisp, clean, and well-delineated wine that should be drunk over the next several years. The three Chardonnays performed well, revealing a buttery, hazelnut character similar to that of a French Meursault. This is particularly evident in the opulent, elegant, attractive 1990 Chardonnay Estate. For $10 a bottle, this is a notable value for a wine that should easily last for another 2–3 years. Montimore's 1990 Chardonnay Winemaker's Reserve will ultimately be a better wine. More oak and higher acids give this tightly knit wine a closed feel at present. It exhibits attractive, smoky, pineapple- and applelike fruit and fine body, weight, and richness. This wine has not budged in terms of evolution, making this a Chardonnay that will benefit from 6–12 months of aging; it will last 4–5 years. The 1989 Chardonnay Winemaker's Reserve indicates how Montimore's wines develop and last. Buttery and rich, with integrated acidity, medium to full body, and plenty of depth and length, the wine tastes exceptionally youthful and fresh. Drink it over the next 3–4 years. Although the light ruby-colored 1990 Pinot Noir Estate does not possess much body, it does offer pleasant, spicy, herbal, fruity notes and a soft texture. Drink it over the next several years. Far superior is the 1990 Pinot Noir Winemaker's Reserve. Boasting a medium ruby color, a big, spicy, herb- and cherry-scented nose, fine body, excellent ripeness, and soft tannins in the moderately long finish, it can be drunk now and over the next 4–5 years. The 1989 Pinot Noir Winemaker's Reserve exhibits more oak and tartness, as well as excellent richness, admirable cleanliness, and an overall sense of balance. It has shed much of its tannin, but given its high acidity, it should last for 4–5 years.

OAK KNOLL* */* * * *

1990 Chardonnay	B	75
1990 Pinot Noir	C	84
1990 Pinot Noir Vintage Select	C	87

I found Oak Knoll's 1990 Chardonnay bizarre and unusual, with no recognizable varietal character. Perhaps it is the clone used. It tastes straightforward and lemony, with some fruit, but there is little to suggest this was made from the Chardonnay grape. Drink it over the next year. The two *cuvées* of Pinot Noir are more reliable. The 1990 Pinot Noir regular *cuvée* exhibits deep color, excellent jammy ripeness, some tough tannins in the finish, but good fruit, medium body, and low acidity. Drink this straightforward, richly fruity Pinot over the next 4–5 years. The 1990 Pinot Noir Vintage Select is a more serious wine, with a toasty, ripe, gamey, raspberry-scented nose, medium to full body, excellent concentration, decent acidity, and soft tannins in the heady finish. It will benefit from another 1–3 years of cellaring and should keep for up to a decade.

PANTHER CREEK* * */* * * * *

1991 Chardonnay	B	78
1991 Melon Stewart Vineyard	B	87
1990 Pinot Noir Canary Hill Vineyard	D	91
1990 Pinot Noir Carter Vineyard	D	90
1990 Pinot Noir First Release	B	87
1990 Pinot Noir Reserve	C	89

Winemaker/proprietor Ken Wright has established himself as one of Oregon's benchmark producers over recent years, especially for his excellent, sometimes outstanding Pinot Noirs, a generally good Chardonnay, and his Melon, one of the tastiest white wines made in Oregon. The 1991 Melon from the Stewart Vineyard is a refreshing, crisp, dry, richly fruity wine that boasts outstanding finesse and a zesty, vividly pure personality. It should be consumed by the end of spring 1994. Panther Creek's light-bodied, diluted 1991 Chardonnay is a straightforward, uninteresting wine—a rarity from this producer. The 1990 Pinot Noir First Release is the least tannic and most flattering of the Pinot offerings. Deep ruby in color, with an attractive, spicy, berry-scented nose, delicious, soft, succulent flavors, and a gentle, velvety-textured finish, it will drink well over the next several years. The 1990 Pinot Noir Reserve enjoys a deeper color as well as a fragrant bouquet of sweet black cherry fruit intermingled with aromas of toast, earth, and underbrush. It is medium to full bodied, with excellent definition, admirable acidity, fine depth, and that pervasive black cherry flavor that can often be found in Pinot Noir. Soft enough to be consumed now, it promises to last for 7–8 years. Panther Creek's two limited-production, single-vineyard wines in 1990 are from the Carter Vineyard and Canary Hill Vineyard, two top sources for high-quality Pinot Noir. Only 100 cases of each wine were made, so chances of finding either are minuscule. Both wines reveal supersaturated ruby/purple colors, more obvious new oak in their aromas, and gobs of rich black cherry fruit. The 1990 Carter Vineyard Pinot Noir is spicy, with superb depth, lovely texture, medium body, firm but soft tannins, and fine length. Acidity gives the wine freshness. Although the tannins are soft enough to make it approachable now, this is a candidate for 5–7 years of aging. The 1990 Canary Hill Pinot Noir is slightly deeper, with more of a black plum/prune aspect. Full bodied, deep, and dense, with outstanding concentration and potential, it should be cellared for another year or 2 and drunk over the following decade.

PONZI VINEYARDS* */* * * * *

1988 Chardonnay Reserve	C	87
1991 Pinot Gris	B	86
1990 Pinot Noir Reserve	C	91

Ponzi always makes a good Pinot Gris. Its 1991 is an aromatic, fruity, lovely wine with excellent ripeness, medium to full body, and a spicy, creamy-textured finish. It should be drunk over the next year while waiting for this winery to release their 1992. The first bottle of Ponzi's 1988 Chardonnay Reserve I tasted was oxidized, but a second bottle was excellent, displaying an attractive, intense, buttery, toasty, ripe nose, rich, medium- to full-bodied flavors, a multidimensional personality, and a deep, crisp, earthy finish. It should continue to drink well for another 2–3 years. Ponzi produced no regular *cuvée* of Pinot Noir in 1990, but fortunately there are 700 cases of the 1990 Pinot Noir Reserve. Once again it is a super wine as well as the most likely candidate for "the Pinot Noir of the Vintage" in Oregon. It displays a deep, saturated, dark ruby color and a dramatic nose of black fruits, herbs, smoked game, and toasty oak. The wine is rich, medium to full bodied, with super purity of flavor and a long, opulent finish. For fans of Ponzi who have followed the bevy of superlative Pinot Noirs he has produced, the 1990 is closer in style to the 1988 than the 1989. However, it is more tannic and structured than either of those vintages and needs 5–8 years of cellaring. Quite impressive! For readers' information, Ponzi released several hundred cases of a 20th Anniversary Cuvée of 1990 Pinot Noir. Because 50% of this anniversary *cuvée* is made from grapes purchased from an Oregon vineyard in which I have a one-third interest, I feel it is a conflict of interest to comment on the wine, but I feel readers should know of its existence. It is being sold for $35 a bottle.

REDHAWK* * * *

1990 Cabernet Franc Reserve Evans Creek Vineyard	C	88
1990 Cabernet Sauvignon Reserve Evans Creek Vineyard	C	87
1990 Chardonnay	C	87
1990 Chardonnay Estate Reserve Unfiltered	C	90
1990 Chardonnay Stangeland Reserve	C	89
1991 Gamay Noir Vintage Select	B	86
1990 Pinot Noir Estate Reserve Pommard Clone	C	86
1990 Pinot Noir Stangeland Reserve Wadensvil Clone	C	88
1990 Reserve Cuvée Evans Creek Vineyard	B	89+

This is an impressive array of exceptionally well-made, intensely flavored wines. Even the 1991 Gamay Noir Vintage Select, which is made in a Beaujolais style, is a rich, supple, elegant, tasty wine with gobs of fruit and personality. Its exuberance and vitality are disarming, but the wine should be drunk over the next 1–2 years. The two Pinot Noirs possess deep colors, soft tannins, and a lovely combination of earthy, berry fruit presented in a medium- to full-bodied format. The 1990 Pinot Noir Stangeland Reserve exhibits more intensity and tannin, whereas the 1990 Pinot Noir Estate Reserve is lighter, in a softer, more gentle style. I would cellar the Stangeland Reserve for 6–12 months and drink it over the subsequent 5–6 years. Although no additional bottle aging is necessary for the Estate Reserve, it will keep for 4–5 years. I tasted three Chardonnays from Redhawk, all of which are among the finest made in Oregon. They are also all unfiltered, which puts winemaker/proprietor Tom Robinson in an elite group of risk takers when it comes to bottling Chardonnay without filtration. The 1990 Chardonnay Stangeland Reserve reveals a lot of oak in its nose that blows off with airing to reveal a full-bodied, superconcentrated, ripe wine with gobs of glycerin, alcohol, and intensity. My score may be low, but I subtracted some points because of the nearly overblown woodiness of the wine. This is a bold, dramatic Chardonnay that should be drunk over the next several years. The 1990 Chardonnay regular *cuvée* displays plenty of rich, hazelnut fruit, a moderate scent of pineapples, butter, and apples, fine acidity, and a chewy texture. It is more restrained and less oaky than the Stangeland Reserve. The best of this trio is the 1990 Chardonnay Estate Reserve. It possesses an exquisite bouquet of smoky nuts, buttery fruit, and toasty oak. Full bodied and opulent, with marvelous richness and density, this expansively flavored, full-throttle Chardonnay is a real attention grabber. Drink it over the next 1–3 years. If Redhawk has the distinction of making very fine Pinot Noirs and some of Oregon's best Chardonnays, it also makes some of that lovely state's most concentrated and ageworthy Cabernet-based wines. The 1990 Reserve Cuvée Evans Creek Vineyard is a proprietary red wine made from 63% Cabernet Sauvignon, 25% Merlot, and 12% Cabernet Franc. The wine needs considerable aging, as it is a closed, broodingly backward, deep wine with all the elements for excellence. The wonderful nose of cassis, tobacco, chocolate, and cedar is followed by a rich, full-bodied wine that cuts a deep line on the palate. The super finish reveals tons of tannin as well as gobs of extract and richness. **Anticipated maturity: 1997–2008.** Redhawk's 1990 Cabernet Sauvignon from the Evans Creek Vineyard is a softer wine, with a fragrant, cedary, herb- and berrylike nose, rich, medium- to full-bodied, supple flavors, and moderate tannins in the long finish. It can be drunk now but promises to develop even more complexity with another 2–3 years of cellaring. It should keep for 10 or more years. I also admired the rich, multidimensional, spicy, and fragrant Cabernet Franc. It is still youthful, but approachable, and capable of lasting 7–10 years.

REX HILL VINEYARDS* */* * *

1991 Pinot Gris	B	85
1989 Pinot Noir	B	86
1990 Pinot Noir Archibald Vineyard	C	87
1989 Pinot Noir Dundee Hills	C	86
1989 Pinot Noir Maresh Vineyard	C	72
1988 Pinot Noir Medici Vineyard	C	78
N.V. Semblanc	A	75

This winery appears to have the right ideas about winemaking and marketing, but the results have been inconsistent. For example, Rex Hill has turned out a delicious 1991 Pinot Gris that displays a smoky, buttery nose, rich, fresh, dry, fruity flavors, medium body, and a tasty, crisp finish. It is ideal for consuming over the next year. Along with Eyrie's and Ponzi's Pinot Gris, it is the best I tasted from the 1991 vintage. However, Rex Hill's cloying, heavy-handed N.V. Semblanc (a 40% Semillon/60% Sauvignon Blanc blend) exhibits a strikingly vegetal nose and sweet, diffuse flavors. Rex Hill has a marketing policy of holding back its wines for several years. I am not sure this is a good idea, as its late-released wines frequently taste dried out and excessively oaky. Because of this policy, I tasted only one 1990 Pinot Noir, the Archibald Vineyard. It possesses a fine color, a big, spicy, gamey, oaky nose, rich, medium-bodied flavors, and a spicy, moderately tannic finish. It should be consumed over the next 6–7 years. The 1989 Pinot Noir regular *cuvée* reveals good depth and a chunky, medium-bodied, corpulent style, as well as spicy wood, herbs, and black fruit notes in its flavor and finish. The 1989 Pinot Noir Dundee Hills offers up a fragrant nose of chocolate candy, herbs, and black cherries. It displays fine richness, plenty of oak, medium body, and a crisp finish. More structured than the regular *cuvée,* it is a worthy candidate for 6–7 years of cellaring. The 1989 Pinot Noir Maresh Vineyard is disappointing. Although the medium color is fine, there is an absence of ripeness in the nose, and on the palate the wine is harsh, astringent, short, completely out of balance, and dominated by acidity, tannins, and wood. The 1988 Pinot Noir Medici Vineyard, which I rated 83 several years ago, continues to display the berry, smoky, earthy nose, but the fruit has faded and astringent tannins have now taken control, giving the wine a narrow, nasty finish. Clearly losing its fruit, this wine will become more attenuated with further cellaring. At the tasting, I also tried two wines I had liked considerably more a few years ago. The 1985 Pinot Noir Dundee Hills and 1985 Pinot Noir Maresh Vineyard have both lost much of their fruit and taken on a hard, tannic, malnourished character as they continue to dry out with the acids and tannins the principle components left. More concentration and less reliance on new oak, in addition to lowering the tannin levels, plus earlier bottling and earlier release dates might solve some of these problems.

ST. INNOCENT WINERY* * */* * * *

1990 Chardonnay Seven Springs Vineyard	C	85
1990 Pinot Noir O'Connor Vineyard	B	87
1990 Pinot Noir Seven Springs Vineyard	C	87
1988 Sparkling Wine	C	82

Oregon's sparkling wines have been unimpressive to date. Although St. Innocent's Sparkling Wine debut release, the 1988, is unlikely to jump off retailers' shelves, it is a pleasant, crisp, light-bodied wine with enough flavor to merit some attention. More body and length would have been welcome. The 1990 Chardonnay Seven Springs Vineyard is a well-made, medium-bodied wine that takes no risks but offers good fruit, purity, a touch of oak, and tasty, lemony, apple flavors as well as a crisp finish. Drink it over the next year. I prefer the two Pinot Noirs, both of which exhibit complexity and a fine touch. The softer 1990 Pinot Noir O'Connor Vineyard is reminiscent of the style of the Domaine Drouhin Pinot Noirs in 1988 and 1989. It offers a Côte de Beaune–like nose of spicy oak, cherries, and floral scents. Ripe and tasty, with a soft, velvety texture, smooth tannins, and a well-balanced, elegant personality, it is a delicious Pinot Noir for drinking over the next 4–5 years. The 1990 Pinot Noir Seven Springs Vineyard is richer, fuller, and more obviously oaky, with a slightly deeper color. Although the wine reaches the limit of too much wood, there appear to be adequate reserves of fruit to support the wine's structure. The nose offers aromas of blackberries, herbs, and spices. The wine is medium bodied, with moderate tannin and excellent concentration. If the oak becomes more subdued and the fruit pushes to the forefront, this wine may deserve an even higher rating.

DOMAINE SERENE* * * */* * * * *

1990 Pinot Noir Reserve Evenstad	C	90
1990 Pinot Noir Reserve Unfiltered	C	87

This newcomer has burst on the Oregon wine scene with two impressive wines. Both are deeply colored, with excellent richness and definition, and, admirably, are unfiltered. The 1990 Pinot Noir Reserve Unfiltered possesses a fragrant, intense, black cherry nose, medium- to full-bodied, deep flavors, soft tannins, and a lush finish. Drink it over the next 4–5 years. The 1990 Pinot Noir Reserve Evenstad offers greater flavor dimension and a more complex nose, with the black cherry component intermingled with aromas of spices and sweet new oak. Rich and full bodied, it exhibits a silky texture and a long, lush finish. It should drink well for 5–6 years. An impressive debut!

SEVEN HILLS WINERY* * */* * * *

1989 Cabernet Sauvignon Seven Hills Vineyard	C	87+
1990 Merlot Seven Hills Vineyard	C	88
1991 White Riesling	A	84

Washington State wine fans should know that the Seven Hills Vineyard is planted on the Oregon side of the Walla Walla appellation. Thus these are wines made from 100% Oregon fruit. The dry 1991 White Riesling offers up a light fragrance of green apples. I would have liked to taste more fruit, but this is a good, solid effort at making a dry, crisp Riesling in an Alsatian style. Drink it over the next year. Seven Hills has consistently done fine work with its Merlot and Cabernet Sauvignon produced from the Seven Hills Vineyard. The 1990 Merlot is close to being a blockbuster. It possesses considerable tannin for a Merlot. The thick, dark ruby/purple color, the rich, chocolaty and cherry-toffee-scented nose, and deep, chewy flavors are a result of modest yields and considerable extraction of fruit. The wine is in a burly stage of evolution, but sweetness and richness of fruit are clearly present. Don't be surprised to see it turn out to be an outstanding wine. Drink it between 1994 and 2003. The 1989 Cabernet Sauvignon Seven Hills Vineyard reveals a saturated, purple/black color and an unevolved but promising bouquet of ripe, jammy, cassis fruit, herbs, and licorice. Dense and rich, with a full-bodied, tannic personality, this big, brawny Cabernet Sauvignon needs at least 3–4 years of cellaring. **Anticipated maturity: 1996–2005.**

SHAFER VINEYARD CELLARS* */* * *

1991 Pinot Noir Blanc	A	85
1991 Riesling	A	85

This winery fares well in wine tastings of Oregon rosés and Chardonnays, but its Pinot Noir is often lacking density and fruit. I liked Shafer's 1991 Pinot Noir Blanc (rosé), a slightly sweet, light, tasty, fresh rosé that combines elegance and fruit. It should have considerable popular appeal. Their 1991 Riesling is made in a dry style, with excellent fruit, a penetrating and fragrant nose of apples and flowers, and a crisp, zesty finish. It, too, should be drunk over the next year.

SOKOL BLOSSER* * */* * * * *

1990 Chardonnay	B	85
1990 Chardonnay Redland Vineyard	C	87
1990 Pinot Noir	B	86
1990 Pinot Noir Redland Vineyard	C	90

This is an impressive quartet of wines. Although Sokol Blosser has made good wines from its founding, the quality of their recent vintages has been noticeably higher. Both Chardonnays merit interest. The 1990 Chardonnay exhibits excellent ripeness, a clean, lovely, fruity nose, and a touch of spice. Medium bodied, well balanced, rich, and tasty, it is ideal for drinking over the next several years. The 1990 Chardonnay Redland Vineyard enjoys greater depth, and an excellent bouquet of buttery fruit and spice. Medium to full bodied, with admirable depth, this elegant yet rich Chardonnay should continue to drink well for another 2–3 years. I also enjoyed Sokol Blosser's 1990 Pinot Noir. It offers a medium ruby color and a big, berry- and cherry-scented nose intertwined with aromas of oak, earth, and herbs. Medium to full bodied, with fine richness, a supple texture, and a long finish, this delicious Pinot Noir should be consumed over the next 4–5 years. The 1990 Pinot Noir Redland Vineyard is a beautiful example of this varietal. Deep ruby in color, with an explosive nose of sweet, toasty oak, berry fruit, smoked herbs, and meats and a subtle touch of vanillin, this rich, full-bodied wine has exquisite balance, elegance combined with power, and superb depth of fruit in the long, lush finish. Drink it over the next 7–8 years. Bravo!

STANGELAND WINERY* *

1991 Chardonnay Estate	B	70
1991 Pinot Gris Estate	B	84
1991 Pinot Noir Estate	B	75

Stangeland's soft, round 1990 Pinot Gris Estate reveals some residual sugar, which gives it the impression of having more body, and a soft, fruity finish. An attractive, commercial example of this varietal, it should be drunk before the fall of 1993. The 1991 Chardonnay Estate is disappointingly light, thin, acidic, and lacking fruit and depth. One can only imagine how high the yields must have been to extract so little flavor. The 1991 Pinot Noir Estate is not appreciably better. It displays a light ruby, almost rust color that is already showing considerable age. The cinnamon- and diluted cherry-scented nose is followed by a wine with some ripeness, vague, undefinable, fruity flavors, and a short, alcoholic finish. It requires immediate drinking.

TUALATIN VINEYARDS* */* * *

1990 Chardonnay Estate	B	72
1990 Pinot Noir Estate	A	82
1988 Pinot Noir Estate	A	82

The acidic, light-bodied, malnourished 1990 Chardonnay Estate is of little interest, but the reasonably priced Pinot Noirs should elicit some consumer attention. Their extremely light colors are deceptive, as they are both fruity, round, tasty wines that only lack depth and complexity. Given how fresh the 1988 is, it should last longer than one might suspect. Clearly of the understated, lighter school of Pinot Noir winemaking, they make for a pleasant drinking experience.

VALLEY VIEW VINEYARD* * *

1990 Cabernet Sauvignon Barrel Select	B	85
1990 Chardonnay Anna Maria Reserve	B	86

Valley View's 1990 Chardonnay Anna Maria Reserve offers up an elegant, fruity nose, medium body, good ripeness, adequate acidity, and a spicy, moderately endowed finish. Drink it over the next 1–2 years. The 1990 Cabernet Sauvignon Barrel Select exhibits a coffee-, chocolate-, cassis-scented nose, medium to full body, some hard tannins in the finish, but overall, fine ripeness and a generally up-front, supple style. Give it another 1–2 years of cellaring and drink it over the following 7–8 years.

WILLAMETTE VALLEY* *

1991 Chardonnay	B	75
1990 Chardonnay	B	74
1991 Pinot Gris	B	74
1990 Pinot Noir	B	85
1991 Pinot Noir Blanc	A	78
1991 Pinot Noir Whole Berry Fermented	A	86
1991 White Riesling	A	84

There is little to get excited about with this mixed bag of wines, save for the two Pinot Noirs. The only other wine of interest is the off-dry 1991 White Riesling, an elegant, floral-scented, tasty, crisp wine that is both a notable value and a competently made example of the Riesling grape. It is ideal for drinking over the next 1–2 years. Willamette Valley's rosé, the 1991 Pinot Noir Blanc, is excessively sweet and cloying, although fresh and fruity. The 1991 Pinot Gris is bland and innocuous. The same thing can be said for both the 1990 and 1991 Chardonnays, two monolithic, straightforward, simple wines with excessive acidity and little flavor depth or concentration. Both wines should keep well for another 2–3 years, but their lack of fruit gives me cause for concern. The 1991 Pinot Noir Whole Berry Fermented is a good wine as well as an excellent value. The flavors are straightforward and grapey, but the dark color and exuberant fruity nose of black fruits and herbs are enjoyable. The wine is supple and medium bodied, with enough concentration and depth to warrant 1–3 years of cellaring. The 1990 Pinot Noir is also pleasant and ripe, although monolithic in its straightforward, oaky, berry-scented nose and flavors. Drink it over the next 2–3 years.

WITNESS TREE VINEYARD* * *

1990 Chardonnay Estate	B	76
1990 Chardonnay Reserve/Estate	B	79
1990 Pinot Noir Estate	B	86

I enjoyed Witness Tree's 1989 Chardonnay, which borders on being too oaky but has tremendous extraction of fruit. However, both *cuvées* of 1990 are too woody. The oak dominates the meager fruit, and the results are two wines that are out of balance, tough textured, and uncharming. The 1990 Chardonnay regular *cuvée* does not possess the depth of the 1990 Chardonnay Reserve. Where's the fruit? Neither wine is likely to get any better, so immediate consumption is suggested. Witness Tree's 1990 Pinot Noir Estate offers an atypical, albeit enticing nose of black fruits, chocolate, and herbs. It is a tasty, meaty wine, with soft tannins, good definition, and a succulent finish. Drink it over the next 5–6 years.

8. OTHER AMERICAN VITICULTURAL REGIONS

Vineyards can be found in every state in America. Most of them are tiny yet boast plenty of local consumer support. Although the great majority of wines I have tasted from areas outside Oregon and California are unimpressive, there are isolated cases of high-quality winemaking as well as potential for the future. Wine consumers should give the following wineries a serious look. Except for Washington State, the products of these wineries are unlikely to be found outside the state of origin. Lamentably, one of the discouraging aspects of local wineries is how poorly local restaurants support them. Unlike European restaurants, which offer regional wineries tremendous support, most American restaurants compile wine lists crammed with imports and California wines but no local products, even with vineyards sometimes just several miles away. The only exceptions are California, Oregon, and Washington. In all of these states, the restaurants aggressively support the local wineries.

Washington State

A number of emerging trends may finally focus attention on the rapidly improving wines of Washington. First, escalating European wine prices, the weak dollar, and increasing international competition for wines of limited availability may force all but the most wealthy wine consumers to look elsewhere for quality wines at reasonable prices. Washington wines could prove to be a significant alternative. Second, Washington has a bevy of quality wines, including Cabernets, Merlots, Chardonnays, and Sauvignon Blancs, priced to compete in the $8–$15 range occupied primarily by budget French imports and Australian or Chilean wines. This segment of the marketplace is ignored by many of California's finest producers, which presents an opportunity for Washington's producers to become more widely known as consumers taste and compare. Third, the giant Château Ste.-Michelle winery has dominated the Washington wine scene in years past. This estate and its sister winery, Columbia Crest, account for 50% of the state's production. For a number of years Château Ste.-Michelle had a spotty quality record, but that has changed given recent dramatic improvements. With a bevy of excellent vintages in the pipeline (1992, 1990, and 1989), optimism is the rule of the day among Washington State's long-ignored winemakers.

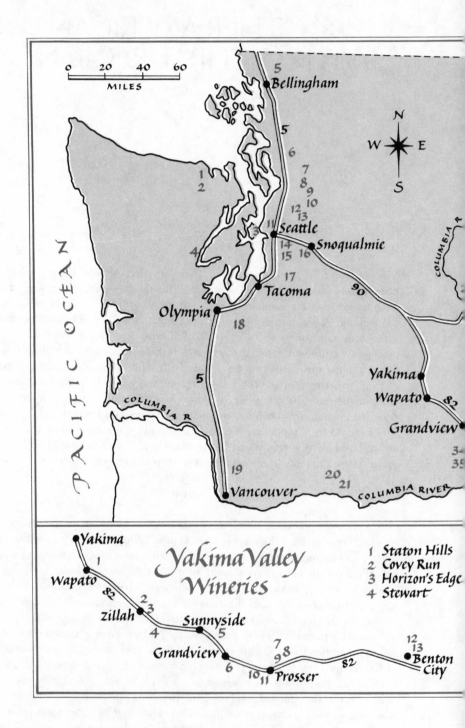

0   20   40   60
MILES

PACIFIC OCEAN

COLUMBIA R.

Bellingham 5

5

6

7

8
9

12   10
13

11   Seattle   Snoqualmie

3

14

15   16

4   17

Tacoma

Olympia

18

5

COLUMBIA R

Yakima
Wapato   82

Grandview
34
35

19   20
21   COLUMBIA RIVER

Vancouver

N
W   E
S

90

Yakima

1

Wapato
82

2
zillah   3

4   Sunnyside   5

Grandview

6

10
11   Prosser   82

7
9 8

12
13
Benton
City

Yakima Valley Wineries

1   Staton Hills
2   Covey Run
3   Horizon's Edge
4   Stewart

Washington

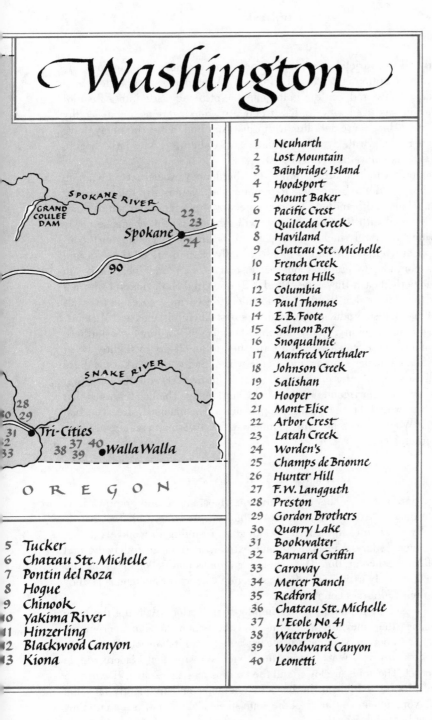

1 Neuharth
2 Lost Mountain
3 Bainbridge Island
4 Hoodsport
5 Mount Baker
6 Pacific Crest
7 Quilceda Creek
8 Haviland
9 Chateau Ste. Michelle
10 French Creek
11 Staton Hills
12 Columbia
13 Paul Thomas
14 E. B. Foote
15 Salmon Bay
16 Snoqualmie
17 Manfred Vierthaler
18 Johnson Creek
19 Salishan
20 Hooper
21 Mont Elise
22 Arbor Crest
23 Latah Creek
24 Worden's
25 Champs de Brionne
26 Hunter Hill
27 F. W. Langguth
28 Preston
29 Gordon Brothers
30 Quarry Lake
31 Bookwalter
32 Barnard Griffin
33 Caroway
34 Mercer Ranch
35 Redford
36 Chateau Ste. Michelle
37 L'Ecole No 41
38 Waterbrook
39 Woodward Canyon
40 Leonetti

5 Tucker
6 Chateau Ste. Michelle
7 Pontin del Roza
8 Hogue
9 Chinook
10 Yakima River
11 Hinzerling
12 Blackwood Canyon
13 Kiona

The Basics

Virtually all the varietals seen in California are grown in Washington. The most notable exception is Zinfandel. However, Washington's answer to this is Lemberger, a fruity, red vinifera grape capable of being made into a Beaujolais-style, non–oak aged wine or, less frequently, into a serious, cellar-worthy wine. A few producers are dabbling with Pinot Noir and, not surprisingly, have failed. Experiments with Syrah, Nebbiolo, and Cabernet Franc have begun, and results to date have been mediocre.

Washington's wineries are banking on Chardonnay, Cabernet Sauvignon, and especially Merlot to bring them to prominence. There is also some hope for Sauvignon Blanc and Semillon. Approximately one-quarter of the state's vineyards are planted with Riesling, but this will diminish in time because newly planted vineyards rarely include this varietal. Fortunately Washington's consumers appear to enjoy Riesling, which is usually bargain-priced ($4–$7), and producers continue to crank it out because it is easy and inexpensive to make—the perfect cash-flow wine. The 1992s appeared on the market within 9 months of the vintage. For Riesling aficionados, these wines represent fine values. Washington also produces this country's best Chenin Blancs and Muscats. Their crisp natural acidity, easily obtained because of Washington's northern latitude, makes these wines, which are finished in an off-dry to slightly sweet style, the ideal summer sipping and picnic wines. Sadly, the market for these wines is limited. For better or worse, the state's future rests with the superstar grapes—Cabernet Sauvignon, Merlot, and Chardonnay. The good news is that these are the wines the marketing people claim consumers desire. The bad news is that Washington State must compete with California in an already congested marketplace.

RED WINE VARIETALS

Cabernet Sauvignon   This is Washington's most successful grape variety. In capable hands it renders an almost opaque purple wine. Cabernet Sauvignon usually ripes fully in eastern Washington, resulting in wines with curranty, plummy, cedary aromas, excellent extract, medium to full body, and good depth and concentration. Overwhelming aromas and flavors of herbs and vegetables are rarely as intrusive in Washington Cabernet Sauvignons as they can be in their California counterparts.

Merlot   Washington producers are hoping that Merlot will bring the state fame. Because the vineyards are young and the winemakers inexperienced, Washington's Cabernet Sauvignon is clearly superior to its Merlot.

To no one's surprise, Washington Merlot yields a wine that is more supple than Cabernet. The acids are lower and the tannins less aggressive. However, a number of Merlots exhibit an herbaceous character and frequently lack the depth of flavor and concentration of the state's best Cabernets. As a group they are pleasant but rarely exciting.

Pinot Noir   This fickle grape variety is no easier to tame in Washington than in California. Nothing tasted to date remotely resembles what Pinot Noir can achieve in Burgundy or selected California and Oregon vineyards.

Lemberger   Originally grown in Germany, this grape is like Zinfandel, highly adaptable and successful in a variety of styles. Just a handful of wineries make Lemberger (vineyard acreage is less than 1% of the total in the state). This is lamentable because the wine is tasty, fruity, and quite quaffable when served lightly chilled and not oak aged.

WHITE WINE VARIETALS

Chardonnay Washington Chardonnay occupies 15% of vineyard acreage and can ripen fully while retaining excellent natural acidity. This has caused an increasing number of producers to barrel ferment it and to encourage their Chardonnay to complete malolactic fermentation. Extended lees contact, in vogue in California, is also favored by many Washington producers. A number of wineries have invested heavily in new French oak barrels and are trying to make a wine in the Côte de Beaune style. Others are going after a fruitier style (à la Fetzer's Sundial), while still others are aiming for something in between. In short, there is a wide range of styles, but the potential for making excellent Washington State Chardonnay exists, although much of it remains unrealized.

Chenin Blanc Washington is capable of making wonderful Chenin Blanc in a slightly sweet style because of the naturally crisp acidity. Yet most wineries seemed surprised that anyone would be interested in tasting this ignored, often maligned varietal. However, at $5–$6 a bottle from producers such as Hogue or Snoqualmie, Chenin Blanc can be a true delight, especially on a hot summer day.

Gewürztraminer Fortunately, plantings of this varietal are rapidly decreasing. It has proven no more successful in Washington than in California.

Muscat Like Chenin Blanc, Muscat grown in Washington can render delicious, crisp, aromatic, perfumed wines that are incredibly refreshing on hot summer days. Latah Creek Winery, Covey Run, Stewart, and Snoqualmie are particularly successful with Muscat. In addition, the price is right.

Sauvignon Blanc When vinified in Washington, the potentially extroverted, herbal, grassy qualities of this grape are held in check. Many estates also give the wines some exposure to oak barrels. As in California, most wineries strive for a safe, middle-of-the-road style that too often results in bland, insipid wines. However, Washington State Sauvignons are priced to sell in the $6–$10 range, which makes then less expensive than their California counterparts.

Semillon This is a grape with excellent potential in Washington. It yields a wine with plenty of body and richness combined with the lively acidity typically found in Washington grapes. Only two wineries seem to be fully exploiting Semillon's potential. L'École No. 41's offerings compete with California's Kalin Cellars for America's best Semillon. Woodward Canyon's Charbonneau white, a Graves-style blend of Semillon and Sauvignon Blanc, is another skillfully rendered wine that prominently displays the glories of Semillon.

White (Johannisberg) Riesling Washington's Rieslings are good but often simple and one-dimensional when compared with the slaty, mineral-scented, aromatic complexity and incredible lightness and zestiness attainable in the best German Rieslings. However, Washington's abundant quantities of Rieslings are practically given away, usually selling for less than $10.

Several producers make superb late-harvest Rieslings. Blackwood Canyon,

Yakima River Winery, and Stewart have been particularly successful, and prices are, again, remarkably modest.

RECENT VINTAGES

1992—A hot, dry year resulted in fine overall ripeness and considerable optimism. This will be a year for opulent, fruity white wines and rich, powerful Cabernet Sauvignons.

1991—This should turn out to be a good, somewhat irregular year because of the relatively high crop yields an irregular growing season. For producers who kept yields moderate and picked physiologically ripe fruit, it should turn out to be a high-quality year. The first releases of Merlot from top wineries such as Woodward Canyon and Leonetti were disappointingly herbal and thin.

1990—Believed to be less successful than either 1988 or 1989, this vintage, according to some enthusiastic producers, may ultimately prove quite good for red wines. Generalizations concerning such a vast, diverse viticultural region are fraught with potential for error. With that caveat in mind, the 1990 red wines tend to be supple, rich, and forward. The hot summer and idea harvest conditions produced fully ripe fruit for producers who harvested at the last moment. The red wines should exceed the quality of the whites and in many cases may prove as good as the highly acclaimed 1988s and 1989s.

1989—Moderate temperatures allowed full ripening of the grapes. The red varietals were deeply colored, perfumed, and richly flavored. The white varietals had full fruit and good sugar levels balanced by excellent acidity. Washington producers all seem to agree that this is a potentially great vintage.

1988—An excellent vintage for both reds and whites, but without the depth and concentration of 1989. However, the reds should be long lived and stylish. The white wines should have been consumed several years ago.

OLDER VINTAGES
(Red Wines)

1987—A vintage of correct, attractive wines without the flesh of 1988 and 1989.

1986—Turned out to be a mediocre vintage. Most of the reds lack concentration.

1985—A tannic vintage in which only the most skilled winemakers made balanced wines. The finest wines are muscular, big, and long-lived.

1984—A poor vintage for Washington and best ignored.

1983—Considered by the top red wine producers to be a superb vintage and, along with 1989, one of the two best years of the decade. The best wines are only now beginning to open up and will need another 5–10 years to reach their apogee. The wines have depth, flavor, flesh, balance, and excellent structure. The 1983 Château Ste.-Michelle Cold Creek Reserve Cabernet Sauvignon is a dazzling example from this vintage.

RATING WASHINGTON'S BEST PRODUCERS OF CABERNET SAUVIGNON, MERLOT, OR BLENDS THEREOF

* * * * *(OUTSTANDING PRODUCERS)

Leonetti Cabernet Sauvignon
Leonetti Cabernet Sauvignon Reserve
Quilceda Creek Cabernet Sauvignon

Woodward Canyon Cabernet
   Sauvignon
Woodward Canyon Charbonneau

* * * *(EXCELLENT PRODUCERS)

Leonetti Merlot
Château Ste.-Michelle Cabernet
   Sauvignon Cold Creek Reserve
Château Ste.-Michelle Merlot River
   Ridge Vineyard

Seven Hills Cabernet Sauvignon
Seven Hills Merlot

* * *(GOOD PRODUCERS)

Arbor Crest Cabernet Sauvignon
Arbor Crest Merlot
Blackwood Canyon Cabernet
   Sauvignon
Blackwood Canyon Merlot
Chinook Merlot
Columbia Crest Cabernet Sauvignon
Columbia Crest Merlot
Columbia Winery Cabernet
   Sauvignon Otis Vineyard
Columbia Winery Cabernet
   Sauvignon Red Willow Vineyard

L'École No. 41 Merlot
Hogue Cabernet Sauvignon Reserve
Hogue Merlot Reserve
Latah Creek Cabernet Sauvignon
Latah Creek Merlot
Preston Cabernet Sauvignon
Château Ste.-Michelle Cabernet
   Sauvignon Cold Creek Vineyard
Château Ste.-Michelle Cabernet
   Sauvignon River Ridge Vineyard
Château Ste.-Michelle Merlot Cold
   Creek Vineyard

* *(AVERAGE PRODUCERS)

Bookwalter Cabernet Sauvignon
Canoe Ridge Cabernet Sauvignon
Cascade Estates Cabernet Sauvignon
Coventry Vale Cabernet Sauvignon
Covey Run Cabernet Sauvignon
Facelli Cabernet Sauvignon
French Creek Cabernet Sauvignon
Gordon Bros. Cabernet Sauvignon
Hinzerling Cabernet Sauvignon
Hogue Cabernet Sauvignon
Hogue Merlot

Hyatt Merlot
Mercer Ranch Cabernet Sauvignon
Quarry Lake Cabernet Sauvignon
Redford Cabernet Sauvignon
Silver Lake Cabernet Sauvignon
Snoqualmie Cabernet Sauvignon
Staton Hills Cabernet Sauvignon
Stewart Cabernet Sauvignon
Paul Thomas Cabernet Sauvignon
Tucker Cabernet Sauvignon

RATING WASHINGTON'S BEST PRODUCERS OF CHARDONNAY

* * * * *(OUTSTANDING PRODUCERS)

Woodward Canyon Roza Berge
   Vineyard

Woodward Canyon Estate Reserve

* * * *(EXCELLENT PRODUCERS)

Blackwood Canyon	Château Ste.-Michelle River Ridge
Château Ste.-Michelle Cold Creek	Vineyard
Vineyard	Woodward Canyon Columbia Valley

* * *(GOOD PRODUCERS)

Chinook	Hyatt
Columbia Crest	Latah Creek
Gordon Bros.	McCrea
Barnard Griffin	Stewart
Hogue	Paul Thomas Reserve
Hogue Reserve	

* *(AVERAGE PRODUCERS)

Arbor Crest	Horizon's Edge
Bookwalter	Kiona
Canoe Ridge	Mount Baker
Caroway	Preston
Cascade Estates	Silver Lake
Champs de Brionne	Snoqualmie
Columbia Winery	Staton Hills
Covey Run	Paul Thomas
French Creek	Tucker
Hinzerling	Waterbrook
Hoodsport	Zillah Oakes

RATING WASHINGTON'S BEST PRODUCERS OF OTHER WINES

* * * * *(OUTSTANDING PRODUCERS)

L'École No. 41 Semillon	Yakima River Late-Harvest Riesling
Yakima River Ice Wine	

* * * *(EXCELLENT PRODUCERS)

Blackwood Canyon Chenin Blanc	Thurston Wolfe Late-Harvest
Blackwood Canyon Gewürztraminer	Semillon
Blackwood Canyon Late-Harvest	Woodward Canyon Charbonneau
Riesling	White (Semillon/Sauvignon Blanc)
Thurston Wolfe Black Muscat	

* * *(GOOD PRODUCERS)

Bainbridge Island Müller-Thurgau	Quarry Lake Sauvignon Blanc
Cavatappi Nebbiolo	Stewart Late-Harvest Riesling

Arizona

Believe it nor not, Arizona has two wineries that merit serious attention. The most interesting is **Sonoita,** started in 1978 by a professor of agriculture at the University of Arizona. The vineyard is planted in a combination of limestone and clay soils. Although I have not tasted its Pinot Noir or Chenin Blanc, I have had five vintages of the Cabernet Sauvignon. The wines exhibit admirable texture and intensity, but the pruny, somewhat baked character evident in several of the Cabernets suggests the grapes were burnt, or raisiny, at the time of harvest. Nevertheless, the 1987 Sonoita Cabernet Sauvignon Private Reserve offers a provocative nose of chocolate, coffee, herbs, and roasted black fruits, as well as a rich, deep, chewy texture. The other winery, **R. W. Webb,** produces straightforward, uninteresting wines. Although they may not have the excesses of the Sonoita Cabernets, neither do they display the personalities of those wines.

Connecticut

The standout winery in this state is **Crosswoods** in North Stonington. Crosswoods has consistently turned out one of the East Coast's better Chardonnays but has had less success with Merlot. Crosswoods is also producing Pinot Noir, Riesling, Gewürztraminer, and a handful of French-American hybrids that I have not tasted. Moreover, it recently purchased **Hopkins,** a winery with which I have had limited experience. Two other wineries that produce average-quality wines are Chamard Vineyards and Stonington Vineyards.

Idaho

One winery again dominates this state's wine production. The **Ste. Chapelle** winery in Caldwell produces in excess of 100,000 cases of wine using grapes from growers throughout the state as well as from Washington. Although its red wines have traditionally been mediocre, recent Reserve Cabernet Sauvignons have exhibited more complexity and richness. Readers should look for the 1988 Reserve Cabernet. The white wines have generally been well made, albeit slightly sweet. There is a good Johannisberg Riesling, an off-dry Chenin Blanc, and some neutral-tasting Chardonnays. Another Idaho winery, **Pintler,** fashions a light, pleasant Cabernet Sauvignon and a woody, crisp, straightforward, tart Chardonnay.

Maryland

There are a number of good wineries in my home state, yet few are known outside the state because of their tiny production. The most famous winery is Dr. Hamilton Mowbray's **Montbray Vineyard** in Westminster. However, the crusty and feisty Mowbray, who certainly produced some of the finest Seyval-Blanc (he calls it Seyval-Villard) in America, and from time to time a hefty, rich Cabernet Sauvignon, has retired and at last notice was seeking a buyer for his vineyards.

Maryland's best Chardonnay is made by Bertero Basignani of **Basignani Vineyards** in Sparks. His lovely, full-bodied, ripe, lush, barrel-fermented, unfiltered Chardonnay usually disappears within months of its release. It is a serious wine. At a 1992 vertical tasting of vintages back to 1983, it admirably demonstrated that as delicious as it is young, it holds its fruit better than a majority of California Chardonnays. Basignani also turns out a fine Cabernet Sauvignon (as with most East Coast wineries, the 1991 will be Basignani's richest and most concentrated because of the dry, hot summer) and a number of super bargains for under $6, including his hybrid red wine blend called Marisa and a proprietary white wine, Elena. Basignani also makes tiny quantities of a dry Riesling that gets high marks from those who have had the good fortune to taste it, as well as Lorenzo, one of the few sparkling Seyvals made in this country. Just about any Basignani wine merits attention.

Basignani has plenty of competition in Maryland. For years the most backward, powerful, richest East Coast Cabernet Sauvignon was produced by **Byrd Vineyard** in Myersville. With hillside vineyards planted in the foothills of the Appalachian Mountains, Byrd's rich, black/ruby-colored, tannic Cabernets seemed to outmuscle the biggest mountain Cabernets of California. Even its top vintages, such as 1980, 1983, and 1986, were not close to maturity when tasted in fall 1992. Byrd's other wines, like those of other small wineries, tended to be overoaked and indifferent. At the time of this writing, this vineyard was also up for sale.

The most successful Maryland winery from a commercial and critical point of view is **Boordy Vineyards,** whose wines have moved from strength to strength in the late 1980s and early 1990s. This estate produces quality Chardonnay and Seyval as well as some pleasant nouveau-style wines from such hybrids as Foch.

Other Maryland wineries of note include **Woodhall,** a Sparks producer that has made considerable progress after a shaky start, and Brookeville's **Catoctin Vineyards,** which has recently produced some good Chardonnays and flavorful, rich Cabernets.

Massachusetts

The **Commonwealth Winery** continues to prove that Chardonnay can prosper in a northeasterly climate. From time to time this winery also turns out pleasant Riesling and a light, washed-out, rusty-colored Pinot Noir. I recently had a well-made Commonwealth Seyval that would have gone beautifully with a plate of fresh oysters. Straightforward, simple wines are made by the **Chicama Winery.** To date, my favorite wine from this producer is the Chenin Blanc.

Michigan

Two Michigan wineries have consistently produced interesting wines. **Château Grand Traverse** fashions one of this country's best dry Johannisberg Rieslings. From time to time it has also turned out a good Chardonnay. **L. Mawby** offers some innovative wines from Michigan's Leelanau Peninsula. The 1990 Vignoles is a dry, crisp, peach-scented wine with lovely freshness and a refreshing fruit character. It could be mistaken for a lighter-style Condrieu. Mawby also produces a well-made sparkling wine. The most recent example I tasted was the Brut Cuvée #5 (a 50% Pinot Noir, 50% Vignoels blend).

Missouri

The star of Missouri is the **Mount Pleasant Vineyard** in Augusta. It produces an interesting portlike wine with none of the funky character that would suggest a blend from hybrid grapes. There is also a surprisingly high-quality Chardonnay and an oaky Vidal Blanc. Mount Pleasant has high aspirations, and its wines are certainly worth trying. Several wineries of note include Hermannhof, Montelle, and Stone Hill

New Jersey

The **Tewksbury Winery** in Lebanon is New Jersey's uncontested leader. Again, the red wines are run of the mill, but the white wines are a different story altogether. Seyval-Villard, white Riesling, Gewürtztraminer, and Chardonnay all merit interest and sell at reasonable prices. Tewksbury also produces some interesting as well as controversial fruit wines. I have also had several delightful Chardonnays from Tomasello Winery in Hammonton.

New Mexico

Believe it or not, there are vineyards in New Mexico. Although the wines of **Anderson Valley** are disappointing, I have been impressed by the sparkling wines from **Gruet.** Both of the wines I tasted, a Blanc de Noir and a Brut, were nonvintage, so one cannot tell how old these *cuvées* are when purchased. I tasted them in the fall of 1992. The Blanc de Noir, from a vineyard called Dealmont, was so rich and well made, with tiny, small bubbles, that I rated it 88 (if you have followed my past reviews of domestic sparkling wines, you'll realize this offering received one of the highest ratings). Even the nonvintage Brut was excellent, with ripeness, a midpalate, and plenty of purity and fruit. Both wines were inserted in a tasting of the finest California sparkling wines, including the Domaine Chandon Reserve and the newest luxury *cuvée* from Schramsberg, the 1987 J. Schram. The Gruet wines came out first and second. This is a winery that merits attention.

New York

After California and Oregon, New York has the greatest number of wineries of any state. The two major viticultural areas are the beautiful Finger Lakes region and Long Island. New York, like most viticultural regions in the Northeast, produces red wines that are generally lean, vegetal, and austere. Many of the best wineries do not even make a red wine, but one producer has miraculously excelled with Cabernet Sauvignon and Merlot, The **Hargrave Vineyard** in Cutchogue, Long Island, makes good, sometimes excellent, Cabernet Sauvignon, one of the best produced in the East. The winery also does an excellent job with Sauvignon Blanc and Chardonnay. Another winery that has begun to demonstrate modest progress with Merlot is **Lenz.**

Elsewhere in New York, Chardonnay, Riesling, and Seyval-Blanc are the most successful grape varietals. For Chardonnay, the finest producer in the East, and one of the best in the country, is **Wagner Vineyards** in Lodi. Its Chardonnays often exhibit remarkable depth of flavor as well as complexity. Wagner also produces fine Seyval. There are a bevy of other fine Chardonnay producers: **Bridgehampton** on Long Island; **Plane's, Casa Larga, Finger Lakes Wine Cellars, Glenora, Hermann J. Wiemer,** and **Knapp** near the Finger Lakes; **Pindar** on Long Island; and **Millbrook, Schloss Doepken, West Park,** and **Wickham Vineyards,** are all reliable. Other than Wagner's explosively rich Chardonnay, New York Chardonnays are more austere, leaner, and less opulently fruity than those found in California.

Several other wineries of note are **Clinton,** a producer of very good Seyval; **Benmarl,** a good producer of Seyval; and the idiosyncratic **Bully Hill,** a good producer of white wine hybrids.

The finest recent vintage for New York's wineries is 1991, an abnormally hot, dry year. The Chardonnays are bold and rich, and most New York producers claim the Cabernets are the finest they have made!

RATING NEW YORK'S BEST PRODUCERS OF CHARDONNAY

* * * * *(OUTSTANDING PRODUCERS)

Wagner

* * * *(EXCELLENT PRODUCERS)

Millbrook   Hermann J. Wiemer
Palmer

* * *(GOOD PRODUCERS)

Bridgehampton   Heron Hill
Casa Larga   Knapp
Finger Lakes   Pindar
Glenora   Sag Pond
Hargrave

North Carolina

One of the South's best kept wine secrets is **Westbend Vineyards** in Louisville, North Carolina. Westbend produces two excellent Chardonnay *cuvées,* a tasty, rich Seyval, a good Sauvignon, and a surprisingly spicy, herbal, cassis- and chocolate-scented and -flavored Cabernet Sauvignon. As fine as these wines are, I am surprised they are not better known outside of North Carolina.

Ohio

Although there is a small but flourishing wine industry in Ohio, the most experience I have had is with the wines of **Markko Vineyard** in Conneaut. They have turned out pleasant Chardonnay and a crisp, acidic, angular Cabernet Sauvignon. **Chalet de Bonne,** a winery situated near Lake Erie, makes a number of wines. The only one I tasted that had some redeeming virtue was the Chambourcin, a red wine made from a French-American hybrid. Last, **Firelands Winery** can make tasty Chardonnays.

Pennsylvania

Two Pennsylvania wineries stand out as a cut above the rest. **Chaddsford** produces what must be the East Coast's most expensive wines. Its disappointing Pinot Noir and Chambourcin are both overpriced. The winery is best known for its Chardonnays, which are usually vineyard-designated by the name Philip Roth or Stargazer. They can possess lavish quantities of oak, but they exhibit excellent varietal character, a steely buttery fruitiness, crisp acidity, and admirable intensity. Readers should be looking for 1991s, a superlative vintage throughout the Northeast. However, do not expect any bargains from Chaddsford; its wines sell for $25 or more.

The other excellent Pennsylvania winery is **Allegro Vineyards** in Brogue, just south of the state capital of Harrisburg. Proprietor John Crouch is a serious winemaker. He has fashioned some elegant, rich Cabernet Sauvignons, as well as fine Chardonnays and a crisp Seyval-Villard. He is also known for being the first to use the name *Opus One* on a proprietary wine. Since he failed to protect the name, he was forced to drop its use when the Mondavi/Rothschild partnership chose Opus One for its luxury-priced proprietary white wine.

Other Pennsylvania wineries have had spotty records. From time to time pleasant and inexpensive wines can emerge from **Naylor's**.

Rhode Island

The **Sakonnet Vineyard** in Little Compton makes fine Riesling and good Chardonnay. Its Pinot Noirs are light and diluted. If you stick to Sakonnet's rosé, Chardonnay, and pleasant, fruity Vidal (a hybrid white wine grape) no older than 3 years, you will find some reasonably good values.

Texas

Texans are unusually chauvinistic about anything grown, produced, or located in that state, but this should not obscure the fact that there are some interesting Texas wineries and, surprisingly, some pleasant wines. The problem is that most of them are priced as if there were an obsession by the world's wine drinkers to acquire them. Values from Texas are an unknown commodity. The following chart profiles the best wines from the top producers.

RATING TEXAS'S BEST PRODUCERS

* * * * *(OUTSTANDING PRODUCERS)
None

* * * *(EXCELLENT PRODUCERS)
None

* * *(GOOD PRODUCERS)

Llano Estacado Cabernet Sauvignon	Pheasant Ridge Cabernet Franc
Llano Estacado Chardonnay	Pheasant Ridge Cabernet Sauvignon
Llano Estacado Sauvignon Blanc	Pheasant Ridge Chardonnay

* *(AVERAGE PRODUCERS)

Cap Rock Sauvignon Blanc	Ste. Genevieve Sauvignon Blanc
Fall Creek Cabernet Sauvignon	Schoppaul Hill Chenin Blanc
Messina Hof Chardonnay Private Reserve	Schoppaul Hill Sauvignon Blanc
Messina Hof Chenin Blanc	Slaughter Leftwich Cabernet Sauvignon
Messina Hof Riesling	Slaughter Leftwich Sauvignon Blanc
Pheasant Ridge Chenin Blanc	

Virginia

I am skeptical about Virginia's overall potential for high-quality wines (Thomas Jefferson's thoughts on this issue notwithstanding), yet I have been impressed by a number of recent efforts from some of that state's vineyards. **Piedmont Vineyards** and the **Williamsburg Winery** have both produced excellent Chardonnays that can compete with not only the best of the East Coast but also the finest from the West Coast. Williamsburg's Chardonnay Acte 12 of 1619 is a particularly impressive wine, as is Piedmont's Chardonnay Barrel-Fermented Special Reserve. Piedmont also excels with Semillon.

The red wines are another story. To date, only **Montdomaine** has demonstrated the ability to turn out a rich, well-balanced, complex Merlot that offers considerable pleasure. Other wineries that have, from time to time, turned out good wine include **Naked Mountain.** It has produced some good Chardonnays as well as a pleasant Cabernet Sauvignon–dominated wine called Claret. **Barboursville Winery** has also begun to fashion an interesting Chardonnay called Monticello Reserve and a Monticello Sauvignon Blanc. Its red wines have been spotty, but I sense a commitment to excellence by the owner, so perhaps improvements will be forthcoming. **Rapidan River Vineyards** has performed well in my tastings. Dedicated primarily to Riesling, and to making wines in both a dry and semidry style, it has proven that American-grown Riesling can make elegant and refined wines. Rapidan River's Rieslings are among the finest made in this country. It has been less successful with Gewürztraminer and Chardonnay. Last, **Meredyth Winery,** one of Virginia's first wineries, makes that state's finest Seyval Blanc, a wine that sells at an exceptionally reasonable price.

RATING VIRGINIA'S BEST PRODUCERS

* * * * *(OUTSTANDING PRODUCERS)

None

* * * *(EXCELLENT PRODUCERS)

Piedmont Chardonnay Reserve
    Barrel-Fermented
Piedmont Semillon

Rapidan River Dry Riesling
Williamsburg Chardonnay Acte 12
    of 1619

* * *(GOOD PRODUCERS)

Barboursville Chardonnay Monticello
    Reserve
Ingleside Plantation Chardonnay
Meredyth Seyval Blanc
Montdomaine Merlot Monticello
    Reserve

Naked Mountain Chardonnay
Rapidan River Off-Dry Riesling
Williamsburg Chardonnay Barrel-
    Fermented Reserve

THE BEST OF THE REST

Australia
New Zealand
Argentina
Chile
Greece
Hungary
Israel
Lebanon
Switzerland

9. AUSTRALIA

Destination Anywhere

You name it and the Australians no doubt grow it, make it into wine, blend it with something else, and give it an odd bin number. Australian wines have been hot for 3 years, and not just in America. The combination of quality and value that many of them offer is the hottest thing in town from London to New York. Australia, like California in America and Alsace in France, labels its wine after the grape (or grapes) it is made from. All the major grape varietals are used here, and amazingly, great wines are turned out from all of them. The major viticultural districts (listed alphabetically) are as follows:

Adelaide Hills   Located in southern Australia, this is a high-altitude, cooler-climate region. Petaluma is its most famous winery. Mountadam makes Australia's finest Chardonnay from vineyards in the Adelaide Hills.

Barossa Valley   In southern Australia, this huge, well-known viticultural area north of Adelaide is home to some of the titans of Austalia's wine industry (such as Penfolds, Henschke, Tollana, Seppelt, Wolf Blass, Orlando, and Hill Smith).

Bendigo   Bendigo is an up-and-coming area, although it has a long history as a wine-producing region. Balgownie is the finest winery there.

Central Victoria   The traditionally styled wines of Château Tahbilk are the best that come from Central Victoria and the Goulburn Valley. The wines from this area are powerful, full bodied, and fruity.

Clare Valley   Located north of Adelaide and the Barossa Valley, this area is known for its white rather than red wines.

Coonawarra   Situated in south Australia, west of the Goulburn Valley, Coonawarra is perhaps the most famous and, according to some, the best red wine–growing area of Australia. Top wineries such as Lindemans (its Limestone Ridge and St. George vineyards are there), Petaluma, Penfolds, Rosemount, Orlando, Reynella, and Mildara pull their grapes from Coonawarra. The two best wineries actually located in Coonawarra are the Bowen Estate and Hollick.

Geelong   Southwest of Melbourne near the coast is the small area of Geelong. The most renowned wineries are Anakie and Bannockburn, but everyone is talking about the potential of Hickinbotham's Anakie, a winery of impecca-

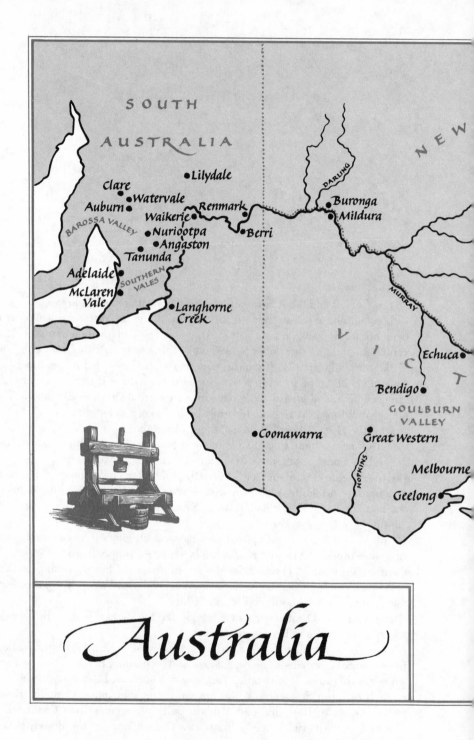

SOUTH

AUSTRALIA

N E W

•Lilydale

Clare
•
•Watervale   •Renmark
Auburn•   Waikerie•
      Waikerie•   •Berri
BAROSSA VALLEY •Nuriootpa
        •Angaston
    Tanunda•

Adelaide•
    SOUTHERN
McLaren• VALES
Vale

        •Langhorne
         Creek

DARLING

•Buronga
•Mildura

MURRAY

V I C

T

•Echuca•

Bendigo•

GOULBURN
VALLEY

•Coonawarra   •Great Western

HOPKINS

Melbourne

Geelong•

Australia

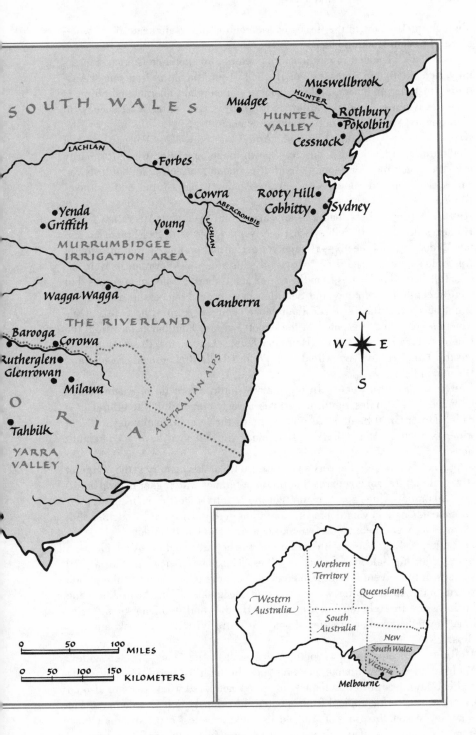

SOUTH WALES

Muswellbrook
HUNTER
Mudgee
HUNTER
VALLEY
Rothbury
Pokolbin
Cessnock

LACHLAN
Forbes

Cowra
Rooty Hill
ABERCROMBIE
Cobbitty
Sydney

Yenda
Griffith
Young
LACHLAN

MURRUMBIDGEE
IRRIGATION AREA

N
W E
S

Wagga Wagga
Canberra

THE RIVERLAND

Barooga
Corowa
Rutherglen
Glenrowan
Milawa

AUSTRALIAN ALPS

O
R
I
A

Tahbilk

YARRA
VALLEY

0   50   100   MILES

0   50   100   150   KILOMETERS

Northern
Territory
Queensland

Western
Australia

South
Australia

New
South Wales

Victoria

Melbourne

ble high quality now in the throes of overcoming the tragic death of its wine-maker, Stephen Hickinbotham.

Glenrowan   Located in northeastern Victoria, this hot area is famous for its inky, rich, chewy red wines, especially the full-throttle Shiraz from one of Australia's historic producers, Baileys. A more commercial Cabernet and Shiraz is made by Wynn's. At nearby Milawa, Brown Bros., one of the most successful high-quality Australian wineries, makes its home.

Great Western   Situated between Ararat and Stawell, to the northwest of Melbourne and Geelong, is an area known for its sparkling wines (primarily from the huge producer Seppelt) and for its smooth, fat, low-acid, but tasty red wines. The top red wine producers are Mount Langi Ghiran and Cathcart Ridge.

Hunter Valley   Less than a 3-hour drive from Sydney is Australia's famed Hunter Valley. It is to Sydney what the Napa Valley is to San Francisco and the Médoc is to Bordeaux—a major tourist attraction and source of some of Australia's most desired wines. Originally this area was known for its rich, exotic, full-bodied red wines from the Shiraz and Cabernet Sauvignon grapes, but more recently Chardonnay and Semillon have proven successful as well. No doubt because of their size and the intense competitive spirit here, this area's wineries are well represented in the export market. Familiar names from the Hunter Valley include Tyrrell, Rothbury Estate, Lindemans, Rosemount, Saxonvale, Lake's Folly, Arrowfield, Hungerford Hill, Brokenwood, Evans, and Wyndham Estate.

Lower Great Southern   In the remote southwestern tip of Australia approximately 150 miles south of Perth is a vast, burgeoning viticultural area called Lower Great Southern. Apple orchards thrive more than vineyards, but wineries such as Mount Barker, Redmond, and Alkoomi have good reputations.

Margaret River   In the very southwestern tip of this country is the Margaret River viticultural zone, an area that produces grapes with higher natural acidities. Australian wine experts claim that the country's most French-like Cabernet Sauvignons and Chardonnays come from here, turned out by such superb wineries as Vasse Felix, Moss Wood, Leeuwin Estate, and Cullens.

McLaren Vale   The traditional fare of this hot area south of Adelaide were thick, rich, high-alcohol Grenache wines. This has changed in the last 10 years with the advent of cold fermentations and the perception that the public yearns for lighter, fruitier wines. Some of the greats of the Australian wine business are in McLaren Vale, including Hardy's and its higher-quality sibling, Reynella. Smaller wineries of note are Wirra Wirra, Woodstock, and Kay Bros.

Mudgee   Located in New South Wales west of the famed Hunter Valley, Mudgee (an aboriginal name meaning "nest in the hills"), with its cool nights and hot days, has proven to be not only a top-notch red wine area, but also an excellent source for tropical fruit–scented, luxuriously rich Chardonnays. For whatever reason, the wines of Mudgee also tend to be less expensive than those from other top areas. One winery, Montrose, dominates the quality scene; two other fine producers are Miramar and Huntington Estate.

Murrumbridgeel Irrigation Area   This area, which has to be irrigated, is in New South Wales about 250 miles due west of Sydney. The region has a mediocre reputation for quality wines that appears justified given what I have tasted, although several producers, such as McWilliams and De Bortoli, have managed to turn out interesting wines. When the wines are good they are a bargain, as prices from this area (called the MIA) are inexpensive.

Padthaway   This southern Australian viticultural area has developed a strong following for its white wines, especially the Chardonnay and Sauvignon Blanc. Padthaway is one of Australia's newest "hot" areas, and two of Australia's largest producers, Lindemans and Seppelt, have shown just how tasty the white wines from this region can be.

Pyrenees   The attractive, rolling-hill countryside of the Pyrenees northwest of Melbourne forms a triangle connecting Redbank, Moonambel, and Avoca. The top wines are the reds from the Cabernet Sauvignon and Shiraz grapes. The best white wines are from the Sauvignon grape. Wineries of note include Redbank, Taltarni, Mount Avoca, and Château Remy.

Riverland   Located in south Australia, Riverland is to Australia what the San Joaquin Valley is to California. This vast source of grapes of mediocre quality is dominated by huge cooperatives and producers who turn out Australia's jug wines and bag-in-the-box generic wines. Penfolds, Kaiserstuhl, Angove, Berri, and Renmano are some of the big enterprises that center their jug wine business here. Although most of the wines from this area are decidedly insipid, some good-value, fresh whites at bargain-basement prices can be found.

Rutherglen   Rutherglen produces Australia's fortified sweet wines, many of which are extraordinary. The famous sweet, nectarlike, ageless ports and fortified Muscats and Tokays of William Chambers, Campbells, and Seppelt are made from Rutherglen grapes.

Swan Valley   This hot, arid area in western Australia just northeast of the coastal city of Perth produces large-framed, muscular red wines and increasingly better white wines. Houghton is the area's most famous winery, but good wines are made by Evans and Tate, as well as by Moondah Brook.

Yarra Valley   This is the viticultural area most in fashion in Australia, and its proponents argue that the climate and resulting wines come closest in spirit to those of Bordeaux and Burgundy in France. I am not convinced. Located in Victoria, this is a cool-climate area outside Melbourne, and every major red and white glamour varietal is planted, from Cabernet Sauvignon, Merlot, and Pinot Noir to Chardonnay, Riesling, and Gewürztraminer. The best wineries are Lillydale, Yarra Yering, Coldstream Hills, and St. Hubert's.

GRAPE VARIETIES

RED WINES

Cabernet Sauvignon   This varietal excels in Australia and generally produces a very fruity, often jammy, intensely curranty, fat wine, sometimes low in acidity, but round, generous, and surprisingly ageworthy in spite of an acid deficiency.

Pinot Noir   There are those who claim to have made successful wines from this infinitely fickle varietal, but the great majority of Australian Pinot Noirs to date have either been raisiny, unusual, and often repugnant or watery, pale, and innocuous. Two wineries that are likely candidates to produce world-class Pinot Noir are Tarra Warra and Coldstream Hills. Except for these two, anyone who suggests Australia is making good Pinot Noir does not have the consumer's best interests at heart.

Shiraz   Despite the obsession with Cabernet Sauvignon, Merlot, and Pinot Noir, this is the grape that makes their greatest wines. The problem is that there is an enormous amount of it, and only a handful of producers treat Shiraz (Syrah) with the respect and care accorded Cabernet. Shiraz can produce Australia's greatest red wine when left to stand on its own, as Penfolds Grange Hermitage convincingly proves, or it can offer more dimension and character to a red wine when blended with Cabernet Sauvignon, as Penfolds and Petaluma have proven time and time again.

WHITE WINES

Chardonnay   The shrewd Aussies, taking full advantage of the wine consumer's thirst for Chardonnay wines, have consistently offered plump, fat wines filled with flavors of apples, pears, oranges, and ripe melons. Although the wines still tend to be overoaked, more and more Australian Chardonnays are fresh and exuberant and bottled early to preserve their youthful grapey qualities. With the advent of centrifuges and micropore filters, many Chardonnays have no bouquet or flavor. The one major disappointment is the aging potential of these naturally low-acid wines, but most consumers are drinking them within several months of purchase, so this is probably a moot issue.

Gewürztraminer   Even though the local salespeople hype the quality of Gewürztraminer, in Australia this grape produces insipid, pale, watery wines that are a far cry from French Gewürztraminers.

Marsanne   Château Tahbilk and Mitchelton are proponents of this grape, which tends to turn out one-dimensional, bland wines.

Muscat   This hot-climate grape excels in Australia and is at its best in the decadently rich, sweet, fortified Muscats that can age for decades. It is also made into a medium-sweet table wine with which Brown Bros. does a particularly admirable job.

Riesling   Australia has proven to be the New World's best alternative to German-made Rieslings. This grape has done extremely well with Kabinett- and Spatlese-style drier Rieslings in the Barossa Valley and Adelaide Hills. Wineries such as Petaluma, Pewsey Vale, Rosemount, and Hill Smith have turned out some spectacular Beerenauslese- and Trockenbeerenauslese-style sweet wines. Overall, this grape gets good marks from me in Australia.

Sauvignon Blanc   The results have been mixed, as the hot climate causes this grape to overripen and take on a grotesque, vegetal, oily, thick fruitiness. There are some fresh, tasty, dry Sauvignons coming from Australia, but for now New Zealand consistently beats Australia when it comes to quality Sauvignon-based wines.

Semillon   This can be delicious, whether it is blended with Chardonnay or Sauvignon or allowed to stand by itself. Semillon produces big, creamy, rich wines loaded with flavor. Wineries such as Rothbury, Rosemount, Montrose, Peter Lehmann, Henschke, and Evans and Tate have been better with this grape than anyone. Some great sweet wines have been made from Semillon affected by the botrytis fungus. Look for those from Rothbury, Rosemount, and Peter Lehmann, which are world class.

FLAVORS

RED WINES

Cabernet Sauvignon   Very ripe, often overripe, sweet, intense blackcurrant flavors, supple, fat textures, and oodles of fruit. When poorly made or overly acidified, the wines are musty, dirty, and tart.

Pinot Noir   Raisiny, pruny fruit flavors with no finesse or complexity represent appallingly bad examples of Pinot Noir.

Shiraz   Intense aromas of cassis, leather, licorice, cedar, tar, and pepper are found in wines that have a healthy dosage of Shiraz. Quite full bodied and rich, with softer tannins than Cabernet Sauvignon, these wines are drinkable young but frequently age better than the more glamorous Cabernet Sauvignons.

WHITE WINES

Chardonnay   Tropical fruit flavors predominate in this creamy-textured, voluptuous wine. Oak is sometimes too noticeable, but better-balanced wines with the fruit in the forefront have been the rule in recent vintages.

Gewürztraminer   Where's the spice and exotic lychee-nut character found in the great Gewürztraminers of Alsace? Watery, thin wines are usually disappointing.

Marsanne   Usually neutral or, as Jancis Robinson says, "reminiscent of glue" aptly describes Marsanne. It generally tastes much better old than young, but because it tastes so uninteresting young, no one ages it.

Muscat   Huge aromas of brown sugar, fruitcake, *crème brûlée*, buttered and baked apricots, and oranges with honey and nuts give this varietal its appeal.

Riesling   The classic Riesling aromas of spring flowers, green apples, and wet stones are present in the drier versions of this wine. As the wines get sweeter, aromas and flavors of oranges, peaches, apricots, butter, baked apples, and honeyed nuts arise.

Sauvignon Blanc   Unfortunately these wines seem to either be feeble, bland, and tasteless or oily, vegetal, and grotesque.

Semillon   In the drier versions, lemon-lime aromas intertwined with honey and toasty oak are often the most interesting. With the sweet versions, buttery nuts and honey-coated raisin flavors take over.

AGING POTENTIAL

Cabernet Sauvignon: 5–10 years
Pinot Noir: 4–6 years
Shiraz: 5–20 years
Chardonnay: 1–2 years
Gewürztraminer: 1–2 years
Marsanne: 4–12 years
Muscat (Dry): 1–3 years
   (Fortified): 5–50+ years
Riesling (Dry): 1–4 years
   (Sweet): 4–10 years
Sauvignon Blanc: 1–3 years

Semillon (Dry): 2–8 years
   (Sweet): 4–12 years

OVERALL QUALITY LEVEL

At the top level, wines such as the Penfolds Grange Hermitage or Bin 707 Cabernet Sauvignon are as fine as any red wine made in the world. Unfortunately there are too few of them in Australia. Australia's overall wine quality is barely average, with oceans of mediocre and poorly made wines. There are, however, plenty of good, agreeable wines at attractive prices, and therein lies the reason for Australia's success in this area—they excel in offering tasty, user-friendly wines at low prices.

MOST IMPORTANT INFORMATION TO KNOW

Given the remarkable diversity, the best thing for consumers to do is memorize the names of some of the better producers and restrict their initial purchases to the surefire successes from that particular winery—usually Chardonnay, Cabernet, and Shiraz. The producers chart for each varietal should be used as a guideline until you have decided which wines and producers you prefer.

1993–1994 BUYING STRATEGY

For 99% of Australia's wines, buy only what you intend to drink over the next year. Except for a few red wines, the open-knit, plump, overtly fruity, low-acid style of Australian wines is ideal for consuming immediately, but their aging potential is nonexistent. For white wines, restrict your buying to 1992 and 1991. For inexpensive red wines, you can safely buy any vintage back to 1986 without worrying about the wine's senility. Furthermore, keep in mind that Australia does indeed produce sensational, world-class, late-harvest and fortified wines at a fraction of the price one has to pay for a German Beerenauslese or Trockenbeerenauslese, a French Sauternes, or vintage or tawny port. These wines, often absurdly low-priced, are well worth seeking out.

VINTAGE GUIDE

As in California, constant sunny weather virtually guarantees at least good-quality wines in Australia, but each year is different as a result of drought, heat or cold waves, and hail. However, the extremes in quality that one often sees in Europe do not exist in Australia.

1992—A cooler than normal year in most of Australia's wine-producing regions has resulted in a significant range in quality. Overall, 1992 should turn out to be an above-average-quality year.

1991—An irregular yet promising vintage, particularly for red wine.

1990—This year has all the characteristics of a top-flight vintage, possibly the finest for Australia's red wines since 1986.

1989—A large, high-quality crop was reported throughout Australia.

1988—Early reports indicate a terrific year for red wines. It was a mixed bag for the whites, which should have been drunk up years ago.

1987—An exceptionally cool and late year all over Australia; the crop size was down, but the quality is considered to be very good to exceptional.

1986—The crop size varied from average to well above average, but the quality is very good to excellent in all major districts. Many producers rate 1986 and 1987 the two best back-to-back years of the decade for red wines.

1985—The second of four straight cool years, the 1985 vintage is highly regarded for its Cabernet Sauvignons. Overall, a good red wine vintage, particularly in New South Wales, but it is far from a great vintage, as most producers prefer 1987, 1986, and 1983 to 1985 (although in the Great Western region, growers felt it was a top-notch vintage). It was a cool, very dry year.

1984—A huge crop everywhere translated into lighter, less concentrated wines. In particular the Hunter Valley suffered because of excessive rainfall.

1983—An exceptionally hot, dry year resulted in some full-blown, now senile, white wines and some rich, intense, outstanding red wines, especially in the Hunter Valley. But overall this vintage looks to be the worst of this decade for quality.

1982—A large crop of good wines was produced. No one has called it great, and most of the successes came from southern Australia.

RATING AUSTRALIA'S BEST PRODUCERS OF CABERNET SAUVIGNON AND SHIRAZ

* * * * *(OUTSTANDING PRODUCERS)

Henschke Shiraz Hill of Grace (Barossa)

Henschke Shiraz Mt. Edelstone (Barossa)

Parker Estate Cabernet Sauvignon Terra Rossa First-Growth (Coonawarra)

Penfolds Cabernet Sauvignon Bin 707 (South Australia)

Penfolds Shiraz Grange Hermitage (South Australia)

* * * *(EXCELLENT PRODUCERS)

Lindemans Shiraz/Cabernet Limestone Ridge (New South Wales)

Lindemans Pyrus Proprietary Red Wine (New South Wales)

Lindemans Cabernet Sauvignon St. George (New South Wales)

Orlando Cabernet Sauvignon Jacaranda Ridge Coonawarra

Penfolds Shiraz Bin 128 (South Australia)

Penfolds Shiraz/Cabernet Koonunga Hill (South Australia)

Penfolds Shiraz Magill Estate (South Australia)

Penley Estate Cabernet Sauvignon

Petaluma Cabernet Sauvignon Coonawarra (South Australia)

Redbank Cabernet Sauvignon Long Paddock (Victoria)

Redbank Sally's Paddock (Victoria)

Rothbury Estate Shiraz (Hunter Valley)

Château Tahbilk Shiraz (Goulburn)

Virgin Hills Cabernet Sauvignon (Victoria)

Wolf Blass Cabernet Sauvignon President's Selection Black Label (Victoria)

Wolf Blass Cabernet Sauvignon Yellow Label (Victoria)

Wynn's Cabernet Sauvignon John Riddoch (Coonawarra)

Yarra Yering Cabernet Sauvignon Dry Red #1 (Yarra Valley)

Yarra Yering Shiraz Dry Red #2 (Yarra Valley)

* * *(GOOD PRODUCERS)

Alkoomie Cabernet Sauvignon
(Western Australia)

Baileys Cabernet Sauvignon
(Glenrowan)

Balgownie Cabernet Sauvignon
(Bendigo)

Bowen Estate Cabernet Sauvignon
(South Australia)

Brand's Laira Cabernet Sauvignon
(Coonawarra)

Brokenwood Cabernet Sauvignon
(New South Wales)

Brown Bros. Cabernet Sauvignon
(Victoria)

Capel Vale Cabernet Sauvignon
(Western Australia)

Cullins Cabernet Sauvignon
(Margaret River)

Fern Hill Cabernet Sauvignon
(McLaren)

Hickinbotham Cabernet Sauvignon
(Geelong)

Hungerford Hill Cabernet Sauvignon
(Hunter Valley)

Huntington Estate Cabernet
Sauvignon (Mudgee)

Tim Knappstein Cabernet Sauvignon
(Clare Valley)

Peter Lehmann Cabernet Sauvignon
(Barossa)

Peter Lehman Shiraz (Barossa)

Leeuwin Estate Cabernet Sauvignon
(Margaret River)

Lindemans Cabernet Sauvignon
(Coonawarra)

Goeff Merrill Cabernet Sauvignon
(South Australia)

Mildara Cabernet Sauvignon
(Coonawarra)

Montrose Cabernet Sauvignon
(Mudgee)

Moss Wood Cabernet Sauvignon
(Margaret River)

Mount Langi Ghiran Shiraz (Victoria)

Orlando RF Cabernet Sauvignon
(South Australia)

Redman Cabernet Sauvignon
(Coonawarra)

Rosemount Cabernet Sauvignon
Show Reserve (Coonawarra)

Saxonvale Cabernet Sauvignon
(Hunter Valley)

Seppelt Cabernet Sauvignon
(Barossa)

Seville Estate Cabernet Sauvignon
(Victoria)

Taltarni Cabernet Sauvignon
(Victoria)

Taltarni Shiraz (Victoria)

Vasse Felix Cabernet Sauvignon
(Western Australia)

Wrights Cabernet Sauvignon
(Western Australia)

Wyndham Estates Cabernet
Sauvignon (South Australia)

Wyndham Estates Shiraz (South
Australia)

RATING AUSTRALIA'S BEST PRODUCERS OF CHARDONNAY

* * * * *(OUTSTANDING PRODUCERS)

None

* * * *(EXCELLENT PRODUCERS)

Clyde Park (Geelong)
Leeuwin Artists Series (Margaret
    River)
Mountadam (Adelaide Hills)
Rosemount Roxburgh (Hunter
    Valley)

Rosemount Show Reserve
    (Coonawarra)
Rothbury Estate Broken Back
    Vineyard (Hunter Valley)

* * *(GOOD PRODUCERS)

Cassegrain (New South Wales)
Cold Stream Hills (Yarra Valley)
Cullens (Margaret River)
Hungerford Hill (Hunter Valley)
Katnook Estate (Coonawarra)
Krondorf (Barossa)
Lake's Folly (New South Wales)
Lindemans Bin 65 (New South
    Wales)
Miramar (Mudgee)
Michelton (Goulburn)
Moss Wood (Western Australia)
Orlando RF (South Australia)

Penley Estate (Coonawarra)
Petaluma (South Australia)
Reynella (Southern Vales)
Rothbury Estate Broken Back
    Vineyard Reserve (Hunter Valley)
Seppelt (Barossa)
Mark Swann (South Australia)
Tarra Warra (Victoria)
Tyrells Vat 47 (New South Wales)
Wynn's (Coonawarra)
Yarra Yering (Yarra Valley)
Yeringsberg (Yarra Valley)

* *(AVERAGE PRODUCERS)

Balgownie (Victoria)
Brown Bros. (Victoria)
Capel Vale (Western Australia)
Cold Stream Hills Four Vineyards
    (Yarra Valley)

Cold Stream Hills Lilydale (Yarra
    Valley)
Mildara (Coonawarra)
Orlando (South Australia)

RATING AUSTRALIA'S BEST PRODUCERS OF DRY
SAUVIGNON BLANC AND SEMILLON

* * * * *(OUTSTANDING PRODUCERS)

None

* * * *(EXCELLENT PRODUCERS)

Henschke (Barossa)

Rothbury Estate (Hunter Valley)

* * *(GOOD PRODUCERS)

Berri Estates (South Australia)
Evans and Tate (Margaret River)
Tim Knappstein (Clare Valley)
Krondorf (Barossa)

Peter Lehmann (Barossa)
Lindemans (Padthaway)
Mildara (Coonawarra)
Rosemount (Hunter Valley)

RATING AUSTRALIA'S BEST PRODUCERS OF SWEET SAUVIGNON BLANC AND SEMILLON

* * * * *(OUTSTANDING PRODUCERS)

Peter Lehmann (Barossa)   Rothbury Estate (Hunter Valley)
Rosemount (Hunter Valley)

RATING AUSTRALIA'S BEST PRODUCERS OF FORTIFIED WINES

* * * * *(OUTSTANDING WINES)

Wm. Chambers Rosewood Tokay and   Seppelt Para Port
    Muscat   Seppelt Show Wines
Morris Muscat and Tokay Liquor   Yalumba Port

AUSTRALIA'S GREATEST WINE BARGAINS FOR LESS THAN $10

Berry Estates Semillon
Brown Bros. Cabernet Sauvignon
Brown Bros. Chardonnay King Valley
Brown Bros. Muscat Lexia
Coldridge Chardonnay
Coldridge Semillon/Chardonnay
Peter Lehmann Cabernet Sauvignon
Peter Lehmann Shiraz
Lindemans Chardonnay Bin 65
Mitchelton Semillon/Chardonnay
Montrose Cabernet Sauvignon
Montrose Chardonnay
Montrose Shiraz
Orlando Cabernet Sauvignon Jacob's Creek
Orlando Chardonnay Jacob's Creek
Orlando Sauvignon Blanc Jacob's Creek
Oxford Landing Cabernet Sauvignon
Oxford Landing Chardonnay
Penfolds Chardonnay
Penfolds Cabernet/Shiraz Koonunga Hill
Roo's Leap Chardonnay
Roo's Leap Fumé Blanc
Rosemount Cabernet Sauvignon/Shiraz Diamond Reserve
Rosemount Diamond Reserve Red
Rosemount Semillon/Chardonnay Diamond Reserve
Rosemount Shiraz Diamond Reserve
Rosemount Diamond Reserve White
Rothbury Estate Chardonnay Broken Back Vineyard
Rothbury Estate Shiraz
Seppelt Cabernet Sauvignon Black Label
Seppelt Cabernet Sauvignon Reserve Bin

Seppelt Chardonnay Black Label
Seppelt Chardonnay Reserve Bin
Seppelt Semillon/Chardonnay
Seppelt Shiraz Black Label
Seppelt Shiraz Reserve Bin
Seppelt Tawny Strafford Port
Tyrrells Long Flat Red
Wolf Blass Cabernet Sauvignon Yellow Label
Wolf Blass Shiraz President's Selection
Wyndham Estates Cabernet Sauvignon Bin 444
Wyndham Estates Chardonnay Bin 222
Yalumba Clocktower Port

10. NEW ZEALAND, ARGENTINA, CHILE, GREECE, HUNGARY, ISRAEL, LEBANON, SWITZERLAND

NEW ZEALAND

The Darling of the Wine Media

Mention the words *cool climate* and many a wine writer will be searching for the next free junket to discover the undiscovered great wines of country XYZ. New Zealand is a case in point. Has anyone noticed the lavish press this country receives from the English wine media? I may be one of the few wine writers left in the world who has not taken a free business trip to New Zealand (or anywhere, for that matter) to taste these "remarkable" new wines from this hot new "cool climate" viticultural paradise. However, I have done my homework, tasting as many of these wines as I can get my lips on. After wading through all the hype, the only positive conclusion I can draw is that Sauvignon Blanc and Chardonnay seem to merit some of the enthusiasm generated by the media.

The Sauvignon Blancs elicit the most excitement. They are surprisingly rich, varying from mildly herbaceous to overwhelmingly green. What makes them stand out is that the well-integrated acidity tastes natural and the best examples possess a stunning midpalate and length. All you have to do is taste a Sauvignon Blanc from Cloudy Bay, followed by Stoneleigh, Kumeu River, Morton Estate, Montana, and Selaks, to see that special wines can emerge from this varietal. However, once past these six wineries, the Sauvignons are often ferociously vegetal and washed out.

As for Chardonnay, New Zealanders have learned to handle the cool-climate acidity by putting their wines through full malolactic fermentation, giving them less contact and plenty of exposure to French oak. However, when yields are not kept low, the Chardonnays taste like a 2-by-4, with enough oak to turn off a wine-loving lumberjack. The finest Chardonnays, showing balance between oak and fruit, have emerged from Cloudy Bay, my pick as New Zealand's finest winery, followed by Kumeu River, Te Mata, Matua Valley, Corbans, Villa Maria (*barrique*-fermented), Babich's Irongate, Delegats, Morton Estate's Hawke's Bay, Selaks, and the Vidal Reserve.

New Zealand's attempts with Cabernet Sauvignon, Merlot, and Pinot Noir continue to be annoyingly herbaceous and/or atrociously vegetal. It is appalling that anyone can find something to praise in these offerings. If you like wines that taste like liquefied asparagus, you will find some merit in them. Although recent vintages suggest New Zealand's wineries are coming closer to purging some of this grotesque character, these wines still possess a nasty vegetal streak. The best red wines to date have come from Te Mata on New Zealand's North Island, where some surprisingly plummy, blackcurrant, herbaceous reds made from Cabernet Sauvignon and Merlot have emerged. As for the other red wines, keep only two words in mind—caveat emptor!

Although there remains considerable enthusiasm for New Zealand's Müller-Thurgau and Gewürztraminer, the only Gewürztraminer that tasted remotely close in quality to those Alsace, France, produces came from another North Island Winery near Gisbourn, Matawhero, which appears to have an uncanny ability to produce wines with that elusive, rose-petal, lychee-nut scent.

Is all the excitement over New Zealand's wines generated by the enormous press coverage it receives warranted? No. However, this country does produce some very fine Sauvignons.

RATING NEW ZEALAND'S BEST PRODUCERS OF CHARDONNAY

* * * * *(OUTSTANDING PRODUCERS)

None

* * * *(EXCELLENT PRODUCERS)

Cloudy Bay   Villa Maria Barrique-Fermented

* * *(GOOD PRODUCERS)

Babich Irongate   Morton Estate Hawke's Bay
Delegats   Selaks
Kumeu River   Vidal Reserve

RATING NEW ZEALAND'S BEST PRODUCERS OF SAUVIGNON

* * * * *(OUTSTANDING PRODUCERS)

Cloudy Bay

* * * *(EXCELLENT PRODUCERS)

Kumeu River   Nautilus
Matua Valley   Selaks
Montana Marlborough   Stoneleigh

RATING NEW ZEALAND'S BEST PRODUCERS OF OTHER WINES

* * * * *(OUTSTANDING PRODUCERS)

None

* * * *(EXCELLENT PRODUCERS)
Matawhero (Gewürztraminer)

* * *(GOOD PRODUCERS)
Te Mata (Cabernet/Merlot)

ARGENTINA

*The Up-and-Coming Star of
South America?*

I suspect few people realize that Argentina is one of the world's leaders in per capita consumption of wine. Not only do these fun-loving people consume wine, but the country is the fifth leading producer of wine, making 275 million cases of wine from 750,000 acres of vineyards. Although Argentina has lagged behind Chile in promoting its wines, it is beginning to become more export conscious.

Are the wines of interest? The white wines from well-known grapes such as Sauvignon, Semillon, and Chardonnay are either uninteresting (sterile and fruitless) or clumsy (oxidized and dirty). On the other hand, the red wines from Argentina's top *bodegas* can possess considerable flavor dimension as well as complex aromatic profiles. In fact, with five red wine *cuvées*, the Bodega Weinert is producing South America's greatest red wines—the qualitative equals of the finest reds in the world! Another winery that is soaring in quality is Etchart. Based on its 1991 Cabernet Sauvignon, this winery is also making far more interesting and complex wines. Interestingly, Etchart hired Michel Rolland, the famed Libourne oenologist, to advise on winemaking and viticultural practices.

Two other wineries for top red wines are Pascual Toso, which makes solid Cabernet Sauvignons, and Trapiche, which is making fine red wines at bargain prices and represents the top-quality wines of the Bodega Navarro Correas. Another world-class producer whose Cabernet Sauvignons rank just behind those of Bodega Weinert and Etchart is Flichman's Caballero de la Cepa.

Argentina's immense potential has not been fully exploited by the American wine trade. Given the high quality of the red wines, this situation will undoubtedly change. Prices for the best wines will certainly escalate once the world begins to recognize what this country has to offer.

RATING ARGENTINA'S BEST PRODUCERS

* * * * *(OUTSTANDING PRODUCERS)

Bodega Weinert Cabernet Sauvignon   Bodega Weinert Malbec
Bodega Weinert Cavas de Weinert

* * * *(EXCELLENT PRODUCERS)

Luigi Bosca Malbec   Nicolas Fazio Malbec
Caballero de la Cepa Cabernet   Navarro Correas Coleccion Paivades
  Sauvignon   Cabernet Sauvignon****/*****
Catena Chardonnay   San Telmo Malbec
Etchart Cabernet Sauvignon (since   Pascual Toso Cabernet Sauvignon
  1991)   Bodega Weinert Carrascal
Etchart Malbec (since 1991)   Bodega Weinert Merlot

* * *(GOOD PRODUCERS)

Bianchi Cabernet Sauvignon   Etchart Torrontes (a white wine)
  Particular   Flichman Cabernet Sauvignon
Bianchi Chenin Blanc (a white wine)   Nicolas Fazio Cabernet Sauvignon
Bianchi Malbec   San Telmo Cuesta del Madero
Humberto Canale Cabernet   (Cabernet Sauvignon/Malbec)
  Sauvignon Reserva   Trapiche Cabernet Sauvignon
Humberto Canale Merlot Reserva   Oak-Aged
Catena Cabernet Sauvignon Reserva

* *(AVERAGE PRODUCERS)

Andean Cabernet Sauvignon   Comte de Valmont Cabernet
Clos du Moulin Cabernet Sauvignon   Sauvignon
Goyenechea (Aberdeen Angus)
  Cabernet Sauvignon

Selected Tasting Notes

CABALLERO DE LA CEPA* * * *

1985 Cabernet Sauvignon	A 86

After the Bodega Weinert, this is probably Argentina's finest winery. I wrote some enthusiastic reviews on its wines several years ago, and I continue to get good reports on its wines from several subscribers in Argentina. Its least expensive Cabernet, the 1985 vintage, is a richly fruity, earthy, spicy wine, with surprising personality, soft tannins, admirable depth, and fine length and complexity. Drink it over the next 5–7 years. For double the price, you might take a look at the Caballero de la Cepa 1980 Cabernet Sauvignon (rated 87). Although it is not the bargain some South American wines are, it is a stylish bottle of fully mature Cabernet Sauvignon.

NICOLAS FAZIO* * */* * * *

1980	Cabernet Sauvignon Mendoza	B	86
1978	Malbec Mendoza	B	87
1977	Malbec Mendoza	B	85

These rich, stylish, complete, and complex wines offer considerable appeal. The 1980 Cabernet Sauvignon reveals excellent richness, deep color, an herbaceous, cassis-scented bouquet, soft, ripe flavors, medium body, and a fine finish. Given the fact that it is already 12 years old, the wine is still fresh and youthful. Drink it over the next 5–6 years. The 1978 Malbec is even better, with a more complete, intense nose of red and black fruits, spices, and subtle oak. In the mouth it is full bodied, rich, and well balanced. Although it is ready to drink, it is capable of lasting for at least another 5–7 years. Even Fazio's 1977 Malbec was as concentrated as the 1978, as well as tasty, interesting, and, yes, surprisingly complex. No wonder Argentina is recognized as producing the finest Malbecs in the world. These are exceptional values.

SAN TELMO* * */* * * *

1987	Cuesta del Madero Mendoza	A	86
1986	Malbec Mendoza	A	87

Here is further evidence that Argentina is making wines far superior to those from Chile. The Bodega San Telmo's 1987 Cuesta del Madero, a blend of 60% Cabernet Sauvignon and 40% Malbec, is a surprisingly rich, intense, chewy wine, with gobs of pure fruit, good body and glycerin, and a fine finish. Although some tannin is present, this is clearly a wine for consuming over the next 5–6 years. The 1986 Malbec may be the best example I have ever tasted of pure Malbec. Very deep ruby in color, with a vividly pure, well-focused bouquet of spicy red and black fruits and subtle oak, this medium- to full-bodied, rich, fleshy wine exhibits enough overall balance to age for 7–10 years, yet it can be approached now for its up-front richness.

BODEGA WEINERT* * * */* * * * *

1985	Cabernet Sauvignon	B	90
1983	Cabernet Sauvignon	B	89
1985	Carrascal	A	88
1983	Carrascal	A	88
1985	Cavas de Weinert	B	90
1983	Cavas de Weinert	B	89
1988	Merlot	B	87

Wonder what my house red wine is? Much of it consists of these wines from the Bodega Weinert (and, of course, Rhônes). The Bodega Weinert is unquestionably making the greatest wines in South America—no ifs, ands, or buts! The wines possess a richness and intensity, as well as a sense of balance, that can come only from brilliant winemaking and low yields. No other South American winery comes close to achieving the richness and complexity of Weinert. Of course, its wines are also South America's most expensive. Some of the Reserve Library Malbec and Cabernet releases from the mid- and late 1970s cost a whopping $50. You will have to spend between $8 and $11 to purchase most of the Weinert recent releases, but they are four to five times as good as just about any other South American wine. In fact, these wines belong in a different category, so overcome your prejudices against all the cheap, diluted, insipid juice coming out of South America and give these wines a try. To further my point, consider the following. One of Bordeaux's most famous oenologists put the 1985 Cavas de Weinert in a tasting against top 1989 Pomerols and St.-Émilions, and the attending French oenologists and winemakers picked the Weinert first—to everyone's shock. These are indeed serious, rich wines. Although released when they display some signs of maturity, they can last for at least 5–8 years in most vintages. The 1988 Merlot exhibits a rich, saturated color and a big, flamboyant nose of black cherries, cocoa, and spices. This wine is medium to full bodied, opulent, voluptuously textured, juicy, succulent, and a joy to drink. It will last nicely for at least 5–6 years. Both the 1985 and 1983 Cabernet Sauvignons reveal big, chocolatey, hickory-, cassis-scented noses; considerable body; a multidimensional, layered texture to their flavors; and long, richly extracted, impressive finishes. The 1983, which is showing some amber at the edge, offers more spice, coffee, and cedary scents than the younger, less-evolved 1985. Both wines are capable of at least a decade of aging. They should be compared with wines costing $20–$25, not $10. Although the 1983 and 1985 Carrascals are lighter than the Cabernets, they are not wimpish wines. Rich, with big, expressive bouquets, medium to full body, soft tannins, and fleshy, rich, chocolate, berry, herb, and coffee flavors, these two offerings should be drunk over the next 5–8 years. The Cavas de Weinert wines represent the winery's top *cuvées* of Malbec, Cabernet Sauvignon, and Merlot. They share much of the same character as the other Weinert wines, with super depth of fruit, excellent ripeness, and a natural, rich, aromatic dimension to accompany their bold, classic flavor profiles. These wines should continue to drink well for 8–10 years. Both have important proportions of Malbec in their blends.

CHILE

Looking for Changes

I began covering Chile's wines in the early 1980s and was probably the first wine writer to praise the values emerging from this country. However, a decade later there is both good and bad news.

The good news is that the wines of Chile are still low-priced. The bad news is that quality has slipped—badly. Every time I do a tasting of new releases from Chile my disappointment grows, along with a disturbing feeling that quality is increasingly being compromised. Consider some of the first Chilean wineries to be successful in America: it is appalling to taste what they are now putting in the bottle. Wineries such as St. Morillon, Santa Rita, Canepa, Miguel Torres, Carta Vieja, and Valdivieso are turning out Chardonnays, Sauvignons, Merlots, and Cabernets that are unquestionably produced from yields of well over 100–120 hectoliters per hectare. These washed-out, insipid, thin, fruitless wines possess no flavor and even at $5–$6 a bottle represent poor values. Worldwide demand and greed are the culprits, reflecting the dangers inherent in popularized press coverage and appalling overproduction. Because they are inexpensive, retailers consider these wines hot items and stack cases of them next to their cash registers. However, the quality is no longer what it once was. Many Chilean producers need a wake-up call!

There are some positive signs that Chile may be bouncing back—an influx of French money from Bordeaux (for example, the Rothschild family of Lafite-Rothschild, Cos d'Estournel's Bruno Prats, and Château Margaux's director, Paul Pontallier). However, consumers should remember that inexpensive wines are not always good bargains. The following chart should put things in perspective.

RATING CHILE'S BEST PRODUCERS

* * * * *(OUTSTANDING PRODUCERS)

None

* * * *(EXCELLENT PRODUCERS)

Concha y Toro Cabernet Sauvignon
  Don Melchor
Concha y Toro Cabernet Sauvignon
  Marques de Casa Concho

Los Vascos Cabernet Sauvignon
  Reserva

* * *(GOOD PRODUCERS)

Concha y Toro Cabernet Sauvignon
  Casillero del Diablo
Concha y Toro Chardonnay Casillero
  del Diablo
Cousino Macul Cabernet Sauvignon

Cousino Macul Cabernet Sauvignon
  Antiguas Reservas
Errazuriz Panquehue Cabernet
  Sauvignon Don Maximiano
Santa Monica Cabernet Sauvignon

* *(AVERAGE PRODUCERS)

Caliterra Cabernet Sauvignon
Caliterra Chardonnay
Canepa Sauvignon Blanc
Carta Vieja (all cuvées)
Cousino Macul Chardonnay
Cousino Macul Sauvignon Blanc
Sage Estate (all cuvées)
St. Morillon Cabernet Sauvignon
Santa Carolina Cabernet Sauvignon
Santa Carolina Chardonnay

Santa Carolina Merlot
Santa Rita Cabernet Sauvignon 120
  Estate
Santa Rita Cabernet Sauvignon
  Medalla Real
Santa Rita Sauvignon Blanc 120
  Estate
Tolva Cabernet Sauvignon
Tolva Sauvignon Blanc
Miguel Torres (all cuvées)

Traverso Cabernet Sauvignon
Traverso Merlot
Undurraga Cabernet Sauvignon
Undurraga Sauvignon Blanc

Valdivieso Sparkling N.V. Brut
Los Vascos Cabernet Sauvignon
Los Vascos Sauvignon Blanc

GREECE

Have You Heard?

The overall quality of Greece's wines has improved since the last edition of this book. Nevertheless there are still too many oxidized, poorly made, bizarre wines that are not likely to enjoy a following outside of transplanted Greek nationals or restaurants specializing in food from this beautiful country. If you want to sample a true Greek wine, check out the Metaxas Retsina, Greece's only legitimate contribution to viticulture. Although most non-Greeks find it akin to chewing on a pine tree, it is considered a national treasure in Greece.

If you want to try a more conventional wine from Greece, consider the following producers. The largest and best-known Greek winery is **Achaia Clauss.** Its Patias white wine is enjoyable. Another producer with somewhat higher standards is **Boutari,** whose top offerings are Naoussa, a relatively forceful, dry red wine, and Santorini, made from vineyards on the extraordinary volcanic island of the same name. The dry wine is called Thira, and the reds are called Santino and Atlantis. There is often a roasted character to the fruit, but I have tasted examples with surprising intensity and personality.

Greece's finest red wine producer is **Château Carras.** Its Limnio and regular *cuvée*, both from the Côtes de Meliton, are excellent wines by any standard. Another medium-weight red wine that is now being aged in oak is **Boutari's** Goumenissa. If you want to try one of the sweet, superconcentrated Greek red wines, a prime example comes from an area called Mavrodaphne. There are numerous producers of this kinky, thick wine, which is something of an acquired taste.

A Greek wine I have been drinking since my hippie days of traveling through the islands is the supercheap dry rosé called Roditys. It is still enjoyable today, and the best is made by **Cambas.** Another inexpensive, competent producer of both white and red wines is **Kuros,** which makes Patias and Nemea that generally sell for well under $7 a bottle.

HUNGARY

It's No Secret

With the fall of communism and the beginnings of a capitalistic society, Hungary's potential for high-quality wine is enormous. This country has plenty of ancient vineyards as well as a historic tradition of wine appreciation.

The greatest Hungarian wine—indeed, one of the finest wines in the world—is Tokaji (Tokay), a famous sweet wine served at the finest European tables prior to the communist takeover. It lives up to its reputation, resembling a mature Sauternes. The wine has different levels of sweetness, designated by something the Hungarians call Puttonyos. The maximum, 6 denotes a phenomenally rich, sweet wine that makes for a decadent experience. Most Tokajis range between 3 and 4 Puttonyos, making them relatively sweet. They can age for 40–50 years.

Some innovative American importers, such as New England Wine and Spirits Co. in North Branford, Connecticut, have been tapping into this unrealized market. One can expect others to follow soon. The French, including Jean-Michel Cazes, Michel Rolland, and Jean-Michel Arcaute, several of Bordeaux's most dynamic and respected businessmen, have invested heavily in vineyards and wineries for making great Tokay.

Hungary is also an undiscovered source for a number of relatively rich, full red wines. Historically the best known is the Bull's Blood red wine, known in Hungary as Bikaver. Today the wine is diluted and far lighter than consumers would expect.

Given the stability of Hungary's government and the blossoming economy, look for some growers to find foreign investors willing to help them break away from the huge regional cooperatives that have long dominated Hungarian wine production. Other growers will undoubtedly sell out to foreigners. Over the next decade, small estates, producing wines with the name of the varietal and the village on their labels, will undoubtedly begin to emerge. Michel Rolland and Jean-Michel Arcaute's estate is Château Pajzos. Presently it is impossible to know what the other producers' names might be.

A number of grapes are renowned throughout Hungary. European authorities have long known that certain varietals have the potential to make wines of surprisingly high quality. Consumers should keep an eye out for these in particular:

Ezerjo   Produces perfumed, fleshy white wine.

Furmint   The classic grape of Tokaji; can also be vinified totally dry.

Keknyelu   Produces relatively full-bodied, fleshy, dry white wines.

Leanyka   Turns out intensely fragrant, perfumed white wines that have immense potential if vinified in a modern style.

Szurkebarat   The Hungarian equivalent of Pinot Gris; results in superrich, full-bodied dry and sweet whites.

Nagyvurgundi   Thought to be a clone of Pinot Noir that is indigenous to Hungary; makes rich, full, expansively flavored wines, particularly from the villages of Szekszard and Villany.

Medoc Noir   Produces fleshy, supple, richly fruity red wines that can be drunk young.

ISRAEL

Hope of Deliverance

Wine production in Israel has moved away from the sweet wines that were so prevalent 20 years ago, to drier styles that offer more international appeal. Although the workmanlike grapes, such as Alicante, Grenache, Muscat, and Carignane, are still in existence, many of the newest vineyards are planted with internationally renowned varietals such as Cabernet Sauvignon, Chardonnay, Sauvignon Blanc, and French Colombard. The three most widely represented brand names in the United States are Carmel, Gamla, and Yarden.

Carmel wines include sticky, sweet offerings with names such as Concord-King David and Sacramental Grape-King David. This producer also makes some drier-style wines, the best of which is the Shiraz Carmel Vineyards, Cabernet Sauvignon Carmel Vineyards, Sauvignon Blanc Carmel Vineyards, and Chardonnay Rothschild.

I have a preference for the wines from Yarden, which include an excellent rosé, called Cabernet Blanc; a fine Sauvignon Blanc; an adequate Chardonnay; and from time to time decent Merlot and Cabernet Sauvignon. Yarden's wines tend to be more expensive than other Israeli wines, so expect to spend $15–$18 for a bottle of Yarden Vineyards wine. They may be the best produced in Israel, but the price differential is not justified.

The best Gamla offerings are its white wines, including a wonderfully fragrant, delicious Muscato de Gamla and a crisp, herbaceous, exuberantly fresh Sauvignon Blanc.

Other producers worth looking at are Golan Vineyards, which produces all kosher *cuvées*, with the best being the Sauvignon Blanc and medium-sweet Emerald Riesling. It also produces an adequate, light Chardonnay and an herbaceous Cabernet Sauvignon.

LEBANON

Not Fade Away

Thirty kilometers (18 miles) from the savage and senseless civil war that has torn apart Beirut is Château Musar, a winemaking estate founded in the 1930s and one that makes superlative wines from a blend of Cabernet Sauvignon, Syrah, and Cinsault. Owner/winemaker Serge Hochar has had vintages wiped out because no harvesters would risk their lives to pick the grapes, but still he continues. His wine training came from his father and a stint in Bordeaux, but the wines remind me of the best and most complex Châteauneuf-du-Papes. They are full bodied, very fragrant, rich, and supple enough to drink young, but if the very good 1966 and exquisite 1970 are any indication, they will last 10, even 20, years. The vintages now on the market are the 1975, 1977, 1978, 1979, 1980, 1981, 1982, 1983, 1985, and 1986. Retailing for less than $15 a bottle, the wines are undeniable bargains given the quality. Musar is still relatively unknown; as long as the disastrous civil war continues to rage, the future is uncertain, but this estate produces distinctive wine.

SWITZERLAND

Frightfully Expensive

The only bargain I have ever gotten in Switzerland was by flying to Geneva, renting my car there, then dropping my car off in Paris at the conclusion of my trip. By originating my rental in Switzerland, I avoided France's prohibitive tax on car rentals.

One does not visit Switzerland on a budget. Like everything else in the country, its wines are frightfully expensive—always have been, always will be. Although one might quibble over the price, the quality of many Swiss wines is very good, especially the fragrant, richly fruity wines made from a grape called Chasselas, which does better in Switzerland than anywhere else. The Chasselas white wines appear not only under the grape's own name, but also under the names Fendant, Dezaley, and Neuchâtel. Switzerland has 35,000 acres of vineyards in every one of its cantons, but the top vineyards are centered either on the steep slopes above Lake Geneva in an area called Vaud or farther east around the town of Sion in an area called Valais. The Chasselas grape, or Fendant as it is called in Valais, produces an aromatic white wine that at its best suggests a Condrieu in bouquet, and a medium-bodied, stainless steel–fermented yet fleshy Chardonnay in texture and weight. If it were not so expensive (usually $20 and up a bottle), it would be quite popular. It is Switzerland's best white wine. Red wine, the best of which is called Dole and is a blend of Pinot Noir and Gamay, is an adequate, serviceable red, though never worth its stiff price tag. Following are the top producers of Switzerland and their best wines:

Domaine du Mont d'Or   Look for the rich Fendant and decent Dole.

Gerard Pinget   The white Chasselas called Dezaley Renard is one of the best white wines of Switzerland.

J&P Testuz   For my money, Switzerland's best winery, making rich, perfumed, delicious Fendant and Dezaley under the Domaine L'Arbalete label. Only the high prices are a problem.

APPENDIXES

RECOMMENDED
WINES FOR
CELLARING OF
MORE THAN A
DECADE

*Don't forget, top vintages are the best
candidates for extended longevity.*

FRANCE

ALSACE

White Wines

Note: Virtually any Alsace sweet wine labeled Vendange Tardive (slightly to medium sweet) and the nectarlike dessert wine called Selection de Grains Nobles can easily improve in the bottle beyond a decade. Some of these wines can last for 20–30 years.

Léon Beyer Gewürztraminer Cuvée des Comtes d'Eguisheim
Albert Boxler Gewürztraminer Brand
Albert Boxler Riesling Brand
Albert Boxler Riesling Sommerberg
Ernest or J. et F. Burn Gewürztraminer Clos Saint Imer Goldert
Ernest or J. et F. Burn Riesling Clos Saint Imer Goldert
Ernest or J. et F. Burn Tokay-Pinot Gris Clos Saint Imer Goldert
Joseph Cattin Gewürztraminer Hatchbourg
Marcel Deiss Riesling Engelgarten Vieilles Vignes

Marcel Deiss Riesling Schoenenbourg
Hugel Gewürztraminer Cuvée Jubilee
Hugel Riesling Cuvée Jubilee
Hugel Tokay-Pinot Gris Cuvée Jubilee
Josmeyer—Joseph Meyer Riesling Hengst
Josmeyer—Joseph Meyer Tokay-Pinot Gris Cuvée du Centenaire
Marc Kreydenweiss Gewürztraminer Kritt
Marc Kreydenweiss Riesling Kastelberg
Marc Kreydenweiss Riesling Wiebelsberg

Marc Kreydenweiss Tokay-Pinot Gris
Moenchberg

Albert Mann Gewürztraminer
Steingrubler

Albert Mann Riesling Pfleck

Albert Mann Riesling Schlossberg

Albert Mann Tokay-Pinot Gris
Hengst

Charles Schleret Gewürztraminer
Cuvée Exceptionnelle

Charles Schleret Tokay-Pinot Gris
Cuvée Exceptionnelle

Schlumberger Gewürztraminer
Cuvée Anne

Schlumberger Gewürztraminer
Kessler

Schlumberger Gewürztraminer
Kitterlé

Schlumberger Riesling Kitterlé

Schlumberger Riesling Saering

Schlumberger Tokay-Pinot Gris
Cuvée Clarisse Schlumberger

Schlumberger Tokay-Pinot Gris
Kitterlé

Schoffit Gewürztraminer Rangen Clos
Saint Théobald

Schoffit Riesling Rangen Clos Saint
Théobald

Schoffit Tokay-Pinot Gris Rangen
Clos Saint Théobald

Domaine Trimbach Gewürztraminer
Seigneurs de Ribeaupierre

Domaine Trimbach Riesling Clos
Sainte Hune

Domaine Trimbach Riesling Cuvée
Frédéric Émile

Domaine Trimbach Tokay-Pinot
Gris Réserve Personnelle

Domaine Weinbach Gewürztraminer
Cuvée Théo

Domaine Weinbach Riesling Cuvée
Théo

Domaine Weinbach Riesling Clos
Sainte Catherine

Domaine Weinbach Riesling
Schlossberg

Domaine Weinbach Tokay-Pinot Gris
Réserve Personnelle

Domaine Weinbach Tokay-Pinot Gris
Clos Sainte Catherine

Willm Gewürztraminer Clos
Gaensbroennel

Zind-Humbrecht Gewürztraminer
Clos Saint-Urbain Rangen

Zind-Humbrecht Gewürztraminer
Clos Windsbuhl

Zind-Humbrecht Gewürztraminer
Heimbourg

Zind-Humbrecht Gewürztraminer
Hengst

Zind-Humbrecht Gewürztraminer
Herrenweg Turckheim

Zind-Humbrecht Riesling Brand

Zind-Humbrecht Riesling Clos
Hauserer

Zind-Humbrecht Riesling Clos
Saint-Urbain Rangen

Zind-Humbrecht Riesling Clos
Windsbuhl

Zind-Humbrecht Tokay-Pinot Gris
Clos Jebsal

Zind-Humbrecht Tokay-Pinot Gris
Clos Saint-Urbain Rangen

Zind-Humbrecht Tokay-Pinot Gris
Clos Windsbuhl

Zind-Humbrecht Tokay-Pinot Gris
Heimbourg

Zind-Humbrecht Tokay-Pinot Gris
Vieilles Vignes

BORDEAUX

Red Wines

L'Angélus (St.-Émilion)
L'Arrosée (St.-Émilion)
Ausone (St.-Émilion)
Batailley (Pauillac)
Beauséjour (Duffau-Lagarrosse)
(St.-Émilion)

Belair (St.-Émilion)
Beychevelle (St.-Julien)
Bon Pasteur (Pomerol)
Branaire-Ducru (St.-Julien)
Cadet-Piola (St.-Émilion)
Calon-Ségur (St.-Estèphe)

Canon (Canon-Fronsac)

Canon (St.-Émilion)

Canon de Brem (Canon-Fronsac)

Canon-La-Gaffelière (St.-Émilion)

Canon-Moueix (Canon-Fronsac)

Cantemerle (Macau)

Les Carmes-Haut-Brion (Graves)

Cassagne-Haut-Canon-La Truffière
  (Canon-Fronsac)

Certan de May (Pomerol)

Chasse-Spleen (Moulis)

Cheval Blanc (St.-Émilion)

Domaine de Chevalier (Graves)

Clinet (Pomerol)

La Conseillante (Pomerol)

Cos d'Estournel (St.-Estèphe)

Cos Labory (St.-Estèphe)

Curé-Bon-La-Madeleine
  (St.-Émilion)

La Dominique (St.-Émilion)

Ducru-Beaucaillou (St.-Julien)

Duhart-Milon-Rothschild (Pauillac)

Domaine de L'Église (Pomerol)

L'Église-Clinet (Pomerol)

L'Enclos (Pomerol)

L'Évangile (Pomerol)

de Fieuzal (Graves)

Figeac (St.-Émilion)

La Fleur de Gay (Pomerol)

La Fleur Pétrus (Pomerol)

Fontenil (Fronsac)

Les Forts de Latour (Pauillac)

Fourcas-Loubaney (Listrac)

La Gaffelière (St.-Émilion)

Le Gay (Pomerol)

Gazin (Pomerol)

Giscours (Margaux)

Grand-Mayne (St.-Émilion)

Grand-Puy-Ducasse (Pauillac)

Grand-Puy-Lacoste (Pauillac)

La Grave Trigant de Boisset
  (Pomerol)

Gressier Grand-Poujeaux (Moulis)

Gruaud-Larose (St.-Julien)

Haut-Bailly (Graves)

Haut-Batailley (Pauillac)

Haut-Brion (Graves)

Haut-Marbuzet (St.-Estèphe)

Lafite-Rothschild (Pauillac)

Lafleur (Pomerol)

Lafon-Rochet (St.-Estèphe)

Lagrange (St.-Julien)

La Lagune (Ludon)

Lanessan (Haut-Médoc)

Langoa-Barton (St.-Julien)

Larcis-Ducasse (St.-Émilion)

Larmande (St.-Émilion)

Latour (Pauillac)

Latour à Pomerol (Pomerol)

Léoville-Barton (St.-Julien)

Léoville-Las Cases (St.-Julien)

Léoville-Poyferré (St.-Julien)

Lynch-Bages (Pauillac)

Magdelaine (St.-Émilion)

Malescot St.-Exupéry (Margaux)

Château Margaux (Margaux)

Marquis-de-Terme (Margaux)

Meyney (St.-Estèphe)

La Mission-Haut-Brion (Graves)

Monbrison (Margaux)

Montrose (St.-Estèphe)

Moulin-Haut-Laroque (Fronsac)

Mouton-Rothschild (Pauillac)

Les-Ormes-de-Pez (St.-Estèphe)

Palmer (Margaux)

Pape-Clément (Graves)

Pavie (St.-Émilion)

Pavie-Decesse (St.-Émilion)

Pavie-Macquin (St.-Émilion)

Pétrus (Pomerol)

de Pez (St.-Estèphe)

Pichon-Longueville Baron
  (Pauillac)

Pichon-Longueville, Comtesse
  de Lalande (Pauillac)

Le Pin (Pomerol)

Pontet-Canet (Pauillac)

Potensac (Médoc)

Rausan-Ségla (Margaux)

St.-Pierre (St.-Julien)

Siran (Margaux)

Sociando-Mallet (Haut-Médoc)

Soutard (St.-Émilion)

Talbot (St.-Julien)

du Tertre (Margaux)

Le Tertre-Roteboeuf (St.-Émilion)

La Tour-Haut-Brion (Graves)

Tour-Haut-Caussan (Médoc)

Tour du Haut-Moulin
  (Haut-Médoc)

Troplong-Mondot (St.-Émilion)   Trottevieille (St.-Emilion)
Trotanoy (Pomerol)   Vieux Château Certan (Pomerol)

Dry White Wines

Domaine de Chevalier (Graves)   Haut-Brion (Graves)
de Fieuzal (Graves)   Laville-Haut-Brion (Graves)

Sweet White Wines

Bastor-Lamontagne (Sauternes)   Lamothe-Guignard (Sauternes)
Climens (Barsac)   Rabaud-Promis (Sauternes)
Coutet (Barsac)   Raymond-Lafon (Sauternes)
Doisy-Daëne (Barsac)   Rayne-Vigneau (Sauternes)
Doisy-Dubroca (Barsac)   Rieussec (Sauternes)
Doisy-Védrines (Barsac)   Sigalas Rabaud (Sauternes)
Fargues (Sauternes)   Suduiraut (Sauternes)
Gilette (Sauternes)   La Tour Blanche (Sauternes)
Guiraud (Sauternes)   d'Yquem (Sauternes)
Lafaurie-Peyraguey (Sauternes)

BURGUNDY

Red Wines

Bertrand Ambroise Corton-Rognet   Leroy Clos de la Roche
Comte Armand Pommard-Clos des   Leroy Clos Vougeot
   Epeneaux   Leroy Latricières-Chambertin
Pierre Bourée Charmes-Chambertin   Leroy Mazis-Chambertin
Pierre Bourée Clos de la Roche   Leroy Richebourg
Chézeaux Chambertin   Leroy Romanée St.-Vivant
Chézeaux Clos St.-Denis   Leroy Savigny-Les-Beaune Les
Claude et Maurice Dugat   Narbantons
   Charmes-Chambertin   Leroy Vosne-Romanée Les Beau
Claude et Maurice Dugat   Monts
   Griotte-Chambertin   Leroy Vosne-Romanée Les Brûlées
Dujac Clos de la Roche   Hubert Lignier Clos de la Roche
Faiveley Chambertin-Clos de Bèze   H. de Montille Pommard Les
Faiveley Corton-Clos des Cortons   Rugiens
A. Girardin Pommard Les Epinots   H. de Montille Pommard Les Epenots
A. Girardin Pommard Les Rugiens   H. de Montille Pommard Les
A.F. Gros Richebourg   Pezeroiles
Jean Gros Richebourg   Ponsot Clos de la Roche Vieilles
Louis Jadot Beaune-Clos des Ursules   Vignes
Louis Jadot Bonnes Mares   Ponsot Clos St.-Denis Vieilles
Louis Jadot Chambertin-Clos de Bèze   Vignes
Louis Jadot Corton Les Pougets   Pothier-Rieusset Pommard Les
Henri Jayer Richebourg   Rugiens
Comte Lafon Volnay Santenots   Domaine de la Romanée-Conti
P. Leclerc Gevrey-Chambertin   Grands Echézeaux
P. Leclerc Combe aux Moires   Domaine de la Romanée-Conti
Leroy Chambertin   Richebourg

Domaine de la Romanée-Conti
  Romanée-Conti
Domaine de la Romanée-Conti
  Romanée St.-Vivant
Domaine de la Romanée-Conti La
  Tâche
Joseph Roty Charmes-Chambertin

Joseph Roty Mazis-Chambertin
Georges et Christophe Roumier
  Bonnes Mares
Armand Rousseau Chambertin
Armand Rousseau Chambertin-Clos
  de Bèze

White Wines

Domaine Robert Ampeau Meursault
  Les Perrières
Domaine de Bongran (Jean Thevenet)
  Macon-Clessé
Domaine J. F. Coche-Dury
  Corton-Charlemagne
Domaine J. F. Coche-Dury Meursault
  Les Perrières
Hospices de Beaune Corton-
  Charlemagne-Cuvée Françoise
  de Salins
Louis Jadot Chevalier-Montrachet
  Les Demoiselles
Louis Jadot Corton-Charlemagne
Louis Jadot Le Montrachet
Domaine Comte Lafon Meursault Les
  Charmes
Domaine Comte Lafon Meursault Les
  Perrières

Domaine Comte Lafon Montrachet
Louis Latour Corton-Charlemagne
Domaine Leroy Corton-Charlemagne
Domaine Leroy Puligny-Montrachet-
  Les Folatières
Domaine Ramonet Bâtard-
  Montrachet
Domaine Ramonet Montrachet
Raveneau Chablis Les Clos
Raveneau Chablis Montée de
  Tonnerre
Raveneau Chablis Valmur
Remoissenet Père et Fils Corton-
  Charlemagne Diamond Jubilee
Domaine de la Romanée-Conti
  Montrachet

CHAMPAGNE

Bollinger
Delamotte
Gosset
Jacquart
Krug
Laurent-Perrier
Joseph Perrier

Ployez-Jacquemart
Pol Roger
Louis Roederer
Salon
Taittinger
Veuve Clicquot

THE LOIRE VALLEY

White Wines

Domaine des Baumard (Quarts de
  Chaume)
Domaine des Baumard-Clos du
  Papillon (Savennières)
Domaine des Baumard-Trie Spéciale
  (Savennières)
Domaine Belle Rive (Quarts de
  Chaume)

Domaine Bourillon-Dorleans
  (Vouvray)
Domaine de Brizé (Coteaux du
  Layon)
Clos de la Coulée de Serrant-N. Joly
  (Savennières)
Clos de la Ste.-Catherine
  (Coteaux du Layon)

Domaine de Closel-Clos du Papillon
(Savennières)
Domaine de la Croix des Loges-
Christian Bonnin (Bonnezeaux)
Domaine Echarderie (Quarts de
Chaume)

Château de Fesles (Bonnezeaux)
Philippe Foreau Clos Naudin
(Vouvray)
Gaston Huet (Vouvray)
Moulin-Touchais (Coteaux du Layon)

Red Wines

Druet (Chinon)
Charles Joguet (Chinon)

Olga Raffault (Chinon)

LANGUEDOC-ROUSSILLON

Domaine L'Aiguelière-Montpeyrous
(Coteaux du Languedoc)
Daniel Domergue (Minervois)
Mas Amiel (Maury)

Mas de Daumas Gassac (L'Hérault)
Dr. Parcé Mas Blanc (Banyuls)
St.-Jean de Bébian (Vin de Pays)

PROVENCE

Domaine de Pibarnon (Bandol)
Château Pradeaux (Bandol)
Domaine Richeaume (Côtes de
Provence)
Domaine Tempier-La Migoua
(Bandol)

Domaine Tempier-La Tourtine
(Bandol)
Domaine de Trevallon
(Coteaux d'Aix-en-Provence)

MADIRAN AND CAHORS

Château d'Aydie-Laplace (Madiran)
Château Montus (Madiran)

Domaine Pichard-Cuvée Vigneau
(Madiran)

THE RHÔNE VALLEY

Côte Rôtie

Gilles Barge Côte Rôtie
Pierre Barge Côte Rôtie
Bernard Burgaud Côte Rôtie
Chapoutier Côte Rôtie Mordorée
Clusel-Roch Côte Rôtie-Les Grandes
Places
Henri Gallet Côte Rôtie
Vincent Gasse Côte Rôtie
Gentaz-Dervieux Côte Rôtie
Guigal Côte Rôtie Côtes Blonde
et Brune
Guigal Côte Rôtie La Landonne
Guigal Côte Rôtie La Mouline

Guigal Côte Rôtie La Turque
Jean-Paul and Jean-Luc Jamet Côte
Rôtie
Robert Jasmin Côte Rôtie
Michel Ogier Côte Rôtie
René Rostaing Côte Rôtie Côte
Blonde
René Rostaing Côte Rôtie La
Landonne
René Rostaing Côte Rôtie La
Viaillere (since 1991)
L. de Vallouit Côte Rôtie Les Roziers
L. de Vallouit Côte Rôtie Vagonier

Vidal-Fleury Côte Rôtie La
  Chatillonne

Vidal-Fleury Côte Rôtie Côtes
  Blonde et Brune

Hermitage

Albert Belle Hermitage
Chapoutier Hermitage Chante-
  Alouette
Chapoutier Ermitage Le Pavillon
Chapoutier Hermitage La Sizeranne
  (since 1989)
J. L. Chave Hermitage
Delas Frères Hermitage Marquise
  de la Tourette
Bernard Faurie Hermitage Le Méal
Ferraton Père et Fils Hermitage
  Cuvée Les Miaux

Guigal Hermitage
Paul Jaboulet Ainé Hermitage
  La Chapelle
Paul Jaboulet Ainé Hermitage
  Chevalier de Stérimberg
  (since 1989)
Henri Sorrel Hermitage Le Gréal
Henri Sorrel Hermitage Les
  Rocoules
L. de Vallouit Hermitage
  Greffières

Crozes-Hermitage

Alain Graillot Crozes-Hermitage
  La Guiraude

Paul Jaboulet Ainé Crozes-Hermitage
  Thalabert

Cornas

Thierry Alemand Cornas
Auguste Clape Cornas
Marcel Juge Cornas Cuvée C
Jacques Lemencier Cornas

Robert Michel Cornas Le Geynale
Noël Verset Cornas
Alain Voge Cornas Cuvée Vieilles
  Vignes

Côtes du Rhône

Beaucastel Côtes du Rhône
  Coudoulet
Fonsalette Côtes du Rhône
Fonsalette Côtes du Rhône Cuvée
  Syrah
Domaine Gramenon Côtes du Rhône
  Centenaire

Domaine Gramenon Côtes du Rhône
  Cuvée des Laurentides
Domaine de la Guichard Côtes du
  Rhône Les Genests
Jean-Marie Lombard Côtes du Rhône
des Tours Côtes du Rhône

Châteauneuf-du-Pape

Beaucastel Châteauneuf-du-
  Pape
Beaucastel Châteauneuf-du-Pape
  Hommage à Jacques Perrin
Beaurenard Châteauneuf-du-Pape
  Cuvée Boisrenard
Henri Bonneau Châteauneuf-du-
  Pape Cuvée des Celestins
Henri Bonneau Châteauneuf-du-
  Pape Cuvée Marie Beurrier

Lucien et André Brunel-Les
  Cailloux Châteauneuf-du-Pape
Cabrières Châteauneuf-du-Pape
  Cuvée Prestige
Les Cailloux Châteauneuf-du-Pape
  Cuvée Centenaire
Chapoutier Châteauneuf-du-Pape
  Barbe Rac
Gérard Chauvin Châteauneuf-
  du-Pape

Clos du Mont-Olivet Châteauneuf-du-Pape La Cuvée du Papet

Clos des Papes Châteauneuf-du-Pape

Eddie Féraud Châteauneuf-du-Pape Cuvée Réservée

Font de Michelle Châteauneuf-du-Pape Cuvée Étienne Gonnet

de la Gardine Châteauneuf-du-Pape Cuvée des Générations

Paul Jaboulet Ainé Châteauneuf-du-Pape Les Cèdres (prior to 1970 and after 1988)

Domaine de la Janasse Châteauneuf-du-Pape Cuvée Vieilles Vignes

Marcoux Châteauneuf-du-Pape Cuvée Vieilles Vignes

La Nerthe Châteauneuf-du-Pape Cuvée des Cadettes

Domaine du Pegau Châteauneuf-du-Pape Cuvée Réservée

Rayas Châteauneuf-du-Pape

Roger Sabon Châteauneuf-du-Pape Cuvée Prestige

de la Vieille Julienne Châteauneuf-du-Pape

Vieux Donjon Châteauneuf-du-Pape

Gigondas

Edmond Burle Gigondas Les Pallieroudas

Domaine de Cayron Gigondas

Domaine de Font-Sane Gigondas Spéciale Fut Neuf

Montmirail (D. Brusset) Gigondas

Domaine Saint-Gayan Gigondas

Domaine Santa Duc Gigondas Cuvée Prestige des Hautes Garrigue

ITALY

Piedmont

Elio Altare Barbera-Vigne Larigi

Elio Altare Barolo

Elio Altare Barolo Arborina

Antoniolo Gattinari Osso S. Grato

Poderi Bertelli Barbera Giarone

Poderi Bertelli Barbera Montetusa

Giacomo Bologna Barbera Bricco della Figotta

Giacomo Bologna Barbera della'Uccellone

Borgogno Barolo

Bruno Ceretto Barbaresco Bricco Asili

Bruno Ceretto Barolo Bricco Rocche Prapo

Bruno Ceretto Barolo Brunate

Bruno Ceretto Barolo Zonchetta

Cigliuti Barbaresco Serraboella

Clerico Arté

Clerico Barolo Briccotto Bussia

Clerico Barolo Ciabot Mentin Ginestra

Elvio Cogno Barolo Brunate

Elvio Cogna Barolo Brunate Canon

Elvio Cogna Barolo La Serra

Elvio Cogna Dolcetto Boschi-di-Berri

Elvio Cogna Nebbiolo Lasarin

Cogno-Marcarini Bruno Brunate

Aldo Conterno Barolo Bussia Soprana

Aldo Conterno Barolo Bussia Soprana Vigna Cicala

Aldo Conterno Barolo Bussia Soprana Vigna Colonello

Aldo Conterno Barolo Gran Bussia

Aldo Conterno Dolcetto d'Alba

Giacomo Conterno Barolo Cascina Francia Riserva

Giacomo Conterno Barolo Monfortino

Renato Corino Barolo Vigna Giachini

Renato Corino Dolcetto

Giuseppe Cortesi Barbaresca Rabaja

Damonte Barbera San Guglielmo

Drago Dolcetto d'Alba

Ricardo Fenocchio Barbera d'Alba
Pianpolvere
Ricardo Fenocchio Barolo
Pianpolvere Soprano
Luigi Ferrando Carema
Fontanafredda Barolo Lazzarito
Fontanafredda Barolo La Rosa
Angelo Gaja Barbaresco
Angelo Gaja Barbaresco Costa
Russi
Angelo Gaja Barbaresco Sori San
Lorenzo
Angelo Gaja Barbaresco Sori Tilden
Angelo Gaja Barbera d'Alba
Vignarey
Bruno Giacosa Barbaresco Gallina
Bruno Giacosa Barbaresco Santo
Stefano
Bruno Giacosa Barolo Falletto
Bruno Giacosa Barolo Rionda
Bruno Giacosa Barolo Villero
Elio Grasso Barolo Gavarini
Elio Grasso Barolo Ginestra
Marchesi di Gresy Barbaresco
Martinenga
Marchesi di Gresy Barbaresco
Martinenga Camp Gros
Marchesi di Gresy Barbaresco
Martinenga Gaiun
Marchesi di Gresy Dolcetto Monte
Aribaldo
Manzone Barolo Le Gramolere
Bartolo Mascarello Barolo
Bartolo Mascarello Dolcetto d'Alba
Giuseppe Mascarello Barolo Dardi
Giuseppe Mascarello Barolo
Monprivato
Mauro Mascarello Barbaresco
Marcarini
Mauro Mascarello Barolo Bricco
Matteo-Correggia Barbera d'Alba
Bricco Marun
Matteo-Correggia Nebbiolo d'Alba
Val Preti
Moccagatta Barbaresco Basarin
Moccagatta Barbaresco Bric Balin
Moccagatta Barbaresco Cole
Monsecco Gattinara
Castello di Neive Barbaresco Santo
Stefano

Armando Parusso Barolo Bussia
Rocche
Armando Parusso Barolo Rocche
Armando Parusso Dolcetto d'Alba
Mariondino
Elia Pasquero Secondo Barbaresco
Sori d'Paytin
Pio Cesare Dolcetto d'Alba
Produttori di Barbaresco Barbaresco
Asili
Produttori di Barbaresco Barbaresco
Moccagatta
Produttori di Barbaresco Barbaresco
Monte Stefano
Produttori di Barbaresco Barbaresco
Ovello
Produttori di Barbaresco Barbaresco
Rabaja
Alfredo Prunotto Barbaresco Monte
Stefano
Alfredo Prunotto Barolo Bussia
Alfredo Prunotto Barolo Cannubi
Renato Ratti Barolo Marcenasco
Renato Ratti Barolo Marcenasco
Conca
Renato Ratti Barolo Marcenasco
Rocche
Francesco Rinaldi Barolo
Giuseppe Rinaldi Barolo
Brunate
Rocca Barbaresco Ronchi
Rocche dei Manzoni Barolo Vigna
Big
Rocche dei Manzoni Barolo Vigna
Mesdi
Rocche dei Manzoni Barolo Vigna
d'la Roul
Rocche dei Manzoni Bricco Manzoni
(Nebbiolo/Barbera)
Luciano Sandrone Barolo
Luciano Sandrone Barolo Cannubi
Boschis
Enrico Scavino Barbera Carati
Enrico Scavino Barolo
Enrico Scavino Barolo Bric del Fiasc
Enrico Scavino Barolo Cannubi
A. & R. Seghesio Barolo La Villa
Filippo Sobrero Barolo
Antonio Vallana Gattinara
Antonio Vallana Spanna

Vietti Barbaresco Masseria
Vietti Barolo Lazzarito
Vietti Barolo Rocche
Vietti Barolo Villero
Roberto Voerzio Barbera d'Alba
  Vignasse
Roberto Voerzio Barolo Brunate

Roberto Voerzio Barolo Cerequio
Roberto Voerzio Barolo La Serra
Roberto Voerzio Dolcetto d'Alba
  Privino
Roberto Voerzio Vigna La Serra
  (Nebbiolo/Barbera)

Tuscany

Chianti, Brunello, Vino Nobile di Montepulciano

Altesino (Brunello di Montalcino)
Ambra (Carmignano Riserva Vigna
  Alta)
Avignonesi (Vino Nobile di
  Montepulciano)
Badia a Coltibuono (Chianti Classico)
Felsina Berardenga (Chianti Classico
  Riserva Rancia)
Biondi Santi (Brunello di Montalcino
  Il Greppo Riserva)
Campogiovanni San Felice (Brunello
  di Montalcino)
Canalicchio (Brunello di Montalcino)
Canalicchio di Sopra (Brunello di
  Montalcino)
Canilicchio di Sopra Pacenti Franco
  e Rosildo (Brunello di Montalcino)
Caparzo (Brunello di Montalcino La
  Casa)
Caprili (Brunello di Montalcino)

Cerbaiona (Brunello di Montalcino)
Costanti (Brunello di Montalcino)
Lisini (Brunello di Montalcino)
Monsanto (Chianti Classico Riserva
  Il Poggio)
Pertimali (Brunello di Montalcino)
Ciacci Piccolomini d'Aragona
  (Brunello di Montalcino)
Poggio Antico (Brunello di
  Montalcino)
Il Poggione–R. Franceschi (Brunello
  di Montalcino)
Castello di Rampolla (Chianti
  Classico)
San Giusto a Rententano (Chianti
  Classico)
Salvioni-Cerbaiola (Brunello di
  Montalcino)
Talenti (Brunello di Montalcino)

Vina da Tavola

L. Antinori (Ornellaia)
P. Antinori (Solaia)
Il Palazzino (Grosso Sanese)

Castello di Rampolla (Sammarco)
San Giusto a Bentennano (Percarlo)

GERMANY

Burgerspital (Franken)
Dr. Burklin-Wolf (Rheinpfalz)
Kurt Darting (Rheinpfalz)
August Eser (Rheingau)
H. H. Eser-Johannishof (Rheingau)
F. W. Gymnasium (Mosel)
Fritz Haag (Mosel)
Von Heddesdorff (Mosel)
Heyl zu Herrnsheim (Rheinhessen)
Immich-Batterieberg (Mosel)

Heribert Kerpen (Mosel)
von Kesselstatt (Mosel-Saar)
J. F. Kimich (Rheinpfalz)
Freiherr du Knyphausen (Rheingau)
Konigin Victoria Berg-Deinhard
  (Rheingau)
K. & H. Lingenfelder (Rheinpfalz)
Monchhof (Mosel)
Egon Müller (Saar)
Muller-Catoir (Rheinpfalz)

Klaus Neckerauer (Rheinpfalz)   Selbach-Oster (Mosel)
J. J. Prüm (Middle Mosel)   von Simmern (Rheingau)
Willi Schaefer (Mosel)   J.U.H.A. Strub (Rheinhessen)
Schloss Schonborn (Rheingau)   Tyrell-Karthauserhof (Ruwer)
von Schubert-Maximin Grunhaus   Dr. Heinz Wagner (Saar)
   (Ruwer)   Werlé (Rheinpfalz)

PORTUGAL

Vintage Port

Vintage port is a sure bet to improve considerably beyond 10 years. In fact, most top firms, such as Churchill, Cockburn, Croft, Dow, Fonseca, Graham, Quinta do Noval, Sandeman, Taylor Fladgate, and Warre produce ports that last 20–35 or more years.

Dry Red Table Wines

Ferreira Barca Velha   J.M. da Fonseca Tinto Velho Rosado
J.M. da Fonseca Garrafeira TE   Fernandes
                                         Quinta do Carmo

SPAIN

Dry Red Table Wines

CVNE Contino   Pesquera Ribero del Duero
Muga Prado Enea Reserva   La Rioja Alta Reserva 890
Marqués de Murrieta Castillo de   La Rioja Alta Reserva 904
   Ygay Gran Reserva   Vega Sicilia Unico Reserva

CALIFORNIA

Cabernet Sauvignon, Merlot, or Blends Thereof

Beringer Private Reserve (Napa)   Katherine Kennedy (Santa Clara)
Caymus Special Selection (Napa)   Laurel Glen Sonoma Mountain
B. R. Cohn Olive Hill (Sonoma)   (Sonoma)
Dalla Valle (Napa)   Robert Mondavi Reserve (Napa)
Dalla Valle Maya (Napa)   Château Montelena Estate (Napa)
The John Daniel Society-Dominus   Newton (Napa)
   (Napa)   Newton Merlot (Napa)
Duckhorn Three Palms Vineyard   Joseph Phelps Insignia Proprietary
   (Napa)   Red Wine (Napa)
Dunn (Napa)   Ravenswood Pickberry Proprietary
Dunn Howell Mountain (Napa)   Red Wine (Sonoma)
Durney (Monterey)   Ridge Monte Bello (Santa Cruz)
Girard Reserve (Napa)   Shafer Hillside Select (Napa)
Grace Family Vineyard (Napa)   Simi Reserve (Sonoma)
Heitz Martha's Vineyard (Napa)   Stag's Leap Cask 23 Proprietary Red
Hess Collection Reserve (Napa)   Wine (Napa)
La Jota Howell Mountain (Napa)   Philip Togni (Napa)

Chardonnay

Chalone
Kalin
Kistler
Matanzas Creek

Château Montelena
Mount Eden
Stony Hill
Talbot

Zinfandel

Lytton Springs Reserve (Sonoma)
Ravenswood Dickerson Vineyard
  (Napa)
Ravenswood Old Hill Vineyard
  (Sonoma)

Storybook Mountain Reserve (Napa)
Topolos Rossi Ranch Old Vines
  (Russian River Valley)

Rhône Ranger Blends

Edmunds St. John Mourvèdre
Edmunds St. John Syrah
Ridge Petite Sirah York Creek

Sean Thackrey Orion Syrah
Sean Thackrey Sirius Petite Sirah
Sean Thackrey Taurus Mourvèdre

WASHINGTON STATE

Leonetti Cabernet Sauvignon
Leonetti Cabernet Sauvignon Reserve
Quilceda Creek Cabernet Sauvignon
Château Ste.-Michelle Cabernet
  Sauvignon Cold Creek Reserve

Woodward Canyon Cabernet
  Sauvignon
Woodward Canyon Charbonneau

AUSTRALIA

Henschke Hill of Grace Shiraz
Henschke Mount Edelstone Shiraz
Parker Estate Terra Rossa First
  Growth Cabernet Sauvignon

Penfolds Bin 707 Cabernet
  Sauvignon
Penfolds Grange Hermitage

ARGENTINA

Etchart Cabernet Sauvignon
Etchart Malbec
Bodega Weinert Cabernet Sauvignon

Bodega Weinert Cavas de Weinert
Bodega Weinert Malbec

CHILE

Concho y Toro Cabernet Sauvignon
  Don Melchor

Los Vascos Cabernet Sauvignon
  Reserva

Explanation of the Charts

Given the number of inquiries I receive about when a particular wine has reached a point in its evolution that it is said to be ready to drink, I have provided an estimated range of years over which specific vintages of the following wines should be consumed. Before one takes this guide too literally, let me share with you the following points.

1. If you like the way a wine tastes when young, don't hesitate to enjoy it in spite of what the chart may say.
2. I have had to make several assumptions, the primary ones being that the wine was purchased in a healthy state, and you are cellaring the wine in a cool, humid, odor and vibration free enviornment that does not exceed 68° F in the summer.
3. The estimates are an educated guess based on how the wine normally ages, its quality, balance, and depth for the vintage in question.
4. The estimates are conservative in the sense that good storage conditions are essential. I have assumed a maturity based on my own palate, which tends to prefer a wine more fresh and exuberant over one which has begun to fade, but which may still be quite delicious and complex.

Consequently, if you have cool, ideal cellars, the beginning year in the estimated range of maturity may err in favor of drinking the wine on the young side. I presume most readers would prefer, given a choice, to open a bottle too early rather than too late, and this philosophy has governed my projected maturity period for each wine.

How to Read the Charts

—   = Not produced.

N/T   = No recent and/or no tasting experience.

Now   = Totally mature, and not likely to improve; this wine should be drunk.

Now–1998 = The wine has entered its plateau of maturity where it should be expected to remain until 1998, at which time it may begin to slowly decline.

Now ?   = Signifies that this wine may be in decline.

1996–2010 = This is the estimated range of years in which I believe the wine will be in its plateau period—the years over which it will be at its best for drinking. Please keep in mind that Bordeaux wines from top vintages tend to decline slowly (just the opposite of Burgundy) and a top wine from an excellent vintage may take 10–15 years to lose its fruit and freshness after the last year in the stated plateau period.

General Vintage

(This vintage chart should be regarded as a very general overall rating of a particular viticultural region. Such charts are filled with exceptions to the rule—astonishingly good wines from skillful or lucky vinters in years rated mediocre, and thin, diluted, characterless wines from incompetent or greedy producers in great years.)

	REGIONS	1970	1971	1972	1973	1974	1975	1976	1977	1978	1979	
Bordeaux	St. Julien/Pauillac St.-Estèphe	90R	82R	67C	65C	68C	89T	84R	73C	87R	85R	
	Margaux	85R	83R	71C	65C	74C	78E	77R	71C	87R	87R	
	Graves	90R	88R	75C	76C	76C	89T	71C	75C	90R	90R	
	Pomerol	90R	87R	65C	70C	75R	94R	82R	72C	84R	84R	
	St.-Émilion	85R	83R	65C	67C	62C	85R	82R	60C	84R	84R	
	Barsac/Sauternes	84R	86R	55C	65C	50C	90T	87R	50C	75R	75R	
Burgundy	Côte de Nuits (Red)	82C	87R	86R	58C	64C	50C	86T	60C	88R	77C	
	Côte de Beaune (Red)	82C	87R	83R	60C	62C	50C	86T	55C	86R	77R	
	White	83C	88C	84C	87C	75C	65C	86C	80C	90R	86R	
Rhône	North-Côte Rôtie Hermitage	90R	84R	86R	72R	70C	73C	82R	72R	98E	87R	
	South-Châteauneuf-du-Pape	88R	82C	86C	74C	70C	60C	75C	70C	97R	88R	
	Beaujolais	—	—	—	—	—	—	86C	50C	84C	80C	
	Alsace	80C	90R	55C	75C	74C	82C	90R	70C	80C	84R	
	Loire Valley	—	—	—	—	—	—	86C	70C	85C	83C	
	Champagne	85C	90C	N.V.	82C	N.V.	90R	90R	N.V.	N.V.	88R	
Italy	Piedmont	84R	90R	50C	70R	85T	65C	67C	67V	95T	86R	
	Chianti	84C	88C	50C	68C	80R	84R	60C	72R	85C	75C	
	Germany	80C	90R	50C	67C	60C	85R	90R	70C	72C	84R	
	Vintage Port	90R	N.V.	78C	N.V.	N.V.	82R	N.V.	98T	83E	N.V.	
Spain	Rioja	90R	74C	67C	86R	65C	84R	86R	70C	84R	79R	
	Penedes	—	—	—	—	—	—	—	—	—	—	
Aust.	New So. Wales & Victoria	—	—	—	—	—	—	—	—	—	—	
California-N.Coast	Cabernet Sauvignon	92R	70C	65C	88R	90R	85R	85T	84R	90R	80R	
	Chardonnay	83C	82C	84C	85C	75C	86C	80C	83C	86C	83C	
	Zinfandel	96C	60C	50C	86R	88C	80C	87C	85R	86R	83R	
	Pinot Noir	—	—	—	—	—	—	—	—	84R	80C	
Ore.	Pinot Noir	—	—	—	—	—	—	—	—	—	—	
Wash.	Cabernet Sauvignon	—	—	—	—	—	—	—	—	—	—	

Guide 1970–1992

Key: 90–100 = Excellent; 80–89 = Very Good; 70–79 = Average; 60–69 = Below Average; Below 60 = Poor.
C = Caution, may now be too old or irregular; E = Early maturing; T = Tannic wines; R = Ready to drink; N.V. = Non-vintage; **Bold Print = The Best Vintages.**

1980	1981	1982	1983	1984	1985	1986	1987	1988	1989	1990	1991	1992
78R	85R	**98E**	86E	78T	**90R**	**96T**	82R	87T	**97E**	**97T**	79R	84E
79R	82R	86R	**95E**	74T	86R	**89T**	81R	85E	85E	**90E**	74R	75E
78R	84R	**88R**	**89R**	79R	87R	**89E**	84R	**89E**	**89E**	88E	74R	75E
79R	86R	**96E**	**90R**	76C	**90R**	87T	85R	**89T**	**95E**	**96E**	65C	85C
72R	82R	**94E**	**89R**	69C	**88R**	**88E**	77C	**88E**	**88E**	**96T**	65C	70C
85R	85R	75R	**88T**	70C	85R	**94T**	70R	**98T**	**94E**	**90T**	70C	75E
84R	72C	82R	85T	78R	**92R**	74R	86R	**88T**	**88E**	**94E**	85E	87C
78R	74E	80R	85T	75R	**90R**	78R	84R	**89E**	**88R**	**92E**	85E	**89E**
75R	86R	**90R**	85C	80R	**89R**	**90R**	79R	82R	**92R**	87R	70C	**89R**
83R	75C	85R	**89T**	75E	**90E**	84T	86E	**92E**	**96E**	**92T**	85E	78E
83R	**88R**	70C	87R	72C	**88E**	86T	60C	**90R**	**96T**	**95E**	70C	70C
60C	83C	75C	86C	75C	87C	84C	85C	86C	**92C**	86R	**90R**	82R
80C	86C	82C	**92R**	75C	**88R**	82C	83R	86R	**93R**	**90R**	75E	82E
72C	82C	84C	84C	68C	**88R**	87R	82R	**88R**	**92R**	**90R**	75R	80R
N.V.	84R	**90R**	84R	N.V.	87E	85E	N.V.	N.V.	**89E**	87E	N.V.	?
70R	80R	**92E**	75C	65C	**92E**	78R	85E	**90T**	**96E**	**93R**	76E	74C
70C	82C	86R	80R	60C	**93R**	84R	73R	**89T**	72C	**90E**	73E	72C
65R	82R	80R	**90R**	70R	85R	80R	82R	**89R**	**90E**	**92E**	85E	**90E**
84T	N.V.	86T	**90E**	N.V.	**90E**	N.V.	N.V.	N.V.	N.V.	N.V.	**90T**	N.V.
75R	87R	**92R**	74R	78R	82R	82E	82E	87E	**90E**	87E	76E	85E
85R	84R	87R	85R	86R	85R	77R	**88E**	87E	**88E**	87E	74E	82E
88C	85C	83C	76R	84R	86R	**90E**	87E	85E	**88E**	**88E**	**89E**	86E
86R	85R	86R	76C	**92R**	**94T**	**90E**	**90E**	75E	84E	**92E**	**90T**	87E
88C	86C	85C	85C	**88C**	84C	**90C**	75C	**89C**	76C	**90R**	85R	87R
82R	82R	80R	78R	**88R**	**88E**	87E	**90R**	82R	83R	**89R**	**89E**	86R
86R	83C	84C	85C	85R	86E	84R	86E	87R	85R	86E	86R	84R
86C	86C	84C	**90C**	65C	**90R**	85R	72R	**88R**	86R	**90E**	87E	**89E**
—	—	78C	**92E**	72C	86T	78R	85E	**88E**	**92E**	87E	85C	87E

BORDEAUX	1990	1989	1988	1987	1986	1985	1983	1982	1981	1979	1978	1976	1975
L'Angélus	1995–2008	1995–2008	Now–2006	–	Now–1998	Now	Now	Now	–	–	–	–	–
d'Armailhac	1994–2003	Now–2000	Now–1998	Now	Now–2002	Now–2000	Now	Now–2000	Now–1996	Now	Now	Now?	Now?
L'Arrosée	1995–2020	Now–1999	Now–2000	Now	1995–2010	Now–2004	Now–2003	Now–2005	Now–1996	Now	Now–1995	–	–
Ausone	2010–2040	2015–2035	2008–2040	Now–2010	1997–2020	Now–2010	Now–2010	2000–2030	1996–2010	1996–2010	1998–2015	1994–2015	Now–2005
Batailley	1995–2010	2000–2018	1997–2008	Now	1998–2010	Now–2005	Now–2000	1995–2010	Now	Now–2000	Now–2000	Now–1994	Now–2000
Belair	1997–2012	1995–2010	1995–2010	Now–1998	Now–2000	Now–1999	1993–2005	1996–2008	Now	Now–2007	Now–1995	Now–1994	Now–1996
Beychevelle	1994–2002	Now–2008	1994–2002	Now	1996–2010	Now–1997	Now–1997	1994–2010	Now–1997	Now	Now–1998	Now–2000	Now–2005
BonPasteur	1995–2005	Now–2003	Now–2008	Now	Now–2005	Now–1995	Now–1997	Now–2005	Now–1994	Now	Now–1995	Now?	Now–1995
Branaire-Ducru	1994–2005	Now–2005	Now–1998	Now	Now–1999	Now–1995	Now–1996	Now–2007	Now–1994	Now	Now	Now	Now–2005
Brane-Cantenac	–	Now–2004	Now–1996	Now?	Now–2005	Now–1997	Now–2005	Now–2005	Now–1995	Now?	Now–1996	Now?	Now–1994
Calon-Ségur	1995–2010	1996–2010	1998–2020	Now–1995	1997–2015	Now–2000	Now–1997	1998–2020	Now	Now	Now	Now?	Now–1997
Canon	2000–2025	1996–2010	1996–2012	Now–1997	1998–2010	1995–2007	1995–2015	1995–2020	Now–2000	1995–2005	Now–2005	Now–1994	Now–2010
Canon-la-Gaffelière	1995–2010	Now–2002	Now–2004	–	Now–2005	Now–1997	Now	Now	–	–	–	–	–
Cantemerle	Now–1999	1994–2010	Now–2005	Now?	Now–1998	Now–1997	Now–2005	Now–2000	Now–1995	Now?	Now–1995	Now?	Now–2003
Cantenac-Brown	Now–2003	Now–2001	Now–2000	Now	1995–2008	Now–2000	Now–2000	Now–2005	Now–2004	Now–1995	Now?	Now?	Now–2000
Certan de May	1995–2010	1994–2006	1994–2010	Now–1997	1995–2015	Now–2003	Now–2010	1996–2015	1994–2005	Now–2005	Now–1996	Now	Now–2000
Chasse-Spleen	Now–2003	1996–2015	Now–2006	Now	1995–2010	Now–2005	Now–1996	Now–2000	Now–1996	Now–1996	Now–2005	Now	Now–2005
Cheval Blanc	Now–2010	Now–2005	1994–2005	Now–1996	Now–2008	Now–2006	Now–2008	Now–2010	Now–2000	Now–1996	Now–2005	Now	Now–2004
Domaine de Chevalier	1997–2008	1996–2015	1995–2008	Now–1998	1995–2015	Now–2005	Now–2005	Now–2000	Now–2000	Now	Now–2005	Now?	Now?
Clerc-Milon	Now–2002	Now–2010	Now–2001	Now	Now–2006	Now–2000	Now	Now–1998	Now	Now	Now?	Now?	Now?
Clinet	1995–2010	1995–2015	Now–2010	Now–2000	Now–2000	Now?	Now?	Now?	Now?	Now?	Now?	Now?	Now?
La Conseillante	1994–2012	1996–2010	Now–1999	Now–1997	Now–2005	Now–2005	Now	Now–2006	Now–2003	Now	Now	Now?	Now–1995
Cos d'Estournel	1996–2012	Now–2009	2000–2020	Now–1997	1996–2010	Now–2010	Now–2000	Now–2008	Now–1996	Now–1997	Now–2000	Now–1994	Now–2000
La Dominique	Now–2005	1996–2008	Now–2001	–	Now–2005	Now–1996	Now–2000	Now–2007	Now–1996	Now–1996	Now–2000	–	Now–1996
Ducru-Beaucaillou	1999–2015	1999–2020	1996–2008	Now–1999	1996–2015	Now–2010	Now–2005	1996–2010	Now–2005	Now–1995	Now–2005	Now	Now–2015
Duhart-Milon-Rothschild	1999–2007	Now–2008	1995–2010	Now	1995–2008	Now–2000	Now–2000	1995–2010	Now–2003	Now	Now	Now?	Now?

BORDEAUX (continued)	1990	1989	1988	1987	1986	1985	1983	1982	1981	1979	1978	1976	1975
L'Église-Clinet	Now–2007	Now–2000	Now–2002	Now	Now–2005	1994–2005	Now–1995	Now–2000	Now	Now	Now	Now ?	Now ?
L'Enclos	Now–2006	Now–2002	Now–1996	Now	Now–1998	Now–2000	Now–1997	Now–2000	Now	Now–1994	Now	Now ?	Now–2002
L'Évangile	1997–2015	1994–2005	Now–2002	Now–2002	Now–2002	1994–2015	Now–2003	Now–2010	Now	Now–1995	Now	Now ?	Now–2005
Figeac	1995–2010	Now–2002	Now–1997	Now	Now–2005	Now–2002	Now	Now–2010	Now–1994	Now	Now	Now	Now–2000
La Fleur de Gay	1995–2003	1995–2008	1994–2010	Now–2000	Now–2003	Now–1998	Now–1998	Now	–	–	–	–	–
La Fleur Pétrus	Now–2005	1996–2009	Now–2000	Now–1996	Now–1998	Now–1997	Now–1997	Now–2000	Now–1995	Now	Now	Now ?	1994–2005
Fonbadet	1994–2003	Now–1998	Now–1996	Now	Now–2003	Now–1996	Now–1996	Now–2000	Now	Now	Now	Now ?	–
Les Forts de Latour	Now–2005	Now–2004	Now–2002	Now–1997	Now–2003	Now–1998	Now–1996	Now–2008	Now–2000	Now–1996	Now–2000	Now	Now–1995
La Gaffelière	Now–2008	1996–2010	Now–2000	–	Now–2006	Now–1997	Now	Now–2000	Now ?	Now	Now	Now	1995–2008
Le Gay	1996–2010	2005–2030	1997–2020	–	1998–2010	1995–2008	Now–2005	1995–2010	Now ?	Now–1996	Now–1999	Now ?	1995–2010
Giscours	1994–2005	Now–2005	Now–1996	Now	Now	Now–1995	Now	Now	Now	Now–2003	Now–2006	Now	1994–2010
Gloria	Now–1999	Now–2000	Now–1997	Now	Now–2002	Now–1997	Now–1995	Now–2000	Now	Now	Now	Now ?	Now–1998
Grand-Puy-Ducasse	Now–1999	Now–2002	Now–1996	Now	Now–2000	Now–1997	Now	Now	Now	Now	Now	Now ?	Now ?
Grand-Puy-Lacoste	1995–2010	1994–2010	1995–2005	Now	1995–2015	Now–2000	Now–2000	1996–2015	Now	Now	Now–2001	Now ?	Now–2000
La Grave Trigant de Boisset	Now–2002	Now–2002	Now–2001	Now	Now–1997	Now–1995	Now–1995	Now–2000	Now	Now	Now	Now ?	Now
Gruaud-Larose	1997–2015	2000–2025	2000–2025	Now–2000	2000–2025	Now–2003	Now–2004	1996–2020	Now–2000	Now–2003	1994–2008	Now	1996–2010
Haut-Bages-Libéral	1994–2005	Now–2000	Now–1998	Now	Now–2010	Now–2005	Now–1996	Now–2005	Now–2000	Now	Now	Now	Now–2003
Haut-Bailly	1995–2005	1994–2012	Now–2005	–	Now–2000	Now–2000	Now–1997	Now–2000	Now	Now–1996	Now–1995	Now ?	Now ?
Haut-Batailley	Now–2005	Now–2006	Now–1998	Now	Now–2002	Now–1996	Now–1996	Now–2005	Now	Now	Now	Now ?	Now–1996
Haut-Brion	1996–2010	1995–2015	1997–2015	Now	1995–2015	1995–2010	Now–2005	1995–2015	Now–2003	Now–2005	Now–2000	Now	Now–1998
Haut-Marbuzet	Now–2005	Now–2002	Now–2003	Now	Now–2003	Now–1997	Now–2000	Now–2005	Now	Now	Now	Now ?	Now–1995
D'Issan	1995–2004	Now–1997	Now	Now	Now–2003	Now–1997	Now–2003	Now–1997	Now	Now	Now–1996	Now ?	Now ?
Lafite-Rothschild	2000–2030	1997–2020	2000–2035	Now–1997	2000–2030	1995–2010	1998–2025	2000–2035	Now–2008	1996–2005	Now–2005	Now–2010	1996–2015
Lafleur	2000–2030	2000–2030	2000–2030	–	2000–2025	2000–2020	Now–2010	Now–2015	Now	2000–2030	Now–2018	Now ?	1995–2035
Lafon-Rochet	1998–2022	1996–2015	1995–2003	Now	1996–2008	Now–1999	Now–2005	1994–2008	Now–1996	Now–1998	Now	Now ?	Now–2000
Lagrange	1996–2010	1995–2010	1997–2008	Now–1996	2000–2020	1995–2008	Now–1998	Now–1996	Now ?	Now ?	Now ?	Now ?	Now ?

BORDEAUX (continued)	1990	1989	1988	1987	1986	1985	1983	1982	1981	1979	1978	1976	1975
La Lagune	Now–2006	Now–2008	Now–2005	Now	1994–2010	Now–2000	Now–2003	1994–2010	Now–1998	Now–1995	Now–2003	Now	Now–2003
Lanessan	Now–2006	Now–2004	Now–2008	Now	Now–2006	Now–1996	Now–2000	Now–2003	Now	Now	Now	Now	Now–2003
Larmande	1994–2003	Now–2001	Now–2002	–	Now–2005	Now–2000	Now–1997	Now–2000	Now	–	Now	–	–
Lascombes	Now–2003	Now–2002	1994–2002	–	Now–2000	Now–1997	Now–2003	Now–2001	Now ?	Now ?	Now ?	Now ?	Now–2003
Latour	2000–2035	1997–2015	2000–2025	Now–2001	1996–2010	Now–2008	Now–2005	1996–2020	1994–2006	Now–2000	Now–2010	Now–1996	Now–2003
Latour à Pomerol	Now–2004	1995–2010	Now–1999	Now	Now–2005	Now–2005	Now–2000	Now–2005	Now–1997	Now	Now	Now	Now ?
Léoville-Barton	1996–2020	1996–2010	1996–2012	Now–1996	1996–2010	Now–2007	Now–2002	1995–2010	Now–1996	Now	Now–1996	Now ?	Now–2005
Léoville-Las Cases	2000–2020	1996–2020	1995–2020	Now–2000	1996–2025	1995–2010	1996–2010	1996–2025	Now–2005	Now–1998	Now–2015	Now–1996	1996–2010
Léoville-Poyferré	1996–2025	1996–2015	1994–2006	Now	1997–2020	Now–1998	Now–2005	1996–2020	Now–1996	Now–1996	Now–2015	Now ?	Now–2001
La Louvière	1995–2006	Now–1998	Now–2002	Now	Now–1997	Now–1996	Now–1997	Now–1998	Now	Now	Now ?	–	Now ?
Lynch-Bages	1994–2010	1996–2015	Now–2010	Now	1996–2020	Now–2005	Now–2000	Now–2010	Now	Now	Now	Now	Now–1998
Magdelaine	1995–2008	2000–2025	1995–2005	–	Now–1998	Now–2003	Now–2003	Now–2010	Now–2000	Now–1995	Now	Now	Now–2005
Malescot St.-Exupéry	1994–2009	Now–2003	Now–2005	Now	Now–2001	Now–1997	Now–2000	Now–1996	Now–1996	Now–1995	Now–1996	Now ?	Now ?
Château Margaux	1997–2020	1996–2015	2000–2015	Now–2000	2000–2050	Now–2008	2000–2030	1995–2025	Now–2010	Now–2010	Now–2010	Now ?	Now ?
Maucaillou	–	Now–2001	Now–1998	–	Now–1998	Now–1998	Now–1996	Now–1996	Now	Now	Now	Now ?	Now–1995
Meyney	1996–2010	1995–2020	1996–2015	Now–1996	1995–2010	Now–2005	Now–2003	Now–2010	Now–1997	Now–1996	Now–2000	Now	Now–2005
La Mission-Haut-Brion	1995–2010	1995–2015	1994–2012	Now–2000	1995–2012	Now–2005	Now–2005	Now–2010	Now–2006	Now–2005	Now–2010	Now	Now–2025
Montrose	2000–2045	1998–2025	Now–2000	Now	1995–2015	Now–2000	Now–1997	Now–2004	Now–1997	Now–1999	Now–1996	Now–1996	Now–2005
Mouton-Rothschild	1999–2010	1996–2010	1999–2020	1998–2008	2000–2040	Now–2010	Now–2010	2000–2040	Now–2000	Now–1996	Now–1998	Now–1997	1996–2008
Les-Ormes-de-Pez	Now–2008	Now–2000	Now–1999	Now	Now–2000	Now	Now	Now–1996	Now	Now ?	Now	Now ?	Now–1996
Palmer	Now–2006	Now–2012	1994–2006	Now–1999	Now–2010	Now–2000	Now–2010	Now–2000	Now–1997	Now–2005	Now–2005	Now ?	Now–1996
Pape-Clément	1996–2008	Now–2005	Now–2008	Now	1994–2010	Now–2000	Now ?	Now ?	Now ?	Now ?	Now ?	Now ?	Now ?
Pavie	1999–2015	1996–2010	1995–2005	–	1996–2010	Now–2005	Now–2005	1995–2010	Now–1995	Now–2000	Now	Now	Now ?
Petit-Village	Now–2005	Now–2000	Now–2000	Now	Now–2000	Now–1997	Now–1998	Now–2000	Now	Now	Now	Now ?	Now ?
Pétrus	2000–2025	2000–2035	2002–2030	1997–2010	1998–2010	1995–2015	Now–2015	1996–2020	1995–2008	1995–2010	Now–2005	Now	2000–2050
Pichon-Longueville Baron	1996–2020	1995–2020	1995–2008	Now–1996	Now–2005	Now–1998	Now–1996	Now–2002	Now	Now	Now ?	Now ?	Now ?

BORDEAUX (continued)	1990	1989	1988	1987	1986	1985	1983	1982	1981	1979	1978	1976	1975
Pichon Lalande	Now–2000	Now–2012	Now–2008	Now	1994–2015	Now–2005	Now–2015	Now–2010	Now–1997	Now–1996	Now–1996	Now	Now–1998
Le Pin	Now–2007	Now–2004	Now–2003	Now–1997	1994–2005	Now–2001	Now–2002	Now–2005	Now–1994	Now–1996	–	–	–
Pontet-Canet	1997–2020	2000–2015	1996–2005	Now–1996	1996–2015	Now–2005	Now–2002	Now–2005	Now	Now	Now–1996	Now ?	Now–2000
Potensac	Now–2003	Now–1999	Now–1996	Now	Now–1998	Now–1996	Now–1993	Now–2000	Now	Now	Now	Now ?	–
Poujeaux	Now–2005	Now–2003	Now–2005	Now	Now–2010	Now–1998	Now–2000	Now–2005	Now	Now	Now	Now ?	Now–1995
Prieuré-Lichine	1995–2005	Now–2005	Now–2003	Now ?	Now–2006	Now–1995	Now–2003	Now–2005	Now	Now ?	Now–1997	Now ?	Now ?
Rausan-Ségla	1997–2020	Now–2012	1997–2012	–	1995–2015	Now–1997	Now–2003	Now–1997	Now ?	Now ?	Now ?	Now ?	Now ?
St.-Pierre	1996–2007	Now–2010	Now–2000	Now	1994–2012	Now–1998	Now–1998	Now–2002	Now–2000	Now–1996	Now–1996	Now ?	Now–2000
de Sales	Now–2005	Now–2003	Now–1997	–	Now–1996	Now–1995	Now	Now–1996	Now	Now	Now	Now ?	Now–1994
Sociando-Mallet	2000–2020	Now–2010	Now–2008	Now	2000–2035	1995–2015	Now–2001	1996–2012	Now–2000	Now–1998	Now–2005	Now–2000	Now–2010
Soutard	1996–2020	2000–2020	1998–2020	–	1997–2015	1996–2010	Now–2003	1995–2005	Now–1996	Now–1997	Now–1996	Now	Now–2005
Talbot	Now–2008	Now–2008	1996–2010	Now–1998	Now–2015	Now–2005	Now–2005	1994–2015	Now–2000	Now	Now–2000	Now–1995	Now–2000
du Tertre	1996–2008	Now–1998	Now–2003	Now–1995	Now–2005	Now–1998	Now–2001	Now–1998	Now–1996	Now–2000	Now–2000	Now ?	Now ?
Le Tertre-Roteboeuf	Now–2010	1995–2010	1995–2010	Now	Now–2002	Now–2000	Now–1999	Now–1998	–	Now–1997	–	–	Now ?
La Tour Haut Brion	Now–2003	Now–2000	Now–2002	Now	Now–2000	Now–1997	Now–2000	1994–2010	1994–2004	Now–1997	Now–2003	Now	1995–2030
Troplong-Mondot	Now–2010	1994–2008	Now–2007	Now	Now–2005	Now–1998	Now	Now	Now ?	Now ?	Now ?	Now ?	Now ?
Trotanoy	1995–2008	Now–2010	Now–2005	Now	Now–2005	Now–2000	Now–2001	Now–2010	Now–2002	Now–1996	Now–1995	Now	Now–2007
Vieux Château Certan	1994–2010	1994–2005	1994–2010	Now–1997	1994–2010	Now–2000	Now–2000	Now–2005	Now–2003	Now–1995	Now	Now	Now–2000

RED BURGUNDY	1990	1989	1988	1987	1986	1985	1983	1982	1980	1979	1978	1976
Bertrand Ambroise Nuits St.-Georges Les Vaucrains	1998–2020	1994–2010	Now–2000	Now–1997	—	—	—	—	—	—	—	—
Domaine de L'Arlot Nuits St.-Georges-Clos des Forêts	Now–2002	Now–2003	Now–1998	Now–1997	—	—	—	—	—	—	—	—
Comte Armand Pommard-Clos des Epeneaux	2004–2034	Now–2002	Now–2002	Now	Now	1994–2005	Now–1997	Now	Now	Now	Now–1995	Now–1998
Robert Arnoux Vosne-Romanée Les Suchots	Now–2002	Now–1998	1995–2002	Now	Now	Now	Now–1998	Now	Now	Now	Now	N/T
Bichot-Clos Frantin Vosne-Romanée Les Malconsorts	Now–1997	Now–1997	1995–2005	Now–2000	Now	Now–2003	Now–1998	Now	Now	Now	Now	N/T
Bourée Père et Fils Charmes-Chambertin	1997–2008	1996–2004	1998–2008	Now–2002	Now–1995	Now–2003	Now–2000	Now	Now	Now	Now–1998	N/T
Bouré Père et Fils Clos de la Roche	1999–2010	Now–1997	Now–2002	Now–2000	Now–1995	Now–2005	Now–2003	Now	Now	Now	Now–1995	N/T
R. Chevillon Nuits St.-Georges Les St.-Georges	1995–2003	1994–2002	1995–2002	Now–1997	Now–1995	1994–2000	Now–2000	Now	Now	Now	Now	N/T
R. Chevillon Nuits St.-Georges Les Vaucrains	Now–2002	Now–2001	1996–2003	Now–1997	Now–1995	1994–2003	Now–2002	Now	Now	Now	Now	N/T
Copin-Groffier Clos Vougeot	1997–2012	Now–2003	Now–2000	Now	Now	—	—	—	—	—	—	—
J. Confuron-Cotetidot Clos Vougeot	Now–2004	1995–2003	Now–2010	1994–2000	Now–1998	—	—	—	—	—	—	—
J. Confuron-Cotetidot Vosne-Romanée Les Suchots	Now–2000	1994–2001	1995–2010	1994–1999	Now–1997	—	—	—	—	—	—	—
Courcel Pommard Rugiens	Now–2000	Now–1998	Now–2000	Now–1996	Now	Now–2000	Now–1995	Now	Now	Now	Now	Now–1998
J. Drouhin Charmes-Chambertin	Now–2002	Now–1998	1994–2002	Now–1997	Now	Now–2000	Now	Now	Now	—	—	—
Drouhin-Larose Chambertin Clos de Bèze	N/T	N/T	N/T	Now	Now	Now–2000	Now	Now	Now	Now	Now–1995	Now–1996
Drouhin-Larose Bonnes Mares	N/T	N/T	N/T	Now	Now	Now–1998	Now	Now	Now	Now	Now	Now
Claude & Maurice Dugat Charmes-Chambertin	1996–2005	Now–1999	1996–2006	—	—	—	Now–1998	Now	Now	Now	Now–2000	1994–2000
Claude & Maurice Dugat Griotte-Chambertin	1996–2008	Now–2001	1996–2006	—	—	—	—	—	—	—	—	—
Dujac Bonnes Mares	1995–2008	Now–1998	Now–1998	Now–1997	Now–1998	Now–2005	Now–1998	Now	Now	Now	Now–2000	1994–2000
Dujac Charmes-Chambertin	Now–2002	Now–1998	Now–1998	Now–1996	Now	Now–2000	Now–1996	Now	Now	Now	Now–1996	Now
Dujac Clos de la Roche	1996–2006	Now–1999	Now–2004	Now–2005	Now–1997	Now–2005	Now–2000	Now	Now	Now	Now–2000	Now–2003
Dujac Clos St.-Denis	1995–2010	Now–1998	Now–2000	Now–2000	Now–1997	Now–2005	Now–2000	Now	Now	Now	Now–2000	Now–2003
René Engel Grands Echézeaux	Now–2000	Now–1998	Now–1997	Now–1996	Now	Now–2003	Now	Now	N/T	N/T	N/T	N/T
Michel Esmonin Gevrey-Chambertin-Clos St.-Jacques	1995–2010	1995–2010	Now–1998	Now–1997	—	—	—	—	—	—	—	—
Faiveley Chambertin-Clos de Bèze	1996–2015	Now–2002	1998–2010	1996–2010	Now	Now–2005	Now–2000	Now	Now	Now	Now	N/T
Faiveley Corton-Clos des Cortons	2000–2025	1995–2005	1996–2010	Now–2010	Now–1997	Now–2002	Now–2000	Now	Now	Now	Now–1996	N/T

RED BURGUNDY (continued)	1990	1989	1988	1987	1986	1985	1983	1982	1980	1979	1978	1976
Faiveley Mazis–Chambertin	1998–2018	Now–2001	1995–2005	Now–1999	Now–1999	Now–2000	Now–1998	Now	Now	Now	Now	N/T
A. Girardin Pommard Les Epenots	2002–2030	1996–2016	Now–2005	1996–2001	1995–2000	—	—	—	—	—	—	—
A. Girardin Pommard Les Rugiens	2002–2035+	1998–2028	Now–2005	1996–2001	1995–2001	—	—	—	—	—	—	—
Machard de Gramont Nuits St.-Georges Les Damodes	1996–2004	1995–2007	Now–2000	Now–1998	Now	Now–2003	Now–1996	Now	Now	Now	Now–1996	N/T
Machard de Gramont Pommard Le Clos Blanc	Now–2005	Now–1998	Now–1998	Now–1996	Now	Now–2002	Now–1996	Now	Now	Now	Now–1996	N/T
Jean Gros Clos Vougeot	1995–2010	N/T	N/T	—	—	—	Now–2000	Now	Now–1995	Now	Now–2000	N/T
Jean Gros Richebourg	Now–2010	Now–2000	Now–1998	Now–2003	Now–1996	Now–2005	Now–2000	Now	Now	Now	Now–2000	N/T
Haegelen-Jayer Clos Vougeot	1995–2010	1995–2002	1998–2006	Now	Now–1998	—	—	—	—	—	—	—
Haegelen-Jayer Echézeaux	1995–2006	1995–2002	1996–2006	Now	Now–1996	—	—	—	N/T	—	—	—
Louis Jadot Beaune-Clos des Ursules	1996–2010	Now–2002	1996–2008	Now–1996	Now–1994	Now–2000	Now–2000	Now	N/T	Now	Now–2000	N/T
Louis Jadot Bonnes Mares	1998–2015	1995–2010	1997–2010	Now–2000	Now–1996	Now–2002	N/T	N/T	N/T	N/T	N/T	N/T
Louis Jadot Chambertin-Clos de Bèze	1998–2025	1995–2008	1998–2015	1994–2002	Now–1998	Now–2008	Now–2003	N/T	N/T	N/T	N/T	N/T
Louis Jadot Chambolle-Musigny Les Amoureuses	1995–2010	Now–2003	1996–2007	Now–2001	Now–1996	Now–2001	N/T	N/T	N/T	N/T	N/T	N/T
Louis Jadot Chapelle-Chambertin	2000–2010	Now–1998	Now–1997	Now–1996	Now–1996	Now–2000	N/T	N/T	N/T	N/T	N/T	N/T
Louis Jadot Clos Vougeot	2000–2020	1995–2010	Now–1998	Now–2002	Now	Now–2002	Now–2005	Now	N/T	N/T	Now–1998	Now
Louis Jadot Gevrey-Chambertin-Clos St-Jacques	1997–2009	1994–2006	Now–2005	Now–1998	Now–1997	Now–1999	N/T	Now	N/T	N/T	N/T	N/T
Henri Jayer Echézeaux	1996–2009	1995–2005	1997–2009	Now–2000	Now–2000	Now–2003	Now–1997	Now	Now	Now	Now–1998	N/T
Henri Jayer Nuits St.-Georges Meurgers	N/T	N/T	N/T	Now–2000	Now–1996	Now–2000	Now–1998	Now	Now	Now–1997	Now–1996	N/T
Henri Jayer Richebourg	N/T	N/T	N/T	Now–2005	Now–2000	Now–2005	Now–2005	Now	Now–2000	Now	Now–2001	N/T
Henri Jayer Vosne-Romanée Les Brûlées	N/T	N/T	N/T	Now–2002	Now–1997	Now–2002	Now–1996	Now–1995	Now–1995	Now	Now–1998	N/T
Henri Jayer Vosne-Romanée Cros Parantoux	1995–2008	Now–2002	1996–2007	Now–2000	Now–1997	Now–2002	Now–1996	Now	Now–1996	Now	Now–1996	N/T
Jayer-Gilles Echézeaux	Now–2007	Now–2006	Now–2005	Now–2000	Now	Now–1996	Now–1996	Now	N/T	N/T	N/T	N/T
Michel Lafarge Volnay-Clos des Chenes	1996–2008	Now–2000	1996–2005	Now–1998	Now	—	—	—	—	—	—	—
Michel Lafarge Volnay-Clos du Château des Ducs	Now–2005	Now–1999	1995–2006	Now–1999	Now	—	—	—	—	—	—	—
P. Leclerc Gevrey-Chambertin Les Cazetiers	1995–2010	Now–2002	1997–2008	Now–2000	1994–1997	1995–2005	Now–2000	Now	Now–1998	Now–1998	N/T	N/T
P. Leclerc Gevrey-Chambertin Combe aux Moines	1997–2015	1996–2007	1997–2010	Now–2000	Now–1997	1995–2008	Now–2000	Now	Now–2000	Now–1996	N/T	N/T

RED BURGUNDY (continued)	1990	1989	1988	1987	1986	1985	1983	1982	1980	1979	1978	1976
R. Leclerc Gevrey-Chambertin Combe aux Moines	Now–2007	Now–2005	1996–2005	Now–1998	Now–1995	1995–2000	Now–1997	Now	Now	Now	N/T	N/T
Lejeune Pommard Les Rugiens	1995–2010	Now–2002	Now–2007	Now–2002	Now–1998	–	–	–	–	–	–	–
Leroy Chambertin	2000–2040	2000–2030	1995–2015	N/T	N/T	1998–2010	N/T	N/T	N/T	N/T	Now–2010	Now–2010
Leroy Clos de la Roche	1996–2030	1994–2025	–	–	–	–	–	–	–	–	–	–
Leroy Clos Vougeot	2002–2030	Now–2010	Now–2010	N/T	N/T	1998–2007	N/T	N/T	N/T	N/T	Now–2005	Now–2005
Leroy Mazis-Chambertin	–	–	–	N/T	N/T	1998–2008	N/T	N/T	N/T	N/T	N/T	N/T
Leroy Richebourg	2002–2035	2000–2030	1997–2020	–	–	–	–	–	–	–	–	–
Leroy Romanée St-Vivant	1998–2028	1998–2015	1995–2020	–	–	–	–	–	–	–	–	–
Leroy Vosne-Romanée Les Beaux Monts	2000–2030+	1997–2010	1998–2010	–	–	–	–	–	–	–	–	–
Leroy Vosne-Romanée Les Brûlées	1996–2010	Now–2010	1996–2007	–	–	–	–	–	–	–	–	–
H. Lignier Clos de la Roche	1996–2010	Now–2000	1996–2005	Now–1997	Now–1996	1996–2005	Now–1998	Now	Now	Now	Now–1998	N/T
Maume Mazis-Chambertin	2005–2025	1998–2008	1998–2010	1994–2002	1995–2002	1997–2010	1995–2010	Now–1998	Now–2002	Now–1998	N/T	N/T
Méo-Camuzet Clos Vougeot	Now–2002	Now–2002	Now–2000	Now–1996	Now	Now	N/T	N/T	N/T	N/T	N/T	N/T
Méo-Camuzet Richebourg	Now–2004	Now–2000	Now–2000	Now–2001	Now–1996	Now–1998	N/T	N/T	N/T	N/T	N/T	N/T
Méo-Camuzet Vosne-Romanée aux Brûlées	Now–2002	Now–1999	Now–1998	Now–1997	Now	Now	N/T	Now	N/T	N/T	N/T	N/T
Mongeard-Mugneret Clos Vougeot	Now–2008	Now–1999	Now–2000	Now–1997	Now–1996	Now–2001	Now–2005	Now	Now	Now	Now	Now
Mongeard-Mugneret Grands Echézeaux	Now–2008	Now–1997	Now–1998	Now–1998	Now–1996	Now–2003	Now–2005	Now	Now	Now	Now	Now
Mongeard-Mugneret Richebourg	Now–2008	Now–1998	Now–2000	Now–1998	Now	Now–1998	N/T	N/T	N/T	N/T	N/T	N/T
H. de Montille Pommard Les Pézerolles	2000–2030	1999–2010	2000–2015		–	–	–	–	1996–2010	–	1998–2015	–
H. de Montille Pommard Les Rugiens	2000–2035	1999–2015	2000–2015	1995–2008	Now–1997	1995–2009	1995–2005	Now–2000	1994–2010	N/T	1995–2010	N/T
H. de Montille Volnay Taillepieds	2006–2030	1998–2010	2000–2015	–	–	–	–	–	–	–	–	–
A. Morot Beaune Les Bressandes	1995–2008	1995–2010	Now–2010	Now–2001	Now	Now–2003	Now	Now	Now	Now	Now	Now
A. Morot Beaune Les Teurons	1998–2018	1996–2010	Now–2010	Now–2003	Now	Now–2003	Now	Now	Now	Now–1997	Now	Now
Mugneret-Gibourg Clos Vougeot	2000–2010	Now–2008	Now–2012	Now–1998	Now–1998	1996–2010	1996–2001	Now	Now–1996	Now	Now–2000	N/T
Mugneret-Gibourg Echézeaux	1996–2008	Now–1996	Now–2000	Now–1999	Now–2003	1996–2009	1995–2006	Now	Now–1996	Now	Now–2000	N/T
Mugneret-Gibourg Ruchottes-Chambertin	1996–2008	Now–1999	1995–2005	Now–2005	1996–2000	1997–2008	1996–2003	Now	Now–1998	Now	Now–2010	N/T

RED BURGUNDY (continued)	1976	1978	1979	1980	1982	1983	1985	1986	1987	1988	1989	1990
A. Mussy Pommard Les Epenots	N/T	Now–1999	Now–1996	Now–1997	Now	Now–1999	Now–2003	Now–1996	Now–1998	1995–2005	Now–1998	1996–2010
Ponsot Chambertin	N/T	N/T	N/T	N/T	Now	Now–2008	1995–2005	Now	Now–1999	1995–2005	1994–2003	1997–2010
Ponsot Clos de la Roche Vieilles Vignes	Now–2001	Now–2003	Now–1999	Now–2010	Now	1995–2007	1995–2005	Now	Now–1998	1995–2005	1995–2002	1996–2012
Ponsot Clos St.–Denis Vieilles Vignes	Now–2000	Now–2000	Now–1999	Now–2005	Now	1994–2007	Now–2005	Now	Now–1997	1995–2005	1994–2002	1997–2010
Pothier-Rieusset Pommard Les Rugiens	Now–2000	Now–2003	Now–2000	Now–1998	Now	Now	Now–2003	Now	1994–1998	1998–2009	1996–2010	2000–2010
Pousse d'Or Volnay-Clos de la Bousse d'Or	Now–2005	Now	Now	Now	Now	Now–1998	1994–2001	Now	Now–1996	1995–2005	Now–2000	1997–2007
Domaine de la Romanée-Conti Grands Echézeaux	Now	Now–2010	Now–2000	Now–1998	Now	Now–2008	1995–2010	Now–2000	1996–2006	1995–2010	1996–2010	1995–2010
Domaine de la Romanée-Conti Richebourg	Now	Now–2012	Now–2005	Now–2000	Now	1995–2010	1996–2012	Now–2003	1996–2008	1998–2020	1995–2015	1999–2015
Domaine de la Romanée-Conti Romanée-Conti	Now	Now–2010	Now–2003	Now–2000	Now	1994–2007	1998–2010	Now–2000	1997–2008	1998–2018	1996–2010	2000–2025
Domaine de la Romanée-Conti Romanée-St.-Vivant	Now	Now–2008	Now–2000	Now–2000	Now	Now–2007	1995–2010	Now–2003	1994–2008	2000–2030	1997–2014	1999–2015
Domaine de la Romanée-Conti La Tâche	Now	Now–2012	Now–2000	Now–2000	Now	1995–2010	1995–2020	Now–2005	1996–2010	1995–2025	1998–2020	1997–2020
J. Roty Charmes-Chambertin	N/T	Now–1998	Now	Now–2000	Now	Now	1996–2010	Now–1996	Now–2000	1996–2012	1995–2005	1998–2010
J. Roty Mazis-Chambertin	N/T	Now–1998	Now	Now–2001	Now	Now	1997–2012	Now–1997	Now–2003	1996–2012	1996–2006	1998–2015
Georges et Christopher Roumier Bonnes Mares	Now–2005	Now–1996	Now	Now	Now	Now–2005	Now–2000	Now–2002	Now–2000	1996–2010	Now–1999	1994–2008
Georges et Christopher Roumier Chambolle-Musigny Les Amoureuses	Now–2003	Now–1996	Now	Now	Now	Now–2003	Now–2000	Now–2000	Now–2000	Now–2005	Now–1998	Now–2004
Georges et Christopher Roumier Clos Vougeot	N/T	Now–2000	N/T	Now	Now	Now–2008	Now–2000	Now–2004	Now–2001	1996–2010	1994–2000	1998–2018
Georges et Christopher Roumier Ruchottes-Chambertin	N/T	Now–2000	N/T	Now	Now	1995–2005	Now–2003	Now–2004	1994–2003	1994–2010	Now–2003	1995–2010
A. Rousseau Chambertin	Now–2000	—	Now–1998	Now–2000	Now	1996–2008	1996–2005	Now–1998	1994–2003	1998–2010	1994–2005	1997–2010
A. Rousseau Chambertin-Clos de Bèze	Now–2000	—	Now	Now–2000	Now	1996–2010	Now–2006	Now–1998	Now–2002	1998–2010	1995–2010	1995–2010
A. Rousseau Gevrey-Chambertin-Clos St. Jacques	Now–2000	—	Now	Now–1998	Now	Now–2006	Now–2000	Now–1996	Now–2000	1996–2008	Now–2006	Now–2002
C. Serafin Gevrey-Chambertin Les Cazetiers	—	—	—	—	—	—	—	Now	Now	Now–2002	1995–2010	1996–2010
Tollot-Beaut Corton Bressandes	Now	Now	Now	Now	Now	Now–2000	Now–1998	Now	Now–1996	Now–1995	Now–2000	1995–2005
Château de la Tour Clos Vougeot	—	—	—	—	—	—	—	Now	Now–1998	Now–2000	Now–1999	Now–2002
Comte de Vogüé Bonnes Mares	Now	Now	Now	Now	Now	Now	Now	Now–2000	1995–2000	1996–2005	1995–2003	1997–2010
Comte de Vogüé Musigny Vieilles Vignes	Now	Now	Now	Now	Now	Now	Now	1995–2001	1995–2002	1997–2008	1996–2005	1999–2020

RHÔNE VALLEY	1990	1989	1988	1985	1983	1982	1978
Beaucastel Châteauneuf-du-Pape	1998–2028	1995–2028	Now–2005	Now–2010	Now–2005	Now	1998–2020
H. Bonneau Châteauneuf-du-Pape Cuvée des Celestins	1996–2020	1998–2020	1995–2010	1995–2008	Now–2005	N/T	Now–2015
Les Bosquet des Papes Châteauneuf-du-Pape	1996–2010	1995–2007	Now–2000	Now–2001	Now–1997	Now	Now–1997
Lucien et André Brunel-Les Cailloux Châteauneuf-du-Pape	Now–2005	1996–2010	Now–2002	Now–2000	Now–1996	Now	Now–2000
Chapoutier Châteauneuf-du-Pape Barbe Rac	1995–2025	Now–2017	N/T	–	–	–	–
Chapoutier Hermitage Chante-Alouette (white)	Now–2010	Now–2010	Now–2005	Now–2000	Now–2005	Now	Now–2000
Chapoutier Ermitage Le Pavillon	2000–2040	2000–2030	–	–	–	–	–
Chapoutier Ermitage La Sizeranne	1998–2025	1997–2015	Now–2005	Now–1998	Now–1997	Now	Now
J. L. Chave Hermitage	2005–2040+	1998–2030	1996–2015	1996–2010	2000–2025	Now–2005	1998–2030
J. L. Chave Hermitage Blanc	Now–2010	Now–2002	Now–2010	Now–2005	Now–2008	Now–2000	Now–2005
A. Clape Cornas	1997–2012	1995–2010	Now–2002	Now–2005	1996–2008	Now–1997	Now–2008
Les Clefs d'or Châteauneuf-du-Pape	1997–2017	1996–2013	Now–2005	Now–2000	Now–1996	Now	Now–2003
Clos du Mont-Olivet Châteauneuf-du-Pape	1995–2010	1995–2015	Now–2005	Now–2008	Now–1997	Now	Now–2008
Clos des Papes Châteauneuf-du-Pape	1997–2017	1998–2010	Now–2004	Now–1999	Now–1998	Now	Now–2002
Coudoulet Côtes du Rhone	Now–2004	Now–2007	Now–2000	Now–2000	Now–1996	Now	Now–1998
Fonsalette Côtes du Rhone	Now–2007	Now–2007	Now–2000	Now–1997	Now	Now–2000	Now–1998
Fonsalette Côtes du Rhone Syrah	2002–2025	2002–2027	1998–2015	1996–2015	1996–2015	N/T	1995–2010
Guigal Côte Rôtie (regular *cuvée*)	1995–2003	Now–2005	Now–2012	Now–2006	1996–2006	Now–1997	Now–2000
Guigal Côte Rôtie La Landonne	1995–2015	Now–2025	2000–2040	1998–2025	1998–2035	Now–2008	1996–2023
Guigal Côte Rôtie La Mouline	1995–2005	Now–2007	Now–2020	1996–2015	1998–2015	Now–2005	1996–2020
Guigal Côte Rôtie La Turque	1995–2008	Now–2007	Now–2025	1997–2010	–	–	–
Guigal Hermitage	1995–2010	Now–2007	1996–2025	Now–2005	1996–2010	Now–2005	Now–2003
Paul Jaboulet Crozes-Hermitage Thalabert	Now–2007	1994–2007	Now–2000	Now–2000	1995–2005	Now	Now–2000
Paul Jaboulet Hermitage La Chapelle	2005–2040+	2000–2035	2004–2020	1996–2008	2000–2030	Now–2008	1998–2020
Jamet Côte Rôtie	1996–2007	1994–2014	1996–2016	1995–2010	1996–2010	Now	N/T
Montmirail Gigondas (Brusset)	Now–2012	Now–2006	Now–2002	Now	Now	N/T	N/T

RHÔNE VALLEY (continued)

RHÔNE VALLEY (continued)	1990	1989	1988	1985	1983	1982	1978
du Pegau Châteauneuf-du-Pape	Now–2018	Now–2007	Now–2012	1995–2010	Now–1997	N/T	Now–1999
Rayas Châteauneuf-du-Pape	1997–2012	1997–2010	Now–2005	1994–2005	Now–2001	–	Now–2003
René Rostaing Côte Rôtie Côte Blonde	Now–2002	Now–2002	Now–2002	Now–2003	1996–2008	–	–
René Rostaing Côte Rôtie La Landonne	Now–2004	Now–2004	Now–2005	1996–2005	1998–2009	–	–
Saint-Gayan Gigondas	1994–2006	Now–2006	Now–2003	Now–1999	N/T	N/T	N/T
Santa Duc Gigondas Cuvée Prestige	Now–2008	Now–2006	N/T	–	–	–	–
Henri Sorrel Hermitage Le Gréal	2005–2040	2000–2035	1998–2005	1996–2008	1998–2008	–	1998–2030
Henri Sorrel Hermitage Les Rocoules (white)	2002–2020	Now–2010+	Now–2010+	Now–2001	Now–2000	–	1995–2009
de Vallouit Côte Rôtie Les Roziers	Now–2004	Now–2000	1996–2010	Now–2004	–	–	–
de Vallouit Hermitage Greffières	2000–2030	Now–2012	2000–2025	1996–2005	Now–2008	–	–
N. Verset Cornas	1995–2008	Now–2000	1996–2008	1995–2010	1998–2008	Now	Now–2005
Vieux Donjon Châteauneuf-du-Pape	1997–2012	1994–2008	Now–1998	Now–2000	Now–1999	Now	Now–2006
Vieux Télégraphe Châteauneuf-du-Pape	Now–2005	Now–2005	Now–2000	Now–2000	Now–2003	Now	Now–2005
Voge Cornas Cuvée Vieilles Vignes	1995–2008	Now–2007	N/T	N/T	N/T	N/T	N/T

California Cabernet Sauvignon	1991	1990	1989	1988	1987	1986	1985	1984
Beaulieu Private Reserve	N/T	N/T	N/T	Now–2002	1995–2005	1996–2010	1996–2010	Now–2000
Beringer Private Reserve	N/T	N/T	1995–2003	Now–1999	Now–2007	Now–2003	Now–2005	Now–2000
Buehler	N/T	N/T	N/T	Now–1998	1995–2004	Now–1996	Now–1999	Now–1997
Burgess Vintage Selection	N/T	N/T	N/T	Now–1999	1995–2004	Now–2000	Now–2003	Now–2000
Carmenet Reserve	1997–2010	1996–2008	N/T	Now–2002	1994–2006	Now–2005	Now–2005	Now–2003
Caymus	N/T	N/T	Now–2000	Now–1998	Now–2002	Now–2000	Now–2005	Now–1998
Caymus Special Selection	N/T	N/T	N/T	Now–2001	Now–2003	Now–2005	Now–2010	Now–2010
Chappellet	N/T	N/T	N/T	N/T	1995–2005	Now–2000	1994–2005	Now–2003
Clos du Val	N/T	N/T	N/T	Now–1997	Now–2006	Now–2002	Now–2000	Now–1996
Diamond Creek (all 3 Vyds.)	1996–2005	1996–2006	1994–2006	Now–2004	1995–2005	Now–2000	Now–1997	Now–2008
Dominus	1996–2015	1995–2010	Now–2010	Now–2008	1997–2010	Now–2008	1996–2015	Now–2005
Duckhorn Merlot	N/T	Now–2003	Now–1997	Now–1997	Now–1994	Now–1998	Now–2005	Now–2000
Dunn-Napa	1997–2008	1998–2012	1996–2008	1996–2005	1998–2010	1995–2008	1995–2009	Now–2000
Dunn-Howell Mountain	1997–2008	1998–2012	1996–2008	1996–2005	2000–2015	1996–2010	1995–2015	1996–2010
Forman	1996–2008	1996–2010	Now–2002	Now–2000	Now–2002	Now–2000	Now–2000	Now–2000
Grgich Hills	N/T	N/T	N/T	N/T	1995–2008	Now–2007	Now–2003	Now–2000
Groth Reserve	N/T	N/T	N/T	Now–2000	Now–2001	1994–2010	1995–2010	Now–1996
Heitz Bella Oaks	N/T	N/T	N/T	1996–2005	1994–2008	1996–2005	1995–2005	Now–2002
Heitz Martha's Vineyard	N/T	N/T	N/T	Now–2003	1997–2010	1997–2010	1998–2012	Now–2010
Wm Hill Reserve	N/T	N/T	1994–2005	1994–2004	1995–2003	Now–2000	Now–2004	Now–2000
La Jota	N/T	1998–2010	1996–2006	1995–2005	1996–2007	1996–2008	Now–2005	Now–2002
Jordan	N/T	N/T	N/T	Now–1999	Now–2002	Now–2000	Now–1997	Now–1998
Kistler	N/T	N/T	N/T	1996–2007	1996–2008	1995–2005	1995–2005	Now–2003
Laurel Glen	1996–2010	1996–2010	Now–2002	Now–2002	1994–2003	Now–2000	Now–2002	Now–1998
Matanzas Creek Merlot	N/T	Now–1999	Now	Now	Now–1997	Now–1995	Now	Now
Mayacamas	N/T	N/T	N/T	N/T	N/T	N/T	1998–2010	1996–2007
Robert Mondavi Reserve	Now–2010	Now–2012	Now–1998	Now–2003	1996–2015	Now–2003	Now–1997	Now–1996
Château Montelena	N/T	N/T	N/T	1998–2008	1997–2025	Now–2006	1994–2010	Now–2005
Monticello Corley Reserve	N/T	N/T	N/T	N/T	1995–2005	Now–2005	Now–2004	Now–2005
Mt. Eden	N/T	1998–2015	1996–2005	1997–2005	1997–2007	1996–2005	Now–2000	Now–2000
Newton Merlot	Now–2005	Now–2005	Now–1997	Now–1998	Now–1997	Now	Now	Now
Opus One	N/T	Now–2005	Now–2001	Now–2001	Now–2002	Now–2000	Now–1999	Now–1997
Joseph Phelps Eisele Vineyard	—	—	—	1995–2002	1996–2006	1995–2005	1995–2010	1995–2002
Joseph Phelps Insignia	—	Now–2007	1995–2003	1994–2000	1995–2003	Now–2005	1995–2008	Now–2005
Ridge Monte Bello	2000–2025	1999–2015	1996–2004	1995–2005	1997–2020	Now–2005	1995–2015	Now–2015
Rubicon	N/T	N/T	N/T	N/T	N/T	1996–2007	1994–2005	Now–2003
Shafer Hillside	N/T	N/T	N/T	Now–1999	Now–2001	Now–1999	Now–2000	Now
Silver Oak (all 3 Vyds.)	N/T	N/T	N/T	Now–1999	Now–2002	Now–2005	Now–2003	Now–2000
Simi Reserve	N/T	N/T	N/T	1995–2003	1996–2008	Now–2005	Now–2005	N/T
Spottswoode	1995–2005	1995–2005	Now–2000	Now–2002	1995–2003	Now–2003	Now–2005	Now–2002
Stags Leap Cask 23	N/T	N/T	N/T	N/T	Now–2008	Now–2000	Now–2005	Now–2000
Philip Togni	1995–2008	Now–2018	Now–2003	Now–2010	Now–2005	Now–1996	—	—
Tudal	N/T	N/T	N/T	Now–2003	1994–2005	Now–2002	Now–2003	Now–2000

1983	1982	1981	1980	1979	1978	1977	1976	1975	1974
Now–1996	Now–2005	Now–1997	Now–2005	Now–2005	Now–1998	Now–1998	1995–2020	Now–1997	Now
Now–1996	Now–2000	Now	Now	Now	Now	Now	N/T	N/T	N/T
Now–1996	Now–1996	Now–1993	Now–1997	Now–1996	1994–2002	—	—	—	—
Now–1995	Now–1995	Now	Now	Now	Now–2000	Now–1997	Now	Now–1998	Now–2000
Now–2000	Now–1998	—	—	—	—	—	—	—	—
Now–1994	Now–1994	Now	Now–1998	Now–1998	Now–1996	Now	Now–2002	Now–1996	Now–1998
Now–1996	Now–2000	Now–1997	Now–2005	Now–2000	Now–2006	—	Now–2010	Now–2005	—
Now–1998	Now–1996	Now–1995	Now–2000	Now	Now	Now	Now	Now	Now
Now–1998	Now–1996	Now–1996	Now–1995	Now–1996	Now	Now	Now	Now	Now
Now–1996	Now–2002	Now–1998	Now–2001	Now–2008	Now–2006	Now	1996–2010	Now–1998	Now
1995–2005	—	—	—	—	—	—	—	—	—
N/T	N/T	Now	N/T	N/T	Now	—	—	—	—
1994–2001	Now–2005	—	—	—	—	—	—	—	—
1994–2005	Now–2008	Now–2002	Now–2002	Now–1995	—	—	—	—	—
Now–2000	—	—	—	—	—	—	—	—	—
Now–1997	Now–2000	N/T	N/T	—	—	—	—	—	—
Now–1997	—	—	—	—	—	—	—	—	—
Now–1998	Now–1997	Now	Now	—	—	—	—	—	—
Now–2005	Now–2003	Now–1997	Now–2004	Now–2003	Now–1995	Now–1997	1995–2010	Now–2005	Now–2010
Now–1995	Now	Now–1996	Now–2004	Now–1998	Now–1998	—	—	—	—
Now–2000	Now–1997	—	—	—	—	—	—	—	—
Now	Now	Now	Now	Now	Now	Now	Now	—	—
Now–1996	Now–1999	Now–1998	Now–1997	Now	—	—	—	—	—
Now	Now	Now–1998	—	—	—	—	—	—	—
N/T	N/T	N/T	—	—	—	—	—	—	—
Now	—	—	—	—	—	—	—	—	—
1996–2005	1994–2010	Now–2005	Now–2010	Now–2000	Now–2000	Now–2000	Now–2005	Now–2005	1994–2015
Now–1995	Now	Now	Now	Now–1996	Now–1998	Now	Now	Now	Now–2000
Now–2000	Now–2002	Now–2000	Now–2002	Now–1996	Now–2005	Now–1997	Now–1998	Now–1997	Now
Now	Now	—	—	—	—	—	—	—	—
N/T	N/T	Now–1996	Now	Now–1998	Now–1998	N/T	Now	Now	Now–2000
Now	Now–1998	Now	Now	Now	—	—	—	—	—
1996–2003	Now–1996	Now–1995	Now–2005	Now–2001	Now–2000	Now–1998	1996–2010	Now	Now–1999
Now–1999	Now–1997	Now–2002	—	Now–1998	Now–2008	Now–1996	—	Now–2005	—
1995–2006	Now	Now–2006	Now–2005	—	Now–2008	1994–2015	Now	Now–1997	Now–2010
Now–2000	Now–2003	Now–1998	Now–1998	Now	Now	—	—	—	—
Now	—	—	—	—	—	—	—	—	—
Now–1996	Now–1998	Now	Now	Now	N/T	N/T	N/T	N/T	N/T
N/T	Now–2000	N/T	N/T	N/T	N/T	N/T	N/T	N/T	Now
Now–1998	Now–1999	—	—	—	—	—	—	—	—
Now–1996	—	—	—	Now	Now–1995	Now	—	—	Now
—	—	—	—	—	—	—	—	—	—
Now–1995	Now–1996	N/T	N/T	—	—	—	—	—	—

INDEX

ROBERT PARKER gave up a career in law to devote himself full time to evaluating and writing about wine. In 1978, he founded *The Wine Advocate*. He lives with his wife, Pat, daughter, Maia, and various basset hounds in the countryside of northern Maryland.

MUCH OF THE MATERIAL in this book is based upon tastings and research done in conjunction with the publishing of *The Wine Advocate*, an independent consumer's guide to fine wines, which is issued six times a year. A one-year subscription to *The Wine Advocate* costs $35.00 for delivery in the continental United States, $45.00 for Canada, and $65.00 for air-mail delivery anywhere in the world. Subscriptions or a sample copy may be obtained by writing to *The Wine Advocate,* P.O. Box 311, Monkton, MD 21120, or by sending a fax to 410-357-4504.